The Worlds of the Indian Ocean

Europe's place in history is reassessed in this first comprehensive history of the ancient world, centering on the Indian Ocean and its role in pre-modern globalization. Philippe Beaujard presents an ambitious and comprehensive global history of the Indian Ocean world, from the earliest state formations to 1500 CE. Supported by a wealth of empirical data, full-color maps, plates, and figures, he shows how Asia and Africa dominated the economic and cultural landscape and the flow of ideas in the pre-modern world. This led to a transregional division of labor and an Afro-Eurasian world economy. Beaujard questions the origins of capitalism and hints at how this world-system may evolve in the future. The result is a reorienting of world history, taking the Indian Ocean, rather than Europe, as the point of departure.

Volume I provides in-depth coverage of the period from the fourth millennium BCE to the sixth century CE.

Professor Philippe Beaujard is an Emeritus Director of Research at the Centre National de la Recherche Scientifique, Institut des Mondes Africains, Paris.

The Worlds of the Indian Ocean

General Editor

Philippe Beaujard
Centre National de la Recherche Scientifique, Paris

Europe's place in history is reassessed in this first comprehensive history of the ancient world, centering on the Indian Ocean and its role in pre-modern globalization. Philippe Beaujard presents an ambitious and comprehensive global history of the Indian Ocean world, from the earliest state formations to 1500 CE. Supported by a wealth of empirical data, full-color maps, plates, and figures, he shows how Asia and Africa dominated the economic and cultural landscape and the flow of ideas in the pre-modern world. This led to a transregional division of labor and an Afro-Eurasian world economy. Beaujard questions the origins of capitalism and hints at how this world-system may evolve in the future. The result is a reorienting of world history, taking the Indian Ocean, rather than Europe, as the point of departure.

Volume I
From the Fourth Millennium BCE to the Sixth Century CE
Philippe Beaujard

Translation edited by Tamara Loring, Frances Meadows, and Andromeda Tait

Volume II
From the Seventh Century to the Fifteenth Century CE
Philippe Beaujard

Translation edited by Tamara Loring, Frances Meadows, and Andromeda Tait

THE WORLDS
of the
INDIAN OCEAN

A Global History

VOLUME I

From the Fourth Millennium BCE
to the Sixth Century CE

A revised and updated translation

Written and translated by

Philippe Beaujard

Centre National de la Recherche Scientifique, Paris

Translation edited by

Tamara Loring, Frances Meadows,
and Andromeda Tait

CAMBRIDGE
UNIVERSITY PRESS

CAMBRIDGE
UNIVERSITY PRESS

University Printing House, Cambridge CB2 8BS, United Kingdom

One Liberty Plaza, 20th Floor, New York, NY 10006, USA

477 Williamstown Road, Port Melbourne, VIC 3207, Australia

314–321, 3rd Floor, Plot 3, Splendor Forum, Jasola District Centre, New Delhi – 110025, India

79 Anson Road, #06–04/06, Singapore 079906

Cambridge University Press is part of the University of Cambridge.

It furthers the University's mission by disseminating knowledge in the pursuit of education, learning, and research at the highest international levels of excellence.

www.cambridge.org
Information on this title: www.cambridge.org/9781108424561
DOI: 10.1017/9781108341004

First published 2019

Translated and updated from the original French edition

Originally published in France as:

Les mondes de l'océan indien.

Volume 1: De la formation de l'Etat au premier système-monde afro-eurasien (4e millénaire av. J.-C – 6e siècle ap. J.-C.)
Volume 2: L'océan Indien, au cœur des globalisations de l'Ancien Monde (7e–15e siècle)

By Philippe Beaujard

© Armand Colin, Paris, 2012

Armand Colin is a trademark of Dunod Editeur – 11, rue Paul Bert – 92240 Malakoff

Published with the help of the Institut des Mondes Africains – UMR 8171 – CNRS /Université Paris 1 / EPHE /Université de Provence

Printed in the United Kingdom by TJ International Ltd, Padstow, Cornwall

A catalogue record for this publication is available from the British Library.

Library of Congress Cataloging-in-Publication Data
NAMES: Beaujard, Philippe, author.
TITLE: The worlds of the Indian Ocean : a global history / Philippe Beaujard (Le Centre National de la Recherche Scientifique, Paris) ; translation edited by Tamara Loring, Frances Meadows and Andromeda Tait .
OTHER TITLES: Mondes de l'ocean Indien. English
DESCRIPTION: Cambridge, United Kingdom ; New York, NY : Cambridge University Press, 2019. | Revised and updated translation of: Les mondes de l'océan Indien, Armand Colin, Paris, 2012 . | Includes bibliographical references and indexes. Contents: Volume I. From the Fourth Century BCE to the Sixth Century CE – Volume II. From the Seventh Century to the Fifteenth Century CE.
IDENTIFIERS: LCCN 2018037957| ISBN 9781108424561 (v. 1) | ISBN 9781108424653 (v. 2) | ISBN 9781108341271 (set)
SUBJECTS: LCSH: Excavations (Archaeology) – Indian Ocean Region. | Indian Ocean Region – Antiquities. | Indian Ocean Region – Civilization. | Indian Ocean Region – Economic conditions. | Globalization – History – To 1500. | History, Ancient.
CLASSIFICATION: LCC DS338 .B4213 2019 | DDC 909/.09824–dc23
LC record available at https://lccn.loc.gov/2018037957

Two Volume Set ISBN 978-1-108-34127-1 Hardback
Volume I ISBN 978-1-108-42456-1 Hardback
Volume II ISBN 978-1-108-42465-3 Hardback

This book is dedicated to my mother Odette Beaujard-Barreau, who died on May 28, 2009, to my father Lucien Beaujard, who died on December 14, 2010, and to my friend Ernest Hudspith, who died on October 22, 2010.

Cargoes

Quinquireme of Nineveh from distant Ophir,
Rowing home to haven in sunny Palestine,
With a cargo of ivory,
And apes and peacocks,
Sandalwood, cedarwood, and sweet white wine.

Stately Spanish galleon coming from the Isthmus,
Dipping through the Tropics by the palm-green shores,
With a cargo of diamonds,
Emeralds, amethysts,
Topazes, and cinnamon, and gold moidores.

Dirty British coaster with a salt-caked smoke stack,
Butting through the Channel in the mad March days,
With a cargo of Tyne coal,
Road-rails, pig-lead,
Firewood, iron-ware, and cheap tin trays.

John Masefield

CONTENTS

Color plates can be found at the following locations:
Plate Section 1: between pages 40 and 41
Plate Section 2: between pages 72 and 73
Plate Section 3: between pages 200 and 201
Plate Section 4: between pages 264 and 265
Plate Section 5: between pages 424 and 425
Plate Section 6: between pages 520 and 521

MAPS AND CHARTS (IN COLOR PLATES)

The information used for the maps was extracted from the ESRI spatial database, world base DWC 1993, and ESRI Data and Maps 2002.

ILLUSTRATIONS (IN COLOR PLATES)

FIGURES

*Repeated in Color Plate Section 4.

TABLES

ABBREVIATIONS

BCE before the Common, Current, or Christian Era
BP before the present
c. century
c. *circa*
CAD *Chicago Assyrian Dictionary*
CE Common, Current, or Christian Era
E. East
g gram(s)
MC Middle Chronology
N. North
PAN Proto-Austronesian
p.c. personal communication
PB Proto-Bantu
PMP Proto-Malayo-Polynesian
S. South
SC Short Chronology
Skt. Sanskrit
W. West

PREFACE

This English edition of my two-volume book *Les mondes de l'océan Indien*, published by Armand Colin, Paris, in 2012, serves several purposes. First of all, of course, it aims to make my work available to English-speaking readers, thus decompartmentalizing knowledge between anglophone and francophone countries. This second edition has also given me the opportunity to update my work, by using books and articles that I had not previously been able to read. These include the second volume of V. Liebermann's *Strange Parallels* (2009);[1] a synthesis on the fourth millennium BCE published by G. Algaze in 2008;[2] and a book edited in tribute to I. Glover (2010).[3] Taking recently published work into account has also allowed me to refine or modify the perspective I propose, on certain points, and to respond to comments made on the first edition. One example that comes to mind is my analyses of the birth of the state in Mesopotamia and of the historical significance of the northernmost part of that region;[4] another example involves the crucial role played by central Asian nomads in the development of South Asia.[5] It was also necessary for me to reflect the dynamism of research being conducted in areas such as China,[6] India,[7] East Africa,[8] continental and

---

[1] V. Liebermann, *Strange Parallels, Southeast Asia in Global Context, c. 800–1830*, vol. II: *Mainland Mirrors: Europe, Japan, China, South Asia, and the Islands*, Cambridge University Press, 2009.

[2] G. Algaze, *Ancient Mesopotamia at the Dawn of Civilization*, University of Chicago Press, 2008.

[3] B. Bellina, E. A. Bacus, T. O. Pryce, and J. Wisseman Christie (eds.), *50 Years of Archaeology in Southeast Asia, Essays in Honour of Ian Glover*, Bangkok: River Books, 2010.

[4] J. Ur, "Cycles of civilization in northern Mesopotamia, 4400–2000 BC," *Journal of Archaeological Research*, 18 (4) (2010), pp. 387–431; J. Oates, "The rise of cities in Mesopotamia and Iran," in C. Renfrew and P. Bahn (eds.), *The Cambridge World Prehistory*, vol III: *West and Central Asia and Europe*, Cambridge University Press, 2014, pp. 1474–1497.

[5] R. Palat, *The Making of an Indian Ocean World-Economy, 1250–1650: Princes, Paddy Fields, and Bazaars*, London and New York: Palgrave Macmillan, 2015.

[6] L. Liu and X. Chen, *The Archaeology of China: From the Late Paleolithic to the Early Bronze Age*, Cambridge University Press, 2012; R. B. Campbell, *Archaeology of the Chinese Bronze Age*, Los Angeles: The Cotsen Institute of Archaeology Press, 2014.

[7] R. Mukherjee (ed.), *Pelagic Passageways: The Northern Bay of Bengal before Colonialism*, New Delhi: Primus Books, 2011; R. Tomber, *Indo-Roman Trade: From Pots to Pepper*, London: Bloomsbury, 2012; Palat 2015.

[8] P. Sinclair *et al.*, "Trade and society on the South-East African coast in the later first millennium AD: the case of Chibuene," *Antiquity*, 86 (2012), pp. 723–737; P. Mitchell and P. Lane (eds.), *The Oxford Handbook of African Archaeology*, Oxford University Press, 2013; N. Boivin *et al.*, "East Africa and Madagascar in the Indian Ocean world," *Journal of World Prehistory*, 26 (2013), pp. 213–281; F.-X. Fauvelle-Aymar, *Le rhinocéros d'or: histoires du Moyen Âge africain*, Paris: Alma Éditeur, 2013; J. Fleisher *et al.*, "When did the Swahili become maritime?," *American Anthropologist*, 117 (1) (2015), pp. 100–115; S. Wynne-Jones, *A Material Culture. Consumption and Materiality on the Cost of Precolonial East Africa*, Oxford University Press, 2016; B. Zhao, "Luxury and power: the fascination with Chinese ceramics in medieval Swahili material culture," *Orientations*, 44 (3) (2013), pp. 71–78; R. E. Dewar *et al.*, "Campements de cueilleurs-chasseurs dans l'extrême nord de Madagascar: travaux préliminaires à Ambohiposa et Lakaton'i Anja," *Taloha*, 21 (2015); J. Hawkes and S. Wynne-Jones, "India in Africa: trade goods and connections of the late

insular Southeast Asia,[9] as well as research done in fields such as the history of cultivated plants[10] and the study of climate change,[11] with the latter seen as a key player in the evolution of societies and in processes of globalization, within the framework of a "systemic logic" as I attempt to show in this book (see the Epilogue).

This edition has given me an opportunity to further develop the concept of the world-system and to expand the study of the processes of dominance and coevolution that accompanied increasing interconnections between cores and other regions.[12] While the present analysis focuses on periods prior to the sixteenth century, it sheds light on the ensuing era, and may also provide some hints as to the possible futures of the system. I disagree with I. Wallerstein by positing the existence of world-systems in periods much earlier than the modern period; in fact, I place their existence as far back as the fourth millennium BCE, to the birth of the state. I also differ from Wallerstein by demonstrating the early existence of trade, not only in luxury goods, but also in raw materials and basic products. I also take a different view from A. G. Frank by clearly distinguishing capitalist practices and capitalism on the one hand, and by setting my work within a framework of global history, on the other: in particular, I take into

first millennium," *Afriques*, 6 (2015), http://afriques.revues.org; M. Wood, "Divergent patterns in Indian Ocean trade to East Africa and Southern Africa between the 7th and 17th centuries CE: the glass bead evidence," *Afriques*, 6 (2015), http://afriques.revues.org.

9 T. Hoogervoorst, "Southeast Asia in the ancient Indian Ocean World: combining historical linguistic and archaeological approaches," Ph.D. thesis, Oxford University, 2012; M. L. Tjoa-Bonatz, A. Reinecke, and D. Bonatz (eds.), *Crossing Borders: Selected Papers from the 13th International Conference of the European Association of Southeast Asian Archaeologists*, Singapore: NUS Press, 2012; C. Higham, *Early Mainland Southeast Asia. From First Humans to Angkor*, Bangkok: River Books, 2014; B. Bellina, "The inception of the trans-national processes between the Indian Ocean and the South China Sea from an early city-state on the Thai–Malay peninsula (fourth–second century BCE)," in M.-F. Boussac, S. Roychoudhury, J.-F. Salles, and J.-B. Yon (eds.), *Proceedings of the International Conference "The Ports of the Indian Ocean, from the Red Sea to the Gulf of Bengal,"* Delhi: Primus Books, 2017, pp. 463–492.

10 Hoogervoorst 2017; D. Q. Fuller and E. Hildebrand "Domesticating plants in Africa," in P. Mitchell and P. Lane (eds.), *The Oxford Handbook of African Archaeology*, Oxford University Press, 2013, pp. 507–526; D. Q. Fuller, "Post-Pleistocene South Asia: food production in India and Sri Lanka," in C. Renfrew and P. Bahn (eds.), *The Cambridge World Prehistory*, vol. I: *Africa, South and Southeast Asia and the Pacific*, Cambridge University Press, 2014, pp. 389–406; R. Spengler *et al.*, "Early agriculture and crop transmission among Bronze Age mobile pastoralists of Central Eurasia," *Proceedings of the Royal Society*, 281 (2014), http://rspb.royalsocietypublishing.org/content/281/1783/20133382.full.html#ref-list-1; A. Crowther *et al.*, "Ancient crops provide first archaeological signature of the westward Austronesian expansion," *Proceedings of the National Academy of Sciences of the United States of America (PNAS)*, 113 (24) (2016), pp. 6635–6640; P. Beaujard, *Histoire et voyages des plantes cultivées à Madagascar avant le XVIe siècle*, Paris: Karthala, 2017.

11 B. Christiansen and F. C. Ljungqvist, "The extra-tropical Northern Hemisphere temperature in the last two millennia: reconstructions of low-frequency variability," *Climate of the Past*, 8 (2012), pp. 765–786; C. Martin-Puertas *et al.*, "Regional atmospheric circulation shifts induced by a grand solar minimum," *Nature Geoscience*, 5 (2012), pp. 397–401; I. G. Usoskin, "A history of solar activity over millennia," *Living Reviews in Solar Physics*, 10 (1) (2013), doi: 10.12942/lrsp-2013-1; J. L. Brooke, *Climate Change and the Course of Global History: A Rough Journey*, Cambridge University Press, 2014; J. Esper *et al.*, "Northern European summer temperature variations over the Common Era from integrated tree-ring density records," *Journal of Quaternary Science*, 29 (5) (2014), pp. 487–494.

12 Cf. also P. Beaujard, "Ancient world-systems and processes of domination, coevolution, and resistance: the example of the East African coast before the seventeenth century," *Actuel Marx*, 53 (2013), pp. 40–62, and "Pour une approche systémique en histoire globale," *Cahiers philosophiques*, forthcoming.

account interactions and dynamics between societies and the environment (here we can speak of a socio-ecological system).[13] Global history is basically characterized by a transdisciplinary approach which transcends the usual thematic and disciplinary fragmentation: global history is not merely a historiographical current, but a "metadiscipline,"[14] anchored in an already long-standing tradition, one which is quite different from what we know as "connected history" or World History.

[13] On this concept, see for example F. Berkes and C. Folke (eds.), *Linking Social and Ecological Systems: Management Practices and Social Mechanisms for Building Resilience*, Cambridge University Press, 1998; E. Sheppard and R. B. McMaster (eds.), *Scale and Geographic Inquiry: Nature, Society, and Method*, Malden, MA, and Oxford: Blackwell, 2004; and A. Hornborg and C. Crumley, *The World System and the Earth System: Global Socioenvironmental Change and Sustainability since the Neolithic*, Walnut Creek, CA: Left Coast Press, 2007. See my Prologue and Epilogue.

[14] L. Berger, "La place de l'ethnologie en histoire globale," *Monde(s)*, 3, 2013, pp. 193–212.

ACKNOWLEDGMENTS

I am grateful to Cambridge University Press for undertaking the publication of this book in its entirety. The present edition includes some new figures and illustrations; various maps have been corrected or completed.

I am grateful to Mrs. B. Bellina, C. Blanc-Pamard, M. Casanova, M.-H. Gates, I. Good, S. Magnavita, C. Michel, S. Ratnagar and Mr. A. Adelaar, P. Bellwood, L. Berger, R. Blench, R. Blust, M. Chauvet, S. Cleuziou, J. Deloche, J. Dercksen, G. Ducatez, C. Eyre, M. Frachetti, D. Fuller, J.-J. Glassner, C. Higham, C. Jouannès, P. Kohl, K. Kristiansen, P.-Y. Manguin, P. Norel, C. Pelras, G. Philippson, G. Possehl, D. Potts, P. Poumailloux, P. Robertshaw, D. Schaps, S. Sherratt, M. Silver, P. Sinclair, F. Thierry, E. Vallet, T. Vernet, D. Warburton, J.-P. Warnier, D. Wengrow, and T. A. H. Wilkinson for the data and the comments they provided on some parts of this text. For the Comoros and Madagascar, I especially thank Mrs. C. Radimilahy and B. Rasoarifetra, and Mr. C. Allibert, R. Dewar, N. Gueunier, Rafolo Andrianaivoarivony, N. Rajaonarimanana, J.-A. Rakotoarisoa, P. Vérin, and H. Wright.

For their help on the illustrations, I am grateful to Mrs. C. Michel, D. Nicholson, C. Radimilahy, B. Rasoarifetra, M. Wood, and Mrs. An Jiayao, Darsot, J. Deloche, J. Fappas, J. Gabin, I. C. Glover, Y. Madjidzadeh, N. Mahajan, Rafolo Andrianaivoarivony, J.-A. Rakotoarisoa, Ramilisonina, H. Ruther and J. Zilberg. I thank the Bodleian Library (Oxford, UK), the Victoria and Albert Museum (London), Dr. Busso Peus Nachfolger, Classical Numismatic Group, Inc., the Centre d'Art and d'Archéologie of Antananarivo, Gorny und Mosch Glessener Münzhandlung, Fritz Rudolf Künker GmbH u Co. KG, Osnabrück, Lübke u. Wiedemann, Stuttgart, Leu Numismatic AG, T. K. Mallon-McCorgray, the Musée d'Art et d'Archéologie of Antananarivo, K. Ponterio/Bowers and Merena, and the University of Pretoria.

Special thanks go to the Institut des Mondes Africains (Paris 1-Ivry-Aix-en-Provence) (formerly Centre d'Études des Mondes Africains) and to the Chiang Ching-kuo Foundation for International Scholarly Exchange (Taipei, Taiwan), which supported the first edition of this book.

I also thank Mrs. T. Loring, Ms. F. Meadows, and Ms. A. Tait, who corrected my translation of the French text.

Prologue

Truth resides in a panoramic view rather than a local view of events.
(Polybius, second century BCE)

Une nouvelle connaissance de l'organisation est de nature à créer une nouvelle organisation de la connaissance.
New thinking about organization can lead to a new organizing of our thinking.
(E. Morin)

Like the Mediterranean Sea, as described by the historian F. Braudel (1949), the Indian Ocean was traversed from the earliest times by men in quest of goods, new lands, or simply the great unknown. These journeys yielded wealth, knowledge, and power. At the same time, terrestrial routes linked far-flung regions of the Ancient World: these included the famed Silk Roads, but also routes between China and India via Burma, routes over the steppes, north–south routes, and more. Over the centuries, exchanges transformed the Ancient World into a unified and hierarchized area, in which the Indian Ocean occupied a central position.

Exchange Networks and Globalization

Trade – primarily long-distance trade – played a crucial role in this process of integration. Trade implies not only an exchange of goods, but also an exchange of knowledge, beliefs, and values. Exchange networks extended far beyond the borders of the Indian Ocean. This ocean should not be viewed as an entity that evolved in parallel to the Mediterranean, as K. Chaudhuri (1985) has suggested, but rather as an area that became integrally tied to the Mediterranean. Over time, from China to Europe and Africa, the routes of the ships and the roads of the caravans gradually built up a wide zone in which events and regional developments occurred *interdependently*. The fact that the various regions of the Ancient World united by trade experienced such a demonstrable synchronization in their development suggests (but is not yet proof of) the systemic nature of their relationship. It is not merely their interconnections nor the size of their networks but the regularity, intensity, and speed of their exchanges which gave rise to the progressive integration and shaping of these varied regions into an

Afro-Eurasian world-system. This probably occurred as early as the beginning of the Christian era (Beaujard 2009, 2012).

What Is a World-System?

Related to the Braudelian model, the concept of the world-system was introduced by I. Wallerstein (1974b) for the modern period. Among the characteristics of his world-system, Wallerstein emphasizes the ever-increasing accumulation of capital, a transregional division of labor,[1] growing imbalances in power between what have been termed "cores" and "peripheries," phases of hegemony – within any given core – that alternate between a single power exercising control and several rival powers vying for control, and lastly the existence of cycles. A transregional division of labor implies the creation of unequal exchanges in which the system's centers (its cores) – taking advantage of an efficient harnessing of the labor force, of their ability to innovate, and of their politico-military power – produce and sell manufactured goods in markets where they are able to establish more or less monopolistic conditions. Conversely, peripheries, essentially, must sell raw materials and slaves in competitive markets. As for semi-peripheries, these are positioned as interfaces between centers and peripheries; the semi-peripheries thus combine organizational and institutional characteristics from both ends of the system's hierarchy.

World-system analysis has been profoundly renewed by recent research that takes into account other areas (Africa, Asia, the Indian Ocean, and the China Sea) as well as other periods, much earlier than those studied by Wallerstein and his followers (Norel 2009b). This research stresses the need to grasp all the interactions among the three levels: local, regional, and global. It also shows that in addition to any matters of economic, political, and ideological dominance, the relationship between core and periphery can lead to processes of co-evolution, with some regions benefiting from the dynamics of the system due to their geographic and human assets. Moreover, peripheries have never remained passive; researchers have generally paid too little attention to the fact that some peripheries have shown a real "capacity for negotiation" with the dominant centers (Beaujard 2013).

Today, the world-system analysis is recognized as one of the major currents in global history (Beaujard *et al.* 2009: 44ff.). A number of researchers have attempted to use this concept to help understand processes of globalization in ancient periods (as early as the Bronze Age), often modifying the notion in order to do so (Schneider 1977; Ekholm and Friedman 1982; Rowlands *et al.* 1987; Kohl 1987; Edens and Kohl 1993; Algaze 1993, 2008; Frank and Gills 1993c; A. Sherratt 1994a, 1994b; Chase-Dunn and Hall 1997; Kristiansen 1998; Ekholm-Friedman 2000, 2005; Friedman 2000; Kristiansen and

---

[1] I will use the notion of spheres of interaction to denote zones where exchanges do not lead to the instauration of a significant transregional division of labor (which is fundamentally different from a world-system). The division of labor allows us to distinguish between a *margin* and a *periphery*: whereas a periphery is structurally interdependent with the other parts of the system, a margin is an area that does not depend on contacts with the system, even in cases where such contacts have begun to transform it (Sherratt 1994b; Chase-Dunn and Hall 1997: 69).

Larsson 2005; Beaujard 2005, 2009, 2010a, 2010b, 2011a; Gills and Thompson 2006; Wilkinson *et al.* 2011). On the other hand, research has emphasized the crucial role played by some regions of Africa and Asia – particularly China – in the evolving Afro-Eurasian world-system. Broadening the scope of reflection has highlighted the Eurocentric character of much of the material published, and has led some to question the origins of the Industrial Revolution and the so-called "Rise of the West" (Abu-Lughod 1989; Frank 1998; Mielants 2007; Norel 2009b).[2]

Based on geographic factors and exchange networks, the Asian and East African maritime zones can be divided into three main areas: the China Sea, the eastern Indian Ocean, and the western Indian Ocean, with the latter area being further divided – except during some rare moments of unity – between the Persian Gulf and the Red Sea. From the first through the sixteenth century, the Eurasian and African world-system was organized around five "cores" – sometimes multi-centered – which held a position of economic, cultural, and sometimes political dominance over their peripheries; these cores were (1) China, (2) India, (3) western Asia, (4) Egypt, and (5) Europe (the Mediterranean, Portugal, and then northwestern Europe). As early as the Tang period, China enjoyed a preeminent position that it would maintain for the whole period under study. Western Europe – except between the first and third centuries – occupied a significant position only from the fifteenth century onward.

From their positions as nodes of networks, and sometimes at the interfaces of maritime and terrestrial routes, cities directed production and exchange according to a hierarchical structure. Within a given core or periphery, there existed a further hierarchical division between each metropolis and its dependent zones. Urban points linked by long-distance trade created a string of conglomerations or relay points – or "archipelagos of towns" to use Braudel's delightful phrase – whose interconnections formed the spine of the system. Throughout the ages, observers of these types of metropolis have underscored their cosmopolitan Tower-of-Babel character as places fostering interrelationships that gave birth to innovative creations (Gruzinski 1999, 2004). Along the perimeter of the Indian Ocean, trade gave rise to the formation of "fringe cultures," a term and concept used by anthropologist P. Ottino (1974a) to account for the similarities in many of the syncretic societies which developed along the Indian Ocean's rim. The unifying movement of the world-system, transcending political and cultural borders, and leading to what McNeill (1990) has called *commonality*, has – as a corollary – a tendency toward differentiation and cultural pluralism (Friedman 2000). Indeed, the system generates both order and disorder, unity and diversity. Here, I take Morin's definition according to which (1) a system represents both a "*complex* unit and the complex of relations between the whole and its parts," (2) a system is made up of cumulative *interactions*, (3) which constitute the *organization* of the system.[3] The character of this organization is, by nature, both complex and dynamic.

---

[2] This research program has also been developed by the Californian School: cf. Wong 1997, Pomeranz 2000, Goldstone 2008. M. G. S. Hodgson (1954, 1963) and W. McNeill (1963) have been pioneers in this field.

[3] Morin 1990: 244–245. The global does not simply generate the local; the local is always the result of interactions between different levels (Friedman 1994; Arrighi 1994). A. G. Frank has been rightly criticized because he did not pay enough attention to the internal economic and social organization of societies or to their specific situations.

Not all coasts benefited from the same opportunities to become trade nexuses. Monsoons and strategic locations gave zones intersecting two subsystems privileged positions, hence the successes of Southeast Asia, South India and Sri Lanka, Aden and Yemen, Hormuz and Oman, respectively. The development of maritime trade also depended in part on the relations established between each coast and its hinterland. The same held true for waterways, such as rivers and streams, for the mouths of large rivers have always served as nodal points in the development of commerce and trade. Likewise, the availability of resources and labor naturally played a role in the construction of a system.

Besides geographic data and economic processes, the hierarchized structure of the system is linked to competition between states and between elites. Exchange must be seen in terms of balance of power; it is connected to ideologies – themselves inseparable from political contexts. The dominance of ideologies along exchange networks helps to build the *desirability* of merchandise and to establish the market value of these goods: thus, studies of world-systems must consider the extent to which the economic is embedded in the cultural and the sacred. Like P. Norel (2009b), we can define a core by what can be termed the "agility" of its merchants, the high desirability of its products, a current account surplus "(at least temporary)," and an ability to transform other spaces. All mechanisms which allow a center (core) to (re-)structure other regions should be taken into account.

The expansion of exchanges was a crucial factor in transforming interconnected societies. This expansion often led to the development of production, triggered increased division of labor and innovation, and favored statebuilding. During some periods, in synergy with the geographic growth of exchanges, a symbiosis between the interests of private entrepreneurs and state elites favored progress in markets (commodity markets and factor markets). This is especially clear for the city-states, which were more inclined than country-states to base their development on long-distance trade. It is therefore not surprising that capitalism emerged in Europe from the fifteenth century on, in a process of globalization accompanied by the financialization of the economy (Arrighi 1994; Beaujard, Berger, and Norel 2009; Norel 2009b).

"The Perspective of the World"[4]

Fundamental transformations are noticeable during at least three historical periods: (1) from 3500 to 2400 BCE in western Asia and Egypt and during the second millennium BCE in China, when the state was born along with private means of accumulation; (2) during the sixteenth century, the period of emerging European capitalism and of the creation of a new space centered on Europe, one that encompassed the Americas and West Africa; and (3) during the early nineteenth century's Industrial Revolution – also an ideological revolution – when the capitalist mode of accumulation first rose to preeminence in a world-system that would henceforth link America, Africa, and Eurasia.

In order to shed light not only on the evolutions or mutations, but also on long-term permanent realities, I have chosen to go back as far as the formation of the primordial

---

[4] Braudel 1984, III: book title.

states of Mesopotamia, Egypt, India, and China, and then follow what I see as the "waves of time," in harmony with Braudel's research proposal. This will lead us to construct a non-Eurocentric history of the Ancient World that should restore to Africa and Asia their "stolen heritage" (Hobson 2004; Goody 2007). In this way, we will grasp the proper origins of the Afro-Eurasian[5] world-system, which began to take form at the start of the Christian era.

A Note on the History of Money

Among specifically focused histories, the history of money is obviously of particular interest. I use the term "money" to denote goods that possess at least some of the functions we take for granted in modern currencies: they were a means of account, a means of payment, and a store of value. Money was the lifeblood of the economy, stimulating transactions and production; it was closely linked to the politico-religious field and – more generally speaking – to the social order; money played a growing role in the construction of the system. "The adoption of money signals that critical changes are taking place within the society" and between societies (Wicks 1992: 7). By lowering the transaction costs, money fosters the credit market and economic specialization, and contributes to economic development (Silver 1995: 157). Public institutions played a crucial role in the rise of money during the third millennium in Mesopotamia (weighed silver), and during the first millennium in western Asia (minted coinage) and in China (cast coinage), all building on the opportunities that money provided for extracting and mobilizing wealth. Coin minting often had motivations other than economic transactions: money expressed a ruler's sovereignty, and established social relations (Aglietta and Orléan 1998, 2002; Breton 2002). Money often served administrative purposes or was used within the context of grants to religious institutions before being used by merchants. Whatever its function, in order to be efficient, money requires either a centralized power or community's authority, which is able not only to promote its standardization and the acceptance of the monetary units, but also to control its issuance.

The geographical area of money or of a type of money provides information on the exchanges and hierarchies present within this area. As early as the fourteenth century, Ibn Khaldun noted the role that money and precious metals played within a global system. The use of money partly helps to compensate commercial deficits. In theory, a money can only be used between regions if the differences in price of the materials from which it is made renders its transport profitable, or if the power that issued this money is able to compel its use, or if this money bears a symbolic message that is universally recognized (as is the case for cowries).

Beyond money, it is the entire financial area that must be analyzed: instruments of credit; the functioning of banks; and accounting techniques. As for money, the use of banking instruments and the rise of credit can develop only within a relatively stable, predictable, and unified environment. Arrighi (1994) has highlighted the existence of successive cycles of accumulation in Europe from the fifteenth century onward, revealing a phase of material expansion followed by

---

[5] Moreover, there were American world-systems, which were almost completely separated until 1492.

> a phase of financial expansion. Seen as "a sign of autumn" (Braudel 1979), the phase of financial expansion corresponds to a period of hegemonic transition within the system. Orchestrated by capitalistic oligarchies, these cycles of accumulation are embedded within the larger cycles of the world-system. We should ponder whether similar cycles can be observed for earlier periods and for non-European regions.

From its origins, the Afro-Eurasian world-system developed and was restructured according to the rhythm of economic cycles lasting several centuries (periods of growth followed by periods of decline). Understanding the nature of these cycles provides a key to unlocking the growth and recession or demise of states and urban centers. We will attempt to define the characteristics of these pulsations through the evolution of exchange networks and interconnected areas,[6] and to determine their origins, thus shedding light on the existence of what can be termed "systemic logic," a question too often largely side-stepped by researchers.

In Favor of a Systemic Approach to the History of the Ancient World

Exchange networks helped generate the system. Studying these networks and their transformations may prove to be more illuminating than the compartmentalization proposed by some civilizational, ethnical, or national approaches, which present only a fragmentary and distorted historical view (Douki and Minard 2007). Responses at the local level are insufficient because the local is always a part of the global, even if it does not simply result from the global. The systemic approach, however, does not merely imply a "search for an explanation at the level of the whole." It calls for an understanding of the dynamic processes of interaction and organization between the parts and the whole.[7] We need to perceive how local trajectories, linked to specific historical and geographical conditions, interact with global phenomena.

Continuing L. Febvre's project of global history, F. Braudel (1958: 734) had already suggested linking specific histories in order to comprehend evolutions over the long term: in his words, "history is the addition of all possible histories," and that of all interactions. The transdisciplinary and systemic approach adopted in this book tends toward what can be termed a "geohistory," a "permanent effort to connect time and space," by linking different scales (Grataloup 2003; Capdepuy 2010). In order to do this, we will have to examine the growth and decline of networks against the backdrop of political events, social and ideological evolutions, geographical factors, technological

---

[6] As R. Mukherjee notes (2011: 9), "investigation into networks" can highlight spatial configurations that are not immediately visible.

[7] Morin rightly stresses that seeking an explanation only at the level of the whole without taking into account the complexity of the system presupposes a vision that simplifies the whole. While "a system is more than the sum of its parts" (Frank 1998: 28, 340ff.), "the whole is also less than the sum of its parts" (Morin 1990: 242–243), something that Frank omitted to note. This omission may explain some biases in Frank's analysis.

innovations, demographic curves, and great epidemics. We will also monitor climatic changes and man's relationship to the environment, each contributing – in connection with other factors – to determine the evolution of world-systems: the latter are truly "socio-ecological systems."[8] This does not imply, however, that ecological factors have always been determinant in the crises of the system (Friedman 2007).

Unfortunately, we have only limited quantitative figures for determining the level of integration of the world-system's various parts for the ancient eras. But the data available from archaeological research and in texts do allow us to estimate the size and intensity of exchange networks and to observe their cycles of expansion and shrinkage. The number and size of the principal cities; their locations; regional urban density; all these provide valuable indications as to the system's general direction of activity (growth or decline) and the system's internal structure. As Morris has done (2013), one can also try to compare social development by evaluating "energy capture," information technology, and war-making capacity.[9] As for archaeological excavations, however, these contain only a portion of the goods traded. Textiles, aromatics, and spices generally left no trace in archaeological layers. Metallic objects, precious or not, were often recycled. As for the movements of people, how can we identify slaves at an archaeological site? Conversely, it is not always easy to understand how and why some goods appear within the contexts where they are found. In addition, some regions have been insufficiently surveyed and excavated. We must take these elements into account when evaluating the data presented.

By situating the analysis at the level of the whole Ancient World, this book will show how the Indian Ocean was progressively unified and became a central space within an Afro-Eurasian world-system. The first volume explores the long path from the formation of the first states (from the fourth millennium onward) to the birth of this Afro-Eurasian system (first through sixth century CE). Data have shed light on the constitution of large spaces that can be considered as systems evolving along cycles. For each period identified, I will first introduce the general evolution of the system(s) under consideration as well as their internal relations;[10] then I will describe the main regions, showing the specificities of their trajectories and the ways in which these regions were shaped by their links with the whole system and – conversely – how these same links acted on the system itself. The second volume traces the expansion of the Afro-Eurasian system until it grew, during the sixteenth century, to include the Atlantic Ocean and a continent previously unknown to the Ancient World: America.

The Formation of a Periphery: The Example of Madagascar

Within the context of this Afro-Eurasian space created by increasing exchanges, Madagascar illustrates a peripheral construction that appeared a few centuries after

---

[8] On this concept, see Georgescu-Roegen 1971; Chase-Dunn and Hall 1998; Berkes and Folke 1998; Sheppard and McMaster 2004; Hornborg and Crumley 2007.

[9] By energy capture, Morris means "the full range of energy captured by humans, above all food, fuel and raw materials" (2013: 53).

[10] Unlike Braudel (1979, III: 16), I do not consider world-economies as closed autonomous spaces, but as opened spaces (cf. also on this point Norel 2004: 197).

the birth of the system.[11] It is a construction that we will follow throughout the cycles of this system. As a meeting point between the Austronesian, Bantu, and Muslim worlds, Madagascar provides a good example of processes affecting other shores, although it was not an important node in the networks. The multicultural encounter characterizing the "fringe cultures" of the Indian Ocean took place in Madagascar under specific modalities, which varied according to regions and periods (Ottino 1974a, 1974b).

Using all the data available up until the arrival of the Portuguese during the sixteenth century (incursions occurring during later centuries, however, will sometimes shed light on various developments), research conducted on Madagascar will be used to grasp the circumstances under which various types of cultural hybridization or *métissage*, their contents, and their "logics," led to the formation and evolution of Malagasy societies. Contrary to an essentialist vision, which paints an image of isolated societies in juxtaposition, this research will emphasize the syncretisms underlying each culture. Identity represents only the "result of a negotiation," at a specific historical time and in a particular place; identity expresses a balance of power – both intra- and intercultural – that forms within the context of a particular configuration of this hybridization (Amselle 1990: 54). The concepts of fringe culture, networks, and hybridization, however, take on their proper meaning only as parts of a systemic approach and global history. It is in this sense that my research goes beyond what are known as the "anthropology of hybridization" and "connected history."[12]

---

[11] Madagascar has been my research field since 1972.

[12] These two currents use similar approaches to propose new interpretations of historical and anthropological facts, with particular reference to either Africa (Amselle 1990; Mary 1992) or America (Bernand and Gruzinski 1993; Gruzinski 1999), with similar approaches. Cf. also Gruzinski (2004) and Subrahmanyam (2005). While these approaches emphasize the importance of transcultural exchanges, they do not clearly explain the genesis of the processes of dominance or coevolution or their impact on the changes observed.

Introduction: The Geography of the Indian Ocean and Its Navigation

> The monsoon unfailingly regulated sea-voyages in either direction in the Far East and the warm seas, thus precipitating or interrupting international encounters between merchants.
>
> (Braudel 1982, II: 126)

The Indian Ocean

The Indian Ocean covers approximately 75 million square kilometers. It is bordered to the west by the African coast and Arabia, to the east by the Thai–Malay peninsula, the Indonesian coasts, and – further south – western Australia. The Asian continent runs along its northern border, with India forming a wide peninsula that divides the northern Indian Ocean into eastern and western parts (the Bay of Bengal and the Sea of India, respectively). The western part of the Indian Ocean extends along both sides of Arabia, with a narrow entrance opening onto the Persian Gulf to the north and the Red Sea to the south. South of India, the Maldive Islands are scattered north of the Equator, while the Chagos Islands lie south of the Equator. The narrow channel of the Strait of Malacca is the crossing point between the Indian Ocean and the China Sea, to the north.

Wind Patterns

Wind patterns, around the world, are determined by the existence of high-pressure zones in the Northern and Southern Hemispheres at both higher and subtropical latitudes. Between these high-pressure zones and the Equator, air flows are deflected by the Earth's rotation (this is the Coriolis effect); it gives birth to the austral and boreal trade winds. The equatorial region is a zone of ascending movements and low pressure. These zones experience seasonal translational movements. The force of these translational movements pushes the trade winds past the Equator; then these winds change direction, toward the southeast for boreal trade winds, and toward the northeast for austral trade winds. In the Indian Ocean, these phenomena give rise to an alternating system of monsoons,[1] which imposes its laws on sailors.

In the Northern Hemisphere, during the boreal summer, Asia's land masses warm more rapidly than the ocean, and an upward movement of air masses occurs on the

---

[1] From the Arabic *mausim*, plur. *mawāsim*, "period of the year, market, fest, season"; in the Indian Ocean, the term acquired the meaning of "navigational season" (cf. in Ibn Mājid).

continent, causing low-pressure systems over Central Asia and northern China. Both the high subtropical pressure systems of the southern Indian Ocean and the low intertropical pressure systems shift northward, and a southwest monsoon wind blows over the northern Indian Ocean. Conversely, when the boreal winter sets in, the land masses cool more rapidly than the ocean, the phenomena are reversed and now it is a northeast wind that blows over the northern Indian Ocean.

In June, the southeasterly trade winds of the Southern Hemisphere cross the Equator, subjecting all of the northern Indian Ocean to the southwest monsoon. In the east, this flow reaches Sulawesi and the China Sea as a south wind: "Ships from the southern seas came to China with the south-west wind . . .; the half year from May to October was the busiest time at the sea ports" (Filesi 1972: 15).

In October, the subtropical high-pressure area begins to shift southward. East of 80°E, the austral trade wind goes no further than the Equator; a zone of doldrums forms over insular Southeast Asia and another over the Bay of Bengal. Conversely, west of 80°E, the austral trade wind continues to cross the Equator, blowing from the southwest. It even blows from the west between the Equator and 10°N as far as the Gulf of Thailand.

In November, the northeast trade winds travel far to the south in the region of insular Southeast Asia; further west, they go no further than Sri Lanka. In East Africa, the monsoon weakens south of the Pangani River. The southeast trade winds remain in the Southern Hemisphere.

In December, a zone of strong high pressure settles over Central Asia. The boreal trade winds begin crossing the Equator, and in January the southeast trade winds take up their southernmost position. Further east, the Australian continent deflects these winds into south/southwesterly winds, that reach the Javanese coasts and islands further east. The northern Indian Ocean and the China Sea come under the influence of the northeast trade winds. These boreal trade winds blow toward the southeast (as northwest winds) beyond the Equator. The Intertropical Convergence Zone, south of the Equator, extends further south into the western part of the Indian Ocean: it reaches Madagascar, which thus receives both north and northwest winds in its north/north-western region, while a portion of the Malagasy east coast remains under the influence of the austral trade winds. The Convergence Zone moves south into the Mozambique Channel, a low-pressure area; the Cape Delgado region and the coast north of it are hit by northeast winds.

In March, the high-pressure systems move northward. The northeasterly trade winds return, reaching only as far as Sri Lanka, Malaysia, and Kalimantan; yet, they still cross the Equator in the vicinity of Sulawesi. A southwesterly airstream blows over Oman and India, as well as over the northern part of the Gulf of Bengal. During this period, the Gulf of Bengal is divided into two zones, each subjected to contrary winds, "on both sides of a line of discontinuity running from the Palk Strait to Arakan" (Donque 1965: 49).

In the north, the April northeasterly trade winds continue to return. Only the southern Philippines and the northeastern Kalimantan still receive northeasterly winds. In the Indian Ocean, the austral trade winds now blow beyond the Equator, becoming southwesterly winds, reaching the Gulf of Thailand. Along the southern coasts of Java and further east, the austral trade winds lose their curve and blow straight from the southeast.

In May, this trend continues. Although the austral trade winds do not yet reach the Equator in the more eastern part of the Indian Ocean, they do cross the Equator west of 90°E. A zone of equatorial calm affects Malaysia, Sumatra, Kalimantan, and the Philippines.

These winds' direction and strength made navigation almost impossible from June to September along the west coast of India. "Most of the Indian harbors were closed at the height of the southwest monsoon. These were preferably reached from the western Indian Ocean ports during the months of August–September, when the ferocity of the monsoon winds and torrential rain would die down somewhat" (Chakravarti 2002a: 49). During the southwest monsoon, as well, it was difficult to sail or berth along the west coast of Malaysia, or on the south coast of Arabia. It was possible, however, to leave at the beginning of this monsoon, around mid-April (according to the Arab pilot Sulaymān al-Mahrī, sixteenth century; Tibbetts 1971: 372). Travel from Oman to India could be undertaken at any time during the year except between May and July. Ships from India's west coast arrived at Aden in April. One traveled from Gujarat to Aden mainly from October to December, with the return journey between March and May. From South India, ships departed between March and June. Ships left Aden to sail to the Malabar coast from October to February, or at the end of the southwest monsoon (late August–September; see below).[2] Between June and October, one could sail back to India along a portion of the South Arabian coastline. Ibn Battūta (fourteenth century) notes that the trip from Calicut to Ẓafār (in Dhofar) lasted one month.

To sail from the west coast of India to the Bay of Bengal and Sumatra, one could leave at the start of the southwest monsoon (the "head of the wind"). "The sailing season from Gujarat toward Malāqa, Shumatra, Tanāsarī, Banjāla and all the 'down-wind' ports," writes Sulaymān al-Mahrī, "[runs] from the 120th to the 160th day from the Nairūz (beginning of the solar year), but the best choice is on the 140th day [this means around April 10, the beginning of the Nairūz at the time of Sulaymān al-Mahrī being around November 21[3]].[4] The sailing season from Manībār [Malabar] toward Malāqa, Shumatra, Tanāsarī, Martaban, Banjāla and all their ports: the 160th day from the Nairūz." One also sailed from the west to the orient at the end of the southwest monsoon: "The sailing season from Aden to Manībār, Konkan and Gujerat: on the

---

[2] Ray 2002: 69–70; Das Gupta and Pearson 1987: 12; Vallet 2010: 218–219, 545–546. See below the comment made by Villiers (1957: 185): "the north-east monsoon is the season of navigation [for the Arabs], [who] can sail both ways with this monsoon." Tibbetts (1971: 360–382) mentions a two-way traffic between India and the Arabian coast several times during the year (cf. Prins 1970: 7, 15, 20; Sheriff 2002: 213). "Eastward voyages in April and May were occasionally possible" (Tibbetts 1971: 368; Margariti 2007). From Oman to Gujarat, "the sea is not closed for any part of the year" (Ibn Mājid, in Tibbetts 1971: 227).

[3] The year starts with Nairūz, from the Persian Nauruz, "New Year," originally celebrated at the spring equinox. The calendar in the Indian Ocean was a 365-day year: it did not take into account the shortfall of a quarter day with the solar year, so the navigator's calendar was "slipping by 25 days every century" (Sheriff 2002: 213, 223, 225 n. 4).

[4] To sail from Gujarat to Malacca, Ibn Mājid suggests a departure between mid-April and May, and during the first part of September, toward the end of the SW monsoon (Tibbetts 1971: 377).

280th day from the Nairûz [around August 28].[5] . . . The sailing season from Gujerat toward Malāqa, Shumatra, Tanāsarī, Banjāla and all the 'downwind' ports: on the first 300th . . . The season for Manībār toward Malāqa, Shumatra, Tanāsarī and all their ports: on the 310th day" (C. Jouannès, p.c.). From Aden to Malacca, according to al-Mahrī, one departed around August 15. For the return journey, from Malacca to Aden, one left between December 28 and February 16. From China, ships left between the end of November and March 1; a November departure made it possible for ships to reach Malacca and to cross the Bay of Bengal in a single journey (Tibbetts 1971).

As for East Africa, in order to reach its coasts, the Omani pilot Ibn Mājid (fifteenth century) recommended a departure from Aden between the 320th and the 330th day of the year [from the Nairūz] [October 8 to 18, when the author wrote his book; see below], from Hormuz around the 70th day [January 31], from India up to the 80th [February 10], and from Sumatra from the 60th day [January 21] (Tibbetts 1971: 234, 360ff., 378; Sheriff 2002: 213). Fortunately for trade, ships arrived on the East African coast when agricultural activities were minimal. The return from the African coast toward Arabia or India could be made between April and May, before the full rise of the monsoon or at the end of the season, in August. During the thirteenth century, Marco Polo describes sailing from the coast of Malabar to Zanzibar in twenty days, but the return journey lasted three months, due to contrary currents.

On the East African coast, once past Cape Delgado, one sailed in a southerly direction at the beginning of the austral summer. Ibn Mājid writes: "The best season from Kilwa to Sufāla is from the first [day] of the Nairūz to the 50th day [that is to say, from November 14 to January 2], but if you set out from Sufāla, you should do it on the 170th day [around May 11], this is the best season of all. Before that date, you encounter the disastrous Kūs wind [southwest monsoon], which is too weak, and later, it becomes too strong in these headlands and you should sail eastward to the open sea [to avoid being driven ashore]." "The sailing season from as-Sawāḥil to al-Qumr [Madagascar] and its isles, and then to as-Sufāl extends from the first [day] of the Nairūz to the 70th. For the pilot of Kilwa the season is on the 90th day . . . The pilots of al-Qumr have two seasons for as-Sawāḥil" (Khoury 1982: 270, 281; Jouannès 2001: 79, 95). To sail from Sofala to Kilwa, one departed between April 17 and May 17.

Moreover, some areas, such as the Red Sea, have special wind conditions. From June to September, winds and currents facilitate journeys to the entrance of this sea, with northerly winds in most of the Red Sea, and a current which sets to the south-southeast; the winds and currents are partially reversed between October and May, with the most favorable season for sailing back to the north being January and February (Meeks 2002: 324; Pearson 2003: 20). The situation is complex, however, with "winds north-northwest in the northern part of the Red Sea and south–southeast in its southern part. Between these two regions, there is a zone of calms or light and variable winds between 18° and 20° North. The current between November and April sets north-northwest in nearly all of the Red Sea. Travel to the north of the Red Sea, therefore, was not easy, and maritime traffic most often stopped in the zone of calms"

[5] McGrail notes: "It would have been prudent to arrive in southern Indian waters in late September" (2015).

(C. Jouannès, p.c.). This phenomenon partly explains the development of ports such as Berenice, 'Aydhab and Jeddah (see Facey 2004).

It was of vital importance for captains to know the system of monsoons, which dictated the movements of ships. The period when the winds became reversed was a particularly dangerous one. Ibn Mājid writes: "He who leaves India [for Arabia] on the 100th day [after the Nairūz, which means March 2 when the author writes his book] is a wise man; he who leaves on the 110th day will be all right; but he who leaves on the 120th day is stretching the bounds of possibility and he who leaves on the 130th day is inexperienced and an ignorant gambler" (Tibbetts 1971: 231).

The Currents

Ship captains also had to take account of the currents, which depend upon planetary mechanisms, and are affected by changes in temperature and winds.

During the austral summer, between 20°S and 10°S, a South Equatorial Current crosses the Indian Ocean from east to west, at a moderate speed (25 to 30 km per day). This current hits Madagascar at the level of Toamasina (Tamatave), and then divides into two branches. The southern branch joins currents running from South Africa to Australia, south of Madagascar; part of this branch, however, flows around Cape Sainte-Marie (at the southern tip of Madagascar) and runs up the Mozambique Channel. The wider northern branch flows around northern Madagascar, hitting the African coast in the vicinity of Cape Delgado, where a new division occurs: a northern current flows along the Tanzanian coasts, while another current makes its way south into the Mozambique Channel. Two currents of opposite directions and uneven forces thus ride this Channel: a south–north current flows along the west coast of Madagascar, and a north–south current flows along the African coast. Their encounter gives rise to numerous crosscurrents.

During the same period, in the northern Indian Ocean, the northeast monsoon favors a North Equatorial Current, whereas south of the Equator an Equatorial Countercurrent develops, along the 7° South latitude. When it arrives near the African coast, the North Equatorial Current curves southward as a result of the northeast monsoon. Further north, in the Sea of India and even more so in the Bay of Bengal, two systems of currents arise, turning clockwise. In the China Sea, a current flows along the coasts of China and Vietnam; then it arcs southward, reaches southern Sumatra and northern Java and enters the Pacific to feed the Pacific Equatorial Countercurrent.

During the southern winter, the southern currents of the Indian Ocean tend to reach southern Australia directly, and the anticyclonic movement of water is therefore less pronounced. It is during this period, however, that the South Equatorial Current reaches its highest speed, thanks to the southeast trade winds, and due to currents from the Pacific, north of Australia. This gives birth to a more powerful current than before in the Mozambique Channel, and to a strong south–north current along the Kenyan and Somali coasts (the Somali Current), favored by the southwest monsoon.

In the Northern Hemisphere, during the summer, the southwest monsoon favors a west–east monsoon current north of the Equator, a southwest–northeast current along the South Arabian coast, and a north–south current along India's west coast. The Equatorial Countercurrent completely disappears at this time. In the Gulf of Bengal, the monsoon current sweeps toward the northeast, and northeast–southwest countercurrents appear along the Coromandel coast. In the Gulf of Thailand, west–east currents dominate and in the China Sea we find southwest–northeast currents. A southeast–northwest current flows from southern Sulawesi to southeastern Sumatra, then curves and flows along the east coast of the Thai–Malay peninsula and then toward the northeast along the Indochinese coast.

As for the Red Sea, a dominant current flows from Egypt to Yemen during the summer, whereas during the cooler season the situation is more complex, with south–north currents along the Yemeni and Arab coasts, but north–south currents in the Gulf of Aqaba and along the Sudanese coast. Moreover, many reefs dot this sea, making navigation unsafe (see Pearson 2003: 17).

In the Persian Gulf, the dominant currents beyond Hormuz are northwest–southeast during the summer, and are the reverse during the cooler season.

These geographical data have imposed their laws on sailors. They have determined the routes followed by ships, and the seasons for navigation. I will return to this point when I speak of the Austronesians' trips to the west.

Madagascar

The island of Madagascar extends from 12°S to 25°S; it is 1580 km long, and approximately 550 km wide at its median part. A central plateau with an average altitude of between 800 and 1400 m descends to the eastern coast through two series of cliffs. To the west, the elevation descends more gently via successive plateaus. Several mountains exceed 2000 m in height: Tsaratanàna in the north, Ankaratra in the center, and Andringitra in the central southeast.

Wind patterns determine two large climatic areas: a windward region, hot and humid, and a leeward region, hot and drier. In the austral winter, Madagascar is hit by a dominant flow of eastern trade winds, which tend to take a northeast–southwest direction in the south of the island (Fort-Dauphin), and a southeast–northwest direction in the northeast (Antsiranana). A diffluence occurs off the east coast near the latitude of Vatomandry. Some of the trade winds cross the eastern cliffs, and then take a southwesterly direction toward the southern part of the island.

During the austral summer, in the western Indian Ocean, the Intertropical Convergence Zone crosses the Equator and reaches Madagascar. A low-pressure area forms in the Mozambique Channel. Northern Madagascar is hit by north monsoon winds. Further south, along the west coast, the winds veer westward, under the effect of the Coriolis force. Less active than during the cooler season, the austral trade wind still manages to reach the east coast. Along the coasts, the days are punctuated by alternating sea and land breezes, which are more pronounced on the west coast than on the east coast, and are also stronger in the summer than they are in the cooler season.

The island is divided into four large phytogeographical zones. The east coast, humid, tropical, fringed with lagoons and dunes, was in the past covered with forest, which has largely disappeared through human activity, except in the northeast and in some parts of the highest cliffs separating the coast and the Highlands. These have given way to zones of pseudo-steppes, with patches of secondary forest where the Traveler's Palm dominates. A series of rivers, necessarily short, range along the coast; the main rivers are the Maningory, Mangoro, Sakaleoña, Mananjary, Faraoñy, Matatàña, Manampatraña, and the Mananara. The extreme northwest (between Nosy Be and the coast south of Antsiranana) also enjoys a humid tropical climate. Along the entire eastern coast north of Manakara, precipitation exceeds 2000 mm annually.

The Highlands, in the past covered by a forest–savanna mosaic, have since been deforested and eroded by human activity (nowadays only residual forests subsist at sacred sites). The Highlands are composed of landscapes of red hills and wetlands, most now converted into irrigated ricefields. Its average annual rainfall varies from 1200 to 1600 mm.

Some large rivers flow down from the Highlands into the western savannas: these are the Sofia, Mahajamba, and Betsibòka rivers, in the northwest, and Manambao, Manambolo, Tsiribihina, and Mangoky rivers, on the west coast. In the latter region, the year is marked by two clearly defined seasons: a very dry "winter" and a humid summer. Annual precipitation is under 1000 mm near the coasts (except in the northwest, which is progressively wetter as one travels further north). The only remaining forest consists of gallery forest along rivers. Several large bays indent the northwest coast, offering harbors for ships.

The south and the southwest of the island experience a semi-arid climate, with sharp irregularities in precipitation averaging from 250 to 500 mm per year. The dry forests of the southwest have also largely been cleared. One finds only one large river in this region, the Oñilahy; it flows to the sea in the Bay of Saint-Augustine, south of Tulear.

The arrival of the first migrants brought enormous changes in the ecosystems of the island, particularly following the introduction of domesticated animals, sheep, goats, and cattle, leading to the progressive disappearance of various wild animals: giant tortoises, dwarf hippos, large lemurs, and giant ratites (*Mullerornis* and *Aepyornis*).

Navigation of the Indian Ocean

> I did not leave one star in the sky that I did not use to guide me.
> (Ibn Mājid, *Sufālīya*; Jouannès 2001: 53)

In order to steer his ship across the ocean, an "ideal pilot" had to know the winds, the currents, and their changes during the year, as well as the lunar mansions, or "the course of the celestial luminaries"; he had to be able to recognize signs and landmarks, the configuration of the coastline, with mountains, capes, islands and their rocks, the color of the water, the birds, the fishes and the seaweeds (Tibbetts 1971: 1–2; Sheriff 2002: 210, 214).

Very early on, sailors learned how to orient themselves by observing the stars, and to assess the latitude of a given place. They invented instruments to measure the positions of certain stars.

Among the Arabs, "latitude" was [notably] measured by gauging the height of the Polaris star (*Jāh*)[6] when the latter was at the lowest point of its trajectory. When a place was situated at Jāh 12, this meant that the Polaris was observed 12 fingers' width above the horizon when this star was 'in its house', in the lowest part of its diurnal rotation . . . Among the Arab pilots of the Indian Ocean, change in latitude had been fixed at one finger [Arabic *iṣbaʻ*], which means 1°45[7] . . . The *tirfā* represented the distance one had to sail in order to observe a variation in latitude of one finger . . . This notion of *tirfā* . . . was known to the three schools of deep-sea pilots who, according to Sulaymān al-Mahrī, sailed across the Indian Ocean: 1. the Arabs, 2. The Indians of Gujarat and Konkan, and 3. the Cholas of the Coromandel coast. (Jouannès 2007b)

When the Muslim world acquired knowledge of the compass from the Chinese, the compass became linked to the rising and setting of certain stars, during the twelfth or thirteenth century (Tibbetts 1971: 3, 290, 295). The Turkish geographer Sidi Ali Çelebi, in his *Mohit* (1554), which is partly based on the works of the *mu'allim* (pilots and scholars) Ibn Mājid (fifteenth–sixteenth century) and Sulaymān al-Mahrī (sixteenth century), describes for the first time a measuring instrument that must have been in common use on ships plying the Indian Ocean. This instrument consisted

of a number of oblong pieces of wood [*loḫ*, 'tablet'] of different sizes with a string or different strings passing through their centers. To measure the height of Polaris in the northern latitudes, or one of the Bears in the southern latitudes, the string was held between the teeth with the wood at a distance from the eye such that while the lower edge [of the wood] was in line with the horizon, [its] upper edge just touched the star. Latitude was calculated in terms of numbers of finger widths (*isbas*) above the horizon. (Sheriff 2002: 216)

"Sidi Çelebi had a system of nine tablets each with a string through it, or with one string through them all. The nine tablets each had a different width corresponding to different angular altitudes on the horizon" (Tibbetts 1971: 316). According to Sidi Çelebi, this was the instrument used by the ancients, but in his own time, he describes "a graduated rod with a small wooden rectangle sliding on it" (see Tibbetts 1971: 316): here we recognize the instrument that the southern Europeans called *ballisti* or Jacob's staff, and which the Portuguese called *balestrilha*, deriving from the Persian *bālā*, "height" and *astar*, "star" (the instrument's origin may go back to Antiquity: during the early third century BCE, the Greek philosophers Timocharis and Aristyllus probably used a Jacob's staff to assess the declinations of some stars). "The *kamal* was improved upon by replacing the different pieces of wood by a single tablet, and the single string was calibrated by a number of knots indicating different latitudes" (Sheriff 2002: 217; 2010: 123) or marking regular intervals of *isba*: here one recognizes the *kamal* described in 1836 by Princep from data provided by a sailor from the Maldives. Note that Ibn Mājid does not use the term *kamal*, and he does not describe the precise way in which the instrument was employed during his time. He mentions only the use by pilots of the Indian Ocean of different "pieces of wood" *khashaba* for measuring stellar altitude (*qiyās*) (the word *khashaba* is sometimes rendered as *khāḍaba* or *ḥataba*)

---

[6] *Jāh* is "an arabization of the Persian *gah*, 'the place'" (Tolmacheva 1980: 186). For Ibn Mājid, it is a star near Polaris (Tibbetts 1971: 122–123).

[7] Following Ibn Mājid, Malhao Pereira gives 1°36 for one *isba* (2003: 22). According to Sulaymān al-Mahrī, it is 1°43 (Tibbetts 1971: 315).

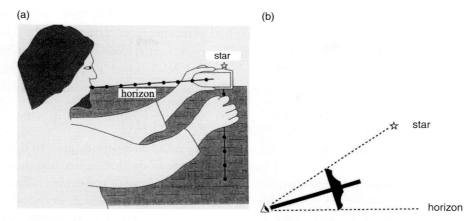

Figure I.In.1 (a) Use of the *kamal* (b) Cross-staff (Jacob's staff). This type of instrument was used in the Greek world during the third century BCE; its use may be older in western Asia. Reproduced from Sheriff 2002: 218,[8] by permission of RoutledgeCurzon Publishers

(Tibbetts 1971: 317). "Ibn Majid takes his stellar altitude measurements using 24 pieces of wood" (Khoury 1985–1986: 215). In his "poem with a rhyme in *mim*" "on the six main *abdāl* methods of using Sharatān (alpha Arietis) and ʿAnaq (Urs. Maj.)" (Tibbets 1971: 19), Ibn Mājid writes: "My instrument of measure (*qiyāsī*) [is composed] of 20 pieces of wood and four more in total and necessarily [verse 19]. When stars appear, I shoot arrows to them that meet their goals [verse 20], they do not miss their target thanks to their mark and to the rope whose ends are between the palm [of my hand] and my wrist [verse 21]. [These pieces of wood are] angels who do not deceive [verse 22]" (G. Ducatez, p.c.). "The *khashaba* boards," confirms Jouannès, "were tablets; their top edges were placed in contact with the star while the lower edges touched the horizon at sea. Whereas for the *kamal*, the variable element was the distance from the board to the eye of the observer (measured by knots on a thread attached to the center of the board); in the other case, arm length was constant. It was therefore the dimension of the board that had to be variable, whence the necessity of having a number of boards" (12, or even 24) (Jouannès, forthcoming). These tablets did not allow sailors to observe stars which were too high in the sky. "Measurements practiced by seamen," writes Sulaymān al-Mahrī, "go from one to twelve fingers [from 1°8 to 21°]." "Fatimi shows that a similar instrument ... may have been in use since the ninth century" (Sheriff 2002: 216). Measurements (*qiyās*) did not consist only in evaluating the height of Polaris or the Southern Cross: Ibn Mājid gives as many as seventy types of measurement in the *Fawāʾid* (Tibbetts 1971: 325ff.).

A Chinese sailor called Ma-Huai-te, who accompanied Zheng He's expeditions during the early fifteenth century, developed an instrument that probably derived from the cross-staff of the Indian Ocean (Fatimi 1996: 289; Sheriff 2002: 217). This Chinese

---

[8] See also J. M. Malhao Pereira 2003: 31, fig. 14. Pereira points out that there is a need for correction when the rope is held by the teeth (the distance between the teeth and the board is less than the distance between the eye and the board), so the *kamal* was graduated for a definite user and could not be used by others (2003: 31–33).

reinvention provides a good example of the knowledge exchanges on the scale of the world-system, exchanges that had in fact been occurring since the dawn of this system. The Gujarati pilot who guided Vasco de Gama from East Africa to India used a Jacob's staff, which Vasco de Gama took back to Portugal in 1499, to be tested by Portuguese sailors ("The Portuguese modified the instrument to read degrees directly instead of the standard finger widths of the Arabs") (Sheriff 2002: 219).

It was thus possible to determine the vessel's latitude, but

Indian Ocean mariners were not able to calculate longitude prior to the introduction of the sextant ... [They] sailed first to the latitude of the destination, and then changing course in mid-ocean [they sailed] due east or west until landfall was made ... Speed of the dhow was calculated by dropping a floating object at the stem of the dhow, and calculating the time it took to reach the stern. East-west measurement of distance was calculated in terms of the *zam* (watch), a standard three hours of sailing [or one-eighth of a degree]. (Sheriff 2002: 217)

The solar calendar of Persian origin was widely used by sailors in the western Indian Ocean, and probably since the Sassanid period.[9] Persia's preeminence during the first centuries of Islam is apparent in boating terminology.[10] This is only one element among others in the elaboration of a culture shared by sailors in the Indian Ocean and the China Sea. Even prior to the Christian era, Arabs, Indians, Austronesians, the inhabitants of southern China, and later the Chinese themselves (from the Han period) were all actively exchanging knowledge and evolving methods of navigational technology. The cosmopolitanism of the ports of the ocean corresponded to that of the crews in the transnational networks.

Exchanges in the Indian Ocean varied according to developments in naval technology. Improvements in the field of shipbuilding allowed ships to travel faster and carry progressively greater loads. We shall see, moreover, that the monsoon system has not remained static over the centuries. In the northern Indian ocean, periods of weak summer monsoons have accompanied phases of low solar activity; conversely, more intense solar activity seems to be correlated with strong summer monsoons. These phenomena are subject to a number of cyclicities.

---

[9] The use of the Persian calendar may date back to Sassanid times, in the sixth century (Sheriff 2002; Tibbetts 1971: 361).

[10] Ferrand 1924. Cf. the Persian origin of terms such as *bandar*, "port," *nakhuda*, "shipcaptain," *khann*, "a rhumb, interval between each star," "i.e. the points of the compass and their intervals on the horizon," *rahnami* (encountered in Swahili), "navigational instruction." According to Fatimi (1996: 285), the word *kamal* also derives from the Persian *kaman*.

PART I

The Ancient Routes of Trade and Cultural Exchanges and the First States (Sixth–Second Millennium BCE)

Introduction

Connections across cultural and other boundaries should serve as an organizing
principle for world history.
(McNeill 1998a: 221)

During the tenth and ninth millennia BCE, western Asia – slightly earlier than China –
witnessed the emergence of the Neolithic, with the cultivation and then the domestication of cereals, pulses, and a fibrous plant (flax), in what has been called the Fertile
Crescent. Animals were also domesticated: goats, sheep, cattle, and pigs.[1] Agriculture
and stockbreeding allowed a sedentarization of the communities, which was accompanied by changes in the social organization and systems of beliefs (Cauvin 1997).[2]

As early as the eighth or seventh millennium, plants and animals domesticated in
western Asia were carried to Egypt, Greece, and then to Crete. To the east, they spread
to Turkmenistan and the Indus valley (Mehrgarh) during the seventh millennium,
along terrestrial and perhaps maritime routes.[3] This diffusion may have involved
movements of population, or have taken place along long-distance exchange networks
that can be detected through the discovery of obsidian from Anatolia in the Levant and
in Mesopotamia, or of shells from the Persian Gulf in Mesopotamia, or from the coasts
of Sind at Mehrgarh, during the fifth millennium.[4] Mehrgarh in this period shows
lapis lazuli from Afghanistan, turquoise, and copper.

Sea voyages probably took place in the Persian Gulf and along the coasts of South
Asia even before the emergence of the Neolithic.

The development of irrigation in Mesopotamia led to progress in agriculture, which
provided the basis for demographic growth. The rise of trading exchanges fostered
innovations such as the breeding of sheep, the wool of which was used in developing
textile crafts (woolly sheep may have evolved in colder regions such as the Pontic-Caspian
steppe [Cunliffe 2015: 74]). At the same time, one notes institutional innovations – a new

---

[1] For the animals, genetic research shows that several domestications usually occurred, in various regions.
Goats, for example, seem to have been domesticated both in western Asia and in Iran or western Pakistan
(Luikart *et al.* 2001). Cattle could have been domesticated early on, in the Sahara, Egypt, and the Fertile
Crescent (Bradley and Loftus 2000).

[2] Hocart (1954) suggests a ritual origin for agriculture, and for the invention of the plow.

[3] J. Diamond rightly speaks of "founding cultures" for the plants cultivated in western Asia, which provided
the basis for the rise of the Egyptian and Indian civilizations (Indus), along with the animals native to the
same region (1997: 188). Moreover, the middle Ganges valley and the Deccan may have represented other
centers of agricultural domestication (rice, millets, and pulses) in the third and second millennia BCE (see
below). In Central Asia, agriculture and stock breeding with West Asian species arrived during the sixth
millennium in Kazakhstan, Tajikistan, and the central Fergana valley (Fuller 2006a: 28).

[4] As early as the PPNB (Aceramic Neolithic, phase B, second half of the ninth millennium BCE), trade
networks developed, as revealed by the find at Jericho of obsidian from Anatolia, jadeite from northern
Syria, and turquoise from Sinai.

social hierarchization was accompanied by the appearance of collective buildings some-times called "temples" – and by the expansion of the 'Ubaid culture (*c.* 5300–4100 BCE) outside Mesopotamia, at least from the Ubaid 3 phase (Oates 2014). This expansion was probably based on the spread of techniques and religious ideas, which explains the homogeneity of the 'Ubaid culture. The exchange networks extended to northern Mesopotamia, northern Syria, southeast Turkey, western Iran, and the Persian Gulf, where the 'Ubaid people introduced domestic animals and domesticated plants, and probably transmitted shipbuilding techniques. They may already have been plying the Persian Gulf to obtain myrrh and incense, which were transported from southern Arabia (Zarins 2002).

The 'Ubaid expansion, which prefigured the flowering of the Sumerian civilization during the Urukian period, expressed new needs, in aromatics, wood, precious stones, and, during its final phase, metals. Copper metallurgy appeared during the sixth millennium in Anatolia, and during the fifth millennium in Mesopotamia, Iran, Pakistan, and southeast Europe, whence it progressed to the north of the Black Sea (4400 BCE), the Middle Danube valley (4000 BCE), and the south of the Iberian peninsula (3800 BCE). Metalworking spread in the Eurasian steppes during the fourth millennium.[5] With copper and then bronze metallurgy, which required access to ores and their transport, trade networks developed on a larger scale, in new social contexts that implied profound ideological and organizational changes.

The end of the 'Ubaid phase *c.* 4100 BCE seems to be linked to a global climatic cooling, accompanied by a process of aridization in the eastern Mediterranean and the Levant.[6]

After the 'Ubaid cultural period, Anatolia and northern Mesopotamia experienced new development, favored by an improvement in the climate. It was marked by the appearance of proto-urban centers (Khirbat al-Fakhar [Hamoukar], Tell Brak . . .), which were connected with Anatolia and with east–west exchange networks extending from Afghanistan to Syria. We clearly observe the development of social complexity from 4400 BCE in northern Mesopotamia, in a process partly distinct from that of southern Mesopotamia. With the town of Tell Brak, northern Mesopotamia shows an incipient urbanization from 3800 BCE, perhaps earlier than in the south,[7] according to some archaeologists (though the earliest levels of Uruk and other sites have never been reached). The recent data from northern Mesopotamia lead Ur to write that "the emergence of the Mesopotamian city must be considered a multicentric phenomenon" (2010: 400). Oates *et al.* (2007: 585) also write: "The 'world's earliest cities' are as likely to have been in northeastern Syria as in southern Iraq, and the model of a core from the south developing a periphery in the north is now ripe for revision." This large northern area, however, appears to have had links to southern Mesopotamia from 3600 BCE, as

---

[5] It is likely that native copper was used first. Hocart (1954) has suggested a ritual origin for copper and bronze metallurgy.

[6] Staubwasser and Weiss 2007. The end of the fifth millennium also saw the collapse of the Chalcolithic culture of the northern Balkans (Kohl 2007: 52). The extent of this climatic change is still debated.

[7] Ur (2010: 400) writes: "Indeed, the possibility is now raised that northern urbanism predates its appearance in the south."

can be seen from sites such as Tell Brak and Hamoukar, in the Jazira, and the south clearly appears to have been dominant throughout the Middle and Late Uruk periods.

Around 3600 BCE, southern Mesopotamia was experiencing new social transformations, which corresponded to the birth of the state. It would be futile to seek any single cause: it was a combination of factors set in specific economic, political, religious, and environmental contexts that led to this transformation (see Testard 2004). The intensification of agricultural practices – with the development of the ard and of animal traction (Sherratt 2006a) – allowed a growth in output and a new rise in population. It was accompanied by increased social differentiation, the development of various crafts and that of urbanization, around 3600 BCE. The agricultural and human potential of Mesopotamia, its geographical situation at the junction of multiple exchange networks, the possibilities of transport offered by water courses and the ethnic diversity of the region, all influenced its political and economic development, characterized – in contrast to Egypt – by the emergence of an "archipelago" of city-states among which the city of Uruk became preeminent (it is possible that Uruk ultimately became the capital of a country-state).[8] Ecological and technological conditions led to the formation of major estates involving the temple.

The "Urban Revolution" was an ideological revolution within society, but also in its relation to the environment. The Urban Revolution was the time of the "great divorce of culture and nature" (Hughes 2001): the motif of the triumph of man over hostile nature is preeminent in Mesopotamian mythology. The rise of cities was to cause rapid deforestation in a region already sparsely wooded. There may have been lower rainfall in Mesopotamia (an aridification of the Sahara from the middle of the fourth millennium onward has been noted [deMenocal *et al.* 2000]), but precipitation seems to have been plentiful in Anatolia: the water from the rivers, downstream, could be used both for simple or more sophisticated irrigation (Burroughs 2001: 244). The spread of sheep bred for wool and the production of fermented drinks (beer and date wine) represented other innovations of the Urban Revolution,[9] which was marked by changes in clothing and food consumption (Sherratt 2004). The production of new goods appears inseparable from the building of urban hierarchal societies and the increased division of labor within cities and between regions. Exports of goods gave rise to asymmetric exchanges with peripheral regions, "production costs falling as the scale of output increased" (Algaze 2008: 36), and they also fostered local development (thus the social context of drinking fermented beverages in Mesopotamia may have led to the growth of viticulture on the Mediterranean shores, as A. Sherratt (2004) has suggested).

Note that some authors have rejected the idea of an "Urban Revolution." Ur (2014), for example, states that "urbanism evolved within the context of a metaphorical extension of the household." Unlike Pollock (1999), Ur does not see cities as developing

---

[8] Algaze (2008: 114–115), however, considers Uruk as a purely religious capital (see below).

[9] The concept of innovation, as mentioned, refers to the use of an invention that may be much older (for example, the production of date wine certainly began prior to urbanization). For the fourth millennium, Sherratt (1981) has postulated a second Neolithic Revolution, that of "secondary products" (milk, leather, wool, the plow). Recent research invalidates the idea of innovations in this period (the use of milk, for example, goes back to the Early Neolithic), but confirms a process of diffusion (Greenfield 2005; Issakidou 2006).

as a result of tributary economies and appears to downplay the significance of increased social stratification (see Adams 1981).

The state – or the great households, in Ur's view – played a crucial role in the organization of production and exchanges and in redistribution of wealth. The Urban Revolution benefited from the growth of long-distance trade, which it helped to develop. "Trade was the earliest spur to population clustering" (Algaze 2008: 30), which, along with political and ideological factors, encouraged economic differentiation. Trade was primarily in textiles, slaves, and copper, which was used for producing weapons and tools. This copper came from Iran, northern Iraq, and eastern Anatolia. Various authors have suggested that the flowering of copper – and then bronze – metallurgy constituted a basis for the emergence of political power (Ratnagar 2001b); the absence of local resources in metals, stone, or wood prompted the Mesopotamian elites to secure their supply. Arsenical bronze and later tin bronze metallurgy spread from the fourth millennium along the trade routes, with a possible transfer of this technology from western Asia (where it appeared between 4000 and 3000 BCE) to China (between 3000 and 2000 BCE). The production of bronze tools increased agricultural productivity, and also military power: competition between cities was not always peaceful, and the extension of conflicts certainly played an important role in the construction of the state.[10] It could also be argued that warfare was both a cause and a consequence of asymmetrical growth. Economic and social development was in part linked to the emergence of a new ideology of political control and to institutional innovations. The newly formed public sector provided the managers necessary for the setting up of entrepreneurial centers: capital accumulation in pursuit of efficiency (it may be too early to speak of "profit-seeking") first developed with the state apparatus and the institutions of the temples, and then the palaces (Hudson 1996). Communal lands belonging to extended families came under the management of "institutional houses." One of the most salient "ideational innovations" of the Uruk world was "the systematic use of various types of dependent labourers receiving rations" (Algaze 2008: 128).

The changes in production and exchanges went along with a radically new division of labor, within societies and between regions, with Mesopotamia positioning itself as a center of gravity (we will see that southern Mesopotamia can be considered as the core of the first world-system [Algaze 1993, 2001]). The Urukian culture extended to Susiana and northern Mesopotamia, Anatolia, and the Levant, acting as an interface with more distant regions. Trade between the shores of the Indian Ocean and western Asia on the one hand, and Egypt on the other, a trade which also involved the eastern Mediterranean world, fostered the rise of states or cities, during the fourth and then the third millennium BCE.[11] New forms of labor mobilization and capital accumulation

---

[10] It is, however, shortsighted to attribute the emergence of the city-states to a matter of defense of the communities, as some authors have proposed.

[11] The usual explanation according to which the management of hydraulic works by an elite favored the building of the state is certainly not valid for all the city-states, even though canals have been discovered at Uruk. Recent research partly invalidates the idea that the Urban Revolution was linked to civilizations based on large hydraulic works. Wittfogel's thesis has been largely abandoned. J. E. McClellan III and H. Dorn (1999: 33–35) have combined the idea of an organization of hydraulics engineering with that of demographic pressure linked to environmental circumscription, a hypothesis perhaps conceivable for Egypt, but unlikely elsewhere. Going against the archaeological data available, McClellan III and Dorn do

developed, involving the use first of servile, and later of hired labor, and the collection of taxes and tributes. Southern Mesopotamia exported textiles and other manufactured goods, and imported mainly raw materials, slaves, and possibly metallic items. The increase in exchanges sheds light on the important role of Central Asia, and the development of Sogdiana and Turkmenistan as early as the fourth millennium and, more importantly, in the third millennium. Mesopotamian influences can moreover be perceived in the Maykop culture (*c.* 3700–3000 BCE), in the western Caucasus (Kohl 2007; Kohl and Trifonov 2014). In the Urals, copper seems to have been exploited at the site of Kargaly as early as the second half of the fourth millennium. On the European side, gold from the Carpathian mountains reached western Asia at the end of the fourth millennium.[12] This expansion was favored by the emergence of political entities in northern Mesopotamia before the middle of the fourth millennium. It was based on economic mechanisms, and also on ideological power and organizational efficiency. "Colonies" and trading posts were established in the north, where cities like Tell Brak and Hamoukar shrank in size and finally came under the control of southern Mesopotamians. Algaze (2008: 117) speaks of an "aborted urbanism" in Upper Mesopotamia.

For Sherratt (2006a), the wheel was probably invented in northern Mesopotamia, Syria, or eastern Anatolia during the Urukian expansion. It was quickly adopted by southern Mesopotamia. This region also enjoyed a more efficient system of communication and transport than the north, through the intensive use of multiple watercourses. Moreover, innovations in one sector led to innovations in others. As Algaze notes (2008: 33), "processes that maximize efficiency in one industry often get adopted by related industries or lead to totally new developments in unrelated fields, thus creating new forms of diversification."

Among the most crucial innovations of the Urban Revolution were techniques of power and new forms of organization. The importance of dependent laborers has already been mentioned. An increasing complexity in glyptics can be noted, with the use of cylinder seals, and imprints of multiple seals, "a glimpse of the number of agents involved in whatever transaction is being recorded" (Algaze 2008: 135). With the progress of exchanges and the development of the state, writing and systematic reckoning appear after 3400 BCE at Uruk in Mesopotamia (writing was first based on "pictograms," then developed into the Sumerian cuneiform during the third millennium), around 3300/3200 BCE in Egypt (hieroglyphic script), and in 3100 BCE in Elam (Proto-Elamite).[13] The development of writing formed one basis for state ideology, and the creation of numerals opened the way to a true "mathematization of the world." There was no direct borrowing from the Sumerian script, but rather a dissemination of

not attribute any role to trade in the process of formation of towns and states. Research today invalidates or leads one to substantially qualify the idea that "the Urban Revolution produced civilizations that depended on large-scale hydraulics engineering" (1999: 41).

[12] J. A. Bakker *et al.* (1999) have suggested that the wheeled wagon spread from northwestern Europe. As P. L. Kohl (2007) emphasizes, whatever the origin of the innovation, it is striking to see how quickly it spread across Europe, the Russian steppes, and western Asia.

[13] I disagree with the idea expressed by J. Ur: "the appearance of writing in the south c. 3200–3100 BCE (Englund 1998, pp. 32–41) was a very late development, likely postdating the collapse of the Uruk expansion" (Ur 2010: 397). See Oates 2014: 1486.

the idea of writing and the development of particular systems, in Egypt, Iran, and later in the Indus valley and Crete. Writing represented a cognitive revolution and, combined with the standardization of weights and measures, became a powerful technique of social control. "The primary function of writing as a means of communication," wrote Lévi-Strauss (1964: 292), "is to facilitate the enslavement of other human beings" (quoted by Algaze 2008: 138). The advent of accounting systems represented a major innovation that gave the state the basis for an effective organization; it also engendered increased social complexity, set in motion by the rise of transregional trade (Hudson and Wunsch 2004). And writing of course allowed for the new accumulation and transmission of knowledge, monopolized by the elites.[14]

In northern Africa, the aridization of Libya and of the eastern desert during the fourth millennium encouraged an intensification of agriculture in the Nile valley. The lands fertilized by the Nile were relatively landlocked; this situation may have favored a centralized political organization and given more stability to the Egyptian system than could the irrigated areas of southern Mesopotamia. Conversely, the latter region benefited from a greater variety of exchange routes: the location and structure of the region of the Tigris and the Euphrates valleys partly explain its instability and dynamism, characteristic of the city-states. The nature of the state in Egypt also derived from the politico-religious features of the societies in which that state originated. The ideological foundations of political power were different from those of Mesopotamia: in Egypt, the figure of the god-king pharaoh was the guarantor of the cosmic and social order, whereas the Mesopotamian "kings" were first and foremost managers and warlords. Order in Mesopotamia resulted from negotiations within cities, between cities, and between urban dwellers and nomads.[15] In Egypt, where urbanization progressed from around 3500 BCE, various competing proto-states dominated sections of the Nile valley and neighboring regions. At the same time, long-distance exchanges developed. Very early on, the Mesopotamian area established indirect contacts with the Nile valley, through the Syrian coast, contacts that were to play a catalytic role in the formation of the state. As was the case for the Urukian world, the expansion of the Nagada culture (native to Upper Egypt) to the south and the north seems to have been motivated at the outset by the search for metals: gold from Nubia and copper from Palestine; this expansion occurred during the Nagada IIc–d phases (3500–3300/3200), and then Nagada III (3300/3200–3100). During the latter period, competition between the first country-states led to the formation of a unified kingdom.

Around 3100 BCE, climatic changes brought about movements of populations in Asia, a disaggregation of the Mesopotamian system and a restructuring of exchange networks.[16] Migrations affected the Caucasus, Anatolia, and northwestern Iran, and

---

[14] This accumulation of knowledge had crucial consequences. "The most important changes," Algaze points out (following Myrdal 1970), "were the creation of economies of scale in production and an increase in the rate of innovation as a result of the expansion of knowledge" (2008: 37–38).

[15] For a comparison between Mesopotamia and Egypt, see Ekholm and Friedman 1993: 64–65; Baines and Yoffee 1998. The term "pharaoh" (from the Egyptian *pr-ʿ3*, "large domain") was used at a later period, from Akhenaton.

[16] In northern China, the Hongshan culture collapsed around 3000 BCE (Liu and Chen 2012: 169; cf. also Schettler *et al.* 2006). W. J. Burroughs (2001: 235) considers that the period *c.* 2900 BCE corresponds to a rise in El Niño–Southern Oscillation (ENSO) phenomena. M. Staubwasser and H. Weiss (2006: 379)

we observe the abandonment of the Urukian "colonies." Relations between Egypt and Mesopotamia nearly ceased *c.* 3100/3000. The links between southern Mesopotamia and the northern and eastern regions weakened. The exchanges involving southern Mesopotamia were reoriented toward the Persian Gulf, where intensive exploitation of copper was beginning in Oman. They were probably accompanied by an improvement in seafaring techniques. East of Sumer, the Susian plain was depopulated, but the city of Anshan, in the Fars region, became the center of an independent Elamite state, whose formation appears linked to a rise in exchanges between Sistan, Afghanistan, and the Indus. Trade routes extended further to Turkmenistan and Tajikistan. This Proto-Elamite space disintegrated around 2800 BCE during an arid phase that affected the Iranian plateau and Mesopotamia. At this time, Susiana was again under the influence of the Sumerian space, divided between competing city-states.

During the twenty-eighth/twenty-seventh century BCE, new links were forged between Anatolia, the Levant, and northern and southern Mesopotamia, prompting the rise of the cities of Mari and Ebla (Syria). However, the area experiencing major changes was in fact much larger. From 2600 BCE, urban expansion – with a rise in the number and size of towns and cities – took place, along with advances in agriculture, crafts, and trade, in Mesopotamia, Iran, Central Asia, and the Indus valley. One notes the spread of the Mesopotamian city-state culture. Written documents (tablets) have sometimes been discovered in these cities, for example at Ur, Shuruppak, Girsu (Telloh), and Ebla. Many temples were built, and this provided a firm ideological basis for the political power in place and played an important role in the cities' economy. The institution of kingship emerged against the background of fierce competition (both peaceful and violent) north of Sumer (Yoffee 1995a; Hudson 1996). Kish seems to have played a particular role (it may have been an early seat of kingship), as did a confederation of southern cities, of which Nippur constituted a religious pole. We can observe attempts by some cities to form country-states, through conquests or alliances.

While a royal ideology was emerging, relations between the temples and political power appear to have been complementary, but also at times conflictual. An incipient process of land privatization was initiated by the king, starting in the north of Sumer: it began at the top of the social pyramid. It was fueled partly by the development of the practices of interest-bearing loans and debt. Texts point to land sales in the north of Sumer as early as the Fara period (2600–2450) (Liverani 2014: 101). The concept of equivalence in value was present during this period,[17] as well as the practice of measuring working time and the use of hired workers, with silver and barley used as currency. Historians have often claimed in the past that the state completely controlled production and exchanges and instituted a system of redistribution. Writing, however, was not confined to the great public institutions,[18] although it represented, for these

---

have identified the period *c.* 3200 as a phase of aridification between the Zagros and Syria and in Anatolia, as well as of a probable weakening of the Indian Ocean monsoon system (the effects are noticeable in Oman and on Mount Kilimanjaro).

[17] In fact, as M. Aubet notes: "The notion of a measurement of value has been present since writing originated" (2013: 148).

[18] Tablets have been discovered in residential buildings that were neither temples nor palaces at Shuruppak (pre-Akkadian), Abu Salabikh (Early Dynastic), and Asmar (Akkadian period).

institutions, an efficient administrative tool and a powerful means of control. A private sector did indeed exist, although its importance remains difficult to evaluate.

This period saw the development of bronze metallurgy, for the production of weapons, tools, and prestige objects. This metallurgy stimulated a growth in trade, through the Persian Gulf and the land routes across Afghanistan and Iran (Boroffka *et al.* 2002).

There was a turning point in exchanges and political developments in the whole of western Asia around 2600/2500 BCE, when interconnections were established between Mesopotamia and the Indus valley, where the Harappan culture flourished.[19] Exchange networks connected these two regions, through the land routes of Iran, and more importantly via the maritime routes passing through Oman and Dharan or Bahrain, regions respectively called Magan and Dilmun in the Sumerian texts. Along these routes, prestige goods, metals, textiles, food products, plants, and animals were transported. These networks made up a new space including, for the first time, the whole of the Persian Gulf, Sind, and the northwest of the Indian peninsula, Turkmenistan, Margiana, and Bactria.[20]

The speed of urban development in the Indus valley has often been pointed out, marked by the appearance of elaborate public architecture, the standardization of weights and measures, the creation of a form of writing (which remains undeciphered), and the growth of export-oriented production (beads and probably cotton textiles). The political power structure and the ways in which production and exchanges were organized, however, remain largely unknown.

On the Mesopotamian side, the port city of Ur benefited from the expansion of trade in the Persian Gulf, as evidenced by the wealth of the "royal" tombs in its cemetery, which yielded a profusion of lapis lazuli and carnelian artifacts from the Indus region. The presence in this cemetery of carts drawn by oxen evokes the great kurgans of the Caucasus and reveals land-based exchanges with Transcaucasia.

The networks extended as far as the Aegean Sea and the Dardanelles Straits. Tin bronze appeared at Troy II, Besiktepe, Thermi, Poliochni, and other sites from 2600/ 2500 BCE. In central Europe, tin bronze was present in Hungary *c.* 2500 BCE, coming from Troy and through the Danube valley (O'Shea 1992).[21] Whereas for these sites the study of copper or arsenical copper objects dating from earlier periods reveals that the ores employed were of Anatolian origin, the analysis of lead isotopes shows another origin for the tin bronzes. The ores originated rather from Uzbekistan, Tajikistan, the Altai, northwestern India or Afghanistan: the development of tin bronze production "coincided with the introduction of new sources of raw material, of tin and, most likely,

---

[19] Kohl (1989), however, considers that the economic developments of the Bronze Age do not represent connected phenomena. The atlas *The Times Archaeology of the World* also writes, about Mesopotamia, Egypt, and Indus, that "each civilisation must be seen as an independent growth" (Scarre 2000: 122). The same claim can be found in McClellan III and Dorn 1999: 32.

[20] Bactria was located in the region of the Middle Amu Darya valley. Margiana is the ancient name for the region of the delta of the Tedjen and Murghab rivers in Turkmenistan.

[21] On the importance of Troy as a node between various areas, see Easton *et al.* 2002: 101ff. Troy probably exported part of an extensive textile production.

also of copper" (Pernicka *et al.* 2003: 163);[22] these analyses thus shed light on the importance of the routes of Inner Asia, along which lapis lazuli and carnelian were also carried. The discovery of a cylinder seal made of ivory at Poliochni and the fact that the weights at Troy and at Poliochni follow a sexagesimal system similar to that of Mesopotamia[23] also reveal the links between the Aegean area and the Levant and Mesopotamia.[24] In the Mediterranean region, the appearance of bronze in the Aegean world – from Anatolia – occurred at the time of the rise of this region, also based on the cultivation of olive trees and grapevines. Around the middle of the third millennium, vineyards extended over the whole Mediterranean area.

The formation of this vast space initiated a new phase of political integration, which was based on kingship by divine right: by gaining the upper hand over the other Sumerian city-states, Akkad (Agade) became the first-ever known empire (2340–2200 BCE). It took direct control of the land networks that brought metals, wood, and slaves to Mesopotamia. The increasing importance of Ebla,[25] Mari, and the Elamite states may have encouraged this Akkadian momentum. Economic growth was based on the development of irrigation, bronze metallurgy, and long-distance trade. The Akkadian Empire exported mostly agricultural products and manufactured goods. For Mesopotamia, and later for the other "cores," textile exports, as we will see, were crucial to the building of regional and transregional chains of dominance. The rise of sheep herding, promoted and controlled by the state for textile production, provided a basis for the development of this activity – perhaps as early as the Urukian period (McCorriston 1997: 521, 534; Kohl 2007: 222).

[22] The mine at Mushiston, Tajikistan (east of Samarkand), contains a natural blend of copper and tin. In theory, it could be at the origin of part of the tin carried to the west; the mine at Karnab (west of Samarkand, Uzbekistan) is another potential source (Pernicka *et al.* 2003; Cierny *et al.* 2005). Evidence, however, is still lacking for the exploitation of these mines during the third millennium. The discovery of an object made of lapis lazuli at Troy (end of the third millennium) strengthens the case for a Central Asian origin of the ores that were exploited; they may have come partly via northern routes even though the routes following the Indus and the Persian Gulf were certainly the most active. Warburton (2003: 143) is obviously wrong when he claims that Anatolia was cut off from the Mesopotamian and Iranian exchange networks during the third millennium. Contacts were only temporarily interrupted, after the collapse or reconfiguring of the Uruk system.

[23] Tin bronze found at Velika Gruda, in the Adriatic, a site dated to the first half of the third millennium BCE, has been compared to pieces from Troy, Behik Tepe (near Troy), Poliochni, and Thermi (Primas 2002, 2007). The tin for these pieces may have come from Central Asia (Pernicka *et al.* 2003). The copper–gold–silver alloy found at the neighboring site of Mala Gruda may also have come from the Aegean world. Silver was exploited as early as the fourth millennium in eastern Anatolia and in Troas, then at Siphnos (Cyclades) and in Laurion (Attica) (Wagner *et al.* 1980). "The knowledge and impetus for silver production in the Aegean Sea came" from Anatolia and the Levant (Pernicka *et al.* 2003: 167). The use of tin bronze spread into Europe from the end of the third millennium, into Spain, Great Britain, and Central Europe (Primas 2002; Kristiansen and Larsson 2005: 112).

[24] An exchange network of prestige goods operated in the Creto-Cycladic area, including western Anatolia and continental Greece; for Persson (2005), this network seems to have collapsed for internal reasons before the turmoil occurring around 2200 BCE. The network extended to the western Mediterranean Sea. It is unfortunate that Persson, in his analysis, does not take into account the fact that some goods are invisible in archaeological layers; these goods, textiles, and weapons, imported from centers such as Crete, and slaves, who came from the peripheries, may have played a crucial role in the construction of the network (cf. Branigan 1970; Ekholm Friedman 2005).

[25] Ebla, however, was destroyed – probably by Mari – prior to Sargon's expansion (see Liverani 2014: 123).

Between Mesopotamia and the Indus, several regions were active in these exchanges. Oman was foremost, thanks to its copper resources. While this region probably did not form a true state, the finds of seals reflect an organized trade. In addition, from 2300 BCE, Oman produced chlorite vessels termed "*série récente*" (showing a "dot in circle" decorative motif); these are found across the entire Persian Gulf, the Indus, and as far afield as Margiana. West of Oman, an urban center on the island of Tarut, was – along with settlements on the Arab coast facing the island – the first Dilmun of the Mesopotamian texts. The city of Qala'at al-Baḥrayn (on Bahrain) then grew in importance from 2100 BCE (Crawford 1998). On the other side of the Persian Gulf, the region of Kerman may correspond to the mysterious kingdoms of Aratta or Marḥashi (also rendered as Barḥashi) mentioned in the Mesopotamian texts. A major urban site has been discovered at Konar Sandal, south of Jiroft, that yielded inscriptions revealing unknown scripts, one of them perhaps the ancestor of the Linear Elamite (Basello 2006).

South of the Indian Sea, exchange networks exporting incense extended along the Arab coasts, and probably part of the African coast, maybe even to East Africa if a pendant unearthed in a tomb near Baghdad, dated to 2500–2400 BCE, turns out to have been made of copal, a resin from the region of Zanzibar.

For the Persian Gulf, archaeology attests not only to contacts between the different countries mentioned, but also to the existence of their own common culture, and the probable settling, in Oman, Bahrain, and Mesopotamia, of communities of craftsmen and merchants from the Indus and other regions. The growth of long-distance exchanges is reflected in the existence of shared beliefs and the extension of syncretisms, as shown by the chlorite vessels of the "intercultural" style, which seem to originate mainly from the region of Konar Sandal (Jiroft), in southern Iran. Some seals also show cultural "hybridization." Pottery and body ornaments provide other evidence for the development of a common culture.

Archaeology and texts also provide crucial information about the ships used in the Persian Gulf and the Sea of India during the second half of the third millennium – these were ships with sewn planks, or reed boats, caulked using bitumen, a substance imported from Iran or Mesopotamia.

It is likely that during these early periods, the organization of long-distance trade on a regular and significant basis (shipbuilding, organizing caravans, funding, and so on) often exceeded the means of private merchants. A private sector, however, coexisted – in a quasi-symbiotic way – with the sectors of the palace and the temple. "The public institutions were the loci through which individual 'entrepreneurs' operated within the temple and palace hierarchies" (Hudson 2004c: 104). Unlike what has often been claimed, during the third and second millennia, the state probably never completely controlled the exchange networks, and long-distance trade was not based solely on prestige goods,[26] even though the overall picture, for the third millennium at least, is that of administered economies, with the development of writing permitting a better organization of production and exchanges, "forward planning and economic cost

---

[26] Ray 2003: 5, 82; Silver 1995. Possehl (2002a: 218) seems to underestimate the importance in trade of basic commodities such as agricultural or raw textile products (wool from Mesopotamia, cotton from the Indus), wood, and dried fish.

rationalization" (Hudson 2004a: 9). The appearance of interest on debts and commercial loans – silver playing a major role here – may have originated in the public institutions (temple and palace) (Hudson 2002), but the private sector was certainly involved in practices that can be observed early on: documents reveal the existence of loans with interest at Girsu as early as the Pre-Sargonic period. Contradicting Hudson, Van de Mieroop (2002) instead places the origin of the loan within the sphere of production. It is noteworthy that "the ancient world provides scant empirical evidence of directly productive loans" (Hudson 2002: 18). Some authors wrongly speak of a "market economy" during the third millennium, although it did not dominate the economic picture (Powell 1977); it would be more accurate to speak of "society with markets" (see below). There was, at least, coexistence of a state sphere and a private sector, the latter partly emerging from within the royal sector (Hudson 1996).

The networks of Inner Asia seem suddenly to have disintegrated or been restructured from 2300 to 2200 BCE, a period of turmoil in Mesopotamia that can be correlated with movements of Indo-European populations from the Balkans to Anatolia, and the possible arrival of Indo-Europeans in the Bactria–Margiana Complex (Bactrian–Margian Archaeological Complex [BMAC]) around 2100 BCE in Central Asia, and later around 2000 BCE in the Highlands, dominating the region of the Indus culture. Domesticated in the steppes during the fourth millennium, the horse was introduced in western Asia at this time. We do not know to what extent these new populations contributed to the destruction of the cities of Poliochni and Troy II observed c. 2300 BCE.[27] The Akkadian Empire disappeared around 2200 BCE, a demise precipitated by Guti invasions out of northern Mesopotamia.

These population movements seem to be linked to a sudden major climatic change, with significantly lower temperatures around 2200 BCE. These climatic conditions lasted – with some oscillations – until c. 1900, and were accompanied by aridization processes that affected northern Mesopotamia, Syria, southern Europe, Iran, and part of the Central Asian steppes around 2200 BCE (Courty et al. 1995; Cullen et al. 2000; deMenocal 2001).[28] Cities in Turkmenistan appear to have declined during this period. Aridization led to different processes of adaptation, with growing mobility of herders in the steppes, and intensification of irrigated agriculture in the oases of Margiana–Bactria and perhaps in Xinjiang (Sin-Kiang) (Hiebert 2000).[29] The rise

---

[27] Tarsus, in Cilicia, was also burnt in this period, while southeastern Anatolia was occupied by populations coming from the east (Joukowsky 1996: 172). Double-spiral-headed pins appeared at Troy around 2300 BCE; we find these pins later in the BMAC culture (this motif, connected to women and maternity, spread to various regions while possibly retaining the same meaning).

[28] deMenocal (2001: 669) connects the collapse of the Akkadian Empire to the growing aridization observed in Mesopotamia and the gulf of Oman around 2100 BCE.

[29] Hiebert (2000) notes a pronounced aridification around 2200 in the steppes between the Aral Sea and the north of the Crimea, this arid phase continuing until c. 1800 (a slower and less pronounced process of aridification may have begun in fact as early as 2500 BCE). Based on dendrochronology from Irish oaks (Baillie 1995), M. Mitchiner (2004: 77) has placed the climatic deterioration as early as 2350 BCE. He stresses that it seems to have been related to an aridification of the steppes between Ukraine and Kazakhstan, and to lower Nile flood levels. Mitchiner evokes as possible causes increased volcanism and/or the impact of a comet, but those events had relatively short-term effects. Indeed, in 2354 BCE, the explosion of the Hekla volcano (Iceland) seems to have had a global impact (Burroughs 2001). For long-term effects, it is more relevant to consider the phases of solar activity and the cycles of the ENSO events.

of the Bactria–Margiana complex, whose aristocracy was perhaps Proto-Aryan, was also founded in crafts and in partial military control of the trade roads. The movements of various groups would, slightly later, be facilitated by the development of the war chariot, borrowed from the Arkaim-Sintashta culture of the Urals. The spread of this chariot was spectacular during the early second millennium in the Eurasian steppes, western Asia, and western Europe. Its extended use went hand in hand with that of new types of weapons and the appearance of warrior aristocracies (Kristiansen 2007: 156). Aridification also affected the Arab peninsula, leading to population movements toward Bahrain during the last centuries of the third millennium, and toward Mesopotamia (Glassner 2002b: 358; Parker *et al.* 2006). Indeed, the changes were global, since they encompassed all of the Indian Ocean (Egypt was indirectly affected),[30] as well as China. Staubwasser and Weiss (2006) bring to light an arid phase that lasted 300 years, from around 2200 to 1900,[31] and Wang *et al.* (2005) also identify a weakening of the Asian summer monsoon between 2400 and 1900 BCE, correlated with low solar activity.

The reign of the Third Dynasty of Ur (2112–2004 BCE) (MC), however, marked a Sumerian revival, which may have been favored by a temporary improvement in climatic conditions as well as a more active maritime trade in the Persian Gulf. A centralized administration partly controlled production and exchanges. The state formed a standing army and a substantial bureaucracy. A private sector, however, coexisted with the state sector. The island of Bahrain (Dilmun) benefited from the trade in the Persian Gulf, and copper extraction remained active in Oman (Magan). Moreover, victorious campaigns in Iran provided the Ur Empire with significant quantities of metals.

The end of the third millennium, however, saw the empire in decline, with the conjunction of various factors such as excessive bureaucracy, decreased agricultural production due to a new phase of aridization and soil salinization, and population movements. An Iranian coalition finally destroyed the city of Ur. The whole of western

---

It is true, however, that unrest in Egypt began under Pepi II's reign (*c.* 2336–2242 BCE). Data collected by Burroughs clearly indicate (though the author claims otherwise) that the climatic changes did not affect western Asia and Egypt alone; around 2200 BCE, China, America, and Nigeria were equally affected (2001: 251, 253) (see below). Research done by Q.-B. Zhang and R. Hebda (2005) based on dendrochronology (Vancouver region) shows a period of lower precipitation in this region between 2200 and the beginning of the nineteenth century BCE. Indeed, the climate change was global.

[30] According to Butzer (1995: 136), Egypt suffered from low Nile flooding between 2200 and 2000 BCE. The low level of Lake Turkana, in East Africa, between 2250 and 2200 BCE confirms Butzer's proposition. Low Nile flooding corresponds with weak monsoons in South Asia (see below). The analysis of ice cores on Kilimanjaro reveals an abrupt climatic change around 2200–2100 (Thompson *et al.* 2002). For the Indus, see Staubwasser *et al.* 2003, Staubwassser and Weiss 2006. In southwestern Madagascar, one notes an arid phase around 2000 BCE (Burney *et al.* 2004: 31).

[31] Staubwasser and Weiss 2006: 380. The variability of precipitation in the eastern Mediterranean Sea appears to be linked in part to the North Atlantic Oscillation (NAO) index. The Caucasus and southern Russia (Khomutova *et al.* 2007) were affected as well as central and southern China. This global climatic change, observed from the twenty-second century BCE, affected a zone ranging from the tropics to the median latitudes; higher latitudes do not seem to have been affected in the same way (Staubwasser and Weiss 2006: 383). Curiously, Bolikhovskaya *et al.* (2004: 215) consider the period 4100–3915 BP as a mild and arid phase in the steppes to the northeast of the Black Sea, whereas lower temperatures are noticeable everywhere during this period.

Asia appears to have been in decline while, farther east, the expansion of the BMAC led to a restructuring of trade networks.

From the end of the fourth to the end of the third millennium, Egypt developed to some extent on its own, following a path different from that of the Mesopotamian "core." Benefiting from the agricultural wealth of the valley of the Nile that flows across the country, and having fewer trade routes with countries abroad, the situation of Egypt, as emphasized, probably favored the emergence of a centralized state, which controlled long-distance trade and production, the latter being stimulated by taxes and demand from the state. Cities formed around administrative and cultural functions that ensured some redistribution of wealth: no city-states ever developed in this context. The importance of the control of production and exchanges by the state, however, is still debated (cf. Warburton 2003). There is little doubt that farmers were owners of their land; texts give evidence of land purchase in the middle and at the end of the third millennium. Texts also show the existence of private trade. Prices were assessed using a monetary standard (copper, gold or silver of a certain weight).

The exchanges mainly operated on a north–south axis, but Egypt enjoyed a privileged position between two seas, the Mediterranean and the Red Sea. Indirect contacts existed with Mesopotamia, through the Levant (the port of Byblos) and the routes linking the latter region and the Nile delta. In addition, land routes (through Nubia and its gold mines) and maritime routes led to Sudan, Arabia, the Horn of Africa, and the legendary land of Punt, the end point of various expeditions by land and sea, the latter benefiting from advances in the rigging of ships during the third millennium. But the role of the Red Sea remained limited: in contrast to the Persian Gulf, this sea became an area of major maritime activity only later, because there was only one core in this region, Egypt, whereas the exchanges in the Persian Gulf had been favored by the existence of two cores, in the Indus valley and Mesopotamia (the importance of Iran should also be taken into account). In addition, Egypt's trade was often carried on through African intermediaries such as Nubia.

Even if Egypt appears to have had weak links with the Persian Gulf, it is striking that the apogee of the Old Kingdom, under the Fourth Dynasty that built the great pyramids, occurred at a time when a globalized space was forming between Mesopotamia and the Indus region. Another parallel is that, soon after the collapse of the Akkadian Empire, Egypt experienced over a century of anarchy, marked by famines ("First Intermediary Period," 2180–2030 BCE), resulting from low Nile flood levels, a phenomenon linked to the global climatic changes from 2200 to 2000 (see above). The weakening of exchanges with western Asia probably accentuated the trend toward political disintegration in Egypt. The entry of populations from Palestine into the Nile delta finally saw the collapse of the Old Kingdom.

In contrast with this global recession at the end of the third millennium, the beginning of the second millennium was a crucial period of transformation and expansion. Unified once again during the Middle Kingdom (c. 2030–1730), Egypt set up links with the exchange networks of the eastern Mediterranean Sea, now developing strongly. An urban civilization appeared in Crete (First Palatial Period), which invented a system of writing.[32] Minoan networks extended into the Aegean Sea, Greece, the Adriatic, and possibly as far as the Black Sea. The pharaohs of the Twelfth Dynasty practiced a policy of expansion into Palestine and Syria, as well as Nubia. Further south, the Nubian kingdom of Kush acted as an intermediary with the African interior. The maritime expeditions of Egypt to the land of Punt (the Horn of Africa, and the coasts of Yemen) went along with growing exchanges in the Red Sea.

In western Asia, weaker political powers after the collapse of the Ur III Empire favored the emergence – on seemingly new terms – of the private sector, which was entrusted with administrative tasks, and the management of agricultural estates and craft workshops; this private sector was able to develop long-distance exchanges, in the Persian Gulf as well as Anatolia. In this region, cities were flourishing during the late third millennium and early second millennium; they may have been the center of macro-states and not proper city-states.[33] Assyrian trading outposts were dotted around Cappadocia. The demand of the Assyrian merchants for tin from Afghanistan or the Samarkand region gave rise to contacts between the BMAC and north Mesopotamia through the roads of northern Iran, with networks expanding toward the Mediterranean.

Farther afield, the invasions at the end of the third millennium opened up contacts between the eastern Mediterranean and Central Europe as of 2000 BCE, on routes that extended as far as Scandinavia and Great Britain (Kristiansen and Larsson 2005), in parallel with the rise of trade in tin, bronze, and amber. Tombs of an elite involved in long-distance contacts have been discovered in southern England, in what has been called the "Wessex culture"; they contain amber artifacts from the Baltic Sea and gold objects from either Armorica or other regions of the continent; this elite probably controlled the tin exports. Elites benefiting from the bronze trade appeared at the same time in Germany and Poland, as shown by tombs found at Leubingen, Helmsdorf, and Łęki Małe.

In the steppes of Central Asia, the increasing mobility of herder–farmers of the Andronovo complexes reflects the development of both metallurgical activities and exchange networks, which extended to the Tarim and East Asia.

At the same time, the period from the twentieth to the eighteenth century BCE saw an "explosive dispersion" of the Bactria–Margiana Complex (Hiebert 1994), and the collapse of the Mesopotamia–Persian Gulf–Iran–Indus space with the abandonment of

---

[32] Several types of writing have been discovered, first the Cretan hieroglyphic and the proto-linear A, then the linear A, presumed to be syllabic and ideographic, in which some authors have seen Luwian influences (Anatolia). These scripts remain undeciphered. Moreover, the Phaistos Disc (c. 1700 BCE) exhibits another undeciphered "script." The Minoan economic organization seems to have been centered on the palace, which included warehouses and workshops. There is not much evidence for the militarization of the "state," which was engaged in commercial activities. Crete had contact with Ugarit, Mari, and the first Babylonian dynasty, as well as with the Cyclades and Anatolia. J. Persson (2005) defends the idea of a proto-state rather than a centralized state for this period of the first palaces. For this author, the isolation of Central Crete at the end of the third millennium led to the creation of competing chiefdoms that erected stone buildings; those chiefdoms would mutate under the influence of contacts with western Asia at the beginning of the second millennium. In addition, Bernal (1991) has proposed influences from Egypt.

[33] In fact, "we are virtually ignorant of the political system" of this region during this period (Hansen 2000a: 23).

Indus cities such as Mohenjo-daro around 1900 BCE and a general decline of urban life in Iran. The reasons for this urban collapse in the Indus valley are still debated: aridization of the climate,[34] Indo-European intrusions, ecological imbalances, tectonic movements, and a falling-off in long-distance trade probably had combined effects. It is obvious that during the period *c.* 2000 BCE many regions were affected by a phase of weak monsoons in the Indian Ocean, which led to increasing aridity. Climatic changes also affected the North Atlantic at that time.[35] Around 1800 BCE, contacts between Mesopotamia and the Indus had all but disappeared. Some trade, however, remained on the coasts of Gujarat, and cultivated plants were transported from Africa to India during the first half of the second millennium BCE, probably via southern Arabia. During the key period from the twentieth to the eighteenth century, while commerce flourished in the western gulf during the Isin-Larsa period (with Bahrain playing a significant role), we observe a gradual shift of the main Mesopotamian centers toward the north. The political integration led by Hammurabi (1792–1750) (MC) from Babylon – marked, as in Assyria in the earlier period, by a symbiosis between the state sphere and a rising private sector – is indicative of the changes taking place; however, it linked the spheres of the Mediterranean and the Persian Gulf for a brief period only.

During the eighteenth century BCE, invasions and economic crises affected various regions. Upheavals in Anatolia led to a breakup of relations between Assyria and Cappadocia. Kassites coming from Zagros entered Mesopotamia *c.* 1740 BCE, soon accompanied by Proto-Indian elements. Groups that came from the northeast of the Balkans introduced the spoked wheel chariot into Greece (it was present in the seventeenth century BCE at the time of Grave Circle A at Mycenae, but various sources contributed to this import).[36] The Greek myth of a sun god in a chariot drawn by horses or swans has obvious Nordic origins (Kuzmina 2007: 123). The Middle Kingdom of Egypt disintegrated against a background of social unrest and foreign infiltrations. From 1780 BCE onward, the Hyksos from Canaan entered Lower Egypt and controlled the Nile delta, while in the south, the state of Kush gained the ascendancy. The period of Hyksos domination during the "Second Intermediary Period" of Egypt, however, was not the time of chaos the Egyptian sources depict. It favored the dissemination of innovations (the introduction of horses, the use of the chariot, the rise of bronze metallurgy, and so forth),[37] and transcultural exchanges fostered the major invention of alphabetic writing.

[34] Burroughs (2001: 255) argues that the collapse of the Indus civilization did not coincide with a phase of aridification, but, as already stressed, a large number of sources show lower temperatures from 2200/2100, and processes of aridification both in Mesopotamia and in India, linked for the eastern part of the Persian Gulf and for the Indian Ocean to a weakening of the monsoon system and a decline in solar activity. The Indus civilization must have been weakened by the climatic changes from 2200/2100 onward. Cf. Staubwasser *et al.* 2003, Gupta *et al.* 2005.

[35] Cf. H. M. Cullen *et al.* 2000, for western Asia; L. G. Thompson *et al.* 2002, for East Africa, C.-B. An *et al.* 2005, for northern China; and S. Nadis 2001, for the North Atlantic.

[36] K. Kristiansen (2007: 157) shows the coexistence of three types of cheekpieces in Eurasia, reflecting vast spheres of interaction. These three types are present in the Mycenaean world. Various authors have suggested that the Mycenaean aristocracy originated from the steppes, but this idea is still subject to debate.

[37] For M. Liverani, however, Hyksos' infiltrations "happened well before the arrival of these new techniques" (2014: 237).

In the Mediterranean, the Cretan palaces were destroyed around 1700 BCE, in circumstances that are unclear.[38] The decrease in trade in the Persian Gulf during the late eighteenth and seventeenth centuries BCE went along with transformations in the networks, which in the period 1600–1400 appear to have been organized mainly along an arc spanning Egypt–Levant–northern Mesopotamia–Anatolia–Greece and the Aegean area.

Major changes also occurred in Europe, with new interactions between the continent and the Mediterranean world. During the seventeenth and sixteenth centuries BCE, the time of Grave Circles A and B at Mycenae, contacts grew between the eastern Mediterranean and the Carpathian mountains, a region that exported gold, copper, and perhaps human beings (mercenaries and slaves), and with the Russian steppes, which provided horses. These contacts accompanied a development of Central Europe marked by the rise of metallurgical activities and the building of fortified settlements (Barca, Spissky Stvrtok, Nitriansky Hradok, in the region of the Carpathian mountains) (Otomani culture) as early as the eighteenth century, but more so during the seventeenth and sixteenth centuries BCE (Kristiansen and Larsson 2005: 162). Disc-shaped cheek-pieces bearing ornaments of Mycenaean type are found from the Danube valley to Kazakhstan (Kuzmina 2007: 122). The exchange networks reached the Baltic Sea, a region that traded amber and furs. The Baltic and eastern Europe were connected to a road linking Mongolia, the Transbaikal region, and Europe; that road explains the diffusion of objects related to the Seima-Turbino complex (c. 1800–1500 BCE), which expanded from a region in Sayan-Altai (Chernykh 1992; Pydyn 2000: 229; Koryakova and Epimakhov 2007: 108). For Kuzmina (2007: 181), however, the spread of metallurgy and art of the Seima complex was first associated with Fedorovo groups from eastern Kazakhstan and Semirech'e: the Altai represents a secondary center of development. Tin may have come either from the Altai or from central Kazakhstan (Hanks 2014: 1950). The expansion of the Seima-Turbino phenomenon, marked by new technology (the use of thin-sided molds and the lost-wax technique) could be the result either of the establishment of trade networks, or the migration of warrior metallurgists, or both. In Moldavia, the treasure of Borodino shows bronze or jade axes (using jade from the Altai), which traveled via this northern route that Chernykh called the "great tin road." Moreover, the fortified site of Monkodonja, in Istria, in the Adriatic, could be viewed as evidence of a Creto-Aegean expansion to the west (Mycenaean pottery has been

---

[38] Internal fighting or invasions have been suggested. Moreover, the explosion of the volcano of Thera (Santorini) occurred around 1628 or 1645 BCE (dendrochronology on Irish and Anatolian trees and the analysis of ice cores in Greenland show a phase of cooling in this period; cf. M. Bietak 2003: 23) (a dating to around 1420 BCE, however, had been put forward previously; see, for example D. G. Sullivan 1988, quoted by M. S. Joukowsky 1996: 186). For W. J. Burroughs (2001), an explosion occurred in 1627 BCE, whose effects must have been felt worldwide (lower temperatures …), but it is not certain that this was due to the Santorini volcano. W. Friedrich et al. (2006: 548) for their part have placed the Santorini explosion between 1627 and 1600 BCE. C. U. Hammer et al. (2003) and H. J. Bruins and J. van der Plicht (2003) favor a date c. 1645 BCE. For M. Bietak (2003: 30), curiously, the dating of the eruption of the Santorini volcano in the seventeenth century BCE does not match archaeological data, which would point to the beginning of the Eighteenth Dynasty and not to the Hyksos period; for him, resolving the conundrum by raising the dates of the Eighteenth [Egyptian] Dynasty, however, is "virtually inconceivable, taking into consideration the Assyrian chronology." Bietak's interpretation of the archaeological documents has been refuted by S. W. Manning and C. B. Ramsey 2003: 112–113 n. 7.

discovered at this site). The greater availability of bronze was accompanied by an increased production of various weapons. Everywhere in Europe, a warrior elite was emerging.

These transformations during the intermediary period of the eighteenth century shed light on the configurations of the Late Bronze Age, marked by the new importance of the eastern Mediterranean and northwestern Asia.

During the seventeenth century BCE, the center of gravity of western Asia shifted toward the north, with the relative decline of southern Mesopotamia and the Persian Gulf, despite the creation of a Kassite Empire with Babylon as its capital. A new sphere of interaction developed, centered on the eastern Mediterranean. By the sixteenth century BCE, both trade and military conflicts increased, between the Egyptian New Kingdom, the Hittite Empire (Anatolia), the states of Mitanni (Upper Euphrates),[39] and Assyria (on the Upper Tigris).[40] This Late Bronze Age space appears to have had links to African, Arab, European, and Asian peripheries. From 1600 BCE, a phase of global warming was accompanied in the eastern Mediterranean by increased precipitation that favored agricultural progress in this region. Crete experienced the flourishing of the "second palatial civilization," from c. 1700 to 1450, marked by trading relations with the Levant, Anatolia, the Mycenaean world, and Egypt. In the north, a Mycenaean civilization flourished, which gave birth to a new writing system, known as Linear B, transcribing Greek. During the fifteenth century, the Mycenaeans took possession of the Minoan cities[41] and, in search of new sources of metals, extended their networks in the western Mediterranean (Italy, Sicily, Sardinia, the eastern coast of the Iberian peninsula). This space was connected to the Atlantic coasts (the exploitation of tin in Cornwall, begun in the early second millennium BCE, grew during this period), to Central Europe, whence tin probably arrived from the Erzgebirge (Germany), and to northern Europe.[42]

Leading a military and trade expansion, Egypt appears to have had close links to the spheres of western Asia and the eastern Mediterranean, as well as the African and Arab peripheries (Nubia and Punt), through which the exchange networks extended toward India. The Egyptian revival was accompanied by social transformations, with the clergy growing in importance, a transformation of the relationship to the divine world (especially under Akhenaton), and the private sector taking on a greater role in craft and commerce.

In all the great centers of the Late Bronze Age space, crafts benefited from advances in metallurgy – with the appearance of iron – and the glass industry, and there was a marked growth in the manufacture of products destined for export. Multiple

---

[39] Called Hanigalbat in Assyrian.

[40] The relative gap in our knowledge for the period 1650–1550 BCE corresponds to a phase of (new) state formation (Liverani 2014: 271).

[41] The date traditionally proposed is c. 1450 BCE, but this is still debated (see below).

[42] Contacts led to the transfer of objects, people, and ideas. Some stylistic or symbolic parallels proposed by K. Kristiansen and T. B. Larsson (2005) between the Minoan or Mycenaean civilizations and northern Europe for objects, rock paintings, or engravings have been questioned by other authors (e.g. Harding 2006). Folding stools and some figurines (for example, that of Schernen, in Poland), however, clearly reflect eastern-Mediterranean influences or represent imports.

exchanges, in which Cyprus and the Levant played the role of hubs, fostered the development of an "intercultural style" in production. These exchanges involved merchants operating for the state – sometimes also as diplomats – or working on their own: the period of the Late Bronze Age represents an era of "internationalism," as clearly shown by the tablets of El-Amarna sent to the pharaohs Amenhotep III and Akhenaton. Political integration was accompanied by a more efficient organization of the armies, which were making use of horses and chariots.

The interregional equilibrium between the main kingdoms changed during the fourteenth century BCE, when Assyria emerged as a dominant power, wiping out the Mitanni Empire and seizing Babylon in 1234. Moreover, the Egyptian expansion into Palestine and Syria following Thutmose III (c. 1479–1425 BCE) led to a major confrontation with the Hittites at Qadesh (Syria) in 1274.

From the thirteenth to the twelfth century, new climatic change played a crucial role in the upheavals affecting the Balkans, western Asia, and Egypt at this time.[43] The Hittite state and the Mycenaean centers were destroyed by population movements that swept over western Asia and the eastern Mediterranean region around 1200 BCE, the "Dorian" invasions in Greece, "Phrygian" invasions in Anatolia, as well as migrations/invasions of the "Sea Peoples" in the Levant and in Egypt. These movements combined with problems internal to both the states and the interconnected area of the Late Bronze Age, and led to the collapse of that entire area. This system of competing imperialist states no doubt formed a fragile edifice, further destabilized by the rise of "interstitial" trade that was taking place beyond the control of those states (Sherratt 2003). There began a long phase of recession, which affected most of the regions until c. 1000 BCE. The collapse of the palatial structures led to the disappearance of writing in Greece. Abrupt changes also occurred in the Eurasian steppes, with the adoption of the practice of horseback riding. Indo-European speakers from Central Asia entered Iran and Pakistan. At this time, India no longer seems to have been connected to western Asia, even though some ports probably remained active on the west coast of India.

In the four millennia during which we have followed the development of states and world-economies in western Asia, East Asia experienced its own trajectory, even though – very early on – contacts allowed the transmission of techniques and products between the Occident and the Orient. China represents, as mentioned, another primary center for the domestication of plants and animals, where sedentary communities organized their territory. The development of rice culture in the Yangtze basin from the sixth millennium BCE provided the basis for a demographic expansion that fueled movements of population toward Southeast Asia. Proto-Austronesian speakers settled in Taiwan as early as the end of the fourth millennium BCE. They reached the Philippines during the third millennium, and eastern (then western) Indonesia during

---

[43] Again, dendrochronology on Irish oaks shows a phase of cooling that was also noted, for a slightly later period, in the Sierra Nevada c. 1130 BCE (Mitchiner 2004: 82). For China, in the central plains, at the beginning of the period of the Western Zhou, the climate became drier and cooler than before. These changes were aggravated by a major volcanic eruption in 1159 BCE (Burroughs 2001), perhaps of the Hekla volcano (Iceland). For K. Kristiansen (1998: 384, 410), a drier climate during the thirteenth century BCE in central Europe may have favored agriculture; conversely, the process of aridification affected the Mediterranean Sea world and part of the steppes.

the second millennium (Bellwood 2005a). Moreover, Proto-Austroasiatic speakers migrated toward continental Southeast Asia during the third millennium BCE, bringing cereal cultivation into this region. They were apparently present in part of western Indonesia before the Austronesians, and entered India during the early second millennium BCE (Proto-Munda) (Blench 2010b; some authors have put their arrival at an earlier date, but this has not been confirmed by the most recent data).

The Yellow River represented another early center of agricultural development, with the domestication of several millets. Very early on, one notes interactions between the Yangtze and the Yellow River valleys, with the presence of rice attested in the latter region during the fifth millennium, and the cultivation of *Setaria italica* millet in the Yangtze valley (Lu 2005; Nasu *et al.* 2007; Fuller *et al.* 2007).

The Yangshao culture, which expanded from the middle valley of the Yellow River during the fourth millennium, reveals an incipient increase in social complexity, which can be more clearly observed during the third millennium. The rise of large agricultural communities and the progress of exchange networks led to the formation of hierarchical societies both in the Yellow River basin (Late Dawenkou culture, *c.* 2800–2500, and later the Longshan culture, *c.* 2500–1900 BCE) and the Yangtze River valley (Liangzhu culture in the delta, 3300–2200 BCE, Qujialing and Quinglongquan cultures in the Middle valley, 3000–2000 BCE). The elites inhabited segregated palatial complexes in large settlements such as Liangchengzhen in eastern Shandong, Taosi in South Shaanxi, and Wangchenggang and Guchengzhai in Henan. In the coastal area of southeastern Shandong, the site of Yaowangcheng covered 367 ha, with a four-level settlement hierarchy (Liu and Chen 2012: 217). The elites controlled specialized handicrafts such as ceramics and jade. The wide geographical distribution of jade artifacts of particular shapes reveals long-distance exchanges and shared beliefs. The abundance of weapons recovered bears witness to the climate of violence that went along with the construction of these first important political entities. Bronze seems to have been present in the main centers of the Late Longshan culture.

The process of urbanization developed in a relatively autonomous way, but external influences played a decisive role in the shift from the Neolithic to the Bronze Age in the third millennium; they came via the oasis routes that led to Bactria and the Indus valley, and via routes farther north. Bronze metallurgy first appeared in the Qijia culture (Qinghai, Gansu) (2200–1600 BCE), which benefited from inputs from both the BMAC and the steppes cultures. Contacts allowed the introduction of barley and wheat into China, as early as the first half of the third millennium. Movement also occurred in the other direction from the Yellow River, for the acquisition of jade and metallic objects.

Various Chinese Neolithic cultures disappeared during the early second millennium, following the occurrence of a phase of marked aridity at that time (An *et al.* 2005), and the political entities centered on Taosi and Guchengzhai collapsed.

During the early second millennium, in the Yellow River valley, new elites adopted and monopolized the use of bronze, not only for the manufacture of weapons and tools, but also for the production of ritual vessels used for ancestor worship. An important kingdom was in place from 1800 BCE in the Middle Yellow River basin (Erlitou archaeological phase). Erlitou developed long-distance exchanges and installed "colonies" as far as the area south of the Yangtze valley, which manifested a desire to control the access routes to natural resources (salt, copper, tin . . .). Travelers probably followed the routes of the Central Asian oases. The communities of Xinjiang and Gansu played the role of interface for contacts between east and west. Gansu and northern China also exhibit influences from the transcultural Seima-Turbino phenomenon (Siberia) (*c.* 1900/1800–1500 BCE?),[44] with forms of weapons and tools that would later be found in Southeast Asia (Higham 1996a).

The arrival of new elites signified the demise of Erlitou. The city of Yanshi emerged near Erlitou, and later a bigger state developed, with the city of Zhenzhou as its center, from 1600 BCE. Probably ruled by the historic Shang dynasty (phase Erligang), this state shows the first signs of a writing system, invented independently from western Asia. The Erligang culture expressed more pronounced expansionist tendencies than those of the Erlitou state, along with the same desire to control resources and trade routes. First the capital, then the regional centers held a monopoly on the production of bronze vessels associated with the royal ancestor cult. The assemblages that have been found in the tombs reveal contacts with southern regions (Lingnan), whence came pearls, turtle shells, and cowrie shells, which would be used as currency in the Late Shang phase.

The end of the fifteenth century BCE was a period of transformation and restructuring marked by the abandonment of sites in the west and the shift of the Shang capital to Huanbei (Anyang), then to Yinxu (Anyang). The urbanization of China increased at this time, as well as its social complexity.[45] Silk weaving – known as early as the fourth millennium BCE – developed, alongside an expansion in trade. Exchanges grew, especially with Sichuan, the Yangtze valley, and regions further south. In addition, the rise of regional cultures at Wucheng (Jiangxi) and Sanxingdui (Sichuan) points to local development, and to increasing long-distance trade toward Southeast Asia and South Asia; this may explain the transfer of copperworking and bronzeworking to Lingnan, as well as to the basins of the Mekong, the Red River, the Chao Phraya, and Upper Burma, along age-old roads.

Contacts continued with Inner Asia via the oases routes and the northern steppes, whence, during the thirteenth century BCE, jade arrived from Khotan and also horse-drawn chariots, which were placed in the royal tombs of Anyang. Iranian speakers may have arrived in Xinjiang. Exchanges transformed the cultures that were in contact with the Yellow River basin. A military elite emerged in the "Northern Complex," north of China (Di Cosmo 2002). The rise of nomadic populations and a deterioration in climate led at last to a disaggregation of the Shang state at the end of the second millennium BCE, and the Zhou dynasty, at the head of a state previously vassal to the Shang, in Shaanxi, came to prominence in 1027 BCE.

For the Ancient World, available data show the existence of two large areas (western Asia–Egypt–the Mediterranean, and East Asia), with only weak connections during the second millennium. A comparison of the evolution of the number and size of towns allows us to assess the interactions between regions and the local dynamics. Urban development followed general demographic trends and the economic expansion (or decline) of regions structured by geographical and human factors, and of the various

[44] Datings "suggest that the Seima-Turbino sites lie within the 22nd to 17th century BC range (Chernykh 2009)" (Higham *et al.* 2011).

[45] The first sizeable city identified by T. Chandler (1987) is Ao, a Shang capital in the Yellow River valley, *c.* 1360 BCE, but other cities have been discovered since the publication of that book.

Map In.1   Wind systems in the Indian Ocean: January and July

January

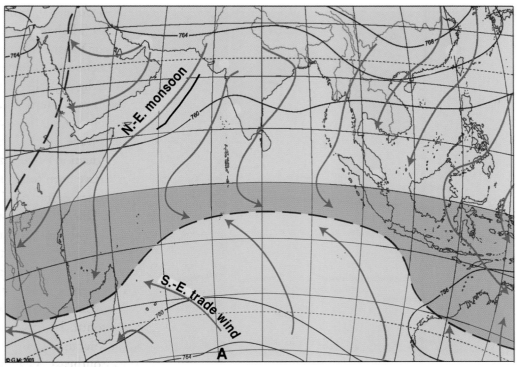

A D   high and low pressure centers

July

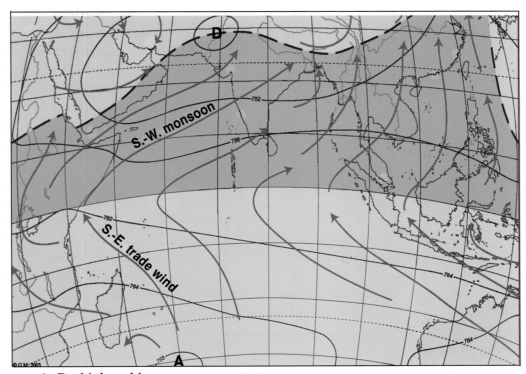

A D   high and low pressure centers

Map In.2   Surface currents in the Indian Ocean: February–March
and August–September

February–March

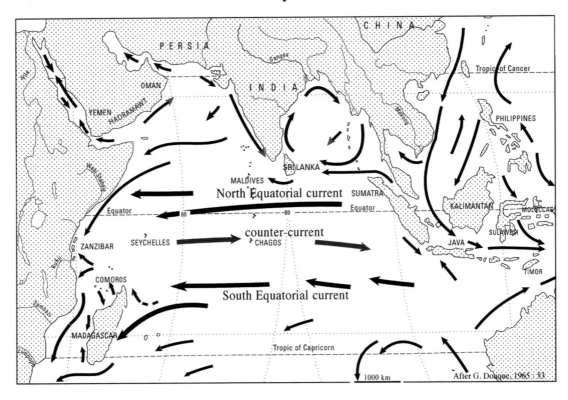

August–September

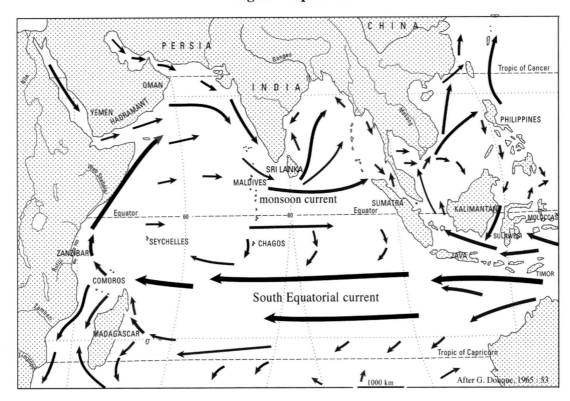

Map 1.1   Western Asia and Egypt 4000–3500 BCE

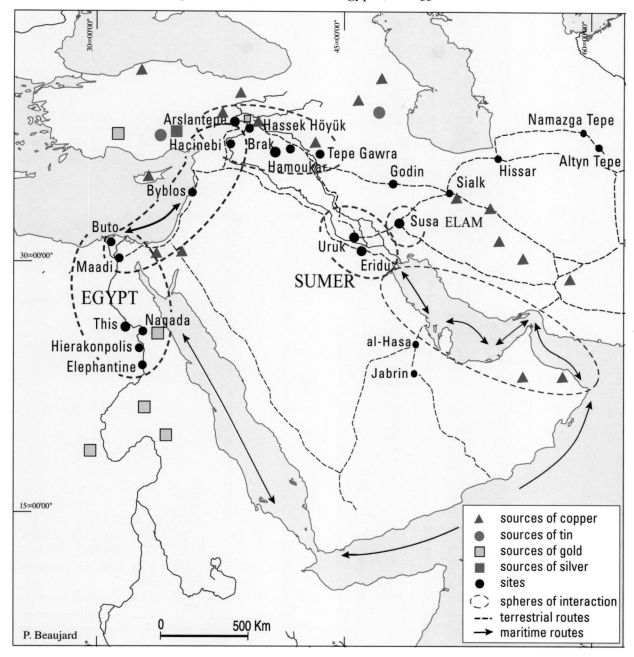

sources of copper
sources of tin
sources of gold
sources of silver
sites
spheres of interaction
terrestrial routes
maritime routes

P. Beaujard

0   500 Km

Map I.2 Western Asia and Egypt 3500–3000 BCE

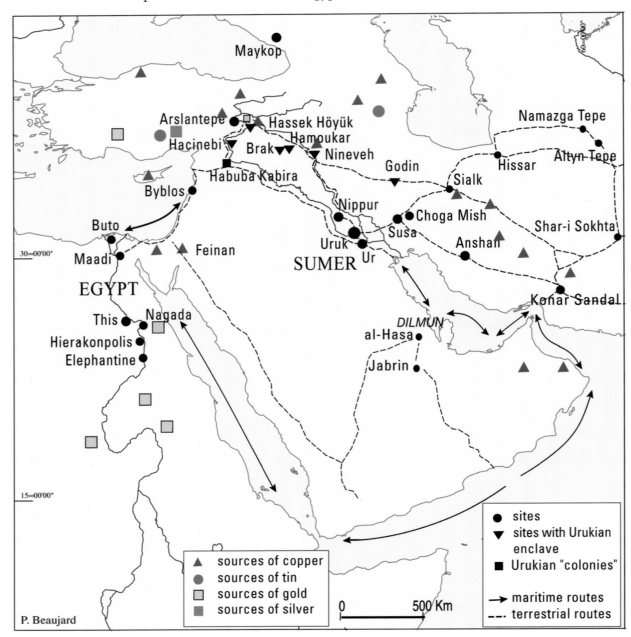

Maykop

Arslantepe
Hacinebi
Hassek Höyük
Hamoukar
Brak
Nineveh
Habuba Kabira
Byblos
Buto
Maadi
Feinan
30∞00'00"
EGYPT
Godin
Sialk
Hissar
Namazga Tepe
Altyn Tepe
Nippur
Choga Mish
Shar-i Sokhta
Uruk
Susa
Anshan
Ur
SUMER
This
Nagada
Hierakonpolis
Elephantine
DILMUN
al-Hasa
Jabrin
Konar Sandal
15∞00'00"

P. Beaujard

▲ sources of copper
● sources of tin
▢ sources of gold
▩ sources of silver

● sites
▼ sites with Urukian enclave
■ Urukian "colonies"

→ maritime routes
-- terrestrial routes

0   500 Km

Map 1.3 Western Eurasia and Africa during the third millennium BCE

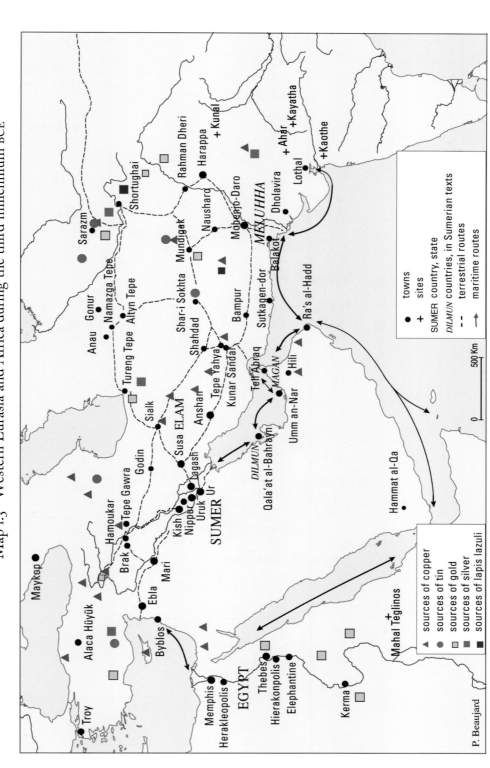

P. Beaujard

Map 1.4 Artifacts showing contacts between Egypt and Mesopotamia during the fourth millennium BCE

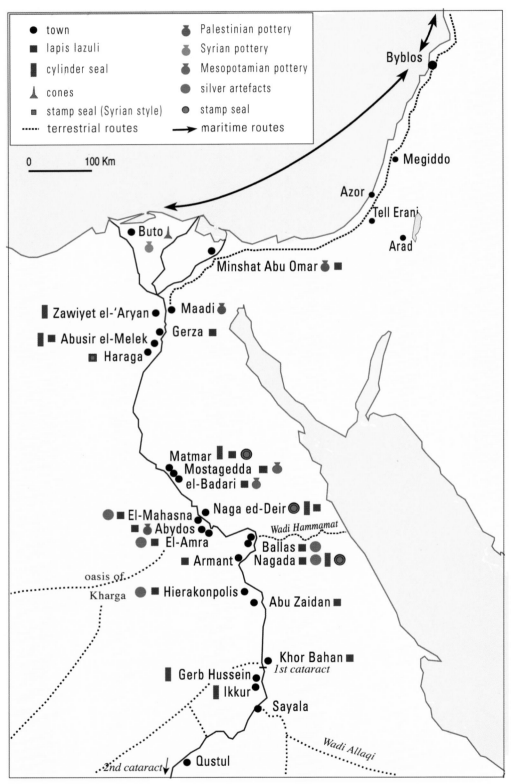

P. Beaujard, partly after P. R. S. Moorey 1995: 192

Map I.5   Egypt during the third and second millennia BCE

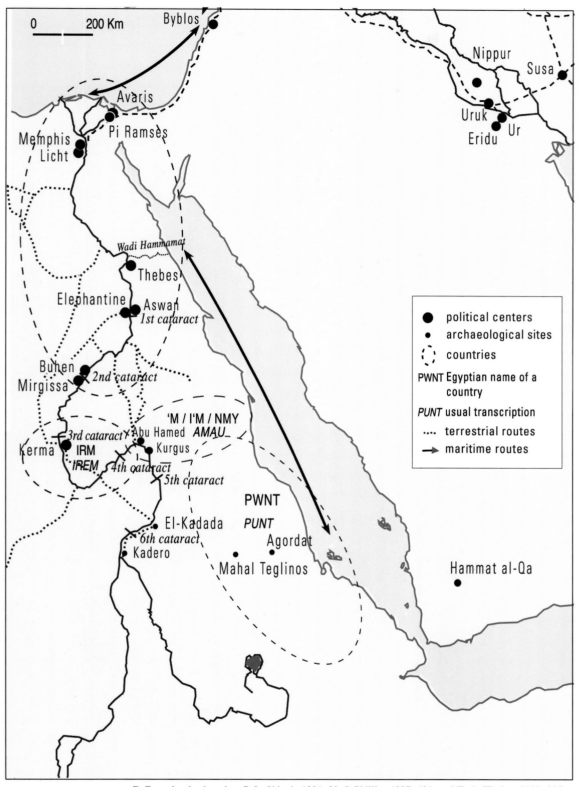

P. Beaujard,   based on P. L. Shinnie 1991: 52, J. Phillips 1997: 424, and K. A. Kitchen 2002: 387

Map 1.6 Western Eurasia and Africa during the second millennium BCE

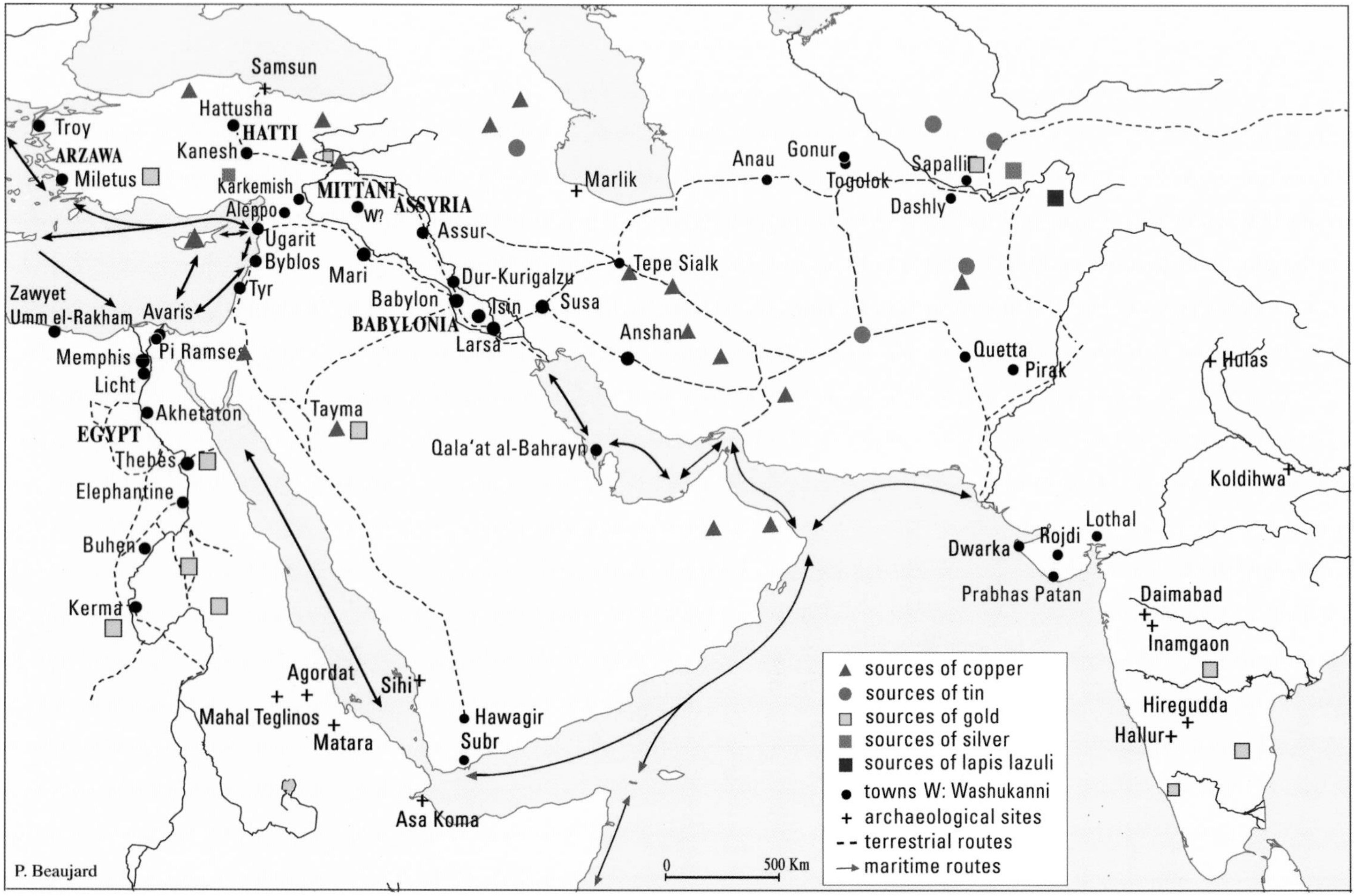

Troy
Miletus
ARZAWA
Samsun
Hattusha +
Kanesh
HATTI
Karkemish
Aleppo
Ugarit
Byblos
Tyr
Zawyet
Umm el-Rakham
Avaris
Pi Ramses
Memphis
Licht
EGYPT
Thebes
Akhetaton
Elephantine
Buhen
Kerma
Agordat
Mahal Teglinos +
Matara
Sihi +
Asa Koma
Hawagir
Subr
Qala'at al-Bahrayn
Tayma
Larsa
Babylon
BABYLONIA
Mari
W?
MITTANI
Assur
ASSYRIA
Dur-Kurigalzu
Isin
Susa
Tepe Sialk
Anshan
Marlik +
Quetta
Pirak
Dashly
Sapalli
Togolok
Gonur
Anau

Hulas +
Koldihwa +
Daimabad
Inamgaon +
Hiregudda
Hallur +
Lothal
Rojdi
Dwarka
Prabhas Patan

towns W: Washukanni
▲ sources of copper
● sources of tin
□ sources of gold
□ sources of silver
■ sources of lapis lazuli
● archaeological sites
+ archaeological sites
- - terrestrial routes
→ maritime routes

0   500 Km

P. Beaujard

Table I.In.1 *The number of cities with more than 25,000 inhabitants, 2250–1000 BCE, according to Chandler (1987) and Bosworth (1995: 212)*

Years BCE	Mesopotamia	Egypt	Levant	Mediterranean	Anatolia	India	China
2250	4	3	1	0	0	0	0
2000	6	3	0	0	0	0	0
1800	3	5	0	0	0	1	0
1600	3	3	1	2	1	0	0
1360	5	4	1	3	2	0	1
1200	5	3	0	2	1	1	2
1000	4	4	1	0	0	1	3

exchange networks. This development was accompanied by flows of populations between the countryside and the cities, and the outbreak of epidemics, generated by the urban phenomenon (McNeill 1998b). Chandler attempted to estimate the size of the urban population from 2250 BCE onward in the largest cities.[46] Because of the fragmentary nature of our knowledge[47] of ancient times, this estimate can only be a questionable approximation. The number of cities reviewed, however, gives some clues about the overall transformations in Afro-Eurasia (see Table In.1).

In the west, Mesopotamia and Egypt represent the centers of areas in which the number of towns varies upwards and downwards – sometimes in opposite directions. A peak in urbanization is seen during the fourteenth/thirteenth centuries BCE, before the collapse at the end of the millennium.

The great poles of civilization fostered the rise of some peripheral regions that benefited from particular assets. Advances in agriculture and exchanges during the third millennium thus encouraged the emergence of complex societies in Arabia, first on the shores of the Persian Gulf (see above), and to a lesser extent on the western side of the peninsula. A bronze culture developed in the Highlands of Yemen during the second half of the third millennium, and proto-urban centers appeared. During the second millennium, whereas the Persian Gulf was in decline, exchanges were increasing in the Red Sea, stimulated by the Egyptian trade with Punt. The Late Bronze Age saw the flowering of the Subr culture on the Yemeni coasts, while the domestication of the dromedary facilitated the organization of caravans toward the Levant.

At the other end of Asia, the contacts of Southeast Asia with southern China and with India were still limited during the third millennium. We know that rice cultivation was introduced by Austroasiatic speakers from a region south of the Yangtze into Thailand and later into the Ganges valley, but not before the end of the third millennium for Thailand and, during the second millennium, in the case of India. During the second millennium, the introduction of copper and bronze metallurgy into continental

[46] Estimates have been done for every 150–200 years until 1000 CE and then every 50 years, until 1800. These estimates were revised by G. Modelski (2003) and I. Morris (2013).

[47] Thus, for the Shang culture (China), texts give about one thousand names of towns and cities, only some of which have been discovered. Moreover, the size of a town or city depends on its pattern of urbanization. Also, the size of the towns imperfectly reflects the dynamics of regions characterized by political decentralization.

Southeast Asia triggered major social transformations, along with a rise in exchanges. No proper urban center can be observed for these ancient periods, however. Despite interconnections between central China, Lingnan, Yunnan, northern Vietnam, Cambodia, and Thailand, and the appearance of local exchange networks in Thailand and in Malaysia, for example, it is difficult to interpret the available data as showing the formation of an integrated area including the whole of East Asia. South Asia (India and Pakistan) and China represent structurally separate spaces, even though links existed between Yunnan, Upper Burma, and Assam, and exchanges developed through Central Asia, seen notably in the introduction of *Panicum miliaceum* millet and rice of the *japonica* type into Pakistan during the early second millennium. Evidence for maritime contacts between Southeast Asia and India during the third and second millennia is marginal. No expansion comparable to that of the Austronesian Lapita culture into the

Table I.In.2 *Comparative chronologies (sixth–third millennium BCE): western Asia, Persian Gulf, and eastern Mediterranean; Egypt and Red Sea, western Arabia; India and Central Asia*

Western Asia, Persian Gulf, and eastern Mediterranean	Egypt and Red Sea, western Arabia	India and Central Asia
c. 6000–4500: ʿUbaid culture	*4400–3800:* Badarian culture	
4600: founding of Uruk?		
4150–3800: Early Uruk	*4000–3600:* cultures of Maadi and Buto (delta), of Nagada I (Upper Eg.), and of "A-group" (Nubia)	*3500–3100:* Namazga II phase in Turkmenistan and in Margiana
3800–3400: Middle Uruk		*3200–2600:* Early Harappan (Indus)
3400–3150: Late Uruk; Urukian expansion into Syria and into Iran; innovation of bronze metallurgy		*3100–2700:* Namazga III phase in Turkmenistan and in Margiana
	3500–3300: Nagada IIc–d: expansion into the delta	
3300?: first writing signs at Uruk	*3300/3200:* formation of hieroglyphic script	
	3300/3200–3100: Nagada III, "Dynasty 0" of Abydos; unification of Egypt under Narmer	
3100: collapse of the Urukian "colonies"; Proto-Elamite state (*3100–2800*) and writing	*3100–2700:* Thinite period (first–second dynasties)	
3000–2340: Sumerian city-states. First Dynasty of Ur	*2700–2180:* Old Kingdom (Third – Sixth Dyn.)	*2600–2000:* Classical Harappan
c. 2500–2350: contacts with Bahrain, Oman, and Indus valley	*2600–:* construction of the great pyramids under the Fourth Dynasty	*2500–2200:* Namazga V phase (Turkmenistan–Margiana–Bactria)
2340: Sargon established the Akkadian Empire, which lasted until *c. 2200*	*2600–2000:* bronze culture of Khawlan (Yemen). Links with Sudan and Ethiopia, and with the Levant	
2300: horse in Syria?		
2300–2200: destruction of Troy II; invasions by Amorite nomads in Palestine and Mesopotamia *c. 2200–:* the Guti invade Mesopotamia *2112–2004:* Third Dynasty of Ur	*2180–2030:* period of anarchy ("First Intermediary Period")	*2200–1700:* culture of Bactria–Margiana (BMAC)

Pacific can be observed for the Indian Ocean (or even for western Indonesia).[48] However, a banana – of an unknown type – was present in the Indus civilization, and the discovery of cloves at Terqa (Middle Euphrates), dated to 1700–1600 BCE, would provide evidence for indirect links between the Austronesian world and the west of the Indian Ocean as early as the second millennium BCE through unknown intermediaries. The possible introduction of bananas into east Africa during the late second/early first millennium BCE – as well as that of taro and water yam? (Blench 2009) – offers another indication of ancient interactions between the eastern and western Indian Ocean.

Table 1.In.3 *Comparative chronologies (third–second millennium BCE): western Asia, and eastern Mediterranean; Egypt and Red Sea, western Arabia; India and Central Asia*

Western Asia and eastern Mediterranean	Egypt and Red Sea, western Arabia	India and Central Asia
2000–1700: first Palatial period in Crete *1900–1830:* Assyrian trade in Anatolia; Isin-Larsa period in southern Mesopotamia	*2040–1730:* Middle Kingdom *2000–1100:* culture of Subr-Sihi in southwestern Arabia	*1900–1700:* Late Harappan *c. 1900:* abandonment of Mohenjo-daro *1900:* Tazabagyab culture (Central Asia)
1800–: "Old Babylonian period." Hammurabi (1792–1750) (MC) *1751:* first Kassite invasion, Babylonian decline	*c. 1780–:* infiltrations of Hyksos from Canaan into the delta, "Second intermediary period" (*1730–1540*)	*1800:* end of Indus/ Mesopotamia contacts, urban decline, Indo-Aryan arrivals *1700:* end of BMAC, Ochre Colored Pottery culture
1700–1450: second Palatial period in Crete *1650:* founding of the Hittite Empire		*1800/1700–1500:* Beshkent-Vaksh culture; African plants introduced into India
1650–1200: rise of the Mycenaean culture *c. 1600:* founding of Mitanni *1595:* formation of the Kassite Empire (Babylonia)	*1540–1070:* Egyptian New Kingdom; expeditions to Punt under Hatshepsut; (*1472*) expansion under Thutmose III (*1479–1425*)	*c. 1700:* the Proto-Munda enter India *1500–1400:* arrival of "Rig-Vedic" Proto-Indo-Aryans Black and Red Ware culture (Ganges)
fourteenth–thirteenth century: rise of Assyria (disappearance of Mitanni, capture of Babylon); Elamite revival *1274:* battle of Qadesh between Hittites and Egyptians	Ramses II (*1279–1213*)	
c. 1200: invasions in Greece (end of the Mycenaean culture) and Anatolia (end of the Hittite Empire); invasions and destruction in the Levant and Cyprus; disappearance of Linear B in Crete	Invasions of the "Sea Peoples"; demise of the Subr culture (Yemen)	*1200–1100:* arrival of new Iranian groups in Central Asia, Iran, Pakistan, and India; introduction of iron metallurgy
1110: destruction of Susa by Nebuchadnezzar I (Babylonian state) *1100:* rise of Assyria under Tiglath-Pileser I; Neo-Hittite kingdoms in Syria and Anatolia	*1070–723:* "Third Intermediary period"	Painted Grey Ware culture (Doab-Ganges)

[48] P. Bellwood (2005: 139) notes that in western Indonesia we do not find the type of red slipped pottery characteristic of eastern Indonesia and the Philippines (Luzon), a pottery also known on the east coast of Taiwan. Western Indonesia had other types of pottery, which may also have originated in the Philippines, but data for this western area are sparse.

Table I.In.4 *Comparative chronologies (third–second millennium BCE): Inner Asia; China; Southeast Asia*

Inner Asia	China	Southeast Asia
3000–2500: Afanasevo culture	Dawenkou culture (Lower Yellow River) Longshan culture (Middle and Lower Yellow River)	
	3000–2500: Qujialing culture (Middle Yangtze)	
	3300–2200: Liangzhu culture (Lower Yangtze) *3000:* Majiayao culture (Gansu)	
2500–1900/1700: Okunev culture	*2600–2400:* Late Dawenkou culture	
2100–1900: Sintashta culture	*2500–1900:* Late Longshan culture. Towns of Taosi, Liangchengzhen, and Guchengzhai	*2500/2000–1500:* Phung Nguyen culture (Red River valley) Ban Chiang culture (Thailand)
2000–: complex of "Andronovo" cultures	*2100?:* bronze metallurgy	
1800–: Fedorovo culture and transcultural Seima-Turbino phenomenon (*1800–1500*)	*c. 2000:* Qijia culture *1950–1550:* Siba culture (Gansu) *1800–1600:* Erlitou state (Yellow River); control of bronze metallurgy	*c. 2000:* Neolithic on Malay peninsula
	1600–1050: Shang dynasty (capitals: Zhengzhou and Anyang); writing *1300:* appearance of chariots drawn by horses	*c. 1500:* bronze metallurgy in Thailand, and the Dong Dau culture (northern Vietnam) (*1500–1000*)
1400–850: Karasuk culture	*1027 BCE*: the Zhou take control of the Shang kingdom	

Table I.In.5 *Chronology of regions and sites of western Asia*

(a) Mesopotamia, Elam, N.E. Iran, southern Iran, Baluchistan, S.E. Iran

Dating	Mesopotamia	Elam	N.E. Iran	Southern Iran	Baluchistan	S.E. Iran
			Tepe Hissar	Tepe Yahya	Bampur	Shar-i Sokhta *sukkalmahs*
4000			(IB)			
	Middle Uruk					
3500		Susa II	IC			
3400	Late Uruk					
3300			IIA			
3200						I
3100		Proto-Elamite Susa III	IIB	IVC		
3000	Jemdet Nasr					
2900						
2800	Early Dyn. I					
2700	Early Dyn. II					II
2600	Early Dyn. IIIA	Susa IVA	IIIB		IV1	
2500				IVB	IV2	
	IIIB–C					
2400		Rulers from Awan			IV3	III
	Akkadian Empire					
2300		Susa IVB			V	
2200						IV
2100	Ur III	Susa V Puzur-Inshushinak	IIIC	IVA?	VI	
2000			IIIC			
1900		Reign of *sukkalmah*s	IIIC?			
1800			IIIC?			
1700						
1500				End IVA?		

(b) Southeastern Iran, Afghanistan, Turkmenistan, Bactria, Pakistan

Dating	S.E. Iran	Afghanistan Mundigak	Turkmenistan	Bactria		Pakistan
	Shar-i Sokhta		Namazga (N)	Sapalli	Shortughai	Mehrgarh
4000			I			
3500		III	II			III
3400						
3300						
3200	I					
3100			III			
3000						VI
2900						
2800		III5–6				VII
2700	II	IV1	IV			VIIC
2600		IV1–2 (?)				
2500		IV3	V		1–2	
2400	III					
2300						
2200	IV	End IV abandoned?	transition			
2100			V/VI	Sapalli	3-4	
2000			VI?	Sapalli		VIII(?)
1900			VI			
1800						
1700				Bostan VI		
1500		V(?)			Yaz I	Pirak II

1 The Birth of the State

The Neolithic Center of the Fertile Crescent

Western Asia was the first primary center of domestication of plants and animals, followed closely by China (Smith 1998; Harlan 1998; Bellwood 2005a).[1] The presence in the Fertile Crescent of vegetal and animal species that could be domesticated, along with the Crescent's situation as hub, were factors favoring the emergence of what has been called the "Neolithic Revolution." During the ninth millennium BCE, cereals (emmer wheat, einkorn wheat, barley), pulses (pea, lentil, bitter vetch, chickpea), and a fiber crop (flax) were grown and then domesticated (Tanno and Willcox 2006; Feldman and Kislev 2007; Colledge and Conolly 2007; Fu *et al.* 2012). Animals (goats, sheep, cattle, and pigs) were domesticated at the same time or slightly later. Agriculture and livestock farming encouraged a process of sedentarization of communities, rendering them able to harvest and to store food that could feed larger populations, and enabling them also to produce textiles and work leather. A change in social organization and a transformation in belief systems accompanied this revolution (Cauvin 1997). Cohabiting with domesticated animals brought in new diseases that would prove to be efficient weapons for the Neolithic centers in their relations with foreign countries (McNeill 1998b; Diamond 1997). From western Asia, cultivated plants and animals arrived in Turkmenistan and in the Indus valley (Mehrgarh) during the seventh millennium; these arrivals reveal terrestrial and perhaps maritime contacts. The diffusion of Asian species occurred as early as the eighth or seventh millennium in Egypt, Greece, and Crete. Even before the expansion of highly stratified societies, long-distance trade was noticeable; obsidian from Anatolia arrived in the Levant and in Mesopotamia, and shells were carried from the Persian Gulf to Mesopotamia, or from coastal Sind to Mehrgarh, during the fifth millennium. Lapis lazuli (originating in northern Afghanistan [Badakshan]), turquoise, and copper have been discovered at Mehrgarh and can be dated to the same period.[2] Lapis lazuli may have been traded as early as the sixth millennium.[3]

---

[1] The Highlands of New Guinea were another primary center for agricultural development in the ancient world. Unlike the Asian centers, New Guinea was too isolated – though Denham (2004) shows that this isolation was only relative – and it was technically limited in its ability to transform New Guinea into a pole of development and future core of a world-system. See Golson 1991; Bayliss-Smith 1996; Diamond 1997: 305ff. It is possible that vegeculture – based on plants reproduced by vegetative propagation – also developed in early times in Insular Southeast Asia, before the Austroasiatic and Austronesian arrivals (Barton and Denham 2011).

[2] Discoveries in the earliest layers at Mehrgarh of beads made of lapis lazuli, a stone originating in Afghanistan, of turquoise, brought from Iran or Central Asia, or of shells, all point to a certain amount of social differentiation and long-distance trade.

[3] Moorey 1994: 85–92. The identification of lapis lazuli at Tell Sotto (Yoffee and Clark 1993: 69) and at Yarim Tepe I (Iraq), around 6000 BCE, has been cast into doubt (Warburton 2003: 121), although these

When did the first maritime journeys in the Persian Gulf and along the coasts of South Asia occur? Probably very early on, if we consider the prehistory of the Mediterranean Sea (on Cyprus, the site of Aetokremnos, inhabited by hunter-gatherers, is dated to the tenth millennium BCE). There is no reason to suppose that the (pre-) Neolithic Arab and Asian societies did not develop the same skills in navigation.

'Ubaid, a Proto-State Phase

Favored by progress in irrigation, visible at Eridu, Larsa, and Choga Mami (marks left by the use of the ard have been discovered, dated to 4500 BCE), demographic and economic growth, and increasing long-distance trade in Mesopotamia: all fueled a first expansionary process from the sixth millennium onward, in the 'Ubaid period (c. 5300–4100 BCE), at least during its phases 3 and 4. This expansion was also based on organizational innovations and a shared ideology, as shown in architecture, and in "seals with near-identical motifs at widely separated sites" (Stein 2009: 135). These changes led to competition between "households" as well as to hierarchies and growing social complexity (Lamberg-Karlovsky 1999: 181), which in turn encouraged the populations to invest in new techniques. A monumental architecture developed with the first proto-urban centers. As Stein expresses it, sites such as Eridu, Uqair (Iraq), and Zeidan (Syria) were "ancient towns on the threshold of urban civilization" (2009: 136). The Late 'Ubaid phases clearly "provide the prototype for the Mesopotamian city" (Oates 2014a: 1484). The successive "temples" at Eridu in particular – public buildings probably serving various functions – marked the emergence of a new type of social organization, overtaking kinship-based structures. Exhibiting niches and buttresses, erected on terraces (prefiguring the later ziggurat),[4] temples became larger during the 'Ubaid 4 period, toward the end of the fifth millennium. It is likely that a private sector already coexisted with a public sector, with interactions and structuring of power relations among the rulers of family households (extended families and their dependants), temples, and councils representing territorial communities. Within the concurrent process of political centralization, control over the temples may have already been a crucial issue (Lamberg-Karlovsky 1996: 82–84). The presence of fine ceramics and of stamp seals as well as evidence for a weaving industry in the "temples" of the urban center of Eridu[5] reveal an economic role that goes well beyond that of "food banks" redistributing agricultural resources.[6] "A Late 'Ubaid cemetery at Eridu, however, reveals little evidence of the social differentiation attested to in the architecture of either Eridu or sites like Zeidan and Uqair" (Oates 2014: 1481).

Agriculture and livestock farming progressed during this period. Culture of the date palm (*Phoenix dactylifera* L.) probably began during the sixth millennium (see below). The fifth millennium saw the development of the olive tree in the Levant, and of grapevine culture in

---

sites did also yield carnelian and turquoise, stones imported from eastern routes. The blue stone at Yarim Tepe is most likely azurite rather than lapis lazuli (Casanova 2013: 24).

[4] Unlike the high terrace of Susa I, however, the Eridu terrace was apparently not stepped (Potts 2014: 26).

[5] Also observed at Tepe Gawra XIII (Pollock 1999: 87).

[6] Matthews 2003: 104, versus Stein 1994: 44. For mass-produced decorated pottery, there is no evidence of any general control by the elite over production, but vessels were indeed produced for this elite (Matthews 2003: 108).

Georgia, southern Turkey, Iran, and the Levant (McGovern 2003). The rise of tree fruit production went along with exchanges. This would become more apparent during the period of urbanization. Moreover, sheep farming developed in Iran and neighboring regions for the production of wool, thus laying the foundation for a textile industry.

The 'Ubaid culture expanded in different directions during the 'Ubaid 3 phase. The Mesopotamians acquired prestige goods and the raw materials they needed by building maritime and terrestrial networks, probably by exporting textiles, leather, and agricultural products. In the Persian Gulf, the Ubaidians practiced fishing and exchanged goods with coastal Arab communities. They brought in domesticated animals and plants, and allowed for the spread of shipbuilding techniques. 'Ubaid pottery has been discovered at over sixty sites in eastern Saudi Arabia and Oman; it is mainly dated to the 'Ubaid 2/3, 'Ubaid 3 periods and to a lesser extent 'Ubaid 4 (Carter 2006).[7] Contacts stopped during the 'Ubaid 5 period. Arab communities played an active role in exchanges, along the coasts and in the Arabian interior (Boivin and Fuller 2009), where trade networks carried myrrh and incense from the Dhofar and the Hadramawt (Zarins 2002). Large quantities of 'Ubaid (3–4, *c.* 4500–4100) pottery have been found at Ain Qannas (al-Hufūf oasis), located inland, as well as some remains of cattle and goats (Potts 1990: 44). Also traded were obsidian (from Yemen or Ethiopia?), shells, shell beads, dried fish, and stone vessels, through the oasis of Yabrin and al-Hasa.[8] Shells of the *Cypraea* type have been discovered in fifth-millennium levels at Chaga Bazar in northern Syria, imported from the Gulf.[9] An interesting result of the excavation on Dalma Island is the discovery of charred date pits (probably from cultivated date palms); these dates may have been brought there via trade exchanges, or perhaps they were cultivated on the island (they are dated to the end of the sixth/beginning of the fifth millennium). Remains of fruit have also been unearthed at as-Ṣabīya (Kuwait) dated to the second half of the sixth millennium (dates would have great importance in food and trade from the third millennium onward).[10] Recent genetic research tends to support a Mesopotamian origin for date-palm domestication (Rhouma *et al.* 2008). The presence of carnelian beads (a stone originating in Iran or the Indus) is noteworthy at Qatari sites, along with Mesopotamian pottery. Carnelian beads have also been discovered in Mesopotamia dating from the 'Ubaid period (Inizan 1999).

At that time, Arabia was undergoing a subpluvial phase (7000–4000 BCE) marked by a strong summer monsoon; the Intertropical Convergence Zone was located 10° north of

[7] Some sites, on Dalma Island for example, may date as far back as 'Ubaid 1/2, end of the sixth – beginning of the fifth millennium (Beech *et al.* 2000: 42–43). However, for Carter (2006: 58), the assemblage of Dalma Island belongs to the 'Ubaid 4 period, and according to H. Crawford (p.c.) to the 'Ubaid 3 period. Gypsum vessels found on Dalma Island, however, are similar to those discovered on Marawah Island, dated to the sixth millennium (Beech *et al.* 2005: 48). A site on Marawah Island yielded 'Ubaid 1 or 2 pottery that may have originated in southwestern Iran (mid-sixth millennium) (Beech *et al.* 2005: 46). 'Ubaid 1–2 pottery has been found at Halili, on the Bushire peninsula (Oates 2014a: 1490).

[8] Zarins 1997: 257–258 and fig. 1, 2002: 428.

[9] A necklace with obsidian beads from Anatolia and cowries from the Persian Gulf has been found at Arpachiyah (British Museum WA 127814). We have evidence of exchanges with Umm Dabaghiyah, in northern Mesopotamia, that show a specialized trade in hides as early as the sixth millennium (onager, gazelle) (Silver 1995: 144). Rice (1994: 217) considers obsidian blades found at the site of Dosariyah as coming from Anatolia.

[10] Beech *et al.* 2000: 42; Tengberg 2004: 59.

its modern position. Weaker monsoons and a southward shift of the Intertropical Convergence Zone were accompanied by growing aridization; this put an end to the use of the inland routes at the start of the third millennium (Zarins 2002: 409ff.).[11]

The first Mesopotamian explorations in what was known as the "Lower Sea" favored the diffusion of shipbuilding techniques. Excavations at as-Ṣabīya (Kuwait, ʿUbaid 2/3 period) have unearthed bitumen which was used to caulk reed ships. The site yielded a terracotta model of these boats, which were of Mesopotamian design.[12] Probably carried on the inland routes of Arabia, obsidian which may have come from Yemen was discovered along with the remains of these boats. As-Ṣabīya yielded a painted disc featuring a boat with a sail supported by a bipod mast (Carter 2006: 54–55 figs. 3 and 4). Clay boat models from the cemetery of Eridu also show the use of a sail at the end of the ʿUbaid period;[13] these models appear to represent wooden ships, as does the model found in Syria at Tell Mashnaqa (Potts 1997: 125). The role of the ʿUbaidians should not obscure the existence of other networks, operated by Arab communities, along the coasts and in the interior of the Arabian peninsula (Cleuziou and Méry 2002: 303; Boivin and Fuller 2009: 126ff.). The location of the sites in the Gulf suggests that the ʿUbaid pottery found beyond Bahrain was probably carried by local communities, who used seagoing ships,[14] as revealed by tuna fishing – tuna was eaten and prepared for export by Omani communities during the fourth millennium. This pottery was considered a luxury item: sites in outlying areas produced imitations of the ʿUbaid pottery (Carter 2006: 59).

The ʿUbaid culture also extended eastward into Khuzistan, where Susa constituted a proto-urban center. It also extended north of Mesopotamia (especially during the Late ʿUbaid phase), toward routes already linking Central Asia, Afghanistan, and the upper valleys of the Tigris and the Euphrates: one finds Ubaid pottery as far as the Transcaucasus region, and lapis lazuli from Afghanistan is present at Tell Arpachiyah and Nineveh, in northeast Iraq; Tepe Gawra yielded lapis lazuli, as well as carnelian from Iran, but the blue stone could be more recent at this site.[15] Pottery from Susa, dated to the late fifth millennium, has been found further east in Iran, in a

---

[11] In fact, the phase of aridization began around 3200/3100 BCE; see below. The abandonment of trans-Arabian routes during the third millennium would be accompanied by the rise of maritime routes (first located on the Arabian coast, Dilmun was situated on Bahrain Island as of the middle of the third millennium).

[12] Carter 2002: 20, 21–23. Bitumen had been mixed with other substances, to make it easier to use. Moreover, the site yielded pits of dates. At ʿAin as-Sayḥ, a coastal site near Bahrain, ships were caulked with Mesopotamian bitumen, during a period lasting from the end of the sixth to the early fifth millennium, but this dating remains uncertain (Carter 2002: 16, 24).

[13] Qualls 1981, quoted by Cleuziou and Tosi 1994: 746. Qualls studied 403 representations of boats prior to 2000 BCE.

[14] Carter 2002: 14, 24 (see the coastal sites with ʿUbaid pottery on Dalma Island and on the west coast of Oman; in the central gulf region, the sites with ʿUbaid pottery "demonstrate a true settlement hierarchy," from the coast to the interior).

[15] Potts notes the appearance of lapis lazuli in Level XIII (4500–3900), but Casanova places it in Level XI (beginning of the Late Uruk, c. 3200 BCE) (2013: 29). Tepe Gawra also yielded alabaster, "steatite" and serpentine, which came via the Khorassan route; Gawra and other sites, such as Sialk, also contain turquoise, probably from Maʿdan (Nishāpūr) as early as 4000 BCE (and even earlier at Gawra). Gold and silver artifacts were present at Gawra during the fourth millennium; copper objects (from melted copper) appear in Level XII dated to the late fifth millennium.

region rich in copper. The quest for copper obviously played a crucial role in 'Ubaid and 'Ubaid-related expansion, as shown by the 'Ubaid "colony" of Değirmentepe, which was located near substantial copper, lead, and silver sources (Oates and Oates 2004).[16] Trade in copper and exotic goods favored a process of social differentiation, not only at Gawra, which Oates (2014: 1481) considers as "a northern Ubaid settlement," but also at Zeidan (12.5 ha), in northern Syria (Euphrates River valley), a site revealing monumental architecture.[17] Zeidan yielded evidence for copper metallurgy and administrative activity (a stamp seal has been found, dated to *c.* 4100 BCE) (Stein 2009: 134). At Susa, a settlement founded around the end of the 'Ubaid period rapidly grew to cover 10 ha. It included a high platform bearing a building (residence, warehouse). Seals and imprints have been discovered, with geometric and sometimes figurative designs (the motif of the "master of animals" is already present) (Pollock 1999: 90ff.).[18] During this period, Mesopotamia formed itself into a "central civilization" (Wilkinson 1995a). This expansion was accompanied by new social complexity in different regions, with the probable emergence of servile labor regulated by family chiefs.[19] One notes the use of stamp seals in Khuzistan, Luristan and Fars,[20] as well as in areas north of Mesopotamia.

The homogeneity of the material 'Ubaid culture implies active exchange networks, at the local level and between regions. Parallels established between the northern temple at Tepe Gawra XIII and buildings at Uruk (tripartite floor plan,[21] orientation, elaboration) reflect some cultural community and shared beliefs. Religion must have played an important role controlling communities and exchange networks. In 1936, 1952, and 1954, A. Hocart had already pointed out the possible religious origin of trade, and of social and state institutions. Moreover, ceramics made on the turnette (slow wheel) and the use of stamp seals can be observed throughout the 'Ubaid area: the diffusion of these technologies contributed to the homogenization of this space (Nissen 2001). A marked increase in the use of seals and mass-produced pottery (suggesting the distribution of rations) signal new social complexity. Seals and other devices reveal administrative activity. At Tell Abada, in east central Iraq, in 'Ubaid buildings, tokens have been found in pottery vessels, probably reflecting the keeping of records (Oates 2014: 1482).

---

[16] 'Ubaid material has also been recovered at Kara Höyük and Norşuntepe.

[17] The site is dated to about 6000 to 3800 BCE (Stein 2009).

[18] A cemetery of this period contained copper material (see below).

[19] McGuire Gibson, http://oi.uchicago.edu/OI/AR/01–02/01–02_Hamoukar. html. Frangipane 2000: 226–227.

[20] Pittman 2001a: 229. A much earlier use of stamp seals can be observed in villages of the Hassuna culture (Syria and northern Mesopotamia). For Lamberg-Karlovsky (1999: 177), this "revolution in communication" intervened "in the 'domestic mode of production,'" at the level of extended families. These stamp seals were later used in the Halaf culture, which came after the Hassuna culture. The Hassuna culture was the first to exhibit social differentiation; Halaf pottery was produced by specialists (Pittman 2001b: 411). Stamp seals were also used in the Samarra culture (as found at the site of Tell es-Sawaan, 5500–4800). The site of Arpachiyah yielded a sealed bulla. The Samarra culture shows distinct "households" (extended families), in tripartite houses with T-shaped floor plans, each containing ten to twelve rooms. These households must have included clients and dependants.

[21] "The standard Mesopotamian tripartite building first appears on the early Pre-Samarran levels of Central Mesopotamia (Tell es-Sawwan). It is also present in the south in the earliest level at 'Oueli" (Oates 2014: 1487).

The expansion of the 'Ubaid culture during the fifth millennium clearly shows the new dimension of the exchange networks, brought about principally by the rise of copper metallurgy. This technology appeared during the sixth millennium in Anatolia, and during the fifth millennium in Mesopotamia, Iran, Pakistan, and southeastern Europe.[22] It then spread to the north of the Black Sea (4400 BCE), and on to the Middle Danube valley (4000 BCE), to Sicily and the southern Iberian peninsula (3800 BCE).[23] This progression provides clear evidence for the expansion of exchange networks. Metalworking reached the Asian steppes from southern Russia during the fourth millennium. It would later spread to northwestern Europe around 2500 BCE. Copper and then bronze metallurgy required a supply of metal ore and an ability to transport it; thus new trade networks were set up on a larger scale, within social contexts that implied profound ideological and organizational changes. The 'Ubaid civilization acted as a catalyst for societies further north and east of Mesopotamia, with long-distance trade now involving a large area.

The end of the 'Ubaid phase *c.* 4100 BCE seems to have coincided with a period of global cooling and aridization in the eastern Mediterranean region and the Levant (Staubwasser and Weiss 2006). In Susiana, "even the Acropole of Susa was abandoned ca. 4000" (Wright 2013: 52). The 'Ubaid period prefigures the flowering of the Sumerian civilization during the Urukian period.

The Urban Revolution and the Development of the State in Mesopotamia

The First Half of the Fourth Millennium BCE

New progress in metallurgy was noteworthy during the fourth millennium. Anatolian sites operated mines (mainly in the region of Ergani) and practiced ore smelting (Çatal Hüyük, Tepeçik, Değirmentepe, Norşuntepe …). There are clues indicating copper metallurgy at Mehrgarh (Pakistan) before 4000 BCE. A wheel-shaped amulet from Mehrgarh has recently been identified as the oldest known artifact made by lost-wax casting (it is dated to between 4500 and 3600 BCE) (Thoury *et al.* 2016). It had been thought that tin bronze was produced at Mundigak (Afghanistan) during the second half of the fourth millennium, but recent reanalyses show no evidence of tin bronze (Pigott 2012a).[24] Feinan (Jordan) has been dated to between 3600 and 3100 BCE for copper ore mining (Hauptmann 2003: 91). This progress in metallurgy and the

[22] Copper metallurgy was present around 6000 BCE at Çatal Hüyük. The emergence of this large village, from 6700 to 5700 BCE, was first based on simple techniques of irrigation and trade exchanges (textiles and a long-distance trade in obsidian). Değirmentepe was another early center of copper metallurgy. Copper metallurgy has been dated to 5000 BCE at Tall-i Iblis (Iran) (Muhly 1995: 1503). As for the copper items of Susa I (dated between 4200 and 3800 BCE), we do not know if these were made from native copper, or from copper obtained after an ore-reducing process requiring a temperature of 1100°C (Benoit 2003: 53).

[23] The southern Iberian peninsula saw the development of a significant copper industry, which spread northward starting in 3500 BCE, reaching northwestern Europe around 2500.

[24] "The lack of evidence for tin-bronzes on the Iranian plateau before the late 3rd millennium BC and the [absence of] early (4th millennium) tin-bronze use at Mundigak mean that Afghanistan should no longer be cited as a possible source of the earliest tin in SW Asia" (Pigott 2012b).

transportation of various goods (not only raw materials but also manufactured products) probably explains why active trade routes were established during this period. These routes would remain of importance throughout the ensuing two millennia. The first bronze tools appear at Beycesultan around 4000 BCE, and at Aphrodisias around 4300 BCE (southwestern Turkey) (Joukowsky 1996: 143). Beycesultan also yields silver items very early on.

After the 'Ubaid period, eastern Anatolia took advantage of improved climate conditions and a fresh increase in exchanges. This region, along with northern Mesopotamia, saw the formation of proto-urban centers (Arslantepe, Hacınebi, Tepe Gawra, and most importantly, Khirbat al-Fakhar and Tell Brak)[25] (see Map 1.1). Societies in Syria and Anatolia were already showing complex organizational characteristics during the first half of the fourth millennium, before "the documentation of regular contacts with the southern Uruk world" (Philip 2004: 209).[26] Public buildings were erected at Arslantepe during phase VII, before the period of contact with the Urukian world.[27] Godin (VI) was also expanding during the first half of the fourth millennium.[28] Hacınebi shows some social complexity during a phase dated 4100–3700 BCE, with stone architecture, administrative activity (stamp seals,[29] also found at Gawra, Tell Brak, Arslantepe, Değirmentepe), and metallurgy. Hacınebi was involved in exchanges between the Mediterranean, the Euphrates and Tigris valleys, and regions further east; it yielded artifacts made from chlorite, a stone imported from a region located 300 km to the east, shells termed "cowries" (Mediterranean shells?), some bitumen (from Mesopotamia), copper items (the metal probably came from the region of Ergani and/or from the Caucasus), and even silver earrings.[30] In northeastern Iraq, Khirbat al-Fakhar was a much larger proto-urban settlement – of low density – covering 300 ha, whereas the total area of the Late Chalcolithic 2 (LC2) (4100–3800 BCE) settlement at Brak reached at least 55 ha (Ur 2010: 395). At this time, Rothman has reported the existence of specialized "temple" institutions at Tepe Gawra (Rothman 2001b: 387–389), Tell Hammam et-Turkman, and Tell Brak (McMahon and Oates 2007: 148–155). "At Tell Brak, adjacent to a monumental building was a structure with abundant evidence for the manufacture of various craft items. The structure itself contained obsidian, spindle whorls, mother-of-pearl inlays, ... " (Ur 2010: 394; see Oates *et al.* 2007). Mass-produced ceramics have been found, along with "a unique, obsidian and white marble 'chalice' " (Oates *et al.* 2007: 591, 594), showing the existence of social differentiation and organized labor.

---

[25] On Hacınebi, see Stein 1999: 125ff. On Arslantepe, see Frangipane 2001.

[26] See Stein 1999: 92, 103; Frangipane 2004a: 124.

[27] The presence of mass-produced bowls signals the existence of a centralized system based on corvée labor (Frangipane 2001: 329; 2004a: 124).

[28] Edens 2002b: 32. It is true that Godin VI exhibits an influence from southern Mesopotamia – or Susa – during the Middle Uruk (Badler 2004: 81) and that the exchanges with the Urukian world may have played a role in the expansion of the site.

[29] As mentioned, stamp seals were already present in villages of the Halaf culture during the sixth millennium. Stein (2004: 150) notes the existence at Hacınebi of two types of seals, possibly indicating the different status of their owners or different functions for the seals.

[30] Stein 1999: 125ff. Stein (2004: 150) also notes the discovery of ceramics comparable to the Amuq F assemblage (Orontes valley region).

These (proto-)urban centers constituted nodes along east–west networks that extended further into Iran and Afghanistan, in one direction, and to the Syrian coast in the other. Lapis lazuli has been found at Iranian sites such as Tepe Sialk, Tepe Giyan (first half of the fourth millennium BCE), Tepe Yahya (3750–3650 BCE), and in northern Mesopotamia, at Tepe Gawra (3200 BCE?), Nineveh, Arpachiyah (4500–3900 BCE) (Casanova 2013: 27ff.). "There was extensive evidence for exploitation of lapis lazuli at Tepe Hissar during the 4th millennium BCE" (Petrie 2013a: 7). The presence of lapis lazuli reveals the existence of routes linking Central Asia, Iran, and northern Mesopotamia; it is rare, however, during the 'Ubaid period and the first half of the fourth millennium. Moreover, trade networks formed with northern regions: obsidian came from central or eastern Anatolia, and "ceramics [from northern Mesopotamia] have been found in eastern Anatolia (Marro 2007) and in Azerbaijan (Akhundov 2007)" (Ur 2010: 395). Interactions between the spheres of Anatolia–Levant and Mesopotamia took place during the flourishing of the 'Ubaid culture; they continued after its demise. On the basis of glyptic art, H. Pittman notes "a shared symbolic ideology" during the Late 'Ubaid–Early Uruk in Syria, northern Mesopotamia, and Khuzistan (2001b: 418).

During the LC2 period, the first proto-urban centers seem to have lacked internal political centralization. But from the LC3 period (3800–3600 BCE), Tell Brak grew into a large urban center, becoming a dense settlement of 130 ha, "prior to the Uruk expansion" (Oates *et al.* 2007, Ur 2010: 396).[31] Another major site was located at al-Hawa, 40 km east of Hamoukar; it may have been as large as 33–50 ha. Hamoukar (near Khirbat al-Fakhar) and Leilan were smaller settlements. According to Algaze, however, Hawa and Samsat – a city now submerged as a result of the construction of the Ataturk dam – truly developed "after the onset of contacts with the Uruk world" (2008: 120).

Domestic structures in Tell Brak "show evidence of high-value items and exotic materials," and of property-control mechanisms. "A cache from a pit included two stamp seals and 350 beads, mostly of carnelian but also silver, gold, lapis lazuli, and rock crystal (Emberling and McDonald, 2003, p. 9)" (Ur 2010: 396). Seals and sealings have also been discovered at Hamoukar (Reichel 2002).

Quoting Algaze (2008: 118ff.), Ur notes that "Brak's urban significance has been downplayed because, unlike the cities of southern Mesopotamia, it was a primate center without intermediate centers in a proper urban hierarchy" (Ur 2010: 399).

The process of urbanization was accompanied by violence: traces of massacres have been discovered in Tell Brak, and structures were destroyed by fire at Hamoukar and Brak. Whether due to internal disorder[32] or attacks by southerners, the origin of this violence is still debated.[33] Also debated is the dating of the Eye Temple at Tell Brak. For Oates *et al.* (2007: 596), it was built prior to the Uruk expansion, in the LC3 period

---

[31] Ur (2010) writes "a few centuries or more" before the Uruk expansion, but this seems to be an exaggeration. Morris (2013: 153) gives an estimate of 8,000 inhabitants in Tell Brak in 3500 BCE, which is probably too low.

[32] Global climate cooling around 3600 BCE may have aggravated the city's internal problems.

[33] Hamoukar was the site of a battle around the middle of the fourth millennium; in 2005, the Oriental Institute of Chicago discovered more than "1200 smaller, oval-shaped bullets and some 120 larger round clay balls" that must have been used in the defense of the city. "It is likely that the southerners played a role in the destruction of this city" (C. Reichel, www-news.uchicago.edu/releases/05/051216.hamoukar.shtml).

(3800–3600 BCE), but other archaeologists date the construction of the temple to 3500–3300 BCE. The temple was decorated with clay cones, copper panels, and goldwork, in a style similar to contemporary temples of southern Mesopotamia. "Eye idols have also been found at Tell Hamoukar (Reichel 2002)" (Oates *et al.* 2007: 596).

The Urukian Expansion during the Second Half of the Fourth Millennium BCE

Interactions with southern Mesopotamia can be seen from 3600 BCE onward, when the latter region experienced major urban development accompanying the birth of the state. As Algaze makes clear, "polities in the north hardly equaled their southern counterparts" (2008: 120). This southern urban development was based on agricultural progress generating demographic growth. Increased irrigation, the use of the ard drawn by oxen and the creation of date-palm plantations led to the creation of large estates; only estates of significant size were able to invest on a scale ensuring surpluses that supported urbanization.[34] Sherratt (2006a) has shown convincingly that the ard was developed along with the urbanization process; it may have been first employed to make furrows for irrigation; it required a major investment, which in turn explains its symbolic link with political power. The use of sledges on rollers to remove seed husks heralded the invention of the wheel.

Urbanization was also based on the progress of various crafts, such as ceramics (the invention of the potter's wheel made mass production possible, and this was linked to new social practices [the use of fermented beverages][35] and organization [distribution of rations]), metal artifacts, and textiles made of flax or wool (see below). Growth in sheep populations is seen at several Urukian sites at the end of the fourth millennium (such as Tell Rubeidheh); this may have been spurred by the state leadership (Kohl 2007: 222).[36] Sheep production certainly represented one driver of the Uruk expansion.[37] Selected in Iran, wool-bearing sheep breeds spread rapidly westward: some of the first-known wool remains, dated to the late fourth millennium, come from El Omari, in Egypt (Good 1998: 658).

The production of new goods was connected to the building of hierarchized urban societies; not only did exported manufactured goods lay the groundwork for an asymmetric exchange with peripheral regions; they also fostered local developments (the social

---

[34] Texts from the late fourth millennium describe extensive palm groves (Tengberg 2004). In 2003, a German expedition partially mapped the city of Uruk, and discovered a complex system of channels.

[35] Sherratt 2004. The potter's (fast) wheel, which speeded up pottery production, may have been a response to two constraints: lack of manpower and increasing demand (Nissen 2004: 9). The wheel was also used in Syria and in southeastern Anatolia. In addition, Pollock (1999: 96) notes the use of the bow drill at this time, for engraving seals.

[36] We will observe this process more clearly during the third millennium, particularly during the Ur III period.

[37] McCorriston 1997: 521, 534. Pollock (1999: 107) also points out "an emphasis on sheep and goat in the southern lowlands [during the fourth millennium] … a sign of the growing importance of secondary products, such as milk, dung, wool, hair, traction and transport." This evolution had little impact on Egypt, where flax remained predominant.

role of fermented beverages in Mesopotamia, for example, may have led to expansion in grapevine culture on the Mediterranean shores, as Sherratt has suggested).

The Urban Revolution benefited from increased long-distance trade, and helped further its development; commerce first involved textiles, slaves, and copper, which was used to produce weapons and tools. The development of copper and later, bronze metallurgy underlay the emergence of political power: "only elites could organize the long-distance procurements of costly copper and tin, as both were scarce," and both proved necessary to social reproduction (Ratnagar 2001a: 355). Bronze was initially an alloy of copper and arsenic,[38] then of copper and tin (the latter alloy being harder than the arsenical bronze).[39] Bronze metallurgy spread from the fourth millennium onward, through the trade routes, with a possible diffusion to China between 3000 and 2000 BCE (Pernicka *et al.* 2003). The production of bronze artifacts increased not only agricultural productivity,[40] but also military power: competition between cities was not always peaceful, and the extension of conflicts certainly played an important role in the building of the state.

The rise in exchanges was partly linked to the birth of a new ideology of political control as well as to institutional innovations. The state played a crucial role, organizing production and exchanges, as well as redistributing wealth.

In conjunction with the rise in exchanges and processes of internal development, southern Mesopotamia experienced a radical new flourishing. Already inhabited *c.* 4600 BCE, the site of Uruk (Warka) grew from 3600 BCE (Middle Uruk) and covered 250 ha *c.* 3100 BCE – which may have represented a population of 20,000 to 40,000 – and 600 ha *c.* 2900 BCE at the end of the Jemdet Nasr period (according to Morris [2013: 153], Uruk had 45,000–50,000 inhabitants by the late fourth millennium). During the Early Uruk period, the city of Warka grew "at the expense of the Nippur-Adab and Eridu-Ur areas" and of Upper Mesopotamia (Algaze 2008: 108, 110; Kouchoukos and Wilkinson 2007): the population of the northern Jazirah decreased, especially from 3500 to 3300 BCE; the same held true for the Fars Plain; northern cities (Tell Brak, Hamoukar) grew smaller, leading Algaze to speak here of an "aborted urbanism" (2008: 117, 121). Other southern cities probably expanded during the late fourth millennium, absorbing rural populations: Nippur, Adab, Kish, Girsu, Ur, Umma, Tell al-Hayyad. None of these cities, however, are comparable to Uruk.[41] Algaze rightly emphasizes that "large settlement agglomerations were almost certainly unable to demographically reproduce themselves without a constant stream of new population" (2008: 29).

---

[38] For Potts (1997: 165), arsenical copper originates from the ores of Anarak, in Iran. Arsenic may have been employed first for the silvery effects it gave to the metal (Sherratt and Sherratt 2001: 34 n. 23).

[39] Early dating (fifth and fourth millennia) had been proposed for bronze objects in a copper-tin alloy found in the caves of Ghar-i Mar and Ghar-i Asp in Afghanistan (Dupree 1972), but this dating has since been put into doubt.

[40] For Ratnagar (2001b: 355 n. 8), "we have no evidence, from any of the great river valleys, that bronze tools were extensively used in agriculture." Metal recycling and the fact that these tools were not deposited in the tombs make them invisible in archaeology. It is likely, however, that the elites largely controlled bronzeworking and the use of this alloy.

[41] We do not know the actual size of these cities during the different Uruk periods. Further investigation is needed.

(McNeill [2000: 204] "pointed out intensified mortality as a result of crowding, with the appearance of a variety of diseases.")

Various authors have stressed the importance of the ideological and organizational changes occurring during the birth of the state.[42] The Mesopotamian agglomerations probably meet the criteria proposed by Wengrow for defining a city: "the existence of a class or classes of individuals not directly involved in agrarian production, a high density of permanent residents, access to ports and trade routes, centralized bureaucracy,[43] a concentration of knowledge and specialised crafts, political and/or economic control over a rural hinterland, the existence of institutions that embody civic identity," and the monumentality of some of its buildings (Wengrow 2006: 76–77). These towns or cities constituted – at one and the same time – political, economic, and religious centers. It is possible that chiefs were primarily religious chiefs. Political power may have emerged as the result of the internal dynamics of the royal system: "It was only when the [various] ritual functions of the [chief] were separated from one another that political power and state organization emerged and developed" (Scubla 2003; Hocart 1970). L. de Heusch also writes: "It is the symbolic construction elaborated on the figure of a magician-chief that allows the genesis of the state, wherever a hierarchy of status or social classes develops" (1997: 230).

Not only was there intensification of labor through biological, technological, and organizational innovations; there was also a more efficient mobilization of the labor force itself. Southern Mesopotamian cities proved better able "to amass and control information, labor and surpluses vis-à-vis those of their immediate neighbors" (Algaze 2001: 70). This efficiency was seen in both economic and political-religious organization. Community lands held by extended families came under the management of "institutional households." The temples, which owned land, craft workshops and herds, were organized as "profit centers" (Hudson 1996: 37). The growing importance of the temple complex[44] paralleled the emergence of a ruling class that was organized as an assembly of community leaders, who managed most of the production and long-distance trade.[45] According to Pollock, the Uruk rulers probably extracted tribute to feed the city. Uruk was the religious capital of Sumer

---

[42] Tosi and Lamberg-Karlovsky 2003: 348. This revolution has its roots during the period 4150–3800 BCE, a time of "experimentation with new modes of political organization … and new strategies and technologies of control," as H. T. Wright suggests (2001: 145). For the third millennium BCE, M. Liverani (2014: 108) points out "the divine foundations of kingship."

[43] See Ur 2014 (below), however, for another vision.

[44] Nissen (2004: 14), however, notes that the exact place of the temple itself in the Uruk economy remains unknown. Little can be gleaned from the texts available. The precise relationship between the temples and the political sphere is no clearer. For Lamberg-Karlovsky (2003: 62, 70), there was a "coevolution" of the temple, writing, urbanization, statebuilding, and the development of crafts, with textiles playing a crucial role. During the Jemdet Nasr period (3100–2900 BCE), the temple of Khafajeh yielded seals, jewels, and kilns (Pollock 1999: 100). For Pollock, there is little evidence to suggest a direct involvement of the temple in production during the preceding period of the Late Uruk (1999: 115).

[45] Means of production such as oxen, seed drills, plows, probably belonged to the various state institutions (Ekholm Friedman 2000: 166). One may not follow J. D. Forest, however, when he argues that "free enterprise has not been invented yet and economic logic cannot be observed. The goods transported did not generate any profit." "The whole system," adds Forest, "was put in place and managed by the elites of

(Algaze 2008: 114), and may also have been the political capital of a Sumerian state (Yoffee 1995b; Westenholz 2002; Matthews 2003).[46] Various elements, however, do suggest the existence of a league of Sumerian cities around 3100 BCE (rather than a single state), a league perhaps headed – as later in the third millennium – by a LUGAL ("great man"), "ceremonial head of the assembly [UNKEN] of city rulers."[47] For Glassner, there was no king yet at the head of the state: an assembly of community leaders was "managing the affairs of the city."[48] Twenty cities are thus mentioned on a seal, from Urum (Tell Uqair) in the north to Ur in the south. Remains of temples and "palaces" have been discovered; they show decorations of niches and pilasters as well as characteristic facade ornamentation using colored "nails" forming geometrical patterns.[49] Algaze (2008: 190), however, believes that kingship was already instituted. The "Titles and professions list" during the Jemdet Nast period starts with a man called NAM$_2$+ESDA, a term translated as "king" during the second half of the 3rd millennium. Moreover, Algaze emphasizes an "iconographic continuity between the 4th and the 3rd millennia for the 'priest-king/city ruler'" (2008: 190, 153). The true nature of the Urukian institutions, in fact, remains unknown.

Some ceramic objects – beveled-rim bowls – were mass-produced and standardized, probably reflecting the distribution of "rations,"[50] in "a system of mass labor" clearly made visible through the size of public buildings;[51] these rations may also have been linked to workshops producing goods for the state such as textiles. "Many of the Archaic texts record disbursement of textiles and grain to individuals. [They may represent] rations given to some sort of fully or partly dependent workers" (Algaze

the South Mesopotamian city-states who were the only authority able to harness energies" (2003: 128–129).

[46] It is not impossible that the great priest EN of Uruk was also a political ruler (Westenholz 2002: 34). Gilgamesh is called "either EN, or LUGAL, according to his activities" (Joannès 2005: 53).

[47] Westenholz, 2002: 34. We cannot exclude the possibility that this league was (re)constituted after the disintegration of a "state" led by Uruk. In line with established practice, Sumerian ideogrammatic terms are written in capital letters.

[48] Glassner 2000a: 267ff., 2000b: 46. LUGAL would mean "king" from the Sargonic period on, according to Westenholz (2002), but the concept of kingship had appeared earlier (see below).

[49] We are only really aware of Level IVA (Late Uruk); there is little to no information about earlier levels. It is difficult to use the finds at Uruk as a basis for establishing a chronology of the potteries, or to date the appearance of bullae, cylinder seals, or written tablets (Nissen 2004: 7ff.). The enclosures of the Eanna, the "House of Heaven," dedicated to the goddess Inanna, and of Kullab, dedicated to Anu, included "temples" and "palaces" (Algaze 2001: 33; Nissen 2001: 154; Joannès 2001: 254–255; Huot 2004: 79ff.). The buildings of the Eanna comprised shrines, storerooms, workshops, and administrative centers (McIntosh 2005: 65). The structure of the Mesopotamian temples derives from the "temples" of the 'Ubaid period. Susa shows the construction of a stepped high terrace, the southern facade of which was decorated with clay nails, as in the Uruk culture ("the high terrace on the Acropole mound at Susa [is] dated to c. 4000 BC … This monumental structure covered 6,400 sq. m" [Potts 2014: 23, 24]).

[50] Pollock 1999: 94–96. Other hypotheses have been proposed: preparation of bread, and votive offerings (Nissen 2004: 9–10). For Pollock, increased demands for tribute and *corvées* imposed on village communities would explain a migration of the inhabitants to the towns and an extension of other processes of centralization. "The combination of increased tribute demands and growth of an urban-based workforce may have promoted the adoption of time and labor-saving technologies and segmented manufacturing processes" (1999: 96).

[51] See the platforms, terraces, and temples at Eridu (Early Uruk period), Uruk (Middle and Late Uruk), and Brak (Middle Uruk); Wright 2001: 141, 143, Nissen 1988: 83–85.

2008: 130). In S. Pollock's view, during the third millennium, the economy moved from a tributary system (tributes were extracted from the rural sector) to a system of "households" employing their own labor forces, servile or not; these "houses" were not only temples and palaces, but also estates belonging to high-level officials or the rulers of extended families.[52] As early as the Urukian period, the archives of the institutional estates evoke the management of land, of herds, and of the labor force (Glassner 2000a: 238ff.), probably with economic viability in mind: here we are outside the context of a simple tributary system.

The emergence of the state and the rise of exchanges brought about the use of new techniques that spread widely, allowing for growing control over the movement of goods, information, and individuals. Calculi and seals on clay bullae containing these calculi represent systems noting quantities that reveal accounting management. They can be found in a vast zone going from Iran to Mesopotamia and Syria: all of western Asia was involved.[53] At Uruk, then at Susa, around 3500 BCE (or slightly later?),[54] cylinder seals appeared (only stamp seals had been used in earlier times) to seal merchandise (bales or jars) and doors.[55] Numerical tablets, each one sealed by the imprint of a cylinder seal, have been unearthed in levels belonging to this period.[56] With the development of cylinder seals, a new iconography flourished that legitimated the power of the elite: it often figures a hero – perhaps already a "priest-king" or deity? (see above) – who is a master of wild beasts, a war leader, a feeder of domestic animals and "a fountain of agricultural wealth" (the hero holds a vase with flowing streams, a symbol of abundance and a possible reference to the role of the state in irrigation systems); he is alternately portrayed as an officiator in religious ceremonies (according to Glassner [2000a], however, versus Algaze [2008], the seals and cultic objects feature different characters, not just one). We can observe this iconography from early periods in Iran and Egypt. For Pittman, in fact, "the characteristic Uruk imagery was first developed and found its richest expression in Susiana" (2013: 295). At Susa and Choga Mish, east of Susa, cylinder seal impressions show temples on high platforms (Oates 2014a: 1491; Amiet 1980: 695).

[52] Pollock 1999: 118–120. This author considers that a "tributary structure" had already been put into place during the 'Ubaid period. The tributary system would have led to migrations of populations, some of them into towns (see above). An increased disequilibrium between rural communities and cities favored technological innovations and finally led to a change in economic organization, with a transition to a system of *oikoi* employing their own labor force (Pollock 1999: 96).

[53] Margueron and Pfirsch 2001: 103. In Syria, hundreds of clay sealings (made with stamp seals) and calculi have been unearthed at Tell Sabi Abyad, within a Late Halaf context (sixth millennium). Calculi in fact appeared at various sites as early as the seventh millennium (see above). Bullae have been found at Susa and at Chogha Mish (Potts 1999: 65). The shape of the calculi indicates their numeric value, according to a system essentially sexagesimal, and secondarily decimal.

[54] Datings proposed at Uruk are problematic, because of the excavations at this site, and more generally speaking – for the whole region – because of problems with radiocarbon dating. Petrie thus points out that "the most problematic factor impacting upon the absolute dating of the late 4th millennium BC is the extended plateau in the radiocarbon calibration curve from c. 3350 to 2900" (2013b: 388).

[55] Technically, Pittman (2001b: 419ff.) links the development of cylinder seals with the invention of the drill, which was also used for the production of stone vessels. The drill would also be used for the decoration of stamp seals. Quoting Pittman (2013), Petrie notes that there is "no overt evidence for the development of cylinder seal technology at Uruk during the Middle Uruk Phase" (2013b: 406 n. 4).

[56] The Urukians used thirteen different types of accounting; the "signs tell what units of measure are employed, [and] they indicate the nature of what is quantified" (Glassner 2000a: 178, 180).

The Susiana Plain was "part of the Uruk world between 3800 and 3150 BC" (Wright 2013: 63); it is likely, however, that during the Early and Middle Uruk periods, "an independent state based at Susa developed in Susiana" (Petrie 2013b: 388). For her part, Pittman (2013) "queries the primacy of southern Mesopotamia in the development of the administrative innovations that took place in the 4th millennium" (Petrie 2013b: 391). For Pittman (2013: 321), Susa was the source of many of the "Mesopotamian" innovations. One notes the appearance "of bevel-rim bowls and other Uruk forms at Ghabristan, Sialk, Tal-e Kureh and possibly Tal-e Iblis" (Petrie 2013b: 13): the question remains to know whether we observe a process of colonization, trade, or emulation/coevolution[57] (at Susa for example, and from Susa) (Rothman 2001b: 21).

Copper metallurgy developed in Iran during the fourth millennium BCE, using crucible-based smelting technology, for example at Tal-e Iblis (periods III and IV), Tepe Sialk (III and IV), Tepe Hissar (II), Tepe Ghabristan (II), Arisman, Godin Tepe (VI.1), and Susa (Weeks 2013). We do not have evidence of ancient mining at Anarak, but local mineral sources must have been used. Iran exported copper and copper artifacts.

The juridical power of the state was constituted at this time. We know from Nissen that "group size and amount and level of conflicts are systematically and inseparably interconnected"; the dimension of Uruk implies the setting up of a system of laws and sanctions, as well as an organization that is able to implement them (Nissen 2004: 14).

Among the crucial innovations of the Urban Revolution figure techniques of power and new forms of organization. Bullae, calculi, and cylinder seals have already been mentioned. The first signs of writing appeared around 3300 BCE at Uruk (the exact period is not known), in response to the growing complexity of commercial transactions and social organization, and to the building of a system of relations between the Sumerian city-states, interacting with a periphery of pastoralist or sedentary populations.[58] The development of writing laid the groundwork for the state's ideology, with the creation of a body of scribes whose apprenticeship must have also been an "indoctrination" (Pollock 1999: 169). Writing quickly acquired a sacred dimension: along with iconography, it brought about contact with the world of the gods. In the economic field, most of the ancient documents contain lists of goods that were received, sent, or stored, such as grains, milk products, wool, textiles, metals ... Some of these documents show attempts at economic planning. They have usually

---

[57] On this concept, see also Chase-Dunn 1988, and Sherratt 1993.

[58] Mainly resorting to metaphor and metonymy, the system is logographic and uses phonetic values and syllabism; "the visual marks of invisible analogies," most of the signs are polysemic and polyphonic (Glassner 2000a: 13–19, 202, 220–224). Stamps, seals, and written symbols reflect a general shift in social relations. They guarantee property rights, transfer of goods or of powers, and they have – in writing especially – an identifying function (Glassner 2002b: 368). Going further, Glassner (2000a: 15) makes the point that the invention of writing cannot be considered simply as a response to increased economic and administrative complexity, as its very existence transformed our relation to knowledge and cultural memory. Obviously, writing was linked to the political and religious spheres (divination, the calendar ...). Considering a "gradual trajectory" from the earliest notational systems (marks on pottery, on bullae ...) to writing (Lamberg-Karlovsky 2003) is a theory that fails to take into account the cognitive revolution writing implies.

been found in the vicinity of public buildings.[59] A vast majority of tablets thus reflect the existence of a centralized and hierarchized administration. Archaic texts from Uruk refer to social differentiation and the organization of various professions.[60] They reveal the existence of slaves of local or foreign origin. "A larger pool of dependent labor available gave a comparative advantage" to southern Mesopotamia (Algaze 2008: 81). Slaves probably worked on irrigation systems and constructions. As Algaze rightly points out (2008: 146–147), "innovations in communication [writing, accounting systems], [transportation] and labor control were fundamental for the Sumerian takeoff." The city of Uruk was crisscrossed by canals used for transport and irrigation.

Slaves also worked in workshops. "The second most frequently mentioned commodity in Archaic texts [after barley] is female slaves" (Algaze 2008: 129). A tablet from Uruk refers to 211 women slaves, who produced textiles for the temple.[61] Many Uruk texts deal with wool and textiles (woven woolen cloth),[62] which probably represented the first exports of the Mesopotamian cities, in addition to leather, agricultural products, perfumed oils, and metal artifacts. During the third millennium, "iconography from cylinder seals and sealings depict various stages of textile production" (Algaze 2008: 81). Archaic texts "attest to the existence of temple/state-controlled sheep herds" (Algaze 2008: 87).[63] It is likely, also, that raw wool imports contributed to the growth of the textile industry in the southern Mesopotamian cities. Wool, notes Algaze (2008: 79), was more easily dyed than linen, and "economies of scale were achievable by using wool as opposed to flax." "The mass production of textiles" financed by elites was clearly "an urban phenomenon" (Algaze 2008: 84). "The earliest economic records and lexical lists also include numerous references to metals" (2008: 93) (see below). In sum, the flourishing of different crafts linked to institutions can be observed. Southern Mesopotamia had at least two other crucial advantages over the north: a higher density of population and efficient water transport, facilitating trade.[64] The Mesopotamian elites ensured the supply of necessary raw materials: metals, stone, and wood. There is

[59] The connection, however, is far from certain; see Nissen (2004: 12) for the site of Uruk. Some documents from private archives have come to light, showing "a minimal use of writing" (Glassner 2000a: 234ff.).

[60] See the lists of titles and professions found during the Late Uruk period and repeated for nearly one thousand years (Nissen 2004: 13). At the end of the fourth millennium, the scribes themselves seem to have been associated with six different professions (Glassner 2000a: 143). "Among the Warka IVA tablets," notes Oates, "there is a surprising number of lexical texts presumably used in teaching, suggesting a longer previous history of writing" (2014a: 1486). It is clear that the public sector was largely at the origin of the growing social complexity in the Late Uruk period, in response to various constraints. The different lists that have been found indicate a willingness "to put the world in order" (Glassner [2000a: 253] speaks of a Sumerian obsession with classification).

[61] Textile workshops employing women in a situation of dependence are well known for the third millennium. It is possible, also, that some communities had a semi-servile status (Wright 2001: 140).

[62] The symbolic importance of weaving has been emphasized by Glassner (2000a: 214).

[63] On the centrality of textiles to the early Mesopotamian urban process, see McCormick Adams 1981: 11 (cited in Algaze 2008: 92). "Of the emergent industries of the time, none would have contributed more to the growth of internal diversification, specialization and overall employment than woolen textile manufacture."

[64] "Waterborne transport in ancient Mesopotamia could have been about 170 times more efficient than the average donkey caravan" (kg/km/day) (Algaze 2008: 61).

little doubt that the state was involved in long-distance trade.[65] During the second half of the fourth millennium, exchanges benefited from innovations in transportation: waterway development, clearly visible at Uruk; improvements in shipbuilding; domestication of the donkey (both in Egypt and in western Asia) and the use of the wheel. A written sign reflects the presence of donkeys during the Uruk period. Recent genetic research shows that donkey domestication first took place in Egypt, from a Nubian subspecies, *Equus asinus africanus* (the first remains of domesticated donkeys were discovered in a Predynastic tomb, at Ma'adi, dated *c.* 4500 BCE). A second domestication occurred from another subspecies related to *Equus asinus somaliense*, but another breed – today extinct – may have lived between Yemen and the Levant; it may have been the ancestor of this second domesticated set (Beja-Pereira *et al.* 2004; Vila *et al.* 2006). Wild donkeys may have been domesticated in Mesopotamia (Uerpmann 2008: 441), where remains are dated to the Middle Uruk period at Tell Rubeidheh, in the Diyala valley. As already mentioned, the wheel was probably developed in northern Mesopotamia, Syria, or eastern Anatolia at the time of the Urukian expansion (Sherratt 2006a).[66] From Anatolia, use of the wheel and the wagon spread along the Danube and the Black Sea. Their arrival went along with the dislocation of the large villages of the Cucuteni-Tripol'ye culture (located between the Dnieper and the Danube) around 3600/3500 BCE, during an ecological crisis brought about by a climatic aridification and a degradation of the environment linked to anthropogenic activities.[67] We cannot exclude a diffusion of wheel and cart through the Caucasus. The remains of a wagon found in a kurgan at Starokorsunskaja (Maykop culture) have been dated to *c.* 3500 BCE (Trifonov 2004; Primas 2007). Clay models of wheels have also been excavated from the earliest levels at the site of Velikent (same period) (northeastern

[65] See the discovery of numerous exotic goods in the foundations of a building of the Eanna (Algaze 2001: 35). Moreover, H. T. Wright (2001: 137) contemplates the existence of mobile craftsmen organized "in guildlike corporate groupings"; this may explain the homogenization of Urukian material styles (ceramics, bricks …).

[66] Models of wheels (made of terracotta or stone) are known at Jebel Aruda and in the Kura-Araxes culture. They show the use of a rigid axle, with wheels turning independently. In addition, a wall painting at Arslantepe (dated to *c.* 3370 BCE) shows a pair of draught animals. The wheel is recognizable on pictograms of the Late Uruk period.

[67] One may wonder whether or not epidemics – favored by settlement size and promiscuity between people and animals – contributed to the dislocation of the great villages of the Cucuteni-Tripol'ye culture; settlements seem to have been abandoned after fires, which were quasi-universal rituals of purification during epidemics. The farmer-herders of the Cucuteni-Tripol'ye culture became mobile pastoralists, with wagons, who moved into the steppes (cf. the Sredni Stog culture, the pre-Maykop culture north of the Caucasus, then the Yamnaya culture [Pit Grave Culture, 3200–2400] …), at the same time continuing to practice agriculture (Kohl 2002: 161, Rassamakin 2002, and Scarre 1999: 148). The wheel seems to have been introduced in the north of the Caucasus soon after the collapse of the Cucuteni-Tripol'ye settlements (Sherratt 2006a: 351). While a west–east movement of population accompanied the dislocation of the Cucuteni-Tripol'ye culture, conversely east–west movements may have occurred at an earlier period, if the identification of buckwheat (*Fagopyrum sagittatum* Gilib., family of the Polygonaceae) among the plants present in the Cucuteni-Tripol'ye culture is confirmed (this identification has recently been challenged). This plant originated in the western Himalayas (Janik 2002: 300ff.). Broomcorn millet *Panicum miliaceum* has been found in Cucuteni-Tripol'ye sites, and in the Late Sredni Stog culture; it was domesticated during an early period in China, but perhaps also in the Pontic steppes. The question of an eastern arrival, however, remains open.

Caucasus) (Kohl 2007: 85). The ard and the wheel spread together and rapidly across Europe along pre-existing trade routes, following the Danube valley and other large rivers, such as the Oder, around the middle of the fourth millennium, probably at the same time as innovations such as wool sheep breeding, the preparation of fermented beverages and the use of bivalve molds for casting metal objects.[68] The adoption of more intensive agricultural practices provided a means of facing the crisis linked to the combination of population surge and climatic deterioration during this period. These diffusions were accompanied by major social transformations. "The use of draught power appears to have been linked to an élite able to mobilize resources; it implied concentration of power and control on herds and therefore on men" (Sherratt 2006a: 345).

The crucial aspect of the invention of bronze has already been emphasized. It allowed for the growing production of weapons: besides trade, war played a major role in forming a dominant political elite and in building the state. Texts from Ur, dated to the end of the Urukian period / beginning of the Early Dynastic, refer to hierarchized military organization.[69] Interestingly, "male slaves [in Archaic texts] are often qualified as being of foreign origin" (Algaze 2008: 129).

The need to maintain an adequate flow of imports to ensure the stability and growth of a type of production destined both for the southern Mesopotamian social space and for export partially explains the Uruk expansion to the north and east: it was a complex phenomenon, variable in both space and time (Rothman 2004: 57). Not only did the city of Uruk take part in this expansion, but so did Nippur, Kish, Ur, and probably other cities, as suggested by the presence of the gods Enlil and Ninhursag at Mari, and of Ningal at Ugarit during the third millennium.[70] Mesopotamia needed to import metals, wood, stone, and luxury goods – as these were indispensable for affirming the power of its elites.[71] Whereas the city had no copper, arsenic, or tin, it managed to develop an elaborate copper and later a bronze industry. The earliest economic tablets

[68] Sherratt 1997, 2006a. The complex of draught power spread as a package (Sherratt 2006a: 346 fig. 5 and n. 49). The tracks or representations of wheels and ards "are distributed between 3500 and 3300 in a vast zone going from the Alps to the Baltic Sea and Great Britain to the northern Caucasus" (Sherratt 2006a: 346). Representations of wagons were found on a pot in Poland around the middle of the fourth millennium, and in Denmark around 3000 BCE. The development of sheep breeding for wool production went along with that of the weaving industry.

[69] Ekholm Friedman 2000: 165, 166. Gat 2002 (for the emergence of city-state cultures). Also Renfrew 1975. Only very few bronze artifacts are known prior to 3000 BCE. Uruk probably used armed forces, not to control trade routes, but to control the Mesopotamian core. The depiction of prisoners on cylinder seals is most likely not merely symbolic. Unlike what can be observed in the Egyptian iconography, the prisoners depicted do not seem to be foreigners. Pittman notes that "scenes of warfare are rare outside Uruk" in the iconography of this period (2013: 309).

[70] Westenholz 2002: 40 n. 9. Moreover, the author notes ancient borrowings from the Sumerian in the Semitic dialects of the northwest. These influences, however, may have resulted from contacts occurring during the third millennium.

[71] The need for Mesopotamia to import raw goods and slaves for building cities and manufacturing products became a motor for building the Urukian world-system (Matthews 2003: 118). H. T. Wright notes, however, that wood was available (2001: 133); but it is likely that the trees did not have the size required for building palaces and temples. The Khuzistan and the middle valleys of the Tigris and the Euphrates provided sources of bitumen (used for vessels and for caulking ships). We should also keep in mind what I refer to as "invisible imports," such as wine.

already contain a pictogram for a smith (Algaze 2008: 77), and the remains of a foundry showing division of labor have been unearthed at Uruk (Nissen 2004: 10). Two types of bronze were used in western Asia: arsenical bronze, found mainly along a north–south axis: the Caucasus;[72] eastern Anatolia; Palestine; southern Mesopotamia;[73] and a type of tin bronze appearing in the early third millennium, along an east–west axis: Afghanistan; Anatolia; northern Syria; Cilicia. Imported into southern Mesopotamia prior to the middle of the fourth millennium, copper came from the Iranian plateau, northern Iraq (Tiyari mountains), or eastern Anatolia. Already known in Palestine, the lost-wax casting technique developed both in Mesopotamia and at Susa.[74] The cupellation process used to separate lead and silver – from galena, a lead ore containing silver – was attested *c.* 3300 BCE at Habuba Kabira, and mid-fourth millennium at Arisman, in the vicinity of the Anarak copper source.[75]

In addition to needs and economic opportunities, ideology probably underpinned both the Urukian expansion and the emergence of ruling elites. Here, as is still the case, religion played several roles: it had an integrative function within a multiethnic population; it represented a kind of sanctification through which leaders could claim legitimacy; and it allowed for the regulation of economic activities when both cooperation and forced labor became necessary.[76] We must take into account not only religion itself, but a system of thought and practices, along with changes in clothing and food consumption accompanying social hierarchization in Urukian society. The role of religious networks in the Urukian world may explain why cultural signs were maintained, differentiating the southern Mesopotamians and their hosts for several centuries, at sites such as Hacınebi (Anatolia), but the "ideological Sumerian capital" also influenced many societies: the spread of "Urukian" potteries may have been linked to the consumption of fermented beverages embedded in new social relations (Sherratt 2004).

The Urukian expansion favored an evolution that had begun earlier in Anatolia and Syria, and built upon it: interactions between the Anatolia–Levant and Mesopotamian spheres took place during the flowering of the ʿUbaid culture, and

---

[72] It is probably no coincidence, notes Kohl (2002: 161), that the Early Bronze Age cultures of the northern and southern Caucasus (Kura-Araxes, Maykop) emerged around the middle of the fourth millennium, "at roughly the same time that the so-called Uruk colonies have been documented in Anatolia on the middle to upper reaches of the Euphrates." Various researchers have shown the links of the Maykop culture and of Transcaucasia with northern Mesopotamia (see below). To the west, solid interconnections are seen between Anatolia, the Balkan region, and the steppes during the Early Bronze Age (Sherratt 1997; Rassamakin 2002: 52ff.).

[73] For Muhly (1995: 1505) and Potts (see above), copper imported from Talmessi (Anarak) in Iran contained arsenic and may be the source of the arsenical copper found in Mesopotamia and Palestine.

[74] Benoit 2003: 59. For Palestine, see the treasure of Nahal Mishmar (*c.* 3500 BCE), consisting of 416 pieces, where arsenical copper may have come from Anatolia (Muhly 1995: 1504; Benoit 2003: 184).

[75] Silver extraction in Anatolia goes back to the early fourth millennium. Silver earrings dated to this period have been found at Hacınebi.

[76] Rothman 2001b: 357ff. For Lamberg-Karlovsky (1996: 94), "the key to understanding the 'Uruk expansion' rests not in the economic sphere but in the political: the establishment of a stratified elite which legitimized itself by a religious ideology, and reserved for itself the right to monitor and control the economic productivity of its subordinate population."

continued after the end of the 'Ubaid period. "Societies from Syria and Anatolia already exhibit complex organisational characteristics in the first part of the 4th millennium, prior to the rise of regular contacts with the Uruk world" (Philip 2004: 209)[77] (see above). At the junction of various roads, Tell Brak exhibits links with southern Mesopotamia already during the Middle Uruk period or even earlier.[78] Tepe Gawra and Arslantepe, though smaller settlements, were craft centers and nodes on exchange networks. Gawra produced textiles. The discovery of annular rimmed vessels which resemble primitive stills implies that perfumes were already being produced in the middle of the fourth millennium (Needham *et al.* 1980: 82). As Algaze points out (2001: 66ff.), however, the complexity of the northern settlements and their techniques of management and communication of information cannot be compared with those of Uruk and the cities of southern Mesopotamia.[79] Lapis lazuli is present at sites in Iran such as Tepe Sialk (Middle Uruk/Late Uruk), Tepe Giyan (already in the first half of the fourth millennium BCE), Tepe Yahya (3750–3650 BCE), and Tepe Hissar (phase 3600–3300, then 3300–3000), where it appears along with silver (perhaps originating in Anatolia, though this origin remains uncertain) (Mark 1998: 37). Lapis has been found in northern Mesopotamia, at Arpachiyah, Nineveh (already during the 'Ubaid period), Tell Brak, Tepe Gawra (Late Uruk?), and Jebel Aruda (before 3200), revealing the existence of trade routes linking Central Asia, Iran, and northern Mesopotamia.[80] This blue stone was also present in the main southern Mesopotamian cities, during the second half of the fourth millennium: Uruk, Ur, Nippur, Khafajeh, and Telloh – but it remained a rarity prior to the Jemdet Nasr period *c.* 3100 BCE. Moreover, "the intrusion [in Pre-Maykop settlements] of northern Mesopotamian cultural elements or peoples (?) predating the subsequent southern Mesopotamian Uruk expansion" signals exchanges with regions beyond the Caucasus (Kohl 2007: 70).

The Urukian expansion from 3600 BCE onward led to a growing connection of the southern Mesopotamian networks with those of northern Mesopotamia, Anatolia, and the Caucasus (see Map 1.2). Trading was active along the Euphrates, a river that played a crucial role in Urukian development. A Mesopotamian influence was felt in the plains of southwestern Iran (Susa II, 3500–3150) and in northern Mesopotamia (Brak, Hacınebi). From *c.* 3500, Uruk – and probably other rival Mesopotamian cities[81] – created "colonies" (built by the state or by small groups independent of the state; this question remains debated): Qraya, Tiladir Tepe, Sheikh Hassan, and later

---

[77] See Stein 1999: 92, 103; Frangipane 2004a: 124.

[78] Oates 2004: 118ff. Oates emphasizes the important role of textile craft as early as the Middle Uruk. Cylinder seals have also been excavated at Brak, dated to the Middle Uruk period.

[79] During the first half of the fourth millennium, the development of a type of painted pottery in Iran probably reflects the extension of exchange networks.

[80] As mentioned, lapis lazuli has been found that is dated to the first half of the fourth millennium in Iran (Tepe Giyan, Tepe Yahya). At Susa, lapis lazuli appears at the end of the Uruk period (Casanova 2013: 36). Throughout the ancient world, magic properties of protection were attributed to lapis lazuli, a fact which partly explains the covetousness that this stone aroused.

[81] This rivalry between city-states may have been at the origin of the Urukian expansion, along with the creation of "colonies." Competition probably went along with forms of cooperation: it is difficult, otherwise, to understand the stability of the expansion process over the long term. Perhaps Uruk was at the head of a kind of federation.

Habuba Kabira and Jebel Aruda.[82] The clear purpose of these colonies was to control access to regions of Anatolia and Iran that were rich in metal ores; to utilize pasture resources (for wool); and to interconnect the southern Mesopotamians with established trade centers and networks in Syria, between Anatolia and the Levant, and on routes crossing Iran. The importance of "outposts" such as Habuba Kabira implies active involvement by the public sector (palace, temple) in the process of creation.[83] Urban planning and the building of its fortifications required a strong community, and therefore state-level organization. The "Urukians" also settled in centers located either at network nodes or near coveted resources. Sites such as Hacınebi (as early as the Middle Uruk period) and Hassek Hüyük[84] thus hosted Mesopotamian enclaves. In the sites where Urukians were present, they usually brought their own administrative techniques (bullae, seals, tablets, weights), ceramics, bitumen, and building techniques. When Hacınebi hosted an Urukian enclave, two administrative systems – Anatolian and Urukian – seem to have coexisted. In an attempt to refute the possible formation of a world-system centered on Uruk and other Mesopotamian cities, Stein alleges – while providing no evidence for it – that exchanges between the Anatolian and Urukian communities were symmetrical; in fact, we do not know what was really exchanged; textiles and slaves, for example, left no trace in the archaeological deposits. In any case, it seems that the Urukian demand stimulated copper production in Anatolia. Stein recognizes that we have little information to go on for understanding the context surrounding the Anatolian elite during Urukian phase B2. He also puts forward the unlikely idea that there were few interactions between the Anatolian and Urukian communities during their two or three hundred years of coexistence (1999: 166)! Moreover, contrary to Stein's assertion, a core's power over a region did not necessarily diminish with distance, nor did exchanges become increasingly "symmetric" when the distance increased – I will come back to this point. Chains of exchanges were formed, along which inequalities could be transmitted and strengthened. While distance and the existence of groups positioned as intermediaries could lead to lower profits for the agents of the core, they did not reduce exploitation of the system's geographic or social peripheries. The fact that the Urukians sought alliances with the local elites does not imply equality in the situation of the two communities within the world-system. Moreover, the Urukians were settled on the highest part of the site, a fact Stein did not take into account. Lastly, Hacınebi was not a "periphery" as Stein terms it, but a semi-periphery: the level of social complexity, development of crafts, and density of its regional population show this clearly. The elites of northern semi-peripheries benefited

---

[82] Qraya, in the Middle Euphrates valley, yielded a date *c.* 3670 BCE, that might be too early (Wright and Rupley 2001: 101). The sealings found, however, go back as far as the Middle Uruk (Pittman 2001b: 410). Tiladir Tepe, near Karkemish, dates from the Middle Uruk period, as does Sheikh Hassan; the other centers are linked to the Late Uruk period. Recent excavations have revealed a substantial Urukian presence on the Upper Euphrates during the Late Uruk period (Algaze 2001: 43).

[83] It is impossible, however, to evaluate the involvement of the state in the process of the Urukian expansion, against the initiatives of private entrepreneurs or agents of the state acting on their own account. See Algaze 2001: 73.

[84] Algaze (2001: 40) suggests that Nineveh was occupied by southern Mesopotamians.

from exchanges with the Urukians within a process of coevolution, but beneficial exchanges are not equivalent to symmetrical relations (Rothman [2001b] commits the same error as Stein when he refutes Algaze's model, arguing that "northern societies must have seen advantages to an exchange relation with Southerners": these advantages recognized by the north did not imply the absence of dominance and exploitation by the southern Mesopotamians).

Other Anatolian sites, such as Tepecik, exhibit Mesopotamian influences without revealing an Urukian presence. This is also the case at Godin (level VI) (Iran) for the Middle Uruk period. The Euphrates River played a pivotal role because it offered access to the metal resources of the Ergani area, the Taurus forests, and the products of the Mediterranean region (the location of the colony of Habuba Kabira is enlightening in this respect).[85] In Syria, the site of El-Kowm, which shows influences from Sheik Hassan from the thirty-fourth century BCE onward, forms the western boundary of the Urukian sphere. Algaze has defined the ensemble formed by the southern Mesopotamian core and the network of Urukian enclaves as an "informal empire" or a "world-system," whose activity and survival depended primarily upon alliance networks with local chiefs.[86]

Moreover, Mesopotamian merchants and artisans may have been present at more isolated sites, located along trade routes (thus Godin Tepe [VI.1],[87] Sialk [III], in Iran, close to copper resources of Anarak).[88] For this "Urukian expansion," we should probably consider the existence of merchant communities operating within indigenous societies.[89] The regional configuration of established Urukian settlements shows dendritic forms that suggest the functioning of a monopolistic system (Algaze 2001: 49) or at least some kind of cooperation.

[85] See also the Urukian settlements found at Hassek Hüyük and Samsat in the Upper Euphrates valley, not far from ore deposits.

[86] For Algaze, the Urukian expansion was that of a first world-system, with the Mesopotamian city-states (core) exploiting various peripheries, in a process similar to that which Wallerstein describes for the modern period, with "a supra-regional system of interaction" which "emerges from the independent efforts of a few fiercely competitive cores" (Algaze 1993: 117). Mesopotamian influences are clearly seen in those societies which had contact with the Urukian enclaves, for example at Arslantepe, Tepecik, or Norşuntepe.

[87] The southerners – from Uruk or Susa – clearly enjoyed a dominant position, since they occupied an oval compound at the top of the hill of Godin during phase VI.1, with a fort built for them, dated to c. 3350 BCE (Badler 2004: 84). The excavations reveal a quasi-absence of Urukian women in the fort. According to Pittman (versus Potts 1999), glyptic art and numerical tablets show links with Susa and Nineveh (2000b: 443). Pittman has argued for the presence of people from Susa at Godin, whereas Rothman alleges that the oval compound was occupied by a local elite: "Godin would find its best analogy with a site such as Arslantepe or Tepe Gawra" (Rothman 2013: 87). However, if there were no "true leaders" at Godin, as Rothman suggests (2013: 89), why was it necessary to use elaborate cylinder seals? (Cylinder seals have been recovered from Godin.) The discovery of some Middle Uruk pottery shows that interactions predated the building of the "enclave" (Oates 2014a: 1491).

[88] Or perhaps these merchants were from Susa (see below).

[89] To interpret the Urukian expansion partly in terms of diasporas is compatible with the fact that this expansion took shape within the context of a world-system (on the concept of diasporas, see Curtin 1984, and Subrahmanyam 1996). Stein (1999) has rejected – generally speaking – the "world-system model" (in doing so, he has failed to consider Wallerstein's perspectives in their integrality) and has presented the "concept of diaspora" as an "alternative" model. Diasporas, however, function as part of the global context of the world-system. Whether these diasporas were politically independent from their cities of origin or not, the diasporas played a crucial role in forming interregional hierarchies.

In Iran, tablets impressed by cylinder seals and bearing numerical notations have been found at Susa, Chogha Mish (Khuzistan), Tal-i Ghazir (between Khuzistan and Fars), and Godin Tepe (in Luristan). According to Potts (1999: 60), the numerical tablets from Godin are similar to tablets from northern Mesopotamia (Tell Brak, Mari, Jabal Aruda), "whereas those from Susiana are most like examples from Uruk"; for Dahl *et al.* (2013: 354), however, "the Godin Tepe tablets are all Uruk-style tablets." "A single tablet (T295) has been classed as numero-ideographic, it bears a pictographic Uruk IV sign" (Matthews 2013: 347). Sialk (IV 1) yielded numerical tablets, prior to the appearance of Proto-Elamite documents.[90] Proto-literate tablets have also been found in northeastern Iran, at Tepe Hissar. At Uruk, proto-cuneiform signs and numerical systems were present together on tablets, but at Susa, it was only at Level III that pictograms appeared, after Susa II and the numerical tablets (Potts 1999: 63). Only "three of the thirteen numerical systems attested at Uruk [Late Uruk and Jemdet Nasr periods] were introduced to Susa [Susa II]" (Potts 1999: 65). But the Proto-Elamite includes a "decimal counting system that is not attested at Uruk (Dahl *et al.*)" (Petrie 2013b: 393). Potts emphasizes that although Mesopotamian scribes probably settled at Susa, it is difficult to view Susa as an Urukian colony. In fact, it is possible that a state centered on Susa maintained its autonomy, and influenced the Iranian plateau (see Petrie 2013b: 399).

The Urukian expansion fostered new development in Anatolia and Syria, where local elites took advantage of the exchanges and adopted some southern Mesopotamian practices such as the use of cylinder seals.[91] They established themselves as intermediaries along the roads of coveted products and organized their own craft production. Arslantepe, where a vast public palace-like structure was built starting in 3500 BCE, appears to have been a minor power center, controlling local or regional production. Many seals have been excavated, that were used in accounting operations. The site shows connections with southern Mesopotamians, but also with Syria and the Maykop culture.[92] As already pointed out, ideology – and ideational technologies – certainly played an important role in the southern Mesopotamian expansion; ideology clearly influenced the northern chiefdoms or proto-states and contributed to their configuration into semi-peripheries of the Urukian world-system.[93] The culture of Maykop, in the northwestern Caucasus, clearly reflects

---

[90] A clay bulla and a tablet dated to the Susa II period have also been found at Tepe Sofalin (Petrie 2013b: 390).

[91] The map presented by Primas (2007: fig. 7) clearly shows the spread of cylinder seals in the fourth millennium, along the Tigris (Nuzi, Nineveh, Tell Brak) with more seals appearing along the Euphrates River (Habuba Kabira, Jebel Aruda, Hacınebi, Hassek Hüyük, Samsat, Arslantepe) and in the Levant (Tell Afis, Judeidah, Catal Hüyük, Ugarit).

[92] Frangipane 2004a: 128; 2004b: 65; Rassamakin 2002: 55. Frangipane, however, does not believe that long-distance trade played a crucial role in the development of northern societies; she mentions growing metallurgical activity at Arslantepe, but considers this as simply production for a local elite. G. J. Stein also seems to agree: for Stein, there is no evidence at Arslantepe for a production oriented toward exports, and long-distance exchange played only a limited role; however, he notes a development of sheep herding for wool production, and borrowings of Urukian symbols of power by the local elites, which went along with societal transformation at Arslantepe (1999: 105–110) (see also Frangipane [2001: 330], who stresses the role of the ruling elites in the sheep breeding). For P. L. Kohl (2007: 223), the development of sheep herding at Arslantepe may have been favored by the arrival of populations from Transcaucasia.

[93] Algaze 2001: 67, 69. The novelty of the sociopolitical organizations in the south refutes Nissen's view (2001: 167) of the Urukian expansion as a simple attempt to reconstitute the exchange networks of the 'Ubaid period.

Mesopotamian influences, first from northern Mesopotamia,[94] with the borrowing of the slow wheel, and later from southern Mesopotamia, as revealed by the discovery of a cylinder seal and a toggle-pin with a triangular-shaped head known at Arslantepe during the Late Uruk period (Kohl 2007: 75; Kohl and Trifonov 2014: 1578). Brought through Iran and the region of Nineveh, lapis lazuli has been unearthed at no fewer than three sites (Maykop, Novosvobodnaya, Staromysatov) (Primas 2007: fig. 9). Carnelian and cotton from India have also been found, as well as turquoise from Tajikistan (Cunliffe 2015: 93). The extension of exchange networks can also be seen in the northeastern Caucasus, where the site of Velikent, which appeared around 3500 BCE, yielded arsenical bronze from its earliest levels.[95] In the Urals, copper at the site of Kargaly was mined as early as the second half of the fourth millennium (Chernykh 2002: 94), and the "royal" kurgans exhibit extraordinary wealth in metals, including gold and silver objects (Kohl and Trifonov 2014: 1579). These interactions would lead to the emergence of new institutions in the Eurasian steppes (Kristiansen 2007: 160). South of the Caucasus, in Transcaucasia, the Kura-Araxes formations expanded from 3500 BCE onward.[96] Some tin-bronze ornaments have also been discovered in the tombs of Velikent; these bronzes would become more abundant during the first half of the third millennium in kurgans south of the Caucasus, and then further west, at Troy II and at Aegean sites and as far as the Adriatic (Velika Gruda). The tin may have come from Central Asia (Afghanistan, Samarkand, or regions further east?).

It would be inaccurate to view the seven hundred years of the Middle and Late Uruk periods as a continuum of growth in space and time: several phases of growth and decline are apparent. A first phase of expansion occurred around 3600/3500 BCE, and another one a few centuries later (Habuba Kabira would come under this second phase). Rothman (2004: 57) discerns three phases of expansion, the first at the start of the Middle Uruk period, the second later during the same period, and the third during the Late Uruk.

Moreover, as already mentioned, authors such as Ur tend to emphasize continuity with preceding centuries rather than "revolution." Ur notes the presence of tripartite houses that were already known during the 'Ubaid period: so-called "palaces" or "temples" retained the same structure. Ur rejects the idea that urbanism results from extending trade and growing tribute demands; he does not believe in the formation of social classes going along with the creation of true bureaucracies. "Urban society in the Uruk period was a dynamic network of nested households," writes Ur (2014: 15). Here, however, he does not discuss the implications of the development of writing and of the impressive division of labor revealed by later lists of professions. For him, "broad social change is more likely to stem from the creative transformation of an existing structuring principle – in this case, the household – than from the revolutionary replacement of

[94] Kohl and Trifonov (2014: 1579) suggest an intrusion by northern Mesopotamian colonists into the southern Caucasus.

[95] Kohl 2007: 106. Produced by means of a potter's wheel, fine ceramics exhibit a Mesopotamian influence. Moreover, metallurgical production in the Caucasus may have been fostered by relations with Iran (Kohl 2007: 70; Avilova 2005: 27). The Maykop culture probably exported wool as well.

[96] The site at Leila-depe contains ceramics exhibiting parallels with Late 'Ubaid pottery, but "the parallels are better made with Early and Middle Uruk ceramics" (Kohl 2007: 68–69).

an existing structure with a completely new one." He notes that "the term for 'palace,' e₂-gal, literally meant 'great house'." However, this may be just a metaphor; and the fact that a city or a temple could remain under the rule of a particular household should not lead us to preclude the idea of new types of political or religious elites. Ur himself notes that some large tripartite houses built on high terraces must indeed be temples; their construction implies a large labor investment. Surely these "households" were not just common households. It is true, however, that when we consider ancient societies, "categories such as 'urban' and 'state' must be able to subsume a great deal of variability" (Ur 2014: 20), and the birth of the state does not imply the disappearance of kinship.

Most of the exchanges between southern Mesopotamians and northern populations are thought to have occurred within peaceful contexts. Military power must have played a role, however, especially when strong political entities emerged in the semi-peripheries of the Urukian area. During the Late Uruk period, settlements such as Habuba Kabira and Abu Salabikh were fortified: this appears to reflect growing conflicts.[97] At Hamoukar, a conquest by southern Mesopotamians has been suggested. "Urukians" also took over Brak – after a period of interaction[98] – and possibly Nineveh. Moreover, slaves may have been exchanged with the northern proto-states and then led to the cities of southern Mesopotamia.[99]

The Urukian expansion extended toward Egypt, via northern Syria. The existence of an Anatolia–Levant sphere of interaction is shown in the participation of Hama and sites of the Amuq in "a Syro-Anatolian glyptic tradition distinct from Mesopotamia," the diffusion of the technology of the "Cananean blades," the use of the pottery wheel, the presence of silver items at Byblos, in the southern Levant and in Egypt, and the relative abundance of copper at Byblos, with silver and copper coming from Anatolia (Philip 2004: 218, 220). This sphere of interaction was already in place at the start of the fourth millennium.

In the Persian Gulf, in contrast to what can be observed in Upper Mesopotamia and Iran, the Urukian presence seems to have been limited, perhaps because the organizational level of Arab societies did not allow for an efficient utilization of resources. It is unlikely that the Mesopotamian influences observed in the Nile delta and in Upper Egypt resulted from the presence of Urukians who sailed around the Arab coasts.[100] Exchanges did occur, however, during the fourth millennium, between Mesopotamia, Iran, and the eastern Arab coast. A clay bulla has been found at Dharan (end fourth millennium); Mesopotamian-type jars with tubular spouts discovered at Umm an-Nussi in the Yabrin oasis and at Umm ar-Ramadh in the al-Hufūf oasis may date to this period.[101] Around 3400 BCE, at Ra's al-Hamra (Masqat), grey ceramic from southeast Iran was used to heat bitumen imported from

[97] On this extension of conflicts, see Wright 2001: 146. Wright notes the growing importance of semi-nomadic communities during this period, especially in Upper Mesopotamia; at the same time, Uruk became preeminent in Lower Mesopotamia. Violence is depicted in the new iconography which developed during the Late Uruk period.

[98] Algaze 2001: 45; Emberling 2002; Lawler 2006. For Oates (2004), it is difficult to discern whether the southern Mesopotamians controlled a part of the site or the whole city, during the Late Uruk period.

[99] The possibility of a slave trade is not taken into account by either Stein or Frangipane.

[100] Oates (2014: 1485), however, does not exclude the possibility.

[101] Potts (1990), however, relates this pottery to the Early Dynastic I.

Mesopotamia (Cleuziou and Tosi 1989: 30). The name of Dilmun (which, during this period, refers to the Arabian coast in the region of Tarut-Dharan, and not yet to Bahrain) appears in a text from the Uruk IV phase: we hear of a "Dilmun tax-collector," which means that Sumerians were involved in trade with Dilmun, and a text from Uruk III refers to a "Dilmun axe" (Potts 1990: 86). Archaic texts from Uruk also mention copper from Dilmun, which may have originated in Oman. It could be that during the final years of the fourth millennium, barley and wheat were taken to Arabia. The term ŠIM, which seems to mean "aromatic essence, incense," already appears in texts of the Uruk IV period. Archaic texts from Uruk mention "an aromatic product for the use of the priests": aromatics certainly reached Dilmun at this time via a route linking Dhofar to Yabrin and al-Hasa (Zarins 1997, 2002). Moreover, the discovery of bowls of Urukian (or Proto-Elamite) type in Baluchistan renewed speculation on the possible role played by contacts with Susa and Mesopotamia in the emergence of the Harappan culture (Benseval 1994, Joffe 2000). Pottery of Urukian style unearthed at Tepe Yahya reflects southeastern Iranian links with Susa. The discovery of cotton fibers on fragments of plaster in a camp at Dhuweila (Jordan) (between 4450 and 3000 BCE) reveals the importation of cotton fabrics, possibly from the Indus region.[102]

Around 3200/3100 BCE, the Urukian "colonies" were suddenly abandoned; we observe a reorganization of the exchange networks as well as social transformations – not yet well understood – in southern Mesopotamia. Various reasons have been advanced. The decline observed in some "colonies" before their abandonment may have had its origin in the core of the system itself. A salinization of the lands – a consequence of faulty irrigation – may have led to weaker agricultural productivity and, therefore, to an increase in conflicts between city-states as well as to internal social problems: one notes "the abandonment of many of the public structures at the very core of Uruk itself."[103] Climate data for the end of the fourth millennium show a decline in oak woodland at Lakes Van and Zeribar, and low water volumes for the Tigris and the Euphrates, reflecting a drier climate.[104] An aridization of southern Mesopotamia may have begun in the middle of the fourth millennium.[105] In addition, one observes a

---

[102] Betts et al. 1994. Remains of cotton threads have also been discovered in the Maykop culture (3600–3200) at Novosvobodnaya (Shishlina et al. 2003).

[103] Algaze 2001: 77. Glassner (2000a: 47) speaks of a "radical redesign" at Uruk, but he also makes the point that no cultural break is observed. For Nissen (2001: 164), the absence of writing at Habuba Kabira and Jebel Aruda could indicate an abandonment prior to the Late Uruk phase: the collapse of the colonies would then have been caused by conflictual political conditions in the north and not by a decline of the south. However, the absence of writing sensu stricto at Habuba Kabira, where numeric tablets, bullae, and other instruments of control and administration of the southern cities have been found, could simply result from the fact that writing was not a requirement for these colonies (H. Wright, p.c.). Carbon dates suggest date ranges between 3340–2890 and 3100–2940 for Habuba Kabira and 3360–2970 for Jebel Aruda (Wright 2001). Moreover, Nissen refutes the idea of a decline at Uruk and in southern Mesopotamia at the end of the fourth millennium (2001: 167, 173) (cf. also Frangipane 2001: 343).

[104] Butzer 1995: 133, fig. 2, 136 (lake levels were probably low between 3200 and 2900 BCE). Pollen analysis at Lake Zeribar shows a decline in oak between 3250 and 2750 BCE.

[105] Wright 2001: 128. For Mitchiner (2004) and for Nissen (2001: 171), the process of aridification had already begun around 4000 BCE, freeing up lands hitherto submerged and stimulating the development of irrigation.

weakening of the summer monsoon system of the Indian Ocean, especially around 3200 BCE.[106] The pressure exerted by cities on their physical surroundings (deforestation …) and the human environment (tributes, corvées, urban migration) may also have been destabilizing factors. It is likely that the activity of the outposts depended in part on products such as textiles delivered from urban centers of the south. The profitability of these outposts could not be ensured within a climate of economic and political deterioration.

In addition, the destruction of the "palace" of Arslantepe by a fire *c.* 3000 BCE leads us to suspect other destabilizing factors which were not solely linked to climate change, but were also the indirect consequences of the Uruk expansion itself.[107] Transcaucasian populations belonging to the Kura-Araxes formations entered the plain of Malatya; they had probably been displaced by the arrival of groups coming from the steppes and the northern Caucasus. These Transcaucasians occupied Arslantepe from 3000 to 2900 BCE.[108] North of the Caucasus, the Maykop culture disappeared around the end of the fourth millennium (Kohl and Trifonov 2014: 1581–1582). We observe a reduction in number and size of the settlements in Anatolia following the collapse of the Urukian colonies, as well as a regional fragmentation.[109] Pontic and Transcaucasian influences are also seen in northwestern Iran during the late fourth and early third millennium, for example at Yaniktepe. At Godin, from 3100 to 2900, the Urukian/Susian influence diminished while at the same time, Transcaucasian pottery came into use (this pottery would become the most commonly used during phase IV).[110] Godin shows evidence of a fire, as does Sialk III, which was destroyed *c.* 3000 BCE. The Kura-Araxes populations also migrated to the southwest, entering the Amuq plain (Syria) then northern Palestine, around 2800–2700 BCE (Kohl 2007). In northern Mesopotamia, the lower town at Brak was abandoned, trade networks faded away, and "the use of tokens and sealed bullae as administrative technology disappeared, and mass production of pottery, on a large scale in the mid- to late-fourth millennium (e.g. Oates and Oates 1993: 181–182), all but disappeared at the end of the Uruk period" (Ur 2010: 401).[111] The

---

[106] Staubwasser and Weiss 2006; see below. For these authors, sharp climate change is noticeable in Anatolia, at Lake Van, and in Oman. Analysis of ice cores from Kilimanjaro also shows a climate change around 3100 BCE (Thompson *et al.* 2002).

[107] These movements can be understood as "one of the long-term consequences of the Uruk expansion" (Algaze 2001: 76). We cannot imply, as did Warburton (2003: 229), that Anatolia collapsed simply due to a decline in southern Mesopotamian demand.

[108] Frangipane 2004b: 63; Huot 2004, I: 174. Sherratt and Sherratt (2001: 34 n. 24) state that these Transcaucasian populations may have contributed to spreading the ritual use of wine. Kohl *et al.* (2002: 127) note the effects of climatic deterioration at the beginning of the third millennium in the north Caucasus–Caspian region. Migrating populations reached Syria–Palestine around 2800/2700 (Lyonnet and Kohl 2008: 32).

[109] Rothman (2001b), however, points to an apparent continuity in the Jazira plain, while a new type of pottery called "Ninivite V" appeared in a vast arch-shaped area. Moreover, Tell Brak, at the beginning of the third millennium, still showed cultural influence from southern Mesopotamia (such as the layout of the Eye Temple) (Crawford 2004: 120–122).

[110] Badler 2004: 82; Burney 1994: 48–50; Kohl 2007: 98. Edens (2002b: 33) gives a date for phase IV at Godin (containing pottery of the Kura-Araxes type, 2600 BCE) that is later than the date proposed by other authors.

[111] Oates (2014: 1485) also suggests the arrival of Semitic people as a possible cause for the abandonment of the Urukian colonies.

Illustration 1

The beginnings of writing

Mesopotamia. Tablet of accounts, probably account of bread distributed to four persons (J.-J. Glasssner, p.c.). The circles represent figures. Uruk, late fourth millennium, Louvre, A029560. © RMN-Grand Palais, Franck Raux

(a–d) Egypt. Bone or ivory inscribed labels. Tomb U-j, Abydos, tomb of King "Scorpio," *c.* 3200 BCE. © German Archaeological Institute, Cairo

(a) Slits representing figures

(b) Offering from the domains (tree) of King Dog (signs with symbolic meaning)

(c) Stork and seat, signs with phonetic value: *ba* and *set*, *baset*, reference to the town of Bubastis in the delta

(d) Signs with phonetic value: *ab* (elephant) and *jou* (mountain), Abjou (Abydos), domain of King Elephant

Illustration II

The influence of Mesopotamian themes and techniques in Predynastic Egypt: the "master of animals," long-necked mythical animals, rosettes, and the use of the cylinder seal (1)

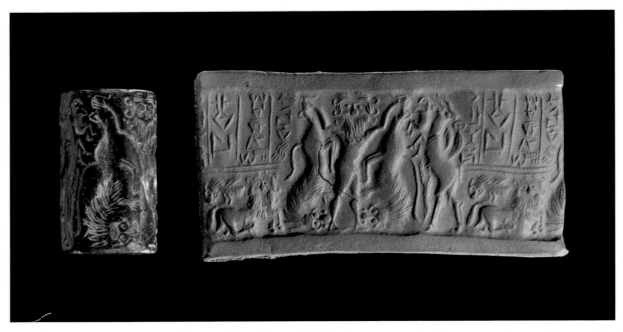

(a) Mesopotamia. Cylinder seal of Ishma-Ilum, Prince of Kisik, featuring a naked hero mastering two lions; made of lapis lazuli, a stone imported from Afghanistan; *c.* 2500 BCE. H.: 3 cm, Musée du Louvre, AO 22299. © RMN-Grand Palais. Christian Larrieu

(b) Egypt. Knife of the Jebel el-Arak; made of flint, with an ivory handle showing an iconography influenced by Mesopotamia, featuring a king mastering two lions, and a lion attacking a horned animal from behind. Nagada III period, *c.* 3400 BCE. H.: 25.5 cm, Louvre, E11517 © RMN-Grand Palais. Cliché Hervé Lewandowski

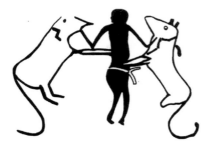

(c) Drawing on a wall of Tomb no. 100 at Hierakonpolis (Nagada IIc period, *c.* 3400 BCE). Hero mastering two lions. After S. Mark 1998: 77 fig. 40. © Texas A&M University Press

Illustration III

The influence of Mesopotamian themes and techniques in Predynastic Egypt: the "master of animals," long-necked mythical animals, rosettes, and the use of the cylinder seal (2)

(a) Mesopotamia. Cylinder seal showing animals with intertwined necks. Uruk period, 3500-3100 BCE. Louvre, MNB 1167. © RMN-Grand Palais. Cliché Hervé Lewandowski

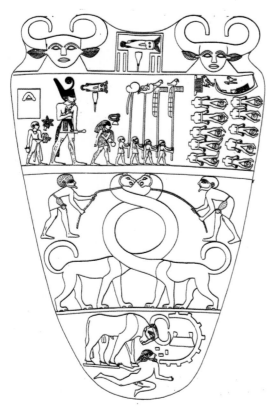

(b) Egypt. Palette of King Narmer, alleged founder of the Egyptian unified kindom, *c.* 3000 BCE. Egyptian Museum, Cairo. H.: 64 cm, L.: 42 cm. The central cup is surrounded by serpopards with intertwined necks, confronting each other. The upper portion shows two bull heads with human faces, a motif known in Mesopotamia. They frame the king's name represented by a fish (*nar*) and a chisel (*mer*). Below, a triumphal procession; to the left of the king, a rosette, another motif well known in Mesopotamia. On the lower portion, the king, featured as a bull, is destroying the walls of a town. Drawing, after A. Mark, 1996: 89. © Texas A&M University Press

(c) Mesopotamia. Drawing of a seal imprint, Late Uruk period. After P. Amiet 1980: 48 no. 680

Illustration IV

Statebuilding and long-distance exchanges

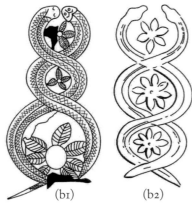

(a) Stone macehead of King "Scorpion," Hierakonpolis. Wearing the white crown (linked to Upper Egypt), the king, holding a hoe, is opening an irrigation canal. It is doubtful that the scorpion refers to the name of the king. Scorpions and rosettes were symbols of fertility, and the rosette may have been a solar symbol. The macehead thus associates two functions of the king, both as warrior and giver of life. Drawing S. Mark 1998: 110 fig. 57. © Texas A&M University Press

(b) Motifs of intertwined serpents and rosettes, (b1) Egypt, (b2) Susa. Symbols of fertility. Iranian and Mesopotamian cultural elements borrowed by Egypt followed a trade route corroborated by the arrival of lapis lazuli in Egypt. Drawing S. Mark 1998: 41 fig. 19. © Texas A&M University Press

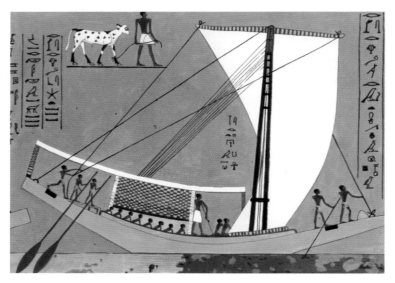

(c) Egypt. Statuette of a naked woman in lapis lazuli (a stone imported from Afghanistan). Hierakonpolis, c. 2900 BCE. H.: 8.9 cm, Ashmolean Museum, E1057. © Ashmolean Museum, Oxford

(d) Ship of the Fourth Dynasty, tomb of Kaem'onkh, Gizeh. After B. Landström 1970: 40 fig. 104

Illustration V
Images of power

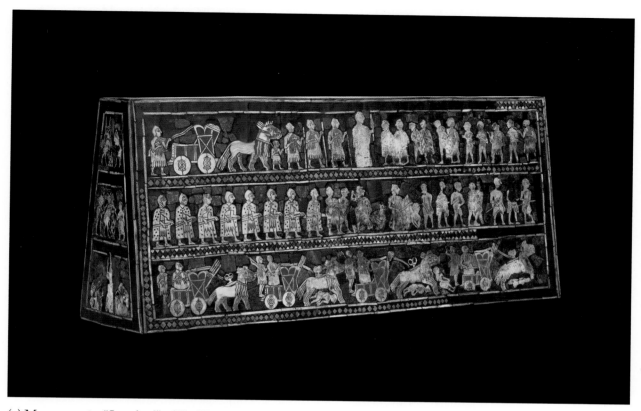

(a) Mesopotamia. "Standard" of Ur, "Royal" tomb PG 779, panel of war. Shell, lapis lazuli, red limestone, bitumen. Top register: the king, of higher stature, stands in the middle. Middle register: foot soldiers; on the right: naked prisoners. Lower register: chariots drawn by donkey-onager hybrids, *c.* 2400 BCE. H.: 20.3 cm, L.: 47 cm. British Museum, London, BM 121201. © The Trustees of the British Museum

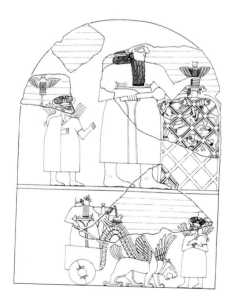

(b) Lion-headed eagle pendant: gold, lapis lazuli, bitumen, and copper. Palace of Mari, *c.* 2400 BCE. H.: 12.8 cm; L.: 11.9 cm. This god appears on a seal of the Late Uruk period. National Museum, Damascus. © Philippe Maillard/AKG Images

(c) "Stela of the vultures," erected at Tello *c.* 2450 BCE by King Eannatum (Lagash) after his victory over Umma. The god Ningirsu holds the lion-headed eagle, which strangles two lions above a large basket in which prisoners are stacked. The lower register shows the chariot of the god Ningirsu drawn by a griffin. A. Benoit 2003: 226, drawing by E. Simpson, after J. Winter 1985: 13 fig. 3

Illustration VI

Long-distance exchanges in the Mesopotamia–Indus world-system

(a) String of carnelian and lapis lazuli beads, with quadruple-spiral gold pendant. Ur, *c.* 2400 BCE. This quadruple-spiral motif has been found from Troy to the Persian Gulf and Turkmenistan, as well as other decorative themes such as flat-disk gold beads with raised mid-ribs (see Aruz 2003: 240, 241). The carnelian stone came from Iran or the Indus, and the lapis lazuli from Afghanistan. © University of Pennsylvania Museum of Archaeology and Anthropology, Philadelphia B17650

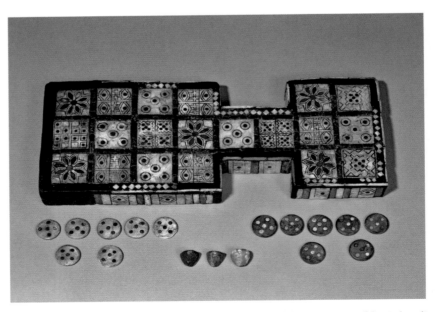

(b) Game board of twenty squares, made of shell, red limestone, and lapis lazuli. From the Royal Cemetery at Ur. PG 513. L.: 30.1 cm, W.: 11 cm. British Museum, London, BM 120834. Known since 3000 BCE, this game spread to Egypt, the Aegean world, and India over the centuries. © The Trustees of the British Museum

Illustration VII
Intercultural theme of horned animals feeding from the tree of life

(a, b) Cylinder seal topped by the figure of a ram, showing the "priest-king" or a divinity feeding two rams from the herd of the goddess Inanna with rosette-shaped flowers. Mesopotamia, Uruk, Jemdet Nasr period, *c.* 3000 BCE. Marble and copper. H.: 5.4 cm. © RMN-Grand Palais / Vorderasiatisches Museum, Berlin, VA10537

(c) Rearing goat with a flowering plant (perhaps the tree of life); gold, silver, lapis lazuli, copper alloy, shell, and bitumen, Royal Cemetery at Ur, PG1237, *c.* 2400 BCE. © University of Pennsylvania Museum of Archaeology and Anthropology, Philadelphia, 30-12-702

(d) Cup from Jiroft, Iran, chlorite, *c.* 2400–2200 BCE. H.: 22 cm. © Y. Madjidzadeh

Illustration VIII

Intercultural style and hybrid seals

(a) Jiroft (Iran). Chlorite vase decorated with a ziggurat topped with a horn, and (b) A "handled weight" featuring an eagle mastering two serpents, chlorite with stone inlays (limestone). So-called "intercultural" style. © Y. Madjidzadeh

(c) Cylinder seal of a scribe of King Shar-kali-sharri of Akkad, *c.* 2183-2159 BCE, made of serpentine. Theme of heroes watering horned animals – here buffaloes imported from the Indus valley – with overflowing vases, a motif known in other regions, such as Jiroft. Inscription in Old Akkadian. H.: 3.9 cm, Diam.: 2.6 cm. Musée du Louvre, 10 22303. © RMN-Grand Palais, Franck Raux

(d) Imprint of a seal from the Indus (M306, Mohenjo-daro) showing the Mesopotamian motif of the "master of animals." © AKGimages/ Nimatallah

(e) Square seal (the shape of the seals of the Indus civilization) featuring a man standing in a boat (motif of the Persian Gulf). Steatite, Failaka, early second millennium. L.: 2 cm. Kuwait National Museum 1129 ADY

(f) Round seal (Persian Gulf), with signs of Indus script. Steatite. Qalat al-Bahrain, late third millennium. L.: 1.45 cm. Bahrain National Museum Manama, 3011-11-90 © Philippe Maillard/AKGimages

Illustration IX
Mutual influences between Mesopotamia and the Indus

(a) Bull with human head. Tello, Ur III period. Steatite and shell. The god wears a horned tiara. The body shows trilobate cavities that would have received inlays. Louvre, AO 3146. © RMN-Grand Palais/Hervé Lewandowski

(b) Seal from Mohenjo-daro, Harappan period. National Museum, New Delhi, DK5075/123. A half-human half-bovine divinity is attacking a horned tiger. © National Museum, New Delhi

(c) "Priest," wearing a cloak with trefoil motifs. Limestone. Mohenjo-daro, twentieth century BCE. H.: 17.8 cm. National Museum of Pakistan. © DEA / A. Dagli Orti/AKG/De Ago

The trefoil motif is also known in Central Asia. A. Parpola (1985) has compared the cloak to the *tarpya* garment of the Vedic ritual (this comparison remains contested).

Illustration X

Objects from Bactria–Margiana showing foreign borrowings

(b) Compartmented seal (here an amulet) featuring a goddess seated on a horned dragon. Silver. Bactria–Margiana culture, *c.* 2000 BCE. The dragon, the cloth on the goddess, and the animals springing out of her shoulders are images borrowed from Mesopotamia. Louvre AO 30226. Diam.: 6.7 cm. © RMN-Grand Palais, Hervé Lewandowski

(a) Composite statuette (chlorite and limestone), possibly representing the Great Goddess, master of the dragon (Francfort 1994), wearing a *kaunakes* of the Mesopotamian type. Bactria–Margiana culture. Musée du Louvre, AO 22918. H.: 17.3 cm. © RMN-Grand Palais, Les frères Chuzeville

(c) Egypt, Eighteenth Dynasty (1550-1295 BCE). Anthropomorphic mirrors appeared in Egypt and in Asia at the beginning of the second millennium. Louvre, E 3745. H.: 31 cm. © RMN-Grand Palais, Les frères Chuzeville

(d) Bactria–Margiana. Copper mirror with anthropomorphic handle. Early second millennium BCE. Louvre, AO 28539. © RMN-Grand Palais, Franck Raux

Illustration XI

Cultural interactions and expansion of the Bactria–Margiana Complex
(late third – early second millennium)

(a) Ceremonial axe. The blade protrudes from the mouth of a horned dragon (this motif would later be found in eastern Asia). Luristan, early second millennium BCE. Well known in the Bactria–Margiana culture, these ceremonial axes have been found in Iran and Mesopotamia. Louvre, 22933. L.: 6.7 cm. © RMN-Grand Palais, Franck Raux

(b) Tell Abraq, United Arab Emirates, *c.* 2000 BCE. Comb decorated with an incised tulip motif imported from Bactria or Margiana. Sharjah Archaeological Museum, TA 1649. © Sharjah Archaeological Museum

(c) Indus, Mohenjo-daro. Bulla or clay amulet with imprints of a Harappan seal on one side, and of a seal of the Bactria–Margiana type on the other (eagle motif). Department of Archaeology and Museums, Pakistan, NMP 50402

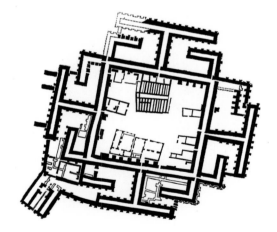

(d) Plan of the "palace" of Dashly 3 (Bactria), *c.* 2000 BCE. After V. Sarianidi 1986: 53

(e) Compartmented seals found in Bactria–Margiana, as well as in Iran and in the Indus valley. After A. Parpola 2002

Parpola (2002) has suggested a relationship between the plans of fortresses such as Dashly, cruciate seals, and mandalas and the Chinese mirrors termed "TLV" from the Han period.

Illustration XII

Possible emergence of the individual during the Middle Bronze Age

(a) Reverse of the envelope of a debt obligation. Kanesh, Anatolia. Debt of one silver mina owed by Shakdunua, son of Sharpa (an Anatolian), to Ashur-taklaku (an Assyrian). The interest amounts to 15 shekels of silver, 5 bags of wheat, and 5 bags of barley. The contract is dated for week, month (II) and year (*c.* 1863 BCE).
The envelope bears the imprint of the cylinder seals of the debtor and of three witnesses.
It features scenes mixing Mesopotamian, Anatolian, and Syrian styles. Text Kt 93/k 550, Museum of the Anatolian Civilizations, Ankara.
Translation and photograph C. Michel

(b) Babylon. Stela, "code" of King Hammurabi (1792-1750 BCE) (texts of law). Diorite. H.: 2.25 m. L.: 55 cm. Found at Susa, where it had been brought by the Elamite king Shutruk-Nahhunte (*c.* 1185-1160).
The upper register shows Hammurabi before the solar god Shamash. The text, written in Akkadian, is meant to be read from top to bottom, in columns. It was written "to demonstrate justice within the land . . ., to stop the mighty exploiting the poor" (Benoit 2002: 289). A "code of laws" had been promulgated by King Lipit-Ishtar of Isin (*c.* 1838-1828). © RMN-Grand Palais, Christian Larrieu

Illustration XIII

Interactions in the world-system of the Middle Bronze Age

(a) Egypt. Pectoral of Princess Mereret, Sesostris III's daughter. Dahchour. Gold, carnelian, turquoise, lapis lazuli, and amethyst. Twelfth Dynasty. The goddess Nekhbet, represented as a vulture, stands on top of the *serekh* (royal cartouche) and two griffins are clawing and trampling vanquished enemies. H.: 6.1 cm, W.: 8.6 cm. Egyptian Museum, Cairo, JE 30875. © Araldo De Luca

(b) Anatolia. Furniture support. Ivory (hippopotamus), gold leaf. Sphinx showing Egyptian influence, H.: 12.5 cm. Metropolitan Museum New York, 32.161.47. © Metropolitan Museum New York RMN-Grand Palais

(c) Silver cup, in the Töd "treasure." This treasure includes objects of various origins, in silver, gold, lapis lazuli, and other stones. The silver items bear witness to Aegean and Cretan connections. Silver was obtained through the Mediterranean trade. Diam.: 10.5 cm. H.: 7 cm, Louvre E 15153. © RMN-Grand Palais, Franck Raux

(d) Byblos, Royal Necropolis, Tomb III, gold pectoral. Decoration influenced by Egypt, featuring the falcon Horus. Eighteenth century BCE. H.: 12 cm, W.: 20.5 cm. Louvre, AO 9093. The pectoral reveals Egyptian expansion as well as privileged connections between Egypt and Byblos. © RMN-Grand Palais, Hervé Lewandowski

Illustration XIV

War, diplomacy, and long-distance trade in the Late Bronze Age

(a) Egypt. The pharaoh leads his army in a victorious battle against Asian enemies. Chest of Tutankhamun (1357–1349), Thebes. L.: 61 cm. Symbolic, the scene does not refer to any specific event. The horse had been introduced from Asia during the Hyksos period.
© Werner Forman Archive/Egyptian Museum, Cairo

(c) Nubians bringing tribute: gold, giraffe tails, wood, leopard skins, and baboon. Tomb of Sebekhotep, *c.* 1400 BCE. © The Trustees of the British Museum

(b) Weighing gold in the Royal Treasure, tomb of Ipouki, Thebes, *c.* 1380 BCE. Gold rings had already arrived from Nubia during the Predynastic period.
© Dagli Orti/Library, Louvre

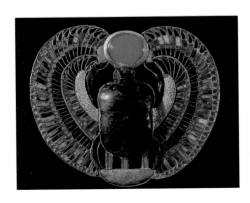

(d) Egypt. The scarab, solar symbol of resurrection. Gold, lapis lazuli, and other precious stones. Tomb of Tutankhamun, Thebes. H.: 9 cm, W.: 10.5 cm. © Dagli Orti/ Egyptian Museum, Cairo

(e) Iran. Pendant, gold and lapis lazuli, Susa, *c.* 1200 BCE. L.: 1.5 cm. Louvre SB 6589.
© RMN-Grand Palais, Christian Larrieu

Illustration XV
Products from Punt and Egypt

(a) Egypt. Pharaoh Thutmose III offers libations and incense to the god Amun. Deir el-Bahari, Hathor chapel, *c.* 1440 BCE. H.: 2.25 m, W.: 1.57 m. Egyptian Museum, Cairo, JE 38574-5. © AKG Images/Andrea Jemolo

(b) Egypt. Casket of the wife of the royal architect Kha, with flasks and jars containing ointments and perfumes, in ceramic, alabaster, and glass. Under Amenhotep III's reign (1386–1349). Museo Egizio, Turin. © AKG Images/Electa. During the New Kingdom, Egypt exported glass, as well as perfumes and ointments.

(c) Egypt. Container for cosmetics and unguents. Naked female swimmer and duck. Wood and ivory. Ducks made of ivory (whose wings formed the lid of the container) were manufactured in the Levant and exported (the Ulu Burun shipwreck has yielded several examplars). Louvre, E 218. L.: 29.3 cm.© RMN-Grand Palais, les frères Chuzeville

Illustration XVI

Egyptian expeditions toward Punt

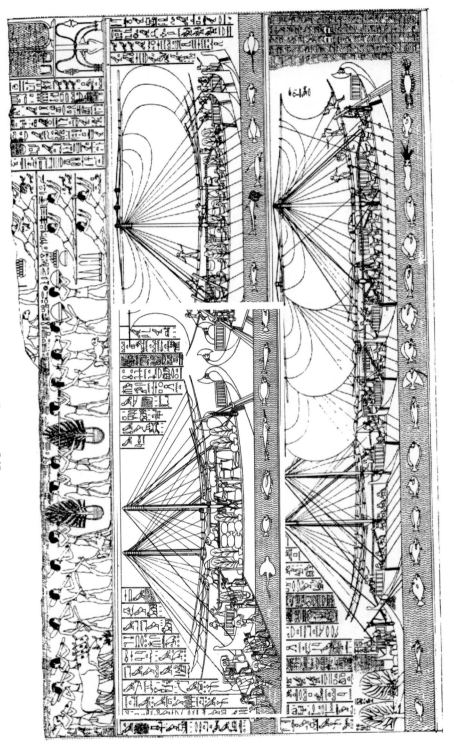

Egypt. Fleet of Queen Hatshepsut in Punt (1472/1 BCE), loading of merchandise: myrrh, incense, myrrh trees, ebony, *tishepes* and *khesyt* wood, ivory, leopard skins, monkeys . . . Drawing after the reliefs of the funerary temple of Queen Hatshepsut at Deir el-Bahari. K. A. Kitchen 1993: 593, fig. 35.2 and D. Fabre 2004: 78-79. © The British Library/Heritage Images

Urukian networks obviously could not survive in a politically hostile environment. Trade relations between Egypt and Mesopotamia practically stopped around 3100/3000. Upheavals in the north of the Urukian sphere of interaction affected not only the north–south relations, but also east–west routes. The abandonment of the northern colonies corresponds to a shift in Mesopotamian trade southwards toward the Persian Gulf, where copper in Oman began to be utilized in a significant way, within a more fragmented political and cultural context.[112]

Changes also occurred in the east. One notes a drop in population in Susiana *c.* 3200. "Sites with Late Uruk material disappear from the Susiana plain, and above the abandoned remains of the last Uruk community at Susa are layers with Banesh-related ceramics [known on the Iranian plateau] and Proto-Elamite texts" (Wright 2013: 68–69). Petrie notes that "the Proto-Elamite period was preceded by a widespread disruption in occupation at all of the excavated sites" (2013b: 400). A distinctive culture then developed at Susa (III), with increasing interaction between Susa and the Iranian plateau.

The State in Egypt: Formation of the First Kingdoms

The Predynastic Period

During the fourth millennium, a progressive aridization of the Libyan desert and of the eastern desert led to movements of populations toward the Nile valley and encouraged more intensive agricultural practices in recession agriculture. Lands fertilized by the Nile formed a relatively landlocked area; this situation may have favored a centralized political mode of organization and may have ensured better stability for the Egyptian system than had the irrigated lands of southern Mesopotamia. In contrast, southern Mesopotamia could have benefited from more varied exchange networks: the situation and structure of the region of the Tigris and the Euphrates rivers partially explain its instability and its dynamism, both characteristic of the city-states. The nature of the state in Egypt was also influenced by the politico-religious features of the societies from which this state originated (Wengrow 2006). One should note that the ritual scene featuring the king striking the heads of his vanquished enemies with a macehead was already represented during the Nagada Ic period (Wilkinson 2003). The ideological foundations of power were different in Mesopotamia and in Egypt. In Egypt, the figure of the god-king pharaoh was the guarantor of cosmic and social order, whereas the Mesopotamian lords were above all administrators and war chiefs. Order in Mesopotamia was the result of negotiations within cities, between cities, and between urban populations and nomads. Egypt became urbanized from around 3500 BCE, with various competing proto-states controlling sections along the river and neighboring regions. Political entities were centered on Nagada, Hierakonpolis (Nekhen), and This (Abydos was the necropolis of the people of This). Upstream from Nagada, the kingdom of Abou (Elephantine)

---

[112] Algaze 2001: 76–77; Crawford 2004: 182. As pointed out above, however, texts from the Eanna IV of Uruk, at the end of the fourth millennium, already mention copper from Dilmun, which may have originated in Oman or Iran.

formed another political entity. Kingdoms also developed in the delta, with Buto and Gerza (Gerzeh) as capitals.[113] During the Nagada IIc–d period, the funerary rituals of the south were adopted in northern Egypt.

At the same time, long-distance exchanges were developing. The dearth of stone and minerals in the valley led to the setting up of commercial networks, with the Nile offering the possibility of transport by boat. Very early on, the Mesopotamian sphere established indirect contacts with the Nile valley, through the Syrian coast.[114] These contacts would serve as catalysts in the formation of the state. The principal domesticated plants of western Asia (wheat, barley, pea, lentil, faba beans) were introduced into Egypt as early as 4500 BCE, and flax around 3500 BCE at the latest (Fuller and Hildebrand 2013). The Nile delta imported olive oil and wine from the Levant; ceramic vessels for both have been discovered. Other ceramics appear to be linked to the preparation of bread and beer, using production techniques clearly adopted from Mesopotamia (Wengrow 2006). This revolution was not only culinary: it went along with the building of the state and with innovations in funerary practices. Iconographic motifs observed in Egypt – especially during the Nagada IIc-d phase – have been linked to Susiana (two intertwined snakes) and Mesopotamia ("the master of animals," serpopards, winged griffons, rosettes),[115] as well as architectural elements (the appearance of a type of monumental architecture using sun-dried bricks shows an influence from western Asia).[116] Moreover, cylinder seals of Mesopotamian type were also in use (Moorey 1995; Mark 1998; Wilkinson 2004; Wengrow 2006), for imprints on jar seals, but were also sometimes used as ornaments. Other objects linked to administrative activity, such as conical "tokens," which have their parallels in Mesopotamia, may have represented elements of accounting (Wilkinson 2004). Lapis lazuli from Afghanistan also arrived in Egypt, probably via the Levantine port of Byblos.[117] Lapis has been found at Nagada (as early as the Nagada I phase), at Abydos and Hierakonpolis. Exchanges became more regular around the middle of the fourth millennium, during the Nagada IIc-d cultural phase (c. 3600–3300 BCE), thanks to the growing use of the

---

[113] Ivory "labels" found in the tomb U-j of the first king "Scorpion" at Abydos (see below) mention three settlements in the delta: Buto, Bubastis, and another unidentified city (Levy and van den Brink 2002: 8, 18). The texts of the pyramids refer to two (neighboring?) cities, Pe (Buto?) and Dep. In a period preceding Nagada IIc, however, tombs in cemeteries of Lower Egypt contain few offerings, compared with the graves of Upper Egypt (Wengrow 2006: 36).

[114] Maritime contacts via southern Arabia appear to have been less likely. It is curious, however, that the major site of Nagada appeared near the road of the Wādī Hammamat linking Koptos and the Red Sea. This route would become the great commercial corridor between Egypt and the Indian Ocean. See Moorey 1995, Mark 1998, Meeks 2002.

[115] Among other motifs originating in Mesopotamia were that of a bird of prey on the back of a quadruped, well known at Hierakonpolis, that of a lion attacking a horned animal from behind, and that of an ibex turning its head (Vertesalji 1992).

[116] A first use of brick has been found for a house at Hierakonpolis dated to the Nagada Ib-c period (c. 3700 BCE). The use of mud-brick in building funerary structures became "a standard feature of high status burials" in the Nagada III period (Wengrow 2006: 78, 171).

[117] There is a necklace from this period, British Museum EA 63077. Tombs in Byblos have yielded silver and copper from southern Anatolia on the one side, and gold, ivory, and Egyptian figurines of the Nagada I type on the other (Aubet 2013: 210).

donkey, domesticated in Egypt,[118] and to the development of navigation. It is during this period that more lapis lazuli was found in Upper Egypt. The Nile Valley also began receiving cedar wood; basalt jars and grinding stones; bitumen from the Dead Sea; carnelian beads,[119] and, more importantly, copper: for the Nagada IIc–d period, Wengrow points to a trade of ingots and copper sheets of a standardized size, a trade revealing contacts with the Levant.[120] In the first instance, the importance of copper in manufacturing weapons probably explains the advance of the Nagada culture into the Nile delta as well as the ensuing Egyptian thrust into the southern Levant. The date palm, domesticated in the Persian Gulf, may have been introduced into Egypt during the Nagada IIc–d period.[121] In exchange for these Asian products, Egypt exported ivory, stone maceheads, palettes, ceramics, stone tableware, gold ingots in rings, and textiles (de Miroschedji 2002). Asians probably lived at Maadi and at Buto even before the middle of the fourth millennium,[122] and Egyptians were already present in the southern Palestine during the Nagada I phase (Levy and van den Brink 2002: 18; Wilkinson 2002: 516–517; Hartung 2002: 446).

Contacts with Mesopotamia progressed when Habuba Kabira and other Urukian colonies developed (at the end of the Nagada II and during the Nagada III periods in Egypt, *c.* 3300–3150 BCE). The discovery of a Nubian shard of the Nagada IIc period at the site of Habuba Kabira is significant. Wright has suggested the possible presence of Syrian artisans in the Nile valley, and that of Egyptians in Syria (quoted by Joffe 2000: 118 n. 7). The discovery of silver at Byblos and in Egypt,[123] and of Mesopotamian-type pottery in Egypt,[124] reveals maritime links between the Nile valley and northern Syria. The presence of Urukian elements at Buto has been inferred from various assemblages. Cones and clay nails found there, for example, have been compared with the cones assembled to form colored mosaics decorating religious buildings during the Urukian period, but this identification has recently been questioned by various authors.[125]

Egyptian influences are also obvious in Lower Nubia during the same period (in the tombs of what is known as the A-group, as well as at Qustul and Sayala), along with imported items such as lapis lazuli and objects featuring an Egyptian iconography. The

---

[118] Moorey 1995: 199. Donkeys were domesticated at Maadi at the beginning of the fourth millennium and perhaps at El-Omari during the fifth millennium (Margueron and Pfirsch 2001: 92). Wengrow (2006: 39) notes increasing interactions with the Levant through "a pack-donkey route" established around the mid-fourth millennium BCE.

[119] Smyth 1998: 7; de Miroschedji 2002: 40. Egypt also received honey and turquoises from Sinai. Egyptian objects in Palestine are more numerous than are Palestinian artifacts in Egypt.

[120] See Wengrow 2006: 39. One notes a growing number of copper artifacts in Egypt and in Lower Nubia during the Nagada IIc-d phase. See also Golden 2002.

[121] de Vartavan and Asensi 1997: 193; Fahmy 1998 (finds at Nekhen, site HK43). Date pits have been discovered in a cave at Nahal Mishmar (Israel), dated to the fifth millennium BCE.

[122] At Maadi, stone structures predating Upper Egypt's Nagada IIc-d period show a Levantine influence that most likely reflects the presence of Asian people. Maadi imported pottery and copper from Palestine.

[123] The cupellation process for separating lead and silver, in use at Habuba Kabira, may have been introduced into Egypt through northern Syria.

[124] Three pottery vessels of Mesopotamian style found at Badari and Mostagedda may be imports (Wilkinson 2004: 238–241).

[125] Cf. Baines 2003; Philip 2004: 221; Wengrow 2006: 97.

contents of some tombs bear testimony to the wealth acquired by a Nubian elite through trade between Arabia and Inner Africa on the one hand, and Egypt on the other, particularly at the beginning of the following Nagada III phase.[126] The Nubian A-group used copper tools and exported copper, gold,[127] and incense (from African *Boswellia*?).

Like the Urukian expansion, that of the Nagada culture (originating in Upper Egypt), to the south and to the north, was based on an agricultural and demographic potential, and seems to have been motivated by the search for metals, Nubian gold, and Palestinian copper; this expansion occurred between 3500 and 3200, within the framework of territorial states in competition. Here again, innovations in means of transport played a crucial role in extending networks. The increasing use of the donkey has been noted above. During this period, many depictions of boats appeared on pottery. As symbols of royal power, boats reflected the scope of the ruler's control over fluvial transport. The first ships were built of reeds, but construction of boats from planks tied by ropes may have begun during the middle of the fourth millennium, a period that witnessed the introduction of the sail (Ward 2006).

"Dynasty 0" at Abydos

Excavations conducted at Abydos have uncovered tombs and inscriptions corresponding to a series of kings forming what is usually known today as "Dynasty 0." Tomb U-j at Abydos, that of King Scorpion (Scorpion I), has yielded 400 jars, mostly for containing wine; some of these jars are of Palestinian origin. Also found were 150 inscriptions, on small bone or ivory plaquettes, or on jars. These inscriptions constitute the first known hieroglyphs.[128] This script, whose creation was probably influenced by the Urukian experience, emerged alongside the formation of the state. Writing was linked to the circulation of goods, and also had a ritual dimension. Both of these aspects of script ultimately referred to the figure of the king. The plaquettes mention the origin of the goods, and some of them bear signs of account; the names *Buto* and *Baset* on labels may attest to tributes sent by these cities. Radiocarbon dating has yielded 3300 BCE, but researchers suggest that the tomb be dated rather to the thirty-second or thirty-first century BCE.[129]

The ninth ruler after King Scorpion I, a king of This, Narmer, at last unified Egypt prior to 3100 BCE (Bard 2000; Watrin 2002). It is likely that the emergence of This/Abydos was based on military organization and an increasing use of violence, as shown

---

[126] The absence of Egyptian objects in Upper Nubia at this time reveals the status of intermediary held by the A-group of Lower Nubia in exchanges.

[127] For Wengrow (2006: 34), "there is no direct evidence of metallurgical knowledge within Egypt until the late fourth millennium BC," although copper items dated earlier have been found. See also Killick 2009b.

[128] Bard 2000: 64; Arnaud and Kiner 2006: 63, 65. The first ruler mentioned in the inscriptions, King Oryx, may date to *c.* 3300 BCE. See also Raffaele 2003: 104ff. The tomb also contained boxes made of cedar imported from Syria.

[129] Joffe 2000: 113–114 n. 4; Braun 2001: 1283. This discrepancy between radiocarbon dating and archaeo-historical estimates is usual for this period and the following one. Krauss and Warburton (2006: 487) propose a later date for Tomb U-j, *c.* 3000 BCE. Raffaele (2003) considers that there was "a time span of *c.* 150–200 years between the owner of Abydos tomb U-j and Narmer."

by the discovery of weapons, which were more numerous from the Nagada IIc–d period onward; the "Towns palette" and the Narmer palette may also reflect this violence: their iconography is unlikely to be merely symbolic.[130] The formation of a unified Egyptian state went along with agricultural intensification and the king's control over transregional exchanges. Tablets became more complex: the name of the sovereign was written down, as well as the year the goods were delivered. It is during this period (Nagada IId–IIIa) that the royal ideology was formulated, accompanied by new religious practices (Wengrow 2006: 265). The purpose of the kings of Abydos seems to have been control of Egyptian gold and of copper resources of the Arava (Timna, Israel). Contacts with the Levant intensified during this period, accelerating the emergence of local hierarchies. In addition, it is likely that centers under Egyptian administration appeared in southern Palestine (Hartung 2002). Besides copper and wine, Egypt imported oil, resins and wood, particularly cedar wood from Lebanon. Originating in the Levant, the grapevine was cultivated in the Nile delta during the second half of the fourth millennium (see below), and Egypt produced wine during the First Dynasty.

Egypt was also connected to the south; the elite of the Nubian A-group culture benefited from its position as intermediary between Inner Africa and the Horn of the continent on the one side, and Egypt on the other (see above).

Egypt, the Interior of Africa, and the Indian Ocean

Ancient routes linked the coasts of the Red Sea and the African interior to Nubia and Egypt. Cowries have been discovered in Nubia that date to the Neolithic period (el-Kadada, Central Sudan), and in a tomb belonging to the A-group culture (Phillips 1997: 427; Haaland 1999: 412–413). Other marine shells have been excavated at Kadero (Sudan) dated *c.* 4000 BCE, and the communities of the Kassala phase (Sudan, 3000 BCE) also had connections with the coasts of the Red Sea. Obsidian from Ethiopia has been discovered in Predynastic tombs of the fourth millennium BCE (period Nagada II, or as early as Nagada I).[131] Two arrows belonging to the Proto-Dynastic period discovered at Abydos are thought to have been carved from ebony (*Diospyros mespiliformis* Hochst. ex. A. DC.), found in Eritrea, Ethiopia, Sudan, and Yemen (Western and McLeod 1995: 80–81, Meeks 2002: 280). A bracelet carved from an Indian shell has been excavated in a tomb in Lower Nubia dating to the end of the fourth millennium BCE (Fattovich 1997a: 480). The cemetery of Qustul (Lower Nubia) yielded stone pots that were used for burning incense.

Central Asia and Southern Asia

From the seventh millennium on, two secondary Neolithic centers formed in Turkmenistan on the one side, and in the Indus valley on the other. Interconnected proto-urban

---

[130] The demise of Maadi was noticeable during the Nagada IIc–d period, and we observe a discontinuity in some settlements around 3300 (for example at Tell el-Farkha and Tell Ibrahim Awad).

[131] Zarins 1989, Bavay *et al.* 2000, Hendrickx and Bavay 2002. The stone used for all the obsidian tools of Hierakonpolis, Abydos, Nagada, and Qaw el-Kebir that have been studied originated in Ethiopia or Yemen. Chemical analysis does not allow us to differentiate between obsidian from the Horn of Africa and obsidian from southern Arabia (Durrani 2005).

settlements appeared in Central Asia, in eastern Iran and in the Indus during the fourth millennium (Tosi and Lamberg-Karlovsky 2003). In Turkmenistan, the assemblages of Altyn Tepe and of the Geoksyur oasis (Namazga III phase)[132] show shells imported from India, and ceramics for which parallels can be seen in pottery found at Shar-i Sokhta I (Sistan, Iran), Mundigak III (Afghanistan), Quetta ("Quetta Ware"), and Mehrgarh III (Pakistan). Spindles unearthed at Anau and Shar-i Sokhta also show links between Turkmenistan and Sistan (Good 2006: 203). The data therefore do reveal connections and interactions among these different regions (Hiebert 1994; Possehl 1999a; Ratnagar 2004). The affinity of the painted pottery from the lower levels of Shar-i Sokhta with pottery from Turkmenistan may indicate that people from this region migrated to Shar-i Sokhta during the second half of the the fourth millennium (Masson 1996a: 232). Global climatic cooling *c.* 3200/3100 BCE may have triggered some movements of populations towards the south, similar to what would be observed more than a thousand years later. In any case, a sphere of interaction including Turkmenistan, eastern Iran, part of Afghanistan and Pakistan, had already formed by this time. Moreover, contacts were made between populations from the steppes and the settlements of Turkmenistan around the middle of the fourth millennium (Lyonnet and Kohl 2008). Shar-i Sokhta also served as an interface for regions near the Indian Ocean. Located on a route leading to Elam and Sumer, Shar-i Sokhta was a regional center linked to Baluchistan (discovery of Nal pottery) and southern Iran. An Elamite seal dated to *c.* 3200 BCE has been discovered in Turkmenistan. East of Shar-i Sokhta, Mundigak received lapis lazuli from Badakshan (northern Afghanistan) and turquoise from either Nishāpūr (northeast Iran) or from Kyzylkum (Kazakhstan). These stones were worked locally into beads. Moreover, Mundigak yielded a single ivory item, imported from India, and ceramics from Baluchistan (Quetta ...).[133] The site was probably connected with settlements of the Indus basin such as Rahman Dheri. The likely center of a chiefdom emerging around 3300, Rahman Dheri became a fortified settlement during the first half of the third millennium.

The expansion of both Turkmenistan culture and long-distance trade was accompanied by the emergence of the site of Sarazm, in the Zeravshan valley (Tajikistan). Its ealiest levels go back as far as the late fourth millennium. It has revealed "close architectural and ceramic parallels with sites in the Geoksyur oasis [Turkmenistan] and even farther south in Baluchistan" (Kohl 1995: 1060; Ratnagar 2004: 15).[134]

---

[132] Connections between Turkmenistan and Iran are already noticeable during the Namazga II phase (Lamberg-Karlovsky 1977: 36).

[133] Jarrige and Tosi 1981, Sarianidi 1996. Mundigak III can be dated to between the second half of the fourth and the first half of the third millennium.

[134] Although Sarazm is located near sources of tin, it contains only copper artifacts. In Turkmenistan, tin was rarely used prior to the Namazga VI phase (Weeks 2003: 176, Francfort 2005: 290 n. 163): it has not been determined whether or not tin was already being mined in Zeravshan during the third millennium (Boroffka *et al.* 2002). The mineworks in this region date to the period 1900–1300 BCE.

2 Early Bronze Age I in Western Asia and Egypt (*c.* 3000–2700 BCE)

Global climate change around 3100 BCE caused population movements in Asia, a dislocation of the Mesopotamian system and a restructuring of exchange networks (Staubwasser and Weiss 2006; Beaujard 2011). Migrations affected the Caucasus, Anatolia, and northwestern Iran, and the Urukian "colonies" were abandoned. Exchanges between Egypt and Mesopotamia diminished around 3100–3000 BCE. Three distinct areas can be distinguished during the early third millennium, centered around southern Mesopotamia, Iran, and Egypt, respectively (Map 1.2). At the same time, Brooke (2014: 183) is probably right in pointing out "a significant intensification of human economies," fostered by climate change between 3200 and 2900 BCE.

Mesopotamia at the Beginning of the Third Millennium: The Opening to the Persian Gulf

From the end of the third millennium onward, northern Mesopotamia and Anatolia had only weak connections with southern Mesopotamia. Anatolia then experienced a period of turmoil, with alternating Syrian and Transcaucasian occupations (Huot 2004, I: 174), and northern Mesopotamia appears to have entered a period of "'devolution' (Schwartz 1994a, p. 154)" (Ur 2010: 401). During this time there was an apparent diminution in social complexity (Akkermans and Schwartz 2003: 216–224), and "the cache of over 500 sealings from the small temple at Tell Brak demonstrates a concern with property control (Matthews 2003[a], pp. 111–113)" (Ur 2010: 403). In the Euphrates valley, many small sites were heavily fortified (Cooper 2006: 71–73).

Southern Mesopotamia's exchange networks began to be more oriented toward the Persian Gulf, where copper exploitation had begun in Oman, while the roads of the Arabian interior fell into disuse. Along with these changes came improvements in maritime techniques. The Jemdet Nasr period (3100–2900 BCE) and the subsequent Early Dynastic period (2900–2400 BCE) correspond to a new boom in the Mesopotamian region, with the development of a writing system and flourishing urbanism – with new cities appearing at Lagash and Shuruppak. The climate may have become wetter in Mesopotamia during the early third millennium, but the data is inconclusive for the Persian Gulf.[1] Uruk reached its

[1] Zarins 2002, Ray 2003: 87. In the Arabian interior, the Awafi lake filled again at the beginning of the third millennium (Boivin and Fuller 2009: 124). Regarding Oman, Cleuziou (2002: 198) points out that there are divergent interpretations of climatic data for the beginning of the third millennium (increased humidity, or aridity?). For Oman, in any case, a 5m decrease in aquifer levels during the third millennium has been noted. Wilkinson (2005: 185) adds that in much of the Fertile Crescent, climatic drying took place after 3000 BCE, with oscillations.

peak size (600 ha) during the Jemdet Nasr period, and remained by far the largest Mesopotamian city. Not much is known about this period, but "a number of texts suggest the existence of a cooperative league of the six cities of Adab, Lagash, Umma, Uruk, Shuruppak and Nippur during the Early Dynastic I [2900–2750] and II [2750–2600]" (McIntosh 2005: 175). The use of silver as currency appears to date back to the Jemdet Nasr period, when "purified silver" is first mentioned, for the purchase of a slave (a boy?) (Gelb, Steinkeller, and Whiting 1991: 277, 295). Archaeology, moreover, has shown the importance of terrestrial trade routes through Iran, where merchants transported lapis lazuli, tin, and gold.

The Proto-Elamite Sphere (3100–2800 BCE)

During the period between 3200–3100 and 2750 BCE, Susiana was oriented more toward the east, and appears to have had only weak connections with southern Mesopotamia.[2] The plain was depopulated, but the city of Anshan (Tall-i Malyan),[3] in Fars (the remains of which cover 200 ha) may have become the center of an independent Elamite state (Potts, however, argues against the idea that Susa was in decline, suggesting that it may have remained an important center [1999: 83]). The period saw abrupt cultural change, with the appearance of new pottery, iconography, and copper-processing technology. Copper production expanded during this period, marked by the move to furnace smelting, for example at Arisman. A system of "Proto-Elamite" writing was created, the origins of which may in part have had links with Susa (Susa III),[4] and which remains little understood. The nature of the state and its extent are also unclear (the controversial term "Proto-Elamite" has been retained for the sake of convenience). It has been noted that "the numero-ideographic tablets at Uruk and Susa order signs and numbers in different ways" (Petrie 2013b: 393). Moreover, "there is a divergence of the Uruk and Susiana glyptic iconography at the end of the 4th millennium BC (Jemdet Nasr/Susa III)" (Pittman 2013; Petrie 2013b: 393). Proto-Elamite may have been a bookkeeping system. "Proto-Elamite societies . . . maintained a structure and system of control and interaction across much of the region that retained some elements of the preceding Uruk phenomenon" (Matthews 2013: 349). Tablets and Proto-Elamite sealings have been found at Susa, Tal-e Ghazir, Tal-e Malyan, Tappeh Sialk (IV), Tepe Ozbaki, Tepe Yahya (IVC), Shar-i Sokhta (I), and Tepe Sofalin (Dahl *et al.* 2013: 353):[5] "the Proto-Elamite civilization was spread over

---

[2] For some archaeologists, the Proto-Elamite period began around 3300 BCE, but "the real [Proto-Elamite] script only began at the end of this period" (Helwing 2013: 93). Studying iconography and tablets, Pittman identifies a transitional phase at Susa, Godin Tepe, Tepe Sofalin, and Sialk (2013: 328).

[3] C_{14} dating at Malyan dates the city back to at least 3300–3200 BCE. "The chronological relationship of the Proto-Elamite settlements remains an unresolved issue" (Lamberg-Karlovsky 2001a: 270). Wall paintings at Malyan suggest links with Central Asia.

[4] Clay bullae were present at Susa before "numeric tablets" (Susa II). The system of Proto-Elamite writing was created slightly later, after the development of the Mesopotamian proto-cuneiform, while Susiana regained its independence from Mesopotamia. The numerical systems in use during the Susa III period are "either identical to or else derived from the systems found in the proto-cuneiform texts from Uruk" (Potts 1999: 75). Cf. also M. van de Mieroop 2004: 28–29. Potts, however, notes a marked "disjuncture," in stratigraphy and in ceramic assemblage, between Susa II and Susa III (1999: 82).

[5] There is some disagreement about the tablets of Godin Tepe (Period VI.1) (see above). According to Pittman, they are related to Susa. With the exception of one tablet, they are only numerical.

the whole Iranian plateau" (Vallat 2003: 89), but this does not necessarily indicate an economic integration of the plateau (Petrie 2013b: 394), and Proto-Elamite writing was probably confined to a very small number of practitioners. The city of Konar Sandal (region of Jiroft, southern Iran) appears to go back to this period, but it is not yet known if it belonged to the Proto-Elamite sphere or if it was a separate entity. The establishment of the Proto-Elamite area was in any case clearly connected to the increased exchanges between Sistan (site of Shar-i Sokhta, phase II), Afghanistan, and the Indus region. Further east, trade routes extended towards Turkmenistan, Uzbekistan, and Tajikistan (site of Sarazm) (Hiebert 2002, Francfort 2005). In the northwest, a road led from Susa to Nineveh through the Hamrin; this road then continued further west toward the Mediterranean (Crawford 2004). The Elamites and the southeastern Iranians also developed maritime exchanges in the Persian Gulf, and a Proto-Elamite port has been found at Sabzabad, on the Bushire peninsula.

This Proto-Elamite sphere disintegrated around 2800 BCE during a period of aridity that affected both the Iranian plateau and Mesopotamia. This episode was accompanied by the migration of steppe populations from north to south through the Caucasus, as confirmed by the appearance of kurgans in Transcaucasia. The ancient Kura-Araxes populations also migrated toward the southwest, into the Amuq plain (Syria), and from there into northern Palestine, around 2800–2700 BCE. These changes were accompanied by a shift to pastoralism. The Proto-Elamite script suddenly ceased to exist, its disappearance reflecting the breakdown of administrative structures (Petrie 2013a: 18). Susiana subsequently fell once more under the influence of Sumer, a region divided between city-states in competition, and it adopted the Mesopotamian cuneiform for the Elamite language. An Elamite kingdom, Awan, was founded on the highlands of Luristan, a region that from 2600 BCE onward became an important center of metallurgical production.[6] The flourishing of this kingdom may have been a reaction to the Mesopotamian presence in Susiana.

The Pre-Harappan Civilization of the Indus

In Pakistan and northwestern India, agrarian communities developed during an "Early Harappan" period that had also mastered metalworking techniques. The climate changes that occurred *c.* 3200 BCE may have been one of the factors triggering the domestication of local millets, cultivated in the summer (plants from Western Asia were cultivated in the winter) (Fuller 2006a, b). Moreover, the water buffalo was added to the other domesticated animal species. The Indus culture extended toward the Upper Ganges as early as the beginning of the third millennium. At the same time, the search for copper may have motivated a thrust towards Rajasthan and Malwa. Domesticated animals spread from the Indus valley to Rajasthan and northern Gujarat during the fourth millennium. Soon afterward, during the third millennium, Gujarat developed a seasonal summer agriculture based on the domestication of local

---

[6] The Awan kingdom was defeated by the armies of the city of Kish around 2675 BCE, but later vanquished the First Ur Dynasty. The site of Pusht-i Kuh has sometimes been proposed as the site of the capital of Awan (Potts 1999: 87ff.).

millets, and of *Vigna mungo*.[7] During the early third millennium, domesticated animals spread toward the south. Sites dated to this period usually show few signs of social differentiation, except at Harappa as early as the Ravi phase (3300–2800 BCE); this site evolved into an urban center during the Kot Diji phase (2800–2600 BCE) (the name of a northern Sind site). During the Ravi phase, at Harappa, the use of non-inscribed seals has been observed, as well as the production of carnelian and lapis lazuli beads. Lapis lazuli is also found at Rahman Dheri, and Nal, in the Amri culture, which suggests interregional contacts. The first signs of "writing" – marks made on pottery after firing, often similar to signs used later in Indus writing – have been discovered at Harappa as early as 3300 BCE.[8] Combinations of signs appear in the Kot Diji phase (though they do not yet reflect "writing"), and stone cubic weights suggest a central structure organizing trade. Harappa, at that time, was a city composed of two walled settlements covering 25 ha. Moreover, "two-wheeled carts pulled by oxen were developed as early as 3700 to 3300 in the Indus region" (Kenoyer 2014: 411): Harappa provides evidence for "an independent development of wheeled carts" (a fragmentary clay model of a cart wheel has been dated to the middle of the fourth millennium BCE) (Frachetti 2012; Kenoyer 2009), and the rise of copper metallurgy is also noticeable there, as well as at other sites (Mehrgarh III, Kalibangan, Sothi, Banawali). "Spindle whorls suggest the development of textile production," and various sites produced glazed faience beads (Kenoyer 2014: 411). In this Kot Diji phase, walled settlements appeared in all regions of the Indus valley. Button seals were used, and especially at Harappa, clay sealing and standardized cubic stone weights "are evidence of some form of elite control" (Kenoyer 2014: 412). Long-distance exchanges developed at this time, on maritime routes toward Oman and as far as Mesopotamia, and on terrestrial routes, toward Afghanistan, eastern Iran, and Turkmenistan, through the Quetta valley. Various objects demonstrate these contacts: carnelian beads in a Pre-Akkadian period in Mesopotamia; shell beads and cups (made of *Xancus pyrum*, a shell found on the coast of Saurashtra) in Iran, at Shar-i Sokhta, around 2800 BCE; and mother-of-pearl pendants (from *Pinctada sp.*) found at Mehrgarh (Pakistan) which may have come from Oman.[9] Maritime connections existed between Oman and the coast of Makran, which would later develop during the Mature Harappan period. Lapis lazuli appeared in the Persian Gulf during the Early Dynastic II period (*c.* 2700 BCE). At the same time,

---

[7] Fuller 2006a: 6, 30, 37ff.; 2007: 406. Domesticated animals coming from the Indus region appeared in Gujarat in the middle of the fourth millennium, and in Rajasthan at the end of the fourth millennium (Ahar culture). The latter culture probably developed a winter agriculture using plants from Western Asia.

[8] These discoveries were made by J. M. Kenoyer and R. H. Meadow, who led excavations at Harappa between 1995 and 2001 as part of the Harappa Archaeological Research Project. www.harappa.com/indus5/index.html; Kenoyer 2006; Kenoyer and Meadow 2008. These marks should be distinguished from pottery marks, which appear as early as 4500 BCE in Baluchistan, at Mehrgarh. It is unclear whether the combinations of signs observed in the Kot Diji phase really do form a writing system. Seals with inscriptions also appear at Kunal and Rahman Dheri during the Kot Diji phase.

[9] Ray 1999b: 6. This author emphasizes the historical importance of fishing communities, too often ignored. These communities played a role in the development of trade, both through the products they collected and transformed, and through their nautical knowledge. When hierarchical societies emerged, trade became more structured, and at this point a distinction should be made between communities of fishermen and those of traders who owned ships or rented space on these ships.

archaeology has revealed the importance of trade routes connecting Mesopotamia, Susiana, northern Iran, Sistan, Afghanistan, and Indus.[10]

Archaeology has also indicated a period of change in the Indus valley at the end of this phase, with numerous sites being abandoned – some, such as Gumla, Nausharo, and Kot Diji, after having been burnt – and the beginning of a short transitional period leading to the Classic Harappan period, a transition not yet well understood (Possehl 2002a). It is probably no coincidence, however, that the Proto-Elamite period in Iran came to an end at this time, partially brought about by a phase of aridification. Another sign pointing to a break with the earlier period is that many sites from the Classic Harappan period were set up on virgin soil. Kenoyer (2014: 412), however, points out that there was continuity at other sites, such as Harappa, Dholavira, and Banawali. There may have been internal causes for the rapid cultural change that can be observed at this time, but what were they, and why did the change occur on such a large scale? An influx of new populations cannot be excluded, which may have combined with domestic factors to produce the ascent of the urban Indus civilization, before trade developed between that civilization and Mesopotamia.

Egypt during the Thinite Period (First and Second Dynasties, 3100–2700 BCE)

Under the first and second dynasties, the capital was at This (Thinis) (Jirja?) then at Memphis; the necropolis remained at Abydos. The state tried to control the production, importation, storage, and transformation of raw products, as well as the distribution of goods. Some authors – for example, Allen (1997) – emphasize the role of geographical factors ("circumscribed" agricultural lands [Carneiro 1970]) in the formation of the Egyptian state, as well as the need for its rulers to control the population. The building and management of irrigation systems probably did not play a crucial role in these developments, unlike what has often been claimed. It is worth noting, however, that the so-called king "Scorpion," on a macehead, brings life to the earth by opening an irrigation channel,[11] and that the rectangle-shaped hieroglyph with a checkered pattern signifying "irrigated land" refers to the royal residence during the Old Kingdom. The control of agrarian surpluses by the elites required the management of complex rural estates by a royal power or institutions such as temples, probably as early as the Predynastic period. The centralized system put in place was based on the creation of nomes (provinces). It was probably during this period that a writing material was created from the pith of the papyrus plant, *Cyperus papyrus* L. The pith was cut into very fine strips that were arranged together to form a sheet. "Dried papyrus sheets were attached end to end to form a roll" (Bloom 2001: 22). The oldest known papyrus is dated to the reign of Khufu, and has been found at a port of the Red Sea (Wadi al-Jarf). In addition, "the first mention of Egyptian documents written on

---

[10] Routes also extended as far as the Levant (see above) as well as northward. Along with expanding exchange networks, there is a notable development in social stratification in regions close to the Black Sea and north of the Caucasus (Scarre 1999: 148).

[11] However, this image can be interpreted as a symbolic depiction of the king as the world orderer, without necessarily implying an involvement of the state in the development of irrigation networks.

leather [parchment] goes back to the Fourth Dynasty" (Diringer 1982: 172). Papyri were an asset for state development and the advancement of knowledge, but the complexity of the Egyptian script limited the spread of its use.

The consolidation of the internal power of the elites was accompanied by external commercial and military expansion. The ascent of the state bore the hallmarks of the fundamental violence of political power – both real and ritualized – as revealed by the iconography of the Palette of Narmer, previously mentioned, showing the king smiting a kneeling vanquished enemy, depicted with Asian features. For D. Wengrow (2006: 211ff.), this representation – which may have appeared as early as 3500 BCE – is not necessarily linked to any specific military victory. The peoples at Egypt's margins symbolized disorder: the pharaoh, responsible for world order, had to vanquish them. On the "Battlefield Palette," the pharaoh, depicted as a lion, is about to devour a Nubian. However, L. Watrin (2002: 459) considers that the Palette of Narmer refers to an actual victory of the king in Lower Egypt (and Palestine?), where populations of Asian origin were probably settled (Wilkinson 2002: 517).

The growth of trade at this time certainly played a role in the rise of the Egyptian state. Egypt maintained links with Ras Shamra, Byblos, and the Palestinian coast (Philip 2004), and continued to extract tributes from Palestine (Watrin 2002: 459; Wilkinson 2002: 517; Wengrow 2006: 146). The Egyptian outposts settled in southern Palestine, however, were abandoned: copper was therefore probably sourced from other locations. In any event, the 700 copper artifacts (including 75 "ingots") found in the tomb of Djer (third king of the First Dynasty) reveal the importance of this metal. Controlling this trade may have been one of the factors that contributed to the building of the state (Marfoe 1987). As a sign of the increasing importance of Byblos for Egyptian trade, Canaanite pottery dwindled in Egypt from Djer onward, and was replaced by pottery from Lebanon (de Miroschedji 2002: 45). The decreasing amount of Canaanite pottery may also have been a result of advances in wine production in the Nile delta: Palestinian wine was no longer a particularly desirable import (Hendrickx and Bavay 2002: 70).

Lapis lazuli was still being imported at the beginning of the First Dynasty, and Syro-Palestinian ceramics are abundant in the Egyptian tombs of this time.[12] From the opposite direction, S. Mark (1998: 43) points out the probable Egyptian origin of monkey figurines found at Tell Brak, in Mesopotamia. This site, from the beginning of the Jemdet Nasr period, was receiving lapis lazuli from Afghanistan, and gold, perhaps of Egyptian origin. After that, lapis lazuli was no longer brought into Egypt: this confirms the transformation of the exchange routes in western Asia during the Early Dynastic I period, marked by the near-total cessation of links between Egypt and Mesopotamia. Silver from Anatolia also does not seem to have reached Egypt during the early third millennium. However, an inscription has been found in Byblos, bearing the name of Horus Khasekhemwy (Second Dynasty, c. 2700 BCE).[13] Under the First Egyptian Dynasty, tombs showing brick superstructures with niched facades recall the Mesopotamian temples, though they might also reflect later influences than those

---

[12] For example, the lapis lazuli in jewels from the tomb of Djer at Abydos.

[13] Byblos was transformed into a genuine town during that period (Aubet 2013: 220). The sites of Ashkelon, Tyre, and Sidon were occupied.

previously mentioned. These architectural forms do not in any event represent an absolute novelty.

Egypt's commitment to maritime trade, as well as its interest in river transport and its regulation, sheds light on the symbolic importance of ships and on their role in legitimizing power. This is apparent in the discovery, in the cemetery of Abydos, of fourteen tombs of First Dynasty ships, the oldest dating to 3050. These ships provide the first known example of "sewn planks" (in this case crosswise to the hull). Though cedar was already being imported from Lebanon in the fourth millennium, the boats of Abydos were made of local wood (Ward 2006). Moreover, Egyptian ceramics found in a cave along the Wādī Sodmein are indicative of an Egyptian presence in the Red Sea (Fattovich 2005a: 15).

Egyptian expansion, however, mainly followed land routes. In the south, the pharaohs of the First Dynasty launched military expeditions that allowed them to control the First Cataract. This Egyptian thrust toward the south was driven by the desire to directly harvest the resources of these regions (gold, copper, stones ...). The same expansion process can be observed west of the Nile (for Nubia, however, we have no evidence of copper production prior to 2600 BCE at Buhen, in Lower Nubia, or at the end of the third millennium at Kerma in Upper Nubia [Killick 2009b]).[14] Deprived of the ability to monitor the flow of trade with the south, and suffering from Egyptian raids and increasing aridity, the kingdom of Lower Nubia collapsed during the early third millennium and the region experienced a drop in population. Lower Nubia thus offers an example of semi-peripheral coevolution during a first phase (until 3100 BCE), followed by a process of incorporation into the core and a new form of peripheralization, this time within the core itself.

Egypt experienced a period of division at the end of the Second Dynasty, during the twenty-eighth century BCE. These internal problems probably reflect a phase of lower Nile flooding corresponding to a weakening of the Indian Ocean monsoon system, itself brought about by the climatic change affecting western Asia during the same period.

---

[14] Killick notes here that copper metallurgy did not spread to the Great Lakes during the third millennium, unlike pottery and stock breeding during the fourth millennium (2009b: 404).

3   Early Bronze Age II (*c.* 2700–1950 BCE)

Urban Bloom and the Emergence of Kingship in Mesopotamia during the Early Dynastic II (2750–2600 BCE)

During the twenty-eighth/twenty-seventh century, northern Mesopotamia and Syria experienced a new phase of urbanization. "Tell Leilan, Tell Mozan, and Hamoukar all grew from around 15 ha to 90–120 ha within a century (Pfälzner *et al.* 2004)" (Ur 2010: 405). Tell Brak expanded to 65–70 ha. In northern Iraq, major cities emerged at Tell al-Hawa, Tell Taya, and Tell Khoshi (Ur 2010: 405). The rise of the cities of Mari and Ebla within the same period resulted from a revival of contacts with southern Mesopotamia, and the development of networks in Anatolia and in the Aegean Sea – Crete being still marginal in these exchanges (Rahmstorf 2006a). Data yield "good evidence for substantial contacts between the Levant, Anatolia and [northern] Mesopotamia" (Philip 2004: 208), with these contacts based in part on pre-existing networks.[1] The founding of Mari (*c.* 2800 BCE?) was linked to the control of caravan and fluvial trade along the Euphrates valley. A wide canal was dug, linking the Khabur River and the Euphrates. Mari was also a processing center for ore from Anatolia (Margueron 2004). A Mesopotamian influence is noticeable in some political and administrative developments, especially at Ebla. It is possible that enclaves of Mesopotamian merchants settled once again along routes leading to Anatolia (Crawford 2004: 184). It is significant that during this period, the cities of Tarsus (Cilicia) and Troy appeared to be using the system of Mesopotamian weights, whose unit was 8.33 g; the Syrian unit (9.4 g), however, was the most usual, as would be the case in the Aegean world slightly later (Rahmstorf 2006a: 24). Other innovations entering the Aegean world show connections to the Syrian area: the use of seals in administration; the adoption of the potter's lathe; common practices in ways of drinking; and body care (Rahmstorf 2006b).

In connection with Egypt, Palestine moved toward urbanization, although the size of its towns remained limited. In addition, the city of Arad prospered through the exploitation of copper ore (in the middle of the third millennium, however, Ebla would import copper not from Arad, but from the Persian Gulf, a change reflecting a reorganization of exchange networks, along with the rise of connections between Mesopotamia and the Indus region).[2]

---

[1] In the case of Arslantepe, Frangipane (2004b), however, notes an interruption of connections with the Syro-Mesopotamian world between 2750 and 2500 BCE.

[2] Metallurgic activity seems to have stopped at Arad around the middle of the third millennium, when the Egyptians controlled the region. Copper then began arriving from Anatolia, and still later from Cyprus,

It was in fact a much larger area, however, that experienced major changes. From 2600 BCE on, an urban flowering – with a rise in number and size of cities – accompanied progress in agriculture, crafts, and trade, in Mesopotamia, Iran, Central Asia, and the Indus valley. One notes an expansion of the Mesopotamian city-state culture. Some cities have yielded written documents (tablets): Ur, Shuruppak, Girsu (Telloh), and Ebla. Numerous temples were built that ensured an ideological basis for the political power in place. As has been noted, Liverani (2014: 108) – and other authors – point out "the divine foundations of kingship." Temples also played a role in the economic life of the cities. It is within the context of peaceful or armed competition between cities that the institution of kingship developed north of Sumer, along with the beginnings of land privatization (Yoffee 1995b; Hudson 1996).[3] Kish – a city partly inhabited by Semitic speakers – may have been the center of a country-state (Steinkeller 1993), but from around 2600 BCE, for southern Mesopotamia, textual data indicate the existence of a kind of confederation of cities – perhaps more religious than political? – the "Kengi league," led by a LUGAL, or "great man" "appointed" by the god Enlil of Nippur, the religious center of the country. The title *lugal Kishi* given to its leader from the twenty-sixth to the twenty-fifth century probably refers either to the particular role of Kish (though the LUGAL was not necessarily from this city) or to the model that Kish represented (there may have been an extension to the south of royal institutions developed in the north) (Westenholz 2002).[4] It is possible that Kish was subjugated by the southern confederation, as suggested by the epic tradition of Gilgamesh, so-called "king" of Uruk, victor of Akka, king of Kish (Joannès 2006a; Lafont 2010). This epic was written starting in the middle of the third millennium (Joannès 2010). The title *lugal Kishi* later became "a way to write 'the king of the whole world' through a play on words that established a correspondance between the ideogram KIŠ and the Akkadian word *kiššatu*, 'totality' (Joannès 2001)" (Capdepuy 2010: 181).

We cannot consider political decentralization in Mesopotamia as a peaceful coexistence of city-states: there may have been constant attempts to form larger political entities, through alliance or conquest (Marcus 1998). It is significant that ancient texts from Ur reveal a hierarchized organization of the army.[5] Around 2500, King Eannatum of Lagash may have conquered the cities of Kish, Ur, Uruk, and Umma, for a while, as

---

during the second millennium. It is doubtful that these changes invariably reflect the adaptation of states and merchants to changing conditions of prices and markets, as Warburton claims (2003: 142); the purported explanation, however, is more convincing for the early second millennium (see below).

[3] Hudson 1996. According to Lamberg-Karlovsky (1999: 183), also, during the first half of the third millennium, "secular households gave rise to nascent dynasties of hereditary lords, while other households turned to the increasing bureaucratization of the sacred."

[4] "The Sumerian king List attributed the earliest 'kingship' to Kish, despite its Semitic nature" (Oates 2014b: 1498). Liverani notes that Kish and Ur were ruled by a *lugal*, while Lagash was ruled by an *ensi*, "estate manager (for the god)," and Uruk by an *en*, "(high) priest" (2014: 106). "The earliest royal inscription" comes from Enmebaragesi of Kish, during the Early Dynastic II, *c.* 2600 BCE" (Liverani 2014: 110).

[5] The armies used hybrids of donkeys and onagers (represented on the "Standard of Ur"). A text from Ebla (*c.* 2300) evokes the production of these hybrids at Nagar (Tell Brak), where they cost forty times the price of a donkey (Oates 2003: 117). During the Ur III period, the donkey-onager hybrid appears to have been four times more valuable than a donkey (Widell 2005: 39n. 3). They were sometimes ridden: an Akkadian seal shows a man riding an equid (Louvre AO22325, Oates 2003: 118).

well as the cities of Elam, while maintaining relations with the temple of Enlil at Nippur.[6] "The text inscribed on the stela of the vultures proclaims Eannatum to have been sired by a high god and suckled by a goddess, a way of stressing the divine legitimacy of royal power" (Winter 2008: 81). Slightly later, Enshakushana, ruler of Uruk, took control of part of Sumer for a brief period.

"Ceremonial head of the assembly [UNKEN] of the rulers of the city-states [ENSI]," the LUGAL was at the same time the ruler of a city. The ENSI (or "estate manager [for the god]") of every city ruled with the agreement of an assembly of elders (we will find the same organization at Ebla soon after the middle of the third millennium), a situation that contrasts with the functioning of the Egyptian state. The degree of political power of the LUGAL prior to the Sargonic period in particular remains a topic for debate (for a different approach from that of Westenholz, see Glassner 2000b: 48).[7]

Unlike what can be observed in Egypt, the relations between the temple and the political power were probably both complementary and conflictual. At Lagash, during the twenty-fourth century, Urukagina (a name usually read today as Uru'inimgina), while pretending to restore original communal forms, aimed at "integrating the administrative and economic structures of the temples into those of the 'houses' of the king, the queen and the royal children" (Joannès 2005). In addition, Urukagina promulgated various reforms, introducing a "protection of debtors, the freeing of debt slaves" and the suppression of taxes (Silver 1995). Here we clearly observe the emergence of a royal ideology, with the ruler as guarantor of social justice. Urukagina, however, "was not the first ruler to implement these kinds of measures. At Lagash, Entemena [the successor of Eannatum] ... remitted interests on debts, and 'established freedom' in Lagash, Uruk, Larsa and Bad-Tibira" (Liverani 2014: 114).

An incipient process of land privatization for the benefit of individuals arose during this period from the king himself and his circle. The king granted land to officials; in theory, these officials were mere users and not owners of this land (Glassner 2002a). At Lagash, for example, in the middle of the third millennium, fiefs were granted to merchants working for the king. Lands were also either granted to farmers or worked using hired laborers.[8] Land sales are documented north of Sumer and in northerly parts of southern Mesopotamia (but not in the far south) as early as the Fara period (Early Dynastic IIIa) (2600–2450 BCE) (Gelb *et al.* 1991: 13, 24)[9] (one does wonder, however, whether there was transfer of a property right or simply the sale of a right to use the land). The difference between north and south, observable until the second millennium, should probably be linked with the emergence of kingship in the north within a non-Sumerian context (during the Late Early Dynastic period, however, one finds

---

6 Some sources suggest that "Lagash for most of its recorded history in the two centuries before 2330 did not belong to ki-engi, the league of cities whose rulers met in assembly" (Westenholz 2002: 33). One notes, however, the existence of a *lugal Lagasha[ki]* in the archaic tablets of Ur (2800/2700?).

7 Michalowski argues that "The Sumerian words *en, lugal,* and *énsi* ... are different local words for 'sovereign,' the first one originally used in the city of Uruk, the second in Ur, and the third in the city-state of Lagash" (2008: 33).

8 Extended families controlled most of the lands that did not belong to the state. See Steinkeller 1999.

9 "A mid-third millennium text of disputed significance from Isin raises the possibility that even a field might be purchased on credit" (Wilcke 2003: 94–96; Silver 2007a: 99).

kings in both the northern and the southern regions). Among the differences between the two regions, Steinkeller (1999) notes that northern Babylonia does not show the existence of what he calls "temple estates" similar to those observed in the south. Conversely, "in southern Babylonia, there is virtually no evidence for the existence of small- and medium-sized holdings of arable land, individually 'owned' and cultivated by nuclear families" (1999: 301).

The development of the practice of loan with interest (as early as the Fara period, 2600/2500), moreover, contributed to a process of privatization of land through debt, a movement counterbalanced by debt cancellations promulgated by the rulers; these cancellations were sometimes linked to ceremonies aimed at restoring the cosmic order (Hudson 1996, 2002). The concept of "working time" also appeared in the Fara period, and the "Instructions of Shuruppak" (middle of the third millennium) mention hired laborers (Silver 2007a).

It has often been claimed that the states controlled production and set up a system of redistribution within the context of what has been called "palatial or temple economies." However, writing was not limited to the great public institutions, although these institutions used it as an efficient instrument of management and control (Pollock 1999) – and the state and private sectors probably coexisted. Tablets from Shuruppak testify to the existence of private property. Moreover, archives show a system of taxation rather than control of the whole production process (the lists of professions mention "tax collectors" for the first time). In the reforms that he promulgated, King Urukagina claimed "to have put an end to the abuses perpetrated by officials who levied taxes in silver and not in kind, making a profit on the difference and seriously penalizing the population" (Lafont 2001: 832). The concept of equivalence values, which had appeared earlier, developed from 2600 BCE on (Englund 2004). Silver and barley were used as means of payment. Copper was also a unit of measure, from the beginning of the third millennium. Silver would progressively become the main reference base for equivalence values, partly because of its religious dimension and its place in contributions made to temples. Independent merchants were probably active on the exchange networks (Lamberg-Karlovsky 1996), but trade was largely controlled by palaces and temples.[10] Texts from Lagash mention a "head of the merchants" toward the middle of the third millennium. A text from Ebla also refers to a "*kārum* man," who may have been in charge of the market.

The development of elites and of highly specialized crafts implied growing social differentiation within the cities, partly linked to the expansion of exchanges. This period saw developments in bronze metallurgy, for the production of weapons, tools, and luxury goods. This metallurgy would provide momentum for the development of trade, toward the Persian Gulf for copper from Iran and then Oman, and toward Iran and Afghanistan, where copper and tin arrived via terrestrial routes (Boroffka *et al.* 2002). Reed boats from

---

[10] Tablets from Telloh describe a domain of 4465 ha belonging to the temple of Bawa, of which a part was leased. The temple estate supported farmers, artisans, scribes, all paid with "food rations" and clothes. "The temple also provided income to the royal family and a part of the city population" (Margueron and Pfirsch 2001: 131–133). In fact, the social organization remains poorly understood. Slavery is not well documented for this time. Notables were able to buy land, which reveals the existence of some type of land market. We do not know the proportion of free farmers vis-à-vis employees of temple and royal estates.

Oman, caulked with bitumen imported from Mesopotamia, transported copper to Mesopotamia, Susiana, and probably to the Indus region (ships made of wood – which was necessarily imported – were also built during the third millennium). Although the arsenic used in the alloy Cu-As is of unknown origin, copper ore with a high arsenic content has been discovered. In Mesopotamia, tin bronze began to replace arsenical bronze during the second half of the third millennium.[11] Tin may have come from Iran (deposits exist north of Shar-i Sokhta), from Afghanistan (south of Herat), or from Uzbekistan (Karnab mine) and Tajikistan (Mushiston mine). But it is arsenical bronze that predominates at Shar-i Sokhta and at other Iranian sites (Weeks 2003: 175). Moreover, there is no evidence of exploitation at Karnab and at Mushiston during the third millennium (see Parzinger 2003; Weeks 2003). An Afghan origin is therefore likely for most of this metal, transported through the Indus valley and the Persian Gulf (Weeks 2003; Rahmstorf 2006b). "Tin-bronze is noticeably rare on the Iranian plateau in the 3rd millennium, with Susa in lowland Khuzistan as a regional exception" (Pigott 2012a), perhaps because it came through maritime routes. Another potential source is Deh Hosain, in northwestern Iran (Pigott 2012a). Tin may also have been exploited at Kestel (Anatolia), but this remains debated. Tin bronze has been found in northern Mesopotamia, Anatolia, Syria, Cilicia, at Troy, and in the Aegean Sea, dated to the first half of the third millennium, a sign of the activity of northern networks (see Pernicka *et al.* 2003; Rahmstorf 2006b, and above). After Edens (1995: 60), Weeks (2003: 176) suggests a route through the Caspian Sea, Transcaucasia, and the Black Sea for the tin bronzes of Troy and of the Aegean Sea, a route used during the late third millennium.

Whereas exchange networks during the Uruk period developed primarily toward the north, southern Mesopotamians were now active in the Persian Gulf. The port city of Ur played a particularly important role. Exports were fueled by the development of the production of woolen clothing in the Mesopotamian city-states of this period (Kohl 1987: 15).

The foreign merchant [GAEŠ, GARAŠ] "is regularly present in the Pre-Sargonic Lagash documents" (Postgate 2003: 211), and archaeological discoveries suggest increasing exchanges in the Gulf. Jemdet Nasr pottery has been unearthed on the eastern Arab coast, Tarut Island, Bahrain, and the Omani peninsula. Various items of Mesopotamian pottery dated to the Early Dynastic (ED) I (2800–2700), ED II (2700–2600), and ED III (2600–2350) have been found in eastern Arabia, at Umm ar-Ramadh and Umm an-Nussi, in the oases of al-Hufūf and Yabrin, and on Tarut Island (Potts 1990: 65–66). The first chlorite bowls appeared in Mesopotamian tombs of the Jemdet Nasr phase, showing links with southern Iran. A large number of chlorite bowls dated to the Early Dynastic II period have been unearthed on Tarut and at Ur; their origin is probably diverse: Tarut, or southern Iran (region of Jiroft).[12] Texts from the Early Dynastic III period of Lagash contain the term ŠIM.GIG, usually translated as "incense."[13] The term

---

[11] A Mesopotamian text from Ur, however, already mentions tin bronze during the ED I period (Weeks 2003: 178).

[12] See Kohl 2001: 220; Crawford 1998: 46. The style of these objects has been termed "intercultural style," but most of them come from southern Iran (see below).

[13] Zarins 1997: 261. In the text DP 513, "the term is used in connection with a silver value and the incense is connected with a specific 'merchant of aromatics' (GARAŠ.ŠIM)" (Zarins 1997: 261). As Zarins notices,

ŠIM.DILMUN appears in a text from Fara *c.* 2500 BCE and a text from Ebla belonging to the same period (the name "Dilmun" refers to the Arabian coast, near Dharan, and to regions of the interior, the core probably being the al-Hufūf oasis).[14]

East of Dilmun, from the end of the fourth millennium onward, Oman developed oasis agriculture, with date palms, and began exploiting mineral resources (copper, hard stones), in connection with exchanges with Mesopotamia. The introduction of cultivated plants belonging to the western Asian package (barley, wheat . . .) and the beginning of copper exploitation occurring at the same time cannot be the mere product of chance (Cleuziou 2002). In addition, the shape of bricks at Hili in phases IIa-C probably reflects not only a Mesopotamian influence, but an actual Mesopotamian presence in Oman. Various types of Mesopotamian pottery have been excavated (Cleuziou and Méry 2002). Archaeological discoveries also reveal links between Oman and Iran and the Indus valley, revealing the formation of a vast sphere of exchanges (see below).

Mesopotamia and the Indus Valley: The First Globalized Area of the Indian Ocean (2500–1950 BCE)

From the Sumerian City-States to the Akkadian Empire

The development of agricultural production and crafts activities as well as expanding exchanges underlay the rise of two civilizational centers, in Mesopotamia and in the Indus region. Their interconnection would lead to the formation of the first globalized economic and cultural space of the western Indian Ocean (see Map 1.3).

The twenty-sixth century marked the beginning of an indirect maritime commerce between these two regions: the silence of texts of the Early Dynastic III period on Meluhha (the Indus region) is likely due to the role played in trade by intermediaries (Ratnagar 2004: 287). The earliest mention of Magan (Oman) and of Meluhha, however, is in a text dated to the Early Dynastic period, which speaks of boats bringing wood (Kitchen 1994: 159). Maritime trade was of course cheaper than commerce over land; it also allowed merchants to bypass the Iranian states. The prosperity of the port of Ur during the First Dynasty of this city (*c.* 2500–2350 BCE),[15] linked to long-distance trade, is shown by the wealth of the "royal tombs" of its cemetery, which have yielded more than 20,000 beads and lapis lazuli artifacts.[16] Lapis lazuli was now imported into western Asia mainly by sea, and in much larger quantities than previously (approximately 500 objects have been recovered for the first half of the third millennium, and more than 30,000 in

---

the use of "the term GARAŠ in opposition to the more familiar DAM.GÀR involves still poorly understood definitions of the nature of capital and long-distance trade in Sumerian society" (1997: 261).

[14] Zarins 1997: 262–263. This term is found again in texts of the Ur III period. Zarins also signals the term ŠIM.MAR.TU, which seems to imply the involvement of Amorites – called MAR.TU by the Sumerians – in the aromatics trade.

[15] Reade (2001: 17), however, proposes a date one hundred years later.

[16] If we consider the total amounts found, Ur is far ahead of Susa and Shar-i Sokhta, which also yielded jewels made of lapis lazuli in significant amounts (Casanova 1999). Cities of Mesopotamia such as Ebla and Mari had workshops using lapis lazuli that were dependent on the palaces or temples. Twenty-three kilograms of raw lapis lazuli have been found in the palace of Ebla. Lapis lazuli was also found in the "treasure of Ur" from Mari. In Iran, besides the towns already mentioned, Shahdad and Tepe Hissar worked the blue stone for export.

sites dating to the second half of this millennium; Casanova 2013). Lapis lazuli is frequently associated with carnelian, also originating from the Indus valley; the alliance of these two stones, symbolizing the masculine and the feminine, respectively, expressed fertility (Winter 1999). Protective virtues were attributed to lapis lazuli; in Mesopotamia as in Egypt, it symbolized the forces of life: "its possession guaranteed political and religious power" (Casanova 1998: 180). Worn by the goddess Inanna (Sumer)/Ishtar (Semitic Mesopotamia), lapis lazuli was a common gift to divinities: one finds it in the foundation deposits of temples, sometimes along with carnelian (Aruz 2003a: 243). It is therefore understandable that the elites controlled the circulation and production of objects in lapis lazuli. Besides Ur, at least two sites worked the lapis lazuli for export: Susa and Shar-i Shokta (Iran) (Casanova 2013: 254). Interestingly, "its distribution was largely restricted to the most important states of the Near East": lapis lazuli was all but absent in Anatolia prior to the second millennium, and it was rare in the Aegean even during the second millennium (Warburton 2013: 287–288). Tombs also yielded gold and silver vessels, which were most likely used for rituals involving the consumption of alcoholic beverages (Sherratt 2006b: 44).

Merchandise was also carried on terrestrial roads. In Iran, Shar-i Sokhta (III) (2500–2300/2200 BCE), however, did not cover 150 ha, as was previously thought, but only around 20 ha (Shirazi 2007: 149). The city hosted crafts that allowed for the export of lapis lazuli and turquoise beads. Shar-i Sokhta and Shahdad were centers for the production of alabaster vessels, which were imported into Mesopotamia during the third millennium.

Sumer was also in contact with northern Mesopotamia and Transcaucasia. This is shown by the discovery, in what is known as the royal cemetery of Ur, of ceremonial, anchor-shaped axes characteristic of groups living in Transcaucasia, as well as oxen-driven wagons (wagons have been found in large kurgans both north and south of the Caucasus) (Kohl 2007: 118, 120).

The various types of progress made during this period spurred economic and demographic growth in the principal interconnected regions as well as a process of urbanization, not only in the centers, but also in some peripheries. From 2500 BCE on, Mesopotamia was again displaying centrifugal trends toward controlling the trade routes and regions that were rich in metals and wood. Unlike what we can observe during the Urukian period, expansion was now based partly on the use of armed force, a mode of control certainly more costly than previous methods, but probably rendered necessary by the fact that Mesopotamian cities were now facing well-established states and highly structured networks. Lugalzagesi, who chose Uruk as his capital, united much of Mesopotamia under his leadership;[17] he went so far as to launch an expedition toward the Mediterranean coasts, perhaps to tackle the growing power of Ebla. The city of Ebla has yielded many tablets dated to the twenty-fourth century; they paint a picture of a highly centralized economy. A council of elders played a political role alongside the king. Precursors of the Assyrian traders, but more dependent on state power, the merchants of Ebla formed a kind of commercial empire during the twenty-fifth and

---

[17] Before him, Lugalannemundu of Adab may have extended his territory to neighboring regions, but the Old Babylonian tablet describing his achievements is a fake (see Liverani 2014: 112).

twenty-fourth centuries. Weights discovered in Ebla's palace G exhibit three units: the Karkemish unit (7.83 g); the "Syrian" unit (9.4 g); and the "Hittite" unit (11.75 g). The Mesopotamian unit (8.33 g) is not present, but has been found at Tepe Gawra (VI) and Tell Brak (around the middle of the third millennium) (Rahmstorf 2006a: 21).

Transactions in precious metals were considerable: the king of Mari, defeated, presented a tribute of five tons of silver and 440 kg of gold to Ebla; these metals came from external trade. The city of Ebla controlled central Syria; it traded with Anatolia, Cyprus, and the Sinai, exporting mainly textiles produced locally ("an Eblaite text shows the import of 17,000 sheep from various cities") (Silver 1995: 143). Ebla received copper from Oman, and not from Anatolia (as occurred later, see Dercksen 1996: 160). In contact with Byblos, Ebla (palace G) yielded objects from the Nile valley and showed the use of Egyptian metrology (Joffe 2000: 119). A cup bearing the name of the pharaoh Khephren, dated to *c.* 2550 BCE, has been discovered, as well as the lid of an alabaster vessel with an inscription bearing the name of Pepi I.

The discoveries at Mari and Ebla reveal the importance of exchanges, not only with southern Mesopotamia, but also via east–west routes. The networks extended as far as the Aegean Sea and the Strait of the Dardanelles. Tin bronze appeared at Troy, in the Aegean Sea, in Hungary and at sites in the Adriatic from 2600/2500. The tin in these bronze pieces may have come from Central Asia, through routes following – or going through – the Caspian Sea and the Black Sea (O'Shea 1992; Primas 2002, 2007; Weeks 2003; Pernicka *et al.* 2003). Whereas during earlier periods copper originated in Anatolia, analysis excludes the same origin for tin bronze. Instead, these indicate ore originating in Central Asia, northwestern India or Afghanistan: with the introduction of tin for bronze production, we appear to be observing – at the same time – new sources of copper; this analysis thus sheds light on the importance of routes through Inner Asia, along which traders also carried lapis lazuli and carnelian. The discovery of an ivory cylinder seal at Poliochni and the fact that as early as the first half of the third millennium the Mesopotamian standard of weight (8.33 g) was known at Troy and in Cilicia, and slightly later throughout the Aegean Sea, also reveal links between the Aegean Sea and Sumer (see above). Moreover, the widespread adoption of the so-called Syrian standard (9.4 g) and of "coil"-shaped weights in the Aegean world signal the integration of this exchange zone (Rahmstorf 2006a: 25, 30). Conversely, it is interesting to note the absence of the Egyptian unit (13.4–13.5 g) in the Aegean Sea.

It was during this period that (arsenical) bronze arrived in Crete, introduced via contacts with Anatolian metallurgists. Besides stamp seals, in use in Anatolia, in the Levant, and in the Aegean Sea, Crete employed cylinder seals during the third millennium, which reveal its connection with the Levant and beyond with Mesopotamia, from 2400 BCE. A tomb in Crete dated to 2200, at Ayia Triada, has yielded lapis lazuli (Mederos and Lamberg-Karlovsky 2004). A tomb at Mochlos contained a silver cylinder seal manufactured in western Asia (Early Bronze Age).

In Mesopotamia, barley, but also silver – necessarily obtained through long-distance trade – constituted means of payment.[18] The conversion rate between silver and barley seems to have varied, but it has not been possible to specify the underlying mechanisms for this variation. Copper was also a unit of measure, as early as the early third

---

[18] Barley was used both as a standard of value and as a means of exchange. Snell 1995: 1491–1492.

millennium. As emphasized previously, the concept of equivalence in value appeared earlier, developing around 2600/2500 BCE (Fara). Public institutions played a crucial role in the appearance of a money of account; the involvement of temples and palaces in trade probably explains the emergence of their monetary role, with silver gaining prominence partly because of its religious dimension and the place it held in contributions made to temples.[19] As of the mid-third millennium, available data show coils and silver rings used as money, as well as the use of what is known as "broken" silver.[20] A temple at Tell Brak, a city located at the junction of roads linking Mesopotamia and Anatolia, has yielded treasure from the Sargonic period containing gold, electrum, serpentine silver ingots, silver threads, a twisted piece of silver, carnelian beads, and lapis lazuli pendants, these stones revealing connections with Iran and Afghanistan (Oates and Oates 1993). Moreover, "the Sumerian sign for shekel seems to be the stylized picture of an axe; in addition, the Sumerian word *gin* not only means 'shekel' but also 'axe'": "it is virtually certain that axes were used as money" (Powell 1996: 238; Michailidou 2005: 21 and fig. 8).[21] It is likely that the use of silver as a means of exchange was still restricted to a fraction of the population (Le Rider 2001; Glassner 2001: 65), but for Silver (2004c), "there is evidence for the dispersal of precious metals in the population. As early as the middle of the third millennium in Ebla (in Syria) silver was used to purchase ordinary goods including clothing and grain as well as wine and semiprecious stones." Taxes owed to the palace and the temples were paid in silver or in grain.

Markets for production factors emerged during the third millennium. Private landed property and a land market appear to have developed, with notable differences between the north and the south of Sumer. According to Gelb *et al.* (1991: 25), "on the basis of the [available data], it can be suggested that the institution of 'private'/alienable landed property

[19] Hudson 2004b: 305, 311–312. Public institutions used silver, a product of long-distance trade, for their expenses and public payments (Hudson 2004b). "Enlil, the chief god of Nippur, bore the title 'trader of the wide world,' and his spouse was called 'merchant of the world'" (Hudson 2002: 21). "The workshops of large institutions advanced textiles and other handicrafts to merchants who traded them abroad and paid the temples in silver or goods that had a silver-equivalent" (Hudson 2004b: 315). Copper, tin and gold played a more limited role. Hudson notes that the temples, "down through classical Greece and Rome, oversaw the refining of metal in order to sanctify its purity and weight" (2004b: 310).

[20] Snell 1995: 1488, 1491–1492. The rings were made of silver, gold, or other metals. The monetary use of metal coils may go back to the fourth millennium: "the symbol for KUG, 'precious metal', may represent a stylized picture of a metal coil or spiral" (Powell 1996: 235–236). Rings from the Diyala region, now in the Oriental Institute Museum of Chicago, may date to 2700 BCE (Powell 1996: 237). A text from the early Akkadian period says: "5 coils of silver, the price of 20 sheep" (*CAD* [*Chicago Assyrian Dictionary*], vol. XV, entry *semeru*, 1984: 224). Texts reveal the existence of metal rings of fixed weight during the Akkadian period (Michel 2001b). A discovery at Tell Taya (near Nineveh) dated to the late third millennium shows small silver ingots, spirals, broken silver, as well as a gold buckle and gold beads (Le Rider 2001: 2).
    In western Asia and elsewhere, many terms used for money, notes Silver, derive from words meaning "to weigh" or "to cut" (1995: 162). The earliest weights known to us also date to the middle of the third millennium (Powell 1999: 17). The use of sealed bags of fixed weight is attested from the early second millennium onward (but their use may go back to earlier times). After 1500 BCE, lumps of silver of equal weight seem to have been in use in Babylonia, as well as sealed bags (see below).

[21] In a text of the Old Babylonian period (second millennium), one finds: "seven minas of bronze, 1/3 mina of the bronze is in axes" (*CAD*, VI, entry *ḫaṣṣinnu*, "axe; used as money," 1956: 134). The shekel was both a weight (8.33 g, or 1/60th of a mina) and a standard of value (see *CAD*, XVII, entry *šiqlu*). Shekel, *šiqlu*, derives from *šaqālu*, "to weigh," and "to pay" (see *CAD*; entry *šaqālu*).

originated in the north, from where it spread to the south."[22] Texts refer to "saleable land," *gan-sam* (Diakonoff 1996: 55). A (limited) labor market existed at least since the middle of the third millennium (Silver 2007a: 98). Diakonoff (1974b: 50) has argued for the existence of wageworkers in agriculture during the Sargonic period, and in a document of the twenty-third century we read: "total: 874 1/2 young men" (Glassner 2001: 62, 69n. 3, citing a text from Nippur, in Westenholz 1975). However, not much can be said about a possible labor market. The late third millennium – at the time of the Ur III Empire – would see a greater use of hired workers.

As already mentioned, the development of loans with interest led rulers to proclaim debt cancellations. As early as 2400 BCE, the ENSI of Lagash, Enmetena, enacted a debt cancellation in the agricultural sector; this cancellation excluded the debts of the commercial sector. According to Hudson, the practice of lending arose in the commercial sector: "Although ancient economies were predominantly agricultural, the practice of accruing interest seems to have been first invented in the commercial sphere of Sumer, apparently with the temples playing a catalytic role" (2000). Thus the loan with interest was first applied to commercial entrepreneurs dealing with the production of great estates. Originally, "the payment of interest may have been viewed as recompense to the gods for a successful voyage" (Hudson 2002: 22). Unlike Hudson, "De Mieroop [2002: 63] places the origin of the loan with interest rather within the sphere of production and individual relations" (Joannès 2006b: 406–407). Interest was paid not only on loans, but also on delayed arrears in the payment of rent and other debts (Van de Mieroop 2002: 64).[23] Rates remained remarkably stable for much of Mesopotamian history. Agricultural rates were different from those in the commercial sector. The rate of 33.3 percent for debts in agriculture derived from the practice of giving a third of the harvest as payment for the use of a field: this was the sharecropping rate. ("Interest rates in the commercial and agricultural spheres remained segregated throughout most of antiquity," notes Hudson [2000]. "Rates for agrarian debts tended to reflect land rents. Rents and agrarian interest rates both tended toward a norm of 1/3 by Ur III times.") As for silver, the annual rate of 20 percent was linked to the metrological system and to the calender (Hudson 2002; Van de Mieroop 2002).[24] Monthly interest was one shekel for one mina (one mina represented 60 shekels). Silver played an increasingly important role until the first millennium, which posed the problem of its supply: silver had to be acquired from foreign countries, through trade or war.

---

[22] However, "in spite of its comparative rarity in the south, 'private' landed property did exist in the region already in very early times" (Gelb *et al.* 1991: 25). Although sale contracts sometimes involved several persons, the buyers were always single individuals (Gelb *et al.* 1991: 17). A Sargonic text from Lagash (ITT1 109) mentions a sizeable quantity of silver for the purchase of land (Silver 2002). Cf. also Lamberg-Karlovsky 2001b and Oates 2014a: 1487.

[23] In fact, the first evidence of loans in the modern sense of the term dates to the Sargonid period (Van de Mierop 2002: 65).

[24] "The earliest interest rates ... were set not economically to reflect profit or productivity rates, but by the dictates of mathematical simplicity of calculation ... Mesopotamia's commercial rate of 1/60th per month aimed at achieving a numerical ease of computing interest regularly at standardized rates. This basic rate found its counterpart in other regions – 1/10th in Greece, and 1/12th in Rome, reflecting their respective systems of calculating fractions ... [During] the Old Babylonian period, [the rate was] 33 1/3 per cent for barley loans ... The barley-loan interest rate may initially have reflected the rent rate ... (in Sumer's case, this was the sharecropping rate)" (Hudson 2000).

Various cities had tried to form vast territorial states, but it was Sargon I of Akkad who formed what can probably be considered the first empire ever created, an endeavor perhaps encouraged by the growing importance of Ebla and the Elamite states. After crushing the LUGAL Lugalzagesi and the "fifty" Sumerian cities that followed him, Sargon united the Mesopotamian city-states under his political authority within the Akkadian Empire (c. 2340–2200 BCE).[25] Attempting to connect the Persian Gulf and the Mediterranean, Sargon undertook direct control, by force, of networks that had formerly brought metals, wood, and slaves to Mesopotamia. The creation of this space initiated a new phase of political integration.

A new political concept of kingship was perhaps introduced in southern Mesopotamia. The Sargonic Empire marked the beginning of the supremacy of Semitic speakers over the Sumerian component of the population (Westenholz 2002: 38).[26] The title LUGAL now clearly referred to the king. Akkadian – a Semitic language – was the official language of the empire. The creation of the Sargonic Empire was accompanied by the founding of a new capital, Akkad (Agadé), probably located at Baghdad, on the left bank of the Tigris (Wall-Romana 1990). The armed expansion of Akkad clearly had an economic aim. Sargon launched expeditions toward the Taurus and Anatolia, to what were known as "the cedar forest" and "the silver mountain" (in Cilicia?): these terms reflect the importance of these regions, which exported coveted goods to Mesopotamia. Sargon's expeditions were most likely aimed at obtaining tribute payments as well as setting advantageous commercial conditions. In addition, Sargon seized Elam, a troublesome intermediary due to its control over terrestrial routes between Mesopotamia and the eastern lands (Indus, Margiana, Bactria). A palace was erected in Susa. It is significant that the most ancient map known to us, discovered at Nuzi, is dated to Sargon's time. His successors would continue the push toward expansion. Manishtushu boasted that he had "been victorious in Iran, on the shores of the Gulf and as far as the country of Meluḫḫa" (Benoit 2003). Naram-Sin led successful campaigns against Ebla and Armanum (Lebanon). Deified, Naram-Sin (2260–2223 BCE) proclaimed himself universal sovereign with the title "King of the Four Regions of the World": the building of the empire went along with the deification of the king. The kingdom was divided into provinces and its script reformed. As proof of his interest in trade, the king set up a standardized system of weights and measures.

The economy experienced a strong expansion, based on the rehabilitation of irrigation systems and the creation of new ones[27] (opening up more land for agriculture); on progress in bronze metallurgy; and on the development of long-distance trade with the Indus

[25] Gasche et al. (1998), however, propose an "ultra-short chronology" in which Sargon takes power around 2200 BCE. Cf. Zettler 2003: 20. Reade (2001) suggests a 2180 ± 40 BCE dating.

[26] Prior to Sargon, other "kings" had already attempted to extend their spheres of power and create territorial states, for example, Lugalzagesi (Thuesen 2000: 59).

[27] Irrigation was mainly gravity-fed. Water was also raised using a shaduf (this system is depicted on a cylinder seal dated to the second half of the third millennium); the shaduf made the irrigation of small areas, gardens or orchards possible. Private landed property may have progressed during this period (Margueron and Pfirsch 2001: 169). However, Weiss (2000) has "turned conventional pictures of the surplus producing irrigation agriculture regime of the southern floodplain 'on its head'," with Akkad seen as a state "dependent on the Khabur's dry farming production" (Zettler 2003: 28).

civilization, from the port of Ur.[28] In this trade, Bahrain and Oman served not only as intermediaries, but also as active agents. Large estates were managed and exploited by the political and religious powers, who were positioned to take environmental risks into account, for example by imposing set-aside measures.[29] The extension of northern institutions throughout the south intensified during the Sargonic period: crown land was created – King Manishtushu acquired (by force?) significant surfaces of land – which was then partially "distributed to royal dependents in exchange for services," and private land holdings were expanded (Gelb *et al.* 1991: 26). Temples sometimes fell victim to the development of royal and private estates. Thus, a "king" of Umma, in the twenty-third century, "distributed to his followers land property belonging to temples."[30] The expansion of sheepherding provided significant support for statebuilding. It was based on the selection of breeds of wool-bearing sheep, and spread quickly over a vast area (Kohl 2007: 223). It seems that during the Akkadian period, the private sector played a significant role, but the palace and the temple may have exercised control over long-distance trade, whose funding required significant resources (Margueron and Pfirsch 2001: 169). It is remarkable, however, that from the middle to the end of the third millennium, most of the loans recorded in the texts were granted to private persons. Some were clearly allocated to commercial ventures (we do not have much evidence, however, for loans intended for investments in production) (see Silver 1995: 109). Quoting Foster (1977), Algaze (2008: 20) notes that the administrative archives do not mention precious stones, wood, or even copper and silver: "they must have been imported by private merchants." Texts from Umma show the existence of entrepreneurs who either were independent, or took advantage of their links with institutions to conduct private business.[31] It is possible that, already at this time, palaces and temples

[28] Following the collapse of the Akkadian Empire, Ur would become the prominent power again. Seventeen references to Meluḫḫa, notes Possehl, come from the excavations of the "workshops" of Ur and correspond to products associated with Meluḫḫa or to the production of "Meluḫḫan style objects" (Possehl 1996: 145). Edens (1993: 408), however, supports the idea that the volume of exchanges under the Akkadian Empire seems to have been lower than it had been during the preceding period (Early Dynastic III), when competition between city-states had stimulated the economy. Edens has pointed out that a parallel did not always exist between economic and political tendencies. In fact, it is difficult to assess the scope of exchanges during the Early Dynastic period. But Edens' remark is certainly pertinent for other periods such as the early second millennium (see below).

[29] Baines and Yoffee 1998: 226–227. For Vargyas (2004: 110), nevertheless, even during the third millennium, "the major part of the population of Babylonia lives outside the sphere of the temples and of the palace." A text from Abu Salabikh found in a temple (Early Dynastic IIIa), however, refers to 14,000 sheep and goats (Postgate 2003: 161). Aside from their role in production and trade, temples also had a social dimension: the temple of Ekur at Nippur, for example, took care of poor people (widows, orphans) in exchange for work.

[30] Glassner 2002a: 131–132. "For the temples, throughout Mesopotamian history, one notes the progressive appropriation . . . of land assets by the beneficiaries of grants and their families, who were the hereditary holders of the main manager positions" (Glassner 2002a: 132). Glassner (2000b: 43) notes also that "at Adab, the ENSI.GAR could dig into the granaries of the temples." Baines and Yoffee (1998: 225) speak of endemic antagonism between the sectors of the palace and the temple, with the palace taking the upper hand during the third millennium. The so-called "model of the temple-city" has long been refuted. One wonders, however, if what Glassner terms "the theocratic slant" was not "a [late] choice [during the third millennium] against the political power and the state" (Glassner 2000b: 43).

[31] Perhaps in contrast with the GARAŠ, the DAM.GÀR were not only agents of the state, but also worked on their own account (Foster 1977: 34). Moreover, the title "chief of the merchants," seen in some texts, seems to imply the implementation of a kind of organization. Foster also shows the existence at Umma of

considered it more profitable to have their products traded by private merchants, a process clearly observed during the second millennium.

The Akkadian Empire exported agricultural goods and manufactured products. For Mesopotamia, more than for the other cores, the export of textiles proved crucial for building regional and transregional chains of dominance. The expansion of sheep breeding, initiated and controlled by the state for textile production, formed one basis for state development – probably as early as the Urukian period (McCorriston 1997; Kohl 2007).

Various Akkadian words were used for places where transactions occurred, revealing the existence of markets (Powel 1999: 10). During the Sargonic and Post-Sargonic periods, silver was more widely used: accordingly, officials were paid in silver. Entrepreneurs "may have silver on deposit at various places . . . The texts reveal the use of silver to pay rents, and purchase slaves, land, animals, and agricultural products."[32] Land sales were recorded, "with equivalences given in units of wool, oil, copper, and silver."[33]

While southern Mesopotamia and Anatolia seem to be only loosely connected, trade routes did link Iran, Syria, and Anatolia. Sargon may have taken direct control over resources and roads, and Naram-Sin may have built a fortress at Brak, precisely in order to secure exchanges with the north. Anatolia and the Aegean Sea saw the flourishing of urban centers, even prior to the Sargonic period: Troy II (c. 2700–2300 BCE); Poliochni (level V), on the island of Lemnos; Thermi (level V), on the island of Lesbos. Gold artifacts excavated at Troy are a testament to the wealth of the elite of this small city, which controlled the Straits of the Dardanelles and the terrestrial roads between Europe and Asia. The discovery of amber beads reveals the trade in this substance from the Baltic Sea.[34] The discovery of an axe made of lapis lazuli shows Anatolia's connection with northern Mesopotamia and Afghanistan – unless the stone had been carried on a route across the steppes. Various artifacts (pins, pendants) exhibit a double spiral motif known at Ur (Sumer), Kuntasi, Chanhu-daro, Mohenjo-daro (Indus), Tepe Hissar II and III (Iran), Mundigak (IV) (Afghanistan), Mehrgarh (Pakistan), Anau and Parkhai

---

a "fund" mainly financed by the state but also by individuals, and used for commercial purposes. Women played a role in the exchanges: at Umma, a female entrepreneur called Ama-é, who had received land from the state, traded grain and metals, by entrusting her wealth to various agents (Foster 1977: 5, 33). Foster (1993) notes the presence at Susa of merchants from Umma who conducted their operations "under the auspices or the protection of the Sargonic administration," but on an independent basis. The relative importance of the private sector remains unknown to us for the Early Dynastic period, but for Foster, the search for profit is clearly apparent in a number of archives. "The slave trade seems to have been a particularly profitable undertaking" (Foster 1977: 37). "As time passes [during the third millennium], the proportion of asymmetrical exchanges, characteristic of the reciprocity put forward by K. Polanyi, went diminishing, and that of symmetrical exchanges, characteristic of merchant economy, went growing" (Glassner 2001: 61).

[32] Silver 1995: 158, who quotes Foster 1977. Hudson (2004b: 314) emphasizes the widespread use of credit, however, rather than cash payments: "most transactions . . . took the form of running debt balances."

[33] Potts 1997: 181. A parcel of land was sold in the city of Adab for 300 gur of barley converted into 5 minas of silver (Glassner 2001: 68). Various authors, however, have pointed out that land was not really considered merchandise during the third millennium (see Ratnagar 2001b: 354; 2004: 291).

[34] Various amber roads are attested from the Baltic Sea to the Danube valley, then on to the Balkans. Amber would arrive in the Mediterranean in greater quantities during the second millennium: in Crete (fifteenth century) and Mycenaean Greece.

(Central Asia).[35] This double-spiral motif appears to have followed the routes of exchange for tin and lapis lazuli (Aruz and Wallenfels 2003: 352).

East of Mesopotamia, merchants were active on the roads of Iran, Central Asia, and Baluchistan. Merchants from Umma settled at Susa. The Iranian coast and the plateau (notably the sites of Tepe Sialk, Tepe Hissar, Tepe Yahya, Shahdad, Jiroft,[36] and Shar-i Sokhta) were part of a vast economic and cultural area connected to the urban sites of Afghanistan and Turkmenistan. In Afghanistan, the most important settlements were Mundigak,[37] already mentioned, and the Harappan "trading post" of Shortughai,[38] in eastern Bactria, located near the sources of lapis lazuli but also near silver mines, and situated on routes leading to Xinjiang and Turkmenistan. In Turkmenistan, towns developed from 2600 BCE (as revealed by the excavations at Altyn Tepe, Namazga Tepe, and Sarazm [IV]). We observe the rise of monumental architecture around the middle of the third millennium, with the construction of religious buildings on high terraces, at Altyn Tepe, Tureng Tepe (Gorgan plain, northern Iran), Sialk (central Iran), and Konar Sandal (southern Iran). These terraces, which we see represented on

[35] Aruz and Wallenfels 2003: 352; Huot 2004, I: 186–187. See below also for jewels with quadruple spirals. The motif of the double spiral has been found in Europe dating from the fourth and third millennia, for example at Font (Switzerland) and at Teglio (north Italy). Pins with double spirals have been excavated in Romania, Bulgaria, and Greece (see Goto 2006: 275–278, who connects this motif to a solar myth). The dating of early Troy II is still debated. In central Anatolia, the "royal" tombs of Alaca Hüyük (2500–2200, or 2300–2100 BCE?) reveal the wealth of this center's elite, who benefited from regional ore deposits, and a location at the junction of east–west and north–south routes. Some pieces reveal links with Troy II. The presence of lapis lazuli shows the insertion of Alaca Höyük into long-distance exchange networks. Besides gold objects, the presence of iron is noteworthy. For Pelon (2001), "the tombs of Alaca belong to a category of burial mounds almost nonexistent in Anatolia, but attested in other regions. Even though there are some claims for a local origin, it is therefore tempting to consider that these burial customs have been imported, probably by a ruling class enjoying religious power; this elite precedes and heralds the arrival of the Hittites in Hatti territory." Other authors consider that Alaca was the center of a Hatti (non-Indo-European population) kingdom. A Hatti king is mentioned by the Akkadian ruler Naram Sin.

[36] In fact, the dating of the assemblage of Jiroft remains debated; it has been related mainly to Tepe Yahya IVB; the beginning of the IVB period is placed in the middle of the third millennium by Madjidzadeh (2003b: 73), *c.* 2200 BCE by Potts (2001: 201), around 2400 (ending *c.* 2100) by Lamberg-Karlovsky, who refutes Potts' arguments and gives a new radiocarbon dating (2001a: 271ff., 276). According to Madjidzadeh (2003a: 26), the cemeteries – largely looted – of the region of Jiroft, may have been used throughout the third millennium. "Plain or painted pottery, similar to that of Shahdad, of Tepe Yahya or of Shar-i Sokhta in Sistan, dated to the IVth or to the first half of the IIIrd millennium" has been unearthed (Madjidzadeh 2003b: 26).

[37] Mundigak IV has been dated between 2600 and 2300, 2200, 2000, or 1800 BCE (the dates are debated) (see Casal 1961; Biscione 1974: 131–132; Pigott 1999: 159; Possehl 2002a: 231; Kuz'mina 2007: 435; Liverani 2014: 182). Phase IV 1 exhibits a "palace" and a "temple"; Phase IV ended with the destruction of the town. The site was later reoccupied (Mundigak V) (with the presence of a "massive building" on a high terrace) and showed links with the Fergana region. Other sites may have been abandoned during the late third/ early second millennium, or were in decline, such as Shahdad, Tepe Hissar and other urban sites (tablets bearing cuneiform script dated to the eighteenth century BCE, however, have been discovered at Tepe Hissar, and Shahdad remained an active center at the beginning of the second millennium (Huot 2004, I: 203). The last phase of the cemetery of Shahdad (1800–1600) contained lapis lazuli (Casanova 2013: 84).

[38] Shaikh (2000: 82) considers Shortughai as a trade "colony" of the Indus region, as well as Ra's-al-Jinz in Oman, a point of view not supported by other researchers, at least for the latter site (cf. Cleuziou 2000).

chlorite vases of the "intercultural style" of Jiroft, are similar to the Mesopotamian ziggurats.[39] The recent discovery at Anau of a seal bearing signs in an unknown script, in a level dated to 2300 BCE, means that a system of writing had probably been developed either in this region (Hiebert 2001) or in Iran. Central Asia was also connected with more eastern regions, and the Indus valley. Two square stamp seals found at Altyn Tepe (Ancient Namazga V period) – one with a swastika, the other one bearing two writing signs – signal contacts with the Indus. The funerary chamber where the seal with a swastika was found also yielded a gold bead and a bronze blade of a Harappan type, as well as four ivory sticks. At Gonur Tepe (Margiana), a bowl with pipal leaves as well as Indus-type stick dice also reveal exchanges with the Indus (Possehl 2002a: 229–230).

The urban developments we observe, occurring simultaneously throughout Central Asia–Indus–western Asia, correspond in part to the building of what Kohl (2007: 223) terms "secondary states." The Mesopotamian texts give us a few names: Marhashi, Aratta (see below).[40] Their organization remains largely unknown, but archaeological finds reveal social differentiation, more limited, however, than in Sumer. The development of cities and states partly resulted from continuous and relatively intense contacts, favored by new possibilities in the transporting of men and goods. Present in western Asia during the fourth millennium and in Oman and the Indus valley during the third millennium,[41] the domesticated donkey became essential for carrying goods from this period onward. What is known as the "Bactrian" camel was domesticated in Central Asia during the first half of the third

---

[39] Possehl 2002a: 230–231; Vallat 2003b; Madjidzadeh 2003b. Recently, Shahmirzadi (2004) has discovered the remains of a ziggurat at Sialk that he considers to be the oldest known (it is dated to the first half of the third millennium), but in fact the high terrace of Susa I was already a stepped building (Potts 2014: 26). Tosi *et al.* (1996: 209) speak of a "new social order" that was taking place (2600–2400 BCE). We do not know, however, which political entities were present in eastern Iran at this time. A crenellated motif, perhaps recalling architectural elements (steps of terraces, niches, shapes of buildings), appears over a vast area during the third millennium: it can be seen on pottery of Geoksyur, Kara Depe, Mehrgarh VII (2800–2600 BCE), Quetta, and on steatite vases; beads take the shape of crenellated crosses (beads from western Central Asia, Tepe Hissar and Susa, in Iran), as well as pendants, seals – compartmented or not (Shar-i Sokhta, Shahdad, Luristan, BMAC, Indus, Bahrain) – and inlays made of Indus shells (During Caspers 1994: 87ff.; Collins, Piotrovsky, Aruz, and Kenoyer, in Aruz and Wallenfels 2003: 353, 354, 358, 359, 360, 383, 399). According to some authors, the practice of building on ancient religious structures – and incorporating them – may be at the origin of the ziggurat; the latter, in Mesopotamia, would already have appeared during the Early Dynastic period (Oates and Oates 1976: 132; Crawford 1977: 27).
The ziggurat built by Ur-Nammu (2112–2095 BCE), at Ur, appears to have been built over more ancient ziggurats. However, as already mentioned, the stepped high terrace at Susa I was founded around 4000 BCE. Some authors have termed "ziggurat" the public buildings of Eridu (fifth millennium), which were successive structures on a platform.

[40] The sites of Shahdad, Shar-i Sokhta, Mundigak, and Tureng Tepe may have had more than 10,000 inhabitants. Tepe Yahya, Tell Malyan, Bampur, Godin Tepe, and Tepe Hissar supported smaller communities (Tosi and Lamberg-Karlovsky 2003: 348). Unlike what has sometimes been written, the development of maritime routes did not lead to an abandonment of sites in Central Asia, Sistan, and southern Afghanistan.

[41] Perhaps as early as 3000 BCE at Hili, in Oman (Cleuziou and Méry 2002: 281). Remains of *Equus asinus* have been identified at Harappa, Ropar, Rangpur III, Kalibangan, and Surkotada, in the Indus civilization, as well as at Shar-i Sokhta, in Iran (Ratnagar 2004: 237).

millennium.[42] J. Schaffer has suggested that the Harappan people came to Shortughai to procure camels (Possehl 2002a: 229). Populations from Turkmenistan used Bactrian camels with harnesses and carts during the early third millennium: "clay models of Bactrian camels attached to wagons have been found in Early Bronze or Namazga IV levels (i.e. early to mid-third millennium BCE) at Altyn Tepe in southern Turkmenistan" (Kohl 2007: 142). The camel seems to have been used very early on in Iran: 2600 BCE at Shar-i Sokhta (Compagnoni and Tosi 1978), and 2500 BCE at Shah Tepe III. A camel head figures on a copper axe from Khurab, dated to 2600–2400 BCE by Lamberg-Karlovsky. While the horse was probably domesticated earlier in the steppes,[43] its domestication spread only during the third millennium (Kohl 2007: 142),[44] as a response to the rise of exchanges between regions (Sherratt and Sherratt 2001; Sherratt 2003). It is possible that "the harnessing of equids and camels was a technologically interrelated development" (Kohl 2007: 142).

More than the terrestrial routes, the maritime routes were economically crucial for this period. From the middle of the third millennium onward, the Persian Gulf experienced a growth of trade obviously encouraged by the rapid urban blossoming of the Indus region.

Why were the Mesopotamians interested in developing trade with the Indus? For Possehl, the development of a complex Mesopotamian society, led by elites who were consumers of exotic goods, led to an increased demand for metals, wood, ivory, and precious stones from 2600 BCE on, fed by competition between ruling social classes.[45] Moreover, different authors put forward the probable presence of a private sector and the functioning of markets in Mesopotamia around the middle of the third millennium BCE, with an interdependance of commerce and production.[46] The institution of the *kārum* ("quay, port," then "merchant outpost, market" during the early second millennium) may have taken shape during

---

[42] According to Potts (2004), the "Bactrian" camel may also have been domesticated very early on in Xinjiang and Mongolia. Kuzmina (2008: 66–67), who refers to discoveries from Anau and Geoksyur, advances the idea that the camel was domesticated at the end of the fourth millennium in Central Asia.

[43] The site of Botai (3600–2800 BCE), in North Kazakhstan, has yielded evidence for domesticated horses raised for meat, milk, and probably for transport (Outram *et al.* 2009). This site has engendered many debates; see Benecke and von den Dreisch 2003 versus Anthony and Brown 2003, and Olsen 2003. Genetic research shows that the horse may have been domesticated, once on a male line, but several times on female lines (Vilà *et al.* 2001). Some of the horses at Botai were probably ridden (Cunliffe 2014: 79–80).

[44] Anthony (2007: 460) claims that horseback riding was already practiced around the end of the fifth millennium west of the Urals; in North Kazakhstan, horseback riding would begin around 3700–3500 BCE (Anthony 2007: 463). Kuzmina (2008: 28) mentions bones of domesticated horses and traces of a horse cult on fourth-millennium sites between the Dnieper River and the Urals.

[45] It would be erroneous, however, to consider that the development of the Indus resulted simply from a growing demand by countries of western Asia, particularly if we adopted a low chronology (Reade 2001: 28).

[46] Oates 1978: 408; Foster 1993. See below. Warburton himself, despite his tendency to consider the "market" as a *deux ex-machina*, recognizes that "It is difficult to demonstrate that market forces operated across the entire ancient Near East during the entire 3rd millennium, as can be seen during the 2nd [millennium]" (2003: 125).

the second half of the third millennium.[47] The presence of a market, however, does not signify the existence of a market economy; global data for the third millennium – structures changed during the early second millennium – suggest rather centralized and administered economies (Hudson 2004a). The formation of stable commercial networks allowed for new integration between regions. The existence of what has been termed an "intercultural style" reflects this integration; it also reveals "that a shared set of beliefs ... was a part of this cultural configuration" (Possehl 1996: 190).[48] As would be the case later with Buddhism and Islam, commerce and shared beliefs may have combined to set up networks linking urban centers and regional states. Relations between regions permitted the establishment of conversion systems for weights (Mederos and Lamberg-Karlovsky 2004: 201). Moreover, the Indus unit was nearly identical to the "Dilmun shekel" (13.5–13.6 g) – known at Ebla – and also, curiously, to the Egyptian *deben* of the Old Kingdom.

The Indus Valley and the Indian Subcontinent

A turning point in the exchanges and political developments of all of western Asia occurred around 2600/2500 BCE, when interconnections were established between Mesopotamia and the Indus valley, where the Harappan civilization flourished. Exchange networks linked these two regions through terrestrial routes in Iran, and more importantly, maritime routes leading to Oman, the regions of Dharan and Bahrain. On these routes, luxury goods, metals, textiles, food, plants, and animals were carried. These networks constituted a new globalized area (Beaujard 2011, 2012), including for the first time the entire Persian Gulf, Sind, and the northwest of the Indian peninsula, Turkmenistan, Margiana, and Bactria.[49]

The sudden flourishing of urbanization in the Indus valley and in Gujarat during the Classical Harappan period (2600/2500–2000 BCE) has often been emphasized. It was marked by the creation of cities on new sites, the emergence of public architecture, and the appearance of assemblages different from those of the Early Harappan period. Kenoyer (2014: 412), however, points to the continuity between the Early and Mature Harappan phases at sites such as Harappa, Banawali, Baror, and Dholavira. Mohenjo-daro (Sindh) and Harappa (western Punjab) covered 100 ha; Rakhi Garhi (Haryana) and Ganweriwala (western Punjab) 80 ha; and Dholavira (Gujarat) 60 ha (Possehl 2002a: 63).[50] Three cities in the Bhatinda district should also be mentioned:

---

[47] A "temple of the quay" (E-Kara) is mentioned at Girsu during the twenty-fourth century. The logogram KI.LAM for the Sumerian *ganba*, "market," already appears at Lagash during the twenty-fourth century, but it refers to a storehouse (Glassner 2001: 67).

[48] Also Possehl 2002a: 216. For Possehl, this shared set of symbols resulted not only from the building of an "intercultural sphere," but also contributed to its formation. More specifically, the expression "intercultural style" is applied to a type of decoration on chlorite vessels that is primarily linked to the Jiroft region (above).

[49] Bactria is located along the Middle Amu Darya valley. Margiana was the ancient name of the delta region of the Tedjen and Murghab rivers in Turkmenistan.

[50] Kenoyer, however, suggests settlements of larger size for Harappa, Mohenjo-daro, and Rakhigarhi (150-250 ha) (2014: 415).

Lakhmirwala, Gurnikalan 1, and Hasanpur 2, none of which have yet been properly excavated (none of these cities, however, can be compared with the 600-ha size of Uruk) (Ratnagar 2001). Urbanization was accompanied by the formation of a "script" that remains undeciphered (but is it a true script?) and by a standardized system of weights and measures; the use of seals on trade goods; the use of bricks of standard size (previously known at Harappa); the introduction of bronze metallurgy; and the rise of various types of manufacturing: ivory and shell carving, the production of beads (especially carnelian etched beads, and long carnelian beads),[51] and cotton textiles.[52] Textiles woven from wild silk were produced; silk has been found at Nevasa *c.* 2750 BCE, and at Harappa *c.* 2450 BCE (the threads are from wild silk from *Antheraea mylitta*) (Good *et al.* 2009, Cameron 2010: 147). Distillation techniques using vessels with annular rims, found in Mesopotamia since the fourth millennium, seem to have been known at that time (Mohenjo-daro). Progress in agriculture provided the basis for this urban flourishing. The Indus civilization benefited from the use of tropical plants (millets, pulses), cultivated in the summertime, and of plants introduced from western Asia (wheat, barley, pea . . .) – during the sixth millennium BCE – which were grown in the winter. The site of Kalibangan shows evidence of the use of the ard (2600 BCE) (probably reflecting a process of diffusion from western Asia).[53] The chicken was added to the animal species of the Pre-Harappan period, in the Indus valley, Gujarat, and northern India.[54] According to Wright *et al.* (2008: 45), climate change worked in favor of agricultural progress: "During the Mature Harappan phase, there was a transition from strong seasonal rainfall to a more uniform moisture distribution."

[51] These beads were produced only at Mohenjo-daro, Harappa, Chanhu-daro, and Dholavira (Kenoyer 2008: 22). Bead production was significant, for example at Lothal and Chanhu-daro. It suggests "highly stratified" trade networks (Kenoyer 2008).

[52] Remains of cotton thread have been excavated at various sites, as well as seeds (Fuller 2008b). It is strange, however, that Sumerian texts do not mention any importation of cotton cloth into Mesopotamia. Flax, hemp, and wool were also woven; Ratnagar 2004: 107ff., 145ff., 159ff.; Kohl 2007: 223. The cotton plant was used at Mehrgarh as early as the sixth millennium BCE (Moulherat *et al.* 2002). At the same site, seeds dated to 5000 BCE have been found: cotton was probably cultivated during this period (Costantini 1984). Cotton thread has also been discovered with a carnelian bead at Shahi Tump, on the Makran coast (Baluchistan), dated to the fourth millennium BCE.

[53] A relationship has been demonstrated among terms referring to the "plow (ard)" in Indo-Aryan, Dravidian, and the Munda languages; they reveal a common substrate, that should be sought in the Harappan culture (Southworth 2005: 80; Fuller 2006a: 15). Blažek and Boisson (1992), however, consider the word as deriving from Sumerian. See Osada 2006. Note that the earliest evidence for the ard in Egypt is dated to the same period (2600 BCE).

[54] Domestication may have taken place during the Pre-Harappan period in northern India. A discovery has been claimed at Tepe Yahya (Iran) dated to the fourth millennium, but it is based on only one bone. For Fuller (2008), the chicken may have been domesticated in the eastern Indus region or in the Middle Ganges valley. "Chickens were probably brought into domestication more than once" (Fuller *et al.* 2011: 551, Kanginakudru *et al.* 2008). Outside India, chickens have been domesticated in China (already in the sixth millennium) and in Southeast Asia (Y.-P. Liu *et al.* 2006b; Kanginakudru *et al.* 2008; Pramual *et al.* 2013). Domestication also occurred in southern China during the late third millennium BCE (L. Liu and Chen 2012: 115–116). Domesticated animals during the Pre-Harappan period included species introduced from western Asia such as goat, sheep, humpless cattle, and species domesticated in the Indus region, such as zebu and water buffalo. It is possible that a second domestication of sheep occurred in Baluchistan, in Central Asia, or at Mehrgarh. Another domestication of the zebu took place further east, perhaps in the Deccan (Magee *et al.* 2007).

The political organization standing behind the coherence of this Indusian area remains poorly understood and has given rise to bitter controversy. Its cultural uniformity, in any case, cannot be cast into doubt, although Wheeler (1968) may have exaggerated it. The careful planning of various cities and the architectural parallels we observe suggest the existence of an administration. The walls of the cities reflect the need to organize their defense, although warfare does not seem to have played a significant role. Different sites exhibit partitions between higher and lower towns (for example Kalibangan, Harappa, and Rakhi Garhi).[55] Water played a major religious role. The sophistication of water control in the Indus cities, for public or private purposes, is well known: there were great baths – probably used for ritual ablutions – as well as dams, tanks, and drains. At Lothal and Kalibangan, moreover, ritual structures have been termed "fire altars" (Ratnagar 2001). Water control was also aimed at promoting agriculture. The main sites had warehouses and what appear to have been granaries. The sociocultural complexity of the Indus is difficult to fathom without presupposing the existence of structured states (Ratnagar 1991). Bead production and trade suggest manufacturing sectors controlled by the state and/or guilds (Kenoyer 2008). It appears problematic to base Indusian cohesion, as Possehl (1998) suggests, entirely on an ideology that remains largely unknown to us. And why was this ideology able to impose itself so rapidly over such a vast area?

The development of long-distance exchanges was certainly crucial to the ascent of the Indus region. The link between political organization and trade development remains difficult to analyze. It is obvious that various materials used by Harappan craftsmen needed to be imported. Metallurgy made use of copper from Rajasthan and Oman, and tin from Afghanistan. Silver came from Iran; gold from Karnataka or Badakshan; precious or semiprecious stones, from western India, Deccan, and Central Asia. The Indus civilization showed an impressive capacity for expansion, a process which did not exclude the development of regional forms, for example in Gujarat.[56]

Harappan exchanges involved not only what we could call the "developed" countries of the Persian Gulf, but also Neolithic and Chalcolithic populations in India and Central Asia, who occupied various ecological niches and were able to provide various resources. Harappan influences are obvious in peripheral regions and margins – these are regions "which provided goods to centers but did not become dependencies, did not specialize in providing certain goods and hence saw no internal stratification" (Ratnagar 2001b: 359): Baluchistan (Nindowari), the Middle Ganges valley, Kashmir (Burzahom),[57] and the Indian peninsula. Interactions with the Indus valley seem to have triggered the rise of copper metallurgy in Rajasthan and in the Malwa region (Madhya

---

[55] Dholavira was divided into three parts built at different levels (Possehl 2002a: 68). In addition, several cities exhibit careful urban planning, with streets forming grid layouts, the building of platforms, and so forth. Mohenjo-daro, however, shows large buildings located in its lower town.

[56] Sonawane (2000: 141) notes that some towns of Gujarat show markers of the classical Harappan culture (some of these towns were clearly Harappan "outposts"). Others, such as Kuntasi, Rangpur, Rojdi, and Zekhada, do not exhibit all these markers. These cities had part of their roots in local Chalcolithic cultures.

[57] The Northern Neolithic already had established links with the Pre-Harappan culture (Possehl 1999: 546).

Pradesh). Discoveries of steatite beads at Neolithic sites located near gold deposits at Maski, in Karnataka, and that of a copper chisel of Harappan type, lead us to suppose that the Harappans acquired gold from this region (Ratnagar 2004: 156). More surprising were the discoveries of seals; an Elamite or Mesopotamian seal excavated at Maski could be dated to the first half of the third millennium; in addition, the Nagpur museum owns a Mesopotamian cylinder seal dated to the late third millennium (Ratnagar 2001b). In the Middle Ganges valley, the discovery of spindles *c.* 2500–2000 at Senuwar reveals weaving craft (Fuller 2008b). Wheat, barley and domesticated animals, imported from the west, arrived in this region during the second half of the third millennium[58] and – for the animals – in Bihar during the early second millennium. Domesticated animals of West Asian stock arrived before 2300 BCE in the Central-South Deccan, where agriculture based on Indian millets and pulses developed.[59]

In the Middle Ganges valley, phytoliths and rice remains at Lahuradewa (Uttar Pradesh) have been observed that could imply rice culture as early as 6300 BCE (Saxena *et al.* 2006: 1550);[60] for some authors, this confirms the idea of a second domestication of rice – of the *indica* type – in eastern India (see Fuller 2006a: 41). Aridification at the close of the fourth millennium may have encouraged the domestication of rice and, in other regions, various types of millet (Fuller 2006a: 45). Fuller, however, refutes an ancient date for rice domestication at Lahuradewa (2007: 397, 404), and considers that *Oryza nivara* may have been exploited on a large scale during ancient periods "without any serious cultivation, or selection of habit changes or domestication traits" (2011a: 80). In any event, Senuwar does represent a site of sedentary rice farmers that is dated to *c.* 2500 BCE (Saraswat 2005; Fuller 2011a: 80). If rice at the site of Kunal (Sarasvati plain, Haryana) was indeed cultivated (Saraswat and Pokharia 2003), cultivated rice may have spread westward from the Ganges valley, as early as the first half of the third millennium.[61] Moreover, several sites in Orissa show the presence of rice during the third millennium.[62] Many sites in central and western India have yielded rice dated to

---

[58] These West Asian plants were integrated into an agricultural system already in place since *c.* 3000 BCE; rice, local millets, and later pulses domesticated in India were grown (Fuller 2007: 403).

[59] Fuller (2008a: 757) suggests an incipient agriculture "perhaps [as early as] 3000 BC" in Gujarat and slightly later in the southern Deccan, based on local millets and pulses. Domesticated animals were introduced during the fourth millennium in Gujarat within societies of hunter-gatherers (Padri and Loteshwar).

[60] The phytoliths come from lake sediments. Analyses done on the neighboring archaeological site of Lahuradewa yielded a dating of 6360 BCE for the earliest level with cultivated rice, where *Setaria sp.* millet seems also to have been present. *Cannabis sativa* appears in more recent layers. An influence of the Harappan world is visible between 2500 and 2000 BCE on ceramics (Lahuradewa), and – for the whole region – through the introduction of barley and ovicaprids (Fuller 2006a: 42; 2007: 404). In addition, during the same period, Indian pulses were introduced from neighboring regions (*Vigna radiata*, *Macrotylema uniflorum*).

[61] Imprints of rice in pottery have been dated to the late fourth millennium at Kunjhun II and Chopanimundo, but this rice could well be wild rice collected and not cultivated (Petraglia and Allchin 2007: 399).

[62] Golabai Sasan, a Neolithic/Chalcolithic site of Orissa, has yielded cord-impressed pottery using rice as temper. Radiocarbon analysis of an assemblage from a layer immediately following yielded a dating of 2300–2100 BCE (Sinha 2000). Most of the site of Golabai, as well as Gopalpur, however, goes back to the second half of the second millennium (Fuller 2006a: 47). Further south, rice arrived from northeast India or from the Ganges valley toward the end of the second millennium BCE (Korisettar 2004: 177).

(a)   (b)

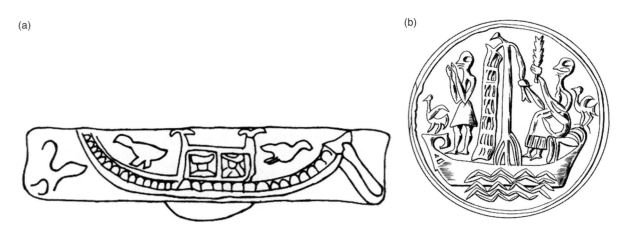

Figure 3.1 (a) Amulet from Mohenjo-daro featuring a reed boat (Deloche 1996: 200); (b) Dilmun seal depicting a sailing vessel (Crawford 1998: 16)

the second millennium BCE.[63] During the Classical Harappan period (2500–2000 BCE), rice (as impressions in bricks or ceramics) may have been present at Lothal A and Rangpur (period IIA), in Gujarat, but the status of this rice (was it collected in the wild, or grown?) remains debated; no rice has ever been discovered in the Indus valley itself prior to the second millennium. Rice of the *(proto-)indica* type also appeared around 2500 BCE in the Swāt valley (Pakistan) in the Northern Neolithic culture,[64] and at the end of the Neolithic at Gufkral (Kashmir).

Several other regions in India became centers for agricultural domestication, especially a region south of the Ganges, then Orissa. Increased aridification, from 2200 BCE on, certainly enhanced this agricultural progress as well as the process of sedentarization, because natural resources were becoming scarcer. An influence from the Indus civilization is also noted.

From Harappan ports, ships sailed to the Persian Gulf and Arabia, but the location of these ports is not known (this may be because these ports were modest in scale, as Boivin and Fuller suggest [2009], or – a more likely hypothesis – because the remains of these ports are hidden below sediments and have not yet been found). Also unknown are the types of seagoing ships that were used. A Harappan seal depicts a type of boat used on the Indus river. The seal also features a bird flying above the boat. This image refers to a practice that we will find later, in India and elsewhere in the Indian Ocean. "The *Baveru Jataka*, [for example], refers to boatmen taking crows with them for finding land."[65] We will find this practice again for journeys made by Arabo-Persians

---

[63] The dating of the rice found at Koldihwa at the junction of the Ganges plains and the Vindhian hills has been moved from the fifth millennium to 1600–1500 BCE. Rice from Chirand, in Bihar, is also more recent than had been proposed initially (second millennium and not 4000 BCE). On the discoveries of early rice in India, see Possehl 1999: 246–249, and Fuller 2006a. Phytoliths of rice have been brought to light at Balathal for the Mature Harappan period, but was this rice wild or cultivated? Further south, some rice has been found at Hallur during the 1800–1200 phase; this may have been wild rice (Fuller 2007: 409).

[64] Imprints in pottery at Ghalegay and grains at Bir-Kot-Gwandhai (Fuller 2006a: 36).

[65] Dhavalikar 1999: 108. There are also seals from Bahrain that depict a ship with birds sitting on the prow and stern (Crawford 1998: 16). In the Epic of Gilgamesh, after the Flood, Utnapishtim (the Sumerian Noah) sent three birds successively in search of land.

and other groups to Madagascar. Lothal has also yielded a terracota model of a boat with one mast and a square stern (Ratnagar 2004: 217).

The Persian Gulf, a Central Corridor between Mesopotamia and the Indus Region

> At the wharf of Akkad he made moor ships from Meluhha, ships from Magan, and ships from Dilmun.[66]

Mesopotamia and the Indus valley were interconnected mainly by sea. This interconnection went along with the development of the intermediary regions, Oman, Bahrain, and southern Iran.

Oman played a major role in these Gulf exchanges due to its copper resources. While it may be that no true state was ever formed (unlike Bahrain, slightly later), communities occupying various ecological niches may have constituted federations of tribes (Cleuziou 2002, 2003a).[67] Discoveries of seals not only imported but also locally made,[68] using systems of writing which derived from the Indus, the Proto-Elamite[69] or the Linear Elamite (*c.* 2150 BCE), however, reflect growing social complexity. Because of the relative importance of the Harappan material found far from the coasts, some researchers have suggested that chiefs of the interior were prominent in the networks, with coastal groups as intermediaries (Boivin and Fuller 2009: 145). Towers made of stone (or brick, at Hili) were used as warehouses and for the defense of communities; they seem to embody centers of regional power. Moreover, from 2300 BCE onward, Oman produced chlorite vessels decorated with a pattern of dots-in-circles (of a type called *série récente* [recent series], these vessels have been found throughout the Persian Gulf, the Indus valley and as far as Margiana [Gonur]).[70] Hard stones such as gabbro and diorite were also exported. The excavations at Ra's al-Jinz (eastern tip of Oman) have shed light on the nature of the boats that sailed in the Persian Gulf and the Indian Sea during the second half of the third millennium: these were sewn plank boats, or reed boats, using a caulking of bitumen imported from Iran or from Mesopotamia (Cleuziou and Tosi 2000).

[66] Kenoyer 1998: 97–98. Meluhha has been identified as the region of the Lower Indus valley, Magan corresponds to the Omani peninsula, and Dilmun to the region of Bahrain. Some authors have established a link between the name "Magan" and that of the coast – *Makran* – of Baluchistan, or with the name *Maka* later given to the region of Oman in Old Persian. See Ratnagar (2004: 99) on the origin of the term Meluhha. The Indo-Aryan *mleccha*, "barbarian, foreigner," has often been related to the name Meluhha.

[67] However, King Naram-Sin, from Akkad, around 2200 BCE, reports that he has defeated "the king of Magan" in a naval battle. Under the king of Ur Amar-Sin (2046–2038 BCE), an administrative document evokes a "prince" (*ENSI*) of Magan, who perhaps bore an Amorite name.

[68] These seals were not distinctive to Oman; they sometimes imitated seals from the Indus or Bahrain.

[69] Glassner 2002b: 366. For some signs found in Oman, parallels can also be established with potters' marks from Shahdad and Tepe Yahya (Glassner 2002b).

[70] Potts 1990: 108ff.; 2001: 205; Hiebert 1994: 106; Shaikh 2000: 86. Among these *série récente* vessels, square bottles with cylindrical necks found at Hili "clearly have Irano-Bactrian affinities" (Cleuziou 2002: 204).

Further west, an urban center on the island of Tarut – along with the Arab coast facing this island, existing prior to Bahrain – represents the Dilmun region of the Mesopotamian texts. A document of the Early Dynastic III period "evokes a gift 'offered' 'according to the custom' by a queen of Dilmun to a queen of Lagaš" (Glassner 2002b: 340, 342, 353). Qala'at al-Baḥrayn took on a growing importance from around 2100 BCE (Crawford 1998).

On the other side of the Gulf, the region of Kerman may have been "the mysterious country of Aratta, envied by the Sumerian potentates" (Madjidzadeh 2003a),[71] unless it represents the kingdom of Marhashi of the Mesopotamian texts (Potts 2002). The myth of *Enmerkar and the Lord of Aratta* (see below) connects this country with the supply of metals and lapis: "My sister, let Aratta fashion gold and silver skilfully on my behalf for Unug [Uruk]. Let them cut the flawless lapis lazuli from the blocks" (Kramer 1952).[72] A major urban site has been discovered at Konar Sandal, south of Jiroft: it has yielded inscriptions showing unknown systems of writing, one of which may be a precursor to Linear Elamite. The objects imported or produced at Jiroft reveal connections between this region and Mesopotamia, the Indus, Bactria, and the Persian Gulf.

Beyond Oman and the Indus culture, towards the southwest, the exchange networks included the Arab coasts (which exported incense) and probably part of the African coast, and even East Africa, if a pendant discovered in a tomb of Tell Asmar, near Baghdad, and dated to 2500–2400 BCE, really is made of copal from the region of Zanzibar.[73] While recent research in Zanzibar has not confirmed a human presence in the Kuumbi cave during the third millennium (Prendergast *et al.* 2016), the involvement of African coastal populations in long-distance trade remains a possibility. The discovery of mango tree wood used in a funerary boat of Khufu suggests some contacts between Egypt and the Indus, via Arab intermediaries, but the identification still needs confirmation (see below). Possehl considers that the bearers of the Harappan culture probably reached as far as Africa (Possehl 2002a: 244).

The archaeology of the Persian Gulf reveals not only contacts between various lands, but also the existence of a common culture, and the probable settlement, in Oman, Bahrain and Mesopotamia, of communities of artisans and merchants from the Indus valley and other regions. The expansion of long-distance exchanges led to a system of shared beliefs and the flowering of syncretisms – the chlorite vessels of the so-called "intercultural style" show this, but these vessels seem to come mainly from the region of Konar Sandal (Jiroft), in southern Iran. Researchers have also focused their attention on seals in order to study interregional contacts. Some seals were clearly imported, whereas others exhibit cultural blending (Parpola 1994a, b; Crawford 1998; Tosi 2001; Possehl 2002a; Aruz 2003a; Cleuziou 2003a). Square seals from the Indus region have been unearthed in Mesopotamia (Ur, Telloh, Kish, Nippur); at Susa, in Iran (Shahdad); and in Oman (Ra's al-Jinz); but one square seal found at Ur in a Pre-Akkadian level bears

---

[71] Liverani connects Aratta with Shar-i Sokhta (2014: 169).

[72] Aubet (2013: 194) argues that the text refers to trading relationships going back to the early third millennium BCE, but this is unlikely. In any case, it had been written during the reign of the Third Dynasty of Ur.

[73] Meyer *et al.* 1991: 296–297. This identification, however, has been cast into doubt; see Phillips 1997: 437.

cuneiform writing. A square seal excavated at Altyn Tepe (Turkmenistan) (at the end of the Namazga V period, *c.* 2200 BCE) bears Indusian signs, but was probably written in a non-Indian language. Round seals exhibiting signs reproducing either an Indian language or motifs from the Indus have been unearthed on Bahrain (in a 2200–2000 BCE context); at Susa, Ur or its region; and at Telloh (round seals appeared in the Persian Gulf around the twenty-third century and spread from 2200 BCE onward, when Bahrain became a major commercial center). Some seals bore Harappan signs, formed into sequences unknown in the Indus valley: these writings may have transcribed a non-Indian – Sumerian or Semitic – language, and reflect the acculturation of Harappans living in the Gulf: this is the case for seals found at Qala'at al-Baḥrayn (*c.* 2000 BCE), Failaka, and Ur.[74] At Tell Asmar (ancient Eshnunna), near Baghdad, a cylinder seal of Mesopotamian type found near an Akkadian house depicts animals from India (elephant, rhinoceros, crocodile); this cylinder seal was likely produced by an Indian artisan who had settled in Mesopotamia (Tosi 2001: 137). A cylinder seal of the Old Akkadian period depicts a translator of the Meluḫḫan language. Another shows two water buffaloes, animals certainly imported from the Indus at this time.[75] Other cylinder seals showing sequences of Harappan signs or Indusian iconography have been excavated at Tell Suleimah (Akkadian period), Ur, Failaka, and Susa. The Mesopotamia of the early second millennium BCE has yielded cylinder seals bearing the design of a bull – portrayed in profile – with a large eye (known in the Kulli culture of Baluchistan, which began *c.* 2600 BCE). One notes the ubiquity of mythical motifs such as "the master of animals," and the importance of the bull in most regions.[76]

Pottery and ornaments show other evidence of contacts and the elaboration of a common culture. Various types of Harappan ceramics have been found in Mesopotamian contexts[77] and on the Arab coasts (Possehl 1996: 163ff.; Tosi 2001: 137). In Oman, Ra's aj-Jinz yielded a large variety of Harappan potteries, revealing the presence of Indus people at this site.[78] Perforated containers, and some jars (found at various sites in Oman), may have been used to transport dairy products. Tombs from the Late Umm an-Nar period were found to contain small Harappan bottles with

---

[74] The site of Saar (Bahrain) has also yielded hybrid seals, especially for the period corresponding to the late third and early second millennia. According to Tosi (2001: 135), a seal imprint from Umma was probably made "for an Indian expatriate."

[75] Aruz and Wallenfels 2003: 413; Potts 1997: 258. The water buffalo no longer seems present in Mesopotamia after the Akkadian period.

[76] Aruz 2003a: 246. One also observes regional particularities. Seals from Central Asia, often compartmented, rarely display the horned divinities that are well attested elsewhere, from Mesopotamia to the Indus (Aruz 2003a: 247). The presence of wings on their shoulders is characteristic of the divinities of the BMAC. Wings appear in Mesopotamia during the Akkadian period as an attribute of the goddess Ishtar, who, like a Bactrian-Margian goddess, is depicted seated on a feline (Aruz 2003a: 206). Compartmented seals featuring zebus have been unearthed at Altyn Tepe, Mohenjo-daro, and Naushario, and observed (as an imprint on a pottery item) at Shar-i Sokhta (Aruz 2003a).

[77] At Tell Asmar, for example. Possehl 1996: 163ff., Tosi 2001: 137.

[78] Cleuziou and Tosi 2000: 22. See Cleuziou and Méry 2002: 291–298 and 299 fig. 8 for a map showing the distribution of imported Harappan artifacts across Oman. The frequency of Indus wares at Ra's al-Jinz is over 40 percent for the period covering the twenty-fifth–twenty-fourth century; then it decreases over the twenty-third–twenty-second century (Cleuziou 2002: 214). It is noteworthy that the appearance of new sites in Oman occurred mainly during the flowering of the Harappan culture.

painted black decorations that seem to have acquired a high symbolic value. Large quantities of pottery from Gujarat have been excavated at Saar (Bahrain), along with other ceramics from the Indus region (dated to the late third millennium).

Mesopotamian pottery has been discovered in Dilmun, in the region of Abqaiq (around the middle of the third millennium), in Tarut and at Qala'at al-Baḥrayn (founded *c.* 2500 BCE), as well as in Oman.[79] Overall, Mesopotamian material appears to have decreased from 2400/2300, whereas objects from the Indus (or influenced by the Indus) increased in number: we seem to have evidence here of a relative reconfiguration of the networks between Mesopotamia and the Indus.

Various types of pottery from southern Iran or influenced by this region have also been unearthed on the Arab coasts: black-on-grey pottery at Bahrain, Tarut, Dharan, and Abqaiq; black-on-red pottery at Umm an-Nar, Hili, and Tarut; and incised grey pottery at Tarut and Hili N.[80] Pottery from Oman has been excavated in Iran at Tepe Yahya (phases IVB to IVA).

Tin is present in objects from Umm an-Nar, Hili, Tell Abraq, and other sites (tin probably came from Afghanistan, through the Indus valley or Southeast Iran) (Potts 1990: 125; Shaikh 2000: 84, 86; Weeks 2003: 178, 181). Tin bronze was known in the Indus valley as early as the twenty-fourth century BCE.

Bitumen was another type of product that was exported from various regions early on. On Bahrain, Qala'at al-Baḥrayn has yielded bitumen imported from Mesopotamia, whereas the bitumen found at the sites of Saar, Karranah, and Buri came from Iran (Connan *et al.* 1998: 177): here we may see clues to private trade. Bitumen was used in the sealing of the brick floor in the Great Bath of Mohenjo-daro (Ratnagar 2004: 141).

Ornaments, in particular, reveal exchanges driven by rulers and notables: exchanges accompanied by the diffusion of symbolic meanings. Beads and other objects made of precious or semiprecious stones were not only ornaments, but also played a role in the magico-religious field. The so-called "royal" tombs of Ur reflect the wealth of the elites of this port city during the period 2500–2400.[81] Gold floral ornaments belonging to "Queen" (NIN) Pu-abi[82] and other women, as well as belts decorated with long carnelian beads, recall ornaments from the Indus civilization. These tombs have yielded lapis lazuli, carnelian etched beads produced in the Indus valley, and copies in gold of segmented faience beads (known at Mohenjo-daro, Harappa ...).[83]

---

[79] Crawford 1998: 51, 54. For a map showing Mesopotamian imports in Oman, see Cleuziou and Méry 2002: 287 fig. 4.

[80] Potts 1990: 104–106; 2001: 203.

[81] Dating would be one century lower if we follow the ultra-short chronology defended by Gasche *et al.* (1998). According to this chronology, Pu-abi reigned *c.* 2350 BCE.

[82] In Pu-abi's tomb "lay soldiers, grooms, maids and musicians" (Glassner 2000b: 48). Unlike Westenholz, Glassner sees the emergence of monarchy at this time.

[83] These beads were known during the Early Dynastic III B period of Mesopotamia (2500–2350 BCE); Possehl 1996: 153–158; 2002: 223. Carnelian beads could have come from other sources (carnelian was exploited in Oman and near Shar-i Sokhta) (Ratnagar 2004: 145). Segmented faience beads have been found in northern Syria (for the Jemdet Nasr period, around 3000 BCE); at Kish (Mesopotamia); Tepe Hissar III (Persia); and even earlier in Egypt (in a Badarian context, a culture dated between 4400 and 3800 BCE). The decoration of the etched beads is of three types: white-on-red, black-on-white, and (more rarely) black-on-red (De Waele and Haerinck 2006: 33).

Carnelian etched beads have also been discovered at Tell Abu Salabikh, dated to the Early Dynastic III;[84] Kish and Tell Asmar (Mesopotamia), during the Akkadian period; in Bahrain,[85] at Umm an-Nar, Tell Abraq, Shimal and Hili (Omani peninsula); at Tepe Hissar (IIIC), Shah Tepe (IIA), Susa, Shahdad (Iran), during the second half of the third millennium; at Jalalabad (Afghanistan), for the middle of the third millennium; at Altyn Tepe (Turkmenistan); and as far as the island of Aegina, in the Aegean Sea (Aruz 2003a: 243, 261). Some bead decorations observed in western Asia were not very popular in the Indus: beads must have been produced either for export or locally by Meluhhans (Kenoyer 2008: 25). The probable presence of communities of foreign craftsmen manufacturing items in the style of their respective countries of origin complicates the interpretation of the data concerning objects that might be considered as imported (Crawford 2004: 177). Barrel-shaped beads, distinctive of the Indus culture, made of lapis lazuli, carnelian, or terracotta (segmented faience beads), have been excavated in Iran and in Mesopotamia (Royal Tombs of Ur). Links can be seen with some cities in particular: long biconical beads made of green jasper mottled with red produced only in the city of Dholavira have been discovered at Ur, where they certainly constitute imports (Kenoyer 2008: 26). In contrast, some of the long carnelian beads perforated with drills made of what is usually called "ernestite" may have been produced in Mesopotamia. Shell bracelets carved in the Indus valley have been found at Ur and Susa, and in Central Asia.[86] Cylinder seals made from the columella of *Turbinella pyrum* shell (found on the coasts of India and Pakistan), excavated in the royal cemetery of Ur, may have been carved locally by Indian craftsmen: it seems that columellae were sent from centers such as Lothal and Nageshwar (Kenoyer 2008: 24). Ivory combs with dotted circle decoration found at Tell Abraq (Oman) may have come from the Indus valley, as well as objects with kidney-shaped ivory inlays found at Tell Asmar. Conversely, a similar comb, but engraved with two tulips, certainly came from the Bactria-Margiana culture (BMAC, Bactria-Margiana Archaeological Complex) (*c.* 2000 BCE) (Potts 2003b: 315).

Other jewels may have taken an opposite route, for example the flat gold beads excavated at Troy; Aegina (Aegean Sea); Eskiyapar (Anatolia); Novosvobodnaya (in the northern Caucasus); Tell Umm el-Marra (Syria); Tell Brak (northern Mesopotamia); Ur; Tepe Hissar; Altyn Tepe (Central Asia); Tell Abraq (Oman); Mohenjo-daro, Allahdino (Indus region), and Lothal (Gujarat). Gold ornaments in the shape of quadruple spirals (the quadruple spiral was a symbol associated with flowing waters and fertility) may also have been carried from west to east, according to J. Aruz. Beads, pendants, and gold or silver pins with this design have been found at Poliochni, Troy; Alaca Hüyük, Eskiyapar (Anatolia); at Tell Brak; Assur (in a tomb dated to the twentieth century BCE that also

---

[84] Abu Salabikh also yielded lapis lazuli, copper, and conch shells from the Indian Ocean (Postgate 2003: 211).

[85] For a list of the carnelian etched beads known for eastern Arabia, see De Waele and Haerinck 2006: 33–35.

[86] The presence of bracelets with chevron decoration, characteristic of the Indus elite, may reveal the presence of women from the Indus valley at Susa and at Ur (Kenoyer 2008: 24). A shell spoon from the Indus has been excavated at Girsu (Mesopotamia) (Kenoyer 2003: 398–400). Susa also shows perforated discs of Harappan type, made from *Turbinella pyrum* shell (Potts 1999: 121).

yielded carnelian etched beads); in the royal tombs of Ur; on Bahrain; at Tepe Nush-i Jan (Iran), and Gonur Tepe (Turkmenistan).[87]

Various Persian Gulf sites have yielded stone weights similar to those used in the Indus valley.[88] At Umm an-Nar, however, some weights seem to correspond to the standards of Ebla (what is known as the "Syrian" unit of 9.4 g). Qala'at al-Bahrain has yielded barrel weights of a Mesopotamian type (Cleuziou 1992: 93). Mesopotamian weights have also been discovered in the Indus (Mohenjo-daro and Harappa) (Ascalone and Peyronel 2003; Rahmstorf 2006a: 29).

Moreover, stone vessels offer other, additional clues to contacts and the formation of a common culture. The Iranian region of Jiroft (Kerman) was the center of production and dissemination of chlorite vases and bowls, which often depicted human and animal figures, and were decorated with precious stones (lapis lazuli, turquoise). From Jiroft, merchants carried these items to Mesopotamia.[89] Lapis lazuli was relatively abundant at Jiroft, brought there from Afghanistan probably via Mundigak. A text from the Early Dynastic III period speaks of a foreign merchant who brings lapis lazuli and silver from the mountains. From 2600 to 2500 BCE, in a large area (including Syria, Uzbekistan, the west coast of the Persian Gulf, the Indus[90] ...), one finds chlorite bowls belonging to the intercultural style (or *série ancienne*), along with nude masculine statuettes, or figurines of monkeys (dated between the Early Dynastic and the Larsa period, during the early second millennium BCE in Mesopotamia).[91] Chlorite-stemmed cups from Jiroft recall ceramics of the BMAC. Shar-i Sokhta exported alabaster vases, which are found throughout western Asia during the third millennium.[92] Outside this region of Jiroft, chlorite

---

[87] The presence, on the same roads, of the motif of the double spiral has been noted. Gold earrings composed of multiple lobes have also been excavated at Troy, Poliochni, in Syria, in northern and southern Mesopotamia, in the Caucasus and in Iran, during the second half of the third millennium (Aruz 2003a: 240–244). This double-spiral motif is known at the beginning of the third millennium in Transcaucasia and at Arslantepe (in a context influenced by the Kura-Araxes culture of Transcaucasia) (Kohl 2007: 93).

[88] For example, Shimal and Tell Abraq (2170–2140 BCE), in Oman (Cleuziou 2003: 146), Qala'at al-Bahrain, and Susa, in the Iranian interior. Harappan weights have been discovered in layers Ib and IIa of Qala'at al-Baḥrayn (2500–2200 BCE) (Ratnagar 2004: 280).

[89] Among the discoveries in Mesopotamia is a box decorated with a zebu and the "master of the animals," from Khafajeh, dated to the Early Dynastic III (2600–2350 BCE), as well as a box found at Ur in the tomb of Queen Pu-abi (British Museum WA 128887 and 121698). As we know, the production of this type of vessel had already begun during a period corresponding to Mesopotamia's Early Dynastic II. Some mythological motifs depicted on the vases of Jiroft may have influenced Mesopotamia (for example, the scorpion-man, found in the myth of Gilgamesh, and the history of Etanna, where an eagle is attacked by a snake which was hidden in carrion).

[90] According to Shaikh (2000: 83), "steatite" vessels found at Mohenjo-daro may be imports. A fragment of vessel may have come from an early level (Ratnagar 2004: 282).

[91] Clay figurines of monkeys are also known, dating to the Old Babylonian period. Monkeys were probably imported from the Indus valley in early times, then from Egypt during the second half of the second millennium BCE (Potts 1997: 259).

[92] Pittman 2003: 81. A cup has also been discovered at Naushiro. In Iran, Shahdad was another production center for vessels. Similarities have been noted between the tall cylindrical cups found at Ur, Kish, Telloh, in the Persian Gulf, and those found in Bactria (Moorey 1994: 46; Ratnagar 2004: 152).

(or steatite) vessels or objects were also produced at Susa and on Tarut Island, using stones of various origins.[93]

As already mentioned, textiles were major exports for the dominant regions. Fabrics often disappear in archaeological layers, but texts and some discoveries do shed light on production and exchanges. In a Sumerian myth written during the Ur III period, the lord of Aratta (Shar-i Sokhta?) calls on King Enmerkar (Sumer) to accomplish three impossible tasks, each of which has a link with textiles: the myth reflects the importance of textile exports for Sumer (Good 2006). Palatial workshops probably worked in part with a servile labor force, as would be the case later, during the Ur III Empire. Under Urukagina's reign, for example, half of the weavers in the house of his wife Shasha were slaves who had been bought (see Maekawa 1987: 53). The excavations at Shar-i Sokhta have shown that this city had produced various textiles, described in the Assyrian trade of the early second millennium (although these textiles were no longer coming from Shar-i Sokhta, as this city had by then been abandoned): here we see evidence for the integration of the world-system, during the third and second millennia. Goat hair and sheep wool were used; moreover, flax was imported, probably from Mesopotamia. Remnants of nets and ropes, in hemp or in *Crotalaria juncea*, a plant from South Asia, reveal long-distance exchanges with Baluchistan and the Indus during periods II and III of the site (2800–2100 BCE) (Good 2006).

Cultivated plants were also exchanged between regions. Sesame, for example, was present in western Asia during the third millennium BCE. A discovery dated to the beginning of the Bronze Age has been reported at Abu Salabikh, in Mesopotamia.[94] Recent research confirms Harlan's arguments about an Indian origin for sesame,[95] which was present in the Mature Harappan culture, at Harappa and Lothal (Possehl 1999a: 251). Recent discoveries have been made in Pakistan, at Miri Qalat and Shahi Tump, for the same period (Zohary and Hopf 2000: 140). Note that the Akkadian and Assyrian term *ellum*, "sesame oil," corresponds to the Tamil and Malayalam *ellu*, Kannada *yellu*. The transfers of plants during this period will be discussed further below. Remnants of dates with a parasitic coleopteran belonging to *Coccotrypes* sp. found at Ra's al-Jinz may suggest an origin of the date palm at the borders of Iran and Pakistan, and its

[93] For Perrot and Madjidzadeh (2005), the expression "intercultural style" "is no longer relevant, since the discovery of Jiroft," but Lyonnet and Kohl (2008: 36) point to the existence of at least four different sources of chlorite for the vessels that have been found; production centers were multiple, but the iconographic style was common. Objects of Tarut and Mesopotamia belonging to this "intercultural style" are dated to the Early Dynastic II–III of Mesopotamia (Cleuziou 2003b: 115, 120, 124). The first chlorite artifacts excavated in Mesopotamia go back to the Jemdet Nasr period (Crawford 2004: 186). The assemblage of the region of Jiroft is still not precisely dated (Cleuziou 2003b: 116; Muscarella 2001); the dating of Tepe Yahya IVB (levels containing most of the intercultural-style vessels discovered) remains controversial.

[94] Charles 1989. Sesame pollen (but is it really *Sesamum indicum*, or even sesame?) has been found much earlier in levels dating to the seventh millennium BCE at Ali Kosh, in southwestern Iran (van Zeist 1985).

[95] See Bedigian 1998. Also Nayar 1995: 405, 406. Sesame was probably domesticated in the Indus region (Fuller 2007: 424). For Witzel (2004: 177), the etymology of the Sanskrit *tila* must be in the "Para-Munda," considered as the Harappan language. Moreover, Southworth reconstructs the term **nū(v)-* for sesame in Proto-Dravidian or Late Proto-Dravidian (2005: 204).

introduction from this region into Arabia.[96] We have evidence for the culture of the date palm at Hili and Umm an-Nar during the first half of the third millennium, but the culture and domestication of this tree in the Persian Gulf go back to the sixth millennium (see above) (Tengberg 2004). Sumerian texts mention imports of dates from Dilmun, Magan, and Meluḫḫa. The reputed dates from Dilmun during the third millennium suggest a selection of the best clones in this region at an early point in time. Another plant of Indian origin, cucumber, may have been present in Mesopotamia during the Akkadian period: seeds have been found at Tell Taya, near Nineveh (Potts 1997). Opium was probably among the products traded (originating in Anatolia, the poppy [*Papaver somniferum* L.] was introduced during an early period in Mesopotamia: a Pre-Sargonic tablet of Nippur calls opium "plant of joy") (Kapoor 1995).

Exchanges between regions also involved animals. The Indian zebu was present in Sistan (Iran), where Shar-i Sokhta has yielded many figurines of this animal (2900–2500 BCE); in Oman around the middle of the third millennium (Potts 1997: 257); and in Mesopotamia during the early second millennium (the animal is depicted on various supports). Moreover, Ra's al-Jinz yielded a chicken bone that is probably of Indian origin (Cleuziou and Tosi 2000: 43).

The increase in exchanges went along with progress in shipbuilding, with the ships built of reeds or planks. This industry reveals social differentiation, and the existence of specialists and of entrepreneurs. One Dilmun seal may depict an alliance in maritime ventures: two individuals, on either side of the mast of a boat, are joining hands, between two branches of a palm tree.[97] The excavations conducted at Ra's al-Jinz have provided information on the ships sailing in the Persian Gulf and the Indian Sea during the second half of the third millennium. The buildings found at this site dated to period II (2500–2300 BCE) have yielded over 300 plaques of bitumen (each residential unit had its own storage area).[98] One face of most of these plaques shows an impression of reed mats or reeds lashed together, and of ropes that must have tied the mats to the structure. Some plaques bear imprints of sewn planks (*c.* 2300 BCE?) (Cleuziou and Tosi 1997a: 69). On the obverse, incrustations of barnacles can be seen along with the bitumen. These bitumen plaques were clearly used as caulking for boats. The analyses conducted show that this bitumen came from northern Iraq.[99] Its transport must have represented an important part of the Gulf trade.[100] Twenty shards of Mesopotamian jars bearing traces of bitumen have been excavated at Ra's al-Jinz. Mesopotamia built ships of various types, identified in Oman (texts indicate sizes

---

[96] Costantini and Audisio 2000. For an opposing view, see Boivin and Fuller 2009: 135 (below). The small size of the fruit found at Shahi Tump and Miri Qalat suggests that wild dates were gathered, not that date trees were cultivated (Tengberg 2004: 60).

[97] Cleuziou 2003a: 145 fig. 6.3, 147.

[98] For Period III (2300–2100 BCE), the buildings also contained bitumen, but less evenly distributed (Cleuziou and Tosi 2000: 63).

[99] The bitumen employed resulted from an amalgamation of organic substances (plants and tallow) and of inorganic material (gypsum was sometimes added) (Cleuziou and Tosi 1994: 755; 2000: 64).

[100] According to a text from the Ur III period, "a 60 *gur* ship at Lagash could carry 120 talents of bitumen" (Potts *et al.* 1996: 302).

ranging from 1.5 tons to 90 tons),[101] made of reeds or (local or imported) wood (see below). The wood used for the boats at Ra's al-Jinz may have come from India. This site was clearly involved in trade with the Indus region, with Harappan traders visiting Oman on a regular basis (Cleuziou and Tosi 1994: 748).

The building of sewn-plank ships, characteristic of the western Indian Ocean, was therefore already known in the Persian Gulf during the second part of the third millennium. The iconography indicates the existence of various types of boats, some with tapered stem and stern, others exhibiting square sterns. The oldest testimonies for plank boats of which I am aware, however, are the Abydos boats[102] and the funerary boats of Khufu from Egypt, buried near the pyramid of Gizeh.[103]

The paucity of objects from western Asia or exhibiting western influences in the Indus valley and neighboring regions contrasts with the abundance of Harappan objects in the Persian Gulf. Some cylinder seals have been excavated at Harappa and Mohenjo-daro; another at Kalibangan; one at Sibri (*c.* 2000 BCE); one at Maski (South Deccan); and a round seal of Late Dilmun type has been found at Lothal.[104] The chlorite vessels have already been mentioned. A jar at Balakot (period II) may have come from Umm an-Nar (Oman). While no cuneiform writing has ever been found in the Indus region, several iconographic motifs have been borrowed, showing that some aspects of the religion and ideology of western Asia may have been adopted in the Indus. A first motif depicts a bull-woman fighting a horned tiger. A second motif shows a hero mastering two animals, a theme also known in southern Iran and in Central Asia.[105] Finally, scenes of a bull fighting with acrobats, "familiar from the art of Syria, Anatolia, the Aegean and Egypt in the 2nd millennium," appear at Mohenjo-daro as well as at Togolok (BMAC) (Aruz 2003a: 246). As Possehl notes (2002a: 229), the apparent imbalance in trade between the Indus and Mesopotamia is probably the consequence of "invisible

[101] Boats had capacities of from 5 *gur* up to 300 *gur*, with ships of 20 or 60 *gur* apparently the most common (Vosmer 2000: 237; Margueron and Pfirsch 2001: 140).

[102] Fourteen pits containing boats have been discovered in the northeast sector of the funerary enclosure from Khasekhemwy (Second Dynasty); they go back to the First Dynasty (*c.* 3000 BCE).

[103] Most of at least one boat had been built out of cedar wood from the mountains of Lebanon (Lipke 1984). See below concerning these Egyptian ships. Seven stamp seals of Failaka (late second millennium BCE?) show single-masted boats made of planks (Ray 2002a: 5–6). A text of the Ur III period mentions 59,290 wooden pegs for the boatyards of Umma (Potts 1997: 127).

[104] In the Indus civilization Possehl (2002a: 227) mentions the discovery of six cylinder seals and of six seals from the Persian Gulf. Mesopotamian weights have been excavated (Mohenjo-daro, Harappa, Dholavira, Lothal), as well as copper toiletry implements similar to artifacts known at Kish and Ur (Harappa, late levels). During Caspers (1994) points to several cylinder seals exhibiting designs that are clearly Indusian; one of these may be an imitation of a seal from Margiana. On the seal from Kalibangan, see also Aruz 2003a: 246.

[105] Possehl 2002a: 146, 227. Eastern Iran may also have borrowed some religious elements from Mesopotamia (as suggested by the find at Shar-i-Sokhta containing a statuette of a woman carrying a pot on her head, a type of figurine associated with rites of foundation in Mesopotamia). Moreover, Possehl signals lotus designs on Proto-Elamite seals and on early Harappan ceramics at Kalibangan (first half of the third millennium). A curious discovery made at Mohenjo-daro and Harappa has also been noted: here, rings were found that are similar to the *kernoi* used in harvest festivals in the eastern Mediterranean Sea (third millennium) (Possehl 2002a: 228).

[West Asian] exports" in the archaeological levels (see also Postgate 2003: 218). The Mesopotamians exported grains,[106] oil, wool, leather, fish, and bitumen, as well as manufactured products, textiles, metallic tools, and jewels. According to Silver, various buildings excavated reveal "capital investment for the production of goods destined for export"; the remains of a building that may have been a textile workshop or a tannery have been discovered at Eshnunna; at Girsu (Telloh), kilns for ceramic production were found as well as the remains of installations associated with a fish-processing industry (Silver 1995: 144).

In addition to archaeology, texts constitute major sources of information. The first mention of Meluhha (the Indus region) and of Magan (Oman and Makran) in Mesopotamian writings goes back to the Early Dynastic period: "May Magan and Meluhha submit to you" says a prayer addressed to a deity or a king. "Boats from the (distant) land of Dilmun carried the wood [for the king of Lagash Ur-Nanshe]," reports a text from the twenty-fifth century: this wood probably came from India. Also worth noting: the standard unit of weight in Ebla was called the "Dilmun *shekel*" (Potts 1990: 88). Texts from Lagash mention the funding of expeditions to Dilmun to acquire copper from Oman during the twenty-fourth century:

The merchant Ur-Enki has received from Subur, the inspector [of the king] Lulaganda, dairy products, grain, oil, balm, resin of cedar wood (?), for exchange in Dilmun.

One year later, wool and six minas of silver were ordered to be sent to Dilmun.

During the Sargonic period, texts reveal that ships from the Indus sailed to Arabia and Mesopotamia. King Sargon, of Akkad (2334–2279 BCE), boasted of the number of ships from Dilmun, Magan, and Meluhha moored in his capital (see above).[107] Relations were not always peaceful trade contacts. According to an inscription, the third king of Akkad, Manishtushu

had ships built to cross the Lower Sea, where a force drawn from thirty-two cities had assembled to do battle. Manishtushu fought and was victorious, subjugating the cities and their lords. The enemy forces from as far away as the metal-mines were rounded up by Manishtushu. [The king] quarried black stone in the mountains, loaded it onto ships, anchored these at Agade, and had a statue of himself made of the stone which he dedicated to Enlil. (Potts 1990: 137)

While this may have been an attempt by the Akkadian kings to control the exchanges directly, we do not have evidence for the existence of an Akkadian enclave on Bahrain, a hypothesis put forward by Larsen (1983). Conversely, Akkadian sources report the presence of Magan people in southern Mesopotamia: a text from Umma evokes the disbursement of beer to a messenger from Magan. Various sources (from Girsu,

---

[106] Potts (1993: 425) has argued for a view opposite to the one held by Edens (1992) on the significant size (alleged by Edens) of barley exports out of Mesopotamia. A text dated to the late third millennium, however, records the export of 714,000 liters of grain to Bahrain (Yoffee 1995b: 1392).

[107] Two texts dated to the Old Babylonian period, copies of inscriptions by Sargon, state that the god "Enlil gave him the Upper [Mediterranan] and Lower [Persian Gulf] seas" (Potts 1990: 136). Two texts from Umma from the Old Akkadian period mention "the disbursement of oil to a gendarme and a passenger (?) of a Meluhha-ship" (Potts 1990: 166–167).

Umma, and Nippur) also signal the presence of people from Dilmun and the sending of ships to Dilmun.

Incense and other resins were among the goods traded. A text from Lagash "suggests that some quantities of resin were transported in bags and delivered by boats." A text from Umma, a city that played a role in the maritime trade of aromatics (Foster 1977: 38), uses the term ŠIM.GIG (Zarins 1997: 261).

Two texts from Gudea, "governor" of Lagash (2141–2122 BCE),[108] list Magan, with Melu<u>hh</u>a, Gubin, and Dilmun, as "one of those foreign countries upon the necks of which he laid his yoke" (Potts 1990: 142). Gudea's ships brought products from Magan and Melu<u>hh</u>a into Mesopotamia: wood, gold, silver,[109] carnelian, alabaster, diorite, copper, lapis lazuli, tin (from Central Asia, transported through the Indus), and ivory. Except for bird figurines, ivory is not listed as part of the trade with Melu<u>hh</u>a but rather with Magan or Dilmun, which also provided wood (from India?) and copper (from Oman). A text dated to this period records the disbursement of 241 garments to a merchant, garments "destined for Magan" (Potts 1990).

From the Akkadian period to the Ur III Empire, ancient references to Magan ships report the transport of copper, wood, "onions from Magan," "Magan reeds," goats, wood (*mesu* wood, *haluppu* wood …), gold dust, carnelian, and ivory (the latter products suggest that Magan served as an entrepôt). For Dilmun, mention is made of pearls, coral, dates, and various products that reveal the intermediary role also played by this region: copper, silver, gold, carnelian, lapis lazuli, ivory. Besides the products already mentioned, Melu<u>hh</u>a exported beads, *mesu* wood,[110] a plant called *gis-ab-ba-me -luh-ha*, various animals, and slaves. The mention of a ship of Meluhhan style (in two texts) reveals peculiar characteristics of the boats of the Indus (Possehl 2002: 220). Yet no text ever mentions the shipping of Mesopotamian products directly to Melu<u>hh</u>a, even though a tablet *c.* 2200 BCE refers to the "owner of a Melu<u>hh</u>an ship" bearing an Akkadian name (Parpola 1977).

It is probably true that during these ancient periods at least, the organization of long-distance trade on a regular and significant basis was often beyond the means of private merchants (it implied shipbuilding, organizing caravans, financing, and so forth). A private sector did, however, coexist – in a quasi-symbiotic manner – with the sectors of the palace and of the temple. The settlement of "Meluhhan" communities in the Gulf and in Mesopotamia does not support the idea of strict control over trade by the states, unless we envision here "colonies" organized by political powers.

---

[108] This ruler probably had a divine status; "sculptures of Gudea were installed in temples and intended to be the focus of cult offerings" (Winter 2008: 82).

[109] In ancient Mesopotamia, gold also came from Egypt and Anatolia (at the beginning of the second millennium in any case). Silver was imported from Anatolia and the Caucasus; for some authors, this was true mainly for the second half of the second millennium, but we have signaled the wealth of Ebla in silver as early as the middle of the third millennium.

[110] *Mesu* wood (Akkadian *musukannu*) may be *Dalbergia sissoo* Roxb (Ratnagar 2004). Imported from Pakistan or Iran, this wood has been discovered at Tell Abraq in contexts dated to 2200 and 2000 BCE: "significant quantities of sissoo wood have been identified at Shar-i Sokhta in Iranian Sistan, at Mehrgarh, Lal Shah, Miri Qalat and Shahi Tump in Pakistani Baluchistan, and at Harappa and Mohenjo-daro in the Indus Valley" (Tengberg 2002: 76). An Omani origin for the *Dalbergia sissoo* found at Tell Abraq cannot be excluded.

Unlike what has been often argued, the state probably never completely controlled the trade networks during the third and the second millennia, and commerce was not based solely on prestige goods, even though the overall picture – for the third millennium in any case – remains that of administered economies, the development of writing facilitating better organization of production and exchanges, economic planning, and cost rationalization (Hudson 2004a).

Turmoil along the Terrestrial Routes during the Twenty-Third and Twenty-Second Centuries BCE (Mesopotamia, Iran, and Central Asia)

Arrivals of new populations were probably a constant in the Mesopotamian area, which needed herders, mercenaries, and a labor force for its manufactures. During a period of ecological and social crisis, these arrivals took on a different aspect.

Toward the end of the twenty-third century, the Guti arriving from northern Mesopotamia tried to control the trade roads along the Tigris; they looted Mesopotamia, especially in the north.[111] They were expelled one century later. These incursions hastened the collapse of the Akkadian Empire (2193 BCE), probably weakened by internal political problems and an agricultural crisis. The text "The cursing of Agade" evokes the staggeringly high prices of grain, oil, wool, and fish at this time, following the disruption of the exchanges and worsening land aridification (this text, however, was not written until around 2000 BCE) (Zettler 2003: 22). The Guti invasions also disrupted incoming supplies of tin from northern and western Iran (Pigott 2012). During the period 2300–2200, the so-called "invasions" of Amorite nomads – who were present in Syria, but who are considered by some authors to be of Arabian origin[112] – led to the collapse of Palestine's urban culture and also affected Mesopotamia, which itself experienced a relative de-urbanization. Byblos was also destroyed *c.* 2200 BCE. The twenty-third century BCE saw the introduction of the horse into Mesopotamia (one sculpture representing a horse has been found in Syria, dated to *c.* 2300 BCE) (Sergent 1997: 221, 450 n. 75).

The invasions by the Guti and other groups (Lullubi . . .) reflect "upstream" upheavals, in the zone of the steppes, the Iranian plateau and Central Asia.[113] The networks of inner Asia seem to have been suddenly either disrupted or restructured from 2300–2200 BCE onward. The turmoil in Mesopotamia was probably indirectly

---

[111] See below. The list of the kings of Sumer mentions twenty-one kings of Gutium, located near Lake Urmiah. They were responsible for the collapse of the Elamite kingdom of Awan. Some authors have considered the Guti as Indo-Europeans, but Witzel relates this name to a Macrocaucasian term meaning "people of the hills" (2004: 109).

[112] The term *MAR.DU2*, Akkadian *amurru*, at the origin of "Amorite," is already present in 2600 in texts from Shuruppak. By the Paleo-Akkadian period, Amorites were established in the main cities of Mesopotamia (Glassner 2002b: 354). See also Yoffee 1995a: 50.

[113] For Kohl (2002: 166), the arrival of Indo-European pastoralists in Central Asia (Turkmenistan, Margiana, and Bactria) occurred with a chronological discrepancy of several centuries vis-à-vis the movement toward Transcaucasia, "the deserts of the Kyzylkum and Kara Kum initially impeding the movement of herders north to south." The possible arrival of Indo-Europeans in western Asia around 2300 BCE has already been mentioned. The infiltrations of Indo-European populations into Anatolia may in fact have begun during the preceding centuries.

connected to movements of Indo-European populations from the Balkans to Anatolia, and the possible arrival of Indo-Europeans in the Bactria–Margiana Archaeological Complex (BMAC) around 2100 BCE in Central Asia, and later around 2000 BCE in the upper Indus valley.

Migrations from Central Europe toward the Mediterranean coasts and western Asia are attested to by the distribution of pins called *Schleifennadeln* in German (Gerloff 1993; Kristiansen and Larsson 2005). The cities of Poliochni and Troy II were destroyed around 2300/2200 BCE, but those responsible for these destructions are not really identified.[114] Double-spiral-headed pins appeared at Troy *c.* 2300 BCE; we observe similar pins later in the BMAC culture (the motif, originally linked to women and maternity, may have preserved its meaning) (Aruz 2003a).

These population movements seem to be linked to a major climatic change marked by global cooling *c.* 2200 BCE. This climatic phase would continue – with some oscillations – until *c.* 1900. It was accompanied by a process of aridification that affected northern Mesopotamia, Syria, southern Europe, Iran, and a part of the Central Asian steppes around 2200 BCE (Courty *et al.* 1995; Cullen *et al.* 2000; deMenocal 2001).[115] Aridification also affected the Arab peninsula, causing movements of populations toward Bahrain, and toward Mesopotamia, over the final centuries of the third millennium (Parker *et al.* 2006). Correlated with low solar activity, these changes were in fact worldwide, since they affected the entire Indian Ocean, as well as China (Butzer 1995; Staubwasser *et al.* 2003; Wang *et al.* 2005; Staubwasser and Weiss 2006).[116] Egypt was indirectly affected and the Old Kingdom disappeared *c.* 2180 BCE.

The trade routes of Iran and Central Asia were disturbed. Tin bronze had become scarce by the end of the Akkadian period, reflecting supply difficulties in tin (Crawford 2004: 190).[117] The cities in Turkmenistan appeared to be in decline at this time.

[114] The concept of invasions (from Anatolia) into the Aegean world and into Greece has recently been rejected (Broodbank 2000; Pullen 2008) (see, however, Doumas [1988] for another interpretation, and Peltenburg [2007] for an intermediary position). In any case, in the Aegean Sea, one does observe strong cultural Anatolian influences; the development of fortified sites before 2200 BCE; and their abandonment at a later stage. These processes suggest intense competition and violence throughout the region. Here again, we should probably consider the combination of external and internal factors in the collapse that we observe. Peltenburg stresses growing contacts between western Anatolia and Cyprus during this period, with a probable migration of Anatolian elements (2007: 154).

[115] Aridification is perceptible through weaker flooding of the Tigris and the Euphrates between 2350 and 2000, and a lower level in Lake Van. Oak pollen diminished at Lakes Van and Zeribar from 2250 BCE on (Butzer 1995: 133, fig. 2, 136). For Rosen (2007), aridification affected the southern Levant, northern Syria, and Turkey. Cullen *et al.* (2000) also show increasingly arid conditions in western Asia around 2200–2000. Hiebert (2000) notes strong aridification around 2200 in the steppes between the Aral Sea and northern Crimea, with this arid phase continuing until around 1800 BCE (a slower and less pronounced process of aridification may have in fact begun as early as 2500). This global cooling was accompanied by more arid conditions or more precipitation, depending upon the regions of Inner Asia (see Frachetti 2004: 247, for Dzungaria). On the basis of dendrochronology from Irish oaks (Baillie 1999), Mitchiner (2004: 77) places the climatic deterioration to around 2350 BCE. This was correlated with aridification in the steppes between Ukraine and Kazakhstan.

[116] Global cooling was accompanied by a weakening of the monsoon system of the Indian Ocean, which led to a decrease in Nile flood levels.

[117] Tin still reached the Caucasus, a rich metalworking area that produced tin bronzes, part of which were exported toward the Eurasian steppes during the late third and early second millennia (Kohl 2007: 122).

Populations adapted to increased aridity, with greater mobility of herders in the steppes, on the one hand, and intensification of irrigated agriculture in the oases of Margiana–Bactria (and perhaps in Xinjiang), on the other (Hiebert 2000). Besides agriculture, the rise of the Bactria–Margiana complex (BMAC), whose aristocracy may have been Proto-Aryan,[118] was founded on crafts development and control over the trade roads. The expansion of this culture went along with the arrival of populations from the steppes and at least some of the inhabitants of the Turkmene cities.[119] The use of seals and bullae indicate control over exchange and perhaps production (Hiebert 1994: 176). Fortified settlements – with circular, square, or cruciform buildings – took shape. This new feature – when compared to Turkmenistan – reflects a context of warfare. The horse, domesticated, entered ritual sacrifices, and chariots with spoked wheels were present (see below) (Sarianidi 2005: 240; 2006). For Sarianidi, the discoveries at Togolok ("temple" of Togolok-21), Gonur (*temenos* and "temple," cemetery) and Dashly 3 (circular "temple") evoke practices later known in Zoroastrianism (the presence of what Sarianidi calls "fire temples," ritual exposure of the corpse, and so forth).[120] Moreover, Togolok and Gonur have yielded remnants of ephedra, poppy, and hemp, substances used to prepare the Vedic *soma*, the Avestic *haoma*.[121] Gonur Tepe may have been the capital of a state of Margiana. The presence

[118]   Various authors believe that the first elite of the BMAC was composed of Proto-Aryan speakers (Proto-Indo-Iranians) (see Parpola 2000: 234; Kuzmina 2007: 324). The population of the BMAC would thus have been progressively "aryanized"; at the same time, the newcomers largely adopted the culture of the BMAC. Scholars, however, disagree on the formative area of the Proto-Aryan, as well as on the process of divergence of the Proto-Indo-Aryan and Proto-Iranian branches from the Proto-Aryan (where did it happen? and when?). Kuzmina (1994, 2007: 297ff.) considers the Andronovo groups (an ensemble of steppe cultures dating back to 2100 BCE) as Indo-Iranians, and the ensuing Fedorovo culture (c. 1800/1700–1500, Kazakhstan) as being at the origin of the Indo-Aryans. Kuzmina suggests that the people of the Srubnaya culture (Lower Volga) ("Timber-Grave Culture," 1900–1300) spoke an Iranian language (Kuzmina 2007). The populations of the BMAC may in fact have spoken several languages: Witzel emphasizes borrowings from a non Indo-European language of the BMAC (thought to belong to the Macro-Caucasian family) into the Indo-Iranian (2004: 22ff., 2006b). For a comprehensive review of the debates on these issues, see Mallory 1998; Renfrew 2002: 8; Lamberg-Karlovsky 2002; Parpola 2002: 236–237, 242ff.; Witzel 2004: 11, 78; Francfort 2005: 255.

[119]   Hiebert 1994: 165, 2002: 241ff.; Masson 1996b: 342 (on Gonur), 345. Francfort (2001a: 152) proposes a dating between 2400 and 1800 BCE for the BMAC, but includes part of the urban phase of the Kopet Dagh. For Kohl (2002: 163ff.; 2007: 200ff.), gradual and continuous arrivals of Indo-European herders from the steppes, who switched over to agriculture, partly explain the emergence of the BMAC. The significance of these flows is obscured by the process of assimilation of these populations from the steppes within sedentary communities. See also Tosi and Lamberg-Karlovsky 2003: 350. The assemblage from the steppes took on greater prominence during the post-urban period 1700–1500 (Francfort 2005).

[120]   Sarianidi 2002: 180ff., 206ff., 252ff. Parpola (2002: 312) establishes a symbolic connection between the presence of chariots in rulers' tombs in some cultures (Sintashta-Arkaim …), the wheel-shaped "temple-fort" of Dashly, and the fire altar of *rathacakra* shape. This symbolism can be later observed in the groundplan of ancient Buddhist stupas, in the wheel of dharma that Buddha turns, and the Indian imperial title *cakravartin*, "the one who turns the wheel." For criticism of Sarianidi's interpretations, see Kuzmina 2007: 301; Francfort 2005: 276–280. The funerary brick buildings (at Gonur), which Sarianidi connects to "the Vedic 'house of the dead'," do in fact have Elamite parallels.

[121]   Sergent 1997: 170; Sarianidi 1994b: 388ff., 2002: 178ff. The Indo-Iranians may have borrowed the use of ephedra from a culture located in southern Central Asia, from Turkmenistan or from the BMAC (Witzel 2004: 145, 2006b: 167, 170).

of bullae bearing imprints of cylinder seals in the "temenos" reveals the activity of an administration. Parpola points out the similarities between the groundplan of the Dashly-3 "palace" and Tantric mandalas. "The mandala pattern of a square with T-shaped projections is found also on many of the geometric seals of the BMAC" (Parpola 2002: 266).[122] This structure and the cosmic notions related to it reached China during the second millennium BCE. The BMAC influenced Xinjiang metallurgy and architecture, through herders of the Andronovo complexes.[123] During the Bronze Age, BMAC people or people in contact with the BMAC were already using what would become the Silk Road network (Kohl 1995; see below).

During the second millennium, the "spread of ideological associations of horses and wheeled vehicles with power and status" is notable throughout Eurasia (Frachetti 2012). The war chariot appeared first in the Arkaim-Sintashta culture of the Urals. Formed during the late third millennium, this culture showed fortified settlements with monumental architecture. Deriving from western Indo-Europeans, it would reflect the emergence of a pastoralist war elite (Kuzmina 2008: 48). Climate aridification led to a process of agricultural intensification,[124] in an economy that also developed metallurgy (the copper mining center of Kargaly, southwest of Sintashta, was probably already active at this time, and perhaps even earlier: at the end of the fourth and during the first half of the third millennium) (Koryakova and Epimakhov 2007: 32).[125] The Sintashta culture spread both westward and eastward during the early second millennium, along with its population. The presence of lapis lazuli at Sintashta and Ushkatta demonstrates connections with networks of Central Asia, as do the discoveries of objects from Margiana and Bactria (Kuzmina 2007: 229, 463, 2008: 3). The development of copper exploitation in the Sintashta culture may have resulted in part from a growing demand on the part of Central Asia (Anthony 2007: 435). Finds in the Zeravshan valley show contacts with the steppes and the Sintashta culture (Cunliffe 2015: 139–140, and below).

The BMAC appears to be the fruit of the encounter of several worlds. Besides influences from the steppes, this culture reveals contacts with South Asia (Baluchistan and the Indus) (Lyonnet and Kohl 2008: 35). Tombs at Sapalli (north Bactria) have yielded silk from the Indus valley (Good 2008). A Harappan seal displaying an

[122] Other sites, such as Sapalli, show buildings of a similar shape. Parpola also emphasizes the parallels between the triple walls of the Dashly-3 "temple" and fortresses in the Vedic myths. He establishes links between a Bactrian goddess, seated on a lion, and the Indian goddess Durga. This motif can be observed later on Kushan coins or intaglios (first–third centuries CE). This feline-escorted goddess "appears to be [ultimately] of Near Eastern origin" (Parpola 2002: 233). Potts (2003c) also connects her to the Mesopotamian goddess Nana. The motif of the goddess seated on a feline/dragon was present in Iran in the middle of the third millennium (see a cylinder seal from Susa; Winkelmann 2008: 195) and in Mesopotamia during the Akkadian period (goddess Ishtar; Aruz 2003a: 206).

[123] Tosi and Lamberg-Karlovsky 2003: 350; see below. According to Witzel (2004: 103), a linguistic influence from Bactria–Margiana (where the main language is thought to have been a non-Indo-European language) is noticeable in Tocharian (cf. Pinault 2003).

[124] Di Cosmo 2002: 27. The site of Arkaim shows evidence of canals and tanks. The aridification of the steppes, particularly east of the Urals, fostered the development of an agro-pastoral economy raising cattle and sheep. Southern Russia was affected by a phase of aridification at the end of the third millennium, with a peak *c.* 2000 BCE; see Khomutova *et al.* 2007.

[125] See also Koryakova and Kohl 2000: 639, 641; Zdanovich and Zdanovich 2002: 253.

elephant has been excavated in the northern complex of what Sarianidi has termed the "palace and the temple" of Gonur (2005: 236). For Francfort (2005: 279ff.), both the iconography and the religious pantheon derive mainly from the Iranian sphere, with obvious Mesopotamian influences due to contacts established within the framework of long-distance exchanges via Iranian roads. A cylinder seal bearing a cuneiform inscription (dated *c.* 2250–2200 BCE) has been discovered in the Gonur cemetery (Sarianidi 2002: 333). A cylinder seal of Trans-Elamite type has been unearthed in the "palace" complex of Gonur, reflecting links with Iran, also revealed by the use of chlorite or steatite. Silver vases of Elamo-Mesopotamian inspiration, however, also show motifs evoking Indo-Iranians (the possible depiction of the Nasatya twins; the presence of a corpse on a funeral pyre), which support Parpola's hypothesis of at least a partially Indo-European origin of the BMAC aristocracy (Francfort 2005: 300). In order to understand these links with Iran and Mesopotamia, we must keep in mind the importance of tin and lapis lazuli routes, from Central Asia to Assyria early in the second millennium. Basing his argument on data from the end of the third millennium, Weeks (2003: 176, after Edens 1995: 60) posits a tin route going through the Caspian area, the Transcaucasus, and the region of the Black Sea. Curiously, the BMAC did not yield much tin bronze, however (Lyonnet and Kohl 2008: 39). The BMAC also exported gold and silver. Using imported materials (steatite, lapis lazuli, alabaster), the BMAC produced luxury goods that would soon be found throughout southern and western Asia (see below).

The upheaval of the twenty-third/twenty-second century affected the entire Sumer-Indus area, and helped transform it. The takeover of the trade routes by people of the BMAC may partly explain the changes observed in Iran, and later in the Indus region. Terrestrial exchanges between the Indus and Iran decreased around 2000 BCE. The Harappan material discovered includes only a single shard bearing a few Indusian signs at Tepe Yahya IVA, and carnelian beads at Hissar IIIB.[126] The drop in trade along the terrestrial routes traversing Iran went along with increased exchanges on the maritime routes, which benefited from a Sumerian revival at the end of the third millennium, at Lagash, then at Ur, where the governor Ur-Nammu built a new empire oriented toward the Persian Gulf. This Sumerian revival, which benefited in part from a temporary climatic improvement, was accompanied by development in Bahrain.

The Third Dynasty of Ur (2112–2004 BCE)[127]

> Along the coast, places of burning flames [lighthouses?] secured the maritime trade.
> He [Ur-Nammu] returned the ships of Magan under Nanna's hands
> [the Moon God].[128]

---

[126] These beads come from what is known as the "Burnt Building" at Hissar IIIB (2600–2200 BCE), which has also yielded material recalling Turkmenistan and the BMAC (Huot 2004, I: 195). Scant further evidence for Harappan material has come to light in Central Asia. In contrast, artifacts from the BMAC are plentiful in the Indus valley during the early second millennium BCE (see below) (Tosi 2001: 143).

[127] Middle chronology. In their "ultra-short chronology," Gasche *et al.* (1998) propose a demise of the Third Dynasty of Ur in 1911 BCE.

[128] Margueron and Pfirsch 2001: 192. These ships of Magan may have been ships from Oman or Mesopotamian ships traveling to Oman.

Around 2112 BCE, the governor of Ur, Ur-Nammu, founded what has become known as the "Third Dynasty of Ur," which marked a Sumerian revival linked in part to trade in the Persian Gulf (the maritime orientation of the Mesopotamian economy was obviously related to the decline of northern Mesopotamia, affected by the Guti invasions). It is probably during this time that the first version of the Sumerian Royal List was written (it has become known through its later versions). Archaeology shows that, unlike the interpretations previously offered, it is likely that the state held only a relative degree of control over the economy, despite centralized administration and a bloated bureaucracy. While the kings became the owners of the temple estates, extended families and individuals also owned land (in the north more than in the south). Available texts, however, no longer mention land sales, and the administration certainly played an important role in the organization of production and exchanges. Most craft production may have arisen from the private sector (Lamberg-Karlovsky 1996: 78), but "we observe, perhaps for the first time in history, a deliberate attempt to systematically plan and manage a kingdom's resources" (Joannès 2006a: 94). Ur-Nammu set up a military organization for the empire, using a permanent armed force. The state committed itself to rehabilitating networks of channels, and organized a system of taxation (*bala*) "by requiring each province to take its turn in supplying large storage centers" (Lafont 2001). Advances on grain or silver loans by institutions may have been attempts at obtaining a labor force, in northern Babylonia at least (Steinkeller 2002: 117; Joannès 2006b: 407). The state ran shipyards, and encouraged the expansion of poles of production by grouping together various industries. These included metallurgic workshops and large textile workshops employing a female workforce. In the district of Lagash, for example, a "house" mustered 6,500 women weavers. At Larsa, also, thousands of persons, women and children, worked in the textile industry. "The province of Ur had an annual production of wool 'sufficient to clothe more than 300,000' [persons], although the province's population would not have exceeded 25,000": here we clearly observe market-oriented production (Warburton 2003: 58) as well as the development of a kind of "state capitalism" based on the use of agricultural surpluses (Postgate 2003: 161). Workshops produced five different qualities of textiles in at least seven cities: Alsharraki, Guabba, Nippur, Puzrish-Dagan, Umma, Ur, and Uruk.[129] Dilmunites may have settled near Eridu and al-Hammar to buy wool directly from the temples. This "textile revolution" was based on the development of livestock production: McCormick Adams (1981) has estimated the sheep population at over 2.35 million, for a human population of between 500,000 and one million (according to Morris [2013: 153], Ur, the capital, may have had about 60,000 inhabitants, but Liverani notes 200,000 inhabitants [2014: 161]; in fact, estimates of city sizes for the third millennium BCE are unreliable). In the workshops, the workers were employees, or dependants (see Silver 1995: 119, 122, 136). Hired labor is also attested to in the agricultural sector, but there was no free labor market (Steinkeller 2002), and documents attest to the importance of slavery in Ur III society (Gelb *et al.* 1991: 14). Religion must have represented a crucial factor in social cohesion, whence the

---

[129] On the importance of textiles in the Ur III Empire, see Waetzoldt 1972; Silver 1995: 143; Potts 1997: 91–95; Sherratt and Sherratt 2001: 32 n6; Algaze 2008: 82.

importance of the construction of sanctuaries (Margueron and Pfirsch 2001: 177). Moreover, a deification of the king is seen during this period. It seems that under Shulgi, who established a new calendar, the sanctuaries, which sometimes played a "banking" role (by lending), then fell under the authority of the royal administration.

Temples and palaces were long considered as enjoying a trade monopoly. Of course, trade was regulated by the state, but the DAM.GAR merchants who worked with the institutions were also private entrepreneurs.[130] It is significant that the DAM.GAR "do not appear on royal rations lists in the Ur III period" (Silver 2007a: 93). The great merchants, however, seem to have been linked to the state and the royal family. Pu'udu, who traded with Oman, commanded a large fleet; his son Lu-Enlilla, was both a judge at Ur and a "sea merchant" working for the state, but he was also "a lucrative business-man in his own right" (Magee 2014: 117). There was clearly a public/private mixture in the Third Dynasty of Ur economy (Steinkeller 2004: 97). Texts from Nippur and Lagash show that some merchants employed by the palace received land allotments (Steinkeller 2004: 102, 104, 109). Moreover, merchants seem to have been used for diplomatic missions. Among these merchants were foreigners.

Whereas the state established theoretical prices for some products, we also have evidence of markets operating on the principle of supply and demand (Silver 2007a; Snell 1991: 135). The state tried "to fix the price of the most common subsistence products [grains . . .] in silver," notes Norel (2004: 81), "while leaving the other prices to vary . . . [However], we [also] have much evidence showing pronounced variations in the price of grains against the price of silver."[131] In fact, "official values were not stable" but varied above and below "standard values" (see Widell 2005: 392, for barley values at Umma), and the theoretical prices stated by the institutions did not necessarily correspond to market prices (van Driel 2002: 11). Barley was used as a standard of value as well as a means of exchange for small transactions. Silver was largely used in payments and transactions involving significant assets. The state ensured the quality of the silver in circulation. Texts mention silver rings or coils (ḫar) (Akkadian shewirum) – without marks – that may have been used as money: the rings weigh one shekel each, or multiples of the shekel.[132] There may also have been "silver ingots that bore the imprints of seals of their owners, a guarantee for the weight and the quality of the silver" (Glassner 2002a: 152). Documents from Umma and Nippur express the existence of credit, private or not; interest rates were 20 percent for silver loans and 33.3 percent for loans in barley (van Driel 2002: 24ff.). However, the overall picture remains that of

---

[130] The Sumerian DAM.GAR derives from a Semitic root *mkr (cf. the name tamkarum).

[131] For Moore and Lewis (2009: 48), goods such as fish, barley, textiles, and wheat "were assigned a fixed value in terms of silver. In contrast to these fixed prices, the prices of many other items – such as copper, tin, lumber, spices, wines and cattle – fluctuated greatly according to their markets." Silver (1995: 103) notes, however, that texts reveal variability in grain and oil prices, and van Driel shows the existence of a grain market at Nippur (2002: 29).

[132] Snell 1995: 1489; Glassner 2001: 69. Although such objects are mentioned in texts from the Akkadian Empire onward, archaeology has revealed their presence as early as the middle of the third millennium (royal tombs of Ur). However, these rings were weighed for transactions. At the time of the Ur III Empire, "such rings were offered . . . to distinguished visitors, strangers or even to the gods" (Glassner 2001: 69).

an administered economy.[133] Instruments of control and planning were perfected with the presentation of "balanced accounts," "putting in place a precondition for double-entry bookkeeping,"[134] and the use of payment orders, precursors of checks or letters of credit (Hudson 2004a: 13–14; Hallo 2004: 92ff., 102).[135] Ur-Nammu promulgated a "law code" that set a monetary standard (mina and shekel of silver), and standardized weights and measures; these texts introduced the protection of widows, orphans, and slaves, a preoccupation we observe once again in the later Code of Hammurabi, but that existed already in the Egyptian laws of the Old Kingdom. Some tax exemptions may have been aimed at fostering free trade.[136]

Trade routes ran north to the cities of Assur and Nineveh.[137] Connections were established with Ebla and Elam. In the Persian Gulf, Ur remained in contact with Bahrain and Oman, using ships of up to 90-ton capacity ("300 *gur*"); large ships "were probably dependent on public institutions, to commission them and to supply the timber with which to build them" (Postgate 2003: 218, 230). Texts from Girsu signal the presence of shipbuilding workshops which worked year round, each with 900 or 1000 workers. One text lists products destined for the building of reed boats, but also for the construction of wooden ships (Zarins 2008: 210ff.).

Indians probably sojourned at Ur and in its region: a text from Telloh dated to 2060 BCE speaks of a "Meluhhan village" in the territory of Lagash, and economic texts from Ur mention "sons from Meluhha."[138] Weights of the Indusian type were in use during the Ur III period, as well as in Dilmun.[139] Mesopotamian cities have yielded what have been called "Persian Gulf seals" (produced in Bahrain) bearing Indusian characters.

In Iran, at the time of Ur-Nammu, Puzur-Inshushinak, "King of Awan," founded an Elamite state that included Susiana and Fars. Under his reign, a new type of writing appeared: Linear Elamite, which has been found on Bahrain, at Shahdad (Iran), and Gonur (Margiana). After the death of this king, Susa came under the control of the Ur administration. Products from Central Asia and eastern Iran (compartmented copper seals, alabaster or chlorite vases) arrived via the roads of Susiana. From his campaigns

---

[133] The number of workers hired by the state "may have reached half a million" (Huot 2004, I: 150). For some authors, the bureaucracy of the state supervised nearly everything. For Diakonoff (1996: 56), though, the documents reveal the existence of "hired workers who could not have belonged to the royal personnel."

[134] Debits and credits are recorded, sometimes in the same text. "Balanced accounts list the receipts and expenditures for a day, a month or a longer period" (Hallo 2004: 96). Similar balanced accounts are known from the Kassite period, from Nippur. "The Kassite accounts use tabulation to separate quantitative from qualitative information" (Robson 2008: 157). The first known tabular document is dated from the Early Dynastic IIIA, and comes from Shuruppak.

[135] "The earliest tables with column headings and a horizontal axis of calculation appear full-fledged already in the Early Dynastic period (24th century), and were well established by the 19th century" (Hudson 2004a: 13).

[136] The series of measures promulgated by Urukagina at Lagash during the twenty-fourth century is also sometimes improperly termed "code of laws."

[137] Traffic on rivers and canals was intense. King Ibbi-Sin received a request for 600 vessels to transport grain from Isin to Ur (Bass 1995: 1421).

[138] Tosi 2001: 136. Various finds from Susa at this time probably come from the Indus (an alabaster figurine of a woman, silver and gold ornaments . . .).

[139] Shaikh 2000: 89. Silver and grain (barley) were used as currencies in Mesopotamia, functioning both as standards of value and means of payment (Snell 1995: 1491). Silver was probably the prominent means of exchange.

in Iran, the king of Ur Shu-sin brought back huge quantities of copper, tin, gold, and silver, which reveal the importance of the Iranian networks in the metals trade. Ur maintained diplomatic relations with Marhashi (Potts 2002),[140] a kingdom located in the east of Anshan, perhaps in the region of Jiroft (see above).

Trade prosperity in the Gulf benefited the island of Bahrain, the "Dilmun" of the Sumerian texts (Weeks 2003). Qala'at al-Bahrayn was an affluent urban center from 2100 BCE on. The Sumerian myth "Enki and Ninhursag," composed around 2000 BCE, mentions the products brought into Dilmun by Ur, Elam, Tukrish (a political entity of the western Iranian plateau), Meluhha, Magan, Marhashi, "the country of the sea," and Zalamgar (?). Pottery found in Bahrain shows links with the entire Persian Gulf. Bitumen was imported from Iran or Mesopotamia (Connan *et al.* 1998). Trade with the Indus valley and the presence of Indian merchants on the island may partially explain the production of Persian Gulf seals (at an earlier time than those known as the "Dilmun seals," which were produced from the end of the twentieth century BCE onward). These seals have been discovered in Mesopotamia, at Failaka, and at Susa, where they have been dated to the end of the third millennium. While the Indus valley has not yielded a single Persian Gulf seal, Dilmun seals have been unearthed at Lothal, and a seal from the Post-Harappan port of Dwaraka shows an iconography similar to that of Bahrain. It has already been observed that some Persian Gulf seals bear signs of the Indus culture in unusual sequences, which reveals the presence on Bahrain of acculturated Indus people. Let us also keep in mind the discovery of Harappan weights on Bahrain. Products from the Indus such as ivory and lapis lazuli were channeled through Dilmun. As early as the end of the third millennium, however, lapis lazuli became rarer in western Asia, a trend that would continue into the early second millennium (Casanova 2013: 195–196).

Various Sumerian texts evoke the importance of trade with Magan (Oman). Under the reign of Ibbi-Sin, a merchant from Ur called Lu-Enlilla was employed by the administration to trade with Magan. He received barley, sesame oil, fish, wool, garments (listed as second-class garments), and skins, for the purchase of copper, but also ivory, semiprecious stones, red ochre, and "a certain drug for the temple of Nanna" (Potts 1990: 145). Ships from Ur may have sailed as far as southern Arabia: texts mention commerce in aromatic resins, "purchased with some difficulty" in "exotic regions" (Snell 1982: 99, 115, 195; Zarins 1997: 261).

Under Ibbi-Sin (2028–2004 BCE), a conjunction of unfavorable factors led to the collapse of the Third Dynasty of Ur, which had been weakened by its conflicts with Elam for control over the tin routes, by the turmoil caused by western Semites (the Amorites),[141] and also by a drop in agricultural production due to the negative effects of intensive agriculture and a new phase of aridification.[142] For Butzer (1995: 145), the

---

[140] Shulgi contracted a marriage alliance with a ruler of Marhashi.

[141] This nomad/city-dweller complementarity broke down during periods that were climatically and economically unfavorable. In addition, Liverani notes that "the disappearance of the Eblaite kingdom had left a power vacuum, which allowed the rise of the Amorites" (2014: 170).

[142] Burroughs 2001: 253; Ziegler 2001: 41. According to Burroughs, the large quantity of sediment in the Persian Gulf from 2000 BCE (over several centuries) signals a new period of aridity in Mesopotamia and Arabia.

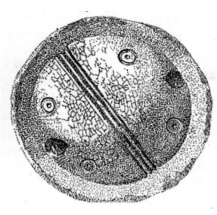

Figure 3.2 Dilmun seal from Saar, depicting a wheel with spokes ending in antelope heads (after Crawford 1998: 92)

salinization of soils in the delta may have led to a movement of population upstream, furthering Babylon's rise to power.[143] The reign of Ibbi-Sin seems to have been marked by price inflation and famines. Excessive administration proved to be another cause of the crisis. Trade recession in the Gulf, following the decline of the cities of the Indus, may also have contributed to the collapse of Ur (tablets from Ur of the Larsa period [nineteenth century], however, mention products supposedly from Dilmun that clearly originated in India, such as *mesu* wood, lapis lazuli, carnelian, and ivory). In 2004 BCE, Ur was captured by an Iranian coalition that destroyed the city and took the king Ibbi-Sin away, as prisoner. The tragic end of the empire's capital is described in striking terms by the *Lament for Ur*:

[The god] Enlil called the storm; winds of abundance he took away from the land . . . [When] the storm was called off from the city, that city was in ruins . . . In its high gate and gangways, corpses were piled. In all the wide festival streets, they lay placed head to shoulder . . . In the open spaces where the country's dances (once) were held, people were stacked in heaps. The country's blood filled all holes, like copper or tin (in molds), their bodies, like sheep fat left in the sun, dissolved of themselves . . . Like gazelles caught in a trap, [men] shoved their noses into the dust . . . The old men and women who could not leave the house were consigned to the flames. The little ones, asleep on their mother's laps, were carried off like fishes by the water . . . On the country's goods, dirty hands were laid. In the country's storehouses, abounding and abounding as they were, fires were lit . . . Into the lofty, untouchable mountain, Ekishnugal's good house, big copper axes chewed like (a pack of) dogs . . . The Sua people and the Elamites, the wreckers, . . . were making the city a mound of ruins. (Joannès 2006a: 90–91; Jacobsen 1987: 458–463)

Population movements and economic recession affected many regions at the turn of the third and second millennia and during the early second millennium. In Syria, urbanization came to a halt. Migrations swept across the Circumpontic area, and Transcaucasia shows a sharp breakup in the distribution of settlements (Koryakova

---

[143] Silver proposes another interpretation, however: at this time, Mesopotamia may have developed palm groves in order to meet a growing demand outside the region, as well as sheep breeding, for wool export. Postgate (2003: 181) expresses doubt about the impact of increased land salinity on the urban decline of southern Mesopotamia during the eighteenth and seventeenth centuries.

and Epimakhov 2007: 97; Kohl and Trifonov 2014: 1583); slightly later, the expansion of the Bactria–Margiana Complex contributed to the collapse of the Indus civilization[144] and to the restructuring of the Iranian sphere. In western Asia, two distinct but interdependent cores – in northern and southern Mesopotamia – experienced a political fragmentation, accompanied by the emergence of a private sector.

Egypt of the Old Kingdom (c. 2700–2180 BCE)

> I am the beginning of men, the end of men … One who finds the solution where it is lacking. As to everyone on whom I placed my hand, no misfortune ever befell him, because my heart was sealed and my counsel excellent.[145]

From the late fourth millennium to the end of the third millennium, Egypt developed partly in an autonomous and specific way, as compared to the Mesopotamian "core." Benefiting from the agricultural wealth of the Nile valley spanning the country, but with a more limited number of trade routes with foreign lands, Egypt's situation, as pointed out previously, probably hastened the emergence of a centralized state. This state had the upper hand over long-distance trade and exercised greater control over an economy driven by taxes and demand from the state. Administrative and religious institutions formed the nuclei of the main cities, with the institutions ensuring a redistribution of wealth. Memphis became the capital of the kingdom from the Third Dynasty onward (the ancient burial ground of Saqqara served as the "necropolis" for Memphis):[146] here there is a marked absence of city-states, in contrast with Mesopotamia. The internal colonization of the country benefited not only from technical innovations originating in the Levant during the fourth millennium (the ard drawn by oxen, tree farming …), but also from favorable climatic conditions marked by high Nile flooding. The state created and maintained the main infrastructures (canals, roads, wells, stopping places …). Pepi I (c. 2390–2360 BCE) boasted about his achievements in irrigation systems: "I made upland into marsh, I let the Nile flood the fallow land … I brought the Nile to the upland in your fields so that plots were watered that had never known water before" (Hughes 2001: 39).

The importance of state control over production and exchanges, however, is still debated. In theory, while land was the property of the god-king, who was responsible for universal order, land could be attributed "to institutions or officials …; through hereditary transmission of offices, early on, great families were probably able to monopolize large estates" (Margueron and Pfirsch 2001: 140–141).[147] During Pepi II's

---

[144] According to the ultra-short chronology put forward by Gasche *et al.* (1998) and advocated by Warburton (2007), the collapse of the Ur III Empire and of the Indus civilization may have been concomitant. See below.

[145] Inscription in the tomb of the nomarch Ankhtifi (c. 2170–2155 BCE), belonging to the Eighth Dynasty, during the First Intermediary Period, marked by famines and social upheaval. Lichtheim 2006, I: 85ff. Dating given for the Old Kingdom is the one most commonly accepted (see Margueron and Pfirsch 2001: 382). Debate on this topic is ongoing. Hornung *et al.* (2006: 490) thus give c. 2543–2120 BCE.

[146] Morris (2013: 153) gives an estimate of 60,000 inhabitants for Memphis in 2000 BCE, but this is just a guess.

[147] For Pirenne (1961: 175), however, there was no "hereditary nobility," in any case, before the Sixth Dynasty.

reign, an inscription on the tomb of Sebni, who led an expedition to recover the body of his father killed in Nubia, reads: "[I took] a troop of my estate, and 100 asses with me, bearing ointment, honey, clothing, oil" (see Eyre 1987: 19). Most of the land was probably cultivated by landowning peasants:[148] we have some evidence for private land property, and documents related to land purchase in the middle and the late third millennium (Silver 1995: 125; Eyre 1999: 41; Warburton 2003: 134). "Every two years, since the Second Dynasty, the state made an inventory of land and gold: . . . it means that land was considered alienable and mobile, and property wealth existed" (Pirenne 1961: 176).

While in a general sense, demographic expansion and technological innovations appear to have been key to economic growth, "the Egyptian example underscores that demand stimulation [by the state] plays a fundamental role in the creation of wealth" (Warburton 2000a: 90): this policy would be pursued until Ramses III. Based on a land register and a survey of the various resources, a system of taxation forced the farmers to increase their production; these farmers were bound to the land they cultivated. State revenues were used to finance building programs (for temples, tombs . . .), the administration, and a class of craftsmen. State policy favored a growing division of labor. In this case, taxation was therefore not merely a levy, by the state, of an existing surplus, but the creation of wealth. The system was obviously dependent on Nile flooding, the efficiency of the administration, and popular support for pharaonic ideology and the values of the state.

Elite craftsmen were under the control of the state. The state supervised shipbuilding and financed expeditions, a phenomenon we will observe throughout pharaonic Egyptian history. Some redistribution occurred through the payment of wages and within the context of temples, but we have no evidence for the existence of large-scale redistribution corresponding to a Polanyian model.[149] Under the Third and Fourth dynasties, the state employed workers on the basis of registered contracts.[150] Individuals (officials or people belonging to the private sector) also used hired work forces, paid in kind. The judge Akhet Heri-Hotep said: "all people who worked for me, they did this for bread, beer, textiles, oil, wheat in large quantity. I have never exploited anyone" (Pirenne 1961: 182).[151] We know today that the construction of the great pyramids was not achieved by mobilizing hordes of slaves, but rather by employing armies of workmen who were salaried by the state.

Some texts also suggest the existence of private commerce. In the late third millennium, a man called Qedes, from Gebelein, owned ships and granaries. "A farmer's letter of about 2000 BCE refers to the sale of emmer and to interest-bearing grain loans"

---

[148] However, Margueron and Pfirsch (2001: 139) write: "during the third millennium, we do not find evidence for a status of free worker for the fellahs."

[149] Warburton 1997: 93, 2007: 184. Polanyi considered the absence of wages as one of the fundamental characteristics of ancient societies.

[150] Under the Fourth Dynasty, "an edict by King Mykerinos [Menkaure'] stipulates that workers hired for the building of a tomb should not have to work more than what is mentioned in the contract." The pharaoh "does not want any man taken in forced labor, but everyone should work to his satisfaction" (Pirenne 1961: 182). Corvée labor existed, but it did not have the importance that some researchers have suggested.

[151] On the wages of craftsmen who worked on building tombs for various notables, see Eyre 1987: 24–25.

(Silver 1995: 108). A production process developed for markets and these were depicted on the walls of various tombs.[152] Documents dated to the mid-third millennium refer to a slave market (Vinogradov 1991: 151). Moreover, Pirenne (1961: 190) noted the sale of annuities.

Prices were gauged against a monetary standard, a "weight of metal whose value and nature varied (copper, gold, silver)" over the centuries (Menu 2001). The Egyptians in particular had an evaluation system which used a unit, the gold *shāti* (*shat*), as a money of account. For Menu, the sign *shāti* has a determinative which may depict a gold or silver ring. It is likely that it is this unit of payment which led to the creation of the *shāti* as a unit of account.[153] In the depiction of a market (in a mastaba of the Fifth Dynasty), three people, including two women, carry small boxes of identical form that may have contained "ingots already weighed, or small jewels." A buyer gives a ring to a greengrocer, telling him: "Here is a good *shat* for you, here is what I owe you."[154] An inscription dated to the twenty-fourth century mentions the payment of craftsmen with copper. Grain was also used as a standard of value and a means of exchange.

The most brilliant period of ancient Egypt was under the Fourth Dynasty, when the great pyramids were built. The construction of great monuments marked a process of unification and centralization of the country. The period 2500–2400 (during the Fourth and the first half of the Fifth Dynasty) saw the greatest territorial extension of the Old Kingdom. As early as the Fifth Dynasty, however, it seems that the creation of the office of "Director of Upper Egypt" corresponded to the need to control the local rulers of nomes. The increasing autonomy of the provinces under the Sixth Dynasty marked a phase of decline which would end in the breakup of the twenty-second century.

Exchanges occurred mainly along a north–south axis, but Egypt enjoyed a privileged position between two seas, the Mediterranean Sea and the Red Sea. Contacts – probably indirect – existed with Mesopotamia, through the Levant and routes linking the latter region and the Nile delta. Commerce with the Levant was essentially operated by sea from 2700 BCE, which led to the development of the port of Byblos. Egypt probably exported textiles, gold, cereals, papyrus (products usually not found in archaeological excavations); the country imported primarily wood: Snefru claimed that he had forty ships come from the Levant, loaded with wood (Marcus 2002b: 408). This wood served to build ships, for maritime and fluvial connections. The practical and symbolic role of these ships – returning from faraway countries carrying prestige goods – in the building of royal power has already been stressed. The remains of five

---

[152] See the tombs of Ti, of Tepemankh, and of Fetekta (Saqqara, Fifth Dynasty) (Peters-Destéract 2005: 107–109). Also Warburton 2000: 79.

[153] Menu 2001a: 75ff. Egypt may have progressed from "a physical object to an accounting instrument" which led to the notion of value. The *shāti* became an "immaterial reference" (Menu 2001a: 88). For Peet (1934: 186), however, "the *š't* or *š'ty* of the Old Kingdom was a metal object already with a given weight." Silver (1995: 162) mentions a market scene in a tomb at Saqqara (tomb of Khnumhotep and Niankhkhnum, *c.* 2400 BCE), in which two merchants offer to exchange fabric for the price of 6 *shāti*, "probably in cash" (see also Michailidou 2005: 27). Note that silver seems to have been more expensive than gold during the Old Kingdom. A volume-unit, called *heqat*, which developed from cereal farming, was also used to measure value. On a debt measured in grain, see a letter by Shebsi (tomb 7695 at Kaw) (Bleiberg 2002: 259–260).

[154] Dykmans 1936: 253–254; Menu 2001a: 77.

ships have been discovered in the vicinity of the pyramid of Khufu.[155] In addition, we have proof that ships were imported from Lebanon from the Fourth Dynasty onward (de Miroschedji 2002: 48). Byblos, which was the main gate for exchanges between Egypt and Inner Asia, yielded Egyptian imports. Gifts to the Egyptian temple of Byblos during Pepi I's reign (*c.* 2289–2225 BCE) mark the importance of this city (Aruz 2003a: 241). Political relations were established between Byblos and Egypt as early as the Second Dynasty. A vase bearing the cartouche of the last pharaoh of the Second Dynasty has thus been discovered at Byblos (Benoit 2003: 163 n314; see above). An axe head found at Byblos bears the name of an Egyptian crew member (dated to around 2500 BCE). During the Fifth Dynasty, in the time of King Sahure, "reliefs record the departure of a fleet and its return with Syrians" (who probably formed the crew) (Bass 1995: 1425). These contacts led to cross-cultural influences. Egypt probably played a significant role in the establishment of a kingship at Byblos, and Levantine people appear to have settled in Egypt.[156] The term *kbn.wt/kpn.wt*, referring to seagoing ships, is sometimes translated as "ships of Byblos" (Meeks 1997; Fabre 2004: 92). Ships from Byblos transported cedar and other products. At the end of the Old Kingdom, Ipuwer "describes Byblos as the source of the finest cedar unguent" (Aubet 2013: 222). Many Egyptian imports have been found in Byblos, for example in temples, especially around 2300 and 2200 BCE. The existence of an Egyptian "colony" in Byblos has been suggested from the middle of the third millennium BCE onward (Aubet 2013: 228, 229, 230ff.).

Diplomatic relations extended to the hinterland of the Levant region. The city of Ebla yielded various objects that were gifts from pharaohs: for example, vases made of diorite or alabaster inscribed with the names of the pharaohs of the Fourth and Sixth dynasties, Khafre and Pepi. A tomb at Dorak (Anatolia) contained an Egyptian seat bearing the name of Sahure (second king of the Fifth Dynasty). In the Nile valley, the Osirian cult flourished under the Fifth Dynasty and especially under the Sixth Dynasty, around 2300 BCE; the cult may have had connections with Tammuz, the Akkadian fertility god (Sumerian Dumuzi).[157] Egypt sent trade – and sometimes military – expeditions toward southern Palestine, where smaller towns developed during the third millennium.

Unlike the case in the Mesopotamian area, the Egyptian state was fundamentally concerned with borders, and the limits between order and disorder. It controlled the desert routes and the oases, both of which were linked to its exploitation of mineral resources. During the third and second millennia BCE, Egypt expanded to the south, into the Red Sea and Inner Africa. Terrestrial (through Nubia and its gold mines) and maritime routes led to Sudan, Arabia, and the Horn of Africa. Egyptian trade was

---

[155] The planks of the first ship studied (43.6 m long, 5.7 m wide) were made of Lebanese cedar. These planks were held together by a system of mortises and tenons, "and with ropes laced through V-shaped mortises" (Bass 1995: 1423).

[156] At the time of Khufu, a man from Byblos was buried at Gizeh, according to the Egyptian custom: he thus had lived in the Nile valley (Wilkinson 2002: 517).

[157] Funerary practices observed in Egypt, at Nagada, Abydos, and Gerza, as early as the Nagada II period, with pre-burial dismemberment of corpses, may also be linked to the Osiris myth (see Wengrow 2006: 118).

partly operated through African intermediaries, such as Nubia. An Egyptian fortress was built at Buhen (second cataract) during Snefru's reign at the beginning of the Fourth Dynasty; copper was probably smelted there.[158] Pharaoh Merenre (Sixth Dynasty) dug five channels to facilitate the crossing of the first cataract, in the vicinity of which Elephantine was at that time a fortified town.[159] An Egyptian presence and the sending of military or commercial expeditions to Lower Nubia are seen in the use of mercenaries. They hailed not only from "Irtjet, Medja, Wawat, Kau, Tjemeh" (Lower Nubia), but also from Yam, located in Upper Nubia, in the Egyptian army.[160] In addition, texts from the Sixth Dynasty mention incense, ivory, ebony, and leopard skins, all imported from southern territories. Beyond Nubia lay the mythical country of Punt, located either on the Eritrean coast and north/northwestern flanks of the Ethiopian Highlands (Kitchen), or on the west coast of Arabia (Meeks). One of the first Egyptian references to Punt (written Pwnt) goes back to the Fifth Dynasty: the Palermo Stone (2450 BCE) reveals that imports from Punt included myrrh or incense ('ntyw) as well as a product called sn-šsmt. In the complex linked to Pharaoh Sahure at Abusir, a scene refers to an expedition to Punt that brought back myrrh and electrum.[161] Sixty years later, under Isesi's reign, the chief of an expedition acquired a dwarf from Punt. If this dwarf was in fact a pygmy, this captive would underscore the connection with regions of Inner Africa and probably the Great Lakes; this interpretation has been cast into doubt by Meeks, however.[162] Around 2270 BCE, under Pepi II's reign, an expedition led by Harkhuf returned from Punt with another dwarf (dng) (or a pygmy?); according to the inscription in Harkhuf's tomb, his presence "filled with joy and love the heart of the Pharaoh." The expedition also brought back ebony and aromatic resins.[163] As already mentioned, incense comes from various Arabian and African Boswellia. In the same way, the term "myrrh" covers resins from various

---

[158] Manzo (1999: 17) suggests that the furnace discovered may have been used for ceramic production. Egyptian outposts may have been present south of the first cataract in earlier periods. Snefru led a campaign into Nubia (Dongola?) whence he brought back 4,000 captives and 2,000 head of cattle (Manzo 1999: 16). This pharaoh also launched an expedition to Libya and conquered the Sinai.

[159] An inscription refers to the exploitation of quarries in Nubia. Egyptian pottery has been excavated in contexts intermediary between the A group and the C group of Nubia, and later in the C group.

[160] These mercenaries are mentioned among the troops led into Palestine by Uni (Weni) under Pepi I. This same Uni was later asked by Pharaoh Merenre to dig five channels at the first cataract (Manzo 1999: 17). Yam may have been located near the confluence of the Nile and the Atbara. Some depopulation of Lower Nubia can be seen, probably linked to Egyptian activities.

[161] One could find electrum in the southwest of Port Sudan, as well as gold.

[162] "The 'pygmy' described by Kherkhouf [Harkhuf] was in fact a dwarf. Petrie found skeletons of dwarves in satellite burial sites of King Qă's tomb (First Dynasty) at Abydos." In addition, "the dwarf brought by Kherkhouf was only described as being identical to the one brought from Punt by the Chancellor Our-Djeded-baou, at the time of King Isesi. His dwarf was said in a vague way to have originated ... from the east" (Meeks 2002: 285–286). Dwarfs were universally believed to be connected to the spirits of the earth; the presence of dwarfs in the entourage of sacred kings has been noted for various regions of Africa. Manzo (1999: 22) argues that pygmies were present in the Bahr el-Ghazal, in southwest Sudan. He relates the Egyptian dng to the Amharic denk and the Tigrinya denkit, "dwarf" (1999: 29).

[163] Four expeditions led by Harkhuf are reported, following various routes (Manzo, 1999: 19). The first expedition reached a region called Yam. For his third journey, Harkhuf wrote: "I descended with three hundred asses laden with incense, ebony, heknu perfume, grain, panthers, ..., elephant tusks, [throw-sticks], and every good product" (Margueron and Pfirsch 2001: 185). The Egyptians probably traveled as

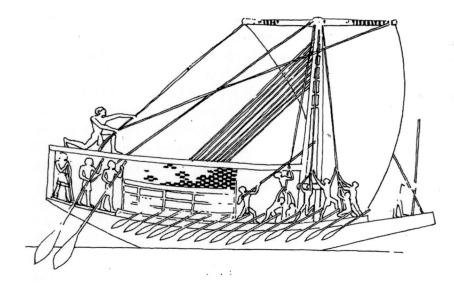

Figure 3.3 Ship from the Old Kingdom of Egypt (after Landström 1970: 42 fig. 109). Ships from the Fourth Dynasty could be as long as 52 m.

Commiphora. The main species was *C. myrrha* (Nees) Engl., native to southern Arabia, eastern Ethiopia, and Somalia. *C. gileadensis* (L.) C. Chr., the "balm of Gilead," was present in Sudan, Eritrea, Somalia, and Arabia. In addition, several other African species are known, especially on Socotra Island (Boivin and Fuller 2009: 139). As early as the Old Kingdom, two types of routes were used to reach Punt: the terrestrial routes followed by Harkhuf, and a maritime route. Pepi II sent troops to recover the corpse of an expedition leader, An-ankhti, killed by nomads as he was on the coast building a ship destined for Punt.[164] Improvements in ships' rigging during the third millennium may have facilitated these voyages on the Red Sea (Fabre 2004: 89ff.; Boivin and Fuller 2009: 137). Under the Sixth Dynasty, around 2200 BCE, a helmsman named Khnumhotep left an inscription in the tomb of Khui at Aswan revealing that he had made several journeys to Byblos and Punt. The site of Mersā Gawāsīs, north of Quseir, was already in use at the end of the Old Kingdom (Fattovich 2005a: 20). Through the coasts of the Red Sea, Egypt could obtain access to products from far-off countries. The role of the Red Sea, however, remained limited:[165] unlike the Persian Gulf, only later would the Red Sea become an area of major maritime activity, because Egypt was the only core in the region, whereas exchanges in the Persian Gulf benefited from the

far as Kerma, where alabaster vases bearing the names of Pepi I and Pepi II have been discovered (Shinnie 1991: 50). The Early Kerma period has yielded Egyptian items made of copper.

[164] According to Meeks (2002: 314), the text says that An-ankhti, called "captain of the sailors and chief of the caravans," was killed by "Asian 'sand dwellers'" (living in the Sinai?). Cf. also Manzo 1999: 19. During the Sixth Dynasty, Punt was sufficiently integrated into the Egyptian world to be personified by a goddess (Manzo 1999).

[165] Lapis lazuli has been found in the temple of Queen Hetepheres I (twenty-sixth century BCE), but it may have come from the Levant. The identification of "ebony from Ceylon," *Diospyros ebenum J. König*, a species known in India and Sri Lanka, in the tomb of Neferirkare (Fifth Dynasty) (De Vartavan and Asensi Amoros 1997: 106; Meeks 2002: 280), still needs confirmation, as does that of mango wood (*Mangifera indica* L.) on a ship from Khufu (*c.* 2500 BCE) (Nour *et al.* 1960; Germer 1985: 111; Asensi Amoros 2003: 181).

existence of two interconnected cores, in the Indus valley and in Mesopotamia, with Iran playing an important role as well.

Unlike western Asia and the Indus region, Egypt did not really develop a bronze industry, although this alloy was known. The tomb of Ti at Saqqara (*c.* 2440 BCE), however, shows the use of a large saw (probably made of bronze) "for cutting a log standing vertical as tall as a man." And "for joining the planks of wheels or boats by clamps, lashing, with wooden treenails, or by the use of gouged out mortises fitted with wooden tenons, the narrow chisel, the hollow gouge, and the rotating drill, necessarily of metal, were indispensable" (Ratnagar 2001a: 109). It is possible that this scarcity in discoveries is due to the practice of metal recycling.

While Egypt appears to have been only weakly connected to the Persian Gulf, it is nonetheless striking to note that the zenith of the Old Kingdom, under the Fourth Dynasty, occurred at the same time as a vast area of exchanges was forming between Mesopotamia and the Indus region. Similarly, soon after the disappearance of the Akkadian Empire, Egypt experienced a period of anarchy lasting for more than a century, marked by famines ("First Intermediary period," 2180–2030 BCE). These famines resulted from lower Nile flooding, a phenomenon linked to the global climatic changes of the 2200–2000 period (see above). The decline in exchanges with western Asia probably aggravated the Egyptian Kingdom's political disaggregation. As early as the end of the Fifth Dynasty, one notes the emergence of regional centers. Some authors describe the formation of a "feudal aristocracy," with officials carving out hereditary strongholds in which land and farmers were inherited (Pirenne 1961: 178). The process of decentralization grew under the Sixth Dynasty. The management of the nomes became hereditary. Various institutions or individuals benefited from tax exemptions that deprived the state of significant resources.

The Old Kingdom finally collapsed, a demise correlated with the entry of "Asian" populations into the Nile delta. This event was in turn linked to the turmoil caused in Palestine and in Mesopotamia by the Amorites. The texts express the chaos of this period in a striking way:

Indeed, the river is blood, yet men drink of it. Men shrink from human beings and thirst after water ... Towns are destroyed and Upper Egypt has become an empty waste ... Indeed, men are few, and he who places his brother in the ground is everywhere ... Indeed, the desert is throughout the land, and barbarians from abroad have come to Egypt ... The palace is despoiled, ... and those who were people [Egyptians] are strangers. (Ipuwer Papyrus, Leiden Museum, no. 1344)

"The plunderer is everywhere," writes Ipuwer, " and the servant takes what he wants." People looted state granaries and tombs (Fagan 2009: 121). The nomarch Ankhtifi claims:

I have kept alive Hefat, Hormer and (?), when the land was in wind ... All of Upper Egypt was dying of hunger, to such a degree that everyone had come to eating his children ... The entire country had become like a starved (?) grasshopper, with people going to the north and south [in search for food]. (Fagan 2009: 120)

CHAPTER

4 The New Spaces of the Middle Bronze Age in Asia and Egypt (*c.* 2000–1750 BCE)

Following the global recession of the late third millennium, the beginning of the second millennium was a crucial period of transformation and expansion. The reunified Egypt of the Middle Kingdom (*c.* 2030–1730) extended its connections with the exchange networks of the eastern Mediterranean, a thriving region in this period. An urban civilization appeared in Crete (first Palatial Period), which invented particular systems of writing.[1] Minoan networks expanded into the Aegean Sea, Greece, the Adriatic, and perhaps as far as the Black Sea. In western Asia, a phase of weaker central powers after the collapse of the Ur III Empire saw the new development of a system of city-states and the emergence – apparently in a new form – of the private sector, clearly visible in the functioning of the Assyrian trade in Anatolia. Trade in the Persian Gulf remained active between southern Mesopotamia and the Indus, with Bahrain acting as an important intermediary. The expansion of the Bactria–Margiana Complex accompanied the collapse of the Indus culture during the eighteenth century, and a restructuring of the Persian Gulf networks, as Oman was also in decline.

Egypt of the Middle Kingdom (*c.* 2040–1730 BCE)[2]

I plowed south to Abu [Elephantine], fared north to the marshes. I stood at the limits of the land, and saw its contour . . . None hungered in my years, none thirsted then . . . All I had decreed was in its correct place. I trapped lions and brought away crocodiles. I subdued the people of Ouaouat, and brought away the Medjay. I made the Asiatics do the dog walk. I made my house adorned with gold, its ceilings in lapis-lazuli, . . . its doors in copper, its bolts of bronze, made for eternity, equipped for everlasting life.
(The teaching of Amenemhat I to his son Sesostris, Joannès 2006a: 133)

The Eleventh Dynasty, originating from Thebes, reunited Egypt around 2040 BCE. The Middle Kingdom experienced its peak under the pharaohs of the Twelfth Dynasty, who were living at Licht. Benefiting from higher Nile flooding than at the end of the third millennium, the Egyptian rulers organized the reuse of abandoned lands and the cultivation of new lands, and re-established the authority of the central administration. A permanent army was set up. The system remained based on taxation: the state thus conducted censuses in the agricultural field, and inventories of metal resources. A middle class of civil servants emerged, particularly under Senusret III, who reinforced the central power with an organization bypassing the nomes (Joannès 2006a: 130).

[1] Several types of writing have been discovered in Crete, notably Linear A, presumably syllabic and ideographic, in which some authors claim to see influences from Anatolia. These writings remain undeciphered.
[2] Hornung *et al.* (2006: 491) give *c.* 1980–1760 BCE.

Egypt benefited at the time from the political and economical expansion of the eastern Mediterranean. The "states" of Minoan Crete – their nature remains a subject of controversy[3] – that formed around 2000 BCE with the building of the palaces of Knossos, Mallia, Zakro, and Phaistos, traded with Egypt, and also with Cyprus, the Levant, and Anatolia. During his visit at Ugarit, King Zimri-Lim of Mari would have "met Cretans who taught him a new way of shipbuilding" (Fabre 2004: 94). For the Old Babylonian period, Mesopotamian cylinder seals have been excavated in Crete, and documents from Mari refer to Cretan artifacts (Potts 1997: 276). In addition, the Minoan system of 65 g weights known for this period may have been inspired by the Egyptian gold unit (5x13 = 65) (Rahmstorf 2006a: 28). The Minoan networks extended into the Aegean Sea, in Greece, into the Adriatic, and perhaps the Black Sea, an expansion fueled by a growing demand for metals.

The Twelfth Dynasty pursued an expansionist policy in Palestine and Syria, with military expeditions under Amenemhat III (*c.* 1850 BCE) and Senusret III (Sesostris III) (1836–1817).[4] Contacts established with Ugarit and Byblos have been revealed by discoveries of artifacts from or influenced by Egypt.[5] Trade developed within the context of a "shared ideology" accompanied by a process of "religious syncretism" (Aubet 2013: 367). At the same time, the Nile delta welcomed large contingents of Asian migrants, both slaves and free men. Syrians, in particular, used to come to trade, and settled there. "The Egyptian texts describe the port of Tell el-Dab'a, the future Avaris, 'with its hundreds of cedar wood ships, full of gold, lapis lazuli, silver, turquoise, bronze axes, honey, oil and all the products of Syria' (Marcus 2002a: 250–252)" (Aubet 2013: 264). Female weavers brought in as a servile labor force may have contributed to the introduction of the Canaanite upright loom.[6] A mixed population was in place in the Nile delta, where Palestinian and Aegean influences were manifest. It was this hybrid culture that influenced other shores of the Mediterranean Sea. Egypt's trading exchanges probably stimulated silver production in Anatolia and the Aegean Sea during this period (Warburton 2007b). The Tôd treasure, buried under the temple of Montou, during Amenemhat II's reign, bears witness to the import of silver into Egypt, as well as contacts with the Levant (it contained lapis lazuli from Afghanistan, seals influenced by eastern Iran, and various Anatolian objects).[7] The attractiveness of

---

[3] See Persson 2005; Parkinson and Galaty 2007.

[4] On the chronology of the Middle Kingdom and the New Kingdom, see Krauss 2003. For Bernal (1991: 332, 383), some expeditions may have gone beyond Syria, and even Cilicia, as early as Senusret I's reign.

[5] Egypt had a strong influence on the royal family of Byblos (see Aubet 2013: 247). A pseudo-hieroglyphic script developed in Byblos.

[6] Smyth 1998: 9–10. Asian workers were present at Kahun at the beginning of the second millennium. During the Twelfth Dynasty, "many great houses belonging to the nobility had Asiatic servants"; some of these came on a voluntary basis (Silver 1995: 120). Silver also mentions voluntary Nubian immigration into Egypt as early as the Old Kingdom. Starting in the twentieth century BCE, the Asian contribution in Egypt became significant (Bietak 2002).

[7] Pierrat-Bonnefois 1999. The treasure contained more than two hundred silver objects, a dozen gold objects, lapis lazuli, as well as fragments of Mesopotamian and Cappadocian seals ranging over the third millennium and the early second millennium. Silver vases have been compared to the ceramic forms of the Middle Minoan of Crete. As a ritual deposit, the treasure thus assembled objects having various origins and belonging to various periods.

lapis lazuli explains the name given to the term "faience maker" (*jrw ḫsbdy*), which derives from the name of this stone (Warburton 2013: 288).

The pharaohs organized the exploitation of the copper mines of Ayn Soukhna, in the gulf of Suez. In the west, they controlled the oases of Dakhla and Kharga, in order to "leave open the roads shortcutting Upper Nubia," a concern already apparent during the Old Kingdom (Manzo 1999: 98). To the south, the Egyptian rulers retook control of Nubia as far as the second cataract. Fourteen citadels were built to protect the borders and provide support for trade expeditions and the exploitation of the region's resources.[8] The Nubians could not trade freely in Egypt, but had to exchange their merchandise at these forts. During the early second millennium BCE, Egyptian ships seem to have been regularly sent to Punt. An inscription in the Wādī Hammamat by the great officer Henu mentions a sizeable expedition launched by Mentuhotep III (Sankhare) (Eleventh Dynasty) around 1975 BCE.[9] Anchors and stelae found in the port of Sa'waw (Mersā Gawāsīs) refer to another expedition, sent by Senusret I (Twelfth Dynasty) *c.* 1930 BCE. An inscription discovered inland reveals that the ships were built at Koptos, in the Nile valley, downstream from Thebes, and transported on a road following the Wādī Hammamat from Koptos to Sa'waw, on the Red Sea, where they were reassembled.[10] The activity of the port of Mersā Gawāsīs experienced an upturn at the time of Senusret I. Another stela found in the valley of the Wādī Gawāsīs evokes an expedition sent during the twenty-eighth year of Amenemhat II's reign (*c.* 1928–1895 BCE). Recent excavations at the site of Mersā Gawāsīs have led to the discovery of the remains of boats, ceramics from the Tihama, and fragments of African ebony (Bard *et al.* 2007). Using imported or local wood, the ships were assembled using a technique of unlocked mortise-and-tenon joints, and sometimes with rope and metal (copper) fastenings (Ward and Zazzaro 2010).[11] It should be noted that myrrh was present under the Eleventh and Twelfth Dynasties (2040–1783 BCE) (but maybe as early as the Fifth Dynasty), and incense (*Boswellia sp.*) under the Eleventh Dynasty at the latest.[12]

---

[8] See the fort of Qubban, at the entrance of the Wādī Allaqi, "the main gold-bearing zone of the Eastern Desert" (Manzo 1999: 22–23).

[9] The inscription mentions the digging of fifteen wells along the Wādī Hammamat, the exploitation of quarries of diorite, and the construction of a ship destined to reach Punt and acquire incense (Manzo 1999: 20–21). Up to 3,000 men took part in these expeditions (Ward and Zazzaro 2010). Fabre (2004: 175ff.) emphasizes the importance of a body of officials, both "messengers" and "explorers," who brought precious goods back from distant countries.

[10] See the stela of the "vizier" Antekofer (Kitchen 1993: 587–591). Sesostris I in fact organized several expeditions. On the links between Egypt and Punt, see also Phillips 1997. Mersā Gawāsīs appears to have been a significant place during the Middle Kingdom. According to Meeks (2002: 326), "the choice of the site of Mersa Gawasis or later of Qoçeir or even of Berenice was linked to the particularities of the navigation in the Red Sea": from the gulf of Aqaba the winds and the currents set the ships on course toward the zone of Mersā Gawāsīs. Meeks (2002: 329) adds that Koptos "combined two advantages: not only was it located at a point in the Nile valley nearest to the Red Sea coast, but the road from Koptos to this coast led to the spot where returning ships were almost naturally forced to berth." From Koptos, it was also possible to go to the Sinai.

[11] The remains of ships dated to this period, assembled using the same techniques, have been unearthed at Ayn Sokhma, near Suez (Mathieu 2004: 690ff.).

[12] de Vartavan and Asensi Amoros 1997: 81–82; Germer 1985: 107; Goyon *et al.* 1999. The ancient Egyptian term '*ntyw* may refer to myrrh (a resin of *Commiphora*) (or perhaps to incense, a resin of *Boswellia*?), whereas *sntr* might mean incense, or be a resin of *Pistacia sp.* For Serpico and White (2000), the *sntr* of

In *The Tale of the Shipwrecked Sailor*, a story dated to the Middle Kingdom, the serpent of Pa'-anch Island (Socotra?), "who calls himself 'The Lord of Punt'," presents the sailor with gifts "[that] include a load of myrrh, *ḥknw*-oil, *laudanum*, *ḥsyt*- spice, *tšpss*-spice, incense, elephant tusks, long-tailed monkeys . . . " (Phillips 1997: 429).[13] Note that Punt probably referred to both the Eritrean/Somali coast and the western Arabian coast. Moreover, cowries arrived in Egypt, as can be seen from a belt represented on a faience figurine.[14] It seems that the pharaoh Senusret III widened a canal located near Aswan (first cataract) that had been dug under Pepi I's reign (Old Kingdom), primarily for military purposes. The existence of a canal linking the Nile and the Red Sea through the Wādī Tumilat under Senusret III remains a matter for speculation.

Further south, taking advantage of the first Egyptian Intermediary Period, a Nubian kingdom (K3š, Kush) emerged around 2100 BCE, with Kerma as its capital. It then expanded, benefiting not only from the control of gold-bearing regions, but also from its situation as a hub on the Nile axis as well as on east–west routes leading to the African interior.[15] The kingdom exported gold, ivory, slaves, ebony, and wild animals. A stela from Mentuhotep at Buhen mentions a military expedition against Kush as early as the beginning of the Middle Kingdom. Senusret III seems to have boosted military activities in Nubia against Kush and other populations.[16] The Egyptian army entered the Kushite territory several times, and the border was pushed south of the third cataract. At first allied to Kush, the country of Yam finally disappeared, probably incorporated into Kush. This state acquired a gatekeeper position for commercial transactions and developed its own production, sometimes imitating Egyptian objects (Manzo 1999: 150, 151). Egyptians were also present in Kush.

During this entire period, the populations of eastern Sudan, who formed a state in the "Gash group," centered on Mahal Teglinos (Kassala), served as an interface between the Horn of Africa and Arabia, on the one side, and Kush and Egypt on the other.[17] The near-exclusive presence of Kerma pottery in the ceramics imported at

---

Punt was a resin of *Commiphora*, whereas that from Syria–Palestine would have beeen a resin of *Pistacia*, perhaps *P. atlantica* Desf. A relief on a tomb of the Fifth Dynasty shows the harvest of *sntr* in a garden (Germer 1985: 110). We know that the pharaohs tried at various times to acclimatize trees yielding aromatic resins, originating in the Horn of Africa and/or Arabia.

[13] The wreck marked the end of an expedition to the "king's mines" (Sinai?). The ship that picked up the shipwrecked man was 55 m long. The "character" of the serpent-king, notes Manzo (1999: 24), evokes the Ethiopian legend of the serpent-king Arwē, a mythical king of Ethiopia, but Manzo also points out that the serpent "in the island of Socotra and in South Arabia," was the "guardian spirit of the aromatic trees."

[14] Paris, Louvre Museum, inventory number E 10942, Ziegler and Bovot 2001: 138.

[15] Three phases have been distinguished: Early Kerma (*c.* 2500–2100), Middle Kerma (2100–1750), and Classic Kerma (1750–1550).

[16] Later traditions refer to sea expeditions: Eratosthenes of Cyrene speaks "about a harbour near the Bab el-Mandeb, called Deiré, where the pharaoh Sesostris is supposed to have gone to Arabia (mentioned in Strabo, XVI 4.4)" (Nalesini 2009).

[17] See below. The period of the Gash culture has been divided into Early Gash (2500–2100), Middle Gash and Classical Gash (2100–1700), then Late Gash (1700–1500/1400). Seals and imprints of seals have been unearthed in five localities of the Gash delta, as well as tokens. Two of the tokens can be related to the "Jebel Mokram Group" (*c.* 1500–500), which succeeded the Gash group. This discovery suggests that "a simple kind of administration survived in the region up to the early 1st millennium BC" (Fattovich 1991: 72).

Mahal Teglinos during the period 2300–1700, however, shows the predominance of Kerma in the exchanges (Manzo 1999: 61).

The Egyptian royal administration managed relations with the Levant and the southern countries, as well as the goods coming from these regions. However, little is really known about the products that Egypt exported (Manzo 1999). A private trading sector coexisted with the state sector, a situation we have already noted at the time of the Old Kingdom. The *Tale of the Oasis Dweller* thus reveals the existence of petty traders coming from oases in order to sell merchandise in the Nile valley (Allam 1998: 149). The existence of private merchants is more strongly attested during periods of weak central authority. Around the middle of the twentieth century BCE, at the beginning of the Middle Kingdom, the letters of a rich farmer, Heqanakhte, refer to the sale of emmer[18] and grain loans at interest;[19] he sent "24 copper *deben* for the lease of land" to his agent (letter II). The *deben* was both a weight and a monetary unit; it may also have been a means of exchange, represented by a metal ring (the original meaning of *deben* could be "ring, circularity").[20] It should be noted that the excavations at Troy and Mycenae unearthed rings that may have been used as currency. Various authors have noted that the ingots and chains from the Töd treasure have a standard weight in silver *deben* (Menu 2001a: 88). Whether the *deben* – weight and monetary unit – was also a means of exchange, represented by a metal ring, remains debated (Menu 2001a; Allen 2004). Bread and measured amounts of cereals were also units of account: Ameny, the leader of an expedition to the Wādī Hammamat under Senusret I, received 200 "loaves" per day, while the "ration" of a simple recruit was ten "loaves" (Peters-Destéract 2005: 321). "Here we are dealing with mere accounting entries that enabled the beneficiaries to capitalize their rations; it allowed these beneficiaries to make a deferred use of these rations by means of transfer." The salaries appear as "receivables convertible into various goods" (Menu 2001a: 81, 93, 96). The salaries mentioned in the inscription from the Wādī Hammamat reveal a scale going from 1 to 20: one sees here the existence of a wide range of wages. The letters from Heqanakhte also indicate various wage levels. Menu argues that a market economy existed, regulated by the state, which "fixed the ratios of equivalence between the various forms of money," silver, copper or grain (Menu 2001a). It should be noted that the Egyptian *mryt* meaning "market" and "commerce" derives, as does the Akkadian *karum*, from a term meaning "quay, landing place" (Vargyas 2004: 113).

---

[18] One reads in letter I, 6–7: "If they will have collected the equivalent value of that emmer that is (owed me) in Perhaa, they should use it there as well [for the renting of land], . . . they should take it valued [*šnʿw*] from Sidder grove and lease land for its value" (Allen 2004: 15, 155). One also finds in letter II, 1–4: "but only when you will have collected the value of oil or anything (else) there" (Allen 2004: 155).

[19] Bleiberg 1995: 1383; Silver 1995: 108, 162. Heqanakhte "loaned grain at interest, paid rent on land in advance and had 'capital' in copper, oil, and cloth" (Bleiberg 1995). We do not have much evidence for the existence of loans with interest, or of credit sales bearing interest at this time (see Bleiberg 2002: 260–262, on the non-payment of the purchase price of his office by a scribe, in the Kahun II Papyrus).

[20] Castle 1992: 263; Silver 1995: 162. During the Middle Kingdom period, the *deben* weighed 27.3 g (Allen 2004: 258). According to Lacau (1949: 14), "the word *deben* has two determinatives": a small rectangle "represents the stone weight with a parallelepiped shape and a vaulted top, and the round O determines the meaning of the verb *deben*, 'to go around in circles'."

The last part of the Middle Kingdom was marked by an economic downturn and a global recession, partly linked to unfavorable climatic changes during the eighteenth century and to internal causes such as cumbersome bureaucracy.[21] Records show "several years of low flood levels between 1768 and 1745, [and] 18 kings presided over Egypt between 1768 and 1740" (Fagan 2009: 140). In the south, the state of Kush took the upper hand and reached its high point (Classical Kerma phase), extending into Lower Nubia. In the north, around 1780 BCE, infiltrations of Hyksos coming from Canaan into Lower Egypt opened up a period of political and social turmoil, which continued until *c.* 1560 BCE [22] ("Second Intermediary period"). However, this was not the time of chaos depicted by later Egyptian sources. It saw, among other things, an increase in private trade and the spread of innovations. In Egypt, the newcomers introduced horses, the use of chariots, the technique of composite bows, the use of leather or metal scaled armours, and the Syrian unit of weight, which would become the standard unit of the Eighteenth Egyptian Dynasty (Mederos and Lamberg-Karlovsky 2004: 201). Remains of domesticated horses have been identified at Thebes, dated to around 1500 BCE and at Buhen, in Lower Nubia, *c.* 1675 BCE (horses may have arrived via the African coast) (Marshall 2000: 212). The Hyksos also established a bronze industry in Egypt which improved the quality of tools. Curiously, bronze was seldom used in Egypt during the third millennium BCE and the early second millennium: we know of only two tin bronze vessels from Abydos, and one piece from Tell el-Fara'in, in the Nile delta (Pernicka *et al.* 2003: 168). In addition, transcultural exchanges fostered a major invention: alphabetic writing, which was apparently born "in the environment of bilingual royal scribes, under the Hyksos domination" around the seventeenth century BCE (Lemaire 2007: 54).

The Hyksos maintained relations with Kush via the route of the oases west of the Nile; this allowed them to bypass Nubia. The period of the Fifteenth Dynasty (Hyksos; seventeenth/sixteenth century BCE) corresponds to a phase of economic development of the Levant, with urban growth in Palestine. Documents describe the wealth of the city of Avaris under the Hyksos: "Hundreds of ships brought cedar, gold, lapis lazuli, silver, turquoise, bronze axes, moringa oil, honey, rosewood" (Smyth 1998: 12 n. 3). The Hyksos dynasties controlled Palestine from their capital of Avaris, and they were in contact with Cyprus, Crete, and northern Syria, outlining what would constitute a central area during the Late Bronze Age period.[23] The end of

---

[21] Baines and Yoffee 1998: 224. The rulers replaced the nome organization by four great regions, which led to a proliferation of new administrative positions.

[22] Or 1530, according to the chronology adopted by Warburton (2007b). The Greek term Hyksos comes from the Egyptian *heka khasewet* or *khasout* ("Rulers of Foreign Lands") which appeared in the Middle Kingdom. At the same time, relations ceased between Egypt and Byblos during the final decade of the eighteenth century. Hornung *et al.* (2006: 492) propose 1759–1539 BCE as the limits of the "Second Intermediary Period." Bietak (2002: 36) gives 1640 BCE as the beginning of the Hyksos period in Egypt.

[23] On the connections with Cyprus, see Eriksson 2003: 419. For Manning and Ramsey, who propose a high chronology for the Aegean Sea, the Late Minoan IA, a flourishing period in Minoan civilization, should be dated to the seventeenth century: it would be contemporary with the Hyksos phase rather than parallel to the Eighteenth Egyptian Dynasty (2003: 114, 117). The dating of the Minoan mural paintings discovered at Tell el-Dab'a (Avaris), however, is still debated: was it during the Hyksos period, or at the beginning of the New Kingdom? Paintings of Minoan inspiration have been found at Tel Kabri, in Israel,

the Middle Bronze Age "corresponds to a golden age of the Canaanite culture which prefigures what the Phoenician world would be" (Benoit 2003: 100).

Western Asia: The Growth of the Private Sector in the Exchange Networks

> The god Assur is continually warning you: you are too fond of money and ride roughshod over your [own] life.
> (Letter written by two women to a merchant; Michel 2001b: 470)

The collapse of Ur opened up a new period of political instability in Mesopotamia, with the cities of Isin and then Larsa becoming predominant.[24] In Iran, a powerful Elamite state developed during the early second millennium, with its capital at Anshan. The ascent of Elam, where the lower country (Susiana) regained the upper hand over the highlands (Shimashki), may partly have been the result of control of the tin routes from Central Asia to northern Mesopotamia and the powerful city of Mari. Susa shows connections with other regions of Iran and with Bactria.[25] It also had trade links with Dilmun and Magan. Led by *Sukkalmah*, "great viziers," a title given during the Ur III period to the Mesopotamian official in charge of the "eastern provinces," Elam exerted a nominal suzerainty over Mesopotamia in the first half of the eighteenth century – the kings Zimri-Lim of Mari and Hammurabi of Babylon called the *Sukkalmah* "father" – until these two kings joined forces to defeat the *Sukkalmah* in 1764 BCE (de Miroschedji 2003: 26 ff.).

In Mesopotamia, kingdoms centered on the cities of Assur,[26] in the Tigris valley, Larsa, in the lower Euphrates valley, and Mari, in the Middle Euphrates valley, acquired dominance. More than 15,000 tablets dated to the first half of the eighteenth century have been discovered in the palace of Mari. The texts reveal the palace as a proper "commercial enterprise," assessing costs, and working in an environment where "boats and workers could be hired," with payment in silver (Warburton 2003: 55, 119). The city paid particular attention to the maintenance of canals (Durand 1998). The palace bought wool – in exchange for silver – and employed 800 workers in textile workshops, for mostly export-oriented production. The city received copper from Cyprus, and tin from Iran,[27] through Anshan and Susa, or via the Mesopotamian city of Eshnunna. It levied taxes on all goods in transit. The question arises whether the Suteans (the "Southerners"), who came from the great oases of northern Arabia, and whom texts from Mari show as being settled in the region of Palmyra around the eighteenth century, operated a structured trade between Arabia and the Middle

---

where they are dated to the seventeenth century. We can connect them to frescoes discovered at Alalakh (Kempinski 1994).

[24] After 2000 BCE, as Morris notes (2011: 195), "no ruler ever again claimed to be a god."

[25] Elam had perforated compartmented seals, animal-shaped hammers, ceremonial axes, stone colonnettes, that probably reflect influences from the BMAC (see below), as well as the motif of an eagle with its wings outspread.

[26] Larsen (2000a: 79–81), however, considers Assur as a city-state. Decisions were made by an assembly, at the head of which was the king (see below).

[27] The true source for this tin is still debated (see Pigott 2012b).

Euphrates.[28] The Syrian kingdoms took advantage of their intermediary position between the Mediterranean and Mesopotamia, especially the kingdom of Yamkhad whose capital was Aleppo, and the city of Ebla, where contacts with Egypt are attested.[29] On the Levantine coast, various ports – Ugarit and Byblos first of all – developed relationships with Egypt.

As in the Levant, competition between Mesopotamian cities fostered a flourishing of private enterprise, against a background of weak political centralization.[30] Agrarian debt developed at this time, leading to the transformation of land tenure, and the formation of large private estates (Hudson 2002: 27). Texts mention loans in grain or silver granted by temples or private persons, sometimes explicitly for profit: for example, a woman from Ur lent three partners barley and silver for hiring crews and boats for a trading venture.[31] The documentation illustrates some variation in the interest rates. Unlike during the Ur III period, a partial "privatization" of the administration can be seen (Van de Mieroop 2004: 88; Masetti-Rouault 2008: 55); one cannot, however, discern any explicit search for economic rationality. Even for cereals, prices appear to have been determined by the market: one king of Uruk was proud of the low price of grain under his reign.[32] For Edens (1993), it was weak regional political integration that fostered the expansion of the private sector. Exchanges were not only commercial, as revealed by the importance of religious pilgrimages to the temples of Terqa and Tattul. At the same time, the state levied heavy taxes on merchants' profits, during the Old Assyrian and the Old Babylonian periods.[33] The privatization of the administration went along with "a more and more important pressure imposed on the population who worked in or for the institution" (Masetti-Rouault 2008: 56).

Everywhere, the private sector was flourishing. It was entrusted with the management of agricultural estates and crafts workshops, and it proved able to develop long-distance trade, in Anatolia as well as the Persian Gulf, where commerce remained active. Dilmun (Bahrain) experienced a "dramatic expansion" in this period (Crawford 1998: 60).[34] At the same time, in Oman, which still exported copper, many tower-houses of the political chiefs were abandoned (these changes may have resulted from an aridification of the Arab coasts). The coexistence in Dilmun of three scripts – cuneiform, Indusian, and Linear Elamite – is indicative of the mix of populations of these

[28] Villard 2001: 62. Like the Egyptian Bedouins, they seem to have been involved in the slave trade (Michailidou 2005: 43).

[29] Evidence includes the discovery of a macehead inscribed with the name of the pharaoh Hotepibrē (Thirteenth Dynasty). Ebla would be destroyed by the Hittites around 1600.

[30] Yoffee (1995b: 1395) gives the example of the small city-state of Dilbat prior to the formation of the Hammurabi Empire. At Mari, a council (*pirishtum*) assisted the king in the eighteenth century. Thuesen (2000: 61), however, notes increased centralization during the eighteenth and seventeenth centuries in Syria. Between the kingdoms, which formed fluctuating confederations, wars of aggression alternated with the use of diplomacy, with agreements sealed by treaties and matrimonial alliances.

[31] Silver 1995: 110. Texts from Ur report silver loans at an interest of 20 percent per month.

[32] One notes seasonal price variations for grain in Babylonia during the nineteenth and eighteenth centuries (Silver 1995: 104–105).

[33] A royal inscription of Assur, however, announces the abolition of taxes for merchants coming from the south (in order to facilitate trade) (Larsen 1987: 52).

[34] "Dilmun now encompasses the island of Failaka. A Paleo-Babylonian text of Ur establishes a distinction between a 'Little Dilmun' and a 'Great Dilmun' " (Glassner 2002b: 338).

regions of the Gulf, at the junction of various networks (Glassner 2002b). Dilmunite caravans went to Babylon and Mari, carrying copper and tin. This could explain some of the Anatolian influence on the glyptic art of Qala'at al-Baḥrayn (Potts 1993b: 191). The merchants of the Indus were active at Dilmun during the twentieth century BCE, as indicated by the adoption of the Harappan weight system, and the presence of Indusian writing on Persian Gulf seals. Dilmun may later have benefited from the disappearance of the Indusian ships, by engaging in the transportation of Indian products to Mesopotamia. Bahrain maintained contacts with Gujarat (Warburton 2007b), and had relations with all the Gulf coasts at this time, and later during the Old Babylonian period, as revealed by the discovery of hundreds of "Dilmun seals" at Failaka, at a site that had been created by Dilmunites, at Ur, Tell Ischali (valley of the Diyala), Susa, in the Gardan Reg (in Afghanistan),[35] and at Lothal (Gujarat). Some of the motifs of these seals show analogies with Syria, Mesopotamia, and even Central Asia. A text and a clay sealing found at Susa bearing imprints of Dilmunite seals show the reception of products (especially copper), on the one side, and the arrival of merchandise sealed at Dilmun and transported to Iran, on the other.

These documents confirm the close links existing between Susa and Bahrain.[36] Perhaps it was via Susiana (or southeastern Iran?) that Central Asian influences reached Bahrain. They may also have come through the Indus valley followed by maritime routes from the Indus. The foundation deposit excavated in the Barbar temple has yielded a series of objects that show affinities with Bactria, which was expanding at that time.[37] The site of Zellaq has also yielded two stone colonnettes, religious symbols found in Bactria and "exported" by this culture. Bronzes from Saar and Bahrain city II show the importation of tin. Lapis lazuli also arrived in the Gulf, probably through the Indus valley. A Murghabo-Bactrian seal has been excavated at Hamad Town. As another clue of contacts with Iran, painted ceramics similar to the pottery of the Kaftari tradition have been unearthed at Bahrain and on the Arabian coast.

The smaller sizes of vessels in Mesopotamia reveal the disengagement of the state: the investors there were temples and private entrepreneurs, perhaps organized in associations, who "lent silver and received a fixed interest on capital invested" (Norel 2004: 78).[38] Objects and texts attest to contacts between Mesopotamia and Dilmun.

---

[35] The presence of copper certainly explains Dilmun's links with this region: "Tosi has suggested a date of about 2000 BC for the copper smelting sites of the Gardan Reg" (Ratnagar 2001a: 113).

[36] Potts 1990: 200, 228, 1999: 179. On Susa-Dilmun connections, see also Glassner 2002b: 349–350. The presence of Elamite speakers in the Gulf, as Glassner has noted, was perhaps greater than previously thought (2002b: 353).

[37] Among these objects: a copper statuette of a man in an attitude of prayer ("similar figures form the handles of copper mirrors" in Bactria), a copper bull's head, a copper figure of a bird, cylindrical vases of alabaster (Crawford 1998: 73–75). The vases could be of Indo-Iranian origin. Susa notably acquired compartmented seals and chlorite vessels from Bactria (Potts 1999: 180–181). During Caspers (1994, 1996) also emphasizes these imports from Central Asia in the Persian Gulf (for example, on seals found at Failaka, on beads, and cruciform seals with stepped crenellations, at Bahrain, Ur, and Susa).

[38] Benoit 2003: 95. See also Michel 2001a: 196ff. M. Silver points to land purchased by merchants of Larsa and Nippur, probably in order to develop sheep breeding, with wool production fueling weaving workshops and exports. Crawford (2005) speaks of "houses or guilds of merchants."

Various texts mention investors who provided silver, sesame oil, and textiles to a merchant called Ea-nasir, for the purchase of copper in Dilmun, under a partnership enterprise. A Sumerian text reveals a conversion system between weights of Dilmun and Ur (Mederos and Lamberg-Karlovsky 2004). A tablet from Larsa dated around 1925 BCE, bearing the imprint of a Dilmun seal, records the consignment of wool, wheat, and sesame to Dilmun (Potts 1995: 1453). The region of Isin exported leather products to Dilmun and Iran (and also to Syria). During the Isin-Larsa period, tablets from Ur show that the merchants of this city "went to Bahrain on a regular basis." The Mesopotamian ships sailed no further than Dilmun, a development that also reflects the changes in the Gulf. Private entrepreneurs worked with the palace and the temple, the latter providing loans.[39] At Ur, for example, a group of merchants delivered 4 tons of copper to the palace; the temple of Nanna bought 9,600 liters of bitumen, exchanged for 1 kilo of silver from a private entrepreneur.[40]

Beyond Bahrain, Oman underwent significant change after 2000 BCE, with a decline in oasis agriculture, and perhaps some return to nomadism.[41] Copper exploitation, however, continued until 1700 BCE, but was less intensive.[42] Then copper from Cyprus was exported to western Asia. Besides possible price phenomena (Warburton 2003: 60), other factors – environmental deterioration, political changes, systemic restructuring – should be considered first as causes for these changes in the commercial networks. Deforestation due to excessive use of wood as fuel for the furnaces probably played a role in the decline of Omani metallurgy, which also occurred – and this cannot be a mere coincidence – when the Indus civilization and the "Indo-Iranian sphere"[43] disintegrated. Chlorite vessels (termed *série tardive*), with handles and incised diagonals or circles, were still being produced and exported: they have been found on Bahrain, Tarut, at Failaka, Bandar Bushire, Ur, and Shahdad, but not in the Indus. Contacts, however, were maintained with the Indus region and Gujarat: jars discovered at Shimal and Tell Abraq have been compared to material of Lothal and Rangpur, dated to *c.* 1900 BCE. A weight of the Harappan type from the same period has been excavated at Shimal. Red Harappan pottery with nail impressions has been unearthed at Hili (period III) and Tell Abraq; and Ra's al-Jinz (phase IV) has

---

[39] Bogaert (1966: 66) has argued that the sanctuaries here were imitating private entrepreneurs: "the merchants during the 3rd millennium invented the loan contract." As already mentioned, the practice of loans with interest may have derived first from the state sector (Hudson 2002).

[40] Baines and Yoffee 1998: 227; van de Mieroop 1992: 92. Warburton (2003: 167) rightly emphasizes that a "local" product (bitumen) was being bought here with imported metal (silver).

[41] Cleuziou (2002: 229) speaks of an abrupt societal transformation during the Wadi Suq period. Inland sites were progressively abandoned from the early second millennium on, while the number of coastal settlements grew at this time (Magee 1998: 51).

[42] One text from Ur dated to the reign of Rim-Sin of Larsa (1822–1763 BCE) reveals the continuing Omani trade in copper: it records the receipt in Dilmun of 18 tons of copper, certainly coming from Oman. "One third of this copper was earmarked for delivery" to the merchant Ea-Nasir of Ur (Muhly 1995: 1506). This copper appears to have been paid for in silver.

[43] Sergent 1997: 190ff. See below. Lamberg-Karlovsky (2001a: 280) speaks of "regional diversity, which after 2000 BC, whether it be in the Gulf, the eastern borders of the Iranian plateau, or Central Asia, sees a clear diminution in civilizational complexity."

yielded post-Harappan pottery from Gujarat.[44] As is the case for Bahrain, some objects exhibit similarities with pieces from Central Asia (for example, silver and gold plaques, with *repoussé* decoration showing animal figures, which must have been sewn on a garment). These Central Asian influences came through the Indus valley, southeastern Iran or Susiana. Mesopotamian cylinder seals dated to the first half of the second millennium have been discovered in Oman.[45] It should be noted that Mesopotamian texts no longer mention Magan as a country, but speak only of objects from Magan. In the end, trade practically stopped between Mesopotamia and Oman.[46] After 1500, in Mesopotamia, "the names Magan and Meluhha came to denote portions of Egypt and Nubia, because the latter regions furnished some of the same exotica as had formerly been obtained from the east" (Potts 1990: 259).

In Anatolia, cities developed during the late third and early second millennia, which may have been the centers of macro-states. Archaeology has revealed the vitality of the exchanges in northern Mesopotamia, and has uncovered the existence of an Assyrian merchant community in Cappadocia in the twentieth and nineteenth centuries BCE, with outposts scattered between Kanesh (Kül Tepe) and the Black Sea,[47] along roads that were probably already active during the third millennium. There were ten main *kārum* (from *kāru*, "quay, market")[48] and ten minor outposts. The 22,000 tablets discovered at Kültepe (Kanesh) attest to the flourishing of this trade between regions. The Assyrian *tamkāru* merchants were either agents of the state or temple, or private entrepreneurs, forming familial firms or kinds of hierarchized guilds that may have been new types of institutions in the political and economic landscape of western Asia (Larsen 2000a; Michel 2001a). The merchant community collected taxes, for example, on caravans leaving Assur. Some merchants acted as bankers and lent money for commercial ventures. Texts mention the practice of debt notes that could be transferred within the merchants' circle (Bogaert 1966), and "the use of notes expressing that the debt had to be paid to the bearer of the tablet, [without mentioning the name of the creditor], the ancestor of bearer checks, moreover, is widely attested" (Glassner 2002a: 150).[49]

---

[44] Potts 1990: 248–249. "Sherds of Harappan type have been identified at almost every site of the Wadi Suq horizon" (Cleuziou and Tosi 1989: 40). A knife found in a tomb at Shimal (SH 99) has been compared with blades from Mohenjo-daro and Harappa (Potts 1990: 253). Another tomb (SH 99) yielded more than 500 carnelian beads.

[45] Four seals, found at Kalba and Tell Abraq (Cleuziou 2003a: 146).

[46] The disappearance of Magan and Meluhha in the texts of the Isin-Larsa period reflects the dominance of Bahrain, but also the decline of Oman and the Indus region.

[47] The Assyrian traders "established a hierarchized network of outposts dominated by a dozen *karum* . . . The *karum* performed multiple functions as banks, storehouses for imported products and products for export, and tax collection centers; they also had judiciary powers in case of conflicts between merchants" (Benoit 2003: 95). On the Assyrian merchants, see Dercksen 1999. There was a *kāru* at Hattusha, the future center of Hittite power. The dating given (twentieth–nineteenth century until 1830) corresponds to the chronology most usually adopted.

[48] The term *mahiru* also denotes a marketplace.

[49] Veenhof 1999: 57ff., 83. "Bonds with anonymous *tamkarum* as creditor could be ceded." These tablets allowed transfers of debt and of claims: "the right to collect the claim was transferred" and/or "the claim itself was transferred, . . . so that the bearer of the tablet had become the creditor" (Veenhof 1997: 355–356,

Some merchants stayed at Assur or Kanesh, while other merchants traveled. A letter says: "Since tin was in short supply we did not take a loan from a moneylender and did not make purchases for you" (Silver 2007a: 101, *CAD* entry *shamû* A.1b). Associations of moneylenders/investors gave certain amounts of silver or gold to merchants going away.[50] They absorbed any losses, but one-third of the profits stayed with the traveling merchant. Interest-bearing loans were also practiced,[51] whereby the traveling trader assumed all risks, but kept the profits. "Common was the practice of entrusting merchandise to agents or traveling salesmen," who signed debit notes which stated their debits in silver (Veenhof 1997: 347). Debtors sometimes repaid the amounts borrowed in labor. Forms of long-term partnership and the existence of *commenda* type contracts (*naruqqu*) have led some authors to make comparisons with what would be found in the European medieval world.[52] Some texts mention long-term silver deposits, bearing interest: "Two minas of refined silver and the interest on it for ten years"; "for thirteen years the silver has been accumulating interest with you" (*CAD* S/ 1a 158–9 entry *sibtu*; Silver 2004b: 72).

Texts reveal the existence of markets – this contradicts Polanyi (1957b, 1981), who held that the authorities would not have let prices fluctuate – and explicit profit-seeking:

As to the purchase of Akkadian textiles, about which you wrote to me, writes a merchant, if . . . there is a possibility of a purchase which allows you profit, we will buy (them) for you and we will pay the silver from our own means. You should take care to send the silver. (Veenhof 1972: 98)

Another merchant wrote: "I saw a chance to get a bargain, so I borrowed money [silver] at interest and bought" (Silver 2007a: 101, *CAD* entry *shamû* A.1c). Texts show rapid price fluctuations, for example involving tin, textiles, or grains, the Assyrian trade

1999: 83). We again find payments to "the bearer of this tablet" during the eighteenth century BCE in Babylonia (Veenhof 1997: 360).

[50] In the *naruqqu* societies, with long-term partnerships (texts mention 9, 10, and even 12 years), investors (*ummeanum*) would put capital at the disposal of a trader; see Veenhof 1997: 345. The texts show the negotiability of shares, which also could be inherited. "The investments made in silver were inscribed in gold at twice the normal rate of exchange, so that a 100% profit was guaranteed from the outset" (Veenhof 1997: 345). Operations were protected by various legal procedures (Veenhof 1997: 347ff.). A man called Amur-Ishtar thus invested 4 gold minas in a *naruqqum* while other people put in 26 minas; as the manager, Amur-Ishtar received one-third of the profits. Starting from Assur, the merchants made two return trips per year. Whereas K. Polanyi (1975) thought that there was no risk-taking on the part of merchants, the data nowadays available, by contrast, reveal the "entrepreneurial" spirit of these merchants. A great merchant thus complains in a letter "that he was losing much profit because of delays in obtaining a loan to finance an enterprise" (Silver 1995: 168). "If textiles are too expensive, instructs a merchant, buy tin" (Silver 1995: 168). Texts say of silver that is not being turned over that it is "hungry" (Silver 1995: 175). On the profit-seeking of the merchants, see Veenhof 1987: 62ff.

[51] An Assyrian merchant could also borrow from an Anatolian: the use of silver as money and the practice of interest-bearing loans were known in Anatolia.

[52] Veenhof 1997: 342, 347. Account keeping can be compared with older Mesopotamian practices (of the Ur III period). In the long-term contracts called *naruqqu*, the manager received one-third of the profits earned during the twelve-year life of the agreement (see above); "the other contributors received the remainder of the profit." If an investor withdrew his capital before the contract had expired, he was denied a share in the profits from the venture, but he could sell his "shares" to another person (Silver 1995: 112).

revealing an adaptation of supply to demand.[53] Purchase by the palace at a fixed price affected only one-tenth of the goods. The state also intervened with the collection of taxes.[54]

The king himself, as head of the merchants' assembly, was involved in commercial activities, and it is clear that in Assur there was no conflict "between personal profit and public interest" (Graslin and Maucourant 2005). Some of the richest merchants belonged to the aristocracy.[55] The temple sometimes invested money in trade, receiving the loan amount and the interest in return.[56] Silver or grain were used as money.[57] The possibility cannot be excluded that sealed silver bags had a monetary use, the bags often adopting standardized weights. The documents speak of "marked" (*uddû*) silver and of "sealed [bags of] silver" (*kaspum kankum*). We have here "the characteristics of a coin" with verified purity, a standard weight and the name of a merchant or an institution.[58] The use of these bags obviated the need to weigh their contents again and

[53] Silver (1995: 141) mentions a letter from a merchant called Puzur Assur who gives indications about the types of textiles that should be produced for export to Anatolia. The great quantities of tin and copper imported into Assyria and Babylonia imply export-oriented [upstream] mining activities (Silver 1995: 142). A letter from a trader at Assur to his agents at Kanesh stipulates: "Sell it at the best price and send me the silver" (Postgate 2003: 213). Polanyi (1957b) was wrong in thinking of Kanesh as an "administered port of trade." Today we can no longer write that "[The] livelihood [of the *tamkārum* merchant] was not dependent on the commercial transaction in hand; it was secured by status revenue . . . The so-called 'Cappadocian' trading colony . . . practiced a riskless type of business under fixed prices, the trader's profit being made on commission fees" (Polanyi 1981: 87, 138–139). The risks were in fact permanent: prices varied, robbers looted the caravans, donkeys died on the road, which forced the merchants to abandon part of their loads, commercial agents disappeared with the merchandise which had been entrusted to them, and debtors died before their debt was paid (Michel 2001a, b). It is true, however, that "the public institution frees up private initiative, a general idea of Polanyi's" (Graslin and Maucourant 2005: 232 and nn. 37, 39).

[54] An assembly played an important role in city management. A letter tells us about the decision of the assembly from Assur to collect 10 minas of silver from each Assyrian outpost in order to rebuild the city walls. As Westenholz has pointed out (2002: 40 n. 20), a royal inscription would surely have indicated that this renovation took place at the king's initiative. This system of a "council of elders" presided over by a king, which we noticed for the third millennium, can be observed for other cities during this period.

[55] For Glassner (2002a: 149), "there are strong signs that the management of the great commercial ventures was in the hands of Assyrian high dignitaries, notably belonging to the entourage of the king."

[56] Curtin 1984: 70. See also Silver 1985: 74. The temples sometimes lent silver to the merchants at a rate of only 15 percent, because these merchants made offerings to the temple (van de Mieroop 2002: 77). Although the temples may have been centers of commerce (for example, at Ur during the Old Babylonian period, and in the Egyptian New Kingdom), seeking to make a profit and working with private agents, they do not seem to have played "a special role in the commercial economies of the Near East" during the second millennium (Warburton 2003: 63).

[57] Tin was also used for the payment of small sums. For silver, the usual rate of interest was 30 percent per year in Assur (Veenhof 1997: 348). In Babylonia, the interest for silver loans (20 percent) was less than that for grain (33 percent) because with grain there was "a loss between the time of the loan and the date of the repayment of the loan" (Glassner 2002a: 150) (Hudson has given another explanation for this discrepancy; see below). There were two types of loans: loans to individuals in need of money, and cash advances to commercial entrepreneurs. Gold, too, was a money of account for large sums. It should be noted that it was forbidden for an Assyrian to exchange gold with an Akkadian, an Amorite, or a "Subarian" (Hurrite) (Larsen 2000a: 82).

[58] Silver 1985: 160; Thompson 2003: 87. The expression "sealed silver" probably means that the bag or the purse was sealed; it does not indicate that the silver itself was marked with a seal (J. G. Dercksen, p.c.). The term *nēpišu* seems to have referred to sealed bags containing silver or gold (see Thompson 2003: 86).

guaranteed the transfer of silver.[59] We are in the presence at this time "of elaborated means of payment: rings or other forms weighed with a good precision . . . Depending on the texts, we find mentioned ingots of 250 g, pieces of silver . . ., rings of 500 g. In these excavations, molds have been discovered, which were used for rectangular and circular ingots, each silver bar weighing 50 g; other molds were used for disks of 250 g, 500 g and 750 g."[60] The use of bracelets or coils of silver for transactions seems well attested, as this complaint by an Assyrian merchant shows: "What silver bracelets did you leave me? When you departed, you did not leave me even one shekel of silver."[61] For Silver (2004c), copper may have been used as money: "Thus, one Dakuku 'owes 12 copper *sadālu* as the price of donkey'" (see Dercksen 1996: 60, n179). The term *sadālu* seems to refer to a copper object used for payments (or to a sack containing copper?) (*CAD*, vol. XVII, entry *sadālu*).[62]

Relations with the Anatolian rulers, who imposed various taxes, were regulated by treaties.[63] The Assyrians exported tin and lapis lazuli, which came from or through Iran, and textiles, which they bought in Babylonia (Babylon, and Sippar, where a colony of Assyrian merchants had settled). From Susa, tin was transported in sealed bags of an average weight of 65 minas.[64] Textiles yielded a higher return than tin.[65] Unlike that of tin, the trade in lapis lazuli was monopolized by the king and a small group of merchants, as was the iron trade. In addition, texts from Sippar and Larsa testify to the importation of slaves from the Zagros, a trade of growing economic significance. Most of the slaves who labored in the palace workshops at Mari during the eighteenth century were female prisoners of war.

The Assyrian merchants received gold and silver in return. Whereas Anatolia may have produced tin during the third millennium, it imported this metal during the early second millennium, just when the use of bronze was spreading. Conversely, silver exploitation in Anatolia was weak during the third millennium, but increased during the second millennium. Warburton (2003: 194) suggests that market mechanisms could explain these changes in production and exchange, with the rising price of silver

[59] "One text records a complaint about silver missing from a sealed shipment" (Thompson 2003: 85).

[60] C. Michel, p.c. See Müller-Karpe 1994: 138ff. For Silver, some molds (probably used for casting silver) bear marks.

[61] *CAD*, XV, entry *semeru* (1984: 223). Objects termed "nails" also seem to have been used as "money," as well as in Mari (*CAD* 1984: 120, entry *samrūtu*).

[62] The text says: "twelve *sadalus* of copper, the purchase price of the ass, are with PN" (*CAD* 1984: 11).

[63] Silver (1995: 174) notes that Assyrian merchants sometimes preferred to take risks by following "dangerous routes" to avoid having to pay taxes; this is consistent with the reasoning of private entrepreneurs.

[64] A text says: "four *šuqlus* of tin, in all 260 minas of tin, under the seals of the City (Assur)" (*CAD*, XVII, entry *šuqlu* Ar'a, 1992: 333) (see also C. Thompson 2003: 85–86). Isotopic analyses show parallels between Aegean bronzes and those of the Persian Gulf; the source of the metal could be in Central Asia (Weeks 2003: 180, 200). Deh Hosein, in Luristan, is another potential source for tin exported to Mesopotamia (Weeks 2003: 193).

[65] See the quotation in the epigraph. The profits reached 200 percent for textiles, and 100 percent for tin (Veenhof 1972: 85, 1999: 56). Fabric bought for 3 shekels of silver in southern Mesopotamia could be sold for 6 shekels at Assur and between 12 and 20 in Anatolia (Larsen 2000a: 81). It would appear that Assur attempted to attract the Akkadians by granting them tax exemptions. An inscription says that the king of Assur established "a free movement [*andurārum*] of silver, gold, tin, grain, wool and other commodities," and of merchants as well (Silver 1995: 196).

leading to the abandonment of the tin mine of Kestel, which might also have been due to exhaustion of the seams. The silver:tin ratio was 1:15 at Assur and 1:7 in Anatolia (Warburton 2000a: 82).[66] The texts express the idea that silver should not sleep but circulate, as quickly as possible. Michel and Warburton rightly emphasize the striking fact that Assyrian traders did not transport copper from Kanesh to Assyria, but purchased and sold this metal within Anatolia, purely for profit. Assur must have received its copper from a region further north – the Assyrian networks extended as far as the Black Sea (Kristiansen 2007) – but perhaps also from Iran and Oman.[67] It is difficult to assess whether the entrepreneurial spirit observed in these trade networks was a historical novelty, or whether this spirit and the organization that went with it existed during earlier periods but were concealed by the lack of data.[68]

At the time of the Assyrian expansion, the Caucasus region saw increased social differentiations, marked by the building of huge kurgans, some of them containing silver and vessels featuring scenes of conflict (Kohl and Trifonov 2014: 1584). Few settlements have been reported for the Middle Bronze Age in this area, and these settlements were usually fortified (Uzerlik Tepe for example).

Around 1830 BCE, a fire in Kanesh marked the decline of the activities of the Assyrian trading posts. Relations between Cappadocia and Assyria ceased around 1780, after the reign of the Amorite king Shamshi-Addu on Upper Mesopotamia, while the arrival of new populations engendered turmoil in Anatolia and northern Mesopotamia.[69] The Hittite king Pithana conquered Kanesh at this time. In addition, a halt to imports

---

[66] Also Yoffee 1995b: 1393. According to the theory of comparative advantages, the differences in prices and competition in markets would ultimately determine the places of production and the direction of exchanges. "By 1800 BC," writes Warburton (2003: 120), "an international market functioned in the Near East, with price differentials (based on silver) changing the distribution of copper and tin production . . . Market forces determined the prices of merchandise in the Near East since at least the beginning of the 2nd millennium." It is possible, however, that tin from Central Asia (Afghanistan) was exploited and exported as early as the beginning of the third millennium, and not at the beginning of the second millennium as Warburton would have it (2003: 193) (see Boroffka *et al.* 2002). Gold and silver were used as standards of exchange in Assyria. Silver (1995: 158) also stresses that "the price of silver [the metal used for payments] in terms of barley was some 7.5 times greater [in Babylonia] than in Cappadocia."

[67] Larsen (1976: 92) indicates imports from a region situated northwest of Assur (Durhumit, a town not precisely located), sometimes involving vast tonnages (15 tons for one caravan, 5 tons for another . . .). According to Warburton (2003: 51), the fact that copper came from Oman or Iran can only be explained by the more advantageous prices of the Iranian or Omani copper against silver.

[68] Veenhof 1997: 338. Tablets from Sippar reveal the existence of an organization of merchants that may have been similar (Veenhof 1997: 340) – Moore and Lewis (1999: 60) interpret it as an Assyrian *kārum*. This trading community "played a role in the civic administration." Here, however, the palace was "an important supplier of capital, for whom the traders worked in a contractual relationship, a situation not attested for Assur" (Veenhof 1997: 340).

[69] Assur was captured by the king of Eshnunna and Ekallatum, Shamshi-Addu (*c.* 1815–1773 BCE), originating from an Amorite dynasty. Shamshi-Addu took Mari and formed a large kingdom in northern Mesopotamia. Importing tin and acquiring silver, he resumed the trade with Anatolia to his advantage, probably on a different basis compared with the Assyrian period, as the creation of a post of "merchant controller" shows. Around 1800, "11,000 pounds of tin were deposited in the palace storehouse of Mari" (Silver 1995: 142). The kingdom seems to have had links to Dilmun. The son of Shamshi-Addu sent a caravan from Mari to Dilmun (Leemans 1960: 141). Around 1765, the Elamites, helped by Babylon, seized Eshnunna. The city was then controlled by Hammurabi (*c.* 1761).

of tin from the east certainly played a role in the collapse of the Assyrian networks. This corresponds to the instability and upheaval that affected Central Asia at this time.

From Central Asia to South Asia: The Expansion of the Bactria–Margiana Archaeological Complex (BMAC)

In the steppes of Central Asia, the growing mobility of pastoralist-farmers of the Andronovo and post-Andronovo complexes corresponds to the development of metallurgical activities and of exchange networks, which extended toward the Tarim and East Asia on the one side, Margiana and Bactria on the other. Contacts between farmers and the steppe intensified during the early second millennium BCE. Near Samarkand, the site of Tugai has yielded ceramics from the Petrovka culture belonging to the Androvovo complex (Kuzmina 2007: 463) and the Zeravshan valley shows contacts with the steppes. In the region of Bukhara, the Zaman-Baba culture which was formed during that period (late third – early second millennium BCE) also reveals interactions between farmers and peoples from the steppe. Groups from the Zaman-Baba culture seem to have moved eastward toward the Tarim.

The period from the twentieth to the eighteenth century BCE saw both an "explosive dispersion" of the Bactria–Margiana Complex (Hiebert 1994) and the collapse of the Indus civilization, along with the dislocation of the Mesopotamia–Persian Gulf–Iran–Indus world-system, marked by the abandonment of Indus cities such as Mohenjo-daro around 1900 BCE and a general decline of urbanization in Iran. Against a background of environmental crisis, Bactrians and populations south of the Caspian Sea took control of the southern trade routes, linking Central Asia, the Indus, Elam, and Mesopotamia.

The causes of the urban collapse in the Indus valley are still being debated: the aridification of the climate (Staubwasser et al. 2003; Gupta et al. 2005), the impact of cities on the environment (deforestation[70] and overgrazing), ecological imbalances, tectonic movements, and a downturn in long-distance trade probably had combined effects (Possehl 2002a). It is obvious that during the period c. 2000 BCE many regions were affected by a phase of weak monsoons in the Indian Ocean, which led to processes of aridification. Climatic changes also affected the North Atlantic during the same period.[71] Around 1800 BCE, contacts appear to have been practically cut off between Mesopotamia and the Indus region.[72] Some trade, however, was maintained along the

---

[70] Chew 2001: 27–29. For the construction of houses, however, baked bricks were only in common use at certain sites such as Mohenjo-daro, Rakhi Garhi, and Harappa (Possehl 2002a: 66, 72, 107–108). Baked bricks were also used for wells, some city walls, and the great baths, as well as for public and private drains, in streets and houses.

[71] See Cullen et al. 2000, for western Asia, Thompson et al. 2002, for East Africa, An et al. 2005, for North China, and Nadis 2001, for the North Atlantic.

[72] Ratnagar (2001a: 116) proposes 1800–1700 as the "terminal" period for these contacts. Texts from the Isin-Larsa period still refer to the importation of carnelian, ivory, and lapis lazuli, coming from Dilmun. Crete, during the Middle Minoan III (late eighteenth century BCE, according to Manning and Ramsey 2003), yielded beads of the Harappan type.

coasts of Gujarat,[73] and cultivated plants were brought from Africa into India, probably via southern Arabia (see below). Climatic deterioration in India led to increased nomadic pastoralism,[74] an abandonment of agricultural settlements and urban decline. There were also marked changes in agriculture, with new strategies of subsistence involving the increased use of Asian cereals – cultivated during summer – and decentralization (Madella and Fuller 2006: 1298).

The influx of Indo-Europeans (Hiebert 1994; Parpola 2002) seems also to have played a crucial role in the collapse of the Indus civilization and in changes to exchange networks. During the late third and early second millennia, bearers of the Margiana–Bactria culture, whose elite may have spoken a Proto-Aryan language, moved toward Turkmenistan, Tajikistan, Iran, southern Afghanistan, and from there toward the Indus valley. The flowering of agriculture in the delta of the Amu Darya (Tazabagyab culture, from *c.* 1900 BCE) also reveals the existence of migrations or the diffusion of cultural influences from west to east (Koryakova and Epimakhov 2007: 112) and from south to north (Kohl 2007: 192).

Trade routes through northern Iran seem to have been active in this period. Demand for tin from Afghanistan or from the Samarkand region by Assyrian merchants gave rise to contacts between the BMAC and northern Mesopotamia, with networks extending towards the Mediterranean. They probably explain the Syrian and Egyptian cultural influences noted in the BMAC area. Amiet (1986: 195ff.) has thus related Bactrian mirrors with anthropomorphic handles to Egyptian forms. Moreover, "the winged disc that appeared in Syria under Egyptian influence is also found in Bactria." Masculine figurines of the BMAC may have links to the myth of Humbaba, the giant guarding the "Cedar Forest" in the myth of Gilgamesh (Amiet 1986: 200). Iron beads found in a tomb at Namazga Tepe (VI) reveal influences from Anatolia.[75] Conversely, a Syrian seal dated to 1800 BCE features a Bactrian camel. The motif of a kneeling god with the head of a bird of prey is attested both in the BMAC and in Syria during the early second millennium (Amiet 1986: 198).

In addition, interactions between the BMAC and the Persian Gulf – through Iran or the Indus valley – are clearly visible. In Central Asia, one finds items called "handled weights" made of chlorite probably originating from Iran,[76] chlorite vessels of the *série récente* type from Oman, and bowls produced in southern Iran (Potts 2003c).

---

[73] The site of Mahegam contains remains dated to 1900–1600 BCE. It could correspond to the port of Bhrgu-kaccha mentioned in the *Mahābhārata* (Deloche 2001: 324).

[74] Nevertheless, Possehl (2002a: 243) notes an increasing number of sites in regions where populations practiced dry agriculture (Punjab, Haryana, northern Rajasthan). This author posits a crisis at the origin of the decline seen within the sociocultural Indus system itself (2002a: 244), whose organization, however, remains largely unknown to us.

[75] The dating of the Namazga VI period remains debated: 2000/1900–1700, or 1700–1500. The first dating appears more probable. However, Francfort gives Namazga VI as contemporary with Bostan VI (Bactria), which ended around 1700/1600 (2001b: 221, 2005: 296). Wheel-thrown ceramics of the Namazga VI type have been unearthed in the far north, for example at Pavlovka, in northern Kazakhstan (Anthony 2007: 450).

[76] A so-called "handled weight" has been found at Soch and there are recent finds at Jiroft (Madjizadeh 2003: 136; Aruz 2003b: 325ff.). A "weight" of this type, coming probably from Iran, has been excavated at Ur in a context dated to *c.* 2500 BCE (see British Museum WA 91700). A "handled weight" has been unearthed at Susa level II, dated to the late fourth millennium (Amiet 1986: 241).

The presence of objects characteristic of the BMAC reflects the expansion of this culture, during the Late Namazga V and Namazga VI phases of Turkmenistan, at the site of Mundigak (V) and in the Fullol hoard (Afghanistan), at Tepe Hissar (IIIC), Tureng Tepe (IIIC2), Susa, Shahdad, Shar-i Sokhta, and Tepe Yahya in Iran, at Khurab, Mehi, Kulli, Shahi Tump in Baluchistan, at sites in the Indus valley, and even in the Persian Gulf (Bahrain, Oman). These objects include stone colonnettes (elements of the religious system), stone "scepters," ceremonial axes, discs, compartmented seals, stepped seals and beads, pins with decorated heads, bronze mirrors with anthropomorphic handles,[77] flasks, stemmed cups, conical vessels, composite feminine statuettes wearing *kaunakes* (a garment of Mesopotamian origin), small trumpets, grey ceramics, and so forth.[78] In a general way, the production of chlorite artifacts (boxes, flasks . . .) in the BMAC was probably influenced by stone working from southern Iran, but the forms adopted and the incised design are particular. Shell beads "of Indo-Pacific origins" have been discovered, for example at Togolok 21 and Gonur, as well as shell beads of Mediterranean origin (Hiebert 1994: 153). The discovery of an ivory comb decorated with an incised tulip – a flower from Central Asia – at Tell Abraq, in the United Arab Emirates, has already been mentioned (see above). Horse bones excavated at Godin Tepe are dated to 2000 BCE.

Parpola distinguishes several waves of migrants coming from Central Asia, who entered Margiana and Bactria during the late third and early second millennia. After the arrival of Proto-Aryans (Indo-Iranians) – who formed the first elite of the BMAC – around 1900 BCE, newcomers, Proto-Indo-Aryans, would have replaced this elite; the Proto-Aryans then moved to Iran, the Indus, and the Ganges valley. The Indo-Iranians of the BMAC thus infiltrated the elite of the Indus culture during the early second millennium. The first Proto-Indo-Aryans of Margiana–Bactria

[77] The handle represents a human body. These mirrors probably contained a high proportion of tin, for the requisite shine and polish (Ratnagar 2001a: 114). The shape of mirrors with anthropomorphic handles from the BMAC could ultimately be of Syrian and Egyptian origin (Parpola 2002: 244, 265, and above). These mirrors were probably borrowed from western Asia and Elam. Amiet (1986, 1997), Francfort (2001a), and other authors have emphasized the importance of the cultural borrowings of the BMAC from the Elamite world. Sarianidi (2002: 100, 223) signals a series of parallels between Anatolia, Syria, northern Mesopotamia, and Bactria–Margiana. He interprets them as evidence that Indo-Europeans arrived from Anatolia or Syria into Margiana, through Iran, which seems less likely than Indo-European intrusions, from Central Asia into Margiana–Bactria, later followed by contacts with western Asia through Iran.

[78] Compartmented seals already had a long history: they appeared at Mehrgarh during the fourth millennium, at Shahi Tump (Makran) and in southern Turkmenistan in the early third millennium, then at Shar-i Sokhta during the first half of the third millennium, in the Nal culture (Baluchistan) (c. 2800), at Tepe Yahya IVB, and during the Namazga V phase of Turkmenistan (second half of the third millennium) (Pittman 2001a: 238; Winkelmann 2008: 187). Crenellated seals of the BMAC type have been found in the Indus valley, in Bahrain, and at Mari. On ceremonial axes, see Parpola 2002: 296ff. Small trumpets characteristic of the BMAC (five at Gonur . . .) have been found in Iran (beginning of the second millennium): at Tepe Hissar (two silver trumpets and one gold trumpet), at Shahdad (a copper trumpet), and at Astrabad (Tureng Tepe). Lawergren (2003a: 88ff.) interprets them as ritual instruments imitating the calls of hunted animals (deer?), and he connects them to ancient Zoroastrian texts which speak of "trumpets that control animals and humans." Parpola suggests that these instruments were used during the second millennium BCE for training horses, but their sound is rather weak. Greyware ceramics known in the BMAC for period 2 (after 2000 BCE) appeared at Tureng Tepe and Hissar IIIC (Hiebert 1994: 85, 177; Kohl 1995: 1061–1064; Sergent 1997: 179ff.; Tosi and Lamberg-Karlovsky 2003: 350).

may then in their turn have entered the Indus River valley during the nineteenth and eighteenth centuries, followed around the middle of the second millennium by the "Rig-Vedic Proto-Indo-Aryans" (see below).

"There was no true military conquest" of the Indus by the Indo-Iranians, "but the expansion of the latter, by disrupting the networks constituting the 'Indo-Iranian interface' led to the decline of the cities and opened up the Indian plains to various populations, . . . who finally took the upper hand at the linguistic and cultural levels" (Sergent 1997: 153).[79] It is interesting to note that for the early second millennium, the Harappan "colony" of Shortugai, in Bactria, presents BMAC assemblage and no longer shows links with the Indus. Artifacts from the steppes, of the Fedorovo type, also appear at this site (Kuzmina 2007: 464; Francfort 1989). "The presence of BMAC artifacts in the upper levels of Mohenjo-daro and Chanhu-daro, which date to circa 2000 BC, seems to indicate the penetration of the BMAC peoples into the [Indian] Subcontinent. [Conversely], there is little if any Indus material in the BMAC homelands" (Possehl 2002a: 231). Ivory worked in Bactria–Margiana, however, is of Indian origin. BMAC assemblages have been discovered at Quetta (treasure, *c.* 2000 BCE) and Damb Sadaat (Quetta valley), as well as at the sites of Sibri and Mehrgarh VIII (early second millennium).[80] Jhukar (north of Mohenjo-daro) has yielded objects showing Margian–Bactrian and/or Iranian affinities.[81] The recent discovery of a "steatite wig" at Harappa in a level dated to 2000–1900 BCE also indicates links with the BMAC, where composite stone statuettes are well known, but some characteristics of the object are strictly Indusian, revealing cultural syncretism (Meadow 2002). "Various authors have considered the bearers of the cemetery H culture [at Harappa] as Aryans" (Sergent 1997: 184–185, 225).[82] Cremation of the deceased appeared in this culture. Seals of the BMAC type have been unearthed in the Indus River valley during the Jhukar period (1900–1500), but also at Somanath, in Gujarat, such as seals with geometric motifs, square seals with stepped crenellations, featuring

[79] The phrase "Indo-Iranian interface" has been used by J.-F. Jarrige to designate the area peripheral to the Iranian plateau, an area unified by exchange networks. It seems today that infiltrations of migrants from Margiana and Bactria indeed accompanied the Harappan decline. The question of a possible link between the expansion of the Bactrian culture and the spread of Indo-European languages, however, remains controversial. Jarrige (1988) notes "the appearance of new elites" "at the Indo-Iranian borders around 2000 BC," and the existence of a culture common to Bactria, southern Turkmenistan, Iran, and Baluchistan, but he does not link these developments to a process of conquest or to the Indo-Europeans (see Sergent 1997: 154). Possehl does not exclude the presence of Indo-Europeans in the Harappan culture, but they were certainly not Aryans, speakers of Vedic Sanskrit. The latter may have entered the Indian subcontinent while "speakers of other Indo-European languages were in the Near East early in the second millennium" (Possehl 2002a: 249). Vedic texts mention the capture, by the Indo-Aryans, of fortresses (*pur*) inhabited by dark-skinned people, the Dasa or Dasyu.

[80] Jarrige 1985. On the treasure of Quetta, Possehl, 2002a: 232–233.

[81] Sergent 1997: 227. The "Jhukar Phase" is dated to 1900–1700 BCE, the phase of cemetery H 1900–1500 BCE, and the period IV of the Swāt valley 1650–1300 BCE (Possehl 2002a: 29). Chanhu-daro and Amri represent key sites of the Jhukar culture. On the similarities of the seals of the Jhukar culture and the BMAC, see E. C. L. During Caspers 1994. Some seals from Shar i-Sokhta are related to the BMAC.

[82] Pottier (1984) sees "evidence of colonization at the sites of Sibri and Mehrgarh VIII." Finds in the oldest part of cemetery H have sometimes been connected to assemblages found in Baluchistan. Baluchistan itself shows objects coming from Central Asia (Kuzmina 2007: 343).

an eagle.[83] The motif on funerary urns of the cemetery H at Harappa of a peacock "carrying people in its stomach to the stars" may also originate in the BMAC and prefigure the Iranian phoenix (Parpola 2002: 303ff.).[84] Moreover, we see the appearance of cylinder seals of the BMAC type, with militaristic motifs, "which however are carved in the Harappan style and carry Indus script with a native Harappan sign sequence" (Parpola 2002: 241, and 244, 259). For Mohenjo-daro (2000 BCE), BMAC material also comprises animal-headed pins, cosmetics bottles, a silver vase, an axe . . . Possehl signals the discovery at Sibri of a copper axe similar to exemplars known in the BMAC of northern Afghanistan, with parallels at Hissar and "farther afield, in Early Minoan II and Troy II" (Possehl 2002a: 227, 232). Ceramics discovered at Djarkutan show similarities with pottery found in Baluchistan and at Mundigak V–VI (c. eighteenth century BCE?), as well as at Pirak and the southern Indus region (Tulamba, Dur-khan, Patami-Damb) (Franke-Vogt 2001; Kuzmina 2008: 86). Figurines of horses found at Pirak (IB, II, and III) (from 1800 BCE?),[85] on a route linking Mundigak and the Indus, could be evidence for the arrival of Indo-Europeans, but the systematic link suggested by some scholars between the presence of horses and Indo-Europeans appears debatable.[86]

The whole of urban life seems to have disintegrated in eastern Iran, in the Indus, then in Bactria itself, between the twentieth and eighteenth/seventeenth centuries BCE. As already mentioned, the urban decline in Turkmenistan and on the Iranian plateau occurred prior to this period. In addition, the chronologies of the various sites remain problematic.[87] In Iran, Shar-i Sokhta "collapsed suddenly at the end of the 3rd millennium."[88] Mundigak was temporarily abandoned between phases IV and V (around

[83] During Caspers (1994) emphasizes that the eagle motif was new in the Indus. Parpola has drawn a parallel between the figure of the eagle with its wings spread (featured on BMAC and Late Harappan seals) and the shape of the Vedic fire-altar. This motif of the eagle was present in Iran during the third millennium (see Winkelmann 2008: 189, 196).

[84] The peacock itself clearly has an Indian origin (see Witzel 2004: 160).

[85] Francfort (2005: 263 n. 55, 274), following Jarrige and Santoni (1979), gives a date c. 1700. Franke-Vogt gives more recent dates for Pirak (1700 for Pirak I, 1300 for Pirak II).

[86] Francfort 2005: 275. At Pirak, Jarrige et al. (1979: 97) note "the presence of a population originating in Central Asia" but they do not connect this population to Indo-Europeans, unlike Parpola (1994a: 155–159). Pirak also yielded figurines of camels. We must recall here that one of the possible original languages of the BMAC may have been Macro-Caucasian. Horses may have been introduced earlier if the identifications of horses in assemblages of Lothal, Kuntasi, and Shirkapur (Gujarat) in the Mature Harappan phase can be accepted (Thomas and Joglekar 1994; Bökönyi 1997). Various Indian scholars, moreover, claim that the spoked-wheel chariot was present during the Mature Harappan period, for example at Kalibangan, Rakhi Garhi, and Banawali (Lal 2002). Other archaeologists refute the identification and/or the dating of the finds involving horses, or the representation of the spoked wheel (Possehl 2002a: 227).

[87] Tosi (2001: 143) places the decline of the cities of Iran and southern Central Asia (Turkmenistan) between 2200 and 2000 BCE; conversely, relations between the Indus and Mesopotamia were at their peak during this period. The forays of BMAC peoples probably did not affect the various regions in the same way. There may have been other reasons for the collapses that we observe at this time.

[88] Sarianidi 1996: 236. The occupation of the "Burnt Building" of Shar-i Sokhta (IV) may be dated to 2200–2000 BCE (Potts 2001: 200; Shirazi 2007). On readjustments of the chronologies, see Potts 2003a (Shar-i Sokhta IV = Bampur V–VI = 2100–1900 or rather 2200–2000 BCE); Salvatori and Tosi 2005; Shirazi 2007. J.-L. Huot (2004, I: 201), however, places Bampur V–VI prior to 2500 BCE, and thus puts the abandonment of Shar-i Sokhta (IV) as early as this period. This chronology has not been widely adopted by researchers.

2300/2200 BCE), and at last progressively abandoned during period VI (seventeenth century BCE?) (Sarianidi 1996: 236). Tepe Hissar experienced a period of abandonment. Anshan was largely empty after the seventeenth century. The discontinuation of trade and the over-population of cities that had to absorb migrants and refugees chased from their lands because of increased aridity and insecurity led to the inexorable decline of the Indus cities, a regional fragmentation and the shift to more rural cultures, often mixing local patterns and elements linked to Central Asia. Mohenjo-daro was deserted around 1900 BCE. At this time – which corresponds to the period of cemetery H – "the size and complexity of Harappa was reduced": this settlement was not a city anymore. There was no trace of long-distance trade (seals were now absent, as well as lapis lazuli). "Important [other] Indus settlements including Chanhu-daro, Kot Diji, Balakot, Allahdino, Kulli, Mehi, Nindowari, Kalibangan, Nausharo, Ropar, Surkotada, Dholavira, Desalpur and Lothal" were abandoned or severely depopulated (Possehl 2002a: 237). Gujarat also shows evidence of de-urbanization from 1900, a process accompanied by the development of semi-nomadism, which reflected growing aridity.[89] Economic breakdown went along with the disappearance of writing, which reveals a significant connection between writing and an ideological, economic, and political system. Conversely, one notes an increasing number of settlements in eastern Punjab, Haryana, western Uttar Pradesh, and northern Rajasthan. In the southern Deccan ("Southern Neolithic"), as well, we observe an increased number of villages of sedentary farmers from 2200 BCE onward (Fuller 2006a: 52).

The urban culture of Margiana–Bactria itself disappeared around 1700 or slightly later (between 1700 and 1500), the victim of increasing incursions by populations from the steppes: Iranian speakers for Sergent, "Rig-Vedic Indo-Aryans" according to Parpola, Indo-Iranians and Indo-Aryans according to Francfort.[90] In Sistan, the site of Shar-i Sokhta, inhabited again since c. 1850, was abandoned around 1700 BCE (Salvatori and Tosi 2005). Anthony (2002) also establishes a link between the collapse of the cities of the BMAC during the seventeenth–sixteenth centuries, the appearance of Indo-Aryan warriors in Mitanni in the same period and the expansion of pastoralist economies in South Asia. Long-distance exchanges involving southern Central Asia all but stopped at this time. However, uncertainty remains about the dating of the de-urbanization of the Bactria–Margiana Complex and the processes by which it occurred. The urban phase of Gonur might have ended in the twenty-first century BCE, whereas there were still major sites in Bactria (Djarkutan, Farukhabad) during the first half of the second millennium. The influx of people from the steppes increased just

---

[89] Sonawane 2000: 142–143. The "post-urban Harappan phase" in Gujarat is dated to 1900–1400 BCE. Imports from Sind disappeared, revealing a decline in exchanges. The cubic Harappan weights were replaced by other types of weights. At Lothal, the acropolis, the entrepôt, and tank were abandoned. Dholavira became a village.

[90] Sergent 1997: 229; Parpola 2002: 245; Francfort 2005: 257. As already mentioned, according to Sergent (1997: 176), the Iranian speakers originated from the so-called "Andronovo culture," which, he considers, spread out "during the 3rd millennium" (?) from the Urals to northern Kazakhstan (it then reached "the Ob and Yenissei rivers, Pamir and Sin-Kiang" during the second millennium). As already noted, however, there was no true "Andronovo culture." Movements of Iranian speakers immediately followed those of Indian groups: "We have indications of Iranian inflows into India as early as the ancient Indian period" (Sergent 1997: 229). An influence by Andronovo communities can be noted in the region of Samarkand (a region with tin-bearing deposits) "from 1900 BC" (Boroffka et al. 2002).

before the middle of the second millennium, with the arrival of populations originating from the Amu Darya delta and other regions.[91]

In fact, the whole of Eurasia was destabilized at the beginning of the second millennium, by climatic changes and population migrations. The war chariot began its spectacular expansion at the beginning of the second millennium in the Eurasian steppes, western Asia, and western Europe. In Iran, tombs with chariots drawn by horses dated to the early second millennium have been discovered at Susa (Francfort 2005: 273 n91).[92] This expansion went along with a proliferation of new types of weapons (composite bow, long sword, lance) and by the appearance of warrior aristocracies as well as social and religious concepts that can be observed from India to Scandinavia (Kristiansen 2007: 156). Climate change and demographic pressure, however, are not the only factors that explain the invention of the spoked wheel chariot. It can be seen as resulting from "continuing interaction in the contact-zone between Near Eastern urbanism and the steppes":[93] it would thus be the product of the encounter between "Mesopotamian military needs and steppe resources and expertise" (Sherratt and Sherratt 2001: 25).[94] For some authors, the practice of horseback riding around the end of the third millennium BCE allowed for the extension of herding;[95] however, horseback riding was largely adopted only at the close of the second millennium; at this time, also, cattle became more important.

[91] Kohl 2007: 202, 208, 211. Hiebert (2002: 243ff.) notes the presence of assemblages from the steppes at sites of the "post-BMAC" period (1800–1500 BCE).

[92] We should recall that the first mention of the horse in Mesopotamia dates from the twenty-first century BCE, in a hymn by Shulgi, king of the Third Dynasty of Ur, but a sculpture found in Syria depicting a horse goes back to an earlier date (see above). A representation of a spoked wheel is known from the Ur III period. A tablet dating to the reign of Shu-Sin, the last emperor of Ur, bears the imprint of a cylinder seal showing a man riding a horse (Oates 2003: 119). However, of 191 figurines of equids found at Tell Brak, at the turn of the third and second millennia, only four might depict a horse (Oates 2001). Remains of horses are rare during the early second millennium (Tell Leilan, Brak, Godin Tepe). The horse could have been introduced slightly later by Hurrites, with whom Indo-Aryan elements from the south of the Caspian Sea became integrated around the seventeenth century BCE (Sergent 1997: 221) (see below). "Horse domestication and horseback riding came from the culture of the Steppes, to which the Bactrian civilization is related, for its main cultural features" (Sergent 1997: 221). According to Kohl (2002: 162), "the riding of horses and their harnessing for lighter vehicles [lighter than the ancient carts] may have begun in the Don-Volga forest-steppe zone, in the second part of the 3rd millennium." As Kohl points out, however, it is perhaps vain to seek a precise geographic origin for this invention, which obviously spread very quickly. The propositions of Di Cosmo on the one hand, and of Sherratt and Sherratt on the other, however, help clarify the process of invention and diffusion.

[93] "State-organized Mesopotamian societies experimented with the harnessing of local equids for warfare, but steppe groups found the solution to this problem by developing a practical method for yoking horses and controlling driven animals with bridle-bits" (Sherratt and Sherratt 2001: 25).

[94] The use of war chariots drawn by horses seems to have preceded the military use of horseback riding (Renfrew 2002: 5). This may have been the first military response of the populations of the steppes to a crisis situation. Cf. Di Cosmo 1999a. According to Drews (2004), the military use of mounted cavalry developed only later, around 1000 BCE.

[95] Mesopotamian texts of the end of the third millennium refer to horseback riding; at the time of the Ur III Empire, the horse was called a "mountain donkey" (Oates 2003: 117). The horse was slow to become a royal attribute: a king of Mari, c. 1800 BCE, was advised not to ride a horse, a practice "unworthy of a king" (Oates 2003: 117). Horseback riding may have been practiced by the Amorites in the early second millennium (Oates 2003: 118).

Inflows of populations from the "Central Asian sphere" seem to have "expelled people of the Iranian plateau, who moved towards Mesopotamia ... or towards Shimashki (Tukrish), then ... Indo-Aryan *avants-gardes* mingled with other people, such as the Kassites" (Sergent 1997: 198).[96] Hurrites (already settled in the Upper Tigris valley during the third millennium, perhaps during the twenty-fourth century BCE)[97] and Kassites (who originated from the Zagros)[98] included Indo-European and "more precisely [Proto]-Indian elements."[99] These [Proto]-Indian elements probably came from the Gorgan plain south of the Caspian Sea. Between the eighteenth and fifteenth centuries, princes with Indo-Aryan names took control of towns in Syria and Palestine. As a continuation of these movements, Hyksos (Canaanite Semites, who may also have included Hurrites) entered Egypt during the same period (*c.* 1780 BCE). The Hyksos arrival, however, "was neither a mass movement nor a military conquest" (Liverani 2014: 237).

During the pivotal period between the twentieth and eighteenth centuries, despite flourishing trade in the western Persian Gulf during the Isin-Larsa period – with Bahrain playing a significant role – we observe a progressive transfer of Mesopotamia's vital centers toward the north. The political integration attempted by Hammurabi (1792–1750) (MC) from Babylon was indicative of the changes that occurred at this time. Babylon, however, connected the areas of the Mediterranean Sea and the Persian Gulf only briefly. The disintegration of networks in Iran and in India went along with a decrease in trade that partly explains the decline of Babylonia after Hammurabi. In the Gulf, Qala'at al-Baḥrayn was abandoned around 1750.[100] The kings of Elam, however, remained powerful even after their defeat by Zimri-Lim and Hammurabi in 1764; their fall became evident later, during the seventeenth century BCE.

[96] Shimashki was a kingdom of the Iranian plateau that disappeared between the third and the second millennia BCE, replaced by the Tukrish entity. Henning suggests a hypothetical connection of Tukrish with the term *Toχri*, the name used by the Uighurs for the Tocharians living in the north of the Tarim around 800 CE. The Greeks in the first century BCE (Strabo) name a population of Central Asia Tokharoi. Cf. also the Sanskrit *Tukhāra-*. Ptolemy mentions several populations in eastern Central Asia whose names appear to be related (Thaugouroi, Taokriaioi, Taguouraioi) (Mallory and Mair 2000: 281). Henning also proposes an improbable connection between Guti, the name of a population, and Kuci (or **kusi*), the name of a state of the region of Kuchā (first millennium CE).

[97] The Hurrian language could be related to relic languages of Dagestan. The arrival of Hurrian-speaking groups may correspond to an extension of the bronze culture of Transcaucasia during the third millennium (Kohl 1995: 1054).

[98] Harmatta (1996) has suggested that the center of origin of the Kassites was located within the Kel'teminar culture, which he places in a territory extending from the Caspian Sea to Tajikistan, whence they would have been pushed toward the southwest by migrations of Proto-Indians.

[99] Sergent 1997: 198. The first Kassite influx can be dated to *c.* 1740 BCE (see below). The Hittite, Kassite, and Egyptian documents mention names of gods and persons of Indo-Aryan origin. The presence of Indo-Aryans is notable from the fifteenth to the fourteenth century in the Mitanni kingdom (Sergent 1997: 203ff.). Tombs of the kurgan type have been described in Syria and in Palestine between the nineteenth and seventeenth centuries. Sergent notes "indicators to an Indian substrate in Iran" (1997: 233). Cf. also Harmatta 1996: 372.

[100] The Barbar temple was abandoned soon afterward. See Crawford 1998: 153. It was not, however, a complete decline: some continuity can be perceived between the Early Dilmun period and the Kassite period.

Dislocations and Regional Restructuring from the Eighteenth Century BCE

The Old Babylonian Period (1800–1595 BCE [MC])[101]

> Anu and Enlil called by name, me Hammurabi, the dutiful prince who fears
> the gods, to bring about the rule of righteousness in the land, to destroy the
> wicked and the evil-doers; so that the strong should not harm the weak.
> (Prologue of the "Hammurabi Code")

In Lower Mesopotamia, an Amorite dynasty settled at Babylon around 1800, and the Amorites founded new cities. Assuming a Sumero-Akkadian heritage, Hammurabi (1792–1750?)[102] brought together the different city-states under his tutelage. The empire was more a confederation of states than a centralized state. Babylon, the capital, may have had about 65,000 inhabitants, according to Morris (2013: 153), but this estimate may be too low. The Hammurabi code mentions the activities of a private sector and the role of the state; the latter maintained irrigation canals, provided loans, and controlled landownership. As was the case during the Isin-Larsa period, the state sector was partially privatized. Salaried employment developed, with fluctuating wage rates being observed.[103] Part of the royal lands was rented out, and another part was granted to officials, thus encouraging an expansion of private landed property. Van de Mieroop points out that "institutions needed to turn the agricultural yield into silver" (2002: 83). Thus, wool was distributed to private entrepreneurs, who paid it back later in silver (Van de Mieroop 2002: 165–166).

Lands granted or leased to tenant farmers "over time, became heritable" (Bogaert 1966: 46). It was forbidden (under Hammurabi's laws) for military officials to pledge the lands that had been granted to them, which shows the importance of private creditors (contrary to the opinion of Hudson 2002). Texts demonstrate the existence of a land market with an overall increase in sales during the Old Babylonian period (Diakonoff 1996: 57). We have clues indicating the existence of a land market, with variations in prices during the second millennium at Nippur and Nuzi (it appears that the ruler at Nuzi forbade land sales around the middle of the second millennium; sales, however, went on, in a disguised way) (Silver 1995: 123, 124, 197). A letter from Mari refers to the complaint of a man concerning land that his father had bought (Heimpel 1997: 65 n. 5; Silver 2007a: 102). There may have been a difference, as had been the case in earlier times, between northern and southern Babylonia, with private property being more developed in the north (Renger 1995: 296, 301; Silver 2002).

A debtor unable to reimburse a debt was forced to dispose of his land, if he owned any, and could lose his status and become a slave. Hammurabi and his successors ordered debt cancellations in agriculture several times (according to Hudson [2002: 28], cancellations during the second millennium were not related to commerce); these decisions shed light on the recurrent problem of debt that affected part of the

---

[101] Or 1704–1499 (ultra-short chronology).

[102] 1696–1654 in the ultra-short chronology proposed by Gasche *et al.* 1998.

[103] See texts from Sippar (Silver 1995: 138). Wages were paid with barley, silver or copper. Even people requisitioned for corvées received a salary.

population (Van de Mieroop 2004: 88, 108; Charpin 2005: 32). The Hammurabi Code reveals that "property rights were recognized and protected and contract security well established." Laws fixed "the divison of profits or losses in a commercial partnership, and the relation and settlement of accounts between a capitalist-trader and his traveling agent" (Veenhof 1997: 344) (most of the reported business activities were already attested in the Assyrian trade in Anatolia during the early second millennium). Laws limited the amount of the interest rates, as well as some prices, fixed the amount of various rents, and established a salary scale, with salaries varying according to the tasks performed. Hammurabi's laws thus reflect a growing economic freedom, the negative effects of which they seek to contain. At the same time, they express the social difficulties within the empire.

Texts from Larsa mention private granaries (this is confirmed by paragraphs 120 and 121 of Hammurabi's Code), and reveal the existence of a grain market (Silver 2007a: 103). Whereas Polanyi has argued that Babylonia had neither market places nor a system of markets of any kind, the documents at our disposal show the opposite (Powell 1999: 10). "At the going market price" (*machīrat illaku*) "occurs frequently in texts of the Old Babylonian period" (Silver 2007a: 101). An "agent of the quay" was responsible for transactions and the proper functioning of the market (Monroe 2005: 163). One notes the growing economic significance of slaves, who were often prisoners of war. Their price seems to have varied from 20 to 90 shekels of silver (by comparison, it cost "around 10 shekels a year to hire a laborer") (McIntosh 2005: 167).

Textiles and other goods were produced for the market. There was also a market for services[104] and a labor market, as illustrated by the term *agāru*, "hired man or woman" (*CAD* entry *agāru* 1a, Silver 1995: 136).[105] Farber (1978) documents wages for hired labor. Interestingly, during Hammurabi's reign, "prices were lower than previously," but "there appears to be an increase in the mean wage paid in both silver and barley" (Farber 1978: 39). Loans granted by institutions or individuals ensured the availability of a labor force otherwise in short supply. The price of wool rose between the beginning of the second millennium and the Old Babylonian period (Warburton 2003: 59), but during the Babylonian period, it "remained stable across many generations, whereas other prices fluctuated" (Algaze 2008: 21).

Commerce appears to have been led by merchants (*tamkāru*) who worked for the state, or developed their own businesses. Administrative texts from Mari reveal the existence of a class of merchants – often foreigners – who were independent of the palace (Durand 1983: 515; Warburton 2003: 64). The Hammurabi Code indicates that some traders traveled abroad. In fact, merchants from Sippar were at the head of *kārum* trading posts at Mari and in other places. Great merchants, also "bankers," undertook "[commercial and diplomatic] missions for the palace" (Glassner 2002a: 148). The *tamkāru* did not always travel with his merchandise (he then used a commercial agent). Brokerage and loans were practiced by temples and individuals (Charpin 2005: 25ff.). A *tamkāru* could finance commerce conducted by other merchants (this can also be observed earlier in Ur), and there was sometimes risk-sharing

---

[104] Michailidou (2005: 31–32) gives examples of washers of clothes or materials from Ur and Eshnunna.
[105] We find in a text: "If a man hires (another) man to supervise his field . . ." (*CAD*, 1964: 146).

among several investors. Under the name *tappûtum*, partnerships of the *commenda* type were set up especially in long-distance trade. "A stipulation in the laws of Hammurabi (*c.* 1750 BCE) reads: 'If a man gives silver to another man for investment in a partnership venture, before the god they shall equally divide the profit or loss'" (Wunsch 2010: 52). As was the case in Assyria a little earlier, we observe a symbiosis between the upper levels of the private sector and state institutions. The palace and temples still participated directly in trade in edible goods, but often employed independent *tamkāru* as agents. The right to sell surplus wool and cereals of the palace and other institutions was granted, in exchange for silver, to a merchant working with his own agents. The state levied taxes on trade and maintained some forms of administration, but exchanges were mainly in the hands of private entrepreneurs.[106] The merchants were organized in guilds "whose leader dealt with the king for the recovery of taxes and for specific purchases" (Margueron and Pfirsch 2001: 170).[107] Commercial practices and enrichment were placed under the monitoring and responsibility of divinities: "The honest merchant who pays loans by the [extra] (?) standard, thereby to make extra virtue, is pleasing to Shamash, He will grant him extra life, He will make (his) family numerous, he will acquire wealth, [his] seed will be perpetual as the waters of a perpetual spring" (Monroe 2005: 160; see Foster 1993: 541, lines 118–121).

Grain and above all silver – the quality of which was verified – were used as standards of value and means of exchange. The Hammurabi Code says that "the conversion rate of grains into silver is fixed by a royal order," but conversely, "a text from Mari dated to the eighteenth century seems to show that the market imposed its will on royal administration" (Glassner 2001: 65). Prices were more often indicated in silver than in barley; in addition, this metal was employed in long-distance trade. As was the case earlier in the Assyrian outposts of Cappadocia, sealed bags of silver are mentioned at Larsa, Babylon, and other cities.[108] A merchant complained in these terms: "You have sent me silver which is not fit for business transactions, I am returning the silver to

---

[106] The state, however, appointed "a trade inspector," who was in charge of the control and proper functioning of the *kārum*. There were also merchants who were completely independent from the palace (Michel 2001b).

[107] At Larsa, during the Old Babylonian Period, notes Silver (1995: 169), merchants were "involved in the collection and sale of tax goods"; they "also engaged in private commercial activities with the goods entrusted to them." Here we perceive the interpenetration of the public and private sectors. "The head of the *kārum*," writes Postgate (2003: 221), "acted as a regulator of the relations between the palace and . . . associations of merchants."

[108] Vargyas 2004: 116, after Stol 1982: 150. Le Rider (2001: 15) translates "with silver marked with seal," but he notes that this "mark" could refer either to the ingots themselves or to the bag that contained them. We experience the same difficulty in interpreting data for other places, for example for the Assyrian outposts of Cappadocia. Many authors reject the idea of a monetary use of sealed bags. In any case, some ingots had their silver content certified (see Silver 1995: 161). We find "purses" in Egypt during the eleventh century BCE. Silver wonders whether the bags tied behind the shoulders of merchants featuring in mastabas (notably in the tomb of Fetekta at Abusir) dated to the middle of the third millennium already represent purses (1995: 160). Ratnagar (2004: 290) notes significant amounts of Anatolian silver imported into southern Mesopotamia, and silver used as money by merchants of Dilmun, during the Larsa period, in connection with the development of Assyrian networks at Kanesh. In fact, Mesopotamia imported Anatolian silver as early as the Early Dynastic during the third millennium.

you. Send me the silver, (in) a sealed bag."[109] A bag of this type contained the treasure found at Larsa, dated to 1738 BCE. Bullae bore "the name of the ruler and that of the official responsible for the weighing" (Vargyas 2004). The documents from Larsa mention a "verifier in the weights office of Ur" who was also a tester: "it means there were weights and measures officers" (Le Rider 2001: 11). In addition, Silver has argued that metal marked by the authorities with a seal guaranteeing its purity may have been circulating. "F. Joannès has shown that Hammurabi paid/rewarded Mari's soldiers with (mysterious) *shamshātum* 'sun discs', gold rings, silver of 5 or 10 shekels, and *small pieces of silver impressed with a seal*" (*kaniktum*).[110] Joannès interprets these small stamped "coins" as decorations; they can be considered as a form of money, in the sense of means of payment of a social debt, and a form of exchangeable object (the value of these medals was clearly defined). Rings (*semeru*) were probably used as money: a priestess of Sippar "referred to land she bought as paid with her 'ring' (money)" (Snell 1995: 1488). "Let them be provided with gold bracelets and provide her with five minas of silver rings," says a letter from the Old Babylonian period. A document from the Royal Archives of Mari mentions "40 shekels of silver for (making) 8 silver rings of 5 shekels each." Another text evokes "1/2 mina of silver in pieces (and) one ring of ten shekels of silver (for the messenger)."[111] Variations in prices are seen over the long term during this Old Babylonian period.[112] It should be noted that it was possible to pay in silver for a service owed to the state.

Mari was destroyed by Hammurabi (1761 BCE), but various cities were active in the east–west and north–south exchanges involving Babylon: Emar, Eshnunna, and Sippar. Wine, wood, and slaves arrived in Babylonia from Syria and northern Mesopotamia (Michel 2001a: 198). Tin continued to be transported on routes coming from Iran. In the Urals, copper resources were intensively exploited at the site of Kargaly between 1700 and 1400 BCE (Hanks 2014: 1951).

Babylonia maintained active relations with Bahrain. This island yielded ceramics of the Babylonian and Kassite types. Sources indicate a trade between Dilmun and Mari (partly with caravans) during the first half of the eighteenth century, evidence of the extension of the Amorite culture from Syria to the Persian gulf.[113] After 1786 BCE, Babylonian sources do not mention any trade of copper from Dilmun, except for one text from 1745 BCE that indicates the importation of copper from Cyprus (Alashiya)

---

[109] *CAD*, VIII, entry *kaniktu* 2 (VAS 16 31: 17) (*CAD*, 1971: 150). In other texts one finds: "I needed (and asked you for in writing) ten shekels of silver under seal" (*CAD*, VIII, entry *kanku*, "sealed document"), "X silver which is placed in its sealed bag," "X silver *ka-ni-ik* PN" (*CAD*, VIII, entry *kanīku*, "sealed bag") (*CAD*, 1971: 153).

[110] Silver 2004a; Joannès 1989. Their nominal value was higher than their intrinsic value (Le Rider 2001: 19).

[111] *CAD*, XV, entry *semeru* (1984: 223), and XVII (2), entry *šibirtu* (1992: 379).

[112] Farber (1978) has shown the existence of parallel price movements and economic cycles. Hammurabi apparently did not try to fix prices (Postgate 1992: 194; Warburton 2003: 64), but his Code fixed norms, which could vary from one region to another. The text of the "Laws of Eshnunna," dated to the reign of King Dadusha (second half of the eighteenth century) gives the quantity of different goods equivalent to a silver shekel (see Joannès 2006a: 228).

[113] Glassner 2002b: 358. A text from Mari refers to the sending of leather sandals, leather bags, oil, sheep, to Dilmun, where a king is mentioned (Potts 1990: 228).

(earliest attestation) and from Dilmun (latest mention).[114] The role of Ur diminished after its capture by Hammurabi. At this time, we can see a decline in exchanges in the Persian Gulf and a restructuring of the networks, in which northern Mesopotamia and Anatolia took the upper hand.[115] A text from Mari refers to refined copper from Teima, "perhaps to be identified with Taymā' in northwestern Arabia. This would imply a trade between the Arabian Hijāz and the Middle Euphrates" as early as the early second millennium.[116] Ivory artifacts were still being imported from Dilmun at the beginning of the Old Babylonian period, but these imports stopped toward the end of the period, revealing an interruption of contacts between Bahrain and the Indus region. It should be noted, too, that after 1750 BCE lapis lazuli became rare in Mesopotamia:[117] Iran's inland routes provided only a weak connection between Mesopotamia and Central Asia, and the Indus was cut off from the most important exchange networks. Northern Mesopotamia was oriented toward the Mediterranean Sea and Anatolia at this time. According to a post-Hammurabi text, "tin was shipped from Babylon to regions to the northwest, and merchants from the northwest [Anatolians?] had settled at Babylon in order to secure this trade" (Leemans 1960: 129).

Trade was maintained in the Persian Gulf during the eighteenth century BCE, as revealed by the prosperity of Failaka at this time. Texts describe contacts between Dilmun and Susa, a city that was expanding. In Susa, an inscription reveals the building of a temple dedicated to Inzak, the main god of Dilmun. Dilmunites were still arriving in Babylonia at the time of King Samsuiluna, Hammurabi's son. A document dated to the reign of the Elamite king Kutir-Nahhunte (c. 1730–1700) indicates the delivery of 17.5 minas of silver in Susa by Dilmunites.[118]

Climatic deterioration increased internal imbalances and induced a state of continual crisis in the empire during the seventeenth century (MC). This was aggravated by inflows of Kassites, accompanied by Proto-Indian groups. The first Kassite invasion is dated to c. 1740 BCE. Another occurred in 1708. The invaders were militarily defeated, but many of them settled in Mesopotamia where they became workers and soldiers. A semi-independant Kassite state formed very early on in northwestern Babylonia (Van Koppen 2004: 22). One notes inflation in barley prices (Powell 1990:

---

[114] Potts 1990: 224, 226. "It is no coincidence," notes Kohl (2007: 232, quoting Weeks 2003: 17), "that [this] text bearing the first cuneiform reference to copper from Cyprus also contains the last reference to Dilmun copper."

[115] Potts 1990. Cleuziou and Méry (2002: 302), however, suggest that the exchange networks in the Gulf remained active not only during the Old Babylonian period but also afterward. Texts from Mari reveal a vibrant tin trade between Iran and northern Mesopotamia during the eighteenth century BCE. It should be noted that in texts from Nuzi dated to the fifteenth century "goods were priced in amounts of tin." During the Middle Assyrian period, this metal appears to have functioned as a monetary standard (Muhly 1995: 1509).

[116] Muhly 1995: 1510. Moorey (1994: 246) also notes that references to copper from Magan in the cuneiform texts stop exactly at a time when we have "the earliest surviving textual indications of copper from Alashiya (Cyprus) reaching Mari and Babylonia." Although the Cypriot copper mines were already exploited during the third millennium, Cyprus did not enter a vast interregional exchange system until the first half of the second millennium.

[117] Potts 1997; Ratnagar 2004: 330, after Moorey 1994: 245.

[118] Crawford 1996: 19. The significance of the relations between Susa and Dilmun during the nineteenth and eighteenth centuries BCE has already been mentioned.

92). The crisis in Babylonia occurred alongside a trade recession in the Gulf, where Dilmun collapsed (Edens 1992: 132; Crawford 1998: 153). In Central Asia, the BMAC culture itself disappeared around 1700 BCE. This decline partly explains the limited role of southern Mesopotamia during this period, but falling crop yields have also been put forward, due to soil salinization.[119] Drier conditions in Mesopotamia between 1800 and 1650 BCE may then have led to a depopulation of the southern part of this region.[120]

Post-Harappan India (1800–1300 BCE)

The urban decline of the Indus region was accompanied by some continuity of Harappan traditions, in the Ganges–Yamuna area and in any event in Gujarat. The latter region may have experienced a greater number of sites between 1700 and 1400 BCE, thanks to a population flow coming from the Indus, and due to a different occupation of the space. Rojdi was rebuilt at the time Mohenjo-daro was abandoned. During the Post-Harappan phase, however, Gujarat shows de-urbanization and economic decline, marked by a shift to semi-nomadism (see above, Sonawane 2000: 142). Significantly, carnelian or chalcedony etched beads disappeared from the archaeological contexts of eastern Arabia during the second millennium BCE; they would reappear only at the end of the first millennium BCE (De Waele and Haerinck 2006: 35–37). Gujarat sites from the Post-Harappan period do not show many exotic artifacts: there was no lapis lazuli, no gold, and not much ivory (Ratnagar 2004: 283). However, it is during this first half of the second millennium that African plants arrived in India (see below): long-distance contacts must therefore have been maintained – and even developed – with southern Arabia. According to S. R. Rao (1999), the underwater fortified city of Dwaraka, mentioned in the *Mahābhārata* as home to Krishna, is as old as the eighteenth century BCE, but this dating is uncertain. It was divided into six sectors, also fortified. Another settlement, also underwater, was in the neighborhood of Dwaraka, at Bet Dwaraka. Both sites have yielded remains of iron artifacts (nails . . .) thus indicating a later date. According to Rao, shards excavated at Dwaraka bear inscriptions in Late Harappan characters that Rao considers as transcribing "Early Indo-Aryan" (?). Finds of triangular stone anchors weighing from 100 to 150 kg show that large ships must have stopped at Dwaraka. The shape of these anchors, with three holes, recalls that of anchors from the Levant and Cyprus dating to the second half of the second millennium BCE. The destruction of sites by the sea may have occurred between 1500 and 1200 BCE.

The Ochre Colored Pottery culture (OCP) (Ganges–Yamuna plain) was contemporary with the Final Harappan culture phase and succeeded it, reaching the Ganges valley during the second millennium.[121] It has sometimes been related to an Aryan

---

[119] Ponting (1991: 72) has shown that by 1800 BC, crop yields were only about a third of those of the Early Dynastic period, and no wheat was grown in southern Mesopotamia.

[120] Crawford 1996: 18. An agricultural textbook dated around 1700 BCE recommends drainage systems and fallow periods in order to address problems of soil salinization. The problem was not new: similar measures had been implemented under Urukagina's reign in Lagash during the twenty-fourth century BCE (Silver 1995: 190).

[121] Ochre pottery is said to have been found in Rajasthan as early as the third millennium (Jodhpura). Some authors attribute an earlier date to the Ochre Colored Pottery culture, as well as to the caches of copper

current (Bellwood 2007). This expansion was accompanied by discoveries of caches of copper or bronze objects. The Harappan culture had developed bronze metallurgy, found at sites connected with the Indus, for example at Ahar, in Rajasthan, and later on in the Kayatha (Madhya Pradesh) and Malwa cultures (Madhya Pradesh and Maharashtra). One might ask whether demand from the Indus did not stimulate copper metallurgy in different regions of India around 1900–1800 BCE, when production in Oman was declining. During the second millennium, copper and bronze metallurgy was widespread in Pakistan and in central India; it appeared in eastern India during the second half of this millennium, in Bihar (site of Chirand), and Bengal (sites of Pandu Rajar Dhabi and Mahisadal). The presence of peculiar swords with antennae-shaped hilts, found in Afghanistan, Pakistan (Mehrgarh VIII, Sibri, Quetta), and in central India (site of Hallur ...), hints at migrations and interactions during the first half of the second millennium BCE. Linguists have proposed a common term for copper or bronze in the Munda, Khmer, and Old Mon languages, but metalworking traditions and artifacts "are quite different" in India and in Southeast Asia (Higham 1996a: 296).

Proto-Munda speakers (Austroasiatics) from the east probably entered India during the first half of the second millennium.[122] Some linguists and archaeobotanists, however, argue that Austroasiatics had been present in South Asia for a long time, including in the Indus valley. They consider that an eastward expansion gave birth to the Mon-Khmer languages. In this scenario – rejected by most researchers – Orissa is considered as the region of origin of the Proto-Munda language. Linked to the Neolithic of the Ganges, speakers of a "language X," perhaps Austroasiatic, are said to have occupied the Gangetic area and to have been responsible for the diffusion of rice, legumes, and cucurbits to northern India.[123] It is likely that the Proto-Munda

items. Bellwood (2007), for example, relates this culture – very hypothetically – to an expansion of Indo-European speakers into the Ganges valley as early as 3000 BCE.

[122] A term for "rice" can be reconstructed in Proto-Austroasiatic. For C. Higham (2004: 49), the splitting of the linguistic branches Munda and Mon-Khmer may go back to the sixth millennium BCE.

[123] Fuller 2007: 414; Southworth 2005; Witzel 2005. The idea of a "language X" has been advanced by C. Masica (1979). According to Witzel, a language other than language X influenced the Early Vedic Sanskrit in the Punjab region. For the Harappan period, we must remember that Witzel (2005), in Punjab, identifies a language – which he has termed Kubhā-Vipāś, or "Para-Munda" – belonging to the Austroasiatic family, whereas the speakers of the related but distinct Meluḥḥan language occupied the south of the Indus valley (see above). Donegan and Stampe (2004) have supported the idea of a Munda center of origin in South Asia. The relations between Munda and Mōn-Khmer languages remain a subject of controversy among linguists. Bellwood has adopted a different point of view, considering the Harappan language as related to the Elamite, and supporting the presence of Indo-Iranians as early as 4000 BCE in Iran and west of the Indus. Dravidian speakers are said to have occupied the lower Indus valley and Gujarat. Bellwood posits that two "Indo-Aryan" currents entered India: the first one moved from the Indus valley to the south c. 3500 BCE, and the second went into the Ganges valley c. 3000 BCE (Bellwood 2005a: 213–215; 2006: 66, 68). Quoting Kuiper (1948), Bellwood, however, points out that contacts between Dravidian and Munda languages seem to have occcured before there was any Indo-Aryan presence. He also recalls (2005a) that in Hindi, according to Southworth, 30 percent of the terms connected to agriculture represent loanwords from languages that are neither Indo-Aryan, nor Dravidian nor Munda; in another publication (2006: 70), however, he casts doubt on the importance given to a pre-Indo-Aryan substratum in the Ganges valley (cf. Bryant 2005: 479). Note that the majority of linguists and archaeologists locate the place of origin of the Austroasiatic languages south of the Yangtze River, with a differentiation of Proto-Austroasiatic around 5000 BCE (Bellwood 2005b, 2006; Sagart et al. 2005).

introduced foxtail millet and rice, but Sagart (2011: 130) notes that the absence of terms of Austroasiatic origin that are specific to rice in the languages of South Asia – Aryan or Dravidian – does not argue in favor of rice being introduced by Munda speakers.[124] For D. Fuller (p.c.), however, "the Munda, who were associated with hill cultivation systems, focused on tubers and I would increasingly guess *aus* rices." The domestication of rice of the *aus* type shows hybridizations between *japonica* and *indica* forms: it could be linked to the Austroasiatic expansion (Fuller 2011a: 87).[125] It should be noted that "in terms of lowland Neolithic, in Orissa (which is probably not Munda in any case) dates really only go back to about 1500 BC" (Fuller 2011a: 87).

Plants and animals of the western Asian stock continued to spread from the northwest at the beginning of the second millennium, following a process already noticed for the Mature Harappan period. Wheat and barley were present in Maharashtra (northern Deccan), and later in the Southern Neolithic, where they contributed little to agricultural production. This South Deccan region also yielded some plants of African origin (see below), as well as the pigeon-pea, introduced from Orissa or a neighboring region. Metal objects and spindle whorls have also been found in southern India around 1500 BCE, and metallurgical terms can be reconstructed in Proto-South-Dravidian (Fuller *et al.* 2011). In the Ganges valley, plants and animals originating from western Asia were introduced as early as the third millennium (Fuller 2007: 403). In various parts of India, from the late third millennium onward, progress in agriculture resulted in population growth and sedentarization (Fuller 2006a: 59, 2008a). Weaving developed during the second part of the second millennium (Fuller 2008b). This expansion led to population movements, accompanied by the differentiation of Central Dravidian prior to 1800/1700 BCE according to Fuller (2007: 427), or around the middle of the second millennium according to Southworth (2006: 133). Using the scenario that locates the Dravidian core in the Indus valley, some authors have referred to migrations of Dravidian speakers from northwestern to southern India. It is likely that movements did take place, but other researchers are more inclined to place the Proto-Dravidian core in peninsular India.[126] The linguistic change was even more dramatic during the second millennium, while new populations arrived in South Asia.

Infiltrations of Central Asian groups had begun during the Late phase of the Harappan culture; they continued after the eighteenth century, as seen in the

Diffloth (2005) and Reid (2005), however, note wildlife of a tropical type and the absence of wet rice culture in the vocabulary that can be reconstructed in Proto-Austroasiatic (tropical fauna may have been present as far as the Yangtze, however, 7,000 years ago).

[124] Sagart (2008: 138) accepted the idea of a diffusion of *indica* rice by Austroasiatics from southern China, which seems very unlikely.

[125] Sagart also writes: "*aus* rice may have been domesticated somewhere in Southeast Asian uplands by the linguistic ancestors of the Austroasiatics and brought west during the Austroasiatic migrations to India (Khasi, Munda)" (2011: 131).

[126] In the region of the eastern Ghats, north of the Krishnā River (Fuller 2007: 420, 422; see above). The Gujarati (Gujarat) and the Marathi (Maharashtra) languages show many borrowings from Dravidian languages. It is possible, as Bellwood has suggested, that Dravidians were present in Gujarat or even in the Lower Indus valley (2005: 214). On this point, Southworth (2005) notes that we find Dravidian names (toponyms . . .) in Saurashtra and Maharashtra, but not so much in Sindh and Rajasthan. He does not, however, exclude an early Dravidian presence in Gujarat and Sindh. See Southworth 2005: 288ff., 328.

assemblage found in the Swāt valley during the first half of the second millennium: this assemblage exhibits affinities with the Vaksh and Beshkent culture (a culture from Tajikistan, where cremation of the deceased was practiced) as well as with sites in Xinjiang (Sergent 1997: 229, 453 n. 152). A horse cult was introduced in the Swāt and the Gomal valleys.

For Parpola (2002: 245), after the arrival of the first Proto-Indo-Aryans in the BMAC and later in the Indus valley during the nineteenth and eighteenth centuries, a third wave,[127] made up of "Rig-Vedic Proto-Indo-Aryans," entered southern Central Asia from *c.* 1750 BCE, where it triggered the decline of the BMAC. This third wave of migrants led to new Indo-Aryan arrivals in India. Kuzmina (2007: 307ff.) convincingly suggests a connection between the Beshkent-Vaksh culture[128] (which incorporated Fedorovo elements), the expansion of this culture into the Swāt and Gomal valleys, and the constitution of Nuristani and Dardic entities in the latter region (these entities are representative of particular branches of the Indo-Iranians) (Kuzmina 2007: 303).[129] The site of Gumla, which shows Harappan influences, was burnt by the newcomers, whose cemetery has revealed practices of cremation, horse bones, and figurines of horses and camels. The same phenomenon can be observed at Hathala. The cemetery at Kherai also expresses "the Andronovo origin of the Swāt culture" (Kuzmina 2007: 314). New (Indo-Aryan and Iranian?) arrivals occurred during the second half of the second millennium in the Swāt valley, which has yielded tombs with horse remains and evidence of a chariot cult (Kuzmina 2007: 338)[130] as well as practices of cremation (besides other funerary rituals). The settlements reflect "the emergence of a sort of central power" (Stacul 2001).

[127] Parpola calls a second wave "'Atharva-Vedic' Proto-Indo-Aryans." They "replaced the Pre-Proto-Iranians as the rulers of the BMAC ca. 1900 BC" (2002: 242).

[128] The Beshkent-Vaksh culture was formed during the eighteenth century, with a triple component from the Zaman-baba, BMAC, and Fedorovo cultures (Kuzmina 2007: 170). Increased pastoralism is noticeable in this culture. Tombs show rectangular hearths for men, and round hearths for women, recalling funerary customs of the Vedic Aryans (Kuzmina 2008: 85). They also exhibit drawings of swastikas and solar symbols. Cremation practices were present here, as well as in the Bostan VI phase of Bactria.

[129] The Nuristani languages, however, could have been separated from the Proto-Indo-Iranian earlier than the Dardic languages (Kogan 2005), but this question remains debated.

[130] Sergent (1997: 229) notes various funerary rites: bodies buried in the flexed position, cremation (these two modes were known in Bactria and in the steppes), and also fractional burial (initially the flesh of the deceased was removed) (this has also been observed in level I of cemetery H of Harappa). Sergent connects this practice to Iranians, but Kuzmina (2007: 343–344) points out that the rite of fractional burial "had been typical to Baluchistan since the Eneolithic."

The Late Bronze Age (*c.* 1600–1100 BCE), an Area Unified around the Eastern Mediterranean

Western Asia and the Mediterranean Region

> And the kings who (are) of equal rank with me, the king of Egypt, the king of Karadunia (Kassite Babylonia), the king of Assyria, ~~the king of Ahhiyawa~~ [Mycenaean kingdom] . . .
> (Hittite document, under the reign of Tudhaliya IV; Bryce 2005: 309)[1]

The collapse of the Indus civilization was accompanied by a decrease in trade both in the Persian Gulf and along the terrestrial routes east of Mesopotamia. The demise of the Sumerian world at this time "cannot be a mere coincidence."[2] De-urbanization occurred at the same time in Iran, while in Babylonia Hammurabi's successors had to deal with a social and economic crisis, aggravated by the Kassite invasions. The "Old Babylonian Period" ended in 1595 with the looting of Babylon by the Hittites (MC) (in 1499 in the ultra-short chronology of Gasche *et al.* 1998).

From the seventeenth century BCE onward, the center of gravity of western Asia shifted northward, and the eastern Mediterranean became the central maritime space of a sphere of exchanges connecting Egypt, the Levant, Anatolia, and eastern Europe. This sphere marked the relative decline of southern Mesopotamia and the Persian Gulf. An era of growth and integration started from the sixteenth century on, with the development of exchange networks – and military conflicts – among various areas: the Egyptian New Kingdom, the Aegean world, the Hittite Empire (Anatolia), the states of Mitanni (Upper Euphrates), and Assyria (Upper Tigris). This Late Bronze Age system was connected to African, Arab, European, and Asian peripheries.[3] From 1600 onward, a warmer climate in the eastern Mediterranean Sea accompanied increased precipitation that benefited agricultural progress in this region.[4] Crete saw the ascent

---

[1] The Ahhiyawan king was later removed from the list.

[2] Margueron and Pfirsch 2001: 165. Sumerian disappeared as a living language, but remained a cultural language. Many texts were written during the eighteenth and seventeenth centuries; they contain mathematical exercises, astrology, and technical briefings (Benoit 2003: 102). Calculations showed how to solve first and second degree equations. The texts reveal the use of "trigonometric lines" (Proust 2006).

[3] Kristiansen (1993: 415) has criticized Frank's proposition that the "central world-system" was in a phase of recession from 1750 to 1500. It is probably necessary to shorten the "B phase" (recession) put forward by Frank. For Muhly (1993: 417–418), as well, "it is not encouraging to be told that the period 1750–1500 BC was a major B phase 'Dark Age' in light of the wealth of material from Akrotiri [Thera], Zakro and Knossos (Crete), the incredible treasures of the shaft graves at Mycenae, and the formation of the Hittite Old Kingdom in central Anatolia."

[4] There were advances in agriculture north of the Black Sea, as well as an increase in cattle herding (Makhortykh 2004: 36; Alexandrovskyi and Alexandrovskaya 2004: 206; Kohl 2007: 157). Kuzmina

of the "Second Palatial Civilization," from 1700 to 1450; this island maintained con-nections with the Levant, Anatolia, the Mycenaean world, and Egypt.[5] The Cretan flowering was partly based on the development of textile production.[6] The palaces exhibited a more hierarchized structure than before, with "an unprecedented expansion of palatial authority into spheres of economic and political life," along with the standardization of writing and other administrative systems (Parkinson and Galaty 2007: 120). In tombs of the elite at Thebes (Egypt), people called "Keftiu" are depicted who appear to have the features of Cretans. Lead-isotope analyses of copper ingots from several Cretan sites show at least five different origins for the metal; it did not originate in Cyprus (Muhly 1995: 1513). Cretans were present at Miletus, in western Anatolia, where an inscription in Linear A has been discovered.

In Greece, discoveries in the tombs of Grave Circle A at Mycenae (seventeenth century) reveal the size of the exchange networks: they include amber from the Baltic Sea; silver from Anatolia; ostrich eggs from Nubia; lapis lazuli from Afghanistan; and ivory from Syria, Egypt or the Black Sea. The Mycenaean civilization gave birth to a new script, Linear B, which was derived from Linear A, but transcribed a Greek language. The Mycenaeans weakened the Cretan networks by trading directly with the powers of western Asia (Parkinson and Galaty 2007), and then took possession of the Minoan cities around 1450 BCE.[7] In addition, the Mycenaeans may have con-ducted raids into Egypt, and attacked Troy. They were probably active in the Black Sea (Bolohan 2005: 162, 163 n.8). Trade contacts with Egypt are well attested. Mycenaean pottery has been discovered at Tell el-Amarna, from the time of the pharaoh Akhenaton (1353–1335 BCE). A Theban tomb shows Mycenaean envoys bringing products into Egypt, and it provides a list of Aegean toponyms. Egyptian objects have also been unearthed at Aegean sites, revealing exchanges between Egypt and the Aegean. In their search for new sources of metal ores, the Mycenaeans extended their networks in the western Mediterranean Sea (Italy, Sicily, Sardinia, eastern Iberian coast); these networks were mainly developed by private merchants.[8] Mycenaean pottery (and/or imitations) has been discovered in southeast Sicily, at the "toe" of the Italian peninsula, in the bay of Naples, in the Po River valley, in Sardinia, and on the southern coast of Spain. Aegeans settled at various sites, for example in Calabria (Schofield 2007: 114), but it is also likely that Cypriot merchants played an increasing role during the thirteenth century. This sphere appears to be connected with the Atlantic coasts (tin exploitation in Cornwall, initiated during the

---

mentions a milder and drier climate at this time in the Dnieper-Urals region (2008: 60). Koryakova and Epimakhov (2007: 11) also point out increasing aridity in western Siberia and west of the Urals from the middle of the second millennium BCE.

[5] For Meeks (2006: 12), "the polychrome faience, that appeared independently in the Near East and in Egypt, at the time of Amenhotep III at least, may result from the slightly earlier development of Minoan polychrome faience."

[6] "References in Linear B Tablets from Knossos and Pylos to female textile workers from Lemnos, Cnidos, Miletus and Aswija (Assuwa?), suggest that western Anatolia had a particular expertise and reputation in this craft" (Easton *et al.* 2002: 105).

[7] This dating is still controversial. The Minoan palaces were burnt down between 1433 and 1415 BCE, according to Manning and Ramsey 2003, thus earlier than the dating 1385/1375 BCE usually adopted.

[8] Kristiansen and Larsson (2005: 104), however, argue that trade was in the hands of the palace.

early second millennium, expanded during this period),[9] Central Europe (which may have exported tin from the Erzgebirge, Germany), and northern Europe (Kristiansen and Larsson 2005; Harding 2006). Located between Europe and Asia, Troy (level VI) shows a revival that demonstrates the vitality of Anatolian metallurgy and the significance of the Mediterranean–Black Sea and Balkans–Asia trade roads.[10]

Between western Asia and Egypt, "contacts were of an unprecedented [intensity]" compared with earlier periods (Moorey 2001: 2). The expulsion of the Hyksos from Egypt and growing exchanges helped disseminate alphabetic scripts developed from the Egyptian innovation (see above).[11] Alphabets did not present the same learning challenges as had earlier forms of writing: they flourished in Palestine and in Phoenicia and seem to have been well adapted to merchant classes in those regions. Two types of linear alphabetic writing can be distinguished, using 27 and 22 signs, respectively; they would later be adapted (especially at Ugarit and in other cities) to cuneiform scripts with 27, 22, or 30 signs. Around the thirteenth century BCE, there were at least "three forms of cuneiform alphabetic writing" (Lemaire 2007: 57). In addition, one notes two different traditions of script learning; the first, a northwestern Semitic version (*abgd*, according to the order of the letters), would be found in the Phoenician, Aramaic, and Hebrew scripts;[12] and the second was a southwestern Semitic tradition (*hlḥm*), characteristic of the North and South Arabian scripts (Lemaire 2007: 57).[13]

These newcomers, who spoke Indo-European languages, played an important role in western Asia from the seventeenth century onward, when a Hittite Empire centered on the Anatolian plateau took shape, with Hattusha (Bogazköy) as its capital. The empire used two systems of writing at the same time (a cuneiform script and "hieroglyphs") that reflect the practice of several languages.[14] This was not just a matter of administrative

---

9   Gold vases exhibiting Mycenaean affinities found in Cornwall (at Rillaton) and Armorica (at Ploumilliau) indicate contacts with the Mediterranean, probably "through Spanish relay stations" (Giot *et al.* 1995: 70, Roman and Roman 1998: 186). Tin was already being mined in Cornwall during the late third or early second millennium (Primas 2002). It is difficult to accept that Mycenaeans were present in Cornwall, as has sometimes been suggested. Tin was exported "down the line" to continental Europe, southern Spain, and the Mediterranean. Tin was also exploited in the Iberian peninsula during the same period.

10   In addition, Kohl (2007: 170ff.) emphasizes the importance of ore extraction and metallurgy in the Eurasian steppes. North of the Caspian Sea, the site of Kargaly reveals intensive exploitation of copper ores between the seventeenth and the fourteenth centuries. Various copper mines were in use in central Kazakhstan (near Atasu for instance), and eastern Kazakhstan benefited from rich tin deposits (Kuzmina 2007: 87–89).

11   The Proto-Sinaitic writing of Serabit al-Khadim has been discovered in a temple devoted to the goddess Hathor, dated to 1600 BCE. This temple was located in the vicinity of turquoise mines exploited by the Egyptians (Benoit 2003: 331). As for Palestine, we know of some short Proto-Canaanite inscriptions, written on various surfaces.

12   This sequence can be observed on tablets from Ugarit. Dated to the eleventh century BCE, one ostrakon discovered at 'Izbet Sartah (in Israel) displays twenty-two signs "that formed a linear alphabet following the sequence of the Phoenician alphabet" (Joannès 2001: 36). This alphabetic linear writing would later be developed by the states of the Levant early in the first millennium (see below).

13   This sequence has been observed on a tablet found at Ugarit (Beth Shemesh).

14   The excavations carried out between 1907 and 1912 have unearthed 10,000 tablets. The use of at least eight languages has been noted. Hieroglyphic Hittite was usually written in Luwian, an Indo-European language belonging to a population living in the region of Arzawa, in west-southwestern Anatolia. Arzawa was an independent political entity after 1500 BCE, whose king sent letters to the pharaoh Amenhotep III (*c.* 1417–1379 BCE). The Luwian language seems to have been a *lingua franca* in the whole

efficiency, but rather an ideological need to ensure the cohesion of a heterogeneous empire. The Hittite Empire aimed at controlling the region's resources (copper and silver mines) and trade routes, along the Euphrates and toward Troy.[15]

The expansionist policy of this empire ran up against the presence of another political entity in the southwest, the Mitanni Empire, founded by a Hurrite and Indo-Aryan warrior aristocracy.[16] The Mitanni dominated Assyria, Syria, and Armenia. This Indo-Aryan aristocracy included a class of horsemen called Marianni, who were horse breeders. Indo-Aryan speakers who may have arrived through Iran made significant incursions into the entire region: Hittite texts dealing with the training of horses have been found, containing terms related to Sanskrit – such terms were borrowed from the Hurrites.[17] The Hittite army used horsemen, for example at the battle of Qadesh. In addition, the Hittites practiced horse sacrifices. Indo-Aryans also brought in the use of the composite bow and of socketed arrows (Kuzmina 2007: 136).

Whereas the Mitanni kingdom had conflictual relations with the Hittites, it maintained friendly contacts with Egypt from Amenhotep II (Amenophis II) onward.[18] Letters from Amarna list the wedding gifts offered for the marriage of a Mitanni princess to Amenhotep III: horses, a chariot plated with gold and inlaid with precious stones, various weapons, armor, shoes, garments, chests covered with gold and silver, golden rhytons, perfumes, jewels made of gold and lapis lazuli, and various ornaments.[19] Finds of Mitannian seals from Iran to Palestine hint at a vast exchange area that went beyond the Mediterranean sphere. Mitanni and Egypt also maintained exchanges with Babylon, the center of a Kassite empire that was formed after 1595 BCE. This Kassite state marked the "end of the city-state in Mesopotamia," at least until the Neo-Babylonian period (Margueron and Pfirsch 2001: 240).

Egypt appears to have had close links with western Asia and the eastern Mediterranean, as well as with the African and Arab regions further south (Nubia and Punt) (see below).

region; it was still a *lingua franca* within the area of the Neo-Hittite city-states after 1200 BCE (Thuesen 2002: 45).

[15] Troy was within the Hittite sphere of influence, if this town corresponds to the Wilusiya/Wilusa of the Hitttite texts (Joukowsky 1996: 198; Bryce 2005: 359; Castleden 2005: 210). According to Wood (1996: 252–254), the Hittite tablets evoke Greek expansion from 1300 BCE and a Greek intervention at Wilusa (Troy) during the early thirteenth century. A Hittite army was also sent to attack Wilusa. Mycenae and the Hittite kingdom thus both seem to have made attempts to control Troy.

[16] In a treaty between a Hittite king and a ruler from Mitanni, during the fifteenth century BCE, the latter made a pledge using the names of Indo-Aryan divinities.

[17] Joukowsky 1996: 236. In another text, a book on horse training, a man named Kikkuli uses Indian figures, and he is called *assussani* (Sanskrit *asvasani-*, "horse trainer") (Lamberg-Karlovsky 2002: 71; Liverani 2014: 272–273).

[18] Thutmose III pursued an expansionist policy in the Levant from 1469 BCE, but his successor Amenhotep II failed to take control of Syria. A peace treaty was then signed with Mitanni, and a royal marriage arranged.

[19] EA22, EA25, Moran 1987: 123–136 and 151–167. The list of gifts sent by the pharaoh Amenhotep IV (Akhenaton) to the Kassite king Burna-Buriash is even more impressive: the manufacture of the gifts listed required at least half a ton of gold and 125 kg of silver (EA14, Moran 1987).

The interregional balance changed during the fourteenth century BCE, when Assyria emerged as a major power. It became dominant during the thirteenth century BCE, removing the Mitanni kingdom from the map and capturing Babylon in 1234 BCE. Assyria could thus control the roads leading to Syria and Anatolia. The archives of Tell el-Amarna (Egypt) contain evidence of contacts between Assyria and Egypt. Elam experienced a revival during the same period. A new capital was created in 1250 BCE at Tchoga Zanbil by a king who married a Kassite princess.[20] The ceramics and alabaster vessels of Elam are rather similar to those found at Assur. They testify to the extension of an international style at the end of the Bronze Age, the result of exchanges and cultural blending. In addition, royal tombs and architectural remains at Tchoga Zanbil reflect contacts with Indo-Europeans (with evidence of cremation of the dead, the remains of a fire temple, the presence of triple walls …). Nomads from the east of the Caspian Sea who entered northwestern Iran around the fifteenth century BCE may have been Iranian speakers. The Marlik culture that developed starting in the fourteenth century BCE south of the Caspian Sea may have been related to these migrants.[21]

Four or five competing dominant regions were thus interconnected, a situation that led to intensification of the military complex. In southwestern Anatolia, the Hittite state faced the hostility of the kingdom of Arzawa (Lydia and the littoral to the southeast). The major threat for the Hittites, however, came from an expanding Egypt, which had controlled Palestine as well as part of Phoenicia and Syria since Thutmose III (Tuthmosis III) (c. 1479–1425 BCE). This expansion led to a major confrontation with the Hittite Empire during the thirteenth century BCE. After the indecisive battle of Qadesh (1274 BCE), a peace treaty was signed in 1270 BCE between the two powers.[22] The military campaigns were aimed at seizing spoils, imposing tributes or controlling territories (the wheat-growing lands of Syria were probably vital for the Hittite Empire). The Hittites and the Egyptians, soon to be imitated by the Assyrians, practiced large-scale deportation of populations in order to ensure the presence of a workforce vital for both production and military purposes. The Assyrian king Tukulti-Ninurta proclaims: "In my first year [of reign], I deported 28,800 people of the Hatti-land from beyond the Euphrates, and I brought (them) into my land" (Liverani 1990: 93). The blinding of slaves, a practice among the Scythians mentioned in the fifth century BCE by Herodotus, probably dates back to this period: Shalmaneser I (1263–1234 BCE) is said to have blinded 14,000 prisoners of war. Insecurity along the Assyrian borders explains the development of fortified settlements, for example in Transcaucasia.

---

[20] The links between Elam and the Kassites may explain an Elamite attack against Assyria in 1224 BCE. See Potts 1999: 231.

[21] The Marlik culture was in contact with Mesopotamia (Huot 2004, II: 70, 88). For Kuzmina (2007: 373), too, horse burials at Marlik may reflect the arrival of Iranian elements. Mallory and Mair (2000: 257) point out the appearance of the "animal style" of the steppes southeast of the Caspian Sea at this time, and the incursion of Indo-Aryans into northwestern India. The metallurgy of Luristan experienced a phase of revival from the thirteenth century BCE.

[22] According to Hittite sources, the Hittites and the Egyptians concluded a treaty as early as the third quarter of the fifteenth century BCE (Klinger 2006: 315–317). Moreover, letters from El-Amarna reveal diplomatic contacts during the fourteenth century.

In both the Hittite Empire and northern Mesopotamia (the economic structures of the Kassite kingdom are not well understood),[23] social evolution can be seen with a growing number of land grants to individuals for services rendered to the state, often in the military field.[24] Besides lands administered by the palaces[25] and the temples, we thus find large estates belonging to a landed aristocracy. There is evidence for land markets, for example at Alalakh (plain of the Amuq), Ugarit, Emar (Syria), and Nuzi (Iraq).[26] The state and individuals controlled workshops which served in part to manufacture goods for export, sometimes using a servile labor force. Textile workshops are mentioned for the Mycenaean world and in Assyria (Faist 2001: 70, 245; Warburton 2003: 58). The period from the fifteenth to the thirteenth century corresponds to a new phase of expansion for crafts, trade, and also war-related activities, with the use of light chariots and horses,[27] the composite bow and iron weapons. In fact, iron metallurgy appeared before 1500 BCE in the Hittite Empire – which might owe part of its preeminence to this technology –, then it spread into Syria between the fourteenth and twelfth centuries.[28] Alongside the progress of metallurgy and the controlled use of fire, a glass industry flourished, notably under the Eighteenth Egyptian Dynasty.[29]

[23] Lamberg-Karlovsky (1996: 97) considers that the weakness of the state in the Kassite Empire favored the flourishing of the private sector.

[24] However, Margueron and Pfirsch (2001: 244) note that there is no well-attested link between land grants and possession of war chariots, as has often been suggested. Lands were granted to state officials, priests, and merchants, for example at Ugarit.

[25] Based on land acquisitions by royal families at Emar and Mari, Warburton (2003: 133) argues – contrary to the generally accepted idea – for increasing land control by the state during the second millennium.

[26] Land sales documented at Emar reveal surprising price fluctuations (Beckman 1997: 100). At Ugarit, "a resident named (C)huttenu sold 3 *ikû* of his fields and his *dimtu*-building and received from Yapsharru 3 *ikû* of arable land and 500 (shekels) of silver" (Heltzer 1996: 180; Silver 2002). Women played a significant economic role, since they appear both as buyers and sellers in texts from Ugarit.

[27] The horse, chariot, and composite bow had already appeared during the late third millennium, but their use spread during the Late Bronze Age, in both central and peripheral areas (Ekholm Friedman 2005: 54). A wall painting in a tomb at Minet el-Beida (Syria) depicts a rider, showing that horses were also a means of transport.

[28] A few iron objects are dated to the third millennium: a dagger found at Tell Asmar (Eshnunna), an iron sword with a gold hilt from a "royal" burial at Alaca Hüyük (Turkey), and "a piece of iron associated with the Great Pyramid at Gizeh" (Muhly 1995: 1514). Small iron objects have also been discovered in Afghanistan at Mundigak (phase IV), at Said Qala Tepe, and Deh Morasi Ghundai (Sarianidi 1996: 236). The king of Purushanda (Acem Hüyük) brought an iron throne and an iron scepter as tribute to the Hittite king Anitta (mid-eighteenth century) (Bryce 1999: 41). Recent discoveries in Georgia also show the existence of craftsmen working iron around 1500 BCE on the eastern coast of the Black Sea (Muhly 1995: 1516). Some iron artifacts have been found in Europe (in Serbia, Slovakia, and Holland) dated to the second half of the second millennium; they suggest long-distance relations with the Aegean world (Harding 1993: 155–157). Starting in the twelfth century, iron technology spread into the Levant, onto Cyprus, and into eastern Europe. Iron can be considered as a by-product in the smelting of chalcopyrite ores (Sherratt and Sherratt 2001: 30). The various centers of metallurgy probably discovered the processes of carburization and quenching that enabled them to improve the properties of the iron.

[29] Outside Egypt, during the second half of the second millennium, centers of glass production were active in northern Mesopotamia, Syria, Palestine, Khuzistan, and perhaps Babylonia (Moorey 1994: 201). Significant development of the glass industry in Mesopotamia may go back to the mid-sixteenth century BCE (Moorey 1995). "An instruction text describing how to make glass" has been dated to the Middle Babylonian period (*c.* 1600 BCE) (Liverani 2014: 276–277). Glass beads had already appeared during the middle of the third millennium in Mesopotamia and Lower Egypt. One finds glass with high magnesia content in Syria, Jordan,

Glass production partly represents an attempt to mimic precious stones from abroad: thus, a type of glass imitating turquoise appeared between 1650 and 1450 BCE, and blue glass resembling lapis lazuli was produced when demand for this stone grew, whereas only limited amounts of actual lapis were arriving in western Asia and Egypt (renewed imports from Central Asia, however, were seen during the Late Bronze Age).[30] As Casanova notes (2013: 197), it is likely that the use of lapis lazuli became less frequent due to the progressive development of substitute materials such as glazes (frit) and glass paste. "Significantly, the Mycenaean word for 'blue glass worker' (*kuwanoworgos*) was ultimately derived from the Akkadian name of lapis lazuli" (Warburton 2013: 288). This glass production went hand in hand with research on dyes.[31] The transfers of technology observed were facilitated by commerce, diplomatic contacts, and wars, which resulted in the capture or disposal of artisans.[32] Written sources also mention itinerant craftsmen, who went from court to court. Interestingly, innovations in dyes and glassmaking were developed not in Lower Mesopotamia, but in Upper Mesopotamia and Syria, thus revealing crucial changes (Liverani 2014: 277–278).

More numerous exchanges promoted the formation of an "intercultural" style in craft production. The Late Bronze Age proved to be a new era of "internationalism," obvious in the texts of the El-Amarna tablets sent to the pharaohs Amenhotep III and Akhenaton. The process was partly driven by the need for copper, tin, silver, and workers in ever-increasing quantities and numbers. Exchanges developed within the context of treaties, which implied the sending of gifts between courts and commercial activities led by merchants working for the state or for private "houses," which often functioned "in interface with the royal bureaucracy" and the temples (Hudson 1996: 41). Merchants were active in the diplomatic game between western Asia, Egypt, and Turkey. Several letters from el-Amarna urgently called for freedom of movement for merchants, thus displaying the importance attached to this freedom: "My brother, let my messengers go promptly and safely so that I may hear my brother's greeting. These men are my merchants. My brother, let them go safely and prom[pt]ly. No one making a claim in your name is to approach my merchants or my ship."[33] The significance of "gift exchanges" between palaces has probably been overestimated in comparison to that of private trade.

At that time, Cyprus served as a hub in eastern Mediterranean trade thanks to its geographic location, the activity of its merchants, and its exports of copper and

---

Israel, and northwestern Iran from the first half of the second millennium (Henderson 2000: 54). Glass with low magnesia content (thanks to the addition of sodium sesquicarbonate from Egypt) has been excavated at Pella (Jordan) and Tell Brak (Syria), dated to the fourteenth century (Henderson 2000: 25, 57).

[30] See the treasure of Nippur, the "Assyrian" tombs of Mari (thirteenth century BCE), and the lapis lazuli and gold dove found at Susa (twelfth century BCE) (Casanova 1999). See also the mentions of lapis lazuli sent by the king of Mitanni and the Kassite king of Babylon to Egypt. Warburton points out that the Mycenaean world did not import lapis lazuli (it was probably too expensive): it imported blue glass instead.

[31] Sherratt and Sherratt (2001: 19) have rightly pointed out the importance of substitutions in the evolution of techniques and exchanges, and the role of cross-innovations from one field to another. Technology, too, follows a cumulative development path.

[32] Moorey 2001: 3–4. Contrary to Kohl's suggestion (1987, 1989), transfers of technology were not always open and accessible to all.

[33] EA39, letter from the king of Alashiya (Cyprus) to the pharaoh (Moran 1987: 208). These merchants were in the service of the king of Cyprus.

manufactured products (perfumes, ships . . .).[34] The singular position of Cyprus encouraged the urbanization (Enkomi) and new social complexity that is clearly reflected in the appearance of the still undeciphered "Cypro-Minoan" script. An anchor of the Cypriot type, made in Egypt, has been found at Karnak, indicating the presence of Cypriot merchants in Upper Egypt. The discovery of Cypriot pottery at Marsa Matruh "strongly raises the possibility of a Cypriot trading post on Egypt's northwestern coast" (Silver 1995: 143).

The Levant also served as a hub for exchanges, the importance of which increased when the Egyptian military power declined from Amenhotep III. The Levantine cities developed luxury craftmanship destined for export: fabric, furniture, jewels, personal care items, and perfumes.[35] Thanks to cedar from Lebanon, Ugarit had long been a center for shipbuilding. Moreover, the city produced textiles, using purple dye from *Murex* shells. Trade was partly governed by international treaties (Heltzer 1999). A strong Egyptian influence was noteworthy at Ugarit and other ports, where vessels from the Aegean world and Anatolia also docked. Relations with the Hittites, who imposed ties of vassalage on Ugarit, gave the Levantine ports access to Anatolian resources and markets. The documents from Ugarit, the main city-state on the Levantine coast, reveal the fluidity of the border between the state and the private sectors. Merchants were organized into a hierarchical structure. Palace or temple trade agents were engaged in private enterprise; conversely, merchants were employed by the palace as controllers or managers and played a role in collecting revenue for the state.[36] This situation is illustrated by the activities of a merchant called Sinaranu who, during the reign of King Niqmepa, was an agent of the state, but also had his own private shipping fleet, which traded in Crete and the Aegean Sea under Niqmepa's royal protection. In addition, he was a tax collector for the king (Moore and Lewis 1999: 82, 85, after Heltzer 1979; Cline 2013: 30). Commercial expeditions seem to have been financed by both the state and the private sector. "'Houses' of merchants" are recorded in Ugarit. These merchants "traveled on behalf of the palace and coexisted with commercial agents who were acting on their own account" (Aubet 2001: 107). The king of Ugarit exercised a monopoly in the copper trade, the wood industries, cereals, and perhaps oil, and the ruling aristocracy was involved in trade. Exchanges were overseen by a "ruler of the harbor."

[34] Cyprus had close links with Egypt particularly during Thutmosis III's reign, while connections with northern Syria and Anatolia grew stronger at the time of the pharaohs Amenhotep III and IV, in parallel to the growing pressure exerted by the Hittite kingdom (Eriksson 2003: 421ff.). See, however, the letter EA35 from El-Amarna, mentioning the sending of 500 talents of copper by the king of Cyprus to Egypt; this king asked for silver and vessels with perfumed oils in exchange (Moran 1987: 200ff.).

[35] Ugarit yielded "a thousand Cypriot flasks intended to contain perfume or essence" (Benoit 2003: 116). Akkadian cuneiform tablets from Mesopotamia dating to between the thirteenth and the eleventh centuries appear to deal with the preparation of perfumes (Needham *et al.* 1980: 82).

[36] The Canaanite equivalent of the Mesopotamian *tamkarum* "would have been an agent of the crown, who received land grants for the payment of his services, and was associated with other traders within a merchant guild having multiple branches abroad" (Norel 2004: 86). On the private entrepreneurs at Ugarit, see also Silver 1995: 169, Niemeyer 2000, and Michel 2001a. The contracts called *tappūtu* seem to refer to a kind of partnership linking merchants in various places; a letter from the king of Tyre to the king of Ugarit thus refers to a *tappūtu* partnership between merchants and royal agents traveling to Egypt to trade (Norel 2004: 86). The system was complex, bringing together agents, partners, and brokers.

The documents reveal prices varying according to supply and demand, for example for raw wool.[37] One episode illustrates the economic and political situation of the city-states of the Levant, where Byblos, Tyre, Arwad, and Sidon were also flourishing ports (Niemeyer 2000: 90). When asked to provide soldiers to help the Hittite Empire in its fight against Assyria, Ugarit preferred to pay 25 kg of gold (a metal that probably came from Egypt, as the result of commercial transactions).[38] Tribute brought into Egypt by Syrians included copper ingots, Canaanite amphorae filled with "incense," and elephant tusks, revealing the long-distance contacts of the Levantine coast.[39] The "incense," however, was probably not Arabian incense, but resin from *Pistacia atlantica*, a species found in the Levant (Serpico and White 2000). Rulers also borrowed money from time to time: "we know that the king of Byblos borrowed huge sums of silver, using ships and their cargo as security" (Van de Mieroop 2002: 81).

Besides silver, which came from Anatolia and the Aegean world, gold "became the standard measure of value in the international exchanges," thanks to Egyptian exports of this metal. Southern Mesopotamia, for example, preferred to use gold, and adopted silver only from 1250 BCE onward.[40] At the same time, one notes the importance of gold in the Aegean world. While the Syrian mina of Ugarit was the result of the encounter of four metric systems (Michailidou 2005: 19), the Syrian system (unit of 9.4 g) was in common use in the Aegean world during the Late Bronze Age. The cosmopolitan character of Ugarit is evident in the use of five systems of writing – some of them alphabetical – that recorded eight different languages. The invention of alphabets was a crucial innovation of this period. Whereas the complexity of ancient writings limited their uses and the number of their users, the simplicity and the efficiency of alphabetic writing transformed not only its social function, but also the relationship of the individual to the various spheres of power. Borrowed by the Greeks from the Phoenicians, the alphabet formed part of the movement of emergence of the individual that would later assert itself during the first millennium BCE.

Excavations on shipwrecks, notably at Ulu Burun (Lycia, Turkey) (end of the fourteenth century BCE) reveal the complex nature of the trade: the wreck yielded 10 tons of copper ingots, 1 ton of tin ingots, blocks of cobalt blue glass, ivory from elephant

---

[37] Silver 1995: 99. This author mentions various documents from Ugarit revealing the activities of private entrepreneurs, for example a letter from a merchant to an associate "advising him of the profitable trade opportunities in Hittite Anatolia" (Silver 1995: 174). See also Monroe 2005: 162.

[38] Agreement between the king of Ugarit Niqmadu II and the Hittite king Suppiluliuma I (second half of the fourteenth century) (MC) (Warburton 2000a: 78). Prior to Suppiluliuma's campaign, the same king of Ugarit was forced to pay 200 kg of silver to the ruler of Amurru (south of Ugarit), in exchange for military "protection." Canaanite ships were active all along the coast. Moreover, Syrian crews were employed on Egyptian ships as early as the Old Kingdom.

[39] Bass 1995: 1426. The documents reveal the large number of ships owned by Ugarit. "During the 13th century, the king of Ugarit was asked to outfit a fleet of 150 ships. During the 12th century, the surprising size of at least some of these ships may be inferred from a request by the king of the Hittites for a ship and crew to transport 2,000 measures of grain – around 450 tons –, in one or at most two trips" (Bass 1995: 1426). Moreover, texts from Ugarit mention the use of standardized, weighed silver money (shekel and quarter shekel) (Snell 1995: 1490).

[40] Snell 1995: 1493. In fact, various currencies coexisted, both locally and in transregional exchanges. In the Hittite Empire, "copper was the most popular money." During the Middle Assyrian period, "fines were paid with tin." At Ugarit, prices were generally given in silver (Snell 1995).

and hippo, ebony, murex opercula, ostrich eggs, turtle shells, shell rings, orpiment, gold jewelry (including a scarab of Queen Nefertiti), a ton of terebinth resin in addition to agate, amber, faience and glass beads, and the remains of figs, coriander, grapes, olives (oil?), various nuts, and cedar. The contents of the cargo are clearly not evidence of exchanges of gifts or tributes, but of state or private commercial activities (the diversity of the cargo suggests private trade). Wooden tablets may have shown the contents of some boxes, and perhaps "the origin and destination of the goods" (Bresson 2000: 142). Moreover, the wreck contained nine different sets of weights (Monroe 2005: 159). It is difficult to establish the "nationality" of the ship, which carried Kassite, Mycenaean, Syrian, Egyptian, and Babylonian seals. It probably came from Ugarit and seems to have been involved in a triangular Levant–Aegean Sea–Egypt trade.[41] "The keel plank and hull were of fir, with mortise-and-tenon joints held together with oak pegs" (Bass 1995: 1428; Pulak 1998). This system was later seen in the Mediterranean Sea – on the Phoenician boats for example – but in fact it could be much older (there is evidence for the use of mortises and tenons in the Egyptian ships of Dashur associated with Senwosret III, during the Middle Bronze Age [Creasman 2005], and in Khufu's ships).[42] The island of Cyprus was probably the source for most of the copper ingots, whereas the tin came from two separate sources, one of them possibly in Afghanistan.

Some copper ingots from the Ulu Burun wreck, rounded or formed into an oxhide shape, bear a mark: they may have been used as currency.[43] The discoveries made between Sicily and the Levant for the second half of the second millennium show an export-oriented production for these copper ingots of standardized shape and weight. Moreover, it is possible that objects representing standard units for payments were in circulation, perhaps in the form of sealed bags. The fact that numbers referring to silver were mentioned suggests a monetary use of silver of verified weight and purity. "The incidence of linen-wrapped silver at twelfth century Beth Shean [in an Egyptian part of the Levant] in an administrative context points to an Egyptian familiarity with the practice of bundling as well" (Thompson 2003: 94). The use of sealed bags has already been signaled during the period 2000–1600 BCE; it is better documented for the first millennium. Silver was actively exploited in Anatolia, and the value of this metal diminished throughout western Asia and Egypt during the Late Bronze Age.[44] Egyptian texts show the working of gold and silver into rings, which could be used in transactions (Breasted 1988: 188, 204).

[41] Bass 1995: 1427; Snape 2000: 81. The presence of a pin, spearheads, and a sword probably coming from northern Italy, that of an axe of the Lozovo/Pobit Kamyt type, carried via the Danube valley and Troy, reveal the extent of the trade networks (Sherratt 2000: 84; Easton *et al.* 2002: 105). Another shipwreck, of a smaller size, off Cape Gelidonya (Lycia) during the thirteenth century, has also been excavated. It was probably a private Cypriot ship (Bass 1995: 1429). It carried weights belonging to seven different systems (Bass 1967: 142; Warburton 2003: 73).

[42] These were river ships. On the ancient Egyptian ships, the tenons were not fixed by pegs, so the ship could be easily dismantled (Ward 2004).

[43] Silver 1995: 164. It was probably usual, as shown here with ingots, for precious products to be presented in specific forms and weights in order to facilitate transactions (Mederos and Lamberg-Karlovsky 2004: 200).

[44] Warburton (2003: 207) emphasizes this fact, which, he feels, had an impact on production. The massive importation of silver, however, did not always have a positive impact on growth, as seen in the case of Spain during the sixteenth century CE.

Pottery was produced for export in various places: Cypriot shapes were copied by Mycenaean potters, but Mycenaean shapes were also imitated in Cyprus, exported to the Levant, and then produced in this region.[45] The distribution of some vessels such as the Canaanite amphorae reveals the breadth of the networks in the eastern Mediterranean.

Written sources (Tell el-Amarna, Ugarit, Emar, Babylon) indicate the existence of a trade in luxury goods (gold, silver, ivory, "Egyptian faience," lapis lazuli),[46] textiles[47] – their crucial role in the relations between cores and peripheries has already been emphasized – as well as agricultural products and wood. Egypt, for example, sent a large cargo of wheat to the Hittite king at the end of the thirteenth century, during a time of food shortage in that empire.[48] Egypt imported wood from Lebanon, Amanus (Nur mountains), and even Crete. The Syrian region of Qatna exported horses. Greece and the Levant produced wine and olive oil. Among the goods produced for trade was opium, which may have been exported from Cyprus to Egypt (Warburton 2000a: 78). Peripheral areas provided reservoirs for slaves, as the slave trade in the Mediterranean Sea grew during the Late Bronze Age.[49] Mercenaries also came from the various peripheries. In addition, in Europe, the expansion of the Urnfield Culture was accompanied by greater metallurgical production during the thirteenth century, and the appearance in the eastern Mediterranean of new types of weapons, pins, and armor, carried on maritime routes (Sherratt 2000).

The volume of goods exported increased (notably for metal), but at the same time the structure of trade changed, with city-states and private entrepreneurs assuming a more significant part in it.[50] Tablets from Alalakh and Nuzi mention silver loans for

---

[45] Sherratt and Sherratt 2001: 29. Mycenaean pottery was also produced at Miletus; this city exported these products to the southern Anatolian coast and the Levant (Joukowsky 1996: 187).

[46] The letters from El-Amarna reflect the links between diplomatic relations and the exchange of luxury goods between the various courts during this period.

[47] Egypt and Mycenae produced linen cloth, Babylonia, Assyria, Syria, and Crete wool cloth (Ekholm Friedman 2005: 61ff.). Tablets written in Linear B show textile production by a servile labor force at Knossos (wool) and Pylos (flax) (Ekholm Friedman 2005, after Chadwick 1976). The crucial role played by textiles in the hierarchization of the world-system can be observed throughout history; textiles were usually produced by the cores, and to a lesser extent by semi-peripheries.

[48] We cannot be sure that this event was linked to an internationalization of exchanges, but it is worth noting that "the price of grain in terms of silver was roughly the same in Babylonia, Syria and Egypt" (Warburton 2003: 204); 100 liters of grain were valued at 2–3 g of silver, a lower price than previously.

[49] Powell (1990: 94 and n. 80) notes that the price of adult slaves seems to have progressively risen from 10–20 silver shekels during the third millennium (between the Pre-Sargonic period and the Ur-III Empire) to 20–30 shekels during the Old Babylonian Empire, over 30 shekels during the Middle Babylonian period, and 60 shekels or more during the Neo-Babylonian period (first millennium BCE). In addition, Silver (1995: 120) mentions a process of voluntary migration into the cores. The peripheries also provided "rare plants and exotic animals" (Ekholm Friedman 2005: 64), which the kings placed in their gardens and zoos. These imports brought with them the vital force associated with foreign parts and symbolized the central place of the king in the cosmos.

[50] Sherratt 2000, 2003. The shipwrecked vessels mentioned above attest to the importance of private trade. The Cypriots appear to have played an active role in the networks leading to the central Mediterranean. Huot (2004, II: 75), however, defends the idea of a strengthening of palatial power during the thirteenth century, which may have played a role – concurrently with external invasions – in the collapse of the urban centers. However, it could be argued that the tightening up of the central states was precisely due to the

commercial ventures.[51] Already attested during the preceding period, negotiable bearer documents (promissory notes) were circulating in Assyria during the fourteenth century. Silver has suggested a "monetary" use for a metal *kakkaru* disc weighing one talent; *kakkaru* also means "loaf," a metaphor used in various western Asian texts during the first millennium BCE.[52] As had been the case earlier during the Ur III Empire period and the early second millennium, loans – from the private or the state sector – were also geared to obtaining a labor force, by forcing debtors to repay their debt in labor (for example, at Nuzi, Alalakh, Assur, and Emar). The ancient practice of debt cancellations in the agricultural sector appears to have been abandoned (edicts of debt cancellations, however, were issued at Nuzi, during the Hurrian period, and the Neo-Assyrian kings applied this measure in order to maintain a free peasant army); small landowners were forced to work as farmers for the new owners, or to leave their land, becoming bondservants, mercenaries, or marauders (Van de Mieroop 2002: 79; Hudson 2002: 27; Liverani 2014: 295–297).

Whereas trade was active in the Mediterranean Sea and in northern Mesopotamia, it seems to have been subdued in the Kassite space, where agriculture was in decline. Intensive exploitation led to land salinization and reduced crop harvests. Loans made by merchants to farmers facing difficulties fostered the accumulation of capital in private hands. Moreover, the Kassite rulers gave lands to high officials.[53] In the Persian Gulf, however, the Kassite Empire controlled Bahrain during the fourteenth century and seized the city of Susa for a short time. Moreover, the Kassite power maintained contacts with El-Amarna (Egypt). Kassite cylinder seals have thus been excavated at Thebes. Cyprus has yielded the imprint of a Kassite seal. The Babylonians, who exported semiprecious stones to Egypt, including lapis lazuli coming from Afghanistan via Iran, imported ivory and gold, a metal that in the Kassite space became "the preferred means of payment along with silver" (Michel 2001a: 198). Nippur, Sippar, and Babylon became the most active centers. During the late thirteenth century, the Assyrian king Tukulti-Ninurta I, victorious against Babylon, brought an end to the Kassite domination of Bahrain and took the title of "king of Dilmun and Meluḫḫa," a title which does not seem to have implied a true Assyrian presence in Bahrain.

It is possible that Bahrain maintained commercial contacts with India: pottery similar to a type of ceramic from Pirak (period II) has been unearthed at Ra's al-

---

   fact that they were losing control over the trade networks. The significant role played by private entrepreneurs would later become more apparent during the Iron Age period.

[51] Silver 1995: 111, 168. A merchant from Ugarit "reminds another that interest is not charged between friends," evidence that this type of loan was in fact common practice (Silver 1995: 49). Silver also mentions for Ugarit, Nuzi, and Khafajeh, types of "contracts of suretyship": "the commercial loan market widened by resorting to suretyship or third-party guarantee of repayment" (1995: 113). A first example would be attested for Lagash during the last half of the third millennium. Silver refutes Polanyi (1981), showing that documents from Nuzi "demonstrate that private lenders made interest-bearing loans for 'business ventures' to merchants" (1983: 803).

[52] Silver 1995: 164. The talent was the equivalent of 60 minas, i.e. some 30 kg. One also finds the term *kakkaru* in texts from El-Amarna and Ras Shamra (*CAD*, VIII). Assyrian lead coins decorated with various motifs found at Assur probably did not function as money, since lead had a low value (Le Rider 2001: 20).

[53] However, various authors have noted the new importance of collective family lands in Babylonia at this time, which may reflect changes in social structures and production, with agriculturists "building up flocks and converting fields into pastures" (Silver 1995: 191).

Qala'at in layers dated to the thirteenth–twelfth centuries (Potts 1990: 155 n. 13). The island, however, was in decline, when compared to previous centuries.

Egypt of the New Kingdom (1539–1070 BCE)

> I came down the river to expel the Asian invaders, my gallant army
> sailing before me, similar to a flame.
> (Pharaoh Kamose, *c.* 1560 BCE; Ballard and Eugene 2005: 87)

The Seventeenth Theban Dynasty undertook the recovery of the lower Nile valley and the delta. Ahmose seized the Hyksos capital, Avaris, and founded the Eighteenth Dynasty (1539–1295). The second pharaoh of this dynasty, Amenhotep I, took back control of the Nubian territories. Under this dynasty, the Egyptian New Kingdom experienced political restoration and economic revival marked by substantial new building programs. Agricultural advances led to a sharp increase in population. The capital, Thebes, may have had 80,000 inhabitants (Morris 2013: 152–153).[54] The use of the shaduf to raise water, probably introduced from western Asia, appears to go back to the fourteenth century BCE, thus facilitating the irrigation of small parcels of land. Political integration was combined with a more efficient organization of the armies, which used horses and chariots. This restoration of Egyptian power was accompanied by significant social transformations. Royal donations to the temples supported the growing role played by the clergy.[55] Moreover, under Akhenaton (1353–1336 BCE), belief systems changed, with the advent of a new approach to the divine, in which the god "specially chooses whom he pleases" (Margueron and Pfirsch 2001: 300). Even though the Egyptian rulers after this pharaoh went back to a more traditional concept, "it was now by a mainly individual approach that the Egyptian man went in search of salvation" (Margueron and Pfirsch 2001: 300).

A new dynasty (nineteenth) ruled from 1292 BCE onward. Seti I and more importantly Ramses II (1279–1213 BCE) were successful rulers. Ramses II established his capital at Pi-Ramses. This city embraced both modern Qantir and Tell el-Daba (Avaris).

Despite the importance of the state and the role played by the temples in production, collection of taxes, and redistribution, these were complemented by a private sector active in agricultural production, as well as in craftmanship and commerce. Land privatization rose through grants made to officials and soldiers.[56] Texts reveal the existence of a land market: "the scribe Amenhotep bought for himself 100 (cubits) of

---

[54] Morris also gives an estimate of 80,000 inhabitants for Babylon (2013: 152–153).

[55] By contrast with Mesopotamia, however, "the institutions of the palace and the temple were not economically separate" (Baines and Yoffee 1998: 230). The situation would be different later at the end of the New Kingdom at Thebes.

[56] This phenomenon has already been observed, much earlier, during the Old Kingdom, but it was much more pronounced during the New Kingdom. From the Middle Kingdom onward, offices of the administration and priesthood seem to have been bought, sold, and turned into family wealth (for Allam [1998: 139], however, the offices were not really sold, but "allocated in the form of an imaginary transaction"). Moreover, the emergence of a military sector was a significant new development during the New Kingdom (Baines and Yoffee 1998: 230).

fallow land" thus reads the Wilbour Papyrus (Twentieth Dynasty) (Warburton 2005: 635). Trade and metalworking were largely in private hands. In fact, "there is no documentation for state control [on craftsmen] in the New Kingdom" (Warburton 2007a: 183). We know that the artisans of Deir-el-Medina were hired by the state for their work in the Valley of the Kings, but they also worked privately, for the Theban elite.[57] Craftmanship was marked by advances in metallurgy – bronze, and early ironworking – and in the glass industry, as well as the increasingly export-oriented production of goods.

Silver and, later, copper were the basic monetary standards. Values of goods were measured in metal weight, *deben* or *shāt(y)*,[58] or expressed in measures of volume of oil or cereals, *hin* and *khar*. Textiles, too, were a standard of value and a means of exchange.[59] The reference to a silver standard in a country that had no silver ores – Egyptian silver necessarily originated from external trade – clearly shows the connection between Egypt (already during the Middle Kingdom) and western Asia.[60] Gold, silver, and copper circulated as currencies. "The mere fact that the tombs were robbed for their precious metals [during the Third Intermediary Period] makes it clear that the ancient Egyptians were conscious of the fact that in their economy silver and gold were money equivalents" (Warburton 1997: 84). Wall paintings in tombs had long depicted gold rings offered by Nubians. One painting features a goldsmith weighing coils – which may represent a currency – with cattle-shaped weights.[61] A treasure found at El-Amarna has been interpreted as a hoard of money (Vargyas 2004: 118). For some scholars, gold or silver rings, and copper blades weighing one *deben* (91 g, during the New Kingdom period), may have been used as a currency. The re-evaluation of the *deben* (-weight) during the New Kingdom, which was worth 10 *kite* (9.1 g) and also 12 *shāt*, would have been carried out with reference to the Babylonian systems (Daumas 1977: 428; Menu 2001a: 81; Warburton 2005: 638). For Rahmstorf (2006a: 16), the standard of 9 g was introduced "between the XIIth and the

---

[57] Warburton (2007) also gives the example (for the Third Intermediary Period) of a sculptor of amulets working for the temple of Amon, who privately sold *shabti* figurines.

[58] The early Eighteenth Dynasty stela of Ahmose from Karnak mentions the transfer of "1010 shat in the form of gold, silver, copper, grain and land" (Silver 2004a). "On the Karnak legal stela published by P. Lacau, conversely, the values are given in *debens*" (Dumas 1977: 428). Allam (1998: 142) mentions the example of the sale of a slave to a cowherd who was probably the owner of a textile workshop, under Akhenaton's reign; the sale was made in exchange for two cows and two veal calves, "equivalent to two *deben and* four *shāti* of silver." He also bought the work of two servant women with garments, goats, and a bull, for the first one, and garments, silver, grain, and goats, for the other. For some authors, the use of scales in Egypt may go back to the Predynastic period (*c.* 3000 BCE), but we do not have evidence of them prior to the Fourth Dynasty (Rahmstorf 2006a: 18).

[59] Menu 2001a: 85, 99. The different units of account were interchangeable.

[60] The divine nature of gold, which was "the flesh of the gods," is not enough to explain the choice of silver: "the pharaohs of the XVIIIth and XIXth dynasties distributed gold necklaces to high officials during public events" (Daumas 1977: 438). The Old Kingdom had already created a standard of monetary value based on gold.

[61] These cattle-shaped weights "may refer to ancient practices of conferring on heads of livestock the role of a paleo-currency" (Menu 2001a: 91). The Grand Treasurer Menkheperreseneb (Eighteenth Dynasty) received gold rings. A relief from the temple of Medinet Habou depicts the pharaoh Ramses III offering gold to a god in various forms: sealed bags, and hide-shaped ingots (Menu 2001a: 90, 92).

XVIIIth dynasties, from abroad" (perhaps by the Hyksos?). "There is also some evidence that a standard weight of 7.6 g of silver existed."[62] E. W. Castle (1992) considered that the unit of silver of 7.6 g (one-twelfth of a *deben*) was sometimes used as a means of payment, as well as the *deben*. The text of one ostrakon says: "Objects of Amenemone which are with the chief policeman Amenemope: 5 *deben* of copper, 2 *rwdw*-garments of smooth cloth, makes 15 [*deben*]."[63] Despite the market scene mentioned for the Fifth Dynasty,[64] according to C. Eyre, however, there is no absolute evidence for the existence of objects with standardized weights used as means of exchanges; the value of rings, ingots or pieces of gold, silver, and copper was calculated by weighing them: "the argument that they are objects created specifically for use in exchange is simply wishful thinking."[65] As in western Asia, however, it seems that sealed bags ensured the weight and quality of the metal. In a letter sent to Amenhotep IV (Akhenaton), the Kassite king Burna-Buriash complained in these terms:

My brother should make a [personal] check, then my brother should seal and send it to me. Certainly my brother did not check the earlier (shipment of) gold that my brother sent to me.

[62] Snell 1995: 1489. The Rhind Papyrus (Second Intermediary Period, but the contents of the manuscript may go back as far as the nineteenth century BCE) indicates that one gold *deben* was worth 12 *shāt*, while one silver *deben* was worth six *shāt*, and one lead *deben* three. In these documents of the New Kingdom, the monetary unit was also written *shenāt, shenāu* (*šn't, šn'w*), and *seniu*. Whereas the gold/silver rate remained 2:1 in Egypt during the New Kingdom, it was 13:1 in western Asia (Menu 2001a: 82). This gold/silver rate seems to have varied, as the Boulaq II Papyrus notes "five silver *shāt* are worth three gold *shāt*" (Daumas 1977: 428). The silver *deben* was worth 100 copper *deben* under Ramses II and 60 under Ramses III (one observes an appreciation of copper against silver) (1 *seniu* – unit of silver – was then worth 5 *deben* of copper) (Janssen 1975: 106).

[63] Janssen 1994: 129. Another ostrakon mentions the gift of "6 *deben* of copper and a *mss*-garment" (Janssen 1994: 134). We cannot be sure, however, that this refers to objects as means of exchange (see below).

[64] Other documents have been cited to support the idea of objects as money. The Brooklyn 35.1453A Papyrus (dated to the Eighteenth Dynasty) refers to the remittance of silver *shāti* to a woman on the "quay" (market). In a tomb at Thebes dated to the thirteenth century, a market scene depicts a man taking a volume of beer or wine in exchange for two white circular objects that may represent *shāti* (Silver 1995: 162). A hoard at Amarna has yielded three metal rings bearing incisions. One finds the expression "active as copper" in the Lansing Papyrus. As had been the case during the preceding period, in the New Kingdom, the *deben* appears to have been worth 12 *shāti*. Among the examples given by Bleiberg (1995: 1377) for this period, a woman acquires a slave; she gives the origin of the goods that were exchanged, and for each of them she mentions an amount in silver or in copper. Some Egyptologists have suggested an uncertain connection between the word *shat(y)* and *š'yt*, "loaf" (Peet 1934: 186); it should be remembered, however, that a currency having the shape of a loaf was seemingly present in some regions of western Asia during the second millennium. In addition, *snw* represents a kind of bread offering (Janssen 1975: 104). However, Silver (1995: 177n. 3) is probably wrong when he considers the expression "(broken) *shayt* 'loaves'" used in the Boulaq II Papyrus (Eighteenth Dynasty) in partial payment as constituting a reference to loaf-shaped money. Whereas for Peet (1934: 198–199) the sign used for *shat*, "coin," "represents a cylinder seal with a string loop to hang it" (quoted by Silver 2004a), for Menu, the sign *shāti* shows a determinative which may represent a gold or silver ring (2001a: 75). However, Menu argues that as early as the Old Kingdom, the *shāti* was "an intangible reference." Peet (1934: 188, 196) interprets the gold and silver *shāt* mentioned in the Boulaq II Papyrus as material objects "of fixed weight" and not only as abstract units. D. Warburton (p.c.) acknowledges the use of rings for transactions, but he believes that these rings were not guaranteed by the state.

[65] C. Eyre, p.c. Cf. also Allam 1998: 136. According to Janssen (1975), also, the *seniu*, which seems to have replaced the *š'ty* or *šn'ty* during the Nineteenth Dynasty, did not correspond to any tangible means of exchange. Silver was probably too rare to have a general monetary use in material form.

It was only a deputy of my brother who sealed it and sent it to me. When I pu[t] the 40 minas of gold that were brought to me in a kiln, not (even) [10, I sw]ear, appeared.[66]

An increasing monetization of the economy[67] went along with the development of loans, in gold or other goods (the Lansing papyrus mentions loans by traders to farmers) (Bickel 1998: 164–166; Fabre 2004: 164). Unlike what can be observed during the first millennium BCE, these loans do not seem to have involved the payment of interest, but penalties could be applied if the loans were not paid back on time (Bleiberg 2002: 268). Wages were usually paid in grain, and sometimes in textiles. Texts demonstrate a concerted effort to control productivity. In the turquoise mines of Serabit al-Khadim (Sinai), workers "were remunerated on a piece-work basis for deliveries of stone beyond the required output quota." *Ostraka* from Deir el-Bahri list rations, records of absences, and lists of supervisors (Silver 1995: 138ff.). The true size of the labor market is still unknown, although Warburton asserts that "the mention of wages establishes the reality of the existence of a labor market" (2005: 640).

"Riverbank markets," can be identified, "where producers, state agents and salespeople exchanged goods."[68] A version of the text "The Satire of the Trades" dated to the New Kingdom mentions "specialists in transactions," agents or brokers linked to the temples or to individuals, or working completely independently (the most ancient versions do not mention traders) (Bickel 1998: 166). The Papyri 10068 and 10053 of the British Museum provide the same clues; they refer to merchants employed by a musician of Sobek, by "the Chief of the Archers of the temple of Ra" and a commander of foreign troops, *Imn-nfr*, involved in long-distance trade; "others seem to be completely free men" (Allam 1998: 153; Fabre 2004: 163–165). The Lansing Papyrus mentions "merchants" (*šwty.w*) "who go up and down the river, and trade with copper; they transport merchandise from one city to another" (Fabre 2004: 159) (the *šwty.w* were in fact "commercial agents, responsible for the organization and management of transactions" (Fabre 2004: 159); they were usually the employees of an institution or an individual, but it is likely that this did not prevent them from conducting their own business) (Bickel 1998: 161; Allam 1998: 156). In the *Onomastica*, the word *šwty* is followed by the terms (of Semitic origin) *mḫr* and *mkri*,

---

[66] Letter from El Amarna 7, Moran 1992: 14, quoted by Thompson 2003: 84–85. There is no proof that the seal was directly applied to the metal.

[67] Silver (1995: 158–159) notes that for gold and silver, "the Egyptians paid taxes and rents, and purchased land, slaves, animals, textiles and agricultural products." The Egyptian word *hedj* means both "silver" and "payment."

[68] Warburton 2000a: 66, 69, 72, 76. Warburton suggests the existence of a "market without money," but money did exist: grains were used as a means of exchange and unit of value, as well as gold, silver, and copper (see above). Taxes were not only paid in grain, but also in other products, as well as in metals (such as silver), or labor (corvée). Taxes on farmers were in proportion to the size of their land, and not based on the harvest: farmers, therefore, were encouraged to produce a surplus. Warburton points out that the prominence of the state is obvious in documents of the late Ramesside period, a difficult time just preceding the collapse of the twelfth and eleventh centuries. On the existence of private merchants – Egyptians and Syrians (see below) – see Silver 1995: 170–171. Whereas the existence of markets is almost certain, the importance of the market remains debated, and it is difficult to assess "whether the prices observed were market prices."

"buyer" and "seller" (*šwty* derives from a root *šwi*, "to unload a ship") (Allam 1998: 151). People produced goods for free market sales and there were also markets for services.[69] Products from the temples were often sold on the market, and in general, state institutions used the market to acquire goods (Warburton 1997: 95, 326). As had been the case as far back as the Old Kingdom, the elite paid artisans to construct its tombs (Warburton 2007a: 190; Müller-Wollermann 1985). There was no significant grain storage by the state, and variations in grain prices have been noted for the twelfth century, which was, admittedly, a troubled period.[70] Foreign merchants were allowed to trade:[71] Syrians, for example, were present in the delta and the Nile valley. The growing integration of Egypt in the transnational market triggered the formation of "a cosmopolitan and multicultural society."[72] In the Turin 2008+2016 Papyrus, a man in charge of the Amon-Ra temple's plans "to trade [the contents of a ship: textiles, sesame oil], by using the Syrian language" (Warburton 2005: 633). The differences in price between precious metals made it profitable to export gold to the ports of the Levant and import silver into Egypt (Allam 1998: 153); this incited tomb looting (Papyri 10053 and 10068 of the British Museum mention tomb robbery involving merchants [Allam 1998: 153; Fabre 2004: 163]).

"The presence of foreign people" (prisoners or migrants) is noteworthy "at the different levels of the court and even in the administration" (Margueron and Pfirsch 2001: 279). During the Eighteenth Dynasty, two craftsmen responsible for naval constructions had Syrian names. Some of the women involved in the textile industry for the Royal House were also foreigners (Moorey 2001: 7).

The period was marked by military conquests, and also by growth in trade toward the Levant and Mesopotamia on the one side, and Arabia and the Horn of Africa on the other. From the Middle Kingdom to the New Kingdom, Egypt managed to control the Levant and Nubia more effectively; this control generated a drain of wealth into the Egyptian "core." Seti I and Ramses II led several military expeditions into the Levant to assert Egypt's domination. Canaan became an Egyptian-administered territory and a place of intense cultural blending. In order to facilitate the control of the Levant, the Egyptians raised children of the Canaanite elite, who were later sent back to their country as officials of the Egyptian state (Ekholm Friedman 2005: 58). Trade with the Levant was at that time crucial for Egypt, which imported tin from

---

[69] Through the sale of textiles, garments, and copper vessels, a woman called Ity-nefer managed to buy a young Syrian slave from a merchant (Cairo 65739 Papyrus). Another woman acquired silver through the sale of goods from her lands (Michailidou 2005: 28, 39). Artisans manufacturing sandals are depicted on tomb scenes and are mentioned in texts. On the services offered, see Michailidou 2005: 29ff. On the renting of slaves for specific periods of time, see Michailidou 2005: 38, 45. See Menu 1998.

[70] Warburton 1997: 327; Silver 1995: 104. At the end of the Ramesside period, the state had to rely on the market in order to acquire grain.

[71] Warburton notes: "it would seem that during the 2nd millennium, trade was not controlled on a national basis, although many restrictions existed" (2000a: 85).

[72] Shaw 2000: 329; Monroe 2005: 165. Egypt practiced a policy aimed at the acculturation of the elites from Nubia and the Levant.

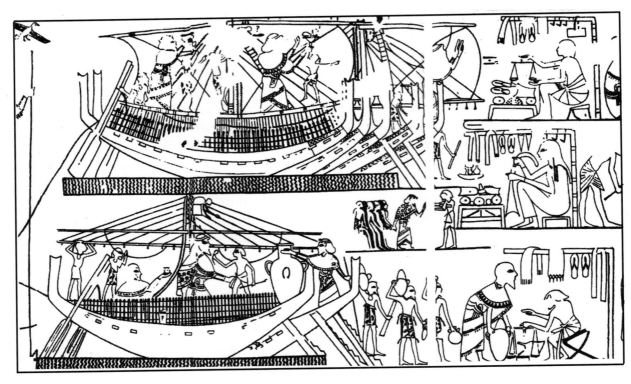

Figure 5.1 Arrival of Syrian merchants in an Egyptian port (Memphis?), relief in the tomb of Qenamon (Eighteenth Dynasty). Market stalls can be seen on the quay (from Basch 1987: 64)

Iran, lapis lazuli from Afghanistan, horses from Qatna (Syria), and copper from Cyprus.[73] The Levant was not only a transit place for merchandise: it was also a region producing goods, some of which were destined for the Nile valley. The Syro-Palestinian coast sent wood, oil, wine, wheat, cattle, copper, mercenaries, and slaves to Egypt (Smyth 1998). Canaanite slaves arrived in Egyptian ports, particularly during the thirteenth century. The "Asians" played a crucial role in transregional exchanges, and also within Egypt. Ramses III built a fleet, many of whose captains were foreigners. In the shipyard built near Saqqara, many workers bore Semitic names, revealing their probable Levantine origin. The captains of ships sailing to Egypt on a contractual basis were usually foreigners, and tomb wall paintings in Thebes depict Syrian ships moored to docks in an Egyptian harbor. Private Egyptian merchants also went to Syria to trade. The means of exchange internationally accepted were silver and gold, with copper used for small transactions (Snell 1995: 1493; Warburton 2000a: 89). State commerce allowed Egypt to accumulate growing quantities of silver, as had been the case earlier during the third and early second millennia. For Egypt, over time, silver became more important than gold (see above). Egyptians sometimes used ships from the Levant, but the reverse was also true: the king of Cyprus (in a letter addressed to Amenhotep III, on

[73] "The Amarna letters attest to the shipment from Alashiya to Egypt of some 54,000 pounds of copper during a period no longer than twenty-five years" (Silver 1995: 142). Tin bronze did not appear in significant amounts in Egypt until Thutmose III's reign (Weeks 2003: 175).

a tablet found at Ugarit) expressed his interest in the purchase of Egyptian ships, which shows that Egyptian vessels "were sufficiently highly esteemed for a foreign sovereign to be inclined to acquire them" (Fabre 2004: 96). A letter from Ramses II to the Hittite king Hattousil III also refers to the building of a ship, to be made on the model of an Egyptian boat from a drawing (Pomey 2006) (it should be noted that "drawings to scale were already in use in architecture during the Old Kingdom") (Pomey 2006: 247). Politico-military and commercial exchanges also fostered technological transfers in the other direction, already initiated slightly earlier by the Hyksos invaders. A glass industry developed under Thutmose III and his successors.[74]

Moreover, a fortress-town, Zawyet Umm el-Rakham, was built on the coast 300 km west of the Nile, to secure the valley from Libyan incursions, and to ensure the safe navigation of ships coming from Crete. At the site of Tell Dab'a, a palace showing Cretan influence has been unearthed; it may have been built to house a Cretan princess, probably destined to marry a pharaoh.

Egyptian expansion also took place southward, beyond the second cataract. It began under Amenhotep I and continued under Thutmose I. This expansion aimed at eliminating Kush, which was a political threat and a troublesome intermediary in trade with countries further south. This expansion also allowed Egypt to directly exploit significant mineral resources. An inscription at Kurgus, between the fourth and fifth cataracts, reveals the annexation of the Kush territory and Egypt's interest in the gold mines of 'Amau and the land of Punt[75] (see Map 1.5). Kush territory was Egyptianized, but not without resistance. Expeditions led by Thutmose III and Amenhotep II came home with captives and booty.[76] Entire populations were deported, from Nubia, and also from Canaan.[77] Military campaigns resulted in the imposition of taxes and tributes, or in the annexation of the occupied territories. From Nubia came "gold, precious stones, construction stones, cattle, wood, ivory, slaves"; from Sudan, "ostrich feathers, aromatics, oil, ivory, and slaves" (Ekholm Friedman 2005: 69). "Nubian tributes, primarily gold, but also products of the African trade now played a crucial role in the functioning of the Egyptian state."[78] Slaves came from the African interior. The temple of Karnak shows tributes brought by the countries of Wawat (gold), Kush (ebony, ivory), and Punt (gold, incense, cattle): the latter region was now directly connected to Egypt via overland routes. The Red Sea also permitted contacts with Sudan and Eritrea, and with the Arabian coast (it has

[74] Shortland 2001: 211–213. Workshops functioned at Thebes, Gurob, and Amarna. Glass was also among the gifts received by Thutmose III, from Babylon and Mitanni. In the crafts sector generally, however, "the juxtaposition of small units does not foster innovation" (Meeks 2006: 11).

[75] Manzo 1999: 26. Very early on, Egypt's policy was aimed at controlling production sites, such as the Wādī Allaqi, and was put into place to cut out the middlemen when trading with regions such as Punt. Punt had connections with Kush. Around 1600 BCE, Punt sent a military force that joined the Kush army to invade southern Egypt (Kitchen 2009).

[76] From Megiddo (Levant), where he was victorious, Thutmose III came back with "silver, gold, precious stones, military equipment (horses, chariots, armor, bows) and prestige goods." He also brought back prisoners, as well as cattle, goats, and sheep (Ekholm Friedman 2005: 68). Amenhotep III stopped this policy of expansion, favoring diplomatic and commercial relationships instead.

[77] People from the Levant also migrated into Egypt voluntarily (Silver 1995: 121).

[78] Margueron and Pfirsch 2001: 275. It is possible that a land route from Korosko to Abu Hamed was used, through the desert. Inscriptions from Tuthmose I and Tuthmose III marking the border have been found at Kurgus (Shinnie 1991: 51).

already been noted that Kitchen locates Punt on the Erythraean coast, east of Irem and south of Amaw, whereas Meeks also locates Punt on the West Arabian coast).[79] In 1472/1 BCE Queen Hatshepsut sent *kpn.wt* ships[80] to the land of Punt, an expedition (the first for 300 years) immortalized by the reliefs of the temple of Deir el-Bahri erected in her memory.

The aim of the Egyptians was clearly to bypass any intermediaries living between Egypt and Punt, by re-establishing direct links with this region. The cost of shipping was also much lower than that of land transport. The Egyptians traveled by sea and by land (one suggested location of the Punt capital was in the hinterland[81]). The ships came back with incense, myrrh, myrrh and incense trees, ebony, "*tishepes* (*tj-shps*) and *khesyt* woods," gold from 'Amau, ivory, leopard skins, dogs, baboons, cheetahs, slaves, and short-horned cattle.[82] The fauna of Punt included domestic as well as wild animals, baboons, giraffes, and rhinos. Meeks notes that the rhino appears to have had only one horn: it must have belonged to the Indian species.[83] In the scenes of the Deir el-Bahri temple, the Puntites are usually represented with light skin similar to that of the Egyptians and Asians. Some had hair that hung to their shoulders, pointed beards and skirt-like garments, a representation suggesting Asian people (from southern Arabia?). Among them, three black figures are depicted. We can see beehive-shaped houses on stilts shaded by trees, some of them palms.[84] In this scene, the Egyptians are offering beer, bread, wine, meat, and fruit to the Puntite chief. The Egyptians may have known that "Punt, or at least T3-ntr ['the land of the god'], extended as far as the Arab coast."[85] After the return of the expedition to Egypt, we see officials weighing gold and

[79] From the Middle Kigdom onward, according to Meeks (2002), the texts locate Punt north or east of Egypt, more often than south. This situation becomes clear during the first millennium BCE. See below.

[80] These ships present some similarities to, but also differences from, the Cretan ships depicted on a fresco at Akrotiri on Thera (seventeenth century BCE) (Fabre 2004: 93). During the New Kingdom, other seagoing ships, the *mnš*, copied from ships of the Levant, were used for trade and as war ships (Fabre 2004: 94) (this type of ship is depicted in the tomb of Qenamon).

[81] Shaw (2000: 324) argues that the Egyptian expeditions by land may have met the Puntites not far from the fifth cataract (Kurgus region). Texts referring to Punt mention "the opening of the two routes" (Manzo 1999: 30).

[82] Kitchen 1993: 592–597. It is possible that unlike what has been claimed, neither *tj-šps* wood nor *khesyt/ khiset* wood represent cinnamon (see below). For Kitchen (2002a: 385), the country of 'Amau was located north of Punt, "perhaps from Abu Hamed at the 5th cataract to the east as far as the mounts close to the Red Sea." We have no proof that the Egyptians ever went further than Punt. A resin called *3hm*, or *imh* or *imh.t*, mentioned before the incense *sntr*, was also imported from Punt (Charpentier 1982). The identification with benzoin, as has sometimes been suggested, is unfounded.

[83] A single-horned rhinoceros is also depicted on a scarab of the New Kingdom found in Canaan (Meeks 2002: 277).

[84] Kitchen 1993: 595–596, figs. 35.3 and 35.4. The fact that the queen of Punt has been represented as a steatopygous woman has been interpreted by some researchers as evidence of a "Hottentot" origin and apparently "reveals" that Punt was located in the Zambezi region; these theories are now abandoned. The physical feature here represented is probably linked to sociocultural factors.

[85] Manzo 1999: 29. The text of Deir el-Bahri includes expressions such as "on the two shores." Note that the inhabitants of the "land of the god" are called Pwntyw, "Puntites", and also Hbstyw, a name that some scholars have tentatively related to Habashat, the population of Ethiopia (Manzo 1999), for whom Conti-Rossini (1906) has suggested a Yemeni origin (Conti-Rossini's proposals, however, have been challenged by many authors). Stephanus of Byzantium (sixth century CE) gives the name Abasēnoi to a population in

ntyw. Scenes represented on the walls of the tomb-chapels of Theban notables show that Puntites also brought their products into Egypt by boat, under the reigns of Thutmose III (1468–1436 BCE), Amenhotep II (1436–1412 BCE), and Amenhotep III (1402–1364 BCE). The Puntites also came via terrestrial routes: the decoration of Amenmose's tomb (no. 89 at Thebes), which dates to the beginning of Amenhotep III's reign, depicts products from Punt and caravans of donkeys.[86] A text from the Sinai (Serabit el-Khadim) engraved under Amenhotep III's reign gives as coming from Punt – perhaps at the port of Merka, on the Gulf of Suez – "ebony, *kȝi* and *tisheps* woods."[87] The name "ebony" may refer to African trees and to Yemeni ebony trees as well, and the identification of Sinhalese ebony in a tomb of the Old Kingdom has already been mentioned. Ramses II grew herbs and trees from the land of Punt in his gardens at Abydos.

The Harris I Papyrus describes a maritime expedition launched by Ramses III (*c.* 1182–1152 BCE), after which Punt vanished from the Egyptian Annals, a disappearance coinciding with the third Egyptian Intermediary Period and marking a decline in relations with Punt. This decline was part of the global recession of the twelfth century. For the first centuries of the first millennium BCE, the fact that Punt is not mentioned rather reflects a shift in trade routes and a better knowledge of the Arab coast.

The Puntites did not bring only goods from their own land. They also transported products from the African interior and from South Asia. The Sinai inscription already mentioned describes the "marvels" of Punt as being a "revenue from lands unknown." The Egyptians knew of many lands besides Punt: in a list engraved at Karnak under

the vicinity of the Sabaeans. Various regions of Yemen contain the root *hbš* in their names, thus the Jebel Habashi.

[86] According to Fattovich (1997b), long-necked pots depicted in a tomb at Thebes dated to Amenhotep II's reign may be compared to ceramics of the so-called "Ona A group" from Eritrea, but this culture is now dated to a later period (see below).

[87] For the location of Punt, Meeks (2002: 296ff.) points to inscriptions found in the Sinai, notably two inscriptions at Serabit el-Khadim dated to the Eighteenth Dynasty. These describe expeditions to Punt. The expedition sent by Hatshepsut also acquired ebony and the *tisheps* wood that stela 238+427 mentions. The pharaoh's envoy declated: "I went to the regions of the Great Green [the Red Sea] to acquire information about the precious goods of Punt and obtain the aromatic gums that the Great Men had [brought] in their ships (?) as contributions of the lands that men [of Egypt] do not know" (Meeks 2002: 311). Kitchen (1999: 183) has translated this text as: "I went forth by the sea-coast to announce the marvels of Punt, to receive aromatic gums, which the chiefs had brought in their *khementy*-boats, as revenue from lands unknown." *Tisheps* was brought back from Lebanon by Amenamhat II (1914–1879/76 BCE). For Meeks, as early as the Middle Kingdom, a northern route to Punt was active via the Sinai, toward the Negev and Arabia Petrea. "The aromatic product called [*khesyt*], [which] figures among the Puntite products of the Hatshepsut expedition, was brought back from Sinai by one of the expeditions sent by Amenemhat II" (Meeks 2002: 308, 309 and n. 241). Some texts mention a "close association" between Punt and Byblos. A text dated to Ramses III designates the Puntites as "sand people" (Arabs) and locates them east of Egypt. "The divinities of Punt," Meeks also writes, "were primarily linked to the eastern part of the Nile delta and to the Sinai" (Meeks 2002: 293). Ships sailing to Punt departed from the Sinai (see above) (Manzo 1999: 33). Manzo also emphasizes that in the list of names of countries found in the temple of Sesebi, between the regions of Kush and 'Irm and that of Punt, we find Asian toponyms; and in the inscription of Ramses II at Karnak, "Punt is still related to the Asian series." The links of Punt with Asia reflect the activity on the maritime routes and the caravan roads of western Arabia (see below).

Figure 5.2 Rafts from Punt arriving in Egypt, tomb 143 at Thebes (from Save-Söderbergh 1946: 24, fig. 6). The ships from Punt appear to have used animal skins as flotation devices. Note the use of a triangular sail.

Tuthmose III (*c.* 1450 BCE), Punt is only the first of thirty names, which are unfortunately difficult to relate to any specific region (Phillips 1997). The exchange networks may have extended as far as East Africa: Egyptian cylindrical blue faience beads similar to those of the Eighteenth Dynasty were discovered in the 1920s in the Juba country (southern Somalia) at a location unfortunately not specified (Manzo 1999: 50). The Eritrean coast, together with Yemen, played an important part in the relations between Asia and Africa, particularly after 1500–1400 BCE.[88] For some authors, the banana may have been introduced to this coast at the end of the second millennium BCE before it was taken to Ethiopia and adopted by farmers cultivating the ensete, who disseminated the banana further west. The early presence of the banana in Africa (this would have been plantain, a *Musa balbisiana* x *Musa acuminata* hybrid, of AAB type) is suggested by the discovery of *Musa* phytoliths in Cameroon (the material was retrieved from refuse pits) dated to between 840 and 350 BCE,[89] but this discovery needs confirmation (Neumann and Hildebrand 2009). Upstream, Yemen and Oman may have been centers of cultivation. Abū Hanifa' al-Dīnawarī (around 895 CE) considered

[88] It is probably no coincidence that the state of Kerma and that of the Gash group disappeared at the same time. The Jebel Mokram Group culture appears to have participated only marginally in exchange networks.

[89] De Langhe and de Maret 1999. This discovery in Cameroon has been questioned by Vansina 2004; see the response from Mbida *et al.* 2004. Moreover, claims have been made for the discovery of *Musa* phytoliths in Uganda dated to the fourth millennium, which would suggest an introduction through East Africa, but the identification of the phytoliths as belonging to *Musa sp.* has been called into question, as well as their dating, see below. In Egypt, the banana may have been present at least since the fifth century (Barakat and Baum 1992).

the banana as native to Oman, whence it would have migrated to the rest of the Muslim world (Watson 1983: 80). We will see, however, that East Africa – and not Eritrea – is the most probable site of the arrival of bananas in Africa, and that plantain did not come from India.

The "Annals" of Thutmose III may indicate direct relations with southern Arabs: among the delegations mentioned who presented tributes when the pharaoh returned from Syria during Year 32 of his reign, are "messengers of the *Gnbtyw* bearing myrrh" and ivory. *Gnbtyw* is probably related to the Gebbanitae of Pliny and other authors, which corresponds to the *Gb'n* found in South Arabian texts (Qatabanites). These *Gnbtyw* may have taken advantage of the trade between Punt and Egypt to pursue their own commercial expeditions to the latter country (Kitchen 2002a: 394). The "Annals" of Thutmose III also signal the presence of "incense" in Syria, but this term does not prove that the caravan routes of Arabia were in use and took incense and myrrh to western Asia: it has already been pointed out that this "incense" may refer to the resin of local *Pistacia*.

Through Arabia, exchange networks extended as far as India. A text from the reign of Thutmose III mentions "the bird that gives birth every day," probably the chicken, which originated in India (Uerpmann 2008). In addition, grains of pepper (*Piper sp.*, the species has not been identified) have been discovered in the stomach and throat of Ramses II's mummy (Germer 1985). Moreover, the arrival of African plants in India at various times during the second millennium has already been mentioned (see above).

The purported attempt by Sethi and Ramses II to dig a canal between the Nile and the Red Sea reflects the significance of maritime trade for Egypt and the idea of connecting the Mediterranean Sea and the Red Sea, especially as terrestrial routes were becoming less safe. Difficulties began with revolts in the south and the "western desert," due to an aridification of the climate.[90] Ramses II launched a campaign against 'Irm (perhaps located in the region of Atbara) and came back with 7,000 captives; other military expeditions would follow, to the south and west of the Nile. One clue to the drop in water level is the fact that this pharaoh found it necessary to re-dig a well on the road leading to the gold fields of the Wādī Allaqi. A rebellion is then mentioned in Wawat (Lower Nubia) under Merenptah, and Ramses III had to launch another campaign against 'Irm. Growing aridity then triggered various population movements (Manzo 1999: 34, 35).

The Cataclysmic Collapse of the Late Bronze Age World

> No land could stand up against their arms, from Hatti, Kodè, Karkemish, Arzawa
> [Anatolia], Alashiya [Cyprus] on, cut off (all) at [once] in one [place]. A camp was
> set in Amurru [south of Ugarit]. They devastated its people and its land was as
> though it had never existed. They were advancing on Egypt while the flame
> was prepared before them. (Inscription year 8 of Ramses III, in his funerary temple)
> (Shaw 2000: 328; Faivre 2001: 646–647)

---

[90] Difficulties may have begun earlier, as shown by a text from Horemheb "who boasts on the walls of the temple of Karnak that he is keeping open the roads leading to the southern resources of Punt" (Manzo 1999: 34). At the beginning of the Nineteenth Dynasty, Sethi I launched a campaign against the 'Irm country.

A sharp cooling in the climate was accompanied by pronounced aridification in the main cores of the Late Bronze Age world during the thirteenth to the twelfth century (Brook 2014: 303). Climate change played a crucial role in the upheavals affecting the Balkans, western Asia, and Egypt at this time.[91] Famines and epidemics struck these regions, triggering social disorder and undermining state structures. The Eurasian steppes were also hit by increased aridification, and the number of archaeological sites between the Danube and the Don rivers fell to one-tenth of their number from the twelfth to the tenth century (Makhortykh 2004: 37).[92] Greece and Anatolia appear to have been the first regions to be affected, as shown by the strengthening of fortifications during the second half of the thirteenth century. In a letter to Ramses II, the king of Cyprus complained that an epidemic had decimated the population, so he was unable to export copper. The Hittite king sent a letter to the ruler of Ugarit, asking him to send grain urgently because his people faced starvation. The pharaoh Merenptah finally shipped wheat to him. In Egypt itself, skilled workers went on strike to obtain delivery of their food rations from the royal warehouses (Ekholm Friedman 2005: 75). The central states reacted to the decline in production and trade with increased control over commerce and manufacturing[93] and restrictions on the movements of foreign merchants. These reactions may also have been a response to the development of an "interstitial" commerce that escaped state control and undermined the foundations of the state.[94] Various sources signal increasing levels of piracy in the eastern Mediterranean Sea. At the same time, one notes renewed conflicts between states eager to take by force what they could no longer obtain through trade. The very structure of the system, centered on a group of imperialist military states competing, in particular, for the acquisition of slaves and mercenaries, explains its fragility. Maintaining military forces involved huge costs that exacerbated social problems. Internal changes, in various states, along with the development of larger estates at the expense of village communities, saw increasing exploitation of the population by the elites. Growing pressure exerted on the social and geographic peripheries (increased taxes, raids, and the formation of a class of uprooted people) logically led to the sudden collapse of the entire interconnected space of the Late Bronze Age (Ekholm Friedman 2005).

---

[91] These changes were aggravated by a major volcanic eruption that occurred in 1159 BCE (Burroughs 2001), due perhaps to the Hekla volcano (Iceland).

[92] Some sources, however, suggest increased humidity in regions north of the Black Sea and in western Siberia (Fagan 2004: 183).

[93] Some authors consider that an excessive expansion of the palatial and temple sectors occurred at the expense of impoverished rural populations (see Ekholm Friedman 2005: 81).

[94] The Hittites prevented Mycenaean ships from reaching Syria, and they also impeded the movements of Assyrian merchants (Ekholm Friedman 2005: 81). In the flourishing of decentralized and "interstitial" trade, which undermined the control of exchanges by the states, Sherratt (2000, 2003) sees the major cause of their decline from the thirteenth century BCE onward (see below). The deposit of small quantities of metals cut into pieces at the end of the thirteenth century in the eastern Mediterranean may reflect a growing decentralization of the networks as well as heightened insecurity.

Conversely, climate change may have been a boon to agriculture in Central Europe in the extensive Urnfield Culture (from 1300 BCE) (Kristiansen 1998: 110). From Italy and the eastern European steppes to Greece and western Asia, population movements by land and sea produced a domino effect that disrupted weakened communities and states. The Mycenaean culture disintegrated around 1200 BCE with the arrival of new Greek populations, known as "Dorian."[95] The collapse of palatial structures led to the disappearance of writing in Greece. Troy (VIIA) was destroyed after a siege, *c.* 1180. The Hittite Empire also disappeared toward 1200 BCE, attacked from the west by the "Phrygians" (Mushki . . .) and from the northeast by the Kashka of the Pontic region. The demise of this empire marked the beginning of a series of upheavals that affected western Asia, with the invasions or migrations of the "Sea Peoples" of the Egyptian texts,[96] a collective name that conceals the heterogeneity of these populations on the move. The towns and cities of the Syro-Palestinian coast (Ugarit . . .) and Cyprus[97] were looted (the Phoenician coast between Arwad and Akko, however, seems to have remained relatively unscathed),[98] and Crete itself was affected. In Arabia, too, the Subr culture (Yemen) vanished during the twelfth century BCE after reaching its peak (Görsdorf and Vogt 2001: 1360).

Within western Asia, entire populations migrated with carts and cattle in search of lands where they could settle. Like the Amorites before them, the Aramaeans, Semites who moved around the margins of Mesopotamia, constituted a permanent threat from the thirteenth century onward; they finally settled in Babylonia and ruled smaller states in Syria, in the area of the Neo-Hittite kingdoms. The collapse of the centralized states led to the disappearance of the alphabetic cuneiform script, but linear alphabetic writing subsisted, although it is not visible in archaeological levels, very probably because it was mainly written on papyri and leather (Lemaire 2007: 59). The Suteans of the Syro-Jordanian desert also invaded Mesopotamia, which experienced a decline in population between the eleventh and ninth centuries. In 1155, Babylon was seized by

---

[95] Authors such as R. Drews (1993) have criticized the migration hypothesis and emphasized the impact of a new kind of warfare, involving infantry and the slashing sword, on the instability of this period. However, this does not eliminate the evidence for migrations.

[96] Some names such as the Lukka of Anatolia (Lycia) appear as early as the fourteenth century BCE: writing to the king of Cyprus, Akhenaton complains about attacks by Sea Peoples from the Lukka country, and the king of Cyprus mentions that every year, "Lukki" take possession of villages on his island. Sirdanu or Sardanu (Sherden in later Egyptians texts) were employed as mercenaries to guard the prince of Byblos Rib-Addi (fourteenth century BCE) and at Ugarit (thirteenth century BCE). Sirdana mercenaries were among the personal guard of the pharaoh Ramses II at Qadesh (1274 BCE), while the Hittites employed "Anatolian contingents originating from the land of Lukka and Dardanya" (Faivre 2001: 645). Elements belonging to the Sea Peoples appear to have been linked to the confederation of Ahhiyawa (Achaeans) mentioned in Hittite texts; this confederation must have been located in Anatolia and Thrace. The populations of Ahhiyawa, like others in this region, were both aggressors and victims.

[97] Exchanges of letters between the ruler of Ugarit Ammurapi, the Hittite king Suppiluliuma II, and the king of Cyprus, attest to their common fear of the advance of the "Sikalayu" and other populations (Faivre 2001: 646).

[98] Niemeyer 2000: 92. Tablets from Ugarit mention attacks coming from the sea (Klengel 1992: 150; Ekholm Friedman 2005: 73).

an Elamite army,[99] but the king of a new Babylonian dynasty, Nebuchadnezzar I (Nabuchodonosor I), destroyed Susa around 1110 BCE.[100] Elam disappeared from inscriptions for three centuries. Regions in the north and the east were also affected. Chernykh notes a collapse of the social systems in the Eurasian steppes and a shift to nomadism in the Irano-Afghan region.[101] Horseback riding probably became widespread in the steppes during this period, along with mobile pastoralism based on sheep breeding rather than cattle breeding.[102] Analogies observed between objects found in tombs of northern Iran and northern Pakistan suggest movements of Indo-European speakers from Central Asia or Iran. During this period, India no longer seems to be connected to western Asia, although some ports probably remained active on the western Indian coast.

From the end of the thirteenth century onward, the Nile valley also experienced a period of disintegration of the Egyptian monarchy, affected by weaker trade and the invasions of the Sea Peoples, whose members had already been identified as mercenaries in Ramses II's army at the battle of Qadesh.[103] Their attacks were repulsed by the pharaoh Merenptah (1230 BCE)[104] and, later, Ramses III. It was during the twelfth century that the Hebrews, coming from Egypt, are likely to have settled in Canaan.[105] Other aggressions came from the western margins. As early as the thirteenth century, the Libyans were threatening Egypt. With the help of other warrior groups, they came to dominate the Nile delta and took over the government of Egypt. Warburton suggests that there were also internal causes for the decline. Ramses III is said to have given one-sixth of Egypt's arable land to the temples, and the state abandoned construction projects.[106] The incentive to produce disappeared as taxes decreased.

[99] It is after this victory that the Elamite king Shutruk-Nahhunte brought back the Code of Hammurabi to Susa, among other Mesopotamian stelae.

[100] For Amiet (1988: 111), this defeat resulted from the decline in the population of Susiana, revealed by the abandonment of towns and villages.

[101] Chernykh 1992: 262, 272, 306; Frank 1993a: 397.

[102] In addition, Kuzmina (2007: 380) notes that the "earliest image of an archer-centaur [featuring the nomads of the steppes] is found on a Babylonian border stone" that may go back to the thirteenth century BCE. The stone is now in the British Museum.

[103] During the second year of his reign, Ramses II opposed an invasion of "Sirdana [Sherden] who came on their warships." They were incorporated into his army and they are mentioned at Qadesh with Lukka (from Lycia), and Peleset, who would later form the Philistines of Palestine. As already noted, the Hittites also employed mercenaries belonging to populations that would be found slightly later among the Sea Peoples. Another attack by the Sea Peoples allied to Libyans occurred in 1208 BCE. Besides the Lukka and the Sherden, an inscription at Karnak mentions the Ekwesh (the Achaeans of the *Iliad*?), the Shekelesh and the Teresh (the Tyrsenoi of the Greek world, located by Hittite sources south of the Troad). Under Ramses III, the Peleset were also mentioned, as well as "the Danuna [Denen, the Danaeans of the Iliad], the Sikala, the Shirdana, and the Washasha. The Danaeans are probably the same population as the Danawo mentioned as enemies of the Iranians in the *Avesta*.

[104] Texts mention an attack by a coalition of Libyans and Sea Peoples (Liverani 2014: 383–384).

[105] Some researchers have wondered whether the mention of Habiru warriors on the statue of King Idrimi (fifteenth century) (kingdom of Kizzuwatna), who reigned at Alalakh as a vassal of Mitanni, referred to the Hebrews; but the text may be dated to the thirteenth century (Benoit 2003: 108). This name Habiru, Hapiru, corresponding to the Egyptian *pr.w*, also appears in other sources. For many researchers, "there is no relation between *'apiru/habiru* and *'ibri*, Hebrews" (Kuhrt 1995: 436).

[106] Warburton 2000a: 69, 2000b: 181. Bleiberg (1995: 1384) also emphasizes the destruction of the Egyptian economy in its classical form during this period, with a disintegration of the redistribution system. Price inflation has been noted at the end of the millennium, under the reign of Ramses VII.

Moreover, data show lower Nile flood levels after 1300 and a series of poor harvests between 1170 and 1100.[107] Decreasing agricultural production caused famines and internal upheaval; the central power split apart, as conflicts arose between the royal power – established at Pi-Ramses (and then Tanis) – and the clergy of Thebes, during the eleventh century. A depopulation of Lower Nubia occurred at this time. The situation in the middle Nile valley, however, is not well understood, as archaeological and textual data are scarce for the late second and the early first millennia BCE: "what happened in Nubia and farther south from the end of the XXth Egyptian dynasty onward remains a historical mystery. Historical sources are silent about the ancient territory of Kush for two centuries. It is only for the 8th century that we find textual elements referring to the southern region."[108] The instability in Egypt was certainly one of the causes of the rapid development of the caravan trade in Arabia.

The recession that had begun *c.* 1200 BCE lingered until around 1000 BCE. In the Mediterranean, after the demise of the Mycenaean power, the Cypriots and the people of the Levant took the upper hand in the western Mediterranean networks (Sherratt 2003). The discovery of a statuette of a Syrian god at Cadiz and a cylinder seal of Cypriot type at Malaga strongly suggests that ships from Cyprus and the Levant sailed to Spain at the end of the Late Bronze Age to acquire copper and silver from the Guadalquivir region.

This traditional reconstitution of the events occurring at the end of the Late Bronze Age, based on a "middle" chronology, has been challenged on several important points. For post-Kassite Babylonia, Cyprus, and Syria, the period between the twelfth and the ninth centuries did not yield many remains and appears to be "not well known." James *et al.* (1993) have proposed placing the Eighteenth Egyptian Dynasty 250 years later than usual[109] – thus eliminating the "hole" of the "dark centuries" (from 1200 to the beginning of the tenth century BCE).[110] Ugarit was destroyed *c.* 930 BCE and there would thus be no hiatus between this Levantine period and the Phoenician flourishing that followed.[111]

---

[107] Butzer 1995: 136; Manzo 1999: 5, based on data near Akasha in Nubia. Tradition tells of the aridification of Lower Nubia and the drying of the eastern branch of the Nile in the delta.

[108] Manzo 1999: 36, 63. This period of "archaeological silence" should probably be shortened.

[109] It is true that radiocarbon analysis for Ramses II and Tutankhamun gave datings 100 to 120 years later than expected, but these datings are not very reliable (Bruins and van der Plicht 2003: 40). In contrast, for Sethi I, C_{14} dating is more or less in line with the "official" chronology. Usually attributed to the armies of the Eighteenth Egyptian Dynasty, the fall of Jericho during the Middle Bronze Age has been dated to 1556 (C_{14}), thus prior to the beginning of the Eighteenth Dynasty (*c.* 1540). More research is obviously needed in the field of dating.

[110] For Mesopotamia, the authors note that the (Babylonian) Poem of Erra (god of war and plague), which describes the destruction of the world order, is believed to have been written around the ninth century or eighth century BCE. Erra incites the inhabitants of Babylon to revolt, bringing ruin and desolation on the city.

[111] The similarities between objects produced during the Phoenician period and assemblages we find at Ugarit for layers traditionally dated to the thirteenth century have often been noted. For James *et al.*, the texts from Ugarit describe Phoenician practices at Tyre and Byblos during the tenth century. The revised chronology for Ugarit would allow us to understand the name of its ruler, Nikmed, prior to the destruction of the city, as being the Greek name Nikomedes. It would also solve the problem of the strange hiatus between the supposed date of the sarcophagus of King Ahiram from Byblos (thirteenth century: objects bearing the cartouche of Ramses II have been recovered in the tomb) and that of the

James *et al.*'s theses have met with much scepticism – to say the least – from most archaeologists and historians.[112] Conversely, the "ultra-short" chronology suggested by Gasche *et al.* (1998) has been relatively well received, but remains a minority view,[113] although Reade (2001, 2008) and Warburton (2007b) have recently advocated this chronology, which lowers historical events between 2500 and 1000.[114]

Moreover, some scholars have cast doubt on the notion of "invasions" by Sea Peoples, even though migrations and attacks, by both sea and land, did occur. For Kuhrt, for example, these migrant populations were primarily mercenaries and refugees, not conquerors.[115] The extensive destruction observed, however, was definitely real.

Central Asia and South Asia

The "Rig-Vedic" Proto-Indo-Aryans entered India on a significant scale around the middle of the second millennium, perhaps "pushed" forward by the arrival of Proto-Iranians into Central Asia, who overwhelmed and assimilated the various cultures of the Andronovo sphere.[116] From Turkmenistan to Bactria, a new culture – called Yaz I-Tyllia-Kuchuk (1500–1000 BCE) – emerged, which demonstrated a knowledge of iron metallurgy and the use of painted pottery made without a potter's lathe. This

---

Phoenician inscription engraved on this sarcophagus (tenth century); James *et al.*'s propositions, however, make for insoluble chronological problems.

[112] See Kitchen 1996: xixff., who also refutes Rohl's arguments (1995); according to Rohl, the duration usually given to the Third Intermediary Period (Twenty-First to Twenty-Fifth Dynasties) should be shortened by at least 141 years.

[113] The occultations of the planet Venus noted under the reign of the fourth successor of Hammurabi (known by texts dated to the seventh century BCE) provide benchmarks in time, with "three major possibilities," hence "high," "middle," and "low" chronologies (Joannès 2001: 187), which place the fall of Babylon respectively in 1659, 1595, or 1531 BCE. Some researchers contest the value of the data concerning Venus. Based on the Hittite chronology, Beckman (2000) has expressed his disagreement with the "ultra-low" chronology put forward by Gasche *et al.* For a discussion on Gasche *et al.*, see Klinger 2006: 309–312.

[114] The First Dynasty of Ur is placed during the twenty-fourth century, and the Guti interlude would have lasted about 40 years and not 145 years. Sargon would have seized power *c.* 2180 (±40).
Dendrochronological data from Acem Hüyük in a building where artifacts associated with Shamshi-Addu have been found appear compatible with an ultra-low chronology, placing this king between *c.* 1712 and 1680 (instead of 1815–1773 BCE). Studies on Syrian (from Terqa) and Kassite seals, as well as texts and artifacts from Alalakh, lead to the same conclusion (Reade 2001). Using data from Alalakh, Zeeb (2004) also opts for a chronology close to that of Gasche. Albright (1956) already used Alalakh to support the hypothesis of a short chronology (thirty-two years higher than the chronology suggested by Gasche). Against Gasche's chronology, see van Koppen 2004: 9 n. 3. Hagens (1999) also proposes an ultra-short chronology for the Iron Age of Palestine, bringing forward the access of Ramses III to the throne to *c.* 1110 (instead of the more conventional date of 1198). On the debates concerning the ultra-short chronology, see also *Akkadica*, 2000: 119–120.

[115] Kuhrt 1994: 390–392. It is likely, however, that mercenaries who were not paid or not well paid might turn into conquerors. The violent destruction of a large number of cities indicates the magnitude of the attacks on the central points of the system.

[116] Parpola (2002: 246) locates the origin of the Iranian speakers in the Pontic steppes. For Frachetti (2004: 212), southward movements of Fedorovo groups (partly Indo-Aryans?) can be seen around the middle of the second millennium, at a time of aridification of the steppes, but these movements had started earlier (Kuzmina 2007).

culture was connected with Indus valley sites such as Pirak II (Kuzmina 2007: 425, 433), and attests to influences from the steppes, which can be seen in metallic objects and the appearance of new types of cheekpieces. Parpola (1995) and Francfort (2005) connect this culture with Iranian speakers. Francfort points out the predominance of the exposure or "laying out" of the dead, which probably explains the virtual absence of tombs in the oasis during this period. The size of bricks, however, remained the same as in the Bronze Age, signaling some continuity. This cultural phase saw a process of re-urbanization, marking the emergence of proto-state entities (Francfort 2001a: 222, 228). Cowries found at the sites of Chirakchi (Burguluk culture, in the Tashkent region) and Yaz attest to possible relations with the Karasuk culture (southern Siberia), itself linked with China (Francfort 2001a: 230). Pakistan and India, by contrast, became de-urbanized.

The timing and manner of the split between the Iranian and Indo-Aryan linguistic families are still debated. Unlike Parpola, Witzel considers that the Indo-Iranian language had not yet split into its Indian and Iranian branches at the beginning of the second millennium, and that the major period of contact between Indo-Iranians and BMAC people occurred *c.* 1500 BCE: the expansion of "Pre-Vedic" and then "Rigvedic" Indo-Aryans into Mitanni and India is perceptible from 1500 BCE onward (2004: 29, 81, 82). In fact, the Indo-Aryan migration into Mitanni probably occurred as early as the seventeenth century (Kuzmina 2007: 322). Southworth also distinguishes successive arrivals in Punjab between the beginning and the middle of the second millennium. The earliest parts of the *Rig Veda* may have been composed *c.* 1500 BCE (Southworth 2005: 47). Branches of Indo-Iranian speakers of the Nuristani or Dardic languages (northwestern Pakistan, eastern Afghanistan) are said to have arrived a few centuries before the "Rig-Vedic" Indo-Aryans. For Southworth, the split of the Proto-Indo-Aryan language happened *c.* 2000 BCE between Bactria–Margiana and the Urals. Fussman (2001: 93) suggests a date between 1800 and 1500 for the split of Indo-Iranian into Proto-Iranian and Proto-Indo-Aryan. As already noted, Kuzmina (2007) criticizes Parpola's hypothesis of an early split of the Indo-Aryan and Proto-Iranian branches and the identification of the Andronovo people as Indo-Aryans: she points out that the language and the culture of the *Rig Veda* and of the *Avesta* are close to each other, which implies a separation shortly before these texts were composed.

According to Parpola, the Rigvedic Indo-Aryans entered India around 1500/1400 BCE, coming from Afghanistan (their economy, as the *Rig Veda* shows, must have been primarily pastoralist). In India, they merged with representatives of the earliest Aryan waves (Parpola 2002: 246; see above). A Black and Red Ware Culture appeared in the Ganges valley,[117] succeeded by the "Painted Grey Ware Culture," from 1200 BCE. During the period between 1200 and 1100 BCE, new Iranian-speaking groups, perhaps coming from the Pontic steppes, arrived in Central Asia, introducing iron metallurgy. These Iranian speakers entered Persia, while others went into India. Through their contact, the Indo-Aryans may have adopted the use of iron *c.* 1100 BCE and a more intensive agriculture developed progressively in the Ganges valley, as well as small

---

[117] Dates *c.* 1500 BCE have been suggested for this pottery in Bengal. Other authors prefer to connect the Rig-Vedic Aryans to the Painted Grey Ware culture.

kingdoms. Relations between this incipient core in northern India and its peripheries at this time are still poorly understood. Interactions with the south of the peninsula allowed rice cultivation to spread from the northeast during the late first millennium BCE.

In the Deccan, the transition between the Neolithic and Megalithic tradition – associated with the presence of Black and Red Ware – testifies to major social transformations, the extension of exchange networks, and perhaps population movements.[118] Iron tended to appear slightly later (although it was already present around 1200/1100 BCE at some sites such as Hallur).

In the preceding chapters, we have followed the evolution of a vast area centered on western Asia and Egypt, where a process of Neolithization occurred during an early period prior to the birth of the state. The formation of the state was accompanied by the development of exchange networks, a process of urbanization, and technical and institutional innovations. In East Asia, communities also domesticated plants and animals very early on. Here too, the "Neolithic revolution" fostered the expansion of exchange networks, demographic growth, and increasing social complexity, with radical innovations that would encourage the formation of states.

---

[118] In some regions such as northern Karnataka, the megalithic tradition starts around 1400–1300 BCE (Fuller, Boivin, and Korisettar 2007: 770). Generally speaking, the Neolithic/Megalithic transition occurred between 1400 and 800 BCE, with the "Classical Megalithic" phase dated to between 800 and 300 BCE.

6 East Asia: From Villages to States (*c.* 5000–1027 BCE)

The Neolithic Cultures of East Asia: Local Developments and First Contacts with Central Asia

During the four millennia that saw the rise to power of states in western Asia and in Egypt, East Asia followed a unique trajectory, though – very early on – contacts led to the introduction of techniques and products from the west. China, where sedentary communities developed, was a primary center for the domestication of plants and animals. The Neolithic communities in the Yangtze valley region developed slightly later than in western Asia, possibly practicing agriculture during the eighth millennium BCE (but more likely during the sixth); a process of rice domestication subsequently began, which led to the development of *japonica* varieties in the east (though it would be more correct to speak of *sinica*) and – for some authors – of *indica* types further south and west.[1] In the Upper Yangtze, rice does not appear to have been present before 3000 BCE.

[1] In fact, the separation of the *indica* and *japonica* subspecies dates back to a period well before rice domestication (Sweeney and McCouch 2007). Genetic data seem to reflect different domestications from subpopulations of *O. rufipogon* Griff. (see also Cheng *et al.* 2003, Garris *et al.* 2005), domestications which are, however, not completely independent of one another (Kovach *et al.* 2007: 584). Genetic research by Londo *et al.* (2006) have suggested that the *indica* varieties were domesticated in the India–Indochina region, and the *japonica* rice in southern China; this contradicts the discoveries of researchers that place the origins of both *japonica* and *indica* types in the region of the Yangtze and of the Huai rivers (Jiahu site) (Bellwood 2005a: 119). Some researchers posit that two domestications of *indica* rice occurred – with the more recent variety being domesticated in eastern India using annual types of *Oryza* (Cheng *et al.* 2003: 72). However, this theory of multiple *indica* domestications has now been abandoned. In contrast, Molina *et al.* (2011a, b) have supported the idea of a single origin for domesticated rice. Note that the *indica* type was not significant in China until 1000 CE (Crawford 2006: 78). Various researchers have suggested a spread of *japonica* rice followed by a process of introgression from local wild populations, in Southeast Asia (Myanmar) and in India (Sang and Ge 2007; Vaughan *et al.* 2008; *cf.* Fuller and Qin 2009). The site of Shangshan (Lower Yangtze) has yielded the oldest discovery of rice that is perhaps partly domesticated (8000–7000 BCE). Rice is well attested in the Pengtoushan culture (Middle Yangtze) (seventh millennium), where the Bashidang site represents the oldest known site with walls and moats. The rice from Bashidang cannot be assigned to a rice subspecies (Crawford 2006: 84). Fuller, Harvey, and Qin (2007) and Fuller and Qin (2009) suggest that the process of domestication occurred much later: rice may only have become fully domesticated around 4000 BCE in the Yangtze River valley. A nascent domestication is, however, perceivable earlier, for example at Kuahuqiao (Lower Yangtze), *c.* 6000 BCE, and at Tianluoshan (Bay of Hangzhou) where domestication was underway between 4900 and 4600 BCE (Fuller and Weisskopf 2011: 47). For these authors, rice cultivation between 6000 and 4500 BCE was based primarily on undomesticated forms. The existence of rice fields is clearly attested at Tianluoshan for the first half of the fifth millennium and at Caoxieshan at the end of the millennium (Jiangshu province) (Fuller, Harvey, and Qin 2007; Liu and Chen 2012).

The Yellow River basin was another center for the emergence of agriculture, with the domestication of several millets.[2] The Yangshao culture, which flourished in the middle Yellow River valley, has provided evidence for growing social complexity. Large sites exhibit public architecture "of a palatial type," for example at Dadiwan (Gansu) and Anban (Shaanxi). The latter site has yielded ceramic figurines representing bearded men with long noses and wearing high hats, doubtless depictions of western foreigners.[3] In Henan, the large walls and moats of the village of Xishan point to competition between emerging political entities, as does the site of Beiyangping, which spread across 90 ha. The Yangshao culture expanded up to Qinghai and Gansu in the west, in its Middle (4000–3500 BCE) and Late (3500–3000 BCE) phases, and into northwest Sichuan (Li 2003: 12). Toward the end of the fourth millennium, population movements from the east coast are noticeable in Henan.[4]

Very early on, there were visible interactions between the Yangtze River and the Yellow River valleys. Rice was present at Lijiacun and Xiawanggang in the Upper and Middle Yellow River valley around 5000 and 4000 BCE. In contrast, in the Yangtze valley, farmers of the Daxi culture (4500–3300) grew *Setaria italica* millet, introduced from the Yellow River basin (Lu 2005; Nasu *et al.* 2007; Fuller, Harvey, and Qin 2007) (it was present at Chengtoushan, a Middle Yangtze site, around 4000 BCE).

In the Yangtze valley, the development of more intensive rice cultivation around 4000 BCE was accompanied by the spread of domesticated rice varieties and the appearance of hierarchized social systems that were capable of mobilizing community labor more efficiently. Social differentiation appeared in the Late Songze culture (3500–3300 BCE), followed by the Liangzhu culture (Fuller and Qin 2009: 99). The site of Lingjiatan (160 ha) (north of the Yangtze, Anhui province), for example, shows evidence of rich elite tombs and of jade manufacturing. This jade was subsequently exported to the south (Liu and Chen 2012: 204).

Starting in the fourth millennium, the emergence of elites, and the existence of long-distance trade linked to the luxury goods on which their power was based, were apparent in different Neolithic cultures in central and northern China:[5] these include the Hongshan culture, on the Liao River, north of the Yellow River valley; the

---

[2] Common millet (broomtail millet) (*Panicum miliaceum* L.), foxtail millet (*Setaria italica* [L.] P. Beauv.), and barnyard millet (*Echinochloa esculenta* [A. Braun] H. Scholz.). The domestication of millets in the Yellow River valley and in Mongolia (site of Xinglonggou) occurred during the early sixth millennium, thus prior to that of rice in the Yangtze River valley (Fuller *et al.* 2007) (conversely, Bellwood [2005b] does not exclude an influence on the part of the Yangtze farmers in the development of agriculture in the Yellow River valley).

[3] Two other clay heads, excavated at Jiangxicun (south of Anban), and at Liujiahe (South Shaanxi, Miaodigou phase, fourth millennium), also show Caucasian characteristics. Figurines from Turkmenistan (Kara Depe, Geoksyur) (during the Namazga III phase, 3500–3000 BCE) exhibit similarities with those from Anban (Liu 2004: 86, 88–91). Even if Liu mentions "palace-like public architecture," at this stage it is not yet possible to discern a segregated elite (which is later observable during the third millennium): the political entities were probably chiefdoms and not kingdoms.

[4] Liu 2004: 167. The demise of Xishan is linked to hostilities marking the emergence of conflicts between groups or chiefdoms.

[5] Liu 2003. Many authors have pointed out that exotic and local "prestige goods" played an important role in the political and economic development of ancient societies, and made it possible to generate and legitimize elite power. The elite tended to control the supply of these goods, and sometimes their manufacture: see Coquery-Vidrovitch 1969; Ekholm 1972; Kohl 1975; Friedman and Rowlands 1977; Schneider 1977; Appadurai 1986; Peregrine 1991; Sherratt and Sherratt 1991; Helms 1993, among others.

Dawenkou culture, in the Lower Yellow River valley during the fourth millennium; and later the Longshan culture, a continuation of the Dawenkou culture, during the third millennium, which covered Shandong and the central plains (Barnes 1999: 109ff.; Liu and Chen 2012: 169ff.).[6] Demographic growth is apparent in central Shaanxi during the first half of the third millennium, with a site of 130 ha at Yinjiacun,[7] and more clearly – throughout the Yellow River basin – during the second half of the third millennium. A cooler and drier climate in the Yellow River valley from 3000 BCE probably led to an intensification of agricultural practices. These new climate conditions also made it possible for previously flooded zones to be settled and exploited.

Advances in agriculture provided the basis for demographic expansion, feeding population movements toward Southeast Asia. At the end of the fourth millennium BCE, Proto-Austronesian speakers were already present in Taiwan. Various origins for these populations have been suggested: the Lower Yangtze valley, Fujian or Guangdong (Bellwood 2004, 2005b), and Shandong (Fuller, Harvey, and Qin 2007, in accordance with Sagart's theory [2008] of a continuum existing between Sino-Tibetan and Proto-Austronesian). Archaeological evidence of rice and millet has been found in Taiwan dating to around 3000 BCE at Nanguanli (Dabenkeng culture, 3000–2500 BCE) (Bellwood 2005a: 134; Tsang 2005). Social change occurring in China may also have contributed to these Austronesian movements. However, contradictions between archaeological, linguistic, and ethnographic data in Taiwan call for a certain degree of caution and suggest that more research is necessary (pottery and tools from the Nanguanli culture have been compared with assemblages from the Hong Kong region, but the ethnographic data surrounding millet cultivation by the Austronesian minorities of Taiwan do not support the theory of a southern origin: this rejection is bolstered by linguistic hypothesis) (Lu 2005: 56, 59; Tsang 2005; Sagart 2005a). Connections with west Taiwan have been found at the Damaoshan site (Fujian) (3000–2300 BCE), which may prove to be part of the Proto-Austronesian expansion (Liu and Chen 2012: 248). Recent genetic analysis shows a link with southern China, in the Liang island region, north of Fuzhou (northwest of Taiwan) (Min-Shan Ko *et al.* 2014).

It is likely that different waves of Proto-Austronesians traveled to the Philippines from Taiwan during the third millennium, and from there reached eastern Indonesia (and later western Indonesia) during the second millennium (Bellwood 2005a). Moreover, Proto-Austroasiatic speakers migrated into continental Southeast Asia during the third millennium BCE, bringing cereal-based agriculture with them. They probably settled in western Indonesia prior to the Austronesians, and entered India during the second millennium BCE (Proto-Munda) (Blench 2010b) (and not during the third millennium as had been

---

[6] See below. Some structures that are part of the Hongshan culture have at times been considered to be "palace" and "temple" remains (site of Dongshanzui).

[7] Liu 2004: 156, 208. A cooling climate and lower precipitation levels in Mongolia probably led to migrations of populations from the north to the Middle Yellow River valley (Liu 2004: 174–175). In comparison with Henan and Shandong, as well as north Shaanxi and Gansu, central Shaanxi, saw a decline in the number and size of its sites during the Longshan period, perhaps due to greater population mobility, in response to climate change or other factors (possibly insecurity). The Wei River valley has revealed relatively few sites belonging to the Erlitou period, and subsequently the period preceding the emergence of the Zhou dynasty remains poorly understood (Liu 2004: 219). The Zhou may have migrated, under the Shang, from the Fen River (South Shanxi) to the Qishan region.

suggested) (see below). The presence of nephrite at some sites in the Philippines (Cagayan valley, Luzon . . .) points to the existence of persistent contacts between Taiwan and the southern seas between 2000 and 500 BCE (Hung and Bellwood 2010: 235).

Urbanization in China began as a relatively autonomous process. The Late Dawenkou culture (*c.* 2800–2500 BCE) shows evidence of marked social differentiation. Various raw materials and artifacts (jade, ivory, turtle shells) attest to long-distance exchanges that became even more apparent during the Late Longshan culture, in the Middle and Lower Yellow River valley (*c.* 2500–1900 BCE). Advances in rice cultivation gave way to a new demographic boom in this region. Paddy field systems were present in the Shandong Province as early as 2500 BCE (Fuller *et al.* 2011: 50). Fortified centers also appeared, for example Chengziyai (Lower valley), Hougang, Pingliangtai, Wangchenggang, and Guchengzhai (Middle valley).[8] At Guchengzhai and the large settlements of Liangchengzhen (272 ha) and Yaowangcheng (367 ha), in eastern Shandong, as well as that of Taosi, in southern Shaanxi (300 ha), palatial complexes and enclosed areas inhabited by elites have been unearthed, whose construction would evidently have required the capacity to mobilize a large labor force. Specialized handicrafts (for ceramics and jade) flourished, partly controlled by these elites (Liu 2004: 114).[9] Not far from possible maritime routes, Liangchengzhen developed jade handicrafts and a type of eggshell pottery. At Taosi (2600–2000 BCE), probably the capital of a kingdom, the elite occupied an enclosed area covering *c.* 10 ha and its members were buried in a segregated cemetery – at least in the Middle Phase of the site.[10] Morris (2013: 164) gives an estimate of 14,000 inhabitants for Taosi in 2250 BCE. The discovery of an observatory shows the Taosi elite's involvement in astronomy (Liu and Chen 2012: 226). For some archaeologists, Taosi or Wangchenggang, and subsequently the city of Xinzhai (central Henan, *c.* 1870–1720 BCE) (100 ha)[11] – it supplanted Guchengzhai – correspond to the ancestral capitals of the Xia dynasty, which historical annals such as *Shiji* (first century BCE) place before the Shang dynasty. Attempting to draw parallels between mythology and archaeology can, however, be problematic. "Some of the goods found in the richest graves match early historical descriptions of royal regalia" (Higham 1996a: 53). The astonishing quantity of weapons (for example, arrowheads) that have been excavated indicate that an increase in warfare and violence coincided with the emergence of these power centers.

[8]   Barnes 1999: 116. Chengziyai had impressive walls covering an area measuring 450 × 390m, 6m high, 13.8m thick at the base, and 9m thick at the summit. The walls of Guchengzhai, erected toward 2300 BCE, reached a thickness of 40m. Liu and Chen (2003) also emphasize the existence of long-distance trade for luxury goods monopolized by elites in chiefdoms of the Late Neolithic. These authors (2006: 55) have shown that ten groups of sites from the Late Longshan culture were present that were either "monocentered" (Taosi, Liangchengzhen) or "multicentered."

[9]   Liu 2004: 108. These palaces enclosed one or several courtyards, whereas public buildings from earlier periods had open courtyards: thus the palace was now designed to separate the elite from the rest of the population.

[10] Curiously, Liu writes elsewhere (2004: 244, versus 110) that the site of Erlitou is the first to have shown segregation both in residential areas and for tombs.

[11] The town was surrounded by three moats. The foundations of a large central building have been unearthed. Fragments of bronze vessels have been found; their design recalls those of Erlitou. Liu (2004: 229) considers the "Xinzhai phase" to have been an intermediary phase between the Late Longshan culture and the Erlitou culture.

Illustration XVII
Knowledge, techniques, and trade during the Middle and Late Bronze Age

(b) Horus falcon, found at Susa, second millennium, silver amulet. Louvre Sb 9201. H.: 2.5 cm. © RMN-Grand Palais, Hervé Lewandowski

(a) Use of the shaduf, tomb of Ipouy, Thebes, Deir-el-Medineh, 1240 BCE. The shaduf made it possible to lift water; it may have been introduced from western Asia during the fourteenth century BCE in order to irrigate gardens. From a drawing by N. de Garis Davies (Plate XXVIII). © Bildar-chiv Preussischer Kulturbesitz / RMN-Grand Palais

(c) Babylonian tablet dealing with problems of geometry, c. 1800–1600 BCE. The second millennium saw advances in mathematics in Mesopotamia. British Museum, WA 15285. H.: 26 cm. © The Trustees of the British Museum

Illustration XVIII
Trade and international art during the Late Bronze Age (1)

(b) Weights in the shape of ducks, Susa, Iran, early second millennium. Carved bitumen. Louvre. © RMN-Grand Palais, Hervé Lewandowski. Systems making it possible to convert weights from various regions already existed during the Middle Bronze Age and perhaps earlier. The Ulu Burun shipwreck (Turkey, Late Bronze Age) has revealed nine different sets of weights.

(a) Gold pendant featuring a goddess above a lion, framed by snakes. She holds two horned beasts. This figure of Ishtar also reveals links with the Egyptian goddesses. Minet el-Beidha. Fourteenth century BCE. H.: 6.5 cm. Louvre, AO 14714. © RMN-Grand Palais, Les frères Chuzeville

(c) Copper ingot found at Enkomi (Cyprus). It is similar to ingots from the Ulu Burun shipwreck. ©The Trustees of the British Museum

(d) Cypriot cylinder seal made of lapis lazuli. The seated goddess wears a helmet of the Syro-Mitannian type. Found at Thebes (Greece), Palace, thirteenth century BCE. H.: 3.5 cm. © Archaeological Museum, Thebes (no. 512)

Illustration XIX

Trade and international art during the Late Bronze Age (2)

(a) "Mistress of the animals," feeding two goats. Minet el-Beidha (Ugarit), thirteenth century BCE. Ivory, pyxide lid. H.: 13.7 cm, W.: 11.5 cm. Louvre AO 11601. Ivory work gained prominence in the Levant. While the dress borrows from Mycenaean elements, the naked torso of the goddess follows a western Asian tradition. The scene repeats an ancient Mesopotamian motif (see above). © RMN-Grand Palais, Hervé Lewandowski

(b) Beaker made of electrum, northern Iran. Decoration depicting a two-headed griffin "master of the animals." The lower part of its body rolls up on itself, repeating an ancient Irano-Mesopotamian motif (see Illustration III). H.: 11 cm, Diam.: 11.2 cm, Louvre AO 20281. © RMN-Grand Palais, Hervé Lewandowski

Illustration XX
Statebuilding and long-distance trade in eastern Asia

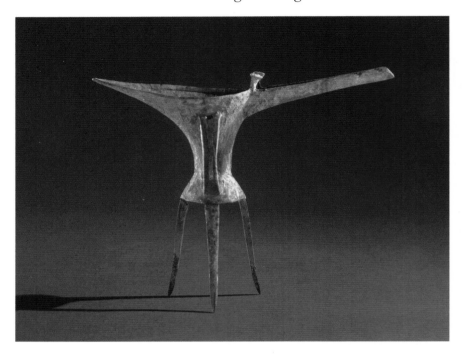

(a) China. Ritual bronze *jue* vessel, a tripod cup for libations, Erlitou phase (1800-1700 BCE). © Dagli Orti / Laurie Platt Winfrey

(c) Bronze plaque inlaid with turquoise, Gedangtou, Yanshi, Henan Province, Erlitou culture. It may feature stylized crouching felines. H.: 14.2 cm. © Cultural Relics Publishing House Beijing

(b) Oracular bone, Anyang, *c.* 1200 BCE (Shang period). H.: 30 cm. © by permission of the Syndics of Cambridge University Library

Turquoise was acquired via long-distance trade. Two similar plaques have been excavated at Sanxingdui in Sichuan, revealing contacts between Henan and Sichuan.

Illustration XXI
Eastern Asia, Shang period

(a) Ritual bronze, *you* wine vessel; it features a man under the protection of a tiger (?). Shang period, *c.* 1200 BCE. H.: 35.3 cm. Musée Cernuschi, Paris. © Musée Cernuschi/Parisienne de Photographie/Roger-Viollet

(b) Bronze *yue*, from a chariot, Western Zhou period, eleventh or tenth century BCE. H.: 16.9 cm. A tiger holds the head of a man with western features in its jaws. Shanghai Museum. © Cultural Relics Publishing House Beijing

(c) Sufutun, Shandong. Bronze ceremonial axe (*yu*). © Cultural Relics Publishing House Beijing

Illustration XXII

Sichuan and trade routes between northern and southern Asia

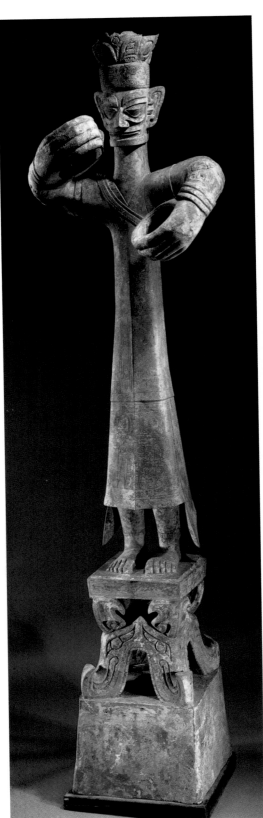

(a) Bronze statue, Sanxingdui, Pit 2 (Sichuan), *c.* 1200 BCE. H.: 2.6 m. © Cultural Relics Publishing House Beijing.

This is the first known statuary in eastern Asia. The figure rests on a base supported by four stylized animals (dragons?). He may have carried an elephant tusk. Pit 2 has yielded 1,300 pieces: bronzes, jades, gold items, cowries, which were found underneath some sixty elephant tusks. This reveals the emergence of a distinctive culture in Sichuan and trade conducted with various regions, central China, the Yangtze basin, and Yunnan.

(b) Ceremonial blade *zhang*, jade, Pit 2, Sanxingdui, *c.* 1200 BCE. H.: 28.2 cm. Sanxingdui Museum. © Cultural Relics Publishing House Beijing

The spread of this type of blade, known since Neolithic times, reveals interactions between regions: blades of this type are found in the basins of the Yellow River, the Yangtze River, Sichuan, at Guangzhou, and in the Red River valley.

(c) *Ge* halberd, bronze, cemetery at Dubaishu, Pi district, fourth century BCE. L.: 25.3 cm. Provincial Museum, Sichuan, Chengdu. © Cultural Relics Publishing House Beijing

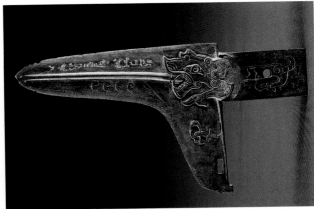

The motif on the blade repeats the theme of an animal spitting out the blade of a weapon, known as early as the second millennium in western and Central Asia (see above). This motif reveals indirect connections between Sichuan and the world of the steppes from the middle of the first millennium BCE.

Illustration XXIII
Statebuilding and long-distance trade (first millennium BCE)

(a) The birth of Horus. Ivory showing Egyptian influence, Arslan Tash (northern Syria), eighth century BCE. Louvre, AO 11465 © RMN-Grand Palais, les frères Chuzeville. The Levant became specialized in ivory work as early as the second millennium. Ivory was imported from Egypt

(b) Amulet revealing Egyptian influence (*udjat* eye), Susa (Iran), *c.* 500 BC. Louvre, SB 10135. © RMN-Grand Palais, Jérôme Galland

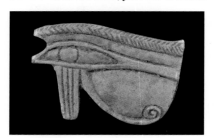

(c)  (d)

(c, d) Imitations of Athenian coins. (c) Egypt, early fourth century BCE, tetradrachm, 16.88 g. © K. Ponterio / Bowers and Merena. (d) Saba (Yemen), silver, with Sabaean N on Athena's cheek, 5.17 g, third century BCE. © Leu Numismatic AG

(e) Daric coin, Persian Empire, gold, 8.36 g, *c.* 375-332 BCE. King running and holding a bow and a spear. © Classical Numismatic Group

(g) Nanda coin, *karshapana*, *c.* 340-320 BCE, silver, 1.4 x 2.2 cm. It bears six symbols, including a sun, a zebu, and a plant on a mountain. © T. K. Mallon-McCorgray

(f) Silver currency, Taxila, 11.3 g (100 *ratti*). Between the sixth and fourth centuries BCE. The *ratti* was the weight of a gunja seed (*Abrus precatorius L.*). © Dr. Nupam Mahajan

Illustration XXIV

Interactions among Persia, Central Asia, and South Asia (1)

(a) Gold rhyton, griffin, Achaemenid Persia, fifth century BCE, National Museum, Tehran. ©National Museum of Iran, Tehran, Bridgeman Images

(b) Gate, Sanchi, first century BCE. The foundation of Sanchi goes back to Ashoka's reign (Maurya Empire, third century BCE). The gate's wings are topped by griffins and lions showing a Persian influence. Note also the motif of the double spiral, and Buddhist vases symbols of abundance. © Massimo Borchi/Atlantide Phototravel

Illustration XXV

Interactions among Persia, Central Asia, and South Asia (2)

(a) Man mastering two griffins. On a gate, at Sanchi, first century BCE. © Massimo Borchi/ Atlantide Phototravel

(b) "The ruler and the dragons" pendant, Tomb II at Tillya Tepe (Afghanistan), first century CE. Gold (from Central Asia), turquoise (from Iran), garnet (from India), and lapis lazuli (from Afghanistan), 12.5 cm x 6.5 cm. The ancient theme of the master of the animals is transposed here onto imaginary animals figuring prominently in the mythologies of eastern Asia and the steppes. © Thierry Ollivier

Illustration XXVI
Southeast Asia and long-distance trade

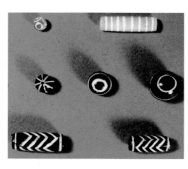

(a) Carnelian lion (a Buddhist symbol); in situ with beads. Imported from India.

(b, d) Etched beads. Ban Don Ta Phet (Thailand). © Ian Glover

(c) Stone pendant in the shape of animal heads, Pa Xua (Vietnam). Sa Huynh culture. Also found at Ban Don Ta Phet. A. Reinecke 1996: 37

(e) Cowry container, Tomb 12 at Shizhaishuan, Yunnan. The lid shows a ritual scene (for an alliance?) with feast and human sacrifice. Many bronze drums are featured. H.: 53 cm. Provincial Museum, Yunnan. © Cultural Relics Publishing House Beijing

(f) Gold ring, featuring a man riding a horse, Prohear (Cambodia). © A. Reinecke

Illustration XXVII
China. States, currencies, and long-distance trade

(b) Coins in the shape of spades and knives 1. Spring and Autumn period (sixth century BCE). 2–5. Warring States (between the fifth and third centuries BCE).

(a) Crossbow mechanism, Han period (second century BCE – second century CE). This weapon was invented during the fifth or the fourth century BCE, within the context of competing states. 11.5 x 18 cm. Bronze and gold. Guimet Museum, MA 3061. © RMN, Jean-Yves and Nicolas Dubois

(c) Sleeve of a silk robe, embroidered with tigers, dragons, phoenix, and flowers. Mashan, Tomb 1, Jiangling, Hubei province, between 340 and 278 BCE. Museum of Jingzhou Prefecture. © Cultural Relics Publishing House Beijing. Elements of this type of decoration can be seen on other materials, jade for example (below).

Illustration XXVIII

Western influences in China

(b) Jade rhyton, featuring a dragon. From the Nanyue king's tomb at Xianggang, Guangzhou, second century BCE. Museum of the Tomb of the Nanyue King, Guangzhou. Like other items from the tomb, this rhyton reveals influences from western Asia that came via land and sea routes. For example, a silver box may have been imported from Persia. © Cultural Relics Publishing House Beijing

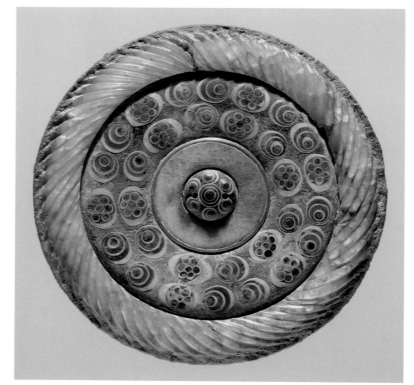

(c) Bronze mirror, with jade and glass inlays. The glass was perhaps imported from western Asia. Jincun, Luoyang, Henan, third century BCE. Diam.: 12.2 cm. © Harvard University, Arthur Sackler Museum

(a) King Goujian's sword, from Yue, fifth century BCE, tomb, Wangshan (Hubei). L.: 55.6 cm. Glass inlays on the pommel. Provincial Museum, Hubei. © Cultural Relics Publishing House Beijing
   This type of weapon was borrowed from the steppes.

Illustration XXIX
How jade traveled

(a) Jade ornament, with dragon and phoenix openwork, tomb of the second Nanyue king, 137-122 BCE, Xianggang, Guangzhou. Museum of the Tomb of the Nanyue King. © Cultural Relics Publishing House Beijing

Dragon-felines, influenced by Iranian griffins, were innovations that appeared around the third century BCE.

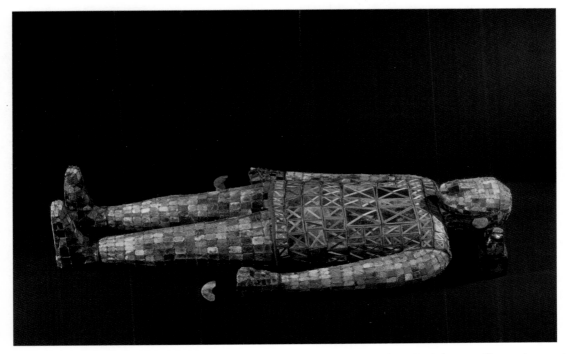

(b) Jade shroud, Tomb of Liu Sheng, at Mancheng, Hebei, 113 BCE. Jade, gold, and gilt bronze. Protection against demons. L.: 1.88 m. Provincial Museum, Hebei. © Cultural Relics Publishing House Beijing

Part of the jade found in China arrived from Khotan, in the Tarim valley.

Illustration XXX

Tabula Peutingeriana, thirteenth-century copy of a Roman map dated to the fourth century (perhaps based on an earlier map)

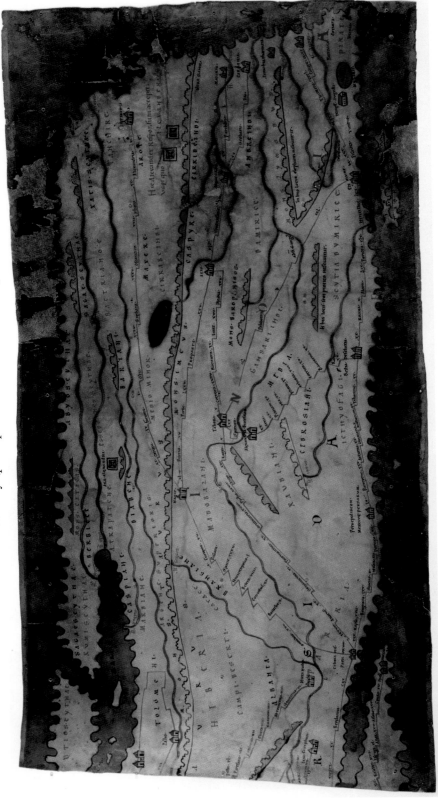

Parchment scroll, 682 x 34 cm, consisting of eleven sections. © Österreichische Nationalbibliothek, Vienna. The map shows roads, rivers, and mountains. Regions of India are mentioned, along with Bactria, various Scythian peoples, a region inhabited by Tokharians, and China (*Sera maior*). Curiously, the island of Sri Lanka (*Taprobane*) faces the mouth of the Indus River, to the west of Muziris. On the left (west), entrance to the Persian Gulf. It shows a "temple to Augustus" at Muziris.

Illustration XXXI

Map of the world published by Leinhart Holle at Ulm in 1482, based on Ptolemy (second century CE)

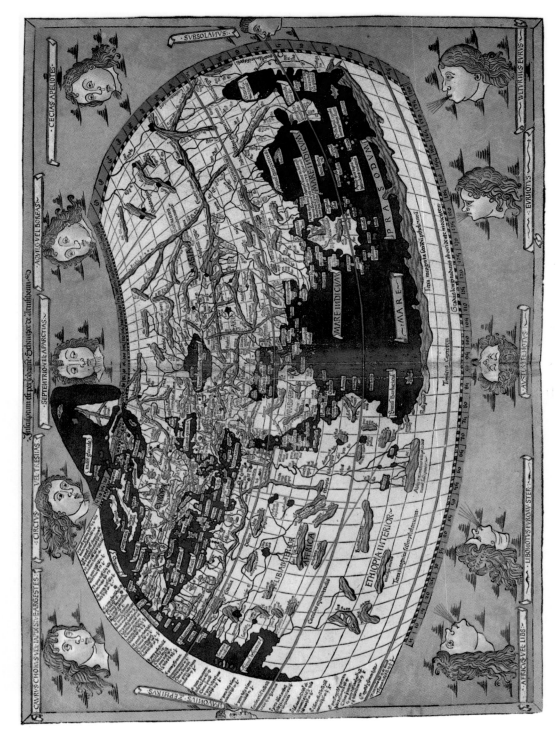

Map by Nicolaus Germanus, Ulm, 1482 (L. Holle, printer). Ptolemy, who viewed the earth as a sphere, improved the techniques of cartographic projection. Earlier maps (by Strabo, for example) saw the habitable world as an oblong island. Ptolemy bordered the "Indian Sea" with an unknown land to the south. This unknown land joins China (*Sinae*) in the east. Note the large size of Sri Lanka (*Taprobane*). To the east of India, the map indicates the *Aurea Chersonesus* (Southeast Asia). Menuthias Island, in the southwestern Indian Sea, may represent Madagascar. In East Africa, the Mountains of the Moon give birth to various sources of the Nile River.

Illustration XXXII

Central Asia, a crossroads linking India, western Asia, and the Roman Empire

(a) Head of a Devata, Hadda site, monastery at Tapa-i-Kafariha, Afghanistan, third–fourth century CE. Stucco. Musée Guimet, MG17141. © RMN-Grand Palais, Daniel Arnaudet

(b) Hand-blown glass vase, with ornamentation of glass rolls, Begram Treasure, second century CE. H.: 22.7 cm. Musée Guimet. © RMN-Grand Palais, Richard Lambert

(c) Women standing under a gateway, ivory, part of a piece of furniture, revealing an Indian influence. Begram Treasure, Afghanistan, second century CE. H.: 14.6 cm, W.: 13.5 cm. Musée Guimet MA321. © RMN-Grand Palais, Thierry Ollivier

In the Middle Yangtze valley, too, the Qujialing culture (first half of the third millennium) saw the development of walled villages or towns, a phenomenon that probably reflects rising conflicts between emerging chiefdoms.[12] Influences from the Longshan culture can be seen from 2300 BCE. Excavations have also produced evidence of walled settlements in Sichuan, for example at Baodun (60 ha) (a C_{14} dating gave 2600–2300 BCE), Yufucun (40 ha), and then at Gucheng (dated to 2200–1875 BCE) (Wang Yi 2003). These sites belong to the Baoduncun culture, one that was in contact with the Middle Yangtze valley and – indirectly, and more loosely – with the Yellow River valley.

In the Lower Yangtze valley, tombs of the Liangzhu culture (3300–2200 BCE) showcase the wealth of some individuals in a highly stratified society.[13] Different centers have been found, notably at Zhaolingshan, Sidun, Fuquanshan, and Mojiaoshan, where walls enclosed an area covering 290 ha (Liu and Chen 2012: 238). Mojiaoshan may well have been the capital of a state. The Liangzhu culture is well known for its considerable jade production (possibly from local sources), and its elite artisans. This culture is also noted for the appearance of pictograms – although these did not yet form a script; many of these pictograms were shared with the Dawenkou culture (Keightley 2006: 179; Liu and Chen 2012: 221, 240).

Social changes in these cultures are concurrent with the development of long-distance trade. Exchange networks followed north–south routes between the Yellow River, the Yangtze and regions south of the Yangtze, as well as east–west routes leading to Gansu and Sichuan. The spread of ritual objects shows that a long-distance trade in prestige goods, which was accompanied by the spread of shared beliefs, was a strong component in building social hierarchy during the Later Neolithic period. Ritual objects made of jade with common shapes across regions (*cong* tube, *bi* disc, *yazhang* scepter) reflect the control of politico-religious power held by interrelated elites with shared religious beliefs.[14] A cultural thrust can be observed towards the Hexi corridor (Gansu). Similarities have been noted between ceramics from the Miaodigou II

---

[12] The Late Longshan period corresponds fairly well to the legendary period of the "ten thousand states," *wan guo*, a term often seen in the later, classical period (Chang 1999: 64). See He Jejiun 1999, on the walled village of Chengtoushan. The remains of human sacrifices have been unearthed under the walls, as well as at sites in the Yellow River basin, for example at Wangchenggang and Taosi. The tombs that have been excavated at Chengtoushan point toward the existence of a social hierarchy. Most of the bodies were buried in a flexed position, in tombs without offerings, but a small number of bodies were placed in a reclining position in tombs containing ceramics and jade ornaments. The excavations have also led to the discovery of irrigation channels and small dikes. At a number of sites, from 2600 BCE on, the walls appear to have served as protection against floods.

[13] The tomb of a young man at Sidun, under a 20 m high tumulus, contained over two hundred jade objects (Higham 1996a: 68). Some tombs in the nearby sites of Yaoshan and Fanshan (north Zhejiang) have yielded many ritual items made of jade, as well as ivory, and a piece of lacquerware (Chang 1999: 60). Jades bearing the *taotie* "animal" mask (with animal and human faces) may reflect an ideological link between rulers and gods or ancestors, and/or shamanistic practices. The richest tombs contained ornamental jade weapons, which were probably symbolic of military and ritual control by the elite.

[14] Liu 2004: 123, fig. 5.4. *Cong* and *bi* have been discovered as far as the Canton region, and in the Qijia culture. Other items such as *yue* axes and drums covered with crocodile skin excavated at Taosi point to long-distance contacts. The same type of drum has been found in tombs of persons of high status on the Shandong coast. *Cong, bi,* and *zhang* reached Sichuan at the same time as the Baoduncun culture (third millennium) (Falkenhausen 2003). It is likely that cloth was also a luxury item, exchanged and redistributed.

context (central Shaanxi, 3000–2500 BCE) and those from the Changshan site – possibly pre-Qijia – (eastern Gansu) (2900–2700 BCE).[15] In Gansu and in Qinghai, the western extension of the Yangshao culture was the basis for the Majiayao (c. 3100–2300 BCE) and subsequent Machang cultures (c. 2400–2000 BCE). There was a visible westward expansion of the Majiayao culture from Gansu into the Jiuquan–Yumen corridor, and a movement further westward of the Machang culture of Gansu – driven by trade aiming to acquire and produce metal objects.[16]

Early on, these various cultural facies benefited from the introduction of cultivated plants, via the routes of Central Asia. Wheat and barley had appeared by 4600 BCE at the Xishanping site, in the Hexi corridor (Gansu) (Li et al. 2007). Other species have been uncovered at the same site, dated to 3000 BCE: rice, millets (from China), and oats (from western Asia) (Li et al. 2007; Liu and Chen 2012: 234). Wheat has also been found at Donghuishan (3000–2500 BCE) (Gansu),[17] and a variety of wheat with small grains appeared in eastern China between 2600 and 1900 BCE, probably from Pakistan (Crawford 2006: 79). At the Tasbas and Begash sites in the highlands of Kazakhstan, wheat and broomcorn millet have been unearthed dated from c. 2800 to 2300 BCE, which suggests that "we have to reconsider the economic basis of Bronze Age Eurasian 'nomads'" (Spengler et al. 2014). Moreover, the discovery of maceheads (in stone [jade], then in bronze) in northwest China "would suggest some cultural contacts between northwestern China and regions to the west. The earliest macehead found so far can be dated to the middle and late periods of the Yangshao culture [fourth millennium], [then] in the context of the Qijia culture" (see below) (Li 2002: 181; 2003: 28).[18] The sheep was also introduced from western Asia during the third millennium,[19] through the Gansu corridor, though it may have arrived in China much earlier: sheep remains have purportedly been found at Peiligang and Dadiwan (from the seventh millennium BCE), and clay figurines that appear to represent sheep and goat heads have also been excavated. These sheep bones found in early Neolithic sites in China, however, are most likely wild species.[20] Liu and Chen mention only dogs and pigs as domesticated animals. Contacts with Central Asia therefore may have occurred at a very

[15] Fitzgerald-Huber 2003: 58. Before the Qijia period, an east–west route linked the region of Xi'an to Gansu and Qinghai (Ledu site) (Fitzgerald-Huber 2003: 60).

[16] Mei 2003: 40. For this author, the Machang culture may have been in contact with the Afanesevo culture through eastern Xinjiang (it may in fact have been a post-Afanasevo culture, given the date of the Machang culture). L. Fitzgerald-Huber (2003: 60ff.) also considers the Qijia culture to have originated in eastern Gansu and in Ningxia. This culture would have later expanded westward, to western Gansu and the Hexi corridor, to link up with networks providing metal items.

[17] At Gumugou and Xiaohe (Xinjiang), wheat has been dated to c. 2000 BCE. The site of Zhaojialai in Shaanxi, which yielded wheat, purportedly dates to the late third millennium BCE. Wheat has been found in a "Xia" context c. 1600 BCE in Henan (Li 2002: 180, 2003: 15). Wheat and barley are present at the Afghan site of Shortughai, linked to the Indus civilization, and also much earlier in the Jeitun culture of Turkmenistan around 6300 BCE.

[18] Maceheads, which were symbols of power, were spread largely throughout western Asia and Iran. They doubtless reached China through Central Asia. A macehead made of ivory has been found at Erlitou (first half of the second millennium BCE). The maps from Li (2003: 28) indicating the discoveries of wheat and maceheads clearly reflect their dissemination along routes through Xinjiang and Gansu.

[19] For Frachetti (2012), "societies living throughout a proposed 'Inner Asian Mountain Corridor' of the Pamir, Tian Shan, Dzhungar, and Altai ranges were key agents of the earliest diffusion of sheep and goat pastoralism to inner Asia around 3500 BC."

[20] L. Liu, p.c. See Debaine-Francfort 2000: 174, 180.

early time.[21] One incentive for establishing long-distance contacts toward the Tarim, as early as the third millennium, may have been to procure jade from Khotan for the populations of Gansu province and for centers in the Yellow River basin.

The pastoralists of the steppes were also metallurgists during the third millennium BCE, and external influences played a key role in introducing copper and bronze metallurgy into East Asia. Routes linking Central Asia and China continued as far as the Indus River valley. Interactions also developed via northern routes. The existence of the Afanasevo and later Okunev cultures (Upper-Ienissei, Minusinsk basin, 3600–2500, and 2500–1900/1700 BCE)[22] point toward population movements in the Asian steppes.[23] It has been suggested that links existed between the Afanasevo culture and the Yamnaya culture (*Pit Grave Culture*) (north of the Black Sea and north of the Caucasus),[24] a scenario now supported by genetic data;[25] Frachetti (2012) notes that sites of the Afanasevo culture are "now calibrated between 3700 and 2500 BC, while Yamnaya sites are confidently dated from 3100 to 2400 BC." Parpola (2002: 236) considers the Afanasevo culture groups to have been composed of Indo-European speakers who came from the Pontic steppes during the fourth millennium (at the same time, other Indo-Europeans moved westward to Europe). Shards of the Afanasevo type have been unearthed at Sarazm (Tajikistan), where a large funerary enclosure has also been linked to this culture (Francfort 2005: 259, 303; Frachetti and Rouse 2012).[26] The discovery of tombs of Afanasevo type in the Dzungar basin demonstrates that contacts existed between this culture and Xinjiang.[27] These pastoralist-farmers, who were also the first metallurgists in the east, may have been motivated to migrate by the search for mineral resources and trade. As early as 2600 BCE metallurgists inhabited the region south of Lake Balkhach (Semirech'ye).[28] In northern Kazakhstan, the lower levels of the site of

[21] A domestication of common millet (*Panicum miliaceum* L.) in Central Asia and its introduction into China as a domesticated plant during the seventh millennium cannot be excluded; however, this type of millet has not yet been found in the Jeitun culture (Turkmenistan); Cohen 1998: 22. Seeds of the melon (a plant originating in western Asia) have been identified at the site of Liangzhu.

[22] C_{14} dating has made it possible to date the Okunev culture between 2500 and 1700 BCE for the Minusinsk basin (Görsdorf *et al.* 2004: 88).

[23] It is possible, as Zaitseva and van Geel (2004: 78) have suggested, that climate change rendered southern Siberia "more attractive" between 2700 and 2200 BCE. Bolikhovskaya *et al.* (2004: 215) consider the period between 2500 and 2300 to have been marked by increased humidity in the steppes to the northeast of the Black Sea. For Shishlina (2004: 94), however, the temperature rose after the middle of the third millennium, and was accompanied by increased aridity in the steppes northwest of the Caspian Sea; in the same vein, cf. also Bokovenko 2004: 29, for the steppes, generally speaking, Alexandrovskyi and Alexandrovskaya (2004: 206), for central Russia, and Levine *et al.* (2003: 17), for the Don basin. Given the ongoing uncertainty on this topic, the idea that temperature and humidity evolved in one way in western Siberia, and in the opposite way in Inner Mongolia and the Minusinsk basin should be treated with caution (Koulkova 2004: 272, and Dirksen and van Geel 2004: 303, who refer to a synchronous evolution of temperature-humidity from 6000 to 2600 BCE for western Siberia and the Lake Baikal).

[24] Chernykh 1992: 183; Kuzmina 2008: 97; Mei 2003: 39 n. 42.   [25] See Gibbons 2015.

[26] However, in his comments on Frachetti 2012, Anthony (2012: 21) writes, "Sarazm does not show material parallels with Afanas'ev."

[27] Frachetti 2002: 164. On the contribution of the Afanasevo culture to the development of the Xinjiang cultures, see also Kuzmina 2008: 95.

[28] Site of Begash (Dzungaria, Xinjiang) (Frachetti 2004: ch. 7). The existence of copper and tin resources in the Altai, the Minusinsk basin, and Dzungaria may explain the emergence of cultures involved in long-distance trade in these regions, a process clearly visible during the second millennium BCE.

Sergeevka probably date to the same period (Levine and Kislenko 2002). The oldest bronze item found in China, belonging to the Majiayao culture, in Gansu, and excavated at the site of Linjia, dates to 2900–2700 BCE, and cannot come from the Afanasevo culture, whose metallurgical skills did not include bronze.[29] The fragment of a bronze knife has been excavated at Yuanyangchi, from the Machang culture of Gansu (2400–2000 BCE), a culture which showed signs of a social hierarchy.[30]

At the time of the BMAC or just before, contacts – probably indirect[31] – intensified between East Asia and Bactria or Margiana, through intermediaries posted on the future Silk Roads. Aridity in Central Asia led to increased mobile pastoralism after 2200 BCE. The establishment of semi-nomadic populations in the corridors of Central Asia appears to be connected to an increase in both trade and in political control over these corridors, after the late third millennium and still more so from the middle of the second millennium BCE onward.[32] Influences also arrived from northern routes, passing back and forth from the Minusinsk basin. In the same vein as Chernykh (2009), Frachetti (2012) proposes "a process of multidirectional diffusion of metallurgical technologies from the late third millennium BC." The introduction of copper and bronze metallurgy is apparent in the Qijia culture (Gansu and Qinghai).[33] Its introduction probably followed several paths, through the Tarim, the valleys of the southern Altai, and a route from Urumqi to Hami. Various techniques – using cast or hammered metal – appear to have been introduced. According to current research, "the earliest metal in Xinjiang is still later than in the Qijia culture" (Liu and Chen 2012: 344); however, the lower strata of a Xinjiang cemetery, at Xiaohe (near Lake Lobnor), have not been dated precisely (perhaps 2000 BCE, the upper strata being dated to 1690–1420 BCE).[34] Moreover, bronze production at Huoshiliang and Ganggangwa, in the Gansu corridor, may well go back as far as 2100 BCE (Liu and Chen 2012: 336).

---

[29] The dating of this knife, however, has been debated (Higham 1996a: 43). The Okunev culture produced tin-bronze objects.

[30] This site has yielded a knife made of bone imitating the shape of a metal knife (Fitzgerald-Huber 2003: 61).

[31] It is difficult to envisage a significant migration of the BMAC people into the Tarim. But some features of the BMAC, such as irrigation techniques, obviously spread into this region through cultures in contact with the BMAC. The question, however, remains an open one (see below for the discovery of ceramics similar to pottery from Margiana in Dzungaria).

[32] Frachetti (2002: 162) suggests that the increasing mobility of pastoralist populations corresponds to the exploitation of new ecological niches, and also represents a form of strategy: settling in the region of the corridors represented a political investment. The foothills of the Tian Shan Mountains were inhabited – and controlled – by semi-nomadic populations, particularly after the middle of the second millennium. Metal resources from the Altai and the Tian Shan Mountains were traded through these corridors, as well as products from the west and the east. Similarities can be noted between the Okunev culture, located between southwest Siberia, the Altai Mountains, and northeast Kazakhstan (2500–1900/1700 BCE), and finds in Xinjiang and the Dzungar basin. The passes north of the Tian Shan Mountains were strongly occupied after the middle of the second millennium (Frachetti 2002: 166ff.). At the same time, the Andronovo groups extended across a wide area: a movement which coincided with advances in metallurgy and a growing mobility linked to the spread of horse-drawn carts or chariots.

[33] For this culture, An Zhimin (1996: 319) gives a range from 2630 to 1800 BCE (C14 dating), Barnes (1999: 157) 2500–1500 BCE, Mei (2003: 34) 2300–1700 BCE, and Liu and Chen (2012: 299) 2200–1600 BCE. See Higham 1996a: 48–49; Mei 2003.

[34] On Xiaohe, see Mai et al. 2016.

Discoveries in various cemeteries have provided evidence for long-distance exchange networks, and population movements. Located 70 km northwest of Loulan, the cemetery of Gumugou (Qäwrighul) (Lobnor) (2100–1500 BCE) has yielded the oldest so-called "mummies" – all Caucasoid – found in the Tarim region. Some were found alongside small bags containing ephedra, a hallucinogenic plant used in rituals in Turkmenistan and in the BMAC (see above). Tombs contained wheat and sheep/goat, horse, cattle, and camel remains.[35] Some copper artifacts are similar to those of the Afanasevo culture. "Clothing, and the complex and structure of the graves resemble those of Afanasevo and Andronovo" (Liu and Chen 2012: 338).

The Qijia culture acted as an interface between west and east. Burials show evidence of a stratified society, with status markers such as jade *bi* discs, pottery drums, and large axes (Liu 2004: 146–147). The human remains reveal a Mongoloid population, but also at the same time "the distinctive Indo-European practice of suttee" (Liu and Chen 2012: 327). This culture is also the source of the earliest remains of domesticated horses found in China. DNA analysis has recently confirmed "genetic affinity of the Qijia people and Tianshanbeilu" (Liu and Chen 2012: 332). The elite, at Huangniangniangtai for example, controlled the production of ritual items made of jade or marble, in part intended for trade. Some researchers have suggested possible connections between Qijia sites and the Kexingzhuang II culture of Shaanxi. Beyond Shaanxi, the shapes of jade artifacts of the Qijia culture may reflect influences from Taosi, which came through the Wei River valley (Fitzgerald-Huber 2003: 66). The discovery in Gansu of *he* ceramic (also attested in Henan) imitating a prototype made of sheets of metal, shows that beyond the Wei river, the Qijia culture's contacts reached as far as the Middle Yellow River valley.[36]

---

[35] Mallory and Mair 2000: 138, 186. The origins of these first Caucasoids (considered to have been Indo-Europeans: Tocharians or Indo-Iranians) remain a topic for debate: be it Bactria–Margiana, or the steppes further north (see below). Barber (1998: 654) considers the arrival of groups from Turkestan to have happened during the early second millennium, whereas the groups arriving a few centuries later may have come from the Caucasus region, via a northern route. Mallory and Mair attribute a Proto-Tocharian language to the first Caucasoid groups: for these authors, the Tocharian speakers of the Tarim identified in manuscripts from Turfan and Kuchā dated to *c.* 600 CE may be derived from some Indo-European groups who arrived during the late third or early second millennium in Xinjiang, groups that had links to the "Afanasevo" culture of the Minusinsk basin (Okunev culture, at that time) (2000: 314–318) (also A. Sherratt 1997: ch. 19; Kuzmina 2007: 252, 2008: 97). The Chinese name for "sheep" derives from an Iranian or Tocharian term (Mallory and Mair 2000: 224). Conversely, Hemphill and Mallory (2004) suggest that the mummies from Alwighul (700–1 BCE) and Krorän (beginning of the Christian era) display affinities with the populations of the urban centers of North Bactria and the eastern Mediterranean (cf. also Kuzmina 2008: 91). Attempting to draw links between languages, names of populations, and cultures, sometimes from different periods, can be an instructive exercise; however, it remains a thought experiment. Recent genetic research on the mitochondrial DNA of human remains (teeth) from Kazakhstan has revealed connections with the Caucasus and the Central Mediterranean Sea for a period prior to the seventh century BCE (Lalueza-Fox *et al.* 2004). Tocharian reveals contacts with various language families (Witzel 2004: 103). Note that barley had a more significant presence in western China between 2000 and 800 BCE with the introduction of two genotypes, revealing separate introductions from western sources (Crawford 2006: 80).

[36] Fitzgerald-Huber 2003: 69. The metal prototypes may have been manufactured "by hammering out the copper around a hemispherical 'form', probably made of wood"; these have not yet been recovered.

Interactions with Bactria and the northern steppes through Xinjiang and Gansu have shed light on the spread of copper and bronze metallurgy toward the central plains of China.[37] In contrast to what would be observed later in Southeast Asia, bronze appeared in complex Neolithic communities in the middle and lower Yellow River valley; their elites monopolized the use of bronze for the production of prestige goods linked to ancestor worship. Bronze metallurgy was present at some sites of the Longshan culture, at Meishan, Wangchenggang (Henan), and Taosi (Shanxi), but "the early use of metal was not [yet] integrated into the existing prestige goods system for expressing social hierarchy ... Not until the Erlitou period did bronze objects become the most valuable ritual goods and status markers associated with high elite groups" (Liu 2004: 111).[38]

Social unrest and competition with a new city built at Fengcheng-Nanshi (230 ha) seem to have triggered the end of the Taosi political entity: the large enclosure was destroyed and the palatial area became a craft production area.[39] Different Chinese Neolithic cultures disappeared at this time, coinciding with a major climatic deterioration (c. 2000/1900 BCE).[40] A decrease in population density and social complexity is seen in the Longshan culture, and a decline in the production of prestige goods marked the end of the Liangzhu culture (Liu 2003: 15; Liu and Chen 2012: 220, 242). Recent

[37]   Gernet has already noted (1999: 45) that "the Bronze Age in China does not seem to have been preceded by the long period during which the pure metals were used that we find in the western parts of the [Eurasian] continent. [Bronze] also appears later than in the Middle East." Thus, a distant influence cannot be excluded for bronze technology, as in the case of other elements of civilization. Various authors argue today that copper and bronze metallurgy arrived via routes that would later be known as the Silk Roads (see Flemings 2002: 113). For Christian (2000: 11), population movements in the Asian steppes led to the spread of Indo-European languages as far as Xinjiang around 2000 BCE. The formation of this area implies exchanges of knowledge, techniques, and goods that are older than the Silk Roads.

[38]   At Meishan, crucible remains holding copper (dated 2290–2005 BCE) have been excavated. A pit at Wangchenggang contained a bronze vessel (dated 2878–2104 BCE). Residues of copper metallurgy have been observed at Pingliangtai (a site dated to 2400–2200 BCE). A bronze bell has been found in a small tomb at Taosi, with no other object; and a human bone from the same tomb has been dated to 2615–1890 BCE. See Higham 1996a: 52. Some Chinese archaeologists have claimed that Guchengzhai was a center for bronze production, but "what have been found so far at the site are fragments of crucibles ... but slag is absent" (Liu 2004: 108).

[39]   Liu 2004: 111. Just as Taosi disappeared, the Yellow River adopted a new course in its lower section, revealing catastrophic environmental changes at this time. Around 3350, the Yellow River had established its bed south of its ancient course; it returned northward c. 2500 BCE.

[40]   Data from Gansu and Qinghai show evidence of an increasingly arid climate around 2000 BCE (An et al. 2005) (cf. also Hsu 1998). Shaowu (2006) similarly indicates increasing aridity in northern China, Gansu, Qinghai, and Inner Mongolia from 2100 to 1800 BCE (there was a perceptibly wetter phase from 2500 to 2100). The quantity of aeolian sediments arriving from Inner Asia in northern China between 2100 and 1600 BCE suggests that there was an arid phase at this time, with peaks occurring at the beginning and at the end of the period (Schettler et al. 2006: 1055–1056). These authors note an intensification of the East Asian monsoon in northern China around 2200 BCE before a dry period that began around 2100. In eastern Shandong, the region of Liangchengzhen was affected by demographic decline between 2000 and 1100 BCE, perhaps due to environmental factors. There was a notable shift of political centers to western Shandong and Henan (Liu 2004: 201). For the Russian steppes north of the Caspian Sea, however, data appear to be contradictory (see Kuzmina 2008: 16) (moreover, unlike regions further south, they show what amounts to a positive correlation between rises in temperature and aridity, and between lower temperatures and increased humidity).

research, however, has led to the discovery of a walled site in northern Shaanxi, at Shimao, which has been dated to around 2000–1900 BCE. It covers *c.* 400 ha, and includes a "palatial" area. The defense system of the city implies the existence of military conflicts during this period. Smaller settlements surrounded the city. A huge amount of jadeware has been discovered, though its origin is still unknown (Zhouyong Sun *et al.* 2014).

Transformations at the Beginning of the Second Millennium BCE

The beginning of the second millennium saw the expansion of a new western world-system to the west, to the south (see above), and to the east. This expansion coincided with closer interconnections with East Asian regions through intermediary groups from Central Asia: groups whose growing mobility was most likely due to economic and political factors. Interactions between regions became more frequent in the Pre-Andronovo and Andronovo groups, along with an increase in metallurgy and in trade (Kristiansen 2007). The late third and early second millennia saw further exploitation of metal resources from the Urals, Kazakhstan, the Altai, and the Yenisei basin. The presence of jade beads in the Urals (Alakul, Ushkatta), in Kazakhstan (Aishrak, Kanai), and in Siberia (Rostovka, Turbino, Okunev) during the second millennium reveals the sizeable dimension of these networks (Kuzmina 2008: 4). This jade may have come from the regions around the Yenisei River and Lake Baikal (Koryakova and Epimakhov 2007: 108). A tomb from Rostovka has also yielded a single lapis lazuli bead. In Xinjiang and in the Hexi corridor, human remains and funerary assemblages have revealed influences from the steppes as well as long-distance exchanges. Koryakova and Kohl (2000: 641, after Linduff 2000) note that copper and bronze discovered in western China belong to assemblages that are comparable to those of the BMAC or "to objects from the eastern Eurasian steppes, especially from the Andronovo area, materials which support a historical relationship between these two metallurgical areas [China and the Eurasian steppes]." In Gansu, copper or bronze items are commonly found for the Qijia (2200–1600 BCE) and the Siba (1950–1550 BCE) cultures. The Siba culture yielded gold and silver ornaments (rings for example) that are also attested in Xinjiang and in Inner Mongolia (in the Zhukaigou culture) (Debaine-Francfort 2001: 62). Caucasoid skeletons have been excavated at Krorän (Loulan), north of the Lobnor; wheat and small bags of ephedra, dated to *c.* 1800 BCE, were given to the dead (Barber 2002: 61). The discovery of a copper-arsenic alloy from the Siba culture may reflect a western influence, this type of alloy being rare in the central plains of China.[41] A socketed axe belonging to the Qijia culture shows similarities with shapes found in the north, in the

---

[41] Qijia and Erlitou contain tin bronze. Without excluding western influences for the arsenical alloy, Li notes the existence of copper ores containing arsenic in the Hexi corridor (2003: 17). For several scholars, however, the presence of arsenic bronze during the early second millennium in northwestern China (Hami, Donghuishan) may have been the result of the material spreading from the Urals, where arsenical copper was produced at this time (Mei 2003: 37). For Debaine-Francfort (2001: 63), who points out that wheat, barley, and bricks have been found in the same assemblages, this spread of arsenical copper may be linked to a Bactrian influence.

Altai and in the Minusinsk basin (Mallory and Mair 2000: 327). Mei and Shell (1999: 572) have also observed that a variety of objects "of Andronovo type" (bronze tools and weapons, as well as ceramics) have been unearthed at several Xinjiang sites, partly introduced through the valleys of the southern Altai (cf. also Linduff 2002: 608). Xinjiang sites such as Krorän have yielded pins with paired spirals on their heads attested in Turkmenistan and in western Asia during the third millennium, and in Tajikistan during the second millennium (Kuzmina 2008: 99). Objects linked to the transcultural Seima-Turbino phenomenon (c. 1900/1800–1500 BCE) reached both Gansu and northern China during the early second millennium.[42] According to Chernykh et al. (2004), the Seima-Turbino complex derived from metallurgical and horse-riding cultures from the Altai. The complex produced socketed spearheads and socketed axes that can be found in China during the Early Shang period, and a little later in Southeast Asia (Thailand ...) (Higham 1996a). Curved knives, with ring handles or bearing animals or human figures, also signal connections with the steppes (Andronovo, Seima-Turbino, and later, the Karasuk complexes). The horse was present south of Lake Baikal and in Central Mongolia around the middle of the second millennium BCE (Honeychurch and Amartuvshin 2006: 259). Soon thereafter, the horse would appear in the Yellow River valley. The cemetery at Xiaohe, near the Lobnor, has yielded human masks with Caucasoid features, as well as thirty Caucasoid "mummies" (Liu and Chen 2012: 340–342). Twigs and branches of ephedra were sometimes placed beside the body. The site also contained *Panicum miliaceum* millet, probably from China, and *Triticum aestivum* wheat from western Asia (Yang et al. 2014).

Moreover, interactions between East Asia and the BMAC are revealed by the adoption of bronze mirrors, found at Xiaohe (here the bronze mirrors had gold rings), Tianshanbeilu (Xinjiang), Qijiaping (Gansu), and Gamatai (Qinghai),[43] or the discovery at Kuchā of a compartmented seal similar to exemplars from Gonur-1 and Shahdad.[44] The Tianshanbeilu and Gamatai mirrors carry a star motif known in the BMAC. At Begash, in the Dzungar basin (Xinjiang), shards similar to ceramics from Margiana have been unearthed.[45] A macehead decorated with four projecting goat heads, found at the site of Huoshaogou (Siba culture), also recalls the BMAC. The same cemetery also shows the practice of horse sacrifice.[46]

Links with the Altai are also visible at Tianshanbeilu (2000–1550 BCE), through ceramics and metal artifacts. Numerous discoveries of copper and bronze objects have

---

[42] Fitzgerald-Huber 1995; Barnes 1999: 124; Koryakova and Kohl 2000: 641; Debaine-Francfort 2001: 63; Sherratt and Sherratt 2001: 26; Mei 2003: 35; Kohl 2007: 168. Concerning the technological "innovations" of the transcultural Seima-Turbino phenomenon (use of the lost-wax technique, probably introduced from the BMAC ...), see also Koryakova and Epimakhov 2007: 39, 106ff.

[43] Fitzgerald-Huber 2003. Mirrors have also been found at Erlitou (Kuzmina 2007: 264).

[44] Similarities between seals of the BMAC and metal "seals" (?) discovered in the Ordos steppes in Chinese Mongolia (Kohl 1995: 1058) have been refuted by Francfort (1990: 122); the Ordos artifacts appear to be more recent (possibly second millennium CE) and show technical differences. The question, however, remains open.

[45] Frachetti 2004: 382–383. In addition, jewels found at this site show that the people of Begash were in contact with southern Siberia and central Kazakhstan.

[46] Curiously, Kuzmina (2007: 256) claims that the Qijia and Siba cultures did not know the domesticated horse, but she admits that the latter was present earlier in the Afanasevo culture.

been made in this cemetery, whose shapes are attested in the steppes, in the Okunev culture and the Seima-Turbino complex – as well as in the Qijia and Siba cultures of Gansu and Qinghai (Mei 2003: 36, 40). Tin in the bronzes of the Seima-Turbino complex came from the Altai or from regions further east. Tianshanbeilu and other sites in Xinjiang were certainly instrumental in transmitting copper and bronze metallurgical techniques to the Gansu corridor and Qinghai. The presence of arsenical bronze – also attested in the Siba culture – "points to connections with cultures farther to the west [Urals] and north." DNA analysis has confirmed that European elements were present in the ancestry of the Xiaohe population, as well as a Siberian component (Li *et al.* 2015).

Clearly, the Qijia and Siba populations both had contacts with Central Asia, southern Siberia, and Mongolia. There was a notable migration of the Siba culture toward western Gansu and eastern Xinjiang. The cemetery at Linya (Hami, Xinjiang) has yielded ceramics and bronze objects similar to those found in the Siba culture, with which it was contemporaneous. As is the case in the cemetery of Yanbulaq,[47] located in the same region, the Linya site has revealed a mixture of Caucasoid and Mongoloid populations. Moreover, some objects from the cemetery of Huoshaogou (Gansu), produced using piece-mold casting techniques, as well as the presence of lead bronzes, seem to reflect technical influences from the central plains of China during the Erlitou and Erligang periods. A Shang-type axe has been excavated in the vicinity of Lake Issyk Kul (Kyrgyzstan). The study of ceramics confirms this double movement – during the third millennium and the early second millennium – of populations from Gansu to the west,[48] and of populations from the steppes to the east.[49] "The presence of nephrite jade objects in China [also] suggests that China had contact with the Tarim basin from as early as the second millennium BCE" (Christian 2000: 13).

Some influences also came from China to South Asia, shown by the discovery of *Setaria italica* (L.) P. Beauv. and *Panicum miliaceum* L. millets during the Late Harappean Phase[50] – *Panicum miliaceum* was domesticated in China, and perhaps in the northern Caucasus (see Zohary *et al.* 2012: 70–71). *Japonica* rice also arrived in northern India. Knives and jade beads found in Kashmir and in the Swāt valley signal Chinese contacts (see below).

After the middle of the second millennium, "large settlements disappeared altogether" along the Gansu corridor, perhaps due to colder and drier conditions (Cunliffe 2015: 149) and the arrival of new populations.

[47] Discrepancies remain concerning the dating for this cemetery (some researchers have suggested two phases, 1750–1300 BCE, then 750–550 BCE, while other researchers see only one phase, spanning the years 1000 through 700 BCE (Mallory and Mair 2000). Some tombs yielded iron tools (see below).

[48] Around 2000 BCE, painted ceramics in the post-Machang style (Gansu) had already appeared at Hami (eastern Xinjiang); people belonging to the Siba culture subsequently migrated toward eastern Xinjiang (S. Li 2003: 12).

[49] S. Li 2002: 174–179, 2003: 13. Li suggests a Caucasoid migration from the Altai region toward Hami, and later toward Lobnor Lake (cemeteries of Gumugou and Xiaohe, *c.* 2000 BCE), and a Mongoloid movement from Gansu, toward Hami and on to Hejing and Urumqi (2002: 180). Remains have been retrieved that can be linked with the cultural Andronovo complex between the Ili River, Dzungaria, and the Lobnor (see S. Li 2003: 25; Mei 2003: 41).

[50] Weber 1998 [1909]: 268; Fuller 2006a: 38, 2007: 406, with some uncertainties for Rojdi.

The Early Bronze Age of China: The Erlitou Phase (1800–1600 BCE)

In the Longshan culture, the systems that were based around a single center such as Taosi and Liangchengzhen did not lead directly to the formation of the first large states. It seems more likely that the Erlitou state appeared within the context of multicentered, competing systems sharing a common culture: "social change tends to take place at focal points of regional social interaction, or in the central sectors of open settlement systems."[51] Erlitou did not belong to the Shang culture.[52] The elites of Erlitou developed the first bronze ritual vessels, which copied the shape of ceramic drinking vessels (Liu 2003). Bronzes were cast using piece-mold techniques that were at the crossroads between several traditions. One technique was linked to the ceramists of the Longshan culture (Yellow River), who "invented" the use of molds and were experienced in the use of high-temperature furnaces.[53] Another tradition was linked to the cast bronze industry from Siberia. It is likely that the artisans of older metallurgical centers from eastern Xinjiang, Gansu, and eastern Qinghai played a role in the flourishing bronze culture of Henan, as did northern groups. Curved knives similar to a type found in the steppes have been unearthed at Erlitou. The cultures that were at the origin of the so-called "Northern Complex" (south of the Mongolian plateau), such as the Zhukaigou culture, contemporary with the first bronzes of Erlitou, may have acquired their metallurgical knowledge directly from the steppes of Inner Asia. "The Qijia people may have brought the metallurgy techniques into the Ordos" (Liu and Chen 2012: 321).[54] These Qijia people also had contacts with the central Chinese plains during this period. Bronze plaques inlaid with turquoise excavated in Gansu thus recall Erlitou artifacts (Campbell suggests that "turquoise inlaying was originally a Qijia tradition" [2014: 39]).

The site of Erlitou (Henan Province), which covered 300 ha, with a central palatial zone surrounded by earth walls (10.8 ha), was the capital of a state, starting in 1800/1700 BCE. The elites controlled the manufacture of ritual bronze vessels[55] linked to ancestor

---

[51] Liu 2004: 246; Liu and Chen 2006: 56. Liu here refutes Carneiro 1970. In her research, Liu used geographical – regional and internal – data relative to the settlements, plus burial finds, to determine the level of social complexity of different societies.

[52] Barnes 1999: 271 n. 11. Some Chinese scholars draw a connection between the site of Erlitou and the mythic Xia dynasty of the ancient Chinese chronicles, but this remains purely hypothetical (see Liu and Chen 2003: 26–28, 148). For these authors, "the Xia dynasty (2100–1600 BC), if it existed, may have started as a chiefdom society during its early period, and then evolved into a territorial state only during the later stages of its development" (2003: 84). A few small copper or bronze objects (rings, knives) have been discovered at Neolithic sites, from an earlier period (Barnes 1999: 119; Liu and Chen 2003: 151 n. 5).

[53] Fitzgerald-Huber (1995: 60–63) has proposed a Bactrian influence in the manufacture of *jue* shape bronzes, but Liu (2003: 23) suggests that their origins lie rather in the white ceramic craftsmanship traditions.

[54] Di Cosmo 1999b: 893ff.; 2002: 48ff.; Barnes 1999: 119, 121. The Northern Complex is characterized by daggers, knives, and enigmatic "bow-shaped" objects. All these objects have distinctive shapes and bear geometric or animal designs. From the thirteenth century on, an "animal style" was dominant in the steppes and in the Karasuk culture of southern Siberia (*c.* 1200–800 BCE, though recently, radiocarbon has dated it to 1400–850 BCE) (Görsdorf *et al.* 2004: 84). The Northern Complex culture – in fact a group of different cultures – expanded eastward, where it entered into contact with the Lower Xiajiadian culture (Inner Mongolia and Hebei), *c.* 2000–1500 BCE (see below). It also influenced the cultures that were already present in Gansu.

[55] Liu (2004: 226) has identified a four-tier settlement hierarchy in the region of Erlitou state, suggesting a "highly integrated and centralized socio-political system." Bronze workshops have been discovered in

worship – and therefore communication with the divine – (other prestige goods such as white pottery, on the other hand, seem to have been offered in tribute to Erlitou) (Liu 2003: 19). Bronze casting workshops were located near the palatial complex, as were turquoise workshops, and ritual bronze vessels were redistributed only within the city of Erlitou. The regional centers of Dongxiafeng and Nanguan produced bronze tools and weapons, but no ritual vessels (Liu 2003: 24).[56] Many jade artifacts have been excavated from tombs (including blades, bracelets, and handle-shaped objects), but there is no evidence for jade working at the site. Erlitou was not fortified, but two walled settlements with bronze and jade objects discovered north and south of Erlitou (Dashigou and Wangjinglou) may have been Erlitou strongholds.

The state of Erlitou was located in a rich agricultural region at the end of long-distance trade routes (excavations have revealed cowry shells from the ocean, objects and decorative motifs which point to links with Central Asia, and *zhang* jade blades attesting to influences from Shandong). An arsenic-copper item points to connections with northwestern regions such as Gansu. Objects and ideas which would influence the whole of eastern and southeastern Asia at this time, and the Shang dynasty later on, originated in Erlitou. Thus, ceremonial *yazhang* jade blades and *ge* dagger-axes can be found in Lingnan and as far as the lower Red River valley.[57] The presence of secondary centers probably initiated by colonization efforts from Erlitou reflects a wish to control the routes leading to natural resources such as salt, copper, and tin (a similar process has been observed for the Urukian expansion in Mesopotamia).[58] This was the case for the centers of Dongxiafeng and Nanguan (South Shanxi), Donglongshan (eastern Shaanxi), and even more so for Panlongcheng (Hubei), in the Yangtze River valley (see Map 1.7). Sites related to the Erlitou culture were even present south of the Yangtze, in the Gan River valley and further east, in copper-rich regions. Erlitou sites also developed in the Huai River valley, between the Yellow River and the Yangtze.[59] Ceramics originating in the Yangtze River valley have been discovered in the Yellow River region

---

the vicinity of the palatial area. Erlitou is the only site which has evidence of ritual vessel production. Bronzes were present in the largest tombs during Erlitou Phase II (1800–1700 BCE). However, they were still relatively rare. Significant changes occurred during Phase III (1700–1600 BCE), with the construction of two palaces, and an increasing number of weapons and funerary offerings – especially complex bronzes, whose manufacture required the use of several molds.

[56] However, Chang (2000) has argued that writing and bronze metallurgy did not play a crucial economic role during the Chinese Bronze Age, but instead helped to ideologically reinforce political power. For Chang, in ancient China – unlike Mesopotamia – control over means of communication was more important than controlling means of production. Though this thesis develops some interesting ideas, it underplays the importance of bronze weapons, and the possibility that writing may have had a wider application, using perishable materials which left no lasting trace.

[57] Liu and Chen 2003: 33; Higham 1996a: 55–56. The jade in Erlitou may have come from Donglongshan (Liu 2003: 16). Other cultures, aside from the Erlitou, were present in the Yellow River basin: the Xiaqiyuan culture (North Henan–South Hebei), and the Yueshi culture (Shandong) (2000–1600 BCE). The latter developed bronze metallurgy. At the site of Shijia, in a ritual pit, oracle bones have been discovered that are incised with glyphs.

[58] In some cases, the expansion of the Erlitou culture may also reflect its appropriation by outside communities (Liu and Chen 2003: 81).

[59] Liu and Chen 2003: 69–79. The copper ores controlled by Dongxiafeng came from the Zhongtiao Mountains. Rich copper mines (Tongling) were located downstream of Panlongcheng in the Yangtze valley. Other Erlitou sites have been found upstream of Panlongcheng (site of Jiangnansi) and in the south

(proto-porcelain developed in southern China has been unearthed at Erlitou). More intensive contacts were to develop in the ensuing period, at the time of the Erligang state. From 2000 to 1500 BCE, the plains of northern China enjoyed wetter and warmer conditions than they do today, leading to progress in agriculture and demographic growth. More than forty glyphs have been noted on pottery vessels, "sometimes similar in form to later oracle-bone inscriptions," but they do not seem to have made up a writing system (Liu and Chen 2012: 263).

Complex pre-state societies belonging to the Lower Xiajiadian culture located in Liaoning Province and Inner Mongolia (2200–1600/1500 BCE), partly contemporary with Erlitou, established fortified sites (the largest covered 23 ha) in the north of China. This culture, in which Di Cosmo (2002: 65, 67) has identified the emergence of a nomad military aristocracy, produced some metal objects that demonstrate links with the Zhukaigou culture of Inner Mongolia. Moreover, the presence of cowries in tombs reveals long-distance contacts reaching as far as the coast (Linduff *et al.* 2002: 61; Sun 2017) (Liu and Chen have even suggested that these cowries may have come from the Indian Ocean [2012: 311]; however, they may also have come from the South China Sea).

The Shang State (1600–1027 BCE): Wider Control over Resources and Long-Distance Exchanges

A step-up in arrowhead production is seen in Erlitou during its late phase, a sign of increased conflicts, connected to the abrupt arrival of newcomers. The sites of the Erligang culture (1600–1415 BCE), different from the Erlitou culture, are often thought to have belonged to the early Shang dynasty.[60] While Erlitou was in decline, the fortified site of Yanshi (200 ha) emerged, 6 km east of Erlitou, and the city of Zhengzhou (2500 ha), 75 km further east, thereafter. Zhengzhou was also fortified, with outer walls 22 m thick at the base; and a rectangular inner city with palaces and temples has been unearthed in its northeastern part.[61] Liu and Chen (2012: 282) give an estimate of 100,000 inhabitants for Zhengzhou (between "78,000 and 130,000"). There was a clear segregation between the elite, who lived mainly in an inner city, and commoners, who occupied the outer city. Zhengzhou was the capital of a state (perhaps the Shang capital given as Ao in the chronicles) whose elites – as was the case at Erlitou – controlled the production of ritual bronze vessels and their redistribution (two bronze foundries have been found). "The scale of bronze production was much greater than in Erlitou . . . Three hoards discovered in the outer city contained 28 bronzes with a total weight of more than 500 kg" (Liu and Chen 2012: 284). The Shang culture is famous for the beauty and quality of its bronzes, which were first of all ritual

---

(Weigang, in the Li River valley). Liu and Chen have noted a standardization process in the ceramics of the Erlitou settlements (2003: 80).

[60] The Proto-Shang may have originated in a region between North Henan and South Hebei, and have belonged to a variant of the Xiaqiyuan culture. Some scholars have also suggested that the Shang state originated in eastern Henan (region of Shangqiu) and western Shandong (Liu and Chen 2003: 85ff.; Liu 2004: 225).

[61] Morris (2013: 164) gives an estimate of 35,000 inhabitants for Zhengzhou, but this estimate may be too low.

drinking and cooking vessels, and its weapons, symbols of the twin foundations of the elites' power (ritual and military). The absence of bronze tools for agriculture has been noted (Liu and Chen 2003: 98); however, the metal may have been recycled. In the outer city, various workshops manufactured bronze, ceramic, and bone objects. Regional centers such as Huaizhenfang (Shaanxi), Panlongcheng (Hubei), Dongxiafeng, and Nanguan produced bronze tools and weapons (Liu and Chen 2003: 133). Thus the idea that "the earliest Chinese cities were primarily ritual and political centers with lesser emphasis on economic functions" (Liu and Chen 2012: 296) – compared to western Asian cities – needs to be rethought.

Two pieces of animal bone, each bearing an inscription, have revealed that the Chinese writing system was already developing, invented independently from western Asia. This script combined semantic and phonetic elements. It was first encountered on animal shoulder blades and turtle shells (plastrons and carapaces), and then on bronzes (during the Late Shang period).[62] For Liu and Chen, however, the inscriptions from Erlitou, Erligang and Xiaoshuangqiao do not yet reflect the formation of "a true writing system" (2012: 294–295), which was in evidence only at Yinxu (see below).

Zhengzhou's elites showed a greater willingness to expand than did those from Erlitou. It was an expansion "driven by the procurement of key resources and prestige items" (Liu and Chen 2012: 284). The Erligang state applied itself to controlling resources and commercial routes, partly by force (Liu and Chen 2003: 102ff.). Fortified outposts were established, at Panlongcheng in the south; at Dongxiafeng, Nanguan, and Donglongshan in the west; at Daxinzhuang in the east, and so forth. In the north, Zhukaigou, which exhibits Shang style bronze ritual vessels, was for a time an Erligang outpost (Liu and Chen 2012: 321). A wider redistribution of prestige goods (bronze vessels, proto-porcelain) to the regional elites around the city of Zhengzhou can be seen (Liu 2003: 26). Erligang material is present north of Zhengzhou, at Baiyan, and at Zhukaigou (south of Inner Mongolia), where a population originating in the heartland (Erligang) probably settled; bronze ornaments similar to those of the steppe cultures have also been found at this site.[63] In the southwest, the regional centers of Laoniupo (Wei River valley) and of Donglongshan probably tried to control the copper ore of the Qinling Mountains. The numerous sites in Shandong that contain Erligang material reflect a process of colonization toward the coast. The presence of some Erligang sites

---

[62] Keightley 2006: 182. The use of bones and shells for divination goes back to the Neolithic (for example, the Dawenkou and Longshan cultures. Turtles made of jade have also been found in Neolithic cultures such as Hongshan and Liangzhu). Their presence indicates the existence of large shared belief systems (Liu 2003: 8); the turtle combines the symbols for the Sky (the disc) and for the Earth (the square). Tombs at Jiahu (seventh–sixth millennium) already contained turtle shells, with small pebbles inside, and bone flutes; some of the shells bore symbols similar to the oracle-bone inscriptions of the Shang period (Liu 2004: 65). The first royal chronicles appear to have been written on silk and on bamboo. Of course, nothing remains of them. Note that the texts written on bones were secondary texts that had been copied. It is likely that the Shang people placed particular value on the act of reading a document engraved on bone and still more on the act of inscribing ("the incising mattered more than the writing"), but above all, the mere presence of the script – a system of symbolic communication with royal ancestors – must have been crucial (Keightley 2006: 188ff.).

[63] Di Cosmo (2002: 48) notes that the Zhukaigou culture (2000–1500 BCE) was one of the "ancestors" of the "Northern Bronze Complex." Evidence of divination practices using bones dated to the early second millennium have been found in this northern region.

along the Si River demonstrates the importance of routes linking the Yellow River to the Lower Yangtze valley. During the Late Shang period, the Shang state probably controlled the production of salt. A significant expansion was still noticeable toward the Middle Yangtze valley, along the Han River and other routes. Knowledge of bronze metallurgy arrived in the south during this period, via the same routes. The fortified site of Panlongcheng was a major city, with outer walls enclosing 290 ha; the inner walls delimited a palatial area (7.5 ha), which demonstrates close affiliation with the north. Panlongcheng controlled the copper mines of Tongling, and produced bronze, but ritual vessels were probably imported from the north. Various Erligang centers were located along the Yangtze River, upstream, and downstream, such as Tonglushan, near copper mines. In the south, a major site was discovered at Wucheng (61 ha), in the Gan River valley, in a zone rich in ore deposits. Shihuishan (Jiangxi) and Zaoshi (Hunan), south of the Yangtze, were producing bronze at this time. The Shang period saw progress in metallurgy and in ceramic production, with the invention of glazes, and the use of kilns reaching a temperature of 1,200°C. Wucheng produced a type of proto-porcelain and glazed stoneware that can be found in the large sites of the north. Products from the far south (Lingnan) also transited through the city, including turtle shells, pearls, and cowries. Cowries were perhaps already used as currency.[64] Wucheng developed a bronze metallurgical technique which, though inspired by the Shang tradition, showed local influences. At Xin'gan (Dayangzhou), 20 km east of Wucheng, the tomb of a high-ranking figure (possibly the ruler of a regional state) contained bronzes (amongst them, the first socketed plowshares attested in China) and numerous jade items (Middle/Late Shang period).[65]

Around 1400 BCE, transformations occurred, with a depopulation of larger sites in the west (South Shanxi) linked to a decline in copper and salt production in this region (a period of warmer and wetter climate appears to have led to a shift in the centers for salt production), as well as an expansion eastward and southward (Middle Shang period). Zhengzhou collapsed,[66] while a large site emerged further east, at Xiaoshuangqiao (150 ha).[67] However, this site was abandoned as well as Fucheng, and a new city, Huanbei, developed at Anyang, with an enclosure of 470 ha (see Map 1.8). Dated between 1420 and 1250 BCE, Huanbei may well have been the Shang capital referred to as Xiang in later chronicles. Marked by political instability, the Middle Shang period seems to correspond to a phase of restructuring, with the demise of some regional centers and the emergence of new poles. Panlongcheng had been abandoned by the end of the

---

[64] At Erligang, one tomb contained 460 cowries. Y.-T. Li (2003), however, has refuted the idea that cowries had a monetary function prior to the Western Zhou period (see below).

[65] The tomb also contained a bronze anvil weighing 20 kg, and four bells, reminders of the Lower Yangtze. Many objects were wrapped in silk (Higham 1996a: 68; Liu and Chen 2003: 121). Further west, sites in Hunan, such as Zaoshi, and sites in Ningxiang county, have demonstrated links with the Erligang culture; they also developed a unique regional style (bells, animal sculptures). Bronzes found at Dayangzhou contain the same lead isotope found in the bronzes of Henan, Hubei, and Sanxingdui (Sichuan). The origin of the copper ore is not yet known, though it may have come from eastern Yunnan or western Guizhou (Liu and Chen 2003: 42).

[66] The historical record mentions a period of chaos and a contested succession.

[67] The status of this city remains uncertain. It was abandoned before the end of the Middle Shang period, as was Fucheng (Liu and Chen 2003: 99, 143).

Erligang period. From 1300 BCE, the Shang capital was at Yinxu (Anyang), whereas Wucheng developed into a more or less independent center.

The excavations at Anyang have revealed the complexity of this society, yielding palace and temple remains, and demonstrating the importance and mastery of bronze-working as well as the extent of exchange networks. The city reached a size of over 3,000 ha at its peak, "with a 'palace-temple' precinct nearly 70 ha in area" (Campbell 2014: 131). Anyang may have had 50,000 inhabitants in 1200 BCE, according to Morris's estimates (2013: 163) (Chase-Dunn et al. [2015] suggest 100,000). This size contrasts with the supposed "political weakness" of the Shang during the Yinxu period (Liu and Chen 2012: 390).[68] In the Xibeigang cemetery (Anyang), the large royal tombs had all been plundered before excavations, but one untouched tomb was found: the tomb of Queen Fu Hao (c. 1200 BCE). This tomb contained more than 200 bronze vessels, 270 bronze weapons and tools, 600 jade artifacts, 7,000 cowries, and many more artifacts.[69] Bronze mirrors, a knife with an ibex head on its pommel, bow-shaped objects (of unknown use), all marked the influence of the northern cultures.[70] Other bronze objects (for example, a pair of *fanglei* wine vessels) point to links with Shaanxi. The stone used in most of the jade objects may have come from Xinjiang,[71] while some pieces have been given southern origins (for example, tubular beads, and a piece depicting an elephant). Tomb 1004 yielded a cauldron weighing 879 kg, and a huge crucible capable of containing 1.5 tons of metal. In a western cemetery, which yielded relatively few bronzes, many tombs contained cowries (Higham 1996a: 59). Moreover, at Xibeigang, more than 1,200 sacrificial pits were excavated; they contained the remains of horses, some elephants, chariot fittings, as well as human victims, notably near tomb 1400.[72] Horses and chariots discovered in the royal cemetery indicate the prestige attached to them; their presence implies close links with the populations of Central Asia. Tin for bronze production may have been procured from Yunnan or Jiangxi (Campbell 2014: 179).

Workshops have been excavated at Anyang that reveal "a two-tiered production organization, with a highly centralized royal production and a more decentralized lineage

---

[68] Campbell (2014: 178) expresses another opinion, although data indicate "troubled northern and western borders."

[69] Barnes 1999: 127; Bagley 1999: 194ff. The jade items include objects probably going back to the Neolithic period, as well as imitations. For Mallory and Mair (2000: 147), most of the pieces were made using jade from Central Asia. Liu (2003: 17) suggests two other possible origins: southern Henan and Liaoning.

[70] The Shang mirrors may also have come from Xinjiang through the Hexi corridor (Kuzmina 2008: 103). "Analysis of the non-standard artifacts from Anyang [shows] that they find their closest analogies in the complexes of eastern Kazakhstan and Semirech'e" (Kuzmina 2007: 262). Mirrors with loop handles, such as those found in the tomb, have also been attested in Manchuria and Xinjiang, in the Karasuk culture, as well as in Kazakhstan, Fergana, and the Tazabagyab culture (Debaine-Francfort 2001: 62). They probably derive from mirrors of the BMAC (Kuzmina 2007: 408, 2008: 103).

[71] Di Cosmo 1999b: 902. With the "Northern Complex" – in fact divided into different cultural regions – armed conflict seems to have increased during the Late Shang period.

[72] Bagley 1999: 192–193. A group of 191 pits southeast of tomb 1400 contained the remains of more than 1,200 human victims. These sacrifices played a crucial religious role for the Shang kings and their society. The largest tombs contained chariots with their horses and charioteers. Horses and chariots have also been found in separate pits. The remains of bronze fittings have been retrieved. Chariot and horse ornaments would remain a mark of high status in later periods, under the Zhou dynasty.

production" (Campbell 2014: 136). Bronzeworking was particularly important, as seen in the remains of six foundries. Bronze vessel production during the time of the kings of Anyang spread to various centers, along with a flourishing of regional styles. The Laoniupo site (50 ha) (Shaanxi) has thus yielded a bronze foundry. Laoniupo was probably the center of a vassal state, which may have "brought Qiang captives as tribute to Yinxu for ceremonial sacrifice" (Liu and Chen 2012: 380).[73] Some of the bronze artifacts found at sites of the Loess Plateau region were probably produced locally (northern Shaanxi, western Shanxi, Inner Mongolia; Liu and Chen 2012: 381ff.). In Jiangxi, the rise to power of Wucheng at this time may explain why Panlongcheng was abandoned.[74] The Late Shang state was surrounded by a number of vassal states and various political entities which were alternately allies or enemies at different periods, such as the Zhou, in Shaanxi (in the west of the Shang domain). Subutun (Shandong) may have been the center of a politically independent entity. Thus, the physical extent of the Shang central state was clearly more limited than the extent of the Shang culture. The characteristics of the Shang state, however, remain a topic for debate.[75] The inscriptions (on divinatory animal bones and turtle plastrons)[76] mention over one thousand names of towns and cities, few of which have been discovered.

Discoveries at Anyang show long-distance trade with regions south of the Yangtze. The Shang state also had indirect contacts with Sichuan and Yunnan (Falkenhausen 2003: 217). Bronze artifacts discovered at Baoshan (Chenggu, South Shaanxi) show concurrent links with Anyang in the northeast and Sichuan in the southwest (Liu and Chen 2012: 376), as well as with Jiangxi in the southeast.[77]

The discovery in Sichuan of a major culture dating from the second millennium has shed light on interactions between the Yellow River and Yangtze River valleys, as well as regions further south. The center of this culture was Sanxingdui, located north of Chengdu, a city with impressive walls surrounding an area of 360 ha, dated to between

---

[73] According to Beckwith (2011), the Qiang may have been of Indo-European origin. The term "Qiang" may mean "charioteer."

[74] Whereas the Shang bronzes were mainly ritual vessels, "the Yangtze traditions of the Late Shang period placed great emphasis on musical instruments" (bells, for example) (Barnes 1999: 122), and also on animal-shaped vessels. A bell weighing 225 kg, the largest currently attested, has been excavated at Ningxiang (northern Hunan). Moreover, a large drum has been found in Hubei.

[75] Qishan, the "predynastic capital of the Zhou," divulged archaeological remains contemporary to those of Anyang. See Barnes 1999: 133, fig. 60, showing the respective sizes of the Shang state and of the Shang culture in the Late Shang period. The core/peripheries concept used by Liu and Chen for the Early Shang period sheds light on what has been observed at the archaeological level. These authors (2003: 134, 146) support the model of a "territorial state" with a strong center during the Erlitou and Erligang periods. The political landscape appears to have become more fragmented during the Middle and Late Shang periods, which is consistent with the *Shiji* written by Sima Qian (first century BCE). For M. E. Lewis (2000: 360), the Shang state had almost no administration: according to him, the Shang and subsequently Zhou areas were formed by a "league of cities" that accepted the authority of a king and of his followers; these were cities ruled by the king's relatives or allies. This authority was primarily founded on religious and military power. However, a bureaucracy did exist, formed through aristocratic lineages (see below for the Zhou period). Keightley (2006: 184) also speaks of the "theocratic nature of the Shang state."

[76] Barnes 1999: 20–21. We know of only a smaller corpus of texts unrelated to divination, written on ceramics, stone, and jade. Of course, the documents written on bamboo strips or silk have disappeared.

[77] See the bronze artifacts found in the Xin'gan tomb (Dayangzhou), located near a large Wucheng-tradition walled site, Niutoucheng (Campbell 2014: 163).

1700 and 1100 BCE.[78] Excavated in 1986, two ritual pits were found to contain ivory (dozens of elephant tusks), gold and jade items, and bronzes (dated to the thirteenth–twelfth century BCE) that differ stylistically from the Shang bronzes. The latter, however, are attested at Sanxingdui: contacts existed between Sichuan and the Shang cultural area, perhaps through the Han River valley and the Middle Yangtze. Among the bronzes discovered at Sanxingdui were statues – the first statuary attested in eastern Asia – these were masks and heads, sometimes covered with gold foil and filled with cowries.[79] Identifying the origins of bronze metallurgy in Sichuan remains an unresolved problem (some researchers have suggested an origin in Gansu, or in the Middle Yellow River valley). Statuary appears to have drawn its influences from the Shijiahe culture (Middle Yangtze, 2500–2000 BCE), which offers representations of human heads in jade.[80] Iconographic elements of the Shijiahe culture must have reached Sichuan at the time of the Baoduncun culture (Falkenhausen 2003: 198). Pottery as well as ritual jades (*zhang* scepters, *ge* dagger-axes, *yu* axes, and collared rings) reveal contacts with the Erlitou culture, and the styles of some jade suggest Qijia influences as well (Chang 1999: 217; Falkenhausen 2003: 203ff., 208ff.; Campbell 2014: 57). Animal-shaped panels of bronze inlaid with turquoise show that influences operated in both directions (Falkenhausen 2003: 212). It has been suggested that lead reached Anyang from Yunnan via Sichuan, but this hypothesis is still debated (Liu and Chen 2012: 372; Campbell 2014: 165). Some scholars have suggested western influences (Central and western Eurasia) – yet to be proven – for motifs of winged animals and for the "spirit-tree" found in a ritual pit at Sanxingdui (Campbell 2014: 218). This culture also had contacts with the Yangtze valley. Sichuan led to Yunnan and the valleys of the great rivers of Southeast Asia. It also benefited from its exceptional underground wealth (gold, silver, and copper). Cowries at Sanxingdui may have come from the Indian Ocean; this route via Sichuan may have been the source of the cowries found at Anyang. Sanxingdui was probably the capital of the Shu state mentioned in Shang inscriptions. The later site of Jinsha appears to have become the regional center after the demise of Sanxingdui.

The second half of the second millennium was a period of greater interaction in the Eurasian steppes, with new surges in metallurgy (see above) and trade in bronze products. Links with Xinjiang developed, at the same time as exchanges "down-the-line" between this region and the steppes, where movements of metallurgists and migrations of populations can be seen. The metal objects found at the sites of Sazi and Tacheng (northwest Dzungaria), Qizilchoqa (1350–1000 BCE), Xintala (southwest of Urumqi) (1700–1300 BCE), and Lanzhouwanzi (Nanwan) (dated 1385 ± 75 BCE) attest to these exchanges (Kuzmina 2007: 254). The Shang state maintained contact with the Northern Metallurgic Complex, and indirectly with the Altai and with Central Asia

---

[78] The foundations of the city walls at Sanxingdui were 40 to 50m thick at the base, and probably 20m thick at the summit. The site has been dated to between 2800 and 1000 BCE (Liu and Chen 2012: 373).

[79] The largest statue is 2.62 m high, and one mask is 1.38 m wide; the fragments of a bronze tree have made it possible to reconstitute a height of 3.80 m. The masks bear the features of humans or monsters. Some human figures bear motifs attested on Shang ritual vessels. Bronzes sometimes recall those of the Middle Yangtze, but were locally produced (Higham 1996a: 69–70).

[80] The jade items of the Shijiahe culture point to influences from the Liangzhu culture. The Shijiahe culture also ended around 2000 BCE, probably due to environmental changes, and also a southward expansion of the Longshan culture (Liu and Chen 2012: 246).

through the Hexi corridor, where the Kayue culture (Gansu and Qinghai) appear to have had links with the cultures of Siberia or Central Asia (Di Cosmo 1999b: 918). The importance of the horse-drawn chariot around 1300 BCE at Anyang has already been mentioned.[81] The Old Chinese terms for wheel, chariot, axle, and wheel hub exhibit borrowings from Indo-European languages, notably Iranian.[82] The abrupt presence of chariots at Anyang implies the arrival of craftsmen and of chariot drivers of foreign origin. New populations, perhaps Iranian speakers, entered Xinjiang, where the horse was now more often seen (Kuzmina 2007: 256). Painted pottery affiliated with the ceramic of the Chust culture has been unearthed at sites in Xinjiang (Kuzmina 2008: 90). In the opposite direction, jade has been found in the Chust culture, marking eastern influences. Chariots, however, may have arrived via different routes. Petroglyphs depicting chariots have been discovered in southern Siberia, in the Altai, in the Tian Shan Mountains, in the Yinshan Range, and in Inner Mongolia (Di Cosmo 1999b: 904). The discovery of disk-shaped cheek-pieces, harnessing elements, documents routes through the steppes (Kohl 2007: 145 fig. 4.9). "Northern bronzes, including [curved] knives and bow-shaped objects, appear in the Anyang archaeological record at the same time as chariots" (Bagley 1999: 208). Socketed axes and spearheads demonstrate increasing contacts with Inner Asia, especially with the Karasuk culture (southern Siberia). The regions of northern China were connected to Siberia, itself in contact with the Central Asian steppes. The discovery of trumpet-shaped earrings, some made of gold (a metal not used by the Shang), at sites in northeastern China, reflects these connections; attested in Siberia, Kazakhstan, Kyrgyzstan, and Fergana, this kind of ornament is associated with the Fedorovo culture (Kuzmina, 2008: 105). The migration of Mongoloid populations to the west can also be observed, where they formed the Dandibay culture in Central Kazakhstan. It coexisted with the Alekseevka culture (Sargary) (post-Alakul) (from 1600 BCE) (Kuzmina 2007: 79; Frachetti, p.c.).

The development of exchange networks was accompanied by the structural transformation of the cultures in contact with the Yellow River region. A military elite emerged in the Northern Complex during the Shang period (Di Cosmo 2002: 50). The Shang alternated between commercial and diplomatic contacts (Queen Fu Hao was a northern princess) and military expeditions with this region (Wang 2001; Sun 2006).

Trade also developed with regions south of the Yangtze. From the southern shores came tortoiseshell, ivory, and seashells. Tombs yielded quantities of cowries. Strings of cowries were used to purchase goods, to reward services or in exchange for work. For F. Thierry (1997: 41), they also represented a standard of value.[83] This use of cowries may go back to an earlier period: the *bei* character, "seashell," appeared in inscriptions in connection with trade operations.[84] Some authors such as Simkin believed that the

---

[81] Gernet 1999: 47; Barnes 1999: 145. See above. The horse-drawn carriage was developed in the western steppes before 2000 BCE.

[82] On the word for chariot, Mallory and Mair 2000: 326.

[83] The expression "rewards of double strings of cowries" is mentioned on oracular bones and on a bronze vessel of the Late Shang period (Thierry 1997: 39). Already present in the Early Shang period, the cowries appear to have been more numerous during the Middle and Late Shang periods.

[84] Hogendorn and Johnson 1986: 13, after Gibson 1940. The *bei* character subsequently appears in words related to the idea of value (Schaps 2007: 18).

monetary use of cowries may reflect ancient contacts between East Asia and the Indian Ocean (Hogendorn and Johnson 1986: 163 n. 101), but the monetary use of cowries is more recent in Bengal than it is in China: it could well be the mark of a Chinese influence. However, Li (2003), as mentioned before, rejects the idea that cowries had a monetary use in China prior to the Zhou period. Note that, from the late second millennium BCE on, silk weaving seems to have developed,[85] but silk fragments have been discovered at Qintaicun (Henan) that are dated much earlier (4500–3630 BCE), at a Neolithic site in Zhejiang, west of Huzhou, dated to 3500 BCE, and at Qianshanyang, a site belonging to the Liangzhu culture (2850–2650 BCE) (Cameron 2010: 147).[86]

The existence of terrestrial routes leading from China to Lingnan, to Yunnan and to Southeast Asia, moreover, explain how bronze technology was transferred to different cultures, from the middle of the second millennium BCE onward (below).

The military activity of the Shang north and west of their territory appears to have increased after the twelfth century BCE. Populations who may have been – at least partly – Iranian speakers migrated eastward around the end of the second millennium BCE. Hoards of metal objects such as that of Agarshin (southeast of Yining) provide evidence of the migration of metallurgists from Kazakhstan and Kyrgyzstan. "The fact they were hidden underground reflects the hostile environment of the steppe at that time" (Kuzmina 2007: 265). Two small heads carved from shell, found at Zhouyuan in a Western Zhou palace complex (dated to *c.* 1000 BCE), "show distinctive Caucasoid facial features." The carvings have conical headgear, and one of them bears the *wu* sign referring to ritual mediators: shamans from Central Asia probably officiated at the royal court (Liu 2004: 91).[87]

Around 1027 BCE, the Zhou, helped by groups hostile to the Shang, put an end to the Shang dynasty. Texts report the subjugation of 750 states associated with the Shang, and give the names of between twenty and seventy Zhou states that recognized the authority of the "royal Zhou state."

---

[85] Along with the spread of mulberry trees. Silk production is already attested "in the divinatory inscriptions of the last centuries of the second millennium" (Gernet 1999: 33): the characters *can* (silkworm), *sang* (mulberry tree), and *si* (silk) were present.

[86] A cocoon was found in 1926 in a Neolithic burial in Shanxi, in the Xiaxian district. According to the *Tribute of Yu*, six regions produced silk at the time of the mythical emperor Yu (third millennium BCE) (Barnes 1999: 173).

[87] These heads with Caucasoid features were used as ornamental heads for hairpins. For Mallory and Mair (2000: 326), the term *wu* may be related to the Old Persian *magush*, which referred to a specialist in the religious field, officiating at the court. Iranian magi may have already been present at the Shang court (Mallory and Mair 2000).

7 The Emergence of Intermediary Spaces

Arabia, an Interface between Continents

The First "Incense Roads"

Arabia was never an isolated region, but from an early stage it acted as a bridge between continents. Affinities between the Ethio-Semitic and the Old South Arabian languages reflect early population movements between Arabia and northeastern Africa. Archaeological data have revealed that Arabia acted as an active intermediary between Asia and Africa. The exchange of plants and animals between Africa and South Asia – via Arabia – offers solid evidence for these contacts.

When Arabia went through a wet phase between the seventh and the eighth millennium, various populations took advantage of the resources offered by lakes and maritime shores (Boivin and Fuller 2009). Coastal groups developed nautical knowledge as early as this Neolithic period. From the seventh millennium onward, Arabia received obsidian from Eritrea and from the Djibouti region, and a regional sphere of interaction was formed between Yemen and the Horn of Africa.[1] By the fourth millennium, these networks extended to the Nile valley (Fattovich 1997a: 480; see above).

Population movements and trade facilitated the introduction of domesticated animals (goats, sheep, and cattle) into the Persian Gulf as early as the sixth millennium BCE (Biagi 2006; Potts 2008; Boivin and Fuller 2009: 133). The presence of 'Ubaid pottery as far as Oman reveals the existence of trade between Mesopotamia and Arabia during the sixth and fifth millennia. The Arab coastal communities took an active part in these exchanges (see above). It is possible that incense and myrrh from southern Arabia were carried to Mesopotamia. Obsidian was also traded over long distances. Obsidian beads excavated from two tombs of the 'Ubaid period in Qatar may have originated in southern Arabia,[2] and obsidian (blades) found at the site of as-Sabīyah (Kuwait) may have come from southwestern Saudi Arabia or from Yemen (Carter 2002: 16). The only plant cultivated at this time seems to have been the date palm: date remains from *c.* 5000 BCE have been found on Dalma Island and in Kuwait. Though "archaeobotanical finds point to an Arabian origin for the date palm" (Boivin and Fuller 2009: 135), some researchers suggest that the plant was domesticated in Sind-Baluchistan (see above).

---

[1] As mentioned previously, chemical analysis does not allow us to distinguish between obsidian from the Horn of Africa and that from Arabia (Durrani 2005: 107). However, obsidian knapping makes it possible to identify affinities between cultures.

[2] Zarins 1990: 531; 2002: 420–421. Obsidian found at Matafah in Dhofar probably originated in southern Yemen (Zarins 2002).

In western Arabia, the obsidian found at sites on the Tihama coastal plain and dated to the sixth millennium may have come from the Horn of Africa, the Eritrean coast, or the Ethiopian Highlands (see above). In addition, terrestrial contacts between the Levant and Jordan, on the one hand, and western Arabia on the other, were present as early as the sixth or fifth millennium. These contacts fostered the arrival of cattle, goats, and sheep in the Yemeni Highlands (Edens 2002a: 50; McCorriston and Martin 2009).[3] An example of rock art depicting cattle standing in profile, with their heads and horns viewed from the front, may go back to the fifth millennium BCE in northern Arabia (Jubba style). Animals were reared in the plain of Tihama during the early fourth millennium.

Climate data point to three phases of aridification in Arabia around 4300, 3800, and 3300/3200 BCE (Boivin and Fuller 2009: 124). During the latter period, the climate more closely resembled its present-day conditions.[4] For the Persian Gulf, the phases of aridification of the fourth millennium led to fewer settlements, on the coast and in the interior, although there was some continuity in the Gulf of Oman. Communities manufactured goods intended for trade, such as shell beads. We have no evidence for the adoption of western Asian plants in this area prior to the third millennium (Boivin and Fuller 2009: 146).

In western Arabia, an agriculture based on plants native to western Asia – which arrived via a north–south or an east–west route – is attested no later than the start of the third millennium (at the sites of Jububat al-Juruf and Hait al-Sawad), though some elements suggest that this agriculture may have been present a thousand years earlier.[5] Terraces have been observed on the Yemeni Highlands that appear to indicate the arrival of these cultivated plants during the fifth or fourth millennium (Harrower 2008a; Boivin and Fuller 2009: 146). The first known terrace, at Ghazwan, south of Dhamar (in western Yemen), goes back to 4000 BCE (Wilkinson 2005: 179). The appearance of stone tombs (circular tombs . . .) seems to reflect a new social complexity, linked to water and land control. Terraces, irrigation works, and tombs represent a symbolic capital which was now being invested in a socialized space (Harrower [2008a: 505] speaks of "symbolic landesque capital"). Moreover, at Al-Rajajil ("the men"), in the Jawf, people from the Bronze Age (third millennium) erected fifty-four groups of rudely trimmed stone pillars. Each group contains 2 to 19 pillars; it is possible that some of the pillars were originally placed to observe celestial phenomena.

In Egypt, during the fourth millennium, drawings of boats on rocks in the Wadi Hammamat portray ancient navigation not only on the Nile, but also in the Red Sea. An indirect trade was established between Egypt and the southern region of the Red Sea, which exported obsidian, myrrh, and incense. The use of these resins was well

---

[3] Cattle breeding in Yemen previous to this period (a date in the seventh millennium has been suggested for the site of at-Tayyilah) remains uncertain (Cleuziou and Tosi 1997b: 124). The same phase of pastoralist expansion from the southern Levant may have contributed to the introduction of goats, sheep, and cattle into Egypt, and into western and eastern Arabia (Boivin and Fuller 2009: 134).

[4] The periods around 4300 and 3200 BCE correspond to periods of global climate change. Cleuziou and Tosi (1997b: 122, 129) note, however, that there are discrepancies in the dates suggested by various authors for the end of the wet period. Mitchiner (2004: 67, 69) suggests that there was a period of severe aridification starting in 4000 BCE in Arabia and Mesopotamia.

[5] Edens 2002a: 51; T. J. Wilkinson 1999: 186; 2001–2002; 2005;. McCorriston et al. 2002; Harrower 2008a, b. Harrower suggests a nascent irrigation system between 4500 and 3500 BCE.

established in Egyptian religious practices as early as the Early Dynastic period (Wengrow 2006: 147; Boivin and Fuller 2009: 131).

Advances in agriculture and trade during the third millennium fostered a new social complexity. In the Persian Gulf, oasis agriculture developed, using irrigation based on the exploitation of water tables, notably in Oman. This agriculture prospered from 3000 to 2000 BCE (see above) (Cleuziou and Tosi 1997b, 2007). "The combination of date palm with introduced winter cereals made oasis cultivation a productive economic system," capable of providing the basis for significant demographic growth in eastern Arabia at that time (Boivin and Fuller 2009: 136). The cereal grown was mainly bread wheat, *Triticum aestivum*, which was also predominant in South Asia (Fuller 2006a). These developments in agriculture, combined with an increase in trade, stimulated the emergence of a new social organization, with the Hafit horizon, marked by the appearance of collective tombs, followed by the Umm an-Nar culture, which was contemporary to the formation of the Indus-Mesopotamia sphere of exchange (see above).

In Yemen too, agriculture progressed during this period, despite the aridification of the climate (Wilkinson 2005). The grain cultivated here was principally emmer *Triticum turgidum* L. *subsp. dicoccum*, which was dominant in Egypt and Nubia.[6] Links with eastern Arabia boosted the spread of the date palm, which was present at the beginning of the third millennium at ar-Raqlah (Costantini 1990b). Irrigation developed in the Mārib region during the second half of the third millennium (Wagner 1993). A bronze culture appeared in the Khawlan (Yemeni Highlands) between 2600 and 2000 BCE, and proto-urban centers have been discovered, such as Hammat al-Qa (end third to early second millennium), a site in the Dhamar region.[7] Metal discoveries are rare in southwestern Arabia, even later, during the Late Bronze Age. Some copper objects, however, have been unearthed from tombs at Ruwaiq and Jidran that date to the early third millennium; others have been unearthed in Hadramawt. Some of the copper may have been imported from Oman (Edens 2002a: 49), but this must be verified. It is said that southern Arabia was in contact with the Levant during the first half of the third millennium, since the Palermo Stone does mention the delivery of myrrh to Egypt from Syria under Sahure's reign; in fact, the text more likely refers to a local resin and not to myrrh from southern Arabia. In any case, between the late third and the early second millennia, parallels in pottery and the existence of sunken-floor dwellings suggest links between Yemen, northern Arabia, and Jordan (Kitchen 2002a: 388, 390); granite anthropomorphic statuettes (third–second millennia) are comparable to material from the Diyala region dated to the mid-third millennium.

Moreover, exchanges are noticeable between the shores of the Red Sea during the third millennium. The similarities between the lithic industries on both the African and Arabian shores in the southern part of this sea point clearly to the existence of

---

[6] T. J. Wilkinson 1999–2000, 2001–2002; Boivin and Fuller 2009. The sites of ar-Raqlah (3000–2500 BCE), Al-Massanah (2500–2000 BCE) and Wādī Yanā'im (2250–2000 BCE), in the Khawlan, yielded various types of *Triticum* wheat, barley, oats (de Moulins *et al.* 2003: 219) and perhaps sorghum (see below).

[7] The walled village of Sibal, older and smaller than Hammat al-Qa, heralds the latter site. Hammat al-Qa and other settlements in this region developed, whereas the Khawlan Bronze Age sites, in the northeast, were in decline, perhaps due to increased aridification.

contacts in this region (Khalidi 2009). In addition, Egypt imported obsidian, which –
at least for Upper Egypt – probably came from Ethiopia. The rock art in northern
Arabia mentioned previously can be observed from the middle of the third millennium
BCE in southern Hijaz, in eastern Ethiopia, and along the Ethiopian Rift Valley as far as
Sidamo. Available data point toward "a movement of people from Arabia to Ethiopia
between the 3rd and the 2nd millennia BC" (Fattovich 1997b: 281). For other authors,
however, the presence of rock art, which is difficult to date, offers no solid proof of
exchange (Durrani 2005: 107).

Yemen was probably involved in trade with the "land of Punt" mentioned in the
Egyptian texts; this area seems to correspond to the African coast south of Port Sudan
(and its hinterland) as well as to the western coast of Arabia (see above). We have little
evidence for relations between southwestern Arabia and Egypt during the third
millennium (Potts 2008: 830); it is likely, however, that the extension of Egyptian
trade toward Sudan and Ethiopia during the third and second millennia stimulated
links between southern Arabia and the Horn of Africa. Incense (*Boswellia sp.*) and
myrrh (the resin of various *Commiphera*) from Punt may have come from the African
coast or Arabia.

A comparison of items of pottery reveals the existence of multiple trade routes
connecting Africa, Arabia, and the African interior. According to R. Fattovich, shards
bearing a wavy impressed decoration along the rim, on the upper part of the pot,
characteristic of the culture of Khawlan, have been found at excavations in the Gash
Group (eastern Sudan) within a context dated to 2500–2300 BCE and in a tomb of the
Nubian C group at Sayala (late third millennium, Lower Nubia).[8,9] In the opposite
direction, ceramics recalling those of the Nubian C-group have been unearthed at
Agordat, in northern Ethiopia, and within the contexts of the Early and Late Gash
Group.[10] Shards found at Mahal Teglinos (southern Sudan) during the Middle and
Classic Gash group phases (2300–1700 BCE) show patterns similar to those of ceramics
unearthed at the sites of Wadi Anaim, Ar-Raqlah 1, and Wadi Rahma 2 in northern
Yemen (Fattovich 1997b: 277).[11] Pottery similar to that of the Gash group has been
found at Lake Besaka (Ethiopian Rift Valley) (scraped ware) and at Asa Koma, near
Djibouti (Fattovich 1997b: 276; Manzo 1999: 53). For several authors, however, the
comparisons that have been made between African and Arabian ceramics for the third
and second millennia are too general for clear interactions to be confirmed between the
two shores of the Red Sea (see below).

In any case, in comparison with the Persian Gulf, there was only limited exchange in
the Red Sea: its integration into a wider exchange network was yet to come.

The significant role played by sailors from the eastern Arabian coasts between Sind,
India, Iran, and western Asia at this time has already been mentioned (see above).

---

[8] Pastoralists arriving from the Sahara may have been at the origin of this culture (Fattovich 1997a: 485).
Other researchers have suggested that their origins lie in the Early Kerma (Manzo 1999: 43). One notes
a growing presence of Egyptian elements in this culture, which finally became fully "Egyptianized" around
1400 BCE (Manzo 1999).

[9] Edens and Wilkinson 1998: 78; Manzo 1999: 55.

[10] These comparisons apply to several types of decoration (Manzo 1999: 54).

[11] The Mahal Teglinos shards may themselves have been imported pottery (Manzo 1999).

Little is currently known about maritime activities along the southern Arabian coast. The discovery of tin bronzes at the site of the sanctuary of al-Midamman, near the Red Sea, may suggest east–west contacts during the late third/early second millennium (Weeks 2003: 178). The copper in these objects, however, is of local origin (Weeks *et al.* 2008). The extent of these connections along the South Arabian coasts is primarily shown by the introduction of African plants into South Asia, starting at the end of the third millennium (see below). The Asian millet *Panicum miliaceum* appears to have been present at sites in Yemen around the middle of the third millennium or a little earlier; this date is surprising, however, since *P. miliaceum* arrived in Pakistan only *c.* 1900 BCE (Fuller *et al.* [2011] accept a date of 2000 BCE for the arrival of *P. miliaceum* in Yemen). It can be found later in Nubia, at the site of Ukma, where it is dated to between 2000 and 1600 (Van Zeist 1987; Fuller and Boivin 2009); this transfer points to contacts between Yemen and the Horn of Africa.

After the demise of the Indus culture, direct contacts are no longer observable between Mesopotamia and the Indus valley, though some links were maintained between Bahrain and Gujarat, as seen in archaeological discoveries and texts from Mari. In addition, exchanges continued between Mesopotamia, Elam, and eastern Arabia, where the towns of Qalat al-Bahrain and Saar flourished during the early second millennium (see above), until the brutal collapse of Dilmun (Bahrain) during the eighteenth century BCE (Crawford 1998: 153). In Oman at this time, in connection with a sharper arid phase, there was a marked decrease in the number of settlements and a recession in trade, as well as social changes (Wadi Suq phase; see above). However, contacts were maintained between Oman and the Indus region or Gujarat, and with Elam, seen in the discoveries of Post-Harappan pottery and Kaftari pottery, respectively (Potts 2008: 832); Indian zebu remains have also been found, but this animal was probably already present during the Umm an-Nar phase (Uerpmann 2001).

During the Late Bronze Age, activities in the Gulf seem to have been in relative decline. Embedded in the Kassite state at the beginning of the fourteenth century BCE, by now Dilmun was only a shadow of what it once had been. Oman experienced a decrease in population from 1600 to 1100 BCE, related to increased aridity. The beginnings of the "Iron Age" in Oman (1300 BCE), however, hint at connections between this region and western Asia.[12] The development of irrigation based on subterranean underground channels (*qanāt*) began around 1100 BCE, perhaps facilitated by this region's expertise in mining activities. This brought about a new phase of agricultural and demographic growth (Magee 2005: 222). It is possible that this technique developed at the same time in southern Iran, a region that had links to Oman (Magee 2005: 228).

Whereas activity in the Persian Gulf began to decline from the seventeenth century BCE onward, the Red Sea experienced an expansion in trade between its shores; further integration of this region can be seen during the Late Bronze Age. It is probably not by chance that cultivated African plants arrived in western India (Gujarat) from the beginning of the second millennium onward, notably from 1600 BCE (see below).

---

[12] Metallurgy in fact remained limited to bronzeworking; the use of iron was practically absent in the region prior to the Seleucids (Potts 1990, I: 383). A cylinder seal and a few Elamite ceramics have been excavated at Tell Abraq (Potts 2008: 832).

Despite the fact that southwestern Arabia was going through a period of greater aridity, one notes an increased number of sites and human activity in the region during the early second millennium (Wilkinson 2003: 161), and data suggest contacts with the Levant via land. Metalworking in the Tihama may signal Syro-Palestinian influences (Keall 1998: 144). Newton and Zarins associate the daggers with crescent-shaped pommels depicted on stelae of the Hadramawt and Mahra with pastoral elites linked to the "Arab Megalithic Complex"; this type of dagger has been compared to shapes recorded in Syria–Palestine and in Mesopotamia during the third and second millennia (Edens 2002a: 50; Newton and Zarins 2000).[13]

Archaeology also provides clues to increasing exchange networks in the Red Sea during the first half of the second millennium. We have seen that the Egyptian Middle Kingdom pursued an active maritime policy in the direction of Punt, thus bypassing African intermediaries. Contacts also expanded between the two shores of the Red Sea. The Tihama yielded a burnished red-brown pottery characteristic of Mahal Teglinos during the period from 1900 until 1200.[14] The region of Kassala (Mahal Teglinos), from the middle of the third millennium to the middle of the second millennium, seems to have acted as an interface between Arabo-African networks and Egypt.[15] It was also connected with Upper Nubia, where the kingdom of Kerma – Kush of the Egyptian texts – developed around 2100 BCE and lasted until 1550.[16] The presence of donkey remains at Mahal Teglinos makes it appear likely that these animals were used for the transportation of merchandise between the Red Sea and the Nile. Black pottery of the Sihi/Subr culture (Tihama) has been likened to ceramics of the C-group in Nubia (2100–1500 BCE) or to ceramics from Kerma (Zarins and Zahrani 1985; Kitchen 2002a: 390). A type of black pottery has also been found at Asa Koma (Djibouti). However, Edens (2002a: 51) sheds doubt on the reliability of these stylistic comparisons between ceramics. "Not until late in the 2nd millennium BC does a little African pottery appear at places like Sabr, along with a few other objects of African origin such as a piece of worked ivory [see below] and an Egyptian faience." In addition, Edens emphasizes that, until the middle of the second millennium BCE, interactions remained fairly minimal between the coast and the highlands of Yemen.

The transportation of domesticated animals from Arabia to Africa presents another clue to links between these regions. One dromedary tooth found at Gobedra in layers dating back to the third millennium BCE may be intrusive, but another one has also been unearthed at Ele Bor (between the end of the fourth and the middle of the second millennium BCE), east of Lake Turkana. Dromedaries seem to have already been domesticated in the Tihama and to have been used as pack animals during the first

[13] Potts (2008: 830) also notes that daggers found in the Wadi Arf and in the Wadi al-Muhammadiyin (Hadramawt) have been compared to pieces from the royal cemetery of Ur and to daggers discovered in Egypt at Dahshur (early second millennium).

[14] Edens and Wilkinson 1998: 85. This pottery should perhaps be dated to the second half of the second millennium; trade intensified between Yemen and the African coast at this time. Besides this red pottery, the Tihama also exhibits a type of black ceramic that has been compared to potteries found on the African coast (see below).

[15] Fattovich 1997a: 480. Shards of Egyptian pottery have been unearthed that are dated to all the phases of the Gash Group.

[16] A kingdom was also present in the Gash Group from 1700 to 1400 BCE (see above) (Fattovich 1997a: 486).

half of the second millennium BCE.[17] The dromedary may have been sporadically present in Egypt as early as the Old Kingdom, but did not play an economic role.[18] It is possible that the increased use of horses in western Asia and the introduction of the horse into Egypt accelerated the domestication of the dromedary in Arabia during the second millennium as well as its use in Egypt. A ceramic statuette of a dromedary carrying two jars goes back to the Nineteenth Dynasty (1295–1186 BCE), and a faience from Abydos representing a dromedary with four jars has been dated to the first half of the first millennium BCE (Lipinski 2004: 208). In addition, the introduction of the Indian zebu into Africa is likely to have occurred at this time (Boivin and Fuller 2009).

Maritime trade in the Red Sea remained limited, however, until the middle of the second millennium, though changes occurred during that period (Edens 2002a: 52). The development of the coastal Subr culture – starting in 2000 BCE – in the "cultural complex of the Tihama" (1500–1100 BCE) may be connected to the expansion of Egyptian trade with Punt around the middle of the second millennium BCE. As already mentioned, Egyptian documents of the New Kingdom attest to links between Punt and Asia, demonstrating that there was growing activity along the maritime and caravan routes of western and southern Arabia. Subr (Sabir) became a relatively significant urban center (1400–900 BCE), covering 75 ha; excavations unearthed a large building 50 m long, made of bricks, with courtyards and rooms for storage. Remains of grains and nuts have been discovered there,[19] as well as faience and a piece carved in ivory (Edens and Wilkinson 1998: 102; Manzo 1999: 50). Finds from the Subr-Sihi culture suggest maritime links with the Eritrean coast, where the port of Adulis may have already been active.[20] According to Fattovich, polished pottery with incised geometric motifs recalls ceramics from Matara (Central Eritrea) and from the Ona culture (Eritrea, region of Asmara).[21] Shards have also been excavated at Yeha

---

[17] Fattovich 1997b: 278. Excavations at the site of Umm an-Nar (Oman) yielded dromedary bones dated to the third millennium (Potts 1990: 129), though these remains are probably those of wild animals. Cleuziou and Tosi (1997a: 58) note that "nothing can yet be said about the state of camel exploitation in Arabia before 2000 BC." The site of Saar (Bahrain) has yielded a few dromedary bones. Around 1400 BCE, Arab troops riding dromedaries attacked Mesopotamian forces. Uerpmann writes (2008: 442) that dromedaries were not domesticated before the end of the second millennium BCE. Curiously, Liverani mentions domestication during the third millennium (2014: 91).

[18] Moreover, the "evidence" for the presence of dromedaries is debatable. Dromedary remains have been found in the Helwan cemetery, but not in a stratigraphic context. The figurines called "dromedary heads" belonging to the Predynastic and Early Dynastic periods (at Maadi, Abydos, Hierakonpolis) are of uncertain identification. A rope "in dromedary hair" dating back to the Old Kingdom (Third/Fourth Dynasty) is in fact made of sheep's wool. Dromedary bones, however, have been found at Sayala (Nubia) (tombs of the C-group) and at Qasr Ibrim. The animal is depicted in the Ramesside art of the twelfth century BCE.

[19] The destruction of the building by fire c. 900 BCE probably indicates a Sabaean expansion at this time. The pottery contained grains of flax, sesame, remains of fruit, and some sorghum (of a wild type) (de Moulins et al. 2003: 220).

[20] A piece from a glass jar similar to products made under the Eighteenth Egyptian Dynasty has been excavated. Copper slag testifies to the existence of local metallurgy (Manzo 1999: 50).

[21] Fattovich 1990: 23; Vogt and Sedov 1998; Edens and Wilkinson 1998: 105. Manzo (1999: 54) describes pottery "with an incised decoration filled with imprints of peas," which is found in the culture of the Tihama, as well as on the African coast, in contexts belonging to the Gash Group near Agordat, and at Mahal Teglinos (Late Gash). "The same decorative style can be observed on the red Ona pottery."

(western Tigray).[22] Trade networks must have extended as far as Nubia and Egypt.[23] Pottery from Subr shows some similarities with ceramics of the Nubian C and of the Pan-Grave culture (Nubia) (*c.* 2000–1500 BCE).[24] Pottery from Subr/ Sihi might also be compared to pottery from the "Late Gash Group" (1700–1500) and with the subsequent ceramics of the "Jebel Mokram Group" (Sudan, Atbai) (1400–800).[25] In addition, lithic tools at sites of the Tihama present affinities with those of the Gash Group of Kassala (Fattovich 1997a: 481, 1997b: 278ff.). However, for the pottery of the Tihama as well as for the pottery of Subr, the stylistic comparisons that have been made recently have been the subject of significant criticisms. "Based on the available data of the Kassala Phase ware, it is difficult to assess the likelihood that it is related to the Sihi assemblage," writes Durrani (2005: 109). The parallels drawn are not specific enough; in addition, the data available on the Gash Group and the Jebel Mokram Group are rather limited. If general comparisons are possible between the assemblages of Sabir [Subr] and the Horn of Africa, "definitive connections are not demonstrated" (Durrani 2005: 112). Moreover, the stone sites of the Ona culture, dated by Fattovich between 1500 and 1000 BCE, should in fact be dated to between 800 and 400 BCE (Schmidt 2006: 261).[26]

Contacts between Africa and Arabia, however, can be regarded as "one of the key catalysts in the emergence of complex societies in Eritrea and Ethiopia" (Boivin and Fuller 2009: 154). The dissemination of objects, materials, and techniques clearly points to the expansion of networks between the Arab and African coasts and the interior of Africa during this period. Moreover, intensive agriculture developed in the Yemeni Highlands, accompanied by growth in trade with the coasts and with northern Arabia during this time. Groups originating in northwestern Arabia may have arrived in Yemen around the middle of the second millennium (Vogt and Sedov 1998: 267). Recent dating of anthrosoils in the southern Arabian foothills shows that irrigation was

---

Fattovich has also pointed out that ceramics of the Late Gash Group (1500–1400 BCE) show a decoration similar to that of pottery found at sites near Wādī Urqʿ on the Red Sea coast of Yemen ("shards decorated with a burnished linear motif") (1997b: 279).

[22] Manzo (1999: 55) draws other parallels (shapes, decoration) between pottery of the Tihama (1500–1000 BCE) and ceramics of Eritrea and of the Ethiopian plateau. Cf. also Fattovich 1997b: 279, especially for big jars with vertical elliptical handles "and/or a deep groove along the rim," a characteristic of the Tihama also found at Matara and Yeha. There are, however, "some striking differences"; "many of the Sabir ceramics were made using the composite technique (part wheel-, part hand-made), which is absent in the Pre-Aksumite assemblages" (Durrani 2005: 111).

[23] The site of Agordat, located in northern Ethiopia, has yielded many objects of Egyptian origin, such as cosmetic spatulas (Manzo 1999: 50).

[24] Pan-Grave tombs may be linked to the Medjay, and not to the Nubian-C group (Barnard 2009: 23), but this is uncertain.

[25] Fattovich 1997a, b; Vogt and Sedov 1998; Edens and Wilkinson 1998: 105. These authors suggest links between Yemen and Egypt around 1400–1200 BCE (at the end of the "Nubian C") (Edens and Wilkinson 1998: 105).

[26] The Ona culture produced stone bull heads that seem to reflect an Arabian influence, according to Fattovich; this theory, however, has been criticized by Schmidt (2006: 269). Note that various sites in the Horn of Africa have yielded cattle remains from *c.* 1500 BCE: Asa Koma (region of Djibouti), Gogoshiis Qabe, Laga Oda (Somalia), and Besaka (Ethiopia) (Durrani 2005).

practiced there between 1850 and 1250 BCE, during a period of increased aridity.[27] In the Highlands, the site of Hawagir developed during the second half of the second millennium on a road linking Yemen and North Arabia. This site was located near pastureland, whereas other sites were situated near arable lands and showed land terracing activities. In the Hadramawt, the first layers at the site of Shabwa, the future capital of a kingdom, go back to the early second millennium. Shabwa became a city during the first millennium BCE.

The increase in trade occurred as much along maritime routes as along terrestrial routes. Researchers have sometimes drawn attention to the incense found in large quantities in Syria during the campaigns of the Egyptian armies of Thutmose III (Germer 1985: 107, 110) in support of the existence of links between the Levant and southern Arabia; as pointed out previously, however, this incense may have been made using local *Pistacia* resins. Some Egyptian texts emphasize the "close association of Punt and Byblos" (Meeks 2002: 309; see above). These contacts grew stronger during the late second millennium BCE, when Egypt took control of Canaan. Egypt's control of Palestine may have accelerated the domestication of the dromedary in Arabia, initiated earlier in the second millennium, and may have facilitated the extension of caravan routes between Gaza and Saba: Egypt probably benefited from the caravan trade with Arabia, and may even have contributed to its emergence.[28] Already around 1400 BCE, Arab troops riding dromedaries intervened against Mesopotamian forces. The formation of the Midianite confederation in the Hijaz attests to links between the Levant and Arabia, as revealed by the discovery of Midianite ceramics at the metal-lurgical site of Timna (Israel) (thirteenth–twelfth century) (Potts 2008: 832). The South Arabian script – observed on monuments from the eighth century BCE onward, but formed earlier – was an alphabetic script using 29 letters whose origin seems to go back to the thirteenth century in Palestine.[29] "Some archaeologists relate new cultural features (painted pottery, houses made of bricks) to the arrival of popula-tions coming from northwestern Arabia during the thirteenth–twelfth century. Others opt for an endogenous evolution" (Breton 2001a: 23). In any case, long-distance contacts with the Levant, Egypt and probably South Asia were a stimulus for new statebuilding in western Arabia. The end of the second millennium was clearly

---

[27] Coque-Delhuile 2001: 20. The datings were obtained using optically stimulated luminescence (OSL-IRSL). Some datings even appear to suggest a nascent irrigation system around 7000 BP (5800 BCE), which would imply the beginnings of agricultural practices in this area much earlier than had been previously thought. A structure downstream from the Mārib dam goes back to 1650 BCE. A hydraulic system was also set up at an earlier time at Baraqish (site of Yathul, which was the Minaean capital around 400 BCE) (Francaviglia 2002: 127).

[28] Meeks (2002: 290) notes "a new period of prosperity of the copper mines of Timna, under Egyptian control." A ceramic bowl found east of the Nile delta may feature a dromedary (but the rear part of the animal is missing) (Meeks 2002: 289 n. 127).

[29] Two tablets bearing alphabetic cuneiform script (thirteenth/twelfth century BCE) found in Ras Shamra-Ugarit and in Palestine exhibit the letter order of the South Arabian alphabet, which differed from the order of the northwestern Semitic alphabet (Bron 2001b: 9; Arbach 2001: 12; Lemaire 2007: 58). A relationship with the alphabetical order of the Egyptian consonants – reconstituted using texts dating from the fourth/third century BCE for the oldest – has been demonstrated (Meeks 2002: 290). According to Lemaire (2007: 58), it is possible to draw links between the Proto-Arabic linear alphabetic tradition and two series of inscriptions found in Jordan (tablets of Deir'Alla and stela of Balu'ua).

a "formative period" for the Yemeni states established in the first millennium BCE (Potts 2008: 831), marked by agricultural intensification using irrigation as of the twelfth century BCE. The great period of the southern Arabian kingdoms and the burgeoning of the caravan trade, however, only began around the eighth century BCE.

Population movements continued at this time between Arabia and the Horn of Africa. "Figures [in art rock of the same style] dating to the 2nd and early 1st millennia BC have been recorded at Jebel Qara in central Arabia, Hararghe in eastern Ethiopia, northern Somalia, and Eritrea. By the 1st millennium BC, this style spread from Eritrea to Nubia, to southern Upper Egypt, and to the Sahara."[30]

The transportation of plants and animals has already been briefly discussed. Archaeobotany and archaeozoology, together with genetic research on domesticated and wild plants and animals, have opened up new perspectives on the interactions between various spaces as well as regional developments.

The Movements of Cultivated Plants and Domesticated Animals between Africa and Asia

The routes taken by cultivated plants provide good evidence for long-standing contacts between regions. Very early on, rulers kept gardens where exotic species were an integral part of royal status. Evidence of this can be found in the transportation of incense trees from the land of Punt on the ships of Queen Hatshepsut, or in this proclamation by the Assyrian king Tiglath-Pileser I: "I brought cedars, boxwood and oaktrees from the countries which I have conquered, trees the like of which none of the kings my forefathers had ever planted" (Renfrew 1995: 193).

The Fertile Crescent was the center of origin for a range of domesticated cereals, pulses and fiber plants. Domesticated barley, emmer, and wheat were transmitted from western Asia to eastern Arabia as early as the beginning of the third millennium BCE. These plants were introduced either from Mesopotamia or the Indo-Iranian region. Moreover, linguistics attests to the introduction of the pomegranate (Arabic *rummān*, related to the Sumerian *nurma*) and of the quince (arabe *safarjal*, Akkadian *supurgillu*) from Mesopotamia at an unknown time. Sesame is called *semsem* in Arabic and *šamašammē*, "oil plant," in Assyrian (sesame, however, is of Indian origin [see above]).[31]

The number of plants that arrived in Egypt from western Asia is much larger, and dates back to an earlier period. Agriculture developed in the Nile valley – with plants from the Neolithic complexes of Mesopotamia and the Levant – around 6000 BCE, when climatic changes in the Levant provoked massive population relocations (Wetterstrom 1996: 29; Gutherz and Joussaume 2000: 295): einkorn wheat, *Triticum monococcum* L.; emmer, *Triticum dicoccum* Schubl.;[32] barley, *Hordeum vulgare* L.; flax, *Linum usitatissimum* L.; pea, *Pisum sativum* L.; lentil, *Lens culinaris* Medic.;[33] and bitter vetch, *Vicia ervilia* (L.) Willd.,

---

[30] Fattovich 1997a: 482. This style appears to go back to the fifth millennium in northern Arabia (see above).

[31] Postgate 1985: 145. Conversely, for Germer (1985: 172), the Egyptian *šmšmt* does not appear to represent sesame. The Sumerian ŠE.GIŠ.I is usually considered to refer to sesame (Blench 2003: 285).

[32] Cf. notably the excavations of Merimde and Fayum. See de Vartavan and Asensi Amoros 1997: 266ff. for *Triticum sp.*

[33] For these plants, see de Vartavan and Asensi Amoros 1997: 127–133, 154–155, 158–159, 208.

were all present in the Egyptian Neolithic.[34] Grapevine (*Vitis vinifera* L.) from the Predynastic period has been discovered at Tell el-Fara'in and at Abusir el Meleq.[35] Safflower, *Carthamus tinctorius* L., originating in western Asia, is known to have been used in Egypt during the third millennium BCE (chemical analyses of textiles going back to the Twelfth Dynasty [2400–2300 BCE] (?) have shown its use as a dye).[36] Pomegranate remains have also been dated to the Twelfth Dynasty (de Vartavan and Asensi Amoros 1997: 218; Zohary and Hopf 2000: 171). The pomegranate, *Punica granatum* L., is part of a set of plants which were domesticated at an early time in western Asia. Garlic has been found in Tutankhamun's tomb (1343 BCE) (originating in Central Asia, southeast Turkey, or the Levant, garlic has been cultivated in Mesopotamia since at least the third millennium BCE) (de Vartavan and Asensi Amoros 1997: 36; Zohary and Hopf 2000: 196).

Cultivated plants originating in western Asia were carried from Egypt to Sudan and Ethiopia,[37] whence they were perhaps transmitted to Yemen (see above).

Further afield, the Arab coast of the Indian Ocean – of which we still know relatively little – must have played a role in the spread of plants and knowledge. As early as 1952, C. Sauer, who wrote about the spread of cultivated plants from Africa to Asia, believed that southern Arabia may have linked the Horn of Africa to the coasts of South Asia at a very early period, constituting "a Great Lost Corridor of Mankind" (Tosi 2001: 147ff.; Boivin and Fuller 2009: 113ff.).

Traces of these links between Asia and Africa are few, but not inexistent (see Maps 1.9 and 1.10). Asian millet *Panicum miliaceum* L. has been found at Jubabat al-Juruf (3000–2200) and Wādī Yanā'im, (2250–2000) (Yemen) (Costantini 1990b; Harrower 2008). These dates, however, are surprisingly early: *Panicum miliaceum* was present only in Pakistan *c.* 1900 BCE (see above). Data for sorghum (an African plant) in Yemen are even more uncertain and still need confirmation (imprints on ceramics from the Bronze Age of Khawlan: a single grain of sorghum at ar-Raqlah, 3000–2500 BCE, and three grains at Wādī Yanā'im, 2250–2000 BCE).[38] The identification of sorghum in Oman (imprints in bricks and carbonized seeds, at Hili 8) and at Abu Dhabi, dated to the third millennium, is uncertain.[39] However, various African plants that reached India during the Harappan, or rather Post-Harappan, period point to links between Africa and South Asia: cereals (pearl millet, *Pennisetum glaucum* [L.] R. Br. and

---

[34] The oldest remains here correspond to the Predynastic period (de Vartavan and Asensi Amoros 1997: 273).

[35] De Vartavan and Asensi Amoros 1997: 154–155. Remains of *Vitis vinifera* have recently been found at Buto II dating to the Nagada IIb–c period (Watrin 2002: 453).

[36] According to Germer (1985: 174) the safflower originated in Africa, but in fact it probably came from Syria, Anatolia, and Upper Mesopotamia (also possibly Iran and Central Asia) (Zohary and Hopf 2000: 211). A site in northern Syria has yielded remains of this plant dating to 3250 BCE (Zohary and Hopf 2000, after van Zeist and Waterbolk-van Rooijen 1992).

[37] Moreover, Ethiopia had already domesticated indigenous plants, such as teff, ensete, and perhaps finger millet, at an undetermined date.

[38] Sorghum has been identified at al-Adhlar; however, it is dated to the first half of the first millennium BCE (Charbonnier 2008).

[39] Cleuziou and Costantini 1980; Costantini 1990a; Edens and Wilkinson 1998: 87–88; Haaland 1999; de Moulins *et al.* 2003; Boivin and Fuller 2009: 147. The discovery of sorghum in Oman (at site RH5) which purportedly went back to the fifth millennium BCE (Nisbet 1985) has now been refuted. The plant found probably belongs to *Setaria sp.* (Potts 1994b: 256). The identification of sorghum at Hili 8 has been cast into doubt (see Willcox 1994; Potts 1994; Rowley-Conwy *et al.* 1997; Tengberg 2003).

sorghum) and pulses (hyacinth bean, *Lablab purpureus* [L.] Sweet, and cowpea, *Vigna unguiculata* [L.] Wal.). These finds are dated mainly to 1600/1500, but some African species may have been introduced as early as 2000 BCE into Gujarat, at the periphery of the Harappan cultural sphere (Fuller 2008a). The spread of domesticated plants may be partly linked to climatic changes. "The 2200 BCE dry event marks the beginning of 200 to 300 years during which long distance exchanges of grains and vegetative crops across mainlands, islands and oceans gather apace" (Rangan *et al.* 2012: 332). Other reasons certainly ought to be taken into account, in particular concurrent social change in India, Arabia, and Africa.

Pearl millet (*Pennisetum glaucum* [L.] R. Br.) has been found at Kaothe (Maharashtra) (2000–1800 BCE?), Rangpur III in Gujarat (1700–1400), at Hallur (1800–1200), and Daimabad (Maharashtra, Jorwe phase 1500–1200), and perhaps at Babar Kot (Gujarat, Mature Harappan, or Post-Harappan phase).[40] The Indian cultivars appear to be genetically related to populations of *P. glaucum* from the east of Lake Chad and from Sudan, which gives us an indication of the route followed by the plant in its spread toward Asia.[41] "Dravidian has a much wider diversity of names [than Indo-Aryan languages], ... it is likely that pearl millet was first adopted in a Dravidian area and only later spread further north" (Blench 2010b).

Sorghum has been found at Rohira, Kunal 1c, Banawali (Punjab) (Sothi-Siswal phase of Early or Mature Harappan, 2500–2000 BCE?), Sanghol (Punjab) (2000–1500 BCE), Hulas I (Uttar Pradesh) (2000–1500 BCE), Daimabad (Maharashtra, phase Jorwe 1500–1200 BCE), and perhaps Kaothe (Maharashtra, 2000–1800 BCE?), Rojdi C (Gujarat, 2000–1700 BCE), and Senuwar (Bihar, 2000–1400 BCE).[42] The presence in India of the five races of sorghum – *bicolor* (found almost everywhere, this one is the closest to wild sorghum), *guinea, durra, kafir,* and *caudatum* – implies that there were multiple introductions, at different times. Moreover, sorghum from the late first millennium BCE has been reportedly discovered in Japan (see below). In Mesopotamia, it has been suggested that an Old Akkadian cylinder seal depicts sorghum, but this theory is unconfirmed (Potts 1990: 81 and n. 92).

An early arrival of finger millet (*Eleusine coracana* [L.] Gaertn.) in India has been refuted by a recent reevaluation of these discoveries. Two finds have been dated to *c.* 1000 BCE at Hallur (one grain only), and between 1600 and 800 BCE at Malhar (Chhattisgarh, Madhya Pradesh), respectively. However, the purported discoveries at

---

[40] Possehl 1999a: 244; Fuller 2003a: 247; 2006a: 50, 53. According to Fuller, the discovery of pearl millet at Babar Kot, and at Surkotada (2000–1700 BCE) (Chanchala 1991) (not mentioned by Possehl) ought to be taken into consideration, though it is not yet confirmed (Fuller 2003a: 248).

[41] Fuller 2003a: 248. Evidence for domesticated *P. glaucum* in Africa goes back to the middle of the third millennium in the Tilemsi valley (Mali) (Funicane *et al.* 2008; Manning *et al.* 2010; Manning and Fuller 2014), and to the early second millennium BCE in Mauritania and Ghana (D'Andrea *et al.* 2001; Fuller *et al.* 2007). Recent research has revealed the monophyletic origin of the *Pennisetum glaucum* cultivated in West Africa (Oumar *et al.* 2008).

[42] The discoveries made at Inamgaon (Jorwe 1500–900), Pirak (1900–1000), and Ahar 1c (2000–1500) appear to be either uncertain or unfounded (Possehl 1999a: 241; Fuller 2003a: 253ff.). Fuller is skeptical about the suggested dating (Mature Harappan period) of the sorghum found at Kunal 1c (2006b: 191) (the dating is also uncertain for Rohira and Banawali). Sorghum dated to the second half of the second millennium has been identified in the middle Ganges valley, revealing a progressive extension eastward from the northwestern part of the peninsula (Fuller 2006b).

sites in Gujarat (Babar Kot, Kuntasi, Rojdi A, Shikarpur, Surkotada) for the Mature Harappan phase have been refuted (they in fact belong to various indigenous millets that were domesticated locally) (Possehl 1999a: 244; Fuller 2003a: 256ff., 2006b: 38). The presence of finger millet at Rojdi C, however, cannot be excluded (Fuller 2007: 406).

Various sites dated to the first half of the second millennium BCE have yielded hyacinth bean (*Lablab purpureus*): Mahorana (Punjab) (2200–1900, or alternatively 1900–1700 BCE), Sanghol (Punjab), Inamgaon (Maharashtra) (from the Malwa phase, starting in 1700 BCE), Hallur (1500–1400 BCE), Hiregudda (1500–1400 BCE) (Karnataka, South India), and Senuwar (2000–1200 BCE).[43] Cowpea (*Vigna unguiculata*) has been found at Hulas (northern India) at a date somewhere between 1800 and 1300 BCE, at Daimabad (Maharashtra) (1700–1500 BCE, Malwa phase) and at Senuwar.[44] In Egypt, cowpea remains have purportedly been discovered in offerings found in the sun temple of Sahure at Abusir (Fifth Dynasty), around 2400 BCE, but this identification appears to be questionable.[45] Moreover, remains of the castor oil plant *Ricinus communis* L. have been reported at Hulas (Late Harappan) (Fuller 2003a: 262, after Saraswat 1993, and p.c.).

The first significant introduction of African millets into South Asia occurred during a period of aridification in northwestern India starting in 2000 BCE,[46] at sites where South Asian millets and pulses were already being cultivated. Experimentation and exchanges mainly took place "after 1700 BC."[47] Plant exchanges between Africa and South Asia (via Arabia?) suggest that during the Bronze Age, ships were already navigating according to the rhythms of the monsoon system (Horton and Middleton 2000: 9). Possehl suggests that "African millets [and perhaps other plants] were probably not traded, but were acquired in the area of the Horn of Africa as foodstuffs for the boat crews to consume on their way back home" (Possehl 2002a: 218). The southern Arabian region therefore was a sphere of interaction linking northeastern Africa and western India starting in the early second millennium.

---

[43] Fuller 2003a: 244–245, 2006a: 39; Fuller and Harvey 2006: 225. This plant has been found at other sites dated to the second half of the second millennium BCE. Curiously, there is no evidence for an older cultivated hyacinth bean in Africa. According to the current state of research, the oldest find has been dated to the first century CE in Namibia. In Egypt, no discovery has been made that predates that of Qasr Ibrim (fourth–fifth century CE) (Fuller 2003a: 246, after A. Clapham, p.c.).

[44] Fuller 2003a: 242; 2006a: 39; Fuller and Harvey 2006: 228. Its introduction is therefore not as recent as has been previously thought (end of the first millennium BCE) (Ng 1995). Southworth, however, only reconstructs the term *ava-rai* at the level of Proto-Tamil (2006: 136). In Africa, a domestic form of *Vigna unguiculata* was cultivated in Ghana c. 1700 BCE (D'Andrea *et al.* 2007), but its domestication must have occurred earlier.

[45] Meeks 1993: 83; de Vartavan and Asensi Amoros 1997: 277. The fact that this is the only "discovery" for ancient Egypt is enough to cast doubt on the find. Researchers support the idea of an original domestication of the plant in the Nigeria region (Ng 1995; Fuller 2003a: 241). Its early arrival in India, however, points to the longstanding cultivation of this plant in a region close to the Indian Ocean.

[46] During the second millennium, the southern Neolithic grew various Asian millets, often of local origin, in addition to Indian pulses (Korisettar 2004; Fuller 2006a).

[47] Fuller 2003a: 264. Fuller thus gives the example of Hallur, where the African millet *Pennisetum glaucum* appears only in small quantities, in samples where Asian millets were predominant.

The African plants introduced into India were evidently domesticated in Africa earlier than what archaeology tells us for this continent. Herders from the Sahel appear to have played an important role in this domestication process (Manning *et al.* 2010). Domestication may also have occurred in a region of Ethiopia–Sudan–Eritrea corresponding to the lands of Yam and Punt in old Egyptian texts (Fuller 2003a: 265). Egypt itself may also have been a center of domestication for some plants originating in the African interior. The route to South Asia followed the Arab coasts, but routes through Egypt and Mesopotamia cannot be excluded, despite the current lack of evidence for this (if sorghum was present in Mesopotamia, it may have been imported from Oman and the Indus). Haaland (1999) has suggested a southern Arabian origin for the domesticated sorghum, following the importation of wild forms from the African coast, but there is no evidence today for the adoption of African plants in Arabian agriculture before they were introduced into India (Boivin and Fuller 2009: 148).

The linguistic reconstructions proposed by F. C. Southworth generally confirm archaeological data. The author has reconstructed a term for sorghum in "Late Proto-Dravidian" (early second millennium BCE), a language he associates with phase II of the Southern Neolithic.[48] He links the word *ragi* for finger millet to Proto-South Dravidian, which is more recent (between 1700 and 1300 BCE), likewise the term **kampu* for pearl millet (*Pennisetum glaucum*).[49]

The tamarind (*Tamarindus indica* L.) – if indeed it is of African origin – also arrived in India at an early period; tamarind remains at Narhan have been dated to 1300 BCE (Blench 2004: 44), and Southworth (2005: 82; 2006: 145) has reconstructed the term **cin-tta* for this plant, at the level of the "Early Proto-Dravidian." For Mayrhofer (1986), however, this word is ultimately of foreign origin. A plant of African origin, the water melon (*Citrullus lanatus* [Thunb.] Mansf.) was introduced into India at an undetermined period. Grains have been found at Raybun (Yemen) in an eighth/seventh-century-BCE – first/second-century-CE context (Potts 1994b: 260; Wasylikowa and Van der Veen 2004: 214). In addition, the winged bean (*Psophocarpus tetragonolobus* [L.] DC.) was carried from Africa to India and Southeast Asia at an unknown date (cf. Blench 2010a). Domesticated in tropical Africa, the yam bean (*Stenostylis stenocarpa* [Hochst ex A. Rich.] Harms) also arrived at an early date in India and in Southeast Asia (Blench 2010a).

In the opposite direction, various plants were carried from South Asia to Africa prior to the first millennium BCE. Besides plantain, already mentioned, one might mention hemp (*Cannabis sativa* L.) and pigeon-pea (*Cajanus cajan* [L.] Millsp.). Pollen from hemp from the Predynastic period (5500–3100 BCE) has been identified at Nagada, and

---

[48] Fuller (2003a: 264) speaks of Proto-South-Central Dravidian, referring to Southworth 1988. Southworth today names this phase Late Proto-Dravidian (2006: 138, 145). He considers Proto-Dravidian to have split into central, northern, and southern branches during the first half of the second millennium (2005: 51).

[49] Southworth 2005: 204. Proto-South Dravidian formed between 1700 and 1300 BCE (Fuller 2007: 424, 427) (see above). Southworth argues that the Dravidian name for finger millet, *ragi*, derives from a Proto-South Dravidian term **iraki* which probably meant "food" or "fodder" in Proto-Dravidian (2006: 128). The root **degi* reconstructed from Bantu languages from South Tanzania and North Malawi may be another possible etymology (Philippson and Bahuchet 1994–1995, quoted by Fuller 2003a: 256). Some authors suggest a link between the Dravidian *kangu* referring to pearl millet (Sanskrit *kangu-*) and the Proto-Bantu **cangu* (Witzel 2006a: 107), but the relationship here is uncertain (Fuller 2006b: 192).

hemp fibers at Kahun date back to the Twelfth Dynasty (de Vartavan and Asensi Amoros 1997: 61). However, an identification of *Cajanus cajan* in a tomb from the Twelfth Dynasty at Dra Abu el-Nega is debatable.[50] These plants may have arrived via western Asia, and the same goes for sesame, present in Egypt during the second millennium BCE (and perhaps already during the Predynastic period).[51] The jujube or Indian plum (*Ziziphus mauritiana* Lam.) was introduced at an early stage into Africa, but the exact period is yet to be determined (Blench 2004: 44). A purported find of sour orange (*Citrus aurantium* L.) in Menthuhetep's tomb at Deir el-Bahri (Eleventh Egyptian Dynasty) seems debatable.[52]

In the Mediterranean, the site of Hala Sultan Tekke, near Larnaca, dated to the second half of the second millennium, has yielded citron remains dated to *c.* 1200 BCE (the dating, however, has been cast into doubt; see Zohary and Hopf 2000: 184).[53] Like other products, citron was probably carried from the western Indian coast into Lower Mesopotamia. From there, merchants would have carried it into the Middle Euphrates valley, and into the Levant. Pepper may have followed the same route; indeed, it has been discovered in the mummy of Ramses II (who died *c.* 1213 BCE).[54] However, it may well also have arrived via Arabia and the Red Sea, a journey opposite to that of the African plants introduced on the west coast of India. On this coast, "in all likelihood, pepper was supplied by hunter-gatherer groups" to coastal communities (Fuller *et al.* 2011: 547). In any case, the transportation of these African plants is evidence for more regular contacts between India and the Red Sea in the world-system of the Late Bronze Age.

Sailors were also instrumental in transporting domestic animals from one region to another. The site of Kalibangan has purportedly yielded dromedary bones dated to the second millennium BCE, as well as zebu, water buffalo, sheep, goat, pig, onager, and perhaps camel remains. The transportation of dromedaries in the opposite direction, from Arabia to Africa, has already been mentioned. Used in Mesopotamia in the Urukian period, the donkey – first domesticated in Egypt – was present at Hili (Oman) during the first half of the third millennium.

While Arabia acted as an intermediary space between Asia and Africa at an early stage, at the opposite end of Asia, Southeast Asia also entered into contact with southern China and India, during the early third millennium at the latest. These connections, still

---

[50] Blench 2003: 284. For Germer (1985: 94ff.), this discovery does not count as proof of the presence of cultivated *Cajanus*. Korisettar (2004: 178) believes, probably wrongly, that *Cajanus cajan* originated in Africa and was introduced into India toward the middle of the second millennium. For Fuller and Harley, *Cajanus cajan* was domesticated in India not long after the middle of the second millennium BCE (2006: 225); this casts doubt on the Egyptian find at Dra Abu el-Nega.

[51] A find of sesame pollen has been reported at Nagada, and in Tutankhamun's tomb (Germer 1985: 172; de Vartavan and Asensi Amoros 1997: 238).

[52] de Vartavan and Asensi Amoros 1997: 79. On the sour orange, see below.

[53] Hjelmqvist 1979; Amigues 2005: 366. Theophrastus (4.4.2) calls it the "Persian or Median apple." The "fruit of the goodly tree" mentioned in Leviticus (23: 40) could be the citron (Amigues 2005: 368). Pollen from *C. medica* from the fourth century BCE has been identified at Carthage (Van der Ween *et al.* 2011: 87).

[54] Lichtenberg and Thuilliez 1981: 328. We cannot totally exclude, however, a passage through southern Arabia and the Red Sea. Moreover, S. Sherratt (2003: 51) has pointed to the increased use of incense in the Mediterranean Sea around the twelfth century, an aromatic perhaps carried by Cypriots.

less known than those in the west, would play a crucial role in the future progress of this region, and of the eastern Indian Ocean.

Southern China, Southeast Asia, and the Eastern Indian Ocean: Developments and First Contacts

Neolithic cultures appeared later in southern China than in the north. Rice reached the southern regions during the fourth millennium BCE, following a coastal route and valleys south of the Yangtze River.[55] In Fujian, the site of Tanshishan has yielded rice dated to 2870–2340 BCE. From the Middle Yangtze region, following the Xiangjiang and then the Beijiang River valley, rice arrived north of the Xijiang River. One of the first known sites is Shixia (3000–2500 BCE), where jade ornaments reminiscent of the Liangzhu culture of the Lower Yangtze have been recovered (3300–2300 BCE). Shixia gave its name to the culture that spread in this region of the Guangdong province in around 2600 BCE (Zhang and Hung 2010: 12, 16, 21). In Guangxi, foxtail millet and rice have been discovered at the site of Gantuoyan c. 2000 BCE (Castillo and Fuller [2010: 99] give 3000 BCE, but this is probably a mistake). Zhang and Hung (2010: 14) give dates in the third millennium (c. 2500–2000 BCE) for the first rice found in Guanxi (Dingsishan and Xiaojin sites) and the second millennium BCE for Gantuoyan.[56]

Austroasiatic populations appear to have brought Neolithic and rice cultivation practices into continental Southeast Asia from a region south of the Yangtze. Pottery of a similar style has been unearthed in Cambodia, Thailand, and Yunnan.[57] From southern China, rice (tropical *japonica*) moved slowly southward, along the Mekong, the Red River, and the Chao Praya valleys, and along coastal routes. Its arrival in continental Southeast Asia cannot have been earlier than the late third millennium, linked with the expansion of Austroasiatic speakers (Glover and Higham 1996; Higham 2003),[58] and subsequently of Tai-Kadai speakers into this

---

[55] Higham and Lu 1998: 871, 874; Lu 2005: 56; Bellwood 2005a: 123, 126. Bellwood does not rule out the arrival of rice cultivation in Guangdong as early as 4000 BCE, though this claim must still be proven (Bellwood 2005a: 126–127).

[56] Lu (2009: 50), however, gives even older dates for rice at Xiaojin and Dingsishan (4500 BCE). Liu and Chen (2012: 208) suggest a date c. 4000 BCE for Dingsishan. They assimilate the presence of rice in this site with a southward expansion of the Daxi culture.

[57] In Cambodia, Samrong Sen site; in Thailand, Ban Kao, Non Nok Tha, Non Pa Wai, and Ban Chiang sites; in Yunnan, site of Baiyangcun, dated to 2462–2014 BCE. See Higham 1996b: 116. Kealhofer and Piperno (1994) argue that rice phytoliths found in the Lopburi region can be dated to 4000 BCE. White *et al.* (2004) have noted environmental disturbances in northeastern Thailand, with an increase in grass pollens and charcoal, after 5500 BP uncal. Societies cultivating plants may have appeared in the region by the mid-fourth millennium BCE cal. (White 1997). Rice cultivation at such an early period, however, appears to be questionable. Higham *et al.* (2011) set the beginnings of rice cultivation at Khok Phanom Di at around 1800 BCE. On this site, see also Renfrew and Bahn 2000: 516ff. and Pearsall 2000: 486–491.

[58] Most linguists and archaeologists locate the original homeland of the Austroasiatic languages south of the Yangtze River, and date the divergence of the Proto-Austroasiatic at around 5000 BCE (Bellwood 2005b, 2006; Sagart *et al.*, 2005; see Sagart 2011: 129 for a discussion of this issue). Proto-Austroasiatic does not display a common agricultural vocabulary with the PSTAN (Sagart 2008: 139). Note that the original Austroasiatic vocabulary reflects the practice of dry rice cultivation on hills, rather than wet cultivation (Fuller 2011a: 87); in addition, this vocabulary refers to tropical wildlife (however, this tropical wildlife may have been present as far north as the Yangtze River 7,000 years ago) (Diffloth 2005; Reid 2005). Higham

region (Sagart 2008, 2011).[59] In northern Vietnam, sites of the Phung Nguyen culture where rice has been found have reportedly been dated to *c.* 2000 BCE. In Thailand, rice appeared after 2300 BCE, but the majority of sites date to the second millennium BCE (Higham 2004; 2009a, b). Rice has been dated to *c.* 1800 BCE at Khok Phanom Di, at Ban Chiang, and in the Lopburi Plain (Thompson 1996; Castillo and Fuller 2010: 106; Higham *et al.* 2011: 11, 13). The earliest foxtail millet found in mainland Southeast Asia is from Non Pa Wai, in central Thailand, where it is dated to 2300 BCE (Weber *et al.* 2010). This expansion led to the development of tropical *japonica*, of varieties of glutinous rice, and perfumed rice (Kovach *et al.* 2009; Fuller *et al.* 2010: 125), Neolithic developments in the Thai–Malay peninsula took place during the early second millennium BCE, with the "Ban Kao culture" (Bulbeck 2004).

The same routes from the Yangtze River – later on in the second millennium – facilitated the spread of bronze metalworking. Knowledge of copper and bronze metallurgy arrived from China, starting in *c.* 1500 BCE, moving from the Yangtze valley to Lingnan along the Xiangjiang and Ganjiang rivers; from Yunnan[60] and from Lingnan to northern Vietnam via the Red River basin and along the Xijiang River; from Yunnan to Cambodia and Thailand along the Mekong and the Chao Phraya rivers; and from Yunnan to Burma toward the Chindwin River valley.[61] The rapid expansion of this metallurgy benefited from the prior existence of exchange networks between these regions and from the ascent of Neolithic societies showing some social complexity.[62] The existence of long-distance trade with the Yangtze River and the Yellow River can be seen in Lingnan and northern Vietnam by the discovery of jade *yazhang* blades, *ge* halberds, and Shang-style bronzes.[63] Pottery at sites of the Phung Nguyen culture (Red River) shows similarities with Yunnan

has refuted the assertions of some authors who suggest an earlier date for the arrival of this cereal in Thailand.

[59] According to Sagart (2008: 133), (Proto-)Tai-Kadai was not in use until 2000–1000 BCE. He considers Tai-Kadai to be a subgroup of PAN: it originated amongst Proto-Austronesian speakers who returned to the continent not long after 2000 BCE (2004, 2005). They subsequently borrowed part of their rice vocabulary from the Austroasiatics (Sagart 2011: 123).

[60] Only two sites date from the Bronze Age in Yunnan. A radiocarbon reading has given the date range 1409–1127 BCE at Haimenkou, but Haimenkou probably belongs to the first millennium BCE. Liu and Chen, however, give 3000–1900 BCE (2012: 249).

[61] The recent discovery of the cemetery of Nyaunggan, in the Chindwin valley, has yielded bronze spearheads with shapes similar to those already documented in eastern regions (Higham 2004: 57). For Moore (2007), the Bronze Age sites of the Chindwin valley could be dated between 1500 (?) and 700 BCE.

[62] Thus in Lingnan, the Late Neolithic communities showed an interest in exotic imports. In addition, Lingnan groups were experienced in ceramic production, using heat control in closed furnaces. In the lower Red River valley, the Phung Nguyen culture (*c.* 2500/2000–1500 BCE) stands out for the quality of its pottery and its stone objects, and the considerable size of some of its tombs (Higham 1996a: 313). Bronze metalworking techniques and finished products show that there were links between Lingnan, Vietnam, Thailand, and Cambodia (Higham 2004: 52).

[63] Higham 1996a: 310ff. See map showing the distribution of jade *yazhang* blades, Higham 1996a: 91. These have been found at Erlitou and at Late Shang sites, in Yunnan (Sanxingdui), at several Middle and Lower Yangtzi valley sites, on the coasts of Zhejiang and Fujian, in Lingnan (Lamma Island, Lantau Island …), at Phung Nguyen and Xom Ren (Red River). Stone *ge* halberds or *zhang* blades exhibiting shapes similar to those at the Shang sites have been found at Sanxingdui, Lung Hoa (Phung Nguyen culture, late period), and at sites of the Fubin culture (eastern Guangdong and south Fujian, *c.* 1100 BCE). The Lung Hoa site has yielded deep, ledged graves, comparable to those made by the Fubin culture. Crafted nephrite and jadeite found at different sites point to links between these cultures and China. It is clear that

ceramics, revealing the existence of trade routes that had most likely been in place throughout the history of these regions. Metallurgical production centers appeared in Lingnan between 1300 and 1000, producing objects already attested in northern China (socketed spearheads and axes) and also developing local forms that imitated the shape of stone items. Bronzes imported from the north were also present, such as bells or vessels.[64] Maritime routes in parallel with the inner routes of China may also have been instrumental in disseminating techniques and objects. In northern Vietnam, "bronzeworking was established" in the Dong Dau culture (1500–1000 BCE), at sites that have also yielded jades imported from the north.[65]

In Thailand, "current evidence suggests that tin-bronze metallurgy appeared rather abruptly as a full-blown technology by the mid-2nd millennium BC" (Pigott and Ciarla 2007: 76). Two routes have been suggested for the introduction of this technology: a direct route from Gansu and Qinghai (Qijia culture) to Sichuan and Yunnan, and an indirect route via Lingnan and northern Vietnam. Thailand produced objects cast in open or bivalve stone molds (such as socketed weapons), like those of the Qijia culture, but this type of artifact has also been found in Lingnan and in northern Vietnam. "Erlitou bronze casting was instead based on the preferential use of a ternary alloy (copper-tin-lead) cast into ceramic piece-moulds to produce vessels of complex shapes derived from earlier ceramic prototypes" (Pigott and Ciarla 2007: 80), but Erligang (and later Anyang) also produced socketed tools and weapons using bivalve mold casting. Contrary to what has been observed in the latter regions, the Bronze Age communities of the Mekong valley and of central Thailand did not show a marked social stratification.[66] In regions of low demographic density, the introduction of bronze, as C. Higham has pointed out, could not trigger an accelerated social hierarchization process; this process would take place later around the middle of the first millennium BCE.[67]

The origins of bronze metalworking in northeastern Thailand have been a subject of controversy (whether it was introduced via China, or developed locally), notably due to

the Red River region maintained indirect contact with the complex societies of the Yangtze and Yellow rivers (Higham 2004: 49).

[64] A number of finds, however, belong to the Zhou period. At the site of Yuanlongpo (middle Xijiang River valley), for example, during the early first millennium BCE, the tomb of a person of high status yielded two vessels imported from the north, and the fragment of a bell (Higham 1996a: 93).

[65] Higham 1996a: 96. The analysis of bronzes from Dong Dau shows that an alloy similar to bronzes of northeastern Thailand was used, but with a higher tin content. Among the objects manufactured were socketed axes and spearheads, showing forms recorded in Lingnan, Cambodia, and Thailand.

[66] At Khok Phanom Di and Phu Noi (central Thailand), in a Late Neolithic context, some graves exhibit more relative wealth than tombs at sites where bronze metallurgy was already widely practiced, in northeastern Thailand (Higham 1996a: 198). Bellwood (1992: 98), however, supports the idea of stratified societies for northeastern Thailand. Ban Na Di, which has yielded bronze bracelets and imported shell or exotic stone bracelets, reveals some social stratification, but datings indicate that these objects belong to the first millennium BCE (Higham 1996a: 204).

[67] The lack of social complexity in Thailand probably explains why the piece-mold technology of the Shang elite was not adopted (Pigott and Ciarla 2007). The cemetery at Ban Non Wat (Upper Mun River valley, Thailand), however, shows evidence of the existence of an elite around 1000 BCE: bronzes have been found in only a few rich tombs (Higham 2004: 55). "During the 11th century, aggrandizers in the Upper Mun valley began actively to seek prestige and status through controlling and deploying exotic materials and knowledge for social advantage" (Higham 2014: 194).

uncertainties surrounding the dating at Ban Chiang.[68] Bronze items found at Non Nok Tha belong to a period between 1500 and 1000 BCE.[69] This site is located 140 km southeast of the copper mines of Phu Lon, already exploited around 1700 BCE. Research in central Thailand has documented a "copper production locus at the major regional center of Tha Kae (Ciarla 2005), as well as in the copper-rich Khao Wong Prachan valley, where an industry is dated *ca.* 1500 BC" (Pigott and Ciarla 2007: 82). Non Pa Wai, located in the vicinity of a copper mine, yielded dates between 1500 and 1000 BCE. Copper appeared at Khok Phanom Di as part of the communities' participation in exchanges with other regions, a phenomenon clearly visible at the nearby site of Nong Nor (1200–800 BCE). Some tombs contained ornaments crafted from jade, marble, serpentine, and carnelian, the stone often imported. Carnelian beads are often considered to have been locally produced,[70] but imports from India cannot be ruled out. Ingots circulated from the mining centers, along long-distance trade routes (marine shells have been excavated 1,000 km distant from the coast) (Higham 2004: 53).

Austroasiatic speakers also reached India: Proto-Munda farmers entered India during the second millennium BCE, bringing foxtail millet with them. Pottery found at Chopani Mando (Uttar Pradesh) has been compared to ceramics from Yunnan (Bellwood 2007), revealing contacts through Burma. The Proto-Munda also probably introduced rice into India (see above). In the Upper Yangtze, rice does not seem to have been cultivated before the middle of the third millennium BCE [71] and its presence in Yunnan is not attested before *c.* 2100 BCE (Baiyangcun site, 2500–2000 BCE; see An 1999; Fuller *et al.* 2010: 125).

The Neolithic cultures of Insular Southeast Asia were long considered to have been imported by Austronesians from Taiwan. In fact, Austroasiatic groups sailing from northern Vietnam probably brought agriculture into Palawan and Kalimantan as early as the third millennium BCE; from there, they reached Sumatra and the Malay peninsula, and perhaps Java and Sumbawa, before the Austronesians' arrival

---

[68] A bronze socketed spearhead has been unearthed for the Early Phase III, which J. C. White (1986) places between 2100 and 1700 BCE. For Higham, a date during the second half of the second millennium is more likely. The Middle Phase (from 900 BCE according to White) has yielded bimetallic spearheads.
The hypothesis for an independent copper metallurgy production center in Southeast Asia appears to be unsubstantiated, in the absence of older dates for this industry (a date from the beginning of the second millennium BCE is nevertheless maintained by some researchers for the Ban Chiang site). The first levels (with bronze) at Ban Takhong (Mun valley) have given a date of 2049–1670 BCE.

[69] Dates suggest an overall date range between 1320 and 1121 BCE (from the Early Phase II to the Middle Phase V). The oldest bronze that has been found is a socketed axe. Crucibles and bivalve molds have been excavated. The craftsmen of Non Nok Tha may have manufactured bracelets using the lost wax technique (Higham 1996a: 189–194). In Cambodia, the site of Samrong Sen has yielded socketed axes, spearheads, a bell, a crucible, bracelets, and shell beads. The correlation between the dating obtained on a shell (1749–1253 BCE) and the bronzes that have been found is uncertain.

[70] Bellwood 1997: 275. Although some tombs appear to have been more richly endowed with offerings than others, Higham (1996a: 281) does not see real signs of marked social stratification at Nong Nor.

[71] But foxtail millet was introduced in Sichuan – from Gansu – during the early third millennium (Zhang and Hung 2010: 20; Fuller 2011a: 87). The site of Karuo (eastern Tibet) contains *Setaria italica* millet, which has been dated to between 3500 and 2500 BCE (Zhang and Hung 2010: 14). Millet was transmitted south through Yunnan.

(Blench 2010b, 2012a).[72] Similarities have been noted between pottery from Gua Sireh (Sarawak) (second half of the third millennium) and ceramics from Vietnam, as well as between stone tools found in Vietnam and in the Niah Cave (Bulbeck 2008). "Bulbeck's analysis (2004: 115) of the early pottery from sites in west-central Sulawesi also draws closer parallels with mainland Asia than with Taiwan" (Anderson and O'Connor 2008: 5; see also Anderson 2006). At Gua Sireh, a grain of rice in a piece of pottery has been dated to *c.* 2300 BCE,[73] but it is unclear whether this rice ought to be linked to Austronesian migrations, or to Austroasiatic populations coming from continental Southeast Asia. Rice has also been found in pottery from the Niah Cave (Sarawak); the earliest dating goes back to the early third millennium BCE, and another dating is from the end of this millennium (Doherty *et al.* 2000: 150). Moreover, genetic research on pigs has shown that the domesticated pig of the Pacific originated in continental Southeast Asia and not in eastern Asia: this means that the Austronesians acquired the domesticated pig in a southern region of Indonesia; they took the pig with them when they migrated to New Guinea and colonized the Pacific (Larson *et al.* 2007; Dobney *et al.* 2008). The earlier Austroasiatic Neolithic wave of migration also brought the chicken (Liu *et al.* 2006a) and the dog; thus Neolithic development in Southeast Asia was more complex than the classical "out of Taiwan" model has described it (Anderson and O'Connor 2008).

Arriving by sail from the Philippines, the Austronesians colonized eastern (and then western) Indonesia during the second millennium[74] and borrowed taro cultivation techniques, and the plant's name, from the Austroasiatics (Anderson and O'Connor 2008) (French-Wright [1983] tentatively reconstructed PMP *tales, "taro," and the Proto-Oceanic *talo).[75] In contrast, Austronesian settlements on the Thai–Malay peninsula and the Vietnamese coast appear to go back only as far as the first millennium BCE for Malayo-chamic speakers.[76] Long-distance contacts were taking shape: the Bukit Tengkorah site (Sabah) has yielded obsidian from New Britain, some 3,500 km further east, that is dated to around 1300 BCE (Bellwood 2004: 29).

We know of only a small number of Neolithic sites in Insular Southeast Asia that date from before the first millennium (Barton and Paz 2007; Spriggs 2011: 517) and rice is rarely present: the arrival of Austroasiatic and Austronesian populations in the

---

[72] An Austroasiatic substratum has been identified in the islands mentioned (Bellwood 1996: 483). For Aceh, however, Sidwell (2005) supports the idea of a Chamic migration coming from the continent and bringing Austroasiatic borrowings.

[73] Datan (1993) dates it to 4840–4100 cal. BP (Barton and Denham 2011: 22).

[74] Pottery appeared in Sulawesi at the site of Uai Bobo between 2410 and 1887 BCE (Higham 1996a: 299). The rapid southeastward advance of the Austronesians may have been facilitated by climatic changes *c.* 2000 BCE (Anderson 2006). A maritime culture was clearly in place around 1500 BCE between the Philippines, Timor, and New Guinea, a culture that would quickly move eastward (Bellwood 2005a: 135–140). Around 1500 BCE, sailors reached the Mariana Islands in Micronesia, and different parts of Melanesia. Polynesia appears to have been settled between 600 and 1250 CE (Bellwood 2005a: 140).

[75] #tales is linked to the Austroasiatic #traw? (the Austronesians probably borrowed the term from Austroasiatics in Kalimantan; Blench 2012: 26). Two centers of domestication have been suggested for the taro: in New Guinea, and in continental Southeast Asia; insular Southeast Asia is another possible center.

[76] However, there is evidence for the existence of other Austronesian languages prior to this Malay migration, but these languages are extinct (Blust 2006).

Equatorial zone was accompanied by the virtual disappearance of rice and *Setaria italica* millet: their varieties were photosensitive, and could not adapt to the new climatic conditions. In northern Luzon, rice from Andarayan is dated only to 2050–1400 BCE (Zhang and Hung 2010: 21). Rice found at Ulu Leang (South Sulawesi) may, however, go back to 2000 BCE (Paz 2005: 112, 113; Donohue and Denham 2010: 234). Glover (1986: 230) found millet (*Setaria sp.*) at Uai Bobo 2 (Sulawesi).

One might speculate on whether or not maritime contacts occurred during the third and second millennia BCE between Southeast Asia and the eastern Indian coast, involving Austroasiatics, Austronesians, and Indians. It is likely that shipbuilding techniques improved in the Austronesian world in the Philippines–Sulawesi area between 2500 and 2000 BCE. Some Austronesian groups – using various types of ships, including catamarans – double canoes – and canoes with one or two outriggers, as well as larger ships, later[77] – may have sailed to the west, as early as the second millennium BCE. These groups probably reached the Indian coasts and settled there.[78] Boats with outriggers are depicted on Mesolithic rock art found on the southern Deccan Plateau, but they are difficult to date (Ray 1999b: 6). Mahdi has recently argued that Negritos from insular Southeast Asia introduced the "double canoe" into India (2016: 39).

For Glover, the similarities noted for pottery (such as cord-impressed pottery) or axes found in eastern India, Southeast Asia, and southern China seem "more likely to be the result of a long-established and continuous distribution of related cultures from southern China and Vietnam, through Thailand and Burma into India, than to be the product of maritime or even land-based trade routes, and there is no evidence I know of for direct long-distance trade between Southeast Asia and India before the Iron Age, which in eastern India begins about 750 BC and a couple of hundred years later in Thailand" (Glover 1996: 372). In Insular Southeast Asia, bronze and iron appear together starting in 500 BCE.

However, the discovery of cloves announced by G. Buccellati and M. Kelley-Buccellati in 1983 at the site of Terqa on the banks of the middle Euphrates, in a stratigraphic context dated to 1700–1600 BCE, would appear to prove the existence of contacts between the Austronesian world and the western Indian Ocean as early as the second millennium BCE. These contacts are surprising, even though the development of exchange networks is notable in Southeast Asia at this time[79] (the discovery at Terqa has yet to be confirmed). Sandalwood remains (*Santalum album* L.), dated to

---

[77] Manguin (1985b) suggests a progressive evolution in the Austronesian world, from ships with stitched planks, "hull with frames and thwarts fixed to lugs" (*lashed-lug technique*), and later using dowels to hold the planks (see below). We do not know when the lashed-lug technique was developed. The first known example, in archaeology, is the boat from Pontian (Malay peninsula); its wood has been dated to between the third and fifth centuries CE (Manguin 1996: 185). The technique is known in the Pacific (Fiji, Samoa, Tonga). It may "belong to the culture of the Austronesian people," unless its introduction occurred after the first Austronesian migrations (Manguin 1985b: 337, 2000a).

[78] The Lapita culture, which originated in eastern Indonesia and – further north – in the Philippines, was present in the Bismarck archipelago around 1300 BCE at the latest. From eastern Indonesia, it spread rapidly further east, reaching Tonga and Samoa (around 1000 BCE). New Caledonia was also reached *c.* 1000 BCE (M. Spriggs, seminar at the EHESS-Paris, April 2002; Bellwood 2005a: 137).

[79] Glover 1996: 373. In Thailand, circular copper ingots have been found, sometimes at great distances from the copper mines (Higham and Thosarat 1998: 99).

1300 BCE, have been unearthed in the Southern Neolithic of India; this is a species that D. Q. Fuller considers to have been introduced from Indonesia (Fuller 2006b: 185) (India, however, may also have been the natural habitat of *Santalum album*). The arecanut tree (*Areca catechu* L.) and the coconut tree may have been introduced during the same period, by sea (Asouti and Fuller 2008; Fuller and Madella 2009). Recent genetic studies, however, show that there were two distinct areas of domestication for the coconut tree, in the western Pacific, and in South India, Sri Lanka, the Maldives, and the Laccadives (Gunn *et al.* 2011). In the Pacific, "coconuts have been recovered from pre-Lapita sites dating to 5,800 years ago, but the first evidence of dwarf characteristics … is from early Lapita sites, *ca.* 1200 BC" (Hirst 2011). In Sri Lanka/South India, the coconut tree was probably domesticated during the first half of the first millennium BCE.

Various Southeast Asian plants arrived in India between the third and first millennia BCE. The banana was present at an early date in the Indian peninsula. According to E. De Langhe and P. de Maret (1999: 385–387), plantain bananas of AAB genome, which are *Musa acuminata* x *Musa balbisiana* hybrids, appeared between the Philippines and the Moluccas between 2500 (Austronesian arrival in the Sulawesi–Moluccas area) and 1500 BCE (implied here are the "African plantains," – the "Pacific plantains" potentially originating "along the north coast of New Guinea or in the Bismarck Archipelago" and perhaps the Solomon Islands) (De Langhe 2009; Perrier *et al.* 2011).[80] In addition, the domestication of *Musa acuminata* appears to have taken place in New Guinea as early as the sixth or fifth millennium BCE (Denham *et al.* 2004; Kennedy 2008).[81] An early distribution of cultivated *Musa* from New Guinea, prior to the arrival of the Austronesians, should not be ruled out.[82] These movements may have triggered the formation of AA diploids through hybridization of the *banksii*

---

[80] Unlike other researchers (see Kennedy 2008), De Langhe (2009) considers "African plantains" and "Pacific plantains" to be the result of hybridizations in different places, and this has been confirmed by recent genetic research (Perrier *et al.* 2009). For De Langhe, "Pacific plantains" are not present west of New Guinea.

[81] Four or five subspecies of wild *Musa acuminata* can be distinguished: *banksii* (New Guinea), *zebrina* (Java), *malaccensis* (Malay peninsula), *burmanica* (northeastern India, Burma, Thailand, southern China), and *microcarpa* (Kalimantan), the latter group being sometimes linked to *zebrina* (Perrier *et al.* 2009: 204). "The A genomes of almost all edible bananas are related to the eastern subspecies *banksii* (New Guinea) and *errans* (Philippines) of *Musa acuminata*, and some cultivars are complex hybrids among *Musa acuminata* subspecies" (Kennedy 2008: 84). For this author, an area shared between New Guinea and the Philippines appears to have been the primary center of domestication ("but where the *Musa acuminata errans* contribution was added [to the *banksii* genome] cannot be determined on present evidence") (Kennedy 2008: 87). For De Langhe *et al.* (2009), "the genetic basis of the distinction between ssp. *errans* and ssp. *banksii* has yet to be established." Perrier *et al.* take the same position and propose a zone between Java and New Guinea for the appearance of various AA diploids (2009: 208 fig. 4). In addition, they show that *banksii* contributed to the formation of most of the AA, AAA, and AAB cultivars, but not of all of them (2009).

[82] In any case, bananas spread from New Guinea, not only toward the east, but also toward the west, probably at different times (Kennedy 2008: 85, 87, 89; Perrier *et al.* 2009). The great yam *Dioscorea alata* was domesticated in New Guinea, and then carried to the west (Lebot 1999; Blench 2009: 371) along with taro and sugarcane (Denham 2010). Linguistic data for the banana support the hypothesis of Papuan migrations prior to the Austronesian arrivals (Donohue and Denham 2010).

and *zebrina/microcarpa* subspecies (Perrier *et al.* 2009: 207).[83] *Musa acuminata* bananas (and possibly AAB hybrids?) may have been carried to India as early as the end of the third millennium BCE, where new hybridization occurred. It is possible that *Musa acuminata* was introduced into India and/or Sri Lanka, and from there crossed with *Musa balbisiana*.[84] According to Fuller and Madella (2009: 338), "an early Holocene hunter-gatherer cave site in Sri Lanka attests to traditions of utilisation of indigenous wild *M. balbisiana*" (the presence of *M. acuminata* has also been suggested, but seems uncertain) (Kajale 1989). Sri Lanka is a region where hybridization may have occurred between wild *M. balbisiana* and domesticated *M. acuminata*, perhaps introduced previously by Austronesian sailors toward the end of the third millennium. *Musa acuminata* seeds may also have been found in Sri Lanka for this period (De Langhe 2009), an identification awaiting confirmation. Because of the uncertainty of the area of origin of *M. balbisiana*, however, it is difficult to reconstruct a history of *M. acuminata* x *M. balbisiana* hybrids (Kennedy 2008: 79, 87). As opposed to Fuller, De Langhe *et al.* (2009) and Perrier *et al.* (2009) consider *M. balbisiana* to have probably been carried by men to South India and Sri Lanka (see also Vrydaghs *et al.* 2013): according to these authors, this species originated in an area between northeastern India and southern China. Various researchers have suggested an Austroasiatic origin for the Sanskrit term *kaḍalī-*, "banana,"[85] but Mayrhofer only notes this word as non-Indo-Aryan, of unknown origin, and Osada considers an Austroasiatic origin improbable.[86] Indeed, Donohue and Denham (2010: 303) have recently shown that the term derives from Indonesia and, ultimately, from Negrito languages of the Philippines (<*kaluay*<*qaRutay*). According to Fuller and Madella (2009: 346), the South Dravidian *vāẓ-a* may have the same origin, but this derivation seems uncertain. The banana was present in the Harappan culture, as seen in paintings on pottery[87] and the discovery of banana phytoliths at Kot Diji (Pakistan) (Madella 2003), Farmana (Haryana) and Loteshwar (Gujarat, Mature Harappan) (Lawler 2012; Vrydaghs *et al.* 2013); however, we do not know which type of *Musa* was used there (one might imagine

---

[83] Perrier *et al.* (2009: 207) emphasize the importance of the Mlali group, found today in Africa, in the Comoros and Madagascar, but originally from an area between Java and New Guinea. The Mlali bananas have been shown to carry contributions from *acuminata* subspecies *banksii*, *microcapra*, and *zebrina* (Vrydaghs *et al.* 2013). Bananas of this type were transported not only to East Africa, but also to the Malay peninsula (where new hybridizations occurred) and India (Perrier *et al.* 2009: 208 fig. 4). Moreover, the existence of AA cultivars showing the contribution of *banksii* in the Philippines (Guyod subgroup) points to movements between New Guinea and the Philippines.

[84] The Indian AAB of the Pome/Prata group were formed through the hybridization of Mlali-type bananas (showing a double contribution of *banksii* and *zebrina*) with *M. balbisiana*. Conversely, in the Indian AAB of Silk type, the *acuminata* contribution derives from the *malaccensis* subgroup (Perrier *et al.* 2009: 211).

[85] Cf. Sakai: *telui*, *kelui*; Nicobar: *talui*; Khmer: *tut taloi*; Palaong: *kloai*, plantain (Turner 1962–1966: 136, no. 2712; Przyluski 1975 [1921]; Patyal 1979). Sanskrit also has the term *mōcha*, "(sweet?) banana," which is at the origin of the Arabic *mauz*, and the Chinese *mao-che* (Fuller and Madella 2009: 345).

[86] Osada 2006: 159–160. For Zide and Zide (1976), the Sanskrit word does not derive from Proto-Munda. Southworth (2005: 211), however, accepts an Austroasiatic origin. For the Dravidian languages, it is possible to reconstruct *vāẓ-a* at the level of Proto-South Dravidian 1 (Southworth 2005).

[87] Lal 1997: 161. The first mention of bananas in India appears in Buddhist texts in Pali which may date to the fifth century BCE (Watson 1983: 51, 172 n. 5). Alexander's army saw the plant in India in the Indus valley in 325 BCE.

a species used for its fibers). According to Achaya (1994: 83), the term *kaḍalī-* referred to plantains, whereas *mocha* was employed for sweet bananas.

It could be suggested that the plantain was carried from India to the Horn of Africa (Murdoch 1959), where it would have entered the continent during the early first millennium BCE, if the discovery of *Musa* phytoliths in Cameroon around 500/400 BCE can be accepted (see above). However, Mbida *et al.* (2001, 2004) argue for an introduction through the Tanzanian coast, bypassing India. Mbida *et al.* (2006) have shown that various data invalidate the hypothesis of a route from India to the Horn of Africa for the AAB plantain. First, they point out the aridity of the coast on the Horn of Africa. Second, in India, a large number of AB diploids and ABB triploids have been found as well as AAB varieties that can be eaten raw, whereas AAB plantains are rare or absent, except in the states of Kerala and Tamil Nadu, which exhibit only a limited number of varieties.[88] According to Vrydaghs *et al.* (2013), "analysis of the African AAB genome details a clear contribution of the *acuminata banksii* and *zebrina* subsp., while the Indian AAB attest to a *malaccensis* contribution," and "the analysis of the B contribution to the plantain genome records differences between the African and Indian ones." Moreover, AAB plantains have not been attested in Ethiopia. We ought therefore to consider a direct oceanic introduction by Austronesians on the East African coast (R. Blench, p.c.), followed by a later transportation of the plant toward Mount Elgon and the involvement of populations cultivating ensete (De Langhe 2007). The two groups of "Pacific plantains" and "African plantains" exhibit a AA genome coming from the subspecies *banksii*.[89] For the African plantains, the introduction of the B genome probably occurred in a zone between the Philippines and New Guinea, at the time of the Austronesian expansion or prior to its expansion (see above, Perrier *et al.* 2009: 209). According to Blench (2009), "plantains arrived in West Africa earlier than 3000 BP along with taro and water-yam." Central west Africa is an area of high genetic diversity for AAB type bananas (plantains), especially in the first zone.

Moreover, the AAA triploids of the Mutika Lujugira group (cooking and beer-making bananas) exhibit a great deal of genetic diversity in the East African Highlands. Their genome derives from a double contribution from *banksii* and *zebrina* (the origin of these bananas has therefore been located between Java and New Guinea) (Perrier *et al.* 2009: 209).[90] For these authors, these AAA bananas may have been

---

[88] Curiously, one finds the term *konDoG* in the Munda languages of northeastern India, but no connection can be established with the African data (Blench 2009: 370). In contrast with the low diversity of the "African" plantains in South India, De Langhe (2009) points out "the surprising diversity of these African plantains among tribal groups of the Philippines."

[89] Denham 2010: 18. The plantains found in the Pacific include two main lineages: the first derives from the subsp. *banksii* (New Guinea) ("Pacific plantains" c.s.), while the second is the result of hybridization between *banksii* and *errans* ("African plantains") (Kennedy 2008: 84) (cf. also Perrier *et al.* 2009: 209). In the Pacific, people also plant bananas belonging to the genus *Callimusa* (*fe'i*), which originated in New Guinea (Kennedy 2008: 81). *Fe'i* and *Musa* were probably introduced separately to the islands east of New Guinea.

[90] Kennedy also notes that cooking bananas (AAA) from the East African Highlands are linked to the subsp. *banksii* by a maternal line, and to the subsp. *zebrina* (Indonesia) by a paternal line (2008: 85). Vrydaghs *et al.* (2013) write that "the AAA highlands are unique to the African continent. Their diversity, with at least 60 cultivars, results from a long phenotypic differentiation and points to a great antiquity as well."

introduced into East Africa prior to AAB plantains (Perrier *et al.* 2009; Denham 2010: 18).

Moreover, the East African coast shows a great variety of cultivars that have probably been introduced more recently (AA, AAA, AB, AAB, and ABB genomes) (R. Blench p.c. and 2009).[91] Sweet AAA bananas – of Gros Michel or Cavendish type – also derive from the subspecies *banksii*, with a genetic contribution from *malaccensis* subspecies (Perrier *et al.* 2009: 209). The discovery of *Musa* banana phytoliths, found in sediment cores from a swamp at Munsa in Uganda, appear to reveal a much earlier arrival of bananas on the East African coast, but the date suggested – fourth millennium – and their identification (banana) has been greeted with great skepticism by most researchers (Neumann and Hildebrand 2009). B. J. Lejju *et al.* themselves remain cautious about their discovery; such an early arrival of bananas cannot be confirmed before new investigations have been carried out.[92]

Two questions remain unanswered: when and where the plantain arrived on the East African coast, and the nature of the carriers' cultural affiliation. The routes taken by the plant between the East African coast and West Africa also remain unknown (Jones's hypothesis [1971] according to which Africa was circumnavigated by Austronesians has been largely abandoned, but it cannot be definitely excluded).[93] One might plausibly see the introduction and spread of the plantain in West Africa as one of the driving forces behind the Bantu expansion – or at least behind a later phase of the Bantu expansion (Blench 2009: 376).[94] "The most prominent reconstructible term for plantain, #*ko[n]do*, occurs across the zone where the greatest degree of somatic variation is found." Vernacular names related to the Proto-Bantu #*ko[n]do* are probably compounds formed with the root #-*kom*, an old reconstructible term in the Benue-Congo languages of West Africa, where it referred to an indigenous (non-edible) ensete, *Ensete gillettii*. "At some point, this name was transferred either to plantain or to the cultivated Musaceae in general," and spread by Bantu farmers during their expansion (Blench 2009: 368, 376).

Moreover, bananas arrived in South India on multiple occasions during the first millennium BCE, with the two branches of the South Dravidian languages showing different words for this plant (Fuller 2007: 424; Fuller and Madella 2009) (*ulu-k*, in Central Dravidian, *ar-Vntii* and *taz/tal* for South Dravidian 2) (Southworth, as mentioned above, also reconstructs *vāẓ-a* at the level of Proto-South Dravidian).

Other plants from Southeast Asia reached India after 1500 BCE: Southworth has reconstructed terms in Proto-Dravidian and in Proto-South Dravidian for the areca tree, the coconut tree, and "the bitter orange *Citrus aurantium* L. (introduced from SE

---

91 The "African center of diversity [of the plantain AAB] is in the zone from southeastern Nigeria to Gabon" (Blench 2009).

92 Lejju *et al.* 2006. The same layer dated to the fourth millennium has yielded phytoliths of *Ensete*.

93 Dick-Read (2005) has recently attempted to revive this hypothesis.

94 The term "Bantu expansion" covers complex population movements, the adoption of Bantu words/languages by hunter-gatherers . . . "Agriculture has been seen as one of the driving forces behind the Bantu expansion" (Bostoen 2014: 130; cf. Diamond and Bellwood 2003). But "apart from the two *Vigna* species [*V. unguiculata* and *V. subterranea*], Proto-Bantu reconstructions for domesticates are restricted to yam species: no names appear to be reconstructible in Proto-Bantu for any of the indigenous domesticated African cereals" (Bostoen 2014: 130). The Proto-Bantu language goes back to the third millennium BCE; its homeland is situated in the grassfields of Cameroon.

Asia via NE India?).”[95] One wonders whether the term *iẓ-e really refers to the bitter orange and not to another *Citrus*.[96] Southworth also reconstructs the terms *māt-aḷ, “citron/lemon,” and *kiccili/kittili, “orange,” in Proto-South Dravidian, as well as *naram-ka in Proto-South Dravidian 1. The reconstruction of these terms, going back to the second and first millennia BCE, may reflect the arrival of different citrus varieties, in connection with the building of networks between India and Southeast Asia. The site of Sanganakallu (Karnataka) has produced mango and citrus remains from levels dating to 1400–1300 BCE (Asouti and Fuller 2008: 134). These plants probably arrived via land routes “from an area Assam/Burma/Yunnan” (Fuller *et al.* 2011). For the coconut tree, the term *tenkay, “fruit of the South” in Proto-South Dravidian, seems to imply an introduction from Sri Lanka.[97]

The sugarcane *Saccharum officinarum* L. reached India long before the Christian era (B. T. Roach [1995] suggests 1000 BCE).[98] Kenoyer places its introduction at around 1500 BCE, because “sugarcane is well documented in the Later Vedic texts which generally refer to the time period at the end of the Indus cities, about 1700 to 1500 BC” (Kenoyer 1998: 169). Southworth reconstitutes a term *cet-Vkk in “Early Proto-Dravidian” and suggests an introduction at the beginning of the second millennium.[99]

Southworth gives an Austroasiatic origin for the Sanskrit names of six other plants:

– betel, which originated in Southeast Asia, Sanskrit *tāmbūla-*;
– more curiously, cotton *karpāsa* and pepper *marīca*;[100]
– the citron tree, *Citrus medica* L., often given as native to Southeast Asia.[101] The sanskrit *nimbūka-*, in fact, may be of Austroasiatic or Austronesian origin;[102]

---

[95] Fuller 2007: 427. For the areca palm, PD *pānkk- may come from an unknown language (Southworth 2005: 82, 211).

[96] Southworth (2005: 215), in fact, gives only the Proto-South Dravidian (?) *iẓ-e, “orange.” Unknown in the wild, the bitter orange, which originated in Southeast Asia, could have derived from hybridization between *Citrus reticulata* Blanco (mandarin) and *Citrus grandis* (L.) Osbeck (pummelo) (Scora 1975).

[97] Fuller 2007: 424; Southworth 2005: 212; Blench 2006. Two terms for coir and coprah can also be reconstructed in Proto-South Dravidian.

[98] The *Atharva Veda* (c. 600 BCE?) mentions sugarcane (Allchin 1969: 119; Mahdi 1998: 401). For some authors, the *Atharva Veda* goes back to 800 BCE at least. Southworth (2005: 44) even thinks that some parts of it may be as old as the archaic texts of the *Rig Veda* (middle of the second millennium BCE), whereas other parts may belong to the Late Vedic period (1000–600 BCE). Note that iron is mentioned in the *Atharva Veda* (Southworth 2005: 59 n. 6), but not in the *Rig Veda*.

[99] Southworth 2006: 146. Sugarcane would then have been present at the beginning of the second millennium BCE at the latest. For the Early Indo-Aryan *ikṣu*, “sugarcane,” Southworth proposes a derivation from the Dravidian *iṭ-cu, “sweet-juice,” perhaps formed from Proto-Dravidian *in, “sweet,” and *cur, “to suck” (2005: 218). The Old Indo-Aryan term *sarkarā*, “sand, sugar,” is related to the Proto-Dravidian *cer-aku, but the two terms could derive from an Austroasiatic language (Southworth 2005: 221).

[100] For betel, Southworth 2005: 211. In addition, he reconstructs *vett-ilay, “betel leaf,” in Proto-South Dravidian 1. For cotton, Southworth 2005: 197. For pepper, Southworth 2005: 216; the Old Indo-Aryan *marīca* is linked to the Proto-South Dravidian 1 *miḷ-Vku.

[101] It was already present in India during the first part of the second millennium (see the Sanghol site, Ganges, 1800–1600 BCE) (Fuller and Madella 2001: 311).

[102] Osada 2006: 162; Southworth 2005: 215. See Malay *limau*, “orange, lemon,” from PAN *limau, Citrus sp. (Beaujard 2015).

– the bottle gourd *Lagenaria siceraria* [Molina] Standl., in Old Indo-Aryan, *alābu-*, related to Malay *labu*; the two terms may be of Austroasiatic origin;
– *Setaria italica* millet, Sanskrit *kangunī*.

For M. Witzel, the Sanskrit name for cotton, *karpāsa*, may derive from the term *yupas* reconstructed in Proto-Burushaki, a language belonging to the Macro-Caucasian family.[103] Before *karpāsa*, the Old Indo-Aryan knew a word *tūla*, related by Southworth to the Proto-South-Dravidian **tū-val* (Southworth 2005: 223). M. Mayrhofer sees the Sanskrit *marīca*, "pepper," as deriving from "a foreign word," and T. O. Osada does not consider it to be of Austroasiatic origin (Mayrhofer 1986–2001; Osada 2006: 162).

Between China, India, and Central Asia, Ancient "Silk Roads"

As touched upon above, evidence of links between western Asia and East Asia can be found throughout the steppes and the Hexi corridor during the fourth and third millennia BCE. At this time, mobile pastoralists with "domesticated cattle, sheep, and horses (along with horseback riding and the use off wagons) ... systematically expanded eastward across the steppe in response to environmental change and the demand for increased pasture" (Frachetti 2012). "By the early 3rd millennium BC, regional modes of mobile pastoralism took shape across the Eurasian steppe zone ... The pastoralist campsites of Tasbas and Begash [eastern Kazakhstan] offer evidence for the use of domesticated grains, [in a period dated] *ca.* 2800 to 2300 cal. BC" (Spengler *et al.* 2014).

It has been suggested that contacts existed between northern India, Central Asia, and northwestern China (with the Majiayao culture [3100–2300 BCE]), on the basis of "similarities" observed in assemblages found in an Indo-Pakistani "Northern Neolithic" (Kashmir, Swāt valley)[104] (other migrations toward India may have occurred from Sichuan and Yunnan). The circular or rectangular structures excavated at Burzahom (Kashmir), for the site's first periods, have at this site coated with red ochre; they have been interpreted as semi-subterranean houses, which were common in northern China. Some semi-lunar stone knives with holes found at this site have also been noted to have a Chinese shape. The occurrence of mat or basket impressions on the bases of some of the pots is shared by three regions: northern China, Kashmir, and the Swāt valley.[105] For Sharif and Thapar (1992: 148), the sites of North Sikkim seem to

---

[103] Witzel 2004: 174. On an Austroasiatic origin, Southworth 2005: 228. Following Southworth, we might consider a borrowing from the "Para-Munda" language of the Indus valley into Sanskrit.

[104] On the "Northern Neolithic," see Possehl 1999a: 543. After an a-ceramic phase (for example at Kanishkapura; see Mani 2004), ceramic appears *c.* 3000 BCE and the number of sites increases toward the end of the third millennium (Fuller 2007: 404).

[105] Sharif and Thapar 1992: 135, 148. The authors also mention bone tools and polished stone axes, which could suggest the Yangshao horizon (?). Semi-lunar knives with holes, of Chinese style, have been excavated in Kashmir. Possehl also signals the discovery of a knife with perforations at Kalako-deray, in the Swāt valley (1999a: 544). Similar knives, but without holes, have been unearthed at the site of Shortughai, in the Amu Darya valley, for the Harappan period (or perhaps Post-Harappan?). Various researchers have put forward the idea that there are affinities between the Northern Neolithic of Pakistan and India on the one side, and North Asian cultures on the other (see Possehl 1999a: 552). Petroglyphs found in the Upper Indus depict figures reminiscent of the Okunev culture (2500–1900/1700) (Francfort

point to Hunan influences "at the beginning of the 3rd millennium BC, via Lungshanoid cultures."[106] Some similarities noted, however, appear to be very general, and various parallels have been cast into doubt by recent research. For example, the semi-subterranean houses appear, rather, to be storage pits (Coningham and Sutherland 1998; Fuller 2006a). The semi-lunar knives with holes (Kashmir), and the jade beads (Swāt valley) could in fact correspond to the first half of the second millennium BCE (see below). Fuller (2006a) states that neither plants nor animals discovered during the first phases of the "Northern Neolithic" suggest introductions from northern China: wheat and barley are present at the beginning of the third millennium, but not East Asian millets. The hypothesis of a westward dispersion of Sino-Tibetan speakers during the middle of the third millennium does not seem very probable (see Van Driem 1998: 76ff., 86, 94, 100). Cereals and domesticated animals came either from the Indus region, or from Central Asia.[107]

Rice of the *indica* type, however, appeared around 2500 BCE in the Swāt valley (Pakistan),[108] and at the end of the Neolithic of Gufkral (Kashmir). As has already been mentioned, various authors have supported the idea of the domestication of *indica* rice in the middle Yangtze valley around the sixth millennium, while other rice varieties had been introduced into India after 2000 BCE by Austroasiatics, from Southeast Asia. For the linguists Pejros and Shnirelman, however, the Dravidians may have borrowed their knowledge of rice cultivation from Sino-Tibetan speakers at the end of the third millennium BCE (Pejros and Shnirelman 1998: 385).[109] Meadow has suggested that rice was introduced via the northwest. Rice may have been carried over several routes to India. The rice of the Northern Neolithic, however, is likely to have come from the Ganges valley (rice was cultivated at Kunal *c.* 2800 BCE, and perhaps earlier in the Middle Ganges valley), and – as outlined earlier – the Austroasiatics did not introduce rice prior to the second millennium (see above).

The discoveries of *Panicum miliaceum* from around 2200 BCE at Tepe Yahya (Iran) (Costantini and Biasini 1975), and earlier during the third millennium in Yemen (these datings appear uncertain; see above), however, reveal long-standing links between

---

2005: 303, and 1993). For Francfort, the analysis of petroglyphs supports the idea that permanent contacts existed between the steppes and northern India via the western Himalayas (2005).

[106] Sharif and Thapar 1992: 148–149. Some of these cultures show a burnished grey-black pottery, that ought to be compared to the burnished grey ceramics of Kashmir (Burzahom) or the Swāt valley (Ghalegay, Loebanr). According to Sharif and Thapar (1992: 148), however, the grey-black pottery of the Swāt valley "is probably connected with the influences originating from northern Iran (Shah-tepe, Tepe Hissar . . .)." Moreover, the authors rightly point out that many features of the Yangshao culture are not found in the Neolithic cultures of Kashmir and of the Swāt valley (1992; see below).

[107] Domesticated goats, sheep, and cattle were present, whereas the domesticated pig, so crucial in the cultures of northern China, was here marginal and of uncertain status (was it wild or domesticated?) (Fuller 2006a: 36).

[108] Imprints in pottery found at Ghalegay and grains at Bir-Kot-Gwandhai (Fuller 2006a: 36). We should speak in fact of "proto-*indica*" (see below).

[109] Van Driem attributes the development of the eastern Indian Neolithic to the "Tibeto-Burmans" (a term which here corresponds to what other authors call the Sino-Tibetans). Van Driem places the eastern Indian Neolithic at an improbably early date (prior to 5000 BCE). According to him, the "Tibeto-Burmans" originally came from the Sichuan region, which is very unlikely (1998, 2005). We do not know of any Neolithic culture in Sichuan at such an early date.

Central Asia and China. This millet left China on westward trade routes during the third millennium BCE: it has been found at Begash in Central Asia as of *c.* 2200 BCE (Frachetti *et al.* 2010; Spengler *et al.* 2014), at Togolok 21 and Gonur in the BMAC, from between 2000 and 1800 BCE (Bakels 2003; Fuller and Boivin 2009).

"Mobile herders in deserts relied on a mixed grain repertoire more heavily after 2000 BC." Data illustrate the increased interconnection "between seasonal pastoralists and regional farmers during the second millennium BC" (Spengler *et al.* 2014). The search for metal resources also led to greater mobility and interactions.

Contacts with Sino-Tibetan groups, implying long-distance exchanges and/or migrations, clearly occurred at the beginning of the second millennium in northern India (Fuller 2006a: 36, 38). "Chinese" semi-lunar knives with holes are present after 2000 BCE (Burzahom II, Gufkral IC). They have also been found in Baluchistan, and at Pirak, north of Mohenjo-Daro, within a Late Harappan context. In addition, Pirak has yielded *japonica* rice dated to 1800 BCE, a type that is of East Asian origin (Costantini 1979; Sato 2005; Fuller 2006a). Asian millets have been discovered, *Panicum miliaceum*, at Shortughai (Willcox 1991), at Pirak and at Babar Kot, and *Setaria italica* at Surkotada, during the Late Harappan period. It is therefore possible to observe the spread from East Asia to India – through Central Asia (Spengler *et al.* 2014) – of several cereals, along with fruit trees (such as peach and apricot) and a variety of *Cannabis sativa* (Fuller 2006a: 38). Domesticated animals were also introduced from Central Asia (such as the horse and the camel). This possible migration of population coming from the northeast appears to have occurred in parallel to the expansion of the BMAC (see above), which facilitated contacts between Central Asia and East Asia.

Hybridizations between local *proto-indica* forms and introduced domesticated *japonica* rice appear to have led to the domestication of *indica* rice in India. This rice may have progressively spread into the whole of the Indian peninsula (Fuller *et al.* 2010: 125; Fuller 2011a: 80–81; Fuller and Weisskopf 2011: 50–51). This scenario is supported by recent genetic research published by He *et al.* (2011) (cf. also Kovach *et al.* 2007), and by linguistic data (Sagart 2011: 130–131; see below).

No proto-term can be reconstructed with certainty for rice at the level of Early Proto-Dravidian: Southworth has reconstructed **var-inci* in Late Proto-Dravidian (2006: 145). In an earlier publication, however, he saw **var-iñc* and **varici* as "Proto-Dravidian" terms (2005: 81). According to Southworth, the Proto-Munda word **ərig*, "millet, *Panicum miliare* [*P. sumatrense*]" (Zide and Zide 1976), was borrowed by Proto-Dravidian speakers under the form **arik(i)* (around 1500 BCE); in South Dravidian, this yielded **arici* (Tamil *arici, ari*). This South Dravidian form is at the origin of the Arabic *aruzz*, from the Greek *oryza, oryzon*.[110] Rice cultivation developed in southernmost India after 1000 BCE (Fuller *et al.* 2010: 126). In Sanskrit, rice appears – only in texts composed later than the *Rig Veda* (*Atharva Veda*, around 1200 BCE)[111] – under the term *vrīhi*, which derives from the Pre-Vedic **vrijhi* and ultimately from the northern Indus

---

[110] Witzel 1999: 26. Earlier, Southworth (1988: 659–660) had proposed an Elamo-Dravidian origin, from the Proto-Elamo-Dravidian **bar*, "grain" (Elamite *bar*, "grain," Proto-Dravidian I [around 2000 BCE] **vari*, "rice"). The relevance of the "Proto-Elamo-Dravidian" remains a subject of debate.

[111] According to Witzel (1999: 26), however, the *puroḍāsa* and *odana* offerings (*Rig Veda*) refer to rice cake and rice gruel, respectively.

form ***(ə)βərij*, a southern Indus form being **vari, (v)ariki* (Witzel 2004: 184; 2006a: 101). In addition, one finds *bras* in Burushaski, *'bras* [əbras] in Tibetan, **ᵇmə-rat-s*, "paddy", in Chinese, and **beRas* in Proto-Austronesian (Sagart 2003; Blench 2005). The Burushaski, Vedic, and Persian borrowings can be explained by contacts with Tibeto-Burman languages (Sagart 2011: 131).

Links were still weak between China and India during the second millennium, both on the roads of Inner Asia and on the maritime routes going through Southeast Asia. For Bellwood (2007), however, the presence of polished stone axes in Assam recalls East Asian technology. In addition, we have seen that exchange networks involving southern China and Southeast Asia led to the spread of metalworking techniques and cultivated plants. The interconnections between the Indian and Chinese spheres brought about during the first millennium would introduce a radically new era. This connection would lead to the constitution of wide spheres of interaction which were the prelude to the formation of an Afro-Eurasian world-system. Are we witnessing a new process of globalization? How ought we to interpret the developments that we have thus far followed in detail?

Since the birth of the state in Mesopotamia, Egypt, southern and then eastern Asia, we have observed the creation and transformation of various spheres of interaction which were more or less intensively linked to one another. Were these interconnected regions incorporated into world-systems through exchange networks? Were they geographically distinct and successive world-systems? Or, as Frank and Gills (1993a) have suggested, are we seeing the development, since the third millennium, of a single world-system comprising western Asia, Central Asia, northwestern India, Arabia, Egypt, and Mediterranean Europe, with the confluence occurring "some time during the early or mid-third millennium BC, that is, by about 2700–2400 BC" (Gills and Frank 1993a: 82; Frank and Gills 2000: 6)?

Were there World-Systems during the Bronze Age?

The birth of the state in regions benefiting from particular geographical and demographic assets (such as Mesopotamia, Susiana, Egypt, and later the Indus and China) was a period during which a partial break occurred from the mode of accumulation inscribed in kinship relationships. Public and private accumulation of capital appeared, along with a new ideology, techniques of power (Mann 1986) – with writing, and the blossoming of institutions linked to the religious sphere – and new forms of labor mobilization, implying tributes and taxes, and servile or hired labor. The birth of the state was accompanied by a spectacular expansion of exchange networks, with exchanges not only of goods, but also of knowledge, beliefs, and values.

How can one explain the concentration of wealth in and around certain poles of development – compared with much less or none in other regions – as well as the variations observed in time and space? The systemic paradigm can provide us with a convincing viewpoint on the data collected for the Bronze Age and Iron Age periods, by taking all interactions at the global, regional, and local levels into account.[1] A world-system approach can help us to recognize and understand five phenomena: 1. the emergence and evolution of an interregional division of labor in certain areas, over the *longue durée*; 2. the connections between events in distant regions, and between the regions themselves; 3. the existence of cycles, both economic and political, in the same areas; 4. shifts in power between competing centers; and 5. changing inequalities, with the processes of both domination and co-evolution set in motion by the system and by local expansions:[2] the growth of the cores favored the blossoming of semi-peripheries, with some peripheries able to benefit from the dynamics of the system.

Different world-systems can be identified, in western Asia and in northern Africa on the one side, and in East Asia on the other. Increasing exchanges would connect these systems to one another, over time.

The World-Systems of Western Asia, Northern Africa, and the Eastern Mediterranean

From the Early Bronze Age to the Late Bronze Age, we observe a progressive integration of the various regions of western Asia and of the eastern Mediterranean through the existence of economic cycles synchronized with political, social, and

---

[1] See Rowlands *et al.* 1987; Kohl 1987; Edens and Kohl 1993; Algaze 1993, 2001; Sherratt 1994a, b; Kristiansen 1998; Gills and Thompson 2005, 2006; Kristiansen and Larsson 2005; Wilkinson *et al.* 2011.

[2] Peripheries were not "passive recipients" (*contra* Stein 1999: 19). See Wolf 1982: 9–10.

ideological evolution, as well as the development of urbanization. For the first time in history, human societies extracted non-renewable mineral resources on a significant and expanding scale. Marked by labor intensification at the core, the exercise of monopolies and monopsonies, and the extension of networks, a growing production-and-exchange organization and its accompanying transfers of wealth helped set up a division of labor within and between interconnected societies.[3] All these exchanges made up unified and hierarchized areas in which regional events and developments appear to have been interrelated. The fact that the various regions united by trade experienced a demonstrable synchronization in their development suggests (but is not yet sufficient proof for) the systemic nature of their relations. The cycles we observe are partly related to climatic variations – around 3200, 2200, 1750, and 1200 BCE[4] – which are an integral part of a "systemic logic" that will be developed in the epilogue of this book.[5] Recession periods were marked by varying degrees of population movements, pressure from (semi)-nomadic groups on sedentary societies, and tensions within these societies. All led to the disintegration of states and of exchange networks.

Long-distance trade clearly exerted a strong influence on the construction and dynamics of ancient societies. The need for metals and wood, the demand for prestige goods, and export opportunities all stimulated production and exchanges. These processes encouraged social transformation in western Asia, northern Africa, and the Mediterranean. The spread of copper and then bronze metallurgy, which required access to metal ore and its transport, was a key contributor to the implementation of new networks and the formation of various systems (Frank and Thompson 2006): the "Bronze Age" would then appear to be an appropriate label for the third and second millennia BCE (Sherratt 1993). Contrary to Wallerstein's opinion, long-distance trade was not restricted to luxury goods of high value compared to their weight; it also involved bulky goods, such as copper, wood, stones, tin, and grain. These products were transported by boat and by land, as is demonstrated by the organization of armed Assyrian caravans that traveled between Assur and the Anatolian trading posts at the beginning of the second millennium. Moreover, commerce in luxury goods had significant social and political implications. Although globally these goods were of only limited economic value, they partially underlay social status. They also encouraged an increase in trade in other, bulkier products (Schneider 1977; Bentley 1996).

Improvements in means of transport were key to the blossoming of transcultural relations, with the development of shipbuilding in Mesopotamia and in Egypt, during the fourth millennium, and in the Persian Gulf and the Indus region during the third millennium. Ships made of planks joined together may have been built in Egypt as

[3] On "transfers of wealth" and the emergence of value in exchanges, see Beaujard 2013. Too often ignored, ideological power played a crucial role in these processes. Warnier (2008) also writes: "The role of imaginative processes is at the heart of the building of the desirability and of the emergence of hierarchies."

[4] Previously, the period c. 4200 saw the end of the 'Ubaid expansion in western Asia and the collapse of the Varna culture (Bulgaria). A 1,000-year cycle is clearly apparent, as is a 500-year cycle. Moreover, Dergachev and Van Geel (2004) point out the existence of 2,400-year and 1,500-year cycles, and Bond et al. (1997) suggest a 1,470-year cycle.

[5] Formulated for the period prior to the sixteenth century, the model seems to be applicable to periods going back to the Bronze Age and the Iron Age.

early as the middle of the fourth millennium.[6] The domestication of the donkey during the fourth millennium in Egypt and in western Asia, and the use of the hybrid donkey-onager in Mesopotamia, were also crucial innovations. The situation of semi-peripheries and peripheries as hubs connecting different spheres or systems[7] was conducive to innovations in these regions: boats from the Syrian coast sailed to the Nile Delta during the fourth millennium, ships from Oman and Bahrain plied the seas between the Indus and Mesopotamia, camels and horses were domesticated during the third millennium in Central Asia and the steppes, and the chariot with spoked wheels was invented in the Caucasus region at the turn of the third and second millennia.[8]

The cores, however, were the first to develop technological and institutional innovations, which – along with military strength and ideological power – allowed them to build up efficient productive sectors and exchange networks where they were globally dominant. Demographic advantage also contributed in great part to the cores' supremacy, allowing for sizeable investments in agriculture, troop mobilization, and the manufacture of products such as textiles, for export. The cores set up asymmetric exchanges with their semi-peripheries and peripheries in less-developed areas, by enhancing what we might term the "desirability" of manufactured products (particularly textiles), which they exported in exchange for raw (or semi-processed) materials and slaves, and by extorting war booty, tributes, and taxes (Beaujard 2013).[9] It is true that the politico-military networks were relatively limited in size during the ancient periods, but trade and information networks were much larger. For reasons both economic and ideological, exchange networks were created by agents of the core and by groups acting as intermediaries between core(s) and peripheries, so that a core's power over a region did not necessarily diminish and exchanges did not grow more "symmetrical" with increasing distance, unlike G. J. Stein's assertion (1999: 62). Even when diasporas were not the direct vassals of a core, they could nonetheless help spread its economic and cultural domination (Beaujard 2013).

With regard to the whole period prior to 1000 BCE, insights into possible world-systems confront major problems of geographical and temporal delimitations, as well as difficulties in interpreting data or a lack thereof. How can we discover the modes of production, and estimate production levels? While it may be true that "dependencies in the modern sense only rarely characterised center-periphery relations in the ancient world" (Edens and Kohl 1993: 31), can we truly ascertain the value of these

---

[6] This does not mean that there were no seagoing ships prior to this period. The migration of populations bringing cattle, pigs, goats, and sheep from the Levant to Cyprus during the ninth millennium has already been mentioned. An active trade developed in the Persian Gulf during the fifth millennium between Mesopotamians of the 'Ubaid culture and Arab communities.

[7] As already mentioned, a "sphere of interaction" refers to a zone where exchanges occur without the subsequent building of a significant transregional division of labor (in contrast to what we observe within a world-system).

[8] The need for greater mobility during arid periods led to the widespread use of the cart at the end of the fourth millennium and around 2800/2700 in the steppes, the innovation of the spoked wheel during the late second millennium, and the adoption of horseback riding at the end of the second millennium and in the early first millennium. Increasing exchanges during periods of global growth also allowed for innovations, for example, the domestication of the donkey, camel, and horse.

[9] Generally speaking, exchanges were embedded within the political and religious spheres. See Appadurai 1986; Aglietta and Orléan 2002: 25, 141.

dependencies and their intensity? How can we assess the global level of trade and the importance of division of labor between regions while a large part of the "products" exchanged (metals – these were remelted –,[10] textiles, slaves, food, narcotics, spices, and aromatics) remain invisible in archaeological contexts? "[Ancient] texts offer little understanding of the cost [of specific goods] or the economic structure that character-ized the trade/exchange" (Lamberg-Karlovsky 2001b: 369). We would need to compare the evolution of the density and size of cities and towns, but many of these have been destroyed or insufficiently excavated. Some regions are practically terra incognita for archaeology. Written sources are often lacking, or give a fragmentary and partial view of societies. Lamberg-Karlovsky thus points out that for the Ur III period, "the texts from Lagash deal primarily with the agricultural economy of the temple, those from Umma with the activities of merchants and state-run agriculture, those from Nippur largely with a private economy, and those from Ur with the manufacture of products" (1993: 416).

Interpretations developed by archaeologists depend not only on available materials, but also on the methodological approaches used. Radically different views have thus been developed concerning individual property (especially for land), the existence or lack of hired labor, and state or private capital accumulation. Many scholars today recognize the importance of private entrepreneurs, of market relations, and of mon-etization processes, as early as the third millennium BCE in western Asia, whereas others adhere to the Polanyian view on ancient societies. The knowledge we have of the nature and evolution of states often appears quite insufficient.

Ongoing discussions on different chronologies, moreover, show clearly how difficult it is to propose periodizations, and to see how sites belonging to different regions can be linked to one another; this hinders an appreciation of the possible cycles of systems into which these regions have been integrated.[11] For example, the discrepancies observed between radiocarbon dating and archaeo-historical data for the Old Egyptian Kingdom and the Levant of the Early Bronze Age have been pointed out,[12] as well as the various chronologies put forward for Mesopotamia.

---

[10] According to Taylor's evaluation (2001), 0.01 percent of the silver in circulation has been found in archaeological excavations in southeastern Europe for the second half of the first millennium BCE. The proportion may be the same for copper.

[11] See the critical evaluations by P. Kohl, K. Kristiansen, C. C. Lamberg-Karlovsky, and A. and S. Sherratt following an article by Frank (1993a) on the phases of growth and recession that Frank has suggested within the context of "his" world-system. Even for the first half of the first millennium BCE, the cycles put forward by Frank and Gills are not readily acceptable within the framework of the system described by these authors. Frank (1993a: 419) has countered these criticisms by stating that a collapse in the center (Mesopotamia) may have been accompanied or followed by the ascent of some peripheries – for example southeastern Europe from 1750 to 1500 BCE.

[12] It has already been emphasized that radiocarbon datings often contradict archaeo-historical data: for example, for the Kheops pyramid, 45 percent of the datings are between 2780 and 2715 BCE: two or three hundred years earlier than had been expected (Hasel 2004: 17, but see Manning 2006: 338–350). Cf. also the various contributions in *Radiocarbon* 43 (1–3), 2001. For Egypt, another problem arises from the discrepancy between some archaeological data, the dating of the Thera volcanic eruption, and the most frequently used chronology (see Kitchen 2000). Conflicting interpretations have also been offered for various regions of Asia during the third and second millennia. For Central Asia, for example, the Namazga V phase would have begun around 2300 BCE according to Masson (1996a,b), and 2500 according

For Frank and Gills (1993a), the existence of an Afro-Eurasian world-system "goes back at least to 5000 BP," but these authors only define phases of growth and decline from the second millennium BCE. Conversely, Frank and Thompson (2006) have suggested the cycles shown in Table I.Con.1 from 3000 BCE onward.

Despite the conceptual problems just pointed out, archaeological data do allow us to identify poles of development, transfers of wealth, and divisions of labor within world-systems for which cycles can be distinguished; see Tables I.Con.2 and I.Con.3.

As early as the Urukian period, southern Mesopotamia appears to have formed the core of a system which included at least part of the Persian Gulf[13] (see Map I.11). The Middle and Late Uruk periods should best be considered not as a single phase of growth and decline, but as two distinct phases (c. 3700–3450 and 3450–3150).[14] A second issue related

Table I.Con.1 *Cycles put forward by Frank and Thompson*

Southwest Asia	Phases of expansion	Phases of decline
	3800–3200	3200–?
	2700–2300	2300–2050
	2050–?	1750–1700/1600
	1600–1250	1250–1000

Table I.Con.2 *Successive cycles in Mesopotamia*

	Phases of growth	Phases of decline
Urukian system	3600–3550?	3550–3450?
	3450–3200	3200–3100
Jemdet Nasr period, ED I and II	3100–2800	2800–2700
ED III, Akkadian Empire	2700–2250	2250–2150
Post-Akkadian period, Ur III Empire	2150–2025	2025–1900
Old Assyrian kingdom, Isin-Larsa period	1900–1750	1750–1600
Late Bronze Age	1600–1200	1200–1000

to Hiebert (1994). See also the chronology-related problems for the Bronze Age and the Iron Age in the Eurasian steppes (Koryakova and Kohl 2000: 642), and the diverging assessments on the dating of Tepe Yahya IVB and Jiroft. Lastly, for western Asia, let us not forget the controversies engendered by the ultra-short chronology advocated by Gasche *et al.* for the last half of the third millennium and the second millennium, which modifies correlations between regions (see above). For an evaluation and recent propositions concerning the chronology of the Egyptian Dynastic period, see Hornung *et al.* 2006.

[13] Algaze 1993, 2001; see above. Yoffee (1995b: 1398) also considers Mesopotamia as the center of a world-system, with the rest of western Asia representing a periphery (fourth–third millennium).

[14] Rothman (2001a, 2004) goes so far as to distinguish three phases of expansion, the first at the beginning of the Middle Uruk period, the second later on during this same period, and the third during the Late Uruk. An arid phase occurring slightly prior to the middle of the fourth millennium may have triggered a temporary decline of the system. The collapse of the gigantic Tripol'ye settlements occurred at this time; "Chalcolithic Transcaucasian sites also reveal a disjunction with the Kura-Araxes remains" (Kohl 2007: 53, 69).

Table I.Con.3 *Successive cycles in Egypt*

	Phases of growth	Phases of decline
Nagada IIc-d	3500–3300/3200	?
Nagada III, Dynasty "o"	3300/3200–3100	?
Thinite period	3100–2800	2800–2700
Old Kingdom, and First Intermediary Period	2700–2200	2200–2030
Middle Kingdom, and Second Intermediary Period	2030–1750	1750–1560
New Kingdom, and Third Intermediary Period	1560–1200	1200–1000

to this Urukian period is the spatial extent of the system. Could the region centered on the Nile valley have been part of the Mesopotamian system, or was it a separate system merely connected to the Mesopotamian area? Interactions with Mesopotamia (through the Levant) certainly played a role in the initial construction of the state in Egypt. For Wilkinson (2004: 245), "the artifacts [from the Uruk world] found in Egypt represent merely the archaeologically visible tip of the iceberg." "There was importation [of goods, techniques and ideas], imitation and emulation." Contrary to Frank and Gills's thesis (1993a) and that of Frank and Thompson (2006), it is apparent that the obvious weakness of the interconnections between Egypt and Mesopotamia prevents us from contemplating the formation of a system uniting these two regions, even if we agree that low-intensity contacts may have had important systemic effects (Hall 2006), and even if we take into account the fact that some of the goods exchanged have rarely left traces in archaeological levels. In the words of A. Sherratt for Europe in the Bronze Age (1993), Egypt "was culturally transformed by trade, but it remained structurally independent." In the north, the search for metal led to an expansion of the system beyond the Caucasus (Maykop culture) and to contacts with the steppes of Central Asia (Sarazm).

A climatic deterioration around 3200/3100 in Mesopotamia and Iran, accompanied by a weakening of the monsoons in the Indian Ocean,[15] probably played a role in the collapse or change of the Urukian system toward the end of the fourth millennium and in the subsequent restructuring of the networks. Commercial links all but ceased between Egypt and Mesopotamia around 3100/3000 BCE. At the start of the third millennium, three systems can be identified, centered on southern Mesopotamia, Iran, and Egypt, respectively (see Map I.12). Mesopotamia consisted of an ensemble of city-states, whereas Iran (the Proto-Elamite entity) and Egypt (Thinite period) held territorial states. During the Jemdet Nasr period, northern Mesopotamia and Anatolia were only weakly connected to the south. Southern Mesopotamia turned

---

[15] See Brooke 2014: 113, 115, 180–181. Global cooling and a weakening of the summer monsoon system in the Indian Ocean probably occurred along with a shift of the Intertropical Convergence Zone further south. An arid phase has been noted north of the Caspian Sea from 3200 onward (Koryakova and Epimakhov 2007: 12). From the fourth millennium onward, Oman constituted the limit of summer monsoon rainfall (Cordova 2005: 113).

toward the Persian Gulf, where copper exports – from Iran and later from Oman – began during the late fourth to early third millennium.

Lower temperatures were accompanied by a gradual process of aridification in Iran and the Levant around 2800/2700 BCE (Rosen 2007: 98).[16] This climate change led to internal disturbance and to movements of populations between regions, and finally caused the disintegration of all the three systems at once. Semi-nomadic groups migrated from the north to the south through the Caucasus; these migrations were marked by the appearance of kurgans in Transcaucasia. Further south, populations of the Kura-Araxes region entered Palestine. Egypt also underwent a period of divisions at the end of the Second Dynasty, during the twenty-eighth century, with the separation of the northern and southern regions. These divisions probably reflected a phase of low-level Nile flooding, corresponding to the climate degradation observed in western Asia, as well as to a weakening of the Indian Ocean's summer monsoon system.

As shown above, from 2600 BCE on, a much larger system took shape, having two cores (the Indus and Mesopotamia) that were connected through the Persian Gulf, but also more indirectly via terrestrial routes which crossed Iran and went northward as far as Turkmenistan and Afghanistan. In the west, the system extended as far as the city of Troy, where trade networks from eastern Europe and the steppes merged (see Map 1.13). The political situation of the Indus civilization is not well understood, but we do know that in Mesopotamia, the first known empire – the Akkadian Empire – appeared during the twenty-fourth century (MC). Archaeological data and texts reveal an interregional division of labor, with the cores of the system exporting manufactured products (textiles,[17] beads, metallic products) and food, and importing raw materials (metals, wood, stone, resins), slaves, and some manufactured products (chlorite vessels, objects made of semi-precious stones ...) from the peripheries or semi-peripheries. As early as the third millennium, existing markets were creating demand which helped increase production (Warburton 1997: 83ff.). Copper was exploited in Anatolia during the fourth millennium, and also very early on in the Negev. The city of Ebla in Syria, however, imported copper from Dilmun (region of Dharan, then of Bahrain) in the middle of the third millennium. Copper would later arrive from Cyprus, during the second millennium. It is doubtful, however, that these changes reflect simply an adaptation of merchants and states to conditions of prices and markets, as Warburton argues (2003: 61, 142).

Although the precariousness of interconnections may have made some systems more unstable than they would be later (Kohl 1987), the Mesopotamia–Indus system and the Egyptian system show a remarkable permanence. It is not certain that the technological gaps were too small and the means of transport too primitive to allow for the building of dependencies between and within societies.[18] Here we must consider

---

[16] More pronounced aridity has also been pointed out in the lower Don Valley and north Kazakhstan as of 2800 BCE (Anthony 2007: 301).

[17] Wool and perhaps flax for Mesopotamia, cotton for the Indus, flax for Egypt, in the Egypt–eastern Mediterranean world-system. On the importance of textiles in the cores' exports and the establishment of relations of dominance, see Schneider 1977, Ekholm Friedman 2005: 61; Good 2006; Beaujard 2009, 2013.

[18] In contrast, P. L. Kohl is correct in pointing out the importance of horse domestication and the use of carts or chariots. These innovations originated in peripheries; they partly contributed to the rapidity of the population movements observed during the late third to early second millennium and the collapse of the Sumer–Indus world-system at that time.

institutional gaps, as well as the ideological power of the cores. It has also been argued that techniques were easily transmitted, thus limiting the installation of long-standing relations of dependence (Kohl 1987). Cores, semi-peripheries, and peripheries actually did share a number of techniques, but not all. A. Sherratt (1994b) rightly notes that techniques linked to an urban environment (e.g. wheelmade pottery production) and complex goldsmithing techniques such as granulation and filigree did not spread out from the eastern Mediterranean to Europe during the Bronze Age, due to the absence of a context favorable to mass production in the first case, and the complexity of the techniques involved in the second. The crafting of etched beads also remained within the bounds of the Indus civilization.[19] The capture and deportation of craftsmen was a systematic practice of the dominant powers from the second millennium onward (and perhaps earlier); this shows that techniques did not spread so easily, at least in some domains (for example, the production of specific high-status objects made of textile, glass, metal, or the construction of buildings or boats).[20]

The synthesis suggested, for this Mesopotamia–Indus system, differs from that of Frank and Thomson on two points at least. The first point concerns links between Egypt and western Asia. The Egyptian area does not seem to have been included in the Mesopotamia–Indus world-system, but was at most connected to Mesopotamia through the Levant, until the end of the Akkadian Empire; then Egypt was practically isolated from Mesopotamia (until the nineteenth century BCE). Moreover, indirect contacts may have been established between Egypt and the Indus, but the identification of wood from South Asia in Egypt has yet to be confirmed. The arrival of Asian millet *Panicum miliaceum* L. in Yemen during the third millennium, however, represents a crucial event. As pointed out, bronzeworking (implying the transport of metals, the use and trade of new weapons and tools) characterized the development of western Asia, part of Europe, and the Mediterranean Sea during the third millennium; conversely, Egypt fully adopted this alloy only from the eighteenth century BCE onward. The absence of the Egyptian unit of weight (13.4–13.5 g) in the Aegean Sea region during this period appears significant. The near-identical value represented by the Egyptian *deben*, the Dilmun shekel, and the Indusian unit of weight, however, is truly troubling. Inscribed weights dated to Snefru's reign (2639–2589) reflect a unit between 13 and 13.6 g, and a dozen types of inscribed weights dated to between the Fourth and Sixth Dynasties, show an average unit of 13.92 g (Rahmstorf 2006a: 14–16).[21] The name

---

[19] In addition, access to raw materials was a limiting factor. Ratnagar (2001b: 363) notes significant differences between regions in the use of tin bronze; she feels that these differences argue in favor of the existence of a world-system.

[20] Kristiansen and Larsson (2005: 41) rightly point out that "the artisan is a connoisseur of secrets, a magician"; his work often implies particular rituals. Artisans also migrated voluntarily.

[21] Several authors have pondered the existence of a gold *deben* of 13.6 g during the Old Kingdom; it would have weighed almost the same as the Dilmun shekel (13.68 g), or twice the weight of the Harappan standard weight (6.84 g) (Warburton 2003: 71; Hafford 2005: 359; Rahmstorf 2006a). S. Allam (p.c.) may be wrong when he claims that the available texts do not confirm the existence of such a *deben*. Peet (1934: 199) had already expressed skepticism concerning the interpretation of the sign that led to attributing 13/14 g to the Egyptian *deben*. Goedicke (1977), however, describes an "object of slightly irregular rectangular shape, made of brown stone," bearing on one of its faces the inscription "Overseer of works K3-tp, 2 deben." This object, which weighs 28.2 g, would represent 2 *deben*, therefore one *deben* here would

deben was used at least starting in the Fifth Dynasty (as revealed by an inscription in a tomb at Saqqara) (Rahmstorf 2006a: 16). During the Middle Kingdom, weights found at Uronarti, in Nubia, reflect a unit varying between 12.2 and 14.42 g. It appears that during the second millennium, the unit of weight at Ugarit (Levant) (the mina) was related to the systems of weight used in Egypt and western Asia; it would also appear that systems of conversion for weights already existed between the Indus and the eastern Mediterranean during the second half of the third millennium.[22] Might a comparison between the size of the Mesopotamian and that of the Egyptian empires shed light on the link between these two regions? The study by Chase-Dunn and Hall shows a discrepancy from 2500 to 2300 (the Egyptian Empire reached its peak between 2500 and 2400, whereas the Akkadian Empire was formed in Mesopotamia around 2300) and opposite tendencies in the two regions during the early second millennium BCE (the Egyptian Empire grew while Mesopotamia, at the same time, was experiencing a phase of political disintegration in 1900 BCE) (see Chase-Dunn and Hall 2000: 106 fig. 4.9). New research based on Modelski's data (2003) does not reveal any significant synchronism between the growth and decline of cities or empires between Egypt and Mesopotamia prior to 600 BCE [23] (conversely, synchronism appears to be the rule starting in 600 BCE). Political data thus do not seem to support the idea of a "fusion of the Mesopotamian and Egyptian civilizations" into a "central civilization," during the Bronze Age – at least during the third millennium.[24] Egypt and Mesopotamia are not readily comparable, however. Data on states and cities can be misleading; first, there is not always a connection between economic growth and political concentration; secondly, knowledge about Egyptian cities is far from satisfactory. Hansen (2002: 13) distinguishes three cycles of city-states in Mesopotamia from the second half of the third millennium onward: between the Akkadian Empire and the Ur III Empire (2200–2110), during the Isin-Larsa period (after Ur III) (2004–1800), and during the Ancient Neo-Babylonian period after the collapse of the Kassite dynasty (1100–750). Did these cycles correspond to periods of economic recession, or not? The answer appears to be positive for the first cycle, inconclusive for the third, but it is certainly negative for the second cycle: at the start of the second millennium, the fragmentation of political power in western Asia went along with intense economic activity, in the Persian Gulf, southern Mesopotamia, and northern Mesopotamia, with the flowering of the Assyrian trading outposts in Anatolia and networks bringing in tin and lapis lazuli from Central Asia and Afghanistan.

Moreover, I diverge from Frank's and Thompson's appreciation of the phases of the Mesopotamia–Indus system. I consider that the periods 2600–2200 and 2200–1900

---

weigh 14.1 g (in the Old Kingdom the *deben* varied from 13.3 to 14.1 g). Thus the question of a connection between Egypt and an international system remains an open one.

[22] Mederos and Lamberg-Karlovsky 2004: 201–204. The mina and the shekel were "weight-metrological terms," and monetary terms (Powell 1996: 226).

[23] Chase-Dunn *et al.* 2006: 129. Following Wilkinson, the authors consider, however, that "the Mesopotamian and Egyptian interstate systems merged around 1500 BC to become a larger single system of states that we call the Central System" (2006: 115).

[24] Bosworth 2000: 273. Frank and Thompson (2006: 142) note: "The expansion and contraction phases were not always found to be Afro-Eurasian wide," an admission implying that several distinct systems did coexist.

were phases of both expansion (2600–2250, and 2100–2025) and recession (2250–2100 and 2025–1900), although the period 2200–1900 shows declining activity overall when compared to preceding centuries (we can speak of a rebound during the twenty-first century, within a long phase of recession). As pointed out, the Akkadian Empire and the Old Egyptian kingdom disappeared *c.* 2200 BCE, partly due to sharp and prolonged climatic deterioration – marked by a weakening of the monsoon system in the Indian Ocean – which led to famines and movements of populations.[25] This climate change affected Turkmenistan[26] and the terrestrial routes of Iran. The dramatic disruptions of this period did not lead to the complete collapse of the Mesopotamia–Indus world-system, but rather to its restructuring, with a shrinking of the West Asian core and a decline in exchanges along the terrestrial routes crossing Iran from east to west (see Map 1.14). At the same time, exchanges increased between Margiana–Bactria on the one hand, and the Indus valley and Persian Gulf on the other. It is interesting to note that data from Lake Van reveal a short period of increased precipitation between sharply arid phases *c.* 2200 and 2000 BCE (Wicks *et al.* 2003): a climatic improvement in western Asia may have fostered a (limited) rebound corresponding to the period of expansion of the Ur III Empire (if Ur III is correctly dated to this period; see below). Moreover, active trade continued along the maritime routes of the Persian Gulf, until the collapse of the Indus civilization in the nineteenth century and even slightly later. The Indus Valley experienced a marked process of de-urbanization at this time, which seems, however, to have affected the Gujarat region to a lesser extent. While climatic changes were not the only cause for this collapse, it is clear that a phenomenon of weak monsoons did affect many regions of the Indian Ocean around 2000 BCE, accompanied by aridification, and leading to population movements.

In the western part of the world-system also, during the twenty-third century, movements of populations took place from Central and eastern Europe towards western Asia. We do not know whether or not these displacements were responsible for the destruction of the cities of Poliochni and Troy II. These movements led to a period of increased contacts between the eastern Mediterranean Sea and Central Europe. The use of tin bronze spread into Central Europe, the British Isles, and southern Spain (El Argar)[27] as of the late third millennium (tin bronze, however, was

---

[25] Many studies have demonstrated the magnitude of the climatic changes between 2200 and 1900 BCE. Bond *et al.* (1997) point to a cold peak in the North Atlantic around 2200 BCE. Cf. also Nadis 2001. Staubwasser and Weiss (2006) assign a duration of at least 300 years, from 2200 to 1900 BCE, to an arid phase in the eastern Mediterranean and in regions of the Indian Ocean affected by weaker monsoons. For East Africa, Thompson *et al.* 2002. Also H. M. Cullen *et al.* 2000. For western Asia, Chase-Dunn *et al.* (2006: 114, 124) have rightly pointed out the role of semi-nomadic pastoralists and semi-peripheral groups in the processes of integration and disintegration of the systems. Climatic changes create an imbalance in the relationships between (semi-)nomads and sedentary populations living in the core of the system. Note that Wang *et al.* (2005) identify a long phase of weak Asian monsoons between 2400 and 1900 BCE. For China, see An and Cullen *et al.* (2005) and W. Shaowu (2006), who indicate an aridification of northern China, Gansu, Qinghai, and Inner Mongolia from 2100 to 1800 BCE. See also Brooke 2014: 292ff.

[26] Further north, one notes a sharp arid phase around 2000 BCE in part of the Eurasian steppes. The steppes may have experienced a cooler and more arid climate after 2500 BCE (Anthony 2007: 389). It would be necessary, however, to study the ways in which each region evolved.

[27] In the Argaric culture, however, tin bronzes represent only a minority of the bronze artifacts, with arsenical bronze being more common. One notes also the circulation of tin beads in Europe during

present *c.* 2500 BCE in Hungary, brought in via a trade route passing through Troy to the Danube Valley). Moreover, the spread of the technologically innovative spoked-wheel chariot, appearing at the end of the third millennium in the steppes, led to growing mobility for the populations of these regions. The chariot spread into western Asia, into the Aegean world, and into western Europe (along with the horse) during the first half of the second millennium.

For Mesopotamia, the middle chronology is used here, although it is being contested nowadays by a number of authors. Following Gasche *et al.*'s theory (1998), Warburton (2007b) thus places the Akkadian Empire between 2190 and 2050, and Ur III between 2019 and 1911 BCE. The ultra-short chronology adopted here largely breaks the correlations established between climate variations and some collapses (the Egyptian Empire, *c.* 2180, and the Akkadian Empire, for example), but other synchronisms then appear: the end of the Ur III Empire would coincide with the end of the Indus civilization (cf. also Possehl 2002a: 23). With this ultra-short chronology, it is harder to explain the formation of the first empire within a period of global recession, but we can imagine Sargon being led to use military means after the ancient order was thwarted by declining trade. It is true also that the emphasis on global cooling and climate aridification around 2200 fails to explain why the Indus civilization seems to have been little affected by this episode (lower Nile flood levels were necessarily correlated with a weakening of the Indian Ocean summer monsoon system, which should have affected the region of the Indus Valley). Moreover, the simultaneous flourishing of the empire of Ur III, Bahrain, and the Indus region during the twentieth century BCE makes perfect sense within the framework of the ultra-short chronology.[28]

Most researchers in any case would agree on the fact that the early second millennium represented a turning point (A. Sherratt 2006b).[29] A new world-system was formed, marked by a shift in the center of gravity toward the Mediterranean Sea and continental Europe on the one side, and the Horn of Africa on the other, foreshadowing the Late Bronze Age situation and the developments of the first millennium BCE. The Mesopotamia–Indus world-system disintegrated when the contacts of Sumer with Meluḫha faded out at the close of the twentieth century BCE. There remained a more limited area whose core was southern Mesopotamia, a region turned toward the Persian Gulf. Mesopotamian networks extended as far as Bahrain, which maintained some contacts with the Gujarat and experienced a "spectacular expansion" (Crawford

the second millennium (Primas 2002; Kristiansen and Larsson 2005: 112). Some tin bronzes appear in northeastern and northwestern Spain during the mid-third millennium; they came from ore naturally containing a mixture of copper and tin (Rovira and Montero 2003). Tin bronzes have also been discovered in the Corded Ware culture and the Bell-Beaker culture (third millennium) (Pare 2000: 22). Lastly, for the Argaric culture, the presence of ivory at many sites reveals contacts with North Africa.

[28] Warburton (2007b: 15) emphasizes the reduction of military activity during the early second millennium. The Ur III Empire, however, was active on the military level. Warburton also claims that "there is no trace of a major alteration in China" (2007b: 18) at the time of the Indus collapse. In fact, various Chinese neolithic cultures disappeared during this time (2000/1900 BCE).

[29] For this millennium, the comparison of cycles suggested by Frank and Gills (1993a) with Chandler's (1987) data on the number and size of cities reveals the difficulties we encounter for periods prior to the Christian era (Bosworth 1995: 226). Chandler's data here appear to be unsatisfactory, partly due to some discrepancies between economic growth and political centralization in western Asia.

1998: 61). Connections with Oman were notably weaker than they had been during the previous period. This sphere was linked to a much larger, multi-centered[30] area encompassing northern Mesopotamia, Anatolia, Greece and the Aegean Sea, Crete,[31] and Egypt (for the first time united with the western Asian world-system)[32] (see Map 1.15). The northern region of the system included the Caucasus, where metallurgic production increased. Tin roads partly controlled by the elite of the BMAC (since the end of the third millennium) may explain the spread of objects and artistic motifs between the Mediterranean and Central Asia, until the disappearance of the BMAC during the seventeenth century BCE.

A number of Amorite dynasties were founded in Mesopotamia (Isin, Larsa, Babylon) by semi-nomads who had lived in Syria during the third millennium (one of the many examples in history in which people coming from a semi-periphery take over the power in a core). The formation of Hammurabi's empire (1792–1750 BCE) (middle chronology) brought to political fruition a fragile and ephemeral unification of both the southern and northern Mesopotamian areas. Egypt exhibited contacts with Crete[33] and Syria; these contacts explain the presence of Babylonian products and lapis lazuli in the treasure of Tôd (Karnak), under the reign of Amenemhat II. This treasure also contained three seals of East Iranian origin, which may have come by land but also via a maritime route circumnavigating Arabia. Between the third and second millennia, in western Asia, gold value diminished as compared to silver, because the Egyptian gold arrived in greater quantities and the demand in silver rose, parallel to its monetary use (Egypt included).[34] The reference to a silver standard in a country which had no resources for this metal – Egyptian silver derived from long-distance trade – shows the integration of Middle Kingdom Egypt with western Asia.

Toward the south, the Egyptian expeditions marked a phase of integration with the Red Sea, which would later accelerate during the Late Bronze Age (an opposite movement of decline was observed in the Persian Gulf). Egypt was more closely linked with Sudan and Ethiopia, while littoral societies established exchanges in the Red Sea, the importance of which may have been significantly underestimated.[35] The journeys of cultivated plants from Africa to India (pearl millet, sorghum, cowpea, castor oil plant) during the first half of the second millennium reflect the setting up of long-distance

---

[30] This phenomenon of pluri-centered cores (here, in western Asia) is not limited to ancient times: one observes it in India from the end of the first millennium BCE onward.

[31] One notes an expansion of Cretan palatial activities in the Aegean Sea during the period 1950–1900 (Broodbank 2000: 317ff.).

[32] Some researchers see Egypt as the center of a system linked, but not integrated into the Mesopotamia–eastern Mediterranean system. Ekholm Friedman thus contemplates the existence of several smaller systems during the early second millennium (2005: 53).

[33] The states of Minoan Crete, which formed around 2000 BCE, traded with Egypt, and also with Cyprus, the Levant, and Anatolia. The script called Linear A appeared at this time. The status of the Minoan states can be debated: did they form a semi-periphery, or a periphery of western Asia and Egypt (Parkinson and Galaty 2007)? These authors consider that the Minoan states represent a semi-periphery only from c. 1680 BCE onward.

[34] Silver value diminished once again, at least in southern Mesopotamia, during the Old Babylonian period (Warburton 2003: 59).

[35] The discovery of a pendant perhaps made of copal in a tomb near Baghdad, dated to 2500–2400 BCE, may imply contacts with East Africa (see above).

networks including southern Arabia, the Horn of Africa, and western India (Gujarat) (some discoveries may even go back to the Harappan period, at the end of the third millennium). Such networks may have been linked to commerce in spices and aromatics. The Indian zebu was probably introduced in Africa at this time. If this were confirmed, the surprising discovery of cloves from the Moluccas at Terqa (Euphrates) c. 1700–1600 BCE would reveal even more distant contacts between Southeast Asia, India, and the Persian Gulf. As for the Post-Harappan Indian world-system which was centered on Gujarat, it disappeared during the eighteenth century BCE, giving way to a vast sphere of interaction connected to Arabia and the Persian Gulf.

The shift of western Asia's center of gravity toward the northwest was a relatively unprecedented event. Accompanied by the rapid spread of bronzeworking, Europe's internal transformation and growing interconnection with the western world-system yielded an even newer situation.[36] As early as the beginning of the fourth millennium, however, available data show a Mesopotamia divided into two regions:[37] southern Mesopotamia, oriented toward the Persian Gulf and Susiana, and northern Mesopotamia, connected to Anatolian networks, northern Iran, the Syrian coast, and the eastern Mediterranean (Babylonia occupied a quasi-central position between these two spaces [Margueron 2004]). Except during the period 3100–2700 BCE, these two regions were united within one system, dominated either by the south (Urukian system, Akkadian Empire, Old Babylonian Empire) or by the north (Late Bronze Age): for part of the Bronze Age, western Asia therefore appears to have been a multicentered core, with power oscillating among different centers (see Table I.Con.4).[38]

---

[36] Interconnections already existed between Greece, the Aegean world, the Adriatic, and the Carpathian mountains during the third millennium (Kristiansen and Larsson 2005: 120), but they were sporadic and of low intensity. A. Sherratt (1994b and d) is correct in observing that Europe remained on the margin of the system and was not a periphery during the second millennium. The spread of bronze is of great importance because this metal was not only technically useful, but also potentially usable in a wide variety of transactions (A. Sherratt 1994b: 338). It may have constituted a form of "proto-money" (A. Sherratt 1994a), as shown by the large spread of annular Ösenring ingots from central Europe that are found at Ugarit and at Byblos, as well as the many "caches" of lumps of metal dated in particular from 1600 BCE. Bronze enabled the development of new forms of long-distance trade. C. F. E Pare (2000) speaks of a "European Metallurgic Province" (parallel to Chernykh's "Circumpontic Metallurgical Province"). At the same time, other techniques spread from the Mediterranean world into continental Europe, such as faience beads, discovered in Slovakia, France, Spain, and the British Isles from the early twentieth century BCE. These beads were often locally produced. Glass bead production would develop later, during the Late Bronze Age (Pare 2000: 33 n. 10; Harding 2000: 268). Northern Italy shows connections with the Aegean world as early as the first half of the second millennium (Barfield 1994: 139). In addition, it is possible that the technique of shipbuilding in the Baltic Sea benefited from influences from the Mediterranean Sea (Kristiansen 1998).

[37] While Frank (1993a) did not note it, Frank and Thompson (2006: 143) have pointed out that "the network structure shifted further west" during the second millennium. Stein (2004), Frangipane (2004a), and M. S. Rothman (2001a, 2004) – among others – have observed the existence, during the early first part of the fourth millennium, of a "northern Mesopotamia–Anatolia" sphere of interaction, which developed in parallel to the southern Mesopotamian system.

[38] Cf. the remark already noted by Sherratt and Sherratt 1993: 418. In addition, the Sumerian Royal List reveals an oscillation of power between the northern and southern regions of lower Mesopotamia.

Table I.Con.4 *Two regions of Mesopotamia*

	Northern Mesopotamia–Anatolia Levant–eastern Mediterranean	Southern Mesopotamia–Persian Gulf
4000–3600	Chiefdoms, city-states	City-states (and/or country-state?)
3600–3100	——Urukian world-system————	
3100–2340	Chiefdoms, city-states	City-states
2340–2200	—— Akkadian Empire —————	
2100–2000	City-states, states of limited size	Ur III Empire
2000–1780	City-states, states of limited size Assyrian tradeposts in Anatolia	City-states (Isin-Larsa period)
1792–1750	———— Hammurabi's Babylonian Empire ———	
1600–1200	Hittite Empire, Mitanni, Assyrian Empire, Mycenaean Empire, Egypt	Kassite Empire

After Hammurabi, the Babylonian Empire went into decline due to invasions and internal problems,[39] and the world-system disintegrated. The two periods of the Middle Bronze and the Late Bronze Age appear to be clearly separated by disturbances occurring *c.* 1750 BCE and continuing over the following century (Van de Mieroop [2002: 78] writes that "the Dark Age that characterizes the 17th and 16th centuries encompassed the entire Near East"). Disorders in Anatolia caused a breakdown in relations between Assyria and Cappadocia. Kassites from the Zagros entered Mesopotamia around 1740 BCE, possibly along with Proto-Indian groups. In the eastern part of the "central system," upheavals were partly linked to the expansion of the Bactria–Margiana Complex and, globally, to climatic changes leading to complex movements of population, in Pakistan, western Asia, and Egypt.[40] The culture of the BMAC itself disappeared *c.* 1700 BCE. The downturn in trade in the Persian Gulf at the end of the eighteenth century and during the seventeenth century triggered the collapse of Bahrain and went along with network restructuring, around an arc composed of Egypt, the Levant, northern Mesopotamia, Anatolia, Greece, and Crete. In Egypt, the Hyksos domination fostered new contacts and innovations. It also led to the "invention" of an alphabetic script which would be transmitted into Palestine, where it would be further developed (Lemaire 2007). It is significant that exports of Cypriot copper increased from the eighteenth century on, precisely at a time when Omani copper stopped reaching Mesopotamia. During the seventeenth and sixteenth centuries, the thrust of the world-system toward the northwest was accompanied by increased contacts between not only the eastern Mediterranean Sea and the Carpathian mountains, which were a source of gold, copper, and perhaps men (mercenaries or slaves), but also the Russian steppes, provider of horses. Exchange networks

[39] Internal and external factors are fundamentally linked, for each period. Their combination is part of the movement and logic of the system.

[40] Climate change appears to have affected various regions of Asia at this time (eighteenth–seventeenth century BCE). Schettler *et al.* (2006: 1055) thus note a weakening of the East Asian monsoon around 1700 BCE. Chernykh (1992: 305) points to a period of turmoil in Inner Asia between the eighteenth and sixteenth centuries BCE.

extended as far as the Baltic Sea, where local groups traded amber and furs. Tin from
Central Asia arrived with more difficulty in western Asia and in the Mediterranean
around the end of the eighteenth century (as already mentioned, the BMAC collapsed
c. 1700); this collapse led the powers of this region to look for other sources of supply,
such as Tuscany, the Erzgebirge Mountains (Central Europe), and the Iberian peninsula.
Moreover, tin from Cornwall – already exploited during the early second millennium –
probably reached the Mediterranean Sea, through middlemen. These contacts would
increase during the Late Bronze Age. Inside Europe, long-distance exchange networks
which were connected to the Mediterranean Sea developed as of the first quarter of
the second millennium (Pare 2000: 32).

The correlations noted between climatic changes from 1750 BCE onward[41] and socio-
political transformations, however, would partly break down if Gasche's ultra-short
chronology were adopted (cf. Warburton 2007b). Hammurabi's empire (1696–1654
BCE) would have flourished during the last part of the global cooling, a phenomenon we
do not perceive through the texts known to us. The Egyptian New Kingdom would
have emerged at the same time as the Hittite Empire, *c.* 1550 BCE, the latter causing the
fall of Babylon in 1499. If this ultra-short chronology were adopted, we should have to
ask ourselves if the effects of the colder periods have not been exaggerated or too hastily
geographically generalized. Conversely, the risk exists of underestimating the dependence of ancient states on their economic bases and therefore their fragility in times of
climate change. And have these periods of global cooling been dated correctly?

Dislocations and network restructuring led to the formation of a multicentered
Afro-Eurasian system during the Late Bronze Age; this included Egypt, northern
and southern Mesopotamia, Anatolia (Hittite Empire), and a Mycenaean area which
took advantage of its location between western Asia and the eastern Mediterranean Sea
on the one side, and an up-and-coming Europe on the other (see Map 1.16).
An increasing demand for metals stimulated a Minoan and then a Mycenaean expansion: from the fifteenth century on, the Mycenaean networks asserted their presence in
the eastern Mediterranean Sea and extended it to the western Mediterranean,[42] which
was connected to amber and tin routes. These routes appear to have adopted the
Mycenaean and then Cypro-Levantine systems of weights (for southern Spain).[43]

---

[41]   Brooke (2014: 298) places the crisis at a later date, "between 1700 and 1500 BC." Climate change was
       accompanied by the spread of plague: bubonic plague may have arrived in Egypt from India before 1600
       BCE, "following a chain of maritime linkages that probably originated in China" (Brooke 2014: 298).

[42]   A dislocation of the exchange networks through the Carpathian mountains, partly due to population
       movements, may have been another cause for the westward shift of these networks, starting in 1500 BCE
       (the Mycenaeans took control of Crete, at the same time, around 1450) (Kristiansen and Larsson 2005:
       127). For A. Sherratt (1994b), this shift of the exchanges reflects competition among various networks,
       particularly between one route following the Oder and another linking the north of the Alps and Jutland.
       Pare (2000: 29) argues that increases in production and exchanges from 1600 on led to a collapse of the
       system of control exercised by local elites and to a transformation of social relations on a continental
       European scale. The arrival of a cooler and wetter climate in part of Europe may also have played a role in
       the social transformations observed, with an expansion toward the east of the Tumulus culture, which
       initially developed in western central Europe (Kristiansen 1998).

[43]   The system of Mycenaean weights (with a shekel of 6.7–6.8 g) appears to have been adopted in Central
       Europe, northern Italy, and Scandinavia. Conversely, the treasures of Villena (southeastern Spain)
       (*c.* 1200 BCE?), Sagrajas and Berzocana (Spain), as well as rings from Ireland and Great Britain reveal

Map I.9   Spread of cultivated plants from Asia into Africa during the third and second millennia BCE

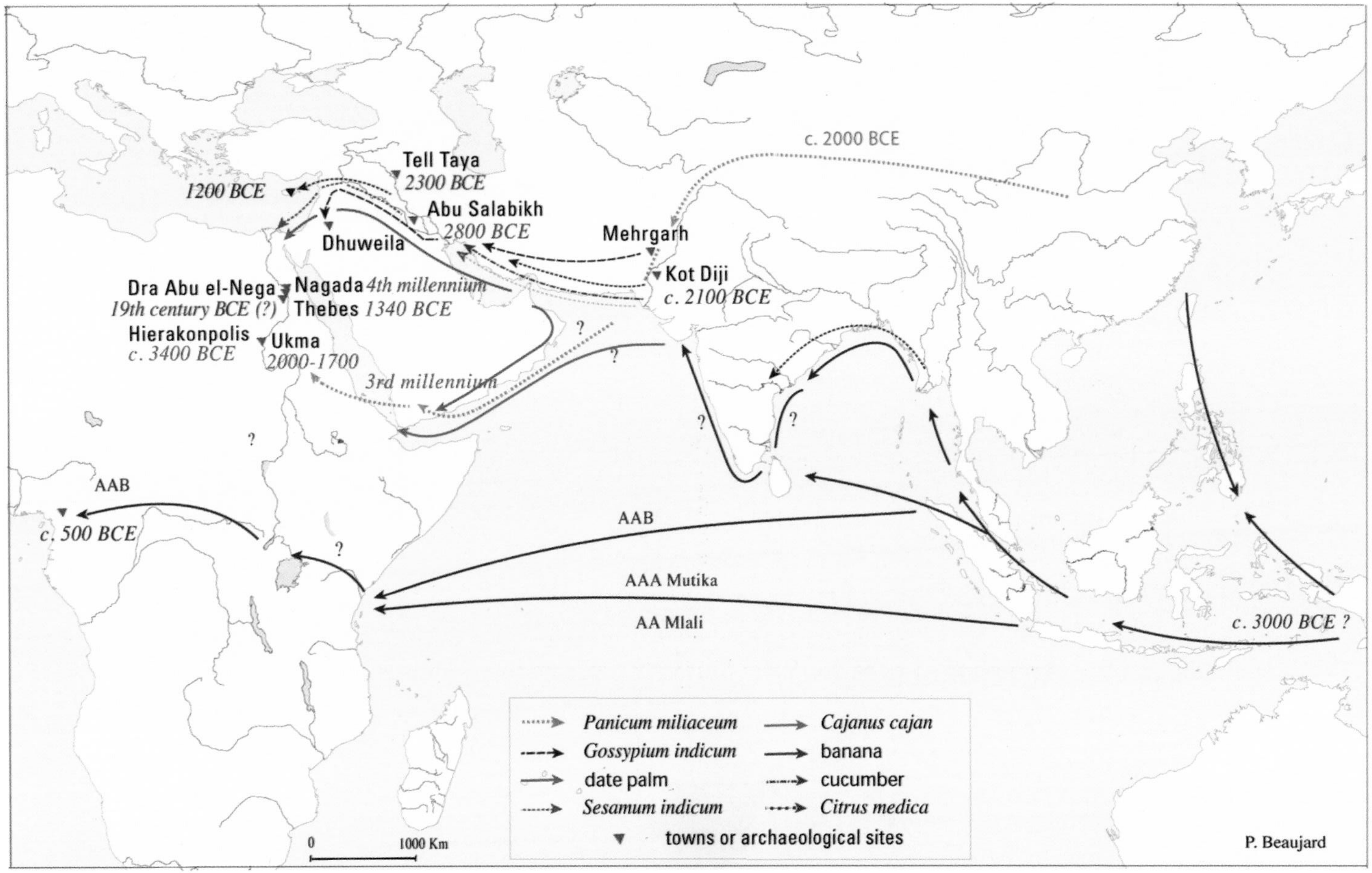

P. Beaujard

Tell Taya
2300 BCE

Abu Salabikh
c. 2800 BCE

Mehrgarh

Dhuweila

Kot Diji
c. 2100 BCE

Nagada *4th millennium*

Dra Abu el-Nega *(?)*
19th century BCE (?) Thebes *1340 BCE*

Hierakonpolis ▼ Ukma
c. 3400 BCE *2000-1700*

1200 BCE

1000 BCE

3rd millennium

c. 2000 BCE

c. 3000 BCE ?

AAB

AAA Mutika

AA Mlali

?

?

?

?

?

?

?

AAB
c. 500 BCE

Panicum miliaceum   *Cajanus cajan*
Grossypium indicum   banana
date palm   cucumber
Sesamum indicum   *Citrus medica*
▼ towns or archaeological sites

0   1000 Km

Map 1.10   Spread of cultivated plants from Africa into Asia during the third and second millennia BCE

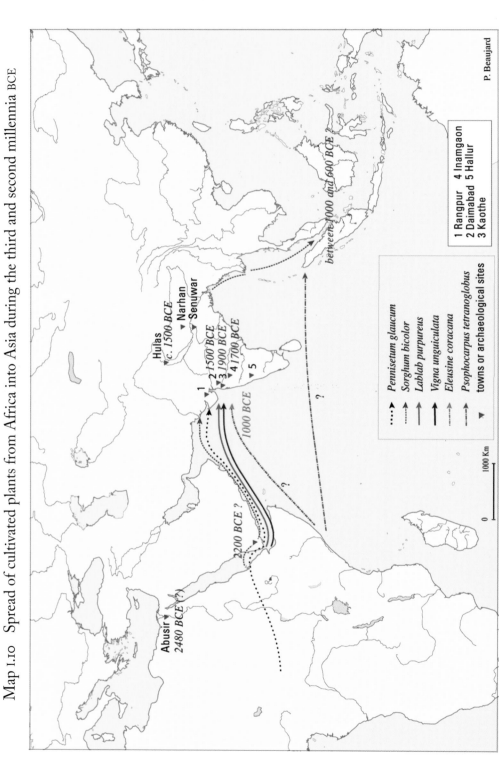

Abusir
2480 BCE (?)

2200 BCE ?

1000 BCE

Hulas
c. 1500 BCE
Narhan
Senuwar

1
2 1500 BCE
3 1900 BCE
4 1700 BCE
5

1000 BCE

?

?

between 1000 and 600 BCE ?

P. Beaujard

Pennisetum glaucum
Sorghum bicolor
Lablab purpureus
Vigna unguiculata
Eleusine coracana
Psophocarpus tetranoglobus
towns or archaeological sites

1 Rangpur   4 Inamgaon
2 Daimabad 5 Hallur
3 Kaothe

0   1000 Km

Map I.II   Western Asia and Egypt 3600–3100 BCE

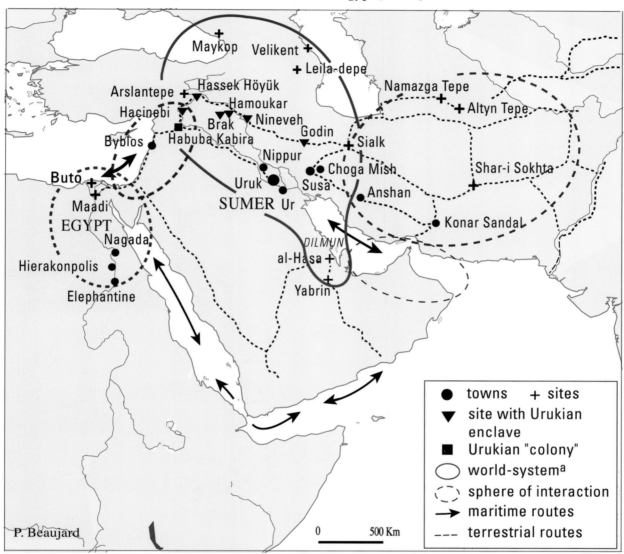

Maykop
Velikent
Leila-depe
Arslantepe   Hassek Höyük   Namazga Tepe
Haçinebi   Hamoukar   Altyn Tepe
Byblos   Brak   Nineveh
Habuba Kabira   Godin   Sialk
Nippur   Shar-i Sokhta
Buto   Uruk   Susa   Choga Mish
Maadi   SUMER   Ur   Anshan
EGYPT
Nagada   DILMUN   Konar Sandal
Hierakonpolis   al-Hasa
Elephantine   Yabrin

● towns	+ sites
▼	site with Urukian enclave
■	Urukian "colony"
◯	world-system[a]
⬭	sphere of interaction
→	maritime routes
- - -	terrestrial routes

0   500 Km

P. Beaujard

[a]The indiction of the boundaries of the world-system is just an approximation.

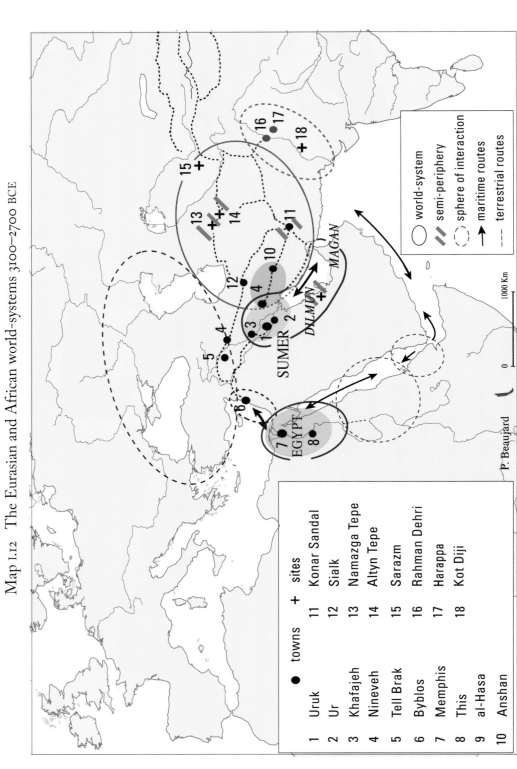

Map 1.12 The Eurasian and African world-systems 3100–2700 BCE

● towns		+ sites

1	Uruk	11	Konar Sandal
2	Ur	12	Sialk
3	Khafajeh	13	Namazga Tepe
4	Nineveh	14	Altyn Tepe
5	Tell Brak	15	Sarazm
6	Byblos	16	Rahman Dehri
7	Memphis	17	Harappa
8	This	18	Kot Diji
9	al-Hasa		
10	Anshan		

SUMER

DILMUN

MAGAN

EGYPT

◯	world-system
▨	semi-periphery
⬭	sphere of interaction
→	maritime routes
---	terrestrial routes

P. Beaujard

0   1000 Km

Map 1.13   The Eurasian and African world-systems 2700–2200 BCE

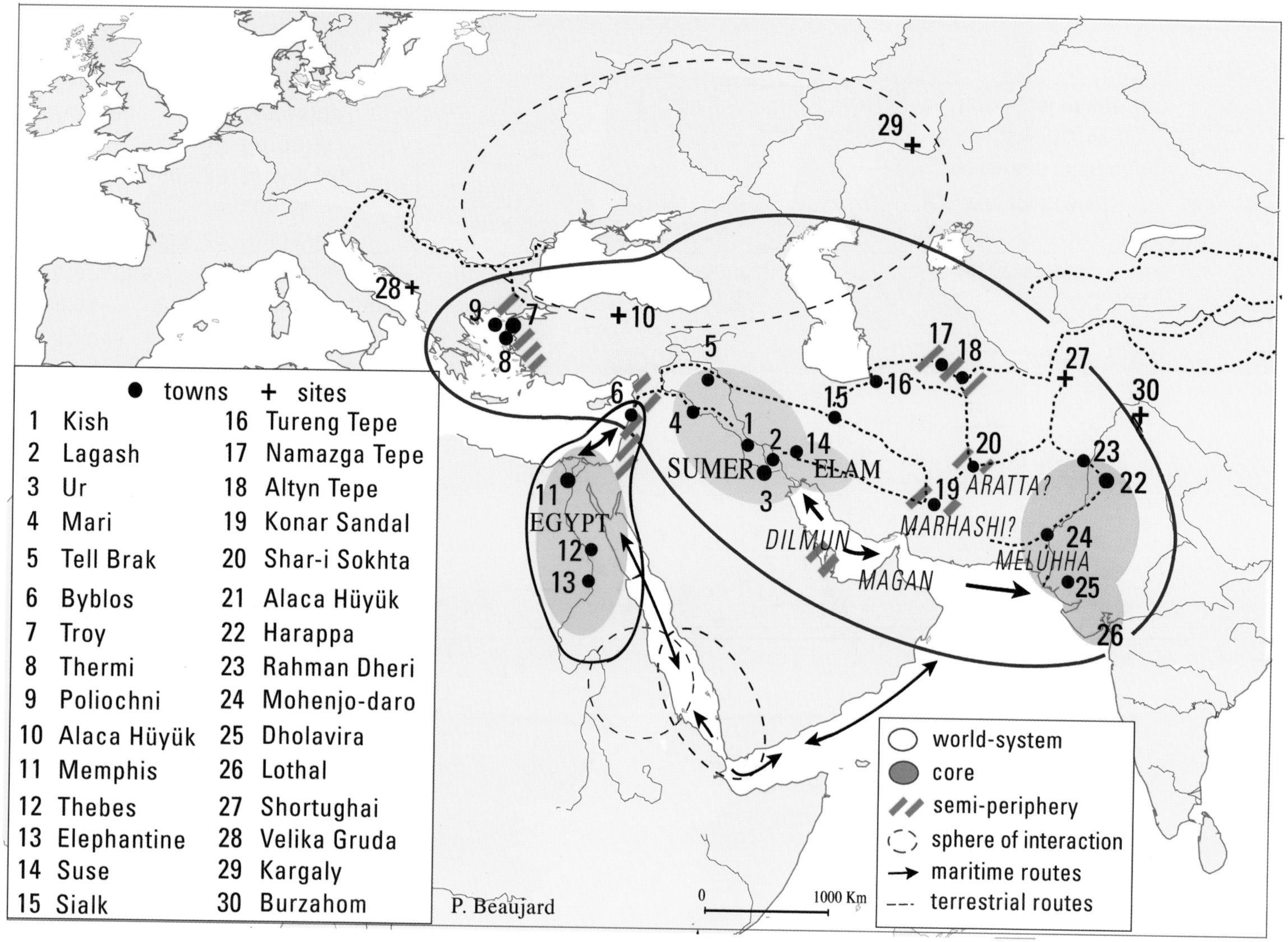

towns			
●	+ sites		
1	Kish	16	Tureng Tepe
2	Lagash	17	Namazga Tepe
3	Ur	18	Altyn Tepe
4	Mari	19	Konar Sandal
5	Tell Brak	20	Shar-i Sokhta
6	Byblos	21	Alaca Hüyük
7	Troy	22	Harappa
8	Thermi	23	Rahman Dheri
9	Poliochni	24	Mohenjo-daro
10	Alaca Hüyük	25	Dholavira
11	Memphis	26	Lothal
12	Thebes	27	Shortughai
13	Elephantine	28	Velika Gruda
14	Suse	29	Kargaly
15	Sialk	30	Burzahom

Legend:
- world-system
- core
- semi-periphery
- sphere of interaction
- maritime routes
- terrestrial routes

0   1000 Km

P. Beaujard

Labels on map: SUMER, ELAM, EGYPT, DILMUN, MAGAN, MARHASHI?, ARATTA?, MELUHHA?

Map 1.14 The Eurasian and African world-systems 2100–1950 BCE

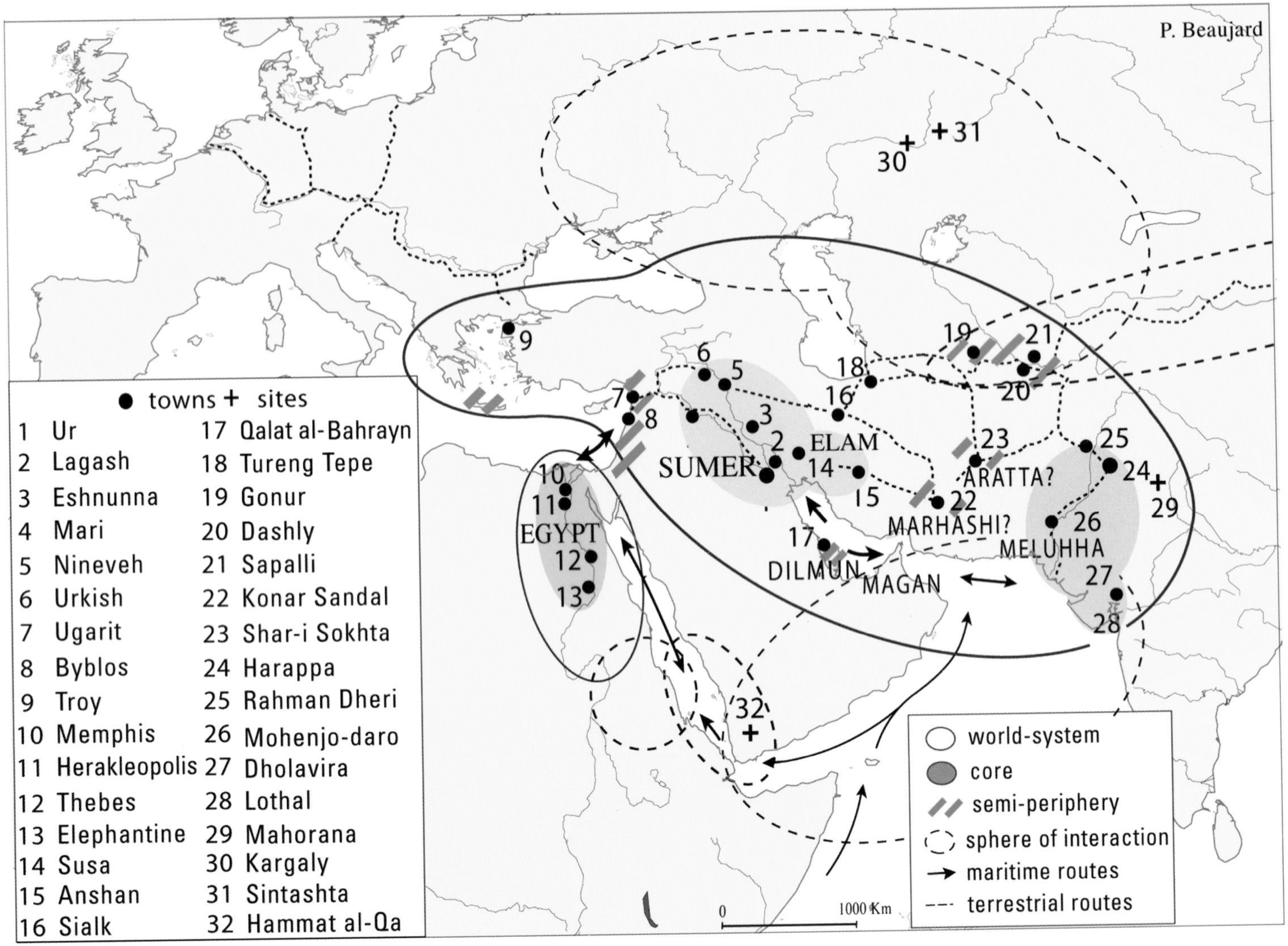

P. Beaujard

● towns + sites

Legend:
○ world-system
● core
semi-periphery
sphere of interaction
→ maritime routes
--- terrestrial routes

0   1000 Km

SUMER
ELAM
ARATTA?
MARHASHI?
MELUHHA
MAGAN
DILMUN
EGYPT

1 Ur
2 Lagash
3 Eshnunna
4 Mari
5 Nineveh
6 Urkish
7 Ugarit
8 Byblos
9 Troy
10 Memphis
11 Herakleopolis
12 Thebes
13 Elephantine
14 Susa
15 Anshan
16 Sialk
17 Qalat al-Bahrayn
18 Tureng Tepe
19 Gonur
20 Dashly
21 Sapalli
22 Konar Sandal
23 Shar-i Sokhta
24 Harappa
25 Rahman Dheri
26 Mohenjo-daro
27 Dholavira
28 Lothal
29 Mahorana
30 Kargaly
31 Sintashta
32 Hammat al-Qa

Map 1.15 The Afro-Eurasian world-system 1950–1700 BCE

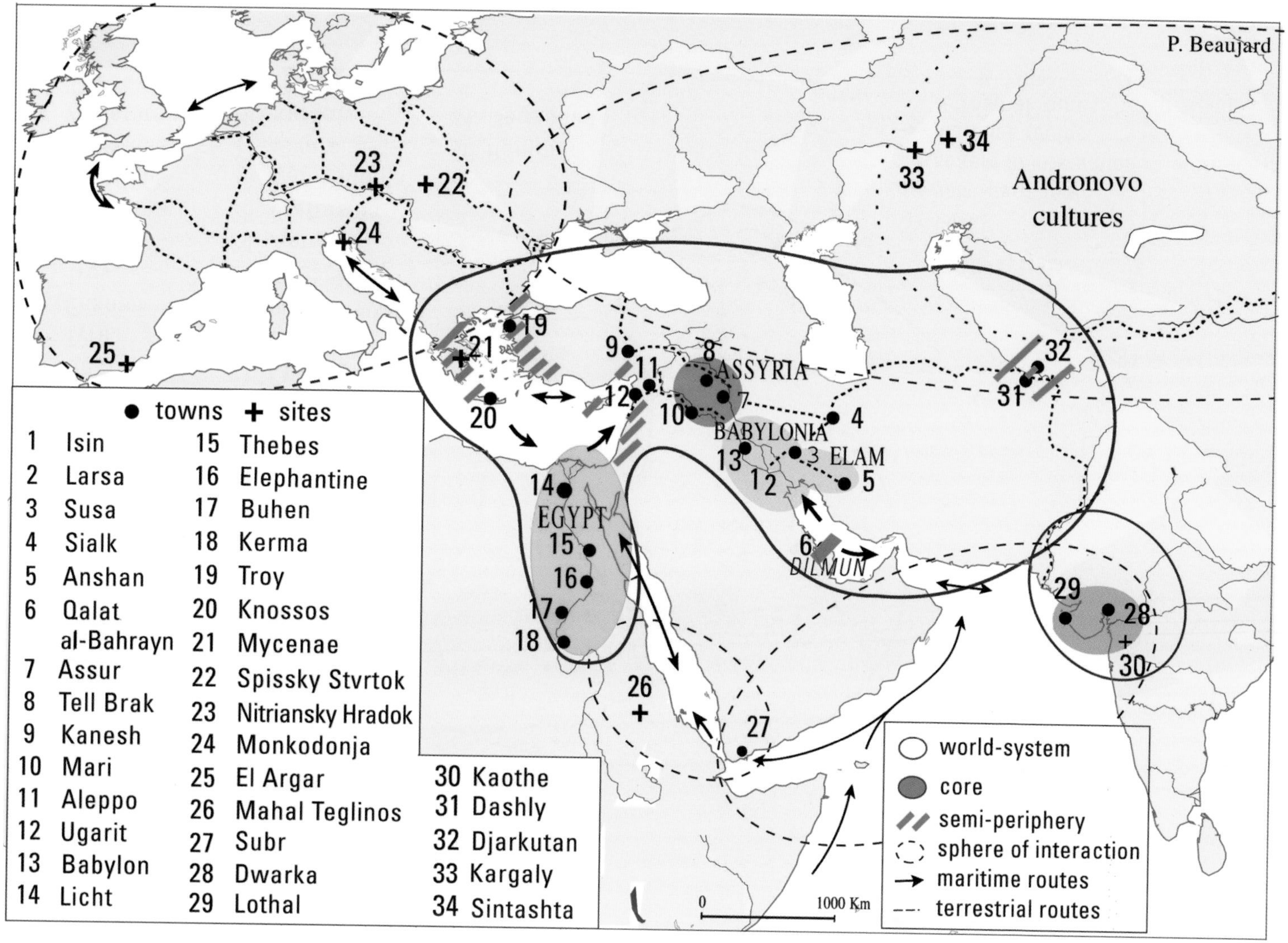

P. Beaujard

Andronovo
cultures

ASSYRIA
BABYLONIA
ELAM
DILMUN
EGYPT

		world-system
	●	core
	▨	semi-periphery
	⬭	sphere of interaction
	→	maritime routes
	----	terrestrial routes

0   1000 Km

●	towns	15	Thebes
+	sites		
1	Isin	15	Elephantine
2	Larsa	16	Buhen
3	Susa	17	Kerma
4	Sialk	18	Troy
5	Anshan	19	Knossos
6	Qalat	20	Mycenae
	al-Bahrayn	21	Spissky Stvrtok
7	Assur	22	Nitriansky Hradok
8	Tell Brak	23	Monkodonja
9	Kanesh	24	El Argar
10	Mari	25	Mahal Teglinos
11	Aleppo	26	Subr
12	Ugarit	27	Dwarka
13	Babylon	28	Lothal
14	Licht	29	
		30	Kaothe
		31	Dashly
		32	Djarkutan
		33	Kargaly
		34	Sintashta

Map 1.16 The Afro-Eurasian world-system 1600–1200 BCE

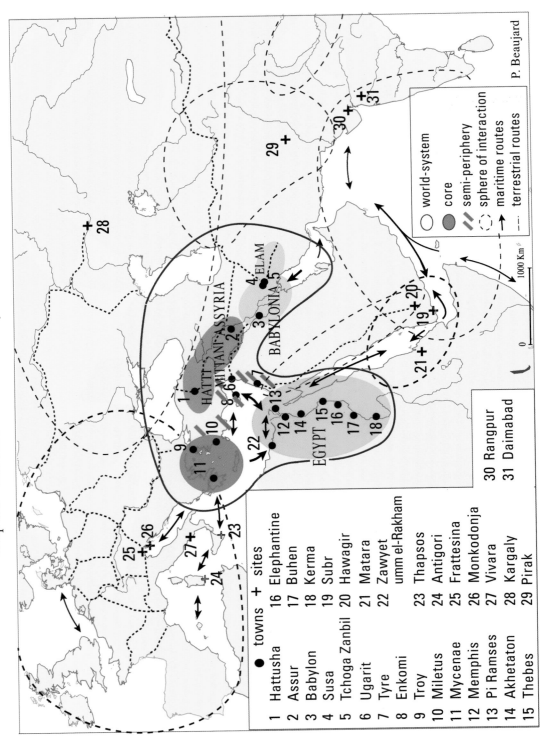

• towns	+ sites
1 Hattusha	16 Elephantine
2 Assur	17 Buhen
3 Babylon	18 Kerma
4 Susa	19 Subr
5 Tchoga Zanbil	20 Hawagir
6 Ugarit	21 Matara
7 Tyre	22 Zawyet
8 Enkomi	umm el-Rakham
9 Troy	23 Thapsos
10 Miletus	24 Antigori
11 Mycenae	25 Frattesina
12 Memphis	26 Monkodonja
13 Pi Ramses	27 Vivara
14 Akhetaton	28 Kargaly
15 Thebes	29 Pirak

30 Rangpur
31 Daimabad

HATTI
MITANNI·ASSYRIA
ELAM
BABYLONIA
EGYPT

world-system
core
semi-periphery
sphere of interaction
maritime routes
terrestrial routes

1000 Km

0

P. Beaujard

Map I.17   Eurasia and Africa at the end of the third and during the first third of the second millennium BCE

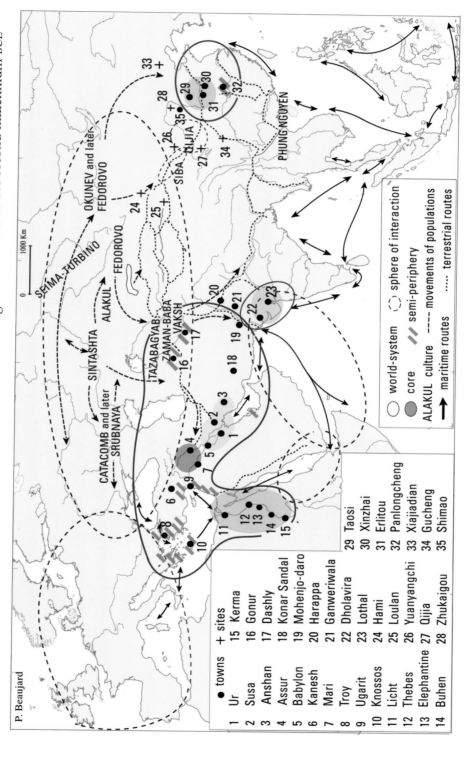

P. Beaujard

● towns   + sites

1	Ur	15	Kerma
2	Susa	16	Gonur
3	Anshan	17	Dashly
4	Assur	18	Konar Sandal
5	Babylon	19	Mohenjo-daro
6	Kanesh	20	Harappa
7	Mari	21	Ganweriwala
8	Troy	22	Dholavira
9	Ugarit	23	Lothal
10	Knossos	24	Hami
11	Licht	25	Loulan
12	Thebes	26	Yuanyangchi
13	Elephantine	27	Qijia
14	Buhen	28	Zhukaigou
		29	Taosi
		30	Xinzhai
		31	Erlitou
		32	Panlongcheng
		33	Xiajiadian
		34	Gucheng
		35	Shimao

Legend:

○ world-system   ⟲ sphere of interaction
⬡ semi-periphery
● core   ⫽ ALAKUL culture

○ world-system
● core

---- movements of populations
⋯⋯ terrestrial routes
↕ maritime routes

SEIMA-TURBINO
OKUNEV and later
FEDOROVO
ALAKUL
FEDOROVO
SINTASHTA
ALAKUL
CATACOMB and later
SRUBNAYA
TAZABAGYAB-
ZAMAN-BABA
VAKSH
SIBA
QIJIA
PHUNG-NGUYEN

0   1000 Km

Map 1.18 Eurasia and Africa 1600–1200 BCE

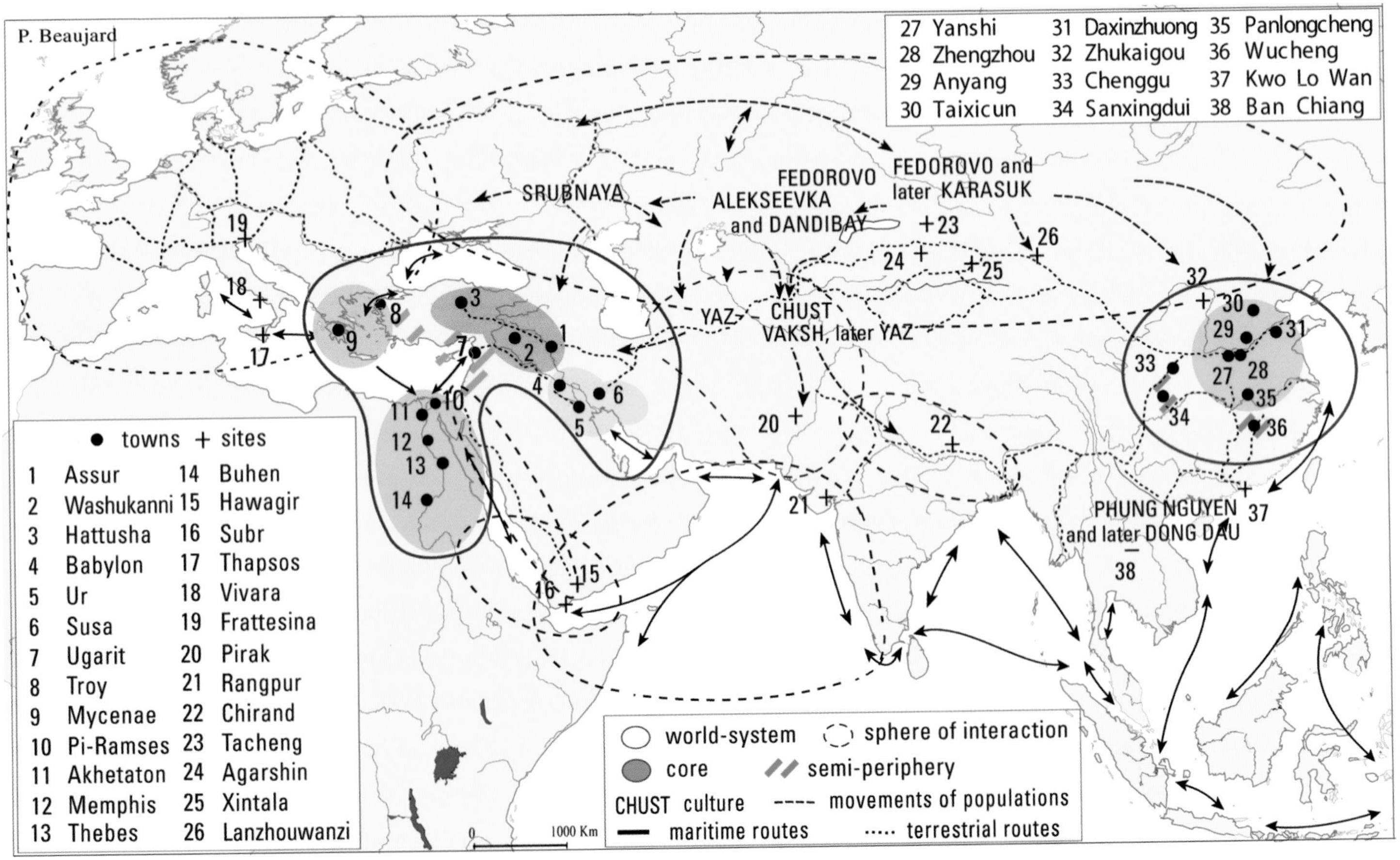

P. Beaujard

27	Yanshi	31	Daxinzhuong	35	Panlongcheng
28	Zhengzhou	32	Zhukaigou	36	Wucheng
29	Anyang	33	Chenggu	37	Kwo Lo Wan
30	Taixicun	34	Sanxingdui	38	Ban Chiang

FEDOROVO and later KARASUK

FEDOROVO
ALEKSEEVKA
and DANDIBAY

SRUBNAYA

YAZ-
CHUST
VAKSH, later YAZ

PHUNG NGUYEN
and later DONG DAU

● towns	+ sites		
1	Assur	14	Buhen
2	Washukanni	15	Hawagir
3	Hattusha	16	Subr
4	Babylon	17	Thapsos
5	Ur	18	Vivara
6	Susa	19	Frattesina
7	Ugarit	20	Pirak
8	Troy	21	Rangpur
9	Mycenae	22	Chirand
10	Pi-Ramses	23	Tacheng
11	Akhetaton	24	Agarshin
12	Memphis	25	Xintala
13	Thebes	26	Lanzhouwanzi

	world-system	◌ sphere of interaction
●	core	semi-periphery
	CHUST culture	- - - movements of populations
——	maritime routes	·········· terrestrial routes

0   1000 Km

Chart 1.Con.1   Bronze Age: climate changes, technological, institutional, and ideological innovations,
and political changes

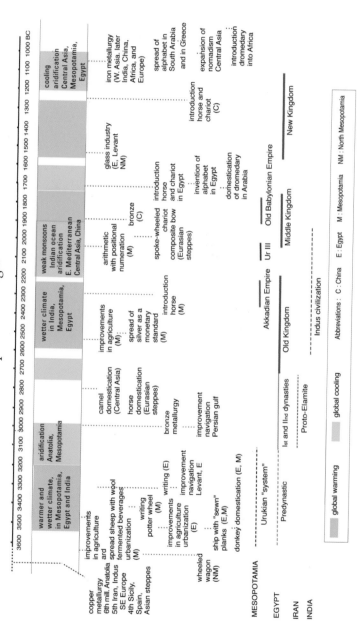

Map II.1 Eurasia and Africa during the sixth and fifth centuries BCE

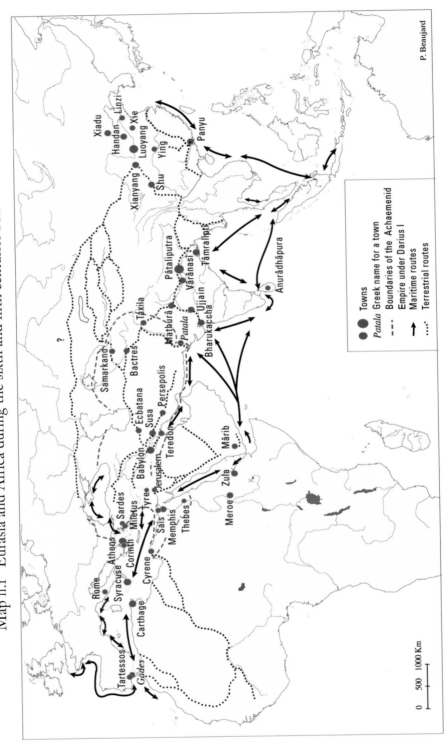

P. Beaujard

Towns

Patala Greek name for a town

- - - Boundaries of the Achaemenid Empire under Darius I
→ Maritime routes
····· Terrestrial routes

0   500 1000 Km

Map II.2 Eurasia and Africa during the third and second centuries BCE

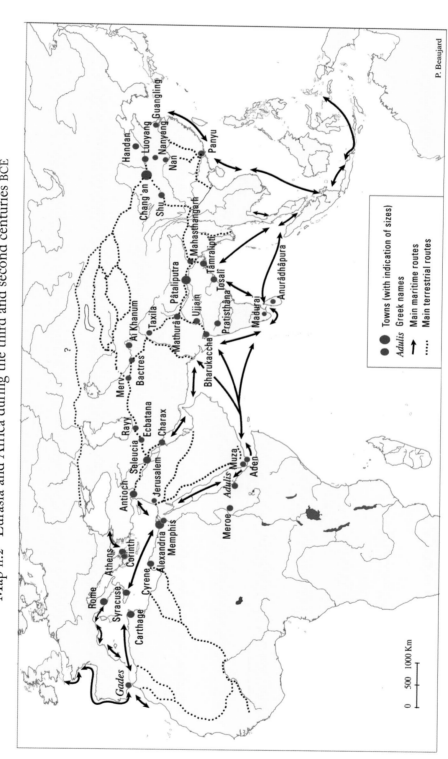

P. Beaujard

Chart II.3   Iron Age: climate changes, technological, institutional, and ideological innovations, and political changes

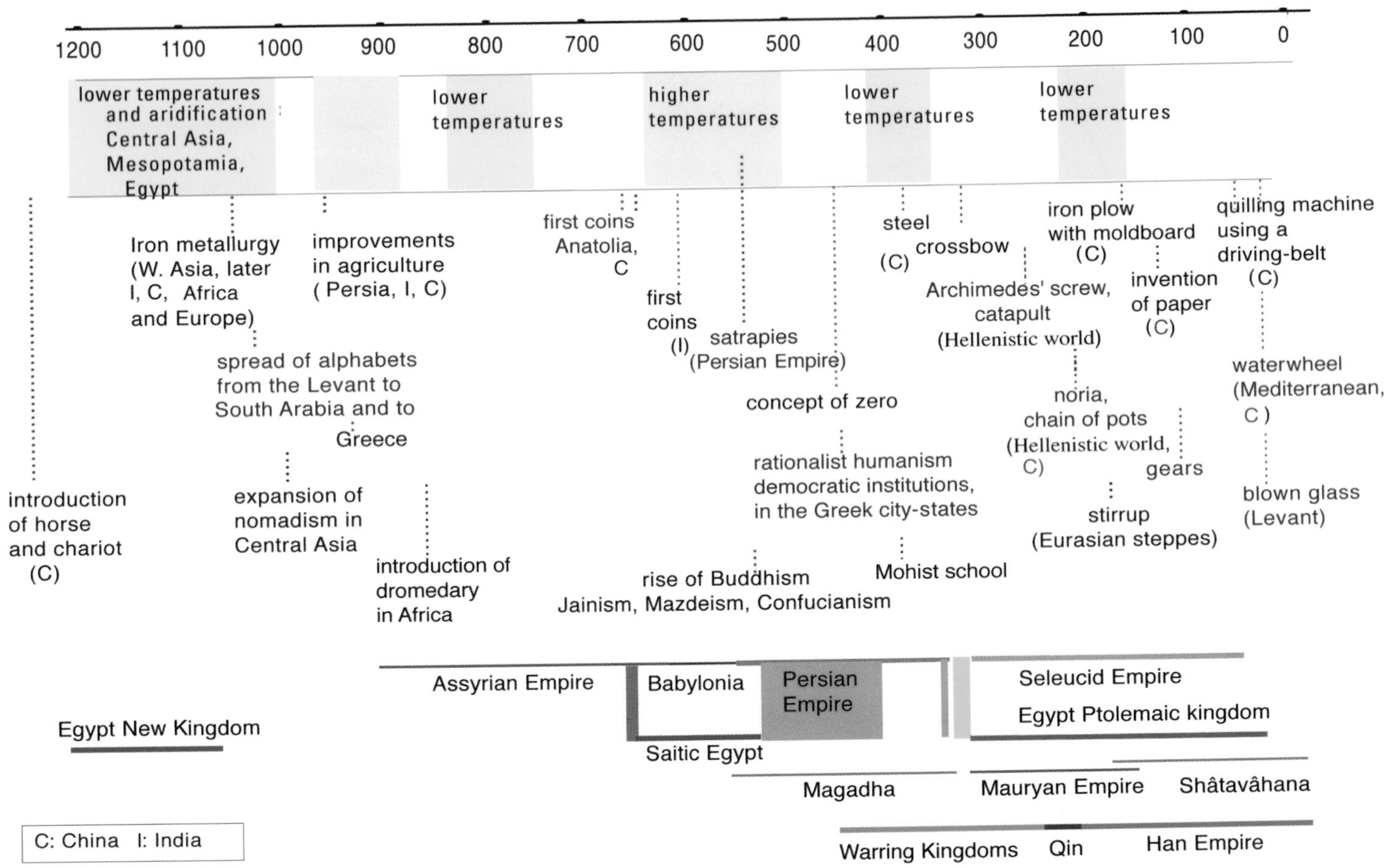

| 1200 | 1100 | 1000 | 900 | 800 | 700 | 600 | 500 | 400 | 300 | 200 | 100 | 0 |

lower temperatures and aridification Central Asia, Mesopotamia, Egypt

lower temperatures

higher temperatures

lower temperatures

lower temperatures

Iron metallurgy (W. Asia, later I, C, Africa and Europe)

improvements in agriculture (Persia, I, C)

spread of alphabets from the Levant to South Arabia and to Greece

first coins Anatolia, C

first coins (I)

satrapies (Persian Empire)

concept of zero

steel (C)

crossbow (C)

Archimedes' screw, catapult (Hellenistic world)

iron plow with moldboard (C)

invention of paper (C)

quilling machine using a driving-belt (C)

nòria, chain of pots (Hellenistic world, C)

gears

waterwheel (Mediterranean, C)

stirrup (Eurasian steppes)

blown glass (Levant)

expansion of nomadism in Central Asia

introduction of dromedary in Africa

introduction of horse and chariot (C)

rationalist humanism democratic institutions, in the Greek city-states

rise of Buddhism

Jainism, Mazdeism, Confucianism

Mohist school

Assyrian Empire

Babylonia

Persian Empire

Saitic Egypt

Egypt New Kingdom

Seleucid Empire

Egypt Ptolemaic kingdom

Magadha

Mauryan Empire

Shâtavâhana

Warring Kingdoms

Qin

Han Empire

C: China   I: India

Amber (beads, and a vessel in the form of a lion) has been excavated in a tomb at Qatna (Syria) dated to 1340 BCE (Mukherjee *et al.* 2008: 49–59). A piece of amber was discovered in Tutankhamun's tomb, on the pharaoh's chest. Conversely, blue glass beads recently found on buried Bronze Age women in Denmark appear to have originated in Egypt (Varberg *et al.* 2014). In continental Europe, an increase in production and exchanges – within the European sphere and between it and the world-system – heralded the transformations of the Iron Age.[44] The Cypriot and Levantine (Ugarit . . .) semi-peripheries grew in importance during this period: the formation of a "Cypro-Minoan" script as of the fifteenth century is significant. The flourishing of linear alphabets in Palestine, extended by cuneiform alphabets in Ugarit and in other cities (fourteenth–thirteenth centuries), were also responses to the progress made in trade relations. Moreover, the Mycenaean presence in the Black Sea highlights the increasing significance of this region.

The Late Bronze Age (*c.* 1600–1200 BCE) heralded a new integration of interconnected regions and an extension of networks. Egypt was now in close touch with the Asian powers of the time, and the relations thus built up led to the incorporation of the Red Sea and western and southern Arabia into the system (the Egyptian expeditions toward Punt and the visits of Puntites to Egypt reflect this incorporation). Arabia functioned as a hinge between the Indian Sea, on the one side, the Persian Gulf and the Red Sea, on the other. Most of the discoveries of African plants in India happened during this period. These contacts fell within the context of a new sphere of interaction linking Gujarat and western India to Arabia and the Horn of Africa. The "Indian" chicken was probably known in Egypt under Thutmose III. The spread of horses in western Asia and their introduction into Egypt by the Hyksos may have hastened the domestication of the dromedary in Arabia during the second millennium, which in turn led to the birth of the Levant-bound caravan trade. The discovery of citrons on Cyprus and of pepper in Egypt during the thirteenth century BCE has been pointed out. Active exchange networks developed across the Red Sea starting in the middle of the second millennium, whereas the Persian Gulf, in contrast, played only a limited role in the world-system of the Late Bronze Age.

From one cycle to another, besides local and/or temporary regressions, one notes global demographic growth, probably stronger in the main cores (Mesopotamia, Egypt); progress in techniques (see Chart 1.Con.1); an expansion of exchange networks and production, particularly bronze for tools (mostly used in agriculture) and weapons. The production of weapons, linked to the growing labor force available and to ideological changes, underpinned the militarization we observe during the Middle Bronze Age and even more clearly during the Late Bronze Age.[45]

---

connections with the Cypro-Levantine system (with a shekel of 11.75 g): the Cypriots, with bases on Sardinia, took over from the Mycenaeans on the trade networks after the collapse of the Greek political entities (Ruiz Galvez 2000).

[44] A. Sherratt (1994b: 341) notes the same expansion in bronze production in other margins or peripheries of the system (the Eurasian steppes, Luristan, Central Anatolia, Caucasus).

[45] Also emphasized by Kohl (2007: 255); for the Late Bronze Age, particularly during the thirteenth and twelfth centuries, many hoards have been excavated, for example in the Caucasus, in eastern Europe, in Kazakhstan (Kuzmina 2007: 246) . . . From the Iron Age on, the dominant power, regardless of its origin,

The State Sector, Communities, and the Private Sector

It was long thought that until the middle of the first millennium BCE at least, palaces and temples administered the economy, and market forces were unknown. From Polanyi's perspective, ancient societies had systems of redistribution, making it possible "to reallocate to the producers the products of the labor of a society which [were] collectively produced, centrally collected and stored" (Renger 1994: 177). In these societies, prices were not determined by supply and demand; there was no search for profit[46] through the production of goods specifically for the market; there was no accumulation of capital; there were no marketplaces; the use of money was negligible; the private sector was nonexistent or weak. Prices for merchandise had no real links with the decisions taken within the production sphere. "The income of the Mesopotamian trader depended mostly on landed property and the payment of rations from the palace stores. Thus, the Assyrian colony in Cappadocia engaged in riskless transactions under fixed prices. The traders made their profit on commission fees" (Silver 1995: 167).[47] According to Polanyi, long-distance trade tended to precede trade over shorter distances. "The traders of the ancient world belonged either to the upper or the lower class. The commercial middle class is a product of nineteenth-century Western capitalism" (Silver 1995: 171).[48]

Various authors have endeavored to refute the assertions of Polanyi and his disciples concerning ancient societies.[49] Archaeological data and progress in the deciphering of ancient texts – especially with regard to the second millennium – have led to a reassessment of the relationships between the state (the palace, the temple) and the private sector, on the one hand, and the role of the state in capital accumulation, on the other. M. Hudson (1996) has convincingly put forward the idea that the public sector provided the innovations that allowed entrepreneurship to develop. Capital accumulation with search for profit developed along with the state apparatus and the institutions of the temples and later of the palaces, as seen in the city-states of the Urukian period, during the Early Dynastic period and the Akkadian Empire, and in the Ur III Empire at the end of the third millennium. Capital accumulation also occurred at the level of households of extended families and of individual entrepreneurs. During the third millennium, a process of land privatization started at the top of the social pyramid,

---

would attempt to connect the Indian Ocean networks with those of the Mediterranean by controlling the lands between these maritime areas and Egypt.

[46] In fact, Polanyi himself did not exclude the possibility of profit.

[47] For Polanyi (1981), "it was only in the Medieval period that long-distance trade became a source of capital for other speculative entreprises": this trade then appears as the mechanism through which the embeddedness of the economy in social life was transformed into an embeddedness of social life in the economy.

[48] Moreover, Polanyi opposed "the idea that commercial activity was 'natural' to men and that markets would thus come into being unless prohibited by the government or other external forces" (Silver 1995: 172; Polanyi 1981: 14–15).

[49] See Veenhof 1972: 348ff., Silver 1995: 95ff., Powell 1999: 8ff.; Warburton 2003: 161, 166. A "historistic" position, intermediary between that taken by the "primitivists" and the "modernists," seems to be the most appropriate; see Masetti-Rouault 2008. The dispute between "primitivists" and "modernists" goes back to the late nineteenth century, with K. Bücher versus E. Meyer, and M. Weber versus M. Rostovtzeff at the beginning of the twentieth century.

initiated by the king and his followers, the institution of kingship itself may have been a northern Mesopotamian innovation. Debts bearing interest first appeared at the interface between public institutions and the communal sector, and also played an important role in this process of privatization. This movement, however, was partly counterbalanced by debt cancellations periodically promulgated by rulers. Whenever state control weakened or disappeared, privatization sometimes progressed. The early second millennium was thus marked by political fragmentation along with an expansion of the private sector.[50] Moreover, in Mesopotamia, the state sector was not monolithic: in contrast to Egypt, there was perceptible partition, and probably competition between the palace and the temples. Although some interpretations by Silver (1995) are debatable, it is clear that Polanyi was wrong about the nature of trade during the second millennium: private merchants who did not belong exclusively to a small elite did take an active part in this trade. The significance of local markets, where prices clearly fluctuated, has been largely underevaluated (see Meijer 2001, for a discussion of Polanyan principles). Even for Egypt, we have no firm evidence for a redistributive economy along the Polanyian model.[51] In fact, a kind of "market economy" was taking place, "which did not have the properties and the characteristics of the modern market" (Masetti-Rouault 2008: 59). Progress in the private sector and markets can be clearly seen during the early second millennium in Assyria (with outposts settled in Cappadocia) and in southern Mesopotamia during the Isin-Larsa phase, then later, during the Old Babylonian period. The lion's share of long-distance trade was handled by businessmen who also worked, quite often, either for or along with the state (Glassner 2002a: 148). Management of agricultural estates and crafts workshops was now largely delegated to the private sector. For various authors, however, the differences between the third and second millennia were not great. The evolution observed between these two millennia may result from gaps in the ancient sources rather than from radical social transformations. Thus, the pursuit of profit may have underpinned commercial activities during the Sargonic period.[52] Moving away from the old idea that the state completely controlled production and exchanges, many scholars today point to the flourishing of a private sector, and the practice of land sales – already in the middle of the third millennium – as well as the existence of markets with price fluctuations – but without the formation of "systems of markets."[53] In western Asia, silver, copper, and barley were already being used as

---

[50] Postgate (2003: 218), Van de Mieroop (1992: 105) and Ratnagar (2001b) note a profound change between the third and second millennia, marked by the ascent of the private sector and the "appearance of 'market forces'." Warburton (2003: 126) suggests a progressive evolution with rising "market forces," which truly emerged only at the beginning of the second millennium: "the conscious exploitation of price differentials for profits may date to the early 2nd millennium BC, and be the direct consequence of the appearance of reliable markets" (Warburton 2003: 136).

[51] As Van de Mieroop (1999: 154) notes, "ration recipients had to work hard for them" (quoted by Warburton 2003: 163).

[52] Powell 1977: 29; Foster 1977: 31. Powell (1999) refutes the idea of a radical change between Ur III and the beginning of the second millennium. As Ratnagar (2001b) points out, it would be absurd, however, to assume that the ancient societies obeyed a purely economic logic, as shown by the burying of precious goods in the tombs.

[53] Norel 2004: 85; McIntosh 2005: 174. A limited land market had existed since the middle of the third millennium, "except [perhaps] in the Ur III kingdom during the 21st century and during the Middle

currencies during the Early Dynastic period, with silver becoming essential by the late third millennium. It is clear, however, that the state, controlling most of the means of production and exchanges, played a crucial role in the accumulation of capital. From the great institutions of the temples and palaces, the states endeavored to use writing and systems of account to organize production, exchanges, and redistribution: the administration, responsible for planning, tried to rationalize costs, by mobilizing the work force efficiently. It would probably be wrong, however, to suppose that modes of organization and management were handled in the same way throughout western Asia – or even within Mesopotamia – or to deny these modes any flexibility and capacity for innovation. In all periods we are dependent on an uneven documentation. It is sometimes difficult to separate the private and public spheres (Aubet 2013: 118; Liverani 2005: 4) and research has shown "how dynamic and heterogeneous ancient Oriental societies were, and that 'what is pertinent for one period or region is not so for others'" (Alster 1996: 1, quoted by Aubet 2013: 122).

Researchers, however, must deal with deficient data, and the interpretations often remain contradictory, particularly for Ur III during the late third millennium, when state control seems to have been stronger; at the same time we discern an interpenetration of state and private sectors. For many authors, Egypt's economy was administered by an omnipresent state. While long-distance trade existed, it would have been strictly overseen by the authorities. "There was no significant market-based regulation before the arrival" of the Greeks (Norel 2004: 68). This vision has been contested by other researchers (Warburton 1997, 2003). In the Egyptian space also, the place of the private sector is now being reassessed, especially during the "intermediary periods," when the disaggregation of state structures allowed private entrepreneurship to flourish, and during the New Kingdom, a time when Egypt's growing integration into the transnational market triggered the formation of a cosmopolitan society, particularly in the Nile delta. The Egyptian state became increasingly decentralized during this period, and we observe the development of a complementary private sector, including in agriculture.

In the entire world-system of the Late Bronze Age, the tendency towards private-sector development continued, although, once again, social relations have proven difficult to reconstruct. The expansion of the private sector went along with "an increasing ability [of the states] to control territories and to extract tax and tribute" (Kristiansen and Larsson 2005: 104). For western Asia and the eastern Mediterranean, these authors note an ever-increasing identification of the rulers with divinities from the third to the second millennium, the ideological basis for efficient power. The states also massively resorted to slavery in the productive sector[54] and to mercenaries in their armies, a trend that continued to grow during the first millennium BCE.

Babylonian period 1595–1155." See Gelb *et al.* 1991: 25; Silver 1995: 126. It is likely that individual property – land and slaves – first concerned members of the elite. Conversely, according to Norel, it is difficult to speak of a proper labor market (2004: 84). See, however, Silver 1995: 132ff., for a slave market and a market for free labor, and Glassner 2001: 62, 69 n. 3.

[54] Also emphasized by Ekholm Friedman 2005: 53, 69ff. Slaves were captured or bought. Egypt even had "breeding houses," where women gave birth to slave-children (Ekholm Friedman 2005: 71).

China's World-Systems and Contacts with the West

The connections between western Asia and the Nile Valley probably played a role in Egypt's development as a core of a world-system. Mesopotamia, Iran, and Turkmenistan also had indirect contacts with complex societies of the Chinese world as early as the fourth and third millennia. In East Asia, these contacts helped accelerate the transformation of chiefdoms into states; they also led to the transmission of domesticated plants and animals, and to the introduction of copper and bronze metallurgy into the Qijia culture (Gansu, Qinghai), through routes of the Tarim and the valleys of the southern Altai. The Qijia culture was in contact with the first Chinese kingdoms (Taosi, Wangchenggang, Guchengzhai), where copper and bronze were present (see Map 1.17). In the Yangtze River valley, the development of more intensive rice cultivation during the third millennium coincided with the rise of hierarchical societies which were themselves in contact with the northern plains. Influences from the Longshan culture (Yellow River) can be seen from 2300 BCE onward. A wide sphere of interaction was formed which was not yet a world-system, despite the birth of the first kingdoms.[55] Various Chinese Neolithic cultures (as well as the city of Taosi) disappeared during the major climatic deterioration occurring at the beginning of the second millennium (Hong *et al.* 2003; Wang *et al.* 2005).

During the first half of the second millennium, new progress in agriculture and trade in East Asia led to a phase of urbanization and statebuilding. The Chinese states centered on Erlitou and later on Zhengzhou and Yin (Anyang) formed the cores of successive

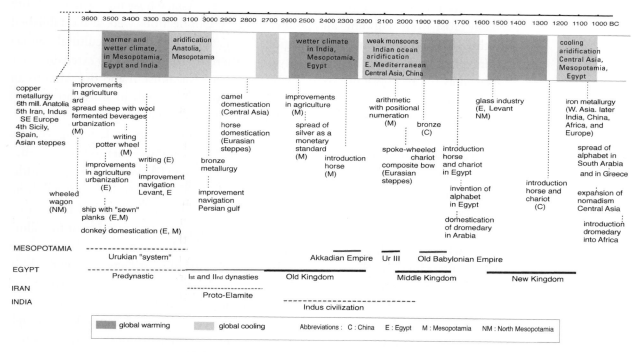

Chart 1.Con.1 Bronze Age: climate changes, technological, institutional, and ideological innovations, and political changes

[55] In Sichuan, the Baodun culture was located outside the sphere of interaction of the Yellow River basin, but had indirect connections with it (Falkenhausen 2003).

Table I.Con.5 *Dominant cultures or states in East Asia*

Yellow River	Dates	Yangtze	Sichuan
Erlitou	1800–1600	Panlongcheng	1700 beginning of Sanxingdui
Erligang Early Shang	1600–1400	Wucheng Phase I	
Middle Shang	1400–1300	End of Panlongcheng	
Late Shang	1300–1027	Wucheng Phase II	Flowering of Sanxingdui Disappearance *c.* 1100

world-systems, which were connected not only to the Northern Metallurgical Complex and to various routes of the Xinjiang, but also to routes leading to the south (Lingnan, Red River, Sichuan, and Yunnan) (see Map I.18). Here again, it is difficult to assess the size of these systems. In any event, the new ritual and practical importance of bronze led the states to control resources in metals as well as supply routes. The middle and the lower Yangtze Valley appear to have been closely linked to the Yellow River as early as the beginning of the second millennium. Several phases can be seen, as listed in Table I.Con.5.

These internal developments in East Asia were accompanied by increasing long-distance trade. During the second millennium, the so-called "central world-system" of western Asia experienced a strong expansion not only to the west, but also to the east. The eastward expansion went along with a greater interconnection of the areas of India and East Asia through intermediary groups in Central Asia, whose increasing mobility probably arose from economic and political factors. Connections were also established with the Altai and the Trans-Baikal region. The extension of the transcultural Seima-Turbino phenomenon signals the vitality of northern tin routes; such an extension may be viewed as the response of groups living in eastern Kazakhstan and the Altai to an increased demand for metals and jade and to an overall growth in Eurasian trade.[56] Eastern Kazakhstan and the Altai were linked to East Asia via Xinjiang.

At the end of the fifteenth century, the demise of the great Erligang centers coincided with a transformation of the system. New capitals emerged further and further to the east, first at Xiaoshuangqiao, then at Huanbei (Anyang) during a Middle Shang period marked by political instability. The Late Shang period saw a flourishing Shang state, with Yinxu (Anyang) as its new capital. This second part of the second millennium saw greater interaction in the Eurasian steppes. The number of metallurgical centers increased, particularly in Kazakhstan and Fergana, and relations with Xinjiang intensified, as shown by the discovery of metallic artifacts similar to those found in the steppes at many sites of this region. Networks providing transport and exchange of various types of ore, ingots, and manufactured products connected the Altai to eastern Europe. The Shang state maintained contacts with Inner Asia through the "Northern Zone Complex," or the Hexi corridor (Gansu), both of which show connections to Siberian or Central Asian cultures. These contacts allowed for the

---

[56] Kuzmina (2007: 180, 253) also views the rise of the Seima-Turbino phenomenon as the result of interactions between the populations of eastern Kazakhstan and eastern Europe, in particular Abashevo, from the beginning of the second millennium onward. Eastern Kazakhstan is particularly rich in tin mines, which were exploited by Andronovo populations (Kuzmina 2007: 87).

introduction of horses, chariots, and the cults that went along with them at Anyang. Interactions also developed with Sichuan, with the Yangtze River Valley and with regions further south, where the city of Wucheng appears to have become the center of an independent state. The size of Sanxingdui, the Sichuan capital, peaked during this period. Copper metallurgy reached Lingnan and continental Southeast Asia. We must wait for the first millennium BCE, however, to see more direct and significant contacts between northern China and the regions of Guangdong, Guanxi, and Vietnam.

The End of the Late Bronze Age: A Systemic Collapse

The western world-system of the Late Bronze Age suddenly collapsed around 1200 BCE, under the combined impact of movements of population – partly triggered by sharp global climatic change and epidemics[57] – and internal conflicts within societies.[58] "All the cores imploded, not only those which were affected by movements of populations" (Ekholm Friedman 2005: 73): the collapse was clearly a systemic phenomenon. In the eastern and central Mediterranean Sea, the growth of "interstitial exchange networks" involving independent itinerant craftsmen jeopardized the control that the centralized states had tried to maintain (S. Sherratt 2000: 90) and accelerated these states' decline and demise.[59] It is likely that the very structure of the system, centered as it was on a set of militaristic and imperialist states in competition – notably for obtaining slaves and mercenaries – explains its fragility. The end of the Late Bronze Age thus provides a good example of correlated processes which, by triggering a vicious cycle, led to the spectacular collapse of the whole system. The demise of the largest states allowed for the rise of political entities and of groups who had previously been in an intermediary situation, such as the Cypriots during the twelfth century, and later the Phoenician city-states (S. Sherratt 2003). Paradoxically, it may be precisely the general breakdown of states and supply networks for copper and tin that led to the development of iron metallurgy[60] and paved the way for the formation of a new world-system at the beginning of the first millennium BCE. In this restructuring, pastoral nomads in

[57] Brooke mentions smallpox and plague (2014: 299).

[58] Frank and Thompson (2006: 143) note that 11 out of the 15 regions studied were affected by the turmoil of the 2200/2100 period and all of them were affected in 1200/1100, a progression signifying an expansion of the system and its further integration. The climate change of 1200/1100 had negative effects for western Asia, but it may have favored agriculture in Central Europe around 1300; the Urnfield Culture expanded at precisely this time. Conflicting data exist for the steppes of western Siberia and north of the Black Sea during the phase of global cooling that characterized the late second and early first millennia BCE; some researchers have observed a process of aridification, whereas others have noted increased precipitation.

[59] For S. Sherratt (2000, 2003), the arrival of bronzes belonging to the Urnfield culture in the eastern Mediterranean Sea during the thirteenth century, after traveling through maritime routes, does not necessarily imply large movements of populations, but does indicate those of artisans. On these trade networks, Cypriots were particularly active. The two interpretations (movement of craftsmen within the context of decentralized trade, and movement of populations) are, in fact, not mutually exclusive. Easton *et al.* (2002) note the decline of Troy during the thirteenth century, when maritime routes toward the central Mediterranean Sea grew in importance.

[60] S. Sherratt has a different explanation for the gradual adoption of iron: the growing quantities of bronze in the eastern Mediterranean Sea would have induced a relative "depreciation" of this metal against iron (2003: 40, 44).

the Eurasian steppes also played an important role, showing the significance of peripheries and semi-peripheries in the evolution of these systems. Movements of population (especially of Iranian speakers) eastward at the end of the second millennium BCE hastened not only the collapse of the Shang state, but also the spread of iron metallurgy. In Sichuan, Sanxingdui also disappeared around 1100 BCE. In China, the Zhou state, previously allied to the Shang state, rose to preeminence at the close of the second millennium, as the core of a new eastern world-system.

PART II

The Birth of the Afro-Eurasian World-System (First Millennium BCE – Sixth Century CE)

Introduction

The Iron Age: From Three World-Systems to a Single World-System

During the Late Bronze Age, a western multicentered world-system formed that included the Mediterranean Sea, Egypt, and western Asia. The implosion of this system, starting in 1200 BCE, along with the collapse of urban life and state disaggregation, broke the long-distance networks that had been in place since roughly 1600 BCE. Then began a long period of turmoil marked by general political fragmentation. We know today that the "dark hole" from 1200 BCE to the start of the first millennium BCE was not quite as "dark" as has previously been thought; it was a period of transformation, and its duration needs to be shortened if we adopt the proposals made by some authors for a shorter chronology. Moreover, long-distance trade may have recovered as early as the twelfth century BCE, on bases that are different from those previously holding sway. At that time, Cyprus took on a leading role in the eastern and central Mediterranean Sea.[1] During the eleventh century, the Phoenician cities rose to preeminence, expanding their networks westward, to Lefkandi (Euboea), Cyprus, and Kommos (Crete). Despite the turmoil of this period, there was also continuity in the Neo-Hittite kingdoms, for example, and in some parts of the Levantine coast, which were engaged in metallurgical and textile industries, as well as ivory work.

A presentation of the main developments from the eleventh century BCE onward, while shedding light on the interconnected trajectories observed for different regions, will also allow us to understand the shift that occurred from near-total chaos to the formation of the first world-system, which included Asia, Europe, and part of Africa,

---

[1] According to S. Sherratt (2003: 42), as mentioned at the end of Part I, not only did Cyprus benefit from the decline of the Bronze Age states, it also contributed to this decline, for Mycenae at least, by "copying" Mycenaean ceramics. During the twelfth century, exchanges existed, linking Cyprus, Egypt, the Levant, and Cilicia; the Cypriots were active in the eastern and central Mediterranean. Ivory was one of the luxury goods transported. Ivory has been found on Cyprus, in Attica (Perati), southern Italy (Torre Mordillo), and northern Italy (Frattesina) (S. Sherratt 2003: 47). The site of Frattesina (twelfth–ninth century BCE) was linked to long-distance exchange networks, as shown by discoveries of amber from the Baltic Sea, and elephant ivory and ostrich eggs from Egypt (Cypriots were probably involved in these maritime networks toward Frattesina). Glass beads were produced and this site worked bronze and iron. S. Sherratt has emphasized the frequent association, in the eastern Mediterranean Sea, of Cypriot assemblage and of artifacts belonging to the Urnfield culture (2003: 42). The region located between the northern Adriatic and the southeastern Alpine zone seems to have adopted "a new system of weights based on an East-Mediterranean unit" (Sherratt 2003: 51).

during the first millennium BCE. The Iron Age (first millennium BCE) proved to be a crucial period for change: it reflected an evolution from three world-systems to a single world-system, through the progressive integration of various regions of the Ancient World (Beaujard 2010a).

At the beginning of the first millennium BCE, states and towns formed once again, production regained buoyancy, and new exchange networks were created in western Asia and the Mediterranean Sea on the one side, and in China on the other. It is possible to interpret these revivals as evidence for the reconstitution of two world-systems, one eastern and one western. Climate warming in China and in western Asia, as well as stronger monsoons in the Indian Ocean at the start of the first millennium, contributed to these revivals, through increased agricultural production. Agriculture also progressed in Oman and southern Iran, thanks to irrigation using systems of subterranean canals (*qanāt*) (Magee 2005).

The Western and Eastern World-Systems: The First Connections (1000–750 BCE)

The collapse of the networks providing copper and tin at the close of the second millennium fostered a rapid expansion in iron metallurgy – the major innovation of this period – and the restructuring of a larger world-system at the beginning of the first millennium BCE, in which the nomadic herders of the Eurasian steppes played an important part. The spread of iron metallurgy after 1200 and later during the first millennium BCE, from western Asia[2] toward the east, the north,[3] and the west, reveals the establishment of new connections. The price of iron certainly influenced its more widespread use; iron was much cheaper than copper during the middle of the first millennium.[4] At the same time, private entrepreneurship developed, at least in some regions. While the production of iron tools and weapons was crucial to the developments observed from 1000 BCE onward, the increasing use of iron did not necessarily reflect its particular qualities: Moorey (1994: 278–292) has pointed out that iron weapons were often no better than bronze weapons, even during the Neo-Babylonian period. G. Childe has noted the social transformations implied by ironworking: "Iron, which was cheap, opened up agriculture, industry and war to all. Any farmer could afford to acquire an iron axe to clear new lands for himself and a plow

---

[2] Cyprus was an active center for the development of iron metallurgy (Sherratt and Sherratt 2001: 31); the island took advantage of the know-how of its craftsmen working bronze and of a growing demand for iron (in Egypt, Tutankhamun was buried with two daggers, one made of gold, the other of iron, probably from meteoric iron). Prior to this period, Anatolia and later the Levant were the first places to experiment with iron metallurgy.

[3] The Caucasus and Transcaucasia became centers for high-quality iron metallurgy from the ninth century on: various types of steel were produced (Koryakova and Epimakhov 2007: 193).

[4] Haarer 2001: 264–265; Warburton 2003: 254. According to Warburton, one observes a price reversal between copper and iron during the early first millennium BCE. For Warburton, "the success of iron cannot be attributed to obvious technological superiority" (2003: 254.). Iron use led to major innovations, however, as seen in the production of iron plows in China and in South Asia, and the development of the crossbow in China.

to break the stony soil" (1961: 161).[5] At the same time, however, the statebuilding processes accompanying the expansion of iron metallurgy in western Asia often came with reinforced social control (for Europe, also, see Kristiansen 1998: 218). Compared to bronzeworking, iron metallurgy introduced "a difference of degree but not of nature in the action of men over matter" (Margueron and Pfirsch 2001: 314). Warfare practices changed, however, with the appearance of new types of weaponry and armor – mass-produced – and the development of an infantry. In Africa, iron tools adopted by the Bantu populations favored these peoples' expansion toward eastern and southern Africa and their agricultural progress.

In the west, the expansion of iron metallurgy throughout Europe "marks the continuation of the shift of the centers of balance toward the Mediterranean."[6] Iron production surged around 1000 BCE in Greece and from the eighth century BCE onward in central and eastern Europe.

The period 1000–850 was one of overall growth in the partly reconstituted western world-system.[7] Four poles emerged during the ninth century: Egypt, whose revival was limited under the Libyan dynasties; Anatolia, with the flowering of Greek city-states

---

[5] For Childe, "a simple craftsman could own a set of tools which made him independent from the houses of the kings, gods or nobles" (1961: 161). Muhly (1995: 1517) adds: "The simplicity of iron-working took metallurgy out of the palace." However, we find many examples of control over iron working by the elites, although this metal was more readily accessible than either copper or tin.

[6] Margueron and Pfirsch 2001: 314. Moreover, in sub-Saharan Africa, iron metallurgy seems to have developed from 800 BCE onward in Central Africa (site of Gbabiri) (Zangato 1999); Rwanda (at Gasiza I); and in the "no date land" 800–400 BCE in Tanzania (Kataruka); Mauritania (Bou Khzama) (McDonald et al. 2009); Mali (Dia-Shoma); Niger (at Do Dimmi 15) (Killick 2004); Burkina-Faso (site of Tora-Sima-Romo 1) (Holl 2009); Senegal (Walalde) (Deme and McIntosh 2006); Gabon (Moanda 1 and 2) (Digombe et al. 1988); Nigeria (Nsukka region) (Okafor 2002); and Cameroon (site of Nkang) (see Woodhouse 1998; Bocoum 2002; Childs and Herbert 2005; Alpern 2005; Killick 2009b; Clist 2012). Even older dates have often been suggested. Zangato and Holl (2010) claim a date of 3000 BP at the site of Oboui (Central Africa). They also accept evidence for an iron metallurgy dated to the beginning of the second millennium BCE in the Termit Massif (Niger) (Quéchon 2002). The Eghazzer basin in Niger has provided a 2200–1500 BCE dating for incipient copper metallurgy (Grebenart 1988). B. Clist (2012) has refuted these early dates (see also Killick 2009). The origin and dating of copper and iron metallurgy south of the Sahara remain controversial. Were they African inventions, or did they result from the spread of techniques, from Egypt or the coasts of northern Africa? Phoenician influences from northern Africa or southern Spain have been suggested; moreover, the Cypriots may have introduced iron metallurgy into northern Africa before the Phoenicians. Berbers may have played a role in its transmission south of the Sahara (McDonald 2011: 75). For a reassessment of the data, see McIntosh 2005, Alpern 2005, Killick 2004, 2009b, and Clist 2012. For the region of the Great Lakes, the oldest datings for iron metallurgy remain uncertain (Killick 2009b). Yemeni or Nubian origins have been suggested (reliable dating from the Great Lakes region gives a date range between 800 and 400 BCE, which corresponds to the period of development of iron metallurgy at Meroe). Schmidt (2006) and Ehret (1998) note that Bantu populations in the Great Lakes region seem to have borrowed the vocabulary of iron metallurgy from speakers of "Central Sudan" languages who settled in the region of the Great Lakes during the first millennium BCE (in this region, "it appears that agriculture, ironworking, cattle keeping and Bantu languages have different time depths," but they spread to southern Africa as a "package" [Killick 2009b: 408]). On the Ethiopian plateau, by contrast, the words used for "iron" are of Semitic origin.

[7] Frank and Thompson (2006) contemplate – wrongly, it seems to me – a global recession between 1000 and 750 BCE. They write that "contraction persisted in most areas through the ninth century BCE," with Egypt remaining in recession until c. 700, and Anatolia until 750 BCE. Frank (1993a) was, I believe, more correct in proposing a period of growth of the "central world system" from 1000 to 800 BCE.

and the founding of the kingdom of Urartu; the Levant, which benefited once again from its position as hub in exchanges both in the Mediterranean Sea itself and between the Mediterranean Sea and the Indian Ocean; and Assyria. A first significant Assyrian expansion occurred during the ninth century, resulting in control over Anatolia's metal resources. Activity remained low in the Persian Gulf until the eighth century, but the same cannot be said for the Red Sea, where the weak Egyptian presence left the field open to the Arabs, who developed relations with the Levant and the Horn of Africa. The Arabs introduced the dromedary into Africa at this time.[8] In the north, the kingdom of Israel dominated the routes leading to Syria and Arabia. Evidence for contacts with the Levant is provided by the South Arabic alphabet, which developed during the eleventh or tenth century from the linear alphabetic "Proto-Arabic" tradition of Palestine and Jordan (Lemaire 2007: 58–59; see above). Israel's alliance with the king of Tyre led to an expansion in joint trade in the Mediterranean and the Red Sea (the expeditions to Ophir attest to this): these were attempts to bypass both the Arab caravan trade and Egyptian control over the gold supply (Aubet 2001: 45). Moreover, a vast area of interaction took shape once again in the Mediterranean Sea.

The place held by the Mediterranean Sea was crucial during the first millennium: it was a sea where the Phoenician, Greek, and later Roman networks would deploy on a grand scale. As most of Part II will be devoted to various regions in the Indian Ocean and to their interactions, this introduction will trace the development of the Mediterranean area in detail.

Cyprus appears to have been a key player at the end of the second and beginning of the first millennium BCE. Fibulae of the "Huelva type" found in southern Spain from the twelfth century BCE onward may derive from a Cypriot type that was also known on the Levantine coast, although it is likely that some oriental exemplars came from Spain (Carrasco Rus *et al.* 2012). The Levantine city-states, followers of Ugarit[9] – Byblos, Sidon, and later Tyre – flourished as early as the beginning of the first millennium, partly stimulated by trade with Assyria.[10] In addition, competition between Sidon and Tyre fostered the maritime Phoenician entreprises during the tenth century, until Tyre at last gained the upper hand (Niemeyer 2000). During the tenth century, an alliance between Tyre and Israel gave the Phoenicians access to the caravan roads and the Red Sea, but it is the Phoenicians' expansion into the Mediterranean Sea which is most noteworthy. As early as the tenth and ninth centuries, the Phoenicians visited southern Spain and the Atlantic coasts, where the treasure of Huelva, the booty from a shipwrecked boat, reveals to the vitality of these networks.[11] During the ninth century, the Phoenicians founded

---

[8] Shaw (1979) has defended the idea of an African domestication of this animal (parallel to the domestication which occurred in Arabia) but his suggestion has received little support. The dromedary is well represented in the rock art of North Africa.

[9] Other city-state cultures developed in the north (Neo-Hittite and Aramaean city-states) and in the south (Philistine city-states) (Thuesen 2000, 2002). Niemeyer (2000: 92) points out that "the length of the discontinuity [the 'Dark Age'] is less long-lasting [than previously thought]."

[10] The Phoenician language and alphabet had already spread into Anatolia (Sam'al, Karatepe) and Cilicia during the ninth and eighth centuries BCE (Liverani 2014: 427).

[11] Ruiz-Galvez Priego 1995; Kristiansen 1998: 126. Note that the chicken spread into the Mediterranean world during the early first millennium BCE; it was found in the Aegean Sea and in southern Spain at that time (Uerpmann 2008: 444).

outposts on Cyprus,[12] Crete,[13] Sicily, and in northern Africa. The ascent of these Phoenician networks and the growth of Egypt both shed light on the sudden emergence of the culture of the Garamantes, which combined agriculture and long-distance trade, from 900 BCE onward, acting as an interface between the Mediterranean Sea and Inner Africa (Pelling 2005). At the site of the Garamantian capital of Zinkekra (900–400 BCE), crop agriculture (with plants from the Mediterranean) and fruit farming (date palm, grapevine, fig tree) appeared at the same time (Mattingly 2011: 53). A tomb from the Wadi Tanezzuft near Ghat (Libya), dated to the end of the second millennium, already contained date pits (Pelling 2005: 401).

Pointing to a possible Phoenician settlement at Thebes at the start of the first millennium BCE, Bernal (1991: 6) has postulated a significant Phoenician influence in the development of Greece from the tenth century BCE onward. The founding of Greek cities in Anatolia, however, began as of 1200 BCE. As early as the late ninth century, the Ionian League was formed as an association of twelve city-states (among them Miletus, Ephesus, and Phocaea): this reveals the progress made by the Aegean world in connection with the Levant. The abovementioned cities also traded with Phrygia, which controlled western Anatolia prior to the Cimmerian invasions of the late eighth century.

To the east of western Asia, the growing integration of interconnected regions was also obvious during the Early Iron Age. During the second millennium BCE, eastern and western Asia were still relatively disconnected spaces. Merchandise and people circulated among these regions, but interactions were neither regular nor intense enough to form the continent into a coherent unit. Increased aridity probably favored the expansion of true nomadic pastoralists within Central Asia from the twelfth century BCE onward; these pastoralists rode horses, using bits and harnesses.[14] Nomadism clearly expanded during the early first millennium BCE. The climatic factor is only one of the elements explaining this evolution, which also derives from increased exchanges and the transformations of steppe societies. These societies, which maintained differentiated modes of production,[15] must have decided to increase their mobility in order to take advantage of trade between rising states. From that point on, pastoralism was based primarily on sheep herding, which allowed for the exploitation of wool products. At the same time, one notes new social differentiation in steppe societies, with warriors as the ruling groups. As early as the late second millennium, there were notable innovations in horse harnessing, weapons, and helmets (Kuzmina

---

[12] This situation is not new: Ugarit already had outposts in Cyprus. Founded by Tyre during the tenth or ninth century BCE, the city of Kition played a highly significant role in its links with Spain, Egypt, Euboea, and the Levant.

[13] Phoenicians appear to have been present at Kommos as early as the end of the tenth century BCE (Shaw 1989).

[14] Horseback riding is certainly older, for herding and for sending messengers, for example along the Assyrian caravan routes to Kanesh (Anatolia) and in the BMAC; a Bactrian seal shows a rider; and figurines of riders have been excavated at Pirak (Baluchistan) (first half of the second millennium). Horseback riding for military purposes developed only during the first millennium BCE (Renfrew 2002: 5–6).

[15] See Honeychurch and Amartuvshin 2006, on the Xiongnu culture.

2007: 358, 388ff.). Central Asia was the likely place of origin for the Scytho-Siberian populations, who spoke Proto-Iranian languages, and who would migrate southward, eastward[16] and westward (they would form the Cimmerian and Scythian populations mentioned in the Greek sources). The movements of these populations helped spread iron metallurgy. Nor can we exclude population movements from the eastern Mediterranean Sea or the Black Sea.[17]

Iron metallurgy was probably introduced in India during the late second millennium. It allowed for the production of new tools and efficient weaponry. Iron thus contributed to agricultural expansion, which in turn triggered demographic growth and fostered a movement of urbanization in the Ganges valley and central India, where various small kingdoms formed. Parallel to this iron metallurgy, a glass industry developed, as well as long-distance exchange networks. These shaped a sphere of interaction centered on the Ganges valley, in northern India: a prelude to the birth of a new world-system.

In eastern Asia, the beginning of the first millennium was a period of development during which a process of urbanization began under the Zhou dynasty. The weakly centralized Zhou state formed the core of a world-system in which various influences from the steppes, Sichuan and regions south of the Yangtze merged. Agricultural development was encouraged (Deng 1999). Iron technology was introduced during the late second millennium BCE in Xinjiang, perhaps from Fergana. It was adopted in the central plains of China around the eighth century BCE. Influences from the steppes (culture of Karasuk, c. 1400–800, and later Scythian culture, from 800 BCE onward) are clearly visible in Mongolia and China, with the discoveries of objects decorated in what is known as the "animal style." The presence of Iranian magi at the Zhou court reflects China's connections with Central Asia and Iran; this connection was still too weak, however, to form the two eastern and western areas into a single system.

Worldwide climatic cooling occurred from 850 to 750 BCE.[18] This played a role in the recession and population movements observed at the time.[19] This climate

[16] Di Cosmo 2002: 31ff. See the Saka culture of Xinjiang. Cunliffe places the appearance "of a new form of pastoral nomadism, focused on warrior leaders able to command multi-ethnic contingents of mounted archers" (2015: 201) during the ninth and eighth centuries.

[17] The custom of holding the jaws of the dead closed with a cloth strip, known in the eastern Mediterranean, appears in the Tarim at Zaghunluk (Cherchen) around 800 BCE and also at Jumulak Kum (Müller 2003: 61). Hemphill and Mallory (2004) suggest affinities between the mummies of both Alwighul (700–1 BCE) and Krorän (beginning of the Christian era) and the populations of the eastern Mediterranean (but also those inhabiting urban centers of ancient Bactria) (cf. also Kuzmina 2008: 91).

[18] Brooke indicates that "solar insolation reached a minimum (the 'Homeric') at 800 BC" (2014: 301) (he also writes "750 BC" [2014: 324]). See also Martin-Puertas et al. 2012; Usoskin (2013) gives 765 BCE.

[19] A decrease in precipitation has been noted for the region of Vancouver at this time (Zhang and Hebda 2005). Bond et al. (1997) point out lower temperatures in the northern Atlantic, with a nadir around 800 BCE. Lower temperatures are reported for Scandinavia between 850 and 760, then again around 650 BCE. The Netherlands also experienced a cooler and wetter climate between 850 and 750 (Dark 2006). The Mediterranean was probably affected by a more arid climate at this time. The period around 800 BCE marks a peak in the production of C_{14}. As already mentioned, a correlation can be established between a high level of C_{14}, weak solar activity and a cooler climate (Kromer et al. 2003: 52–53). Liu et al. (2002) emphasize more severe aridity and lower temperatures in Inner Mongolia as of 900 BCE. Wang et al.

change was marked by increased aridification in some regions, but also by increased precipitation in parts of the steppes such as the regions of Tuva and Minusinsk, western Siberia, north of the Black Sea (Koryakova and Epimakhov 2007: 10–11). For some authors, this period of increased precipitation may have boosted demographic growth of the "Scythian" population and its expansion outward from this region (Van Geel *et al.* 2004).[20] This expansion must also be understood within the context of the general progress the system had made so far. Indo-European migrations occurred in the steppes of southern Siberia and in the Tarim (Müller 2003: 61). Attracted by the wealth of the agrarian states, various nomadic populations appeared to be willing to take by force what they could no longer obtain through exchange. In China, attacks from the steppes forced the Zhou to move their capital, thus reducing the power of their state. Further west, a series of movements in Central Asia led to the migration of "Cimmerians," who were living north of the Black Sea. Their invasions reached Anatolia at the end of the eighth century and during the first half of the seventh century, and affected eastern and central Europe from 800 BCE onward (Harding 1994; Kristiansen 1998).[21] In 707 BCE, a letter from Sennacherib records that "the king of Urartu has been defeated in battle by the Gimirrai" (Cunliffe 2015: 194). Iranian speakers entered India at this time. The second half of the ninth century was a period of recession, clearly noticeable in Assyria and even more so in Egypt. The Nile region was affected by a weakening of the Indian Ocean monsoon system, which began *c.* 850, at the death of Osorkon. In 853, although Egypt was divided, it was still able to send mercenaries to Syria; allied with the Hebrews, these mercenaries stopped the Assyrian armies at the battle of Qarqar. The participation of Arab cameleers in this battle is evidence of the profitable commerce already linking Arabia and Syria at this time.[22]

(2005) suggest a weakening of the monsoon around 800 BCE. Morgunova and Khokhlova (2006: 314) also note a short period of aridification in the region of the Urals during the eighth/seventh centuries BCE. Cf. also Hsu 1998: 687 and Fagan 2004: 201. Global warming occurred after 750 BCE. For the Russian steppes, Kuzmina (2008: 12) describes a period of climatic cooling between the ninth and seventh centuries, with a wetter climate (Alexandrovskyi and Alexandrovskaya 2004: 207). Curiously, Bokovenko (2004: 29) indicates a humid phase and global warming during the ninth and eighth centuries BCE in the Eurasian steppes.

[20] Cunliffe (2015: 186) notes that "humidity increased [and] the overall temperature decreased [in the steppe] from the 12th to the 10th centuries, while in 9th and 8th centuries BC the humidity continued to increase while the temperature became significantly warmer." A royal tomb at Arzhan, displaying archaic Scythian features, is dated to *c.* 800 BCE. E. Kuzmina (2007) has emphasized the importance of the Altai region and Kazakhstan in forming the Scythian cultural complex. In contrast, the Urals were depopulated at this time. The tombs at Arzhan demonstrate knowledge of iron metallurgy around the eighth century BCE.

[21] Cimmerians were employed as mercenaries by the Assyrians, but later they fought alongside the Medes against the Assyrians. They are mentioned under the name "Gomer" in the Bible. Kristiansen (1998: 74) notes a decline in production as well as a crisis of the elites' legitimacy in northern Europe during this period.

[22] Kitchen 1994: 117. A confederation of Qedarite Arab chiefs was formed during the first half of the first millennium BCE.

The Development of Three Interconnected World-Systems (750–350/300 BCE)

The Western World-System from the Eighth to the Sixth Century BCE

The western world-system saw a new phase of growth and integration during the second half of the eighth century (here, I agree with Frank and Thompson [2006]). Climatic improvement probably had a hand in this process.[23] This period of growth was marked by a new blossoming of the Assyrian Empire (from Tiglath-Pileser III, 745–727); a Phoenician and Greek expansion in the Mediterranean and the Black Sea; and the constitution of the kingdom of Saba in Yemen. The Saba kingdom exerted a strong influence on the pre-Axumite entity of Daamat (central Eritrea and western Tigray) (was it a kingdom or a confederation?), which was formed around 700 BCE. The growth of networks and states continued during the seventh century, and was strengthened by crucial technological and institutional innovations such as the development of iron metallurgy, agricultural progress, and the diffusion of alphabets within the new states of the Levant, the Aegean Sea, and other areas. Kristiansen (1998: 133) writes of a "commercial explosion" in the Mediterranean and western Asia from 700 BCE onward.

The construction of the Assyrian Empire meant creating a new capital and organizing provinces; it was marked by a twofold movement: the Assyrianization of conquered lands and the Aramaization of the core (Beaulieu 2005). After Ur III and Egypt, Assyria was the first state to maintain a standing army. The emperors undertook massive deportations of populations, and at the same time adopted Aramaic as their *lingua franca* and the Aramaic script in their administration. Institutional innovations of the empire – often borrowed from Syria and the Levant (Allen 2005) – explain its unequaled size. The centralization set up by the rulers and the creation of a class of managers and military officers did not prevent a private sector from developing: various documents reveal the existence of prices fixed by supply-and-demand conditions (Silver 2004b). In addition, the city of Kar-Assurnasirpal provides an example of a region developed by an Assyrian official on his own initiative and for his personal interest (Masetti-Rouault 2008). This is proof of the changes taking place at this time (although the regional development conducted by this official was later viewed as a crime of lese majesty).

Assyrian imports of slaves, luxury goods, and metals, whether exchanged or extracted as tributes, furthered the development of the Levantine cities. A Tyrian influence was obvious at Karkemish, the capital of a Neo-Hittite kingdom near the Euphrates, and in Cilicia. The example of the Phoenician city-states and of the Greek cities belies Weber's idea that ancient cities did not produce significantly for export and did not invest their revenues in productive activities.[24] The Phoenician coast developed

---

[23] Climate improvement – notably in western Asia – may have played a role starting in 700 BCE, when data from Lake Van show a relative increase in precipitation (Wicks *et al.* 2003).

[24] Weber contrasted these ancient cities with medieval European towns (see above). The Egyptian and Mesopotamian states of the third and second millennia already reveal the development of industries producing goods destined for export, notably textiles. Weber probably overestimated capital instability in the ancient *polis*, as well.

export-oriented industries, accompanied by labor intensification in the manufacture of crimson, textiles, and luxury objects such as worked ivory, precious inlaid furniture, and glass items. Various monetary devices made use of weighed silver (Thompson 2003), a practice that Powell sees as reflecting the existence of a "market economy" as early as the second millennium BCE (Masetti-Rouault 2008). At the level of the system, the Levantine area occupied a core position, despite the political domination of Assyria over the Phoenician cities, which triggered an influx of wealth to Nineveh and Assur.

Through its needs, above all for metals, and its growing politico-economic pressure, Assyria contributed to Phoenicia's expansion westward, where capital accumulation escaped Assyrian control (Aubet 2001: 278; Allen 2005: 85). Unsafe routes toward the Indian Ocean during the ninth century and the economic needs of Egypt also aided this Phoenician ascent in the Mediterranean. Most of the Phoenician trading posts were founded during the eighth and seventh centuries BCE.[25] This was the case for Carthage, built *c.* 814 BCE according to tradition. This dating appears to be confirmed by discoveries linked to iron metallurgy going back to the first half of the eighth century (Gras *et al.* 1995). Gadir (Cadiz)[26] was founded during the same period, in a region of Spain where the kingdom of Tartessos provided silver in ever-increasing quantities (see Herodotus, Book I). Assyrian demand for silver, the standard currency of the empire, obviously stimulated this trade with the Iberian peninsula. Silver from Spain paid the fleets of Tyre and the armies of Nineveh (Moore and Lewis 1999: 118; Diodorus of Sicily, V: 35, 2–5). The western Mediterranean Sea was no longer a margin but a semi-periphery of the world-system for the eastern Mediterranean Sea, and was connected to peripheries on the continent, where one notes the formation of various alphabetic writing systems.[27] "It is not by chance that we find the greatest concentrations of [imported] prestige goods

[25] Tyrian development in the Mediterranean Sea was partly triggered by Assyrian control of western Asia. See Niemeyer 2000: 102. As early as the ninth century, Tyre and Sidon offered tributes to the Assyrians, in gold, silver, textiles, and purple (murex-shell dye). During the eighth century, Assyrian controllers settled at Tyre and Sidon.

[26] The period during which trading posts such as Carthage and Gadir were founded is still debated (Niemeyer 2000: 100, 104). Three different schools clash as to the dates of Phoenician colonization in the western Mediterranean, placing it in the eighth, tenth, or eleventh century BCE (Gilboa and Sharon 2001: 1346–1348). For these authors, the data suggest a "low chronology" for the Iron Age of the Levant: a Phoenician expansion during the eleventh century seems uncertain. This low chronology has already been put forward by Finkelstein (1998, 2003), who suggests lowering the dates of the Iron Age of the Levant by 75 or 100 years. Torres Ortiz *et al.* (2005) see a first Phoenician colonization in Spain from the last quarter of the ninth century BCE onward. Various discoveries of iron objects go back to the end of the tenth or beginning of the ninth century (Ria de Huelva), or perhaps even to an older period (Moreirinha, dated between the thirteenth and ninth centuries) (Javaloyas Molina 2006). The Guadalquivir basin was already attracting Mediterranean traders during the Late Bronze Age because of this region's copper and silver deposits. Excavations in Portugal have revealed the presence of merchants hailing from the western Mediterranean Sea during the early first millennium BCE (Harrison and Mederos Martin 2000: 139–140). For the region of Malaga, the site of Morro de Mezquitilla has yielded dates between 894 and 835 BCE (Aubet 2001: 375). The importance of Gadir is well attested for the period of the eighth through sixth century (Aubet 2001: 261–262).

[27] The Phoenician system of weights (with a unit of 7.5–7.9 g) was adopted along networks of the Iberian peninsula, and also in the Alps (see the molds of Zurich-Alpenquai) (Ruiz-Galvez 2000: 275–276). Alongside social complexification, Ruiz-Galvez notes the appearance of various writing systems, for

in native burials situated in the territories that were richest in metal ore: southern Etruria, the lower Guadalquivir and Huelva" (Aubet 2001: 137). The Phoenician networks extended along the Atlantic coast of Morocco (a colony of people from Gadir settled at Mogador)[28] and the coasts of the Iberian peninsula, where gold arrived from western Sudan and tin from the British Isles (Cornwall), with the Phoenicians trading at least indirectly with this region.[29]

Some authors have conjured the possibility of a circumnavigation of Africa during the sixth century BCE,[30] but this remains uncertain. The Phoenicians may not have ventured regularly much beyond the region of Mogador. The question of contacts by Phoenician colonies with sub-Saharan populations has been debated, as well as that of an early gold exploitation in western Sudan (Herodotus wrote about the "silent barter" of the Carthaginians through which they acquired gold on Morocco's Atlantic coast). "The so-called 'chariot route' of the central Sahara, originating in the Fezzan, already led to a place near the site of Gao around 500 BC" (Coquery-Vidrovitch 1993: 127). The Nok culture (central Nigeria) may have learned iron metallurgy "from Carthaginian influences filtering down from the north through the 'chariot route' of the central Sahara (Tassili n-Adjer and Adrar of Iforas)" (Coquery-Vidrovitch 1993: 52). We may also consider a Cypriot influence from northern Africa. Copper metallurgy can be observed at Takedda (Niger), the site of a sizeable deposit, during the first millennium BCE.

One wonders whether the trans-Saharan routes were truly active before the end of the first millennium BCE or from the beginning of the Christian era, when the dromedary was supposedly introduced from Egypt. Improved climatic conditions from 1500 BCE in the Sahara, however, seem to have facilitated the use of these "chariot routes" linking Tripolitania and Cyrenaica to the Niger River valley. Parietal art exhibits many drawings of carts, drawn by oxen rather than by horses,[31] accompanied by figures of men armed with spears and daggers (MacEachern 2005: 443; Alpern 2005: 54–56). While scholars today no longer refer to "chariot routes" (Alpern 2005; Vernet

example in Spain and in southwestern France (2000: 277–278). In southern Spain, the introduction of writing resulted from an adaptation of the Phoenician script c. 800 BCE (Lemaire 2007: 63).

[28] Aubet (2001: 301) dates Mogador to the seventh/sixth century BCE. The site of Lixus (Oued Loukhos) appears to go back to the Punic period. Sala (Rabat) was also a Punic settlement.

[29] It is possible that from Gadir, the Phoenicians reached the British Isles. Carthaginian coins have been found in Devon. According to the *Ora Maritima* from Avienus (fourth century CE), "The Tartessians," Avienus adds, "were accustomed to carrying their merchandise to the borders of Oestrymnides [Brittany and/or Cornwall]; also the colonies of Carthage and the communities dwelling within the Pillars of Hercules used to frequent these seas." During the fourth century BCE, the Greek merchant Pytheas, from Massilia (Marseille), reached the British Isles and northern Europe. He was the first to give the name of Thule to an island north of Great Britain (see Strabo, I. 4) (Roman and Roman 1998: 187ff.). According to Casson (1991: 125–126), Thule may refer to Norway. The Phoenician system of weights may have influenced Brittany (Ruiz-Galvez 2000: 276).

[30] The completion of another periplus, the so-called Periplus of Hanno (c. 470 BCE?), has also been debated (Desanges 1981; Warmington 1984; Gonzalez-Ponce 2008: 92–115). Hanno may have sailed along the coasts of western Africa and reached the Gulf of Guinea (see Casson 1991: 121–123). The story of Eudoxus (late second century BCE) reported by Strabo suggests that sailors from Gadir sailed around the Cape of Good Hope and had some knowledge of this route.

[31] This could "indicate use of carts for haulage, rather than chariots in warfare" (MacEachern 2005: 443).

p.c.), trade routes did exist. The Dhar Tichitt region (southern Mauritania) and the Middle Niger may have been connected to Mediterranean networks during the first half of the first millennium BCE (Holl 1993; McDonald 2011). The Tichitt settlements disappeared *c.* 500 BCE, possibly the victims of Berber attacks from the north (McDonald 2011). Herodotus refers to the population of the Garamantes, and that of the Nasamonians, who sent an expedition from Libya that reached a "black town" perhaps located in the Niger valley. According to Herodotus, the Garamantes used chariots drawn by four horses to go after Troglodyte Ethiopians. It is remarkable that several Phoenician ports of trade were created along the Tripolitan coast (Sabrata, Oea, Leptis Magna). We have "evidence for black slaves in the Mediterranean as early as the 6th century BC"; the representations are "mainly of children" (Fentress 2011: 66). "Punic Carthage was a beneficiary of [the slave] trade from the beginning. Frontinus tells us that black auxiliaries served in the Carthaginian army from the 5th century on. However, this trade was not fully underway before the end of the 5th century BCE, when the urban site of Garama started to take off and the quantity of representations of Black Africans multiplied (Mattingly 2003: 348)" (Fentress 2011: 68). "Leptis Magna provided the most direct route to the Mediterranean. Another route [mentioned by Herodotus] cut upward from the Libyan oasis of Augila to 'the land of the Lotus Eaters' [Nile valley]" (Fentress 2011). Towns influenced by the Punic culture were founded in Morocco (Siga, Volubilis, during the third century BCE), and coins were struck (Callegarin 2011). In western Mauritania, Akjoujt yielded copper objects, some of them showing similarities to artifacts found in northern Africa (Childs and Herbert 2005: 280; Bisson 2000: 90). The mines of the Akjoujt region were exploited between 800 and 200 BCE (Alpern 2005: 59–60). Here, influences from Morocco – and perhaps from southern Spain – have been suggested. In Mauritania, "habitation sites of varying sizes existed in a four-level settlement hierarchy between about 1500 and 500 BCE. Such hierarchies indicate some degree of political centralization" (MacEachern 2005: 447; see Vernet 1993). Near Lake Chad, the fortified site of Zilum (*c.* 500 BCE), linked to the incipient Sao culture, shows that evolution occurred, which may have been linked to long-distance exchanges (Magnavita *et al.* 2006). Moreover, the Phoenicians developed a route between Tunisia and Egypt; it was little used, however, prior to the late seventh century CE (Sherratt and Sherratt 1993: 367). The discoveries of carnelian and amazonite beads at Akreijit (Tichitt) and Kolima South (Mali, first millennium BCE) appear to reflect long-distance trade (McDonald 2011: 73–74). Around 250 BCE, according to Burroughs (2001), increased aridification in the Sahara led to the introduction of the dromedary, used by the Garamantes. It is likely that this introduction, however, had occurred at an earlier time. Herodotus (IV.169) speaks of people called the Giligamae in Libya, "people of the dromedaries" (Lipinski 2004: 211). A rock sculpture featuring a dromedary found at Erdi (Chad), has been dated to the mid-first millennium BCE (2004: 209). Gold transported from Ophir (possibly Opiros, on the Libyan coast) may have come from western Africa (see below).

Up until the third century BCE, the Phoenicians and then the Carthaginians did not seek to control resources directly, but they did forge connections with local proto-economies which they helped develop through trade and transfers of techniques, for example in metalworking (Norel 2004: 88).[32] Treaties must have been negotiated between Phoenicians and the indigenous powers. It is possible that autochthonous populations converted to Phoenician cults. The role of temples and religion in the Phoenician settlements, emphasized by P. Norel (2004), with merchants grouped together in what we might term "brotherhoods" under divine protection, remains a topic for debate. It is true that religion was often a crucial factor of cohesion among trade networks, as demonstrated later with Buddhism and Islam. The Phoenician merchants were probably bound by divine oaths (sworn to a divinity). Temples were places of exchange,[33] acting as interfaces between agricultural or craft production and trade, particularly long-distance trade. Here again, it is difficult to evaluate the true role of the temples within the system in place, although at Gadir, the temple of Melqart – patron of seamen – was clearly crucial to capital accumulation and the financing of trade expeditions. For Aubet (2001: 278–279), "the temple was the pivot and protector of the commercial diaspora" (see also Allen 2005: 86). For various authors, trade was first organized on the basis of familial firms or merchant guilds placing agents in various outposts.[34] The great merchants belonged to the ruling oligarchy. According to Isaiah (23:8): "[The] merchant princes [of Tyre] were the most honored men on earth." The Phoenician kings themselves were involved in long-distance trade.[35] Moreover, Phoenician growth was based on war fleets, utilized also by rulers in trading operations.[36] Crews were multiethnic and the army made use of mercenaries. As at Ugarit in earlier times, the state and private sectors were closely linked to one another,[37] with the merchants involved in public affairs. The king of Byblos mentions a "Council of state" who ruled the city with him. The power at Tyre and Carthage relied upon a "Council of Elders," the suffetes (Phoenician *sptm*, "judge") (Aubet 2001: 117), and Carthage formed an oligarchic republic as of the fifth century BCE, with suffetes elected for one year. Eusebius of Caesarea and Flavius Josephus mention suffetes governing Tyre between 564 and 556 BCE (after the city was captured by King Nebuchadnezzar II of Babylon).

---

[32] See Moore and Lewis (1999: 116–118) on the growing exploitation of silver mines in southern Spain, driven by Phoenician demand. The Iberians exploited the silver mines of the Huelva region even before the arrival of the Phoenicians in southern Spain, and imported tin from the British Isles. However, it is probably inaccurate to say that "the Phoenicians of the western Mediterranean Sea had very little influence on the indigenous local cultures" (Graslin and Maucourant 2005).

[33] Sherratt and Sherratt (1993: 375) also felt that "temples and sanctuaries formed important meeting points between the different economic systems of Phoenician and indigenous groups."

[34] Gamito 1988: 54. Also Aubet 2001: 118–119.

[35] There were kings in Phoenicia, but kingship never existed at Carthage, which was ruled by a governor (*skn*) (Ferjaoui 1993: 41). For this author, there is little evidence that the temples organized trade, or even played a major role in trade. The cities founded in the western Mediterranean Sea paid tithes to the kings of the mother-cities, at least during the first centuries; then, these payments dwindled (Ferjaoui 1993: 30–31, quoting Diodorus of Sicily, XX.14, 1–2).

[36] The settlement in Sardinia, around the middle of the eighth century, seems to have been made with the help of armed forces. The Phoenicians were interested in copper resources, which were already being traded during the Late Bronze Age.

[37] The treaty signed by the Assyrian king Esarhaddon and Tyre during the seventh century shows that "the merchant fleet of Tyre was the property partly of the king and partly of the 'elders of the country', that is, the shipowners and merchant princes" (Aubet 2001: 117).

The network of Phoenician cities set up a geographical division of labor, where Sidon and Tyre and later Carthage played prominent roles. Tunisia and Sicily delivered grain, Sardinia silver and lead, and Iberia silver and copper. From 700 BCE onward, silver extraction (mostly from Tartessos, in southern Spain), became the major export activity of the Iberian peninsula. Silver financed this expanding Phoenician network, as well as that of Tyre and Assyria, for which this metal was a crucial import (Allen 2005: 88).

Tyre and Phoenicia were under Assyrian suzerainty, but they also took advantage of this status. During the ninth and eighth centuries, Phoenician ships maintained the upper hand on maritime routes in the Mediterranean, except in the Aegean Sea. Later, the Phoenician and Carthaginian ports were forced to compete with Greek cities.

During the eighth and seventh centuries, Greek trading posts were founded throughout the Mediterranean: Pithekoussai (Bay of Naples), around 775 BCE; Syracuse (Sicily), in 734 BCE; Naucratis (Egypt), c. 650 BCE; Cyrene (Libya), in 630 BCE; and Euesperides (Libya) and Massilia (Marseille, southern France) c. 600 BCE. From Massilia, the Greek networks would expand into the Rhone valley, and toward the Atlantic, whence tin came from the Cassiterides Islands (British Isles).[38] Moreover, Miletus set up outposts on the Black Sea: Trapezous (Trebizond), during the eighth century BCE; and Istros and Pantikapaion (Kerch) during the seventh century BCE. Greek colonists from Megara founded Byzantium in 657 BCE. The Greek and Phoenician networks were intertwined; "quantities of Greek products have been found in early layers at Carthage" (Cunliffe 1994: 339). The reasons for this first Greek expansion are still debated; for some authors, it was propelled by demographic growth and the need for new lands and not so much motivated by trade: often, the "colonies" kept no links with their "mother city." This demographic pressure explains the presence of Greek artisans in Babylonia during the seventh century and that of Greek mercenaries in the Egyptian, and later the Neo-Babylonian and Persian, armies. Trade – especially in cereals, precious metals, and slaves – certainly provided an added impetus for this expansion.

In Anatolia, the Greek cities were obliged to take Lydia into account. Lydia was a significant power during the seventh and sixth centuries, and a bridge between the routes of Asia and the Mediterranean world. Taking advantage of the gold exploited in the Pactolus River, the Lydian capital Sardis became the richest city in Anatolia.[39] According to Herodotus, the Lydians colonized Etruria c. 800 BCE (central-western Italy), an episode still unconfirmed, though Lydian influences are still noticeable. The formation of Etruscan city-states, which benefited from the resources of Tuscany in iron,[40] also resulted from local and regional development, stimulated by Etruscan

---

[38] The discovery of the Greek vase of Vix in the foothills of Mont-Lassois (late sixth century BCE), of Greek and Massiliot ceramics, and of a "palace" showing Hellenistic influence on Mont-Lassois show evidence of these networks (Roman and Roman 1998; Chaume 2007), as do the discoveries at Heuneburg (Bavaria) and other sites. The rich tomb of a Celtic prince containing several Greek artifacts has recently been found at Lavau, near Troyes (Aube). The tomb is dated to the early fifth century BCE.

[39] Croesus's reign (561–547 BCE) corresponds to the peak of Lydian power. Croesus built an alliance with Sparta, Egypt, and Babylonia against Persia, but the Lydian troops were defeated by the Persians led by Cyrus II in 547 BCE.

[40] In general, iron production increased in Europe as of 700 BCE.

connections to Mediterranean networks.[41] As was the case in Iberia, writing came about due to external connections: here, it arose from contact with the Greeks, who were active on the maritime routes along the Italian coasts.

The growth of trade with the continent's interior led to the integration of part of central Europe ("Hallstatt culture") into the world-system. This region exported metals, hides, salt, slaves, and horses, with Etruria acting as an interface with the Greek outposts (Sherratt 1993; Kristiansen 1998).[42] Beyond, amber routes connected Italy and Scandinavia.

Between the Mediterranean Sea and the Indian Ocean, an active trade also flourished on various routes. The blossoming of the Assyrian Empire during the eighth and seventh centuries amounted to the first attempted take-over of the whole area between these seas. The Assyrians also endeavored to control the Arab caravan trade to western Asia, a trade based on the exportation of incense, especially from the eighth century onward. Trade progressed in the Red Sea, parallel to that in the Persian Gulf. A marked process of urbanization occurred in Syria, Palestine, and western Arabia at this time. The Assyrians went so far as to invade Egypt, but failed to maintain their grip on the country. In any event, the invasion of Egypt in 671, then again in 664 BCE, became the first time the "bread basket" of the Nile valley became incorporated into an Asiatic empire. This Assyrian expansion reveals a new phase of integration within the western world-system; it led to a stronger link between the Mediterranean Sea and the Indian Ocean. In western Asia, Assyrian military operations triggered the crystallization of a Mede confederation, which would play a major role in the Assyrian collapse by allying itself with Babylon. This marked a shift in power toward southern Mesopotamia.

Egypt then experienced a revival after Psamtik I (663–609 BCE) managed to throw off the Assyrian yoke. The army included a large number of Greek mercenaries, and interactions with the Greek world developed, through the trading post located at Naucratis. Phoenicians were also present in Egypt, and the Nile valley had trade links with Carthage. As a sign of growing exchanges and of Egypt's entrepreneurial spirit, Psamtik's successor, Nechao II, dug a canal between the Red Sea and the Nile, and launched a fleet operated by Phoenicians, intent on circumnavigating Africa. These changes went along with a new monetization of the economy, founded on silver. Markets developed, including a land market, with army officers receiving land grants in exchange for their military services.

The Formation of an Indian World-System during the Seventh Century BCE

From 700 BCE onward, we observe a parallel enlargement of not just two, but three world-systems. Connections would multiply over the following centuries, both within and among these world-systems. In India and Pakistan, cities were formed and states emerged, in the central plains of the Ganges; in Gandhara (region of Peshāwar and Taxila); in Afghanistan (Kamboja); in Madhya Pradesh; Maharashtra; Saurashtra; and

---

[41] The Etruscan language was a non-Indo-European language. Its sole well-established connections are with inscriptions found on the island of Lemnos (Aegean Sea).

[42] The transformation of the interior of the continent into a periphery of the system went hand in hand with the formation of political entities and the appearance of true industrial centers such as Stichna (Slovenia) (iron metallurgy) and Hallstatt (Austria) (exploitation of salt).

Bengal: ancient Buddhist and Jain sources refer to sixteen states at the end of the seventh century BCE. Among them, Magadha (Middle Ganges) asserted its prominence during the sixth century, partly due to its control over iron resources. The Ganges valley and the Ujjain region formed the core of an Indian world-system, which was connected to western Asia via terrestrial routes running across Bactria, Margiana, and northern Iran. Maritime routes through the Persian Gulf also grew in importance. An Assyrian fleet was built, during the seventh century, with the help of the Phoenicians. Toward the east, links were established through the Gulf of Bengal with various regions of Southeast Asia. The western Indian Ocean was now connected to the East Asian world, with the different coasts of the Indian peninsula actively participating in transregional exchange networks. Trade between Mesopotamia and the Indian subcontinent included spices and aromatics from insular Southeast Asia and perhaps China as early as the seventh century BCE. The carriers appear to have been diverse: Indians, Arabs, Persians, and Phoenicians in the west, and Indians, Austronesians, and Austroasiatics in the east, where the situation at that time is still poorly understood.

The Eastern World-System during the "Spring and Autumn" Period

Trade routes also developed between India and China through Central Asia, where more favorable climate conditions made it easier for merchants to move about. At this time, China was evolving rapidly. Iron metallurgy developed, and agriculture benefited from a warming climate after 700 and even more so after 500 BCE. This progress provided the basis for urban development during what has become known as the Spring and Autumn period (722–481 BCE). Chandler's estimates of the number of towns and cities with populations exceeding 25,000 (1987) (see also Bosworth 1995: 212) clearly reflect this Chinese expansion, and to a lesser extent that of India (see Table II.In.1).

While political fragmentation characterizes this period, larger kingdoms began to form around the periphery of the Zhou core, with the states of Qi (Shandong), Jin (Shanxi), Qin (Shaanxi and Gansu), and Chu (Middle Yangtze). These developments were accompanied by growth in trade and crafts. At the same time, innovations were introduced in the functioning of the state, with the establishment of administrative districts in the kingdom of Chu, and the first forms of land taxes, in the states of Lu and Zheng. Debates were conducted on the interest of state intervention and on its forms, as opposed to an economic *laisser-faire*. The transformation of the state prompted the crucial invention of a fiduciary currency – in bronze – at the beginning of the sixth century BCE; there was no correspondance between the coin's nominal and the intrinsic value: one did not trust "a material but the issuing power" (Thierry 2001: 126). This helps us understand why, during the tenth century of the Christian era, China became the first country to issue paper notes (Testard 2001: 10).[43] During the sixth century BCE, law texts written on bronze also appeared.

---

[43] The coins issued by Wang Mang, in particular, bore no indication of weight, only face values (1, 25, 50, 100, 500, 1000); they were the bronze equivalent of the paper notes issued from the tenth century onward (Thierry 2001: 135).

Table II.In.1 *Towns and cities with populations exceeding 25,000, 1000–650 BCE*

BCE	Mesopotamia	Egypt	Levant	Mediterranean	India	China
1000	4	4	1	0	1	3
800	4	3	2	0	1	5
650	5	2	1	1	2	6

The state of Chu acquired a special importance after its victory over Jin in 597 BCE. It developed iron metallurgy, which allowed it to manufacture weapons and tools. Other neighboring maritime kingdoms flowered: Wu, at the mouth of the Yangtze, and Yue on the coasts of Zhejiang, which annexed the state of Wu in 473 BCE. The rapid development of Chu and of its neighbors between the seventh and fifth centuries BCE fostered interactions with the south and marked a broadening of the Chinese world-system. The appearance of a glass industry and of imported glass, moreover, reflects increasing connections with the west through what would become the Silk Roads, and also through a Yunnan–Burma–India route, revealed by the discoveries of glass beads in Chu tombs from the fifth century BCE; this was a route already known during the second millennium BCE. The artistic motifs on various ornaments, found between Central Asia and China, also show the importance of transregional interactions (Wu Xiaolong 2004), as does the introduction of the peach tree into the Mediterranean world during the seventh century BCE (Zohary and Hopf 2000).

Social and political mutations at the end of this period shed light on the emerging figure of Confucius, whose teaching – known through later texts – tried to promote the idea of the "virtuous man," mindful of social harmony.

The Restructuring of the Western World-System during the Second Half of the Seventh Century BCE

Around the middle of the seventh century BCE, attacks by nomads affected the Chinese states, leading to the formation of coalitions between kingdoms. During the same period, movements of populations brought significant changes to the western world-system. Scythian invasions from Central Asia and the steppes north of the Black Sea did not affect the entire system, but they did lead to a certain amount of restructuring. Migrations reached eastern Europe, and Scythian mercenaries entered the service of princes of the Hallstatt culture (Kristiansen 1998: 287).[44] These movements had a hand in shifting the trade routes from central Europe toward the western area of the Hallstatt culture. The new populations who settled north of the Black Sea forged successful contacts with the Mediterranean world. In Anatolia, the Scythian invasions led to the demise of the Urartu kingdom, and to a decline of Assyria, which was also affected by domestic turmoil. This Assyrian decline helped shift power toward southern Mesopotamia during the late seventh century BCE. A Chaldean dynasty allied itself with the Medes of northwestern Iran against the Assyrians; Assur and Nineveh were

---

[44] The Scythians maintained contacts with the east: Chinese helmets have been found in a Scythian burial at Kelermes (Kuban region, northern Black Sea steppe) dated between 800 and 600 BCE (Cunliffe 2015: 199).

captured in 612 and Assyria disappeared. Babylon built an empire (610–539 BCE) that succeeded the Assyrian Empire, with the same purposes, but on a lesser scale. Egypt backed off before the Babylonians in the Levant, but protected the Nile delta from invasion; in the south, the capture of Napata by the Egyptians in 590 BCE opened access to the gold mines of Nubia.

The early sixth century marked a turning point for the balances of power in the Mediterranean. Babylon's control over the Phoenician cities led to the decline of the whole Levantine coast, which in turn triggered Carthage's emancipation; it also furthered Greek expansion overall.

The Key Period of the Sixth and Fifth Centuries BCE

Trade expanded throughout Eurasia during the sixth and fifth centuries BCE, a period of general economic growth during which the population of the Ancient World may have doubled (Bosworth 1995: 214). A movement of urbanization and new statebuilding was shaping up, marked by the impressive rise in power of Persia (with the formation of the Achaemenid Empire), China and India, and by the expansion of Carthage and the Greek cities in the Mediterranean. Everywhere, one notes "a change of scale in the interconnections" (Harding 1994: 334). As in the Bronze Age, the cores of the various systems (the western Asia–Egypt–Mediterranean area; northern India; China) exported textiles and other manufactured products (metallic objects, glass) and imported raw or semi-manufactured goods and slaves from more or less distant peripheries. Between the two ends of the chain of exchanges, semi-peripheries flourished, whenever they were able to benefit from the dynamics of the system (their elites, in any case, were beneficiaries) (see Map II.1).

The sixth and fifth centuries were a crucial time because major technological and institutional innovations transpired in the political, religious, and economic domains. This was also a crucial period due to social transformations. The Achaemenid area did not merely replace the Assyrian and Babylonian empires; it became the first truly "universal empire" by virtue of its size and institutional innovations.[45] In China, a transformation of the state was initiated (see above), which was the prelude to more radical mutations during the following period of the "Warring Kingdoms." Coinage guaranteed by the state appeared in Lydia and in China, resulting from parallel political developments.[46]

From China to the Mediterranean, social transformation gave rise to new views on the universe and society, and this went hand in hand with the emergence of individualism. We witness this in the sudden appearance of great philosophical and religious doctrines claiming universal truths (Jainism and Buddhism in India; Confucianism in China; Zoroastrianism in Persia),[47] as well as the flourishing of rationalist humanism

---

[45] These innovations, however, were partially inherited from earlier developments, which had occurred during the last phase of the Assyrian Empire.

[46] Although the ultimate origin of money is probably religious, as Hocart (1952) as suggested. On the "religious origins of money in 'Homeric society'," see Laum (1924), Peacock (2013: 84ff.). See also Theurl 2004: 38–41 and below.

[47] Zoroaster is generally considered as having lived c. 600 BCE (Mallory and Mair 2000). Other estimations place his birth earlier, around the eighth century, or even during the late second millennium (see Kuzmina 2007: 448–449). Moreover, the Hebrew Bible was partly written during the fifth century BCE.

in the Greek world; a scientific rationalist current in China (the Mohists); and a political rationalist movement in India (with the *Arthasāstra*, perhaps written during the fourth/third century BCE,[48] which places the quest for profit above any other goal in life) (Glover 2000: 95). These simultaneous evolutionary pathways most likely reflect a higher level of integration for the Afro-Eurasian area (Frank 1993a). The new status of the individual was linked to major political and economic changes. Babylonia and the Persian Empire enabled the deployment of "capitalistic" firms such as the "House" of Egibi; these firms often worked in connection with the state. The Phoenician city-states also allowed entrepreneurship to expand, along with an interpenetration of the state and private sectors. The private sector often took an active part in long-distance trade and the internal economy of the states – including the management of assets belonging to public institutions, for example in the Neo-Babylonian Empire.[49]

The Greek world was the first, however, to contribute to the most radical innovations in the western world-system. Here the emergence of markets occurred in connection with a freedom of thought leading to reflections on the world, on city governance, and even on divine laws. These changes can be seen – mainly from the fifth century BCE onward – in a flowering of rationalistic humanism[50] and democratic institutions,[51] marked by the appearance of a new concept of citizenship in the city-states. These innovations benefited in part from contacts with western Asia and Egypt, an influence which remains poorly understood (McNeill 1963: 602, 609). The Greeks borrowed the alphabet from the Phoenicians (around 800 BCE), probably institutional principles as well, and "perhaps even the idea of the *polis*" (Niemeyer 2000: 109).[52] The *polis* appears to be linked to religion, to a legalistic vision (the citizen only obeyed the laws of the city), and to the "hoplite revolution" which rendered it possible (from *c.* 750 BCE on) to form citizens' armies made up of well-trained infantry regiments using the phalanx formation. Foreigners and of course slaves were non-citizens: they took no part in the political life of the city. As already mentioned, however, Tyre and Carthage relied upon a council of notables; Carthage organized itself into an oligarchic republic from the fifth century BCE

---

[48] Mittal 2004 (*contra* Trautmann 1971, who argues that the text is a compilation dated to the third century CE). The text may actually have been written during the first centuries of the Christian era and be based on older texts.

[49] Van Driel 2002: 164. "The institutions [themselves] were forced into a more market-oriented economy" (van Driel 2002: 165).

[50] As early as the seventh century, the Milesian School (from Miletus) developed a form of rationalist thought (see below). Some thinkers, notably Xenophanes of Colophon (who may have died around 470 BCE), developed the concept of religious skepticism. The majority of the population remained committed to cults that proliferated and were being privatized, becoming the property of families who ran them as enterprises (Moore and Lewis 1999: 155). Greek art expresses these social transformations.

[51] It would be wrong, however, as Hansen rightly emphasizes (2000b: 165–166, 2000c: 599), to consider the Greek *polis* as a democratic state. "Some *poleis* were democracies, some were oligarchies, and some were monarchies." In addition, the system was based on the massive use of slavery.

[52] To the Phoenician alphabet, the Greeks added signs to indicate vowels. For Hansen (2000b: 147), "the emergence of the *polis* in the colonies influenced *polis* formation in the homeland" in Greece and Anatolia. Ancient sites such as Lefkandi, in Euboea (1000–700 BCE), were probably not *poleis*. According to Morris (1987) (quoted by Kristiansen 1998: 141), who underplays the Asian inheritance, the Greek *polis* resulted instead from internal processes where class conflicts (farmers against the landed aristocracy) played a driving role in change.

onward, with suffetes elected for one year (Aubet 2001). This Carthaginian organization would influence the Roman republic, which was led by two consuls.

The Western World-System (Sixth and Fifth Centuries BCE)

The rapid development of the western world-system from the sixth century BCE on was partly based on favorable climatic conditions in the cores.[53] With the exception of the Levant, Palestine, and Susiana, victims of Babylonian imperialism, the sixth century clearly appears to have been a period of expansion, noticeable in the Mediterranean as well as in the Persian Gulf, where trade was growing when the Achaemenid Empire took shape in 550 BCE. The formation of this empire, open to three seas, marked a new phase of integration for the system.

Exchange networks extended into the western Mediterranean Sea and beyond, into the Atlantic. This expansion was the result not only of a systemic logic, but also of political events in western Asia. After the occupation of the Levantine cities by the Neo-Babylonian emperor Nebuchadnezzar II in 573/572, Carthage, partly cut off from Tyre, acquired new importance, founded on control over access to the Iberian silver mines and the Atlantic routes.[54] Links were maintained between Tyre and Carthage, however (Ferjaoui 1993). The Phoenician cities of the western Mediterranean Sea now relied upon Carthage for their defense (Niemeyer 2000). A Carthaginian movement of colonization occurred in northern Africa, Sicily, Sardinia, and Spain, starting in the fifth century BCE. Ibiza became a major Phoenician center as of 550 BCE in connection with the new significance of southeastern Spain; this was accompanied by the relative decline of Tartessos. While from 800 to 600 BCE trade activities were usually peaceful, competition grew arduous from 550 on for control over resources and trade routes; in some cases, this led to conflicts between Carthaginians and Etruscans on the one side, and Greeks on the other.[55]

At the same time, major changes were occurring in Greek society. Around the seventh century, the political system of "tyranny" (from the Lydian *turan*) appeared, where one man held supreme authority, a development perhaps linked to the upsurge in "capitalist" practices in the cities (these practices would later be considered as characteristic of capitalism). The idea of the equality of all citizens before the law would emerge progressively at the end of the sixth century (Carlo 2001). During this period, Greece saw the development of markets for goods and factors of production. Abandoning cereal crops, large estates began growing fruit, for the production of olive oil and wine for export, whence the necessity for the Greek cities to import more and more grain: in the following centuries, Athens usually imported half of its consumption

---

[53] The climate was generally milder and wetter than it had been during the eighth/seventh centuries. One also notes increased rainfall in parts of the steppes, for example in the south of the Urals, after a period of aridity (Davis-Kimball and Yablonsky 1995; Thompson 2005).

[54] The incorporation of the Phoenician city-states into the Babylonian empire also facilitated Greek expansion overall (Kristiansen 1998: 126).

[55] In 535 BCE, an Etrusco-Carthaginian alliance inflicted a great deal of damage on the Phocaean Greeks from Massilia and Corsica at the battle of Alalia (Aleria, in Corsica), the first serious conflict in the western Mediterranean Sea. A second large naval battle occurred in 474 off Cumae, which saw a victory of the Greek forces over the Etruscans. On the changes in this period, see Cunliffe 1994: 340–341.

of wheat (Bresson 2000: 205). This shift toward large estates would continue during the fourth century, marking a "capitalization of agriculture" (Friedman 2000: 139). Some estates resorted mostly to servile labor, as did industry and the silver mines. "A large number of freemen [however] had a salaried status," even though slavery remained a fundamental feature of the economy.[56] In addition, "slavery was entirely enmeshed in commercial activities": there was no opposition between slavery and the "market,"[57] which played a vital role in the economy. For the fourth century, Norel notes the possibility of selling land (non-citizens, however, could not buy land), and the payment of workers "in proportion to their work and not to their status"; he emphasizes capital accumulation by "sea merchants" (2004: 102), "the extensive use of money and the obligation for every citizen to acquire [sufficient] monetary means to buy the equipment he needed as a hoplite . . .:] the market necessarily features prominently in the Greek economy from the Vth century" (2004: 105).

Growth in industry and trade characterized this period. Greek cities imported grain – especially from the sixth century onward – from Anatolia, Syria, and Egypt, as well as raw materials (ore from Thrace, wood from the Balkans) and slaves. They delivered oil, wine, silver, and manufactured products such as wool textiles, weapons, ceramics, while pursuing an active export policy. A form of regional specialization seems to have been taking shape. During the sixth century, the production of ceramics adapted itself to suit specific markets (Moore and Lewis 1999: 149–151). Xenophon emphasizes the link between price levels and production activities, revealing the emergence of markets, where movements of prices steered production (Bresson 2000: 294). Plato himself, anticipating Adam Smith, observes that "division of labor within the city avoids wasting everyone's time, at the same time ensuring the production of objects of better quality" (Bresson 2000: 118). Workshops produced leather, textiles, metallic objects, and ceramics. Pericles (495–429 BCE) captures the opulence of Athens in these terms: "The magnitude of our city draws the produce of the world into our harbor, so that to the Athenian the fruits of other countries are as familiar a luxury as those of his own" (Thucydides II.38; Hansen 2000c: 615).

Trade within the Greek cities was somewhat different from trade involving western Asia or Egypt: in Greek cities, trade was based mainly on the activity of individual merchants and not upon firms and/or merchant-princes linked to the state and the temple.[58] Private merchants provided Athens' wheat supply. As early as the seventh century, craftsmen from the island of Euboea, or Athens, or Corinth inscribed their names on their products, thus starting the "practice of labelling their work" (Moore and Lewis 1999: 143). Maritime traders, operating privately, each owned one or several ships. Partly financed by bankers (see below), long-distance trade was secured by the

---

[56] Norel 2004: 105. For Descat (2004), half of the population of Athens was composed of slaves during the fourth century BCE. A text by Pseudo-Aristotle (c. 320–310 BCE?) indicates that a slave is the possession that allows one to achieve maximum profit (Descat 2004). Slaves were widely used in urban workshops, but not as much in agriculture, except in olive growing.

[57] Friedman 2000: 137. Friedman points out that slaves received the equivalent of a "salary" and could themselves rent other slaves.

[58] Changes also occurred in Egypt; at the beginning of the first millennium BCE, the scribe Any wrote: "If wealth is placed where it bears interest, it comes back to you redoubled" (Silver 1995: 115).

"possibility of establishing contracts having an absolute legal value in the community where they were issued." Loans by merchants trading over long distances were the result of rational calculation aimed at maximizing profits (Bresson and Bresson 2004: 101–102). Long-distance trade and even crafts were often in the hands of foreigners, a fact that contrasted with the restrictions placed on foreign traders in Asia and at Carthage. The state exerted control and oriented trade flow, by extracting various taxes,[59] by controlling prices to prevent large fluctuations, and by negotiating contracts between cities or with country-states (Bresson 2000: 122ff., 149). Some redistribution of wealth took place through "the payment of services rendered to the collectivity, the use of 'liturgies,' which were instances of spending in the public interest by individuals" chosen among the richest citizens,[60] distribution of cereals to citizens, and the sharing of war booty: there was therefore "a crucial intertwining between private income and public income" (Norel 2004: 102, 106; Bresson 2000). The state borrowed money from temples, from non-citizens, and even from other states. It placed its reserve fund in the temples, which ensured the fund's growth: "the sanctity of these places helped ensure the depository function" (Bresson 2000: 256).

For Hudson (2002), the introduction of Syrian and Phoenician commercial practices into a Greek world that had not created the same public institutions as western Asia, with institutions able to regulate the system by proclaiming debt cancellations,[61] had dramatic results: the development of slavery for debt, the appearance of an oligarchy of great landowners, and deeper social inequalities, while the economy grew increasingly monetized. The new polarization of society, with a private sector whose wealth rose at the expense of the public sector, led to the emergence of reformers such as Solon (c. 640–558) (Athens) (Hudson 1996: 35, 54, 2004b: 318). Solon succeeded in implementing both innovative economic and social legislation, by adopting a new system of weights and measures, removing debt bondage, and releasing mortgages affecting the lands of farmers (Schmitt 1987: 43). According to Aristotle, Solon imposed a law limiting the area of land a person could acquire, evidence for the existence of a land market at this time.

The use of money in the form of coins appeared during the sixth century in Anatolia (Lydian and later Ionian coins),[62] and spread into Greece, Mesopotamia, Persia, and India. Minting was in fact the continuation of the practice of seals affixed by palaces,

---

[59] There were no property taxes, but indirect taxation "that primarily affected the *metic* professions" (Friedman 2000: 139).

[60] It is possible to consider the liturgy, in fact, as the transformation of economic capital into symbolic capital.

[61] Syrian and Phoenician merchants may also have introduced the practice of interest-bearing loans in Etruria. Debt cancellations, however, are no longer attested in Babylonia during the first millennium BCE (but edicts of *andurārum*, "return to previous status, freedom," were issued in the Neo-Assyrian Empire). Only some remissions of taxes for limited periods of time are observed: for example, the remissions promulgated by the usurper Bardiya in the Persian Empire (Jursa 2002). Conversely, the idea of debt cancellation entered Jewish law with the "Jubilee year" (Hudson 1996: 35). Note that interest rates in Greece complied with the decimal system: the *dekate* was 10 percent per year. According to Hudson (2000), "already in their Linear B records the Mycenaean Greeks are found using a decimal system, probably reflecting Egyptian influence via Crete."

[62] The first true coins were issued by the Lydians, and follow the Mesopotamian value ratio of 60 shekels to one mina. On monetary forms guaranteed by authorities during the second millennium, see above.

temples, or merchants on bags of specific weight containing lumps of metal of guaranteed purity, known perhaps since the beginning of the second millennium;[63] however, minting was also a crucial innovation that occurred within a context of states in competition, of societies in mutation, and of growth in production and trade. The first coins in western Asia and in Greece had political significance and a role that was both social and economic. They were first meant to be used in local exchanges, but convertibility was established among various silver currencies. The state monopoly on coin minting and the iconography displayed thereon strengthened the collective identity (Aglietta 2009). This was a true innovation: with the ancient system of bags or ingots guaranteed by merchants or by the state, "weight measures goods and services and allows exchange to take place" whereas "coins tend to become a mere sign expressing value" (Le Rider 2001: 23). This was also the case for Chinese money. During the fifth and fourth centuries BCE, the political preeminence of Athens and the extension of exchange networks made that city's money (the tetradrachm depicting the owl of Pallas Athena) the first international money; it circulated within the Persian Empire and was imitated by the Egyptian pharaohs; its commercial value was higher than its intrinsic (metallic) value.

In the Greek cities, minting and the occupation of money changer were part and parcel of the developing banking system, which was still limited during this time. These ancient bankers issued credit bills that merchants could cash in another town, a practice long known in western Asia. The Greeks probably borrowed the practice of paying deposits from Phoenicia (and ultimately from Babylonia), as well as the charter contract.[64] For Bogaert, however, the custodian bank using silver entrusted to it may have been a Greek innovation, with the interest rate freely set (Bogaert 1966: 135ff.).[65] Bankers compensated depositors either indirectly, by giving them "access to trade opportunities," or directly, by paying interest. According to Bogaert (2007), loans granted by banks were usually spent on consumption rather than used for productive purposes, and maritime loans did not originate with the banks. Conversely, Silver (1995: 173) points out that bankers often lent money for profit-oriented activities.

[63] See above. For the first millennium, see the silver bags of Dor, in the Levant. During the first millennium, marks may sometimes have been stamped on the metal itself (see below). Balmuth (1975) sees links between the legend of a jasper seal dated to the eighth century, found at Megiddo, and the legend of a coin made of electrum from Ephesus, dated to the sixth century. For Le Rider (2001: 27), however, "the concept of a stamp seal is different from that of a coin, contrary to Balmuth's opinion." In any event, Thierry (2001: 121) rightly emphasizes that the practice of Lydian/Greek and Indian minting was not "a sudden innovative and decisive break," but the result of a long process originating in Mesopotamia. Moreover, it may be within the context of increasing exchanges between Anatolia and Egypt that the system of so-called "Ionian" figures was formed: Greek alphabetic figures may thus have been borrowed from Egyptian demotic figures as early as the first part of the sixth century (Chrisomalis 2003).

[64] Bogaert 1966: 147, 151. The author has stated that Phoenician practices in these domains were derived from those of cities such as Ugarit and Alalakh, during the second millennium, and quite often, they ultimately originated in Babylonia.

[65] However, as already mentioned, there were long-term silver deposits, bearing interest, in connection with merchants during the Old Assyrian period. During the second millennium, Babylonian temples maintained deposit accounts (Bogaert 1966: 151). Greek temples also accepted deposits, and made loans, at least during the classical period (Bogaert 1966: 130).

He thus mentions one loan from a banker to a captain who wanted to buy a ship on credit, and a loan of 2,000 drachmae to acquire mines.

The mutations in Greek society outlined here led to the extension of a movement that had begun previously. During the sixth and fifth centuries BCE, for economic reasons and to solve the problem of a large surplus population, the Greek cities of Greece and Anatolia continued to create outposts in the Mediterranean Sea, and in the Black Sea, at the endpoints of routes either running along the valleys of great rivers (the Don, the Volga) or leading to Central Asia. Largely based on the use of a servile labor force and mercenaries, the development of Greece led to the establishment of trade networks that helped structure and geographically broaden European peripheries. In a process of coevolution, increasing contacts between Greeks and Scythians fostered the formation of kingdoms as well as an incipient urbanization in Ukraine during the sixth century BCE, as seen in the site of Belsk (Taylor 1994). Herodotus's writings (484–420 BCE) reveal the existence of a steppe route east of the Black Sea, toward Central Asia. In addition, south of the Black Sea, the port of Trapezous marked the end of a trade road out of Iran. A considerable slave trade operated from what was called "Scythia" to the Greek world (from the Scythian capital of Gelonus [Belsk] toward the Greek colony of Olbia, in Ukraine, for example); this trade would persist into the Roman period (Taylor 2001: 34). Other slaves came from the Danube valley and western Asia. The first millennium BCE was the first historical period to see massive population transfers – whether labor forces or mercenaries – from peripheral regions and margins toward central regions. From the sixth century on, one observes a growing militarization of the societies in the steppes, triggered by a rising slave trade in the west, and the Achaemenid expansion in the east.[66] The Scythian region also exported wheat, gold, furs, and horses; this trade extended as far as the Adriatic. These goods were exchanged for wine, oil, and metallic vessels. In the western Mediterranean Sea, the Greek presence also grew, marked by the creation and rapid growth of Massilia. At the same time, an Etruscan thrust toward the Po valley, at the end of the sixth century, triggered the flowering of the ports of Spina and Adria, where Greek merchants from the Adriatic went to trade. These Greek and Etruscan developments led to a strengthening of exchange networks with northern Europe through the Swiss Alps and the Rhone valley. They were accompanied by a relative shift of the main trade roads from the eastern Hallstatt region to a western space,[67] where chiefdoms emerged. These chiefdoms benefited from positions as interfaces between northern margins (the Marne, the Rhine-Mosel region) which exported slaves, tin (from the British Isles), and furs and amber (from the Baltic Sea) on the one side, and Mediterranean centers which delivered wine and metallic vessels, on the other.[68]

---

[66] Darius sent an expedition to Scythia around 512 BCE. It reached the Danube but was ultimately not successful. At the same time, fortified settlements appeared in the societies of the forest zone north of the steppe (Koryakova and Epimakhov 2007: 253).

[67] As pointed out above, the Scythian expansion in eastern Europe (as far as Hungary, Moravia, and Silesia) may have also influenced the shift of the trade roads toward the western area of the Hallstatt culture.

[68] Fortified settlements appeared, for example at Mont-Lassois, Heuneburg, and Châtillon-sur-Glâne, showing the emergence of elites as interface between the southern and northern worlds, as well as violent competition that would increase during the fifth century BCE (Kristiansen 1998: 141).

One also notes a growing involvement on the part of the Greeks in Egypt, where merchants and mercenaries poured in. After a decline during the first half of the seventh century BCE, Egypt experienced a revival under the Twenty-Sixth Saite Dynasty (664–525 BCE), which resulted in an Egyptian expansion into the Levant, and into southern regions, at the expense of the Kushite kingdom. Egypt pursued an active policy in the Red Sea until 525 BCE, the date of the Persian invasion. Southern Arabs also played a major role both in the caravan trade toward Gaza and along the maritime routes of the Red Sea. Moreover, caravans transporting incense crossed Arabia toward Gerrha (perhaps Thaj, but this is debated). Several political entities shared Yemen: Saba, the Minaean kingdom, Qataban, and the Hadramawt kingdom, which was centered on Shabwa.

The political and economic flourishing of the Greek cities accompanied the blossoming of philosophy, science, and history, and the emergence of rational thinking. The development of "the first monetized market economy in history" (Bresson 2000: 307) was linked to new patterns of freedom of thought involving all the intellectual domains – Migeotte (2007: 150) refers rather to an "economy with markets," emphasizing that factor markets and commodity markets were still weakly interconnected.[69] Parallel to their reflections on political power and social organization, the Greeks seem to have been the first to develop abstract theoretical research,[70] first on the Anatolian coasts (Miletus)[71] and later in Italy (Pythagoras and his disciples) during the sixth century BCE.[72] Due to a division between scientific theory and practice, but also to the prevalence of slavery, little technical progress was made, however, in production.[73] During the fifth and fourth centuries, ideas spread throughout Greece and Asia. Athens, the home of Socrates (c. 470–399), Plato (c. 428–348), and Aristotle (c. 384–322), appears to have been a center

[69] See also Maucourant (2008: 17): "The idea that the existence of markets implies the reality of a market economy is highly debatable, because the latter is characterized by markets which are closely connected, thus constituting a system with self-regulating properties." "More than the Greek world, it was the Roman world that engaged in the commodification of social relations" (2008: 25).

[70] Babylonian and Egyptian mathematics tended to seek solutions to concrete problems; astronomy progressed in relation to the establishment of calendars and astrological concerns (Babylonian astronomers, however, used abstract models of mathematical cycles to calculate the appearance of the new moon). But the pursuit of knowledge of nature *per se* and the development of abstract speculations about the cosmos and nature would be innovations of Greek thought (McClellan and Dorn 1999: 52–54).

[71] Thales (c. 625–545 BCE) – said to have introduced Egyptian and Babylonian geometry into the Greek world – is seen as the leader of "the school of Miletus." He was the first to study magnetism. Anaximander (Anaximandros) (c. 610–546) introduced a cosmological model and put forward the idea of infinite and eternal matter. The Greek thinkers thus developed the novel concept that nature is governed by rational laws.

[72] Pythagoras (sixth century BCE) was born in Samos, but lived at Crotone (Italy). The Pythagoreans elaborated the idea of a mathematical harmony of the world. They introduced the concept of mathematical proof. However, the deductive reasoning and the use of mathematical proof only developed later, with Euclid (thirdcentury BCE).

[73] In addition, in agriculture, the type of landed property (along with the existence of both great landowners and small peasants) did not foster technological innovation (Bezbakh 2005: 13). The split between science and practice should be qualified for the ensuing period and the School of Alexandria. The water mill seems to have been an innovation originating in the eastern Mediterranean during the late first millennium BCE. Unlike the Chinese mill, showing a horizontal wheel, the Mediterranean mill used a vertical wheel.

for thought.[74] The rediscovery of Plato and Aristotle, thanks to translations done in the Muslim world, would influence Europe's path from the eleventh and twelfth centuries on.[75] Stoicism founded by Zeno (fourth–third century BCE) would find an echo in the writings of Cicero and of Marcus Aurelius.[76] Thucydides (c. 460–400 BCE) introduced the critical method in history; authors such as Polybius, Sallust, and Tacitus would make use of his contribution. Schools were created, with no state support. In Athens, Plato founded the Academy in 387, and Aristotle the Lyceum in 335. Aristotle was one of the first philosophers to ponder an equitable distribution of wealth. He condemned "the accumulation of money for itself," as is the case for interest-bearing loans.[77] The fear expressed by Aristotle of "an extension of the merchant sphere that would undo traditional social relations" coupled with his criticism of "the way to acquire goods" within a profit rationale are precise reflections of the progress made by this merchant sphere (Norel 2004: 103; Latouche 2005: 59–60). At the beginning of the fourth century BCE, Xenophon "presents the *oikonomia* as knowledge to increase his own wealth" (Migeotte 2008: 72):[78] some economic rationality was clearly developing at this time (Bresson and Bresson 2004). This change came from both the state and from individuals: all were attempting to augment their revenues (Bresson 2000: 243ff.). Traders "held a very accurate accounting," and various documents onboard ships followed the movements of their cargoes (Bresson 2000: 144). As would be the case in Rome, a parallel was drawn between the wealth of the state and that of individuals (Bresson 2000: 259).

In western Asia, too, in a continuation of trends that had emerged during the second millennium, the private sector was often active in long-distance trade and internal state economy – including the management of property belonging to public institutions, as was the case in the Neo-Babylonian Empire. This empire was formed when the Assyrian Empire collapsed, and quickly revealed its urge to expand. After a victory over the Egyptians at Karkemish in 605, Emperor Nebuchadnezzar II (604–562 BCE) conquered Susa in 595/596 BCE, Jerusalem in 586 BCE, and then overcame the resistance of Tyre in 584 BCE. Attempts to invade the Nile valley were all repelled by the Egyptians.

---

[74] First a pupil of Plato, Aristotle was Alexander the Great's tutor for a while at the Macedonian court. The holistic approach of Aristotle and his disciples emphasized the sensible qualities of things, whereas the Platonists developed quantitative and transcendental approaches (see McClellan and Dorn 1999: 72).

[75] See below. Moreover, a philosopher from the Ionian School, Heraclitus (Herakleitos) (576–480), has often been considered as the father of modern dialectical thought. In contrast, the atomistic, materialistic, and mechanistic cosmology of Leucippus (Leukippos) (c. 460–370), Democritus (Demokritos) (c. 460–370), and Epicurus (Epikouros) (c. 341–270) would fade into obscurity, although this was reiterated by the poet Lucretius (98–53 BCE) at Rome. Texts by the physician Hippocrates (460–377 BCE), who introduced clinical observation and a theory of humors, as well as many other Greek texts, would later be translated in the Muslim world.

[76] Stoicism asserted the existence of a natural law (an idea that Cicero would borrow) and defined man as citizen of the world ("It is interesting," notes J. Friedman, "that of the many philosophies of the period, stoicism is adopted by expanding Rome" [2005: 99]). Stoicism developed a logic different from that of Aristotle: it was not based on syllogism (deductive reasoning) but on chains of consequences.

[77] Bezbakh 2005: 11. Aristotle's thinking on the equitable distribution of wealth led him to bring up the problem of value; thus he considered the value of labor and the notion of utility value (Bezbakh 2005).

[78] In its original sense, *oikonomia* means "household management."

The Neo-Babylonian Empire installed a hierarchical administrative structure similar to that of the Assyrian Empire, and adhered to the Assyrian policy of deporting conquered populations. It is possible that at this time, Jews emigrated to the west coast of India. Babylon became the largest city in the Ancient World. The emperors improved the existing channels, thus promoting agriculture and trade. The state and private sectors were closely interlinked. The great Babylonian temples, whose administration was supervised by the king, entrusted the management of their assets to private contractors, in exchange for royalties. They rented portions of their land, and sold their products on the market. The temples paid in silver for the purchase of local products, and also to remunerate outside employees. Thus, a limited labor market was born. Some texts show the development of firms working in symbiosis with the state, such as the House of Egibi, which managed farmland and irrigation channels, while at the same time collecting taxes, and making interest-bearing loans. Monetization and the expansion of credit – with the use of debt notes – fostered progress in trade. State institutions lent money to businessmen, who often formed trading companies. According to Joannès (2000), almost no silver loans were made by temples,[79] whereas entrepreneurs acted as "bankers" – this was attested during the Old Babylonian period – with widely varying interest rates. While for Bogaert (1966), the custodian bank arose in the Greek world (see above), authors such as Silver (2004b) claim that while Neo-Babylonian entrepreneurs lent money by using deposits, they were not really bankers.

The Neo-Babylonian Empire was linked to Mediterranean exchange networks. It also developed trade in the Persian Gulf, by subjecting Bahrain and the Oman peninsula, whence copper, Arabian aromatics, as well as spices and dyes from India were shipped. Beset by difficulties in Mesopotamia, Emperor Nabonidus launched an expedition into northern Arabia, occupying Hijāz as far as Medina and settling in the oasis of Taymā'.

Neo-Babylonian hegemony was of short duration. At the end of the sixth century BCE, a new empire was formed whose source was in Iran. More innovative than the Babylonian Empire, this new Persian Empire managed to unify a transnational area of unmatched size. Moreover, its control over the routes toward Central Asia reveals the new importance of the Central Asian area: it was a hub between India and western Asia, as well as a gateway to the Orient.

After the conquests of Babylon by Cyrus II in 539, and of Phoenicia, Cyprus, and Egypt by Cambyses II in 525, Darius organized the empire on the basis of a system of provinces (satrapies), ruled by members of the Persian aristocracy or members of the local elites, a flexible system expressing an innovative vision of the state. "The satrap was rewarded with the income from a royal estate assigned to him" (Cunliffe 2015: 209).

---

[79] See Jursa 2002: 208. However, Stevens mentions loans of silver from the temple archive of Eanna at Uruk (2006: 152), but these are more the exception than the rule: "Three and two-thirds shekels of silver out of the silver of Sin-iddin, the keeper of the property of the Belit of Erech and Nana, charged against Nabu-sum-liser, the son of Marduk-nasir, son of Kuri, in the month of Silvan he shall pay" (after Dougherty 1933).

This allowed the Persian Empire to become the first large "universal" empire, "a synthesis harmoniously constituted of diverse political and cultural systems."[80] The multinational character of its army, the use of different languages, and religious tolerance, all were expressions of this "universal" character, also manifest in buildings and in art. The empire drew most of its revenues from taxes levied on the agricultural sector. Members of the elite managed large estates. Moreover, from other polities, the empire borrowed the ancient system of land grants in exchange for military services. As in the Neo-Babylonian Empire, private "firms" worked closely with the state – the Egibi and Murashu "houses" are well-known examples. Transactions were primarily effected in silver, which was weighed, according to the ancient Babylonian custom, but the emperors also issued gold and silver coins, that had an ideological as well as economic dimension (Huyse 2005).

The formation of a large empire opening onto four seas clearly signals a new phase of integration of the system. In order to facilitate military transport and trade, the Achaemenids built roads across the empire. They promoted maritime trade in the Persian Gulf and the Red Sea, at times calling upon the skills of the Phoenicians and Greeks in order to do so.[81] Darius (re)dug a channel between the Nile and the Red Sea, revealing the importance of the Indian Ocean trade, which provided Mesopotamia with the precious products of India. Trade routes with India also crossed Central Asia. Persian control of the regions of Kandahar, Charsadda (Pushkalāvati), and Taxila triggered the appearance of both the written word and minted coins in southern Asia.

In Anatolia and in the Aegean Sea, however, Persian expansion was blocked by the Greek city-states, now rivals of the Phoenician cities. Confrontation between the Persian Empire and the Greek world broke out during the sixth century after Cyrus II, the Persian emperor, had conquered Lydia (546 BCE). Starting in 499 BCE, the Ionian cities revolted. Led by Athens, the Delian League successfully fought off Persian attempts to invade Greece. Athens rose to preeminence after the Persian defeats – on sea and land – in 490, 480, and 479 BCE, at Marathon, Salamis, Plataea, and Mycale.[82] The naval battle at Salamis was also a victory over the Phoenicians, who were allied with the Persians: the Athenian navy was now all-powerful in the eastern Mediterranean. In 460 BCE, the Greek victory at Eurymedon secured freedom for the cities of Ionia. As Wiesehöfer rightly points out (2009: 74), the Persian wars helped create "pan-Hellenic identities." Athens created military outposts, called *klerouchía*,[83] that occupied strategic locations. It captured Cyprus in 450 BCE, thus obtaining control over the island's copper resources. Moreover, through private operators, Athens exploited the silver mines of Laurion, in Attica, where as many as 20,000 slaves

---

[80] Adams 1979: 403; Matthews 2003: 148. Matthews rightly emphasizes the unprecedented size of this empire, accompanied by the organizational invention of the satrapies, an invention linked to a "change in the ideology and the practice of bureaucratic control." On the size of empires, see Taagepera 1978: 121.

[81] Curiously, Frank (1993a) has proposed a phase of recession between 800 and 550 BCE. As for the period 1750–1600, Frank has mooted the idea that a decline of the "center" (Mesopotamia) was accompanied by the rise of a "periphery" (the Mediterranean). For criticisms of Frank's periodization, see Kristiansen (1993: 415), Muhly (1993: 418), and Sherratt and Sherratt (1993: 418).

[82] Victorious again in 465, Athens even attempted a military intervention against the Persians in Egypt in 454 BCE, but this strategy failed. In 448 BCE, the Persians recognized the independence of the Ionian cities.

[83] Initially, *klerouchía* refers to the assignment of a plot of land to a citizen-soldier.

labored.[84] Ephialtes and Pericles strengthened Athenian democratic institutions, with the aristocratic council of the Aeropagus losing part of its prerogatives to the benefit of an assembly of citizens (*ekklesia*), the Council of Five Hundred (*boulē*), and of a supreme court including 6,000 citizens (*heliaea*).[85] All citizens except women voted and were eligible. Slaves and foreigners, who represented 200,000 and 70,000 of the 400,000 inhabitants of Attica respectively, were excluded from the political system.[86] From the fifth century BCE onward, a mode of alliance representing a step toward the formation of larger political units developed in the Greek world: this was the federation of city-states. "The federal institutions were in charge of foreign policy, defense and coinage, and included a federal court ... A further development was a genuine federal citizenship" (Hansen 2000b: 171).

The tensions between Persians and Greeks did not truly hinder the deployment of exchanges. Exotic goods arriving in Greek markets included products from the Indian Ocean such as Indian beads during the fifth century BCE; pepper, mentioned during the fourth century BCE at Athens; black pepper (*Piper nigrum* L.) and long pepper (*Piper longum* L.) (Amigues 2005: 371), signaling of the growing interconnections of the Indian sphere with the western world-system. The unprecedented intensity of the interactions taking place during the sixth and fifth centuries BCE may explain the appearance of new diseases such as the plague, which decimated the Athenian army in 430–429 BCE and affected Persia.[87] The Bible emphasizes the frequency of epidemics during certain periods of the first millennium BCE.

An Indian World-System Connected to the West

India also experienced spectacular growth during the sixth and fifth centuries BCE. A strong urbanization movement clearly took place in the Ganges valley and central India. While this resulted primarily from regional developments, it is remarkable that the expansion of Magadha occurred precisely at the time of the Achaemenid conquest of Pakistan as far as the Indus valley, through which Persian and Babylonian influences entered the Indian peninsula: writing developed from systems in use in the Achaemenid Empire. The upswing in exchanges was bolstered by the issuance of money (another western influence) and the establishment of a system of standardized

---

[84] Silver was also exported by the island of Thasos, and by Thrace. According to Thucydides, Seuthes, the king of Thrace, was able to extract an annual tribute of 400 talents (more than 10 tons of silver) (Taylor 2001: 32–33).

[85] Prior to Pericles, Cleisthenes (end of the sixth century) had introduced a democratic constitution, forming an assembly of citizens, and allowing the election of ten *strategi* (magistrates) by the population. At the beginning of the sixth century BCE, the legislator Solon is said to have initiated a democratization of institutions (see above).

[86] Ancient authors such as Ctesicles go so far as to propose a higher number of slaves for Attica; figures of 400,000 slaves have also been suggested for Aegina and Corinthia. These estimates have often been seen as improbable (Taylor 2001: 29). Bezbakh (2005: 11–12) rightly notes that the freedom of the citizen had as corollary the labor of the slave. Illustrating "the entrepreneurial nature of Greek economy," the life story of Pasion, at the end of the fifth century, shows, however, that a slave could become a banker and ultimately a citizen (Moore and Lewis 1999: 166). Pasion's activities were diverse: he invested money in a shipping company and in a workshop manufacturing weapons. He later bequeathed his bank to his former slave Phormio.

[87] McNeill 1998b: 120. The disease may have spread from Upper Egypt.

weights. The Indian coasts were active in long-distance trade. Greek and biblical texts mention spices and aromatics arriving not only from southern Arabia, but also from India and beyond: from Southeast Asia and even China. Various Indian texts refer to a maritime trade between Babylon and India during the seventh and sixth centuries BCE. This trade probably involved Dravidians, Aryans, Arabs, and Persians. Wood, precious stones, beads, spices, and aromatics from India arrived in Mesopotamia (Salles 1996a: 256), as did iron and steel. Archaeology has also shown evidence of this trade. Examples include the discovery of a cinnamon flower in the Heraion of Samos (Amigues 2005: 374). In addition, finds of cowries in Punic tombs reveal connections with the Indian Ocean via Egypt and the Levant.[88]

The core of the Indian world-system was located in the Ganges valley and in central India, but terrestrial and maritime networks extended out from this core. Sri Lanka was linked with northern India, as shown by the discovery at Anurādhāpura of shards bearing Brāhmī letters in levels dated between 510 and 340 BCE.[89] "From the very start, the language was a form of Prākrit of North Indian origin" (Coningham *et al.* 2006: 435). The expansion of Buddhist networks accompanied the expansion of internal and external trade, especially toward Southeast Asia. Exchanges took place across the Bay of Bengal as early as the middle of the first millennium BCE. Indians probably settled in Southeast Asia from the fourth century BCE onward, as the site of Khao Sam Kaeo makes plain: the "indianization" of this region began earlier than usually thought (Bellina-Pryce and Silapanth 2008). Pepper was traded: a protoform *amrec (deriving from Sanskrit) has been reconstructed in Proto-Chamic. Conversely, it is worth noting that the *Arthasāstra* mentions aloeswood under a name of Malay origin. The appearance of iron metallurgy originating in China and India in continental and insular Southeast Asia reveals the extension of maritime and terrestrial routes as well as the progressive formation of a global Asian sphere. Progress in iron metallurgy as well as that of various interactions between 500 and 200 BCE in the Strait of Malacca and the Java Sea triggered the development of more complex societies and urban centers. These also resulted from internal evolution, which was partly founded on advances in wet rice culture (Wisseman Christie 1995: 251).

Central Asia progressively became a vital artery for the Eurasian world (see also Christian 2000: 6). Briant (1982: 36) places the formation of a proto-silk road, controlled by Scythian chiefs, at this time.[90] One wonders whether the flowering of the cities of Samarkand, Balkh (Bactres), and Taxila around the seventh and eighth centuries, and the thrust of the Persian Empire toward Central Asia and the Indus – showing the vitality of exchanges in these regions – might reflect the formation of a world-system

---

[88] Because contacts existed between northern Africa and the sub-Saharan regions, the question arose as to whether or not cowries arrived in this area during the first millennium BCE (Hogendorn and Johnson 1986: 15). The current state of research holds that the earliest cowries discovered so far are dated between the fifth and seventh centuries CE (Burkina Faso) (S. Magnavita, p.c.).

[89] Ray 2003: 114 n. 4. In addition, etched carnelian beads have been discovered in an Iron Age "megalithic" cemetery in the northern plain of Sri Lanka, dated between the seventh and fourth centuries BCE (Coningham 2002: 104).

[90] Further west, new Scythian populations arrived north of the Black Sea, where Kamenskoe became a major political and economic center.

encompassing the spheres of western Asia (Egypt and the Mediterranean) as well as northwestern India and Central Asia. Gills and Frank (1991: 68) go one step further, and contemplate an interconnection between eastern and western Asia during the sixth and fifth centuries BCE, leading to the formation of a world-system covering the entire Eurasian world and part of Africa. It is astonishing that minted or cast currencies appeared simultaneously in Lydia, India, and China during the sixth century. Their issuance signals crucial social mutations, with the rapid development of states in competition, changes in the nature of the state, and increased interactions. However, unlike what has been suggested previously, the discoveries of silk at Kerameikos (Greece) and in tombs of the Hallstatt culture (Hochmichele, Hochdorf, Germany) (sixth and fifth centuries BCE) do not correspond to the introduction of Chinese silk, but rather to the development of a craft using raw silk from European lepidoptera (Good, p.c.); or perhaps the pieces found are not silk at all (Margariti *et al.* 2010, for Kerameikos; Banck-Burgess 2012: 142, and 1999: 128, 234, for the German sites).[91] Moreover, the discovery of wool cloth fragments from "cashmere goats" at Lattara, near Montpellier (dated to 470–460 BCE), may come from a goat breed from the Pyrenees: this is not proof of contacts between Europe and Central Asian networks (Amigues 2005: 362; Good forthcoming). Chinese silk did arrive in India, however. Ancient Indian texts such as the *Rāmāyana* (possibly written during the fifth century CE from texts partly going back to the fourth century BCE) indicate silk as a product coming from abroad, and the *Arthasāstra* mentions raw silk among materials spun by weavers (Boulnois 2008: 161). Hebrew texts mention silk at least twice under the terms *dmeshek* (Amos 3:12) (cf. Arabic *dimaks*) and *meshi* (Ezekiel 16:10), referring to transparent silk (Gills and Frank 1993b: 160, 194).

It is curious, moreover, that a type of crossbow was used by the Ancient Greeks, at Syracuse for example in 397 BCE. Hero of Alexandria left the description of a crossbow. Needham believes that this weapon was introduced from China, which invented it no later then the fifth century BCE. The mobility of the nomadic populations of Central Asia fostered exchanges, which were certainly of benefit to them; however, it is premature to consider eastern and western Asia as united under one system. While it is obvious that there were interconnections among the various spheres of eastern Asia, India, and western Asia during the sixth and fifth centuries BCE, these relationships seem neither intense enough nor regular enough to be termed systemic: it is difficult to demonstrate synchronous evolution and interdependence among these regions during this period, unlike what can be observed later.[92] The expansion that we perceive in China from 700 BCE onward resulted more from internal processes in eastern Asia than from connections forged with western Asia and southern Asia.

The Eastern World-System during the Fifth and Fourth Centuries BCE

Higher temperatures from 500 BCE on led to advances in Chinese agriculture, laying the groundwork for new urban growth. Around 430 BCE, China had 7 of the 25 largest cities in the world (Chandler 1987). The fragmentation of the "Spring and Autumn"

---

[91] *Contra* Good 1995: 966.

[92] See also Christian 2000: 16. For Chase-Dunn *et al.* (2006: 115), however, there was a "synchrony between East and West Asia that emerged around 500 BCE."

period was followed by a phase of political reconcentration starting in the second half of the fifth century, during the period of the "Warring Kingdoms" (481–221 BCE). As was the case within the context of the Greek city-states and much later in Europe, competition between these kingdoms fostered institutional innovations, with a radical change of the state influenced by the Legist school. State bureaucracies were put into place, removing the old noble families from power. Competition also brought about a flourishing of thought, technical innovation, and overall economic progress, although one notes a relative recession in northern China between 400 and 350 BCE, during a phase of climate change affecting all of the Ancient World.[93] The states of Wu and Chu were the first in the fifth century BCE to develop large-scale iron metallurgy, with the production of cast iron. One process of steel production goes back to this period, as does the invention of the crossbow. The use of efficient harnesses for horses was another major innovation.

Large kingdoms were formed, on a new basis: Yan, Qi, and Zhao, in the north; Qin, Han, Wei, in the center; and Chu, in the south. While expressing little interest in the moral virtues of the princes, in various kingdoms, legists did focus on building efficient states, whose good functioning was guaranteed by "the institution of objective rules." In other words, common law should apply to everyone (Gernet 1999: 88). The power of the state had to be based on social and political institutions. The transformation of the state was clearly apparent in the kingdom of Qin: here, hereditary aristocracy was abolished, and the state promoted the emergence of a meritocratic elite, a new military organization, and a tax system. Agriculture was the primary source of economic and military power, which is why farmers had access to land and benefited from land rights. At the same time, land could be sold, and a land market developed. An economic reflection emerged, connecting the roles played by the state, money, capital accumulation, and the importance of the market. The logician school of thought of the Mohists, who advocated an egalitarian society, appeared at this time (fifth–fourth century), but this school would not have a legacy equal to that of other Chinese schools of thought, or the Greek rationalist currents, due to a very different political and social context in China (in a powerful central state influenced by the legists and later by Confucianism).

The changes occurring during this period drove expansion in production and trade, between the regions of China and with the outside world. Exchanges thus progressed with Central Asia and South Asia, along the roads of the Tarim and Sichuan, and on routes further north (Christian 2000; Wu Xiaolong 2004). The state had a vested interest in production. At the same time, a class of rich merchants developed, who combined trade and craft enterprises. The *Zhouli* (*Rites of Zhou*), composed during the fourth or third century BCE and borrowed from older traditions, mentions the development of a silk export industry: "the Chinese government [as early as the Zhou period] supervised the production of silk in every detail and specialties of design, ornament and embroidery were already monopolized by different families" (Schoff 1974: 263; see Gernet 1999: 84). Growing interactions with Inner Asia triggered the emergence of two neighbors of Chu. The first was the state of Qin, whose development was also impelled by the internal dynamics described above. The second was the

---

[93] Brooke (2014: 309) notes intense winter monsoons from 475 BCE onward.

kingdom of Shu in Sichuan, a good example of the formation of a "secondary state," enjoying a favorable position as the interface between several areas; this highlights the significance of the trade routes linking Sichuan to the Yangtze, the Yellow River, and Southeast Asia. The wealth of the tombs of the Lake Dian region from the fifth century BCE onward also reveals the growing use of routes connecting China and South Asia through Yunnan (these discoveries would become more spectacular during the final centuries before the Christian era). The introduction of iron plows may have resulted from contacts with India, via this route. Animal-drawn plows seem to have spread in connection with iron metallurgy (Sherratt 2006b) but in fact iron technology was probably introduced into Southeast Asia from China. With Southeast Asia, contacts extended via terrestrial routes – toward the Pearl River – and via maritime routes. Objects found in northern Vietnam and the Lower Mekong valley point to clear connections with southern China during the Warring Kingdoms period (Higham 1996b: 114, 211; 2002: 173). Chu's armed forays into Yue provide ample evidence for the new importance of coastal exchanges. Sailors from Zhejiang and Guangdong were in contact with Southeast Asia, and in northern China, the kingdom of Yan established diplomatic relations with Japan.

The Recession of the Late Fifth and Early Fourth Centuries BCE

Growth in the western world-system remained significant during the early fifth century BCE,[94] except in Egypt. The entire world-system entered into recession during the second half of the fifth century BCE, however, for systemic reasons, partly linked to a brief period of lower temperatures between 400 and 350 BCE.[95] Epidemics also affected various regions.[96] The decline in trade was accompanied by a process of hegemonic transition: the Macedonian semi-periphery took advantage of the weakening of the cores, and some peripheries of Inner Europe expanded. Greece experienced a significant decline, with less commercial competitivity and a process of decentralization of wealth accumulation (Friedman 2005). Wars against Sparta (431–404) also hastened the decline of Athens, which attempted to increase silver extraction in order to obtain the grain and goods it could no longer produce competitively. The lack of silver led to the issuance of bronze coins, at Corinth, Syracuse, and later Athens (Aglietta 2009).[97] Movement of capital – wealth, artisans, mercenaries – occurred from the Greek city-states toward Egypt, western Asia, and northern Greece.[98] Moreover, military

---

[94]　Morris gives an estimate of 24,000 kcal/cap/day for energy capture in 400 BCE (2013: 61). He gives an estimate of 22,000 kcal/cap/day for China during the same period (2013: 111). Estimates of energy capture appear highly speculative, especially for these ancient periods.

[95]　Brooke notes a moderate solar insolation minimum at 400 BCE (2014: 301). Later, he writes "325 BC" (2014: 324). Usoskin (2013) gives the date of 360 BCE. Brooke points out intense winter monsoons in China from 475 BCE onward for two centuries.

[96]　There was "plague" in Athens in 430 BCE, and epidemics affected the Carthaginian army in Sicily in 405 and 396 BCE (Morris 2009: 114).

[97]　Deteriorating confidence is reflected in price increases.

[98]　J. Friedman 2005: 96–97, 103. For this author, the phenomena observed during this period are similar to those described during phases of hegemonic transition of the capitalistic world-system from the fifteenth century on, with a weakening of productive capacities of the dominant core, a process of financial expansion, and the transfer of capital.

activities increased in the steppes, both to the west and the east of the Urals, which were experiencing growing aridity. The use of heavy cavalry developed soon afterward, during the fourth and third centuries (Koryakova and Epimakhov 2007: 243). In western and central Europe, declining trade led to social unrest and the collapse of the western Hallstatt culture at the hands of new warrior elites expanding in the northern peripheries of Champagne, Rhine-Moselle, and Bohemia (La Tène culture) (Cunliffe 1994: 358ff.; Kristiansen 1998: 291–293, 321ff.). It is customary to speak of "Celtic" migrations with regard to the movement of populations and cultural expansion that would affect all of Europe from the fifth to the third century BCE. Various kinds of confederations took part in organizing these migrations. As early as the end of the fifth century, the "Celts" settled in the Pô valley, and made progress in the middle Danube valley; in 387 BCE, they reached Rome, which was partly looted and burned. During the fourth century BCE, Celtic armies also conducted raids in Illyria, and led attacks in Bulgaria at the beginning of the third century. These movements were finally blocked further south by the Macedonian power.[99]

The beginning of the fourth century was also a period of relative decline for northern China: this decline was linked to shifts in balance of power between the northern and southern Warring Kingdoms on the one hand, and attacks or migrations from the steppes, on the other. In addition, the recession occurred during the abovementioned spell of global cooling for western Asia. By contrast, the sphere of exchange linking South China and Southeast Asia saw growing interactions between regions. During this period, ships of the Yue people living on the coasts of Zhejiang and Guangdong probably sailed to Southeast Asia, and may even have ventured into the Indian Ocean (Needham 1970), although archaeological evidence for these contacts remains elusive.

The phase of decline in northern China proved to be brief. During the second half of the fourth century, production and trade took on new momentum, both within and outside China. Merchants traveled along the routes of Central Asia and from Yunnan to Burma, taking silk to India and the Seleucid Empire.

Growing Interactions among the Three World-Systems (c. 350–1 BCE)

Toward the Unification of the Western World-System with the Indian World-System

After a general phase of decline during its first half,[100] the late fourth century saw a new economic and political awakening in southeastern Europe. This was brought about not by the Greek city-states, but by a state unified in 338 BCE by Philip II of Macedonia. In 334, Philip's son Alexander unleashed his armies to conquer Asia. Alexander's epic march broke Persia's hegemony and opened up the "marvels of India" to the

---

[99] Celtic attacks did occur, however, around 280 BCE. In 279, Celts launched a raid into Greece and looted Delphi. Some of them entered Anatolia, and settled in Phrygia. Celtic warriors then went to Egypt to become mercenaries in the service of Ptolemy II.

[100] Whereas the "revolt of the satraps" (366–360 BCE) corresponds only to local upheavals, with no links to one another – they did not have the organized character that the Greek sources describe (Briant 1996: 675ff.) – the Persian Empire does seem to have experienced serious difficulties under Artaxerxes II's reign (404–359 BCE).

Mediterranean world. Alexander built cities at the nodes of trade networks, with the clear aim of controlling them. In Egypt, Mesopotamia, Persia, the Indus valley, and Central Asia, "Alexandria" cities were created. In Alexander's footsteps, artisans and artists took the Greek culture to Asia. The pillaging of Persian treasures allowed the government to dispose of hoarded precious metals (the Achaemenid treasures have been "variously recorded as 170,000–190,000 talents = 4.67–5.22 million kilograms of silver"; van der Spek 2006: 309). The tetradrachm called the "Alexander," minted by its namesake and his followers, circulated throughout the empire and then in successor states, easing exchanges within the context of a growing monetization of the economy.

After the sudden death of Alexander in 323 BCE, the empire's African and Asian sectors were divided between the Seleucids (western Asia)[101] and the Ptolemies (Egypt), who would soon be fighting each other for control of the Levantine interface. This partition of the system's two cores (Macedonia and Greece, ruled by the Antigonids, were mere semi-peripheries by the third century) led to competition between the Persian Gulf and the Red Sea, while the Arabs were busy asserting their position as intermediaries between the Indian Ocean and the Mediterranean. Dominated by the Gerrheans, the Arab caravan roads running to Petra and Babylon were thus key to long-distance trade (Salles 1996).

The Hellenistic period was marked by increased economic and cultural integration. A new cosmopolitan culture emerged that was linked to elites who often were no longer Greek.[102]

The Mediterranean area became a world market for perfumes, spices, drugs, ivory and jewels from central Africa, Arabia, and India; for gold, furs and forest products from central Russia; for amber from the Baltic; and for metals from the British Isles and Spain. Among the most prized commodities of international trade were human beings. To the great international slave mart of Delos, victims were brought from Britain, Ethiopia, south Russia, Morocco, Iran and Spain. They were distributed to Seleucia, Antioch, Alexandria, Carthage, Rome, Athens, and Pergamon. Among them were not only laborers and prostitutes, but doctors, scientists, artists and craftsmen, who carried their ideas, traditions, and skills along wherever they went . . . Alien merchant colonies could be found in every port. We read, for instance, of an Indian merchant, resident in Egypt, who actually held a priesthood there; of a guild of Syrian merchants who maintained a regular hostel on Delos providing lodgings, stock-rooms, a council chamber, and a chapel; of an Italiote bronzeworker who transferred his business from Lucania to Rhodes; and of a silk manufacturer from Antioch who died in Naples. (Bozeman 1994: 99, quoted by J. Friedman 2005: 100–101)

The two main empires show some parallels, but also differences due in particular to the history of their respective territories.

The Seleucid Empire inherited both the administrative model of the Greek cities and the oriental royal model. As would later be the case in the Roman Empire, large estates were formed, at the expense of a class of smaller landowners. The social consequences were great: in the past, according to the Greek model, "cultivators had been obliged to provide corvée labor, serve in the army and pay taxes to the

---

[101] Moreover, the Attalids would reign over a kingdom centered on Pergamon.
[102] Friedman 2000: 130. Greece itself was in decline at this time.

palace in exchange for holding land." With the emergence of a new aristocracy who no longer paid taxes, the palace grew impoverished, forcing the state to replace its soldier-farmers with mercenaries (Hudson 1996: 35–36, 54). The state was soon faced with huge military expenses.

Exchanges developed between India and Mesopotamia along the maritime routes of the Persian Gulf, strengthened by the active Seleucid policy. After a military clash, diplomatic and economic relations were established between the Mauryan Empire in India and the Seleucids. Various products then reached the Greek world from India.

The Ptolemaic Empire, for its part, enjoyed a twofold legacy, Egyptian and Greek. Because silver – originating in foreign trade – was used to pay soldiers, sailors, and mercenaries, the empire introduced what amounted to a mercantile system. To maintain a positive trade balance, it invested significantly in the agricultural sector. The state also played a key role in industry and trade – by imposing monopolies on various products – while a private sector was active as well. In addition, the state pursued a building policy in the Pharaonic tradition. The bureaucratization of the empire brought with it heavy taxation and corvées. The use of silver filtered down to society in general, as well as that of payment orders.

As had been the case in China, from the fourth to the second century BCE, an arms race between cities or states stimulated technological research and development in the Greek world.[103] A mixture of naphta, sulphur, and burning pitch may have been used in incendiary arrows as early as 429 BCE during the Peloponnesian War, and Arrian mentions the use of fireships using bitumen and other substances in 332 BCE (Partington 1999: 1, 28). Note that the Greek *naphta*, "petroleum," derives from the Persian *naft*. Scientific thought and research remained fruitful until the Roman period.[104] For the first time in Greek civilization, the Ptolemies sponsored scientific research, founding the Museum and the Library of Alexandria (this official support would last until the fifth century). Euclid developed abstract mathematics and introduced the idea of "proof." Engineers such as Ctesibius and Hero invented or improved upon hydraulic machines, automatons and weapons, using systems of cams, gear trains, and augers.[105] During this period in Egypt and western Asia, agriculture benefited from the development of two types of norias (Arabic *nā'ūra*): these were waterwheels with either compartmented bodies or compartmented rims (Jacomy 1990: 116–117). The *saqiya*, a waterwheel (scoop-wheel) with a gear system, powered by oxen (or men), was also used to lift water. This device may have originated in India, as well as the norias –

---

[103] The possibility that steel was produced in Greece and Rome is still debated (Craddock 2003: 249). The main sources are Pliny (Book XXXIV), and Pausanias (second century CE) (*Description of Greece*, 3.12.10 and 10.8.16).

[104] The major figures were Archimedes (Syracuse) (see below), and Aristarchus (Aristarkhos) (Samos), who was one of the first – long before Copernicus – to put forward the model of a universe having the sun in its center, with the earth turning on its axis daily and around the sun yearly.

[105] They are heirs to the first great engineers such as Archytas of Tarenta (early fourth century BCE), who invented the auger and the pulley (Jacomy 1990: 45). Braudel's opinion must be qualified: whereas in Alexandria, inventions were oriented toward technical applications, "the Hellenistic society," argues Braudel, remained indifferent to the inventions of its engineers (Braudel 1984: 543-544).

according to Needham, but other authors have proposed Iran. The astrolabe, which used a mathematical model of the sky, may have been invented around the second century BCE.[106] The Greeks invented the waterwheel in order to mill grain[107] (we do not know, however, whether the waterwheel was truly an invention of the Hellenistic world or a borrowing from China, via Persia). Greek proto-chemists developed new forms of stills, used at Alexandria to prepare perfumes (the Arabic *al-anbīq* derives from the Greek *ambikos*).[108] Pliny and Strabo would later mention the use of naphta (distilled naphta?) in Babylonia, used in lamps (Partington 1999: 4).

During this period, contacts strengthened with the African interior. South of Egypt, the flourishing of the Meroe kingdom signaled the incorporation of new regions of Inner Africa into the world-system, as well as the connection of northeastern Africa with Arabia and the Indian Ocean trade (the Meroitic script was formed at this time). Farther west, from the mid-fourth century BCE onward, the Libyan region inhabited by the Garamantes was connected to the Punic networks, Egypt and Meroe on the one hand, and sub-Saharan Africa, on the other. The Garamantes kingdom enjoyed a second phase of growth, marked by the introduction of new plants from the Mediterranean world (wheat, pomegranate tree, olive tree), from Egypt (cotton), and from sub-Saharan Africa (millet *Pennisetum glaucum* and sorghum of the *caudatum* race) (Pelling 2005, 2008). It also developed a *qanāt* system of irrigation, introduced from Egypt when the Achaemenids were ruling the Nile valley. Agricultural labor in this Garamantes kingdom was probably accomplished by slaves. "The tombs of the Fezzan have provided evidence for the presence of sub-Saharan Africans (Mattingly *et al.* 2009: 118)" (Fentress 2011: 69). A Libyan script derived from the Punic/Phoenician alphabet developed as of the third century BCE. As noted above, the dromedary was introduced around the middle of the first millennium BCE (possibly along with the chicken). The expansion of the Garamantes state went along with regional developments in western Africa, notably in the Niger valley.

In the western Mediterranean, Carthage held a preeminent position, but the expansion of Rome soon threatened it. The city of Rome appeared *c.* 800 BCE; it became a republic in 509 BCE. Two magistrates (consuls) were elected each year, according to the Tyrian and Carthaginian model of the suffetes. Plebeians obtained the legal right to access the highest hierarchical positions at the government level, thereby creating a community of interest between the Roman social classes that would

---

[106] Turner 1997: 88. More sophisticated than astrolabes, the astronomical Antikythera mechanism (late second century BCE), discovered in 1900 and the focus of recent research, seems to have been designed "to calculate astronomical positions and eclipses of the moon and the sun, and of some planets" (X. Moussas, *Le Monde*, June 9, 2006). In addition, its meshing gears predicted eclipses, and the dates of the Olympic Games (J. Goudet, August 4, 2008, www.futura-sciences.com/fr/news). This mechanism may have originated from the school of the philosopher Poseidonios of Rhodes, according to Goudet.

[107] The Greek Antipaster of Thessalonica (first century BCE) was the first to refer to this device in the Mediterranean world.

[108] According to Partington, "distillation in which the vapour from a flask was condensed in an upper part and ran into a receiver through a spout, was invented by the first chemists in Alexandria in the first to third centuries AD" (1999: 31), but this dating is probably too late. Alcohol distillation does not seem to have been known in the Hellenistic world, but this question remains debated. See Needham *et al.* 1980: 124ff. A bronze distiller may have been unearthed in Liu He's tomb (China), dated *c.* 59 BCE. See below.

underpin the city's expansion. Rome quickly built itself into a militaristic state. A situation of ongoing war offered both a principle for economic and social organization and a source of identification. The *equites* (members of the equestrian order), an army corps, became a social class. Rome extended its power into Italy during the fourth and third centuries BCE, following the subjugation of the Etruscan cities and other populations. When the Roman sphere of power – which Hansen (2000c) considers as an empire of city-states, until the first century BCE – encroached on the territory of Carthage, confrontation was inevitable. In 264 BCE, the Romans entered Sicily, responding to a Carthaginian intervention at Messine. Then began the first Punic War; after several defeats, Carthage was forced to ask for a cessation of hostilities, in 241 BCE, at the cost of a heavy war indemnity and the abandonment of Sicily. It also lost control over Sardinia and Corsica. These steps backward led the Carthaginians to adopt a new strategy, marked by the territorial conquests of General Hamilcar Barca in Spain. Hannibal's capture of the town of Sagunto – allied with Rome – triggered the second Punic War (218–201 BCE), which ended with the peace treaty of Tunis, which forced Carthage to abandon Spain.

The transition between the fourth and third centuries BCE was also a period of growth for India and Central Asia. Established in Magadha, the first Maurya ruler, Chandragupta, built an empire starting in 322 BCE, just after Alexander the Great's retreat from the Indus valley. Under Ashoka, this empire extended south beyond the Kistna River. A Seleucid envoy at the Maurya court described a strongly centralized state, which promoted production and trade. Recent research, however, has cast into doubt the idea of state control over the economy, and has qualified its supposed centralization. The state did benefit from trade, but trade was operated primarily by private merchants and guilds (Ray 1996, 2003). Great merchants were also "bankers," sometimes lending money to rulers. The Mauryan expansion into the Indian peninsula accelerated a process of urbanization in the south, and at the same time helped Buddhism and trade expand, particularly toward Southeast Asia.

To the west, there were interactions with the Seleucids, as described above. A royal edict from Ashoka mentions Ptolemy Philadelphus, revealing the existence of contacts with Egypt, also attested to by Agatharchides. In addition, the ascent of the Greco-Bactrian kingdom, around 250 BCE[109] is a significant event, reflecting the vitality of the trade routes of Central Asia: it became an interface between India and western Asia (see Map II.2). Around 200 BCE, many "cities associated with Alexander's project were prominent," for example, Seleucia, in the Tigris valley, Balkh, in Central Asia, Rayy, in Iran, and Alexandria, the third largest city in the world (Bosworth 1995). For the first time, China could boast the largest city (Chang'an, pop. 400,000);[110] the second largest was in India (Patna, pop. 350,000). Morris gives an estimate of 300,000 inhabitants for Alexandria in 200 BCE (2013: 152). The Greek expansion accentuated militarization in the steppe societies as well as their involvement in long-distance trade. At this time, Central Asia was more

---

[109] The formation of this state was in part the result of the expansion of the Parthian kingdom in northern Iran, which cut off the Seleucids' access to Bactria.

[110] Morris (2013: 155), however, gives an estimate of "only" 250,000 inhabitants for Chang'an in 200 BCE, but 375,000 in 100 BCE.

strongly connected to northern China, which was then undergoing deep transformation. The Silk Roads (several itineraries were in use) following chains of oases in Central Asia (between western Gansu and the Syr Darya and Amu Darya basins) linked the kingdom of Qin to India and Persia. People and merchandise also took a road running from Sichuan and Yunnan to India via Upper Burma; this road became active during the first millennium while the cultures of the Ganges valley were flourishing. For this period we do not yet have proof of direct maritime contacts between India and China, but we do know that the Indian and Chinese spheres of influence overlapped in Southeast Asia.

The Western World-System in Crisis during the Second Century BCE

The second half of the third century and the second century BCE saw a decline of the Egyptian and Mesopotamian cores, weakened by the six so-called "Syrian Wars." This decline was accompanied by growing internal conflicts. In 274 BCE, epidemics and famines struck Babylonia.[111] The western world-system experienced a new period of hegemonic transition during which the center of gravity of the Mediterranean area shifted westward: Italy, and more precisely the city of Rome, then rose to preeminence. The Phoenicians and Greeks had begun transforming the Mediterranean Sea into a unified space. Rome achieved this unification, not only through trade but also on a political level, by the second and first centuries BCE. Carthage was finally razed to the ground in 146 BCE at the end of the third Punic War (it is no coincidence that Corinth was plundered during that same year, following an uprising against Rome). Corinth would later be rebuilt as a Roman city.

The decline and demise of Carthage, allowed Rome to become the new core of the Mediterranean system. This is clearly shown by the Roman victories over Macedonia in 197 and 168 BCE, and over the Seleucid emperor Antiochus III at Magnesia in 190, as well as the submission of Antiochus IV to the orders of the Roman ambassador Gaius Popilius Laenas, who urged Antiochus IV to leave Egypt and Cyprus in 168 BCE. During the second century BCE, the Roman state conquered Spain, southern Gaul, the Dalmatian coast, Greece, western Anatolia, and Cilicia. Roman expansion led to an increased demand for slaves and iron. Growing interactions with Rome and the processes of internal development – marked by progress in agriculture and crafts – led to the appearance of the first towns in continental Europe: at the same time, *oppida*, which were political, industrial, and trade centers, were built from southern England to Serbia (Danebury, Bibract, Manching, Magdalensberg, and so forth), within a context of competition and violence. These first urban centers north of the Mediterranean Sea reflect the emergence of chiefdoms that took advantage of their positions as intermediaries between Rome and more distant peripheries. The border zones – where middlemen were thriving – would be pushed further north during the first century BCE: most of the *oppida* disappeared, due to the German expansion and the collapse of the

---

[111] Vargyas (2001: 56), however, indicates favorable grain prices during the second century BCE, prior to the Parthian invasion (which may have been the result either of good harvests, a silver shortage, or a reduction in population size). There was a "relationship between the level of the Euphrates and the level of [grain] prices, . . . but water levels were not the only determinant" (Van der Spek 2007: 306).

Celtic politico-economic entities, under attack by Rome. Rome then took possession of Gaul[112] and central Europe as far as the Danube River. The Rhine and the Danube became Rome's borders with the German world. In the eastern Mediterranean Sea, Rome occupied Syria, Palestine, and later Egypt. The capture of the Treasure of the Ptolemies resulted in a decrease in interest rate from 12 to 4 percent at Rome; and a correspondingly large increase in land prices. Tributes were imposed on those defeated, and these conquests allowed Rome to directly exploit various resources, such as silver from Iberia (40,000 slaves would work in the mines located near Cartagena);[113] copper from Cyprus; wheat from Egypt, as well as wood and wheat from northern Africa. Provinces were created in the newly conquered territories, each headed by a governor. The position of governor was not salaried, but usually lucrative. Defeated by the Parthians at Carrhes in 53 BCE, Rome failed to take control of Mesopotamia; through Egypt, however, Rome gained access to the Red Sea and the Indian Ocean. It secured inland routes from Upper Egypt – and access to the gold mines – after a victorious war against Meroe, in which the city of Napata was burned to the ground in 22 BCE. An embassy from Meroe was later sent to Augustus.

In the Roman state, in theory, "politics is *res publica*. All the citizens serve in the army, pay taxes, elect the magistrates, vote laws and deliberate on the question of peace or war" (Deniaux 1987a: 58, quoting Polybius). Citizens were not equal before the law, however: an oligarchy held power, and the military sector played a central role due to its economic and political importance. In the footsteps of the armies, firms were flourishing, often led by *equites*, who engaged in mass production using partnership arrangements. During this period, Rome kept to a "minimalist approach to administration," by governing with volunteers and local elites (Burbank and Cooper 2010: 30). In the provinces, "a specific procedure was implemented to collect tax revenue, which was bestowed on private entrepreneurs called publicans, who formed powerful societies, some of them quasi-'public limited companies,' for more than two centuries" (Nicolet 2000).[114] The publicans were involved in banking activities; they formed associations in order to fulfill contract requirements. Thus, a class of private entrepreneurs developed, that was closely linked to the expansion of the state. The private sector and leading political class were closely interwoven: the Roman aristocracy was heavily involved in the long-distance wine trade (Roman 2009b), and senators were shipowners. In western Asia, unlike what could be observed previously, "the major creditors no longer were public institutions, but private individuals" (Hudson 2002: 38). The system was largely based on servile labor and on the availability of slaves,[115] which fueled its expansion. From the third century BCE on,

---

[112] Caesar reached the Rhine's left bank in 54 BCE. The threat exerted by the Germanic tribes was one reason for the Roman expansion northward. Teutons would be recruited *en masse* into the Roman army. The development of commerce at the borders worked in favor of new Germanic entities, such as the Frankish confederation, during the second and third centuries CE.

[113] For Gibbon, "Spain was to Rome as Peru and Mexico were to the Old World" (Cunliffe 1994: 370).

[114] Publicans often belonged to the class of the *equites*. They managed their businesses through agents who settled in the provinces.

[115] The Italian population grew from 5 million to 7.5 million between the third and first centuries BCE, partly thanks to the influx of slaves. Slave revolts occurred periodically. The revolt led by the gladiator Spartacus (73–71 BCE) in Italy was the most successful.

the influx of slaves working for rich landowners transformed Italy's agrarian structures[116] and "freed" a labor force, who entered the army, worked in industry and engaged in urban trade. These sectors also employed slaves: at the turn of the Christian era, out of one million persons living at Rome, 400,000 were slaves; Italy counted 2 or 3 million slaves for a total population of 6 or 7 million inhabitants (although some authors give lower percentages of slaves; see below). Produced on large estates worked by slave labor, wine was one of Rome's main exports, and the quantities exported were considerable (one million amphorae were sent to Gaul each year, which corresponds to 2.5 million hectoliters, according to Olmer [2008] [Roman 2009b: 261]): in continental Europe, "the Italian merchants transport the wine by boat . . . and by wagon, and receive in return for it an incredibly high price. For one amphora of wine, they get in return a slave" (Diodorus, quoted by Cunliffe 1994: 413). Commerce, with a flow of Italian products at prices lower than the prices of Greek products, triggered a "romanization" of Gaul from the third century BCE onward – a process prepared by the Greek networks – prior to the Roman occupation of the first century BCE (Roman and Roman 1998):[117] in western Europe in any event, "political and military unity [at the beginning of the Christian era] was largely facilitated by [earlier] trade contacts that had a clearly cultural influence" (Cabouret-Laurioux *et al.*, 2009: 24).

Roman growth was accompanied by social tensions during the second and first centuries BCE because the rewards of the empire were unequally distributed. Tiberius Gracchus proposed land redistribution, but he was murdered in 133 BCE. In 123 BCE, free or low-price grain distributions were introduced; grain was imported from Sicily, Egypt, and later northern Africa. More than 300,000 people benefited from these measures in 58 BCE, and 200,000 under Augustus. The creation of colonies was promoted in remote regions of Italy and abroad. Mass overseas colonization responded to the mass immigration of slaves (Hopkins 2009: 180). At the beginning of the first century BCE, civil wars led Rome to grant Roman citizenship to all Italians (in 91 and then again in 89 BCE).

While the social disruptions in Italy during the second century BCE had internal causes, they also reflected greater worldwide unrest. With the exception of the incipient Roman Empire, the whole western world-system was affected by a silver shortage during the second century BCE;[118] this shortage resulted from the monopolization of the Iberian metal by Rome, and from declining trade in the Mediterranean Sea. The weakening of the ancient cores and the economic recession went along with growing insecurity on land and sea in western Asia during the second century BCE: "the whole [eastern] Mediterranean Sea and the Pontic Sea were infested with pirates, and the situation worsened at the beginning of the 1st century" (Sartre 2001: 436). In the

---

[116] The search for profit on landed estates was accompanied by the implementation of technological advances, albeit limited. These were often borrowed from Greece, along with the grafting, hybridization, crop rotation, and the use of manure or compost (Nicolet 1988).

[117] At the same time, a process of monetization developed in part of Gaul: a "denier zone" thus appeared around the Aedui territory (Roman 2009b: 261).

[118] For another opinion, see Le Rider and De Callatay 2006: 202ff. Several rulers, however, were led to reduce the weight of their tetradrachms. These rulers included Perseus (Macedonia), Eumenes II (Pergamon), and Antiochus IV (Seleucid Empire).

western Mediterranean Sea, fights conducted by Rome led to a disruption in merchant networks, resulting in a slowdown in trade. In Egypt, lower seasonal Nile flooding triggered a decline in agricultural production. A stela erected near Elephantine, reporting a period of seven years of famine under King Djoser (Third Dynasty), has been dated to the reign of Ptolemy V (204–181 BCE):

I was in mourning on my throne, those of the palace were in grief . . . because Hapy had failed to come in time. In a period of seven years, grain was scant, kernels were dried up . . . Every man robbed his twin . . . Temples were shut, shrines covered with dust. Everyone was in distress.

This period of low Nile flooding was related to worldwide climate changes triggering population movements in Central Asia, and later in Afghanistan, Iran, and northwestern India during the second century BCE, leading to endless political changes in these regions at the close of the first millennium BCE.[119] As early as the second half of the third century, Sarmatians arriving from the north of the Aral Sea took control of the Scythian territories north of the Black Sea.[120] The rise to power of a Xiongnu proto-state in the eastern steppes (Mongolia and neighboring regions) from 204 BCE on was another trigger for the population movements observed in Central Asia.[121] This development came in the wake of changes occurring in China with the expansion of the state and later the empire of Qin. In 176 BCE, the Xiongnu nomads[122] forced the Yuezhi, who controlled the Hexi corridor, to migrate westward toward the Samarkand region. Like falling dominoes, the confrontation of the Yuezhi with the Saka ("Scythians") led to the Saka's displacement, and then to the displacement of other groups further west. The decline in trade spurred Scythian attacks against the Greek colonies of the Black Sea during the second century BCE.

In India, the collapse of the Mauryan Empire around 185 BCE favored the expansion of the Greco-Bactrian kingdom, and later of an Indo-Greek kingdom,[123] when the king of Bactria, Demetrius I (c. 200–180), invaded northern India. Greco-Buddhist art then developed, notably in Gandhara, and would have an impact throughout the Indian subcontinent.[124] In Iran, a Parthian empire was formed c. 171 BCE. Eucratides,

[119] Morgunova and Khokhlova (2006: 314) signal a period of sharp aridification during the second century BCE that continued until the first century CE. A depopulation of the steppes south of the Urals has been noted (Barbarunova 1995: 122). Schettler et al. (2006: 1055) also point out a weakening of the East Asian monsoon around 200 BCE.

[120] For Koryakova and Epimakhov (2007: 11), the first Sarmatian movements occurred earlier, during a period of aridification of the steppes that began around 500 BCE. This aridification was more pronounced in the Asian than in the European part. In the region of the Fergana valley, Chinese chronicles mention a state called Kangju, that was tributary to the Yuezhi in the south and the Xiongnu in the east. In the northwest lay the Yancai territory, inhabited by nomads who have been linked to the Alans, a Sarmatian people.

[121] While it is usual to speak of a "confederation" of "nomads," archaeological research shows that the Xiongnu space included more than nomads, and that "the Xiongnu polity was founded on a more developed system of statecraft than is generally supposed" (Honeychurch and Amartuvshin 2006: 268). The Xiongnu territory shows an articulation of nomads and farmers, who were in contact with centers of handcraft and trade (Di Cosmo 2002: 169ff.). See below.

[122] The term "Xiongnu" refers to a culture and not to an ethnic group.

[123] There were several Indo-Greek kingdoms after Menander's death in 130 BCE.

[124] "The plaster casts used in the production of metalwork provided a very direct means of transmission for images and motifs from the Mediterranean world to Gandhara" (Mairs 2012).

king of Bactria, was forced to abandon Herat to the Parthians in 167, and in 130 BCE, the kingdom of Bactria collapsed following invasions of nomads from Central Asia. These political reconfigurations do not seem to have led to marked economic recession, although the migrations of the Yuezhi and the Saka into Sogdiana, Bactria, and later Parthia and India during the second and first centuries BCE, indicate volatile political situations during the closing years of the millennium.[125] Between 141 and 122 BCE, the Parthian kingdom occupied Mesopotamia and Persia, but was itself the victim of Scythian raids. The Parthian emergence put an end to the Seleucid Empire and cut off Greek access to the Persian Gulf. In the western Indian Ocean, competition between the two seas bordering Arabia turned in favor of the Red Sea: heavy taxes imposed by the Parthians, who held the upper hand on the Persian Gulf (second century BCE – third century CE), led to a relative shift in trade toward the Red Sea and Egypt – where the Ptolemies maintained their power until the Roman domination in 30 BCE – and toward the Arabian caravan roads, where the Nabataeans of Petra controlled trade (the discovery of Nabataean ceramics and coins at Thaj and Qatif [Potts 1991] shows that the Nabataean networks extended to the Gulf) (Seland 2014). From the second century BCE onward, both the Greeks and the Romans began to use the monsoon winds to travel to India from the Red Sea. The Parthians, however, maintained significant commercial activity in the Persian Gulf, where they ensured their suzerainty over the port of Spasinou Charax. Parthian pottery has been found on all the coasts of the Persian Gulf, but also at Ras Hafun, on the Horn of Africa.

Basing their argument on the decline of western Asia and the collapse of the Mauryan Empire (185 BCE), Gills and Frank (1993b: 163) suggest a "B phase" (phase of recession) for a world-system unifying India and the western Asia–Mediterranean sphere "between 250/200 and 100/50 BC." It is indeed tempting to link the dislocation of the Mauryan Empire to the weakening of the Seleucids and the restructuring of the western world-system. Conversely, these authors rightly note that China was then in expansion and therefore not "in sync" with this B phase of the western world-system. Eastern Asia thus formed an area connected to the west, but structurally separate.

The Ascent of an Eastern World-System Centered on China

In eastern Asia, crucial transformations occurred during the third and second centuries BCE. The reforms implemented by the legists in the state of Qin led to the creation of a centralized state, with an efficient administration, promoting agriculture and forming a powerful army. The king of Qin managed to take the upper hand over his rivals and to unify China in 221 BCE; his armies reached as far as the Pearl River and the Red River, where commanderies were formed. The king took the title of Shi Huangdi, "First Shining God [Emperor]," which implied his divine character (*di*). An empire was founded based on new political bases, one that benefited from the increase in exchanges. Responding to the Chinese unification, the peoples of the steppes (Xiongnu) formed a "confederation" in 204 BCE, a sign of the importance of trade and military contacts on

---

[125] A crucial innovation appeared in the steppes during the late first millennium BCE: the stirrup. It would signal a new phase of warfare development and enhance the negotiating capacities of the nomadic populations. The Chinese would borrow and improve the stirrup around the third century CE.

what would become the Silk Roads as well as along a more northerly steppe route, revealed by finds at Pazyryk, in the Altai (third century BCE). The kurgans of Isakovka, belonging to the Sargat culture, in the region of Omsk, in Siberia, have yielded Xiongnu artifacts dated to the third century BCE, as well as silver bowls bearing Chorasmian inscriptions (two vessels) and Parthian inscriptions (one bowl), evidence of trade routes running north–south and east–west (Koryakova and Epimakhov 2007: 311). The involvement of the Sargat elite in trade certainly explains the wealth of its tombs; it also reveals probable competition for control over the exchanges. Many Chinese swords, silk, and lacquered artifacts have been excavated in the steppes or the forest-steppe zone.

The Qin dynasty did not survive the bloody dictatorship and excesses of Emperor Shi Huangdi: it disappeared soon after his death. The advent of the Han dynasty in 206 BCE ushered in a new phase of expansion for a unified China, where institutional, ideological, and technological innovations and major public works fostered production and trade. The adoption of Confucianism did not prevent a legist inheritance from continuing to influence political thought. One notes the invention of paper; the appearance of iron plows with various types of moldboards; the invention of a multi-tube seed drill; a rotary winnowing fan (functioning with a crank handle); the invention of the drive belt, used by the textile industry in winding machines; the development of various waterwheels, for grinding grain or activating furnace bellows – all of these, and more, laid the foundation for the first energy revolution.[126] This empire would initiate Chinese expansion to the west and to the south, where a Chinese officer, following the collapse of the Qin Empire, would proclaim himself king of Nanyue (Guangdong) and would subjugate northern Vietnam in 208. Emperor Wudi (141–87 BCE) sent missions to Central Asia and Parthia. Embassies from Gandhara and Parthia also arrived in Han China (Needham *et al.* 1980: 332). The second half of the second century BCE saw the first great deployment of the Silk Roads, secured by the Han Empire later, during the first century BCE, when the Chinese took control of a corridor stretching from Mongolia to Turkestan. Through these roads horses, jade, metal artifacts, furs and silk were traded. The discovery of etched carnelian beads (in the Tarim and east of Khotan) reveals the interconnection of Central Asia with networks linked to India. A large part of Yunnan was incorporated into the Chinese state from 109 BCE onward: the region was rich in precious metals, and a trade route went through Yunnan toward South Asia. The Han Empire also sent armies southward. The conquest of the Nanyue Kingdom, in 111 BCE, triggered an increase in trade with Southeast Asia. During the reign of Emperor Wudi, Chinese envoys went via the southern seas toward Huangzhi (Kāñchī, on the southeast coast of India), on board Austronesian ships. Taking advantage of the growing exchange networks, ships from Southeast Asian populations, which probably benefited from various technical innovations, sailed to the Chinese coasts (already known)[127] and to ports in eastern India and Sri Lanka. The Nanyue region was in contact with the Malay world: after the conquest of this kingdom,

---

[126] Pacey (1990) considers the waterwheel and the water mill to be borrowed by the Chinese from Persia (and, beyond, from the Mediterranean; see above). On the other innovations of Han China, see below.

[127] Mahdi 1999b: 215. On the Han mission, see the *Qianhanshu, History of the Former Han*, written by Ban Biao, then by his children Ban Gu and Ban Zhao, finished *c.* 121 CE (Needham *et al.* 1971: 443; de la Vaissière 2002: 31).

"among the most remarkable plants brought into North China were young plants of the arecanut palm *Areca catechu*," referred to as *bin-lang*, from the Malay *pinang* (Salmon 2009: 183).[128] The tomb of the Nanyue king Wendi (137–122 BCE) contained imported items, such as a silver box from Persia, similar to boxes known in the sixth or fifth century BCE at Ecbatana (Salmon 2004: 25). Clearly, a vast Asian sphere was taking form with China at its core, a sphere connected to the Indian and West Asian world-systems through the roads of Inner Asia and via maritime networks.

Conclusion

The first millennium BCE was a period of growth – more rapid than in the Bronze Age – of networks and states, through major technical and institutional innovations. Exchanges developed on a vast scale along terrestrial and maritime routes (Maps II.4 and II.5). Morris notes that "the rate of increase in energy capture accelerated in the first millennium BC, [while] city sizes grew even faster" (2013: 170).

The systemic approach provides a convincing perspective on the data available for this period, although the paucity of quantitative data prevents us from assessing the level of integration among regions. Exchange networks reveal a transregional division of labor, and the systems that have been discussed evolved in a converging manner. Frank and Thompson (2005, 2006) have based their analysis of this period on firmer theoretical bases than had Frank and Gills (1993c),[129] by examining observable trends in fifty-year phases for various regions.[130]

Their research has been continued here, with the addition of Central Asia and western Arabia. The results are often similar, but at times differ from those of Frank and Thompson.[131] By presenting trajectories of the main regions of the western

---

[128] After the *Sanfu huangtu*. The original text may have been written at the end of the Eastern Han period (Salmon 2009: 183). The *Yiwu zhi*, going back to the same period, mentions both the areca nut and the betel (Salmon 2009: 184).

[129] A study re-examined by Bosworth (1995). The comparison between the evolution of the number and size of towns and cities and the phases of expansion and recession proposed by Frank and Gills (1993c) shows some divergences and reflects the difficulties inherent in this approach (in addition, and unfortunately, Chandler's estimates for the largest cities of the world jump from 200 BCE to 100 CE).

Phases of growth (Frank and Gills)	Support by Chandler	Phases of recession (Frank and Gills)	Support by Chandler
1000–800	strong	800–550	contradictory
550–450/400	strong	450–350	weak
350–250/200	strong	250/200–100/50	weak/inconclusive
50/100–200	strong	200/250–500	strong

[130] Frank and Thompson 2005: 146–147, table 9.3. It is regrettable that the space available for their article did not allow the authors to connect an extensive bibliography and the global results that are put forward in a more precise way.

[131] The divergences probably come from different assessments of sources that are difficult to interpret. Briant (1996) thus notes for the Persian Empire how dependent we are on biased Greek sources; the documents are insufficient for periods such as Artaxerxes II's reign. Sartre (2001) also points to an incomplete and inconsistent documentation for the Levant during the Hellenistic period.

Table II.In.2 (a) *Growth and recession in various regions of Africa and Eurasia*

	Egypt	Israel Palestine	Syria Lebanon	W. Arabia	Anatolia	Greece	N. Africa	Italy	N. Mesopotamia
1000–900	+	+	+	+	?	+		–	?
900–850	+	+	+	+	M	+		+	+
850–800	–	+	+	+	–			–	–
800–750	–	+	+	+	+	–		+	–
750–700	–	–	+	+	M	+	+	+	+
700–650	–	–	– ?	+	–	+	+	+	+
650–600	+	+ ?	M	+	–	+	+	+	–
600–550	+	–	–	–	+	+	+	+	+
550–500	+	+ ?	+	+	+	+	+	+	+
500–450	–	+	+	+	+	+	+	–	+
450–400	–	–	+	+	–	M	+	–	+
400–350	M	–	M	M	+	–	+		–
350–300	M	M	M	M	+	+	+	+	+
300–250	+	+	+	+	M	M	–	+	+
250–200	+	M	M	+	M	M	+	–	+
200–150	–	–	–	–	M	–	+	+	–
150–100	–	–	–	–	M	–	–	M	–
100–50	–	–	–	–	M	–	–	M	+
50–1	M	M	M	+	+	–	M	+	+

+ growth; – recession; M intermediary situation; ? uncertain situation

world-system, Table II.In.2 clearly shows that all regions did not follow the same path on the one hand, and that some areas were directly influenced (positively or negatively) by the expansion of dominant cores on the other. We see three long cycles, marked by processes of hegemonic transition between competing regions. Recessions were partially triggered by climatic changes of varying magnitude (with an overall decrease in temperatures) around 800, 400, and possibly 200 BCE[132] (see Table II.In.3).

---

[132] Brooke (2014) does not note any climatic deterioration around 200 BCE, however. He writes of "the improvement of monsoon conditions" during the Qin dynasty in China (2014: 309). By contrast, Lamb writes of a colder regime returning in eastern China by 200 BCE (1995: 150). Usoskin *et al.*'s (2012) reconstruction of decadal solar sunspot activity over the Holocene suggests only limited global cooling around 200 BCE; a large volcanic event has been registered in Greenland in 210 ± 30 BCE (Baillie 1992). The Weather Science Foundation pinpoints a colder phase centered on 170 BCE (www.longrangeweather .com/200bc.htm). Tree rings from Central Europe show low summer temperatures around 350 and 50 BCE, and later between 350 and 600 CE (Büntgen *et al.* 2011).

Table II.In.2 (b) *Growth and recession in various regions of Africa and Eurasia*

	S. Mesopotamia	Iran	W. Central Asia	N. India	S. India	S.-E. contin. Asia	N. China	S. China
1000–900	−						+	?
900–850	+						+	?
850–800	−		−				−	?
800–750	−		−				−	−
750–700	−	+	+				M	−
700–650	−	M		+			+	+
650–600	+	+	+	+			+	+
600–550	+	M	+	+			+	+
550–500	+	+	+	+			+	+
500–450	+	+	+	+			+	+
450–400	+	+		+			+	−
400–350	− ?	−		+	+	+	M	+
350–300	+	+	+	+	+	+	+	−
300–250	+	+	+	+	+	+	+	+
250–200	+	+	+	+	+	+	+	+
200–150	M	+ ?	M	M	+	+	+	+
150–100	M	−	−	M	+	+	+	+
100–50	+	M ?	+	− ?	+	+	+	+
50–1	+	+	+	− ?	+	+	−	+

Table II.In.3 *Western world-system*

Phases of growth	Phases of decline and restructuring
1000–850	850–750
750–450	450–350
350–200	200–1

The cycles of the Indian world-system that came into being around the seventh century BCE are more difficult to ascertain, due to more limited data on the one hand, and the peculiarities of South India on the other. It is an area that appears to fall "out-of-sync" with the rest of the world-system from time to time: due to the geographic complexity of the Indian peninsula and its connections with multiple areas, its various regions do not necessarily evolve at the same pace. It is possible to contemplate a union

Table II.In.4 *Chinese world-system*

Phases of growth	Phases of decline and restructuring
1000–850	850–750/700
750/700–450	450–350/300
350/300–50	50–1

Table II.In.5 *Indian world-system*

Northern region	
Phase of growth	Phase of decline and restructuring
700–200?	200–1?
Southern region	
Phase of growth	Phase of decline and restructuring
200–1	

of this Indian system with the world-system including western Asia and part of Africa and Europe, from 350 BCE onward. The growing relationships of this Indian world-system with Southeast Asia and China starting in 200 BCE seem to run counter to the decline of western world-system networks; South India was apparently enjoying a phase of growth at that time (see Table II.In.5).

The eastern world-system centered on China developed along three cycles (see Table II.In.4). The first two cycles are clearly parallel to those of the western world-system (Table II.In.3); such parallelism does not reflect a fusion of these two systems, however, but rather the probable influence of global climatic factors (with variations in mean temperature) in the cyclic logic at work here and there. Although the general trends and their global effects seem rather well documented today, new studies would be useful for dating these climatic changes more precisely, and for assessing their impact on the various regions under consideration.

The third cycle appears to be totally different from that of the west: the eastern world-system was undergoing a phase of growth until the middle of the first century BCE. The terrestrial and maritime Silk Roads that were laid out set the scene for the following period.

From one cycle to another, in the different systems, we observe a process of globalization characterized by an increase in production and exchanges, which in turn fostered a growing division of labor between regions and within the interconnected societies. This dynamic was accompanied by the formation of larger and more complex states, demographic growth, and increasing urbanization. Institutional and technical innovations were crucial to these developments. Demographic pressure, burgeoning trade, and statebuilding provided incentives for innovation. The close relationship between technology and military institutions has often been emphasized.

During phases of globalization, the markets for goods progressed, as, to a certain extent, did markets for factors of production (land, labor) – the importance of which is not always easy to assess. This progress in the main states paralleled a process of monetization of the economies and an expansion of credit. These evolutions yielded a certain amount of disembedding of the economy. These markets could only develop where the state exerted a positive effect, however, and where some symbiosis had occurred between state elites and private entrepreneurs. While the investments made by the state often contributed to economic growth in a first phase, later, overextension of this state, the development of social inequalities, and external issues usually led to recessions, which were accentuated by unfavorable climatic conditions. During phases of recession, the world-systems did not disappear, but underwent a phase in which their networks were restructured, as were their states and the societies involved. Recessions were accompanied by processes of hegemonic transition between competing dominant powers.

As has been observed for the Early Bronze Age, expansion of production and exchanges was founded on two processes: statebuilding and the expansion of a private sector. "Capitalist" practices[133] developed within the state and within the context of private entreprises. Whereas at times one notes an opposition between the state and private sectors, their coordination is clearly visible in the Greek and Roman empires. In China, the Han state was wary of merchants, who nonetheless prospered under the empire. In the Roman world, the state tended to make use of traders, and the richest merchants often belonged to the ruling elites.

The end of the first millennium BCE saw an increase in large-scale exchange networks, on terrestrial and maritime routes. The Greek and later Roman thrust toward the Indian Ocean reflects the growing importance of trade in this ocean, particularly in the Bay of Bengal, and the desirability of products such as pepper and silk; it was not the Greek and Roman ventures that led to a surge of trade in the Indian Ocean, as has too often been said, but the opposite: the flowering of Indian commerce with eastern Asia and the expansion of Han China explain this increase in trade. The various forms of evolution over the final centuries BCE thus mark a milestone for the integration of the Mediterranean, Indian, and Chinese areas and the interconnection of these three worlds. They herald the turning period of the first century CE, when the intensity of exchanges led to an interdependence of the different parts of what now formed a single world-system, stretching from eastern Asia to western Europe and Africa.

The Birth of the Afro-Eurasian World-System

The First Phase of Integration of the World-System

> "You, Roman, be sure to rule the world (be these your arts), to crown peace with justice."
> (Virgil, *Aeneid*, VI, 851–853)

---

[133] This refers to practices that would later be considered as characteristic of capitalism (see above).

The Roman expansion during the first century BCE was the fruit of internal changes and of a favorable international context. The military reforms of Marius in 107 BCE – with the creation of a professional army – led to the emergence of war chiefs and to a transformation of the political system into a quasi-monarchy from Augustus onward, under the Principate. Chief of the Roman civic religion, the emperor was first of all the holder of *imperium maius*: he commanded the armies and the provinces, and decided matters of peace and war. Grants of land to soldiers as rewards fed Rome's expansion. Control over the Egyptian wheat granary in 30 BCE proved to be a turning point in this expansion. The emperor took immense territories for himself. Rome's power reached its peak during the first and second centuries CE, but the extension of the empire held the seeds of its own decline. In central Europe, the Roman Empire extended as far as the Danube (14 CE). In the west, it occupied a part of Britain after Agricola's campaigns (77–84 CE). In the south, after Tunisia, the rest of northern Africa was annexed in 44 CE. In Asia, a victorious war against the Parthians allowed Trajan to enter Armenia (114 CE). In 116 CE, this emperor conquered Mesopotamia and obtained access to the Persian Gulf, but his successor Hadrian decided to evacuate these territories in 117. The overextension of the empire was becoming too costly. Already during the first century CE, as McLaughlin points out (2014: 218), while "the expense-cost of the empire was about 1,000 million sesterces per annum, over 700 million sesterces [were] spent on the military." The Roman historian Appian notes:

Since [the emperors] control the best regions of the earth and sea, they wisely wish to preserve what they have rather than to extend the empire endlessly by including barbarian tribes, which are poor and unprofitable. (Appian, *Roman History*, Preface 7, quoted by Hopkins 2009: 185)

Trajan's capture of Petra in 106 CE appears to have triggered a partial regression in the caravan routes crossing the Nabataean territory in western Arabia (the tribute exacted by the Romans – one-fourth of imported merchandise – certainly had something to do with this regression); in addition, the rise to prominence of Palmyra during the second and third centuries reveals the vitality of the trade routes linking the Persian Gulf to Syria and the Levant, the most productive provinces of the Roman Empire.[134] Inscriptions from Palmyra "document caravan ventures from AD 19 to the 260s AD" (McLaughlin 2010: 17). Palmyra was also connected to the Silk Roads of Central Asia (Liu 2010: 30–31). In Egypt, Trajan re-excavated the canal between the Nile and the Red Sea, and Hadrian made arrangements for its maintenance. This canal appears to have been used until the fifth or sixth century (Tomber 2012a: 66).

The empire was built not only on impressive infrastructures (roads, bridges, forts, walls), but also on progress in navigation, a unified system of weights and measures, the development of a law of universal value, and a limited – and later general – extension of Roman citizenship as of 212, when Caracalla granted this status to all free inhabitants of

---

[134] Palmyra, which had come under the control of Rome during the first century CE, became a free town in 129. The fiscal legislation of Palmyra, dated to 137, provides a list of the taxes levied on 28 articles traded. First on the list were slaves, second "dry products" (including spices), then aromatics (myrrh in alabaster vases, and so forth) and oils, purple fabrics, and animals (Keay 2005: 88).

the empire, for both fiscal and political reasons (Simonnot 2002: 63–64).[135] The Roman Empire expressed "a tendency toward homogenization," as shown by "the practice of taking other people's gods into the imperial pantheon" (Burbank and Cooper 2010: 12). Rome offered an impressive material culture[136] – with its planned cities, water-channeling systems, public baths, and amphitheaters – as well as its non-material culture. In the empire, the spread of a shared ideology was crucial; it included "a civilized way of being and living" (*humanitas*) (Burbank and Cooper 2010: 38). The Roman Empire was "a unitary symbolic system" (Hopkins 2009: 186). At the same time, the Roman way of life and Roman beliefs and customs spread throughout the empire. The Roman Empire was divided into senatorial and imperial provinces (where armed forces were stationed). The extension of imperial administration led to a diminished role for the publicans, as taxes were directly collected by employees of the state.[137] The administration remained minimalistic, however: "in the 2nd century, there was only one Roman elite administrator for 400,000 inhabitants of the empire, whereas in 12th-century China there was an elite administrator per 15,000 people" (Hopkins 2009: 184). The Senate was politically weakened, while the *equites* rose in the social hierarchy, as did some freedmen who had been enriched through trade and finance. "The aggregate wealth and income of the aristocracy was probably greater than the tax income of the central government" (Hopkins 2009: 184).[138] The emperors, however, extended taxation and imposed new taxes: a poll tax (from which the plebs of the cities of the Orient were exempted);[139] a tax on trade and transport (*vectigalia*); duties on imports and exports (*portoria*); inheritance tax, and so forth. The mines became state property; they were leased out or managed directly by officials. "By the late 1st century AD, bullion production provided Rome with between 120 and 200 million sesterces per annum. This was about a sixth of the revenue that the Roman Empire needed to meet its basic costs (1,000 millions sesterces per annum)" (McLaughlin 2014: 13). A courier and transportation service was created, and was already in use during the Republican period (Molin 2009: 215). The empire had a legislative system;[140] an administration; a fiscal

---

[135] "The concept of citizenry corresponds to a cosmopolitan orientation of the Roman elite" (J. Friedman 2000: 131). Under the Antonines (96–192 CE), notes Deniaux (1987: 60), "the senators of Rome come from Spain, Gaul, Greece, from the Orient, as well as from Italy." Alongside the idea of unity of the Roman world, a growing acceptance of diverse religious beliefs was gaining ground. Moreover, the "role of the Greek sophists in the fusion of the Greek and Latin worlds" has often been emphasized (Grimal 1993: 135ff.).

[136] Morris gives an estimate of 31,000 kcal/cap/day for energy capture during the first and second centuries in the Roman Empire, a figure that would later be reached in the West only in the seventeenth–eighteenth century (2013: 61). He gives an estimate of 27,000 kcal/cap/day for Han China for the same period (2013: 111).

[137] For Rostovtzeff (1998: xii), "an alliance between the Italian bourgeoisie and the Italian proletariate" under Augustus "resulted in the collapse of the hegemony of the two privileged orders of Rome, the senatorial and the equestrian" and marked the end of the influence of the magnates of the late Republic.

[138] During the first century, six senators were reputed to own most of Tunisia (Hopkins 2009: 190). The aristocrats' wealth increased over time: during the fourth century, "a middling senator had an income of 6–9 million sesterces per year," seven times more than during the first century (Hopkins 2009).

[139] While Roman taxes were relatively low, "many Egyptian peasants struggled to pay their poll taxes in cash" (Hopkins 2009: 184).

[140] The emperor himself derived his power and his legitimacy from the law.

system; an army; and population registers for sociopolitical and fiscal purposes. For these reasons, the Roman Empire has sometimes been considered as "the matrix of the modern state" (Nicolet 1988: 313). The empire carried out land surveys, and maps were drawn. The state allowed the private sector to develop, by securing property rights, and by leasing out some of its activities. While private banking developed,[141] loans destined for productive investment remained in the minority (Andreau 2010: 150ff.). "The Roman capitalists," observes Nicolet, "were 'state annuitants' rather than 'entrepreneurs'" and Roman growth was first the fruit of "the looting of the world."[142] Nicolet also notes, however, that the landowners using slave labor were "concerned with performance" (1988: 194); Rostovtzeff (1998: xiv) evokes a "capitalist management" of land during the Republican period starting in the third century BCE, but also writes that during the Empire "the prevailing outlook of the municipal bourgeoisie was that of the rentier." This may have been true for Italy. In contrast, however, authors such as Simonnot (2002: 51) have emphasized the entrepreneurial spirit of the elites.[143] As we have observed in the Greek world and the western Asia of earlier times, assignment of credit claims was a common practice; a claim to be paid could be transferred to a third party. The state fixed a maximum loan rate at 12 percent, but rates varied according to supply and demand (Andreau 2010: 158, 161). The rate might be high for a maritime venture, a practice inherited from the Greek maritime loan: it was a contract including "both sponsorship and guarantee" (Nicolet 1988: 91). The *annona*, a tax on grains extracted from the provinces to feed Rome, led not only to unequal taxation, but also to greater production. The state subsidized the transport and storage of grain, and controlled prices. For wheat, oil, stones, and metals, the state contracted private haulers, as there was no state-owned fleet. Taxes in kind were replaced by monetary taxes that forced the provinces to borrow from Roman "bankers." The Roman world went further than the Greek world in the "monetization of social relationships" (Maucourant 2008: 25). The existence of a single gold currency (*aureus*) and silver currency (*denarius*) fostered exchanges throughout the empire (there were, however, local issues for copper coins, and Antioch and Alexandria maintained the minting of silver coins) (Rostovtzeff 1988: 143).[144] During the second century, "seven billion silver coins were in circulation, more than four times the estimate for 50 BC ... The total value of the coinage system grew twelve times from the 1st century BC to the 2nd century AD" (Hopkins 2009: 197, 199). This growing monetization corresponded to an

---

[141] Unlike those of the Greek world, Roman temples did not play a truly banking role: they did not develop the practice of monetary loans.

[142] Nicolet 1988: 98; Norel 2004: 115. In addition, the prevalence of slavery helped limit innovation (see below). Roman societies – in which political power and merchant power merged – developed by using the people and the capital of preexisting networks (Moore and Lewis 1999: 241, 242, 246). Note that the institution of slavery was more complex than is usually described. We find "slaves who are businessmen or managers"; the fact that some slaves were the property of several owners led to the creation of "societies"; there were also slaves who depended on other slaves (Andreau 1999). Some "businessmen" of servile origin engaged in maritime trade (Aubert 1999).

[143] People who were only merchants, however, could not become senators, and bankers could not obtain access to the Senate or the order of the *equites*.

[144] "The denarius was introduced in 211 BC and produced in enormous quantity from the silver captured in the sack of Syracuse the year before" (van der Spek 2015). The *aureus* was regularly issued from the first century BCE to the beginning of the fourth century CE, when it was replaced by the *solidus*.

increase in trade. At the center of the empire, the Mediterranean Sea became a vast sphere for exchanges, which largely functioned according to the rules of a "market economy" (Temin 2001). Here again the expression "economy with market(s)" (*économie à marché[s]*) used by Bresson (2000) and Migeotte (2007) might be more appropriate: we are not in the presence – as Simonnot (2002: 54) also claims – of an "immense unified market" (see Andreau 2010: 176ff.). It is true, however, that products and people from Africa, Europe, western and eastern Asia arrived in Rome. The importance of the Mediterranean resulted in part from the fact that "transport by land cost fifty to sixty times as much (per ton/km) as transport by sea" (Hopkins 2009: 186).

Slaves came mostly from northern and eastern Europe,[145] from Upper Egypt, and from Africa (through trans-Saharan routes).[146] There is increasing evidence for a precocious trans-Saharan trade (see above; Mattingly 2011; MacDonald 2011). It appears that the Romans acquired ivory and slaves from West Africa through the Garamantes, who traded with Tripolitania (the population of their capital Garama would reach 4,000 inhabitants *c.* 150 CE). In addition, the culture of African cotton in Fezzan around the fourth century reveals contacts with Nubia (Pelling 2005: 406). The Garamantes acted increasingly as an interface between the Mediterranean Sea and the African interior, exporting slaves, wild beasts, and ivory to Rome. "Large quantities of Roman trade goods have been found at Garamantian sites and in their burials." The Garamantes produced and exported textiles and beads to the interior (Mattingly 2011: 57). Cowry shells from the Indian Ocean have also been excavated. "The Roman general Julius Maternus[147] accompanied the king of the Garamantes on a slave raid as far as the Niger at the end of the 1st century AD" (Fentress 2011: 69).[148] "In return for slaves, carnelian and wild beasts, they imported textiles and [wine]. Wilson [2005] estimates the number [of slaves traded] at 50,000 between the 2nd century BC and the 2nd century AD" (Fentress 2011). As Fentress notices, "the slave trade [with the Mediterranean world] must have had a knock-on effect on societies along the Niger" (2011: 69). Liverani has suggested a link between an early trans-Saharan trade and increasing social complexity south of the Sahara (2005: 447). Jenne-jeno formed a conurbation with nearby sites during the first century BCE. Glass beads from the Mediterranean have been found at this site. The size of Jenne-jeno went from 12 ha in 100 CE to 25 ha in 400 CE (Hansen 2000a: 15; MacIntosh 1999). Moreover, gold may

---

[145] On Delos, according to Strabo, as many as 10,000 slaves were sold every day.

[146] This trans-Saharan trade was already in place during the first millennium BCE, but it certainly expanded following the introduction of the dromedary around the end of the first millennium BCE (see above). The site of Kissi (Burkina Faso) has yielded glass beads dated between the first and third centuries CE (Magnavita 2003: 133), as well as cloth remains made of dromedary wool (dated between the first century BCE and the eighth century CE) – whether this cloth was imported or locally produced could not be determined (Magnavita 2008).

[147] Ptolemy (*Geography*, 1.18, 1.20) speaks of a first expedition, led by Septimius Flaccus, who was probably a governor of Numidia (in the 80s CE. See Cassius Dio 67.5.6). A few years later, there was an expedition by Julius Maternus, whom Desanges thought to be a rich merchant (1975: 397). Julius Maternus's march southward with the Garamantian king took four months.

[148] An inscription from Sousse reads: "The dregs of the Garamantes have come to our lands, and the uncouth black man glories in his pitch-black body" (Desanges 1975: 412).

have come from West Africa: Carthage struck gold coins from 296 onward (McDonald 2013: 72). Some Roman objects have been found in the Sahara: coins east of Akjoujt (Mauritania); remains of amphorae at Gourma (Mali) (fifth–sixth centuries); and an oil lamp, a Greco-Roman bead, and a glass vessel in a tomb at Abalessa (western Hoggar) (fifth century) (MacDonald 2011: 75–76).

The Roman state also imported gold from Spain and central Europe. Copper came from Cyprus, Anatolia, Spain; silver from Spain and central Europe. Large family firms and companies in partnership were established on all the shores of the Mediterranean Sea, with agents at Ostia, the port of Rome. Long before Ibn Khaldun and Adam Smith, "Pliny the Younger observes the benefits of trade in these terms: '[Trajan] has linked the various nations by trade so that natural products in any place seem to belong to all countries' and if abundance reigns in Rome, famine no longer exists, anywhere" (Andreau 1994: 95). This said, "the elite did not take global measures to promote exchanges, because economic activity was considered private" (Andreau 1994) (Cicero, nevertheless, writes in *De imperio Cnaei Pompeii*: "Our ancestors have often waged war because of insults endured by our merchants and our shipowners") (Andreau 2010: 208).

Weber has emphasized the lack of rationality of "ancient capitalism," whereas Rathbone (1991), after studying the archives of a large private agricultural estate in Fayum, has shown the emergence of a form of economic rationality: "the choices that were made responded to profitability calculations and tended toward profit maximization, cost reduction and risk minimization, [through] a centrally planned management of the estate" (Andreau and Maucourant 1999: 50). For Rathbone, "production choice and supply of labor would both be market-driven" (1991) (Andreau and Maucourant, however, do qualify the supposed rationality of estate management, and refuse to extend the facts from the Fayum to the whole Roman Empire or even to Egypt, 1999: 65, 94).[149] Choices made on the estate express an alternative, already present in western Asia as early as the second millennium BCE: is it better to "work directly" or "let

---

[149] Sombart (1926: 273) has pointed out that "the greed for gain, and economic rationalism, were already developed in the books from Xenophon and Roman writers" such as Columella. For Weber, a form of "ancient capitalism" did exist (1998 [1909]), but it was different from medieval capitalism: this capitalism was structurally dependent on the political sphere and remained "irrational," using techniques that limited its development (see Capogrossi 2004; Bruhns 1998, 2004). In fact, "capitalist" entrepreneurs took advantage of the links set up with the politico-military sphere, benefiting from the demand in luxury goods, slaves, and equipment for the armed forces. Lands and licenses for the collection of taxes were granted to them. Weber, however, recognized the importance of the market in the economy of agricultural estates using slaves: these estates produced for the market, and they did represent a kind of capitalistic enterprise (1998 [1909]: 100; Descat 2004). "The largely capitalist character of entire periods of antiquity seems . . . quite plausible" writes Weber. However, Weber sees the political and military orientation of the ancient city (where industry destined for export was nonetheless present) as essentially different from that of the medieval city, where a set of factors (geographic, political, institutional, juridical) promoted the development of rational behavior and the appearance of "bourgeois corporate capitalism": "medieval urban development [was] a crucial factor [in] the birth of modern capitalism," an idea already expressed by Adam Smith (Bruhns 2001: 62–63) (this medieval development may be linked "to the [apolitical] cities of both the Hellenistic period and Late Antiquity," Bruhns 1998: 47; see Weber 1998 [1909]: 384). Rathbone (2003), however, sees "strong rights ensuring private property, an effective and flexible juridical system, a political and social system that was stable and open, and a governance of *laissez-faire*" in the Roman world (Maucourant 2004: 85).

out work" (by leasing out the land or using a labor force)? Moreover, Rathbone (2004: 142) refutes the idea of any preeminence of the slave system: "free hired labor was dominant throughout the Roman Empire, surpassing servile labor by at least two to one." Italy, however, had about 3 million slaves, or 30 or 40 percent of the population between the first century BCE and the first century CE according to Andreau (2010: 74), whereas Scheidel (1999) advances an estimate of "only" 10 or 15 percent. Slavery is usually seen as an obstacle to the extension of hired labor, but in some cases slavery "contributed to its development" (Andreau 2004b). In addition, the extent of slavery varied according to region (Roman and Roman 1998), and the number of slaves diminished in Italy during the empire.

Despite the system of the *annona* and political decisions aimed at protecting Italy, the vision of an empire centered on the city of Rome and dominated by Italy should be qualified: the empire was in fact a multicentered core. As early as the first century, the building of the empire triggered a centrifugal movement of people, marked by the settlement of legions and colonies in distant lands, and capital was largely invested in the provinces (Friedman 2000: 131). It is significant that Trajan decided to force each senator to invest part of his fortune in Italy. Emperor Hadrian, in particular, tried to develop the provinces and improve border fortifications. The emperors themselves often had parental or matrimonial links outside Italy. A trend reversal occurred in exchanges between Italy and the provinces between Augustus's reign and the 2nd century AD. This trend can be seen in table ware, wine, oil, oil lamps, and is probably relevant to other products, such as glass and textiles (Andreau 2010: 185ff.). While Rome was the seat of political power, economic power resided increasingly with the provinces, particularly in the east, which benefited from assets such as agricultural wealth, human capital, and technological knowhow, as well as from trade with Asia and Africa. Early on, the merchants of the eastern Mediterranean gained the upper hand in trade. "Very rich men are now to be found ... chiefly in the provinces, not Italy," such as the Lycian Opromoas and the Athenian Herodes Atticus (second century) (Rostovtzeff 1998: 151); the imperial aristocracy originated mainly in the urban bourgeoisie of the west and the east. "By the end of the 2nd century, half of the central Roman Senate was of provincial origin" (Hopkins 2009: 186). A decentralization of economic power was thus noteworthy, and trade from province to province would grow from Augustus onward. Various factors combined to lead to Italy's relative and progressive downturn, which triggered an impoverishment of its urban "bourgeoisie." The productivity of rural people also declined in Italy, and supply from the provinces grew. Provincial growth was also spurred by demand from Rome as well as from the armies stationed in some provinces. The expansion of markets favored a development that first benefited local elites who "served as a transmission belt for the new political order" (Dumasy 2005).[150] Romanization allowed for the diffusion of techniques: grapevine culture spread into Gaul and Iberia, Italian ceramics were copied in Gaul and other regions, and so forth. Taxes also led to increased production and trade in some provinces (Andreau 2010: 190ff.). The southern Iberian peninsula

---

[150] According to Pliny, in northern Africa, "six landowners controlled half of the country prior to Nero's confiscations" (Leveau 1978).

exported oil and a fish sauce; Catalonia sold wine; Gaul wine, ceramics, and bronze vessels;[151] for the Syria–Palestine region, Anatolia and Egypt, it was textiles, leather items, precious pieces of furniture, glass (raw glass, and glass products), carpets, and spices. Moreover, Rome's trade with the Indian Ocean was largely in deficit, causing a massive hemorrhage of precious metals toward the Orient.

We can speak of a Smithian growth for the western part of the world-system, with expanding long-distance trade supported by both the state and the private sector, but – in contrast to eastern Asia – innovations would play a minor role in the overall growth of the Roman Empire. It has often been pointed out that whereas the technical achievements of the Romans were impressive, they produced little theoretical scientific work and innovations were limited, except for the improvement of cement[152] (used increasingly from the first century BCE onward). The water mill and the screw press were inventions of the Hellenistic world,[153] as were various devices for lifting water, such as the bucket chain, bucket wheel, and Archimedean screw (Bouet 2005). With few exceptions,[154] in the technological and scientific domains, the great names of the Roman period come from the Greek tradition, for example Galen (*c.* 131–201, born in Pergamon), a physicist at Rome at the court of Marcus Aurelius, and Ptolemy (*c.* 90–168), a mathematician, astronomer, and geographer from Alexandria, whose cosmological geocentric system would remain the reference model in the western world until the sixteenth century. In the military field, various ancient authors describe weapons reflecting the use of *naphta* in incendiaries, for example Herodianos (around CE 240) during the siege of Aquileia (Partington 1999: 4). "Tacitus [56 CE – after 117] speaks of fire-lances thrown by machines" (Partington 1999: 2), but these weapons were probably borrowed from the Greeks. Scientific curiosity seems to have vanished, and even the desire to conserve ancient knowledge died out. Of course, heavy reliance on slavery did not auger well for technological innovation or a broadening of the division of labor. Science was "weakly socialized and institutionalized in the ancient world, and it largely lacked an ideological or material basis of support in society" (McClellan and Dorn 1999: 93). Moreover, science was meeting with ever-increasing hostility from Christians. Saint Augustine (354–430 CE) thus spoke out against "those named physicists by the Greeks." The assassination of Hypatia, the first female mathematician, by Christian fanatics in 415 marked the end of the Museum of Alexandria.

Yet the Roman world was not as deficient in the fields of innovation and technological progress as has often been claimed. Improvements were made in maritime transport: "the Romans had large seagoing vessels, sometimes as large as those of the

---

[151] "Gaul was able to impose its products in the Roman world under Claudius or Nero's reign" (Roman 2009b: 246).

[152] Cement was already being used in Egypt by the final centuries of the first millennium BCE. M. Barsoum (Drexel University, Philadelphia) goes so far as to advocate the idea of cement use in the construction of the Great Pyramids, an idea refuted by most Egyptologists.

[153] Mazoyer and Roudart 1998: 296–297 (after Amouretti 1987). Some large hydraulic mills were built during the Roman Empire. As mentioned above, the water mill appeared in the eastern Mediterranean during the final centuries BCE. The screw press, called a "Greek press" by Pliny (XVIII. 37), may have been developed in the Hellenistic world around the first century BCE and perfected during the first century CE.

[154] These exceptions were Lucretius, the naturalist Pliny the Elder (24–79 CE), and the engineer Vitruvius (first century BCE), who wrote a book on architecture that would be used by the Renaissance architects.

Genoese during the 15th century, steered with two huge side rudders, coupled by a bar" (Roman 2009b: 250). The development of sail led to improved rigging (Marlier and Pomey 2008).[155] Terrestrial transport was also improved, with the use of oxen and mules, and to a lesser extent horses. Lefebvre des Noêttes (1931), followed by generations of researchers, believed that the strap of the so-called "throat-and-girth harness" choked the horse and that the yoke hurt the horse's withers. In fact, as Raepsaet points out, this reconstruction, erroneous, confused two ancient types of harnesses: "that with neck yoke[156] and that with shoulder collar" (Camps 1978; Spruytte 1977).[157] Moreover, a double-shafted vehicle was developed, that was adapted to mule and donkey, thus introducing draft using a single animal; this system used a "single yoke" placed on the animal's neck (Raepsaet 2008a: 95–96). The Romans applied the theoretical discoveries of Hero of Alexandria in hydraulics (Leveau 2008: 155). Agriculture also made significant progress, as a book by Columella (first century CE) reveals. Long before Islam, the Roman world had practiced systems of crop rotation and selective breeding. It had developed irrigation, and promoted the diffusion of plants such as durum wheat and rice (Decker 2009: 189ff.).[158] The crank, known prior to the Christian era, was used in tools and machines: a sarcophagus at Hierapolis (Turkey) features two water-powered stone sawmills, combining a crank with a connecting rod. In the textile industry, craftsmen invented a vertical loom with horizontal bars (Andreau 2010: 238). In fact, "the assertion of a stagnation in techniques, of a standstill and of poorly developed manufactured production in the Roman world does not really make sense and is but fantasy" (Roman 2009b: 250). Furthermore, arguing against the idea of stagnation in techniques due to the significance of slavery, Rostovtzeff (1988: 253) has pointed out that stagnation in fact occurred precisely when the number of slaves began diminishing. While Roman "globalization" favored both the spread and synthesis of techniques, the fact that markets remained relatively "localized" and insufficiently linked to one another tended to limit innovations.

The extension of the Roman Empire to Egypt, the Levant, Anatolia, and the western and southern shores of the Black Sea multiplied the links of the Mediterranean world with the large states of Central Asia, India (the Kushan and Shātavāhana empires, the South Indian kingdoms,[159] and China (the Han Empire).

[155] This development in sails "has to be linked not only to a diversification in the types of ship, but also with an increase in gross tonnage of the biggest units" (Marlier and Pomey 2008: 114–115). Ships were able to sail against the wind (Marlier and Pomey 2008).

[156] Like Spruytte, Raepsaet (2008a: 94) points out that "the yoke rested on the curve of the back, behind the shoulders, and was attached to a girth strap that exerted force on the shoulder joints and not on the throat."

[157] "Traction was exerted by a breast-strap harness [girth-strap]" (Camps 1978) (see also Molin 2009: 211–212), but this was not yet the true "breast collar harness," a Chinese innovation that arrived later in Europe (see below).

[158] It is significant that Diocletian's *Edict on prices* (third century) gives a price for the rice (Decker 2009: 197).

[159] For the beginning of the Christian era, contacts between Egypt and India are attested by Diodorus, Strabo, then the *Periplus* and Pliny on the one hand, and by the Tamil Sangam literature on the other (Salles 1996; Thapar 1997).

The Indo-Roman trade expanded mainly via the Red Sea. It fostered the emergence of the Axumite kingdom, which became a partner of the Roman Empire and a mandatory intermediary between the Indian Ocean and the Mediterranean Sea. Axum occupied the port of Adulis, and dominated trade in southern Arabia. The Axumite kingdom was also able to develop because it controlled the routes leading to the African interior, toward the Blue Nile.

China was the second major pole of the world-system. The Han Empire, however, experienced an internal crisis at the end of the first century BCE, a crisis generated by its rapid expansion and accompanying social transformations. General Wang Mang then attempted to impose radical reforms, but was made destitute and killed during a revolt. Under the eastern Han who reigned afterward (25–220 CE) from their capital at Luoyang, the empire enjoyed a new phase of expansion, but also underwent a process of decentralization marked by the formation of large estates, the ascent of a private trade sector, and the emergence of local elites. In connection with this rise in trade, new technological innovations appeared, fostering growth in production especially in agriculture and iron metallurgy. Luoyang had about 420,000 inhabitants in 100 CE, with Chang'an remaining a large city (120,000 inhabitants in 200 CE) (Morris 2013: 155).

The Han Empire extended both toward the south, where it occupied the Red River valley, and into Central Asia, where the Chinese took control of the oases once again. Buddhism entered China during this period, via the Silk Roads. The Han carried on significant diplomatic activity, receiving embassies at Luoyang, and sending emissaries to India and Parthia. With the nomads, the conclusion of agreements – through large gifts of silk – became "a fundamental strategy" (Burbank and Cooper 2010). Another trade route led to the Black Sea: bronze mirrors from the Han period have been excavated in Ukraine, and fragments of silk textiles have been found in tombs in Crimea. Lapis lazuli from Afghanistan arrived via the Black Sea route: "the best *cyanos* [lapis], writes Pliny, is that from Scythia" (de la Vaissière 2002: 46). Products of the Roman Empire arrived in China, carried first of all along the terrestrial Silk Roads. Contacts intensified with Southeast Asia, which partly explains the progress made in Chinese navigation at this time. While the Chinese probably did not venture far into the southern Sea, sailors from Southeast Asia traded in Chinese ports. It is difficult to share Adshead's view that the world-empire of the Han "constituted a world apart in a planet of separate worlds" (1995: 1).

Central Asia and northern India played crucial roles in building connections between eastern and western regions. Originating in Central Asia, the Kushans had occupied Bactria since 135 or 130 BCE; they extended their empire by taking over northern India. Under their greatest king, Kanishka I, at the beginning of the second century, they controlled a territory from the Oxus River to Vārānasī and included Gujarat in their empire. On the routes leading to China, the Kushans controlled the country west of the Tarim; several times they had to fight Chinese armies. The Kushan kings promoted exchanges with the west, but also between India and China. The precise organization of the empire is not well known, but it probably borrowed the Persian system of satrapies. Inscriptions show a complex administrative hierarchy; standardized coins were minted, revealing some centralization of the state, as well as the religious tolerance of the Kushan kings. Their support for Buddhism reflects the insertion of the empire into a large Asian sphere of exchange. The kings moved their courts among several capitals, with Peshāwar (Purushapura) and Mathurā representing the empire's administrative centers. The treasure of Begram (found on the site of Kapisa, the summer capital of Kanishka I, in Afghanistan) and the rich contents of the tombs at Tillya Tepe reflect the extent of the exchange networks, with objects from as far as China, India, and the Roman world. The trade routes extended into the steppes. The Kushan Empire had contacts with Sri Lanka, through Gujarat. In addition, Kushans were present in Orissa and in Bengal, as shown by the development of the Kharoṣṭī script, also found in Southeast Asia, as far as Bali.

In the Indian peninsula, the Shātavāhana kingdom formed another major polity, whose formidable army was described by Pliny. Exchanges within India and with foreign countries reveal the power this kingdom held during the second century CE. The kingdoms of South India – Chola, Pāndya, and Chera – were also active in maritime exchanges, as was Sri Lanka.

The global role of South Asia during this period should be reassessed. It is clear that Indian merchants were present in the western Indian Ocean, particularly in the Red Sea, and that the Indian influence in Southeast Asia is older than was previously thought. As an interface between the China Sea and the Indian Ocean, Southeast Asia also benefited from local and regional developments. Centered on the Lower Mekong valley, Funan was the first major state that was able to combine agricultural and military progress, craft production, and commerce; its elite made use of the techniques of power (religion, system of government, writing) and luxury goods from India. Along with Funan, the Malay peninsula, the Cham coast, and most particularly the islands of Austronesian Southeast Asia were also active participants in the burgeoning trade between the China Sea and the Indian Ocean. Metals (tin from the Malay peninsula, gold from Sumatra and Kalimantan) and Moluccan spices began to take on importance. Ships from Southeast Asia sailed to China as early as the third century BCE. The discovery of Indian beads and Dong-Son-type bronzes reveal the extent of the networks in the Pacific, to as far as western New Guinea, probably to acquire feathers of birds of paradise.

The Austronesians also sailed to India and further west. In a likely attempt to trade directly with the western Indian Ocean, without resorting to Indian intermediaries, they settled on the East African coast (other Austronesians would later reach the Comoros and Madagascar). It is precisely during this period that a Pre-Swahili culture developed on the East African coast. Arab, but also Greek, Roman, or Parthian ships sailed to this coast: at the start of the Christian era, Arabs from Yemen were forced to abandon their virtual hegemony in trade, and the port of Aden was opened to foreign ships.

With increasing Roman demand and Han China's interest in goods from the southern seas and the west, trade networks now extended from the Mediterranean Sea to the China Sea via the Silk Roads and along maritime routes. This interconnection gave rise to the first large-scale world-system. This system, already traced by the development of the terrestrial[160] and maritime[161] routes of previous centuries (see Map II.6), covered three continents (Asia, Europe, and Africa). Trade in silk, iron, aromatics, and perfumes was key to this process, as well as transfers of precious metals. Interactions among different "world-economies" led to the "economic integration by trade of most of the inhabited world" (Glover 1996: 368; 2000: 96).[162] Archaeological data and texts reveal the setting up of a transregional division of labor. Essentially, the cores or centers of the system exported manufactured products, above all textiles (silk textiles and silk yarn for China; silk and cotton materials for India; linen cloth for Egypt; wool or linen textiles for the Levant and Anatolia); these cores imported raw goods and slaves. An unfavorable trade balance with Asia triggered a flow of precious metals from the Roman Empire to India and China. Needham and Wang Ling (1954: 109) note that Tiberius prohibited the wearing of silk in Rome just after the Han Empire decided to call in gold metal in exchange for bronze coins (Schneider 1991: 57). Obviously, the demand for precious metals – from India first of all – was essential to the growth of the system. In this case, ought we to view the flows of bullion as simply the result of a trade imbalance?

The Roman expansion toward India was first of all the result of Asian dynamism, particularly between India and China. It is certain that the desirability of goods from the Roman Empire was weak in the Indian and Chinese cores (with the exception of gold and silver); however, Roman demand and the connections that were established did stimulate the economy of Asia and the transformation of its societies, also through exchange of knowledge.

Driven by an increasing demand for luxury goods, the "commercial revolution" was also linked to the extension of iron technology. Ironworking spurred progress in agriculture, which also resulted from various social processes (Ray 2003: 6). This expansion provided the basis for urban development and overall growth; it also led to improvements in weaponry. During this period, new states emerged all around the Indian Ocean.

Demographic growth accompanied economic development. Chandler (1987) estimates that around CE 100, Rome was the world's foremost city with one million inhabitants (Luoyang, in China, placed second), and five of the Ancient World's ten largest cities were under Roman domination. Born from Judaism, Christianity appeared during the first century in Palestine and then spread throughout the Roman Empire (Anatolia, Greece, Rome, Alexandria, and so forth). Its expansion in Egypt during the second and third centuries went along with the disappearance of the

---

[160] The Han emperor Wudi was not responsible for opening up the Silk Roads, as has so often been claimed: these routes had been in existence long before the Han dynasty.

[161] The cities of Sri Lanka are a testimony to these maritime routes. Ray (2003: 6–7) situates a general expansion of trade networks in a Pre-Maurya period; these were still operated largely on a regional basis. For Ray, two major systems emerged during the second–first century BCE: one in the Bay of Bengal, the other in the western Indian Ocean.

[162] Chase-Dunn and Hall 1997: 249–250. McNeill (1998b: 129) has also noted "the new importance of maritime and terrestrial exchanges" during the two first centuries of the Christian era. For Bentley (1993: 29ff.), however, integration began during the third century BCE. Bellina and Glover (2004: 83) also argue that "by the late centuries BC, Southeast Asia was already part of a world trading system linking the civilizations of the Mediterranean basin and Han China."

ancient Egyptian religion and the religion of the traditional political elite. Gnostic sects flourished alongside Christianity; these were particularly active in Egypt. It is probably not by chance that the idea of a saving and merciful figure (*boddhisattva*) appeared at this time in the Buddhism of "the Great Vehicle" (Mahāyāna), which developed in India during the first century CE.[163]

The World-System Recedes (Third–Sixth Century)

As a consequence of increased exchanges and of population migrations, epidemics spread as early as the second half of the second century CE in both Rome and China, preceding an economic recession that would begin during the third century.[164] In the Roman world, an epidemic of exanthematic typhus or smallpox broke out in 165; it was called the "Antonine plague." It was brought in by the armies of Cassius who had sejourned in Mesopotamia. However, the first outbreak had occurred in China in 162 (see McLaughlin 2014: 210ff.). There was a major recurrence of the disease in Rome in 189, and an even more devastating epidemic of smallpox or cholera occurred from 252 to 254, followed by a "disease called 'anthrax' by Eusebius of Caesarea in 302," and an epidemic of smallpox in 312 (McNeill 1998b: 130, 165ff.; Acot 2003: 133). A crucial role was played by climatic change in northern China and in Central Asia from the second century on, marked by lower temperatures and increased aridity in some regions, inducing a decrease in resources and undermining population health. McCormick *et al.* also point out that "the three to five major volcanic eruptions that clustered from *c.* 235 to 285 potentially triggered commensurate episodes of rapid climate change" (2012: 186).[165] These climatic changes, from the end of the second to the fifth century, gave rise to vast movements of populations: the Xiongnu in the east, and Goths and Huns in the west, with the latter in turn causing the displacement of other groups.[166] The Silk Roads were cut off as early as the end of the second century. Substantial global cooling occurred, especially around 300 and 540/550 (Burroughs 2001; Moberg *et al.* 2005).[167]

[163] Venerated as deities, the *boddhisattvas* are men who temporarily renounce Buddhahood and access to the nirvana in order to help other human beings in their process of achieving Buddhahood. Buddhism has also influenced the Gnostic and Neo-Platonist movements, as well as Christianity (Conze 1968; Amore 1978; Sterling Berry 1997).

[164] According to Adshead (2004), smallpox may have come from Arabia or the Horn of Africa, and originated in the mutation of a bacterium affecting dromedaries. However, the dates of the first outbreaks in China point to an Asian origin for the disease.

[165] As Brooke points out, "in sum, it would not appear that Malthusian overpopulation fundamentally drove the collapse of Old World antiquity"; this collapse was triggered by climate change and epidemics (2014: 349). However, there were also causes that were internal to the empires.

[166] We know that a branch of the Xiongnu migrated westward as early as the second century CE (Koryakova and Epimakhov 2007), but the equation Huns=Xiongnu has been criticized by various authors (see, however, de la Vaissière 2006). The Hun names are partly of Turkish and sometimes of Iranian origin; the origin of other names has not been determined. The Goths migrated from the Baltic Sea toward the Black Sea during the second and third centuries.

[167] The level of Lake Issyk Kul dropped by 20 m between the first and fifth centuries CE. The Aral Sea also seems to have fallen to a low level around 400, and arid conditions were observed in the Karakum desert and the Tianshan mountains (Treydte *et al.* 2006; Austin *et al.* 2007). The level of the Dead Sea declined from 300. Research led by Q.-B. Zhang and R. Hebda (2005) based on dendrochronology in the Vancouver region points out two periods marked by lower precipitation in this region: between 150 and

We know that Nile flooding intensified between 100 BCE and 100 CE, but its waters abated from the second through the sixth century (higher flooding resumed after 600) (Butzer 1995: 136). Data collected by Chandler show declining population in the twenty-five largest cities of the world between 100 and 350. The drop was particularly severe in China, whose place on this list was halved (Bosworth 1995). In the Roman Empire, after Hadrian, the creation of cities became increasingly rare (Rostovtzeff 1998: 135). Arab cities also underwent decline both in the east (Kennet 2007) and in the west (Schiettecatte 2010). Conversely, we observe demographic expansion in western Asia and in India from 200 to 600 (McNeill 1998b). The recession caused major political dislocations: at virtually the same time, three empires disappeared: the Han (in 220), the Parthian (226), and the Kushan (c. 240), although a Kushan state survived in Bactria and Gandhara until the end of the fourth century. The first significant invasions of the Roman Empire occurred around 169 from the Danube valley, and "the manpower shortage forced the Emperor Marcus Aurelius to adopt a risky new policy towards the German tribes. [He] granted land to German allies . . . as a reward for their military service" (McLaughlin 2014: 217).

The collapse of the Han Empire had both external and internal causes. A decline in trade occurred at the end of the second century in the provinces and along the Silk Roads, which were no longer safe. Nomads threatened China's northern and western borders. At the same time, decentralization of the empire became more pronounced, with provincial governors increasing their powers. The empire's revenues plummeted, and military expenses escalated. Social inequalities, aggravated by famines, led to the outbreak of revolts, such as the Yellow Turban Rebellion which started in 184, while various factions at the court fought with one another. The central power at last lost control of the provinces, and in 220, the Han Empire broke into three kingdoms: Wei, Wu, and Shu.[168] The third and the fourth centuries were marked by decline in trade, demonetization of the economy, de-urbanization and increased political fragmentation, following a very short reunification of the empire by the Jin dynasty starting in 280. Centered on the Yangtze, the kingdom of Wu (222– 280), however, welcomed exchanges with Southeast Asia. The *Weilue*, or *Brief Account of the Wei Dynasty*, compiled during the third century by the Chinese scholar Yu Huan, contains a chapter entitled "Peoples of the West"; however, its references to Mesopotamia suggest that part of the data was actually based on reports collected between 116 and 165 CE (McLaughlin 2010: 21; Hill 2004). In the north, sinicized populations from the steppes

190, and between 540 and 560. For southern Russia, T. E. Khomutova *et al.* (2007) have identified an arid period during the second and third centuries. Conversely, from 400 to 900, an area running from the eastern Mediterranean to the Aral Sea may have experienced a milder and wetter climate (linked to a negative phase of the North Atlantic Oscillation) (Sorrel *et al.* 2007). Some areas of the Asian steppes, particularly in the north, may also have benefited from more precipitation, as revealed by data collected at Lake Kutuzhekovo (Bokovenko 2004) (see also Fagan 2004: 204, for western Europe). Like Biraben, Brooke notes that "between AD 200 and AD 400, the populations of the Old World plow cultures and empires declined by 30 percent" (2014: 323). Brooke indicates "a deep cold temperature spike after AD 636" (2014: 325).

[168] Brooke connects this decomposition of the Han Empire to "a century-long monsoon failure beginning around AD 170" (2014: 326).

dominated what were known as the "Sixteen Kingdoms" (304–439). Although the period of the "Southern and Northern dynasties" (317–589) was a time of political chaos, some technical progress did take place; moreover, Buddhism developed, especially from the beginning of the fifth century onward. The regions south of the Yangtze changed with the arrival of northern populations, driven off their lands by famines and social disorders, mostly at the beginning of the fourth century. Economic growth was still present, however, at the end of the fifth century in the Wei Empire (386–534), which reunified northern China in 439, as well as in the southern states. The Sogdians led a trade revival with Central Asia. During the same period, the Southern Song (420–479), the Qi (479–502), and then the Liang (502–557) dynasties maintained relations with Southeast Asia, and embassies from Indian and Sinhalese kingdoms visited China; at this time also, Sassanid activity was expanding, and indianized Southeast Asian insular states developed.

Although it occurred in parallel to that of the Roman Empire, the demise of the Han Empire would not have the same long-term negative effects. Eastern Asia remained a core of the world-system, whereas Europe (except for its southeastern part) lost its preeminence. As was the case for China, external pressures, declining foreign trade, and internal crises combined to lead to the collapse of the Roman Empire. Indeed, from the second century onward, internal contradictions worsened when this empire stopped growing.[169] "The army could not 'feed' anymore on the conquests," now limited, because "the costs of territorial expansion now outweighed the benefits" (Nicolet 1988: 277; Simonnot 2002: 56). It is significant that Hadrian and Antoninus abandoned territories conquered by Trajan: the two leaders were probably aware of the price they would have had to pay for such conquests. The army had 450,000 men for borders more than 10,000 km long following the invasion of Dacia (and these borders had an unfavorable rectangular configuration) (Simonnot 2002: 80–81). The army was not large enough to defend the empire, but was too much of a financial burden: "during peacetime, the army absorbed at least 40% of the state budget" (Nicolet 1988: 305).[170] The empire was now failing to acquire enough slaves (Weber 1998 [1909]); what is more, the progress of Christianity favored the freeing of slaves. The functioning cost of the empire forced the emperors to debase their silver coinage, which led to recurring inflation (the nominal pay of soldiers was raised at the end of the first century, at the end of the second century, and again during the third century, but real pay – in silver – probably diminished). The decline of mining and exchanges led to a shortage in precious metals. Fewer revenues were collected, whereas state expenses kept rising. During the third century, taxation in kind (to ensure the supplies for the armies and the state bureaucracy) allowed local commanders some control over this taxation and gave them the ability to institute powers that could compete with Rome (Rowlands 1987: 10). Moreover, taxes were used to recruit mercenaries. This economic recession was accompanied by political dislocation: twenty-five emperors succeeded one another

---

[169] Chew (2000: 223) has also emphasized the ecological degradations caused by Rome's development. Moreover, M. Weber has noted the difficulties of moving from a (primarily) maritime empire to a continental empire (1998 [1909]: 78).

[170] Hopkins gives an estimate of 50 percent (2009: 194).

between 235 and 284, and one Gallic empire briefly seceded (260–274), as did Palmyra.[171] Under Diocletian (284–305), Italy lost its exemption from the land tax. A militaristic and autocratic regime was put into place, putting an end to the autonomy of the cities and reducing individual freedom (Rostovtzeff 1988: 335ff.).[172] The army became "the emanation of the less Romanized peasant classes" (Andreau 1988: lxi) (in fact, the Roman military already seems to have been "barbarized" under Trajan's reign, and even more so from the time of Marcus Aurelius onward). The increasing reliance on liturgies, which could be considered as compulsory gifts to the state, extended to the whole empire, and this discouraged production (for the cereals sector, see Silver 2007b): Rostovtzeff (1988: 381) has rightly described this system of taxation as "an organized system of plunder." Weaker domestic markets led to a decline in industry, accompanied by deurbanization and a loss of political and economic power for the urban bourgeoisie (Rostovtzeff [1998]: xv] here speaks of "the collapse of city-capitalism" and "the growth of state capitalism"). The colder climate provoked a decline in agricultural production from the second century onward, especially in Egypt, a region already affected by demographic decline (Bagnall 2003). Investments were now limited, and the large agricultural estates appear to have been less productive. The model of the slave-based villa died out from the third century onward. The trend was toward a concentration of lands, which were often rented to tenant farmers or sharecroppers: the former spirit of quest for maximal profit disappeared. Transformations went along with increasing social hierarchization, and a reduction in the assistance given to the poorest families. All these changes probably led to a loss of faith in the empire. In addition, climatic changes worsened environmental degradation and deforestation, due to urbanization, the development of metallurgy, and the production of pottery and bricks (Hughes 2001: 73ff).

Historians have often pointed out the lack of technical innovations during this period, as well as its decline in production, and the imbalance between the east, richer, more urbanized, more populated, and the west; it is an imbalance that sheds light on the ensuing centuries. Trade became mainly interprovincial, partly going back to a configuration known prior to the Roman period. Overall, Rome's exchanges with the Orient declined over the third and fourth centuries. And the Ethiopian kingdom of Axum for the Red Sea and the new Persian Empire built up by the Sassanids in the Persian Gulf – constituted in 226 at the expense of the Parthians – now controlled the movement of people and merchandise.

Foreign trade also played a part in Rome's financial problems. The empire was dependent upon imports from the Indian Ocean: these provided high revenues

---

[171] Under Queen Zenobia (266–272), Palmyra controlled Syria, Anatolia, and Egypt for a short time. In 272, Palmyra was taken by Emperor Aurelian, who captured Zenobia.

[172] "The constitutional monarchy of the Antonines, according to Rostovtzeff (1998: xii), rested on the urban middle class throughout the Empire, ... [but] this urban middle class was not strong enough to support the fabric of the world-state"; moreover, the monarchy was too closed, the ruling groups becoming "more and more exclusive": the gap between *humiliores* and *honestiores* and between the cities and the country could therefore not be reduced.

through taxes. When this eastern trade went into decline (due either to a weaker offer, or to weaker demand – mining production in precious metals was also in recession) state revenues were affected.

The reign of Constantine, who became emperor in 306, marked a watershed for the Roman Empire. The emperor established freedom of religion in 313, and favored Christianity. The conversion of Constantine to Christianity reflects the progression of this religion as of the second century, despite persecution under Diocletian and later Galerius (until the edict of tolerance promulgated by Galerius in 311). Constantine convened the first Council of Nicaea in 325, which brought together the various Christian currents and attempted to impose an orthodoxy. Three bishops were excommunicated, including Arius. The decline of official pagan cults has often been noted as having encouraged the birth of new religions in the Roman space. The fact that Christianity was better equipped than paganism to provide answers for the unpredictable nature of epidemics striking both rich and poor may have acted in favor of its expansion. Another factor may have been the solidarity of the Christian community, which brought together people of different social classes (McNeill 1998b: 135–137). At the same time, however, society was becoming more rigid. The pauperization of the middle and lower classes fed exoduses that led Constantine to issue edicts forbidding population movement.

In 324, Constantine decided to build a new capital at Byzantium, on the Bosphorus, at the junction of Europe and Asia: this is the city that would become Constantinople. In a few years, its population reached 100,000. The administrative reforms enacted by Constantine gave rise to a significant bureaucracy. An economic rebound seems to have occurred in the empire during the fourth century. In any case, the economic situation of northern Africa and Anatolia appears to have been favorable at this time, and we observe no decrease in city size in the eastern Mediterranean (Andreau 2010: 231). Constantine was nonetheless obliged to increase taxes, and this led to reduced trade. The emperor created – or expanded – the chrysargyrium, a tax on industry and trade paid in gold, silver, or bullion. He confiscated temple properties and stabilized the monetary system by issuing a gold *solidus* of 4.54 g (the *aureus* weighed 6.54 g under Caracalla and 8 g at the time of Augustus). Part of the gold probably came from Ghana (McDonald 2013: 72). "The flow of gold from Ghana from the period of Constantine onward was a direct consequence of [the slave trade], using the slaves themselves to carry the gold" (Fentress 2011).

The divergent trajectories of the various regions of the Roman Empire led to its division into two blocs as of 395, marked by the emergence of Constantinople (Byzantium), which ruled Egypt and replaced Rome as the largest city in the world. Christianity took precedence over the other cults of the empire (mithraism, manicheism, the mystery cults, the Isis cult, the worship of Baal) and became the state religion in 380, under Theodosius I and Gratian. It was a crucial unifying force for the multinational space of the Empire, but in the east as well as in the west, the expansion of Christianity was accompanied by a decline in intellectual life, although schools remained active during the fourth century at Constantinople, Alexandria, Athens, Antioch, Beirut, and Gaza (Goody 2007: 72, 223). Nisibis and Edessa became well-known centers for the translation of Greek texts into Syriac, during the fifth century in particular. The Nestorian Christians also maintained schools in Sassanid Persia, such as the university of Gondeshapur (Goody 2007: 231).[173] In the Red Sea, the Church was involved in Indian Ocean trade (Tomber 2012a: 169–170), and cooperation developed between the Byzantine Empire and the Christianized kingdom of Axum.

On the other hand, the founding of the Sassanid Empire marked the beginning of confrontations between this state and the Roman Empire and later the Byzantine Empire. These confrontations did not exclude interconnections between the Persian and the Byzantine worlds, however. Persian court practices were thus adapted by the Byzantine Empire, which by the end of the fourth century had an army of 600,000 men – largely recruited among "barbarians" from the empire's margins – but the empire employed a mere 30,000 to 40,000 officials (Burbank and Cooper 2010: 66). While Byzantium, despite its ups and downs, remained a core of the world-system until the twelfth century, western Europe became a simple periphery of this system for 700 or 800 years.[174]

Increased climate cooling – perhaps with growing aridity (data here are contradictory) – was perceptible in southern Russia during the second half of the fourth century (Brown 2001: 73).[175] This precipitated movements of populations: the Huns crossed the Volga River around 370, subjugated the Ostrogoths in 375, and led the Visigoths to settle in Roman territory. In 378, the Visigoths defeated the Roman army at Andrinople, killing the emperor Valens; they entered Dalmatia and then Italy, where they looted Rome in 410.[176] Further west, Gaul and later Spain were invaded successively by the Alans, the Suevi, and the Vandals from 406 onward, followed by the Franks, the Burgundians, and the Alamans, while Angles, Saxons, and Jutes landed in England in 450. The dislocation of the western portion of the Roman Empire worsened during the fifth century. Many emperors succeeded one another; they were simple puppets in the hands of "barbarian" generals. In addition, "a duality arose between temporal and spiritual power" (Simonnot 2002: 78). In the northern part of the remaining Roman world, the Huns built an empire between the Rhine and the Caucasus, under the rule of Attila (434–453), to whom Theodosius II paid tribute. The defeat of the Huns at the Catalaunian Fields in 451, however, stopped their advance,

---

[173] Nestorianism was one of the major schisms to appear in the fifth century, with the Monophysite movement. Nestorius, Patriarch of Constantinople from 428 to 431, believed in the separation of the two natures of Christ: divine and human. In contrast to Nestorianism, Monophysitism proclaimed the unity of the (divine) nature of Christ. Monophysitism was influential under Theodosius II, but after his death, the fourth Ecumenical Council of Chalcedon (in 451) condemned the Monophysites. This condemnation resulted in persecutions and social unrest in Palestine, and later in Egypt.

[174] There was, however, a "reassertion of Romanitas by the Latin military aristocracy of Illyria, and later by latinized Slavs such as Justinian himself and Belisarius, against the Greek east of Alexandria and Antioch" (Adshead 1995: 64). After Diocletian (284–305), who created a centralized bureaucracy, and with the rise to prominence of the Christian Church and its bishops, not much was left of the ancient institutions of the city-states (Hansen 2000b: 149).

[175] Esper *et al.* (2014) indicate that northern European summer temperatures were low around 220, 540, and 660 CE, and very low around 340 CE.

[176] Rome was plundered once again in 455 by the Vandals led by Genseric, who had founded a kingdom centered on Carthage.

and Attila's death in 453 initiated the collapse of this empire (Beckwith 2011: 96ff.). In the east, "barbarians" were incorporated into the army, and an Alan chief, Aspar, played the role of "emperor maker." The Ostrogoth ruler Theodoric then became the military chief of the empire, and took Italy in 488. Curiously, at this time, in sub-Saharan Africa, the Nok culture seems to have vanished.

By contrast, during this phase of recession of the world-system, the eastern coast of India remained buoyant, thanks to trade with Southeast Asia, in an area perhaps less afflicted by the climatic changes observed in Central Asia, western Asia, and China. Commerce expanded further in the eastern Indian Ocean during the fourth and fifth centuries, while an empire led by the Gupta dynasty reunited the various territories of northern India. Buddhist and Hindu networks developed toward Southeast Asia and China. The Gupta Empire was probably weakly integrated, but the minting of gold and silver coins reveal the wealth of this state, which encouraged progress in wet rice cultivation. Cities flourished in the Ganges basin, along the southern coasts of the Indian peninsula, and in Sri Lanka. The Indian Ocean experienced a period of relatively stronger monsoons during part of the fifth century, and this boosted agriculture in South Asia and Egypt. The decline and abandonment of numerous towns in Arabia (Taymā', Hegra ...), however, show that there was a general tendency toward greater aridity (Schiettecatte 2010). "The cessation of Khor Rori [Sumhuram: Moscha Limēn in the *Periplus*] and the reduction in Indian wares at Qanī [Kanē] reflect a decline" in the South Arabian trade. Red Sea ports such as Aila, Aqaba, Berenice, and Adulis remained active, however (Tomber 2012a: 162). Increased infrastructure at Berenice and finds of Roman coins dated to the fourth and fifth centuries in South India and Sri Lanka reveal an "ongoing investment and Roman participation in Indian commerce" (Tomber 2012a: 164). Seland (2014) points out "the relative prosperity of port sites from the third to the seventh century AD" in the western Indian Ocean, but this does not contradict the observation of an overall decrease of the system.

The decline of the Mediterranean Sea and the Red Sea seems to have affected Axum, Yemen, and the East African coast. Most commercial activity shifted toward the Persian Gulf. Excavations at the ports of Sīrāf and Sohar have revealed significant Sassanid levels, showing the importance of this region prior to the Islamic period. After the Persians took control of the Red Sea during the sixth century, most westbound maritime traffic went through the Persian Gulf, a situation that would last until the tenth century. Controlling exchanges in the western Indian Ocean, the Sassanids sent their ships to Southeast Asia and probably as far as China: the discovery of Chinese stoneware at Sīrāf, Sohar, and Zanzibar dated to the fourth–fifth century may corroborate these journeys.

The commerce of the Sassanids obviously benefited from India's prosperity under the Gupta dynasty. But at the end of the fifth century, the White Huns (or the Hephtalites, a term used by Procopius to set them apart from the Huns) trounced the Sassanids and invaded northwestern India, contributing to the fall of the Gupta Empire *c*. 535. A Hun empire then formed, with its capital at Bāmiyān; this empire would later be defeated by the Turks around 560. These events lent a greater importance to the maritime routes of the Indian Ocean and the China Sea. As for the Silk Roads – particularly their southern branches – they became active once again thanks to the Sogdians. "Adapting themselves to the successive Turk empires," the Sogdians, mixing commerce and diplomacy, extended their networks across the Eurasian steppes: "between the fifth and eighth centuries, the Sogdians had a quasi-monopoly on the caravan trade between China and the west, and the Sogdian language became *lingua franca* on the Silk Roads, in particular on their northern branch. Political glory went to the Turks, and economic benefits to the Sogdians. A Byzantine document shows one Sogdian organizing an expedition thousands of kilometers away in order to sell silk recently extorted from Chinese courts at Constantinople, showing a clear and explicit awareness of the political and economic issues at stake on a continental scale" (de la Vaissière 2008). In the west, the Sogdians founded the port of Sogdaia (Southak), in Crimea, during the seventh century (de la Vaissière 2002: 238ff.). In China, Sogdians were merchants, as well as artisans and soldiers. Their role would grow even stronger there at the start of the Tang dynasty.

Although a worldwide recession occurred toward the end of the fifth century, it did not affect all the regions of the Ancient World equally: in India, for example, the decline was felt primarily in the northern and western parts of the peninsula (many towns were abandoned during the post-Gupta period), but not so much to the east, where the dominant Pallava state was involved in increasing exchanges with Southeast Asia. In this region, the demise of Funan – at the same time as the Gupta Empire – allowed for the formation of smaller states on the Thai–Malay peninsula; this was even more the case on the Indonesian islands, which took the upper hand in trade between the Indian and the Pacific oceans. Since the beginning of the Christian era, in fact, East Asia, centered on its Chinese "core," was one of the world-system's most active regions. An economic upturn occurred in northern China (in the empire of the northern Wei) during the late fifth century and in southern China (under the Liang dynasty) during the early sixth century. Climatic deterioration (with cooler or colder periods), famines, and epidemics then marked the mid-sixth century, from northern China to Europe; these phenomena also affected northern India, Egypt, and Yemen.[177] In northern Africa, the Garamantian culture

[177] Basing his study on oak dendrochronology from Ireland (Baillie 1999) and Argentinian data, Mitchiner notes the worldwide dimension of the climate cooling occurring between 536 and 545, perhaps accentuated by a volcanic eruption (Krakatoa? Or Ilopango, in Salvador?). Brooke (2014: 348) points out "a spike of cold temperatures around AD 540," after "a massive volcanic eruption in 536." Meteorites, abundant during the fifth century, may also have contributed to this global cooling (a large meteorite formed the Sirente crater in Central Italy, and substantial impact craters are known in northern Australia). This phenomenon combined with a longer-term episode of global cooling and a weakening of the monsoon. The Nile experienced repetitive, very low flooding. Chinese chronicles also describe poor harvests and famines at this time (on Chinese climatic data, see An and Thompson 1998: 20). These perturbations appear to be connected to a frequent occurrence of the El Niño phenomenon, especially around 590. Data presented by Jones and Mann (2004) suggest global warming in the Northern Hemisphere around 500, and then colder temperatures after 500, with a nadir around 550–560.

disappeared at this time, "perhaps because of falling water levels in the aquifer" (Mattingly 2011: 57).

As already mentioned, during part of the fifth century relatively strong monsoons held sway in the Indian Ocean, resulting in major Nile flooding (Brown 2001: 79). Christiansen and Ljungqvist (2012) state that Northern Hemisphere temperatures increased around 400. Byzantium, which occupied Egypt, was then poised to benefit from improving agricultural production in the Nile valley. Agriculture in Greece also saw favorable conditions. From 400 to 900, the region from the eastern Mediterranean to the Aral Sea enjoyed a milder and wetter climate (linked to a negative phase of the North Atlantic Oscillation) (Sorrel et al. 2007),[178] except during a period of severe global cooling from 540 to 560. In contrast to the general trend of the world-system, the Byzantine Empire appears to have been in expansion during the first half of the sixth century – for a shorter period. Emperor Justinian (527–565) retook northern Africa (533),[179] Sicily, Italy (535–540) and southern Spain (554).[180] The Mediterranean Sea then became "a Byzantine sea" (Ahrweiler 1966). The Greek fleets also held the upper hand in the Black Sea, as far as Trebizond. This Byzantine flowering was expressed in the religious and artistic domains with the building of Hagia Sophia at Byzantium (537) and the Basilica of San Vitale in Ravenna (548). Significant legislative work was published, such as "Justinian's Code" (*Codex Justinianus*), which quoted and adapted older texts. This code provides the basis for Roman Law, as it would come to be known in western Europe as of the twelfth century. Byzantium had nearly 500,000 inhabitants at the beginning of the sixth century, but what became known as the "plague of Justinian" in 541–542 resulted in the death of 40 percent of the population;[181] the plague also affected Egypt, Yemen,

---

[178] Laiou and Morrisson (2007) emphasize an increase in the number of settlements, which is linked to milder winters for the northern Mediterranean, and wetter conditions in the south, during the fifth and the early sixth centuries. According to Hirschfeld (2004), areas under cultivation and settlements expanded at the end of the fifth century in Palestine. Conversely, for the northeastern part of the Black Sea, Bolikhovskaya et al. (2004: 215) mention increased aridity between 450 and 700.

[179] The development of some sites south of the Sahara, such as Niani and Jenne-Jeno, involves regional processes, but a trans-Saharan commerce seems to have been active during the sixth–seventh century, as demonstrated by the site of Maranda (Marandet) in the Aïr, located on the caravan road from Egypt to Gao (Coquery-Vidrovitch 1993: 68). In Fezzan, the Garamantes formed a centralized state. Glass beads at the site of Kissi (Burkina Faso) are dated to the fifth–seventh century; while their provenance remains uncertain, the Sinhalese site of Mantai is one possible origin (Magnavita 2003: 133–134). Cowries dated to between the fifth and the seventh centuries CE have been discovered in Burkina Faso. Kissi has also yielded remnants of wool textiles dated to the same period (Magnavita 2008). Through Libya, "traffic diminished, however, in the Late Roman period, when Garama declined noticeably, and sites such as Aghram Nadharif were abandoned" (Fentress 2011).

[180] From approximately 470 on, the Visigoths established a kingdom in Spain. After 493, the Ostrogoths controlled Italy (and its capital Ravenna), where they had been sent by the Byzantine emperor Zeno. Visigoths, Ostrogoths, Burgundians, and Vandals adhered to Arianism. By contrast, the Frankish kingdom, formed in northern Gaul since Clovis's conversion (c. 496), adhered to orthodox Christianity. By 600, this kingdom had become the most powerful state in western Europe.

[181] Morris gives an estimate of 450,000 inhabitants in 500 CE, and only 150,000 in 600 CE (2013: 151).

western Asia, and Persia,[182] and later the western Mediterranean Sea. By the end of the sixth century, the population of Europe was half of what it had been around 200 CE. The period saw a setback in education; as early as 529, Justinian closed the Academia Platonica of Athens (Goody 2007: 223); Greek scholars then traveled to Persia. After Justinian's death, under threat of raids by Slavs and the arrival in Europe of the Avars (Asian nomads), the Byzantine Empire once again slid into decline.[183] Threats also came from the Sassanid Empire. Between 614 and 618, Byzantium lost Syria, Palestine, and Egypt, but won victories at Nineveh and Ctesiphon in 627 and 628; these victories made it possible for Christians to carry the remains of the True Cross – taken by the Sassanids in 614 – to Byzantium. The endless wars between Sassanids and Byzantines at last weakened both empires. The Byzantine decline also had various internal causes, including the overextension of the state under Justinian and the high cost of the military sector. Opposition developed at the court between the military elite and civilian dignitaries. It is during this period of defense of an empire under threat that Emperor Heraclius I (610–641) changed the official language from Latin to Greek. Heraclius initiated efficient reforms of both the administration and the army, going back, through land donations, to the old Roman tradition of the soldier-farmer.

The Avar invasions affected eastern Europe, but they also introduced the stirrup and the trace harness, as well as new breeds of horses. The horse collar harness seems to have been brought from Central Asia slightly later, during the seventh century. These innovations (along with horse shoeing, and growth in size through selective breeding) would play an important role in the agricultural progress of Europe during the Middle Ages.

A combination of external and internal factors, within the context of specific dynamics, must be taken into account in the regional trajectories we have observed. The empire of the Kök Turks (the "Blue Turks") emerged in the mid-sixth century: at this time, no powerful state existed in China, and the Byzantine Empire, in decline, was attempting to bypass the Persian obstacle by using northern routes. The Turks very quickly obtained a tribute of 100,000 bales of silk from the Northern Zhou (557–581), a clear expression of the Turks' militaristic approach.[184] This silk was carried to the west

---

[182] Brown 2001: 92. McNeill 1998b: 137. According to this author, the origin of the plague may have been central Africa (?) or northeast India. East Africa has also been suggested (see Phillipson 2012: 206–207; Brooke 2014: 348). Adshead (2004: 71) is in favor of a "Mongol" origin between Lake Baikal and Lake Issyk Kul. China appears to have been less affected by these plague epidemics that were ravaging western Asia and Europe at this time, recurring over more than a century (see the testimony of Gregory of Tours, in his *History of the Franks*).

[183] The Avars may have been related to the Rouran (Joujan) established in Mongolia during the fifth–sixth century (this hypothesis, however, does not meet with unanimity among historians). The Joujan/Rouran confederation was defeated by the Kök Turks around 552; some Rouran escaped to China, but most migrated to the west. For more on this confederation, see Kradin 2005. The Avar movements toward Europe were precipitated by the defeat of the Hephtalites (White Huns) against the Sassanids and the Turks in the years 550–560.

[184] Di Cosmo has convincingly demonstrated that militarization of pastoralist societies should sometimes be understood as a response to a crisis situation and that this may partially account for the formation of the state in the steppes (1999: 14ff.).

by Sogdians. It is also possible that global cooling at this time resulted in increased precipitation in parts of the steppes, reinforcing pastoralism.

The waning years of the sixth century saw China reunified under the Sui dynasty, initiating a rebound in the world-system that corresponded to fresh climatic change, marked by milder and wetter conditions in northern China (An and Thompson 1998). Temperatures in the Northern Hemisphere appear to have risen around 590–600 (Mann *et al.* 2008; Christiansen and Ljungqvist 2012). The seventh century would prove to be a period of major development, with China's prosperity under the Tang dynasty and the appearance and expansion of Islam, which would usher in not only a new phase of growth, but also a whole new era for the Indian Ocean and the Mediterranean Sea.

Table II.In.6 *Comparative chronologies (first millennium BCE – first century CE): western Asia and the Persian Gulf; Egypt and the Red Sea; East Africa and Madagascar; the Mediterranean and Europe*

Western Asia and the Persian Gulf	Egypt and the Red Sea	East Africa and Madagascar	The Mediterranean and Europe
Period of turmoil in Mesopotamia Neo-Assyrian Empire *722–705:* Sargon II *705–681:* Sennacherib *668–630:* Assurbanipal Neo-Babylonian Empire *604–562:* Nebuchadnezzar II	*1070–723:* "Third Intermediary Period" *671, 664:* conquest of Egypt by the Assyrians *610–595:* Nechao II, digging of a Nile–Red Sea canal *c. 600 BCE:* circumnavigation of Africa by Phoenicians?		*1000–800:* supremacy of Phoenician cities in the Mediterranean Sea *c. 814:* the Tyrians found Carthage *eighth–seventh century:* expansion of Greek city-states in the Mediterranean Sea
539 BCE: Cyrus II captures Babylon. Emergence of a Persian Empire *521–486:* reign of Darius	*525 BCE:* conquest of Egypt by the Persian Cambyses *486, 460, 404 BCE:* Egyptian revolts against Persians; independence of Egypt in 403		*499–479 BCE:* wars between Greeks and Persians *478 BCE:* Athens dominates the Delian League
334–324 BCE: conquests by Alexander the Great	*331 BCE:* founding of Alexandria		*338 BCE:* unification of the Greek states by Philip II of Macedonia *336–323:* Alexander the Great
323 BCE: dynasty of the Seleucids *c. 170 BCE:* Parthian Empire *53 BCE:* Roman defeat at Carrhes	*323 BCE:* dynasty of the Ptolemies *third century BCE:* new digging of the Nile–Red Sea canal *119 BCE:* Eudoxus of Cyzicus travels to India	*first century BCE:* Bantu arrivals on the East African coast; iron, agriculture	Formation of a Roman state in Italy *264–241:* 1st Punic War *218–212:* 2nd Punic War *146 BCE:* Carthage is razed by the Roman army

Table II.In.7 *Comparative chronologies (first millennium* BCE *– first century* CE*): India and Central Asia; Southeast Asia; China and East Asia*

India and Central Asia	Southeast Asia	China and East Asia
1000 BCE: use of iron tools and weapons		*1027–256 BCE:* Zhou dynasty
seventh century BCE: development of kingdoms in the Ganges valley	*From* c. *600 BCE:* Sa Huynh culture (central and southern Vietnam)	*eighth century BCE:* raids by peoples from the steppes led the Zhou to transfer their capital further east
sixth century BCE: urbanization of Magadha	*500 BCE:* classical period of the Dong Son culture (northern Vietnam)	*722–481:* "Spring and Autumn" period; political disaggregation
sixth century BCE: birth of Jainism and Buddhism		*sixth century BCE:* spread of iron metallurgy
320 BCE: Chandragupta founds the Mauryan Empire	*fourth–third century BCE?:* Indian presence at Ban Don Ta Phet (central Thailand) and Khao Sam Kaeo (southern Thailand); contacts with India, Vietnam, and Taiwan (Dong Son drums)	*481–221 BCE:* period of the Warring Kingdoms; transformation of the Qin state
302 BCE: treaty between Seleukos I and Chandragupta		
273–237 BCE: reign of Ashoka in India		*221 BCE:* unification of China by the Qin king (*Shi Huangdi*, First Emperor)
250 BCE: creation of a Greco-Bactrian Empire; expansion of Buddhism toward Southeast Asia and Central Asia		*204–43 BCE:* Xiongnu confederation (Mongolia, Central Asia)
185 BCE: demise of the Mauryan Empire		*206 BCE – 26 CE:* dynasty of the western Han
		second century BCE: Han embassies to Seleucia and Kāñchi
		110 BCE: China annexes the Yue and Nanyue kingdoms

Table II.In.8 *Comparative chronologies (first–seventh century* CE*): western Asia and the Persian Gulf; Egypt and the Red Sea; East Africa and Madagascar; the Mediterranean and Europe*

Western Asia and the Persian Gulf	Egypt and the Red Sea	East Africa and *Madagascar*	Mediterranean and Europe
116 CE: Trajan conquers Mesopotamia but Hadrian leaves Mesopotamia in *117*	*31 BCE:* control of Egypt by Rome	*first century CE:* Rhapta port visited by Yemenis and Romans *Human presence in southwestern Madagascar*	*58–52:* conquest of Gaul by Caesar
226 CE: founding of the Sassanid Empire	*165–180 CE:* Antonine plague		
	254–265 CE: low Nile flooding, and epidemics of "the plague of Cyprian"		

Continued

Table II.In.8 *Continued*

Western Asia and the Persian Gulf	Egypt and the Red Sea	East Africa and *Madagascar*	Mediterranean and Europe
		Pre-Swahili culture as far as southern Mozambique	*312:* conversion of Constantine to Christianity *330:* founding of Constantinople
471 and *484:* the Persians are defeated by the Hephtalites; death of Emperor Peroz	*395:* Egypt province of the Byzantine Empire; the Roman Empire splits in two	*fifth century: human presence in northern Madagascar (Andavakoera)*	*410:* Rome is looted by the Visigoths *first half of fifth century* Hunnic invasions; creation of the Hun Empire (Attila *434–453*)
562: peace treaty between the Sassanid Empire and Byzantium *563:* Khosrau I's victory over the Hephtalites	*527–565:* Justinian; Byzantium reconquers Libya and Tunisia *619–629:* Persian domination over Egypt *642:* Muslim conquest	*Possible human presence in the Malagasy Highlands during the seventh century*	

Table II.In.9 *Comparative chronologies (first–seventh century* CE): *India and Central Asia; Southeast Asia; China and East Asia*

China and Inner Asia	India and Central Asia	Southeast Asia
26 CE: Eastern Han *89–105* CE: Indian embassies to the Han *220* CE: disappearance of the Han Empire *220–264:* the Three Kingdoms (Wu in the south [*222–280*], Shu-Han in Sichuan, Wei in northern China) *266–316:* Western Jin	*first century – middle of third century:* Kushan Empire in northwestern and northern India, Shātavāhana Empire in central India	*first–sixth century:* prominence of Funan *first–second century:* Indian pottery on Java and Bali, Indian beads on Palawan *132:* embassy of the Yediao kingdom to China (Jambi, or a kingdom from Java?) *230–240:* Funanese embassy travels to India *c. 250:* arrival in Funan of Indian envoys and Chinese ambassadors
fourth–sixth century: Northern Wei *fourth –sixth century:* South: Six dynasties	*fourth century:* emergence of the Pallava (Southeast) *320–480:* Gupta Empire *335–375:* Samudragupta *375–413:* Chandragupta II	*fourth–fifth century:* sizeable Indian presence in Southeast Asia

Continued

Table II.In.9 *Continued*

China and Inner Asia	India and Central Asia	Southeast Asia
Rouran Empire in Inner Asia (402–552)	*c. 430:* the Hephtalites invade Sogdiana and Bactria	
552: creation of a Turkish Empire, divided into two khanates	*early sixth century:* the Hephtalites conquer the Indus basin and loot northern India	*sixth century:* disappearance of Funan. Smaller states along the Thai–Malay peninsula, in eastern Sumatra and Java
581: reunification of China by the Sui dynasty		
618: founding of the Tang dynasty	*c. 535:* end of the Gupta Empire	*seventh century:* emergence of Srīwijaya

8 The Beginnings of the Iron Age

> I brought back the exhausted people of Assyria [who] had abandoned [their cities
> and their houses], [driven] by hunger and famine, [those] who had gone up to
> other lands. I settled them in cities and houses that were
> suitable and they dwelt in peace
> (inscription of Ashur-dan II, 934–912; Roaf 2001)

The Assyrian Hegemony

After the collapse of the centralized states of the Late Bronze Age, Cyprus came to preeminence in new exchange networks during the twelfth century, followed by a similar ascent on the part of the Phoenician city-states. The papyrus entitled "The Story of Wenamun" tells us how Wenamun, a dignitary of the temple of Amun, visited Byblos, where he had been sent to buy wood in exchange for gold, silver, flax, oxen hides, papyri, ropes, and lentils, and found twenty seagoing ships in the port of Byblos in "commercial association" with Egypt. There were fifty more at Sidon, sailing under the orders of a man called Werket-el, who seems to have been a foreign shipowner at the head of a seafaring business, transporting merchandise for Smendes, the vizier of Lower Egypt (de Spens 1998).[1] This imaginary account[2] shows business records being kept by the king of Byblos, as well as the symbiotic relationship between the state and the private sector, with contractual bonds between the ships' captains or shipowners and the ruling institutions (Aubet 2001: 116; Fabre 2004: 155).

Around 1100 BCE, led by King Tiglath-Pileser I (1115–1076 BCE), the first Assyrian expansion occurred in Cappadocia, Cilicia, and on the Phoenician coast, with the royal troops reaching Byblos, Sidon, and Arwad, attracted by the prospect of substantial booty. Under the successors of Tiglath-Pileser I, Assyria experienced a downturn and we know little about the kings of the second half of the eleventh century. Similarly, Phoenician cities remained active during the early eleventh century, as the story of Wenamun suggests, but their history from then until the following century is uncertain. The end of the eleventh century, however, saw the rise of Tyre, which built commercial links in the Mediterranean, "towards Cyprus and beyond" (Sherratt 2003).

In the central region of what may be considered as a "western world-system," the first centuries of the first millennium BCE were a period of turmoil, both in Egypt

---

[1] According to the text, the journey of Wenamun would have taken place around 1075 (MC). Wenamun was the victim of pirates: insecurity in the eastern Mediterranean Sea explains the investment of Tyre and other cities in warships.

[2] It has been recognized that "The Story of Wenamun" is not an actual historical account, but a literary text (Egberts 2001). A Twenty-Second Dynasty date (945–715 BCE) has been suggested for its composition. It may, however, have used historical elements.

(Third Intermediary Period) and Mesopotamia. Aramaean infiltrations led to chronic instability in western Babylonia, where political fragmentation was accompanied by a revival of a city-state culture,[3] even during the period of Assyrian domination over Babylonia during the eighth and seventh centuries. The Assyrian kingdom around 930 BCE was modest in size, but it became more prosperous at the end of the tenth century, partly due to an increase in rainfall. Chaldean groups entered Mesopotamia; they would later play an important role in Persian Gulf trade and in political life in Babylonia. In response to the deteriorating climate at the end of the second millennium, various regions in Assyria, Anatolia, and Syria, invested in irrigation systems. Moreover, ironworking developed during this period, at a time when copper and tin were in short supply following the collapse of the exchange networks around 1200 BCE. More labor-intensive than copper, iron metallurgy then became profitable, iron being a hundred times more plentiful than copper (Muhly 1995: 1515). Though they had no monopoly, the Philistines became known as specialized ironworkers.

The Assyrian kingdom experienced its first period of expansion in the second half of the ninth century, under Shalmaneser III, around 830 BCE (Roaf 2001), when this king took control of Anatolia's metal resources. The kingdom appears to have gone into relative decline during the ensuing century (850–750 BCE), because of external threats from the Urartu kingdom and the Cimmerians, climate change, and internal conflicts between the old aristocracy and new elites linked to state power. During the second half of the eighth century, however, first Tiglath-Pileser III (745–727) and later Sargon II created a vast empire, thanks to victorious military campaigns. The Assyrian Empire maintained a standing army (Allen 2005: 78). It seems that the Assyrians used naphta, probably mixed with burning pitch and sulphur in incendiaries (fire-pots) in sieges of towns (Partington 1999: 28). The figure of the king represented both a hero and the symbol of the state. The building of the empire was accompanied by major innovations, with the creation of a new capital and the transformation of former vassal regions into provinces[4] (their governors were appointed by the king). It was marked by a dual trend of "Assyrianization" of the conquered territories and of "Aramaization" of the core (Beaulieu 2005). The administration employed the Aramaic script, and the Aramaic language became the *lingua franca* of the Assyrian world, partly because "the merchants of the western regions [were] the merchants of the empire" (Allen 2005: 80). Other innovations also represent borrowings from Syria and Palestine (including the use of stamp seals, the use of the system of weights of Karkemish, as well as other systems). A class of managers and military officers was in place. The Assyrian Empire promoted more intensive agriculture, and was underpinned by an efficient army, which seized large

---

[3] Larsen 2000b. The governors, who submitted to the Assyrians, were supported by a popular assembly (*puhru*).

[4] Allen (2005) distinguishes three phases on the basis of the administrative techniques deployed, with each of them reflecting a particular response to the problems caused by the increasing size of the empire. The first phase dealt with the organization of the core and the establishment of tributary relations with neighboring vassal regions. The second saw the transformation of previously vassal regions into provinces (eighth century), the adoption of Levantine techniques and the employment of merchants from that region. During the third phase, the empire tried to control the elites of the marginal regions and set up trading posts (*karu*) in those regions. Assyrian administrators were sent into the vassal states as "advisers" and to collect taxes. The marginal states were thus partly incorporated into the bureaucratic structure of the empire.

amounts of booty from the conquered territories and practiced massive deportations of populations. The victims of these abuses were eastern Anatolia in 865 BCE, Babylonia during the campaigns of Tiglath-Pileser III (742–741 BCE), and Israel in 720 BCE when Sargon II annexed the country. Over 4 million people were deported in just two centuries. As early as the ninth century, 20 percent of captured populations had been deported (Joannès 2000: 42; Allen 2005: 80). Within its own borders, the Assyrian Empire benefited from various taxes and duties, "collected by specialized administrative officers, and established on the basis of a land survey" (Lafont 2001: 833). Lands were granted to generals and officials of the empire. At the same time, the state committed itself to road building. All along the royal roads, "the state maintained a communication system for state letters and envoys traveling on state business," with well-organized post stations (Radner 2012). The military garrisons at the borders of the empire "were places where trade was encouraged . . . The fact that ports and road junctions were freed from taxes shows that there was a private trade" (Glassner 2002a: 149). The Assyrians exacted tributes from the smaller Anatolian and Syrian kingdoms, which were finally incorporated into the empire during the ninth and eighth centuries. Moreover, in 665 BCE, the decision of the Lydian king Gyges "to seek Assurbanipal's protection against the Cimmerian threat provided Assyria with an excellent channel to spread its influence to western Anatolia" (Parpola 2003: 102). Lydia then paid a tribute, as Phrygia had done since Sargon II's reign. Through Lydia, Assyria exerted a cultural influence on the cities of the Ionian coast (Parpola 2003).

During the final phase of the empire in particular, the Assyrian emperors established direct administration of the vassal regions, which probably permitted intensified exploitation of these regions, but would ultimately prove to be a source of weakness when external and internal threats increased. Either way, this process of integration, developed during the middle of the seventh century, was an innovation that the Achaemenids would later imitate more systematically in building their own empire. At the same time, the Assyrian power "was culturally open to foreign elites and external influences" (Joannès 2000: 51). The creation of a royal library by Assurbanipal served the need to develop an imperial culture and reflected the idea of an emperor sitting at the center of the world. The scribes of the empire wrote in Aramaic as well as Akkadian or Egyptian. The consolidation of the Assyrian Empire went hand in hand with the expansion of long-distance exchanges by land and sea. The empire exported manufactured products and imported raw or semi-manufactured goods (metals, dyes, resins ...), horses, and slaves. Slavery played a significant economic role; even soldiers could keep prisoners as private spoils of war. The Assyrians held sway over Phoenician maritime trade, and also contributed to its rise. Moreover, two Assyrian ports were created on the Mediterranean coast, one near Sidon, and the other, farther north, in the region of Arwad. The growth of the town of Ekron as a center for the production and export of olive oil and textiles provides another example of coevolution of a region located at the margins of the empire (Beaulieu 2005). More indirectly, the Ionian cities also benefited from a process of coevolution with Assyria during the seventh century, as did the vassal kingdom of Judah (Parpola 2003: 103–104).

The Assyrian Empire did not merely fulfill the dreams of Sargon I of Akkad or Hammurabi to unite all the lands between the Mediterranean Sea and the Persian Gulf under their rule. The Assyrian thrust extended toward Arabia and northern Africa. The Assyrians, who reared large numbers of dromedaries, controlled the caravan trade with northwestern Arabia,[5] a trade going back to the second millennium. Assyria's prominence was probably not to the Bedouins' liking. At the battle of Qarqar (853 BCE), between the Assyrian king Shalmeneser III and an army of Syrian, Levantine, and Egyptian coalition forces, the Arab king Gindibu (who may have settled in Transjordan) is said to have sent 1,000 camels and meharists against the Assyrians.[6] In addition, the Assyrians acquired "Bactrian" camels: according to a tablet belonging to Assur-bel-kala (1074–1057 BCE), the king sent merchants to buy she-camels. The Assyrian kings systematically hybridized dromedaries and camels.[7] Moreover, cavalry units were set up as early as the beginning of the first millennium, under the influence of steppe cultures. Sargon II (722–705 BCE) expressed his support for trade between Assyrians and Egyptians, but in 671 and then in 664 BCE, the Assyrians took control of Egypt, for a brief period. For the first time, a west Asian power had attempted to incorporate Egypt into its empire. In the Persian Gulf, the Assyrians took advantage of the Babylonian trade networks, Babylon having been integrated into the empire. Several Babylonian revolts were harshly repressed (notably in 689 and in 650 BCE). Under the reigns of Kings Sennacherib (705–681 BCE) and Assurbanipal (668–630 BCE), an Assyrian fleet was formed, with the help of the Phoenicians, and – according to Assyrian texts – the "king of Dilmun" paid tribute to these kings. During this period, Nineveh became the largest city in the world (Morris [2013: 152] gives an estimate of 100,000 inhabitants, but other estimates have been higher).

Commerce during the Neo-Assyrian period was conducted both by royal trade agents, who cooperated with the army, and private merchants (Radner 1999a: 101; 1999b: 138). Not only Assyrians were involved in trade, but also merchants belonging to other "ethnic" groups: Arabs, Anatolians, and so on. Entrepreneurs formed partnerships that could involve loans, with or without interest ("interest rates varied enormously," the "ideal" rate being "an increase of 1 shekel per mina per month, i.e. 20 percent in decimalized terms") (Van de Mieroop 2002: 82). Copper, bronze, and silver – especially after the victorious campaigns of Sargon II (the king brought home a huge amount of silver in 712 BCE after the capture of Karkemish) – were used as currency, as well as written documents. Within the empire, private traders marketed the products of the palace and the temples, and acted as lenders, including to kings (Sargon borrowed from merchants for the construction of his new capital Dur-Sharrukin). The temples also played the role of "bankers of the empire" and guaranteed

---

[5] The Assyrians tried to integrate the nomadic groups into a tributary system. Relations with the Arabs, however, were often conflictual. Tiglath-Pileser III led a campaign around 733 against the Arab queen Shamsi; aromatics were among the spoils seized. The alliance of the Qedarites with Babylon resulted in reprisal raids by Sennacherib and Assurbanipal (Retsö 2003a: 154ff.). It was forbidden for Arabs to buy iron (Villard 2001: 63). Arabs were present in Lower Mesopotamia around 700 BCE. The Qedarites would later help Cambyses conquer Egypt.

[6] Retsö 2003a: 126. The Arabs had been riding dromedaries since 1400 BCE (see above). Stelae from Karkemish and Tell Halaf dated to c. 900 BCE depict cameleers (Retsö 2003a: 191). The stela from Tell Halaf shows a cameleer seated on a box-shaped saddle.

[7] Potts 2004. The hybridization of these two species, which produced stronger animals, may have been developed first in Iran and Mesopotamia.

the purity of metals (Allen 2005: 78, 85). Demand for labor seems to have been the triggering factor for some loans, at this time as before.

To the east of the Assyrian space, a new Elamite "empire" grew up, though with no visible urbanization.[8] Moreover, as early as 821 BCE, a small kingdom called Parsūash appeared in northeastern Elam, probably founded by Iranian speakers.[9] The discovery of spindle-shaped bone cheekpieces with three holes (known in the steppes), at Sialk VI and Hasanlu IV, may reflect the arrival of Proto-Iranians in northern Iran at the beginning of the first millennium BCE (Kuzmina 2008: 65). Moreover, the Assyrian expansion led to the crystallization of a Median confederation into an organized state in the region of Ecbatana.[10] Several wars pitted the Elamites against the Assyrians, who seized Susa in 653 and 646. The Assyrian interest in Elam was partly due to the formation of the kingdom of Urartu during the ninth century BCE in the region of Lake Van, a kingdom blocking the Assyrians' access to iron mines south of the Black Sea and the Transcaucasus region.[11] The defeat of Urartu by the Assyrians during the eighth century was followed by Scythian invasions, which led to the disappearance of Urartu during the seventh century. The Scythians looted Assyria, and Egypt avoided invasion only by paying a significant tribute. The Assyrian decline led to a new shift in power to Babylon at the end of the seventh century, with the help of the Medians.

In the west, on the Levantine coast, the rise of Phoenician city-states (especially Sidon and Tyre)[12] at the beginning of the first millennium was encouraged by local factors and by the position of interface we have already observed during the two preceding millennia. This rise was favored at the same time by developments in Anatolia, the Assyrian expansion, the relative Egyptian revival, and the growth of the Arab caravan trade. Derived from a Proto-Canaanite linear alphabet, the Phoenician alphabet appeared, already fully formed, during the tenth century on King Ahiram's sarcophagus at Byblos.[13] As early as the ninth century, this alphabet was adopted in both Cilicia and Phrygia

---

[8] As Liverani notes, "the gap in the evidence between the Middle and Neo-Elamite kingdoms remains an unresolved issue" (2014: 526).

[9] Medes (Madai) and Persians (Parsua) are already mentioned under the Assyrian king Shalmaneser III in 843, along with other peoples who controlled the roads of the Urals and Iran. They may have brought to Assyria the lapis lazuli found in the royal tombs of Nimrud. The Persians occupied the region of Kermanshah around 692 BCE (the king of Elam who reigned in 693–692 was the last to bear the title of "king of Susa and Anshan"). The ancient Elamite province of Anshan was ruled by Kurash (Cyrus I), the grandfather of Cyrus II, cited in an Assyrian text as "king of Parsuwash." Coming from northeastern Iran (and perhaps also from the Scythian plains, across the Caucasus, along routes that the Cimmerians would follow during the eighth century BCE), speakers of western Iranian languages probably arrived in Iran in different waves around the end of the second millennium and the beginning of the first millennium BCE (see above).

[10] Contrary to Herodotus's assertions, archaeology has shown that this Median state was weakly structured (Kuhrt 1995: 654–656). Stimulated by trade and Assyrian demand for tributes during the seventh century, the Median centers went into decline following the Assyrian collapse.

[11] Urartu (Uruatri), however, was already mentioned during the reign of the Assyrian king Shalmaneser I (1274–1265 BCE).

[12] Tyre was not a new port: the site had already been occupied during the third millennium, as revealed by recent surveys (Huot 2004, II: 97).

[13] Margueron and Pfirsch 2001: 294. H. Frankfort (1969) has suggested dating the tomb to the thirteenth century, and the inscription to the tenth century. Artifacts going back to the reign of Ramses II have been found in the tomb.

(Lemaire 2007: 61–62). Dominating the maritime routes, the Phoenician cities created outposts all across the Mediterranean, even venturing beyond the Straits of Gibraltar in search of silver and tin (see above). Phoenician merchants and artisans settled in the Greek cities (Eretria [Euboea], Athens, Pithekoussai [in the bay of Naples], and so forth). In Palestine, fortified cities appeared, in connection with Arabian trade and cities. Weighed silver was used in transactions. A significant number of treasures containing silver have been unearthed on the West Bank of the Jordan, dated between 1200 and 600 BCE.[14] Thirty-three out of thirty-four reported finds were wrapped in cloth bags, and at least twenty-one were sealed. The sealings must have indicated the weight of the bags and ensured that the quality of the metal had been verified. The weights of bags, at Keisan and Dor for example, sometimes corresponded to standards: thus, the bags exhibited "fundamental qualities typically associated with coinage."[15] In addition, the hoards of the West Bank of the Jordan (at Beth Shean and Akko, for example) show the use of "pre-portioned" ingots – also found at Troy, in Cyprus, at Zinjirli (Zincirli) (Turkey), at Eretria (Greece), and at Nūsh-i Jān (Iran) – spiral rings, sometimes weighing one mina, oval silver pieces, "often of a predetermined size," and kinds of "tokens" (at Tel Dor, Eshtemoa, and Eretria).[16]

Phoenician cities developed export-oriented labor-intensive crafts. They produced purple (the name "Phoenicia" comes from the Greek *phoinix*, "purple"), from *Murex* collected in the Aegean Sea and on the African coasts; they exported textiles, ivory objects, and furniture parts made of ivory,[17] metal cups, timber, glass artifacts, and perfumed oils. A type of glass called "Syro-Palestinian" was manufactured around the eighth century throughout western Asia and Egypt.[18] Opium, the use of which is mentioned by Homer (eighth century BCE) in the *Iliad* (Book VIII) and the *Odyssey* (Book IV), was probably among the products traded.

[14] Several hoards have been dated to the eleventh–tenth century, for example those of Dor, Arad, Ashkalon, Megiddo, Shechem, and Tell Keisan (Thompson 2003: 93). These hoards contradict the idea of a "dark age" on the West Bank of the Jordan during the late second and early first millennia. For this region, the hoard of Tell Ajjul, dating to the sixteenth century BCE, provides the first evidence of the use of broken silver for monetary purposes (Vargyas 1999).

[15] Thompson 2003: 83. The seven bags from Dor (tenth century), placed in a pot, weighed one mina (500 g, the equivalent of 60 "Babylonian" shekels, one shekel weighing 8.33 g), and those of Keisan (eleventh century) weighed 25 g, representing 3 shekels. The sealings that have been found do not mention any name, except at Larsa, where the name of an official who weighed silver is mentioned. The Second Book of Kings (12:9–10) indicates that silver accumulated in the chest of the temple of Jerusalem was "put into bundles" and "counted" (Thompson 2003: 86). This passage, however, has been translated in different ways, expressing the idea that the silver itself was marked and counted (Silver 1995: 160). Note that the Muslim world still used sealed purses bearing an indication of the value of their contents (Udovitch 1979: 267).

[16] The weight of the ingots, at Nūsh-i Jān and Amathus (Cyprus), reflects a choice (Thompson 2003). Vargyas (1999) mentions "a piece of round silver, very similar in form and of identical weight with the much later Persian *siglos*" in the early tenth-century Dor hoard. The Levant used various standards of weights (cf. the discoveries of ingots at Cretan sites) (Thompson 2003: 91). *Šibirtu*, "broken," "eventually came to denote something in the order of 'ingot'": "texts from the mid-first millennium speak of *šibirtu* silver as being precisely one mina each" (Powell 1996: 237).

[17] Huot (2004, II: 95) has termed the ninth and eighth centuries in Phoenicia the "Ivory Age." The ivory used in the Phoenician workshops was primarily elephant ivory, probably imported from Egypt.

[18] Soda-lime glass produced from natron (Dussubieux 2001: 49).

From the ninth century BCE onward, the Assyrians controlled the coast, but the Phoenician ports enjoyed a state of semi-independence until the unsuccessful revolt of Tyre and Sidon against the Assyrian power during the seventh century. The Phoenician city-states "developed into a kind of service society for Assyria" (Niemeyer 2000: 103). The Neo-Assyrian demand for silver and tin was obviously crucial to Phoenician expansion (Niemeyer even speaks of a "political and economic symbiosis" between Phoenicia and Assyria). As already pointed out, the majority of the Phoenician colonies were created during the eighth and seventh centuries BCE. King Tiglath-Pileser III authorized the Tyrian merchants to cut and sell wood from Lebanon, "but they were not allowed to sell it to the Egyptians and to their Palestinian allies" (Graslin and Maucourant 2005). The existence of "mutual benefits" in these exchanges does not mean that there was "equality." If it is true, for example, that King Mattan II of Tyre presented 4.3 tons of gold to the Assyrian king Tiglath-Pileser III in 732, then the amounts paid by the Phoenician cities in tributes must have been huge (Graslin and Maucourant 2005). The treaty with Tyre allowed the Syrian ambassador to be present at all general assemblies of the city when political decisions were made (Radner 2009). In 709 BCE, Assyrian troops were sent to Cyprus on board Tyrian ships. The growing pressure exerted by the Assyrians explains the revolt of the Phoenician cities during the seventh century. It resulted in the partial destruction of Sidon in 677. Trade through the Phoenician ports was weakened after that, and strictly supervised by Assyria. During the sixth century, when the Levantine coast came under Babylonian rule, the empire of Tyre crumbled.

The Phoenicians, moreover, had to compete with the Greek cities, which between the eighth and sixth centuries BCE founded colonies in the western Mediterranean, along the coasts of Africa and around the Black Sea. Minted coinage appeared first in Lydia and Ionia during the late seventh or the early sixth century, and later in Greece during the sixth century, and the Phoenician city-states in the fifth century. The practice of coinage – an extension of the use of sealed bags that dated back at least to the early second millennium BCE, was also an innovation. Coinage may in fact have begun "as a way of certifying the weights of bits of metal" (Snell 1995: 1494). The first "coins" were merely round pieces of metal with no pattern or inscription, but with a punched mark to indicate their weight. Later coins bore a design on the obverse. Several series can be distinguished, attributed to the kings of Lydia (the Sardis workshop).[19] It is significant that this innovation came about against a background of competition between states (the same situation occurred in India and China). Coins, note Snell, allowed states, among other things, "to standardize payments ... to

---

[19] Some of them bore inscriptions (Le Rider 2001: 51, 55ff.). Punched globules made of electrum (possible symbolic representations of the eye) can be considered as the first forms of minted coins (Le Rider 2001: 51; Nicolet-Pierre 2002: 113; Herrenschmidt 2004). The earliest discovery was made in the Artemision of Ephesus; it includes electrum ingots, small round pieces of metal, blank on both obverse and reverse, round pieces without designs but with punched marks, and coins with both designs and punched marks. "The dating is still debated, but it may be placed prior to 560. The birth of coinage thus may be placed around 590–580 BC" (Le Rider 2001: 65). The first Greek coins can be dated to around 550. Very early on, one finds very small silver coins in Ionia, convenient for minor transactions (Le Rider 2001: 68, 70).

mercenary soldiers";[20] they also encouraged the extension of commodity trading and lowered transaction costs.[21] These factors, however, are not enough to explain the appearance of coinage. In the case of Lydia, C. Herrenschmidt (2004) has postulated that the birth of minted coinage was linked to the cult of Artemis and its temple at Ephesus; when substituted for the sacrificial victim, coinage may initially have represented the payment of a debt to the goddess. Hocart has already stated that money originated as an offering to the deities (Hocart 1952: 97ff.). Moreover, it should be noted that the expansion of coinage was a state initiative: "when the state saw in the coinage a possible source of fiscal income, it monopolized the minting of coins by marking them" with a relevant picture and inscription (Le Rider 2001: 81).[22] The state benefited on various levels from controlling the minting of coins. The first was fiscal, through a twofold decision: that the nominal value of the currency issued was higher than its intrinsic value, and that state-minted coinage was the only valid currency within its territory. This forced foreign merchants to exchange their precious metal, providing a source of profit for the state. Moreover, minted coinage bore a political message and was an instrument of unification. The growth of coinage was fundamental to the building of a new social order and ideological transformations. The Greek world clearly established a link between currency (*nomisma*) and law (*nomos*), accepted by all. "The monetary institution was one of the aspects of the regulation of the internal structures of the society."[23] The first Lydian coins were made of electrum,[24] found in Lydia; later under Croesus, gold and silver were minted.[25] Greek cities used only silver, a practice probably influenced by their trade with the Levant, which employed this metal for exchanges.[26] The discovery of very small silver coins in the Greek cities reveals the existence of denominations facilitating low-value exchanges.

[20] Schaps (2007: 36–37) shows how armies may have contributed to market development. Van der Spek (2015) also points out that "the production of coinage by states in Antiquity was not motivated by economic reasoning, but by the wish to pay soldiers and laborers on public works and finally to facilitate taxation."

[21] But "the minting of coins did not result from a spontaneous extension of exchanges" (Aglietta and Orléan 2002: 140–141). Note that the Phoenicians did not adopt the use of coins until later (mid-fifth century BCE), under Greek influence.

[22] Prior to Lydia, "no state had ever monopolized any currency through minting and its direct control to ensure fiscal resources" (Le Rider 2001: 82). Le Rider notes that the other states primarily earned their income from land, whereas Lydia and the Ionian cities were more trade-oriented. But there is more to it than that: as pointed out above, the Phoenicians did not at first adopt minting.

[23] Will, quoted by Le Rider 2001: 78. Money is the product of a decision accepted by all. Aristotle writes in the *Nicomachean Ethics*: "Money has become by convention a sort of representative of demand; and this is why it has the name 'money' (*nomisma*), because it exists not by nature but by law (*nomos*) and it is in our power to change it and make it useless" (quoted by Thierry 1997: 36–37).

[24] Some authors have considered that the objective of coin minting was to stabilize the value of electrum; its gold:silver ratio was somewhat variable. See Schaps (2007: 26ff.) for a criticism of this hypothesis. Vargyas considers the round "coins" (without any mark) found in Israel as prototypes for the future coins of Anatolia and the Greek world (quoted by Le Rider 2001: 36).

[25] Coins called "croeseids." The attribution of these coins to Croesus, however, is uncertain (Le Rider 2001: 101ff.).

[26] Thompson 2003: 95. Note that the silver mines of Laurion were exploited during the seventh century (and probably even earlier; see above): silver from three objects at Tell Miqne-Ekron (West Bank) may have come from these mines; silver in other objects came from islands in the Aegean Sea. The search for new

As pointed out above, prior to the innovation of minted coinage, the states of western Asia had instituted the practice of marking sealed bags containing silver. Moreover, according to M. Silver, in the Neo-Assyrian Empire, "stamped ingots of a weight fixed by the government" may have been used as means of exchange. "Assyrian loan contracts of the eighth to seventh centuries refer to a silver *aklu* 'loaf' and a *(c)huchuru* 'round loaf' that possess 'the high degree of fineness of (the goddess) Ishtar' (Lipinski)" of Arbela.[27] It is not clear, however, whether the ingots from Arbela were inscribed or not, and a number of researchers reject the interpretation put forward by Silver. During the Neo-Assyrian period, we know of an official responsible for weighing silver (*bel hi'ati ša sarpi*).[28] From the same period (seventh century), ingots with incised or stamped inscriptions have been found at Zinjirli and Nūsh-i Jān, southeast of Hamadan (Iran).[29] The ingots at Zinjirli, in the shape of loaves, bear the engraved name of the king, preceded by the Aramaean letter *lamed* ("belonging to," or possibly "in the name of"). Like M. Silver, M. Powell (1996) and C. Thompson (2003) consider it possible that they were used as money. G. Le Rider (2001) and D. Schaps (2007) take an opposite view:[30] that the inscription signified royal property and therefore the storage of wealth. Schaps, however, points out the significance of the discovery of the treasure of Nūsh-i Jān (seventh century BCE), which has yielded silver ingots of specific weights (cast in molds), rings, beads with double or quadruple spirals, and pieces of silver, one of them bearing cuneiform signs: the silver bar from which this piece had been cut must have

sources of silver may have played a role in the Greek expansion in the western Mediterranean. "In the Hebrew Bible most prices are given in silver" (Snell 1995: 1494). Terrestrial routes also played a role: according to Curtius (*Hist. Gr.* 1.76), "The Lydians became on land what the Phoenicians were by sea, the mediators between Hellas and Asia" (Thompson 2003: 96).

[27] Silver 2004a, after Lipinski 1979: 574. The temple probably ensured this metal's purity, but we do not have evidence for inscription on the silver "loaves." Lipinski translates: "Twelve reliable silver minas of Ishtar of Arbela, that are loaves of the god's house." He concludes: "The words *aklu* [loaf] and *huchurru* [round loaf] seem to refer to ingots of a specific weight. The *aklu* would be the ingot of one mina as in the text from Nineveh." Kwasman and Parpola (1991: 186), however, propose another translation: "Twelve minas of silver, first fruits of Ishtar of Arbela, of the bread of the temple, belonging to S., at the disposal of Z." The discussion is in fact centered on the word written SAG.MEŠ, interpreted by Lipinski as "silver of reliable quality [of Ishtar]" (J.-P. Dercksen, p.c.). The circulation of ingots of guaranteed quality may go back to the second millennium, if we give this interpretation to the expression "silver of the gods" found in texts at Mari and Amarna (Malamat 1998: 185; Silver 2004c).

[28] J.-P. Dercksen, p.c. These officials were already known in the Ur III period (KUG.LA; see above).

[29] Snell 1995: 1489. "Ingots in the shape of bread, unearthed at Zincirli," notes Lipinski (1979: 574), "resemble the 'breads' and 'loaves' mentioned in the texts." Some authors argued for the existence of marked silver as early as the beginning of the second millennium in the Assyrian area. According to Silver (1995: 163; 2004a), texts from this period already mention "heads of Ishtar" or "of Shamash," but Silver's interpretations have been questioned: the word "head" should perhaps be interpreted as meaning "capital" (of the temple) (see above).

[30] Le Rider (2001: 27) rightly points out that the silver disks of King Bar-Rakib were not stamped, but engraved: "the inscription indicates that the silver belongs to the king, which is confirmed by the sign *lamed*." "The marking shows that the object belonged to the king; the purpose of the inscription was to ensure royal ownership. Why should we think that the purpose of the imprint was to ensure its free circulation?" (D. Schaps p.c.). One might ask whether the shape of ingots of various origins could have been related to Croesus's offering to the Apollo temple at Delphi of "a statue of a baker" (*artoskopos*) (Herodotus). Herrenschmidt (2004) sees several plays on words in this name, linking it to a word referring to a "silver beater" on the one hand, and to Artemis, on the other.

borne an inscription.[31] The same remark can be made for a piece of silver bearing a fragmentary Elamite inscription found in Afghanistan (treasure of Chaman Huzūri, Kabul)[32] and dated to the fifth century BCE. The silver bars of Nūsh-i Jān may well have been used as such for transactions; they may be the precursors of the curved bars found in India (Le Rider 2001: 3, 4). The question of whether there was minting of precious metal by the state or merchant groups during the early first millennium BCE for monetary use thus remains open to debate. This minting did not directly show a value – as the later coins did – but probably guaranteed the degree of purity of the metal. Bars of precious metals continued to circulate, at the same time as coins, the use of which slowly progressed from the sixth century onward. In addition, legal documents could be used as "money" to make payments (Radner 1999b: 137).

Phoenician expansion was not limited to the Mediterranean Sea. The alliance formed under King Ahiram (the "Hiram" of the Bible) from Tyre between Phoenicians and Hebrews may have originated from the desire for access to the networks of the Red Sea and the Indian Ocean, with the Hebrews acting as middlemen in exchanges with this area.[33] The exact role of the Phoenicians in the Indian Ocean space is difficult to assess, but we cannot accept Toussaint's opinion whereby "the Phoenicians were the first to really expand maritime exchanges, which before them were very limited, among the main regions of the Indian Ocean" (Toussaint 1961: 20). Indian, Arab, Mesopotamian, and Persian navigations did not need to wait for the Phoenicians to provide the impetus for their development. The Phoenicians did, however, play a significant role between the tenth and fourth centuries BCE "thanks to their skills in shipbuilding and steering seafaring vessels" (Lemaire 1987: 60). They appear to have worked in constant association with the rulers of countries controlling access to the Indian Ocean.

The founding by Solomon (970–931?)[34] of the port of Ezion-Geber, at the head of the Gulf of Aqaba, probably marks the entrance of the Phoenicians into the Indian

---

[31] Bivar 1971. This author considers that the pieces of silver that have been found correspond to various standard weights of western Asia, but the weight of the pieces seems rather to be a matter of chance (Le Rider 2001: 9).

[32] This treasure also contained forty-three Indian punch-marked silver coins, Athenian coins, and Achaemenid coins. For Le Rider (2001: 28), the question remains whether the inscriptions noted in the hoards of Nūsh-i Jān and Chaman Huzūri represent marks certifying the quality of the metal, or only indicate its royal ownership.

[33] The maritime routes of the Red Sea and of the Indian Ocean extended toward the interior of Africa. J. E. Dayton (University College London, 2003), on the basis of isotopic analysis of lead content in tin ingots found at Haifa in 1982, suggests locating the origin of the tin in Uganda at the beginning of the first millennium; this remains to be confirmed (see Chami 2006: 138)

[34] The date of Solomon's reign is still debated. No archaeological remains can be attributed to his reign with certainty, and we do not have any Hebrew inscriptions for this period. Both the Aramaean stela of Tel Dan and the stela of the Moabite king Mesha, written in a Proto-Hebrew alphabet, mention "the house of David" and are dated to the ninth century BCE. A large number of *ostraka* dated from 900 BCE have been excavated in the kingdom of Israel. The absence of any written document going back to the kingdom of Solomon and the lack of archaeological evidence for contacts with neighboring countries are in sharp contrast with the biblical text, as is the relatively small size of Jerusalem at this time (the city experienced a phase of major growth only around 700 BCE). Finkelstein (1998, 2003) and other authors have suggested lowering the dates of the Iron Age in the Levant by some 75 to 100 years. For another interpretation based on the data from Tel Rehov, see Bruins *et al.* 2003.

Ocean. They agreed to build him a "fleet of India" and in 945 they led it to a region known in the Bible under the name "Ophir," from which they brought back gold, silver, ivory, monkeys, and slaves:

King Solomon built ships at Ezion Geber, which is near Elath in Edom, on the shore of the Red Sea. And Hiram sent his men – sailors who knew the sea – to serve in the fleet with Solomon's men. They sailed to Ophir and brought back 420 talents of gold [about 16 tons], which they delivered to King Solomon . . . Hiram's ships brought gold from Ophir; and from there they brought great cargoes of almugwood [al-muggīm, sandalwood?][35] and precious stones. The king used the almugwood to make supports for the temple of YHWH and for the royal palace, and to make harps and lyres for the musicians. So much almugwood has never been imported or seen since that day . . . The king had a fleet of Tarshish at sea along with the ships of Hiram. Once every three years it returned, carrying gold, silver, ivory, and apes (qohīm), and peacocks (tukkiyīm).[36]

The search for Ophir has attracted a great deal of interest. Some authors have set it in Southeast Asia, but Ophir has usually been located in Africa (products from Ophir have been likened to those brought from Punt into Egypt) or in Arabia: Kitchen suggests the region of Asir in western Arabia, north of the Wādī Baysh (Kitchen, 2002a: 396), and a location in Libya has also been suggested (see below). The Book of Genesis (10:29) locates Ophir between Saba and Havilah (southern Palestine). If Ophir was in the south, the expeditions of Hiram and Solomon were probably aiming to bypass the Arab caravan trade that transported spices, aromatics, and other luxury goods from the Indian Ocean to western Asia overland, and to evade Egypt's control of the gold supply. The capture of Jerusalem by the pharaoh Sheshonq in 930 may have marked the end of the expeditions to Ophir: Tyre later developed a new trade axis aimed at Cilicia (Aubet 2001). The interpretation of the texts is made difficult by the use of rare words such as al-muggīm or tukkiyīm. The latter has sometimes been related to an Indian word referring to the peacock (Tamil togai, Sanskrit cikhi). Basham (1967: 230) tentatively connects al-muggīm and the Sanskrit valguka, one of the names for sandalwood. Flavius Josephus (37–100), Eusebius of Caesarea (c. 265–340), and Hieronymus (348–420), all located Ophir in India.[37] J. Schreiden also supports this hypothesis; in the Septuagint[38] he notes other spellings for Ophir: Sopeir, Soupeir, Soupir, which he associates with the

---

[35] The Ecumenical Translation of the Bible translates it as "sandalwood" (1976: 645). Almuggīm represents a plural; the radical should be mug.

[36] Book of Kings I, 9:26–27, 10:11–12, 22, Chronicles II, 8:17–18, 9:2, 10–11. The translation of tukkiyīm by "peacocks," notes the Ecumenical Bible, is "traditional" (1976: 647 n.x) (links to Indian terms referring to the peacock, however, have been put forward; see below). Lemaire (1987) quotes a translation that gives "baboons" instead of "peacocks."

[37] According to Flavius Josephus, Phoenician pilots went "along with [Solomon's] own stewards to the land that was of old called Ophir, but now the Aurea Chersonesus [Golden Chersonese], which belongs to India, to fetch him gold." One might ask whether the Golden Chersonese here refers to the region in Sumatra or, as R. N. Saletore suggests (1994: 244), a region close to India. Moreover, gold arrived from Arabia, along caravan routes. Archaeological excavations have identified a gold mine at Mahd ad-Dahab, exploited during the early first millennium BCE (Heck 1999: 381).

[38] Greek translation of the Hebrew Bible, Alexandria, third and second centuries BCE.

name of the Indian city of Sopārā[39] (mentioned in the *Mahābhārata* under the form Shurpāraka,[40] and in the *Periplus of the Erythraean Sea* under the name Suppara), north of Bombay. Ophir has also been linked to the name Sauvīra given in ancient times to the Lower Indus valley. The *Milinda-Pañha* (fourth century CE; see below) speaks of Sauvīra as "one of the trade centers which a shipowner had to visit from Alexandria down to China along with Vanga and Takkola" (Saletore 1994: 244).[41]

During the ninth century BCE, Jehoshaphat, the king of Jerusalem, who controlled the Edomite territory, attempted to reactivate trade in the Red Sea:

Jehoshaphat made ships of Tarshish to go to Ophir for gold: but they didn't go; for the ships were broken at Ezion Geber [in the Gulf of Aqaba]. (Book of Kings I, 22:48–50)

The kings of Samaria, allied with the Phoenicians of Tyre, seem to have been involved in the trade between the Red Sea and the Mediterranean until the annexation of Samaria by the Assyrians (722 BCE). "Phoenician and northern Hebrew inscriptions found at Kuntillet 'Ajrud, between Qardesh-Barnea and Elat, mention the alliance of the Phoenicians and northern Israelites," under King Jeroboam II of Samaria (790–750 BCE) (Lemaire 1987: 52). Chapter 27 of the Book of Ezekiel refers to the trade of Tyre, partly with the Indian Ocean:

The men of Dedan were your traffickers; many islands were the market of your hand: they brought you in exchange horns of ivory and ebony . . . The traffickers of Sheba and Raamah, they were your traffickers; they traded for your wares with the chief of all spices, and with all precious stones, and gold . . . The ships of Tarshish were your caravans for your merchandise: and you were replenished, and made very glorious in the heart of the seas.[42]

It could well be that there were several Ophirs, connected to the gold trade. Recent research on Ophir places it in Africa and suggests a West African origin for the gold (Lipinski 2004: 204). "On the Borgian planisphere or Velletri Table (in the Vatican Library) dating to the early 15th century, Ophir is placed at the edge of the world, near the southern ocean, from which it was separated by a range of mountains" ((Lipinski 2004: 194–195). Ophir is mentioned ("30 shekels of gold from Ophir") on an ostracon found at the port of Tell Qasile (Israel), and "a harbour called Opiros on the *Tabula Peutingeriana* is located on the western side of the Greater Syrtis, in Libya" (Lipinski

---

[39] Schreiden 1979: 2. One finds in Arrian the form Uppara, "probably an Iranian form of Sopārā." Warmington also mentions Sovīra (1928: 56). Cf. also Basham 1967: 230.

[40] In its current version, the *Mahābhārata* may date back to the fifth century CE; the text, however, was written over several centuries.

[41] Other authors have proposed locating Ophir on the coast of Sofala, in Mozambique. The interpretation of the term Tarshish is also problematic. For the Ecumenical Bible, this "undetermined geographical place" could be located in Spain (Tartessos, in the region of Gibraltar), in Tunisia, or on the Black Sea. We find in Ezekiel (27:12) "The people from Tarshish traded with you because of your great wealth. You sold to them and they paid you with silver, iron, tin, and lead." The identification of Tarshish seems to vary according to the texts. While Aubet (2001: 123, 205) excludes the identification with Tartessos and the western Mediterranean, Lipinski (2010: 267) and Liverani (2014: 424) accept it. Flavius Josephus identified Tarshish with Tarsus, in Cilicia.

[42] Ezekiel 27:15, 22, 25. The text also depicts trade on terrestrial routes, through the Levant, Arabia, and Mesopotamia. This passage (27:12–24), notes M. E. Aubet (2001: 121), seems to describe the situation of Tyre during the ninth century BCE: it was introduced in a text written during the sixth century.

2010: 267). This location, however, is not in agreement with the mention of the Gulf of Aqaba in the Book of Kings (see above).

Moreover, Assyrian tablets reveal that the Assyrian king Sennacherib asked Phoenicians to build and command a war fleet that he sent against the Arabs in the Persian Gulf. It is possible that Phoenicians sailed to the coasts of India at that time. The ivories of the Ziwiya hoard (end eighth–seventh century), in Kurdistan, bear testimony to the links between western Asia and India.[43]

Assyria was in decline during the second half of the seventh century, stricken by a financial crisis caused by diminishing income and military expenses. Maintaining control over an oversized empire, weakened by Scythian attacks and internal revolts, came at too high a price. Its decline would facilitate a transition of hegemony to southern Mesopotamia.

The Neo-Babylonian Empire

Assyria managed to incorporate Babylon into its empire, but at the end of the seventh century BCE, Lower Mesopotamia reaffirmed its prominence. A Chaldean dynasty established an alliance with the Medes against the Assyrian cities. Assur and Nineveh were captured in 612 BCE and the Assyrian state disappeared. King Cyaxarus unified the various Scythian and Persian tribes, and made Ecbatana the capital of a "Median empire," but it was short-lived: his successor, Astyages, was defeated by the Achaemenid king Cyrus II in 549 BCE. The vision offered by Herodotus of a great Median empire has been put in doubt by archaeological excavations, which rather suggest the existence of various urban centers, each of them under the leadership of a monarch.[44] In Mesopotamia, Nabopolassar founded a Neo-Babylonian Empire and his son Nebuchadnezzar II (604–562 BCE) made Babylon the largest city of the Ancient World (it covered 850 ha); Morris gives an estimate of 125,000–150,000 inhabitants (2013: 152). Nebuchadnezzar was victorious over the Egyptians at Karkemish in 605, conquered Susa in 595/596, Jerusalem in 586 BCE and managed to overcome the resistance of Tyre in 584 BCE. The position of the Phoenician and Palestinian cities, caught between the Babylonian and Egyptian powers, was indeed difficult; the Levant was affected by no fewer than eight Babylonian military campaigns from 604. Attempts to invade the Nile valley, however, were repulsed by the Egyptians.

The Neo-Babylonian Empire used the administrative structure of the Assyrian Empire and repeated the Assyrian policy of deporting conquered populations in order to exploit them more directly (as was the case for Jerusalem).[45] It is possible that Jews migrated to Gujarat when the kingdom of Israel collapsed (721 BCE), and to

---

[43] At the same time, Ziwiya has yielded gold plaques showing a decoration "comparable to the Scytho-Siberian animal style" (Cunliffe 2015: 172).

[44] Hansen 2002: 8. In the west, the Lydians managed to seal a peace treaty with King Cyaxarus when the latter invaded Anatolia.

[45] Craftsmen and specialists were present at the royal court (Moorey 2001: 7). This was nothing new. Moorey signals that according to a Sumerian poem, one king of Uruk, victorious over the king of Aratta, deported the goldsmiths from that country.

the west coast of India during the Neo-Babylonian period:[46] to this day, the Jews of the Cochin region still play a type of board game that was known in Babylonia at the time of Nebuchadnezzar II. This king set up a hierarchized administration, and extended the existing system of canals for irrigation and transport, greatly benefiting agriculture and trade. As Jursa points out, there was "a massive royal investment of the 'spoils of empire' in the agrarian and urban infrastucture" (2015: 103).

The Neo-Babylonian Empire shows increasing connections between the state and private sectors. Traders under the command of a chief of the royal merchants were in charge of provisioning the palace and selling its products, without being part of the palace administration (Michel 2001a: 196). Under Nebuchadnezzar, the leader of the palace merchants was a high official called Hanon, "a typical name of Phoenician derivation" (Aubet 2001: 119). "Privatisation of the exploitation of the institutional assets is a fact in this period" (van Driel 2002: 164). The great Babylonian temples relied on outside businessmen, who acted as managers for the temples, against the payment of a fixed annuity (the businessmen therefore had an interest in developing production). Though not having the same importance as in the past,[47] the temples still played a significant economic and administrative role. They leased part of their land, and sold wool and dates on the market through private intermediaries (see Jursa 2010).[48] The temples used refined silver – of guaranteed quality[49] – not only as payment for local products, but also to reward services (Joannès 2005: 38; Vargyas 2001: 12). They relied on outside workers (Lerouxel and Zurbach 2006). Texts show advances in hired labor, with fluctuating wages that appear to reflect the existence of a labor market (Jursa 2005, 2010; Silver 2007a); a land market also developed. The economic system was strongly market-oriented, and "most parts of Babylonia in the sixth century formed a single and comparatively well-integrated economic space" (Jursa 2010: 140). During what is known as "the long sixth century" (c. 605–480 BCE), however, "the land market was not fully synchronized with the commodity markets" (Jursa 2015: 97).

"The institutional sector of the economy could not have functioned without Babylonian businessmen" (Jursa 2010: 767). Texts reveal the emergence of what has sometimes been termed "capitalist" firms, working with the state and other economic actors, notably the House of Egibi. "The agents of the Babylonian firms of Egibi bought slaves on the Elamite markets, imported agricultural products and sold grains or wool cloth" (Huyse 2005: 98). Taking advantage of its relations with the political sphere, the House of Egibi took charge of irrigation canals and agricultural production, collected taxes, and lent money, with interest. The documents relating to this house

---

[46] Jews were also present very early on in Arabia, where they arrived via the caravan routes.

[47] For the period he calls "the long sixth century," Jursa (2010: 759) notes that "the temples were of course important landowners, but they did not dominate the rural landscape by any means."

[48] "Commercial agents were primarily involved in the marketing process of the goods of the temples or the royal palace; however, they also practiced private transactions." As in the Paleo-Babylonian period, the temples practiced a pre-sale system, exchanging their surplus wool and other products against silver (Joannès 2005: 46–47).

[49] The silver alloy *bitka* had a guaranteed quality of one-eighth pure silver (0.875) (Vargyas 2001: 14). Other degrees of purity are mentioned from the sixth century (Vargyas 2001: 14, 35).

cover five generations; it remained active under the Persian Empire, notably under the reign of Darius (see below).[50]

Trade expansion benefited at this time from the use of contracts of suretyship (Silver 1995: 113), and, more importantly, from increased circulation of money and the extension of credit.[51] Around 600 BCE, the maximum interest rate on grain loans was lowered to 20 percent, the same rate as for silver loans. More taxes had to be paid in silver than in kind (Jursa 2010: 657–660). "A comparison of prices of dates and barley during the second millennium BC with Neo-Babylonian prices shows that the purchasing power of silver had fallen by 50 to 65%" (Jursa 2014: 120). Prices were high from 550 BCE onward, because of the increased quantity of silver in circulation due to the spoils from Assyria and Syria (Jursa 2010). Jursa also points out the higher standardization of the silver in circulation. Besides money, the texts show the existence of "promissory notes" (u'iltu) – acknowledging debts – arising from various operations. Debt notes were not traded, but texts show that "interest-bearing debt notes were counted among the inheritable assets of the creditor's family. Claims were transferable ... and could be ceded by the creditor to a third party" (Wunsch 2002: 249). Besides funds made available to the tamkāru who worked for the state, state institutions lent to businessmen – who often formed associations – "money that these businessmen could use for their own account; knowing that the interest to be paid was set at 20%, it is obvious that the [expected] profit must have been considerable" (Glassner 2002a: 149). Loans were often secured by pledges. Temples were no longer in the habit of lending silver (although they did make loans in grain).[52] Entrepreneurs acted as "bankers," however, as had already been attested during the Old Babylonian period. They lent money with interest rates varying from 5 to 240 percent. Benefiting from the rise in exchanges, partnerships between merchants ([c]harranu) developed that could involve sizeable silver loans.[53] Did these "bankers" lend money taken from deposited funds? For Bogaert (1966: 105–118), the Egibi and other firms used neither the silver that had been deposited in their "house," nor borrowed silver, for loans that would have allowed them to make a profit: the deposit bank would appear later, in the Greek world (around the fourth century BCE). Wunsch (2002: 248) observes that the Egibi had to pay interest in one case on a deposit,[54] but she acknowledges that "the essential characteristic of taking money as a deposit and lending it out at a higher rate cannot be found" within the Egibi archives (2010: 59): entrepreneurs such as the Egibi were not really bankers. However, Silver (2004b: 72) points out that the verb qiāpu means both "to grant a loan" and "to deposit" (CAD Q/A 3–4 95–7 entry qāpu).[55] Silver also notes that "Oppenheim (1969) calls attention to cuneiform sources of the first half of the second millennium

---

[50] The archives of the House of Ea-iluta-bani (Sippar) also cover six generations, from 687 to 487 (Joannès 1995: 1478–1479).

[51] Unlike what can be observed during the second millennium, we have no evidence at this time of the existence of debt bondage, or debt cancellation by the ruler (Jursa 2002; see also Wunsch 2002).

[52] Merchants working for the temple, however, could receive silver for their own businesses; then they were obliged to pay 20 percent interest (Joannès 2000).

[53] Moreover, the use of insurance contracts fostered trade expansion.

[54] The use of a deposit may have been considered similar to borrowing.

[55] Under the entry qāpu A, the meanings given are "to entrust silver or goods for trade or on consignment," "to make a qiptu loan" (CAD 1982: 93). According to C. Michel (p.c.), the verb qāpu, in the Assyrian

and the seventh to sixth centuries that refer to sealed bags of silver *(kaspum kankum)* deposited with persons who used the silver in various transactions" (1995: 115). We can clearly see the development of "capitalist" practices in the cities, based on the use and trade of silver and other goods.

The Mediterranean networks were crucial for the Babylonian Empire, which imported copper (from Cyprus), iron (from the Aegean Sea and Syria), alum (from Egypt), dyes (from Phoenicia), ivory (from Egypt via Phoenicia), and so forth. Moreover, the Persian Gulf gained new prominence. The Neo-Babylonian kings extended their control over Bahrain and the Oman peninsula, rich in copper and the "gateway to India" as some Arab authors would later call it.[56] Nebuchadnezzar II founded the city of Teredon, near Bassora, "where merchants brought incense and aromatics" from Oman and India (the city is called Diridotis in Arrian, VIII.41.7; Salles 1996a: 256). Plants were also introduced. Already under the reign of the Assyrian emperor Sennacherib, "wool trees" (cotton plants) were cultivated in Mesopotamia (the introduction of the cotton plant may be older, as cotton is mentioned in a tablet of the Babylonian king Nabu-apla-iddina, 887–855 BCE). The Hebrew *(karpas)* and Greek *(karpasos)*[57] names for the cotton plant derive from the Sanskrit *karpāsa*. Rice was cultivated in Mesopotamia and in northern Iran.[58] Herodotus writes that the Babylonians grow a type of millet *(kenkhros)* "as big as a tree": this seems to refer to sorghum. Note that the Persian name for sorghum is *juar i hindi*, "Indian millet."[59] Moreover, the Neo-Babylonian kings tried to control the Arab caravan trade. Nabonidus thus launched an expedition into northern Arabia, occupied Hijaz as far as Medina and built a palace in the oasis of Taymā' (his departure from Babylonia may also have been motivated by political difficulties in Mesopotamia as well as religious considerations [Liverani 2014: 544]).

Various texts bear witness to the existence of maritime trade between Babylon and India during the seventh and sixth centuries BCE, in which both Dravidians and Aryans were involved. The *Baveru Jātaka* mentions connections between Bharukacha, Surparaka (Sopara), on the coast of Gujarat, and Baveru (Babylon), which imported peacocks. The *Purāna* mention Nineveh, under the name of Shonitapur, as well as the Asuras (Assyrians) and their king Asura-Bana (Assurbanipal). Indian merchants probably settled in Babylon. "Trade relations [of Babylon] with the east, however, did not leave many traces in the private Babylonian archives known to us" (Joannès

archives of Kanesh (early second millennium BCE), means 1. to entrust silver or goods for trading operations or a deposit, 2. to make a loan *qīptu* (see Dercksen 1999).

[56] Bahrain does not seem to have played as important a role as Oman during the period between the eighth and the sixth centuries BCE. One "king of Dilmun" paid tribute to Assyria at the end of the eighth and the beginning of the seventh century. "In the Neo-Babylonian period, a document dating to the reign of Nabonidus (545) signals the presence of a Babylonian 'governor' in Dilmun" (Glassner 2002b).

[57] Herodotus (III.106) described the cotton of India in these terms: "the trees, in the wild, bear a fruit which gives a finer and stronger wool than the wool from sheep; thus these trees provide clothing to the Indians" (Barguet 1964: 265). Cotton is mentioned once in the Bible (Esther 1.5–6).

[58] Rice was present at Hasanlu (Iranian Azerbaijan) during the seventh century BCE, and is mentioned in texts from the Neo-Assyrian period (Akkadian *kurangu*); it was grown in Susiana in 318/317 BCE (Potts 1997: 273).

[59] Hindi: *jowar*, sorghum, Prākrit *juāri*, "kind of grain, millet," from the Sanskrit *yavākāra*, "of the same kind as barley" (Turner 1973: 603 no. 10437). On the reliefs of the palace of Sennacherib, plants that have sometimes been taken as sorghum instead depict the reed *Phragmites communis* Trin. (de Wet 2000: 156).

1999: 186).[60] The mention of indigo in Neo-Babylonian texts and of recipes for combining indigo and dyer's madder (*Rubia tinctorum* L.) reflect the importation of indigo and perhaps the indigo plant into Mesopotamia at this time (Balfour-Paul 1997: 8) (the Greek *indikon*, which gave "indigo," means "Indian, from India").

Phoenicians may have been present in the Gulf, but they were more active in the Red Sea. According to Herodotus, they circumnavigated Africa from east to west around 600 BCE, an expedition commissioned by the pharaoh Nechao II; however, doubts have been cast – perhaps wrongly (Lemaire 1987: 58) – on whether this voyage ever took place. Herodotus writes:

> When [Nechao II] had finished digging the canal which leads from the Nile to the Arabian Gulf, he sent Phoenicians in ships, instructing them to sail on their return voyage past the Pillars of Hercules until they came into the northern sea and so to Egypt. So the Phoenicians set out from the Red Sea and sailed the southern sea . . .; after two years had passed, it was in the third that they rounded the pillars of Hercules and came to Egypt. There they said (what some may believe, though I do not) that in sailing around Libya they had the sun on their right hand. (*Histories* IV.42)[61]

We know that Nechao II, when threatened by the Babylonians, pursued an active naval policy "by building triremes in the Arabian Gulf to sail to the Eritrean Sea" (Herodotus, *Histories* II.159; Lemaire 1987: 56).[62] It is not certain that the digging of the canal linking the Nile and the Red Sea was ever completed; in any event, the project reveals the importance of trade between these two seas. Inscriptions at Abu Simbel dated to 591 BCE and Phoenician graffiti at Abydos dated between the fifth and the third centuries BCE provide convincing evidence that there was a Phoenician presence in Egypt. They confirm Herodotus's indication of a Phoenician colony at Memphis.[63] The Phoenicians may have tried to bypass the Arab confederation of the kings of Qedar, who controlled southern Palestine, the Sinai, and the port of Gaza (Herodotus, *Histories* III.5; Lemaire 1987: 55). The Phoenicians dominated trade between the Red Sea and the Mediterranean until the capture of Tyre by Alexander in 332 BCE and the founding of Alexandria in 331. Moreover, Liverani (1991) points out that Tyrian commerce during the sixth century was conducted more on land than by sea.

Starting in the sixth century BCE a new empire emerged. More enterprising and innovative than the Neo-Babylonian Empire, with the concept and organization of a transnational territory, it would succeed in uniting western Asia and Egypt, and linking the Indian Ocean and the Mediterranean, something that the

---

[60] "Babylon does not seem to have been a major place for the near eastern trade." The city of Opis was the gateway for the eastern trade of Babylonia, but "at the moment, references to Opis provide the only tangible documentation linked to this eastern trade" (Joannès 1999: 186).

[61] See also Casson 1991: 118. During the fifth century, a Persian called Sataspes, sent by Xerxes, may have reached the coasts of Senegal and Guinea (Casson 1991: 120).

[62] "Some of his ships of war were built in the northern sea, and some in the Arabian Gulf" (Herodotus, *Histories* II.159).

[63] Herodotus, *Histories* II.112. The presence of Phoenicians in the region of Memphis is also confirmed by a papyrus found at Saqqara. Aramaean and Phoenician texts have been discovered at Saqqara. Phoenician wine jars of the Neo-Babylonian and Persian period have been unearthed at Tell el-Maskhouta (the Wādī Tumilat region) (Lemaire 1987: 56, 58).

previous Mesopotamian empires had attempted but failed to fully achieve. In addition, for the first time, a western empire took control of the routes leading to Central Asia, a sign of the future linking of the spheres of western Asia, India, and East Asia.

Achaemenid Persia: The First "Universal Empire"

> [Marduk] inspected and checked all the countries, seeking for the upright king of his choice. He took the hand of Cyrus, king of the city of Anshan, and called him by his name, proclaiming him aloud for the kingship over all of everything.
> (Cylinder of Cyrus II, from Babylon, written in Akkadian; Kuhrt 1995: 601)

> The cedar timber, this was brought from a mountain named Lebanon. The Assyrian people brought it to Babylon; from Babylon the Carians and the Yaun [=Greeks] brought it to Susa. The *yak*-timber was brought from Gandara and from Carmania. The gold was brought from Lydia and from Bactria . . . The precious stone lapis lazuli and carnelian which was wrought here, this was brought from Sogdia. The precious stone turquoise, this was brought from Chorasmia, which was wrought here. The silver and the ebony were brought from Egypt. The ornamentation with which the wall was adorned, that from Yaun was brought. The ivory . . . was brought from Kush and from India and from Arachosia. . . . The stone-cutters who wrought the stone [of the columns], those were Yaun and Lydians. The goldsmiths who wrought the gold, those were Medes and Egyptians. The men who wrought the wood, those were Lydians and Egyptians. The men who wrought the baked brick, those were Babylonians. The men who adorned the wall, those were Medes and Egyptians.
> (Foundation charter of the palace of Darius I at Susa; Huyse 2005: 62–63)

During the second half of the sixth century BCE, Assyrians, Babylonians, and Elamites disappeared from the political scene; their places were taken by the Persian Empire that would soon extend from the Indus to the Mediterranean Sea, and from the Caucasus to the Indian Ocean.[64] A kingdom was first founded in Persia by the Achaemenid ruler Teispes; his great-grandson Cyrus II, making "alliance with Babylonian groups dissatisfied with the role of Nabonidus," took Babylon in 539 BCE and captured King Nabonidus (Wiesehöfer 2009: 70). In 525 BCE, Cambyses II forged alliances with Arab tribes, who helped him to cross the Sinai. A victory at Pelusium in 525 BCE opened up the route to Memphis for the Persians (Wiesehöfer 2009: 71). Egypt remained occupied until 403 BCE. After a crisis due to financial and political problems, Darius (521–486 BCE) developed an imperial organization that subsisted until the appearance of Alexander the Great in 331 BCE. It was founded on a system of provinces (satrapies),[65] in which the local elites often held executive functions, though the empire was primarily administered by

---

[64] The Elamite culture would nevertheless have a great impact on Persian culture. Elamite was still the language of administration in Fars during the fifth century BCE.

[65] Huyse 2005: 79. The satraps enjoyed broad autonomy, since they kept their own treasure and could raise troops. Royal inspectors, however, were charged with the task of monitoring the satraps (Briant 1996: 355). The "central" region (ideologically) of Persia was under the king's direct administration. All the satrapies paid annual tributes, in silver or gold, but "the Arabs, the Ethiopians, the Colchians and the Persians of

members of the great Persian aristocratic families.[66] "Institutional variety" was a characteristic feature of the empire (Wiesehöfer 2009: 85): its lack of unity was both an asset and a weakness. The Achaemenid Empire was probably the first universal empire, its universal dimension having been introduced by Cyrus II and symbolized by the construction of the palaces of Darius at Susa and Persepolis,[67] the multinational character of the Persian armies,[68] the religious tolerance of the emperors,[69] the eclecticism of Achaemenid art, and the use of Old Persian, Elamite, Neo-Babylonian, and Aramaic in inscriptions. There was no serious attempt to "Persianize" the subjects, in contrast to what the Assyrians had attempted. The deportation of populations existed, but was not as systematic as in the earlier empires. Relative tolerance and flexibility in the exercise of power explains the greater stability of the empire compared to its predecessors (Beaulieu 2005: 59–60). A unitary system of weights and measures, inherited from the Babylonian sexagesimal system with some adaptations, was imposed throughout the empire.[70] Darius moved between various capital cities: Susa, Persepolis, Pasargades, the older capital of Cyrus II, and Ecbatana. Particular attention was paid to agricultural progress. The Achaemenids promoted irrigation systems using underground channels (qanāt) in various regions of the empire.[71] Dams were built, and Herodotus describes systems of waterways. Management of irrigation channels was in principle a prerogative of the royal administration, which made the users pay for it. Taxes levied on agricultural products provided the major source of revenues of the empire (Huyse 2005: 95). The king leased out land to small farmers in exchange for services and taxes. Large domains were

Persid" were exempted from this payment (Huyse 2005: 86). Various taxes had to be paid. Some "satraps" were actually client-kings, whose power had been acknowledged by the Persians.

[66] Briant 1996: 362. In Babylonia, notes Joannès (2000: 146), "finances, the army and royal law were directly controlled by Persian administrators." Babylonian officials exerted power at a local level. R. J. van der Spek (2015) points out a relative decline of Babylonia, "much of the surpluses being now drained off to the Persian capitals."

[67] The building of the palace of Susa brought together artisans and materials from the whole empire. The foundation charter of the palace is a hymn to the world-empire (see above). "The text mentions sixteen populations and countries that provided raw materials (or a labor force); the skills of artisans from eight countries were used on the worksites" (Briant 1996: 184).

[68] Elite troops, however, were Persian. Darius formed a standing army, in which cavalry played an important role. Royal garrisons were settled throughout the empire, composed of soldiers of various origins.

[69] The emperors, however, used Avestan concepts for political purposes (Huyse 2005: 138). As for the Avestan corpus, see Huyse 2005: 167ff.

[70] The Persian system influenced the Athenian units and those of the Greek cities of Anatolia. For Wiesehöfer, however, "the Persians did not attempt to standardize weights and measures" (2009: 84).

[71] The technique is necessarily older, since it can be observed in the Garamantes culture (Libya) from the eighth century BCE onward (Pelling 2005). Magee (2005: 228), however, considers that it represents an independent Libyan invention. It is possible that a type of qanāt was developed in Bahrain during the Dilmunite period (Crawford 1998: 144, after Konishi 1994). In Oman, the system of irrigation, called falaj, consisted of draining groundwater aquifers from the mountains and transporting the groundwater to the foothills region through underground channels. This technique appears to go back to the period 1100–600 BCE, before the Achaemenid domination (Magee 1998: 52; 2005: 222). The first known example in Iran may go back to the eighth century BCE: Sargon II observed this technique at Ulhut, during its eighth campaign (Magee 1998). We cannot, however, exclude the possibility that this method was used in Iran prior to this date. The assemblage found in Oman for the beginning of the first millennium BCE has many parallels in the Iranian Iron Age. The reoccupation of sites such as Tepe Yahya around 800 BCE in southeastern Iran is worth noting (Magee 2005: 227).

granted to members of the elites. Moreover, lands were assigned to military officials, often foreigners, who in return provided soldiers and sometimes chariots, a system which "has some correspondences" in the Old Babylonian Empire.[72] From the fifth century onward, these lands were incorporated into the *hatru* system, which fulfilled territorial, administrative, and fiscal functions. The beneficiaries of land grants often "leased [the land] to 'entrepreneurs' who sublet [it] to tenants" (Wiesehöfer 2009: 80). During the fifth century, despite increased production, price inflation must have been caused by demographic growth and the expansion of exchanges (Joannès 2000: 152). "Capitalist" firms worked with the state, for example the "houses" of Egibi, until Darius's reign, and then Murashu, during the second half of the fifth century BCE, combining financial, commercial and agricultural activities.[73] Management of land and of some revenues by private "business houses" made possible a migration from taxes paid in kind into taxes paid in precious metal.[74] Documents mention agents of the Egibi at Ecbatana, Babylon, and Persepolis, where they bought slaves (Briant 1996: 452, 760). These financial operations and commercial transactions were the subject of contracts, in which the amount lent, lender, and rate of interest were specified.[75] By the fifth century, in Mesopotamia, "the prevailing interest rate on loans of both grain and silver was 40%" (Stevens 2006: 152), thus higher than it had been during the Neo-Babylonian period (note that prices for barley and dates were also high; see van der Spek 2006: 304).[76] Belshunu, who was at once governor of Babylon and a "businessman," provides a good example of how state power and the private sector overlapped. For transactions, people primarily used silver,

[72] Joannès 1995: 1482; 2000: 146–150. These families did not own the land but enjoyed the agricultural income. It was this system that the Muslim Empire would later borrow with the *iqtā'* system. Over time, the tendency was toward privatization of the land granted, with transmission of the domains by inheritance (Joannès 2000: 151). "The system of land grants in exchange for military services goes back at least to the end of the 3rd millennium in Mesopotamia" (Joannès 2000: 149). On military tenures, see also Briant 1996: 615. From Xerxes I onward, military service was often converted into a silver tax (519–465 BCE). The Persians would increasingly call on Greek mercenaries from Artaxerxes I (465–424 BCE).

[73] Yoffee 1995b: 1397. See also Joannès 1995: 1483–1484; 2000; Briant 1996: 605, 615, 618–619; Abraham 2004. Like the Egibi family in earlier times, the House of Murashu took advantage of its links with the Achaemenid power; it accumulated means of production, managed large domains, leased irrigation canals to the administration, collected taxes, and lent money at interest (Briant 1996: 501). Babylonian merchants were notably present at Susa, in Media, and in Syria (Briant 1996: 390).

[74] The Murashu paid rents to the owners of the land in silver and paid all the taxes owed to the crown in silver. See Briant 1996: 418, 618–619, 1005; Joannès 2000: 155, 158. "Thanks to the businessmen belonging to the urban gentry, who controlled the marketing channels, the administration ended up with a regular income in silver, without having to involve itself directly in the collection of taxes or the marketing of the products taxed" (Joannès 2000: 159).

[75] Joannès 1995: 1476–1477. This type of contract was already known in Hammurabi's time. The author notes that international trade, in Babylonia, was largely in the hands of non-Babylonians; most of the merchants had West Semitic names.

[76] Hackl and Pirngruber (2014: 115) note rates between 20 and 80 percent (471–177 BCE). Note that it is always round numbers that are involved: 20, 40, 60, 80 percent. "The tendency towards rising interest rates continues into the early Seleucid period during which rates of 40 per cent p.a. are attested quite frequently" (Hackl and Pirngruber 2014: 115).

which was weighed, as had been the case in Babylonia in the past.[77] However, Cyrus II and Cambyses II issued gold and silver coins in Anatolia that imitated "croesid" coins.[78] Darius and his followers minted new coins in Anatolia featuring the king as an archer: gold darics and silver *sigloi*. For Huyse, this coinage had "an ideological rather than an economic function" (2005: 104). *Sigloi*, however, were used for financing military operations, and the fact that the use of silver money became especially widespread in the empire under Darius seems to indicate the extent of commercial transactions.[79] Quantities of coins with the effigy of the Achaemenid kings have been discovered in India. Moreover, Greek coins were in circulation in Egypt from the sixth century onward.

The extension of the Achaemenid Empire reached its peak under Darius, with control of Cyrenaica, Thrace, and the Indus valley.[80] It also made a treaty with Athens in 507–506 BCE. After occupying pivotal regions between the Mediterranean Sea and the Indian Ocean as well as on the Asian continent, the empire tried to develop both terrestrial and maritime routes. The Persians appealed to the Phoenicians,[81] and also to the Greeks. Darius offered a Carian shipmaster, Scylax of Caryanda, the leadership of a maritime expedition that departed from the Indus and reached Arsinoe, in the Gulf of Suez, after a voyage lasting two and half years. Scylax wrote a report on his expedition, which was unfortunately lost. The above narrative is based on Herodotus. Panchenko (1998, 2003), however, argues that Scylax in fact traveled down the Ganges, and sailed to Taprobanē (Sri Lanka). A hieroglyphic inscription found at Suez attests that under Darius's reign, ships sailed from Egypt to Persia by circumnavigating Arabia. The Achaemenids did not really initiate commercial activities in the Red Sea – rather they "took advantage of existing systems"[82] – but Darius completed Nechao II's project for a canal between the Nile and the Red Sea

---

[77] See Joannès (2000: 152) for Babylonia. Tributes were presented in (weighed) silver. Farmers from Judah complained around 450 BCE that they had to mortgage their land to pay their dues (Briant 1996: 418). Different degrees of purity are attested for the Achaemenid period (Vargyas 2001: 14-15, 48-49).

[78] For some authors, it was Cyrus II and Cambyses II who in fact issued the first "croesid" coins (Le Rider 2001: 119-120).

[79] See Powell 1999: 21-22. However, under Darius the court's employees were paid in kind. "The tablets that have been unearthed provide information on 15,000 persons coming from one hundred different localities"; they have revealed the use of an elaborate "salary scale" (Huyse 2005: 107). In addition, the circulation of debt notes meant that people could avoid carrying silver (Bongenaar 1999: 163). For Vargyas (2001), who defends the idea of a mint not only at Sardis but also at Babylon, the *siglos* was widely used in the economy of the Persian Empire, but Le Rider (2001: 30-35, 139, 169-174) takes the opposite view. For this author, no silver *sigloi* were issued in Babylonia, where cut silver was still in use. However, excavations at Babylon have unearthed what could be a "reserve of monetary metal" ready for exchange, including seven Persian *sigloi*, a few Greek coins from the fourth century BCE, and pieces of silver (Le Rider 2001: 4). For Vargyas (2001: 25), the *sigloi* probably correspond to the expression *kaspu ginnu* ("*ginnu* silver") in Mesopotamian texts. We find the Sumerian GI.NA, "verification," inscribed on weights, as early as the third millennium (Vargyas 2004: 117).

[80] Darius was less successful in his attempt to invade Scythia in 513 BCE.

[81] Especially when they attempted to invade Greece. A Phoenician–Persian fleet was defeated by the Athenian navy in 480 BCE at Salamis. The Levantine ports benefited from the Persian expansion, especially Tyre and Sidon; Sidon, however, was partly burnt in the crackdown following its revolt in 345 BCE. The Phoenician merchants were intermediaries between the Mediterranean Sea and Babylonia.

[82] Herodotus (III.97), followed by Pliny (XII.80), says that the Arabs paid an annual tribute of 1,000 talents of incense to the Persian king.

(Herodotus, *Histories* II.158), perhaps in order to undermine the confederation of the kings of Qedar, with whom the Achaemenids, however, maintained a special relationship: during the fifth century BCE, Qedar had the upper hand in the caravan trade with Hijaz (see above; Lemaire 1987: 55, 56). The canal gave the Greek and Phoenician traders more direct access to the Red Sea. The entire Persian Gulf, on the Persian side as well as the Arabian side, was under Achaemenid control, a situation inherited from the Neo-Assyrian and Neo-Babylonian kings. The history of trade in the Achaemenid and Hellenistic period, notes J.-F. Salles, in fact goes back to the first half of the first millennium BCE (Salles 1996a: 252–253). The Achaemenid kings not only benefited from growing trade in the Persian Gulf, but successfully developed it still further. Darius founded the emporium of Aginis (Ampe) near Baṣrah, to which he deported the inhabitants of the Ionian city of Miletus, who had revolted.[83] Babylon continued to import steatite and copper from Makka (Oman), precious wood from Oman, the Makran coast and India (Meluhha, which was also the name of Nubia and/or Ethiopia at that time), "parrots, precious stones, pearls, spices" and aromatics,[84] as well as iron and steel.[85] Caravans carrying incense crossed Arabia to Gerrha (perhaps Thaj), but incense and myrrh also came from South Asia, along with other products.[86] When Alexander and his troops entered southern Baluchistan (Gedrosia), "they discovered myrrh trees higher than anywhere and the Phoenician mercenaries who accompanied him began to harvest myrrh" (Salles 1996a: 257). Indian beads were known in Greece during the fifth century BCE and pepper arrived in Athens during the fourth century BCE: black pepper (*Piper nigrum* L.) and long pepper (*Piper longum* L.) (Amigues 2005: 371). In addition, the bas-reliefs of the Apadana at Persepolis feature Indians bringing cotton, an import that the *Periplus of the Erythraean Sea* would later emphasize.

As J.-F. Salles points out, we do not know what cargoes the ships coming from the Persian Gulf carried to India. The *Periplus* would later mention slaves, textiles (embroidered fabrics), gold and silver plates, glass objects or vessels, raw glass, wine, dates, coral, and purple.

According to Herodotus, after the exploration of the Indus by Scylax, "Darius demanded the submission of the Indians and made use of their sea," a remark which seems to imply a kind of older Indian hegemony in the Arabian Sea. The contacts with India brought about the transmission of Babylonian knowledge, notably in astronomy

[83] Herodotus, *Histories* VI.20. Like their Assyrian and Babylonian predecessors, the Achaemenids practiced a policy of deportation of rebellious populations. Barkaeans were sent to Bactria; Carians and Beotians to Susiana (Briant 1996: 522, 779-780, who quotes Herodotus III.93).

[84] Salles 1996a: 256. Salles emphasizes that "there are no arguments to say that these products [mentioned in cuneiform texts] came from East Africa, although this region was also known under the name of Meluhha [as northwestern India]" (1996a: 256). Wood imported from Oman and the Makran coast probably came from India.

[85] Schoff 1974: 70-71. Ctesias mentions two marvelous steel swords from the court of the Persian king. A book by Zosimos of Panopolis (southern Egypt), who lived during the third century CE, describes the production of crucible steel. "The process," writes Zosimos, "was discovered by the Indians and exploited by the Persians," notably giving the famous "Damascus" steel blades (Craddock 2003: 243-244). Works by Zosimos were later quoted in Arabic texts.

[86] Incense is the product of various *Boswellia: B. sacra* Flueck. (found in Somalia, Yemen, and Oman) (oliban, *frankincense*), *B. serrata* Roxb. ex Colebr. (India) (*Indian frankincense*), and the African *Boswellia* already mentioned.

and astrology. The Persian presence in the satrapies of Kandahar, Charsadda (Pushkalāvati), and Taxila triggered the appearance of coins in the northern part of South Asia (Sinopoli 2006: 328).

The Persians already dominated Central Asia during the reign of Cyrus II, who, however, suffered a defeat in 530 BCE against the Massagetae (Alans, according to Ammianus Marcellinus), given as living east of the Caspian sea (Herodotus I.177, 201, 205–214). Darius repressed a revolt in Margiana in 522 and led a campaign against the Saka Tigrakhauda ("Saka with pointed hats") in 519–518 BCE. The Persian occupation of Afghanistan and northwest Pakistan shows the importance acquired by the terrestrial routes linking India and Central Asia. The Achaemenids controlled Taxila, in northern Pakistan, Bactria, and as far as the Syr-Darya: citadels were built in Bactres, the capital of Bactria, and Maracanda (Samarkand), in Sogdiana, where satraps were installed.

The emperors undertook the construction of roads, for example from Babylon to Ortospana, near Kabul, and the renowned "Royal Road" from Susa to Ephesus (2,400 km), by adopting Assyrian techniques including resting posts, landmarks, royal stores, and ferry services for crossing rivers. Vital for such a large empire, these routes permitted the transmission of royal messages with couriers and the swift transport of troops. Merchant caravans also used the roads, sometimes accompanied by armed men. In western Asia, the Aramaeans were particularly active; Aramaic became the administrative language of the empire and its trade language.[87] Moreover, around 460 BCE, parchment replaced clay tablets for administrative documents (the use of "parchment skin," which is not true parchment, is already attested in Egypt during the second millennium BCE) (Wissa 2006).

The Persian expansion into Anatolia and the Mediterranean led to a confrontation with the Greek world, marked by Persian defeats at Marathon, Salamis, Plataea, Mycale, and Eurymedon. For the Achaemenids, the threats came not only from the outside world, but also from the interior. The cost of the military buildup designed to maintain the cohesion of the empire triggered a decline in money supply, price inflation, and tax increases in its final years (Margueron and Pfirsch 2001: 349). In 486, then in 460, the Egyptians, supported by Athens, had already revolted against the Persians, who crushed the uprisings. A revolt in Babylon in 484 BCE was also put down. Egypt revolted again in 404 BCE and this time the Persians lost control of the country until 343 BCE. The Indus region became separated around 380 BCE. During the fourth century, centrifugal tendencies were visible throughout the Achaemenid Empire, with the so-called "satraps' revolt" between 366 and 360 BCE a series of disturbances that proved to be unrelated and less significant than what Diodorus would have us believe.[88] The gap was, however, growing between rich and poor. Artaxerxes III and Darius III tried to maintain order in the provinces, and it is not certain that the Persian Empire was truly in decline during the second half of the fourth

---

[87] The presence of Aramaean copyists was noted at the Assyrian court of Assurbanipal in 668 BCE. The use of Aramaic by the Achaemenids reflects how important this language had become. The inscriptions by the Indian emperor Ashoka at Kandahar and Taxila during the third century BCE were in Aramaic.

[88] See Weiskopf 1989 and Briant 1996: 675ff. Not much is currently known about the long reign of Artaxerxes II (405-359). Upheavals ("Cadusian Wars") did occur in Anatolia and Persia (Briant 1996: 374).

century (Briant 1996; Sartre 2001; Wiesehöfer 2009), although climatic deterioration between 400 and 350 BCE probably did shake its foundations. The irruption of Alexander's army into western Asia would in any case mark the sudden end of the empire. The weakness of central authority and the superiority of the Greek army explain the empire's sudden collapse following Persian defeats at Granicus (334 BCE), Issus (333 BCE), and finally Gaugamela (331 BCE).

Egypt, between Political Fragmentation and Foreign Dominance: An Independence under Threat

After the incursions of the "Sea Peoples," Egypt was in a weak position. With the political fragmentation of the country, the centers of power that asserted themselves during the New Kingdom – the clergy and the military sector – took on a leading role (Baines and Yoffee 1998: 224). The Twenty-Second Libyan Dynasty restored royal authority during the tenth century BCE and installed an active foreign policy by subjugating Palestine once again and developing links with Phoenicia. Phoenician merchants settled in the Nile delta. The practice of interest-bearing loans reported under Takeloth II's reign (844–819 BCE) attests to Egypt's socioeconomic transformations during this period, with a stronger monetization than in the preceding periods and a pronounced search for profit (Bleiberg 2002: 270), transformations that went hand in hand with the growing integration of this country into the transregional trade of the Mediterranean Sea. According to Diodorus of Sicily, the pharaoh Bakenranef (720–715 BCE) was forced to limit the amount of indebtedness and prohibit enslavement for debt, probably because farmers were potential soldiers (Hudson 2002: 37). It seems that between 950 and 700 BCE, Egypt benefited from stronger Nile flooding than in the previous period.[89] During the eighth century, however, it experienced a phase of political disintegration that facilitated the conquest of the valley by the kings of Kush, whose capital was at Napata, an interface zone between Egyptianized Nubia and more southerly regions; a Nubian dynasty reigned from 717 to 664 BCE. Criticisms made by Herodotus of Egyptian traditions concerning the Nile and the mountain of Punt show that the Egyptians knew that there were snowy mountains and a great lake at the sources of the Nile.[90] Contacts with the Horn of Africa and the Arab coasts led to the introduction of the dromedary at this time. Dromedary remains dated to the first half of the first millennium BCE have been discovered at Qasr Ibrim, in southern Egypt (Rowley-Conwy 1988, 1991). From Egypt, the dromedary spread to the Sahara (the ancient route between Nubia and Lake Chad should be mentioned here: it was probably used as early as the Egyptian New Kingdom). A Roman text mentions the dromedary in the African interior around 45 BCE (MacDonald 2000: 13).

Whereas during the third and second millennia, Egypt had never been conquered by an Asian power, it fell under the domination of the Assyrians in 671 and 664 BCE.

---

[89] Butzer 1995: 136. Manzo (1999: 4) also mentions high flooding around 1000 BCE (?) and 700 BCE.

[90] Herodotus rejects the idea that Nile flooding may have come from melting snow, or an inflow of water from a river called Ocean, which he considers fictional (II.20-23). Kitchen (2004: 28) does not exclude the possibility that the country known to the Egyptians as Punt included lands as far away as the East African coast.

Assurbanipal described the Nile valley as a constellation of cities ruled by "kings," referring to a decentralized state (which may also be an interpretation of Egypt in "Mesopotamian" terms). This period probably saw a decline in maritime trade in the Red Sea, alongside an increasingly prosperous Arab caravan trade.

Egypt then went through a period of revival under the Twenty-Sixth Saite Dynasty (663–525 BCE), after Psamtik I (663–609 BCE) reunified the country and rejected the Assyrian protectorate. It welcomed Greek, Lydian, Carian, and Syro-Palestinian contingents into its army. War chiefs received land in exchange for military services. The pharaoh re-established the ancient administrative system of nomes. Greeks settled in the emporion of Naucratis, which permitted exchanges between the Greek world and Egypt, an emporion controlled by the pharaoh.[91] As mentioned above, Psamtik I's successor, Nechao II, built a channel between the Red Sea and the Mediterranean, and launched a Phoenician expedition to circumnavigate Africa. These initiatives reflect flourishing trade in this period and the eminent position held by Egypt. Besides Greeks, other foreign communities were active: Herodotus later mentioned a Tyrian area at Memphis (during the Persian period), and graffiti show the presence of Cypriot merchants and mercenaries at Abydos (Fabre 2004: 161). Relations also developed with Carthage, where many Egyptian deities were mentioned, which is evidence for the settlement of Egyptians in that city (Fabre 2004: 160). A process of monetization is noticeable at this time. The country used silver bars and rings, worth 1 *deben* and 1 *kite* (one-tenth of a *deben*), respectively: "Silver was melted and weighed in the temples and marked with the name of a god, such as Harsaphes at Thebes, and Ptah at Memphis." "At Memphis, contracts for silver loans stipulated that the amount borrowed would be paid back in silver of the same provenance": here we are close to a minted currency.[92] Unlike F. Daumas and B. Menu, P. Vargyas (2004: 119) considers that silver issued by the temples was put into bags of standardized weights, without any imprint directly stamped on the metal. At least two discoveries reveal the use of sealed bags, notably that of the Elephantine treasure (eighth/seventh century BCE), wrapped in three bags of the same weight.[93] From the Saite period on, the merchant system was very similar to that of Classical Greece. During the mid-fifth century BCE, Herodotus found Greek merchants everywhere in Egypt. Athenian coins ("owls") were imitated as early as the beginning of the fourth century, initially for the payment of mercenaries. Moreover, gold coins with the hieroglyphs *nb nfr* and showing a prancing horse were minted

---

[91] The institution of the Naucratis enclave was established after ethnic conflicts broke out in the delta. The enclave hosted various Greek sanctuaries, built notably by the cities of Miletus, Samos, Chios, and Aegina (Fabre 2004: 161).

[92] Menu 2001a: 82. One reads in a papyrus from the British Museum (10113) dated to 568 BCE: "From you, I have received one *deben* of silver from the Treasury of Thebes . . . If I don't pay it back in the year XXI month of Choiak, it will begin to bear interest, at a rate of one-third of a *kite* for one *deben* of silver per month." Papyrus E 3228e from the Louvre, written at Thebes under King Chabaka, mentions the sales contract for a slave, ceded by the lady Tefiouiou to the choachyte Petoubastis. The latter acknowledges: "I have received from you the amount of 2 *deben* 2 1/2 *kite* [of silver] from the Treasury of Harsaphes." The sales contract for a slave dating to 688 BCE also involves silver from the Treasury of Harsaphes (Papyrus E 3228d from the Louvre) (Malinine 1953: 17, 37, 43).

[93] However, no sealings have been found on the bags. Vargyas emphasizes that out of 200 hoards buried at various times in the ancient Near East, a quarter have been unearthed in Egypt.

during the second half of the fourth century (Daumas 1977: 434); their weight (8.4 g) was only slightly below that of Daric coins and Attic staters (8.56 g). After a limited occupation of Palestine from 620, Egypt was engaged in confrontations with the expanding Neo-Babylonian Empire. Psamtik II (589–570 BCE) was probably responsible for the fall of Jerusalem, which he had encouraged to revolt against the Babylonians. Egypt, however, managed to protect its border east of the Nile delta.

Under Amasis (570–526 BCE), who was allied with Croesus and the tyrant of Samos (who provided soldiers), Egypt once again enjoyed growth, indirectly helped by the Persian expansion that threatened the Babylonian Empire. Cyprus came under the rule of Amasis, who owned a sizeable commercial fleet. Syria became a tributary region during this period, but under his successor, the country was unable to resist Cambyses's armies: Persia absorbed Egypt into its empire between 525 and 404 BCE.

The Persians turned the country into a satrapy and forged links with local elites. Temple revenues were cut off, and increasing taxes imposed on the population. Two major revolts burst out in 486 and 460–454 BCE, which were crushed by Persia. Taking advantage of the battles for succession in the Persian Empire at Darius II's death, a warrior chief from the delta named Amyrtaeus allowed Egypt to recover its independence; Egypt would remain independent under the Twenty-Eighth, Twenty-Ninth, and Thirtieth Dynasties.

During the period of independence from 404 to 343 BCE, the major historical figure was the pharaoh Nectanebo I (380–362 BCE). Many buildings were erected at that time, reflecting Egypt's economic wealth during his reign, despite Persian threats to the country. After several failed attempts in 380, 373, and 351, the Persians took control of Egypt again in 343 BCE; they ruled the Nile valley until the arrival of Alexander.

After Alexander's death, Egypt was ruled by the Ptolemies (see below) and later incorporated into the Roman Empire in 31 BCE. Successive invaders aimed to control the trade routes through Egypt, and also to take advantage of the "bread basket" of the Nile valley.

9   The Roads to the Orient

The Europeans in Asia and in Egypt

The Greeks in the Footsteps of Alexander the Great

> The sun never sets on my empire.
> (attributed to Alexander the Great)[1]

From 334 to 324 BCE, Alexander conquered Persian possessions as far as the Indus.

> The first to use this ingenious plan since Darius, Alexander built a universal empire by organizing transnational routes of economic importance around urban centers. In a few years, seventy Alexandrias had been created. Thus, the great roads of Central Asia were laid out for the future. But the main artery of the Empire was the sea, on whose coasts the largest centers would take shape. (Pirenne 1944, I: 201; Toussaint 1961: 29)

Alexandria was founded in Egypt in 331 BCE. In the region of Baṣra, Alexander built an Alexandria that would become Antiocheia and ultimately Spasinou Charax.[2] At the other end of the empire, another Alexandria was also founded in the Indus valley.[3] In Central Asia, four Alexandrias appeared, pointing to Bactria's importance as a hub of exchanges. In addition, according to the Greek historian Arrian (95–175 CE), Alexander organized various maritime expeditions. In 326 BCE, a fleet of 400 ships led by Nearchos departed from the Indus River; near Hormuz, Nearchos reached "a friendly country" and received the assistance of a pilot who spoke Greek, an episode suggesting that Greeks were present and had influence in the region prior to Alexander.[4] Nearchos finally arrived at Diridotis, in the Persian Gulf, in February 325 BCE, "where the merchants gather the incense produced by the neighboring region and the other aromatics of Arabia" (Briant 1996: 781). In 324/323 BCE, Alexander sent an expedition to Arabia (west coast) led by Anaxicrates.[5] During the same period, he built forty-five ships in Phoenicia whose parts were destined to be transported to Babylon for assembly. Nearchos was supposed to head this fleet in order to circumnavigate Arabia, but Alexander's death aborted the project.

---

[1] In fact, this "quote" has been well attested only as far back as the seventeenth century, for the Spanish Empire.

[2] Charax was located near Apologos. According to Schoff (1974: 149), it was at the confluence of the Karun and the Shatt el-Arab rivers.

[3] Northwestern India was in a state of great political fragmentation at that time, considering that the Greeks recorded as many as twenty-eight political entities in this region.

[4] Arrian VIII.27.1; Strabo XVI.3.7; Salles 1996a: 256.

[5] There were also the expeditions of Archias to Bahrain, of Androsthenes (also in the Persian Gulf), and of Hiero, who reached Cape Musandam.

The empire was divided. Antigonus I took control of Anatolia, and his son seized Macedonia. One of Alexander's lieutenants, Seleucus (Seleukos), founded the Seleucid dynasty in western Asia, and chose Antioch as its capital. Another Greek general, Ptolemy, founded the Ptolemaic dynasty in Egypt. Thus, the Red Sea and the Persian Gulf became competing international trade routes (see Map II.9).

The Seleucid Empire encouraged agricultural progress. The use of norias – wheels with buckets or pallets – to lift water, facilitated the spread of irrigation (norias were also in use in Egypt before the Roman era). In Mesopotamia, agriculture also benefited from "well organized canal building, sophisticated sowing systems and crop rotation" (van der Spek 2004: 304). Prices were largely driven by supply and demand. A corpus of price data has been retrieved from astronomical diaries from Babylon. These diaries probably served as a database for astrological research (Jursa 2010; Van der Spek and Van Leeuwen 2014).

The empire appears to have been centralized to some extent, with treasuries and royal warehouses, which does not mean that cities – notably the Greek cities – or regions were not autonomous; a conciliatory policy toward regional populations gave local rulers a relative amount of freedom within the system of satrapies. As had been the case previously, the temples played an important role in the economy and in local societies – at least this was the case in Mesopotamia (Joannès 2000: 160). Archives found at Babylon show that businessmen were integrated into the structure of the temples, but at the same time they conducted their own private affairs.[6] It is worth noting that the zero appeared in Mesopotamia during the third century BCE.[7] The empire "was standing at the junction of two traditions: the administrative and financial model of the Greek cities and the royal model, whether it be in this case the Macedonian or the eastern model." For some historians, the Seleucid state, just like the Achaemenid state, was first of all a collector of tribute. It might be described as a hoarder and a redistributer, corresponding to P. Briant's so-called "tributary mode of production" (Briant 1994; Chankowski 2004). Other authors present a different model, one based on money. Chankowski (2004: 13) writes:

Unlike the Ptolemies, the Seleucids did not consider their coinage to be the only legal currency of their kingdom. Non-Seleucid coins could freely circulate, and the state did not collect fees for the exchange. Moreover, the Seleucid currency seems to have represented only a limited part of the money supply in circulation . . . According to G. Le Rider, this absence of state control on the imports of money, which was also the Achaemenid approach, . . . must correspond to a certain idea of economic and financial activity. This interpretation prompts one to question the significance of royal coinage: was it made for specific state functions (fiscality, army)?[8]

---

[6] See the archives of Murānu (277–253 BCE), and those of Rāhimēsu during the Parthian period (94–93 BCE) (Joannès 2000: 173).

[7] Though it was not yet a number used in calculation, the zero marked an empty space in the sexagesimal positional numeral system (in China, too, around the fourth century BCE [Needham and Wang Ling 1959: 146], the zero was "a vacant position" within a decimal system; however, its invention may well have been an independent phenomenon). The Mesopotamians used a positional numeral system, inherited from the Sumerian world (it was attested in the Old Babylonian period): the value of the symbol varied according to its location within a given numeral. The sexagesimal system has been inherited by the modern world for the division of time (one minute: 60 seconds) and it is still used to measure angles.

[8] See also Le Rider 1997. Money issued by the Seleucids benefited from an added value in comparison with other currencies, as was the case for the "Alexander coins," whose exchange value was higher than their

Indeed, the Seleucids went on to place great importance on the army. They continued the Achaemenid system of military colonies; land was granted in exchange for military service. The empire multiplied military posts for the protection of territories originally stretching from the Indus valley and from Bactria to the Mediterranean Sea. With the influx of migrants from Europe, these posts sometimes became Greek cities. The military expenses for them very quickly rose to astronomical proportions: they have been estimated at 6,000 talents during the fourth century BCE based on a total income somewhere between 10,000 and 15,000 talents. The Seleucid state paid its personnel in cash (unlike the Achaemenid state) and the economy became increasingly monetized (Aperghis 2004; van der Spek 2004). Taxes were paid in cash or in kind.[9] The Seleucid Empire had been thought to experience a silver shortage after the defeat of 190, but the impact of the treaty of Apamea imposed by Rome (see below) is now minimized by some researchers.[10] Coinage increased under Antiochus IV (185–164 BCE) and Antiochus V (164–162 BCE) in an attempt to cover war expenses. The Parthian king Mithridates I seized 10,000 talents from the treasures of Elymais in 140 BCE. However, a reduction in the weight of the royal tetradrachms can be observed under Antiochus IV, and a deflation in Babylonia *c.* 188 BCE.[11] The quantity of minted silver diminished during periods of recession, for example during the second half of the second century and at the beginning of the first century BCE.[12] Moreover, Le Rider and de Callatay (2006: 126) note that "the silver minted was not the most important element in trade."

While the Mediterranean littoral very quickly became a disputed region between the two empires – who fought no fewer than four "Syrian wars" – the Seleucids tried to consolidate their positions in the east, with mixed success. Alexander viewed the Persian Gulf as "a potentially new Phoenicia": Arrian's words have often been cited "to underline the active policy of the Seleucids" in the region (Salles 1996a: 260), who in fact were following the same path as the Persians. The Seleucids thus created a "Satrapy of the Eritrean Sea" near the Shatt el-Arab river, and founded a new capital in the Tigris valley, the city of Seleucia, which became a veritable storehouse of oriental products. The Seleucids attempted to control trade with India from Failaka and Bahrain (Potts 1990, II). Seleucus I Nicator became embroiled in a conflict with the Maurya Empire: the

intrinsic value (Le Rider and de Callatay 2006: 114–116, 118). One can question, adds V. Chankowski, "the relationship between monetary issues and price movements. If we accept the possibility that the Seleucids were liberal in their monetary policy, this policy may have induced inflation due to the absence of control on the monetary mass in circulation. But conversely, in a time of silver shortage, did the Seleucid state adopt a more interventionist policy to ensure some stability by using its regional [minting] workshops?" (2004: 14). The two models suggested (intervention of the state, and "liberalism" on a monetary level) are not necessarily incompatible. In addition, "while taking into account its Achaemenid legacy, the Seleucid Empire certainly must have used Greek knowledge . . . The notions of partnership and financial networks may help to shed light on the functioning of the [Seleucid] system" (Chankowski 2004: 15).

[9] Le Rider and de Callatay 2006: 264–266. On the contrary, Aperghis (2004) believes that the taxes were paid in cash.

[10] Le Rider and de Callatay 2006: 202–203. The Romans seized a large quantity of coins after their victory in 189 BCE, and imposed an exorbitant tribute.

[11] In contrast, prices rose after the capture of Babylon by the Parthians (Le Rider and de Callatay 2006: 229). Antiochus IV tried to seize the temples' treasures (Grainger 1993: 116–117).

[12] Epidemics have been reported for 144, 108, 106, and 94 BCE (van der Spek 2006: 296).

conflict ended in 302 BCE with a peace treaty stating that the Seleucids would leave the Indus valley, Gandhara, and Arachosia to the Indian king Chandragupta, and that Seleucus could keep Bactria. This policy was ultimately successful, and in 288/287 BCE Seleucus was able to present the Apollo temple at Didyma with "ten talents of incense, one talent of myrrh, two minae of cassia, two minae of cinnamon, and two minae of *costus*."[13] In addition, Chandragupta sent him 500 war elephants, probably via Bactria. Cassia, cinnamon, and *costus* evidently came from India, or from more distant lands. Ivory was also a coveted product; after their triumph at Magnesia, the Romans seized 1,231 elephant tusks. There was a visible flow of oriental products into the Greek world at this time. Textiles remained a significant export product for Mesopotamia.

However, Arab sailors were fierce competitors for the Seleucids. The Gerrheans, in particular, who controlled the caravan trade to Petra and to Babylon, would also travel to Oman and probably to India to acquire Asian products; they acted as intermediaries for the Seleucids as well as the Ptolemies. Various authors have underlined their significant role in exchange and their wealth. "No people," wrote Agatharchides, "seems to be wealthier than the Sabaeans and the Gerrheans, who profit from [or 'act as the warehouse for'] everything from Asia and Europe, and who have made Ptolemy's Syria rich in gold, procuring markets for the Phoenicians [or 'the Phoenicians procuring markets for them']."[14] Moving up the Euphrates valley, the Gerrheans brought commodities that were conveyed to Babylon. The Seleucids established a military garrison on Failaka, where a naval force was stationed. Pliny reports that Antiochus III in 205, and Antiochus IV in 165 BCE, launched expeditions against Gerrha, to force the city to direct its trade toward the Seleucid Empire rather than toward the Ptolemies.[15] Greeks were involved in trade at this time; a Greek community settled at Bushire, on the Persian coast, and Greek graffiti have been discovered at Qala'at al-Bahrain; we know that some of the inhabitants of Bahrain spoke Greek. Greek artifacts have been unearthed at Thaj (eastern Arabia) and at Mleiha (United Arab Emirates). A Greek presence is also attested at ed-Dur (United Arab Emirates) and at Bidya (at the mouth of the Gulf) (Salles 1993: 501). Moreover, there were successive Greek ambassadors at the court of the Maurya kings: Megasthenes (sent by Seleucus I to Chandragupta's court), and Deimachus (an envoy of Antiochus I to

---

[13] Salles 1996a: 260. The term *costus* derives from the Sanskrit *kushṭha*, Aramaic *qushṭā*, and refers to a product made using the root of *Saussurea costus* [Falc.] Lipsch., Asteraceae family, a plant originating from Kashmir and Punjāb. In English, it is called *putchuk*, from the Malay *puchok*. "Dioscorides distinguished three varieties: the best was the 'Arabian', next was the 'Indian', and thirdly the 'Syrian'" (Miller 1998: 85). As Parker (2002: 43) points out, however, the identifications proposed by Miller probably point erroneously toward a single botanic species.

[14] Agatharchides, quoted by Photius (250.102) (Salles 1996a: 261; Crone 2004: 38). Gerrha began to trade with Petra during the second century BCE (according to Agatharchides). "They sail between Somalia and South Arabia using large rafts" (?) (*On the Erythraean Sea*, Book V, 103a, quoted by Ray 2003: 175). On Gerrha and the activities of the Gerrheans, see Strabo XVI.3.3, who quotes Eratosthenes and Aristobulus: the author claims that the city was inhabited by Chaldeans who came from Babylon (perhaps *c.* 700 BCE). Gerrha probably corresponds to the site of Thaj. Gerrha's port was at al-Jubayl. The city flourished from the end of the fourth century BCE until the first century CE, after which it went into recession following the rise of both maritime routes and the port of Spasinou Charax.

[15] According to Polybius (XIII.9.5), the Gerrheans gave Antiochus III 1,000 talents of incense and 200 talents of liquid myrrh (Salles 1996a: 260).

King Bindusāra [297–272 BCE]). Maritime exchange led to the growth in the port of Antioch in the Characene region during the second century BCE, and to the near-autonomous development of southern Mesopotamia (Joannès 2000: 171). The minting of a large number of bronze coins under Antiochus IV at Susa reflects the desire to promote trade in the Persian Gulf at this time. It has long been recognized that most of the Greek terms related to Indian traded products are of Sanskrit or of Tamil origin: precious stones, spices and aromatics, sugar, rice, and so forth. In the opposite direction, some Greek terms entered the Sanskrit language, for example names of coins, and words pertaining to mathematics and warfare (some of these terms were borrowed from the Latin, via the Greek, therefore during Roman times) (Basham 1967: 230).

Greek amphorae and other Mediterranean ceramics were present in southeastern India (Arikamedu ...) as of the second century BCE at the least (see below). These contacts between southeast India and the Greek world do not necessarily imply that Greek sailors or merchants themselves brought merchandise, but Greeks and Romans were certainly present in India and perhaps even further east. It has been suggested that the Maurya alliance with the Seleucids may have played a role in the rise of Arikamedu; however, some Greek ceramics were probably imported from the Red Sea. Moreover, "Arikamedu looked east far more than it looked west":[16] it was the importance of the eastern trade, as much as the wealth of western India, that attracted the Romans to the Malabar coast.

Greek influences also entered India via Bactria, at that time under Seleucid administration.[17] The city of Bactres expanded, and a new capital was created at Ai Khanum. In 240 BCE, Diodotus, a satrap of Bactria and Sogdiana, rebelled against Seleucid rule and founded a Greco-Bactrian kingdom that extended into northern India after the collapse of the Mauryan Empire. Discoveries in Buddhist sanctuaries show that "Greeks actively participated in the enshrinement of Buddhist relics and worship of the Vasudeva cult" (Ray 2003: 181).[18] Silk probably arrived as early as the third century BCE on the roads of Central Asia. According to Apollodorus of Artemita (writing in 87 BCE), the king of Bactria, Euthydemus (successor to Diodotus), carried out a series of successful campaigns that allowed him to extend his empire as far as the country of the Seres (China), in 220 BCE.[19] He then became vassal to the Seleucid Antiochus III who, writes Florus (first century CE), "erected in Euboea tents of cloth of

---

[16] Frank 1993a: 400. In addition, Arikamedu was settled along the Ariyankuppam River. O. Bopearachchi (2002: 95) rightly emphasizes that the main ports of South India and Sri Lanka were located at river estuaries, facilitating "transactions with the interior regions."

[17] Note that Ashoka erected a stela with a bilingual inscription in Greek and Aramaic near Kandahar in 248 BCE.

[18] See the finds at Taxila (third–second centuries BCE) and Sirkap (first century BCE – first century CE). Written during the first millennium CE (possibly fourth century), "the *Visnu Purāna* refers to the Yavanas as living in the west of the country" (Ray 2003: 181). Under the Maurya, as well as during later periods, Yavanas were sometimes in charge of provinces, for example in Gujarat and the Konkan (Ray 2003: 181–182).

[19] A large number of silver and bronze coins featuring the effigy of this king have been discovered in Afghanistan, reflecting the extent of his power. His successors, during the second century BCE, issued bilingual coins (Greek/Prākrit), written in Brāhmī and later in Kharoṣṭī script (Ray 2003: 186). The metal (copper-nickel alloy) used to mint the coins of Euthydemus's successors may have come from Yunnan (Adshead 1995: 24).

gold and silk" during a military campaign in Greece in 190 BCE.[20] Apollodorus was the first to use the term "Seres," in reference to communities linked with the silk trade. The Greek *serikos* (*ser/ikos*), "silk," is related to the Mongol *sirkek*, and the Chinese *si*, "silk."[21]

Based on archaeological finds, it had been claimed that silk was transported to Europe and Egypt during the early first millennium BCE; however, this theory has recently been refuted. Though silk threads, possibly of Chinese origin (absence of sericin), have purportedly been found in the hair of a female Egyptian mummy dated to *c.* 1000 BCE (Lubec *et al.* 1993), this discovery has yet to be confirmed. Silk unearthed in Greek tombs dated to the fifth century BCE appears to have been of Mediterranean – and not Chinese – origin.[22]

Vanquished by the Romans at Magnesia, the Seleucids were forced to accept the peace treaty of Apamea in 188 BCE. Antiochus III had to abandon Anatolia and pay considerable war compensation to Rome (15,000 talents of silver). This indemnity would in consequence increase the burden of taxes on the provinces of the empire, which appeared to be in decline during this period. During the Sixth Syrian War, Antiochus IV (175–163 BCE) managed to take control of Egypt, but at the request of a Roman embassy had to leave Egypt and Cyprus. Soon afterward, the Parthian expansion brought about the demise of the empire at last. However, the Seleucids continued to control Syria until 68 BCE. The Parthians would dominate western Asia until the third century CE. As Salles notes, "the failure of the Seleucids was not so complete, since the Characenians were able to take over the trading system in the Persian gulf by the beginning of the first century BC" (1996a: 260).

Bordering the Seleucids, the Ptolemies (or Lagids) formed a rival power, centered on Egypt, and built an empire that would remain in place until the Roman conquest in 30 BCE. They introduced a system of radial irrigation, and Greek colonists came to settle in the Nile valley. Durum wheat (*Triticum durum*) cultivation was encouraged (Decker 2009: 193). The economic system stands out as compared with earlier periods. Farmers often had to pay a fixed amount rather than a share (often one-third) of the harvest as had been the case before (the system was therefore an incentive to maximize production) (Manning 2003: 199). Rotations alternating cereals and pulses were also practiced.[23] The gradual spread of the waterwheel during the Late Ptolemaic period and the Roman Empire facilitated the irrigation of new lands with the creation of

---

[20] Boulnois 2001: 18. The Greco-Bactrian kingdom maintained its unity until 130 CE, when it gave way to the Kushan Empire. The "Greek" elites of this kingdom probably fled southward into the Indo-Greek kingdoms.

[21] Cf. also the Korean *sir*. The name "Seres" was later applied to various populations of Asia and even of southern Arabia; see below. In Latin texts, "Seres" appears for the first time in Virgil's *Georgics* in 29 BCE. The two categories of Seres distinguished by an author like Pausanias clearly correspond to the terrestrial and maritime "silk roads."

[22] I. Good, p.c.; Boulnois 2001: 22 (according to Lubec *et al.* 1993, a discovery in the cemetery of the king's workers at Thebes), 23. See above.

[23] This agricultural technique in Egypt appeared well before the Hellenistic period. It was transmitted to the Greek world and then to the Roman world, before being practiced in the Byzantine and Arab empires (Mazoyer and Roudart 1998: 318). Thanks to biannual crop rotation, cultivated grasslands were developed, alternating with cereal cultivation, thus bringing about an advancement in animal husbandry (G. Gal 2004, www.univ-tlse2.fr/multimedia/bazthal/thales/concours/Thales2.htm).

vineyards and orchards. For the first time in the history of Egypt, several harvests per year were possible on some lands. In exchange for grain exported to Greece and Anatolia, the state acquired slaves and silver. This metal was used to pay sailors, soldiers, and mercenaries, whence the need for a positive trade balance and efforts to promote agriculture: a kind of mercantilist system was in place as of Ptolemy II (Hölbl 2001: 28). Large estates were owned by temples or individuals.[24] Private landed property, which had already existed before the Lagids, was increasing; however, its importance is difficult to measure – in any case, it was far from being the dominant form of landownership, and the land market remained limited (Manning 2003: 193, 233). Like the pharaohs – who had already been doing so during the New Kingdom – the Lagids settled soldiers – Greco-Macedonians, and later Egyptians – on lands, as klerouchs: in exchange for these land grants, they had to provide military service[25] (the institution also aimed to promote the development of new land through irrigation). Soldiers and bureaucracy formed the basis of Lagid power; conversely, temples, as institutions, were in decline at this time, even before the Roman period (Manning 2003: 237).

Even more so than in the Seleucid state, the bureaucratization of the Ptolemaic Empire was accompanied by heavier taxes and requisitions, with the organization of so-called "liturgies." As much as half of each farmer's harvest was absorbed by tax charges.[26] The state played an important role in craft production and trade – it instituted absolute monopolies over oil, beer, natron, salt, and the importation and exportation of aromatics, as well as partial monopolies over flax, papyrus, and other products (Bogaert 1998–1999: 77ff.). However, there was also an active private sector, which paid taxes to the rulers. Private merchants and ships transported most of the grain. At the end of the first millennium BCE, associations or "corporations" of traders appeared, often formed around a shared ethnic basis (groups of this kind, "usually composed of sea peoples from abroad," "simultaneously professional, religious and cultural," had developed earlier in the Greek world of the eastern Mediterranean Sea) (Fabre 2004: 171). Money was limited to the payment of salaries for mercenaries and to trade with the Greek or the Achaemenid worlds, but its use would expand during the Ptolemaic period.[27] From 300 BCE, the Ptolemies issued large quantities of silver coins, different from the Attic standard; like the Greek cities, they forbade the use of any foreign currency on their territory. This forced the merchants to carry out transactions which allowed the Ptolemies to impose an onerous tax of 17 percent on them. In addition, Ptolemy I chose to overvalue his gold staters.[28] The Ptolemies also issued bronze coins. At the same time, the administration ensured the stability of wheat prices. Royal banks were set up in twenty-two cities. They acted both as state coffers,

[24] Warburton (2000a: 93–94) points out that this new situation reflected the repercussions of policies implemented at the end of the Ramesside period.

[25] "Originally, a kleroukhia was only valid for a lifetime, but it would later become hereditary at the same time as military service" (Gal 2004; see n. 23 above).

[26] Préaux 2002: 371. The sale of standing crops was also practiced.

[27] Valbelle 2005: 732. One notes the development of minting, notably under Ptolemy II (Le Rider and de Callatay 2006: 229). Taxes on salt and oil products were paid in cash; conversely, land taxes were paid in kind.

[28] Le Rider and de Callatay 2006: 112–113, 141, 144, 146–148, 153.

which collected taxes and the revenues from monopolies,[29] and as organisms of control. In addition to these royal banks, there were leased banks and private banks, which carried out exchange operations, received deposits, and lent money with interest. The banks also traded for their clients. Various documents reveal the existence of payment orders that might be defined as "checks."[30] Before Alexander, there were no banks in Egypt; "the first banks were certainly private establishments operated by Greek immigrants."[31] During the second century BCE, "almost all classes [farmers excepted] used private banks for their payments" (Bogaert 1998–1999: 138).[32]

The state controlled or supervised agricultural and mine production (in the Sinai for example), and it also played an important role in the economy through a policy of major building projects, following the Pharaonic tradition. Moreover, the Greek rulers decided to sponsor scientific research by founding the Museum and the Library of Alexandria (280 BCE). This state support would continue until the fifth century. Paid by the state, scholars enjoyed genuine freedom of thought, and freedom in their research. Another great library existed in the Greek world at Pergamon (Ionia). At Athens, the Academy founded by Plato and the Lyceum of Aristotle also acquired official status. Alexandria developed abstract mathematics, with Euclid (third century BCE) representing one of the prominent figures in this domain.[33] Alexandria was also famous for its mechanics school, primarily represented by a mathematician and an engineer, Ctesibius (third century BCE), and Hero (second or first century BCE). The latter invented or perfected various hydraulic devices such as clepsydras and pressure pumps, war machines, and automata, using systems of cams, gear trains, endless screws, pulleys, and even steam.[34] The Syracusan Archimedes (c. 287–212 BCE)

---

[29] The state leased out tax collection for the profit of private entrepreneurs, but the collectors were civil servants. Among other state revenues were income from real estate (leased lands, sale of royal properties, sale of sacerdotal offices), the proceeds from the sale of slaves by the king, the income of royal fisheries, and so forth (Bogaert 1998–1999: 90). The royal banks covered the expenses of the state; they also lent money to notables and kleroukhs, apparently without interest (Bogaert 1998–1999: 111).

[30] "The check as it is known today [however] is not attested under the Ptolemies untill the 1st century BC" (Le Rider and de Callatay 2006: 212).

[31] Bogaert, 1998–1999: 131. As for temples, their coffers "received much silver through the collection of taxes, operating grants, and the purchase of offices by priests, but the sanctuaries did not conduct banking activities to make their assets grow": the deposits accepted by the sanctuaries do not appear to have been used for loans (Chankowski 2004: 10).

[32] The number of private banks, however, was limited: they were only present in five large cities. For Bogaert, these checks of the Lagid period were the first known in history (1998–1999: 136–137, 141) (as pointed out above, however, payment orders already appeared in the Assyrian world during the early second millennium BCE, and credit notes were used in Babylonia during the first millennium BCE). There is no evidence of deposits bearing interest. For loans, interest was legally limited to 24 percent (1998–1999: 144). There were also private accounts in state banks (1998–1999: 113–115).

[33] The director of the Library of Alexandria, Eratosthenes (c. 276–194 BCE) was another major figure. An astronomer and mathematician, he gave the first estimate of the earth's circumference.

[34] The aeolipile was a reaction steam turbine (Jacomy 1990: 83). There were automatic door-opening systems in temples. Many devices described in Hero's treatises were borrowed from Ctesibius and Philo of Byzantium (c. 200 BCE), but Hero also invented new mechanisms. From Ctesibius to Hero, progress was made not so much in terms of the originality of the mechanisms, but rather in terms of the scientific approach developed (Jacomy 1990: 80). In the armaments sector, Hero invented the chirobalist (a kind of crossbow) (Jacomy 1990: 86). McClellan and Dorn (1999: 86) have overemphasized the fact that at

prolonged Euclid's research in mathematics, and pioneered innovations in various theoretical or practical fields (he wrote the first scientific treatise on statics, and invented or perfected war machines).[35] From the fourth to the second century BCE, the arms race was clearly a stimulus for technical research. Alexander made great use of "neuro-ballistic artillery to conquer his empire" (Jacomy 1990: 84).

Alexandria became a sizeable cultural and commercial city. By engaging in ship-building, the Egyptian rulers promoted the growth of maritime trade not only in the Mediterranean, but also in the Red Sea (toward the Indian Ocean), to the detriment of the Arab caravan trade (see below).[36] Egypt was in close contact with Carthage under Ptolemy II and after.[37] It annexed Cyrene (Libya), occupied Cyprus and the Phoenician cities during the third century BCE, and increased its presence in southern Anatolia. New ports were founded, for example Ptolemais Theron, near Aqiq, Philotera, at the mouth of the Wadī Gawāsīs; Berenike (Berenice) (Ras Banas); Ampelone, north of Jeddah, built under Ptolemy II, and Adulis, founded by Ptolemy III.[38] The Ptolemies began to fight the Nabataean "pirates" and forged alliances with the Minaeans of the region of al-Ula.[39] Although the state did not become directly involved in trade, it contributed to its development through various interventions. The routes passing from the Red Sea to the Mediterranean were protected and maintained. Merchandise could be transported from Berenice and onward from Myos Hormos (Quseir al-Qadim), as far as Koptos on the Nile; from there, one could sail down the river to Alexandria. Other ports were in use on the Red Sea coast, but "discussions on the location of the arguably most important of these ports, Ptolemais Theron, still rely on literary evidence" (Bukharin 2011; Seland 2014). Eunuchs and ivory are said to have been subject to taxation in this town. The canal of Darius between the Nile and the Red Sea appears to have been re-dug by Ptolemy II Philadelphus (285–246 BCE) and may have been in use for a span of 200 years before becoming silted up. In 275 BCE, the Egyptian state led an expedition into Nubia to take control of the gold mines of the Wādi Allaqi. Cosmas Indicopleustes copied the (Greek) text of a stela erected at Adulis by Ptolemy III Euergetes (246–221 BCE): this text referred to a military campaign led by this king into Asia and mentioned the occupation of Adulis and the significance of this port. The expeditions in the Red Sea were aimed notably at capturing or otherwise acquiring elephants, needed by the

---

Alexandria (and in the Greek world generally speaking), "the study of mechanics was, like its kindred sciences, almost completely detached from the wider world of technology."

[35] Hero is reputed to have invented the endless screw (the so-called "Archimedes screw"), but it was perhaps already known in the Greek world (Jacomy 1990: 76).

[36] Ptolemy Soter (305–285 BCE) sent ships under the command of Philo to explore the Red Sea. Around the middle of the third century BCE, a text by Eratosthenes of Cyrene describes this sea. The text of Agatharchides of Knidos, around 150 BCE (*On the Erythraean Sea*), explores its coasts (his sources are in fact "in the previous century") (Phillips 1997: 448).

[37] Egypt remained neutral during the first Punic War (264–241 BCE). In 273 BCE, envoys had been exchanged with Rome.

[38] Wind conditions partly explain the creation of ports such as Berenice and Myos Hormos (Quseir), located relatively far south along the coastline (Facey 2004: 11).

[39] The Nabataeans were in fact caught between the Seleucids and the Lagids.

army (the Seleucids obtained their elephants from Asia).[40] These expeditions also helped to strengthen connections with more distant networks. In his inscription, Ptolemy III boasted of sending a fleet and land forces to Arabia and of succeeding in subduing "the whole coast from Leucē Cōmē to the country of the Sabaeans." Agatharchides (second century BCE) writes this of trade between India and Egypt: the Egyptians used to go to Aden and Muza, and would exchange their products for merchandise sold by the Indian merchants from the Indus region. Texts mention spices and aromatics (incense, myrrh), ivory, elephants, turtleshell, gold, and precious stones.[41] Chicken bones in Egypt appear to go back to 330 BCE.[42] According to Pliny, Ptolemy II sent an ambassador to the court of a Mauryan king (possibly Ashoka), and he also received an Indian embassy. The six wars waged against the Seleucids during the third and second centuries BCE for control over the Levant probably prompted the Ptolemies to secure the routes of the Red Sea. The important role of the state under the Ptolemies has already been outlined earlier in this book; however, a private sector was active, and owed taxes to the rulers. Trade, notes Casson (1989: 36), was partly "in the hands of private individuals, but the spices and aromatics they brought back became crown property, purchased at rates fixed by the government."

While it is unlikely that Egyptians and Greeks often ventured beyond the entry of the Red Sea prior to the second century BCE, expeditions were certainly launched to India and the East African coast.[43] A Greek garrison was present at Adulis, and Greeks settled on Socotra. Ptolemaic coins have been excavated in India (Tchernia 1997: 261). At the end of the second century BCE, at the same time as the Parthian Empire was emerging and had partly cut off direct access between the Hellenistic world and the Indian Ocean – by controlling the Persian Gulf – the Greeks "discovered" the direct maritime route between East Africa and India, by making use of the monsoons (myth of Hippalos/Hippalus, which was the name for the southwest wind [Mazzarino 1997]), a route already used by Arab and Indian ships.[44] The lateen sail characteristic of Arab ships may have already been in use during the first millennium BCE in the Persian Gulf and the western Indian Ocean.

[40] Elephant tusks have been recovered from Berenice. According to some scholars, the Ptolemies appear to have employed mahouts from India, but evidence for this is still missing.

[41] Salles 1996a: 259. Arabs also traveled to Egypt: a text dated to 125/124 BCE engraved on the wooden sarcophagus of a Minaean at Saqqara indicates that he had "provided the temples of the Egyptian gods with myrrh and calamus oils" (Robin 1997a: 42).

[42] MacDonald 1993: 587; Chami 2002. The chicken was perhaps already present at the time of Thutmose III (see above). The presence of the chicken in other parts of Africa is attested for a more recent period. "While some chickens may have first entered Africa overland, moving up the Nile from Egypt to Nubia, historical linguistic data suggest perhaps three separate introductions, including two from the north across the Sahara, and one from the Indian Ocean and the east coast of Africa (Williamson 2000)" (Fuller *et al.* 2011: 551). Chicken remains have been unearthed at Qasr Ibrim in Sudanese Nubia dated to the fifth–sixth centuries CE, and slightly later in East Africa (see below). Remains of chicken are also attested at Sanga (Congo Kinshasa) around the tenth century, and at Jenne-Jeno (Mali), *c.* 900 CE (a seventh–eighth-century dating has been proposed at Tegdaoust, but the identification of the bones is dubious) (MacDonald and MacDonald 2000: 142).

[43] See the discovery at Mafia of shards similar to ceramics from southern Egypt (dated to *c.* sixth century BCE), and Persian activities in Egypt under Darius's reign.

[44] Pliny (VI.100–101) indicates that a westerly wind had the native name of Hypalus; it was used to sail from Arabia to Patala (Sind) (De Romanis 1997: 85).

Agatharchides refers to Socotra as a stopping point for maritime travelers between India and Arabia. Diodorus, quoting Agatharchides, wrote: "The merchants from all parts resort to these islands, especially from Potana [Patala, "founded" by Alexander the Great not too far from the mouth of the Indus River]." In addition, "ships from Persia, Carmania [Kerman, eastern Persia] and from this whole region" also came to Socotra. The names Socotra and Dioscuridēs (in the *Periplus of the Erythraean Sea*) derive from the Sanskrit *Dvīpa Sukhādāra*, "Island Abode of Bliss."[45] According to Strabo, Eudoxus of Cyzicus sailed to India in 119 BCE, guided by an Indian he met on the coast of the Red Sea.[46] It is possible, however, that Arabs and Indians sailed instead with the northeast winter monsoon, from October to April, whereas the Greeks may have also used the southwest summer monsoon from June to September to sail from Africa to India.[47] In 78 BCE, the *epistrategos* of Thebaid was in charge of the Red Sea and the Indian Sea. The "discovery" of the monsoon appears to coincide with an increase in tonnage of ships: "For the first time in the history of west–east navigation, the Indian Ocean received its true dimensions" (Salles 1996a: 252).[48]

Despite a victory over the Seleucids in the Fourth Syrian War (217 BCE), won by Ptolemy IV, Lagid rule was evidently in some difficulty after 200 BCE, marked by money devaluation, and an increase in debt and taxes, which led to social unrest. Copper money experienced a gradual depreciation, which, according to G. Le Rider and F. de Callatay, cannot be accounted for by a lack of silver. Egyptian commerce, however, was in decline during the second and first centuries BCE, although Strabo estimates the income of Egypt at 11,500 talents under Ptolemy VI in the first century BCE; this amount can be compared to the sum given by Diodorus for the Seleucids during the fourth century BCE.[49] The decline of Egypt made it possible for the southern Arabs to dominate trade in the Red Sea and along the African coasts. The *Periplus of*

[45] Schoff 1974: 133; Salles 1996a: 255. Certain reservations should be expressed, notes Salles, concerning the supposed taboo for Indians against entering the Red Sea. Diodorus of Sicily also wrote that the island of Panchaea (possibly Socotra) "had a foreign population of 'Oceanites, Indians, Scythians and Cretans'" (Oldfather 1939, III: 215 and V: 42; Pankhurst 1979: 107). Mas'ūdī (1965: 332) reports on a tradition according to which, in order to exploit aloes, "Alexander dispatched a certain number of Greeks [to Socotra] [where they] subdued the Indians who were established there." Aloe is described as "Indian" in classical and Muslim sources, a term that reflects a probable commercial use of the plant by Indians from Socotra (Crone 1987: 61). The name Panchaia or Pancheia and the traditions linked to it derive from Egyptian stories related to Pa'-anch (see above). It appears in Diodorus of Sicily, who quotes Euhemerus (third century BCE), and later in Pliny and other authors.

[46] Returning from a second journey to India, in 114 BCE, Eudoxus was forced by the winds toward the East African coast south of Cape Guardafui. There he purportedly found the end of a wooden prow, with a horse carved upon it, which was brought back to Alexandria. It was recognized as "the bow of a ship from Cadiz that sailed to countries far away south and never came back. Eudoxus then decided, leaving from Cadiz, to undertake the circumnavigation of Africa, but his attempt failed" (Toussaint 1961: 35). In fact, we do not know exactly what happened to Eudoxus and to his companions (Cary and Warmington 1963: 126).

[47] For some researchers, it was the robustness of the Greek and Roman ships that allowed them to undertake this crossing. "The southwest monsoon wind was probably not used by the Arabs, as it is dangerous to sail downwind with it in heavy seas" (Pirenne 1970: 103). The ships used only the southwest monsoon wind once its intensity had eased off (August–September); see above.

[48] The monsoon system was in fact used as early as the Bronze Age (see above).

[49] At its peak during the second century CE, the Roman Empire had an income of over 37,500 talents, representing 900 million sesterces (Le Rider and de Callatay 2006: 171, 173). The decline in the income of

the Erythraean Sea notes that the city of Rhapta, probably located on the Tanzanian coast, was tributary to the Yemeni king who controlled the port of Muza (see below). In addition, the struggles for the succession of the Lagid throne allowed the Romans to intervene in the affairs of the kingdom, the rulers having been politically weakened by the emergence of powerful local families (Manning 2003: 239). In 55 BCE, for the first time, Roman armies entered Egypt. "The Lagid monarchy was now basically just a hand puppet in the hands of the Romans" (Gal 2004). When Octavius gained control of Egypt in 30 BCE, he found a country in a disastrous economic state, though several periods of low Nile flooding had also played a role in bringing about this situation (notably between 51 and 49 BCE).

Rome and Indian Ocean Trade: The Periplus of the Erythraean Sea

> The merchants of Alexandria are already sailing with fleets by way of the Nile and of the Arabian Gulf as far as India . . . I learned that as many as one hundred and twenty vessels were sailing from Myos Hormos to India, whereas formerly, under the Ptolemies, only a very few ventured to take the voyage and to carry on traffic in Indian merchandise.
>
> (Strabo 2.5.12)

> India, China and the Arabian peninsula take one hundred million sesterces from our empire per annum at a conservative estimate: that is what our luxuries and women cost us.
>
> (Pliny XII.41, 84)

In 189 BCE, the Romans, allies to the king of Pergamon, gained a victory over the Seleucid army at Magnesia. This allowed them, with the support of the Greek cities, to dominate western Anatolia. They went on to occupy or control Phrygia (103 BCE), Cilicia (101 BCE), Syria and Palestine (64/63 BCE): thus the Roman conquest brought the Seleucid monarchy to an end.

As of the second century BCE, the Romans were participating alongside the Greeks in the commerce of the Indian Ocean, not only in its western part, but also beyond. However, it is not the arrival of the Greeks and the Romans that put the Indian Ocean at the center of the world-system, but rather the centers of gravity of the world-system located in the Indian Ocean that drew the peoples of the Mediterranean eastward (see also Chakravarti 2004: 307). Roman commerce began to develop in full swing during the second half of the first century BCE and the first century CE (Syrian, Hebrew, Greek, and Roman merchants took part in this movement). It is during this period that the notion of the "Orient" started to appear (in Tacitus for example), in opposition to the Greco-Roman world. Pliny is the first classic author who uses the term "Indian

---

the Egyptian state was relative. According to Suetonius, "during his Alexandrian triumph in Rome, Augustus exhibited the treasure of the kings of Egypt, which made money so plentiful in Rome that the rate of silver diminished, while the price of land rose considerably" (Le Rider and de Callatay 2006: 215; Philippson 2013: 424, *Augustus* 41).

Ocean." Whereas the Persian Gulf had been preeminent during the first millennium BCE, the Red Sea now became the most important exchange route between the Mediterranean Sea and the Indian Ocean.

In 31 BCE, Augustus established Rome's control over Egypt and united the Mediterranean world. At the beginning of the Christian era, Roman ships were present not only in the Red Sea, but also on the East African coast, as far as the city of Rhapta (and perhaps Madagascar). The development of maritime trade through the Red Sea was a necessity for the Roman Empire in order to bypass and weaken the Parthians,[50] who had the upper hand on land routes to Central Asia and to the Orient (it is through the Parthians that silk appeared for the first time at Rome during the first century BCE).[51] The Romans were severely defeated in 53 BCE at Carrhae (near Harran, in the Upper Euphrates valley): here they discovered the efficiency of the Parthians' heavy cavalry and their archers. Florus and Plutarch later described "the standards shining with gold and silk" of the Parthians, and praised the quality of their weapons "made of a Margianian iron glittering clean and bright" (Boulnois 2008: 34). It is worth recalling that Margiana (where Antiochus I built an Antioch at the site of an older Alexandria) lies west of Bactria, at the junction of two branches of the Silk Roads. The iron from Margiana may have been of Chinese origin, or produced using Chinese techniques. "Of all the different kinds of iron, the palm of excellence is awarded to that which is made by the Seres, who send it to us with their textiles and skins; next to which, in quality, is the Parthian iron," writes Pliny.[52] Indian iron was also renowned.[53] Among the 10,000 Romans taken prisoner by the Parthians, a number were deported to Central Asia. Former Roman prisoners may have lived in Zhezhe (in the Talas River valley, in Kyrgyzstan); they were taken to China when the Chinese seized the town in 36 BCE (Boulnois 2008: 42–43).[54]

A frankincense road tightly controlled by the Nabataeans[55] linked Arabia to the Roman world. The presence of Nabataean pottery at Mārib, Qanī (Bi'r 'Alī), and Sumhuram attests to the existence of a caravan trade extending to southern Arabia. The Nabataeans were also present in the Red Sea, where they maintained two major

---

[50] Rome, however, did not abandon its project to seize Mesopotamia, as shown in Trajan's offensive in 114–117 CE (see above), followed by those of Marcus Aurelius in 165–166 CE and Septimius Severus in 195 CE.

[51] Parthian traders had already been selling silk to the Greeks during the second century BCE (Christian 2000: 16).

[52] Boulnois 2001: 23, 24. The Seres to which Pliny refers were probably peoples from Central Asia (he places them east of the Caspian Sea, between the Scythians and the Eastern Sea). As for the fur trade, it operated along north–south routes, in Siberia.

[53] Schoff 1974: 70–71. M. Lombard (1971: 197) considers "Seric iron" to have come from the Dravidian country of the Chera, a region that in fact was a part of the "Seres countries." The mention of "furs," however, is a clear reference to northern Asia.

[54] During the third century CE, the city of Kharakhoja hosted Roman soldiers or Christians from Ephesus. Conversely, Armenian families claimed to be descended from Chinese people who had perhaps arrived during the Han period (Adshead 1995: 34–35).

[55] Their capital, Petra, enjoyed a period of prosperity from 100 BCE to 150 CE, after which it went into decline due to the rise of maritime routes and Roman domination. Diodorus of Sicily had already mentioned the wealth of the Nabataeans during the fourth century BCE in relation to the transportation of spices and aromatics from *Arabia Felix* (see below).

ports, at Aila and Leuko Kome. According to Pliny, they had established a colony on the Horn of Africa: "cassia, cancamum and tarum are brought by way of the Nabatæan Troglodytæ, a colony of the Nabatæi" (XII.44). Nabataea had become a client-kingdom of Rome in 62 BCE, and was finally incorporated into the empire in 106 CE. It was more profitable (or rather, less costly) for the Romans to use maritime transport and to try to draw nearer to the most coveted goods. The emphasis put on the Indian ports of Barbarikon, Barygaza, and Muziris in the *Periplus of the Erythraean Sea*, ports which were connected to Arabia and the Red Sea, is significant. Direct Roman trade with India and East Africa affected the Arabian cities of the interior. Various ports, however, developed on the Arabian coasts.

The Roman demand for luxury products (ivory, spices, textiles, pearls) and iron – along with the parallel emergence of the Chinese Han Empire – led to a considerable increase in trade across the whole Indian Ocean, which brought about the formation of the first Afro-Eurasian world-system (see above; see Map II.10 for its western part). The Greek geographer Strabo (c. 26–24 BCE) notes that, by the time of Augustus, up to 120 ships were setting sail every year from Myos Hormos (in the Red Sea) for India, whereas formerly, under the Ptolemies, only a very few ventured to undertake the journey and carry out traffic in Indian merchandise (*Geography* II.5, 12, and XVII.1, 13). Various routes were successively used, with changes motivated by economic reasons (notably with the desire to draw closer to the pepper-exporting region) (De Romanis 1997: 86ff.). Greek inscriptions mention Callimakos, a "Commander of the Red and Indian Seas," who held this position between 78 and 51 BCE. This is the first mention of the "Indian Sea." According to Pliny (VI.26, 104), a ship leaving from Berenice or Myos Hormos could reach Muziris (on the Malabar coast) in forty days.[56] In earlier periods, trade may have been organized by the state or by the private sector. During Pliny's time, however, it was primarily run by private entrepreneurs: the *Pax Romana* made it possible for them to conduct their business (high-level officials were involved in this trade). The state benefited from this situation, notably by levying duties (25 percent on imports at Alexandria),[57] but according to Tomber, "the lack of substantial infrastructures in the ports" makes it clear that there was no Roman imperial control (2012a: 154), a statement that probably needs to be supported by further proof. Adulis became the principal port between Egypt and India. "Vessels from the Mediterranean world [have been excavated], with an emphasis on the late period, as well as amphorae of the Aila/ Aqaba type which also are found at Qana, Zafar, and Axum" (Peacock and Blue 2007a; Seland 2014). The Romans exported coins, vessels made of precious metals, and glass. The glass industry underwent a revolution at the end of the first millennium BCE in the Levant, with the development of glass-blowing technology (in addition to glass

---

[56] Casson (1980) argues that the journey may have been shortened to twenty days.

[57] Casson 1989: 14. For this author, "the historical record reveals no measures taken by the emperors which unquestionably were part of a policy for promoting maritime trade with the East" (1989: 39), but Sidebotham (1996) has emphasized that the Romans were careful to maintain the roads between the Nile and the Red Sea, and a second-century papyrus (P. Lond II.328) mentions camels being requisitioned for the caravan service to Berenike (Adams 2007: 234). Warehouses were built in both Koptos and Alexandria. "Taxes were levied at the seaports (Myos Hormos and Berenike), but also at Coptos and Alexandria" (van der Ween *et al.* 2011: 66).

molding).[58] Mediterranean coral was also massively exploited (see Pliny XXXII.23). According to Pliny, the Ethiopian ports exported ivory, rhino horns, and slaves. A hoard of money found at Debre Damo in 1940 contained Kushan coins of Kadphises I, Kanishka I, Huvishka, and Vasudeva I (Fauvelle-Aymar 2013: 130), that possibly date to sometime in the third century (however, they were found in a sixth-century context; Tomber 2012a: 93).

The existence of the Indo-Roman trade is now solidly documented by archaeological data, numismatics, epigraphy, and ancient texts. In the same period, exchanges were developing between the Red Sea and the Mediterranean. The internationalization of these networks is highlighted in a text from Alexandria dated to the second century BCE concerning a loan agreement to finance a trading venture to the "spice-bearing land" (perhaps Somalia). The five borrowers had Greek names, but one of them came from Sparta, and another one from Massilia. The lender's name was also Greek. The banker who handled the funds was probably a Roman. Four of the five guarantors belonged to the army; one came from Massilia, another was from Thessalonica, a third from southern Italy; and the fifth guarantor – a traveling merchant – was Carthaginian. Rich families from Egypt and other countries kept agents in the main ports (Casson 1989: 31–33). A papyrus kept in Vienna (Vindob G40822), dated to the second century CE, deals with the shipment of goods from Muziris to Alexandria, with a loan agreement between two Greco-Roman merchants; the contract was probably drawn up in Egypt (the "financier" was based in Alexandria). It mentions the export of nard (between 300 and 800 kg), ivory (2.1 tons), and cotton textiles (350 kg) to Alexandria. The cargo was of tremendous value: 1,154 talents of silver and 2,852 drachmas: more than 10 million sesterces. The document mentions the transport of the merchandise from Myos Hormos to Koptos, and on to Alexandria, and the payment of taxes (25 percent) there. The loan was to be repaid after the return trip, and the borrower pledged the goods purchased.[59] The Latin *carbasina*, from the Sanskrit *karpāsa*, referred to cotton materials; the term appears in Pliny's work during the first century CE. Thus "wealthy financiers recruited merchants to undertake trips" (Tomber 2012a: 153).

Between the Red Sea and the Nile valley, private companies used caravans to transport merchandise, as revealed by the "Nikanor archives," which record "the commercial activities of one family over a period of sixty years (Adams 2007: 221–34)" (from 6 to 62 CE) (Seland 2011).

Merchants from Egypt (Greeks, Jews …) and from the Levant sailed to India, but foreigners also settled in Egypt. Documents signal the establishment of a colony of Indian merchants at Alexandria during the second century CE (met by the Greek philosopher Dio Chrysostom [*c.* 40–120 CE]),[60] and the presence at Koptos of an association of shipowners from Palmyra and of a merchant from Aden. Indians

---

[58] At Axum, the *Periplus* (paragr. 6) signals imports such as copper and iron artifacts, glass of the *millefiori* type, textiles, some Italian wine, olive oil, and "for the king, silverware and goldware" (Casson 1989: 53).

[59] Casson 2001; Parker 2002: 64. This maritime loan is comparable to a loan mentioned by Demosthenes (Casson 2001: 241). Curiously, the document does not mention the shipment of pepper, which was probably of interest to other investors (part of the document, however, has been damaged and may have mentioned pepper).

[60] See McLaughlin 2014: 107.

certainly visited the Red Sea on a regular basis. Besides the presence of the Indian shipwreck survivor who guided Eudoxus, the discovery of three *ostraka* in Tamil and Brāhmī script dated to the first–second century CE at Berenice and at Leukos Limen (Quseir al-Qadim) should be noted.[61] At Berenice, a graffito in Tamil-Brāhmī was actually written on a Roman amphora (Tomber 2012a: 74). Interestingly, "the [Tamil] name 'Kanan' appears as a mark scratched on Indian pottery fragments found at Arikamedu; and this name is also found on shards recovered from Myos Hormos" (McLaughlin 2014: 201). The remains of an "Indian" domestic cat have been recovered from Berenice (Ottoni *et al.* 2013). Inscriptions in Brāhmī script have also been found on Socotra. A sanctuary recently discovered inside the Hoq Cave on the northeast coast of the island contained "a large number of graffiti in South Arabian, Indian Brahmi, Ethiopic Geez, and Greek script, as well as an inscribed tablet in Palmyrane Aramaic, giving a date corresponding to AD 257–258" (Dridi 2002; Strauch and Bukharin 2004; Strauch 2012; Seland 2014). Pottery found at Kosh, "near the western point of the island, revealed close affinities to material excavated at Qana" (Vinogradov 2011; Seland 2014). Pliny signals the arrival of Indian traders in Europe in 62 BCE. Objects of Indian origin have been excavated in Italy, notably an ivory figurine found at Pompei. For the first century CE, Martial and Juvenal signal the presence of Indians at Rome (see McLaughlin 2014: 107). Though petty merchants may have traded along the African coast, commerce with India required the mobilization of large ships and enormous sums of money for the purchase of luxury goods; thus this trade was only possible for powerful investors.[62] Knowledge also circulated; Indian influences, for example, are obvious in Greek medicine and in Gnosticism (Needham 1970: 139).

Investigations at the harbor of Berenice,[63] on the Egyptian Red Sea coast, have divulged the remains of sixty-five cultivated plants, six of them originating in India. Large quantities of black pepper (*Piper nigrum* L.)[64] show that contacts existed with the Malabar coast (one Indian jar contained 7.5 kg of black pepper [Tomber 2012a: 76]). Pepper has been found at other Egyptian sites, in smaller quantities (Shenshef, Quseir al-Qadim, Mons Claudianus), and also in Europe, at the borders of the empire

---

[61]   Salles 1996a: 259; Parker 2002: 64; Rajan 2002: 88. For Chakravarti (2002a: 60 n. 8), "the names of Indian merchants mentioned seem to have been those typically of early historical Deccan," but Rajan proposes rather that they are of Tamil origin (2002: 88). A so-called "Sophon the Indian" (perhaps Subhanu) left a brief inscription in a temple at Redesiye (Basham 1967: 228).

[62]   Casson 1989: 34–35. Goods were not the only thing transmitted from India. On four Hellenistic tombs dated to the second century CE, Casson signals the discovery of reliefs depicting a ship with a kind of spritsail, a technique surely imported from the Indian Ocean (Needham *et al.* 1971: 615).

[63]   The port was active from the third century BCE to the early sixth century CE. Archaeology and texts provide data mainly for the first and second centuries CE. The port seems to have been in decline during the third century CE and then in expansion again at the beginning of the fourth century (Wendrich *et al.* 2003: 48ff.).

[64]   Written sources mention the trade in long pepper (from northern India) and black pepper (exported from the Malabar coast). Berenice has yielded only black pepper (Cappers 1999: 56; Wendrich *et al.* 2003: 69). It is interesting to note that "when the city of Rome was blockaded by the Visigoths under Alaric, in 408, the Senate offered him, together with 5,000 lbs. of gold, 30,000 lbs. of silver and no less than 3,000 lbs. of pepper" (Zosimus, *Historia nova* 5.35–42, quoted by Parker 2002: 45). Four thousand pieces of silk also appear to have been promised.

(Oberaden, in Germany, grains dated to 11–8/7 BCE, and Straubing, on the Danube). Berenice has also provided evidence of rice. The *Periplus* tells us that northern India (Barygaza) and the Malabar region exported rice to the Somali coast and the island of Socotra, where it was loaded onto ships from Egypt.[65] In Europe, rice has been unearthed at Neuss, in Germany (196 grains, dated to the first quarter of the first century CE). However, rice was already being grown in Egypt during the second century CE. Citing Aristobulus, Strabo claims that rice was cultivated in Babylonia, Susiana, and Syria (Decker 2009: 195). Coconut fragments from various locations at the site of Berenice demonstrate that this nut was not a rarity.[66] The discovery of fragments from the inner wall of the *Phyllanthus emblica* L. fruit (a plant which is not mentioned by written sources) also point to its importation; the Arabs used to trade this fruit for its supposed medicinal properties. *Phyllanthus emblica*, the "Indian gooseberry," native to India, is a sacred tree for the Hindus, and is often planted on the southern side of a temple or a house. Dozens of *Vigna radiata* (L.) Wilczek grains, a pulse of Indian origin, have been excavated in an area of the Berenice site. The fact that the finds were grouped together suggests that it was probably an import. A hard fruit belonging to a wild form of "Job's tears" (*Coix lachryma-jobi* L.), a plant of South Asian origin, has also been unearthed (these fruit are used to make necklaces of protective "beads"). *Coix* has been found at eight archaeological sites in India.[67] Sorghum and (fruits of the) tamarind, given by Cappers as originating from northeast Africa, could well have been imports from India: Pliny (first century) notes that a new "black millet" (sorghum) had recently been introduced into Egypt (*Natural History* XVIII.10; Blench, 2003: 278). Remains of citron (*Citrus medica* L.) and of sesame and cucumber (*Cucumis sativus* L.), have also been found; these plants are of Indian origin (and not Mediterranean as stated by Cappers).[68] Rice, *Vigna*, *Phyllanthus*, and coconut, though not mentioned in written sources, were probably imported by Indian merchants. Grains of *Abrus* were imports from South Asia, from Arabia or East Africa. Finally, teak (*Tectona grandis*) is one of the three most common wood species found at Berenice; the *Periplus* designates

[65] *Periplus*, ch. 31. For the rice found at Berenice, a western Asian origin cannot be excluded (Berenice yielded amphorae from Syria), but an Indian origin seems more likely (Cappers 1999: 56).

[66] Curiously, coconut is mentioned neither by the *Periplus*, nor by Marcus Aurelius. The latter, in a text written between 176 and 180 CE, listed fifty-six goods subject to customs duties at Alexandria, half of which were plant products (Cappers 1999: 52). Cappers rightly notes that a comparison between written sources and archaeological remains at Berenice does not reveal many common botanical species. The fact that some plants may have been destined to remain at Berenice may explain their absence in written documents. The absence of other plants in archaeological discoveries from Berenice is doubtless due to conservation issues and research deficiencies in archaeobotany (Cappers 1999: 60).

[67] Notably Ahichchhatra and Balathal (Cappers 1999: 59). The *Coix* was an important plant in Indochina, southern China and insular Southeast Asia, for food and in medico-religious practices. Soft-shelled varieties were selected and cultivated in ancient times.

[68] The *Citrus medica* is an ancient import in the Mediterranean region. Theophrastus calls it the "apple from Media or Persia" and considers it to be a native plant from this region. The citron is mentioned in *Boiotis* from Antiphanes (*c.* 330 BCE) and was therefore present in Greece at this time (Amigues 2005: 365). As mentioned above, citron remains have been excavated on Cyprus, dated to *c.* 1200 BCE, and the Romans knew of it in 300 BCE. The citron tree was the first *Citrus* introduced into Egypt; remains dating from the Ptolemaic period have been unearthed at Thebes (Germer 1985: 106). Cucumber seeds have been found in Egypt, but not prior to the Greco-Roman period. Sesame has been present since the third millennium BCE at least in Mesopotamia, and it was commonly grown in the Greco-Roman world.

it as an export notably from Barygaza. The presence of teak at Berenice may suggest that wood recycling from old ships was practiced; however, ships were probably built in Egypt from imported wood (Sidebotham 2011: 203–205). Shipbuilding technology was certainly exchanged between India and Egypt.

Indian ceramics have been recovered at Berenice, and have also been attested at Qanī, Sumhuram, Koptos, and Myos Hormos (Ballet 2001: 38; Tomber 2002: 25, 29). Among these, the coarser pottery can be distinguished from the fine ceramic, in particular Rouletted Ware (RW), probably a personal possession of Indian merchants from Arikamedu. Rouletted Ware and related vessels reveal "the predominance of the Red Sea routing [over the route to the Persian Gulf]. They occur at Berenice, Coptos, Myos Hormos (Quseir al-Qadim) and at Qana and Sumhuram, but are not traced at the Gulf sites" (Schenk 2007: 65). Some Indian red ware seems to have come from South India (Arikamedu) or Sri Lanka (Schenk 2007: 67–68), and paddle-impressed jars came from eastern India. Tomber (2012a: 155) points out the important role of South India in these imports, but black ware from Gujarat has also been unearthed at Berenice, Myos Hormos, and Aila. In the opposite direction, Mediterranean amphorae containing fish sauce (*garum*) from Spain, wine and oil, found at Berenice, show that these products were exported to Arabia and India.[69] Berenice has also divulged southern Arabian and Axumite ceramics (Tomber 2012b). Rock crystal, diamonds, lapis lazuli, and other semiprecious stones also came from Sri Lanka and India, from the ports of Muziris and Nelkynda (Malabar coast), Barygaza (Gujarat), and Barbarikon (located at the mouth of the Indus), and southern Arabia exported alabaster. Glass beads of an "Indo-Pacific" type, probably from Mantai (Sri Lanka), have been excavated. One glass bead seems to have been imported from Java, but belongs to the early seventh century (Francis 2007: 254–255). Fragments of cotton cloth, including sails, have also been recovered. Z-spun yarns and resist dyes reveal an Indian origin and suggest importations (Wild and Wild 2007; Cameron 2010: 142). The cotton plant was cultivated in Palestine and in Egypt, but the Levanto-Egyptian fabrics were manufactured with S-spun (left-hand spin) yarns (Decker 2009: 199–201). Berenice has so far "yielded evidence of 12 written languages, including South Arabian, Palmyrane Aramaic, and Tamil-Brahmi" (Sidebotham 2011: 74–75; Seland 2014). Moreover, several temples and a church have been excavated at Berenice (Sidebotham 2011: 81ff.). An inscription found on a route between Berenice and Edfu shows that Indians also traveled inland. All of these data create a compelling image of Berenice as a cosmopolitan hub – a cosmopolitanism also evident at Myos Hormos, and in Hoq (Socotra) (Strauch 2012). "Thomas (2012), using proxies such as diet, occupation, and tableware, has argued that groups of different origins resided in different quarters of Egyptian Red Sea ports" (Seland 2014: 381). These recent finds "underline the multicultural nature of ancient Indian Ocean trade" (Seland 2014: 382).

Along with Adulis and Berenice, Myos Hormos (Quseir al-Qadim) was another major port, where "finds partially parallel those from Berenike" (Seland 2014: 381). Rice and black pepper from India (Van der Veen *et al.* 2011), basalt from southern Arabia,

---

[69] Wendrich *et al.* 2003: 78. Some of these amphorae have been found at Qanī (Kanē) and at Ras Hafun. Grapevine imports are mentioned in the Indian text *Purananūru* (De Romanis 1997: 152 n. 164).

Roman glass (Peacock 2011), as well as sailcloth made from Indian cotton, woven using Indian techniques (Handley 2011) have all been found. "Pottery with texts in South Arabian, Palmyrene Aramaic, and Tamil-Brahmi echo the heterogeneous cultural environment of Berenike (Tomber 2011), and ceramics from the Adulis area also have been found" (Seland 2014: 381). Interestingly, two vessels from Myos Hormos belong to the Indian Red and Black Megalithic Ware, providing evidence for early contacts during the Ptolemaic period (Tomber 2012a: 75). The distribution of the pottery found suggests that "foreigners lived in separate quarters" (Tomber 2012a: 75). Some Indian cotton sailcloth was found attached to a brailing ring made of teak (revealing that a Roman technique was used): it is possible that Roman-style ships were built or that Roman ships were repaired in India (Tomber 2012a: 73).

In India, archaeology has confirmed the presence of amphorae from the Mediterranean (Greek *koan* dating back to the second or first century BCE as well as Italian pseudo-*koan* assigned a date somewhere between 50 BCE and 79 CE) at many sites in the subcontinent, notably at Arikamedu (Will 1992: 151ff.) and Pattanam (Muziris) (the third largest assemblage is at Nevasa [Tomber 2012a: 156]).[70] The existence in Egypt of pottery from Knidos (first century BCE), Kos, and Rhodes, shows that amphorae must have reached Arikamedu from the Red Sea. They contained Greek and Italian wines, oil from the Adriatic, and fish sauce from Spain, signaling the likely presence of "Romans" at Arikamedu. Apart from the amphorae, a red gloss pottery called *Terra Sigillata* from Italy and the eastern Mediterranean has been discovered; it has been dated to between 10 BCE and 50 CE (Tomber 2012a: 136), the pieces often bearing names stamped on their undersides. Early Sigillata Ware has also been discovered at Karur (Tamil Nadu), and at Mantai (Sri Lanka) (Schenk 2007: 69). Arikamedu probably contained a Roman enclave at the beginning of the Christian era. Rouletted Ware from Arikamedu is widespread in India (along the coast of Coromandel, and further north, in Andhra, Orissa, and Bengal)[71] and also in Sri Lanka. It has been unearthed at sites in Egypt (Myos Hormos, Koptos, Berenice), Yemen (Qanī), Oman (Khor Rori), Vietnam (Tra Kieu, Go Cam), Indonesia (Sumatra [Palembang], Java [Buni complex], Bali [Sembiran]), and Malaysia (Bukit Tengku Lembu) (Schenk 2006: 146). Schenk (2006: 141) connects the spread of this pottery with the Mauryan period and the expansion of Buddhist networks. It was made in India, but the decoration of some RW types may have been influenced by Mediterranean wares as early as the second century BCE or even earlier (Begley 1992: 4).[72] At Arikamedu, this pottery is generally

---

[70] The presence at Mathurā of an amphora fragment bearing a Latin inscription shows that imported goods traveled within the subcontinent. Apart from Roman pottery, ceramics from Hadramawt have also been recovered from Pattanam and Arikamedu.

[71] Schenk (2006: 142–145) has listed 124 sites where Rouletted Ware was present: in Tamil Nadu, Andhra Pradesh, Orissa, Bengal, Bangladesh, Karnataka, Maharashtra, and Sri Lanka. See also Gogte 2002, Ford *et al.* 2005, Magee 2010.

[72] There are several different types of Rouletted Ware. Both Black and Red pottery (from South India) and Rouletted Ware (three of the five major types) (fourth–third century BCE) have been found at sites in Sri Lanka such as Pilapitiya, near the mouth of the Kelani River (Bopearachchi 2002: 99). Various types of Roman-style artifacts were produced in India.

dated between the second century BCE and the third century CE, but dates between 350 and 275 BCE have been put forward for pottery found at Anurādhāpura in Sri Lanka.[73] Magee (2010) makes a distinction between two groups of fine wares, including RW. He concurs "with Coningham that prior to the 2nd century BC, the production of fine wares was centralised within southern India and Sri Lanka." Along with "an intensification of maritime trade, two fine ware traditions emerged in the 2nd century BC. One branch of Group A production is represented by IRW which is decorated in a fashion that clearly betrays foreign influence . . ., while the other branch continues the Greyware production typical of the period before 200 BC. It is at this time that Group B production also emerges, characterised by IRW and Type 10 fine ware production in Sri Lanka" (2010: 1052).

Roman bronzes have also been discovered, notably at Kolhapur (first century CE for most of them), in the ruins of a Roman merchant's house, as well as Roman lamps in ceramic,[74] at Ter, at Vallore (near Coimbatore), and "Roman" glass, at Taxila (Pakistan), Begram (Afghanistan),[75] Ter, Rajghat, Alamgirpur, Paithan, Nevasa, Arikamedu, Karakaidu (India), Ridiyagama and Anurādhāpura (Sri Lanka).[76]

[73] Tomber 2002: 28, according to Coningham and Allchin 1995: 167. According to Schenk (2006: 141), RW was manufactured between the third and first centuries BCE at the latest. Gogte has proposed that this ceramic originated in the Lower Ganges, but this hypothesis is still debated (it has been accepted by Schenk [2014], but Magee [2010] suggests that there are probably multiple production zones for RW: the RW found in South India came from local production centers) (Schenk admits "the emergence of local imitations during the 1st century BC," for example at Tissahama [2014: 140]). Bellina and Glover (2004: 78) note that the amount of RW shards found in Bengal is rather small. They are cautious about the early dating of this pottery at Anurādhāpura.

[74] Most of "the ceramic lamps, however, derive from Hellenistic rather than Roman models" (Tomber 2012a: 132).

[75] Some of the glass came from Egypt (Mairs 2012).

[76] Basa and Behera 1999: 20. A statuette of Poseidon may be older than the first century CE. Kolhapur has yielded a cache of 102 bronzes, of which "at least ten are Roman imports" (Parker 2002: 66). At Arikamedu, a carnelian ring possibly inscribed with the portrait of Augustus has also been found. The site of Taxila has yielded many objects of Mediterranean origin or influence such as a silver emblem representing Silenus or a satyr, glass vessels, and engraved gems. Kolhapur has divulged a great variety of glass beads, including "gold-glass beads," certainly imported: P. Francis Jr. (2002: 91) thinks that this technique originated in Egypt, but the only known workshop was on Rhodes Island (100 BCE – 400 CE) (Lankton and Dussubieux 2006: 57, 106). The importation of glass vessels from the Mediterranean world has been dated to 100–200 CE at Paithan, to the second–third century CE at Nevasa, and between the second and fifth centuries CE at Arikamedu. On the glass beads of a "Syro-Palestinian" type (mineral soda-lime glass using natron and limy sand), see Dussubieux 2001: 111–113, 199–202. This author has demonstrated the existence in India and in Southeast Asia of other soda-lime glasses that are distinct from the Syro-Palestinian type and may not have been imported (this type of glass was also known in China) (2001: 113). Moreover, types of glass of composition similar to that of the "Islamic glasses" (vegetable soda glass, using limy sand) but dating to the late first millennium BCE or the early first millennium CE have been found at various sites in India (Ahichchhatra [third century BCE – second century CE], Nevasa [second century BCE – second century CE], Taxila [undated], Nālandā [fifth century CE]), in Sri Lanka (Giribawa, Ridiyagama [fourth century BCE – seventh century CE], Kelaniya [fourth century BCE – second century CE], Anurādhāpura), in Cambodia (Angkor Borei), and in Vietnam (Oc Eo). This type of glass was known prior to the eighth century BCE in western Asia and in the Mediterranean world. Its manufacture may have continued in workshops yet to be identified (examples of these glasses have been attested in the Mediterranean between the first century BCE and the first century CE). Dussubieux has identified this type of glass in a port of the Red Sea where it is dated to the fourth–sixth century CE (2001: 126, 202).

At Sisupalgarh, a gold medallion reveals Kushan influences on one of its faces, and features a "Roman head with a Roman legend on the reverse."[77] Raw "Roman" glass arrived in South India and probably in Southeast Asia, where it was used for the production of beads (at Arikamedu, for example).[78] Moreover, a type of red Indian moldmade ware, with a decoration in relief of either Acanthus leaves or radiant lotus petals, seems to have taken inspiration from Megarian bowls and from Greek or Egyptian metallic forms going back to Achaemenid prototypes; produced in northwestern India (in Gujarat and Maharashtra) as early as the end of the third century BCE, this ceramic has also been discovered in the western Deccan, notably at Nevasa (dated to the first century BCE), Ter, Kondapur, and Kolhapur.[79] A stamped ceramic attested at Arikamedu (Wheeler's type 10) shows a decoration pointing to a Roman influence; this ware has been found at Alagankulam (the Salour [Saliyur] of Ptolemy, southeast India), Anurādhāpura, Kantarodai (Sri Lanka), Chandraketugarh (western Bengal), and Sembiran (Bali).[80]

There have been discoveries of Roman coins in two main areas: the district of Coimbatore (Tamil Nadu), a source of beryl that may have interested Mediterranean traders, and the Krishnā River, in Andhra Pradesh; the hoards sometimes also contain imitations of Roman coins (see McLaughlin 2014: 202). Coins from the Republican period are rare; conversely, there was a notable inflow of silver denarii as of the Julio-Claudian period, and then of gold aurei (dated to the first and second centuries CE). Their distribution, which was wider than that of the denarii, implies a diversification in trade.[81] Shātavāhana coins (a dynasty that ruled the Andhra state from the second century BCE until the third century CE) were in use in the Deccan, but in South India there was a preference for Roman coins. Roman coins have also been found in Orissa (Mayurbhanj and Koraput districts). Pliny (23–79 CE) emphasized that India drained Roman wealth, which went into the trade in luxury goods (silks, semiprecious stones, pearls, ivory, turtleshell, and more importantly, spices and perfumes), described by Gibbon as "splendid and futile": "In no year does India drain our empire of no less than five hundred and fifty million sesterces," Pliny has lamented, "giving back her own

---

[77] Behera 1999a: 165. One face shows the Kuṣāna design of a standing king, with a Brāhmī legend; the other side features a Roman head and a Roman legend (possibly third century CE). Sisupalgarh has also yielded clay *bullae* "embossed with heads resembling that of Silenus" (Behera 1999a: 165).

[78] Glass was also produced at various places, for example at Nevasa (from 150 BCE). This site has yielded many beads from between 50 BCE and 200 CE.

[79] Begley 1992: 157ff.; Bellina 1999: 170. Hellenistic molded bowls have been unearthed at Taxila, where they are dated to the second/first century BCE.

[80] Bellina 1999: 166. According to Begley, this pottery appeared during the second century BCE and was made until the third or fourth century CE. Another stamped ceramic, attested in north and central India from the final centuries BCE, appears to derive from an Indian type (Bellina 1999: 167–168). The "so-called amphorae from Chandraketugarh are local" and not Roman (Tomber 2012a: 129).

[81] Tchernia 1997: 264; Basa and Behera 1999: 20. In addition, terracotta or metal copies of Tiberius and Augustus coins have been unearthed in Maharashtra (Ter, Paithan, mentioned by the *Periplus* under the respective names of Tagara and Paithana), Andhra Pradesh (Kondapur), Karnataka, Uttar Pradesh (Rajghat), Orissa (Sisupalgarh), and western Bengal (Tamluk). Meyer (2007) rightly notes that while the presence of coins is a poor indictor of transactions between Rome and India, they can tell us about the sociopolitical conditions in India: if the hoards were not recovered, it means that their owners were probably killed or forced into exile.

wares in exchange, which are sold among us at fully one hundred times their prime cost."[82] Similarly, Solinus (third century CE) bemoans: "It was the passion for luxury that led first women, and now even men to use these fabrics which serve to reveal the body rather than to clothe it" (Drège 1986: 18). In a text where he refers to beryl, Tacitus ascribes a criticism of women's extravagance to Tiberius, speaking of "that luxury of women which, for the sake of jewels, diverts our wealth to strange or hostile nations" (*Ann.* III.53; De Romanis 1997: 97). During the second century CE, Aelius Aristides, a Greek sophist who was born in Anatolia, writes:

> You can see so many cargoes from India or, if you wish, from Arabia Felix, that you might think the trees in those countries had been left permanently bare and that the inhabitants would have to come to Rome if they needed anything, to beg for their own goods. Clothing from Babylonia and ornaments from foreign lands beyond arrive here in greater quantity and more easily than goods shipped from Naxos or Cythnos or Athens. (Drège 1986: 17)

The futility of this trade, of course, is only an outward show: "What we term 'luxuries' were no more than the necessities of the rich and powerful, whose import interest determined foreign economic policy."[83] Large amounts of money were invested in the trade with India by a political-financial oligarchy,[84] a trade that also generated money for the state through taxes. Rome imposed a 25 percent import tax called the *tetarte* on all international goods crossing the imperial frontiers; international "commerce raised more than 250 million sesterces" for the Roman state every year (McLaughlin 2014: 14). "Foreign goods were crucial to the economic foundations of the empire" (McLaughlin 2014: 27). For Rome, control of Egypt was essential: Egypt was the "bread basket" of the empire, and received all the spices and aromatics from the Horn of Africa, Arabia, and Asia.

Pliny acknowledged that long-distance trade could be useful for a few products:

> There should be a perpetual interchange going on between all parts of the earth, of productions so instrumental to the welfare of mankind! Results, all of them, ensured to us by the peace that reigns under the majestic sway of the Roman power, a peace which brings in presence of each other, not individuals only, belonging to lands and nations far separate, but ...their plants and their various productions! (XXVII.1)

---

[82] Pliny VI.26. In another passage (XXII.41), Pliny gives the amount of 100 million sesterces exported every year (see above); Boulnois 2001: 106. For a discussion of Pliny's monetary evaluations, Parker 2002: 75. The revenues of the Roman Empire during the second century CE have been estimated at around 900 million sesterces per year (see above); they were only 4–8 million sesterces per year in 250 BCE, and 50–60 million in 150 BCE (Hopkins 2009: 185). Nicolet, for his part, gives the Indian imports as representing one-tenth or one-fifteenth of the expenses of the state ... and a quarter of the capital of the freedman Narcissus (1988: 208). Recipes left by Apicius show that eastern spices and aromatics had largely entered Roman cooking during the first century CE. Andreau (1994: 93) notes that Pliny "fails to give the trade balance: the differences between imports and exports."

[83] Polanyi 1975: 135. Silk appeared in Rome during the first century BCE and its use spread during the first century CE. For Pliny, Seneca, and other authors, silk symbolized extravagant luxury spending and moral decline. According to Lucan, Chinese silks were sometimes unravelled and then rewoven according to western tastes by Egyptian artisans to produce the light fabrics coveted by the Romans (Adshead 1995: 37–38).

[84] This went along with an increase in borrowing and a rise in interest rates that partly explain the financial crisis of 33 CE (De Romanis 1997: 126; Tchernia 1997: 272).

However, Pliny qualifies the positive aspect of economy and trade in his days by pointing out that: "so much more comprehensive was the diligent research of our forefathers, or else so much more happily employed was their industry" (XIV.I) (Nicolet 1988: 109). However, he also writes in the same passage: "in days gone by, the sway and the destinies of states were bounded by their own narrow limits, and consequently the genius of the people was similarly circumscribed as well."

A large quantity of coins has also been discovered in Sri Lanka (50 or 60,000 coins), signaling the importance of this island as a focal point for trade networks, an importance also paralleled in the size of Sri Lanka depicted in Ptolemy's work (compared to the Indian subcontinent, which appears to be flattened).[85] The coins were Roman (silver denarii from the first centuries CE, and copper or bronze coins of the fourth and fifth centuries CE), but also Indian, Kushan, and later Persian, Sassanid, and Byzantine. Roman coins have also been found in a shipwreck from the Laccadive Islands; "this hoard contains a higher percentage of Republican coins than anything yet found on the subcontinent" (Parker 2002: 67). India hosted not only merchants, but also artisans from the Roman world.[86]

What relationship did the Greek or Roman merchants have with the Indian networks? Inscriptions mention donations by Yavana merchants to Buddhist or Jain establishments in Maharashtra, for example at Karla, Nasik, and Junnar (Dhavalikar 1999: 109). Conversely, no donation has been mentioned in South India. For H. Ray (1988), in the north, the Yavana (Mediterranean people; see below) needed to integrate local merchant networks, whereas in the south, they participated more directly in these networks. Ray links this interpretation to another comparison, in regard to currencies. The north had strong local currencies, and "absorbed" the Roman imports, by melting them; the south did not issue major currencies, and either adopted the Roman coins or imitated them.

Coins and objects of Roman origin have been discovered further east, in mainland Southeast Asia, probably brought there by Indian merchants (see below), but perhaps also by travelers from the eastern parts of the Roman Empire. According to the Chinese chronicle *History of the Liang* (*Liangshu*) (sixth or seventh century), merchants from Da Qin (earlier spelled Ta-ch'in, Ta Ts'in) ("the Great Qin": the eastern Roman world) often went to Funan, Jenan, and Jiaozhi, "whereas few people from these countries have been to Da Qin" (Malleret 1963, III: 393). The historian Florus, however, mentions Seres (possibly Chinese or men from Central Asia) visiting during the Augustan period.

Various Latin and Greek authors wrote about India and trade: Strabo, Pliny the Elder, Arrian, Ptolemy, and later Cosmas. According to Strabo, a Pāndya king sent an embassy whom the emperor Augustus met at Athens around 20 BCE. Augustus also welcomed embassies sent by the Saka king Azes from Barygaza in 26 and 22 BCE (at this

---

[85] Eratosthenes (third century BCE) had already attributed a large size to Sri Lanka (Arnaud 2012: 53).

[86] According to the apocryphal *Acts of Saint Thomas* (late second – early third century), Thomas traveled to India as a carpenter during the first century CE along with a merchant called Habban; he was employed by the Indo-Parthian king Gondophares, who controlled the Indus valley as far as Taxila (Parker 2002: 87; Chakravarti 2002b: 105). Thomas would then have sailed to Socotra, and finally returned to the Malabar coast, at Muziris, probably following usual trade routes. He died in the region of Madras. Jews also arrived in India during the first and second centuries, fleeing the Roman yoke.

time the Saka were being threatened by the Parthian Empire and were probably seeking help from the Romans). Suetonius, during the first–second century CE, Florus during the second century CE, and Aurelius Victor during the fourth century CE mention the arrival of Indian delegations. Trajan welcomed one of these embassies at Rome in 107 CE. Sri Lanka sent envoys under the reign of Claudius (41–54 CE),[87] and perhaps during the Augustan period (27 BCE – 14 CE). Embassies from Bactria visited the emperors Hadrian and Antoninus Pius during the second century CE. Elagabal and Aurelian during the third century, and Constantine in the fourth century, also received Indian emissaries. In 361 CE, a Sinhalese embassy was received by Emperor Julianus. Tamil texts belonging to the Sangam literature[88] (*Silappadikāram, Manimekhalai, Nakkirar, Akanānūru*) write that Yavana (Westerners) resided in India,[89] where they worked as merchants, carpenters, guards, and so forth. The *Akanānūru* speaks of the ships of the Yavana that bring gold and leave with pepper (see below). A Yavana settlement is signaled at Kāveripattinam (Puhar), at the mouth of the Kāverī River (Ptolemy's Khaberis), in the Chola kingdom. The port is described in these terms in the *Silappadikāram*, a text dated to the first centuries CE:

The sun shone over the open terraces, over the warehouses near the harbour and over the turrets with windows like the eyes of deer. In different places of Puhar, the onlooker's attention was caught by the sight of the abodes of the Yavanas, whose prosperity never waned. At the harbour were to be seen sailors from many lands, but to all appearances, they lived as one community.[90]

The presence of Roman enclaves or even of Roman residents, however, has been put into question by some scholars. The *Silappadikāram* can be dated to around 450 CE (Seland 2007: 72); during that period, the "foreigners" it mentions could also be Persians, Arabs, or even Axumites. However, the text does refer to a Chera king from the end of the second century. Seland puts forward other, more interesting arguments. The Romans had few economic incentives to sail beyond Cape Comorin, due to the price of food, of the duration of loans (granted for a navigation season), and the problems caused by the monsoons.[91] In addition, it is unlikely that the South

---

[87] Diplomatic contacts are also referred to in early Buddhist annals such as the *Mahāvamsa* (see McLaughlin 2014: 198–199).

[88] "Sangam literature was named after the 'academies' (*sangam*) of Madurai and its environs, where poets worked under the patronage of the Pandya kings" (Kulke and Rothermund 1995: 103).

[89] The name refers to the region of Ionia and its inhabitants. One finds *yona-* in inscriptions from Ashoka – from the Old Persian Yauna – and *yavan* (pl. *yavanim*) in Hebrew, *iamanu* (or *iavanu*) in Assyrian, $y^e v^a n$-(n)*a* in Egyptian. In ancient Sanskrit and Pāli literature, the term is applied to Greeks and Indo-Greeks; in Tamil literature, it refers more often to people from the Roman world, and later to Arabs (Ray 1988, 2002a: 25; Parker 2002: 63 n. 43).

[90] Kulke and Rothermund 1995: 107. Kāveripattinam seems to have been inhabited between the third century BCE and the twelfth century CE.

[91] Bopearachchi (2011) has "suggested that the Greco-Roman merchant ships never sailed as far as Sri Lanka because they had to take advantage of the monsoon winds for the voyage to India in July from the Red Sea, and thus reaching the Indian ports by September/October with the return journey to be taken in November to take advantage of the northeast monsoon. Such timing meant that the Roman merchants had only a month to exchange their wares in South Asia, and this is not considered to be enough time by Bopearachchi" (Chew 2018). However, Greek/Roman merchants were certainly present in the eastern Indian Ocean, and Bellwood *et al.* have shed light on a Mediterranean influence seen on boats found in Vietnam (2007) (see below).

Indian kings would have allowed Roman ships to venture into the Bay of Bengal. The *Puranānūru* refers to a Chera king in these terms: "he runs his ships, that carry gold, so that no other vessels dare to travel those waters" (Seland 2007: 76–77). It is true that Roman knowledge of Sri Lanka was still minimal during the first century, even though Pliny (VI.24) writes of merchants who visited the island under Claudius (see McLaughlin 2014: 197), but this would no longer have been the case in the ensuing centuries. It is likely that the Roman merchants used Indian ships to travel to the ports of the Coromandel coast; they may also have followed transpeninsular roads (Ray 1988; Casson 1989: 24ff.; Young 2007: 31–32). If the Roman presence in the East was really as "infrequent, or even exceptional" as Seland suggests (2007: 79), why then did the *Periplus of the Erythraean Sea* bother to list six places on the southeast coast of India?[92]

A kind of guide for merchants and mariners, the *Periplus*, an anonymous eyewitness account of the first century CE[93] written in Greek, describes the ports and towns of Arabia, the African coast, India, and mentions East Asia. It examines the main products that were traded. Besides spices, aromatics, and other luxury goods, it mentions manufactured products (glass, ceramics, various textiles, sewn ships …), raw goods (wood, copper and so on), and food. Depending on the places, it notes the existence of barter-trade or exchange for money. It also mentions the rulers of a few trading places, thus highlighting the links between politics and commerce (the author, however, shows no interest in religion). Half of the book is dedicated to trade between Egypt and India, which shows the importance of exchanges between these regions. The *Periplus* repeats the legend of Hippalos, and details the routes followed by ships sailing to India: from Kanē (Qanī, port of the Hadramawt) or other ports in Arabia, or from the Cape of Spices, ships sailed either directly to Dimirikē (Tamilikam, "Tamil Land"),[94] in the southwest and the south of India, or to Barygaza, in the northwest, whereas the Arab ships – according to the *Periplus* – formerly followed the coasts.[95]

The journey began in Myos Hormos, continued on to Berenice and then Adulis, on the Erythraean coast. From there it was possible to sail to Muza, Eudaimôn Arabia (port of Aden – its foundation may go back to at least the fifth century BCE) (Yemen), or Avalites, Mosyllon, Aromata, and Opônē (Somali coast). Muza appears to have been a significant stopping point, where merchants could buy myrrh, using coins from

---

[92] The fact that, for these places on the Coromandel coast, the *Periplus* lists only the exports and does not mention the imports, probably implies that Roman ships did not sail there, but it does not prove the absence of Roman merchants on this coast.

[93] The dating of the *Periplus* has been fiercely debated. Most scholars today accept a date between 30 or 40 and 50 CE. The text mentions a Nabataean king, Malichus (Malik), who lived at that time, as well as Charibael (Karib'il Watār Yuhan'im), "king of the Homerites [Himyarites] and the Sabaeans" (Casson 1989: 7, 63, 189; Robin 1997c: 58; Parker 2002: 62). The Indian data lead Fussman (1997: 70) to date the text "between 30 and 50." The only known manuscript of this text, held in Heidelberg, is dated to the tenth century. The author has often been considered as being a Greek merchant; however, Arnaud (2012) has pointed out that the author belongs to "a Hellenized Latin sphere" (thus, he uses the Latin names for the months of the year), and that the work is a compilation. Arnaud also shows that the text is not merely a guide for merchants, but reflects a "literary ambition."

[94] *Periplus*, ch. 53, has "Lymirike," but for Schoff (1974: 205), this "is a corruption caused by the scribe's confusing the Greek d and l"; he notes that Ptolemy writes "Dimirike." For a different opinion, see Casson 1989: 213, who transcribes it as Lymirikē.

[95] *Periplus*, ch. 57; Schoff 1974: 45; Casson 1989: 87.

Egypt. In contact with East Africa, Muza was also the starting point for caravans going to the north. From there, Arab ships sailed to Eudaimon Arabia ("Prosperous Arabia": Aden) and Barygaza (Broach, northwestern India).[96] In Aden, merchants from Egypt and India used to meet to exchange their products. It "was called Eudaemon when, since vessels from India did not go on to Egypt and those from Egypt did not dare to sail to the places further on but came only this far, it used to receive the cargoes of both" (*Periplus*, paragr. 26; Schoff 1974: 32; Casson 1989: 65).[97] On the southern coast of Arabia, Kanē (Qanī, site of Husn al-Ghurab), the port of "the frankincense land," was also connected to the Red Sea, the Persian Gulf and India (Barbarikon, Barygaza, Muziris-Nelkynda) (*Periplus*, paragr. 27 and 28), as well as Moscha Limēn (coast of Hadramawt).

Qanī was founded at the end of the first century BCE. The activity of this port was at its peak between the second and the fourth centuries (Sedov 2010a,b). A stopping-point for Roman ceramics exported to India, Qanī witnessed the rise of maritime connections between India and the Greco-Roman world (Sedov 2001: 33). Moreover, as the *Periplus* (paragr. 27) points out, "all the frankincense grown in the land is brought to Kane." Frankincense was collected by royal slaves and convicts (paragr. 29), and the king of Hadramawt probably controlled a large part of its trade. Trade in myrrh at Muza was also controlled by the political power. The text mentions the importation of wheat and wine from Egypt (paragr. 27). Sigillata ware from Arezzo and Campanian Dressel 2–4 amphorae (also found on the Horn of Africa, at Heis [Mundu in the *Periplus*] and Damo, on the Somalian coast) have been excavated, as well as amphorae and eastern Sigillata from the Aegean Sea and Anatolia, and Nabataean bowls (the Nabataean city of Petra was an important entrepot between Arabia and the Red Sea on the one side, and the Mediterranean on the other). Egyptian amphorae and jars (which probably came via Myos Hormos and Berenice) and Indian pottery reveal an expanding Indian Ocean trade (Ballet 2001: 38). A coin of Kanishka I and an Indian bronze statue have also been excavated. Indian merchants or craftsmen probably lived in Qanī. Ships from Persia and India arrived at the port in November, while ships from the Red Sea reached it in October (McLaughlin 2014: 141). "From Qana it was a voyage of at least 30 days back to Egypt" (McLaughlin 2014: 245).

In another testimony to the internationalization of trade during the first century CE, the *Periplus* tells us that the inhabitants of Dioscuridēs Island (Socotra) were "foreigners, a mixture of Arabs, Indians and Greeks, who have emigrated to carry on trade there" (*Periplus*, paragr. 30; Schoff 1974: 34; Casson 1989: 69).[98] The island, famed for its "dragon's blood" (a resin from *Dracaena cinnabari* Balf. f. and *D. ombet* Kotschy & Peyritsch), was under the rule of "the king of the frankincense country" (the Hadramawt).

After Kanē, the *Periplus* mentions the "frankincense-bearing land," and the ports of Syagros and Moscha Limēn (Sumhuram/Khor Rori), "a designated harbour for loading the Sachalite frankincense. Some vessels are customarily sent to it from Kanē."

---

[96] *Periplus*, paragr. 21; Schoff 1974: 30–31; Casson 1989: 63. Pliny (VI.104) writes that Greek merchants stopped at Muza to acquire frankincense and aromatics; ships bound for India did not stop at this port.

[97] Cf. also Pliny XII.82–88, and Agatharchides.

[98] On Socotra, see above. On the king of the "incense country," *Periplus*, paragr. 27, and Schoff 1974: 117–119.

Ships from the Malabar coast or Barygaza "that passed the winter there . . . take on, in exchange for cotton cloth, grain and oil, a return cargo of frankincense" (paragr. 32; Casson 1989: 71).

On the Somalian coast, Opōnē "was a redistribution point, not only for slaves [and cinnamon, *Periplus*, paragr. 13], but for rice" (Tomber 2012a: 159). Investigations at Ras Hafun (Opōnē in the *Periplus*) have revealed the existence of two sites. A smaller site, with remains from 150 BCE to the beginning of the Christian era, contained first Egyptian pottery, some South Asian Wares, and later Parthian ceramics. A second site, dated between 100 and 500 CE, has yielded ceramics from Gujarat and the Persian Gulf (and only a few Egyptian shards), and in a second phase mainly Sassanian pottery (Smith and Wright 1988). "Unidentified materials may include Ethiopian sources" (Tomber 2012a: 97).

The *Periplus* names only a few places in the Persian Gulf (paragr. 35, 36, 37): Apologos, near the mouth of the Euphrates, and Omana (perhaps the archaeological site of ed-Dur; see below), located on the Omani coast but controlled by Persia. From there, ships sailed to Barbarikon, at the mouth of the Indus River, and to Barygaza, in Gujarat (Pliny [v, XXXII] also mentions a port called Acila, which could be Qalhat). Omana and its region exported pearls, gold (possibly from Egypt), "purple cloth, native clothing, slaves," and agricultural products (wine, and dates "in quantity") to India and southern Arabia.

It is obvious, however, that the author of the *Periplus* was not familiar with the Gulf, which was a Parthian territory, though he knew the routes between the Red Sea and India quite well. Indian products are given in detail, and the *Periplus* reflects a good knowledge of the cities and routes to the interior. Barbarikon was located in a country called Skythia (Scythia) (in Sind). Its capital, Minnagar, was located inland, and "the throne [was] in the hands of Parthians."[99] Barbarikon offered *costus*, *bdellium* (also exported on the Makran coast),[100] *lykion*,[101] nard,[102] turquoise, lapis lazuli, cotton cloth, "Seric skins," silk yarn (these goods reveal connections between China and northwestern India),[103] and indigo.

The port of Gujarat, called Barygaza, owed its wealth to its location at the end of a route starting at the city of Ozēnē (*Periplus*) (Ujjain) in the interior, where goods from

99　*Periplus*, paragr. 38; Casson 1989: 74–75. Indeed, the Parthians took control of the Indus region at the expense of the Saka ("Scythians") at the beginning of the Christian era (Casson 1989: 186). The *Periplus* mentions another town called Minnagara (paragr. 41), a Saka capital, located northeast of Barygaza (Casson 1989: 199).

100　*Commiphora wightii* (Arn.) Bhandari (=*Commiphora mukul* Engl.), Burseraceae (see Miller 1998: 69). The plant is originally from India (Gujarat, Karnataka, Madhya Pradesh, Rajasthan) and Pakistan-Sind.

101　Various species of *Berberis*, growing in the Himalayas. Some authors, however, have proposed *Acacia catechu* Willd., a tree from India (Casson 1989: 192–193).

102　The term "nard" has been applied to different plants. Schoff identifies the nard of Barbarikon as coming from the rhizome of various species of *Cymbopogon* (including *C. jwarancusa* [Jones] Schult.) (Gramineae) (perhaps also the *Cymbopogon martini* (Roxb.) J. F. Watson, *ginger-grass*). It ought to be distinguished from the nard or *spica nardi* which is *Nardostachys grandiflora* DC., from the Valerianaceae family, a plant from the Himalayas. See Schoff 1974: 42; Miller 1998: 88ff.; Crone 1987: 72–73. The Greek *nardos* comes from the Sanskrit *naladā*, *Nardostachys grandiflora* DC., Hebrew *nerd*. Miller (1998: 90) associates these terms with the Assyro-Babylonian *lardu*, but this proposition has not been accepted by Assyriologists.

103　Silk yarn imports supplied the weaving industry in the Levant.

the Ganges valley and the Himalayas arrived. Other routes indirectly linked Barygaza with the cities of Ter and Paithan (Pratishthānapura), the capital of the Shātavāhana.[104] Barygaza exported "cotton cloth of all kinds," silk cloth, agate and carnelian, ivory, spices and aromatics (nard *spica nardi, costus, bdellium, lykion*).[105] Copper, sandalwood, ebony, and teak were also sent from Barygaza to Omana and Apologos on "big vessels" (*Periplus*, 36). Aryakē (Gujarat) sent iron and steel, cotton fabrics, and lacquer to Adulis (*Periplus*, 6). The export of agricultural products is also mentioned for Barygaza – long pepper, "wheat, rice, sesame oil, and reed honey called *sacchari*" (cane sugar) – to Moscha Limēn and Somalia, whence these products were shipped onward to Egypt.[106] The production of Indian sugar appears to have been diversified, since Kautilya gives six kinds of sugar. Wheat and rice from Barygaza and the Tamil kingdoms also arrived on Socotra, as well as [cotton] textiles and "a few female slaves" (*Periplus*, 31; Schoff 1974: 69; Casson 1989: 69). Whereas authors such as I. Wallerstein have argued that long-distance trade in ancient times dealt only with luxury goods, L. Casson rightly observes that India was a supplier of raw materials and foods to the Persian Gulf and Arabia (Casson 1989: 18). The *Periplus* notes that Indo-Greek coins of Apollodotos and Menander were circulating in Gujarat.

Barbarikon and Barygaza imported commodities such as wine (primarily Italian), metals (lead, copper, tin), coins, red coral,[107] storax,[108] antimony, glass, embroidered cloths,[109] frankincense (at Barbarikon), arsenic sulphide (at Barygaza and on the Malabar coast), and topaz (according to Pliny, topaz came from Ethiopia and from islands in the Red Sea).

Market prices seem to have facilitated the importation of Egyptian copper into Barygaza; however, this city also exported copper (produced in northwestern India) to Apologos. Precious metal prices also encouraged the importation at Barygaza of money from Egypt made of gold and silver, a currency that commanded "an exchange at some profit against the local currency" (*Periplus*, paragr. 49).

Along the southwestern coast of India, the *Periplus* mentions eleven ports (and two large cities in the interior: Paithana and Tagara), and then the major ports of Muziris (Pattanam), and Nelkynda (possibly near Kottayam), located in Dimirike/Damirica, "the land of the Tamils," which was divided among four main kingdoms: the Chēra,

---

[104] *Periplus*, 51. Contact was indirect, as the Saka of Barygaza were at war with the Shātavāhana (Casson 1989: 213).

[105] *Periplus*, 49; Schoff 1974: 42; Casson 1989: 81. A carnelian ring bearing an inscription in Brahmī script has been found at Adulis (Pankhurst 1979: 107).

[106] *Periplus*, paragr. 14, 32, 41. The *Periplus* lists thirty-four plant species or plant products (Cappers 1999: 53). It is sometimes difficult, however, to match the terms given by the text with specific botanic species (for example, the term *cassia*). Depending on the context, the term *aloe* can correspond to various parts of different plants (Cappers 1999: 60). The name for cane sugar comes from the Sanskrit *sarkarā*.

[107] Pliny (XXXII.11) notes the significance of coral for the Indians, who used it for amulets to ward off evil (Boulnois 2001: 173–174), a practice also widespread in Italy. The religious dimension of coral can be observed in Christian iconography. Part of the coral arriving in India must have been sent to Central Asia and China (see below).

[108] A resin from *Styrax officinalis* L., originating in western Asia (Syria, Lebanon) and the eastern Mediterranean Sea (Greece) (Styracaceae family), or the gum of *Liquidambar orientalis* L., from Anatolia (Hamamelidaceae family).

[109] Pliny (VIII.74) wrote of embroidered fabrics from Babylon, called *polymita* (the same term used in the *Periplus*) (Schoff 1974: 167).

Figure 9.1 Silver tetradrachm of the Indo-Greek king Menander, 160–145 BCE. Bust/ Pallas standing © Bob Reis

the Pāndya, the Satiya, and the Chola. Muziris and Nelkynda were the main trade markets for pepper. The Romans, writes the *Periplus*, "send large ships to these market-towns [on the Malabar coast]," bringing glass, metals, embroidered linens, and "a great quantity of coin, on account of the great quantity and bulk of pepper and *malabathron* [from the Sanskrit *tamalapatra*, 'leaf of *tamala* [cinnamon]', or 'dark leaf']," imported from the interior (*Cinnamomum tamala* Nees and Eberm. is purportedly native to the Himalayas).[110] Money was used for carrying out transactions on the Malabar coast. The rise of Roman trade is more obvious when one compares the *Periplus* with Strabo. Strabo had knowledge only of ports in northern India, between the Indus and Bombay; however, the Ganges delta was already (vaguely) known (XV.1, 4; De Romanis 1997: 131 n. 14; see below). Muziris and Nelkynda probably hosted small Greco-Roman colonies. On the ancient map *Tabula Peutingeriana* (fifth century), a "temple of Augustus" is marked at Muziris,[111] and the city's importance is emphasized (the religious building may in fact have been a Hindu temple; see Ray 1988: 314). Recent analysis of human bones has shown the cosmopolitan nature of Muziris: only 40 percent of the skeletons studied belonged to "Indians"; the remains of three people from western Asia or eastern Europe have been found, as well as a man from the Baltic Sea, another from Central Asia, a man related to Jews from Kerala, and so forth. Excavations conducted since 2007 at Pattanam (Muziris) by the Kerala Council for Historical Research have led to the discovery of Mediterranean glass, Roman *Terra Sigillata* pottery and amphorae, dating to the first century BCE through to the second century CE (Seland 2014). Hoards of Roman coins have been discovered, and Rouletted Ware and Paddled-Impressed Ware from eastern India show that there were

---

[110] *Periplus*, paragr. 54, 55, 56; Schoff 1974: 44–45, 205; Casson 1989: 83–85, 241.

[111] The *Tabula Peutingeriana* was named after Konrad Peutinger, from Augsburg, to whom the humanist Konrad Celtes of Vienna left this map in 1507, a map that Celtes had discovered in the monastery of Benediktbeuren. It lays out the routes and the main cities of the Roman Empire and the limits of the known world. Long and narrow, the map is drawn on a parchment 6.83 m long and 0.34 m wide. The parchment goes back to the twelfth or thirteenth century, but the data on the map, according to E. Weber (1999), could date back to the fifth century. Some authors, however, have proposed earlier sources, going back to a map from Vipsanio Agrippa, who lived at the time of Augustus.

connections with the Coromandel coast (Tomber 2012a: 143). Sassanian and Sassano-Islamic ceramics have also been excavated (Kennet 2009).

Travel along the west coast of India was not without risk, and Roman ships had archers on board. Pliny warned against pirates in the region of Muziris and advised sailing instead to Becare (Bakare), further south. The *Periplus* and Ptolemy also mention that pirates were active on this coast. Greek mercenaries employed on ships sometimes settled in South Asia: the *Silappadikāram* describes Yavanas employed as guards in Madurai, the capital of the Pāndya kings (De Romanis 1997: 104). It is likely that Yavanas who settled in India converted to Buddhism (Thapar 1997: 35).

Muziris and Nelkynda also exported nard from the Ganges,[112] silk, ivory, large quantities of fine-quality pearls, precious stones (diamonds, sapphires), and tortoiseshell imported from the island of Chrysē (Sumatra, the Thai–Malay peninsula)[113] and islands along the coast of Damirica (Tamil Nadu). It is evident that ports in southwestern India served as storehouses for products arriving from the Ganges, Southeast Asia, and China. In terms of trade with the Orient, however, the Coromandel eclipsed the Malabar coast. Data given by the *Periplus* show that whereas the state controlled trade at Barbarikon and in South Arabia, in contrast, trade on the Malabar coast was in the hands of private traders.

In South India, Balita, Komar, and Colchoi, a region "that belongs to the Pandya kingdom," are named by the *Periplus*. Colchoi was a pearl-fishing site; pearls were sold on the market of Argaru "and nowhere else," a city which also exported muslins.[114] The text also mentions, on the southeast coast of India, the names of Kamara (Karikal, mouth of the Kāverī River), Podukē (Pondicherry), and Sōpatma (Supatana, or Madras),[115] where ships came in from the west coast, and also from the Ganges and Chrysē. "There is a market in these places [of the Coromandel coast] for all the [western] trade goods imported by Lymirike and, generally speaking, there come to them all year round both the cash originating from Egypt and most kinds of all the goods originating from Lymirike and supplied along this coast" (*Periplus*, paragr. 60; Casson 1989: 89).[116] The text here clearly mentions the use of coins from the Roman world to finance the trade with the East.

The *Periplus* distinguishes between two types of boats from this region: the *sangara*, "made of single logs bound together" (two canoes joined together – "double canoe" – called *jangār* on the Malabar coast), and the "very large" *kolandiophōnta* that sailed to Chrysē and the Ganges. Several interpretations have been provided for this name. Its

---

[112]   Miller 1998: 88ff.; Wheatley (1961: 18 n. 4) identifies the *malabathron* as *Pogostemon heyneanus* Benth., from the Lamiaceae family, or patchouli, found wild from India to the Philippines.

[113]   Chrysē, in the *Periplus* (paragr. 63), corresponds to both continental and insular Southeast Asia.

[114]   Schoff (1974: 241–242) has suggested identifying Argaru with Uraiyūr, the early Chola capital. Slaves were used for pearl-diving (*Periplus*, paragr. 59), and the king controlled its commerce.

[115]   "Many centuries later, European trading factories were put up near these places," note H. Kulke and D. Rothermund (1995: 107): the Danes settled at Tranquehar, near Karikal; the French at Pondicherry; and the British at Madras.

[116]   Contrary to what what has been asserted by J. Keay (2005: 76), the *Periplus* does not say here that merchandise was transported on roads crossing the southern end of the Indian peninsula, although transpeninsular roads were indeed active, and were probably used by merchants of the Roman world, as revealed by the presence of coins and Roman objects found, especially in the district of Coimbatore, rich in precious stones.

origin may be Dravidian: from the Tamil *kulinta*, "hollowed," and *oṭam*, "ship" (Huntingford 1980: 163). Moreover, the word *kola* means "ship" in the Buddhist Sanskrit texts, as does the term *kalam* in Tamil texts from the Sangam period. Though he does not specify his reasoning, Rājendralāla Mitra makes a connection with the Sanskrit term *kolāntarapota*, "ships for going to foreign shores" (Schoff 1974: 246). The term *pōta-*, "ship," exists in Sanskrit (Kumauni: *pot*, id.), and Hornell notes that *küllan* refers to the outrigger on Austronesian boats or to the outrigger canoe in Tamil: *kolandiophōnta* could thus be translated as "ship with outrigger" (Hornell 1920: 215; Turner 1962–1966: 477). J. Moudiappanadin (Inalco, Paris) prefers to break the word down into *kolu* ("paddle") + *undiya* (the past participle of the verb *unda*, "pushed, led") + *pōdam* ("boat," from the Sanskrit): "a boat conducted with paddles" (Moudiappanadin, p.c.). A. Christie considers *kolandiophōnta* to be "a Greek representation of the [Southeast Asian] term which the Chinese rendered as *kun-lun [bo]*" (*k'ouen-louen po*),[117] which means "Kunlun ship," *Kunlun* being the name given by the Chinese to southern people, and above all to Austronesians (see below). Pelliot (1925: 261) notes that as early as the fourth century "the term K'ouen-louen was in use in China and referred to dark-skinned people." Sima Biao, who lived from 240 to 305 CE, writes: "The large seagoing ships are called *bo*." However, the term *kunlun bo* is only attested during the Tang period (cf. a text from Huilin dated to 817 CE) (Pelliot 1925: 258–259).

None of these etymologies appears to be completely satisfactory; however, the *kolandiophōnta* mentioned by the *Periplus* could well be the large ships – without outriggers – that the Portuguese found when they arrived in the Malacca Strait. They correspond to the *bo*, seagoing ships already described by a Chinese chronicle (*Nanzhou yiwu zhi* by Wan Zhen) during the third century: "The large ones are more than 50 m in length and stand out of the water four to five meters. They carry from six to seven hundred persons, with 10,000 bushels of cargo [from 250 to 1,000 tons, according to various interpretations]" (Manguin 1980: 275).[118] For the *K'un-lun bo*, a text by the Buddhist monk Huilin notes that coconut tree fibers were used "to bind the parts of the ship together," and that they possessed "several thicknesses of side-planks," needed no nails, were divided into "three sections," and caulked using a kind of resin (Pelliot 1925: 259–260). These characteristics were later noted by the Portuguese, as was the use of wooden dowels to join the planks together,[119] the presence of double quarter-rudders, and of two masts in addition to the bowsprit. The ships used several sails, "woven with tree leaves."

[117] Christie 1957: 353. G. Coedès (1968: 273 n. 78) writes that Christie "considers *kolandiapha* to be a Greek transcription of the Chinese *k'ouen-louen po*." More precisely, Christie writes that: "It now seems to me best to consider *kolandiophonta* as a corrupt form which originally represented some compound of the same general order as *kun-lun po*": the original term was Austronesian.

[118] According to the *Guangya*, a dictionary compiled *c.* 230 CE by Zhang Yi, the "*bo* is a seagoing ship." These ships, writes Huilin, "lie six or seven feet deep in the water. They are fast and can transport more than a thousand men, aside from cargo. They are also called *K'un-lun bo*. Many of those who form the crews and technicians of these ships are *K'un-lun* people" (Pelliot 1925: 258–259). See also Christie 1957: 348; Manguin 1980: 275.

[119] Besides ancient characteristics, the ships observed by the Portuguese exhibited more recent features, partly the result of Chinese influences during the Song period (see below).

This type of ship had probably been sailing between the Orient and the West since ancient times. According to P.-Y. Manguin, one of the ships depicted in the frescoes of Ajanta (Maharashtra) during the first half of the sixth century shows a number of similar features. The drawing of this ship does not appear to display the "sewn-plank" technique common in the western Indian Ocean.[120] Indeed, in the Insulindian lashed-lug and stitched-plank technique,[121] the stitches are not visible on the vessel's exterior.[122] The strakes of the hull are fastened on the interior, in a discontinuous manner; lugs carved out of the inner side of the planks support crosswise thwarts that maintain the hull. The lugs are also used to fasten "thwarts, frames and strakes" together with fibers.[123] As noted above, the planks are also fastened together by way of wooden dowels.

[120] Manguin 1980: 274. The ship mentioned by Manguin is depicted in Deloche 1996: 203 fig. 3d. It may represent a hybrid image of various vessels – or reflect the hybridity of some of the Indian Ocean vessels. The ship is decorated with two eyes at the bow and at the stern. It possesses a bowsprit, and three rectangular sails that may be sails of a Chinese type, made up of an assemblage of battens and mats (Deloche 1996: 205). G. Yinzeng considers this Ajanta image to represent a Chinese ship (2006: 120). Another painting from Ajanta features a ship with three masts bearing a dais in the middle (Deloche 1996: 203, fig. 3c). Ships with two masts and steered by quarter-rudders were already depicted on second- and third-century Andhra coins; the type of sails used is still unknown. See also the relief from Aurangabad (sixth century CE) depicting a ship with two masts (Deloche 1996: 201 and 202 fig. 2a–d, e). Manguin (1985a: 12) has pointed out similarities between the sails depicted on the Ajanta ships and those on the boats depicted on bas-reliefs at Borobudur.

[121] See Manguin 1996. The oldest known ship in Southeast Asia, built using the lashed-lug and stitched-plank tradition, has been excavated at Pontian, on the Malay peninsula. A radiocarbon dating gives a period between the third and fifth centuries. Other discoveries of ancient ships have been made at Kolam Pinisi (Palembang), dated between the fifth and seventh centuries, and at Sambirejo (downstream from Palembang), dated between the seventh and eighth centuries (Manguin 1996: 185–186). A ship found at Butuan (Mindanao) has been dated to the third or fourth century; this dating has been rejected by Manguin (1996), but accepted by Bellwood *et al.* (2007). Other ships found at Butuan are of a more recent date (between the thirteenth and fifteenth centuries). Ship remains have also been excavated at Khuan Lukpad (first millennium) and at Kota Cina (between the twelfth and fourteenth centuries). Ropes were usually made using sugar palm fibers (*Arenga pinnata*, an ancient use already mentioned in a Chinese text written in 304 CE) or coconut fibers (Manguin 1993: 261). The ancient ships of the Solomon Islands (without outriggers) called *mon* show some affinities with the Pontian boat. They were built using a mixed technique: "their planks were sewn together (not edge-dowelled)," and "lugs were left protruding from the carved planks, to which solid timber frames were lashed" (Manguin 1985b: 337). The Solomon Islands may have been in contact with eastern Indonesia and the Philippines during the Iron Age (Manguin 1985b: 338; Bellwood 1978: 269).

[122] In a few cases, on Southeast Asian ships with sewn and lashed hulls, the (noncontinuous) lashings or stitches are visible on the outside of the hull (Manguin 1985b: 326 fig 20.6D and E). Ships from the Pacific use techniques where the planks are held together with (continuous or noncontinuous) stitches visible from the outside of the hull (Manguin 1985b: 337). It is possible that the technique with hidden lashings on the inside of the hull and the practice of noncontinuous stitches were a development occurring after the Austronesian dispersion throughout the Pacific. However, ships from Fiji, Tonga, and Samoa display stitches on the inside of their hulls (Manguin 1985b). Whereas the ships of the western Indian Ocean of which we are aware possessed continuous stitches, that were visible from the hull's exterior, the lashings on the Egyptian boat of Khufu (see above) were on the hull's interior (Manguin 1985b: 338).

[123] In addition, wooden dowels are inserted between the strakes. Dowels were rare on ancient ships; they would become more common during the second millennium, while the lugs began to disappear (Manguin 2000a: 39–40; see below).

The scale of ancient Indian navigation ought to be emphasized here. It has long been underestimated, as has long-distance trade, and this in turn has perpetuated the idea of an agrarian, static, and unchanging Indian subcontinent. The *Paṭṭinappālai*, a Tamil text of the second or third century, mentions horses being transported by boat. The Sanskrit lexicon *Amarakosha* (sixth–seventh century) and some other glossaries mention various names of ships and parts of ships (Chakravarti 2002a: 42). *Pota* designates a large ship. The Sanskrit terms *citra* and *alekhya* may refer to nautical charts (Ray 2002b: 78). Under the term *bo* (*po*), Chinese texts describe Austronesian vessels, but also sometimes refer to Indian ships. A passage in a book by Kang Tai, lost but quoted in the *Taiping yulan* (982), indicates that: "From Chia-na-t'iao [western India] (one could) board a large *p'o* which has seven sails, and sail for a month and a few days with the seasonal wind to enter the country of Ta-ch'in [Persian Gulf]" (Wang Gungwu 1958: 39 n. 32).[124] Pliny (VI.24) spoke of Sinhalese ships "of 3000 amphorae" (75 tons). According to the *Jātaka*, some vessels transported from 500 to 700 people, and the Sinhalese chronicles such as the *Mahāvamsa* speak of the large fleets that the Tamils were already capable of fitting out during the last centuries BCE (Filliozat 1956; see below). During the fifth century, the Chinese pilgrim Faxian traveled from Sri Lanka to Java on a ship carrying 200 men. "A recent perusal of ancient Tamil literature has brought to light at least eighteen terms suggesting the rich varieties of indigenous vessels in South India" (Chakravarti 2002a: 41).[125] Jacq-Hergoualc'h suggests that Indian techniques spread into the western Indian Ocean were characterized by the use of teak, sewn planks, caulking using the coconut tree, and sugar palm fibers, "triangular and high sails woven with coconut or cotton threads" (Jacq-Hergoualc'h *et al.* 1998: 285). Quoting Eratosthenes, Pliny reported that boats made of reeds sailed between the mouth of the Ganges and Sri Lanka in twenty days. Indian ships went to ports on the Persian Gulf and the Arab coasts. In the western part of the Ocean, however, most of the trade was controlled by Arab intermediaries. Triangular "lateen" sails that allowed vessels to tack close to the winds may have been used by Arab sailors several centuries prior to the Christian era,[126] but Manguin notes that "all observers thus appear to agree that the late medieval Arabo-Indian vessels did not sport lateens. What they had was a boom-less 'canted square-sail' (actually a rectangular sail) or, in other words, a 'dipping lug-sail'" (2012: 605).

Words relating to ships testify to exchanges between the East and the West, for example in the Bay of Bengal. Of foreign origin, the Chinese *bo* has sometimes been linked to the Tamil *padao* and the Malay *perahu* (Dravidian languages also have *padahu*, *patavu*).[127] *Perahu*, however, does not appear until the ninth century in Austronesian languages, in an inscription in Old Balinese (Manguin 1996: 192).

---

[124] See also Wolters 1967: 43–44, who locates "Chia-na-t'iao" near the Indus valley instead. Pelliot (1925: 252) considers Kia-na-diao to be the transcription of the term *Kanadvīpa*.

[125] "The largest of these South Indian vessels, called *matalai* (also *kalam*), [were] generally used for long-distance voyages" (Chakravarti 2002a: 41).

[126] Pearson 2003: 67. Pearson suggests a Persian origin for the "lateen" sail. This type of sail may have been present in the Mediterranean Sea as early as the beginning of the Christian era and most likely during the ninth century (see below). Similar sails appeared independently in eastern Indonesia. The sail featured in the Kelenderis mosaic (sixth century) is not a lateen sail (Z. Friedman 2007).

[127] Fuller *et al.* (2011: 553) also note the Hindi term *parwa*, and the Sinhalese *paruva*, which can be connected to the Javanese *prau*.

The word seems to be of Austronesian origin.[128] Moreover, Mahdi rejects the idea that the Chinese term *bo* derived from the Malay *perahu*; he considers the pronunciation of *bo* to have probably "sounded something like *bak*," which seems to reflect an Austronesian term derived from a proto-form *qabaŋ* (see Mentawei *abak*, whereas the Favorlang *abak* appears to be a loanword: it has an irregular final –*k* where one would expect *aban*) (1994b: 458; 1999a: 165–166).[129] Note, though, that the Sriwijayan stela at Telaga Batu, in its inscription in Old Malay, shows the term *puhawang*, "shipmaster."

For P.-Y. Manguin, the Chinese did not have transoceanic ships prior to the eighth or ninth century; however, ancient Chinese texts clearly state otherwise. It is true, however, that Chinese monks traveling during the seventh century did not do so on Chinese ships, but on ships from Srīwijaya. The Chinese junk may have been influenced by *kunlun* ships. Evidence of a Southeast Asian loanword present in India can be found in the Austronesian term *wangkang* appearing in Indian texts from Sangam literature dated to the beginning of the first millennium (*Maduraikancci*) under the form *vangkam* (some authors have suggested that the term *wangkang* was borrowed from Dravidian languages, but the opposite appears more likely).[130] One also notes the existence of a Malay term *kapal* and the Dravidian *kappal* (Manguin 1996: 192). In the *Jātaka*, one of the words referring to a sail, *lakara*, is considered to be of foreign origin: it may be an Austronesian term.[131] In addition, an ancient Indian term (Middle Indic, first millennium) *layara* is obviously derived from PAN *layaR*, "sail" (Turner 1966: 636). The Maldivian term *baraa*, "outrigger," is also derived from an Austronesian term (see the PAN *baRat*, "crossbeam"; Fuller *et al.* 2011: 553). It is sometimes difficult to identify the direction taken by a loanword. In any case, this community of terms expresses the scale of exchanges between India and Southeast Asia before and after the beginning of the Christian era as well as the existence of shared traditions, also illustrated by representations of ships (Ajanta, Borobudur).

Along the southern coast of India, double canoes joined by deck-platforms are mentioned in the *Periplus* under the term *sangara* (see above). Schoff notes the existence of double canoes on all the coasts of southern India (Malabar for example), in Sri Lanka, and of course in Polynesia,[132] where Hornell mentions their presence in a simpler form in Andhra Pradesh (mouths of the Kistna [Krishnā] and the Godāvarī rivers); he also mentions double-hulled barges on the Ganges (Hornell 1946: 191, 248, 263). Mahdi suggests that the *sangara* were of Austronesian origin (but the word can be

---

[128] Mahdi 1999b: 169ff. The author reconstructs an Austronesian term *pəDaHu/ paDaHu*, suggested as a loanword from the Nagas of eastern India, but ultimately of Austronesian origin (Mahdi 1994b: 462). See also Manguin 2016: 64.

[129] J. Lo (1970) also proposes "an ancient pronunciation *bahk*" for *bo*. Mahdi notes that an Austronesian term derived from *qabaŋ* has been borrowed in Old Mon under the form *kbaŋ*, "ship" (Mahdi 1994b: 458).

[130] Manguin 2016: 64. We find the same problem as has been pointed out for *perahu* (Manguin 1996: 192; 2004a: 281). A. Christie (1957: 349) has noted the Car-Nicobar *ku-pōk*.

[131] Ray 1996: 361. Ray adds that "many of the catamarans on the east coast [of India] carry sails which are said to have an Indonesian origin" (she quotes here Bowen 1953: 110).

[132] One finds the term *jangār* on the Malabar coast, *jangāla* in Tulu, and *samghādam* in Sanskrit, "raft" (Schoff 1974: 243).

linked to the Tamil *sangādam*, "a double canoe") (Mahdi 1999a: 152).[133] In southeastern Madagascar, on the Matatāña River, the Onzatsy clan used "double canoes" (*lakaña hamba*), joined by crossplanks forming a kind of deck (the Onzatsy carry the corpses of their chiefs to their collective tomb with this kind of boat). They are mentioned as being commonly used "on the rivers on the west coast" (Oñilahy and Tsiribihina) of Madagascar at the beginning of the 20th century, where they are called *vata hambaña* ("twin boxes") (Grandidier and Grandidier 1928: 368).

Let us return to the journey of the *Periplus* where we left it, south of India. The island of Sri Lanka is mentioned under the name of Palaisimundu, "called by the Ancients Taprobanē [from Tamraparni]."[134] "It produces pearls, transparent stones, muslins and tortoiseshell" (*Periplus*, paragr. 61). Pomponius Mela said of the island that it was "the beginning of another world," which expresses well the way in which Sri Lanka acted as a link between two oceans. On the eastern coast of India, beyond the regions of Masalia (Masulipatam) (where "great quantities of muslins" were produced) and Dēsarēnē (Orissa), which provided ivory, one arrived at the Ganges River, where a city of the same name was located at its mouth (= probably Tāmralipti, today called Tamluk). The Ganges exported *malabathron*, nard, pearls, and "muslins of the finest sorts. It is said that there are gold-mines near these places, and there is a gold coin which is called *kaltis*" (*Periplus*, paragr. 63; Schoff 1974: 47, 255ff.). Prior to the *Periplus*, Strabo, in his *Geography*, had already written of the Ganges. The delta of the Ganges was at the far end of the earth, but Strabo notes that: "As for the merchants who now sail from Aegypt by the Nile and the Arabian Gulf as far as India, only a small number have sailed as far as the Ganges; and even these are merely private citizens and of no use as regards the history of the places they have seen" (Strabo XV.1.4).[135] During the second century CE, Arrian knew of Palimbothra (Pātaliputra), referring to it as a city located near the Ganges.

On Chrysē, "an island in the ocean just opposite the Ganges," "the last part of the inhabited world toward the east, under the rising sun itself," the *Periplus* does not provide much detail except the fact that this country exports "the best tortoiseshell of all the places on the Erythraean Sea." However, it does reveal knowledge of Southeast Asia acquired from the Indians. "After this region [Chrysē], under the very north, the sea outside ending in a land called This, there is a very great island city called Thinae, from which raw silk and silk yarn and silk cloth are brought on foot through Bactria to Barygaza, and are also exported to Damirica by way of the river Ganges" (*Periplus*, paragr. 64). Another route went to China: "Every year there turns up at the border of Thina a certain tribe, short in body and very flat-faced, called Sēsatai, they come … bearing great packs resembling mats of green leaves

---

[133] Mahdi (2016) links it ultimately to the boat technology used by the Negritos of Insular Southeast Asia.

[134] The *Geography* of Ptolemy gives the island the name of Salikē. Palaisimundu comes from the name of the capital, given by the Sinhalese embassy under Claudius's reign.

[135] Before Strabo, Diodorus of Sicily, referring to Megasthenes, writes of the Gangaridai, mentioned next to the Prasioi (Magadha) (see below).

[*malabathron*]."[136] The author of the *Periplus* thus knew of two main routes between China and India through Central Asia and Upper Burma.[137] The land of "This" (Casson reads Thina) probably refers to Qin, a western region of China.[138]

The *Periplus* thus offers an almost complete panorama of the areas in the Indian Ocean where the merchants of the Greco-Roman world used to trade. In his *Geography* (written in 156 CE, but in its present form the *Geography* may have been compiled by a Byzantine author of the tenth or eleventh century),[139] Ptolemy, a Greek from Alexandria, leads us along the roads of Central Asia en route to China. He used a chronicle by Marinus of Tyre (*c.* 100 CE) based on the notes of a Macedonian merchant called Maës Titianos, who did not complete the whole journey. The last section, toward Kattigara, is based on the account of a man called Alexandros, not known elsewhere.

The route began in Cilicia, crossed Mesopotamia, Assyria and Media, to Ecbatana and the Caspian Sea; through Parthia and Hyrcania to Antiochia Margiana (Merv), thence though Aria into Bactria. Thence the route passed through the mountainous country of the Comedi, and through the territory of the Sacae to the 'Stone tower', the station of those merchants who trade with the Seres (Tashkurghan, on the Upper Yarkand river in the Chinese Pamirs ...). Thence to the Casii (Kashgar) and through the country of the Thaguri [Tocharians], until after a seven-months journey from the Stone tower, the merchants arrived at *Sera metropolis* [the capital of the Seres]. (Schoff 1974: 269)

These Seres lived north of the Sinai, whose capital was Sinai (or Sinae) or Thinai.

Two branches of the "Silk Roads" in fact merged at Merv, departing from Kashgar (Chinese Shule). One could leave Merv on a northern route through Sogdiana toward

---

[136] *Periplus*, paragr. 65; Casson 1989: 91, 93, 241–243. For the population that lived near the Chinese border, "somewhere between Assam and Sichuan" (G. Coedès), and traded with China, Ptolemy writes of the Saēsadai or Bēsadai. In the *Periplus*, Schoff transcribes the name as Besatae.

[137] Pliny does not know the origin of silk, but he writes of the Seres that they are "famous for the woolen substance obtained from their forests; after a soaking in water they comb off the white down of the leaves, and so supply our women with the double task of unravelling the threads and weaving them together again" (VI.20). He also evokes the Cirrhadae, "who cover themselves with a down plucked from the leaves of trees," showing some knowledge of a silk road going through Upper Burma and Assam (Schoff 1974: 267). There is obviously confusion in Pliny, as L. Boulnois notes, concerning the origin of silk and the use of "a white down which forms on the leaves of the white *tong* tree, a variety of *wutong* [*Sterculia platanifolia* L.]. The manufacture of this cloth was a specialty of the ancient Burmese kingdom of Piao, on the border with Yunnan" (Boulnois 2008: 103). Virgil also speaks of "the fine fleece of the leaves" of the forests of the Seres (Boulnois 2008: 103).

[138] "The land of This," the *Periplus* also writes, "is not easy of access; few men come from there, and seldom." From the kingdom of Qin came the king who unified China before the Han Dynasty (221–207 BCE). The city of Thinae has been given various locations, sometimes at Chang'an, the capital of the Han. The Thinae of the *Periplus* did not necessarily correspond to the Sinae or Sinai of the *Geography*. Some authors have related Thinae or Sinae to the name "Theinni, the Burmese form of Hsen-wi, or the Northern Shans" and to the name Tien given to Yunnan by Marco Polo. These linguistic comparisons have been rightly criticized by Schoff (1974: 273–275) for the Thinae of the *Periplus*, but are perhaps valid for the Sinae of Ptolemy.

[139] Wheatley 1961: 138, who agrees with Bagrow (1945). For Freeman-Grenville (1975: 3), the version of the text known to us may be a compilation dating to the early fifth century. Mathew (1975: 153) argues that the parts concerning Southeast Asia and East Africa were probably additions made by geographers at the end of the fourth century CE.

Maracanda (the future Samarkand); this road joined the upper valley of the Syr-Darya and the country of Fergana and then arrived at Kashgar. A southern branch – which Maës or his informers must have followed – went through Bactres and Bactria and then northward, to Kashgar. In addition, from Bactres, a road went down to Taxila and northern India. Ptolemy also signals the existence of two routes from China, one to Bactria, and the other to India through Palimbothra. The Sinai referred to by the author could have been the inhabitants of Sichuan or Yunnan (see above). In Serica, he lists fifteen towns, which are difficult to identify.

The *Geography* also discloses new knowledge on maritime routes.[140] Ptolemy mentions that Roman merchants visited two harbors in Sri Lanka called Modurgi and Talacori (see McLaughlin 2014: 199). He gives data not present in the *Periplus* for the eastern coast of India. The discovery of Roman coins at the mouth of the Krishna River may indicate a Roman presence, a movement "correlated with the Shatavahana shift" to that river (Tomber 2012a: 144). Products from eastern India reached Rome: "Martial describes how the emperor Domitian had Bengal tigers displayed in the Roman arena" (McLaughlin 2014: 204). For Southeast Asia, Ptolemy probably used data from a book written by a Greek merchant, Alexandros, that described Roman voyages to the Malay peninsula (McLaughlin 2014: 201). Roman merchants traveled as far as the Burmese city of Tamala, and Ptolemy indicates that a road went from Tamala to the Gulf of Thailand: "they traverse from Tamala over the Golden Peninsula on a crossing that is 1,600 stades (176 miles)" (McLaughlin 2014: 205). For Southeast Asia, the *Geography* mentions various toponyms, notably Iabadiou, a transcription of a Prākrit form Yavadivu, from the Sanskrit Yavadvīpa (Java, or Sumatra), a site called Barousai, probably Barus, in the north of Sumatra (Guillot 1998: 113), the peninsula of the "Golden Chersonese" (Thai–Malay peninsula and Sumatra) (see below) and beyond, the city of Kattigara (a port of the Sinai on the shore of a large gulf, Kattigara has not been precisely located: perhaps Kauṭhāra, in Champa, or Luy Lau, in Jiaozhi [Chiao-chih, Hanoi], in the Red River valley, or Oc Eo, on the Gulf of Thailand). According to Ptolemy, Masalia (Masulipattanam) was the port of departure for ships sailing to *Chryse chora* and *Chryse chersonesis*, names which may refer to the Suvarnabhūmi and Suvarnadvīpa of ancient Indian literature (Ptolemy, *Geography* VII.1.15; Chakravarti 2002a: 41). References to several rivers on the Thai–Malay peninsula probably point to a knowledge of the use of transpeninsular routes between the Gulf of Bengal and the Gulf of Thailand. At the same time, a port called Sabara is mentioned near Singapore, showing that there was some familiarity with maritime routes going around the Malay peninsula.

A comparison between the *Periplus* and the *Geography* on the one hand, and more recent texts such as the accounts of Marco Polo and Ibn Battūta on the other, shows that as early as the first centuries of the Christian era, the main nodes around which trade was organized were already in place (Barbarikon and Barygaza foreshadow the ports of Daybul and Cambay; Muza, Eudaimōn Arabia, and Kanē [Qanī] herald the future roles played by Aden and Shiḥr, and so on). Journeys between the Red Sea and the coasts of India were undertaken regularly during the second century. Apart from

---

[140] It is clear, however, that the *Periplus* and Ptolemy's *Geography* have sometimes used the same source(s) (see Arnaud 2012: 48).

some products such as wine and oil, shipped by the Roman world, there was a continuity in the types of products exported: cotton cloth, silk, indigo for textiles and dyes, incense from Arabia, myrrh from Arabia and India, cinnamon from South and East Asia, pepper from India for spices and aromatics, precious metals (gold, silver), iron, slaves, ivory, glass, leather, and so forth. In later centuries, however, products would become more and more diverse, and a significant increase can be observed in the volume of trade.

A drop in Roman trade to the east has been noted during the third and fourth centuries. Berenice went through a marked decline at this time (Sidebotham 2011: 259). In Egypt, epidemics broke out; the Antonine plague of 165–180 CE may have killed a third of the population, and the plague of Cyprian, probably a smallpox pandemic, coincided with a period of low Nile flooding during the third century. During the late fourth and fifth centuries, however, Egypt began to recover, under the influence of more significant Nile flooding linked to stronger monsoons in the Indian Ocean during a part of this period.[141] Many Roman coins or imitations dated to the fourth and fifth centuries have been discovered in Tamil Nadu (region of Madras, and Tirukkoilur) and in Sri Lanka, revealing a revival in trade at this time.[142] Raschke (1975: 244) observes that "there are more Egyptian textual references to Indian spices in the 3rd and 4th centuries than earlier" (Tomber 2012a: 161), and Tomber emphasizes ongoing Roman participation in Indian commerce during the fifth century (2012a: 164, and above). At the end of the fourth century, Ammianus Marcellinus notes that silk was now worn by all social classes,[143] and that Chinese goods were present at the annual fair of Batanea in the Euphrates valley, around 360 CE. Late Roman pottery of the fifth–sixth century has been found in Gujarat, and in Maharashtra (at Elephanta) (Tomber 2012a: 166).

Direct contacts between Rome and India, however, became rarer during the third and fourth centuries. Instead, intermediaries stood between the Orient and the Occident: Axum first,[144] and later the Sassanid Empire – which, at its peak during the sixth century, controlled the Persian Gulf and part of the Indian Ocean trade – and more importantly, from the seventh century onward, the "Muslim screen."[145] Axumite pottery is most common in Berenice during the late Roman period (Tomber 2012b: 204). Myos Hormos was abandoned during the third century,[146] perhaps for local reasons, as was Berenice c. 550, after a period of growth during the fifth century (Sidebotham 2011). Until

---

[141] This revival benefited Constantinople. During the fourth century, "Egypt's corn trade began to shift from Rome to a burgeoning Constantinople" (Brown 2001: 77).

[142] Basa and Behera 1999: 25; Mitchiner 2004: 98. The most recent coins found in Sri Lanka are coins of Honorius (395–423) (Pirenne 1970: 115).

[143] At Byzantium, St. John Chrysostom (*Homily* XXV) tells us that silks were no longer costly (Adshead 1995: 37).

[144] The *Periplus* already mentions the "city of the Axumites" as a place where "all the ivory is brought from the country beyond the Nile"; it that was then transported to the port of Adulis (paragr. 4; Schoff 1974: 23; Casson 1989: 53). According to D. W. Phillipson (2012: 64), "the Greek-speaking King Zoscales mentioned in the *Periplus* [parag. 5] ruled in the coastal region [Adulis] rather than – as has usually been assumed – at Aksum." Ties were formed between Byzantium and Axum, marked by the Ethiopian conversion to Christianity (see below).

[145] Lombard 1990, II: 26. Late Roman and Byzantine coins have been unearthed in Gujarat, Andhra Pradesh, and Tamil Nadu, however.

[146] For Seland (2014: 383). however, "the overall trend seems to be that ports of the northern Red Sea gained importance in late antiquity."

the rediscovery of India by Marco Polo, the West's image of this region was based on descriptions by Roman and Greek authors.[147] During the sixth century, precious goods did reach Alexandria, from western Asia, the Mediterranean, Arabia, India, or from lands further east. A list of fifty-four items attributed to a third-century jurist, Aelius Marcianus, is quoted in the *Digest* promulgated by Emperor Justinian in 533 CE, listing "articles subject to duty" upon entry in Alexandria (meaning that these products still arrived in Alexandria, though the transporters may have changed):

cinnamon, long pepper, white pepper, *folium pentasphaerum* [unidentified spice], Barbary leaf, putchuk (*costum* and *costamomum*), spikenard, Tyrian cassia, cassia bark, myrrh, amomum,[148] ginger,[149] cinnamon leaf, *aroma indicum* [unspecified Indian spice], *galbanum*,[150] asafoetida,[151] aloewood,[152] barberry, astragalus,[153] Arabian onyx, cardamom,[154] cinnamon bark, fine linen, Babylonian furs, Parthian furs, ivory, Indian iron, raw cotton, *lapis universus* [unspecified Indian stone], pearls, sardonyx, bloodstones, *hyacinthus* [perhaps aquamarine], emeralds, diamonds, lapis lazuli, turquoise, beryls, tortoise stones, Indian or Assyrian drugs, raw silk, garments made completely or partly from silk, painted hangings, Indian eunuchs, lions and lionnesses, leopards, panthers, purple cloth, cloth woven from sheep's wool, orchil, Indian hair [?], etc.[155]

---

[147] The myth that all luxuries originated in India has been of great significance for the West, and even for the history of the world. "The quest for India," noted Hegel, "is a moving force of our whole history. Since ancient times all nations have directed their wishes and desires to that miraculous country whose treasures they coveted. These treasures were the most precious on earth: treasures of nature, pearls, diamonds, incense, the essence of roses, elephants, lions, etc. and also the treasures of wisdom" (quoted by Kulke and Rothermund 1995: 105).

[148] *Amomum subulatum* Roxb. (Zingiberaceae), Indian cardamom, originating from China (Yunnan, for example), Nepal, Bhutan, India (Assam, Sikkim, Bengal), and Myanmar; but the term *amomum* can refer to other plants, for example *Amomum aromaticum* Roxb., native to eastern India, Bhutan, and Nepal.

[149] Dioscorides claims that ginger was imported from Eritrea and Arabia, where it was cultivated. Ginger was grown in the Indus during the third millennium BCE (traces of ginger and turmeric have been found in a pot, and on the teeth of humans and animals [cows] at Farmana, Haryana) (Lawler 2012). The Austronesians also developed ginger cultivation (it is possible to reconstruct the PMP *laqia*). Southworth (2005: 83, 213) has reconstituted the term *cinki* in Proto-South Dravidian 1, a term of uncertain origin.

[150] *Ferula gummosa* Boiss. (=*Ferula galbaniflua* Boiss. and Buhse), Umbelliferae family, a plant native to Persia and Turkmenistan (Miller 1998: 99). The plant was probably already being exported from India at an early time.

[151] *Ferula asa-foetida* L., *Ferula foetida* (Bunge) Regel. This plant was imported as a substitute for *silphium*, a related plant exported from Libya that had already disappeared before Pliny's time.

[152] *Aloeswood: Aquilaria malaccensis* Lam. (also called eaglewood) and other species of the Thymelaeaceae family. Found in Bhutan and in Southeast Asia. The Sanskrit *agāru-* gave the Hebrew *aḥāloth* and the Greek *agalokhon* (in Dioscorides, first century CE) (Miller 1998: 65–66). The Malay *garu* points to a Southeast Asian origin for the tree. Quoting Mayrhofer, R. L. Turner, however, sees a Dravidian origin for the Sanskrit term. Southworth reconstructs *akil* in Proto-South Dravidian 1 (the split between Proto-South Dravidian 1 and 2 appears to have occurred *c.* 1100 BCE at the earliest) (Southworth 2006: 133).

[153] The *Astragalus* genus encompasses many species originating from Asia (but also from other regions).

[154] *Elettaria cardamomum* (L.) Maton (Zingiberaceae), found in India and in Southeast Asia. Pliny distinguishes four different kinds. Dioscorides and Pliny link the *cardamomum* to Arabia, indicating here not the place of origin of the plant, but a trade route (see Miller 1998: 71–73). It is also possible, as P. Crone (2004) would have it, that the term in fact referred to one or more plant(s) from Arabia and western Asia.

[155] Parker 2002: 41–42. Also Schoff 1974: 289. In the *Digest* XXXIX, XV. 5, 7. The list includes neither camphor, nor incense, which is surprising for the latter; however, the text may be incomplete. Note that eunuchs from India were subject to taxes, while African slaves were not mentioned.

The list also mentions cloves and sugar. As we can see, aromatics and spices made up a significant part of luxury imports. These substances are invaluable clues to understanding the makeup of exchange networks and their evolution.

Spices and Aromatics

> Who is this coming up from the wilderness, like a column of smoke, perfumed with myrrh and incense made from all the spices of the merchant?
> (Song of Songs 3:6)

Spices and aromatics appeal to our sense of smell and taste. Bringing humankind closer to the Divine, they are a part of rituals and used for various medicines. Across most societies, fragrant plants or substances are associated with divinities and ancestors, whereas stinking plants or substances pertain to the field of evil spirits, refuse, and death. The fragrance of exotic perfumes and aromatics are indicators of their magic powers, and the "qualities associated with distant places" (Helms 1988: 124–125). At the beginning of the Christian era, the trade in spices and aromatics played a crucial role both in the "indianization" of Southeast Asia, and in the unification of Indian Ocean networks. This trade explains why the Europeans were so interested in the Indian Ocean; it would also become a significant factor during the Muslim expansion. As Glover notes regarding cloves, "the western demand for an aromatic flower bud of rather little value to the native peoples of the Moluccas transformed, in the long run, the economic and political face of Asia" (1996: 369).

Shipwrecks and the mummy of Ramses II have shown that pepper was being imported into the Mediterranean Sea as early as the second millennium BCE, "probably by the Phoenicians" (Parker 2002: 43). Sappho (at the end of the seventh century BCE) and the Bible in the Book of Exodus (possibly written in the fifth century BCE) both mention that spices and aromatics came from southern Arabia, India, and perhaps Southeast Asia or even China. Exodus thus shows that aromatics from distant countries were used to make anointing oil – see below – and the "incense" of the priests (Exodus 30:34–35), composed of "myrrh, onycha, *galbanum* and pure incense."[156] The Book of Numbers (24:6) in the third of the seven oracles of Balaam mentions the term *aḥalim*, which may refer to aloeswood.[157] Genesis (2:12) and Numbers (11:7)

---

[156] As mentioned above, incense can be made using different species of *Boswellia*, from Arabia or Africa. Different ingredients are identified for its composition, depending on which version of the Bible is consulted. In the New International Version: "The Lord said to Moses: 'Take fragrant spices – gum resin, onycha, and galbanum – and pure frankincense, all in equal amounts, and make a fragrant blend of incense, the work of a perfumer. It is to be salted and pure and sacred'" (Exodus 30:34–35). The Hebrew term used for *galbanum* is *ḥelbenah* (also present in the Book of Sirach 24:15) (in Aramaic *halbane*, in Greek *chalbane*). In different religious rituals, clouds of incense symbolized the hidden presence of God. "Incense," a mixture of fragrant substances that were burnt, was also used in Greek and Roman religions. The practice was resumed by Christianity. The "Three Magi" brought myrrh and incense to Bethlehem. Onycha was prepared using the operculum of a Red Sea mollusk.

[157] Or *oḥalim* (Negev 1990: 355); Miller 1998: 66. The date assigned to this document by Miller (between 900 and 722 BCE) appears to go too far back; the fifth century BCE is a more plausible time frame. In Psalms 45:8, Proverbs 7:17, and Song of Songs 4:13, the Hebrew term corresponding to aloes is *aḥaloth* or *oḥaloth*. See above for the etymology of this term.

mention the *bdellium*, rendered in Hebrew as *b'dolah*, related to the Assyro-Babylonian *budulhu*,[158] "both transcriptions of a non-Semitic word" (Miller 1998: 69). According to the first Book of Kings (10:11–12), "Hiram's ships brought gold from Ophir; they also brought a very great amount of *almug* wood [sandalwood] and valuable stones. With the sandalwood the king made supports for the Lord's temple and the royal palace, and lyres and harps for the singers."[159] Cardamom was introduced into Greece during the fourth century BCE from South India (and possibly Sri Lanka), and perhaps also directly from Indonesia (see below). These products were transported to the Persian Gulf, on the one side, and to Yemen and the Horn of Africa, on the other. The name of the island of Socotra, which is derived from the Sanskrit, is probably reminiscent of travels from India to the Red Sea in ancient times (see above). Moreover, the Song of Songs mentions nard three times (*nerd, naird, nard*), which is *Nardostachys grandiflora* DC., a plant from northern India.[160] In connection with cinnamon and nard, the same text mentions *karkom* saffron, which seems to be the Indian saffron *Curcuma longa* L. The *khroma* dye given by Theophrastus as a root from Syria is probably *Curcuma longa*. The plant was imported from India into western Asia as a substitute for true saffron as early as the seventh century BCE.[161] "A fragrant reed" (see below) also came from India. This was in addition to incense (Hebrew *lebonah*, Arabic *luban*, southern Arabic *libān*) from Arabia and East Africa, and myrrh (Hebrew *mor*, Arabic *murr*), brought from Arabia, Africa or Baluchistan.[162] Biblical texts also mention the balm of Gilead, which was a kind of myrrh, native to Arabia and the Horn of Africa, but cultivated in Judea (it was introduced into Egypt during the Roman period).[163]

It is clear that spices were already arriving in Mesopotamia under the Assyrian and Neo-Babylonian kings. According to Arrian, merchants brought incense and aromatics to the port of Teredon; ships took cinnamon and other spices to Cape Maceta (Ras Musandam, in the Strait of Hormuz), which were then exported to Assyria from there.[164] Several texts attest that Persians of the Achaemenid court were experts in perfumes; texts attributed to Hippocrates (fifth–fourth century BCE) mention pepper as an "Indian drug,"[165] and the

---

[158] One finds *balchos* in Dioscorides, and *brochos* in Pliny. The *Atharva Veda* mentions it under the name *guggulu* ou *gulgulu*. Potts *et al.* (1996) have suggested a link with the Akkadian *guhlu* (unconfirmed). For Crone (1987: 68), the term *bdellium* probably refers to several distinct species.

[159] The text adds: "So much *almug* wood has never been imported or seen since that day." Sandalwood (if the wood did belong to this species) probably came from India.

[160] See also Mark 14:3 and John 12:3. On Indian nard, see above.

[161] See "the *kurkanù* dye of the Assyrian 'herbaria'" (Amigues 2005: 380).

[162] For incense, see also Nehemiah 13:5. For myrrh, see Psalms 45:8 ("All your robes are fragrant with myrrh and aloes and cassia"). The Greek terms *libanos* and *myrra*, "myrrh," are already present in Sappho.

[163] In Greek *balsamon*, Latin *balsamum*, Hebrew *basam, basaam, bosem, besem*. These terms "appear more than forty times in the Bible and the Apocrypha" (Zohary 1982: 198). The *Mishna* (first part of the *Talmud*) has *balsamon, opobalsamon*. Cf. Arabic *balasam, balšam, basm, bašam*. The queen of Saba arrived with *besāmīm* and *zāhāb* (which refers not to gold but to an aromatic). According to Müller (1997: 199), one finds *bšm, bšmt* in ancient South Arabic, but only in proper names. For Crone, however, what would later be known as balm of Gilead was not made using the Arabian *C. gileadensis*; it could refer to a cultivated species (1987: 63–64).

[164] Arrian VII.32.7, VIII.41.7, quoted by Salles 1996a: 256, and Amigues 2005: 375.

[165] The Greek *peperi* and the subsequent Latin *piper* derive from the Sanskrit *pippali*, a word referring to long pepper. *Peperi* would later also be applied to *Piper nigrum*, black pepper (see De Romanis 1997: 99).

Greek author Theophrastus (372–288 BCE) writes that spices and aromatics (pepper, incense, myrrh, cassia, cinnamon, nard) come from Asia.[166] Incense was used by the Delphic cult at this time (Retsö 2003a: 256). Of course, spices and aromatics were destined to be more widely used in the Greek world after Alexander's conquests. The Seleucids and the Ptolemies, too, had inherited Persian and Egyptian merchant networks and their knowledge. During the third century BCE, a letter from the Syrian king Seleucus I (288–287 BCE) mentioned a list of offerings to the Apollo temple at Didyma which included Arabian incense, *cinnamum*, and *costus speciosus* from India.

In the centuries preceding the Christian era, the Mediterranean demand for spices and aromatics contributed to an increase both in the trade of these products, and in the movements of merchants and sailors. For the eastern Indian Ocean, Mahdi has suggested that the names of spices and aromatics such as cloves (*Syzygium aromaticum* [L.] Merrill and Perry, Myrtaceae family) and camphor (*Dryobalanops aromatica* Gaertn., for Sumatran camphor) allow us to date to the "2nd century BC the first sailings to India of spice traders using Malay as principal language of communication . . . It is remarkable that the earliest iron as well as the first appearance of onyx beads [probably of Indian origin] in archaeological sites along the spice-trade route between Maluku and the Straits of Malacca has also been radiocarbon dated to the second century BC, e.g. in the Tabon Caves site of Palawan, and in north Maluku."[167] Contact between the Austronesian world and India, however, had already occurred much earlier (see above).

The *Rāmāyana* contains the first known mention of cloves, using the Sanskrit term *lavanga*, a loanword from the Malay *buŋa-lawaŋ* ("flower-nail": *lawaŋ* < *laBaŋ*, "nail"), through a Dravidian intermediary.[168] If the text of the *Rāmāyana* can be "dated to the 1st century BC," the reference to *lavanga* implies a trade in cloves via the Malay world at least during the second century BCE.[169] At the same time, the Austronesians transported cloves to China. Burkill has noted that according to the *Annals of the Western Han*, courtiers had to put cloves in their mouths when speaking to the emperor. Contact with southern countries occurred under Emperor Wudi (141–87 BCE), and the *Annals* of the Han dynasty note that Chinese envoys did not use their

---

[166] Salles 1996a: 257; Amigues 2005: 373; see Pliny XIII.3, Theophrastus, *Hist. Plant.* III.107 and 110–111, IX.7; Parker, 2002: 43. These spices were used for more than culinary purposes. Theophrastus reveals that they were used in fragrant powders, cosmetics, and as antidotes to poisons. Gourmet recipes from Apicius (first century) mention nine spices from South and Southeast Asia: "pepper [by far the favored spice], ginger, putchuk (*costum*), *folium* [possibly nard leaf], *malabathrum*, nard, *asafoetida*, sesame seed, and turmeric" (Parker 2002: 44).

[167] W. Mahdi, 1999b: 219. It has been noted that the clove tree, originally, only grew on the Ternate, Tidore, Moti, Makian, and Bacan islands, in the Moluccas.

[168] In Sanskrit, *lavanga* can also refer to the fruit of the cinnamon tree (M. Chauvet p.c.). This can be attributed to the fact that the term *lawan*, in the Moluccas, was used for cloves, as well as for a "kind of cinnamon" (< *lawan*, "bark"); in western Indonesia *lawaŋ* can refer to both spices (Mahdi 1994a: 195).

[169] Mahdi 1999b: 213. Some scholars have suggested that the *Rāmāyana* texts can be dated to the fourth century BCE (see above); however, it is actually very difficult to date them. M. Winternitz thought that the *Rāmāyana* could have been written during the third or fourth century BCE, but Books I and VII, and some interpolations of Books II–VI were added around the end of the second century CE (Wheatley 1961: 204). For other authors, the *Rāmāyana* was compiled during the fifth century CE from texts going back to the fourth century BCE, but various parts were added later. Charaka, a physician at the court of the Kushan king Kanishka, mentions cloves at the end of the first century CE.

own vessels, but instead ships that would later be called *kun-lun bo*, "ships of the *Kunlun*," *Kun-lun* designating southern people, and notably Austronesians (see above; Burkill 1935: 961; Mahdi 1999b: 215).[170] We know that contacts had in fact existed much earlier. Wudi's policy of territorial expansion was in part a consequence of increasing relations through trade at this time.

The Sanskrit *karpūra*, "camphor," and Prākrit *kappūra*, derive from the Malay *kapur*, "lime" (<*kapuR*). Austronesian, as well as Indian ships, most likely transported camphor to India.[171] The first mention of the term *karpūra* can be found in the Sanskrit medical treaty *Sushruta Samhitā* (a version from the seventh century CE has been preserved, but the original text may go back to the last centuries BCE) (Mahdi 1999b: 216ff.). Conversely, an older medical treaty, the *Charaka-Samhitā*, does not mention the *karpūra*. At an unknown time, Indian languages also borrowed the Malay *damar*, "resin" (Hindi *kaladamar*: "resin of *Canarium strictum*," or *karuppu-damar*, in Tamil).

For the East African coast, the *Periplus of the Erythraean Sea* mentions a kind of cinnamon (*kasia*) traded in the ports of the Guardafui Cape region: at Malaō,[172] Mosyllon,[173] at the "Cape of Spices" (where the text indicates five different varieties), and Opōnē ("in it the greatest quantity of cinnamon is produced" [*Periplus*, paragr. 13]; this place knew of two varieties).

It is likely that Austronesians were active in the importation of cinnamon. But what kind of "cinnamon" was it, and which roads did they use? Even today it is still difficult to determine exactly which species were being referred to when ancient Greek and Latin authors used the terms "cassia" and "cinnamon" (Amigues 1996: 657–664),[174] and the trajectories of these plants remain a subject of debate.

Cinnamon comes from the Latin *cinnamomum* or *cinnamum*, Greek *kinnamomon*, *kinnamon*, itself derived from a Phoenician word, and from the Hebrew *qinnāmon*; Syriac had *qunnāmā*.[175] A suggested link with the Malay *kayu manis*, "sweet wood" is

---

[170] According to Wilensky, *kunlun* later denoted a black person. "In the *Jinshu* (History of the Jin dynasty [265–420]), Empress Li, a concubine of Emperor Xiao Wuwen (373–397), is described as being black-colored. 'All the people in the palace used to call her *kunlun*'" (Wilensky 2002: 4).

[171] Mahdi notes the Malay term *kapur Barus*, "camphor from Barus" (1994b: 191). Some researchers have even suggested that the analysis of an Egyptian mummy dated to 170 + 70 BCE has revealed the presence of *Dryobalanops aromatica* Gaertn. camphor from Sumatra or Borneo. This identification does not seem to have been confirmed.

[172] *Kankamon* and *makeir* could also be found at Malaō (*Periplus*, paragr. 8). On *kankamon*, see below. *Makeir* (*macir*, in Pliny) could be the bark of an Indian tree, imported via Malaō, *Holarrhena antidysenterica* Wall. (Casson 1989: 126).

[173] Emphasizing the difference between the two spices, Dioscorides (middle of the first century CE) notes that the best cinnamon comes from Mosyllon, where cassia can also be found.

[174] More recently, Amigues (2005: 373) identifies cassia as *Cinnamomum aromaticum* C. Nees (=*Cinnamomum cassia* Blume), exported from China into Southeast Asia at an early period. According to Amigues, the *kasia* mentioned by Herodotus and among the products used for embalming in Egypt may refer to this plant. For Germer (1985: 14), however, "no plant remains that can be identified as *Cinnamomum*, whatever the species, have ever been found in Egypt" (Amigues 2005: 373 n. 367).

[175] Koehler and Baumgartner 1983, III: 1041. Olck (1899) transcribes it as *kūnema*. The Sanskrit or Prākrit *cīna-*, "Chinese," does not seem to be a plausible etymology for the first part of the words. Olck notes, however: "At Alexandria, the cinnamon [from the Red Sea] was sold under the name of *cinnamomum*, one could say *amomum* from China" (1899: 1638).

improbable. One finds *kakynnama*, "cinnamon," in Sinhalese; the term *kurudu*, however, of Sanskrit origin, is much more common; *kakynnama* is probably a loanword (possibly from the Syriac). The Hebrew term may derive from the root *qanan*, "to shelter, to protect," or from the root *qnh*, "cane, tube."[176] Cinnamon was a component of the anointing oil used by the Hebrews. In Exodus (30:23–24), one finds: "The Lord spoke to Moses: 'Take the following fine spices: 500 shekels of liquid myrrh, half as much (that is, 250 shekels) of fragrant cinnamon, 250 shekels of fragrant calamus, 24500 shekels of cassia. Make these into a sacred anointing oil."[177] The Song of Songs (4: 13–14) mentions cinnamon when comparing the beloved to perfumes and spices from distant lands: "A garden enclosed is my sister, my spouse. Your shoots are an orchard of pomegranates, with all choicest fruits, with henna and nard, nard and saffron, calamus and cinnamon, with every kind of incense tree, with myrrh and aloes, and all the finest spices." The "Complaint of Tyre" (Ezekiel 27: 19, King James version) mentions cassia: "Dan [possibly in Syria] also and Javan [Ionia] going to and fro occupied in thy fairs: bright iron, cassia, and calamus, were in thy market."[178]

Cassia is the Latin *cas(s)ia*, Greek *kasia*, attested since Sappho[179] (late seventh to early sixth century BCE), derived from the Hebrew *ketzi'oth*, *kezī'ah* (Olck 1899) or *qsy'wt* (De Romanis 1996). According to De Romanis, the word may come from the Egyptian *šš3t/ḫs3t*. Olck, who transcribed the Egyptian term as *khisīt*, was not in favor of this etymology. He drew a link between the Hebrew *kezī'ah* and "the Chinese *kei-schi* [?], twig of cinnamon" (*gueizhi*).[180] For Amigues, the discovery of a "cinnamon tree flower (*Cinnamomum cassia*) in the Heraion of Samos confirms Sappho, but this biological identification is uncertain."[181] Moreover, traces of

---

[176] See Löw 1924–34, II: 105; Mahdi 1994: 478 n. 162.

[177] Also Proverbs (7:17): "I have perfumed my bed with myrrh, aloes and cinnamon." The "sweet cane" or "sweet Calamus" is also mentioned in Ezekiel (27:14), Isaiah (43:24), and Jeremiah (6:20): "What do I care about incense from Sheba or sweet calamus from a distant land?" The Hebrews called the plant *kaneh bosem* and *kaneh hat-tob*. According to Miller (1998: 92–94), the name refers to *Acorus calamus* L. (Araceae). This plant is native to temperate and tropical Asia (from China to Turkey for the former; Bhutan, northern India, Nepal, and Pakistan for the latter). Zohary (1982: 196) identifies these aromatic reeds as different kinds of *Cymbopogon*. Some researchers have cast doubt on the idea that the plant given as *qinnamon* by the Hebrews and the Phoenicians was a *Cinnamomum*. See, for example, Schoff 1920 and Crone 1987.

[178] In the New International Version: "Damascus did business with you because of your many products and great wealth of goods. They offered wine from Helbon, wool from Zahar and casks of wine from Izal in exchange for your wares: wrought iron, cassia and calamus."

[179] Sappho writes of incense, myrrh, and cassia burnt during the wedding ceremony of Hector and Andromache.

[180] Olck 1899: 1640; Amigues 1996: 659. Besides *ketzi'oth* (plural form), *kezī'ah* (singular) (Psalms 45:9; Job 42:14), the Bible has *kiddah* (Exodus 30:24; Ezekiel 27:19; Book of Sirach 24:15). The inhabitants of South Arabia brought *kiddah* to Tyre (Ezekiel). The origins of the Hebrew terms are still debated. A link with the Cantonese Chinese *gwai sam* or the Mandarin Chinese *guì xìn* (which refers to *Cinnamomum cassia* Blume) remains to be confirmed. Some authors consider the Hebrew to derive from the name Khasi given to Austrosiatic populations living in northeastern India and – in the past – in Assam and Burma. These populations may have been active in the transportation of cinnamon along routes from Yunnan, but this etymology remains very hypothetical.

[181] Amigues 2005: 374. "Two centuries later, the fruit of the cinnamon tree is mentioned twice in the Hippocratic texts, and then it disappears from the sources" (Amigues 2005: 374).

cinnamaldehyde, the organic compound that gives cinnamon its flavor, have been found in ten flasks dated to the tenth century BCE and coming from five different sites, notably Tel Dor (Israel) (the type of cinnamon could not be determined) (Namdar *et al.* 2013).

The *Periplus* does not differentiate between cinnamon and cassia (it mentions only this latter term), but the Ancients made a distinction, and at the same time associated the two plants with each other. For the Romans, cassia sometimes referred to a cinnamon of lower quality, from different barks. Dioscorides (writing *c.* 65 CE) mentioned several kinds of cassia. Cinnamon was also known to the Greeks and the Romans. It is mentioned for the first time in Herodotus, and later Hippocrates, Theophrastus, Dioscorides, Pliny, and others. The term "cinnamon" probably referred to various plants, perhaps including *Cinnamomum aromaticum* C. Nees (=*Cinnamomum cassia* Blume) and *Cinnamomum zeylanicum* Breyn (from Sri Lanka).[182] However, some authors such as P. Crone (1987), argue that the cinnamon and the cassia of the ancient texts were plants growing on the shores of the Red Sea (she notes that Theophrastus and Pliny have described the plants). Burkill has also rejected the idea that Chinese cinnamon was imported into Europe during this early period, noting that according to Laufer, "the first Chinese description of the Chinese 'cassia' was written during the 3rd century CE" (Burkill 1935: 544; Laufer 1919: 543; see also Haw 2017).

The presence of cinnamon on the Somali coast could be quite ancient, if we accept the hypothesis that this aromatic was mentioned in the Egyptian inscriptions of Deir-el-Bahri linked to an expedition sent by Queen Hatshepsut in the fifteenth century BCE. For further information, see Naville (1895–1908), who accepted Loret's translation of *tj-šps* as "cinnamon wood," an import given as "one of the marvels of the land of Punt" (see above). Most scholars, however, reject this thesis of a Sinhalese, Indonesian, or Chinese cinnamon in Egypt at the time of Queen Hatshepsut or later. R. Germer has convincingly refuted the identification of this *tj-šps* from Punt as cinnamon.[183] It is curious, however, that the term *ḳnni* (or *ḳni, ḳnn*), generally considered to refer to an oil prepared with *Acorus calamus* L., a plant of Indian provenance, is mentioned along with *tj-šps* in various Egyptian texts.[184] The Persian name for cinnamon, *dār chīnī*, "Chinese bark" (also termed "sweet wood," the equivalent of the Malay *kayu manis*, "cinnamon"), may suggest that Chinese cinnamon was traded in ancient times.[185] Herodotus indicates the use of *kasia* in Egypt for embalming corpses, and Diodorus that of

---

[182] Note here that a single term can refer to various different botanical species, and conversely, various parts of a plant can be given different names; cinnamon, for example, refers to the bark of various *Cinnamomum*, and *malabathrum* could be the name of the leaves of *Cinnamomum tamala* Nees and *Cinnamomum bejolghota* (Ham.) Sweet.

[183] Germer 1979: 344–346; 1985: 14. Burkill has emphasized that there has been no evidence to demonstrate that Chinese cinnamon was at the origin of the barks that arrived in Egypt at the time of the exodus (1966: 545).

[184] See Charpentier 1982: 728–729, entry 1205 (and entries 1209, 1210, 1259, 1300).

[185] During the fifth century CE, the Armenian Moses of Chorene knew that "*darazenic [dara sini]* comes from China" (Olck 1899: 1642). The word **dār-i čēnik* was known in Pahlavi (Middle Persian) at the same period, and this term is present in the Talmud (Crone 1987: 268, 262).

kinnamomon.[186] At Deir-el-Bahri too, Naville claimed to have found nutmeg among offerings going back to the Eighteenth Dynasty, but no botanist has ever examined this find (Germer 1985: 15).

The identification of *cassia* and cinnamon from Antiquity has preoccupied generations of researchers. There is also passionate debate about the routes that were taken, and about those who carried the goods. According to J. Pirenne, cinnamon came from India:

> According to Pliny, the casia and the cinnamon transported by the Gebbanite Arabs [from Qatabān] originated in an 'Ethiopian' land, that M. Filliozat has demonstrated to be in Ceylon or eastern India. (Pirenne 1970: 103)

As noted above, Theophrastus indicates the existence of a trade in aromatics between India and the Mediterranean during the fourth century BCE, and Arrian gives the Ras Musandam, "a promontory at the extremity of Arabia," as a place where "cinnamon and other similar goods" arrived (probably from India) (Amigues 1996: 662–663, also Olck 1899: 1641). During the second century BCE, Agatharchides writes that cinnamon "grows on the Arab coast." Authors such as Strabo (born in 58 BCE) and Apuleius claim that cinnamon originated in India.[187] "It cannot be excluded," notes J. Filliozat, "that Indians and Sinhalese participated in the navigation from India to the Occident. The Buddhist texts, as S. Lévi has pointed out, contain many references to maritime Indian commerce, and Pliny collected information on Indian sailors. He indicates that the Sinhalese sailed on boats with two bows having a gross tonnage of 3,000 amphorae, around 75 tons, without observing the stars, and carrying birds that they released to follow them flying to the coast."[188] The Sanskrit text *Yuktikalpataru* also mentions this practice.

It is difficult to know precisely when spices such as cloves and nutmeg arrived in India for the first time (though perhaps not prior to the last centuries BCE). Nothing is known about their presence in the Indus civilization, "though they are mentioned in the Later Vedic texts as important ingredients in food preparations."[189] Indians and Malays, as mentioned above, undoubtedly contributed to the spread of these spices.

Cassia and cinnamon probably traveled along several routes. The cinnamon that arrived in the Horn of Africa may have come from India (directly or via Arabia), from Sri Lanka, or from insular Southeast Asia, via the Maldives. Herodotus suggested that cinnamon came from "the land where Dionysus was raised," which refers to Sri Lanka:

[186] Herodotus II.86; Diodorus I.91, quoted by Olck 1899: 1640. For Germer, however, the fact that Diodorus mentioned *qinnamon* does not prove that the term refers to cinnamon. Theophrastus also names as "cinnamon" the ingredient used to make an Egyptian oil (Germer 1985: 14).

[187] Strabo XVI.782; Apuleius, *Florides* I.6, quoted by Olck 1899: 1641. Onesicritus also writes that cinnamon originated in South India. "Aristobulus noticed that the cinnamon grew in South India, as well as in Arabia and in Ethiopia" (Crone 1987: 255).

[188] Filliozat 1956: 8–9, quoted by Pirenne 1970: 103. On this practice, see above.

[189] Kenoyer 1998: 170. Let us recall, however, that cloves have been found at Terqa (Iraq), dated to 1700/1600 BCE.

As for cinnamon, the Arabs gather it in an even stranger way. Where it comes from and what land produces it they cannot say, except that it is reported, reasonably enough, to grow in the places where Dionysus was reared. There are great birds, it is said, that take these dry sticks which we have learned from the Phoenicians to call cinnamon and carry them off to nests stuck with mud to precipitous cliffs, where man has no means of approach.[190]

Pliny (x.4) also recounts the legend in which the phoenix built its nest with twigs of *cassia* and of frankincense trees. "This fable probably comes from the relation established – through popular etymology – between the Semitic *qinnamon* and a word referring to a nest, *qinnu*" (M. Chauvet, p.c.). Strabo (xv.695) asserts that most *cassia* comes from India. According to Claudian (ep. 2.15), the phoenix brings *cinnamum* from East Asia (quoted by Olck 1899: 1641). Ptolemy writes that "above Kirradia [located east of India, perhaps in Burma] is the region in which, they are said, to produce the best cinnamon."[191] Cinnamon from East Asia was probably transported in Austronesian ships: the Chinese did not seem to venture very far from their coasts at this time. However, trade was probably also carried out along terrestrial roads.

J. I. Miller suggests that a "cinnamon route" went to Egypt via Madagascar and the African harbor of Rhapta (a very improbable route; the *Periplus* does not mention cinnamon at Rhapta) (Miller 1998: 147, 149, 153ff.). It is true, however, that Pliny describes what seems to be the importation of cinnamon into Arabia by seafarers arriving from Southeast Asia:

The cinnamon as well as the cassia originate from that part of Ethiopia where the Troglodytes intermarried with the local inhabitants. The Troglodytes buy it from their neighbours and [others] convey it over the wide seas in ships that are neither steered by rudders, nor propelled by oars or drawn by sails, nor assisted by any device of art . . . Moreover, they choose the winter sea about the time of the shortest day, as the Eurus wind [East wind] is then chiefly blowing. This carries them on a straight course and from gulf to gulf, and after rounding a cape [of Arabia], the Argestes wind [a west–northwest wind] brings them to the harbour of the Gebbanites called Ocilia. On this account that is the port most resorted to by these people, and they say that it is almost five years before the traders return home, and that many perish on the voyage. In return for their wares, they bring back articles of glass and copper, clothing, and buckles, bracelets and necklaces . . . The king of the Gebbanites exerts monopoly power on the cinnamon, he rules its sale and market by decree.[192]

In his comments, A. Ernout, citing P. Fournier, notes: "The bold sailors whom [Pliny] mentions were probably Malays."[193]

---

[190]   Herodotus III.III. Commentary on the text of Pliny, ed. A. Ernout 1949: 93. For J. Keay, this report from Herodotus may indicate that the Greeks "had heard rumors about the edibility of certain birds' nests" (2005: 5).

[191]   Ptolemy, Book 7, ch. 2, p. 156, ed. Stevenson. It is surprising that Cosmas Indicopleustes (sixth century), when writing about Sri Lanka, did not mention cinnamon. Kirradia (as well as the Kirradai mentioned by the *Periplus*) can be linked to the name Kirātas given to the Mongoloid people of northern and eastern India in Indian literature (Casson 1989: 234). On the possible presence of Kirradai from Arakan in Orissa, see Salles, 2004: 215 n. 62.

[192]   Pliny XII.42–43, ed. Ernout 1949: 47–50, 92–94; Miller 1998: 156.

[193]   Pliny XII, ed. Ernout 1949: 94. The "rafts" may have been catamarans, with two hulls linked by a deck.

We have no proof of an early presence of cinnamon in Madagascar. The Swahili name for cinnamon, *darasiny* (which derives from the Persian), is known in northern Madagascar, but it has only been recently introduced into this region.

Ptolemy, in accordance with Strabo (II.95), also makes note of a "land bearing cinnamon" in eastern Africa, north of the Great Lakes at the sources of the two Niles, suggesting knowledge of an African cinnamon.[194] Miller interprets this as evidence of a cinnamon route going from the African coast into the hinterland, and from there to the Red Sea or the Nile. From the Mombasa region, a land route proceeded north, to the Maji region in southwestern Ethiopia. "Here the road forked, one route running east . . . to Avalites," on the Red Sea, "the other turning west" to the Nile. Other roads converged at Avalites, one from Sarapion (Mogadishu region) and another from Opōnē (Miller 1998: 146 [map 6] and 147ff.). F. Chami argues that a route from Rhapta went along the Rufiji River and up to the Great Lakes; it would then have followed the Nile, toward Meroe (see below).

In addition, spices and aromatics were transported via the Persian Gulf, offloaded in Oman, Bahrain, or at Apologos, and from there carried by caravans.

For the Arabs, as the principal transporters of spices, some benefit lay in confusing the issue, which may explain in part the contradictions between the various sources available, and the fact that they often resorted to surreal imagery.

The different types of cinnamon were not the only coveted spices. Pliny adds that:

From the confines of the country which produces cinnamon and cassia, cancamum[1] and tarum[2] are imported; but these substances are brought by way of the Nabatæan Troglodytæ, a colony of the Nabatæi . . . Thither, too, are carried serichatum and gabalium, aromatics which the Arabians rear for their own consumption, and which are only known by name in our part of the world, though they grow in the same country as cinnamon and cassia. Still, however, serichatum does reach us occasionally, and is employed by some persons in the manufacture of unguents. It is purchased at the rate of six denarii per pound. (Pliny XII.44–45, ed. Bostock and Riley)

The recipe for the royal ointment of the Parthians, according to Pliny, contained *cassia*, cinnamon, *amomum*, *comacum*, cardamom, *malabathrum*, *serichatum*, nard, *costus*, myrrh, and *ladanum* (Pliny XIII.2; Schoff 1974: 112). Several different plants have been identified as the *cancamum* (Greek *kankamon*), mentioned by Dioscorides as the resin of a tree from Arabia. The *Periplus* (paragr. 8) claims it to be an export from Malaō (port on the Somali coast, on the Red Sea), that was imported into Arabia. Miller identifies it as the benzoin of Southeast Asia (*Styrax benzoin* Dryander, family of the Styracaceae) and considers *tarum* to be aloeswood. However, W. W. Müller has recently demonstrated that *cancamum* can be linked to the ancient South Arabic *kmkm*, which is often preceded by *ḍrw* in inscriptions, a term at the origin of *tarum*. *Ḍrw* may be the bark of *Pistacia lentiscus* (cf. Arabic *ḍaru*, *Pistacia lentiscus* or *Salvia nudicaulis*), and *kmkm* the wood of the same tree. It appears, in fact, to be a plant from

---

[194] Ptolemy, Book 4, ch. 7, p. 108, ed. Stevenson. Other authors claim that cinnamon and cassia are of
        African origin: Artemidorus (first century BCE), for example, writes of "cinnamon and pseudo-cassia"
        (Strabo XV.4:14; Crone 1987: 255–256, 261). Moreover, Strabo mentions an "Indian land producing
        cinnamon" (*kinamomophorou indikes*).

Arabia and not from Southeast Asia. Casson, on the other hand, suggests that *kankamon* can be identified as *Commiphora kataf* (Forssk.) Engl. (=*Commiphera erythraea* [Ehrenb.] Engl.), found in Somalia, Kenya, and Tanzania.[195] Concerning *serichatum* and *gabalium*, Ernout has pointed out that thus far only unreliable identifications have been made (*laka* wood,[196] for the first, camphor for the second). The term *serichatum* must be related to the ancient South Arabic *slḫt* (cf. Arabic *salīkha*, cassia, Chinese cinnamon). *Gabalium* can be connected to the Sabaean *qbltn* (Müller 1997: 208). Though not supported by much evidence, Miller considers the Austronesians to have supplied the western world with aloeswood, benzoin, camphor, ginger, cloves, nutmeg, and mace. Camphor is mentioned by Galen (second century CE) as being used in one medicine. The Greek name for ginger, *zingiberis*, appears during the fifth century BCE, attesting to connections between India and the Mediterranean at this time. This term comes from the Sanskrit *sṛmgavera*, itself derived from the Proto-South Dravidian **cinki-ver*, "root of ginger" (Southworth 2005: 251); one finds *zangebīl* in Aramaic and in Syriac, and *zanjabīl* in Arabic. Cloves from the Moluccas reached Rome *c.* 70 CE. Pliny mentions cloves for the first time, as a product from India, under the name *Caryophyllum* – of Greek origin (*karyophyllon*), itself from the Sanskrit (*kalika-phala*, "fruit-bud").[197] Conversely, cloves are mentioned neither by the *Periplus*, Theophrastus, nor Dioscorides. It has already been pointed out here that cloves and nutmeg (perhaps the *comacum* of Pliny)[198] originate respectively in the Moluccas and the Banda Islands, south of Seram. These islands' involvement in the spice trade (a trade route went through Bali, Java, and continued to India and the Maldives) could explain East Indonesian influences in Madagascar (these influences probably occurred much later than the first Austronesian arrivals on this island). For cloves, the Betsimisaraka dialect uses the word *karafoy*, from the Swahili *karafuu* (from the Arabic *qaranful*),[199] a term that is certainly of recent introduction.

In the first known dictionary of the Malagasy language (1606),[200] F. de Houtman indicates a Malagasy name for nutmeg: *rarà*. Today, the nutmeg tree, *Myristica fragrans* Houtton (Myristicaceae), a tree recently introduced into Madagascar, is known under the name *rarambazaha*, "*rarà* of the White Men [or 'of the foreigners'],*" and on the east coast *rarà* refers to various trees of the Myristicaceae family, the fruits of which yield a fragrant oil: *Mauloutchia chapelieri* (Baillon) Warburg, *Mauloutchia*

---

[195] Casson 1989: 124–125. It has also been suggested that *kankamon* can be identified as copal resin from *Hymenaea verrucosa* Gaertn. (*Trachylobium verrucosum* [Gaertn.] Oliv.).

[196] *Dalbergia parviflora* Roxb., a liana with an aromatic wood, native to Southeast Asia (Miller 1998: 57).

[197] Miller 1998: 49; Pliny XII.15, ed. Ernout 1949: 28; on cloves and the Roman Empire, see also Warmington 1974: 199–200.

[198] "Syria also produces the kind of cinnamon called comacum," writes Pliny; "this is a juice squeezed out of a nut, and is quite different from the juice of the true cinnamon, although it is almost equally agreeable" (Pliny XII.63, Ernout 1949: 62). For *comacum*, notes Ernout, "Pliny has read Theophrastus too hastily, who among the aromatic plants imported from Arabia distinguishes between the *comacum*, the cinnamon and the casia." "Some authors, without any evidence, have related the comacum to the nutmeg" (Pliny XII, commentary Ernout 1949: 105–106). Amigues 2005: 375ff.

[199] The Arabic is itself related to the Greek *karyophyllon*. Cf. Sanskrit *kalika-phala*, Hindi and Gujarati *phul*, "flower," and Dravidian *kirampu*, from *pu*, "flower."

[200] The lexicon compiled by Houtman was recovered in Sumatra from a Malagasy slave who came from the Bay of Antongil. Published by A. Grandidier *et al.*, *COACM* (vol. I).

rarabe (Perrier de la Bathie) Capuron. These trees "secrete red tanno-gums," which probably explains the name *rarà*, "like blood" (from *ra*, "blood") (Boiteau *et al.* 1999, III: 198).

Miller (1998: 86–87) also suggests that sandalwood (*Santalum album* L., Santalaceae) exported from Barygaza (Broach) (see the *Periplus*) was an import from the Malabar coast and from Indonesia (sandalwood was found between East Java and Timor; it was also present in South India, as Miller notes).

Archaeological discoveries in Egypt have led to the possible identification of benzoin (*Styrax benzoin* Driander) during the Greco-Roman period, at Hawara (de Vartavan and Asensi Amoros 1997: 244). The Egyptian process of embalming involved the use of fragrant substances. According to the Gospel of St. John, Jesus's corpse was embalmed using "a mixture of myrrh and aloes ... as the custom of the Jews is to bury."[201] For Roman funerals, "incense" (a mixture of various fragrant substances), was burnt in excessive amounts, according to Pliny.[202]

Archaeology, ancient texts, and linguistics can thus provide us with a map of the complex exchanges involving spices and aromatics, but more research is needed to be able to grasp the true dimension of this trade and its antiquity.

Persia, and later the Muslim Empire apparently stood as obstacles that prevented direct access to the aromatics of India or the silks of China, for Rome and later Byzantium; but these empires also appear to have been intermediaries and key players in a larger system that was taking shape.

Parthians and Sassanids: The Occident of the Silk Roads

First settled in the southeastern regions of the Caspian Sea at the time of the Seleucid Empire, from 160 BCE on, the Parthians expanded their control over Bactria and Persia, and seized Babylonia from the Seleucids in 141 BCE. The Parthians were ruled by the Arsacid Dynasty, who were Scythian Dahae from the eastern Caspian Sea: here again, we have an example of a (semi-)periphery taking possession of a core. Note that the Seleucid colony of Failaka, linked to the control of trade with the east, was abandoned around the middle of the second century BCE. The Parthians established their capital at Seleucia and later at Ctesiphon, a city facing Seleucia, on the other side of the Tigris. Hecatompylos (Shar-i Qūmis) and Nisā (modern-day Ashgabat) were other capitals, while Susa remained an important city. As early as 122 BCE, the Parthians subjugated the territory of Mesene-Characene and its port of Spasinou Charax. Parthian power was soon threatened, in the northeast by peoples from the steppes (King Phraates II was killed by Yuezhi in 129 BCE, as was Artaban I in 124 BCE),[203] and in the west by the Roman Empire, from the first century BCE. The border between the two powers, established along the Euphrates River by the treaty of 66 BCE, kept moving as the conflict shifted, but Rome would never manage to keep a durable hold on Mesopotamia.

---

[201] John 19:39–40. The aloes could be *Aloe vera* L. (Zohary 1982: 204).

[202] Pliny notes that Arabia did not produce in a whole year the quantity of perfumes that Nero burnt at the funeral of Poppaea (*Natural History* XII.18.83).

[203] In 90 BCE, Scythians (Saka) invaded Iran.

The Parthian Empire, which received an envoy from the Han emperor Wudi in 115 BCE, benefited from the increase in exchanges along the roads of Inner Asia. It used a silver currency based on the drachm, and copper coinage for minor local transactions. "Wages and prices were now given in silver" (Huyse 2005: 108). Vassal states in Persia, Elymais (Susiana), and Characene issued their own money. The Parthian Empire tried to develop production and trade in the territories it controlled, but the prices found on the tablets of Babylon show inflation during the second and first centuries BCE, leading to a fall in living standards for the population. A set of negative factors came together during this period: Arab raids, Elamite invasions, and civil wars (Grainger 1999). The Parthians, however, generated huge revenues from the taxes imposed on merchandise that was carried through their territory. Toward India and Central Asia, they briefly dominated Taxila, at the beginning of the first century CE, but the city was later incorporated into the Kushan Empire. The Parthians controlled a large part of the trade between the Mediterranean and Central Asia. The text *Stathmoi Parthikoi*, "The Parthian Stations," by Isidore of Charax (first century BCE – first century CE), lists the halting points of the caravans along a route running

from Zeugma, on the Euphrates, to Alexandria in Arachosia (Qandahar) via Doura, Palmyra, Seleucia, Ctesiphon, Kermanshah, Hamadan (Ecbatana), Ray (Rhagai), Nisā and Merv (Antioch in Margiana), where the route divided into two branches. A northern branch went through Sogdiana, and a southern branch [the most frequented] led to Bactres and the Indian plain ... At the time of Ammianus Marcellinus, an annual fair was taking place at Zeugma where local merchants offered Indian and Chinese products.[204]

Babylonia, the economic core of the empire, acted as a hub between Anatolia, the Levant, and Egypt on the one side, and Persia and the territories located further east, on the other. Spices, aromatics, "Seric iron," ivory, and silk were imported from the east; and olive oil, wine, horses, Pyrola dye, flax, gilded or silvered vessels, brass, glass, and ceramics were carried from the Mediterranean Sea or the Parthian territory over terrestrial and maritime routes. Maritime networks extended as far as Burma: rubies in the eyes of a statuette from Ishtar found at Hillah (Babylon) – dated to the first century BCE – appear to have been imported from this country.[205]

Prestige goods were not the only thing carried on the roads of Central Asia:[206] agricultural products and cultivated plants also went the same way. Thus fruit trees such as the peach tree[207] arrived in Persia, as well as the apricot tree, from China and Tibet. The peach tree was thought to have been introduced into Greece around the third or the fourth century BCE; however, peach remains recently identified on the island of Samos appear to go back to the seventh century BCE (Zohary and Hopf 2000:

---

[204] Huyse 2005: 99. The territory of the Parthian Empire yielded many objects attesting to these exchanges, for example about sixty ivory rhytons found at Nisā, of Greek style, but possibly produced by a local workshop (Huyse 2005: 208).

[205] *Le Journal du Net*, 2006.

[206] "In Persia, the Chinese acquired Iranian eyebrow makeup, Babylonian carpets, precious stones from Syria and Egypt, fabrics from these same countries and narcotics from Central Asia" (Toussaint 1961: 47 n. 1).

[207] *Prunus persica* (L.) Barsch. Postgate (1987: 129–130), however, supports the idea that the peach tree was present in Mesopotamia during the early first millennium BCE (under the name *hahhu*).

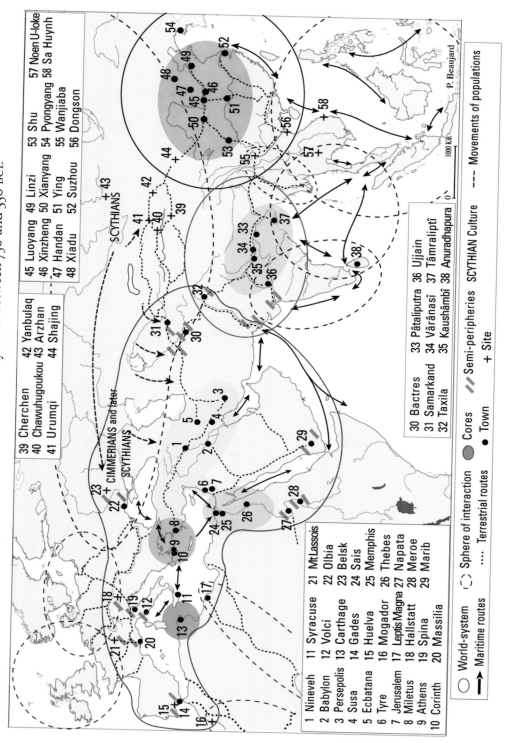

Map II.4 Afro-Eurasian world-systems between 750 and 350 BCE

1 Nineveh	11 Syracuse	21 MtLassois
2 Babylon	12 Volci	22 Olbia
3 Persepolis	13 Carthage	23 Belsk
4 Susa	14 Gades	24 Sais
5 Ecbatana	15 Huelva	25 Memphis
6 Tyre	16 Mogador	26 Thebes
7 Jerusalem	17 Leptis Magna	27 Napata
8 Miletus	18 Hallstatt	28 Meroe
9 Athens	19 Spina	29 Marib
10 Corinth	20 Massilia	

30 Bactres	33 Pâtaliputra	36 Ujjain
31 Samarkand	34 Vârânasî	37 Tâmraliptî
32 Taxila	35 Kaushâmbî	38 Anuradhapura

39 Cherchen	42 Yanbulaq	45 Luoyang	49 Linzi	53 Shu	57 Noen U-loke
40 Chawuhugoukou	43 Arzhan	46 Xinzheng	50 Xianyang	54 Pyongyang	58 Sa Huynh
41 Urumqi	44 Shajing	47 Handan	51 Ying	55 Wanjiaba	
		48 Xiadu	52 Suzhou	56 Dongson	

SCYTHIANS

CIMMERIANS and later
SCYTHIANS

P. Beaujard

1000 Km

○ World-system   ◠ Sphere of interaction   ● Cores   ╱╱ Semi-peripheries   SCYTHIAN Culture
→ Maritime routes   ···· Terrestrial routes   ● Town   + Site   --- Movements of populations

Map II.5 Afro-Eurasian world-systems between 350 BCE and the end of the first millennium BCE

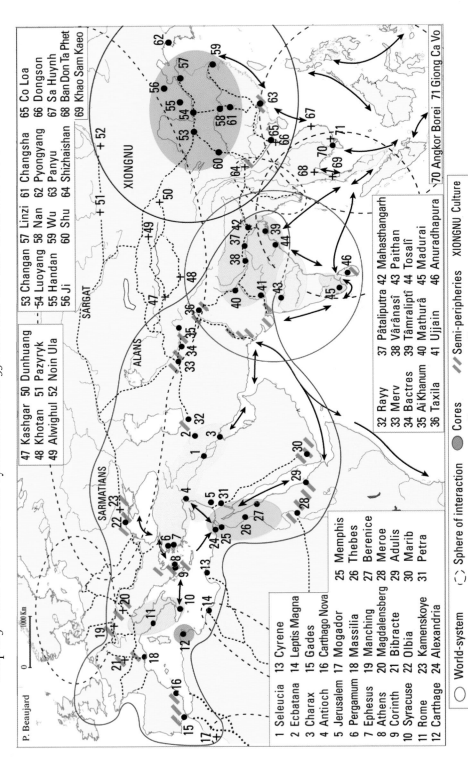

P. Beaujard

1 Seleucia	13 Cyrene
2 Ecbatana	14 Leptis Magna
3 Charax	15 Gades
4 Antioch	16 Carthago Nova
5 Jerusalem	17 Mogador
6 Pergamum	18 Massilia
7 Ephesus	19 Manching
8 Athens	20 Magdalensberg
9 Corinth	21 Bibracte
10 Syracuse	22 Olbia
11 Rome	23 Kamenskoye
12 Carthage	24 Alexandria

| 25 Memphis |
| 26 Thebes |
| 27 Berenice |
| 28 Meroe |
| 29 Adulis |
| 30 Marib |
| 31 Petra |

32 Rayy	37 Pâtaliputra	42 Mahasthangarh
33 Merv	38 Vârânasî	43 Paithan
34 Bactres	39 Tâmraliptî	44 Tosalî
35 Aï Khanum	40 Mathurâ	45 Madurai
36 Taxila	41 Ujjain	46 Anuradhapura

47 Kashgar	50 Dunhuang
48 Khotan	51 Pazyryk
49 Alwighul	52 Noin Ula

53 Changan	57 Linzi	61 Changsha	65 Co Loa
54 Luoyang	58 Nan	62 Pyongyang	66 Dongson
55 Handan	59 Wu	63 Panyu	67 Sa Huynh
56 Ji	60 Shu	64 Shizhaishan	68 Ban Don Ta Phet
			69 Khao Sam Kaeo
			70 Angkor Borei 71 Giong Ca Vo

SARMATIANS
ALANS
SARGAT
XIONGNU

World-system
Maritime routes
Sphere of interaction
Terrestrial routes
Cores
Town
Semi-peripheries
Site
XIONGNU Culture

0   1000 Km

Map II.6 The Afro-Eurasian world-system from the first to the third century CE

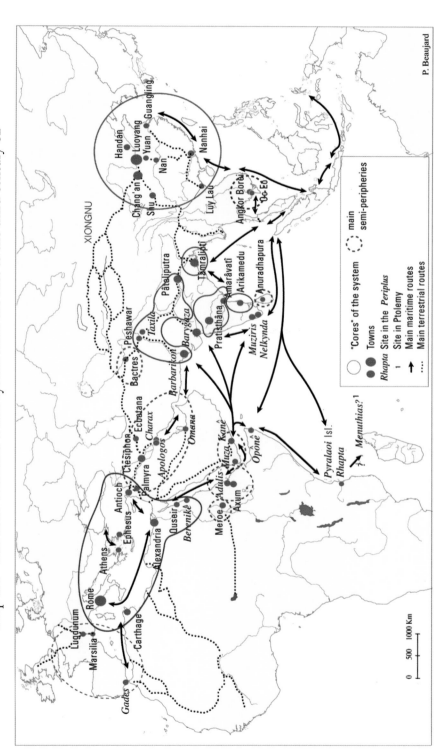

P. Beaujard

"Cores" of the system

Towns

Rhapta Site in the *Periplus*

1 Site in Ptolemy

↑ Main maritime routes

····· Main terrestrial routes

main

semi-peripheries

XIONGNU

Handan · Luoyang · Yuan · Guangling
Chang'an · Shu · Nan · Nanhai
Luy Lau
Angkor Borei · Oc-Eo

Taralipti
Amarāvatī · Arikamedu
Pātaliputra · Pratiṭṭhāna · Anuradhapura
Taxila · *Muziris*
Peshawar · *Nelkynda*
Bactres
Barbarikon
Barygaza

Ecbatana
Ctesiphon · Charax
Antioch · Palmyra · *Apologos*
Ephesus · *Omana*
Athens · Quseir · *Adulis* *Muza* *Kanē*
Rome · Alexandria · Berenikê · *Opone*
Lugdunum · Berenikē · Meroe · Axum
Marsilia · Carthage · *Pyralaoi* Isl.
Gades · *Rhapta*

Menuthias? 1

0 500 1000 Km

Map II.7   Madagascar: climatic areas and isohyets

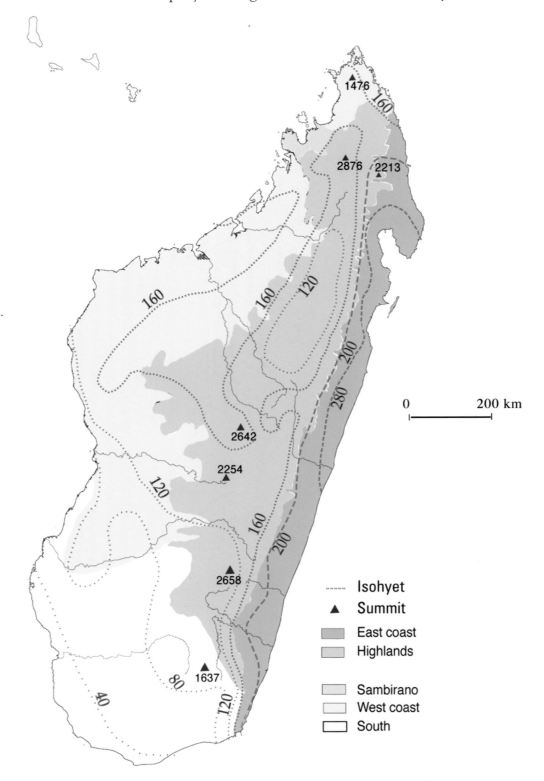

Isohyet

▲ Summit

East coast

Highlands

Sambirano

West coast

South

After J.-L. Guillaumet (1995) and the map of isohyets
from the Service de Cartographie National de Madagascar (1984)

Map II.8 Western Eurasia and Africa during the sixth and fifth centuries BCE

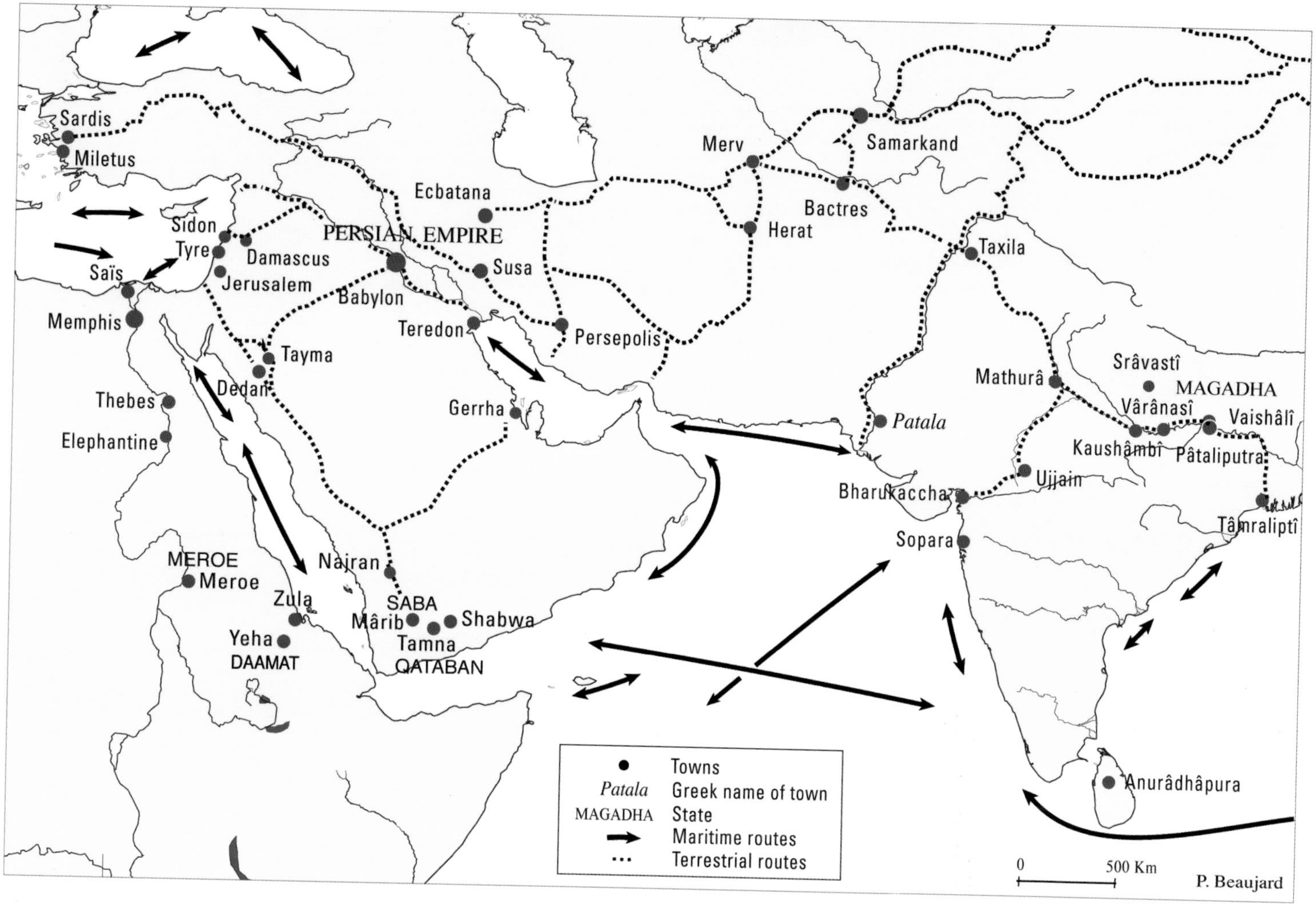

P. Beaujard

Legend:
- Patala — Greek name of town
- MAGADHA — State
- ● — Towns
- ↑ — Maritime routes
- ⋯ — Terrestrial routes

Places:
Sardis, Miletus, Sais, Memphis, Thebes, Elephantine, Tyre, Sidon, Damascus, Jerusalem, Tayma, Dedan, Najran, MEROE, Meroe, Yeha, DAAMAT, Zula, SABA, Mârib, Tamna, Shabwa, QATABAN, Gerrha, Teredon, Babylon, Susa, Ecbatana, PERSIAN EMPIRE, Persepolis, Merv, Herat, Bactres, Samarkand, Taxila, Patala, Bharukaccha, Sopara, Ujjain, Mathurâ, Srâvastî, MAGADHA, Vârânasî, Kaushâmbî, Vaishâlî, Pâtaliputra, Tâmraliptî, Anurâdhâpura

0 500 Km

Map II.9 Western Eurasia and Africa during the third and second centuries BCE

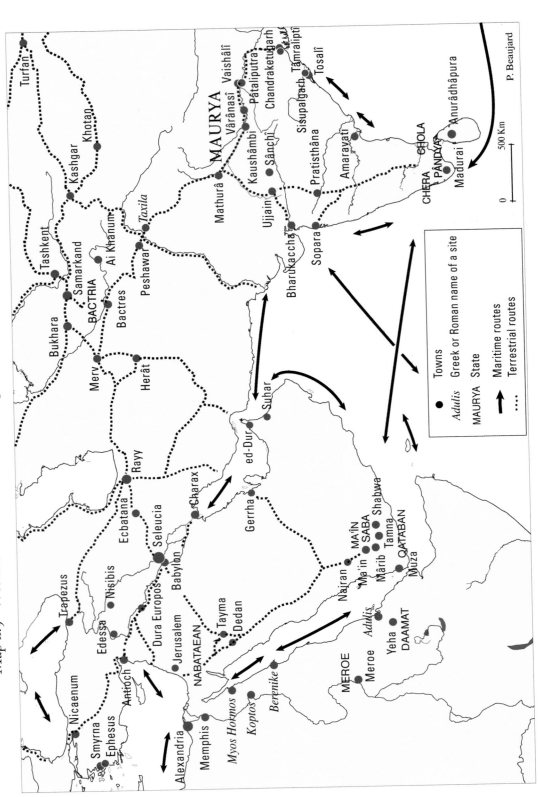

Map II.10   Western Eurasia and Africa from the first to the sixth century CE

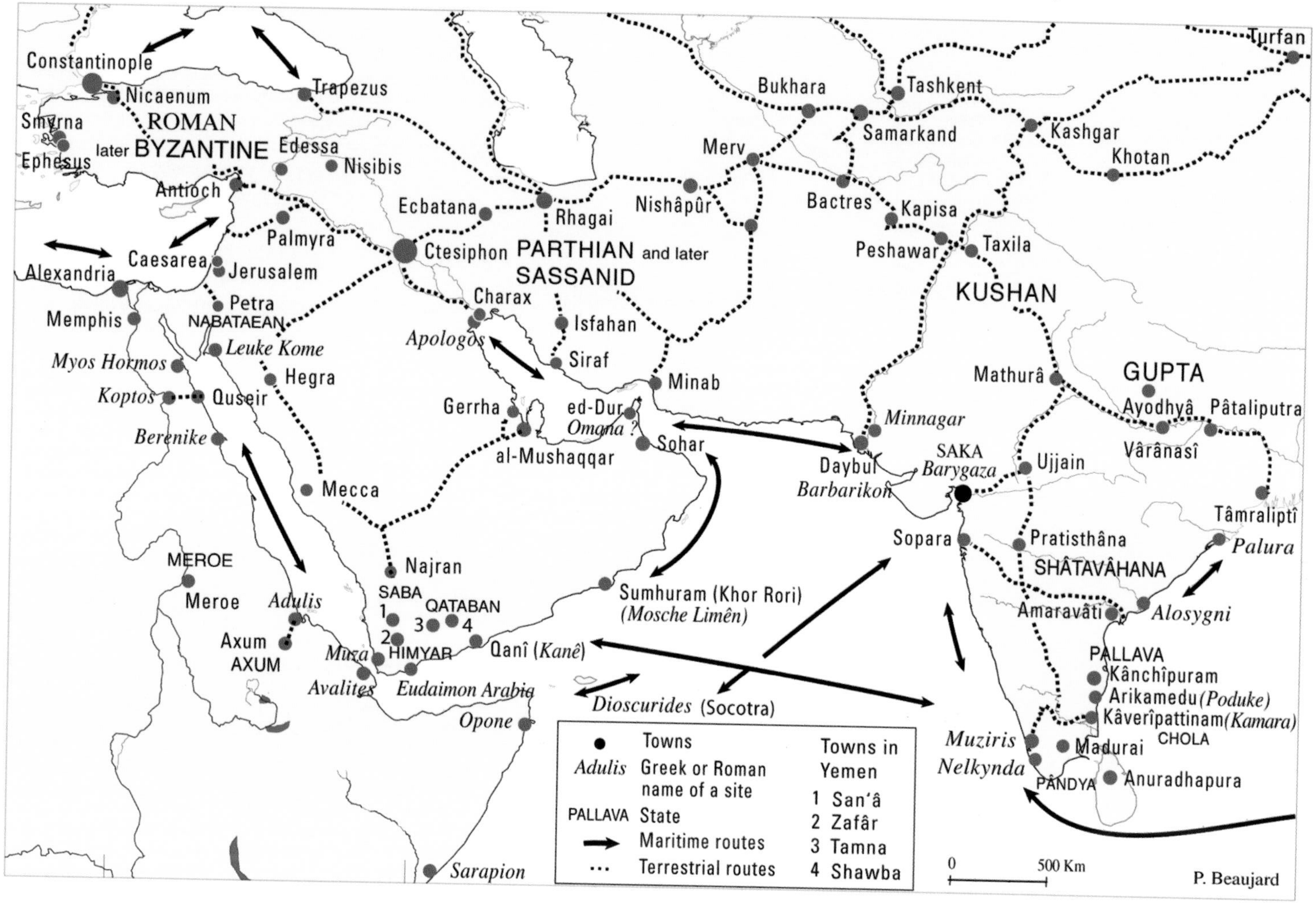

Map II.11   Main archaeological discoveries bearing witness to exchanges between India and Southeast Asia and within Southeast Asia (late first millennium BCE–sixth century CE)

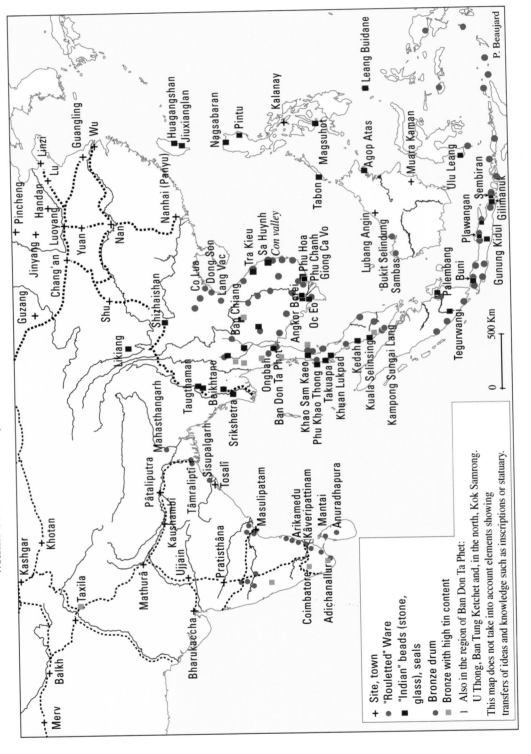

+   Site, town

●   "Rouletted" Ware

■   "Indian" beads (stone, glass), seals

●   Bronze drum

●   Bronze with high tin content

■   Also in the region of Ban Don Ta Phet: U Thong, Ban Tung Ketchet and, in the north, Kok Samrong.

This map does not take into account elements showing transfers of ideas and knowledge such as inscriptions or statuary.

P. Beaujard

Map II.12 Main archaeological discoveries showing exchanges between China and Southeast Asia (late first millennium BCE – sixth century CE)

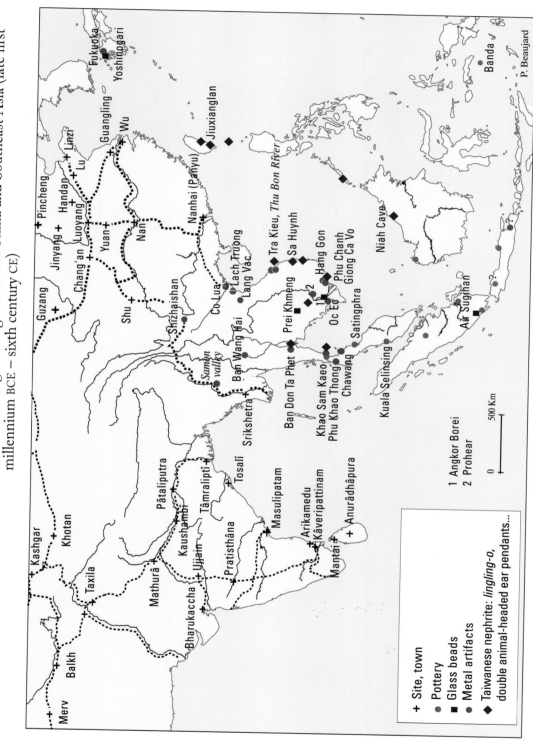

P. Beaujard

Legend:
+ Site, town
● Pottery
■ Glass beads
● Metal artifacts
◆ Taiwanese nephrite: *lingling-o*, double animal-headed ear pendants...

1 Angkor Borei
2 Prohear

0 ——— 500 Km

Labels on map:
Merv, Balkh, Kashgar, Khotan, Taxila, Mathurā, Bharukaccha, Ujjain, Kaushambi, Pratisthāna, Pātaliputra, Tāmralipti, Tosalī, Masulipatam, Arikamedu, Kāveripattinam, Mantai, Anurādhāpura, Srikshetra, Ban Wang Hai, Samon valley, Ban Don Ta Phet, Khao Sam Kaeo, Phu Khao Thong, Chawang, Satingphra, Kuala Selinsing, Air Sughan, Niah Cave, Banda, Giong Ca Vo, Phu Chanh, Oc Eo, Hang Gon, Prei Khmeng, Sa Huynh, Tra Kieu, Thu Bon River, Lach Truong, Lang Vac, Co Loa, Jiuxianglan, Fukuoka, Yoshinogari, Guangling, Wu, Linzi, Handan, Lu, Pincheng, Jinyang, Luoyang, Yuan, Nan, Chang'an, Guzang, Shu, Shizhaishan, Nanhai (Panyu)

Map II.13   Routes crossing the Thai–Malay peninsula during the first millennium CE

Muang Fa Daet

FUGANDULU

Sri Thap

Chansen
Muang Sema
Lopburi

U Thong

Ban Don Ta Phet
DVARAVATI

Pong Tuk
Nakhon Pathom
Phum Snay

DUNSUN
Ku Bua
Muang Phra Rot
Ishanapura

Angkor Borei

Khao Sam Kaeo
Oc Eo

PANPAN
Chaiya

Takuapa
Takola
TAMBRALINGA

Ligor
(Nakhon Si Thammarat)

Khuan Lukpad
Satingphra

LANGKASUKA
Pattani

Kedah
Katâha
CHITU
Kuala Trengganu

Kuala Selinsing
DANDAN

Kelang

Kampong Sungai Lang

P. Beaujard

Malayu

●	Town, site
Takola	Indian name of town
TAMBRALINGA	State
DANDAN	Chinese name of state
.....	Main terrestrial routes

0   500 Km

Map II.14 China and Southeast Asia at the beginning of the first millennium BCE

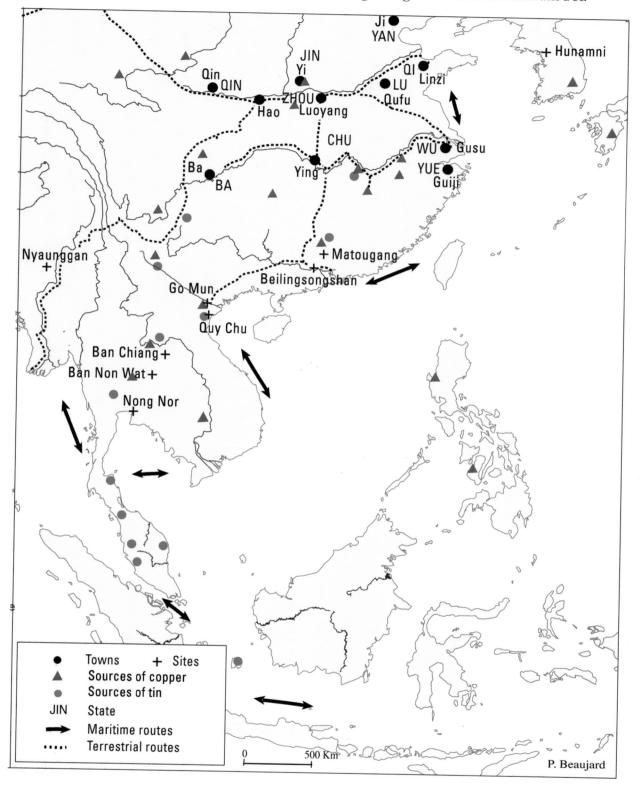

Ji
YAN
Hunamni
JIN
Yi
Qin QIN
QI Linzi
ZHOU
LU
Hao Luoyang
Qufu
CHU
WU Gusu
Ba
YUE
BA Ying
Guiji
Nyaunggan
Matougang
Go Mun
Beilingsongshan
Quy Chu
Ban Chiang
Ban Non Wat
Nong Nor

● Towns   + Sites
▲ Sources of copper
● Sources of tin
JIN State
→ Maritime routes
···· Terrestrial routes

0   500 Km

P. Beaujard

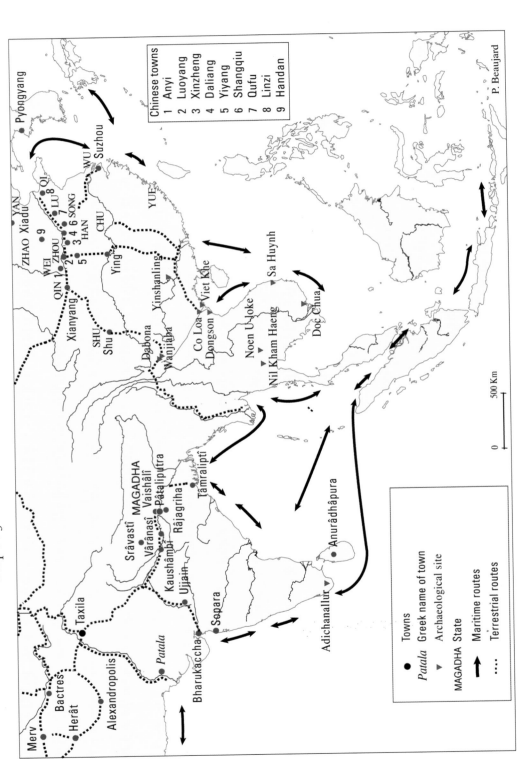

Map II.15   East Asia from the sixth to the fourth century BCE

Chinese towns
1 Anyi
2 Luoyang
3 Xinzheng
4 Daliang
5 Yiyang
6 Shangqiu
7 Qufu
8 Linzi
9 Handan

P. Beaujard

500 Km

● Towns
Patala Greek name of town
▶ Archaeological site

MAGADHA State
→ Maritime routes
····· Terrestrial routes

Map II.16   East Asia during the third and second centuries BCE

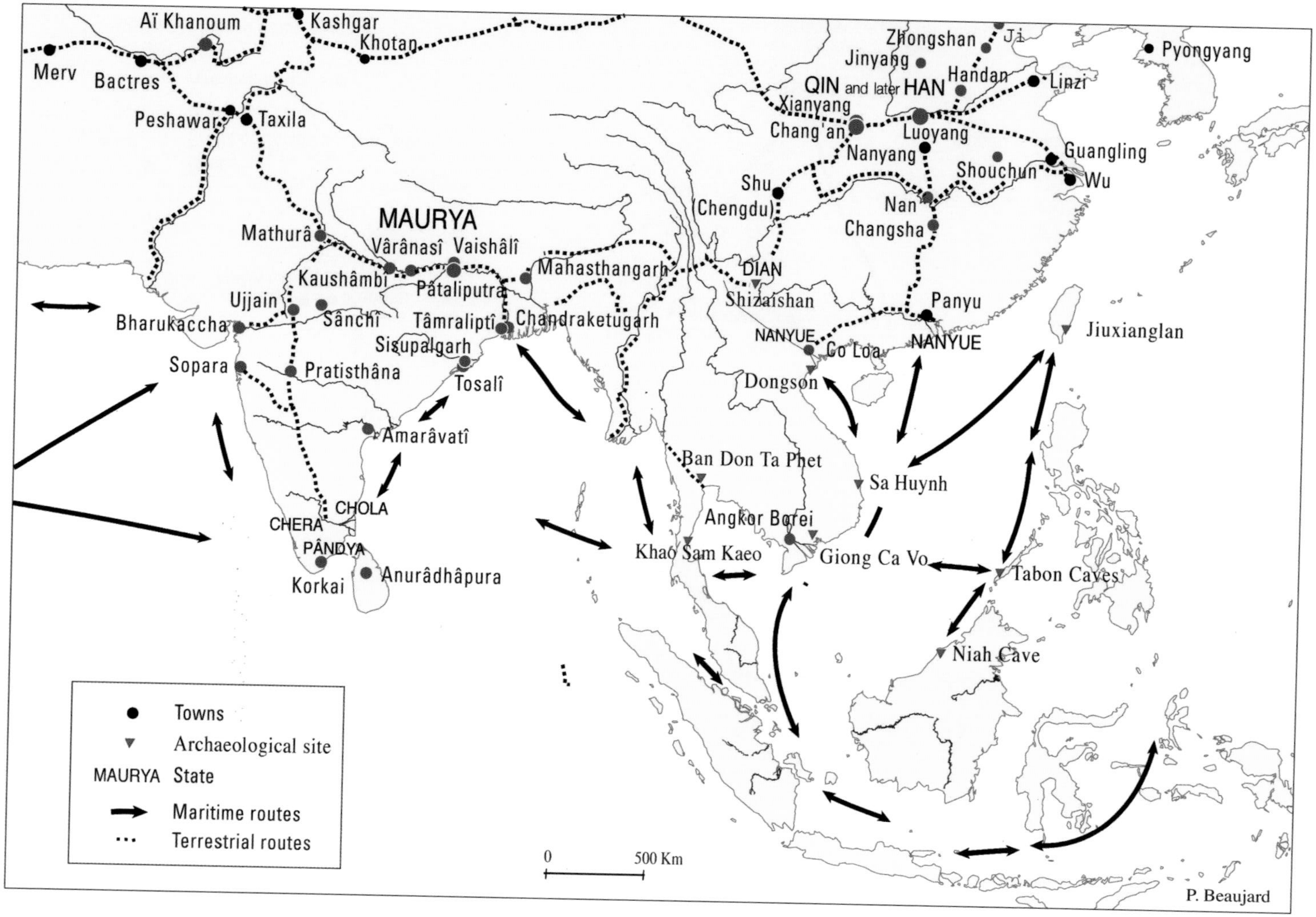

Pyongyang

Zhongshan
Jinyang   Handan
Linzi
Ji
Guangling
Wu
Shouchun
Luoyang
Nanyang
QIN and later HAN
Xianyang
Chang'an
Nan
Changsha
Shu
Chengdu
DIAN
Shizhaishan
NANYUE
Co Loa
Panyu
NANYUE
Dongson

Jiuxianglan

Tabon Caves
Niah Cave

Sa Huynh
Giong Ca Vo
Ban Don Ta Phet
Angkor Borei
Khao Sam Kaeo

MAURYA
Vaishali
Varanasi
Pataliputra
Mahasthangarh
Chandraketugarh
Kaushambi
Sanchi
Tamralipti
Sisupalgarh
Tosali
Amaravati
Pratisthana
CHOLA
CHERA   PANDYA
Korkai
Anuradhapura

Mathura
Ujjain
Bharukaccha
Sopara

Kashgar
Khotan
Taxila
Aï Khanoum
Bactres
Peshawar
Merv

P. Beaujard

500 Km
0

● Towns
▼ Archaeological site
MAURYA State
↑ Maritime routes
⋯ Terrestrial routes

Map II.17 East Asia from the first to the sixth century CE

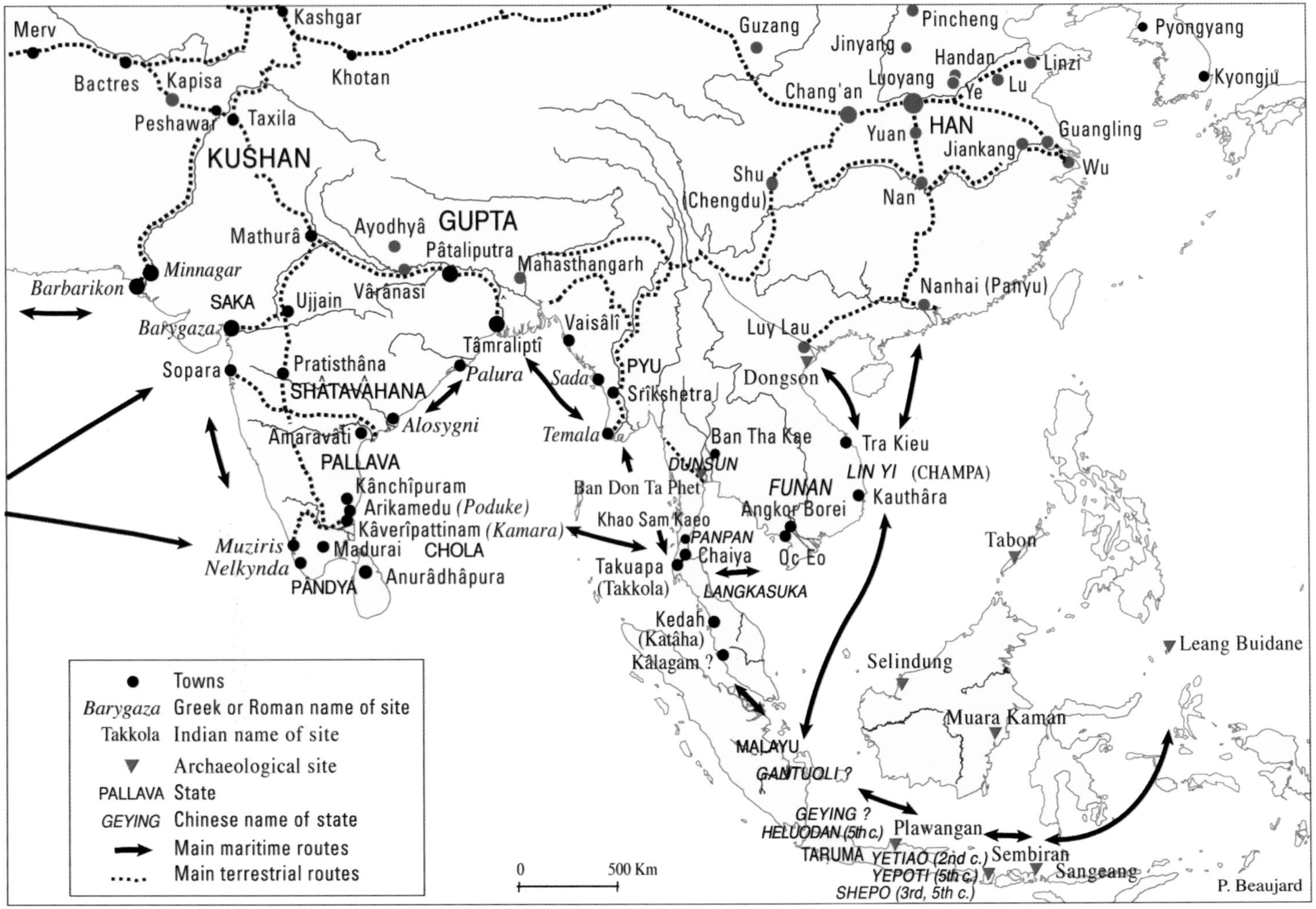

P. Beaujard

Map II.18 East Africa and Madagascar (first–sixth century CE)

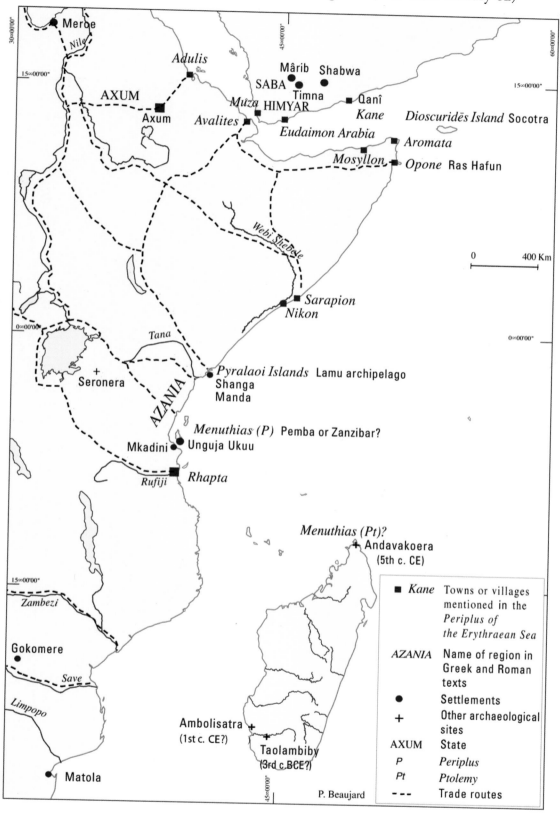

Meroe

Nile

Adulis

AXUM

Axum

SABA

Mârib

Shabwa

Timna

Mûza HIMYAR

Avalites

Qanî

Kane

Dioscuridēs Island Socotra

Eudaimon Arabia

Aromata

Mosyllon Opone Ras Hafun

Webi Shebele

0   400 Km

Sarapion
Nikon

Tana

Seronera

AZANIA

Pyralaoi Islands Lamu archipelago

Shanga
Manda

Menuthias (P) Pemba or Zanzibar?

Mkadini Unguja Ukuu

Rufiji *Rhapta*

Menuthias (Pt)?

Andavakoera
(5th c. CE)

Zambezi

Gokomere

Save

Limpopo

Ambolisatra
(1st c. CE?)

Taolambiby
(3rd c. BCE?)

Matola

P. Beaujard

■ *Kane*	Towns or villages mentioned in the *Periplus of the Erythraean Sea*
AZANIA	Name of region in Greek and Roman texts
●	Settlements
+	Other archaeological sites
AXUM	State
P	*Periplus*
Pt	*Ptolemy*
- - -	Trade routes

Map II.19 Madagascar: first cultural contributions

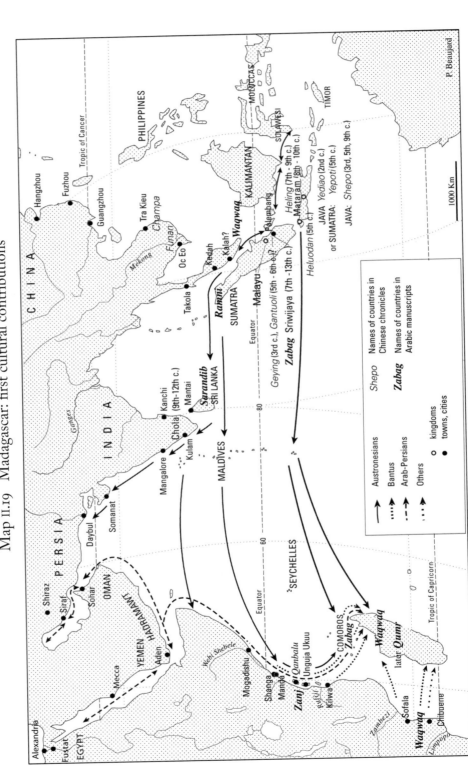

182, after Kučan 1995). The peach tree was known in India as a fruit from China (*cinani*), whereas the Greeks and the Romans knew it as a fruit of Persian origin (*persicum*).[208] In Egypt, the introduction of the peach tree goes back to the period of Persian domination and that of the apricot tree goes back to the Late Ptolemaic period (De Vartavan and Asensi Amoros 1997: 215, 216). The data are less clear for the apricot tree, which may have been introduced from Persia or Armenia into western Asia during the first century BCE.[209] Curiously, the pear was known in India under the name *cinarajaputra*, "fruit of the king of China," during the Kushan period, even though it is a plant that was domesticated at an early period in western Asia and in the eastern Mediterranean (Adshead 1995: 36). Plants also traveled from western Asia and/or Central Asia to China. The Chinese medieval name for spinach is "Persian vegetable."[210] A Chinese name for the walnut tree, *po-lo-ši*, derives from the Sanskrit *pārasī*, which comes from the name given to Persia. Under the Han or after the Han, garlic, carrot, alfalfa, pomegranate, grapevine, sesame, and linen (called "hemp of the *hu*") arrived in China from Central Asia (Boulnois 2008: 91).

Contacts between cultures also facilitated the exchange of knowledge and ideas. Various authors have thus pointed out an influence of Chinese alchemy in Persia, and subsequently in the Greek world (Adshead 1995: 44–46).

The Parthians would not turn out to be as actively involved as the Seleucids in the trade of the Persian Gulf. However, they occupied some regions of the Arab coast, triggering the decline of Gerrha. A text by Pliny mentions a victorious expedition conducted by Numenius, the Seleucid governor of Mesene (Charax region), against the "Persians," in the Ras Musandam region. This has sometimes been interpreted as evidence for a Parthian presence in Oman around 135–130 BCE. The *Periplus* designates Omana as a "market-town of Persia." It was mainly after 131 CE – when a Parthian prince was placed on the throne of the kingdom of Charax – that the Parthian hold on Bahrain and Oman appears to have become effective. As the departure point of a caravan route toward Palmyra[211] and Syria, Charax played a crucial role in the Gulf during the first centuries CE, which may explain the spread of the Aramaic language along the Arab coast at this time.[212] Ceramics found in the Gulf between the second century BCE and the third century CE attest to the existence of a true common culture, influenced by the Parthians (Potts 1996: 270ff.). Beyond Arabia, Parthian ceramics have been found at Opōnē, on the Horn of Africa. A Parthian presence in Arabia may

---

[208] The peach was called "Persian apple or plum" in Greece from the end of the fourth century BCE (Amigues 2005: 360, 363).

[209] Zohary and Hopf 2000: 182. Apricot tree: *Armeniaca vulgaris* Lam.

[210] Laufer 1919: 393. In 647, it figures among the donations given by the court of Nepal to Emperor Taizong.

[211] Palmyra was one of the main entry points for merchandise from Central and eastern Asia into the Roman world. People from Palmyra were present in Parthia, at Charax, and in the Persian Gulf (for example, on the island of Kharg). In 131 CE, a merchant from Palmyra called Yarhai was appointed satrap at Tylos (Bahrain) by the king of Charax. The Palmyrenians chartered ships; a text carved in stone mentions traders from Sind.

[212] Potts 1996: 276. During the Parthian period, Aramaic was still the usual vehicular language, along with Greek; Parthian was the language spoken at the Arsacid court and the language of the administration. The Sassanid emperors had trilingual inscriptions engraved, in Middle-Persian, in Parthian, and in Greek.

explain why an expedition was launched by the first Persian king, Ardashir I, the founder of the Sassanid dynasty and of an empire which would be much more enterprising than the Parthians in controlling and developing trade routes.

The Parthian Empire was progressively weakened by the wars conducted toward both the east and the west,[213] as well as by conflicts between the king and the aristocracy. The decline of central power allowed "vassal" kings to emerge. In 228 CE, the Persians seized Iran from the Parthians; King Ardashir I rebuilt an empire almost as large as the Achaemenid Empire. Some regions were placed under the authority of a king; others were satrapies.[214] More than the previous Persian Empire, the Sassanid Empire, as was the case in the Byzantine Empire, closely associated politics and religion, which constituted the foundations of its power. The preeminence of the Sassanids would last until the Arab conquest during the seventh century.

The Persians improved irrigation in Mesopotamia: around 500 CE or slightly later, two 200-km-long canals, the Nahrwan and the Katul al-Kisrawi, were dug in order to bring water from the Tigris into arable lands. A network of smaller canals made it possible to enclose irrigation basins. A large dam was completed at Shūshtar (the "Dam of the Emperor"), built with a labor force deported from the Roman Empire.[215] The irrigation systems in Mesopotamia were probably at their peak during the Sassanid period (Decker 2009: 190). Rice agriculture was developed in Mesopotamia and the Levant (Decker 2009: 195). There was also a notable increase in the cultivation of cotton, primarily in Khorassan (Merv) and in Azerbaijan. These regions were able to export cotton cloth: the cotton fabrics in the Byzantine Empire were manufactured with Z-spun (right-hand spin) yarns, as was the case for the Sassanid Empire (in line with the Indian tradition) (Decker 2009: 200). The rulers ensured that roads were maintained; at their intersections, cities flourished, such as Nisibis, Artaxata (in Armenia), and Ctesiphon. The latter became the capital of the empire, where the king of kings was crowned. Increased gains in agriculture underlay a sizeable demographic expansion. In parallel with urbanization, craft production progressed in various regions of the empire, accompanied by an increasing division of labor, with craftsmen organized into corporations, during the Late Sassanid period. The state drew a large part of its revenues from land taxes and head taxes, and it also collected customs duties on goods. In the domain of finance, Toussaint notes "the creation of banks" and "the expansion [of a precursor] to the bill of exchange" (1961: 47–48); however, we have seen that banks and notes of credit did in fact develop in Mesopotamia as early as the early second millennium. Though the Sassanid Empire had no silver mines, it issued significant quantities of silver dirhams on a regular basis, even during the late period, and took on ancient Parthian denominations and norms.[216] The Sassanid economic system has often been described as marked by a tight

---

[213] Unlike the Achaemenid Empire, the Parthian Empire did not have a standing army. The army was above all based on light cavalry and heavy cavalry, with soldiers and horses protected by scale armor (Huyse 2005: 73). The Sassanid Empire would later resort once again to a standing army, which included an efficient cavalry (armor had become lighter compared to the previous period, and allowed for greater mobility).

[214] The organization of the empire changed during the sixth century; it had three levels: counties, provinces, and regions, under the direction of a commander.

[215] Slavery developed to a significant degree under the Sassanid Empire.

[216] Daryaee (2003: 11) gives four locations where coins were minted, in Fars. The drachm was the main nominal value. Shapuhr II made the decision to pay his troops with coins; this explains why the Sassanids

state control, and by the introduction of a number of taxes, which appear to have held back the growth of commerce. Production and trade, however, were in the hands of private entrepreneurs, and there is not much evidence that the state had control over long-distance trade (Daryaee 2003: 16).

Whereas the Zoroastrian clergy was unsympathetic toward merchants, the kings expressed their support for traders (Panaino 2004). The Sassanids tried to promote the development of trade along the Silk Roads, secured during the third century. Sogdiana – which remained independent – also had an important role to play, which would become even more significant from the fifth century onward. Silver Persian coins have been discovered in particular on the northern branch of the Silk Roads running through Kucha and Turfan (several hoards unearthed at Turfan contained Sassanid coins dated to the fourth century). The Fars province was especially dynamic in the manufacture of fabrics, perfumes, and carpets, which were exported to China. Eggs stolen – possibly in Central Asia – around 410 CE (or perhaps earlier) made it possible for the silk industry to expand in Persia, an industry that was also fed by yarn imports[217] and by the occasional deportation of weavers.[218] Silk production developed in Khuzistan. The Persians held a monopoly over the sale of raw silk until the sixth century.[219] During the early seventh century, the Chinese pilgrim Xuanzang (Hsüan Tsang) notes that Persia produces "fine silk brocade, wool fabrics and carpets" (Huyse 2005: 97). Xuanzang recounts a legend in which a Chinese princess purportedly introduced *Bombyx* eggs into Khotan around 400 CE, but silkworm breeding in the oases of Central Asia may go much further back. Sericulture is said to have appeared during the fourth century CE in the Fergana valley (Boulnois 2008: 186). The Sogdians transported Persian silk to China, as well as their own silk products, decorated with Sassanid motifs (riders facing each other, *simurgh*, ducks, and so forth), produced at Zandan (near Bukhara) during the sixth century (Liu 2010: 82).[220] Persia also exported pearls from the Red Sea, corals, narcotics, steel blades,[221] glass, and Syrian fabrics to China.

minted large amounts of coins from the fourth century onward. Gold coins (dinars) were also issued, but primarily for prestige. The dinar was based on the Roman *denarius aureus* (Huyse 2005: 106).

[217] Boulnois (2008: 160), citing A. Mazaheri, mentions another tradition acording to which the Sassans, an Indo-Iranian family, introduced silkworm breeding into the south of Fars province (possibly from worms imported from Tchinapati) as early as the third century. A Chinese text mentions foreign silk thread woven in the Hexi corridor during the fourth century, as well as an offering of "silk from Da Qin" at Kucha around the end of this century (Liu 1988: 67). Japan purportedly imported silkworm eggs during the second century CE, as did Korea during the last centuries BCE (Boulnois (2008: 161).

[218] In 360 CE, the Persian king Shapuhr II apparently "captured the silk workers of Roman Syria and moved them near to Susa" (Boulnois 2008: 205). The capture and deportation of artisans was a common strategy in wars.

[219] Previously dependent on Persian imports, Byzantium was able to produce silk during the sixth century, from eggs stolen around 552 CE (according to Procopius) and thanks to imported mulberry trees. Justinian had already sent Byzantine silk in 565 CE. As for the people who originally brought Bombyx eggs to Byzantium, different traditions have been reported (monks "from India" according to Procopius; a Persian arriving from the country of the Seres, according to Theophanes) (Boulnois 2001: 245).

[220] Remnants of Sassanid or Sogdian silks have been discovered in religious institutions in Europe, and on a road crossing through the Caucasus (Liu 2010). Some *zandaniji* fabrics probably came from the Tarim, and the Chinese also produced copies of Sogdian or Iranian models (de la Vaissière 2002: 235).

[221] The Babylonian Talmud (compiled between the third and fifth centuries) mentions crucible steel *hinduan* (the term *hinduwani* was later used by Muslims for "Indian steel"). "The Talmudic reference

Zoroastrian Persians traveled along the roads of Central Asia and influenced Buddhism, which was still a major religion: the enormous Buddhas of Bāmiyān were probably carved during the third and fifth centuries, respectively. The Buddhas in the caves of Yungang, in Shanxi, carved during the fifth and sixth centuries, mark the opposite end of the Silk Roads. Manicheans and Christians were also present on these roads, having been persecuted in Persia during the fourth century, within the context of the war against the Roman Empire (note that in the Roman Empire, pagan cults were prohibited after 392 CE).[222] Persia, however, hosted the Nestorian Church, condemned by the Council of Ephesus, in 431 CE. Many Syrians also left the region of Antioch, affected by an earthquake in 526 CE (the region later experienced a series of plague epidemics), and Khosrau I employed a fair number of Nestorian Syrians in his administration.[223] These Christians brought with them elements of Greek science, translated into Syriac. Christianity expanded into eastern Arabia during the fourth and fifth centuries (it also progressed into Yemen at this time [Robin 2005–2006]). The Nestorians would also go on to extend their trade networks throughout the Asian continent. Christians and Jews[224] were affected by renewed persecutions during the fifth and sixth centuries, when Zoroastrianism became the state religion in Persia.[225] Merchants of the Sogdian diaspora, for their part, were first Buddhists, and later became Manicheans or practiced a variant of Mazdeism (de la Vaissière 2002: 133).

Very early on, the Sassanids engaged in military campaigns against Rome along the western flank of their empire. In 256 CE, Antioch was taken by Shapuhr I, who had taken Emperor Valerian prisoner in 260 CE, near Edessa. In the east, part of the Kushan Empire was conquered. During the third century, Rome managed to regain lost ground, but during the fourth century, under Shapuhr II, the Sassanids again had the upper hand. A peace treaty was signed in 384 CE between Shapuhr III and Theodosius I, who was the last ruler of a unified Roman Empire; peace would last until Bahram V's reign (420–438 CE). Despite these conflicts, commercial and cultural links were established. King Shapuhr I employed Byzantine artisans for the construction of his monuments and had Greek texts on science and philosophy translated.

The end of the fifth and the early sixth centuries was a difficult time for the Sassanid Empire; repeated famines, coupled with the burden of additional taxes levied in order to finance renewed warfare with Byzantium, led to popular revolts against the nobility.

suggests that trade between India and Persia was controlled by Jewish merchants . . . The Persians then traded at least some of this steel onward to the Roman Empire" (Craddock 2003: 244).

[222] Christians were present in Persia as early as the third century, for example at Baith Lapāt (Khuzistan). The populations deported from the Levant by Shapuhr I included a good number of Christians. The Manicheans, disciples of the Parthian Mani, whom the Zoroastrians considered to be a heretic, formed a large community in Sogdiana. Manicheism would go on to become the "state religion" of the Uighurs during the eighth century (see below). Manicheism shows both Christian and Buddhist influences: Mani was considered to be an "apostle of Christ" and a "Buddha of light."

[223] Rejected by Byzantium during the fifth century, the Nestorians were less mistrusted than the Orthodox Christians, who were often accused by the Persians of being agents of the enemy.

[224] Fleeing Roman persecution, many Jews went to Persia during the second century.

[225] Huyse (2005: 141–142) rightly points out that this was not the case before the fifth century, although the Sassanid kings instrumentalized Zoroastrianism by claiming that they were of divine origin. The emperors made (land) grants to Zoroastrian religious leaders, whose power grew when the empire encountered difficulties, during the fifth and sixth centuries.

The rebels, who followed the Zoroastrian schism of Mazdakism, attacked the social barriers that differentiated the various classes (Huyse 2005: 78). At the same time, in the east, nomad incursions that had begun around 350 CE took on a new dimension: the Hephtalites, who had settled in Central Asia, severely defeated the Sassanid emperor Peroz twice, in 471 and then in 484 CE, when Peroz died in battle. The Hephtalites had become a direct threat to Sassanid power and the latter was forced to pay hefty tributes, at least until the reign of Khosrau I (531–579 CE) (de la Vaissière 2002: 117). For several centuries, Sassanid silver coins from these tributes would be common currency along the northern branch of the Silk Roads,[226] and this wealth would in turn benefit the Sogdians (de la Vaissière 2002: 117, 170). Whereas Bactria was going through a long-drawn-out decline, Sogdiana was strengthened under the Kidarite dynasty: this was a "Hun" branch originally from Bactria.[227] The region made progress in agriculture, and cities such as Nasaf (150 ha), Samarkand, and Pendjikent developed. This prosperity was accompanied by artistic development influenced by Bactria. During the second half of the fifth century, the Kidarites lost Bactria to the Hephtalites, who eventually seized power in Sogdiana, in 509 CE, but the Sogdian merchants adapted themselves to this new power. The Hephtalite Empire arrived at its zenith around 520 CE, controlling a region from Turfan to Merv and Gandhara. The fifth and especially the sixth century witnessed a spectacular Sogdian expansion, marked not only by a commercial boom, but also by colonization that led to urban development, notably in the north, along the Syr Darya (city of Kanka), and in the east, for example in Semirech'ye (sites of Navaket and Suyab). "All sectors of Sogdian society were affected by emigration" toward the Tarim and Gansu, and this emigration "covered the whole region," with well-structured communities enjoying a great deal of autonomy (de la Vaissière 2002: 140). Though the Persians were potential competitors with the Sogdians, they joined the Sogdian caravans, and Sassanid embassies reached the capital of the Northern Wei, Pingcheng (Datong) – by land – in 455 and 522 CE. The arrival of the Huns and a decline in trade led to the de-urbanization of Bactria and northwestern India, where the city of Taxila was deserted.

The Sassanid region, however, enjoyed a new period of growth during the sixth and the early seventh centuries. Emperor Khosrau I repressed the Mazdakist schism, which believed in social justice, in opposition to the great landowners, but he also set up social, economic, and military reforms which bore fruit (these endeavors may have been influenced by previous Byzantine reforms under Diocletian [284–305 CE]). Embassies were sent to Chang'an in 553, 558, and 578 CE, evidence of the search for a Sino-Persian political axis to confront the threat coming from the steppes (Gernet 1999: 178; Salmon 2004: 30). Three tributary "Persian" missions also traveled to China during the Liang

---

[226] The southern branch of the Silk Roads, at the time without minted money, seems to have been in decline between the fourth and seventh centuries. Conversely, Thierry (2000: 125) emphasizes that silver and copper coins have been found along the northern branch, which was then the most active. "Of the 1,500 Sassanid coins unearthed in China, 1,000 were excavated in Serindia, of which 947 in the treasure of Ulugh Art," in the region of Kashgar, in Xinjiang. The kingdom of Kuchā issued its own coinage between the fourth and sixth centuries. Silk was also used as currency.

[227] The "identity" of the Kidarites remains uncertain. The *Weishu* calls them Yuezhi (Kushans). They ruled Bactria, then Gandhara and Sogdiana. They clashed with the Sassanids under Bahram V (420–438) then Yazdigird II (438–457) and with the Hephtalites, who expelled them from Bactria *c.* 467 (Grenet 2005).

period, probably by sea, in 530, 533, and 535 CE (Salmon 2004: 3). In the war against Byzantium, the Sassanid armies regained the upper hand. Khosrau I destroyed Antioch and deported its inhabitants (532 CE). In 562 CE, a "fifty-year peace" was established with Byzantium, which was obliged to pay tribute. Helped by the Turks, the Sassanids then turned against the Hephtalites, and defeated them in 563.

Byzantium tried out various strategies in an attempt to bypass the Sassanid obstacle. Through Egypt, it entered into contact with the distant Axumite kingdom, via Adulis. A coin from the Ethiopian king Aphilas (fourth century) and some Ethiopian graffiti have been found at Berenice. South of Berenice, "the site of Shenshef shows the continuation of Indian imports during the 5th and 6th centuries," but "Indian ceramics are less common during the Late Roman period" (Tomber 2012a: 76–77). In Asia, after the founding of the empire of the Kök Turks in 552 CE,[228] a silk road running north of the Caspian Sea was reactivated by the Sogdians and the Byzantines. According to the Byzantine historian Menander Protector, the Sogdians – then subjects of the Turks – first attempted to enter the Sassanid market, at the heart of the empire: at this, the Sassanid emperor bought the silk that they had brought and had it publicly burned. This act, which intended to protect the Persian merchant class,[229] also targeted the Turkish political rulers. The Sogdians subsequently advised the Turks to rely on Byzantium for trade (de la Vaissière 2002: 223–224). Turco-Sogdian envoys were sent to Byzantium in 568 CE, carrying silk. The Byzantines, in turn, sent an embassy to the Altai that same year, then sent another in 576 CE (de la Vaissière 2002: 230ff.; Boulnois 2008: 240). This policy was nothing new for Byzantium; the Pseudo-Zacharias of Mytilene (sixth century) tells us that as early as the fifth century, a merchant from Apamea (Syria), a Byzantine ambassador to the Hephtalites, encouraged the latter to attack Persia (de la Vaissière 2002: 229).

The challenges present on the routes of Central Asia along with diminishing trade with Byzantium led the Sassanids to prefer the route that went via the Persian Gulf and explains their interest in the Indian Ocean, leading to the conquest of Arabia in 571 CE (see below). This interest in the Ocean, however, was not new. From the early days of the empire, the Sassanids had already asserted their maritime power, attempting to control and organize trade, a policy later reported by Muslim historians. The first king, Ardashir, invaded Bahrain and Oman. Hamza mentions the names of eight ports founded or developed on the Gulf or along rivers that flow into the Gulf, notably Rev Ardashir, on the Bushire peninsula (Būshehr, on the Iranian coast), Batn Ardashir (ancient Gerrha, on the Arabian coast), and Artarabad Ardashir, which replaced Charax. At the end of a land route, Sīrāf was already by that time a port that traded with Minab, at the entrance of the Gulf, and with Sind (Daybul – probably the Barbarikon of the *Periplus* – was a major port before the Arab conquest) and

---

[228] The term "Blue Turk" is found in inscriptions written in Old Turkic; a Sogdian inscription from 582 CE speaks of "Turkit Ashina," from an East-Iranian or Tocharian term meaning "blue." The empire was divided into two khānates: eastern (552–630 CE) and western (552–659 CE) (Golden 2005: 21).

[229] "The Iranian state," notes de la Vaissière, "did everything in its power to monopolize the sale of silk to the Greeks for the benefit of its merchants" (2002: 224). This policy of control was already noticeable during the Parthian period. Sogdian merchants, however, were present in the eastern Sassanid Empire, particularly at Merv.

Gujarat. A coin of the Roman emperor Theodosius I (376–394 CE), struck at Alexandria, as well as Roman glass dated to the fifth century have been found at Sīrāf. Chinese stoneware also goes back to this period, as does Red Polished Ware from Gujarat. On the Persian coast, although the main harbor was Rishar (Rev Ardashir),[230] Persian ships bound for India departed from Oman, which explains why this region was occupied by Ardashir. The remains of a Sassanian settlement that had a military function have been discovered at Jazirat al-Ghanam, an island off the Musandam peninsula. The Sassanids had fortresses at Sohar, Dama, and Jurrafar. V. Piacentini notes the existence of a maritime Sassanid administrative structure still in place at the time of the first caliphs (2002: 166ff.).

Sassanid ships sailed to India on a regular basis, especially to the port of Barygaza, and to Sri Lanka, where they met merchants from Southeast Asia; Persian ships probably also sailed to Southeast Asia and China. Zoroastrians were present in Sind prior to Islam. The fact that torpedo jars from Mesopotamia were the most common type of amphorae imported into northwestern India is significant, suggesting the considerable scale of Sassanian commerce (Tomber 2012a: 126). On the Konkan coast, torpedo jars have been unearthed at Elephanta, along with some Late Roman amphorae (Tomber 2012a: 128). Torpedo jars and blue-green-glazed ware have also been found in Anuradhapura (Sri Lanka), as well as a Pahlavi inscription, on a ceramic piece bearing a Nestorian cross. During the fourth century, Palladius, and subsequently the *Nestorian Annals*, at the time of Yazdigird I (399–421), speak of Persian travels. Ṭabarī tells us that King Bahram V (421–438) married an Indian princess and received the port of Daybul and its region as a dowry (Whitehouse 1996: 344). He brought in two groups of people, the Zoṭṭ and the Sayābiga (a name referring to Sumatra; see Volume II) from the Lower Indus region, whom he employed as mercenaries (Hamza, Firdawsī, and al-Ta'ālibī speak of singers belonging to the Zoṭṭ or the Luri tribe, who may have been the predecessors of the European Roma). The expansion of Sassanid trade benefited from the political and economic consolidation of India under the Gupta dynasty. Sugarcane imports made it possible to cultivate this plant in Persia around the fifth century. As a result of contacts between Persians and Indians, Manichaeism influenced Indian Buddhism, which itself played a role in the iconography of Manicheism in Central and eastern Asia. Nestorians from Persia settled in Indian ports, in particular along the Malabar coast[231] and in Sri Lanka. In addition, Christians were active on the eastern Arab coast (bishops were present in Bahrain and in Qatar at the beginning of the seventh century). Greek and Sanskrit texts were translated into Middle Persian (Pahlevi), indicating the interest of the Sassanids in other cultures. This also shows the role of hinge played by their empire between Europe and India. Sassanid art reflects the impact of Byzantine and Levantine art, in

---

[230] A town (*polis*) called Hieratis by Arrian already existed on the Bushire peninsula at the time of Alexander the Great (Whitehouse 1996: 342).

[231] Cosmas mentions their presence on this coast and at Kalyan (near Bombay). Persecution led Christians from Persia to emigrate to the Malabar coast. Stone Nestorian crosses dated to the sixth century have been found in South India: two at Kottayam, south of Cochin, and one near Mylabore, in the Madras region (Boulnois 2001: 270). In addition, Nestorians appear to have been present on Socotra, a stopover on trade routes leading to the Red Sea.

reliefs, glass, and cameos, as well as Indian and Central Asian influences. During the Sassanid period, masonry using cement was introduced from the Mediterranean world. A Roman influence is noticeable in the techniques used for building bridges and dams (Huyse 2005: 201). In the opposite direction, a Sassanid influence has been described in Byzantine art, in the Romanesque art of western Europe, "on Coptic textiles and in Ethiopian miniatures" (Huyse 2005: 196). Generally speaking, Persian fabrics influenced the styles produced in Europe and Egypt. The Persian Empire developed indigo cultivation; this plant was also grown in Palestine during the second century CE (Balfour-Paul 1997: 10, 13).

Regarding Persia, other – Byzantine – sources can be found in the writings of the historian Procopius (c. 500–565) and of Cosmas Indicopleustes in his *Topographia Christiana*.[232] Cosmas was a Greek merchant from Alexandria; he became a monk in the Sinai, and traveled to India. He emphasized Sri Lanka's key role in the maritime trade during the sixth century (see below).

Ṭabarī, Hamza, and Ṯaʿālibī have claimed that a Sassanid fleet sent by Khosrau I conquered the island of Sri Lanka. The reality of this expedition has been cast into doubt; it was mentioned neither by the Byzantines nor by eastern sources. In any event, this tradition suggests the power of the Sassanids: trade was largely in the hands of the Persians during the fifth and sixth centuries. According to Procopius, "it was impossible for the Ethiopians to buy silk from the Indians, for the Persian merchants always locate themselves at the very harbors where the Indian ships first put in ... and are accustomed to buy the entire cargoes" (*Wars*, 1.20.12; Whitehouse 1996: 345). Sri Lanka yielded Sassanid coins, as well as Partho-Sassanid and Indo-Sassanid pottery.[233]

At the head of the Persian Gulf, Ubullah (the ancient Apologos of the *Periplus*) was the largest Sassanid port. According to Dīnawarī, Balāḏurī, and Masʿūdī, this port welcomed "ships from China" (see below). The Persians were probably present in Southeast Asia and ventured as far as East Asia prior to the Arabs. Glass beads were manufactured on the Thai–Malay peninsula (Khlong Thom) and in insular Southeast Asia using glass from the Sassanid Empire, especially hexagonal bicone beads made of m-Na-Ca glass (see Lankton *et al.* 2008: 355).[234] Chinese stoneware found at Sirāf, Sohar, and on the East African coast (Unguja Ukuu) appears to demonstrate (perhaps direct) links between Sassanid Persia and China, where Persian communities may have settled, at Canton, Hongzhou, and Yangzhou (Salmon 2004: 30) (the discovery of Chinese jars dated to the fourth century at Sohar – in stratigraphy – may be significant [Kervran, p.c.], but other researchers have dated this material to the Tang period). Sassanid coins dated to the fifth century have been discovered in Sri Lanka, in southern Thailand (at Yarang, in the Pattani region), and in China. They have been found in northeastern, eastern, and southeastern China, the former brought on the Silk Roads,

---

[232] Conversely, Persian sources are scarce for the Sassanid period.

[233] Coins from Yazdigird I (399–420), Shapuhr II (309–379), Hormoz IV (579–590), and a Kushano-Sassanid coin (c. 300–325) have been discovered. For O. Bopearachchi (2002: 111), the layout of the site of Sigiriya, associated with the Sinhalese king Kasyapa (477–495), was influenced by Persian tradition.

[234] The m-Na-Ca glass found in Southeast Asia had a different origin, probably Egyptian (Lankton *et al.* 2008).

and the latter brought partly via maritime routes.[235] Silver or silvered vessels produced in Persia or in Central Asia also reached China; those that have been unearthed near the southern coast were doubtless brought by ships.[236] What motivated the Persian merchants to travel to China? Schafer (1985) mentions the use of brazilwood (from Indonesia) as a dye in Sassanid Persia. Merchants probably also brought silks, spices, and aromatics back from the Orient. When the Muslims took Ctesiphon in 637, in the palace of Chosroes II they "discovered large jars full of [Indonesian] camphor," and during the fourth century, camphor was commercialized in China by Sogdians (Guillot 2004: 164). Ferrand has pointed out that the Persians acted as forerunners along the routes to China. The sailors who joined the caliphs[237] were mainly Persians, and several toponyms of Persian origin have been noted in the most ancient Arab chronicles related to China. The Chinese term Dashi (Ta-shih) referring to the Arabs probably derives from the Middle Persian *tāzīk/g* or from the Middle Parthian *tāžīk/g*, meaning "Arab" (from the name of the Arab tribe of Ṭayyi'), a term that Persian or Parthian merchants took with them to Central Asia (Sogdiana, for example).[238]

The Chinese texts attest to the frequency of contacts between Persia and China. Products that had previously been linked to Da Qin (the eastern Roman Empire) by the *Houhanshu* (*Book of the Later Han*, a fifth-century work compiled by Fan Ye, based on data from the first century CE), were now being associated with Bosi, Persia, as can be attested in the *Beishi* or the *Suishu* (Boulnois 2008: 169).

Amongst the Persians traveling to East Asia were Nestorian Christians, whose presence is reported in Sri Lanka by Cosmas.[239] Among the bishops who attended the synod in 410 CE was the "Metropolitan of the Islands, Seas and the Interior, of Dabag [possibly Java], Chin and Macin [various regions of China]": these were Nestorians who came by sea on Persian, Indian, and Austronesian ships, or by land on the Silk Roads, and probably settled in Southeast Asia and in China.[240] Persian-speaking Christian communities lived in Kerala and in Tamil Nadu around 600 CE (Ray 2003: 186). At the time of the Catholicus Ishoyahb III (647 or 650–657/658), the Metropolitan of Rev Ardashir was in charge not only of the Church of Fars, but also of India, from the border of the Sassanid Empire to a place called Qlh, located at a distance of "1,200 parasangs." This was probably the port of Qalah mentioned by

---

[235] Daryaee (2003: 13) mentions the discovery of Sassanid coins dated to the end of the fifth, sixth, and early seventh centuries at three sites close to the sea in Southeast China (Kukgong, Yingdak, and Suikai). Other coins issued in the name of Kawad I have been found in Guangdong province. See also Salmon 2004: 32.

[236] As well as glass bowls (see below). Silver vessels may have been "gifts," made in the context of diplomatic exchanges (Huyse 2005: 209). A tomb dated to the fifth century on the Leizhou peninsula (Guangdong) has yielded an assemblage of silver and gold artifacts of Persian origin (Salmon 2004: 32).

[237] Conversely, Ibn Manzūr mentions that "the king of the Persians Ardchīr Babakān recruited sailors among the Arabs of the Azd tribe, living in the city of Chihr in 'Umān" (quoted by Hamidullah 1974: 201).

[238] Shahid 2000: 62. The Arabs of the Ṭayyi' tribe (Syriac Tayyāyyē) were employed as guards by the Lakhmids of al-Ḥira during the sixth century, but the term is certainly older. Non-Muslim Turks adopted the term, giving it the meaning "Muslim."

[239] A baked-clay *bulla* found at Mantai (sixth–seventh century) bears a Persian inscription, the image of a Bactrian camel and a Nestorian cross (Bopearachchi 2002: 110).

[240] Nestorians were present in the oases of Central Asia, for example at Dunhuang (Bentley 1993: 106).

Arab geographers in the following centuries on the west coast of the Thai/Malay peninsula (Whitehouse 1996: 345) (see also Guillot 2004).

In the commerce of the western Indian Ocean, the Persians' competitors were not the Byzantines, who were never very active in that ocean, but the Axumites, who however received the support of Byzantium, in hope of breaking the Persian hold on trade. Axum minted its own gold, silver, and copper currency from the third century onward (using the Greek, Sabaean, and Ethiopian languages). It conquered Meroe, which was then in decline, during the fourth century. In 529 CE, an Axumite troop of 70,000 men invaded Yemen and occupied the region for about forty years, until the Persians, after expelling the Axumite merchants from Sri Lanka, dislodged the Axumites from Arabia in 570 CE. Khosrau I sent a fleet of eight ships and 4,000 troops, who appointed a Sassanid governor. The Sassanid ships based at Aden were able to control entry to the Red Sea. They probably also traded along the East African coast. A Sassanid governor was present in Oman. At this time, and for four subsequent centuries, the merchandise of the Orient was far more likely to go through the Persian Gulf than through the Red Sea.

The Sassanid expansion continued under Khosrau II, who conquered Egypt in 619 and besieged Byzantium in 626 CE. The Byzantine reaction under Heraclius, however, was to mark the end of Sassanid preeminence. On the eve of the Arab conquest, the Sassanids controlled most of the trade routes of the western Indian Ocean, but the empire was undermined from within by the cost of wars against Byzantium and by famines triggered by periods of increased aridity; the state was in continuous internal turmoil after 628 CE, marked by a revolt of the nobility, after which a period of anarchy began. The Sassanids could not withstand the Arab armies and were defeated, notably at Nihāvand (Media) in 642 CE.

10 India: The Birth of a New Core

All enterprises depend on finance, therefore particular attention should be paid to Treasury [of the state] . . . Mines are the source of treasury; from treasury comes the power of government; and the earth whose ornament is treasury is acquired by means of treasury and army. (*Arthasastra*, quoted by Schaps 2006)

Wealth, and wealth alone, is important . . . Wealth earned should not be stored but spent . . ., the path of rectitude requires us to work relentlessly for the acquisition of wealth and profits. (*Arthasastra*)

The Emergence of Empires: Buddhist Networks and the Rise of Trade

The Persian presence in Sri Lanka reveals this island's hingelike function between the western and eastern parts of the Indian Ocean. At the continental level, however, it was the entire Indian subcontinent which played a pivotal role between eastern and western Asia. Of course, India (or rather, the interconnected Indias) was no simple intermediary, but a set of active powers, each of which developed its own productions, transmitted its own worldview, knowledge, and values, and launched its ships on the trade routes.

The *ārya* clans who entered India during the second millennium BCE in a sequence of waves slowly spread throughout northern India, imposing their language (Sanskrit, which in turn gave rise to various Prākrit languages and dialects), as well as their religion and social system. After the Earlier Vedic period, "the epicentre is no longer in the Indus valley but further east, between the Punjab and the Upper Yamunā River, in the Doāb" (Sergent 1997: 245). Linked to Indo-Aryans, the Painted Grey Ware culture appeared in the Doāb region and the Ganges valley as of 1100 BCE (Sergent 1997: 245; Chakravarti 2002b: 64 n. 15).[1] Tripathi (2001) sees the rise of a first Iron Age alongside the expansion of Painted Grey Ware. Then from 800/700 BCE onward appeared the

---

[1] Curiously, Sergent notes that the Indo-Aryans had made only a slow advance between the seventeenth and eleventh centuries BCE, from the region of Pirak toward the Ganges. But were they really the same Aryans? Beads made of lapis lazuli and violin-shaped figurines suggest links between the PGW culture and Afghanistan (1997: 248). Possehl (2002a: 239) notes that "the interface between the assemblage [of Painted Grey Ware] and the Late Harappan in the Punjab has been documented at such places as Dadheri and Bhagwanpura," whereas "the interface between the cemetery H assemblage and Painted Grey Ware has not yet been defined in Pakistan"; the Indo-Aryans of the Ganges did not come from the west, but from the northwest: from Punjab and Afghanistan. Possehl also notes that "the Aryans may have come to the Punjab over a long period of time" (2002a: 249). For Masson (1996b: 354), the grey ceramic found at Bhagwanpura, in Haryana, in a Post-Harappan context would signal the first occurrence of this pottery in northern India, but this identification with PGW is not yet proven.

Northern Black Polished Ware culture, found in northern and central India: it was linked to new developments in iron metallurgy and the flowering of large kingdoms. The use of iron tools such as plows from the end of the second millennium BCE onward spurred progress in agriculture[2] – particularly rice culture – in the middle and lower Ganges valley, leading to demographic growth. Iron metallurgy also allowed for the manufacture of more weapons, and many sites – including megalithic sites across peninsular India – reveal the importance of iron weapons (Chakravarti 2002b: 38). This metallurgic know-how was introduced from 1200/1100 BCE on with populations entering India, and continued after 800 BCE.[3] The development of an intensive rice culture during the first millennium in northern India may partly explain the greater number of Indo-Aryan speakers (Fuller 2011a: 87). The "agricultural revolution" first applied to northern India; it became noticeable in the south only during the second half of the first millennium BCE (Franke-Vogt 2001). In Sri Lanka, however, rice culture developed around 900 BCE and iron was used at Anurādhāpura between 900 and 600 BCE (Coningham *et al.* 2006: 648; Fuller 2008a: 765) (see below). In addition, this Iron Age culture developed a glass industry during the early first millennium.[4] Exchanges also dealt in gold: the mine of Hatti, in Karnataka, was already operating during the eighth century BCE (Ray 2006b: 114).

It has often been thought, albeit without much proof, that it is during this time, called the "Late Vedic," that a caste system crystallized (Boivin 2007: 349). Recent genetic research seems to support the idea that Indo-Aryan migrants imposed themselves on indigenous populations (tribes) by introducing this caste system (Bamshad *et al.* 2001; Basu *et al.* 2003; Cordaux *et al.* 2004). Cordaux *et al.* write: "Indian caste paternal lineages are largely descended from the linguistically and archaeologically inferred dispersal of Indo-European-speaking pastoralists who migrated from Central Asia some 3,500 years ago. Conversely, paternal lineages of tribal groups are predominantly derived from the original Indian gene pool" (unlike caste and tribal groups, which are homogeneous with respect to mitochondrial DNA variation, which marks inheritance in a female line). For various authors, however, interpretations based on these works are problematic for several reasons, such as insufficient sample size, debatable sample choices, and gaps in knowledge concerning the paternally inherited Y chromosome. Also, these interpretations fail to take into account the fact that Caucasian influences were multiple and occurred over a long period of time (Boivin 2007: 354). Other genetic studies have reached opposite conclusions, showing a common origin for caste and tribal groups (Kivisild *et al.* 2003; Metspalu *et al.* 2004). Endicott *et al.* (2007: 239) note that

---

[2] Heavy iron plows were implemented very early on. Indian texts dated to the beginning of the Christian era mention plows drawn by teams of twenty-four oxen. Irrigation techniques were known to the Indo-Aryans of the Pirak region.

[3] Authors such as D. K. Chakrabarti (1992: 171ff.), however, argue for an independent origin of iron metallurgy in India, building on datings earlier than 1000 BCE in Malwa (Nagda, Eran), in Rajasthan (Ahar), in Karnataka (Hallur), and *c.* 1000 in Bihar (Barudih) and western Bengal (Mahisadal). D. P. Agrawal and J. S. Kharakwal (2003) remain cautious regarding this assumption and regarding dates going back to the middle of the second millennium that are sometimes put forward for iron metallurgy in India.

[4] The most ancient glass has been excavated in the upper Ganges valley, in Haryana state, in association with the Painted Grey Ware culture (sites of Rupar, Hastinapur, Alamgirpur, Bhagwanpura) (Dussubieux 2001: 53), with various objects, beads, rings, pendants, stamps, and seals.

some data (concerning the R1a haplogroup of the Y chromosome) also indicate movement in the opposite direction, from northwestern India to Central Asia. In addition, for these authors, "there is no strong genetic signal for a major genetic component accompanying the spread of Indo-Aryan languages or the caste system into India" (2007: 239).

Late Vedic texts reveal that trade was active from 600 BCE onward.[5] States formed not only in the central Gangetic plains and Bengal, but also in Gandhara, Afghanistan (Kamboja), Madhya Pradesh (region of Ujjain), Maharashtra (region of Paithan), and Saurashtra. According to early Buddhist and Jain sources, there were sixteen major states at the end of the seventh century BCE. Among them, Magadha emerged as the most powerful around 500 BCE (control over the iron trade routes out of southern Bihar partly explains this state's rise to power) (Basham 1967: 225–226). The monarchical system was dominant, but we also find "republican" institutions, for example in the state of Vajji (Vaishālī, Bihar) (Chakrabarti 2000: 382). A class of rich landowners appeared in the Ganges valleys. A possible climatic amelioration during the sixth century BCE may have spurred progress in agriculture and an accompanying second urbanization phase in the subcontinent, first in the Ganges valleys and then further south (urbanization developed slightly later in Deccan and in southern India). Towns and cities such as Ujjain and Kaushāmbī were surrounded by walls, a sign of intense competition. This period saw the flowering of various crafts, organized via a system of guilds (the *Gautama Dharmasūtra*, for example, clearly shows their importance). Trade flourished both within India and toward more distant regions. As mentioned above, relations were established with the Babylonian Empire throughout the Persian Gulf, led from ports such as Broach, Sopara, and Kalyan. These developments were encouraged by the rise of the Persian Empire, which controlled Gandhara and Sind. From these regions, Persian and Babylonian influences entered northern India, especially in the field of astronomy.[6] The expansion of the Magadha kingdom, which had Rājagraha as its first capital, occurred when the Persians conquered northwestern India (Kulke and Rothermund 1995: 56–57). Writing developed, from systems already in use in the Achaemenid Empire (see below). The kingdom of Gandhara, with the city of Takṣasilā (Taxila), was proof of the vitality of roads leading to Central Asia and Iran. Contacts between India and China occurred early in the first millennium: remnants of ramie (a native plant in China) discovered at Narhan, north of the middle Ganges valley, can be dated between 1300 and 600 BCE (Fuller 2008b; Saraswat *et al.* 1994).

---

[5] Prior to this, the *Rig Veda* mentions Panis, whose language was not understandable (Dravidian speakers?), making long journeys which were sources of wealth: perhaps these were merchants engaged in long-distance trade. During the Later Vedic period, the term *vanij* denotes small merchants. The *Atharvaveda* refers to three types of exchanges: bartering (*prapana*), exchanging merchandise (*pratipana*), and buying and selling (*vikraya*). The *Satapatha Brāhmana* mentions *kusīdin*, "usurers," and the *Taittirīya Samhitā* uses the word *kusīda*, with the meaning of "borrowing." The smallest unit of weight, the *māna*, represented 1.8 times the seed of *Abrus precatorius*; Later Vedic texts mention a unit of weight of one hundred *māna* (*satamāna*), in gold or in silver (coins did not yet exist) (Chakravarti 2001a: 20–23, 42–44).

[6] Remains of stills have been unearthed at Taxila dated to the first century CE and at Charsadda (Pushkalāvati, another Saka capital), that may have been used to distill alcohol. The knowledge of distilled alcohol in ancient India has been argued by various authors on a linguistic basis, the word *sunḍa*, which means both "elephant trunk" (side-tube of the still) and "alcoholic drink," being found already in the *Rāmāyana* (Needham *et al.*, 1980: 131). We know that the Hellenistic world developed stills, but without achieving alcohol distillation. The still was associated with alchemical practices and the preparation of perfumes.

During the sixth century BCE, sizeable trade and increasingly competitive states led to the minting of coins issued by merchants and kings in the Ganges valley and at Taxila,[7] and to the setting up of a system of standardized weights. Coins were bar- or cup-shaped, and consisted of punch-marked silver pieces; the use of this imported silver as a standard of value shows Mesopotamian influences – via Iran – prior to the founding of the Achaemenid Empire.[8]

The growth of urbanism came with a mix of populations fostering the emergence of unorthodox religious movements (Chakravarti 2002b: 62). The sixth century saw the emergence of Jainism and Buddhism, which spread across the Asian continent, indicating profound social change.[9] This expansion led to a weakening of the Brahman orthodoxy and encouraged commercial exchanges. The black burnished ceramics produced in the Ganges valley spread to other regions: they have been found in Kalinga, at Ujjain and at Peshāwar. After 500 BCE, maritime trade networks must have encompassed the entire Indian subcontinent (Coningham 2002: 103) and social transformations were obvious in South India (Ray 2006b). India's main regions were linked by trade roads: one went from Bharukacha (Broach, Gujarat) to the Ganges valley; another route, from the Ganges to the Indus, connected Tāmralipti and Taxila. A city such as Kaushāmbī, for example, developed thanks to its situation on a trade route as well as its region's mineral wealth. In southern India, routes crossed the Deccan.[10] The simultaneous production of high-tin bronzes in Tamil Nadu (the Nilgiri cairns, Adichanallur), Maharashtra (Mahurjhari), and the Taxila culture during the first half of the first millennium BCE reflect an exchange of ideas between northern and southern India, during a period predating the spread of Buddhism. Carnelian and lapis lazuli found at Kodumanal (Tamil Nadu) were imported from northern India and Afghanistan (Srinivasan 2010). The presence of cotton at sites such as Hallur (c. 800 BCE) signal the growth of a craft industry geared toward long-distance exchanges (Fuller et al. 2007). Urban development occurred in the Kāverī delta during the fifth or fourth century BCE with Uraiyūr as the main city. Maritime routes linked India with Mesopotamia (see above), Arabia, and the eastern coast of Bengal Bay.

Very early on, Sri Lanka acted as a hub for various areas of the Indian Ocean. Around the ninth century BCE, ironworking was introduced to this island, as well as a

---

[7] According to D. Rajgor (1998), seventeen states issued silver money between the sixth century BCE and the Maurya period, in Bengal (they feature a ship), Kalinga, in the Ganges valley, Gandhara, in the kingdom of Avanti (Ujjain, Madhya Pradesh), on the coast of Konkan (western India), in the regions of Junagadh (Saurashtra) and Paithan (Maharashtra) (Chakrabarti 2000: 383). Copper coins were also issued. They do not show inscriptions but bear marks on the metal. The most ancient coins may have been issued by guilds. Known in Indian literature since the fifth/fourth century BCE, the term *putabhedana* "signified a center of exchange with facilities for the storage of commodities" (Chakravarti 2001a: 24–25, 53, 55; Ray 2003: 186).

[8] Schaps 2007: 8–9. The discovery of Nūsh-i Jān in Media (seventh century BCE) provides an example.

[9] Various datings have been proposed for Buddha, between the sixth and fifth centuries. Moreover, the medical treaty of the *Âyurveda* was codified around the sixth century BCE. As Chakravarti suggests (2002b: 39), the rise of Jainism and Buddhism, "protestant religions," probably "lessened the importance of the priestly community in statecraft."

[10] The products transported included not only luxury goods, but also food and raw materials. According to the *Vinaya Piṭaka*, "on his way to Rājagṛaha, the Buddha is said to have met Belaṭṭha Kaccāna, who was traveling with 500 wagons carrying many jars of sugar" (Chakravarti 2001a: 30).

Black and Red ware characteristic of the Indian Iron Age.[11] Sri Lanka was also initiated into rice culture and livestock breeding (cattle, horses). The first settlement at Anurādhāpura is dated to between the ninth and fifth centuries BCE; it had become a fortified city covering approximately 100 ha by the fourth century BCE (Coningham *et al.* 1999: 54). The discovery in Iron Age levels dated to between 510 and 340 BCE of shards bearing Brāhmī letters implies contacts between Sri Lanka and northern India in a Pre-Mauryan period,[12] via the western or eastern coasts of the peninsula. According to traditions such as the *Mahāvamsa*, the first Sinhalese kingdom was founded by a prince called Vijaya, who came from Kalinga. Megasthenes, the Greek ambassador of Seleucus at the court of the Maurya king Chandragupta (third century BCE) reports that Sri Lanka exported elephants to Kalinga. Kalinga and Sri Lanka would maintain links over the centuries. Onesikritos, a commander in Alexander's fleet, was the first Greek to speak of Taprobanē (Sri Lanka), which reveals contacts between Sri Lanka and Sind. Further south, exchanges developed with the Maldives, where the cowries found in the middle Ganges valley had originated (see below). Very early on, the Maldives also exported coir.

The kings of Magadha finally ended up extending their rule over all of northern India; under the Nanda dynasty (fourth century BCE), their capital was established at Pāṭaliputra (Patna). This dynasty was overthrown by Chandragupta, who founded the Mauryan Empire in 320 BCE. He added the Deccan, a region rich in mineral resources, to the empire. Mauryan expansion southward – as far as the gold mines of Kolar, in Karnataka – encouraged the diffusion of northern Indian cultural features, the development of trade, and urbanization.

A peace treaty signed in 302 BCE between Seleucus and Chandragupta multiplied exchanges between India and the West in the Persian Gulf and the Indian Sea. Megasthenes described Pāṭaliputra as a very large city – twice the size of Rome under Marcus Aurelius – and portrays the organization of a strongly centralized Mauryan state. The Maurya promoted agricultural progress, by extending irrigation,[13] and by clearing new land (perhaps thanks to the deportation of populations from Orissa). This Mauryan expansion led to new urban growth, in the capital as well as at Māthura, Kausambi, Sisupalgarh, and other cities. The state created and maintained infrastructures and services that promoted production and commerce: roads (for

---

[11] This ceramic is well known in the megalithic complexes of India (Ray 2003: 117–119). The site of Anurādhāpura already covered 10 ha in 800 BCE.

[12] Ray 2003: 114 n. 4. Bopearachchi (2002: 107) notes that the Sinhalese sites of Ridiyagama (dated to the fourth century BCE – first century BCE) and of the "megalithic" cemetery of Ibbankatuwa (in the northern plain of Sri Lanka) (770–395 BCE) both exhibit Black and Red ware and carnelian etched beads (also Coningham 2002: 104). Iron metallurgy can be seen at Anurādhāpura as early as the K period (possibly sixth century BCE): smelting was carried out elsewhere, and "prepared billets of metal were brought into Anurādhāpura for smithing into artifacts" (Coningham 2002: 105).

[13] Megasthenes notes than more than half of arable land is irrigated, permitting two harvests per year. "A special department of state supervised the construction and maintenance of a well-developed irrigation system with extensive canals and sluices, and the same bureau planned and directed the settlement of uncultivated land" (McClellan and Dorn 1999: 143). According to Megasthenes, farmers paid rent to the king, with the state taking a quarter of their production. This vision of state control of the economy by the Maurya departs from that of other researchers: for H. P. Ray, this control was confined to the core of the empire, in the north.

example, a royal road linked Pāṭaliputra with Taxila and Pushkalāvati/Peshāwar), guard posts, wells, riffles, and a postal service.[14] The state controlled weights and measures, and market prices. It appointed officials to take charge of towns and cities: these formed six five-person boards. Other officials were placed in charge of the army. State establishments were installed in the textile industry, the mines, and metallurgy.[15] According to Megasthenes, the Mauryan state levied taxes on artisans and merchants, as well as a poll tax (McCrindle 1877: 84–88). It held a monopoly on shipbuilding, an indicator of its interest in maritime trade, confirmed by inscriptions by Ashoka found at Sopara and Orissa (Chakravarti 2001a: 56). Megasthenes mentions spices and pearls imported in Bihar as coming from southern Indian kingdoms. The manufacture of weapons was also under state monopoly. The silver currency *kārṣapāna* of the Maurya was "universally accepted."[16] Coins were issued by the state, or by guilds. Some coins from the third/second century BCE found at Taxila bear the legend *negama*, "guild" on the reverse; a guild of perfumers issued coins at Kaushāmbī during the second century BCE (Singh 2008: 405). The Brāhmī script appeared fully developed at the time of Ashoka; this script had probably been elaborated within an environment of Sanskrit grammarians influenced by Persia, around the fifth or fourth century BCE; these grammarians created an innovative system of vowels. As early as the fourth century BCE, merchants introduced this script into Sri Lanka. A system of decimal numeration is attested at the time of Ashoka, and this allowed mathematics to evolve.[17] The Kharoṣṭī script, derived from Aramaic, the official script of the Achaemenid Empire, was introduced after the conquest by Darius I of part of the Punjāb and of

---

[14] According to Megasthenes, "officials in charge of the countryside were entrusted with the construction and maintenance of roads." "A category of municipal officers had the joint responsability of looking after the markets, harbours and temples" (Chakravarti 2001a: 54, 57). The *Arthasāstra* of Kautilya refers to a "Director of Trade" and a "Director of Tolls and Customs," who collected taxes and controlled the merchants (we know, however, that the *Arthasāstra* was probably written several centuries after the Maurya period). The text encourages the promotion of foreign trade. "Foreign merchants should not be sued in a court of law for disputes in money matters," and "sailors and caravan merchants coming from abroad are allowed certain fiscal remissions" (Chakravarti 2001a: 55). Along the royal roads and in the cities, there were houses hosting travelers.

[15] The *Arthasāstra* advocates "state intervention in all spheres of activity": he tells the king to "extend facilities for irrigation, encourage trade, cultivate wasteland, open mines, look after the forest" (Kulke and Rothermund 1995: 64). It supports control of prices and production by the state, which holds some monopolies.

[16] Deyell 2001: 414. Pānini (fourth century BCE) mentions different coins (*satamana, sana, vimastika, kārshapāna*) as well as gold *nishka*, that are either coins or ornaments used as money. The *Laws of Manu* (first–second century?) refer to a series of coins whose weight is measured against a seed of *Abrus precatorius* (*gunja, rati*) (0.13 g). The gold coin *suvarna* weighs 80 *rati*, the copper coin *kārshāpana* has the same weight, the *purāna* is a silver coin of 32 *rati* (Pusalker 2007: 29). The *suvarna* represents 16 *māsā*, and one *nishka* is worth 4 *suvarna*. The denominations vary according to the texts. A source from the Gupta period gives the equivalence of 20 *māsā* for one silver *kārshāpana*, and one *suvarna* (*dīnāra*) is worth 12 *dhānika* and 48 *kārshāpana* (Sarkar 2003: 21). The gold:silver ratio is 1:12 or 1:16.

[17] A system of positional numeration was adopted during the first century BCE (the Jain text *Anuyogadvara-sutra* refers to positions of numeration). A Chinese or Babylonian origin has been proposed for this innovation. The manuscript *Bakshālī* (possibly third or fourth century CE) shows the development of knowledge in arithmetics (fractions, square roots) and algebra (quadratic equations, arithmetic, and geometrical progressions).

Sind in 518 BCE. This script became the official alphabet in Gandhara and in north-western India between the third century BCE and the fourth–fifth century CE.[18]

Recent research, however, challenges the idea of Mauryan government control over production and trade. This research has also qualified the centralization of the state, and points to an "internal variability in its administration" and "the discontinuous geography" of the empire, which was primarily interested in controlling the mineral resources of some regions as well as the main commercial routes (Sinopoli 2006: 331). The Gangetic core, however, was administered by the state (here the tax on harvests, usually amounting to a quarter [according to Megasthenes] or one-sixth of production [see Manu and Kautilya], implied censuses, in agreement with Kautilya's views [*Arthasāstra* II, 35]). Four "viceroys" lived at Taxila, Ujjain, Tosalī,[19] and Suvarnagiri. For H. P. Ray, the state derived revenues from trade, but trade itself was largely conducted by private merchants and guilds; specialized merchant communities developed in the middle Ganges valley.[20] Each guild (*sreṇī, nigama*)[21] of artisans had a comparatively free hand, and carried out various economic and administrative functions, as well as banking activities and charitable works.[22] Based on the *Manu Samhitā* and the *Arthasāstra*, P. Baishya (1997) discerns the existence of what he terms a "putting-out" system at this time. The expansion of Buddhism was key to this flourishing trade. In this field, Buddhists' views were very different from those of Hindus. For the latter, visiting foreign countries led to impurity; Manu forbade sea travel.[23] Buddhism rejected ideas of racial purity and "favored interest-bearing loans, which were condemned by Hindu law books."[24] Buddhism and Jainism accepted wealth accumulation and the reinvestment of capital, and money began to be used

---

[18] The Kharoṣṭī script was in use along the Silk Roads. It was written from right to left, whereas the Brāhmī script was written from left to right. All the Indian writing systems derive from the Brāhmī script, which may have originated from the Phoenician or the Aramaic script. After the collapse of the Achaemenid Empire, the Aramaic experienced processes of "localization" and gave birth to various writing systems in Central Asia, Afghanistan, and India.

[19] This city was perhaps not Sisupalgarh, as was previously thought.

[20] Ray 1991; Basa 1999: 55. "Long-distance trade was handled by rich merchants though the rise of the Mauryas meant a more successful and organized control over labour, means of production and surplus distribution" (Ray 1996: 354). The grammarian Pānini gives several terms referring to different types of merchants (including sea merchants), the leader of a caravan, and the members of a guild. According to I. Fiser (2001: 194), during this period, "trade could be carried on by any member of the three highest *vannas* if he owned sufficient means for it." The Maurya state seems to have paid wages to the tax collectors, but after the Maurya period, the collectors were no longer salaried, and kept part of the sums levied for themselves.

[21] The grammarian Kātyāyana (third or second century BCE), who speaks of Pānini, also gives the term *pūga* for a guildlike organization of merchants (Pusalker 2007: 29). One also finds the name *gana*, in Pānini and in Pāli canonical texts. An epigraph of Karle dated to the second century BCE mentions an association of merchants under the name of *vaniggrāma*, a name found again in sixth-century inscriptions in Gujarat (Chakravarti 2002b: 26).

[22] The guilds received silver and practiced moneylending (Thaplyal 2001). For this author, the guilds developed from the sixth century BCE onward as a result of the rise of Buddhism and Jainism; the guilds' decline started in 300 CE.

[23] The concept of *āpaddharma*, however, allowed people of all classes to engage in trade in times of difficulty. See Jain 2001: 347. But the practice of usury was forbidden for the Hindus.

[24] Basa 1999: 56. See Ray 1994. Like Buddhism, Jainism does not espouse caste discrimination.

much more frequently. The *Arthasāstra* of Kautilya goes so far as to view the search for profit as more important than life's other goals. It recognizes trade as a significant potential source of revenue, and shows a special interest in foreign merchants, calling upon rulers to allow foreign merchants into their countries (in contrast, Kautilya is suspicious of local merchants).[25] In addition, the *Arthasāstra* reveals the possible use of guilds by the government.

Ray considers that merchants acquired new importance during the Mauryan dynasty, whereas Chakravarti (2002b), on the other hand, believes that the emergence of a significant private sector, with great *seṭṭhi* merchants,[26] occurred only during the post-Mauryan period. It is true that Kautilya never uses the word *seṭṭhi*, and that inscriptions from the Mauryan period mention only small merchants (*vānijā*) and guilds (*nigama, gosthi*).[27] "The *seṭṭhi* figures prominently for the first time in the Pāli canonical literature as the merchant par excellence," in close contact with the rulers, whom he assists financially whenever the need arises (Chakravarti 2001a: 49).[28] The *Arthasāstra* describes trade administered by the state, with taxes levied at the entries of towns and ports, and protection granted to caravans, but in contrast, "the Buddhist *Jatakas* [referring mainly to the first centuries of the Christian era] describe an economy only marginally under state control" (Ray 2003: 192). Landowners, referred to as *seṭṭhi-gahapati*, invested in trade.[29] "A loan (*ina*, i.e. *rna*) is viewed in the Pali canons as essential for launching and maintaining an enterprise" (Chakravarti 2001a: 50) (these texts were written during the first century BCE, based on earlier traditions). Loans and debt notes are mentioned by the *Arthasāstra* and the *Jātaka*; their rates varied according to the caste of the borrower and the risks inherent in the enterprise, but they were usually 15 percent (Sarkar 2003: 27); they reached 20 percent per month for sea merchants, which gives an idea of the profits expected from maritime expeditions. According to the *Tipitaka*, two merchants, Tapassu [Trapusha] and Bhalluka [Bhallika], linked to the Utkala region (Orissa), were the Buddha's first two disciples.[30] It was also within the class of the sea merchants that the Buddha found one of his most famous disciples: Purna, from Surparaka (north of Bombay), who had sailed six times

---

[25] There is ongoing controversy surrounding the date of the *Arthasāstra* (Basa 1999: 54). The text probably includes multiple strata. The most ancient parts go back to the fourth or third century BCE, but the main part of the text may be dated to the third century CE (see Trautmann 1971).

[26] The term *seṭṭhi* (Sanskrit *sreṣṭhī*) refers to various categories of traders, according to the periods considered. Generally speaking, it refers to a rich merchant; the *sātthavāha* is a caravan trader, and the *vānijā* a petty merchant (Chakravarti 2001a: 49–50). The reading of the *Jātaka* reveals that the *seṭṭhi* became entrepreneurs, great traders as well as bankers, who employed trade agents (in contrast, the term *vānijā* always refers to individual merchants). The king usually maintained a privileged relationship with a rich *seṭṭhi*, who could lend him money (Fiser 2001).

[27] The *Arthasāstra* speaks of merchants who sell goods belonging to the king, under the supervision of the state; these merchants may have existed, but the text first presents an ideal model.

[28] According to a later text from the *Avadāna*, a merchant advanced loans to Kosalan king Prasenajit during his war against Magadha in the sixth century BCE (Chakravarti 2001a: 110 n. 2).

[29] *Gahapati* refers to a landowner. In fact, it is likely that a class of great merchants had already emerged during the Maurya period (see above).

[30] De Casparis 2000: 53. De Casparis mentions the Sanskrit inscription at Tiriyay, where merchant guilds at the origin of a foundation compare themselves to "Trapussa and Bhallika" (2000: 53). The name Trapusha derives from *trapush*, "tin."

across the "great ocean."[31] As mentioned above, the older Buddhist literature of northern India contains many references to powerful landowners who invested capital in trade ventures. The Sangam literature would later emphasize the role played by rich merchants in coastal trade during the first centuries of the Christian era. The Buddha was reborn several times as a merchant or caravan trader.[32]

Tangible relations between India and China may have begun around the fourth century BCE. The *Rāmāyana* (perhaps written during the fifth century CE from texts partly going back to the fourth century BCE) and the *Laws of Manu* (possibly first–second centuries CE) refer to silk as a product from foreign countries, and the *Arthasāstra* mentions silk thread among the materials given to weavers (*china-patta*).[33] A pot found at Masaon (middle Ganges valley) contained 3,000 cowries (a find dated between 600 and 200 BCE).[34] We must admit the possibility that ancient contacts between India and China led to the adoption of cowrie shells as money in India (the monetary use of cowries in China may go back as far as the Shang period, and in any event to the Zhou period). The production of vessels made of cast metal (and therefore breakable), mentioned by Nearchos for India (quoted by Strabo), probably describes an East Asian inheritance (Sherratt and Sherratt 2001: 35 n. 27). A Yunnan–Burma–Assam road was already active at this time, bringing in silver, gold, and silks. Several routes led to Bangladesh.[35] A first route left the Upper Irrawaddy and ran down along the Brahmaputra River as far as the city of Pundranāgara (Mahasthangarh), which was an emporium set up by the Maurya no later than the early second century. Another route linked the Irrawaddy to the Barak River, through Imphal. A third route followed the Irrawaddy River to its mouth; here the merchants could take a boat for Chittagong and western Bengal.[36] The appearance in the kingdom of Chu (southern China) of punched-mark, square-shaped gold coins, issued between the fifth and third centuries BCE (see below), may reflect an Indian influence, arriving via Yunnan or by sea.

---

[31] See Tatelman 1999. Surparaka was an active port, whence ships departed to the Occident or the Orient: Purna's brother is said to have embarked in this port with a troop of merchants in search of red sandalwood (in Timor?).

[32] Bentley (1993: 44) has also rightly insisted on the "doctrinal flexibility of Buddhism," which allowed it to adapt to different cultural contexts.

[33] See above. Pānini mentions a fabric called *kauseya* "that originates from the envelope of the cocoon": this may refer to wild silk (Basham 1967: 199; Lévy 1995: 25; Boulnois 2001: 161). The use of wild cocoons seems to go back to early times in India, in Assam – here perhaps due to Chinese influences – and also further west: silk fibers have been discovered in the Indus valley (Harappa, Chanhu-daro), dated to the third millennium, and in Maharashtra (Nevasa) for the second half of the second millennium BCE (Good *et al.* 2009; see above).

[34] Ray 2003: 31. An inscription from the third–second century BCE at Mahasthangarh (Bangladesh) "refers to aid in the form of *kākanīs* and *gandakas*, i.e. low denomination coins and perhaps cowries, respectively" (Ray 2003: 31).

[35] Mitchiner 2000; Salles 2004: 208. Also Deyell 1994: 128.

[36] Mitchiner 2000, quoted by Salles 2004: 208; see map, Salles 2004: 207; Deyell 1994: 128, 134. Based on Megasthenes, Diodorus of Sicily (first century BCE) mentions the Gangaridai with the Prasioi (Magadha, Maurya Empire). These Gangaridai or Gangaridae, living in the region of the Ganges delta, are often mentioned in Greek and Roman literature. According to Greek and Roman authors, Prasioi/Prasii and Gangaridai/Gangaridae (the Maurya?) could mobilize 200,000 infantrymen, 20,000 horsemen, and 3,000 elephants.

Exchanges both within and outside India progressed during the third century BCE, especially under the reign of Ashoka (273–237 BCE), the greatest of the Mauryan emperors. It is not by chance that a Greco-Bactrian kingdom emerged in 250 BCE at the peak of Mauryan power. Moreover, Persian influence was noticeable in various fields over the entire Mauryan period.

Ashoka's empire extended over the entire subcontinent – and west of the Indus – with the exception of southern India (Kalinga, today Orissa, which had resisted Ashoka's predecessor, was conquered in 261 BCE at a cost of 100,000 victims and 150,000 deportees).[37] The Maurya clearly intended to control mineral resources and major trade routes. Throughout his empire, Ashoka had symbols of his power engraved on pillars and rocks: these edicts expressed his adherence to Buddhism, and were inscribed in Prākrit and at times in Aramaic or Greek. The inscriptions found along the coasts (in Orissa, and further south, in the lower Krishnā valley) reflect the significance of trade in the Bay of Bengal. Moreover, they often appear associated with "Megalithic sites on the one hand, and Buddhist shrines on the other" (Ray 2006b: 125). Ashoka maintained friendly relations with the eastern Greek world, and the Seleucids sent several embassies to the Mauryan capital, Pātaliputra, which was the largest city in the world at that time.[38] Promoting Buddhism,[39] the Mauryan emperor may have dispatched missionaries to South India and Sri Lanka, "to Suvarnabhūmi" in Southeast Asia,[40] and to the Occident (Syria, Egypt, and Epirus), in order to spread the message of "righteous behavior." From northwestern India, Buddhism entered Central Asia, whence it later reached China via the Silk Roads, around the first century CE. The growing wealth of northern Indian cities was based partly on trade, over maritime and terrestrial routes (to Taxila,[41] Pushkalāvati, and Bharukacha, in the northwest, and to Tāmralipti, at the mouth of the Ganges). This trade was stimulated by the elites' demand for luxury goods. Regions rich in mineral resources such as precious stones and gold became integrated into the exchange networks.

The trade routes connecting Bengal, Upper Burma, and Yunnan (see above) became more active as of Ashoka's time. The use of cowries in Yunnan goes back at least to the second century BCE, when cowries constituted both a measure of value and a medium of exchange.[42] "Etched carnelian beads are regularly found by villagers at Han period sites

---

[37] The interest of the Maurya in Orissa probably came from the exchanges of this coast with the Orient.

[38] The occupation of the coasts of Gujarat and the Konkan by the Maurya, notes R. Chakravarti (2002b: 36), must have stimulated exchanges with the Occident.

[39] Buddhism provided its political conception of *dhamma*, which refers to ethical conduct and righteousness and offers a theory on royal behavior, and the idea of universal sovereignty (see Ray 2003: 133).

[40] Reported in the *Sasanavamsappadipika* (Glover 2000: 95). Ashoka probably played a crucial role in the spread of Buddhism; for Ray (2006), however, the importance of the state in the expansion of Buddhism may have been overestimated.

[41] Two Aramaic edicts of Ashoka were found in Laghman province in Afghanistan, along a "Royal highway" (Chakravarti 2001a: 58–59).

[42] Wicks 1992: 39, 63, 168. "Large quantities of imported cowrie shells as well as a number of Chinese cash were recovered from [the tombs of the elite at] Shizhaishan" (second and first centuries BCE) (Wicks 1992: 29; see below). In addition, cowries have been excavated from prehistoric sites in Thailand (Central and Northeast), Cambodia, and Laos. "Prehistoric cowries from Thailand and Cambodia have had their backs cut off, perhaps to make them easier to string together or fasten to clothing" (Wicks 1992: 308). The circulation of cowries in China is well attested during the seventh century BCE (see below). They were

in Yunnan" (as early as the second century BCE) (Glover and Bellina 2001: 202).[43] Burma was in contact with both Yunnan and India. The culture of the Samon valley, in particular, shows close links with the Dian region of Yunnan, through items such as halberds similar to the Chinese *ge*, and bronze musical instruments. The site at Hnaw Kan has yielded a tomb associated with the deposit of a horse, recalling the equestrian Dian aristocracy (Moore 2007: 95). Several discoveries of bronze drums recalling the Heger I type known in Yunnan have been signalled at Sin Bo, Win Maung, and Bagan. Indian influences can be seen – perhaps from 500/400 BCE (Moore 2007: 122) – through the use of carnelian and etched glass beads; some of these, probably of local manufacture, have been found at Taung Thaman, Srīkshetra, Prome, and Beikhtano.[44] The site of Myo Hla (Samon), dated to the Iron Age, has yielded carnelian beads, zoomorph carnelians, and glass beads. Cast bronze vessels hint at contacts with southern China.[45] The appearance of fortified sites in Burma along a route leading to China may indicate evolving chiefdoms and the adoption of Indian norms by local rulers (B. Hudson 2004).

This period also saw a significant development in southern India and Sri Lanka. Major irrigation systems were implemented under state control, not only in Mauryan India, but also in Sri Lanka, around Anurādhapura. Small states appeared in southern India centered on large river valleys that were favorable to intensive rice culture. These states were also sea- and trade-oriented. Many archaeological sites dated to this period have been discovered in Karnataka, Tamil Nadu, and Andhra Pradesh. The first urban centers then emerged in South India, such as Banavāsi, in Karnataka, and Dhānyakataka ("rice bowl") [Amarāvatī], in the Krishnā River valley.[46] The large number of arrowheads and other iron weapons excavated signals the rise of interstate conflicts. At the end of the fourth century BCE, Megasthenes mentioned the wealth of the Pāndya kings of South India, mainly derived from the export of pearls. The capital

---

probably used in Yunnan earlier than the second century BCE; cowries were first considered prestige items, appropriated mainly by elites. It is possible that cowries were imported from northern Vietnam. Annam is given in the fifth century CE as an area of production for cowries (*Cypraea annulus*) (Vogel 1993: 235).

[43] Beads have been found in the princely burials of the Dian culture. See below.

[44] The site of Taung Thaman, in the Irrawady River valley, near Amarapura, has provided evidence for cast iron. The site is dated to between 710±200 and 410±35 BCE (Pautreau *et al.* 2005: 52–53). The tombs have yielded iron knives and swords, *c.* 500 BCE. An unfinished etched bead has been excavated at Prome (Glover and Bellina 2001: 205–207; Gutman and Hudson 2004: 156–157).

[45] Pautreau *et al.* 2005: 54–55. Zoomorphic carnelian figures come from some rich tombs that reveal a stratified society; these figures feature tigers, lions, tortoises, and crocodiles. The motif of a tiger holding a tiger cub in its mouth recalls the decoration of Zhou bronzes (Moore 2007: 116). The assemblages included iron weapons (such as swords) and tools, bronzes (vases, small bells, toiletry implements), and ivory rings. Carnelian beads have been found at another site in the valley, at Ywa Htin. At Hnaw Kan, tombs have yielded glass grains, one cowry, and some carnelian (Pautreau *et al.* 2005: 56). Glass flat discs or rings from the Samon culture are reminiscent of objects found in eastern Cambodia and western Vietnam (400–200 BCE) (Moore 2007: 113).

[46] These developments attest to growth in agriculture, craft, and trade. Mineral resources were exploited (stones). "The largest concentration of sites is along the rivers Krishna and Kaveri" (Ray 2003: 113). See below, on the region of Coimbatore. "The large-scale exploitation of mineral resources, especially iron, within a protohistoric context, in a region which provides no indication of Mauryan presence, challenges Kosambi's interpretation regarding the introduction of iron and plow agriculture by the Mauryas" (Ray 2003: 115 n. 6).

of the Pāndya was the port of Korkai; the capital was moved to Madurai during the initial centuries of the Christian era. As far down as its early levels (third century BCE), the site of Alagankulam shows a "burnished black ceramic" revealing contacts with northern India. Relations with northern India, Gujarat, and Bengal paralleled the arrival of Buddhist and Jain monks, who played key roles in the political and economic evolution of the southern states. Various authors have pointed out the joint role of trade and religious institutions – Buddhist, Hindu, but also Jain in the region of Madurai – in the emergence of South Indian states from the Mauryan period (Ray 2006b: 123). A textile industry was developing: the *Arthasāstra* refers to "the fine textiles of Madurai" (Ramaswamy 2002: 429). Chola, Pāndya, and Chera are mentioned in Ashoka's inscriptions of the third century BCE, in some Tamil inscriptions of the second century BCE and in an inscription by Kharavela, a king from Orissa who ruled over a short-lived empire during the second century BCE. Megasthenes attributed an improbable armed force of 400 elephants, 4,000 horsemen, and 130,000 infantrymen to the Pāndya kingdom. In Sri Lanka, the building and digging of walls and moats at Anurādhāpura between 360 and 190 BCE reveals transformations in social structure as well as major expansion. A more centralized political structure was taking shape; at the same time, Buddhism was becoming more influential, and iron metallurgy, glass bead production and trade were developing (with Sri Lanka exporting high-quality iron). Finds of inscribed shards – with Brāhmī scripts – from vessels or lids at Anurādhāpura reveal links between traders and Buddhist settlements (Ray 2006a: 313). Exchanges brought a type of Indian grey ceramic,[47] carnelian, lapis lazuli, and the first coins onto the island.[48] Cultural connections were clearly stronger than they had been during the previous period (Coningham 2002: 103–104). Bronze coins with a high tin content – a metal certainly imported from the Malay peninsula[49] – appeared at this time in the

---

[47] For Coningham (2002: 105), however, the grey ceramic found at Anurādhāpura as early as 510 BCE, a ceramic thought to be the "ancestor" of Rouletted Ware, does not represent an import from northern India but a parallel production, influenced by northern India (cf. the shards with writing, mentioned above). A shard from period I (fourth–second century BCE) shows an incised drawing of a seagoing ship (with one mast) (Coningham 2002: 106). The Northern Black Polished Ware of northern India is present at Anurādhāpura in a level dated to the fourth–second century BCE, as are lapis lazuli and carnelian: these discoveries reflect contacts with Gujarat (Coningham *et al.* 2006: 165).

[48] Ray 2003: 119–120; Coningham *et al.* 2006. A Buddhist inscription in Brāhmī script in the Mihintale Cave is dated to the third century BCE. The same inscription has been found at Anurādhāpura on a shard. Note that the ports of Mantai (Sri Lanka) and Kāveripattinam developed around the third century BCE. Horse remains have been excavated on the island that are dated to this time. Many coins of the Maurya period have been unearthed at Anurādhāpura and in the ports of Sri Lanka. Coins of the Maurya dynasty remained in circulation perhaps until the third century CE; an inscription of the end of the third century BCE refers to their circulation in the island: trade was already operating not only through barter but also with money (Bopearachchi 2002: 105). In the first half of the second century BCE, Sri Lanka shows coins influenced by the Pāndya region. The island would issue its own money in 28 BCE, when it became politically independent again after a period of Pāndya domination. Some Sinhalese coins have been found in South India (Bopearachchi 2002: 101, 122 n. 42). The discovery at Ruhuna of a coin inscribed with *mahacatan* (probably "great merchant") reveals the minting of money also by merchants (Rajan 2002: 94).

[49] Wisseman Christie 1995: 247. Cf. also the importation of high-tin bronze vessels, produced in the region of U-Thong (Thailand), and also found in South India, in the Deccan, and as far as Taxila (see below).

urban centers of South India. Moreover, according to B. Cain, a Proto-Maldivian language split off from its original Prākrit language during the second century BCE, and became the *lingua franca* of various groups (Cain 2000: 3).

After Ashoka, a relative decline occurred in northern India, marked by coin debasement. Yet even after the collapse of the Maurya in 185 BCE, trade and coastal traffic continued to thrive. The Shunga dynasty maintained an empire in the Ganges valley and in eastern India (185–73 BCE), with Pātaliputra and later Vidishā (Malwa) as its capital.[50] Trade expanded, not only due to increasing demand from the Mediterranean world and East Asia, but also from internal developments in India. The *sreni* guilds seem to have benefited from the disappearance of the Mauryan state. The extension of Rouletted Ware along the coast of the Bay of Bengal (see above) as well as that of clay seals and coins reveal the importance of exchanges. The city of Mahasthangarh, the capital (Pundranāgara) of the early Pre-Maurya kingdom of Pundravardhana, experienced an economic boom until the middle of the first century BCE, and to a lesser extent until the second century CE, a prosperity linked to exchanges not only with the Ganges valley and Gandhara, but also with Yunnan, via Upper Burma (Salles 2004: 196ff., 208). The earliest levels at Chandraketugarh have yielded copper coins depicting a ship. This site, 35 km northeast of Calcutta, may have been the capital of a state. An inscription on a seal (third century CE) gives the name of a shipowner, thus revealing the activity of private merchants (Chakravarti 2002a: 51). Epigraphs from the first century BCE at Amarāvatī mention donations from merchants to Buddhist monastic settlements. Tamil inscriptions in Brāhmī also refer to merchants. Other inscriptions, in northern Sri Lanka, signal donors linked to a community of South India (first century BCE). They also mention the importation of horses, probably from northwestern India[51] and from Persia,[52] perhaps via Bengal. Silk from India has been found in the stupa of Deliwala (Cameron 2010: 147). On the other hand, discoveries along India's eastern coast show the presence of Sinhalese.[53] The name *barata* found in Brāhmī inscriptions of Sri Lanka appears to refer to a merchant community with a high social status: its shipmasters (*tissa*) sometimes served as royal emissaries (Rajan 2002: 94).

In the northwest, the Hellenized kings of Bactria controlled the port of Patala (in the Indus valley), and the ports of Gujarat; Menander (*c.* 160–140 BCE?) unified a large part of northern India. His reign saw an increase in maritime trade between Gujarat and western Asia, and with Sri Lanka.[54] Menander and the Indo-Greek kings issued a

---

[50] The Shunga dynasty was defeated by the Shātavāhana king Sātakami I. The Kanva dynasty then succeeded the Shunga (73–26 BCE).

[51] Ray 1996: 355, 356. According to the *Mahāvamsa*, the first Tamil rulers of Sri Lanka may have been the sons of a horse merchant (Rajan 2002).

[52] The Median plain was already famous during the Achaemenid period for the abundance of its horses. Strabo (58 BCE – 25 CE) speaks of more than 150,000 horses in the Persian stud farms of this region.

[53] Dated between the second century BCE and the first century CE, shards found in the Kāverī valley show inscriptions that could be in Old Sinhalese (Ray 2003: 114 n. 4, after Mahadevan 1996); the same may be true for shards found at Arikamedu and Alagankulam (Bopearachchi 2002: 101). The Sinhalese site of Ridiyagama produced stone and glass beads. Similar beads have been found in the major sites of South India (Arikamedu, also a great production center for beads, as well as Karakaidu, Uraiyūr, Alagankulam).

[54] The Sinhalese chronicle of the *Mahāvamsa* (sixth century CE) "mentions Buddhists from Greek territories of [northwestern India] among the foreign delegations invited by the Sinhalese king Dutugamunu, a close contemporary of the Indo-Greek Menander [*c.* 161–137 BCE], to the inauguration of the great stupa

great quantity of coins that would influence all the coins of ancient India.[55] From the late second century BCE onward, the Indo-Greek kings were progressively wiped out by the Saka, who were Scythians originally from Central Asia. In Central Asia, the Saka, in turn, were displaced by the Kushans (or Kuṣāna), one of the groups that the Chinese chronicles call Yuezhi (Yüeh-chih). Also from Central Asia, the Yuezhi occupied Bactria as early as 135 BCE.[56] The Indo-Scythian rulers of northwestern India, however, would soon have to pay allegiance to the Indo-Parthian king Gondophares I (20–10 BCE), who placed his capital at the Gandharan city of Taxila.

Under Kanishka I, the greatest Kushan king (late first – early second century CE?),[57] the empire stretched from the Oxus in the west to Vārāṇasī in the east, and from Kashmir in the north to Gujarat in the south.[58] On the routes leading to China, the Kushans occupied the western part of the Tarim basin. They were defeated in 90 CE by the Chinese general Ban Chao, but were victorious in 114–116 CE; Kanishka I then may have taken Chinese workers back to India and settled them in a town called Tchinapati.[59] The goal of the Kushan kings, who tried to promote exchanges, was to control trade routes linking Rome and India on the one hand, and India and China on the other. The building of the Kushan Empire reflects an extension of trade along the roads of Inner Asia, where the Gāndhārī language (a form of Prākrit including borrowings from other languages) became the *lingua franca* in the Tarim basin until the fourth century (de la Vaissière 2002: 90). Silk was no longer carried across Iran; its trade was diverted by the Kushans to ports in the Indus valley and northwestern India. Roman aurei were melted down in order to mint Kushan money.[60] The Kushans were probably the first rulers to issue gold coins in India. The standardization of these coins

Ruwanvali Dagoba" (a *yona* from Alasandra [Alexandria] was also present) (Bopearachchi 2002: 104). Coins of King Menander have been found in Sri Lanka (Bopearachchi 2002: 106).

[55] The Kushans, however, adopted Roman standards for the weight of their coins, and the Gupta will introduce an "Indian standard" (Kulke and Rothermund 1995: 75).

[56] The Yuezhi were defeated by the Xiongnu and forced to emigrate to the west. Some of them occupied Bactria and eastern Iran, while others went to settle directly in the Indus valley. The elite of the Kushan Empire may have used an Indo-Iranian language, but several authors argue that the Yuezhi originally spoke a Tocharian language (Beckwith 2011). The Kushans correspond to the clan called *kuei shang* by Chinese sources; we find *küsän* in Old Uighur (Beckwith 2011: 85). Yuezhi or Saka invaders were responsible for the burning and abandonment of the Bactrian city of Ai Khanum around 130 BCE.

[57] Kanishka was the successor of Kadphises II, who conquered northern India. His dates are not readily ascertainable: some historians propose 78–130, others 120–144 CE.

[58] The discoveries of a large number of Kushan coins in Bengal and in Orissa (Purī . . .) dated to the first three centuries of the Christian era imply a strong Kushan influence in these two regions. See below on the Murunda dynasty.

[59] A tradition mentions the introduction of silkworms by these Chinese, but this tradition is doubtful since the Chinese pilgrim Xuanzang, who went across the region (Xuanzang names the town Zhinapudi), does not mention silkworms (Boulnois 2001: 158–159). Tchinapati is a term already present in the *Arthasāstra* where it refers to a fine fabric, notably made of silk, coming from the country of Qin (Tsin) (Boulnois 2001: 162). *Pati*, "fabric, silk."

[60] According to Kulke and Rothermund (1995: 79), "after the debasement of Roman silver coins in 63, gold became the most important medium of exchange for the Roman trade with India," but the processes involved were probably more complex. For transactions, notes Meyer (2007), the Indians asked for coins of the same quality and weight as the ancient coins. Moreover, it would be useful to know how the ratio gold/silver evolved between Rome and India (McDowall [1996: 92] notes ratios of 1:12 in Rome and 1:10 in India).

Figure 10.1 Silver tetradrachm of the Indo-Scythian king Vonones (75–65 BCE). Horseman with a spear/ Zeus. The motif of the horseman-king would be used on coins of Afghanistan and India until the thirteenth century. © aryanaencyclopedia

Figure 10.2 Coin of the Kushan king Kanishka I. The reverse features a hellenized Buddha. On the right: the *tamgha* symbol. Gold, 7.93 g. © Classical Numismatic Group, Inc.

reveals a high degree of state control over the minting process. The Kushans also issued coins of lower denomination; these facilitated basic transactions. Expressing astonishing syncretisms, the coins of Kanishka I depict Hindu gods, Buddhist, Greek, and Persian figures, or Sumero-Elamite divinities, thus expressing a universalist ideology: as many as thirty different divinities have been identified on Kanishka I's coins (Klimburg-Salter 1999: 9). The legends are in Greek. As had been the case earlier during the Achaemenid Empire, the religious tolerance manifested by the ruler ought to be viewed as a technique of power, allowing him to exploit the cultural diversity of his empire (Honeychurch and Amartuvshin 2006: 276). The king himself may have converted to Buddhism; according to Buddhist texts, Kanishka I played a significant role in the expansion of this religion (Klimburg-Salter 1999: 10). Kushan coins clearly reflect the building of a powerful imperial ideology (Sinopoli 2006: 337).[61] With Wima

[61] Sinopoli (2006) notes for the Kushan Empire a greater visibility of the state than in the Deccan, with the effigy of the king already struck on the coins for the first ruler.

Kadphises and Huvishka, the figure of Shiva became preeminent. The Kushan kings' links to Buddhism and some Hindu gods underscore the importance of religious legitimation for rulers of foreign origin. Moreover, temples at Mat (near Mathura) and Surkh Kotal express the divine nature of the royal lineage (Liu 2010: 46).[62]

The promotion of Buddhism also reflects the rulers' interest in trade. During this period, Mahāyāna Buddhism was expanding, expressing a deification of the Buddha, and emphasizing the significance of offerings of perfumes and of "the seven precious substances" on one's path to salvation.[63] Silk and gems decorated stupas and monasteries. Mahāyāna Buddhism thus had a role to play in the exchange of luxury goods carried on the Silk Roads (Liu 2010). In the Kushan Empire, the Buddhist monasteries themselves engaged in exchanges and provided services to merchants. Documents from northwestern India in Saka territory dated to the third century show that monasteries functioned as financial institutions, receiving deposits and practicing moneylending with interest (Liu 1988: 125).

Inscriptions reveal a complex administrative hierarchy. The empire adopted the system of the Persian satrapies, but we do not know exactly how the state levied taxes, nor the source of its revenues. It is possible that the Kushan state controlled certain products such as alcoholic beverages. The kings traveled between several capitals: Surkh Kotal in northern Afghanistan, in the valley of the Kunduz Ab, Bactria; Termez, in the Amu Darya valley; and Mathurā. Peshāwar (Purushapura) and Mathurā were the empire's administrative centers. The sites at Sirkap (Taxila), Charsadda (Pushkalāvati), Hastinapur, Atranjikhera, Kaushāmbī, Shrāvastī, Ahichchhatra, and Vārānasī have also yielded Kushana remains (Sinopoli 2006: 337). Towns developed further north: Dal'verzin tepe, north of Termez, and Toprak Kala in Khwarezm, in Uzbekistan. The discovery of the Begram treasure (in the ancient Greco-Bactrian city of Kapisa) in 1938 in Afghanistan (on a road linking Taxila and Bactria) revealed the extent of the networks and the interconnection of land and sea trade routes, with discoveries such as Chinese lacquer bowls, sculpted ivories, Roman glass and bronzes, plaster emblemata, red coral branches, a bronze statue of Hercules cast in Alexandria, and a painted vase from Alexandria (first–second century).[64] In 1978, graves of Kushan notables at Tillya Tepe, northwest of Balkh, yielded artifacts made of gold and precious stones, showing a mixture of "Greek, Iranian, Indian, and Scythian influences": "Greek style cameos and intaglios, Parthian coins, and Chinese

---

[62] As the heirs to Hellenistic and Iranian ideas of deification of the king, the Kushan emperors played a role in the evolution of the Hindu ideas of kingship (Kulke and Rothermund 1995: 86).

[63] Mahāyāna (the "Great Vehicle") Buddhism encourages everyone to become a *bodhisattva*, "enlightened being," one who vows to attain enlightenment, not just for oneself, but for the benefit of all beings. The cult of the *bodhisattvas* developed from this period. The term "Mahāyāna" appeared for the first time in the *Lotus Sutra*, written between the first century BCE and the first century CE.

[64] The objects of Begram were stored at a time between the first and fourth centuries. They partly originate in taxes levied by the kings or the viceroys of Kapisa. Whitehouse (1989) has reassessed the dating for some of the glass artifacts: they were deposited during the first century CE (see also Dussubieux and Gratuze 2001). Some of the ivories were also produced during the first century CE, but others are of a later date; interestingly, several of the ivories "show a close affiliation with the South Indian tradition" (Stone 2008: 48).

bronze mirrors" (Boulnois 2008: 408).[65] Deposits in Buddhist sanctuaries (foundation deposits, reliquaries) also reflect the extent of exchanges and the cultural syncretisms achieved along the trade networks.[66] Merchants and missionaries spread Buddhism throughout the oases of Central Asia, where they founded monastic communities. Documents in Kharoṣṭī script have been discovered in oases such as Khotan and Niya. Because the oases depended economically upon merchants, many inhabitants converted to Buddhism. Moreover, the trade routes extended far northward: Kushan and Han coins have been unearthed in the forest zone north of the steppes, along with Syrian or Egyptian beads and silver items from Central Asia or the Mediterranean world. In addition, tombs of the Sargat culture have yielded lacquered objects, remnants of silk with gold embroidery, and Roman coins. At the end of the first millennium BCE a northern east–west route was therefore active, as were north–south routes, confirmed by the arrival of furs at Barbarikum, at the mouth of the Indus (Koryakova and Epimakhov 2007: 274, 311).

The Kushan area of northwestern India maintained links with Sri Lanka, as shown by the Kushan coins, carnelian beads, lapis lazuli, and intaglii discovered on this island.[67]

In use in western Bengal from the first through fifth centuries (in addition to the Brahmī script), the Kharoṣṭī script signals the arrival in this region of Kushans using the Prākrit language of northwestern India.[68] Kushan traders appear to have been involved in maritime activities, importing Central Asian horses and exporting them to Southeast Asia, probably from the mouth of the Ganges; these traders were active in Thailand, Cambodia, and as far as Bali, as shown by inscriptions in Kharoṣṭī script discovered in various places (see below). A seal impression dated to the third century found at Chandraketugarh depicts a ship transporting horses and featuring a man wearing a high hat of the "Scythian" type (Chakravarti 2002b: 121). The Chinese chronicle of Kang Tai mentions the importation of Yuezhi horses into Geying (Southeast Asia) (see below). A bronze drum from Sangeang Island, near Sumbawa, features a horse and men in Kushan costumes. The Sangam texts reveal that South India was also seeking horses. Many Kushan coins, both authentic and imitations, have been discovered in Bengal and in Orissa. The Vanga (Bengal) country, which issued copper money following the standard of silver *kārshāpana* of the Mauryan Empire, produced imitations of Kushan coins, during the second century, it issued

---

[65] Kushan architecture, moreover, reflects a Greco-Bactrian heritage.

[66] Thus, the deposit for the foundation of the stupa of Ahinposh (district of Jalalabad) included three Roman aurei, besides eighteen Kushan gold coins (Ray 2003).

[67] Bopearachchi (2002: 106) signals the discoveries of ten coins of Soter Megas, grandfather of Kanishka I, coins of Kanishka II (one of these was buried at the foot of the frontispiece of the Jetavanarama stupa, a frontispiece which also shows traces of lapis lazuli), and of Vasudeva II. The site of Jetavanarama has yielded a "Hellenistic" type of pottery that probably came from northwestern India. Note also the discovery at Kataragama of a carnelian intaglio depicting a figure holding a flower. Inscriptions refer to a corporation of Kambojas, a name applied to an Iranian-speaking group settled in Arachosia. They are often mentioned along with Yona ("Ionians," Greeks), with Gandhara people and with Saka. An inscription of Bagavalena in late Brahmī mentions a sailor called Mala, who goes to Bharukacha (the Barygaza of the *Periplus*) (Bopearachchi 2002: 107ff.). S. Paranavitana (1961: xci) did not exclude the presence of Saka on the island. Parpola (2002: 247) indicates the influence of Iranian speakers in South India during the fifth/fourth century BCE.

[68] See above. Inscriptions also show a mixed Kharoṣṭī-Brahmī script.

"Kushan-Vanga" coinage, bearing Kushan motifs, but using its own metrological system (Mukherjee 2001: 216–221).

Bengal had a large port, Tāmralipti, which may be the Gangēs of the *Periplus* and Ptolemy's Gangē, the capital of a kingdom.[69] The Ganges valley exported textiles (the *Periplus* praises its muslins), as well as glass artifacts, such as a type of glass produced in particular at Kopia (Uttar Pradesh).[70] Translucent green beads of prismatic shape imitating beryl from South India have been excavated at Taxila, Ahichchhatra, Kaushāmbī, and Nahran. Hexagonal green beads, similar to beads produced at Arikamedu and also present at Mantai (Sri Lanka)[71] have been excavated at sites in northeastern India (Harinarayanpur, Chandraketugarh, and Deulpota); these sites have also yielded gold beads showing a technique used in the Mediterranean world. According to Jahan (2002), the Indo-Pacific beads found in Bengal may have been produced by Tamil craftsmen who settled in this region. Bengal also exported rice; several seals found at Chandraketugarh depict ships bearing symbolic stalks of grain, or baskets with stalks of grain (Chakravarti 2002b: 125).

Kushan merchants also settled in Orissa. The significance of this region for long-distance trade grew as of the second century, since – according to Ptolemy – ships sailing to Chrysē departed from one of its ports.[72] At the close of the second century, Orissa issued coins called "Puri-Kushan," imitating coins from Vanga. These coins remained in use until the fifth century. A dynasty of Kushan origin seems to have reigned in Orissa during the third century, a period during which the names of two "Murunda" kings are known (they are written on a gold coin found at Sisupalgarh, and on a stone inscription at Bhadrak, Orissa).[73]

In the center of the Indian peninsula, the Shātavāhana emerged as an independent power from 230 BCE onward. Pliny describes a large Andhra kingdom (the *Andarae*), which included thirty fortified towns, and could mobilize an army of 100,000 men, 2,000 horsemen and 1,000 elephants. The extension and organization of the Shātavāhana Empire remain topics of debate, as does its political cohesion; the empire certainly experienced phases of expansion and centralization, but also of recession and fragmentation: the period 25 BCE – 86 CE, for example, was a phase of disintegration; the empire appears to have been politically stronger from 100 to 25 BCE and even more so from 86 to 187 CE (Sinopoli 2006: 334). Prolonged conflicts opposed the Shātavāhana

---

[69] Casson 1989: 91, 236. See above. B. N. Mukherjee (2001: 201–202), however, considers that Tāmraliptī should be distinguished from another port, Gangā, located on the Yamuna branch of the Ganges.

[70] The site is dated to the third century BCE – third century CE (Dussubieux 2001: 54).

[71] See above; Dussubieux 2001: 49, 57. The sites of northeastern India, however, exhibit a majority of red or orange beads. Gold beads have been excavated also at Arikamedu, Kolhapur (India), Anurādhāpura (Sri Lanka), and Khuan Lukpad (Thailand). They are probably imports. However, at Bara (Pakistan) (first century BCE – first century CE), gold beads were locally produced, using the Mediterranean technique (Dussubieux 2001: 184, 210). The glassmakers of Bara also borrowed and transmitted the *millefiori* technique. For Mantai, see Francis 2002: 132.

[72] See also the *Periplus Maris Exteri* of Marcianus (around 400) (Mukherjee 2001: 214–215). Moreover, Mukherjee (2001: 212) suggests a link between the name Minnagara – "located by Ptolemy on coastal Orissa," according to the author, but this interpration is uncertain – and the Saka or Indo-Scythians (the *Periplus of the Erythraean Sea* mentions two Minnagaras, in Pakistan and northwestern India; see above).

[73] Murunda corresponds to a royal title. This dynasty of Kushan origin is mentioned by the Chinese envoy Kang Tai (see below).

and the Saka ("Western Kshatrapa") kings who reigned in Gujarat, in northern Konkan, and sometimes as far as Ujjain, with both sides vying for control over the ports of Broach, Kalyan, and Sopara; however, the Shātavāhana recovered territories to the detriment of the Saka under the reign of King Gautamīputra Sātakarni (from 78 to 102 CE) (Singh 2008: 383). For the control of their empire, the Shātavāhana "divided it into districts headed by imperial officers," and military garrisons were distributed throughout the empire. The Shātavāhana did not truly rely on a centralized bureaucracy, however, but "incorporated local lords into the state hierarchy" (Kulke and Rothermund 1995: 102). According to Pliny (XI. 11.1), the Shātavāhana state "derived even greater revenue from salt mines than from those of gold and pearls" (Chakravarti 2002b: 53). Moreover, the second century CE provides the first inscriptions mentioning land grants to Buddhist monks or Brahmins; these grants came with various privileges, such as tax exemptions and immunities. We know of many coins issued by the Shātavāhana kings, in copper (for the lower denominations), and sometimes gold and silver. The coins of Yajnashri Satakarni (165–195), the last great Shātavāhana king, depict one- or two-masted ships. Their empire was obviously a key player in India's exchanges with regions abroad. Amarāvatī was one of their capitals, after Pratishthānapura (Paithan). The empire exported textiles in particular: these were produced at Pratishthānapura and at Tagara (Ter). On the Konkan coast, Ptolemy mentions Semylla (Chaul) as an emporium.

The first two centuries CE were a period of intense cultural and economic contacts, that benefited from the importance of Buddhism,[74] and from the networks built by the Indo-Greek, Saka, and Kushan kings in the north, as well as by the Shātavāhana, and later the Chera, Pāndya, and Chola, in the south. Thapar (1997: 35) emphasizes interconnections among the royal families, the Buddhist *sangha* community, and the *sreni* guilds of craftsmen and merchants. An inscription at Nasik (Maharashtra) dated to 42 CE thus reveals an investment by the son-in-law of the Indo-Scythian king Nahapāna ("Western Kshatrapa") with guilds of weavers, with the interest being passed on to the monks of a monastery (Sarkar 2003: 25–26; Thapar 2007: 266–267). During the first century CE, the *Periplus* gives the names of Indian ports, and the products exported (see above): here the importance of perishable goods for the west coast should be noted. Other ports should be mentioned such as "Dwarka (Gaur *et al.* 2006), Kamrej (Gupta *et al.* 2004), and Elephanta Island (Tripathi 2004), as well as the inland center of Nevasa (Gupta 1998; Gupta *et al.* 2001). [These ports] appear to have been significant focal points for regional and long-distance exchange" (Seland 2014). On these sites, "imported pottery is not limited to Mediterranean and Mesopotamian wares but includes vessels of Arabian (Selvakumar *et al.* 2009: 34) and probably Axumite origin" (Seland 2014 373; cf. Phillipson 2012: 200; Tomber 2005). Trade in the Bay of Bengal reached its peak at the end of the first century and during the second century CE, when the circumnavigation of India by ships from the western Indian Ocean seems to have grown more common.[75] It is during this period also that the power of the Shātavāhana kings grew, from the western Deccan to the Lower Krishnā

---

[74] Notably after the birth of the Mahāyāna school, the "Great Vehicle," during the first century: Buddhism, then became "the first true ecumenical religion" (Adshead 1995: 167).

[75] According to H. Ray (1988), the connection of the southeastern coast of India with the Indo-Mediterranean trade may have occurred at this time, but this connection certainly developed earlier.

valley. With their empire now stretching from the west to the east coast, the Shātavāhana were key players in the transnational trade between the Occident and the Orient.[76] Inscriptions (notably in the lower Krishnā River valley) stating donations to Buddhist monasteries reveal the wealth of some groups of merchants. While some merchants traded in precious goods (gold, aromatics), an inscription in the monastery of Nagarjunakonda (end of the third century CE) mentions a guild of merchants dealing in betel leaves. One inscription sheds light on the multiple international connections of this monastery: Kashmir and Gandhara, Yavana (Greeks from northwestern India), Banavasi (western India), Kirata (the *Cirrhadae* of the *Periplus*, west of Sikkim), Tosalī and Vanga (Bengal and part of Orissa), Damila (Tamil Nadu), the island of Tamrapani (Sri Lanka), and China (Kulke and Rothermund 1995: 103).

The active role played by southern and southeastern India has already been emphasized. During the second century, in this region, the Chola had the upper hand over the Pāndya and the Chera. The Tamil text of the *Pattinappālai* highlights the wealth of the Chola port of Kāverippūmpattinam (Puhar); horses, merchandise from the Ganges, Sri Lanka, Kālagam [Thai–Malay peninsula], pearls from Korkai, coral from the eastern seas, gold, gems, and pepper from the interior: all arrived there (De Romanis 1997: 115). This port was most likely created by the great Chola king Karikāla, celebrated by the *Pattinappālai* and whose dates of reign remain uncertain. The discovery at Kodumanal (district of Peiyar) of shards inscribed with the word *nikama* (*nigama*) signals the existence of a guildlike mercantile organization (Chakravarti 2001a: 23). A metallurgical center, this site has provided clues indicating steel production.[77] It also produced stone beads and textiles (Rajan 2002: 86). The cities of Uraiyūr, Madurai, and Kānchīpuram were centers for textile production, probably partly for exportation. Puhar kept a prominent position until the fifth or sixth century, when Nāgapattinam became the main Chola port. As already mentioned, pearl fishery was important in the Pāndya kingdom, where, according to the *Periplus*, prisoners of war were employed as divers.

Sri Lanka was connected with both the western and eastern parts of the Indian Ocean, as shown by the diversity of the artifacts (beads, ivories, intaglii, bronzes, and so on) found in the treasure of the Jetavana stupa, at Anurādhāpura: these objects are dated to the second century BCE through the third century CE.[78] In Sri Lanka, M. Wheeler found fragments of "Roman" glass bowls as well as shards of Mediterranean amphorae. Recent excavations at Anurādhāpura have yielded other traces of trade with the Mediterranean world,[79] as well as Partho-Sassanid ceramic (Coningham

---

[76] The presence of Mediterranean lead in Shātavāhana coins has been pointed out (Glover 1996: 369; Bellina and Glover 2004: 72). The museum of Hyderabad owns 38,000 coins, 24,000 of which come from Peddabankur, in the Andhra region (Ray 2003: 153).

[77] In northern India, artifacts from Taxila also attest to the knowledge of crucible cast steel manufacturing employing a process of carburization of wrought iron. Decarburization of cast iron must also have been known. In addition, the technique of co-fusion, in which cast iron (with a high carbon content) and wrought iron (with practically no carbon content) were melted together, was probably in use in ancient India, but the period has not been determined (Craddock 2003: 244–246).

[78] Ray 2003: 233. The stupa itself may have been built between 276 and 303 BCE.

[79] Among pottery imported from or influenced by the Greek or Roman world, one can mention a type of black slip ware (mainly from 200 BCE to 130 BCE at Anurādhāpura), knobbed base bowls with central cones (same period), and a type of grey ware of "Arikamedu 18" type (same period) (Coningham *et al.* 2006).

2002: 101). The island produced mineral soda–alumina (m-Na–Al) glass (at Giribawa) and also imported various types of glass.[80] On the northern coast, the port of Mantai developed as of the third century BCE. Another major port was located on the southern coast, at Godavaya, near mines of precious stones, and the political center of Tissamaharama (Ruhuna) (its remains give dates of occupation between the fourth/third century BCE and the eighth century CE; Godavaya was in decline after 500 CE). Some 75,000 late Roman coins have been found in pots in the region of Godavaya. The fact that one king issued an edict demanding a transfer of duties from the market center of Godavaya to a monastic site is significant: it reveals that Buddhist networks were involved in trade during the second century CE (Ray 2003: 202).[81] A shipwreck was discovered in 2008 off the ancient port of Godavaya. Its cargo "is still under excavation, but preliminary publications and news reports have announced finds of glass ingots and metal, possibly of Indian provenance" (Carlson 2010; Lawler 2012; Seland 2014).

Trade with Rome brought many gold coins into India. The Kushan kings probably melted these coins, while the kings of South India merely defaced them for reuse. The quest for Roman gold is reported by the *Periplus*, and also by a Tamil text of the second or third century CE:

The beautifully built ships of the Yavanas came with gold and returned with pepper, and Muciri [Muziris in the Greek and Roman texts] resounded with the noise [of the merchants]. (*Akanānūru*, 149, 7–11; Kulke and Rothermund 1995: 107; De Romanis 1997: 98)

A graffito on a shard of Rouletted Ware found at Alagankulam may be an image of the three-masted ships described in Greco-Roman texts (Tchernia 1999).

Prices varied with the movements of the ships, but according to early Buddhist literature "a practice was for local merchants to book a share of the incoming cargo by paying money in advance," a "practice which could be manipulated in order to control prices" (Ray 2002b: 70; see *Jātaka*, Book I, no. 40). For prestige goods such as gold or pearls, the king would fix their price, helped by the experts of his court (Ray 2001; *Jātaka*, Book I, no. 5).

Roman trade certainly stimulated production and exchanges, especially along the Malabar coast, although its role should probably be downplayed (Thapar 1997: 24, 30). The Greco-Roman sources mention three great categories of Indian exports: aromatics and spices, precious stones, and textiles. The *Silappadikāram* describes streets bordered by the shops of textile merchants, and refers to thirty-two kinds of cotton fabrics (Herodotus had already associated cotton with India [Herodotus III.106; Parker 2002: 48]). India also exported Chinese silk (in both its raw and textile forms) (the *Periplus* mentions silk for the main regions of India dealing in long-distance trade). Perhaps

---

[80] Beads in the shape of a stupa (Sri Lanka) have been produced with different types of glass: Syro-Palestinian glass, glass made with soda from plant ashes and limy sand (v-Na-Ca), and soda-alumina glass (m-Na-Al) (Dussubieux 2001: 219). Glassworking goes back to the first century BCE at Anurādhāpura (Coningham *et al.* 2006). Glass beads found in Southeast Asia (opaque monochrome beads) – for example in eastern Java – may have been made with glass from Giribawa (Lankton *et al.* 2008).

[81] In India, the transfers applied only to agricultural revenues.

India already had its own silk industry. Various kinds of wood used for shipbuilding were also exported (see above).

This period of multiplying exchanges saw a general trend toward urbanization in India. Chakravarti (2002b) has correctly pointed out that this urban growth was only possible because agriculture itself had progressed, in the areas of both food and cash crops. Texts reveal the expansion of coconut groves at this time (see an inscription at Nasik, from King Nahapāna) and of the culture of pepper, clearly boosted by foreign demand. Archaeology and epigraphy reveal that rulers tried to promote irrigation and regulate the rivers. Rudradāman I (*c.* 150 CE), king of the Western Khsatrapa, repaired the water tank at Sudharshana (Gujarat), which had been built by the Maurya; the Chola king Karikāla undertook the building of dams in the Kāverī delta, and the *Gāthāsaptashatī* refers to the use of norias (waterwheels with pot garlands) (Chakravarti 2002b: 51).

As pointed out above, the third century CE was a period of recession in the world-system. The Kushan Empire collapsed during this time, when the Sassanid king Ardashir I conquered Bactria and the rest of the Kushan domain in Central Asia (Thapar 1984: 98). Rulers of northwestern India, vassals of the Sassanids, issued silver coins termed "Indo-Sassanid"; these coins could be found in various regions of the subcontinent, where they were often imitated, a sign of their success on the trade networks.[82] The Shātavāhana Empire also disintegrated during the third century, giving way to various principalities, which are known by their coins. New dynasties set up smaller kingdoms, such as the Vākāṭaka dynasty of the Deccan (*c.* 250–500), whose capital was at Vatsagulma (Maharashtra); the Kadamba dynasty (345–525) in Karnataka (with Banavasi as capital); the Ikshvāku of Andhra, who chose Nagarjunakonda (in the Krishnā River valley) as their capital; the Abhīra in western Maharashtra, and so forth. At this time, land donations to Brahmins increased, for example during the fourth century in the territory of the Ikshvāku, who were none-theless Buddhists. "Kosambi (1956), Sharma (1987), and others have suggested that after the decline of long-distance maritime trade during the third and fourth centuries CE, grants of land were made to the brahmanas by the newly emerging elite in its bid for legitimation," as the Buddhist monasteries were in decline. Ray (2003: 141, 144) goes on to emphasize the procedural complexity of what she calls a "consolidation" of political power during this period. Land grants would become more widespread during the seventh and eighth centuries in peninsular India.

The decline of India should not be overestimated. Merchants did maintain an active trade on the coasts, for example along the Malabar coast. Sassanian shards are known from Amreli and from a site near Barygaza in Gujarat (Schenk 2007: 57–58), and "specimens of Sassanian-period (CE 224–651) torpedo jars from Mesopotamia, late Roman (fifth to seventh century) Aila/Aqaba amphorae, glazed Partho-Sassanian pottery, and shards of probable South Arabian origin are reported" from Pattanam (Muziris) (Cherian 2011; Seland 2014). The context of these discoveries fits within a framework spanning the second through fourth centuries CE. The amphorae probably

---

[82] Smith 2002: 142. In Gujarat, the "Western Satraps [Khsatrapas]" of the Kārdamaka dynasty (of Saka origin) maintained their power until the fifth century. Then the Gupta took control of Gujarat.

contained *garum*, wine, and dates. The decline in trade with the Mediterranean region at this time as well as internal problems probably contributed to the abandonment of some urban centers in northern India and the western Deccan. On the other hand, sites along the east coast continued to flourish, notably in the lower Krishnā River valley.[83] During the fourth century, the Pallava gained power in Tamil Nadu and occupied the region of the Krishnā and the Godāvarī deltas, where they appointed a governor. The capital of the Pallava, Kāñchīpuram, remained active in long-distance trade. The reverse of one type of Pallava coins found at Kāñchīpuram features a ship. A coin of this type has been unearthed at Khuan Lukpad (Khlong Thom, in the province of Krabi in peninsular Thailand). A brick structure – possibly a quay – dated to this period has been excavated at Kāveripattinam (Ray 1996: 358). The Pallava were in decline at the end of the fifth and at the beginning of the sixth century, however, and a significant resurgence of the Pallava kingdom did not occur before the late sixth century (Champakalakshmi 1996: 16). In the extreme south of the peninsula, the Pāndya kingdom seems to have been prominent. The reign of the great Pāndya king Nedunjeliyan II, celebrated in Tamil texts, should probably be dated to the third century. The southern Tamil country, however, experienced a so-called "dark age" from the fourth to the sixth century, under the domination of a poorly identified population called Kalabhra in the texts; this was a population who may have come from southern Andhra Pradesh. In Sri Lanka, by contrast, Anurādhāpura benefited from a "golden age" between the third and the sixth century. Sri Lanka's relative prosperity resulted from progress in both rice cultivation and trade. Sri Lanka maintained exchanges – probably indirect – with the Roman world, as shown by the discovery of thousands of coins (see above). The port of Mantai also yielded Red Polished Ware, which most likely originated in Gujarat (Ray 2003: 201). Shards of Sassanian glazed ware have been found with local pottery dated from the third to seventh century CE at Anurādhāpura and Tissamaharama, where some shards go back as far as Parthian times (first century BCE up to the first half of the first century CE (Schenk 2007: 58). More significant was the growth of trade with Southeast Asia across the Bay of Bengal. Over the following centuries, along India's southeastern coast, similar developments would lead to the consolidation of political entities centered on the main river valleys.[84] Western Bengal was also active in transnational networks. Various seal impressions dated to the third century from Chandraketugarh show vessels with tripod masts,[85] which are different from the ships depicted on the Shātavāhana coins; one ship may feature a furled lateen sail, while another ship transporting grain (see above) appears to carry a steering mechanism on its stern.[86]

---

[83] R. S. Sharma enlarged upon the supposed de-urbanization of India after 300 CE, notably in the post-Gupta period, but this urban decline has recently been toned down by researchers (Champakalakshmi 1996: 13). Similarly, the demonetization of the economy was not as pronounced as some suggested.

[84] It is significant, note H. Kulke and D. Rothermund (1995: 98), that "Ptolemy [already] mentions not only the ports of South India but also the capitals of rulers located at some distance from the coast." Champakalakshmi (1996) considers, however, that a decline in trade led to a situation of crisis in the "chiefdoms" of South India and to an urban recession and processes of recomposition during the period from the third to the sixth century.

[85] Ships with tripod (or bipod) masts are represented on bas-reliefs of Borobudur (Manguin 1993: 263).

[86] Chakravarti 2002a: 37–40. The mixed Brāhmī-Kharoṣṭī script of the first seal impression gives the name of the ship as *trapyaka*, similar to the *trappaga* mentioned by the *Periplus*. The second inscription "suggests

Northern India was reunified by the Gupta dynasty (320–480), originating from Allahabad or Vārānasī. Conquered by Samudragupta (335–375), who was proclaimed "universal sovereign," Pātaliputra became the capital of this empire, and one of the largest cities in the world. Kings in Bengal and Orissa submitted to the Gupta. Under King Chandragupta II (375–413/415), who annexed the Saka territory in Gujarat, the empire stretched from the mouth of the Ganges to the Indus River valley, and from northern Pakistan to the mouth of the Narmada River.[87] Ujjain became its new capital. As is the case for the Mauryan period, two opposing views exist with regard to the Gupta period: that of a strong, centralized state, obtaining its income from land taxes and controlling the economy, or – a more likely scenario – that of a weakly integrated state. The empire, in fact, may have been less centralized than the Mauryan Empire (Thapar 2004: 290–291). The core of the empire was under direct administration; beyond the core, tributary kings enjoyed some autonomy. While the emperors sponsored the Hindu religion,[88] donations also went to Buddhist monasteries, which acted as "banks" (Kulke and Rothermund 1995: 95). The first copper plates recording donations to religious institutions go back to the mid-fourth century, for northern and central India (Ray 2003). The fourth and fifth centuries saw a flowering of palace and temple construction, as well as the development of various aspects of Indian culture, along with the administrative and literary use of Sanskrit,[89] and advances in mathematics and astronomy.[90] The spread of "Sanskrit culture [from the Ganges basin] facilitated both horizontal integration and social differentiation," helping create "a coherent civilizational zone" (what Pollock has called "the Sanskrit cosmopolis") (Lieberman 2009: 662). Several rulers undertook hydraulic works during the fourth

that it was fit to undertake journeys in 'three directions'": it was therefore a seagoing vessel. On another inscription referring to a ship, the latter is said to belong to King Juja, "the conquering king." The ship carrying a basket with stalks of grain is called *jaladhisakra*, "Indra of the ocean."

[87] Diplomacy and alliance through marriage – for example with the Vākāṭaka dynasty, which became prominent after the collapse of the Shātavāhana – also played a role in the establishment of the so-called "Gupta peace."

[88] Gold coins of Samudragupta depict horse sacrifice. The first temples that were built appeared toward the third century. Adshead (2004: 56) considers that the donations to religious institutions weakened the state more than they strengthened it. Land grants to Hindu temples, however, often concerned uncultivated land, which the grantees had to develop. In the south, also, the spread of Hindu traditions can be observed (see below). The flexibility of Hinduism allowed it to incorporate local divinities and groups who were outside the system of varnas.

[89] The drafting of the Law Code of Manu during the first or second century marked a revival for the Sanskrit language. Poets such as Kālidasa were present at the Gupta court.

[90] Astronomy benefited from Babylonian and Greek inputs. Chinese influences are likely in the mathematical domain (Needham and Wang Ling 1959: 146–147). Two names emerge here. Aryabhata (born *c.* 476), an astronomer and mathematician, used the decimal system and the zero; he suggested that the earth rotates on its axis. The mathematician Brahmagupta, born in 598, defined the zero, and calculated the circumference of the earth. He led research on topics such as algebra, trigonometry, negative numbers, and *pi*. The Indian numerals *nagari*, which the Muslim world would borrow, go back to the fifth century. "Indian mathematics focused on arithmetic and algebra, not so much on geometry" (Ronan 1988: 276–277). Indian medicine was also renowned (see the *Charaka samhita*, first century CE). The Buddhist center of Nālandā promoted the development of medicine. In the field of alchemy, Ronan (1988: 278) notes that the Indians used a still of Chinese type "more often than the still of Alexandrian type," a borrowing probably linked to Buddhist voyages between China and India.

and fifth centuries, a period of prosperous Indian agriculture. Cities blossomed, such as Kāshī (Vārānasī) and Mathurā, where jewelry, metalworking and textile industries were booming (in contrast, the Chinese pilgrim Faxian signals the decline of other cities). Many guilds developed (artisans, merchants), and great merchants emerged: a man by the name of Saddalaputta owned 500 workshops for potters in addition to boats that traded on the Ganges (Thapar 2007: 265). At this time, merchant-financiers and caravan chiefs were politically active on the boards of cities and regional governments.[91] The gold and silver coins minted by the Gupta expressed the wealth of the state.[92] The *dīnāra* (named after the Roman coin *denarius*) was both an abstract measure of value and, as a gold coin, a means of payment.[93] Gold coins "initially followed the Kushan weight standard" (Thapar 2004: 299). The discovery of sixteen hoards all over the Gupta territory demonstrates the widespread use of currency in the empire (Sarkar 2003: 22). In addition, Faxian recorded the monetary use of cowries at Mathurā around 400.[94] Shell-shaped "tokens" were also in circulation. The Gupta maintained relations with Sri Lanka (mainly through the port of Mantai) and with kingdoms in Southeast Asia, where a major Indian influence held sway for this period (Burma, Thailand, Funan). Gold exported by insular Southeast Asia may partly explain India's growing interest in this region: the gold trade, whether from Bactria or Europe, was hampered at this time by wars and disturbances. The empire's access to the ports of India's eastern and western coasts led to increased trade, also spurred by the dynamism of the Sassanid Empire on the one hand, and the development of Sogdian, Persian, and Indian networks in Central Asia, Southeast Asia and China, on the other.[95] In the northwest, a road connected India to Central Asia through Kashmir. Faxian arrived in India through Central Asia and what is today Pakistan,[96] and we know that Sogdian merchants traded in the upper Indus valley between the third and fifth centuries (de la Vaissière 2002: 87; Liu 2010: 68). The main ports were Broach (Barygaza), in the west, and Tāmralipti, in the east, where merchants and pilgrims boarded ships bound for Southeast Asia and China.

[91] According to V. K. Jain (2001: 358 n. 99), "a number of documents of the Gupta age refer to *sreṣṭhīs* [wholesalers and financiers] and *sārthavāhas* [caravan chiefs] as important members of the boards which assisted the provincial governors and district officers in administration." During the Maurya period, board members were appointed.

[92] S. A. M. Adshead (2004: 93), who does not reveal his sources, suggests that at that time, India "possessed both the largest economy in the world and the highest per capita distribution from it," notably thanks to its textile (cotton) and sugar production.

[93] Wicks 1992: 67, 69. During the fifth century, the gold:silver ratio appears to have been 1:16 (Wicks 1992: 71). In Bengal, cowries were used for smaller transactions, as Faxian notes when he was there.

[94] Xuanzang (*c.* 640) also refers to the use of cowries in Orissa. Mas'ūdī, in the tenth century, writes that the cowries in India are the common currency. Their use would later stay preeminent, in particular in the Bengal economy.

[95] I do not agree with Gills and Frank's idea (1993b: 170) according to which the rise of the Sassanids and the Gupta [only] came from the weakness of other regions (within a context of economic recession). There was indeed an economic decline in the east (China) and the west (Mediterranean, Egypt), but the Indian Ocean (from Persia to Southeast Asia) did not experience the same kind of decrease in trade.

[96] Despite a revival of the ancient Hindu institutions of kingship under the Gupta, and the devotion of the kings Chandragupta II and Kumaragupta to Vishnu, religious tolerance was still the rule. The Buddhist monasteries received donations and "retained their functions as banks" (Kulke and Rothermund 1995: 88, 92–93).

During the first centuries of the Christian era, the center for Buddhist scholarship was Taxila. During the fifth century, the university of Nālandā was created, to which visitors flowed from Southeast Asia and China. Chinese sources mention 162 visits by Chinese Buddhist monks to India between the fifth and eighth centuries, but there were certainly other pilgrims (Kulke and Rothermund 1995: 156).

As was the case for other regions of the world-system, northern India experienced a decline during the fifth and sixth centuries. From the middle of the fifth century onward, invasions by the White Huns (Hephtalites), who had entered Transoxiana and Bactria before 450, weakened the Gupta Empire and disrupted transregional trade. Central Asian cities (Balkh, Taxila . . .) fell into decline. Various revolts broke out in the Gupta Empire, which finally disintegrated at the beginning of the sixth century, a period also marked by weaker summer monsoons that affected the harvests and therefore the income of the state, further drained by the fight against the Hephtalites.[97] A process of distinct de-urbanization occurred at this time in the Ganges valley. (For Chakravarti [2002b], the existence of market-centers *mandapikā* in northern India, however, contradicts the idea of de-urbanization in post-Gupta India, but the author gives no example prior to the eighth century.) The Hun leader Toramana managed to occupy most of northwestern India, for a brief period (as early as 533, his son was expelled from northern India). Transoceanic trade, however, remained active, as cotton fabrics from northwestern India have been excavated in Egypt (Barnes 2004a,b). Gujarat retained a significant role during the fifth and sixth centuries, as seen in the spread of its red pottery and the discovery of copper plates with inscriptions recording donations to a temple by merchants from other regions such as Mathurā, Ujjain, and Kanauj (Ray 2003: 200). A kingdom led by the Maitraka dynasty (475–767) that had appeared in the fifth century in Saurashtra controlled all of Gujarat during the sixth century, with their capital at the port of Vallabhi. An inscription referring to the donation of a village by the king in 571 mentions several administrative levels, with units above villages, *peṭha*, that were "below a new and higher administrative tier, namely the *sthalī*" (Chakravarti 2002b: 206). In eastern India, Orissa and Bengal formed independent states. Eastern Bengal, called Samatata, acquired new importance as of the seventh century, with its main port at Samandar (Chittagong). The Chinese pilgrim Xuanzang mentions six regions with links to Samatata: "Shi-li-cha-ta-lo [Srīkshetra], Kia-mo-land-kia [Kāmalanka, Pegu], To-lo-po-ti [Dvāravatī], Mo-ho-chen-po [Mahacampā, Vietnam] and Yen-no-na-chien [Yamanadvīpa, location not identified]" (Chakravarti 2002b: 134).

In the south, the Pallava dynasty became a major regional power at the end of the sixth century. The sixth and seventh centuries were a time of religious and political change for peninsular India, with "an amalgamation of the Buddhist and Hindu

---

[97] As noted above, climatic disturbances affected the whole northern hemisphere, and contributed to the collapse of the Funan state. For this period, S. A. M. Adshead (2004: 94) mistakenly considers that cooler conditions were accompanied – generally speaking – by a wetter climate. On the contrary, as pointed out above, the Indian Ocean and the China Sea experienced weaker summer monsoons. J. L. Brooke (2014: 353) notes that the Gupta Empire collapsed following harsh droughts. A part of the Eurasian steppes, in contrast, enjoyed a wetter climate (see Bokovenko 2004: 28–29; Koulkova 2004: 266).

concepts,[98] . . . a more direct involvement of the kings in the construction of temples to Hindu deities, donation of land to Brahmanas, elaboration of the origin myths of the rulers, and the emergence of complex administratives structures" (Ray 2003: 149).[99] From the Gupta period onward, Hinduism was radically transformed to include local divinities and the development of devotional *bhakti* cults – first in Tamil Nadu[100] – where Vishnu and Shiva (and their various manifestations) held prominent places, while at the same time the texts of the *Purāna* were being written. During the Gupta period, India was already producing images of divinities in increasing numbers, whereas "Vedi brahmanism had excluded icons" (Thapar 2004: 315).

The entire Indian subcontinent was active in long-distance exchanges. In Kathiawad (Gujarat), "a port in or near Lohatagrama (under the Maitraka rulers of Valabhi) emerged, if one takes into account an inscription from 592 CE" (Chakravarti 2012: 76–77). This inscription refers to a body of merchants (*vaniggrama*) and to seagoing vessels *vahitra*. The Greek Cosmas describes a pepper trade on the Malabar coast, and mentions the textiles of Khambat (Cambay), Kalyan, Chaul; he also points out the centrality of Sri Lanka – "called by the Indians Sielediba [the Arabic Serendib is obviously related to this name] and by the Greeks Taprobanē." Sri Lanka functioned as a hub for international trade. The island received elephants from India, ivory from Africa, horses from Persia, and products from China and Southeast Asia. It was visited by ships from India, Persia, Ethiopia, and it also traded with its own vessels:

From all parts of India, Persia and Ethiopia come a multitude of ships, [because this island] is placed as it were midway between all lands; and it sends ships likewise hither and thither in all directions.

From the inner regions, that is, from Tzinista [Tzinistan, "the country of Tzin," Qin] and from the other market-towns, are brought silk cloth, aloe-wood, cloves, sandalwood and other

---

[98] The preceding centuries have already revealed a spread of Brahmin traditions. The migration of Brahmins southward was accompanied by a hardening of the caste system in this southern region. It also helped spread "Gupta style court terminology, architecture and art" (Lieberman 2009: 660).

[99] According to Ray, the first reference to taxes levied by a king – Pallava – from various corporations may go back to the fifth century (in fact, an inscription dated to the middle of the fourth century at Hirahadagalli, in Karnataka, already mentions officials who collect taxes in a market-center *mandapika*; Chakravarti 2002b: 198). Before that period, the inscriptions that we know of do not refer to any levy: for Ray, the Indian states before the fifth–sixth century were weakly integrated, with a limited administrative apparatus, which explains the importance of the religious networks with their integrative capacities for the kings (Ray 2003: 131, 144ff.), as well as the importance of rituals and religious ideology. In addition, kings obtained support from local vassal rulers. Privileges were granted to guilds (see the trade charter promulgated by the king Vishnusena in western India in 592) (Jain 2001: 369). Unlike Ray, other authors have stated that systems of taxation were already well developed earlier, notably under the Maurya, and even under the Nanda who preceded them. Later Vedic texts (before 600 BCE) alluded to an occasional tax called *bali* (Chakravarti 2001a: 21). Data reported by Megasthenes has been mentioned above. According to Arrian, who quotes this author in part, "the farmers . . . pay the taxes to the kings and to the cities such as are self-governing . . . The herdsmen pay taxes from their animals . . . The artisans and shopkeepers . . . pay tribute from their works, save such as make weapons of war" (Arrian VIII.11–12, trans. E. I. Robson 1933).

[100] This development, from around 500 CE, can partly be seen as a reaction against the spread of the Sanskrit culture, which implied a "Sanskrit monopoly on creative written expression, brahmanic ritual leadership and the notion of Aryavarta (northern India) as a privileged zone" (Lieberman 2009: 660). See Volume II, Chapter 3. The *bhakti* cults would later spread from south to north.

products . . ., and it forwards them to those of the outside . . .[to western markets]. And in return, it receives other things from all these places, which it transmits to the inner regions, with its own products likewise.[101]

From Sri Lanka, ships sailed to Malē (on the Malabar coast), "which has five ports where pepper is brought," to Calliana (Kalyan), on the coast of Konkan, "a large market-town" near Bombay, whence brass, ebony, and cloth were exported to Sindu (mouth of the Indus?), which in turn provided musc, costus root, and Indian nard, and on to the Persian Gulf or the Red Sea. Pulakeshin II (609–642), the Chālukyan king of Vatapi, controlled the Konkan coast, and sent diplomatic missions to the Sassanid king Khosrau I.[102] Pulakeshin II's conquest of southern Gujarat must be viewed within the context of these relations with the Persian Gulf.

Also mentioned among the large market towns of India are: Orrhotha, Sibor, Male, and Marallo, in the south. "And then is Kaber [Kāverī River, in the east], shipping alabandenum, and then the country from which cloves are shipped; and then Tzinista, which sends silk cloth; within which there is no other land, for the ocean encircles it on the east" (Schoff 1974: 251). Ships from "the country of Tzin" (China) may have reached Sri Lanka, but Cosmas does not state this clearly.[103] In 428, a king of this island sent a diplomatic mission to the Chinese court.

Toussaint notes that "the rise of trade did not attract the Indians to Egypt and the Occident in the way it had encouraged the Romans to go to India and [the Indians to go to] the Orient," and wonders why (Toussaint 1961: 41). A first answer for Toussaint might be that the Indians did indeed travel westward, although it is true that they traveled more frequently to the Orient. And other arguments can be put forward: the origin of the goods coveted by the West (Chinese silk, spices from the Moluccas and the Banda Islands, Sumatran camphor, and so forth), the fact that goods from the West had little interest for India and East Asia (except precious metals and glass); the role played by Buddhism from Bengal or the east coast of India in the development of trade networks involving Southeast Asian populations (relations grew between India, Lower Burma, Central Thailand, Malaysia, and the islands of the region that would be named Insulindia); and the Indian demand for spices and gold from Southeast Asia. The first and foremost reason, however, was the fact that East Asia – China – represented the "core" of the world-system.

Relations between India and Southeast Asia

The ways in which the relations between India and Southeast Asia are viewed have changed over the course of the twentieth century. In light of recent archaeological

---

[101] Cosmas Indicopleustes, Book XI, quoted by Schoff 1974: 250–252. Cosmas records the joint arrival of ships from Adulis, with a "Roman" called Sopater, and of Persian ships. The first Tzinista mentioned by Cosmas, because of the indication of "inner regions," has sometimes been identified as Sichuan or Yunnan, beyond Burma.

[102] Chakravarti 2000b: 263. On the Konkan coast, Cosmas also mentions Souppara (Sopara), and Semylla (Chaul).

[103] Needham (1954) adopted this hypothesis, quoting S. Lévi (1900), who nevertheless spoke only of Sinhalese embassies in China.

finds, we know that these connections began earlier than previously thought. Moreover, they can no longer be considered truly unilateral. It is difficult to accept Coedes's point of view that the Insulindian states were simple imitations of Indian models.[104] While partly linked to the expansion of trade in the Indian Ocean and in the China Sea, the first states of Southeast Asia also arose from internal processes. Southeast Asia was not the passive recipient of ideas and objects coming from a dominant Indian culture, but rather an active agent in ongoing processes;[105] neither the indianization of the elites, nor the presence of Indian merchants and scholars turned Southeast Asia into an "Indian colony" (de Casparis and Mabbett rightly emphasize the ambiguity of the term "indianization," "which may suggest a conscious effort on the part of Indians to spread their culture over major parts of Southeast Asia. This was indeed the view expressed by most scholars until a half century ago ... It was based mainly on analogies with Greek, Roman or western expansions").[106] The process of indianization was also conducted by men from Southeast Asia who had studied in India. It is an almost universal phenomenon that the assertion of a link with an external power validates the status of the elite (see Helms 1988). There were "local appropriation and a re-invention of Indian models" (Wolters 1999; Bertrand 2007). However, the "deconstruction" of the concept of indianization has probably been taken too far, at the same time erasing the idea of the economic and ideological ascendance of the Indian cores. The processes of coevolution that we observe – those that led to the building of Southeast Asia as a semi-periphery of the world-system (for these processes of coevolution, Chase-Dunn [1988] speaks of the *spread effects of development*) – and the fact that the region was not "passive" in the processes initiated by the various exchange networks do not imply that the cores failed to exert any dominance. Moreover, whereas much research has been conducted on the Indian presence and influence in Southeast Asia, only a few scholars have studied the opposite journeys of Austroasiatics and Austronesians to the coasts of India and Sri Lanka. The presence of Southeast Asian sailors and merchants in the trade of the Indian Ocean – and notably along the coasts of India – has not been taken seriously enough by researchers, with the exception of pioneers such as Hornell, Jones, and Miller.

[104] "The discourse by Coedès and his fellow orientalists ... was bound by many of the representations conveyed by foreign sources dealing with Southeast Asia and of the perception of the world in which those scholars lived" (Manguin 2004d: 294). Conversely, the approach of historians like J. C. van Leur (1955) focuses on indigenous social developments in Southeast Asia. It leads them to deny any significant role to the contributions coming from the cores, and to ignore the processes leading to domination through trade and religious networks.

[105] De Casparis and Mabbett 1992: 281. De Casparis (1983: 18) has suggested moving from the "somewhat simplistic" view of initial indianization to the idea of a complex network of relations that built up over long-lasting relationships between the Indian subcontinent and Southeast Asia. This change in the perception of Southeast Asian societies – which has obvious political implications – can be compared to the evolution of the analysis concerning the birth and development of the societies of the East African coast.

[106] De Casparis and Mabbett 1992. Wolters (1999: 15–26) has also emphasized that borrowings from India were embedded in local cultures.

People from Southeast Asia on the Coasts of India?

It is unlikely that the trade networks that we see established as early as the fourth century BCE (see below) between India and Southeast Asia worked in only one direction. Austronesians certainly sailed to the coasts of India during the first half of the first millennium BCE, taking part in what is known as the "Commercial Revolution" initiated in the Indian Ocean at the time. Moreover, visits of Buddhist pilgrims from Indonesia may have begun early on in India.

W. Mahdi, in particular, supports the idea of regular contacts between Southeast Asia and India, and of Austronesian settlements in India during the first millennium BCE (see also Ray 1999a: 226). According to Mahdi, the use of funerary urns was introduced from Southeast Asia into South Asia, notably in Sri Lanka, prior to 400 BCE (1999: 227). Southeastern India may have borrowed other funerary customs from Indonesia, for example reburial after excarnation of the bones. A key feature of Indonesian megalithism, the cult of the *Ficus benjamina* tree may have been introduced into India, according to Mahdi, where it intermingled with that of *Ficus religiosa*. Indonesian "megalithism," however, reflects links established with South Asia, as shown in finds of beads, and the presence of iron metallurgy (Bellina and Glover 2004: 79–81). Without attempting to draw conclusions other than the possible exchange of ideas through various contacts "from the middle of the first millennium BCE," P. Bellwood observes that urn burial (sometimes "mouth-to-mouth urn burial," a type of burial referred to in the *Manimekhalai*) "and specific features of this tradition, such as the practice of secondary burial with grave goods in the urns, the use of bone boxes and legged coffins, and the occasional occurrence of stone jar lids (as in some Philippines sites), have definite Indo-Malaysian parallels" (Bellwood 1997: 307).[107] Bellwood also notes, however, that metal objects and pottery are quite different in each of the two regions. In Southeast Asia itself, there is no unity in megalithism and the notion of a "megalithic culture" should probably be abandoned. Moreover, Bellwood points to similarities between ceramics from tombs of the Yayoi period on Kyushu Island (third century BCE – second century CE) and Southeast Asia; beads of the "Indo-Pacific" type have occasionally been unearthed in these tombs (see below). S. Gupta has recently suggested that the funerary urns of Kyushu and those from Adichanallur in South India reflect the oriental and western ends of a sphere of exchange where Southeast Asians sailors were active.[108] Recent excavations at Adichanallur have unearthed Mongoloid-type human remains which may

---

[107] K. P. Rao (2000) discerns similarities between megalithic statues of South India and the cult to which they belong (in the Moria and the Savara populations, for example) and the anthropomorphic statues of the Iron Age of Java. Moreover, P. Bellwood notes that jar burials appeared in southwestern Japan in the Late Jomon Period and in the Yayoi period. He also points out parallels between the Yayoi pottery and ceramic of the Philippines, and does not exclude some contacts between the two regions during the first millennium BCE (Bellwood 1997: 306–307). The bearers of the Yayoi culture, however, came from Korea, with rice, introducing bronze and iron metallurgy around 500 BCE.

[108] Gupta 2005: 22. If the first levels of Adichanallur go back at least to the beginning of the first millennium BCE ("pre-Megalithic" phase), the burial jars should perhaps be dated to the middle of the first millennium BCE (Gupta 2005: 28 n. 5), or slightly earlier (see below), something future excavations could tell us. Sites with burial jars have also been found in northern Sri Lanka (Gupta 2005).

indicate maritime links with Southeast Asia "around 700 BCE."[109] Burials using double urns have also been observed along the Kerala coast and in Neolithic contexts at Nagarjunakonda (Andhra Pradesh) and Wargal (Karnataka) (from the second to first millennium BCE). Moreover, S. Gupta places special emphasis on discoveries made at the site of Sankarjang, near Bhubaneshwar, which have yielded polished axes and stone bars probably representing lithophones, well-known instruments at Vietnamese sites. A C_{14} analysis returned the date of 740 BCE (Yule *et al.* 2000; Gupta 2005: 23).

While major reservations are held regarding comparisons initiated by W. Mahdi, the idea of Austronesian settlements in India remains a plausible and attractive one. These Austronesian migrants, who adopted Aryan or Tamil cultures, may have been involved in exchanges between India and Southeast Asia. Plants from this region arrived in India very early (see above), brought in by Austronesians and/or Austroasiatics. R. Blench notes that the word for coconut tree in Sanskrit, *nārikela*, may derive from two Austronesian terms *niur* and *kelapa*, but this etymology appears uncertain.[110] Mahdi, curiously, paid scant attention to the Austroasiatics. At the end of the Bronze Age some societies in continental Southeast Asia were becoming increasingly complex. Significant social differentiation, however, occurred only from 500 BCE onward, at a time when trade connections intensified (see below).

Bronze vessels with a high tin content, found at Coimbatore, Adichanallur, and as far as Taxila, have been viewed as imports from Southeast Asia, brought either by Southeast Asians or by Indian merchants who went to trade in this region (Glover 1989; 2000; Basa 1999: 40); in fact, their production in India predates exchanges with Southeast Asia (Srinivasan 2010). These vessels are well known in Thailand (Ban Don Ta Phet, Ban Chiang, Ban Na Di, and Tham Ongbah, dated to the second century BCE) and in the Malay peninsula (tombs of southern Perak and northern Selangor).[111] During the final centuries BCE, high-tin bronze ingots – excavated at Khao Sam Kaeo, on the Thai-Malay peninsula – may have been exported to India (see below).

The possible exchanges of shipbuilding techniques have been emphasized above. For Horridge (1995: 146), "the westward spread of the Austronesian triangular sail into the Indian Ocean [may have occurred] about 200 BC." According to this author, this may be the origin of the Arabic "lateen" sail, but this proposal remains speculative. On the other hand, Horridge believes that systems using fixed mast, quarter rudders, trapezoid sails, and the dowelling technique (to hold the planks of the hull together) were introduced into Indonesia from the Indian Ocean at an undetermined period (1995: 146), but this also is hypothetical. The use of pegs seems to have been known in

---

[109] The excavations, led by T. Satyamurthy (2004–2005), yielded Black and Red pottery, red pottery, black pottery, bronze figurines, iron tools and weapons, and carnelian beads; some shards bear letters that seem to be in early Brāhmī script. The remains of a fortified town have been discovered in the vicinity of the funerary site.

[110] F. C. Southworth (2005: 82) gives as origin of *nārikela* the Proto-Dravidian **nar(i)*, "fiber," and the Tamil *kēḷi*, "coconut palm."

[111] I. C. Glover (2000: 109) mentions the discovery of high-tin bronze bowls featuring engraved scenes, at Khao Jamook, on Thailand's border with Burma; these bowls are similar to vessels found at Ban Don Ta Phet and Gundla (in this case, a vase) in northwestern India. A bowl from Ban Don Ta Phet with an incised frieze features a procession of cattle, a buffalo, and a horse.

the Pacific, for example on the boats of the Tuamotu Islands (Manguin 1985b: 340) and they may be an independent invention in the Austronesian world.

Tamil and Sanskrit traditions often mention a people called the Nāgas ("snakes"), who were sometimes involved in piracy. These Nāgas may have included Austronesians and Austroasiatics. In the first book of the *Mahābhārata*, the ocean is said to be "the domain of Nāgas," whose country is Ramanīyaka, a name Mahdi links to "country of the Mons" (Ramañña-desa): Ramān or Rmān would be an earlier name for the Mons. The Arabs used the name Rāmnī for the northern part of Sumatra, a region (along with other islands) probably inhabited by Austroasiatic populations in the past (see Blench 2010b). Some Tamil traditions indicate that the Tamil country was once conquered by the Nāgas. According to W. Mahdi, cultural elements that seem to be linked to the Nāgas, such as "buffalo sacrifice, head hunting [?] and megalithism," can be ascribed to Austronesian influences.[112] The parallels seen by Mahdi, however, would require a more refined analysis of the cultural ensembles envisioned. The female deity Kali may "reflect matrilineal traditions widespread among Austronesians. In some areas of South India, stone monuments depict the serpent deity as half-snake, half-woman. The female gender of the divine serpent is a fundamental feature of early Austronesian cosmology" (Mahdi 1999b: 175). Passages from the *Mahābhārata* and the *Mahāvamsa* mention some matrilineal customs of the Nāgas.[113] These people seem to have inhabited Sri Lanka at an early time (the *Mahāvamsa* calls the island or the Jaffna peninsula Nāgadīpa), and Nāga kingdoms may have had a hand in converting the island to Buddhism during the third century BCE.[114] According to legends collected by the Chinese pilgrim Faxian (413–414 CE), "there just were spirits and dragons living here [on Sri Lanka], merchants from various countries carried on trade [with them]" (Mahdi 1999b: 177). On the basis of Tamil texts, J. Hornell has already surmised that the Nāgas reflect an ancient Austronesian presence on the southeastern coast of India. He refers to the legend of a punitive naval expedition by the emperor Ashoka (third century BCE) against Nāga pirates who had looted Indian ships (Hornell 1920: 232). According to the Buddhist text *Bodhisattvāvadāna Kalpalatā* of Kṣemendra, written in the tenth century, it was only following Ashoka's conversion to Buddhism that the Nāgas returned the confiscated goods (Mahdi 1999b: 178). The Tamil text *Manimekhalai* gives the capital of Cāvakam, "country of the Malays," the name of Nāgapuram, "City of the Nāgas," and specifies that the language spoken there is Tamil: thus one may imagine a Tamil *emporium* (possibly with "Tamilized" Austronesians) in the Strait of Malacca region. For the kingdom of Kalinga, a name that seems to be of neither Dravidian nor Indo-Aryan origin, the question of a link with Austroasiatics or Austronesians remains unanswered.

---

[112] Mahdi 1999b: 175. In fact, in India, we have no evidence for the ancient existence of "head hunting" similar to what is known in insular Southeast Asia.

[113] Mahdi 1999b: 175–176, 178. The Sinhalese chronicle *Mahāvamsa* may have been written in Pali by Mahānāma during the sixth century CE (Wheatley 1961: 208–209).

[114] The *Mahāvamsa* (ch. 1) mentions three (mythical) visits by Buddha to Sri Lanka, where he would have met Nāga chiefs, notably a king who inhabited Kelaniya.

The origin of the Malays of the Thai-Malay peninsula and of Orang Melayu Asli groups such as the Temuan and the Jakun lies in Sumatra or west of Kalimantan; movements toward the peninsula are dated to the first millennium BCE. Unfortunately, any links between this Austronesian expansion and (limited) archaeological data are difficult to assess (Bellwood 1997: 287). R. Blust (1988b, 2005) considers that the so-called "Malayo-Chamic" languages were disseminated from a center of origin situated in southwestern Kalimantan around 300 BCE, a spread that may be linked to the transmission and development of iron metallurgy.[115]

Concerning the spice and aromatics trade, it has been pointed out above that various clues signal the transportation of cloves from the Moluccas and of Sumatran camphor by the Javanese and the Malays from the second century BCE onward, a period of growing transregional commerce. It is around this time that the first Indian beads and ceramics were found in insular Southeast Asia (on Bali and on the Talaud Islands) (Bellwood 1997: 300). The Austronesians were also active in the transportation of cinnamon to the West (see above).

With the expansion of Buddhism during the succeeding centuries, pilgrimages to Indian sanctuaries lent new importance to routes between Southeast Asia and India. H. Kulke (1990) and O. W. Wolters (1999 [1982]) have suggested that state developments in India and Southeast Asia involved two-way exchanges of ideas and technologies.

Indian Trade in Southeast Asia

Archaeological data, numismatics, and texts all support evidence for trade between India and the East, and suggest an Indian presence in Southeast Asia prior to the Christian era: a system of exchanges through the Bay of Bengal was in place as early as the middle of the first millennium BCE. Recent research helps us better understand the nature, and even the organization of this commerce. In Southeast Asia, the Indians were seeking gold,[116] spices, camphor, and various types of aromatic wood. They exported beads and other ornaments, and probably cotton fabrics as well; these items that left few traces in the sites excavated. Beyond Southeast Asia, increasing exchanges with China shed light on the Indian as well as the Malayo-Javanese and Funanese expansion.[117]

The rise of trade and the expansion of Buddhism appear to be closely linked (Ray 1994: 121ff.). Buddhism spread through regional and transregional trade networks, and

---

[115] See also K. A. Adelaar 1985: 239, 1995: 84. Bellwood (2005: 271) suggests a date "around 500 BC or later." J. T. Collins (1998) advocates various Malay migrations from western Kalimantan after 100 CE. The name Melayu appears for the first time in Ptolemy, on the west coast of his "Golden Chersonese" (Melayu Kulon, "Western Melayu', in Javanese") (Reid 2001: 297), and later as a kingdom in southeastern Sumatra that sent an embassy to China in 644 (Andaya 2001: 319).

[116] Cf. the names Suvannabhūmi, "the gold country" (Mōn country?), where Ashoka may have sent Buddhist monks, and the "Golden Chersonese" of Ptolemy. For K. R. Hall (1992: 186), gold arrived from Siberia during the Maurya period, but the trade routes were cut off, and the Indians were therefore forced to seek other sources. It is likely that Indian interest in gold from Kalimantan or Sumatra intensified after the Roman emperor Vespasian prohibited the export of gold in 61 CE (Higham 2002: 233).

[117] Contrary to what some authors still write, it was not "the Roman demand for spices and luxury goods" that drove the Indian movement towards Southeast Asia (Thapar 2007: 274).

also thanks to the existence of smaller states located at the nodes of these networks. Routes that had been opened centuries earlier by Austroasiatics and Austronesians on the one hand, and by Indians on the other, certainly had roles to play in the expansion of Buddhism; they offer a new perspective in understanding the "indianization" of Southeast Asia from the beginning of the Christian era.[118]

Trade involved not only the eastern coast of India (and Sri Lanka), but also the Kalinga kingdom (Orissa) and the mouth of the Ganges. The invasion of Kalinga by Ashoka during the third century BCE certainly aimed at controlling its resources as well as its maritime trade. This invasion has sometimes been viewed as triggering an exodus of Brahmins toward Sri Lanka and Southeast Asia: an unlikely scenario. In fact, contacts between Kalinga and Sri Lanka appear to have begun before Buddhism arrived on this island (Vitharana 1999). The significance of Kalinga "is [later] reflected in the name of Kling used by the Malays and the Cambodians to refer to the Hindus."[119] Moreover, "the appellation Talaing, applied to the Mōns by the Burmese, seems to indicate that at a certain epoch Telingāna, or the Madras region, maintained particularly active relations with the Mōn country" (Coedès 1964a: 64).[120] The biggest ports of India's western coast were also connected to Southeast Asia during the first centuries of the Christian era (see below).

Besides Buddhists, Jain and Brahmins maintained active contacts with Southeast Asia and helped transmit cultural values in religious and political domains, spreading the notion of Hindu divine kingship and bringing their knowledge to the art of governing.[121]

For some researchers, exchanges across the Bay of Bengal go back to the beginning of the first millennium BCE.[122] Carnelian beads dated to between 1200 and 800 BCE have been excavated at the site of Nong Nor and – dated to 700–500 BCE – at Nile Kham Haeng, in central Thailand.[123] These dates indicate either the local working of carnelian, or early contacts with India. Another possible clue to early contacts is sorghum, a plant of African origin, which may have spread from India to Southeast Asia between 1000 and 600 BCE.[124] In eastern Timor, in 1966–1967, Glover discovered goat bones – goats may have come from India – dated to the beginning of the first millennium BCE (1996: 377–378).[125]

Some of the oldest dates for contacts between India and Southeast Asia come from Ban Don Ta Phet in Thailand (early fourth century BCE – fourth century CE). This site

---

[118] The magnitude of "indianization" during the 1st millennium CE can partly be explained by this long period of regular, less intense, less visible, contacts, in preceding centuries (Glover 1996: 366; Ray 1999a: 226).

[119] For B. N. Mukherjee (2001), however, for trade with Southeast Asia, the Kalinga only became important from the second century.

[120] This Tamil trade has also been emphasized by J. Filliozat (1975, 1980).

[121] P.-Y. Manguin (2002) has criticized H. P. Ray for underestimating the importance of Vishnuites in the networks that were put in place.

[122] Ray 1999a: 226, who quotes Solheim 1983.

[123] Bellwood 1997: 275, after Higham (1996a). Tombs at Nile Kham Haeng also show iron bracelets (700 BCE). For Glover (2000: 113 n. 17), eastern India could be the source of the introduction of iron metallurgy into this region of Southeast Asia.

[124] Mahdi 1999b: 220, with linguistic arguments.

[125] According to Bellwood (1997: 231), however, these bones should be assigned a more recent dating.

may have controlled the eastern part of the road to the Three Pagodas Pass linking "the Chao Phraya plains and the gulf of Martaban and finally India."[126] Various types of Indian beads have been found at this site: red glass beads,[127] dark blue cubic beads,[128] hexagonal beads,[129] and agate or carnelian beads, sometimes decorated with white lines (etched beads).[130] Ban Don Ta Phet has also yielded a carnelian pendant "carved in the form of a leaping lion," a symbol of Buddha, "lion of the Sakya clan" (*sakyasimha*).[131] Carnelian beads or pendants in the form of a lion have been found at other sites: Tha Chana, Ban U Taphao, Khuan Lukpad, and Khao Sam Kaeo (Thailand). Such items have also been found in Chinese tombs of the Han period (Bellina and Glover 2004: 73). Other feline pendants have been unearthed in Burma. Still other excavations have yielded a Buddha head in the Gandhara style, high-tin bronze bowls decorated with incised scenes of people, houses, horses, and buffaloes, and bronze vessels whose bases feature a conical boss within concentric incised circles (possibly picturing the Meru Mountain), that may be linked to Buddhist rituals.[132] This type of "knobbed-base" vessel, however, was known in India prior to the spread of Buddhism. Similar containers have been discovered at various Indian sites: high-tin bronze vessels at Taxila and in megalithic tombs in the Nilgiri mountains; ceramic vessels along the Ganges valley, in Orissa, western Bengal, Bangladesh, Andhra Pradesh, and Tamil Nadu (Arikamedu); and silver and stone vessels at Taxila (Glover 1996: 388ff.).[133] Others have also been

---

[126] Higham 2004: 59. Rice in pottery has been radiocarbon dated to the fourth century BCE, but B. Bellina has proposed a third–second century BCE dating for the earliest level of the site, based on stylistic comparisons (Bellina and Glover 2004: 84 n. 20).

[127] Red beads in India date to the sixth century BCE at Rajghat, and to the fifth century BCE at Taxila; others were produced at Arikamedu from the fourth to third century BCE. According to Francis, these beads, which the Indonesians would name *mutisalah*, were also manufactured at Mantai and Anurādhāpura as of the first century BCE, as well as in continental and insular Southeast Asia (Bellina and Glover 2004: 74) (see below).

[128] This type of bead has also been found at Taxila around 50 CE. Similar beads are known in Egypt, Mesopotamia, and Persia (Basa 1999: 32).

[129] Manufactured at Arikamedu and in northern India, also found at Ban Chiang, in northeastern Thailand, and at Oc Eo, green glass beads in the form of hexagonal prisms imitate beryl crystals from South India, "which were so popular in the Buddhist cultures of North India as well as the Roman world" (Glover 1996: 381). Arikamedu and its region would later remain a major center for the production of "Indo-Pacific" glass beads until the sixteenth century (Francis 1989).

[130] Known in the Harappan period (see above), this technique "reappeared" in the Ganges valley between 600 BCE and 200 CE. Glover notes that the etched beads found at Ban Don Ta Phet "most closely match those" produced in the provinces of Uttar Pradesh and Bihar (northern India), and at Taxila (Pakistan). These beads would become fashionable again in Muslim communities, particularly between Iran and Sind (Glover 1996: 382–383). On the beads of Ban Don Ta Phet and other sites of Thailand, see Glover and Bellina 2001: 197–202.

[131] Glover 1989: 28; 1996: 374. Bellina (2002) compares these carnelian lions to finds in the Gandhara culture.

[132] Bellina and Glover (2004: 77), however, suggest that the form could originate from Greece, where it was known in the third century BCE. J.-F. Salles refutes the link suggested by Glover (1996) between the expansion of Buddhism and the diffusion of knob-based vessels (2004: 188).

[133] Knobbed-ware pottery is common mainly during the last centuries BCE. Ban Don Ta Phet has also yielded a bronze bowl with a possible depiction of a horse (we know that the Kuṣāna of Bengal and Orissa traded horses in Southeast Asia) (Behera 1999a: 166).

found at Dong Son (northern Vietnam)[134] and at Bon Tai (southern Vietnam). An ivory comb in the Amarāvatī style (first–fourth century) bearing Buddhist symbols[135] has been excavated at Chansen (central Thailand). Further east, the Andhra art of Amarāvatī was present at Oc Eo.[136] Ban Don Ta Phet has also yielded cotton cloth from India (Cameron 2010: 142).

Glass beads (often red, or orange-red) and agate or carnelian stone beads – imported or locally manufactured – have been recovered at other sites in Thailand (at Ban Chiang, dated between 300 BCE and 200 CE, Ban Na Di, Chombeung, Don Khlang, Noen U-Loke, Ban Non Wat, Non Muang Kao, U-Thong, Kok Samrong, Khao Sam Kaeo, Tha Chana, Khuan Lukpad [137]), and also in

– Cambodia (Phum Snay, Prohear, Bit Meas, Lovea);[138]
– Malaysia (Pangkalan Bujang, Kuala Selinsing);
– Vietnam (Giong Ca Vo, Giong Lon, Giong Phet, Go O Chua, Go Mun, Hang Gon, Lai Nghi, Phu Hoa, Sa Huynh, Oc Eo, from the first century CE onward);[139]
– the Philippines (Manunggul Chamber B, dated to 190±100 BCE, and Chamber A,[140] on Palawan Island; at the beginning of the Christian era at the Pintu rockshelter, on Luzon Island; at Nagsabaran, in the Cagayan valley, Luzon; at Magsuhot, on Negros Island, where beads and iron tools found in burial jars have been dated to the beginning of the Christian era);

---

[134] They were found in brick-built tombs of Chinese Han style dated to the first century CE (Bellina and Glover 2004: 75).

[135] This comb is decorated with horses, a *hamsa* goose, and "the vase of inexhaustible abundance." One can also observe a motif called *srīvatsa*, often found in the art of the caves of Orissa, and on later coins from Southeast Asia. The *srīvatsa* is an ancient Indian motif; "emblem of Lakṣmī," it can be seen marked on Vishnu's or Krishna's chest; it is also worn by Shiva, and used by the Jains as an emblem of the tenth jina (Malleret 1959, I: 132–133; Behera 1999a: 166).

[136] See a gold foil showing a female figure playing a bow-shaped harp (Malleret 1959, I: 43).

[137] On this major site, see Glover 1996: 374–375; Glover and Bellina 2001: 199; Dussubieux 2001: 111, 135. Dussubieux has highlighted the presence of beads similar to glass items produced at Arikamedu at Chombeung (southeast of Ban Don Ta Phet) and at Khuan Lukpad. A bead from Khuan Lukpad contains gold in fine particles; it can be compared to a type of bead known in the Roman world (Dussubieux 2001: 184). The assemblage found at Khuan Lukpad spans from the second to the ninth century. A. Srisuchat (1996: 245), however, mentions a first period of settlement dated to between the first century BCE and the second century CE.

[138] Phum Snay, a significant Iron Age settlement located between the Mekong and the Chao Phraya rivers, has revealed carnelian, agate, and gold beads (Higham 2002: 214–215), as well as glass beads. Phum Sophy has yielded many stone beads. Some tombs at Prohear contained glass beads in large numbers. The sites reflect the existence of social hierarchy, and a hierarchy between sites can also be seen (Carter *et al.* 2013).

[139] Sites with burial jars dated between 700 BCE and the first century CE. The beads at the site of Giong Ca Vo are dated to the fourth century BCE according to Bellwood (1997: 294), between the third and second centuries BCE according to Glover and Bellina (2001: 202). Other sites of this region have revealed carnelian or agate etched beads: Go Hang, Go Dung, Go Gon (Nguyen Kim Dung 2001). Giong Ca Vo also yielded glass ear pendants and gold beads. In Funan, only one etched bead has been excavated at Oc Eo. Sites in Funan (Go Hang, Go De) contain decorated beads of a type unknown in South Asia (Glover and Bellina 2001).

[140] Chamber A has yielded a dating going back to the early first millennium BCE. Stone beads in burial jars show links with the mainland.

- Taiwan (Jiuxianglan, Beinan, Huagangshan) (see below);
- southern Sumatra (Pasemah Plateau);
- eastern Sabah (Gua Sireh, Agop Atas Cave, northern Kalimantan);
- northern Kalimantan (Lubang Angin, Sarawak);[141]
- the Buni complex (northwestern Java), at Plawangan, at Lamongan (northern Java),[142] in the region of Gunung Kidul (central Java),[143] at Besuki (eastern Java),
- Sulawesi (Mallawa);
- at Leang Buidane, on Salebabu Island (Talaud Islands, beginning of the first millennium CE);[144]
- on Bali Island.

At Tegurwangi (southern Sumatra), a green hexagonal bi-conical bead, of a type known in India (notably in the south) and Thailand (Ban Don Ta Phet, Khao Sam Kaeo) has been discovered in a stone cist. Beads of similar shape have been found at Ulu Sungai, in southeastern Kalimantan (van Heekeren 1958; Basa 1999: 34). Beads were locally produced at various sites from imported raw materials, notably at Oc Eo, which has yielded the largest number of glass beads in Southeast Asia.[145] I will return to this point.

Glass of the *Syro-Palestinian type* (eighth century BCE – eighth century CE) has been excavated in India (Karaikadu, Arikamedu), Sri Lanka (Ridiyagama, Anuradhapura), and one bead was found at Khuan Lukpad, in southern Thailand (Dubussieux 2001: 202). Angkor Borei, Oc Eo, and Sri Lankan sites have yielded glasses of the *Islamic type* (v-Na-Ca glass) but dating from the first half of the first millennium; they probably represent other imports from western Asia (possibly Persia), but the source remains uncertain.

High-alumina glass (m-Na-Al) is one of the most common types of glass in South and Southeast Asia. For Southeast Asia, two subgroups have been distinguished: a low-uranium–high-barium group (m-Na-Al 1), and a high-uranium–low-barium group (m-Na-Al 3). The m-Na-Al 1 type of glass (*c.* fourth century BCE – fifth century CE) was manufactured in Sri Lanka (Giribawa) and perhaps in India, although neither

---

[141] Glass beads and fragments of iron items have been found together. The datings (C$_{14}$) fall between 700 BCE and 500 CE. See Bellwood 1997: 239.

[142] Sites of the Buni cultural complex have yielded carnelian and gold beads. At Plawangan, glass beads were found with a child buried inside a bronze drum. The Lamongan drum contained remains of a child with carnelian, glass, and gold beads (Bellwood 1997: 292).

[143] Bellwood 1997: 290. Slab graves have yielded glass and carnelian beads, with iron or bronze items, not precisely dated.

[144] Among the discoveries in Palawan and the Talaud Islands (Leang Buidane) are etched agate beads similar to beads of northern India (Orissa, western Bengal, Taxila, and Kaushāmbī) dated to the last centuries BCE or to the first century CE (Bellwood 1997: 295, 300). The sites of Agop Atas and Leang Buidane have yielded pottery decorated in the style termed "Sa Huynh-Kalanay" by Solheim, copper/bronze and iron objects, and Indian beads. Moreover, burial jars at the Uattamdi cave on Kayoa Island (northern Moluccas) contained glass beads, fragments of iron and bronze, and undated Chinese coins. "Dates for this assemblage run from about AD 1 to 1200" (Bellwood 1997: 300).

[145] Beads were also produced – probably from imported raw glass – at Khuan Lukpad, U-Thong, and Khao Sam Kaeo (Thailand), at Kuala Selinsing (Malaysia), and at Muara Jambi (Sumatra) at the beginning of the Christian era (Glover 1996: 375; Bellwood 1997: 277; Bellina and Glover 2004: 74). In addition, Ardika (1999: 87) mentions Pangkalan Bujang (Kedah, Malaysia).

type was common at Arikamedu (Brill 1999; Dubussieux 2001; Dussubieux and Gratuze 2010: 250). The type known as m-Na-Al 3 glass is unknown in South India and Sri Lanka, but has been found "in large quantities at Khao Sam Kaeo, but also at other sites located in Thailand, Cambodia and South Vietnam" (Dussubieux and Gratuze 2010: 250).[146] Dated to a period prior to the seventh century, mineral soda-alumina glass is found in all regions of Southeast Asia: at Ban Don Ta Phet, Ban Wang Hai, Chombeung, Takuapa, Khuan Lukpad (Thailand), Kuala Selinsing (sixth–tenth century) (Malaysia), Oc Eo (Vietnam) (Oc Eo probably manufactured glass of this type), Giong Ca Vo (fourth–second century BCE), Tra Kieu (middle of the first millennium, in Vietnam), Air Sugihan (Sumatra) (fifth–sixth century), Gilimanuk (Bali), Ulu Leang (dated between 200 BCE and 200 CE) (Sulawesi) (Dubussieux 2001: 203–208).[147] The m-Na-Al 1 type of glass "dominates the glass assemblages from all the sites studied" for the post-fifth-century period (Dussubieux and Gratuze 2010: 255).

Another category of glass found in Southeast Asia is glass "with higher lime concentrations" and "soda derived from plant ashes or mineral deposits" (Na-Ca-Al) (Dussubieux and Gratuze 2010: 249). It accounts for 30 percent of South Indian glass, with most samples found at Arikamedu. This m-Na-Ca-Al glass appears similar to Syro-Palestinian glass, but has higher uranium concentrations. In Southeast Asia, "half of the samples come from the site of Phu Kao Thong, on the western coast of the Thai-Malay peninsula" (Dussubieux and Gratuze 2010: 254). This type of glass has also been found in Sri Lanka (Anurādhāpura, Ridiyagama), in southern Thailand (Khuan Lukpad), Cambodia (Angkor Borei), Vietnam (Dong Son [Than Hoa]), and Indonesia (Ulu Leang) (Dubussieux 2001: 215–216). A few red beads from Ban Don Ta Phet may correspond to this type from Arikamedu. Black beads similar to beads from Arikamedu have been found at Chombeung and Khuan Lukpad. "Some green, red and black glass samples have a distinctive composition (called Arika composition)"; this glass is known from Arikamedu, Alagankulam (South India), and Kelaniya (Sri Lanka, third century BCE – second century CE).

Dussubieux has also pointed out the existence in Southeast Asia of "an alumina glass with a mixed alkali composition," represented by disc-shaped red glass beads, and smaller annular orange glass beads." Known in Sri Lanka (Kelaniya, third century BCE – second century CE, Ridiyagama, fourth–first century BCE) and India (Alagankulam, third century BCE – third century CE, Kodumanal, third century BCE – third century CE, Karakaidu, first century CE, ...), this type of glass has been found at Chombeung (Thailand) and Giong Ca Vo (southern Vietnam).

Interestingly, recent research shows that the red beads excavated in Southeast Asia are usually made of alumina glass. This type of glass is rare at Arikamedu, whose red beads are made from a type of Na-Ca-Al glass to which an ingredient containing magnesia and potash was added in order to lower the melting point of the glass. "These finds undermine the assumption of a spread of Arikamedu red beads (the *mutisalahs*) throughout Southeast Asia" (Dubussieux 2001: 211). (Bellina [2003–2004: 381] has also

---

[146] This glass type disappears during the period second century BCE – fifth century CE, "except for the site of Chombeung."

[147] For the 204 samples studied by the author for Southeast Asia, mineral soda–alumina glass represents over 50 percent for all regions, with a peak of 84 percent for Malaysia.

criticized P. Francis's tendency to overestimate the importance of Arikamedu in exports toward Southeast Asia). Red beads made of soda–alumina glass may have come from other sites in South India (such as Karakaidu, Alagankulam, Kodumanal), Sri Lanka (where half of the glass is of the soda–alumina type), or northern India.

Whereas these discoveries suggest links with India or Sri Lanka, as well as the probable presence of Indian communities, for example at Khuan Lukpad, the high lead content of glass beads found at Angkor Borei (Cambodia) and Hitam Cave (western Kalimantan) indicates a likely Chinese origin.[148] Discoveries of objects from China are relatively few in Southeast Asia (see Map II.12, and below). Exchanges were probably just as intense as those with the Indian Ocean, however. We must keep in mind that silks exported by China, for example, usually leave no traces in archaeological layers. Moreover, as noted above, aromatics give some clues to ancient contacts: Chinese cinnamon may have arrived in the Persian Gulf as early as the seventh century BCE, and cloves reached China during the second century BCE, as well as areca nut (the Chinese *bīnlang*, which reflects the Malay *pinang*, is attested in 110 BCE) (Blench 2006).

Potash glass, found at the earliest sites in Vietnam (Dong Son, Giong Ca Vo) and Thailand (Ban Wang Hai), is another type of glass that may have been imported from China. Widely distributed in China, it was also known in Korea and Japan, and has been found in Central Asia. Beads made of potash glass have been excavated at Ulu Leang (Sulawesi) and Gilimanuk (Bali). However, potash glass is also abundant in South India (44 percent at Arikamedu, 15 percent of the glass reported in South Asia), and it is present in northern India and in Sri Lanka.[149] This type of glass seems to be absent from Oc Eo and Angkor Borei. Angkor Borei has yielded only m-Na-Al 1 glass, from Sri Lanka and South India. While Glover and Henderson have argued that production of potash glass in China resulted from an Indian influence, Chinese researchers have put forth an opposite hypothesis. In sum, the provenance of Southeast Asia's potash glass remains uncertain.[150] Four subgroups of potash glass (with varying lime and alumina concentrations) have recently been identified; all are present in Southeast Asia (Dussubieux and Gratuze 2010: 252). Research into strontium isotopes shows that "potash glass may have been manufactured in at least three locations" (Dussubieux and Gratuze 2010: 252). These types of glass seem to vanish as of the third century CE.

[148] These glass beads have been excavated in a cemetery of Angkor Borei (Vat Komnou, 200 BCE – 200 BCE) (Dussubieux 2001: 136–137, 202–203).

[149] Thus potash glass has been found at Ter, Nevasa, Udaigiri, Kaushāmbī, and Hastinapur (Dussubieux 2001: 212).

[150] For an Indian origin, see Glover and Henderson 1995. For a Chinese origin of the potash glass, see Shi Meiguang *et al.* 1987; Brill *et al.* 1992: 86; Fukang 1992: 161–162 (with uncertainty, however, for the red potash glass) (Brill argues that the saltpeter used is the source of the potash found in this type of glass). See Dussubieux 2001: 212–215. The cobalt that some types of glass contain could provide a clue to their possible origins. However, a deposit of asbolane (a mineral containing both cobalt and manganese) located between the Krishnā and Godāvarī Rivers may have supplied Arikamedu. In China, deposits of asbolane have been reported in Yunnan, Zhejiang, and Jiangxi (Dussubieux 2001: 176). Gratuze and Dussubieux (2005) suggest "a Southeast Asian origin," *sensu largo*, for these types of glass. Khao Sam Kaeo, in fact, has yielded two types of potash glass (see below).

Although etched beads (often agate beads) were also manufactured in Burma, Thailand, and perhaps Vietnam, those that have been excavated are usually imports from India.[151] For B. Bellina, the older stone beads, of higher quality, are imports or locally crafted by Indian artisans. For the Sa Huynh culture and the Philippines, the beads' diameter of perforation is identical to that of the South Indian beads.

The discoveries of Indian beads coincide with the distribution of other prestige goods (Dong Son drums, bronze bowls) and the presence of a thriving industry of iron metallurgy (see below). The fact that "common status markers were used as a means of legitimization by different Southeast Asian trading communities ... may account for the cultural similarities these communities have shared during more recent historical periods" (Bellina 2003: 292).

Textiles – and plants connected to their production – were certainly exported by the Indians early on. Remains of cotton fibers have been identified at Ban Don Ta Phet (Cameron 2010: 142). For J. Wisseman Christie, cotton (Javanese *kapas*, from the Sanskrit *karpāsa*) was transmitted to Java around the middle of the first millennium BCE. The earliest remnants of cotton cloth in Indonesia come from the site at Pontanoa Banka (South Sulawesi), where they have been dated to 500 CE (Cameron 2010: 142). Indigo *Indigofera tinctorius* L. (Old Javanese *nīla*, *nula*, from the Sanskrit *nīla*) may have been introduced during the first centuries of the Christian era.[152] Moreover, pepper was traded prior to the Christian era. As mentioned above, the form *amrec* can be reconstructed in Proto-Chamic (from the Sanskrit *marīca*; Headley 1976). The importation of Indian pepper stimulated the export of the Javanese long pepper (*Piper retrofractum*) during the early centuries CE. The Malay term for pepper, *cabai*, comes from Old Indo-Aryan *cavi*, *cavya* (the Old Javanese has *cabya* for "a kind of pepper"; the name for the Javanese long pepper is *cabe* in Semang, *sabiya* in Tagalog (Hoogervoorst 2012: 183).[153]

The development of exchanges between India and Southeast Asia also led to the introduction of *indica* rice and new hybridizations. Yet the site at Khao Sam Keao has yielded tropical *japonica* rice, but no *indica* (Fuller *et al.* 2010: 126–127).

The presence of objects of Indian origin does not necessarily mean that Indians lived in all the places where discoveries have been made. It seems, however, that Indian communities were present in various centers. Research shows that during the early periods the Indian – and then Southeast Asian – centers were already adapting their

---

[151] They are related both to northern and southern groups of South Asian beads (Glover and Bellina 2001: 192, 209 n. 13). On the techniques used, see Glover and Bellina 2001: 191 n. 2. On the basis of chemical analysis, Theunissen *et al.* (2000) consider, however, that carnelian or agate beads from Noen U-Loke may have been produced locally, using a source located in Central Thailand, but there is no evidence for the manufacture of this type of bead in Southeast Asia prior to the Iron Age (Bellina and Glover 2004: 73). Theunissen *et al.* note that stone beads from Ban Don Ta Phet that have been analyzed appear to be similar to material from Anurādhāpura: Sri Lanka may have exported stones to Thailand (Bellina and Glover 2004: 100). The importation of exotic stones may have initiated local manufacture, sometimes of lower quality (Bellina and Glover 2004: 101).

[152] Wisseman Christie 1999: 239. For J. G. de Casparis (1988: 60), the Javanese *kapas* does not come directly from the Sanskrit, but from a "Proto-Neo-Indian" term.

[153] In Minangkabau, *cambai* means "betel" (*Piper betle*); the Malay *cabai* is at the origin of the Malagasy *sakay*, "ginger, chilli."

exports to demand, conforming their production of beads to the tastes of local elites. In Southeast Asia, beads were probably made by Indian craftsmen who worked under the protection of local rulers.[154] Production must also have been exported to other centers; the beads of Khao Sam Kaeo, Giong Ca Vo, and Tabon are quite similar (they show potash glass containing calcium and aluminum that is known from India to southern China).[155] "During the more recent period corresponding to the middle of the first millennium of the Christian era [a time which also saw the building of religious monuments influenced by India and social transformations], local production, after adapting Indian techniques or models, took precedence over Indian production and reveals an intensification of trade" (Bellina 2005: 77). Later we observe mass production of lower quality, which must have been used by the elites of the city-states for trade with the non-indianized populations of either the interior or certain islands. "Conversely, the elites of the city-states kept on purchasing high quality Indian beads for themselves"; these beads were imported or locally produced (Bellina 2005: 77; 2003: 291, 293–294).

Items such as etched stone beads (see above) that differ from beads produced for India, and carnelian seals bearing inscriptions in the Brāhmī script of northern India both indicate the probable involvement of Indian artisans. These beads and seals have been found at Khuan Lukpad,[156] Khao Sam Kaeo,[157] Kuala Selinsing[158] (Perak, West coast of the Thai–Malay peninsula), Chaiya (East coast of the Thai-Malay peninsula), Oc Eo, and in Kharoṣṭī or mixed Kharoṣṭī-Brāhmī script, discovered at U-Thong and Oc Eo. At Oc Eo, inscriptions in Brāhmī script on carnelian seals and gold objects have been dated to the third–fourth century CE.[159] A tin seal matrix, probably manufactured locally, shows a mixture of Kharoṣṭī and Brāhmī letters that can be dated to the third century CE.

The arrival of Kushan merchants in Bengal and Orissa at the close of the first century has been mentioned above. The inscriptions in Kharoṣṭī or Kharoṣṭī-Brāhmī scripts

---

[154] Bellina (2002, 2005) demonstrates this process for the site of Khao Sam Kaeo. B. Bellina is correct in noting that this presence, in itself, must have been a symbol of power for these elites.

[155] So the origin of these beads is not clear.

[156] A touchstone bearing the inscription *perum pathan kal*, "the stone of the great goldsmith," is dated to the third century (Karashima 1995; Rajan 2002: 89). Khuan Lukpad has yielded a seal showing a Brāhmī script dated to between the first and third centuries CE.

[157] Bellina 2002: 335; Bellina-Pryce and Silapanth 2008. Several seals may go back to the turn of the Christian era. A gold seal whose four faces feature a lion, a bull, a star with six branches within a circle, and a Sanskrit inscription, is dated to the fourth–fifth or the sixth–seventh century.

[158] Kuala Selinsing was an estuarine pile village; see Bellwood 1997: 286. The sites of Kuala Selinsing were occupied from 200 BCE to 1000 CE. Pottery from western Asia has been found for a period 600–1000 CE.

[159] Basa 1999: 42, 50. On the Sanskrit inscriptions at Oc Eo, see Malleret 1963, IV: 311. These inscriptions are not only related to trade: they are also found on amulets (for example, on tin rectangles). Moreover, agate cameos recall amulets worn in India (Malleret 1962, III: 302). Carnelian intaglii show feminine figures reminiscent of India, as well as two women drawn with a stylus on gold sheets. See also a glass intaglio featuring a zebu bearing a disc between its horns, a motif known on Andhra coins (Malleret 1963, IV: 363, 371–372). Many objects at Oc Eo recall the Middle and Upper Ganges basin, for example, glyptic art. It is likely that not all of these pieces were imported, because a glyptic industry existed at Oc Eo. Malleret mentions decorative motifs such as six- or eight-lobed flowers on a tin plaque at Oc Eo, motifs known at Taxila on copper or bronze objects (Malleret 1963, IV: 376). Hindu symbols such as the conch, the trident, the *vajra*, the elephant goad (*ankusha*), the bull Nandi, the drum of the ascetics, the sacred vase *kumbha*, a vase with flowers, or an overflowing vase, can be observed on various objects excavated at Oc Eo.

found in Thailand, Cambodia – see above – and as far as Bali, as well as various objects (at Oc Eo, for example, engraved jewels showing figures with Iranian headdresses)[160] provide evidence for the presence of Kushan communities in Southeast Asia, who remained in contact with their ports of origin.

On the Vietnamese coast, Indian inscriptions at Vo Canh (Nha Trang) are dated to the third century CE; they have been compared to inscriptions from Andhra Pradesh for the same period.[161]

The Indians transmitted objects from the Roman world, but a – limited – presence of merchants arriving from Egypt or the Levant cannot be excluded and McLaughlin argues that "during the mid-2nd century, Roman ships began sailing around the Malay Peninsula to reach markets in Thailand" (2014: 206). A Roman medallion with an inscription of Antoninus Augustus Pius dated to 152 CE has been unearthed at Oc Eo,[162] as has a coin of Marcus Aurelius (161–181 CE). A copper coin of Victorinus (268–270 CE) has been found at U-Thong (western Thailand).[163] A figurine of Poseidon of a "Lysippan" type discovered at Tra-Vinh (Vietnam) is comparable to another statuette unearthed at Kolhapur, in India.[164] Two Roman carnelian intaglii, dated to the end of the first or beginning of the second century CE, have been excavated at Khuan Lukpad, as well as blue glass similar to "Roman" glass.[165]

Ceramics also shed light on long-distance exchanges. Fragments of "Attic vases" have been excavated at Bukit Tengku Lembu (state of Perlis, Malay peninsula).[166] Various sites in Southeast Asia have yielded *kendi* vessels linked to Hindu and Buddhist rituals, molded ceramics, and Rouletted Ware. Known from Sri Lanka to Bangladesh, Rouletted Ware is a good marker of Indian influence and presence in

[160] Mukherjee 1999: 201; Malleret 1963, IV: 363–364 (on rock crystal or carnelian intaglii). Kushan influences in Funan certainly came from eastern India, but western influences via Sri Lanka cannot be excluded. Mukherjee (2001: 207) also relates the name Thagora – given by Ptolemy to a port located on the Gulf of Thailand – to the name of the original language of the Kushans, Tocharian, but this hypothesis is uncertain. Mukherjee argues that Kushan merchants settled in Southeast Asia may have traded horses as far as China.

[161] De Casparis 1979: 382. Pollock (1996), however, suggests a dating in the fifth century or even later.

[162] Malleret 1962, III: 115. Malleret has suggested a link between composite figures called "grylles," found on intaglii at Oc Eo, and gnostic currents active in Iran, at Alexandria, in Rome, and in Babylonia. This motif can be observed on objects from Begram (Afghanistan) (1962, III: 281–285). According to Malleret, too, gold eye beads and granulated beads found at Oc Eo may indicate Mediterranean influences – via India (1959, I: 33; 1962, III: 388–389).

[163] In addition, P. Paris may have seen a coin from Antoninus at Quang Ngai. A silver drachm featuring Alexander has been discovered at Phnom Penh. Other ancient coins have been found in northern Vietnam, west of Hanoi: one sesterce in the name of Antoninus, a coin from Constantine dated to the fourth century, and a Byzantine coin from the fifth century (Malleret 1962, III: 383).

[164] Moreover, a bronze of Maximinus (third century CE) has been discovered near My Tho (Malleret 1962, III: 380). Note also the discovery of a bronze lamp at Pong Tuk, that does not date to the second century CE as previously thought, but is in fact a Byzantine lamp from the fifth or sixth century CE (or even seventh/eighth century). Ceramic lamps of similar shape have been unearthed at Tha Kae, U-Thong, and Ku Bua (Basa 1999: 42, who quotes Brown and MacDonnell 1989).

[165] Glover 1996: 374–375. Khuan Lukpad has also yielded a worn Roman coin, and a Pallava coin. See Bellwood 1997: 277; Indrawooth 2004: 125. On the Roman glass at Khuan Lukpad, see Dussubieux 2001: 180, 184, 202.

[166] Coedès (1964a: 42 n. 4) placed them in the fourth or fifth century BCE. Glover speaks of black "Greek" or "Indo-Roman" pottery, but this material "lacks a good context" (1996: 376).

Southeast Asia.[167] It has been unearthed at Bukit Seguntang (Palembang, Sumatra); Kobak Kendal, Cibutek and Cibango (Buni); Batujaya (20 km east of Buni, Java); at Pacung and Sembiran (Bali); and at Sa Huynh and Tra Kieu (Vietnam).[168] Textiles made using asbestos – imported from the Roman world – have also been found at Batujaya dated to the late first millennium BCE/early first millennium CE (Cameron *et al.*, 2015: 162).[169] According to Ardika, the first and second centuries CE are likely datings for the Indian pottery of Sembiran, but curiously, an accelerator mass spectrometry measurement done on rice husks found in a shard has yielded an approximate dating of the eighth century BCE. Sembiran contained glass beads that chemical analysis has shown to be very similar to beads from Arikamedu,[170] shards of pottery from Arikamedu,[170] and a shard with a black slip bearing a line of Kharoṣṭī characters. Gilimanuk (Bali) has also yielded glass and semiprecious stone beads, and many iron, copper, and bronze ornaments.[171] At this site, gold leaf covered the eyes of a skull, a practice found at Rengasdengklok (Buni, western Java), on Panay Island (Philippines), at Santubong (Sarawak) and in the megalithic tombs of Adichanallur, on the Tamil coast.[172]

For the Indonesian area, early Buddhist influences are visible. However, bronze Buddhas found in Sulawesi (at Sikendeng), Sumatra (west of Palembang), and Java previously thought to be connected to the Amarāvatī tradition (Andhra, between the second and fifth centuries CE)[173] have now been dated to the seventh–eighth century (Manguin 2010: 173).

[167] Moreover, paddle-impressed ware known in South India and Sri Lanka shares some features with pottery excavated in the Buni complex (Java) and on Bali (Sembiran, Gilimanuk). Solheim (1990), however, thought that this pottery originated in South China (Bellwood 1997: 295). Curiously, Bali is only mentioned in a late Indian text, the *Manyunnulakalpa* (*c.* 800 CE).

[168] An Indian gold seal (perhaps showing a Hellenistic influence) has also been discovered in the region of Pekalongan (northern coast of Central Java); it has stylistic affinities with pieces from Khuan Lukpad and Oc Eo (Manguin 2004d: 289). The site of Oc Eo has not yielded a single shard of Rouletted Ware. But the excavations conducted since 1997 led to the discovery of a type of black burnished Indian pottery, also attested at Karang Agung (Sumatra) and Batujaya (Java), as well as pottery of *kendi* shape influenced by India. In addition, clay roof tiles which must have covered the roofs of some houses were produced using a technique that is probably of Indian origin (Manguin 2004d: 292).

[169] "Chinese sources of the mid-first millennium CE also repeatedly state that asbestos came to Funan," and asbestos has been found at the Noen U-Loke site (upper Mun Valley) dated to the early first millennium CE (Cameron *et al.* 2015: 170).

[170] Notably a stamped ceramic (Arikamedu type 10). Its decoration has been said to be a Roman import, but "an ancestral link has been demonstrated between Grey Ware, Rouletted Ware, and Arikamedu Type 10 (Ford 2005)" (http://community.dur.ac.uk/, "The Arikamedu Type 10 Project"). Ardika 1999: 81–87. Moreover, Burma and Central Thailand (Chansen) show another stamped ceramic that seems to reflect "the adoption and adaptation" of Indian pottery (see above) (Bellina 1999: 167–168).

[171] Glass beads were locally produced, probably from imported raw glass. Some beads are made of soda-alumina glass of Indian type; others are made of potash glass of undetermined origin (Glover and Henderson 1995; Dussubieux 2001). Carnelian or agate beads (of Indian origin, or produced in Southeast Asia) have been found at various sites on Bali (Sembiran, Gilimanuk, Nongan) and at Plawangan (Java).

[172] Ray 1989: 51; Bellwood 1997: 292, 294; Ardika 1999: 88. Similar gold eye and mouth covers have also been discovered at Pangkungliplip (West Bali), at a site with sarcophagi.

[173] Coedès 1964a: 24, 43, 106–107; Pelras 1996: 25. The capital of the Andhra kingdom, the city of Amarāvatī was a major Buddhist center.

Discoveries of objects linked to India reflect exchanges with the whole Southeast Asian area (Bellina and Glover 2004: 80–82); however, Manguin (p.c.) notes that the total number of shards of Indian origin in Southeast Asia does not exceed 2,700. These finds sketch out different sets of maritime routes that would later prove to be the routes followed by other foreign traders such as Persians, Arabs, and Chinese (see Map II.11). From the Indian Ocean to the China Sea, a route ran along the Vietnamese coast and onward to Chinese ports. Another route followed the western Kalimantan coastline, Sabah, entered the Sulawesi Sea and continued as far as the Moluccas.[174] It is unlikely that Indians were present along this northern route; no Indian pottery has ever been found in the Sulawesi Sea, unlike what can be observed further south: Rouletted Ware and beads of an Indian type reveal the existence of a route along southern Sumatra, the northern Javanese coast and Bali; this route led to the Moluccas, the source of cloves and nutmeg, and to lands further east (see below), perhaps as early as the second century BCE. This commerce grew between the first and fifth centuries (Glover 1996: 138; Bellwood 1997: 275, 295ff.). Besides spices, Indian traders probably sought metals (tin from the Malay peninsula, gold from Sumatra and Kalimantan). Tin ingots have been unearthed at Abhayagiri, in Sri Lanka (Rajan 2002: 90).

Indian or Greco-Roman literature also informs us about links between India and the West on the one hand, and India and the Orient, on the other. Various toponyms in Indian texts refer to Southeast Asian lands. In the centuries before the Christian era, Indian texts confirm connections between India and Southeast Asia. The *Rāmāyana* of Vālmikī mentions Yavadvīpa (the "island of barley" or the "island of millet,"[175] the "Iabadiou" of Ptolemy), where seven kingdoms lay, rich in gold and silver mines, and Suvarnadvīpa, ("the golden island"), a name that more likely refers to Sumatra than to Java (Mahdi 2008). Wicks has made a connection between the Indian toponyms evoking a "golden land or island" and the importance of this metal in societies of insular Southeast Asia.[176] In a passage from Book 4 of the *Rāmāyana*, King Sugriva gathers his vassals; among them is a people who "on the milky sea's beach, and in *tamāla* woods live, and of coconuts eat, their number is countless."[177] The *Rāmāyana* does not name this people, but includes it among the Vanara, "monkeys" who form the bulk of King Sugriva's army.

The *Arthasāstra* mentions Suvarnabhūmi (in Pali Suvannabhūmi) as a place where aromatic aloeswood (Skt. *agāru*, cf. Malay *garu*) could be found (on the *Arthasāstra*, see Wheatley 1961: 206). The Buddhist texts of the *Jātakaṭṭavannanā*, part of which may go back to the final centuries before the Christian era, mention relations between Indian ports – including Bharukacha – and Suvannabhūmi, "the land of gold," which must

---

[174] Discoveries of carnelian beads also shed light on inland routes, leading to Yunnan, where carnelian beads similar to those of Ban Don Ta Phet and to beads of northern India have been excavated at Shizhaishan and at Lijiashan, during the Western Han period (Glover and Bellina 2001: 202).

[175] Millet was probably a major food crop; its importance diminished when wet rice culture developed; rice production was better suited to feeding the artisans, officials, and merchants of the flourishing towns.

[176] Wicks 1992: 304. Sumatra has yielded gold coins dating to the ninth century. Conversely, the first coins found in Java (eighth century) are in silver (Wicks 1992: 233–234, 248).

[177] Mahdi 1999b: 168–169. According to Mahdi (1999b), the name *tamāla* could refer to a tree from insular Southeast Asia, *Aegle marmelos* Correa (Rutaceae), but this tree is also present in India. In addition, R. L. Turner (1962–1966: no. 5690) gives Sanskrit *tāmala*-: "dark-barked tree, *Xanthochymus pictorius*" (cf. Skt. *tamāla*-, "dark").

correspond to the Chrysē in the *Periplus of the Erythraean Sea*.[178] One of the texts in the *Jātaka* notes that the journeys of Indian ships from Bharukacha to Suvannabhūmi "responded" to visits of merchants from these countries (Wheatley 1961: 184).[179] Suvannabhūmi is mentioned in other Buddhist texts in Pali, such as the *Milinda-pañha* ("Questions of Milinda [King Menander]"), written during the fourth century CE (a translation into Pali of a Sanskrit or Prākrit text from northern India dating back to the beginning of the Christian era), or the *Mahāniddesa*, part of the Pali Buddhist canon dating to the second or third century CE.[180] The *Mahāniddesa* describes a maritime journey to "Takkola, Java, Tamali, and Suvannabhūmi." The *Paramatta-Dipani*, written by Dharmapāla around the fifth century CE, gives the city of Pātaliputra as an *emporium* preeminent in the trade with Suvannabhūmi. The Pali literature of Sri Lanka also refers to Suvannabhūmi. The Sinhalese chronicle of the *Mahāvamsa* (sixth century CE) mentions Ashoka sending the missionaries Sona and Uttara to Suvannabhūmi.[181] Unfortunately, none of these texts gives us a description of this "land of gold," which has been associated with Burma (Mount Kelasa), Thailand, the Malay peninsula, and Sumatra.

The name Takola mentioned in the *Mahāniddesa* finds an echo in Ptolemy's *Geography*: Takola is the first name used for the Golden Chersonese. This port must have been situated along the west coast of the Malay peninsula, but scholars disagree on its precise location (perhaps Takuapa, north of Phuket). According to Wheatley, the name is probably linked to a local term designating white cardamom (*takur*).[182] Takola may correspond to the Geguluo (Ko-ku-lo) or to the Touzhuli (Zhuli) of Chinese texts.[183] Tamali has been linked to Tāmbralinga, a port and state on the east coast of the Thai–Malay peninsula, perhaps located south of Samui Island, at the latitude of Takola (Wheatley 1961: 271; Coedès 1964a: 79). The *Mahāniddesa* also mentions Tambalingam, which is the transcription for Tāmbralinga. A road here allowed travelers to cross the peninsula.

[178] Mahdi 1999b: 215; Basa 1999: 45. The *Sankha Jātaka* thus reports the journey of the Brahmin Sankha from Vārānasī to Suvannabhūmi. The *Jātakamala*, a Sanskrit version of the *Jātaka* tales, composed by Arya Sura during the third or fourth century CE, mentions Surparakara (on the northwestern coast of the Deccan) as a port where ships bound for Suvarnabhūmi stopped. The *Baveru Jātaka* (Book XXI) evokes a prince who decides to carry on trade and puts merchandise and merchants on board a ship bound for Suvarnabhūmi (Ray 2003: 195). The *Jātaka* represent a collection of Indian Buddhist tales, written in Pali, recounting episodes concerning the previous births of the Buddha. The oldest of these tales go back to the third century BCE.

[179] The *Jātaka* (Books I, X, XI, XVI) "describe a variety of social groups who were involved in seafaring activity" (Ray 2001: 408).

[180] Basa (1999: 54) dates it to the third century BCE, a dating that seems too early. The *Mahāniddesa* mentions twenty-four places, among them Vanga, Javadvīpa, and Suvannabhūmi. The name Vanga refers to Bengal and not to the island of Bangka situated near the southeastern Sumatran coast, contrary to what has sometimes been curiously argued (Coedès 1964a: 107).

[181] Wheatley 1961: 181; Coedès 1964a: 40. Coedès notes that Suvannabhūmi has been "generally identified, rightly or wrongly, with the ancient land of the Mon, and especially with the town of Thatön" (1968: 17).

[182] Wheatley 1961: 271. It may also be related to the Arabic *qāqullah*, "cardamom," pehlevi *kākura*. On Tak(k)ola, see also Coedès 1964a: 80.

[183] Two different interpretations have been proposed; see below. For the first name, see the *Xintangshu* (Wheatley 1961: 270–271); for the second, see the *Liangshu*, which repeats a testimony from Kang Tai giving the itinerary of Funanese envoys to Tianzhu (Bengal) (Mukherjee 2001: 205).

The *Raghuvamsa*, written by Kālidāsa around the fourth century CE, mentions, in connection with the Kalinga coast, winds that bring the fragrance of clove tree flowers (*lavanga*) from Dvīpāntara. Here the name seems to designate the entire Insulindian archipelago.[184] In a Sanskrit–Chinese lexicon of the seventh or eighth century CE, Dvīpāntara is given as a synonym for the Chinese *Kunlun*, a term referring to Southeast Asian populations, and more precisely to Austronesians.

Puranic texts provide other names, such as Kaserudvīpa, Malayadvīpa, Kaṭāha ("the seat of all felicities," according to the later text of the *Kathāsaritsāgara*).[185] Kaṭāha is surely related to Kedah (the Jiecha of Chinese chronicles), on the Malay peninsula. Other texts also mention Karpūradvīpa, "the island of camphor"; this may be western Kalimantan (Wheatley 1961: 285).

The Tamil poem *Paṭṭinappālai*, composed during the second or third century CE, speaks of a flourishing trade between South India (Kāveripattinam) and Kāḷagam, which can be linked to the Kalāh of the Arab geographers, a major port from the eighth to the tenth century that was already known during the fourth century (Geluo [Ko-lo], in Chinese chronicles [Wheatley 1961: 55ff.]). Kāḷagam was located either on the isthmus of Kra, or north of Kedah on the Malay peninsula, or perhaps at Kelang, not far from Kuala Lumpur. The *Silappadikāram* mentions "aloes, silks, sandal, spices and camphor, put by the residents of Tondi [east coast of the Thai–Malay peninsula?] on board a fleet of tall roomy ships." The same text signals silk coming from Kāḷagam (Wheatley 1961: 182, 279).

Buddhist literature notes that various communities were involved in overseas trade, and that merchants, religious men, and princes engaged in these long-distance journeys.[186]

In western literature, one of the first references to Southeast Asia lies in Pomponius Mela (43 CE): *De Chorographia* mentions Chrysē, "the land of gold," and Argyre, "the land of silver," corresponding to two areas (probably insular and continental Southeast Asia) where gold and silver respectively were the metals fundamentally used in transactions.[187] While the *Periplus of the Erythraean Sea* (see above) sheds light on relations between South India and Southeast Asia during the first century CE, it does not give the name of any port in Southeast Asia. According to Ptolemy, ships sailing to the Golden Chersonese left from the port of Alosygni (probably at the mouth of the Godāvarī River) and from Palura (Lake Chilka).[188] At that time, other ports were

---

[184] Wolters 1967: 66. The poem *Raghuvamsa* is based on the *Rāmāyana* and some *Purānas* (Wheatley 1961: 207).

[185] On Kaṭāha, see Wheatley 1961: 279–280. The *Kathāsaritsāgara* contains tales and stories put together by Somadeva in 1040 CE "for the amusement of Sūryavati, wife of King Ananta of Kashmir" (Wheatley 1961: 205). "It may be regarded as a Kashmiri recension of the *Brhtatkathā*," an older book in Prākrit.

[186] Ray 1999b: 9. The author quotes the *Jātaka*, I, 4, X, 439, 442, XI, 463, XVI, 528, XXI, 539.

[187] Wicks 1992: 303, 306. The "island of silver," Argyre, may correspond to the Arakan and the Lower Irrawaddy, with the metal coming from Yunnan and Upper-Burma (see Salles 2004: 215 n. 62).

[188] Excavations at Manikpatna – possibly the "Palura" of Ptolemy – led to the recovery of a shard dated to the second century bearing an inscription in the Kharoṣṭī script related to the Kushans (Mukherjee 2001: 212). The site has also yielded Rouletted Ware, fragments of amphorae, and a type of white-glazed pottery (called "eggshell ware") reflecting links with Arabia (Nabataeans). This pottery is dated to a period running from the sixth to the seventh century at Ras Hafun, on the Somali coast (see below).

actively trading with Southeast Asia: Tāmralipti, at the mouth of the Ganges; Supatana (Sōpatma in the *Periplus*, Madras); Arikamedu (Podukē in the *Periplus*, Pondicherry); Kāveripattinam (the Kamara of the *Periplus*; and the Khaberis of Ptolemy); and on the west coast of India Bharukacha (Greek Barygaza), Shurpāraka (Suppara/Sopara), Pattanam (Muchiri, Greek Muziris), and so forth.

From Palura, ships sailed to Sada (Ptolemy, *Geog.* I.13) on the Burmese coast (Sandoway), and then reached Temala, near Cape Negrais. On the Golden Chersonese, the *Geography* mentions successively "the *emporium* of Takola, the promontory situated beyond this town, the estuary of the Khrysoanas River, the *emporium* of Sabara, the estuary of the Palandas River, Cape Maleoukolon, the estuary of the Attabas river, the town of Kole, Perimula, and the Perimulikos gulf."[189] It then lists cities in the hinterland: "Kalonka, Konkonagara, Tharra, and Palanda." These names must refer to rivers and towns on the Malay peninsula. Takola has already been mentioned (see above). Sabara (Sabana) lay in the southern part of the peninsula, and Kole possibly on the northeast coast. The other locations are highly speculative.[190] Ptolemy still mentions Zaba, a twenty-day sail from Temala, perhaps in the Gulf of Thailand. The last known Asian port was Kattigara, which Ptolemy situates on what he considers to be the eastern coast of the Indian Ocean, facing Rhapta; for him, the Chinese coast bent toward the south, and finally joined the continuation of the African coast: he saw the Indian Ocean as an enclosed sea. As Toussaint points out, the *Periplus* here was better informed, since it wrote that after Rhapta, "the unexplored ocean curves around towards the west."[191]

Indian ships probably sailed to the China Sea during the first centuries of the Christian era. According to the Chinese chronicles, the first embassies in China seem to have come from India, and not from Southeast Asia: from Huangzhi (Huang-chih, identified by G. Ferrand with Kāñcī [Kanchi], on the southeast coast of India), under the emperor Pingdi, in 2 CE, and later from the Tianzhu (T'ién-chu) kingdom, in northern India, in 159 and 161 CE.[192] Funan and Champa would send embassies only from 226 CE onward. In addition, in 405, Shize (Shih-tse) (Sri Lanka) dispatched envoys who carried some products from western Asia to the Song; other Sinhalese embassies arrived in China in 428, 430, and 435. There would be another embassy in 527 to the Liang (Lévi 1900). These Indian and Sinhalese delegations may have traveled on Southeast Asian ships.[193] During the first years of the Liu-Song

---

[189] Ptolemy Book VII, ch. 2; Wheatley 1961: 140. The term *emporium* here refers to a market defended by walls.

[190] Kokkonagara or Konkonagara may be a corruption of the Sanskrit Kukkutanāgara (Mahdi 1999b: 222), but this tells us nothing about its location.

[191] Toussaint 1961: 40. See *Periplus*, 18; Schoff 1974: 29.

[192] The *Houhanshu*, *Chronicles of the Later Han Dynasty*, mentions trade between Tianzhu and Da Qin, Anxi, Funan, Jinan, and Jiaozhi (here Indochina, generally speaking) (Hirth and Rockhill 1911: 113). The *Houhanshu* was compiled by Fan Ye (398–446). "There are several dozens of kingdoms other [than the main kingdom]. At this time [around 125 CE], they all depended on the Yuezhi [the Kushan Empire]" (*Houhanshu*; Chavannes 1907: 46–47).

[193] Wang Gungwu 1958: 20, 28, 37, 119–120. It is odd that A. Toussaint wrote (1961: 4) that "the Sinhalese never meant to become a maritime power." Moreover, the Shan country (Burma?) sent an embassy in 132 CE, according to the *Houhanshu* (Wolters 1967: 80).

dynasty (420–479 CE), four missions arrived in China from Sri Lanka, and two from India. Indian traders were present in China at the beginning of the sixth century (and certainly much earlier) (Wang Gungwu 1958: 50; Schottenhammer 1999: 284).

The Chinese chronicle *Liangshu* goes so far as to suggest the existence of regular trade with Da Qin, the Roman Empire, during the third century, through South India. "Da Qin" sent two "embassies" to China, one in 226 (the "envoy" arrived in Jiaozhi, and then was sent to Nanjing, capital of the Wu kingdom) and another was sent in 284, to Luoyang. As for Marcus Aurelius's so-called envoys in 166, it is likely that these were merchants from the eastern Roman world.[194] Roman coins (16) from Tiberius (first century) to Aurelian (third century) have been found in Shaanxi. The *Liangshu* also tells us that Da Qin merchants were active in regions corresponding to Cambodia and Vietnam (Young 2001: 33).

India's influence on continental and insular Southeast Asia increased from the fourth century onward, with the adoption of Hindu practices – Buddhism was also quite active – as well as the appearance of Sanskrit inscriptions on stone or copper plates, usually to register donations. According to Malleret and Coedès, Samudragupta's conquests in the Ganges valley and South India may have triggered a new Indian exodus to the east, in particular that of the Kuṣāna people from Bengal.[195] But Indian expansion was founded primarily on trade and also involved South India. As had been the case earlier, the variety of scripts and languages in these inscriptions reflects the diversity of the communities crossing the Bay of Bengal. Khlong Thom has yielded inscriptions in the Pallava script (South India) and in Sanskrit dated between the fifth and seventh centuries CE. Near the mouth of the Muda River (province of Kedah, Malaysia), an inscription in Sanskrit and in Pallava script dated to the fifth century CE has been unearthed. It was written by a shipmaster called Buddhagupta following the successful completion of his voyage. This mariner lived in the Indian city of Raktamrttikā, on the Bagirathi River (western Bengal).[196] Besides the Chinese

---

[194] Wang Gungwu 1958: 28, 32, 40; Wolters 1967: 40–41. According to the *Houhanshu*, the "embassy" of a so-called envoy of Marcus Aurelius Antoninus arrived in Annam in 166 CE. This embassy, however, brought only ordinary products from Southeast Asia. R. McLaughlin, however, believes that these Roman diplomats were genuine (2014: 209).

[195] Coedès 1964a: 92, 446. The Kushans and the Iranian world may have influenced Funan during the fourth century (a glass cabochon bearing a Sassanid effigy was discovered at Oc Eo, with a figure wearing a Scythian cap, who inhales the fragrance of a flower) (Malleret 1963, IV: 365, 372; Coedès 1964a: 94; Guillot 2004). According to Malleret, these influences may have resulted from the presence of Indo-Scythians who found refuge in Funan when the Gupta established their empire; Indo-Scythians may have ruled Funan for a short time. The *History of the Qi Dynasty* states that, in 357, "the king of Funan, the Hindu Chan-t'an, sent an embassy to China" (Pelliot 1903: 257). For S. Lévi (1936), "Chan-t'an" was the royal title *chandan* in use among the Yuezhi, "and especially among the Kushans in the line of Kanishka" (however, see Vickery 2003–2004, below). Malleret also points out parallels between figures known at Oc Eo and in India, for the position of their legs (the "royal posture"). It is likely that as early as the second century CE, Kushan communities settled in Southeast Asia (see above).

[196] L. Y. Andaya (2001: 325), however, relates Raktamrttika, meaning "Red Earth," and the Chinese Chitu (same meaning), which referred to a state located on the eastern part of the Thai–Malay peninsula. See also de Casparis 2000: 56. Similar texts have been discovered in western Kalimantan, at Batu Pahat, on a tributary of the Kapuas River, and along the coast of Brunei; they may correspond to a state called Jinlipishi (Chin-li-p'i-shi, perhaps Vijayapura) in Chinese sources (Manguin 2004d: 302); for Wisseman

Annals and archaeological data, epigraphy attests to the flowering of Southeast Asian states from the fourth century onward. These states, whose elites were indianized and where an Indian presence was well attested, took control of trade between the China Sea and the Indian Ocean (see below). At Muara Kaman, in the region of Kutei (eastern Kalimantan), seven Sanskrit inscriptions (in Pallava script) on sacrificial pillars, engraved in the name of Mūlavarman, go back to the beginning of the fifth century. They reflect the enrichment of a local elite, probably through the gold trade.[197] Inscriptions – also in Sanskrit – of Pūrnavarman, the king of Tāruma, in western Java, date to the same period (see below). The various Champa states adopted Sanskrit names and Hindu cults during the fourth century, with Shaivism sometimes preeminent, as is the case in the Middle Mekong valley (the first known temple is that of My Son, founded by the king Bhadravarman [fourth or fifth century], who left several Sanskrit inscriptions).[198] Many Buddhist or Vishnuite vestiges have been discovered in Funan (see below). Ships plied between Sri Lanka and insular Southeast Asia, as shown by Faxian's journey from Sri Lanka to Java during the fifth century.

From the end of the Gupta period in 480, economic conditions in northern India deteriorated, and trade appeared to decline. The *Devi Bhāgavata* mentions a "one hundred year" famine. According to the Javanese chronicles, *c.* 603 CE, "a ruler of Gujarat was warned of an approaching calamity and the consequent destruction of his kingdom. He therefore dispatched his son along with five thousand followers, in six large and a hundred small vessels to Java. They laid there the foundation of a great civilization" (Mookerji 1999 [1912]: 51).

As has been emphasized above, the emergence of complex societies in Southeast Asia was not simply the result of external influences, however; it arose from internal developments that were connected to progress in rice cultivation and to the rise of regional and long-distance exchange networks.

Christie, they suggest the existence of a common Buddhist cult supported by Malay networks (1995: 256–257).

[197] Wisseman Christie 1995: 261; Coedès 1964a: 103. The father of King Mūlavarman also bore a Sanskrit name; by contrast, his grandfather's name seems to have been purely Indonesian. Vestiges of various Buddhist communities have been discovered along the Mahakam River (end first – early second century CE) (McKinnon 2000: 229–230). For McKinnon, Kutei was probably within the orbit of networks centered on Java. The letters of the Kutei inscriptions already show discrepancies from Indian writing: the script must have been introduced earlier, but used on plant materials, which have since disappeared (Miksic 2004: 237).

[198] Coedès 1964a: 94ff.; Higham 2002: 275. It is not pure chance, notes Coedès, that this region would later bear the name of Amarāvatī. Shaivism seemed to be prominent, mixed with Vishnuism and Mahāyāna Buddhism. The great Indian figures merged with local divinities.

CHAPTER

11 Southeast Asia, an Interface between Two Oceans

> The eastern frontier of Dunsun is in communication with Chiao-chou
> [Tonkin], the western [frontier] with T'ien-chu [India] and An-hsi
> [Parthia]. All the countries beyond the frontier come and go in pursuit
> of trade . . . At this mart East and West meet together so that daily there are
> innumerable people there. Precious goods and rare merchandise
> – there is nothing which is not there.
> (*Liangshu*; Wheatley 1961: 16)

> Foreigners call ships *bo*. The biggest are 20 *chang* or more in length, and
> 2 or 3 *chang* above the waterline. Seen from above they resemble covered
> galleries. They carry six to seven hundred men and a cargo of 10,000 *hu*.
> (Wan Zhen [3rd century], quoted in the *Taiping yulan* [1983]; Christie 1957: 347)

> Many of those who form the crews and technicians of these ships [*bo*] are *K'un-lun*
> people. With the fibrous bark of the coconut tree, they make cords which bind
> the parts of the ship together . . . Nails and clamps are not used . . . The ships are
> constructed by assembling several thicknesses of side-planks . . . Their length is over
> 60 meters.
> (Chinese text of the eighth century; Manguin 1980: 275;
> Pelliot 1925, II: 243ff.; Needham *et al.* 1971: 600–601)

The Emergence of Complex Societies during the First Millennium BCE

Southeast Asia is a clear example of how new techniques (both of power and production) and products "generate new social forms" (Higham 2002: 291). In Vietnam, Yunnan, and Thailand, the development first of bronze, and later iron metallurgy, led to exchanges and migrations, and fostered the intensification of agriculture as well as the emergence of powerful chiefdoms; the attendant process of militarization can be seen from the large amount of weapons recovered.[1] Bronzeworking began in northern Vietnam, northeastern Thailand, and central Thailand as early as the second millennium BCE. In northern Vietnam, the Go Mun culture, which succeeded the Dong Dau culture, was characterized by the production of a large repertoire of bronze objects, ritual vessels, and weapons as well as agricultural implements such as hoes, shovels, and sickles (1000–600 BCE).[2] Further

[1] Higham 2004: 57. This tendency is particularly noticeable, of course, during the Chinese Han advance to the south during the first century BCE.
[2] Higham 1996a: 99–100. The valleys south of the Red River Valley (Ma, Ca) show the same kind of assemblage. Use of the lost-wax technique is evident.

south, the Quy Chu sites, which preceded the Dong Son culture, show a type of pottery comparable to that of Shixia (Guangdong) (Nguyen Khac Su *et al.* 2004: 195).

At the same time as relations were increasing with India and China, complex societies were emerging in Southeast Asia during the first millennium BCE; these were embedded in what can be viewed primarily as an eastern world-system, and later were part of a global world-system, in which Southeast Asia became a semi-periphery. The pace of change accelerated throughout the region, starting in the mid-first millennium BCE. In northern Vietnam, bronze metallurgy flourished from 500 BCE onward in the Dong Son culture, which was famous for its drums decorated with war scenes and rituals. High-status burials reveal differentiation among the elites.[3] The transition pointed out by Bellwood (1997: 271) "to a highly stratified and partly urbanized society" was based on intensive rice cultivation in irrigated fields, worked with plows drawn by buffaloes. Wet rice agriculture spread across the whole region.[4] Here again, the spread of animal traction was accompanied by the centralization of power and increased social stratification (see Sherratt 2006a). A drum weighing 72 kg discovered at Co Loa contained 96 socketed bronze plowshares. Plows found within the Dong Son context are quite similar to those known in China (Higham 2002: 178). Moreover, the Dong Son culture was associated with a maritime tradition. The spread of bronze drums of Heger type I throughout Southeast Asia (Map II.12) reflects the participation of this culture in long-distance exchange networks. The necropolis of Viet Khe (*c.* 500–300 BCE) shows various bronze objects, some of them similar to those found at Guangdong and Guangxi sites.[5] The Viet Khe necropolis has yielded several boat-shaped coffins. At least one of these was carved from a boat; it shows bulkheads and holes for lashing: "its plank-joining technique was lashing," without the use of dowels or tenons (Bellwood *et al.* 2007: 16).

Iron appeared at this time along with spearheads and a cast iron hoe, reminiscent of the forms found in Lingnan.[6] Many weapons have been excavated, evidence of extended conflicts. Co Loa, a sizeable moated site with three walls, was probably the capital of the kingdom of Au Lac for a short time during the third century BCE, though defensive structures at Co Loa have yielded a date in the fourth century BCE (Higham 2014: 204). As early as 208 BCE, this kingdom fell under the power of the Nanyue ruler (Guangdong), Trieu Da (Zhao Tuo in Chinese), who divided the country into two commanderies.[7] Northern Vietnam then became a Chinese protectorate in III BCE and

---

[3] Bellwood 1997: 269–270. Drums have been found at Dong Son, and throughout the region of the Red River valley, as well as at Lang Vac, further to the south. The Dong Son elite probably controlled metalworking. A crossbow trigger mechanism found at Lang Vac "indicates knowledge of Chinese weaponry" (Higham 2014: 208).

[4] Whereas the Phung Nguyen sites have yielded only long-grain rice, round-grained and glutinous varieties have been found for the Dong Son period (Nguyen Khac Su *et al.* 2004: 201).

[5] Higham 1996a: 111–114. The various cemeteries show burials in boat-shaped wooden coffins. Three datings for the Viet Khe cemetery indicate the third century BCE (Higham 2002: 173). No iron has been found in either Viet Khe or the site of Lang Ca, dated between 382 and 195 BCE, which has yielded bronze items (including a drum). Iron appears to have been less abundant in northern Vietnam than in central Thailand (Higham 1996a: 119).

[6] Bellwood 1997: 271. Iron is quite rare in the Dong Son sites. It was cast using Chinese technology. The Co Loa drum also contained a bimetallic spearhead (with an iron blade and a socket made of bronze). The site at Dong Son has also yielded a bimetallic sword and a bimetallic spearhead.

[7] Zhao Tuo became king of Nanyue after the collapse of the Qin dynasty in 207 BCE.

Figure 11.1 Tympanum of a Dong Son bronze drum found in 1893 at Nhu Trac, Nam Ninh province, diam.: 79 cm, National History Museum of Hanoi. After Pham Huy Thong *et al.* (eds.), *Dong Son Drums in Vietnam*, Editions of Social Sciences of Hanoi, 1990

a Chinese province in 43 CE. Tombs in necropolises near Lach Truong and Bin Son contained many Chinese artifacts or artifacts influenced by China.[8] Finds of glass beads, and also agate and carnelian beads, show the region's participation in South Asian exchange networks. Further evidence is provided by the export of Dong Son bronze drums (of the Heger I type), found far away to the south (see below), a spread that clearly reflects active exchanges in Southeast Asia, using both terrestrial and maritime routes. The tradition of these bronze drums originated in Vietnam and may have been transmitted to the Dian culture of Yunnan, a region in contact with the Dong Son culture (Moore 2007: 103; Calo 2008: 211; see below). Daggers with human- or animal-shaped handles and other bronze artifacts reveal the influence of the Dian culture (Nguyen Khac Su *et al.* 2004: 200). Drums of the Heger I type have also been found in Xilin (western Guangxi), in a tomb dated to the Later Han period.

In fact, Higham correctly states that "a series of increasingly complex polities [were developing] along the southern margins of the expanding Shu, Chu, Qin and Han states"; all these states exchanged goods and technologies (Higham 1996a: 133–134; Bellwood 1997: 318 n. 2).

Further south, the Sa Huynh culture (central and southern Vietnam) flourished from *c.* 600 BCE (or even possibly from the beginning of the first millennium BCE) up to the first century of the Christian era. For Bellwood, the Sa Huynh culture was linked to an Austronesian-speaking (Chamic) population, originally from Kalimantan or perhaps the Malay peninsula. This hypothesis gives rise to a problem of dating, with R. Blust placing the arrival of Malayo-Chamic groups on the continent only during the third century BCE.[9] The Chamic settlement was preceded (and encouraged) by contacts between the Philippines and northern Kalimantan on the one hand, and the Vietnamese coast on the other: burial jars were present in the caves of Tabon (Palawan Island, South Philippines) and Niah (Sarawak, northern Kalimantan), and also at the site of Long Thanh (near Sa Huynh), at the beginning of the first millennium BCE.[10] Note that the ancient ships using the lashed-lug technique within an area Vietnam–Hainan–Philippines form a coherent set (Manguin 1985b: 327, 337). The sites of the Sa Huynh culture, with their burial jars and decorated pottery

---

[8] Bronze items (vases, mirrors, bells, belt buckles), terracotta (incense burners, lamps, house models), weapons (crossbows, halberds), coins, lacquered objects, and silk. Tombs from the Han period have also been unearthed at Ke Noi (near Co Loa) and near Haiphong. Various other sites have yielded Chinese coins, for example Xuan La, at the mouth of the Red River. A crossbow bolt has been excavated at Lang Vac. Tam Tho Phu shows the remains of furnaces used for producing ceramics in the Chinese style (Higham 2002: 283–286).

[9] Should we contemplate an earlier Cham arrival on the continent? Or ought we to consider the possibility of other Austronesians arriving prior to the Cham migrations? Blust does not exclude an earlier date for the Chams on the mainland (p.c.). He pointed out, a few years ago, that ironworking, and the Malayic innovation *besi* "iron," spread to the mainland with the Chamic expansion, and during this process the word was borrowed by the Mon and perhaps other Mon-Khmer speakers (see Blust 1976).

[10] Bellwood 1992: 130. Funerary jars and evidence of the practice of cremation, both typical of the Sa Huynh culture, can be found from the southern borders of Vietnam to the mouth of the Red River. Moreover, Donohue and Denham (2010: 301) propose a link between *baRat*, an ancient term from the Philippines, for which related terms are also known in Kalimantan (referring to wild bananas), and *priit*, reconstructed in the Austroasiatic languages of Indochina (the vowel change, however, poses a problem for this hypothesis).

(incisions and shell impressions), also show affinities with sites along the Sulawesi Sea (Leang Buidane for example), suggesting likely contacts (Bellwood 1997: 303). The "Sa Huynh-Kalanay [pottery] style" influenced a wide area including eastern Kalimantan, Sulawesi, and the Moluccas; the similarities that we observe may reflect processes of transmission and the existence of trade routes (Bellwood 2004: 36). Similar incised and stamped pottery has recently been found in peninsular Thailand, while Mindoro jade has been found at Khao Sam Kaeo (southern Thailand) (Hung and Bellwood 2010: 243).

The linguistic affiliation of the Chams and the exchange networks existing at the time must have facilitated the spread of metallurgical techniques (notably for iron) toward insular Southeast Asia. The sites of the Sa Huynh culture are spread across 700 km of coastline, as far as southern Vietnam, where Phu Hoa appears to have been inhabited as early as the first half of the first millennium BCE.[11] These sites reveal both growing social complexity and a substantial amount of long-distance trade, which may explain the Austronesian expansion along the coasts. Besides burial jars, two types of ear ornaments (rings called *ling-ling-o*, and double animal-headed pendants), often made of nephrite, are items representative of the Sa Huynh culture. They have been found near the mouth of the Mekong (Hang Gon, Giong Ca Vo,[12] Phu Hoa), at sites in the Philippines (province of Batangan, Luzon, in the Tabon caves of Palawan), in Sarawak (Niah caves), and also at U-Thong, Ban Don Ta Phet, Khok Phlap, and Khao Sam Kaeo (Thailand), at Samrong Sen (Cambodia), at Hong Kong, and in Taiwan (Jiuxianglan, Changguang, Lan-yu Island).[13] Much of the nephrite used to make these earrings "originated in eastern Taiwan" (Hung and Bellwood 2010: 235), revealing a sphere of interaction encompassing Taiwan, the western Philippines, the Vietnamese coast, and western Kalimantan. Excavations have provided evidence of local working of this nephrite in the Philippines, southern Vietnam (Giong Ca Vo), and southern Thailand (Khao Sam Kaeo) (Hung and Bellwood 2010: 238). In southeastern Taiwan, the sites of Jiuxianglan and Beinan have revealed carnelian and glass beads, dated to the last centuries BCE; at Huagangshan (eastern Taiwan), Indo-Pacific glass beads are dated to the first centuries BCE (Hung and Bellwood 2010: 240, 241).

Moreover, imported carnelian, agate, and glass beads at a number of sites show connections with Thailand, Burma,[14] and India (Bellwood 1997: 275). These imports often led to changes in "artistic and stylistic preferences" (Hung and Bellwood 2010: 242). The site of Hoi An (Tra Kieu region, Thu Bon valley) contained thousands of beads associated with burial jars, including agate, carnelian, jade, glass, and gold beads.

---

[11] The Cham people also expanded into inland regions (Higham 1996a: 307).

[12] Nguyen Kim Dung 2001. Some at least of these ornaments were locally produced, in jade, carnelian, or glass.

[13] Reinecke 1996; Bellwood 1997: 217, 273–274; Higham 2002: 180–182; Hung and Bellwood 2010: 236–237. The double animal-headed pendants found at Giong Ca Vo are made of stone or glass. The Arku cave (Cagayan valley, Luzon) has yielded stone ear ornaments that recall the *ling-ling-o*, dated to the first millennium BCE (Bacus 2004: 264). Note once again that the introduction of bronze and iron at Tabon occurred parallel to the importation of beads of the Indian type (Chamber B, Manunggul cave, *c.* 200 BCE). Copper and tin were brought from the mainland, and bronze was cast in Palawan (Higham 1996a: 303).

[14] The raw materials for the beads found at Nagsabaran (Cagayan valley, Luzon) probably came from Burma (Hung and Bellwood 2010: 241).

Two etched agate beads appear to be similar to Indian beads. The Lai Nghi cemetery, near Hoi An, has "yielded 10,000 beads, over 1,000 of which are of semiprecious stones . . . Most glass beads would have been made locally, but etched beads [probably came] from India" (Lam Thi My Dzung 2009: 71, 73). A tiger-shaped carnelian bead has been discovered in Lai Nghi, that "is remarkably similar to a carnelian tiger pendant from Binnaka" (central Burma) (Glover and Bellina 2003). A relationship has been suggested between Myanmar carnelian tigers and bronze Qin Dynasty tigers which "served as symbols of military office" (Lam Thi My Dzung 2009: 74). It is likely that gold beads and earrings were also imported. "Lai Nghi bronze vessels include typical Chinese forms and decoration. Several bronze mirrors of Western Han provenance have been found at Lai Nghi" and other sites. "A number of bronze coins (*wu shu* and *wang mang* types), bells and other ornaments have been found . . ., mostly from Lai Nghi. A large number of iron knives with loop handles, presumably local imitations of Western Han knives," have also been excavated (Lam Thi My Dzung 2009: 73). In the Sa Huynh region, the cemetery at Go Mun contained agate, carnelian, glass, and gold beads. Bronzes also reveal the existence of relations with the Dong Son culture. On Ly Son Island, the Suoi Chinh site has yielded Han ceramics from the second century BCE. Jar burials contained glass beads and iron tools (Higham 2014: 214). Sa Huynh sites have also been found inland. The Thu Bon River valley was a major center for the Sa Huynh culture. The site of Binh Yen was located 70 km inland; it contained a bronze mirror from the Western Han period (70–50 BCE) as well as carnelian, agate, and nephrite ornaments (Higham 2014: 214). At Tien Lan, 115 km from the coast, a burial revealed a Chinese bronze bowl, and a Dong Son drum was found in the vicinity (Higham 2014).

The Plain of Jars culture (Laos) may partly represent an extension of the Sa Huynh culture. The site of Phon Savanh has yielded iron objects, bronze bells, cowries, and carnelian and glass beads (Higham 2002: 183–184).

As already mentioned, beads have been discovered at Hang Gon and Giong Ca Vo in southern Vietnam, where C_{14} measurements have yielded datings between the fourth and first century BCE. At Phu Hoa, the dates are 350 ± 140 BCE and 540 ± 290 BCE (Nguyen Kim Dung 2001: 107; Higham 2002: 180–181). Ironworking has been documented at these sites. The site of Giong Lon, located near the Bay of Vung Tao, contained rich burials housing ornaments of garnet, glass, carnelian, and rock crystal; three gold death masks were also recovered, and "one of the masked individuals was buried with an iron sword" (Higham 2014: 218–219). The discovery of a *wu shu* coin reveals Chinese contacts (Reinecke and Luyen 2009). At Go O Chua, an Iron Age cemetery has yielded iron items, glass beads, and "amulets in the form of tiger's teeth (Reinecke 2012)" (Higham 2014: 218). In southeastern Cambodia, the site of Prohear contained graves showing "unparalleled" wealth in Southeast Asia. The first phase (400–100 BCE) has revealed glass beads. The second phase (100 BCE – 100 CE) has yielded stone beads, glass beads, bronze drums, bronze bells, and many gold and silver ornaments (one is decorated with an image of a horse, and a ring features a man riding a horse – "the first evidence for cavalry in Southeast Asia") (Higham 2014: 219–220). Reinecke *et al.* (2012) have suggested that groups emigrating from Guizhou Province and Yunnan may have been responsible for the changes observed during the second phase at Prohear (2012: 222).

Not all stone and glass beads were imported from India. They were also produced locally in Southeast Asia. The sites of Giong Ca Vo (Vietnam) and Khao Sam Kaeo (Thailand) have revealed glassworking soon after 400 BCE. During the first millennium CE, Oc Eo (Vietnam) became one of the main production centers for Indo-Pacific beads (see below). In Taiwan, Jiuxianglan was "a workshop for the production of glass beads" and bronze (tin came from mainland Southeast Asia); some stone molds are identical to molds known at Thai sites (such as Chansen) and the Oc Eo sites (Hung and Bellwood 2010: 241).

The presence of bronze drums at various points along the Vietnamese coast[15] signals exchanges with the Dong Son culture.[16] Moreover, iron metallurgy in Vietnam reflects a Chinese influence.[17] The Chinese impact becomes even more apparent in the south of the continent under the Han dynasty, which gained a limited foothold on Rinan, a region south of the Ca River. The earliest roof tiles (of Chinese style) in central Vietnam appeared during the first century CE, but Chinese merchants rarely ventured into the southern seas at this time. However, Han pottery has been found in southern Sumatra – in uncertain contexts[18] – and recently at the site of Khao Sam Kaeo.[19] Southeast Asian seafarers, and perhaps non-Chinese sailors from southern China, transported Chinese products.[20] The *Qianhanshu*, however, refers to journeys made by Chinese traders organized by the state (see below), and it would certainly be wrong to assume that the Chinese were absent from the southern seas. During the second and

---

[15] In the provinces of Quang Tri, Gia Lai, Phu Yen, Nha Trang, Bin Phuoc, Binh Duong, Ba Ria, and Kien Giang (Yamagata *et al.* 2001). Nine drums have recently been discovered in the Con valley (Higham 2002: 179).

[16] Bellwood (1992: 130), however, points out the apparent weakness of the relationships between the Dong Son and Sa Huynh cultures. The Sa Huynh culture shows more links with the West (Thailand and the Thai–Malay peninsula) (and with Taiwan, and perhaps southern China).

[17] Bronze items are relatively rare in burial jars, whereas iron is more common.

[18] Gernet (1999: 117) also mentions discoveries in eastern Kalimantan and western Java for the first century CE, probably a borrowing from Needham *et al.* 1971: 443, who quote Van Orsoy de Flines (1949) (collection of the Museum of Jakarta). In addition, bronze items – some perhaps older than the Han period – are present in private collections; they reputedly come from looted graves in the region of Lumajang in eastern Java. Contacts, however, seem to be rare before the Tang dynasty (Bellwood 1997: 316).

[19] See *Southeast Asian Ceramics Museum Newsletter*, 5 (3), May–June 2008.

[20] A sword manufactured in China has been found at Hang Gon (Mekong delta, north of Giong Ca Vo). Coins dating from the reign of Wang Mang (9–23 CE) have been discovered at Hau Xa (province of Quang Nam). Sa Huynh burial urns excavated at Go Cam (near Tra Kieu, region of Da Nang) contained Chinese mirrors (first century BCE); the same site has yielded Chinese seal imprints, tiles and ornaments, fragments of Han jars, glass objects, imprints of Chinese coins of the *wuzhou* type on ceramics, as well as crossbow bolts (Southworth 2004a: 217). Six Chinese vessels and two bronze mirrors were unearthed at Lai Nghi (Quang Nam province) in 2003 (Nguyen *et al.* 2017). Three bronze mirrors dating from the end of the Former Han period were also discovered in 1998 and 1999, two of them in burial jars of the Sa Huynh type, at Binh Yen and Go Dua, southwest of Da Nang, and the other in a bronze drum of the Heger I type at Phu Chanh, north of Ho Chi Minh City (Yamagata *et al.* 2001). The jars from Binh Yen also contained glass, agate, and carnelian beads. Similar mirrors have been found at Sa Huynh, Lang Vac (Nghe An province), Thieu Duong (Thanh Hoa province), in northern Vietnam, and at Chawang (Nakhon Si Thammarat region), in southern Thailand (Yamagata *et al.* 2001). In addition, Han coins have been retrieved in Sa Huynh burial jars at Hoi An.

third centuries, revolts against the Chinese presence in northern Vietnam resulted in the creation of an independent political entity known as Linyi in the Chinese chronicles (see below).

Another region, on the continent, played a crucial role in long-distance exchanges between China and South Asia: this was Yunnan, where various political entities developed. These had connections with Sichuan (Shu kingdom), in the north, and benefited from substantial mineral and agricultural resources, as well as local crafts and the control over various roads. We can appreciate their wealth and the power of their elites through the tombs of the Dian culture.[21] This culture emerged prior to the middle of the first millennium BCE. It shows influences from ancient Shang China and from Zhou China, transmitted through Sichuan (Falkenhausen 2003: 217), revealing the activity of ancient trade routes linking northern China and regions further south. Chiou-Peng discerns the penetration of cultures from the steppes into the Upper Jinsha River (Sichuan and Yunnan) and the region of Lake Erhai (western Yunnan) around 1000 BCE. Graves from the Dekin region (northwestern Yunnan) show the introduction of horses (Chiou-Peng 2004: 306; 2008a: 234). From the seventh century onward, other influences, from the Middle Yangtze, are apparent in shaft tombs containing bronze weapons, bronze agricultural tools and kettledrums (Chiou-Peng [2008a: 235] sees these as ancestors to the Dian drums, but see Calo 2008). During the last centuries BCE, the hybridized Dian culture appears to have been ruled by an equestrian warrior elite. Bronze plaques created using the lost-wax casting process and featuring the "animal style" of the steppes reveal a distant influence of nomads from the north (2008: 226), as do representations of a "proto-stirrup": "some figures on horses are riding with either a toe-ring or looped device attached to their feet. A bronze tool shows a 'qiang' nomad leading a horse which has a ring-shaped device dangling from its saddle" (2008: 232). Pirazolli-t'Serstevens (1988) has also emphasized parallels between certain objects from western Yunnan and artifacts from Gansu, Qinghai, and Mongolia, revealing the importance of exchanges along north–south routes. Bronze figures from the Dian culture sometimes show Caucasoid features and wear clothes similar to those discovered in the Tarim. For Moore (2007: 123), the Dian aristocracy seems to have resulted from the introduction of horsemen into a sedentary population, perhaps at different times. We know that when the Yuezhi displaced the Saka, the latter migrated to the south. Some of them may have gone to Yunnan during the final centuries BCE.

In 109 BCE, Han armies invaded the Dian country. The Chinese thrust into Yunnan had economic and strategic motives: the control of Yunnan allowed them to bypass Nanyue and the Xiongnu "empire" (see below). Moreover, "the *Huayang Guozhi* (fourth century) states that thirty thousand head of horses and cattle were gathered for the Han court from the Dian region" (Chiou-Peng 2004: 306). Tomb 6 at Shizhaishan contained a gold seal of the "Dian king," granted by the Han emperor, as well as other artifacts imported from China or influenced by China (remains of a horse harness,

[21] The chiefdoms of Yelang, in the east, and Kunming, in the west, have also yielded vestiges from this period. Bellwood and Glover (2004: 11) link the Dian culture to speakers of the Tai-Kadai group of languages. An army from the state of Chu managed to conquer the Dian country as early as the beginning of the third century BCE; blocked by the armies of Qin, the Chu general stayed in Dian and became its king.

lacquered coffins, a bronze mirror, crossbow mechanisms, bells, and jade ornaments). This tomb also contained drum-shaped bronze containers for cowrie shells with lids showing scenes of battles or ceremonies,[22] as well as bronze drums, and agricultural tools. Turquoise, agate, and carnelian beads were imported from the south; cowries may also have come along the southern routes.[23] Similar discoveries have been made at other sites of the Dian lake region, and in the northwest (Wanjiaba, Dabona).[24] In its phase 2 (perhaps during the period of the Warring Kingdoms),[25] Wanjiaba shows jewelry made of exotic stones, drums, bells, halberds, hoes, axes, and socketed spearheads. Phase 3 (Qin/Han period) has also yielded very rich tombs.

Calo (2008) has shown that the Dian elite imported Heger I bronze drums from northern Vietnam, as well as cast drums sharing features with containers for cowrie shells. Some bronze drums were converted into containers for cowries. We do not know whether Dian bronze casters imitated the Vietnamese bronze drums, or if foreign bronze casters from the Dong Son area settled in Yunnan around the second century BCE. Dian drums have been found in Yunnan (Shizaishan, Lijiashan, Tianzimiao, for example), in Sichuan (Huili) and outside the Dian sphere of influence (in northern Vietnam, and Burma), a fact that Calo links to the expanding Han presence in the region (2008: 217).

Extensive exchanges took place between the Red River valley and Yunnan. These two regions were also connected to more southerly areas, themselves linked to the networks in central Thailand and Cambodia. In northeastern Thailand, silk has been found at the site of Ban Na Di, reflecting Chinese influences (Cameron 2010: 146). With the spread of iron metallurgy around 500 BCE, centers developed in the Mun valley, surrounded by moats, with systems of canals and tanks, within a context of agricultural intensification. Ringed by five moats, Noen U-Loke (12 ha) appears as one of the most significant sites; it was much smaller, however, than the nearby site of Non Muang Kao (50 ha). Salt extraction was a major activity at Noen U-Loke and other sites, as salt was part of long-distance exchanges. Besides locally produced bronze

[22] The custom of filling bronze vessels with cowries finds parallels at Sanxingdui (Sichuan). The shape of these vessels, as well as that of the bronze drums from Southeast Asia, may derive from *zun* wine vessels from Shang China (von Falkenhausen 2003: 217). The depiction of complex ritual scenes on these vessels shows links between the cultures of Sichuan and Yunnan, as does the use of gold sheets to cover statues or figures of ritual scenes.

[23] An etched bead has been unearthed at Shizhaishan, and another at Lijiashan (Glover and Bellina 2001: 202). Other tombs have yielded cowrie containers, some belonging to the first phase – without iron – of Shizhaishan (fifth century BCE). Despite their presence in the richest tombs, cowries may have been used as currency (which runs contrary to Pirazzoli-t'Serstevens's argument, 1992, quoted by Higham 1996a: 148). According to H. U. Vogel (1993: 218), most of the cowries belong to the *Cypraea annulus* L. species.

[24] See also Tianzimiao (300–100 BCE), near Lake Dian. Various sites have yielded bimetallic swords, in shapes known in Sichuan. A tomb at Dabona (dated to 566–334 BCE from the wood of a coffin) contained a bronze coffin weighing 257 kg. Bronze technology in Yunnan used techniques known in China and Southeast Asia: casting in bivalve molds, the use of multiple-piece molds, and lost-wax casting. Gilding was developed using a mixture of gold and heated mercury. Knowledge of ironworking came from northern China; however, iron was rare in the Dian and Yelang states.

[25] A dating between 791 and 467 BCE has been proposed for Phase 2, but this appears to be too early, as are the datings ascribed to Phase 3 (523–192) (Higham 1996a: 177). The first levels at Dabona have yielded dates between 532 and 332 BCE.

bracelets, belts, and bells, and bronze or iron tools, Noen U-Loke shows the importation of glass beads, agate, and carnelian beads (from 100 BCE onward), as well as bracelets, which tended to replace the older bangles and shell beads, revealing this region's insertion into exchange networks with South Asia via central Thailand and the Lower Mekong region.[26] Weapons were rare during the earliest phases of Noen U-Loke, contrasting with the situation prevailing in northern Vietnam, Yunnan, and Lingnan. The profusion of iron weaponry during the last phase of Noen U-Loke (perhaps dated to 300–500 CE), however, reflects growing conflicts. Rich tombs signal the emergence of an elite; at precisely the same time, the state of Funan was growing in prominence (see below). Brick temples appeared in the Mun valley during the fourth–fifth century. The discovery of bronze drums at various sites in the Mekong valley also reveals interconnections with either Yunnan or the Vietnamese coast. Bronze drums have been found in the region of Savannakhet, at Don Tan, Ban Na Pho Tai (at the confluence of the Mun and Mekong rivers), and on Sane Island in the Mekong River (Nitta 2007). Moreover, along the Mekong River, we observe the spread of funerary rituals using lidded jars.

An Iron Age cemetery at Ban Non Wat shows evidence of indirect contact with India, demonstrated from the fourth century BCE in the form of glass, carnelian, and agate jewelry (Higham *et al.* 2014: 39). Another moated site has recently been excavated in the upper Mun valley, at Non Ban Jak. The manufacture of socketed iron plowshares went along with what Higham *et al.* call an "agricultural revolution" in the Mun valley during the first half of the first millennium (2014: 40).

Several Bronze Age and Iron Age sites have been found in the Lower Mekong valley. They show indirect contacts with China (bronze halberds, found at Doc Chua, Hang Gon, and Long Giao), at the time of the Warring Kingdoms and the Han Empire (Nitta 2007; Higham 1996a: 211). An Iron Age cemetery has been discovered at Angkor Borei, a site that corresponds to a capital of the state of Funan (see below).

In central Thailand, bronze production and exchanges grew during the period before and after the introduction of iron (no later than 500 BCE). The site of Nong Nor reflects these developments (see above), as does the site of Nile Kham Haeng, near Non Pa Wai. The site of Ban Don Ta Phet, mentioned in connection with Indian imports into Thailand, illustrates the changes occurring at this time. The manufacturing of iron hoes and pruning knives accompanied an intensification in agriculture; iron spearheads were among the weapons produced in large numbers. Moated sites go back to this period,[27] reflecting a process of political centralization and social complexification that

---

[26] Glass, agate, and carnelian appeared after iron, during the second phase of the site. Higham (2004: 61) suspects that the agate and carnelian may have come from mines located in Thailand. Some glass beads may have been produced locally. Many other moated sites have been discovered in the Mun valley and its region (Higham 1996a: 212), and further north, in the Chi valley, where Non Chai has yielded glass beads (four were dated to the third century BCE) (Higham 1996a: 188). Seventeen furnaces producing wrought iron have been excavated at Ban Dan Phlong (Mun valley), revealing the importance of iron metallurgy during the final centuries BCE.

[27] For example, Ban Tha Khae, Khok Plord, Sab Champa I, Lopburi (Higham 1996a: 282). Imported goods followed the rivers upstream, as shown by the discoveries made at Ban Lum Khao, Noen Ma Kok, and other sites.

is also seen in cemeteries such as that of Ongbah. Note that both Ban Don Ta Phet and Ongbah were located along the Three Pagodas road linking Burma and Thailand. Much further to the northwest, the site of Bang Wang Hai (province of Lamphun) demonstrates not only exchanges with the south, with the discovery of cowries, glass beads, agate, and carnelian beads, but also Chinese influences, especially noticeable in the presence of an iron sword.[28] Silk found at Ban Don Ta Phet was probably a Chinese import (Cameron 2010: 148).

Ban Don Ta Phet has yielded early discoveries of objects of Indian origin. While iron metallurgy may have come from India, iron items (tools, weapons) at sites such as Ban Don Ta Phet and Ongbah Cave are hard to compare with those known in eastern or South India.[29]

Ornaments at Ban Don Ta Phet and other sites also reveal links with Vietnam. They show double animal-headed ear pendants made of nephrite, well known in the Sa Huynh culture.[30] A bronze bucket is "closely paralleled in the Dong Son culture" (Higham 2014: 223). Bronze drums from the Dong Son culture have been excavated in Thailand (at Ongbah Cave,[31] in central Thailand, and Khao Sam Kaeo, Taling Phang, and other sites in southern Thailand); in Cambodia (Prohear, Bit Meas, Lower Mekong); and in various places on the Malay peninsula: Kelang, Kampong Sungai Lang (Selangor),[32] Batu Pasir Garam (Tembeling valley) (second century BCE), and Kuala Trengganu. Near Ban Don Ta Phet, the site of Doembang Nang Buat has yielded remains of a bronze drum as well as a fragment of cast iron, a Chinese technique unknown in Thailand (Higham 2002: 220). These imports reflect a new demand from emerging aristocracies.

On the Thai–Malay peninsula, knowledge of gold, copper, and bronze metallurgy came together during the first millennium BCE (Higham 2004). The wealth of tin in the peninsula partly explains its connection with the trans-Asian networks of the time. Located at the narrowest point of the Isthmus of Kra, near to regions rich in tin, Khao Sam Kaeo, ringed with walls enclosing 54 ha, developed not along the coast but inland: it clearly functioned as part of a network linking the Bay of Bengal and the Gulf of Thailand, along routes crossing the peninsula. The site was occupied mainly between the fourth and first centuries BCE. Glassworking and stoneworking (chalcedony, nephrite) were located in two distinct quarters, with Indian craftsmen probably present

---

[28] Pautreau *et al.* 2005: 63–65. The site is dated between 200 BCE and 200 CE. South of Bang Wang Hai, not far from the future capital of Sukhothai, the site of Ban Wang Hat has yielded agate, carnelian and glass ornaments (Higham 2002: 223).

[29] Glover 1996: 372. As mentioned above, this author does not exclude an Indian influence for the introduction of iron metallurgy, however (Bellwood 1992: 284–286).

[30] Higham 1996a: 288; Glover 1996: 384. Found in a bronze bowl. A similar find has been reported for U-Thong. See above. A metal vessel with a high lead content discovered at Ban Don Ta Phet may have originated in the Dong Son culture (Glover 2000: 108, 120 n. 82).

[31] A rich iron industry was discovered at both Ongbah Cave and Ban Don Ta Phet. Ban Don Ta Phet has also revealed wooden boat-shaped coffins (200 BCE) (Bellwood 1997: 286). Similar coffins have been excavated at other sites, such as Kuala Selinsing (Malay peninsula).

[32] This site has yielded four of the eight Dong Son drums found along the west coast of the Thai–Malay peninsula, and three of the four bronze bells known on this coast. Their datings reveal an occupation during the first half of the first millennium (Bulbeck 2004: 322).

(Bellina-Pryce and Silapanth 2008).[33] They brought in Indian plants, sesame, and pulses, mungbean *Vigna radiata*, and horsegram *Macrotylema uniflorum*, also found on the nearby site of Phu Khao Thong (Castillo 2013). The artisans produced bracelets (similar to those found at Ban Don Ta Phet) as well as beads.

Four types of glass have been identified:

- A mineral soda glass containing aluminum (m-Na-Al 3) and uranium came from the Ganges valley. Guilds of Indian Buddhist craftsmen may have been involved in its importation.
- A potash-rich glass containing calcium and aluminum (m-K-Ca-Al) is known from India to southern China. It has been found in Vietnam at Giong Ca Vo and other Sa Huynh sites.
- A potash-rich glass containing aluminum (m-K-Al), different from the previous one, was not present in India, but was found from Myanmar to China. In eastern Asia, it is associated with Dong Son sites. Drawn beads at Khao Sam Kaeo belong to this type.
- A fourth type of glass, containing a mixture of mineral alkali (soda) and potash from plants, was probably produced locally (Lankton and Gratuze 2013).

Bronze bird figurines and a bronze bowl with high tin content (and showing a central cone) reveal imports or influences from India, as do seals inscribed with Indian Brāhmī script dated between the first century BCE and the first century CE (see above). Three Dongsonian bronze drums, a swallowtailed bronze axe of a type known in China during the Warring Kingdoms period,[34] arrow heads, a bronze mirror, Han pottery, and a Han dynasty seal were imported from Vietnam and China (Pryce *et al.* 2006). Gold beads are comparable to beads from Giong Ca Vo (southern Vietnam), and a gold rosette may be connected to jewels found in the Tabon caves (dated between 500 BCE and 300 BCE) (Palawan Island), while a pendant decorated in filigree is similar to pieces from Oc Eo and Sirkap (Taxila). A piece of S-shaped gold foil also recalls jewels from Sirkap dated to the first century CE (Pryce *et al.* 2006: 308ff.). In addition, a gold polyhedral bead matches beads found at Pyu sites, in Burma. The internal organization of the Khao Sam Kaeo site already shows parallels with what would be observed later at urban sites with links to long-distance trade: it probably reflects the formation of a proto-state. Artisans worked iron, but there is no trace of local ceramic production. Pottery and the various metallurgical techniques associated with copper alloys reflect connections with India and eastern Asia. The presence of high-tin bronze ingots shows that this metal was exploited for export (Murillo-Barroso *et al.* 2010).

Phu Khao Thong, southwest of Khao Sam Kaeo, on the Andaman Sea, has yielded Indian ceramics (Rouletted Ware), and stone and glass beads. One shard bears a short inscription in the Tamil language and Brahmi script. Roman intaglios, glass, and ceramics have also been recovered. One intaglio features a horse. Two fragments of mirrors dating to the Eastern Han dynasty hint at eastern contacts (Bellina *et al.* 2014; Higham 2014: 233).

---

[33] As evidenced by the discovery of "trumpet"-shaped iron instruments known in India in the production of glass beads (Pryce *et al.* 2006: 300).

[34] This type of axe has been found in Java, dated to a later period.

The coasts of Vietnam, the Gulf of Thailand, and the Thai–Malay peninsula were connected to insular Southeast Asia. On the islands, bronze, and iron appeared together during the final centuries of the first millennium BCE, revealing the recent integration of this part of the world within an incipient Asian system.[35] Centers emerged very early on in southern Sumatra and in Java; they dominated the exchange networks and controlled access to imported goods. J. Wisseman Christie points to an "explosion of commercial activity" between 500 and 200 BCE in the two interconnected sectors of the Strait of Malacca and the Java Sea.[36] Bronze drums (or fragments of drums) have been excavated in Sumatra;[37] at Kota Waringin and Bukit Selindung in western Kalimantan;[38] in western, north-central and eastern Java; on Bali; on islands in the Flores Sea (notably a drum from Selayar Island featuring elephants and peacocks, and a drum from Sangeang Island, near Sumbawa, which shows a horse and figures wearing Han dress and Indian or Kushan costumes); on the southern Moluccas; and as far away as western New Guinea (on the Kai Islands, in the south, and in mainland New Guinea), where traders went to acquire feathers of birds-of-paradise.[39] Most of these drums appear to have been imported from Vietnam, during or after the period of Chinese domination. For the Sangeang drum, R. Heine Geldern (1947) has suggested a cast in the Funan state around 250 CE (Bellwood 1997: 278). According to M. Spriggs and D. Miller (1988), the drums of Heger I type found in eastern Indonesia, of which there are at least fifteen (Glover 1996: 377), may be dated to the third century CE. Their distribution "does overlap in the west with that of the earliest recorded Indian contacts" in the Indonesian world: they appear to have been "transported – long after their date of manufacture – within the trade (especially spice trade) networks of the earliest historical states in the Malay peninula and western Indonesia" (Bellwood 1997: 278–279). H. Loofs-Wissowa (1991) has suggested that these drums were bestowed on local chiefs as symbols of kingship, a compelling sign of the advent of complex

---

[35] Prajekan (Java), Gilimanuk (Bali), Dong Son (Vietnam), and sites in Yunnan revealed bronze-handled iron daggers, also known in India (at Majurhari, in central India, for example) (Bellwood 1992: 121; Ray 2003: 122). Ban Chiang (Thailand) has also yielded spearheads with iron blades and cast-on bronze sockets. It is significant, Ray points out (2003: 122–123), that "many of the early Metal phase sites (e.g. the Buni sites, Gilimanuk and Sembiran) have provided evidence for contacts with the Indian subcontinent around the beginning of the Common era."

[36] Wisseman Christie emphasizes that Dong Son drums in Java are concentrated in regions near the coasts (1995: 250, 251).

[37] Notably a fragment of drum found at Kota Agung, in the Sunda Strait. Dong Son drums also appear on stone reliefs at Batugajah and Airpurah (Sumatra), and on a painted wall in a megalithic chamber at Kotaraya Lembak (Bellwood 1997: 288). Moreover, Malleret (1962, III: 176) has noted the similarity between glass beads with high lead content found in southern Sumatra (district of Pasemah) and beads found at Oc Eo and in northern Vietnam (high lead content is characteristic of Chinese beads). However, bronze flasks bearing a "decoration that is outside the Dong Son repertoire" have been discovered at Kerinci and Lampung (Sumatra), and on Madura (Bellwood 1997: 281). In addition, the megalithic sites of Pasemah contain red pottery of the *kendi* type (ritual vessels) (Manguin 2004d: 288). Wisseman Christie points out that in the Sumatranese provinces of Selatan and Jambi, prestige goods seem to have reached the interior regions of Pasemah, Lebong, and Kerinci directly, these being regions that produced gold, whereas in the south (Lampung), imported goods were mainly found at the estuaries (1995: 250).

[38] McKinnon 1994. Western Kalimantan has also yielded carnelian beads (Collins 1998: 5).

[39] Swadling 1996; Sherratt 2006b: 51. Socketed axes were deposited in Sentani Lake (northern coast of western New Guinea).

societies. Their sides often show representations of boats. In some cases, a drum contained a skeleton: at Plawangan (central-northern Java), a drum of Dong Son type placed upside down contained the bones of a child, along with a bronze spearhead, a bracelet, glass beads, and gold foil that covered the eyes and the mouth of the deceased (see above). The Plawangan cemetery has also yielded Indian beads. At Kradenanrejo (near Lamongan, northern Java), a child was placed inside a drum of Pejeng type, along with carnelian, glass and gold beads, gold umbrella-shaped ornaments (perhaps revealing a Buddhist influence), two bronze cups, and various iron objects; a Dong Son drum was used as a protective cover.

Other copper or bronze objects may have been imported from the Vietnamese coast: these include a statuette of a man from Satus, near Bogor (western Java); a miniature drum from Cibadak (western Java); and a lidded bronze vessel from Lamongan (eastern Java). Moreover, sarcophagi belonging to the Early Metal Age in Bali have yielded socketed bronze weapons (small axes and spearheads) and "socketed bronze tools with crescentic and heart-shaped blades" showing similarities with objects from central Thailand (at Nile Kham Haeng) dated between 700 and 500 BCE (Bellwood 1997: 294). It is not certain, however, that these objects were imported into Bali. At the beginning of the Christian era, insular Southeast Asia saw the flourishing of many metalworking centers, on Bali (see the drums of Pejeng type),[40] Sumatra, Java, Sabah (northern Kalimantan), on the Talaud Islands, and elsewhere. We thus observe the expression of "shared artistic vocabularies, codes and values," that would later facilitate "the adoption of an Indian cultural package" termed "indianization" (Manguin 2010: 177). In addition to the bronze drums, copper or bronze tools and ornaments found in eastern Indonesia and in New Guinea confirm the extent of exchange networks. Though copper sources are abundant on the continent, copper ores are rare in Insular Southeast Asia: copper can be found on some islands of the Philippines, in Sumatra, and Timor. There is plenty of tin in the Malay peninsula. Iron ores are more widely distributed, but are rare in Java and Bali: these regions imported most of the metals they used. The elites oversaw the importation of metals and metal objects (Wisseman Christie 1995: 246, 251). The inclusion of Java in long-distance exchange networks and its control over the spice routes (the Moluccas) and the wood trade from Timor largely explain the relatively abundant discoveries on Java. For Java and Bali, the absence of metal resources provided an incentive for developing their exports. Java's high population density and agricultural potential were also crucial to the emergence of influential states. This island seems to have been the source of various types of bronze axes that can be found in insular Southeast Asia, especially east of Java, as well as bronze drums. Alongside the control of prestige goods by the elites, we note the development of megalithic traditions in various regions, showing collective mobilization on the part of the new powers.

The introduction of metallurgy partially transformed shipbuilding. Manguin (1985b: 339–340), however, has criticized Horridge's proposal (1982: 1, 57) linking the introduction of metal to the development of a technique whereby dowels are inserted between

---

[40] Bellwood 1997: 281. Higham (1996a: 303) notes that axes and bracelets were made of a ternary alloy (Cu-Sn-Pb) that was often found on the continent at the turn of the Christian era.

Figure 11.2 Horse and elephant on the Sangeang bronze drum

planks (Manguin points out the use of dowels in boats of the Tuamotu Islands; see above). By contrast, the remnants of two boats used for burials at Dong Xa and Yen Bac, in the Red River Valley, reveal a technique using mortises and locked rectangular tenons to fix together planks that were laid on the boats' hulls (these two boats are thus quite different from the older boats found at Viet Khe). The implementation of this locked mortise-and-tenon technique may reflect a Mediterranean influence via the Indian Ocean (Bellwood *et al.* 2007) (yet a mortise-and-tenon technique was indeed known in carpentry during the Chinese Neolithic, for example at Hemudu; it is not attested in shipbuilding anywhere else but at Dong Xa and Yen Bac in eastern or Southeast Asia). The grave at Dong Xa, dated to the first century BCE, has yielded two Chinese coins and a cup made of red lacquered wood. The grave at Yen Bac held carnelian beads, blue glass beads, a glass pendant, and a jade ear pendant (the jade may have come from Sichuan or Jiangsu) (Bellwood *et al.* 2007: 5–6).

The Integration of Southeast Asia into the Afro-Eurasian World-System

We have seen that a global trading system took place progressively in the Indian Ocean during the final centuries BCE. Halfway between the Mediterranean Sea and China, the Indian subcontinent was able to benefit from the expansion of eastern maritime routes at this time. In China, disturbances in Central Asia encouraged the Han rulers to look kindly upon maritime trade with the West via Southeast Asia. After the collapse of the Han dynasty, this policy would be pursued by the kingdom of Wu, which ruled southern China and northern Vietnam, and whose capital was at Jiangning, in the lower Yangtze River valley.

The Insulindian archipelago and continental Southeast Asia were favorably located at the junction of two seas. During this period, they had ships well adapted to ocean sailing (see Manguin 1980: 275). They had access to products coveted by India, western Asia, and the Mediterranean world on the one hand, and China on the other. At the top of the list figured spices, which the Indians went and fetched as early as the late first millennium BCE, as well as tin and gold from the Malay–Thai peninsula, and also gold from Sumatra and Kalimantan. Southeast Asia acted as a hub between the Chinese Empire, India, and – beyond India – the Greco-Roman world from the second century

BCE onward. The involvement of Southeast Asian cultures in trade before "indianiza-tion" has been emphasized above: networks had been in place between India and Southeast Asia before the formation of "indianized" states in the latter region.

The Han dynasty emperor Wudi (141–87 BCE) sent an embassy to Huangzhi (India). The *Qianhanshu* ("History of the Former Han," written by Ban Gu around 80 CE) notes:

There are interpreters, who recruit crews and go to sea to trade for brilliant pearls, glass, strange gems and other exotic products, giving in exchange gold and various silks. Merchant ships of the Barbarians transport them home again. But these Barbarians also, to get more profit (sometimes), rob people and kill them. Even if nothing (of this kind happens), they are away for several years.[41]

At this time, merchants and holy men from southern Asia or China traveled across the isthmus of the Malay–Thai peninsula on foot and sailed to India from ports located on the west coast of the peninsula, or from the Burmese coast. The *Qianhanshu* thus describes a crossing between Shen-li (on the Gulf of Thailand) and Fugandulu (Fu-kan-tu-lu), on the Bay of Bengal "on foot, in ten days." From there, the travelers would have had a two-month road journey to Huangzhi.[42]

Another mission was sent to Huangzhi by the regent Wang Mang, between 1 and 6 CE. This mission did not travel on Chinese ships. This time the whole voyage was made by sea, via a port called Pizong (P'i-tsung) located near Johor, on the Malay peninsula, or in Sumatra (Wheatley 1961: 11–12). The Chinese envoys returned through the country of Siqengbu (Ssu-Chheng-Pu), located "south of Huangzhi," which some authors have associated – based on no evidence – with the Axumite Empire or with a region in East Africa. Huangzhi sent a tribute in return, including a live rhinoceros.

Many archaeological sites reveal traces of Southeast Asia's insertion into the networks connecting China and the Indian Ocean. Oc Eo (Vietnam) has been mentioned above – a place to which we shall return later – as has Ban Don Ta Phet (Thailand). Central Thailand was linked to Indian networks via the terrestrial road of the "Three Pagodas Pass" and also via maritime routes. U-Thong, an early Buddhist center, was an active port; its site has yielded beads, seals, amulets, some of them from India.[43]

---

[41] Needham *et al.* 1971: 443; Ferrand 1919: 445–46; Wang Gungwu 1958: 19–20; Wolters 1967: 33. See below. P. Wheatley's translation is slightly different: "There are chief interpreters attached to the Yellow Gate who, together with volunteers, put out to sea to buy lustrous pearls . . . The trading ships of the barbarians transfer [the Chinese] to their destination. It is a profitable business [for the barbarians], who also loot and kill" (1961: 8). Note that "a Chinese coin – estimated to be dated to the 2nd century BC – was found in 1909 in excavations at Candravalli, [near] Mysore" (Malleret 1963, III: 392).

[42] "From the barriers of Jih-nan [northern Vietnam], Hsü-wen and Ho-p'u [Guangdong], it is about a five-month voyage to the country of Tu-yuan. [And] a further four-month voyage to the country of I-lu-mo, and yet another twenty odd days' voyage to the country of Shen-li [Chao Phraya River valley?]. It is rather more than ten days' journey on foot to the country of Fu-kan-tu-lu [Fugandulu], whence it is something over two months voyage to the country of Huang-chih [= Kanchi]" (Wheatley 1961: 8).

[43] Indrawooth 2004: 128. U-Thong shows the remains of a Buddhist building going back to the third or fourth century. Ku Bua was another significant coastal site, where a Dong Son drum has been excavated. A Buddhist construction stood in the center of the site. A clay-baked relief depicts a man with a high

On the Thai–Malay peninsula, Khuan Lukpad, and Kuala Selinsing exported tin and gold, and probably locally produced carnelian and glass beads as well. Kuala Selinsing has yielded artifacts of Indian origin (beads, seals), and also Chinese ceramics and a pottery reminiscent of Oc Eo. Various sites dated to this period have been discovered in the vicinity of places rich in tin in the Kelang region, an area that was already trading with the gold-producing regions of the interior (Upper Pahang) during the fifth–fourth century BCE.[44] Most of the bronze drums discovered in the Malay peninsula come from the Kelang region, which has also yielded bronze bells.[45] Moreover, land routes linking the Gulf of Thailand and the Indian Ocean went across the Thai–Malay peninsula; merchants followed these routes at least until the sixth century (see below).

As for insular Southeast Asia, the sites of southern Sumatra, Java, and Bali (Gilimanuk, Sembiran) are clearly situated along roads leading to the Moluccas and their spices. Other sites, in the Sulawesi Sea (Leang Buidane), the Sulu area, and the China Sea show links between the Moluccas, northern Kalimantan (Agop Atas), the southern Philippines (Tabon Caves in Palawan), and the Vietnamese coast (see above). Tools and bronze ornaments found in eastern Indonesia and New Guinea suggest the existence of trade routes going back at least as far as the second century BCE (Glover 1996).

The adoption of more intensive agricultural practices led to demographic growth. These advances, coupled with increasing trade, fostered the emergence of hierarchized societies.[46] For Wisseman Christie, "trade appears to have been the key to economic growth; control of trade appears to have provided the key to political development" (1995: 277). Connected with Indian networks, the Southeast Asian proto-states evolved, with the appearance of true urban forms and kingdoms presenting Indian features.[47] Complex societies were emerging, whose rulers adopted the Hindu or Buddhist religions, the Sanskrit or Pali language, script, and the notion of a divine king, on contact with Indian traders and missionaries. Indian concepts of kingship allowed Southeast Asian rulers, who invited priests and scholars into their court, "to legitimize their rule and enhance their status" (Indrawooth 2004: 123; Helms 1988: 140).[48] Brahmins, as religious specialists, who knew "the Sanskrit codes regarding law,

pointed hat reminiscent of that of the Saka of western India (100–400 CE). We know that the Saka used to send merchants to Southeast Asia (Indrawooth 2004: 130).

44 Wisseman Christie 1995: 248–249. The artifacts locally produced on the coasts were probably partly destined for trade with inland sites, whereas the goods imported from India or other distant countries were mostly kept by the coastal elites (Wisseman Christie 1995)

45 Bellwood 1997: 281. In addition, a bell has been found at Kampong Pencu near the Muar River (Bellwood 1997), dated to the third century CE. These bells derived from North Vietnamese models.

46 Slamet-Velsink (1995: 84–85), with whom Ray (2003: 124) appears to agree, linked the appearance of various types of "megalithic traditions" to these developments, in insular and continental Asia, and to assemblages containing bronze or iron objects.

47 In Funan and other states, "India," writes Malleret (1963, vol. IV), "brings a system of beliefs, political organization, and urban concepts." The importance of non-indianized elements has since been emphasized for the political traditions of Southeast Asia.

48 "The adoption of Brahmanical ritual by predominantly Buddhist societies," notes Ray (1994: 134), "led to the coexistence of the Buddhist monk and the Brahmana . . . Brahmanical ritual suited the requirements of the ruling elite better than that of Buddhism." The kings often provided patronage for both these

the art of government, art and architecture," were invited by local chiefs, and certainly played a role in the development of the state, along with Buddhist and Jain monks, especially from the fourth century onward (Kulke and Rothermund 1995: 153).[49] Sanskrit became the language of bureaucracy and government (Helms 1988: 145). In much the same way, Arabic, along with Islam, would later enter the languages of the semi-peripheries of Southeast Asia (and East Africa). Throughout Southeast Asia, writing brought about crucial changes in the spread of cumulative knowledge and the storing and transmission of information (Goody 2001: 144; Ray 2006a: 304). Shared beliefs "allowed the elite to communicate, interact and compete within a fully intra-regional [and supra-regional] context" (Manguin 2010: 171). The development of religious communities, urban centers, and state elites was accompanied by new patterns of consumption.

Various kingdoms flourished during the first centuries of the Christian era; their wealth was founded on trade, crafts, and intensive rice agriculture: the main kingdoms were Funan[50,51] in mainland Southeast Asia (southern Cambodia and Vietnam) from the first to the late sixth century CE, and the Cham kingdoms on the Vietnamese coast from the end of the second century onward,[52] where the languages spoken belonged essentially to the Austronesian family. Funan itself may have included a linguistic and cultural Austronesian component, but the main language spoken there was probably Mōn-Khmer.[53] Various researchers have suggested that the rulers of Funan claimed an Indian origin through the mythical marriage – a metaphor for "indianiza-tion" – of a princess and the Brahmin Kauṇḍinya.[54] In fact, the name of the "foreigner"

religions. "Though the earliest material traces of 'indianization' are Buddhist, by the fourth century AD, it was Saivism that dominated the royal capitals of the lower Mekong valley" (Ray 1994: 136).

[49] The inscriptions appeared from the fourth century onward. The Brahmins brought both "moral support" and their knowledge of administration. The state was built not only with support from an ideology that legitimated its power, but also through the assimilation of local cults (Kulke 1993; Ray 2003: 131). It is clear that in Funan, during the fifth and sixth centuries, beliefs were "mainly Brahmin," although Buddhism was present: at the turn of the fifth and sixth centuries, two Buddhist monks from Funan went to China (Pelliot 1903: 284–285).

[50] Variant: Banan (Pelliot 1903: 252, 284). This is the name of the state in the Chinese chronicles. It is probably the transcription for "an Old Khmer word bnam, today phnom, 'mountain'." For Coedès (1964: 74), "the kings of this country bore a title meaning 'mountain king'." According to M. Vickery (2003–2004: 103), however, "this was only a speculation by Finot," and C. Jacques has shown that there is no solid evidence for it. Vickery prefers another etymology for Funan: fu + nan, "south" (2003–2004: 126). Moreover, third-century Chinese texts mention the title fan for Funanese rulers, which seems to correspond to the Khmer title poñ, found in inscriptions and used for regional leaders and persons of high status (Vickery 1998: 190–204; Higham 2002: 252).

[51] According to J. Fox and J. Ledgerwood (1999), rice cultivation in Funan was a flood recession culture, assisted by the construction of retaining works.

[52] The Chinese texts place the founding of Lin-Yi (Champa) in 192 CE (Coedès 1964: 85). Like Funan, Champa developed an intensive rice culture, using iron plows, and waterwheels for irrigation.

[53] Blust 1994b: 50, 63. Vickery 2003–2004: 123ff. G. Thurgood (1999), however, argues that Funan belonged to the Austronesian domain.

[54] Various parallels to this legend can be found in Southeast Asia and in India (notably for the Pallava dynasty). Kaundinya was the name of a Brahmin lineage in South India (Kulke and Rothermund 1995: 153). During the thirteenth century (1296), a Chinese envoy at Angkor reports that "the population believes that the Khmer king sleeps with a nāga princess," the result of their union ensuring the kingdom's prosperity.

who married this princess reads as *hun* in the Chinese chronicles, a term which may represent a local title, according to Vickery: if so, then it is unlikely that *hun-dien* corresponds to an Indian name such as Kauṇḍinya (Vickery 2003–2004: 108–110).

The development of wet rice cultivation was inextricably linked to that of major political entities in the Javanese and Balinese kingdoms as well. Neither in Java nor in Bali did the formation of the state seem to have a direct connection with irrigation. The state did have the means, however, to build hydraulic networks and accumulate enough surpluses, allowing it to feed both the inhabitants of the cities and the merchants who needed to sojourn there for months while awaiting a change in wind direction. In fact, it was population growth, favored by the introduction of iron, that triggered the intensification of agriculture, and here water control was crucial. The use of buffalo-drawn plows and harrows may have been introduced from India prior to the creation of Funan.[55] Various irrigation techniques (such as the use of tanks) also seem to have benefited from Indian influences (Ludden 1999).

Funan

Although Funan's economy was primarily based on agriculture, its emergence (like that of the insular states) also resulted from the growth of transregional trade between the China Sea and the Indian Ocean. The true nature of the Funanese state is poorly understood. Power may have been founded – as was the case later in Srīwijaya – on systems of alliance: Funan should not be seen as one great, centralized state, but rather as "a network of ports and small states" (Lieberman 2003: 217).[56] For Funan and the region around the Gulf of Thailand, Manguin (2000d: 175) suggests a culture of city-states, parallel to that of the Malay world (the state of Dvāravatī would later repeat this configuration). The region, however, does not exhibit the same geographical fragmentation as the Malay world or the Vietnamese coasts; therefore various political entities found it possible to impose their dominance during certain periods of time. The hydraulic complex linking Oc Eo and Angkor Borei by channels reveals a state able to mobilize a substantial labor force, probably through a system of corvées and perhaps using slaves. The oldest levels at Angkor Borei go back to the fifth–fourth century BCE. Most of the building of the hydraulic networks probably occurred from the third century CE, when Buddhist and Vishnuite religious monuments were first erected.[57] The city of Angkor Borei covered 300 ha, ringed by walls. It was the capital

---

[55] Their adoption indicates a population density sufficient to enable intensification of agricultural practices in some regions. The use of plows, however, may have been limited to rulers. Moreover, in the case of the flood-recession rice cultivation described by Fox and Ledgerwood, the use of plows was unnecessary.

[56] See Wolters (1979); Vickery 1998: 18–19, 61ff.; Higham 2001: 23ff. Other authors think in terms of the building of a true state, with an army and administration.

[57] Spouted vessels of the *kendi* type also appeared at this time; they played a role in rituals. On the first results of the excavations led in 1997–2002 in Oc Eo and its region, see Manguin 2005. At Linh Son, on Ba The hill, the oldest levels of the site (dated to 100 BCE – 100 CE) have yielded a vessel containing a carnelian bead and some gold; the upper levels (200–850) have shown brick structures. For Angkor Borei, the Lower Mekong Archaeological Project (LOMAP) has been conducting research since 1995 (see Stark and Sovath 2001). The radiocarbon datings at Angkor Borei are between the fourth century BCE and the tenth century CE, during a period postdating the collapse of Funan: the site, therefore, had not been abandoned at the

(or one of the capitals) of Funan.[58] The Chinese texts mention the implementation of taxation and military expansion. At the beginning of the third century, writes the *Liangshu*, "with his powerful troops, Fan Shih-man attacked and subjected the neighboring kingdoms; all acknowledged themselves his vassals. Later, he had large ships built, and sailing all over the Chang-hai [the Gulf of Thailand] he attacked more than ten kingdoms, including Chü-tu-k'un, Chiu-chih [Zhuli] and Tien-sun [Dunsun]. He extended his territory by five or six thousand *li*."[59] The Chao Phraya region was located within the sphere of Funan, as shown by the assemblages excavated at Ban Tha Kae (glass, agate, and gold beads, seals), a site covering 40 ha, Muang Phra Rot and, for phases 3–4, Chansen.[60]

The interest Southeast Asia and China held for India resulted in part from the arrival on the Indian subcontinent of products from the region the Chinese called Da Qin (Roman western Asia and the Persian Gulf). Trade networks between the Mediterranean Sea and India were in fact interconnected with those of the eastern Indian Ocean and the China Sea, and Chinese chronicles seem to indicate the existence of regular trade with Da Qin during the third century (see above).

Various states on the mainland, the Thai–Malay peninsula, and insular Southeast Asia sent ships overseas. The Chinese annals left us the names of these states, but they are not always easy to locate. During the first centuries of the Christian era, however, it is probable that Funan dominated the maritime routes (and the land routes crossing the Thai–Malay peninsula). A Chinese book, the *Liangshu* ("History of the Liang"), written in the seventh century, speaks of the large ships of a Funanese king during the

time of those political transformations. For the Funanese period, brick structures belonging to temples – the founding deposits of which have been extensively looted – have been discovered (Stark 1998: 191, 193–194). Near Oc Eo, recent excavations at Nen Chua "uncovered a brick and stone foundation for a temple which contained a linga and gold ornaments" ("radiocarbon dates indicate use between AD 450–650") (Le Xuan Diem *et al.* 1995; Higham 2002: 239). East of the Mekong, a cemetery dated between 400 and 600 CE at Go Thap has yielded stone and glass beads, and gold leaf decorated with images of Hindu divinities has been found in the foundations of brick structures; a statue of Vishnu has been discovered. Gold leaf has also been found at Go Xoai (*c.* seventh century), east of Oc Eo, in the brick foundations of a stupa (Higham 2002: 240), showing archaic elements from northwestern India (Le Thi Lien 2005) (one fragment of gold leaf bears an inscription). A Vishnuite inscription dated to the fifth century has been excavated at Thap Muoi, northeast of Oc Eo; Thap Muoi has also yielded Buddhist ruins (Manguin 2004b: 303). East of Oc Eo, Da Noi also revealed gold plaques with representations of linga, and an inscription (fifth–sixth century) (Le Thi Lien 2005).

[58] The location of this capital has generated intense debate. Coedès (1964a: 74–75) has argued that the Chinese Temu given as the name of the capital (during the sixth/seventh century) is the transcription for a Khmer term *dmāk*, rendering the meaning of Vyadha (pura), a city that he located at Ba Phnom. Coedès acknowledged that Angkor Borei was the capital of the last king of Funan, who may have settled there after an attack from Zhenla (Coedès 1964a: 130). On the location of the capital, Vickery 2003–2004: 125ff.

[59] Pelliot 1903; Coedès 1968: 38. These kingdoms, probably situated on the Thai–Malay peninsula and in central Thailand, have not been precisely located.

[60] Higham 2002: 254–255, 259. Ban Tha Kae is situated not far from Lopburi. The lower levels of the site go back to the Bronze Age; later, iron is present; the median levels show Indian imports, whereas the upper levels exhibit links with Oc Eo. At Chansen, "eight bowls in a metallic black ware with parallels in Sri Lanka" have been excavated: they may be imports (Higham 2002: 255). However, Vickery has refuted the idea that Fan Shih-man dominated southern-central Vietnam (2003–2004: 122).

third century.[61] During this time, Funan engaged in trade with the Moluccas in order to acquire cloves, which were then exported to China or to the West (Wolters 1967: 39). A fifth-century Chinese text refers to Funanese people who hired vessels that were probably Indonesian. Chinese ceramics dated to the fifth century have been recovered in the Banda Islands, far earlier than the Song pottery of the tenth century (Lape 2002: 484). The *Jinshu* ("History of the Jin"), written around 645, signals that between the third and fifth century "taxes, in Funan, were paid in gold, silver, pearls and perfumes": Funan was clearly involved in international trade, which favored its development.[62] The *Yi yuan*, written in the middle of the fifth century, notes that the inhabitants of Funan "use gold in their transactions." Zhang Yue (seventh century) speaks of "the big seagoing junks of Funan that come from western India and sell mirrors of *biboli* [transparent glass]" (Hirth and Rockhill 1911: 228). The Chinese chronicles mention two Funanese ports on the Malay peninsula: Dunsun, on the northeast coast, and Douzhuli, which has sometimes been identified with the Takkola of Ptolemy (Takuapa), on the west coast.[63] Dunsun was the name of another region (see below).

Archaeological work conducted in the Mekong delta has revealed the importance of Oc Eo (first–seventh century) in transregional exchange networks. Surrounded by four ditches and five walls, the city covered 450 hectares. Oc Eo has yielded objects from the Greco-Roman world, Persia, and India (see above).[64] Silver coins from Burma, Thailand, and India have been unearthed, and coins may have been minted locally.[65] According to the *Jinshu*, "many of the utensils used by the people from Funan for their meals are made of silver," a metal that must have been imported, possibly from China

---

[61] Wheatley 1961: 15; see above. "The inhabitants of Funan were able to build ships of closed construction using large crews" (Pelliot 1925: 252–263; Malleret 1962, III: 393).

[62] Wicks 1992: 184, 186. Gold and silver were probably imported into Funan.

[63] It was from this port that the Funanese envoy departed for India. P. Wheatley has argued against this identification, however, placing Douzhuli in the estuary of Kuantan. This would correspond to the Kōle of Ptolemy (Coedès 1964a: 80). Dunsun cannot correspond to Khlong Thom as proposed by Higham (2002: 262).

[64] Besides the assemblages already mentioned, Malleret (1963, IV: 313) notes the discovery of stone artifacts such as a mitred Vishnu and three lingas. One of the lingas, "of an archaic type," evokes the style of Travancore (South India). A Sūrya from Bathē (dated to the sixth century) exhibits a costume of Iranian aspect, which Malleret connects to "Indo-Scythian" influences (going back to the Murunda dynasty) which were noticeable in India until the sixth century (Malleret 1963, IV: 320). Recent excavations at Oc Eo reveal a phase of abandonment of the sites at the turn of the third and fourth centuries, prior to a new period of occupation that extended until 650. Remains of buildings, as well as inscriptions and statuary show the coexistence of Buddhism and Hinduism (Manguin 2004b: 298). The abandonment of the site of Oc Eo during the mid-seventh century may have been linked to environmental problems caused by a volcanic eruption, but a change in interregional trade routes and a shift of political power to Zhenla, located inland, seem to have been more relevant causes (Manguin 2004b: 300–301). The site of Angkor Borei remained inhabited after the tenth century, although one notes a drop in its population from the seventh century onward and a hiatus in statuary during the eighth and ninth centuries (Stark and Sovath 2001: 91).

[65] But one Chinese text mentions gold for transactions in Funan (see above). Silver coins show the Vishnuite conch, or sun, on one face, and the *srīvatsa*, on the other, an ancient Indian symbol, especially common in Amāravatī art (Malleret 1959, I: 132–133). Coins from the Oc Eo region "have been compared to coins issued at Chandravalli, Karnataka and to a type found between the Krishna and Godavari rivers" (Ray 1989: 52; Stark and Sovath 2001: 93).

(Pelliot 1903: 254; Malleret 1962, III: 410).[66] While trade with China, via the Vietnamese coast, has been detected, Oc Eo provided only a few Chinese objects, especially fragments of mirrors belonging to the eastern Han dynasty period (25–220).[67] Funan sent many embassies to China. The first one, in 225, offered Indian or Mediterranean glass.[68] A king by the name of "Fan Hsün may have sent three delegations to the Jin court between 285 and 287" (Southworth 2004b: 530). In 484, a Funanese embassy presented "a chiseled gold picture of the throne of the king of the dragons, an elephant made of white sandal wood, two ivory stupas, two lengths of cotton fabrics, two glass *sou-li*, and a tray for betelnuts made of tortoiseshell"[69] to the Chinese emperor, and asked "the emperor at the same time for help in conquering Línyì [north of Champa]" (*Nan Qi Shu*). In 519, the tribute brought by one of the six embassies sent by the Funanese king Rudravarman between 517 and 539 included "*hou-ts'i* beads, Indian saffron, storax and other perfumes."[70]

Funan was the only political entity of Southeast Asia to receive an embassy from a Chinese empire: in 245–250, the kingdom of Wu (lower Yangtze) dispatched Kang Tai and Zhu Ying (Chu-Ying), perhaps to gather information on maritime routes to India and the Roman world (Wu was cut off from the Silk Roads of Inner Asia, and therefore interested in maritime trade routes). At the court of Funan, the Chinese met the ambassador of a Muruṇḍa king.[71] Kang Tai learned about the existence of trade between Funan and India, and the possibility that a "seagoing junk using seven sails" could go from Chia-na-tiao to Da Qin in one month and a few days with favorable wind.[72] Kang Tai and Zhu Ying pointed out the use of a script originating in India: "They like to engrave ornaments and inscriptions. There are books and depositories of archives. The characters of their script resemble those of the *hu*."

Funan also maintained official relations with India. Around 230–240 CE, the kingdom of Tianzhu (India) received envoys from Funan, who arrived at the mouths of the Ganges and sailed up the river (perhaps as far as Pāṭaliputra). The kingdom of Tianzhu later sent

---

[66] The texts indicate local crafts: "They manufacture gold rings, bracelets and silver plates . . . Bronze idols are cast" (Pelliot 1903: 261, 269). A Chinese text, however, mixes imports and local goods in its description: "Funan produces gold, silver, copper, tin, aloeswood perfume, ivory, peacocks, kingfishers, and parrots of five colors" (Pelliot 1903: 263).

[67] Malleret (1962, III: 173–174) has also mentioned the discovery of a *capstan bead* of Chinese origin. In addition, he has noted two Buddhist statuettes "related to the Chinese aesthetics of the Wei" (sixth century).

[68] Ferrand 1919: 179. Malleret writes (1962, III: 410) that China received opaque glass from Funan (thus in 225, and later in 229 and 231), a type of glass that the Chinese texts also mention as coming from Da Qin.

[69] Pelliot 1903: 269. On the promise of an alliance, the king of Funan agreed to give five gold *polo*, the equivalent of several hundred kilos. The Indian monk Nagasena was sent by Funan in 484 as ambassador to solicit China's assistance for a military invasion of Champa. Between 434 and 438, the king of Funan "Shih-li-t'o-pa-mo (Sri Indravarman)" had already sent offerings to the emperor Wen (Song dynasty), because at the time he planned to launch an attack on Champa.

[70] Malleret (1962, III: 410) indicates that the beads are *gilded beads*, "with a metal lamella inserted between glass beds." Similar beads have been discovered at U-Thong, Kedah, and other sites in Southeast Asia. They were certainly imported from the Roman world; they are known in India, the Mediterranean, and Egypt (as early as the fourth century BCE). See above.

[71] This testimony by Kang Tai and Zhu Ying has been preserved in the *Liangshu* (Wheatley 1961: 14; Coedès 1964a: 84–85).

[72] See above. Wolters, as previously mentioned, locates Chia-na-tiao toward the Indus.

Figure 11.3 Coins found at Oc Eo (Vietnam) with *srivatsa* on one side, conch or sun on the other; these are similar to coins from Burma and Thailand (after Malleret 1962, vol. III, pl. XLIV)

emissaries to Funan. "The king of Funan sent one of his relatives [Su Wu] in embassy to India to the court of the Meou-louen (Muruṇḍa) ruler who reigned on the Ganges, and the Murunda in return sent four Yue-tche horses as a gift to the king of Funan."[73]

The States of the Thai–Malay Peninsula

The Thai–Malay peninsula, as pointed out above, formed an active interface between the Indian Ocean, the Gulf of Thailand, and insular Southeast Asia. Small states emerged very early on, whose development resulted, on the one hand, from their situation as intermediaries on trade routes between oceans and, on the other hand, from the exploitation of tin, gold, and forest products. The Indian text of the *Mahāniddesa* uses the term *Tambalingam* to refer to Tāmbraliṅga (see above), whose capital was Ligor (near Nakhon Si Thammarat). In addition, the Chinese texts mention Langyaxiu (Langkasuka, centered on Pattani-Yarang), situating its founding around the second century,[74] and Dunsun (Tun-sun), from the Proto-Mon *dun sun*, "five cities" (Tennasserim, north of the Thai–Malay peninsula), which may have been a Mōn kingdom with a capital located near Pong Tuk or P'ra Pathom. According to the *Taiping Yulan* (seventh or eighth century), which quotes a book from the fifth century entitled *Funan zhi*, in this kingdom of Dunsun there were "five hundred families of *hu* from India, two *fo-t'u* and more than a thousand Indian Brahmans. The people from Tun-sun practice their doctrine and give them their daughters in marriage; consequently many of the Brahmans do not go away."[75] The *Liangshu* (see

---

[73] Coedès 1964a: 92. "Ch'en Sung was sent to Funan with four Yuezhi horses by the ruler of Tien-chu (possibly the Murunda dynasty)" (Wang Gungwu 1958: 40 n. 35, after the *Liangshu*). On the Murunda dynasty, see above.

[74] The *Liangshu* says that Lang-ya-hsiu "was founded more than 400 years ago" (Wheatley 1961: 253; Coedès 1964a: 79). The same chronicle mentions Dunsun as a vassal kingdom of Funan (Wheatley 1961: 15–16). Chinese ceramics have been excavated north of Pattani at Satingphra from 100 CE onward.

[75] Wheatley 1961: 17, text and n. 2. According to Pelliot (1904: 279 n. 4), the *hu* were probably part of a class of merchants. The *fo-t'u* may have been Buddhists. The term *hu* is usually applied to people from Central

epigraph above) points out the central position of Dunsun between the Indian Ocean and the Gulf of Thailand, a region vassal to Funan.[76]

Geluo (Kolo) was another significant city-state of the peninsula. According to parallel sections of the *Tongdian* (written by Du You, 732–812), the *Taiping huanyu ji* (published in 979), and the *Wenxian tongkao* (finished in 1317), "Kolo first became known during Han times" (Wheatley 1961: 56; Gernet 1999: 302). As noted above, the Tamil poem *Paṭṭinappālai* mentions trade between South India and Kāḷagam, which may be related to the terms Geluo in the Chinese chronicles and Kalāh used by Arabo-Persian geographers. Kalāh was especially active from the eighth to the tenth century, when it was brought under the rule of Srīwijaya (as was Kedah). Its location is still debated: the isthmus of Kra, Kedah, and Kelang have all been suggested.[77] The *Wenxian tongkao* mentions – in the itinerary of Jia Dan (730–805) – Kokulo (Takola) as being located west of Geluo (Keluo, or Ko-lo), which situates the latter south of the isthmus of Kra.

As already mentioned, during the early third century, Funan extended its domination over Dunsun, in order to control trade between the Indian Ocean and the China Sea. It has often been thought that from the third to the sixth century, the ports of Chaiya (north of Tāmbralinga), Tāmbralinga, and Langkasuka (Pattani), on the eastern Malay coast, were under the tutelage of Funan, as well as inland roads leading to these ports. The city-states of the Thai–Malay peninsula, however, sent their own embassies to China (Manguin 2004b: 296). P. Wheatley notes as many as ten transpeninsular trade routes between the China Sea and the Indian Ocean. According to the *Qianhanshu*, Dunsun controlled routes from Shenli (Chao Phraya valley) to Fugandulu (on the Bay of Bengal) (see above, Wheatley 1961: 8–9). A route ran from the estuary of the Tennasserim River in the west, to the east coast at the same latitude. Another crossed the isthmus of Kra. Further south, a route linked Takola and Chaiya. From Trang, a route led to the region of Ligor. Kaṭāha (Kedah) was connected to Pattani. A path linked the valleys of the Perak and Pattani rivers, and another Muar and Pahang. Finally, in the south of the peninsula, a route ran across Johor, between Batu Pahat and Endau (Wheatley 1961: xxvi–xxvii) (Map II.13). Some researchers have questioned the significance of these routes, however, because few artifacts have been excavated for that period.

Asia, who used a script of Indian origin (Coedès 1964a: 85). Lombard (1990, II: 28), despite the mention of India, sees in the term *hu* a reference to Persians who had settled in the kingdom of Dunsun, during the Tang period. For Manguin (2004b: 297), these were more likely to be Sogdian and Bactrian merchants.

[76] "More than 3,000 *li* from the southern frontier of Funan is the kingdom of Dunsun . . . The [main] city is ten *li* from the sea. There are five kings who all acknowledge themselves vassals of Funan" (Wheatley 1961: 16). See also Guillot 2004.

[77] Wheatley 1961: 56–59; Wolters 1967: 163; Streck 1978: 488–489; Lombard 1990, II: 26. On the different locations suggested for Kalah, see Tibbetts 1979: 118–128. Ferrand places Kalah on the isthmus of Kra, as does Wheatley, who suggests a location at Mergui; Kern considers Kalah as having been located at Kedah, as does Nilakanta Sastri (1949: 66) (Sastri sees the Zabag–Kalah pairing in the Arab texts as parallel to the Srivisaya–Kaḍāram pairing in the inscriptions from South India). The Chinese term "Golofujalo" may correspond to the same place. The Arab geographer Mas'ūdī (tenth century) mentions mountains rich in tin located between Pahang and Kalāh; this may indicate a location either at Kedah or Kelang. For Jacq-Hergoualc'h *et al.* (1998: 266), "Kalah was probably an umbrella term for various Muslim ports of call on this coast."

The Chinese chronicles mention the states of Panpan (P'an-p'an), located on the Malay peninsula north of the Kra isthmus, with the town of Chaiya as its center,[78] and Dandan (Tan-tan), a southern polity located in the region of Trengganu.[79] The *Liangshu* contains the oldest mention of these states in a text concerning Funan. Panpan sent embassies to China during the fifth, sixth, and seventh centuries and Dandan during the sixth century (see below). Moreover, at the beginning of the seventh century, a Chinese embassy traveled to the "Land of the Red Earth," Chitu (Ch'ih-t'u), a Hinduized region probably located south of Langkasuka. They brought "five thousand kinds of gifts" for the king, and received gold and camphor from Barus in exchange.[80] The *Xintangshu* mentions Luoyue, in the southern part of the peninsula, during the seventh century: "traders passing back and forth meet there; every year merchants embark on junks and come to Kuang-chou [Canton]" (Wheatley 1961: 58). Indian and Chinese texts also speak of Kedah (Indian Kaṭāha, Chinese Jiecha [Chieh-ch'a], mentioned for the first time during the seventh century by Yijing).

Archaeological discoveries have complemented the textual data. Cultural vestiges at Chaiya are mainly Hinduist prior to its domination by Srīwijaya, marked by the implantation of Mahāyāna Buddhism; older Buddhist items have been discovered, however.[81]

During the 1970s, the region of Nakhon Si Thammarat yielded a treasure containing hundreds of silver coins of the "rising sun" type, also known in central Burma and Thailand. Remains of smaller Hindu temples have been found that are dated to a period between the fifth and seventh centuries, revealing statues of Vishnu and *linga*,[82] as well as Buddhist vestiges (statuettes of Buddha, votive tablets) going back as far as the seventh century. A Sanskrit inscription dated to the seventh century in Pallava script mentions donations both to Brahmins and to the Buddhist *sangha*, showing the good relations that existed between the different religious communities. Several Buddhist monuments dated to the sixth and seventh centuries have been discovered at Yarang (Jacq-Hergoualc'h 2002).

[78] Jacq-Hergoualc'h *et al.* 1996: 361. According to Chinese traditions, Panpan was said to have been founded during the third century by a Funanese general who had conquered this region.

[79] Wheatley 1961: 47–55; Coedès 1964a: 102–103. In contrast, O. Wolters situates Dandan in Java (1967: 204–206).

[80] See the *Suishu*, Wheatley 1961: 26–36; Coedès 1964a: 148–150. The *Liangshu*, completed in 635, also mentions camphor as a product from Langyasiu (Langkasuka) in the sixth century (Hirth and Rockhill 1911: 194). Shen Fuwei (2002) situates Chitu at Palembang, but his arguments are inconclusive (Yang Shao-yun n.d.).

[81] Jacq-Hergoualc'h *et al.* 1998: 245ff. "Mitred" Vishnus have been discovered in the region of Chaiya and further south; the oldest is dated to *c.* 400 CE. A small Vishnuite complex dated to the sixth century has been unearthed at Khao Sivichai, near Chaiya. Among Buddhist statues excavated in the region of Chaiya, the oldest, from the site of Wiang Sa, may date from the end of the fifth century and seems to have been influenced by the Gupta school of Sārnāth. Another Buddha, from the sixth century, is similar to pieces from Funan; it shows influences from the art of the Krishnā River valley or Sri Lanka. Mahāyāna Buddhism was present even before any influence from Srīwijaya; it probably arrived with merchants and pilgrims from eastern Asia (Jacq-Hergoualc'h *et al.* 1998: 255).

[82] M. Jacq-Hergoualc'h *et al.* 1996: 368ff. The authors mention the discovery of a foundation deposit including a turtle cut from a gold sheet, as well as silver and gold lotus flowers. Similar deposits are known from Oc Eo, Kedah and other sites (Jacq-Hergoualc'h *et al.* 1998: 376).

On the west coast, finds of objects from India or the Roman world at Khuan Lukpad have been signaled above. Here, many local gold coins, based on the Pegu conch/*srīvatsa* prototype have been unearthed, in association with glass remains (the site may have been a manufacturing center for glass beads between the second and the sixth–seventh centuries). These gold coins were probably used in exchanges. The various coin types suggest that "coinage had a relatively long development in the region of Krabi" (Wicks 1992: 222).[83] The assemblage at Khuan Lukpad resembles those at U-Thong and Oc Eo and surely dates to the same period. Although the conch/*srīvatsa* type from Pegu influenced other types of Southeast Asian coinage,[84] it is worth mentioning that these coins were "struck to local weight standards and limited in geographical distribution."[85] Many remains of sanctuaries have been discovered in the region of Kedah, reflecting the adoption of Indian traditions by local elites.[86] Recent excavations show ironwork at the site of Sungai Batu (Kedah); they have yielded a date of 110 CE.[87]

As noted above, the majority of the Dong Son bronzes discovered on the Thai–Malay peninsula came from the region of Kelang, where a small kingdom appears to have developed very early on. It probably controlled a route leading to Kuala Trengganu, as well as the export of tin (the Kalāh/Kāḷagam of the Arab and Tamil texts may be located here).[88]

Champa and Jiaozhi

Centered on a river valley, the kingdoms of the Thai–Malay peninsula provide us with models for the states that we also find in Champa, on the east coast of Sumatra or on the coasts of Kalimantan. Beyond a kingdom's fluvial system, its ruler's power depended upon his military strength and first and foremost, upon his ability to build alliances. The changing location of the capital among various urban centers founded at the mouths of different rivers reflected a transfer of hegemony from one fluvial system to another (Hall 1992: 254). This favored different regions in turn: there was no strongly institutionalized state system, but rather a setting up of alliance networks. Very early on, the Vietnamese coast appears to have forged a cosmopolitan culture, in connection with its various neighbors. "Champa (i.e. central Vietnam) was a gate to the Chinese world for Malay-Indonesian people, and also a gate to the indianized world for the

[83] A first variant of these coins is reminiscent of the silver coins from Pegu. Another variant shows a *swastika* instead of the *srīvatsa*.

[84] Many of these silver coins have been found at P'ra Pathom, as well as coins featuring the rising sun (Malleret 1959, I: 136). As mentioned above, P'ra Pathom was perhaps the center of a Mōn kingdom. Rising sun coins were often cut into pieces: "cut portions would have served as fractional coinage" (Wicks 1992: 162).

[85] Wicks 1992: 313. The same may be said of sandalwood flower coins from Java or Sumatra, which have been found in various places along trade networks.

[86] Even when involved in trade with India, the small states were not all "indianized." Wisseman Christie (1995: 254) mentions the port of Tanjung Rawa, in the region of Kuala Selinsing, during the third through fourth centuries, as "the core of a merchant-state" that was apparently not indianized.

[87] Mokhtar Saidin, conference at Penang, December 18, 2010.

[88] Wisseman Christie 1990: 50–51. The tombs of the Kelang region reveal the existence of a stratified society. Ibn Khurdādbeh says of Kalāh that it "owned the renowned tin mines *kala'i* and plantations of bamboos."

Philippines and Vietnam" (Lam Thi My Dzung 2009: 68). Indian Rouletted Ware and *kendi* vessels have been found at Tra Kieu, a significant political and economic center throughout the first half of the first millennium CE. Excavations have also revealed Chinese influences: Tra Kieu has yielded Han seal impressions, bronze crossbow-bolts, and roof tiles decorated with human faces, in the Chinese style (associated with Wu and the western Jin, third–fourth century); these are also known at Co Luy, Than Ho, Nha Trang (central Vietnam), Lung Khe, and Tham To (northern Vietnam) (Southworth and Prior 2010: 191; Yamagata and Nguyen Kim Dung 2010: 194). For Southworth (2001), Tra Kieu was the capital of the Xitu kingdom, located south of Xianglin, a region that rebelled against Han China around 192 CE. Tra Kieu was occupied until the seventh century, and again from the tenth century onward. Co Luy has also yielded Han-style stamped jars.

For Yamagata (2007), however, Tra Kieu was the capital of a state known as Linyi by the Chinese ("city of the forest"); its Vietnamese name was Champa from the sixth century onward (and Zhànchéng in Chinese records). The Chinese chronicles place the founding of Linyi in 192 (Coedès 1964a: 85). Linyi alternated between diplomatic missions and looting raids. It sent two embassies to China during the third century (to the Jin, in 268 and 284), three embassies during the fourth century (to the Jin, in 340, 374, 380), no less than thirteen during the fifth century (eleven of these to the Song),[89] and again fifteen during the sixth century (nine to the Liang, four to the Chen, and two to the Sui).[90] The *Shuijing Zhu* (sixth century) describes Lam Ap, the capital of Linyi. Trade with India and China (Guangzhou region) grew over these final centuries. Sanskrit inscriptions found in Quang Nam province and – 500 km further south – in Phu Yēn province mention the name of a king, Bhadravarman, who founded a sanctuary dedicated to Shiva located at My Son, near Tra Kieu. Here Bhadravarman probably built his capital.[91] In 605, after conquering northern Vietnam, a Chinese army entered Linyi and took its capital, discovering eighteen inscribed gold tablets, and 1,350 Buddhist texts "in the Kunlun language." These discoveries reveal the significance of Buddhism at the time (Southworth 2004a: 224).

Excavations have yielded evidence of exchange networks between the coast and the mountains, with the discoveries of Indian carnelian and agate beads and two-headed animal ornaments at the inland site of Tabhing (Quang Nam province) (late first millennium BCE to early CE).

---

[89] In reprisal for the Cham raids in Rinan (northern Vietnam), *c.* 440, a Chinese army sacked the fortress of Qusu, then the capital of Linyi, perhaps located in the region of Hue. "The recorded removal of as much as 48,000 kg of gold is some indication of the wealth which the rulers of Linyi had amassed" (Higham 2002: 275). In 445, the Linyi offered "10,000 *jin* of gold, 100,000 *jin* of silver and 300,000 *jin* of copper as tribute." Part of this metal must have come from long-distance trade.

[90] Wang Gungwu 1958: 120–123. The first tributary missions came from a northern kingdom (region of Hue, and later of Tra Kieu); they went to Jiaozhi in 220–230, then to China from 268.

[91] A region later known by the name Amaravati. Tra Kieu has yielded several rupestrian inscriptions, one in a Chamic language. A bronze Buddha showing a "Gupta influence" has been discovered at Dong Duong (Coedès 1964a: 96) (it has been dated to the fourth century, but may in fact belong to the ninth century). See above. The oldest levels at the site of Tra Kieu go back to the third or second century BCE. As already mentioned, a fragment of Indian Rouletted Ware has been unearthed. Funan may have controlled the southern regions, at least at certain times. An inscription by a Funanese king has been found in the Nha Trang region.

Between Champa and China, northern Vietnam was a region active in maritime trade very early on (see above). The Red River Valley was dominated by the Nanyue kingdom (203–111 BCE), and later by Han China (111 BCE – 222 CE) and the kingdom of Wu (222–280). Through its relations with Funan on the one hand, and the region of Canton and the Lower Yangtze on the other, this valley welcomed many foreigners. One of the translators of Indian texts into Chinese, Kang Senghui, who arrived at Nanjing in 247, was born in Vietnam to a family of Sogdian merchants, who had come from India (Gernet 1999: 190). From the third to the fifth century, however, maritime routes seem to have gone from southern China and Champa, bypassing northern Vietnam. This change in the routes may have been facilitated by the development of naval technology, with the appearance of larger ships (Nishimura 2005: 106).

Insular Southeast Asia: State Development during the Fifth and Sixth Centuries

Various states also formed in insular Southeast Asia. At the beginning of the third century, a kingdom that the Chinese called Geying (Ko-Ying) or Zhaying (Cha-ying) traded with Yuezhi (Kushan) merchants originating from northern India: horses bought from the Yuezhi arrived at Geying.[92] This kingdom may have been located on the Malay peninsula (Pelliot 1925: 250) or the southeast coast of Sumatra, or in Java, as Wolters (1999) suggests. Geying may be the transcription of the Indian name Kalinga, which during the Tang period referred to Sumatra-Java (Pelliot 1925: 250). Chinese envoys in Funan during the third century also allude to the Sidiao kingdom, located 3,000 li southeast of Geying (Nan zhou yi wu zhi). An Austronesian trade developed toward China. The Chinese text Houhanshu mentions an embassy from the Yediao kingdom in 132; the term Yediao corresponds to the Prākrit form of the Sanskrit Yāvadvīpa and may refer either to the region of Melayu/Jambi on the eastern Sumatran coast or to a Javanese kingdom (Mahdi 2008: 114).[93]

Recent excavations have unearthed two sites along the southeastern coast of Sumatra dating to the first half of the first millennium. North of Palembang, Karang Agung has yielded glass and bronze bangles, metal pendants imported from India or from Oc Eo, shards of Indian pottery with a pinkish grey paste, red-slipped ceramics of the kendi type (ritual vessels); gold foil that probably covered the eyes of a corpse; and

---

[92] These merchants sailed from a port that the Nan zhou yi wu zhih calls Kunu (Wolters 1967: 59). The name Geying is mentioned in the Wushi waiguo zhuan of Kang Tai and Zhu Ying, and in the Nan zhou yi wu zhi of Wan Zhen, both written during the third century; although these books are lost, they have been quoted in a tenth-century compilation entitled Taiping yulan (Wolters 1967: 24, 47, 49–50, 59–60). The design of the bronze drum from Sangeang Island attests to this horse trade (Malleret 1962, III: 403 n. 9; see above).

[93] Sidiao may be "a typographical error for Yediao," see Mahdi 2008: 114, 116. According to Mahdi, Sidiao was more likely located in Java. Ferrand (1919: 178) had already supported the idea of "indianization" during the first centuries of the Christian era. He interpreted the name Tiao-Pien attributed to the king of Yediao who sent an embassy to China in 132 as the Chinese transcription of the Sanskrit name Devavarman (?). Pelliot (1925: 251) has refuted any equivalence between pien and varman.

beads. East of the mouth of the Musi River, glass and bronze bangles and two Chinese ewers have been excavated at Air Sugihan (fifth–sixth century).[94]

When the Hephthalites cut off the terrestrial Silk Roads during the fifth century, China and Persia turned to maritime trade. Southern China's demand for luxury goods from the West promoted trade between China and western Asia (Wolters correctly observes that this was a greater factor for growth than was the demand for Chinese silk from India, Persia, and the Mediterranean Sea [Wolters 1967: 82; Basa 1999: 48]). This progress in maritime trade benefited the Southeast Asian states. Closer relations between Funan and China brought prosperity to the states controlling the routes crossing the Malay peninsula, and insular Southeast Asia also took an active part in this commerce. During the fifth century, 24 embassies from Southeast Asia arrived in China: 4 came from Funan; 2 from the Panpan kingdom (on the Malay Kra Isthmus); 8 from Pohuang (southern Sumatra?); 1 from Gantuoli (Kan-t'o-li) (Sumatra?);[95] 6 from Heluodan (Java); and 3 from Poda (P'o-ta) (Java ?). During the sixth century, China welcomed 38 embassies from these regions: 12 from Funan; 9 from Panpan; 4 from Langkasuka; 7 from Dandan (on the Malay peninsula); 4 from Gantuoli; and 2 from Poli (Panei, in Sumatra, as well as Bali, have both been suggested).[96]

Various states from insular Southeast Asia competed with Funan along the main trade routes. "Western Java [especially] may have profited from the third–fourth century Funan paramountcy over the perimeter of the Gulf of Thailand by serving as a base for shipping to China via the alternative route over the Java Sea, Strait of Macassar, and the Philippines" (Mahdi 2008: 122 n. 31). The kingdoms that the Chinese called Gantuoli – a state preceding Śrīwijaya – and Heluodan (Ho-lo-tan, or Ho-lo-t'o, or He-le-tan) (western Java) were both in contact with South India.[97] Heluodan sent an embassy in 430 which brought with it cotton cloth (*gu-bei* and *bo-die*) from Tianzhu (India) (Salmon 2009: 188; Ferrand 1919: 179, data based on the *Songshu*). Heluodan's final embassy to China is dated to 452. In a letter, the king expressed concerns as his country was being attacked on all sides; he then requested help from China (soon thereafter, Tārumānagara succeeded Heluodan) (Wolters 1967: 151). The presence of Chinese jars that may be dated to the fourth–fifth century (Sassanid period) at Sīrāf in Persia and Sohar in Oman has been mentioned above; they may have been transported by Sassanid traders (or other merchants) (Rougeulle 1996: 159). The Southeast Asian states certainly played a part in this trade (Wolters 1967: 153, 158). During the fifth and sixth centuries, Insulindian ships, with foreign merchants probably on board, were carrying western products to China. Maritime archaeology has provided evidence for

---

[94] Manguin 2004b: 287. Circular gold earrings have also been found at Air Sugihan; molds discovered at Oc Eo made possible the manufacture of similar ornaments. An analysis of a black glass bead from Air Sugihan reveals an alumina glass probably of Indian origin (Dussubieux 2001).

[95] Wolters 1967: 160–164; Lombard 1990, II: 18ff. Mahdi (2008: 122) relates Gantuoli to Kendari, the name of a region located in Southeast Sulawesi. Conversely, Gerini (1909) has suggested that the term Gantuoli was a Chinese transcription of Kanturi, located near Chaiya, on the east coast of the Thai–Malay peninsula. Shen Fuwei (2002) connects Gantuoli to the name of Sinkel Kandari given by Ibn Mājid in 1462 to a port in Sumatra. Consequently, Gantuoli's location remains uncertain.

[96] The *Suishu* relates that one reaches Poli after passing Chitu and Dandan (Wheatley 1961: 31).

[97] Wang Gungwu 1958: 55 n. 44, according to the *Songshu* and *Liangshu* chronicles.

the type of ship used along the Southeast Asian coasts. The remains of a ship with "stitched fastenings and cleats to which ribs had been lashed" have been excavated at Kolam Pinisi, west of Palembang, dated to the fifth century CE (Manguin 1993: 257; McGrail 2001: 298).[98] In 412, the Chinese pilgrim Faxian returned from Sri Lanka (where a ship from Tāmralipti had left him) via Yepoti – this is a transcription of Yāvadvīpa, the region of Melayu/Jambi on the eastern coast of Sumatra.[99] From here, Faxian took a ship sailing to Canton; the presence of Brahmins on the same ship reveals that Indians traveled to China (Wheatley 1961: 41). Yepoti does not seem to have ever sent a single embassy to China. In contrast, the kingdom of Poda sent envoys in 435, 449, and 451. Various Chinese texts also mention Shepo (Chö-p'o or Sheh-p'o) (during the third, fifth, and ninth centuries). Shepo may be a Javanese pronunciation of "Jawa."[100] Embassies from Shepo arrived in China in 433 and 435. The monk Gunavarman, a prince of Kashmir, preached Buddhism there before 424.[101] Heling (Ho-Ling) (perhaps in central Java) is signaled for the first time in 640; it dispatched three embassies during the seventh century (640, 648, and 666); after a long pause, Heling was mentioned again from 767 onward. The "New Tang Annals" (*Xintangshu*) note that "Heling is also called Shepo." The name Po-li appears four times (517, 522, 616, and 630) (Wang Gungwu 1958: 119ff.). According to the *Liangshu*, "the people of Poli (possibly Bali) as well as those of Gantuoli wear *gu-bei* [cotton] as a stole, and use *gu-bei* to make sarongs." Cotton – imported from India, or cultivated and woven locally – is mentioned in connection with the countries of Linyi, Dandan, Gantuoli, Langyaxiu, and Poli: it was brought to the Liang court as a gift (Salmon 2009: 188). We know that eastern Java was active in long-distance trade: "Jatim" glass beads produced in eastern Java have been found in Korea in the Silla kingdom, where they are dated to between the fifth and seventh centuries (they were probably made of imported glass, and, in the case of millefiori beads, show influences from Egypt) (Lankton *et al.* 2008).

The importance of Indian influences (attested by the remains of sanctuaries and inscriptions) in the states of Southeast Asia, especially from the fourth/fifth century onward, has already been mentioned. This was a period of blossoming for the Gupta

---

[98] Manguin 1996: 185. The remains of three ships built using the same technique have been excavated at Sambirejo, 10 km downstream from Palembang; one of the three ships has been dated to the seventh or eighth century (Manguin 1996: 186).

[99] Mahdi 2008: 112. Wheatley (1961: 39) situates Yepoti in northwestern Kalimantan, however. See also Coedès 1964a: 108. According to Faxian, Yepoti is a country "where heresies and Brahmanism were flourishing, while the Faith of Buddha was in a very unsatisfactory condition" (Wheatley 1961: 38).

[100] Lombard 1990, II: 18, 314 n. 41, and Ferrand 1987: 1182. L. Dabut has noted the difference between Yepoti and Shepo, reflecting the Sanskrit Yawa (Yava) and the term Jawa (Java) respectively (1964a: 126–127). Moreover, in the *Liangshu*, we find the variants Zhubo and Shebo, "apparently renderings of an early vernacular Malay term *Jabaka, representing the Prākrit Jāvaka, an adjectival derivation of Java, also reflected in Tamil as Cāvakam and in Arabic as az-Zābağ" (Mahdi 2008: 116). "The Malay *Javaka seems to have had a doublet variant, probably *Jəbaka, rendered in Chinese as Qibo. We find it in another version of the passages quoted, such as the one given by Guo-po (276–324 CE) as follows: 'Ten thousand *li* to the east of Funan is the kingdom of Qibo. More than five thousand *li* further east is the burning mountain kingdom . . . '" (Mahdi 2008: 116).

[101] Coedès 1964a: 107. Gunavarman may have come from India via Sri Lanka (Wolters 1967: 35–36), on an Indian ship. He belonged to the Sarvastivada school, which developed missionary activity outside India (Ray 2006a: 316).

Empire and the Pallava kingdom.[102] Moreover, relations between India and Southeast Asia were inseparable from the maritime orientation of the states in southern China, at a time when the roads of inner Asia were more or less cut off. Indians settled in Sumatra, Java, and on the Malay peninsula; they imported and produced cotton cloth and beads, also made by local craftsmen. An indianized culture developed, reflected in archaeological remains. At Cibuaya and Batujaya, for example, on the northwest coast of Java, vestiges of Vishnuite temples and Buddhist stupas, constructed from bricks, have been unearthed.[103] Similarities have been noted with the stupas and temples of central Thailand (Manguin 2010: 176). These sites likely belonged to the state (*nagara*) of Tārumā mentioned in Sanskrit inscriptions dated to the fifth century and drawn up in the name of King Pūrnavarman. The stone inscription of Tugu (Jakarta East) indicates the digging of canals and grants to Brahmins. This kingdom, mentioned under the name of Duoluomo (To-lo-mo) by the *New History of the Tang*, sent embassies to China in 666 and 669.[104] The association of Buddhism and Vishnuism, that we observe in the state of Tārumā, became the rule in Southeast Asia between the fifth and seventh centuries. Vishnuism "appears to have been intimately linked to kingship and statehood"; it clearly "played a major role in the process of state formation from the fifth to seventh century" (Manguin 2010: 174). "Mitred" Vishnus have been found in Thailand, Cambodia, and southern Vietnam. In Insular Southeast Asia, Vishnu statues are known from western Java (see above) and Bangka (early seventh century), among others. Mitred Vishnus reflect the shared adoption of sectarian Vishnuism across Southeast Asia. The inscriptions that have been discovered "often refer to devotional (*bhakti*) practices" that were developing in

[102] The *Liangshu* alludes to the spread of Indian influences. For example, it relates the arrival in Panpan (a state then under the control of Funan) of an Indian Brahmin called Chiao Chen-ju (Kauṇḍinya), who established Indian laws in the country. Funan later invited him and he ascended the throne in that country, "at a time of political unrest." This mythical figure symbolizes "a second wave of indianization" of the Thai–Malay peninsula and Funan (Pelliot 1903: 269; Kulke and Rothermund 1995: 155–156). Moreover, the *Liangshu* and the *History of Qin* mention an Indian "usurper" – prior to Chiao Chen-ju – named Zhu Chandan (Chu Chant'an) (or Tianzhu Chandan), a title that has been linked to the Indo-Scythians of northern India (see above) (Vickery [2003–2004: 112–113], however, objects to this interpretation, developed by Coedès [1964a: 91ff.]). This king may have sent trained elephants to the Jin court, in China. During the fifth century, King Jayavarman seems to have taken the title of Kaundinya: in this period, the Funanese appear to have adopted a legend of origin involving an Indian with the name of Kaundinya (Vickery 2003–2004: 114–115). An inscription at Go Thap records the consecration of a footprint of Vishnu by Gunavarman under Jayavarman's reign.

[103] McKinnon *et al.* 1994. Statues of Vishnu as well as lingas linked to the Shaivite cult have been discovered. Footprints of Pūrnavarman, compared to those of Vishnu, have been carved in the stone of Ciuraton, near Bogor, south of Jakarta (*c.* 450 CE); nearby, one can see the footprints of his elephant. The coastal site of Cibuaya is located near the former Tarum riverbed. The building techniques of a recently discovered brick platform are reminders of what can be observed at Oc Eo (fifth–sixth century). At Batujaya, a lower layer has yielded a radiocarbon dating between the second and third centuries. The following period shows glass and stone beads as well as Indian type ceramics, including shards of Rouletted Ware. On the Buddhist complex of Blandongan (Batujaya), the first architectural phase spans the fifth to eighth century. The site was then abandoned and later rebuilt after 800, and abandoned once again during the tenth century (Manguin 2004b: 302; 2005b).

[104] Coedès 1964a: 106; Wisseman Christie 1995: 257, 259. According to Manguin (1988), however, "it was not To-lo-mo [Tārumā] but Tan-tan [=Dandan], that sent an embassy in 666–669." Wang Gungwu (1958: 122) signals only an embassy from Heling to China in 666.

India at this time (Manguin 2010: 175); devotional forms of Vishnuism "had strong ties to both the economic and the political spheres" (Manguin 2010: 178). Buddhism also retained its importance. Gupta or post-Gupta statues of Buddha have been found in continental Southeast Asia, and also in Kalimantan (region of Kutei, eastern Kalimantan; Candi Laras, southern Kalimantan; Santubang, Sarawak) and eastern Sumatra, along the Musi and Batang Hari rivers (Manguin 2010: 173).[105] Figures of the Bodhisattva Avalokitesvara have also been excavated in southern Cambodia (Angkor Borei), and southern Sumatra (Palembang, Bingin). While the Shaivite cults also played a significant role, they would figure more prominently among the elite during the eighth century.[106] These Indian religions were associated with ancestor cults and local divinities: this is clearly visible throughout the ensuing centuries.

At this time, traders from the Persian Gulf and southern Arabia arrived in the ports of Southeast Asia and China. Persians from the Sassanid Empire appear to have already reached Funan during the third century, while the Chinese envoys Kang Tai and Zhu Ying were visiting that country. According to Wolters, it is unlikely that Persian ships went directly to China prior to the eighth century; however, the Buddhist pilgrim Yijing did embark on a Persian ship that sailed from Canton to Foshi (Palembang) in 671, if we assume that the term "Bosi" (Posi, Po-sse), a Chinese transcription of Parsa, Persia, associated with the ship, effectively refers to Persia: Arab and Persian ships were certainly present in China during the seventh century. It is true, however, that the description of the ship given by Yijing, with spars one hundred cubits long (?), may refer to an Austronesian or Indian ship (or to a type of *fuzhou* junk built from the Tang period onward).

Before that time, Sri Lanka may have lain at the end of the journey for ships coming from the West. During the sixth century, Cosmas emphasized Sri Lanka's central position in Indian Ocean trade, between West and East. The island imported Chinese silk and spices from eastern lands; these goods were sent to all parts of India and to other countries. We know that Persians settled in Sri Lanka, but Wolters notes that during the late fifth century, Chinese texts reflect the existence of a "Persian" commerce that was in fact in the hands of Austronesians. Note that the term Bosi seems, in some cases, to refer to regions in Southeast Asia: a fourth-century Chinese text tells us that Bosi produces ebony, and a fifth-century book situates Bosi in the Nanhai, the southern Seas (Wang Gungwu 1998: 59). However, Hu from "Daqin" (probably Syrians or Persians from the Persian Gulf) introduced two varieties of jasmine into Canton at the beginning of the fourth century,[107] and for the eighth, ninth, and tenth centuries, the Chinese chronicles and Arab and Persian sources all mention the presence of Persians and Arabs in China (see below).

---

[105] "Amarāvatī style" Buddhas are no longer dated to the third–fourth century, but to the seventh–eighth century (see below) (Manguin 2010: 173).

[106] For example in Zhenla and Champa. According to Wheatley (1983), the king identified with the figure of Shiva. Lingas have also been found in Kalimantan and on the Thai–Malay peninsula (sixth century).

[107] Mentioned in the *Nanfang caomu zhuang* written c. 304 by Chi Han.

Changes during the Sixth and Seventh Centuries

During the sixth century, Funan declined and disappeared. Global climate changes likely played a role in this demise; moreover, we cannot exclude the possibility that the plague that reached the western Indian Ocean shortly before the mid-sixth century also spread eastwards to countries as far as Funan and southern China. Moreover, this period saw a restructuring of international trade. Several states were formed in continental Southeast Asia, but they would not attain the importance of Funan in maritime trade. According to Chinese texts, a Khmer kingdom called Zhenla was set up in the middle Mekong valley, and took control of the Funanese capital, Angkor Borei, in 550;[108] however, "three embassies were still sent between 559 and 588, as well as others at the beginning of the seventh century" (Southworth 2004b: 530). Recent research shows that there was not just one state, but multiple political entities whose preeminence benefited from Funan's decline, alongside that of the maritime trade. During the seventh century, we see a consolidation of centralized authority within lineages centered on Ishanapura (Sambor Prei Kuk) (King Ishānavarman) and Purandarapura (King Jayavarman I). Some of the reservoirs and the moated enclosure at Ishanapura were probably constructed during the seventh century (Higham 2014: 291). The emergence of these smaller states went hand in hand with the construction of brick and stone temples, whose decoration reveals some parallels with motifs known at Ajanta, Ellora, and Mamallapuram (500–650).[109] Cults combined Hindu and local divinities. Various inscriptions refer to the founding of sanctuaries dedicated to Shiva by King Ishānavarman. "An inscription [thus] records the installation of a *linga* by a Brahman in the service of the king" (Higham 2014: 291). Ma Duanlin (1245–1322) reported a description of King Ishānavarman's "sumptuous court" at Ishanapura. Under Jayavarman's reign, "inscriptions reveal the replacement of *pon* [*poñ*, a Khmer title attached to rulers and individuals of high status, the *fan* of Chinese chronicles] by royal appointees," revealing the setting up of an administration.

The Mōn state of Dvāravatī, originating in the south of the Menam basin, developed when Funan disintegrated (it might previously have been a vassal state of Funan). Its place in transregional trade is still difficult to assess, but during the seventh century it controlled part of Tennasserim, and seems to have played a significant role in the expansion of Buddhism.[110]

In Burma, the Pyu "kingdom" emerged during the sixth century, formed by a population of Tibeto-Burman speakers who arrived around the first century CE.[111]

---

[108]   An ambassador of the Chinese emperor Wu of the Liang dynasty arrived in Funan as late as 535, and King Rudravarman of Funan sent his final embassy to China in 539. At Angkor, the cemetery of Prei Khmeng (first–seventh century) shows glass beads with a high lead content (Pottier 2005), which may have come from China. Vickery in fact demonstrates the relative continuity between Funan and Zhenla (2003–2004: 134).

[109]   Temples at Thala Borivat, Ishanapura, and Ampil Rolum (Higham 2002: 249, 250–251). The Buddhist Caves of Ajanta were created between the second century BCE and sixth century CE, and those at Ellora between the fifth and seventh centuries.

[110]   De Casparis 2000: 58. This author notes an influence of Theravāda Buddhism from Sri Lanka as early as the beginning of the Dvāravatī period.

[111]   In order to avoid an ethnicist approach, E. H. Moore (2007) is probably correct in preferring to speak of "Pyu culture." Various Tibeto-Burman groups were present.

This may have been a confederation of city-states. Its main city (perhaps its capital), Srīkshetra, was located near Prome, in the Irrawaddy valley. Beikthano, Halin, Maingmaw, and Tagaung were other major centers, containing the remains of religious buildings.[112] These sites covered from 222 to 300 hectares (Stark 2006). Revealing possible links with Sri Lanka, inscriptions in Pali on gold plaques found near Prome provide the oldest evidence for Theravāda Buddhism in the region, dated to the beginning of the fifth century. From the eleventh century onward, Theravāda Buddhism would become the dominant form in Burma, and later in the rest of continental Asia.[113] A similarity has been noted between the Brāhmī script of Sri Lanka and the Pyu script, between the fourth and seventh centuries (Karashima 2002: 177). Pyu art appears to be linked with both the Amarāvatī and the Gupta culture. Connections with Yunnan are also evident, for example at Maingmaw (figures of horsemen …) (Moore 2007: 194). Tagaung has yielded clay roof tiles that are similar to Vietnamese finds influenced by China and dated to the first centuries of the Christian era (Moore 2007: 190). Located south and southeast of the Pyu state, smaller Mōn states, sometimes vassals of Funan, such as Dunsun, were active in trade.[114] A network of fortified sites was linked by trade and religion (Srīkshetra, Kyaikkatha, Thaton, Thagara, and sites further east) (Moore 2007: 208). The Mōn minted silver coins with a conch/*srīvatsa* pattern that would become the prototype for coinage issues by various regions during the first millennium (the *srīvatsa* was seen as a symbol of prosperity and good fortune). The Pyu also issued silver (and gold) coins, with the *bhadrapitha* (symbol of a throne), the rising sun, and *srīvatsa*; these seem to reflect an influence from Andhra Pradesh arriving around the second century CE (Moore 2007: 143–144). Coins of the rising sun/*srīvatsa* type were the most common among ancient coins of continental Southeast Asia: they have been found in Thailand (U-Thong, Nakhon Si Thammarat), Cambodia, and southern Vietnam (Oc Eo). These coins are still poorly situated in time, but they may well be the earliest.[115] For minor transactions, Burma imported cowries. Coins of a Pyu and Mōn type have been

[112] The Pyu sites show the presence of moats and display inner walls delimiting the residential area of the elite. The oldest dating that Beikthano has yielded is 180 BCE – 260 CE. The Halin site is dated between the late first century and the ninth century CE. It has yielded Indian Rouletted Ware. Srikshetra is said to have had thirty-two gates, corresponding to the thirty-two provinces of the kingdom and the thirty-two gods of Indra's realm.

[113] De Casparis and Mabbett 1992: 293; de Casparis 2000: 54. Aung-Thwin (2005) has emphasized the development of Theravāda Buddhism already during the Pyu period. Moreover, Pyu art shows traces of Mahāyāna Buddhism: the Pyu were familiar with a Sanskrit Buddhist canon that may have come from northeastern India. In addition, agate seals bear a South Indian script (fourth–fifth century CE). The Pyu kingdom later sent embassies to China in 802 and 807. The Chinese pilgrims Xuanzang and Yijing (seventh century) mention Srīkshetra as a Buddhist kingdom. Note that later Mōn inscriptions from Thailand used a script derived from the Pallava script, reflecting various types of religious and commercial exchange networks.

[114] It would be better to speak more generally of Austroasiatics, and not just of Mōn. Lower Burma seems to have been sparsely populated at this time; however, only limited research has been conducted in this region. Aung-Thwin (2002) places a significant influx of Mōn populations into the region after the demise of Dvāravatī (tenth century) (Lieberman 2003: 90 n. 4; Moore 2007: 216).

[115] Moore 2007: 143–144. Malleret feels that these coins are more recent than the coins of the conch/*srīvatsa* type (1959, I: 134). Cf. Wicks 1992: 86, 112–113, 116–118. All the Mōn coins have been discovered on the coasts. For the Pyu country, Deyell (1994: 124) also mentions half-moon-shaped silver bars. The silver originated in upper Burma and in Yunnan.

discovered in the Pegu region, the Arakan kingdom, Bengal, Thailand (at sites of the Dvāravatī culture), Vietnam (near Ho Chi Minh City), and on the Malay peninsula (Khlong Thom), thus delineating the contours of a vast area of exchanges.

Insular Southeast Asia began taking on an increasing share of international trade. Even before the emergence of Sriwijaya, ships from insular Southeast Asia traveled to Sri Lanka and India to acquire products coming from Europe, the Persian Gulf, Arabia, or Africa, and transported them to China (Wolters 1967: 139–172). From the sixth century onward, most international traffic used a maritime route via the Strait of Malacca. This circumnavigation around the Malay peninsula was linked to the decline of Funan and the rise of states located in the southern Malay peninsula (Kedah, Kelang) and in Sumatra or Java. It was also connected to increased demand (mostly from China) for forest products coming from the interior of various islands. Pine resin, benzoin, and camphor were substitutes for western Asian products such as frankincense, *bdellium*, and myrrh (Wolters 1967).[116] Wisseman Christie has convincingly demonstrated that in Sumatra especially, the links forged between the coast and the interior, and the possibility for inland groups to trade with various fluvial systems, necessarily led, on the one hand, to the building of alliances between the coastal states and hinterland societies (a policy of redistribution of wealth amongst client groups must have played a key role), and the control of several fluvial systems, on the other. This resulted in the expansionary policy of coastal states (or city-states) such as Sriwijaya (Wisseman Christie 1990: 45; Manguin 2000c, 2000d). As was the case with the interior, coastal expansion was often achieved through alliances rather than coercion.[117] Three categories of products circulated along the networks, in different ways:[118] imported goods, products manufactured in coastal centers, and raw materials coming from the interior. At the regional level, the growing dichotomy between continental Southeast Asia, influenced by Hīnayāna Buddhism, and insular Southeast Asia, where Mahāyāna Buddhism was preeminent, probably reflects different (though interconnected) trade currents. Influences from Mahāyāna Buddhism coming from northeastern India (Bihar, Bengal) became evident in Indonesia from the seventh to tenth century.[119] Sriwijaya offers a good illustration of the links between Buddhism and trade at the time.

Rather than the Thai–Malay peninsula, the eastern coast of Sumatra now acted as a hub between the China Sea and the Indian Ocean. Various inscriptions in Old Malay (three located near Palembang, one at Karang Brahi, in the upper valley of the Batang Hari

---

[116] Camphor was already being exported earlier, as was benzoin (see above).

[117] Manguin has shown that several functional models were in use simultaneously: a model in concentric circles (from the king and his residence) (2000b: 162 fig. 1), and a downstream/upstream model (in which the downstream region was prominent) which combined with the interconnection of both complementary and competing fluvial systems (Manguin 2000b: 163 fig. 2). These models will be discussed further below: they shed light on the political constructions of southeastern Madagascar.

[118] Depending on the products, but also depending on the regions: few products imported from abroad went into the inland regions on the Thai–Malay peninsula, but this was not always the case in Sumatra. "Overseas importing," writes Wisseman Christie (1990: 47), "played only a minor role in upriver exchanges," but see Wisseman Christie, 1995: 250, for Sumatra.

[119] At an earlier time, Buddhist influences came from Andhra Pradesh and Sri Lanka (de Casparis 2000: 61).

River, one on Bangka Island[120]) attest to the emergence of the kingdom of Srīwijaya on the southeast coast of Sumatra during the seventh century. An inscription at Sebokingking (Telaga Batu) (686 CE) signals the presence not only of foreign merchants, but also of sculptors, ships' captains and local merchants. That of Kota Kapur on Bangka (686 CE) ends with the mention of an expedition led against the restive land of "Java" (*bhumi Jawa*), perhaps the ancient kingdom of Tārumā[121] (Mahdi [2008: 119–120] instead suggests an attack on Keling, a state he locates on the Malay peninsula). In addition, an inscription in Old Malay perhaps dating to the seventh century has been discovered at the site of the Candi Laras sanctuary, at the estuary of the Barito river (southern Kalimantan) (Manguin 2000b: 174), testifying to a Malay presence in this region; this fact can be related to the existence on the stelae already mentioned of a text written in a language related to the Southeast Barito languages (see below). Srīwijaya sent a mission to China for the first time in 695. Embassies were later dispatched in 702, 716, and 724 (Pelliot 1904: 334, 335).

The preeminence of Srīwijaya is emphasized in the chronicles of the Chinese pilgrim Yijing, which report the lives and travels of sixty Buddhist pilgrims, most of them Chinese, who undertook pilgrimages to India during the second half of the seventh century. Yijing departed from Canton and reached Foshi (Fo-shih) (Srīwijaya) in 671. He spent six months there before going on to the country of Moluoyu (Melayu, Malayu = Jambi), and later Jiecha (Kedah). During the twelfth month, he boarded a ship belonging to the king bound for India; he arrived in Danmolidi (Tan-mo-li-ti) (Tāmralipti). His return journey took him through Kedah, where he took a ship from Srīwijaya sailing to Melayu, "that had become Foshi" (it was then controlled by Srīwijaya). Later, sailing northward, Yijing reached Guangfu (Guangdong, Canton region). His chronicles show the existence of other routes, from China to the Mekong estuary, and then Langjiashu (Langkasuka), whence people crossed the Thai–Malay peninsula to Kedah. From there, ships sailed to Tāmralipti, Najiabodana (Na-chia-po-ta-na) (Nagapattinam, or Negapatam) or Sri Lanka.[122] From the Gulf of Thailand, routes also led to Heling (possibly in Java) or Bupen (south of Kalimantan).

For the first millennium BCE and until the sixth century CE, archaeological and textual data reveal the emergence of two areas, in continental and insular Asia that were not merely connected, but were also in competition with each other. In these two areas, the structuring of political entities and the cristallization of towns occupying nodal positions along networks appear to be due both to internal development and the

---

[120]   Site at Kota Kapur. Kota Kapur has yielded remains of two small Hindu temples dated to the sixth–seventh century (one contained statues of Vishnu, the other a linga), and those of an Iron Age settlement (third–fourth century) (Manguin 2004: 304). Kota Kapur may have been the center of a small state (*maṇḍala*) that was incorporated into Srīwijaya during the seventh century. Inscriptions located in the Batang Hari River valley and the extreme south of Sumatra may also have marked the control of peripheral *maṇḍala* by Palembang (Manguin 2000b: 162) (see below).

[121]   Coedès 1964a: 158. The Kedukan Bukit inscription (Palembang) is dated to 683. An inscription dated to 684 CE was engraved on the occasion of the founding of a public orchard at Talang Tuwo. On these inscriptions, see below.

[122]   The "sailing routes through the South Seas as illustrated by Yijing's biographies," Wheatley 1961: 44. The Chinese pilgrim Xuanzang, who visited Orissa during the seventh century, referred to a coastal city called Che-li-ta-lo as "a resting place for sea going traders and strangers from distant lands" (Mukherjee 2001: 226).

growth of long-distance trade, via land and sea. South of the Thai–Malay peninsula and the lower Mekong, the insular region (Sumatra, Java) dominated the Southeast Asian interface. At the northern end of the sea roads, China's immense area, made up of various interconnected spheres (such as the Yellow River and Yangtze River valleys, the coasts of Zhejiang, Fujian, and Guangdong, and the Pearl River), formed the core of the world-system. Without necessarily directly controlling the routes to Southeast Asia, the kingdoms of East Asia acquired dominant positions on the networks early on, through their commercial and political power. The spread of Buddhism and the demand of the Chinese elites for prestige goods from the southern seas and western Asia stimulated trade along the first Silk Roads, on both sea and land. A Buddhist monk thus advised the ruler of Gantuoli to send a tribute to China so that his land would become "rich and happy, and travelers would multiply a hundredfold" (Manguin 2004b: 304).

Illustration XXXIII

India and Central Asia: the state, religion, and long-distance trade (first–sixth century)

(a) Coin of the Kushan King Vima Kadphises (100–127). Gold, 13.93 g. The king is seated and holds a laurel branch in his right hand. The legend is written in Greek. Reverse: the god Shiva holds a trident in his right hand, and places his left hand on the bull Nandi. On the left, the symbol of the Buddhist *triratana* ("three jewels"). © Classical Numismatic Group, Inc.

(b) Buddhist temple, Karla Caves (Maharashtra), first century CE. Prayer hall with stupa, H.: 16 m, L.: 40 m, W.: 15 m. © Massimo Borchi/Atlantide Phototravel

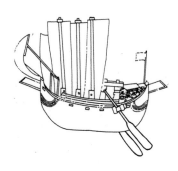

(c) Drawing of a ship depicted on a wall in the Ajanta Caves (Cave 2), sixth century. This ship may show some Indonesian features. J. Deloche 1996

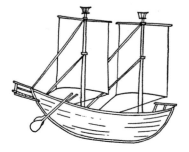

(d) Drawing of a ship depicted on Andhra coins, first century CE. J. Deloche 1996

Illustration XXXIV
The Funan state (Cambodia) and Indian Ocean trade

(a) Figure holding a flower (?), seated in the *lalitasana* ease posture. Seal imprint, Oc Eo, first half of the first millennium CE. © Photograph École Française d'Extrême-Orient, fonds Cambodge, Ref. 01847

(b) Coin, Chandragupta II (India, Gupta period), 380-414. Gold, 7.81 g. The goddess Lakshmi, seated on a lion, in the *lalitasana* ease posture, holds a diadem in her right hand and a lotus flower in her left hand. © Gorny und Mosch Glessener Münzhandlung, March 9, 2009

(c) Tin amulet decorated with a vase containing flowers. Oc Eo. India borrowed this ancient motif from western Asia (above). Tin came from the Thai–Malay peninsula. L. Malleret 1962, vol. III

(d) King smelling a flower, Iranian motif. The headdress is similar to that of the Sassanid kings. This "exaltation of the flower" gesture can be seen on Indo-Greek and Kushan coins. © Photograph École Française d'Extrême-Orient, fonds Cambodge, Ref. 01849

(e) Engraved carnelian, Mediterranean intaglio. © Photograph École Française d'Extrême-Orient, fonds Cambodge, Ref. 01849

Illustration XXXV
Insular Southeast Asia: an interface between two oceans (1)

(a) *Boshanlu* censer: incense burner, with lid featuring the sacred mountain base of the eight Immortals. First century CE. Korinci, central Sumatra. Imported from China. In China, it is found in tombs of the Han period. H.: 19 cm. National Museum, Jakarta, no. 3159. © National Museum, Jakarta, D. Harahap

(b) Offering bowl with dragon-shaped handle. First century CE. Sambas, Western Kalimantan. Imported from China. H.: 11 cm. L.: 32 cm. National Museum, Jakarta, no. 1519. © National Museum, Jakarta, D. Harahap

Illustration XXXVI
Insular Southeast Asia: an interface between two oceans (2)

(a) Stone at Ciuraton, near Bogor (western Java, Highlands), fourth century CE. The inscription, written in the Pallava script, reads: "From the valiant lord of the earth, the illustrious Purnavarman, the ruler of Taruma, the pair of footprints, similar to those of Vishnu." © École Française d'Extrême-Orient, Paris

(b) Bronze drum of the Dong Son type, found at Sangeang, Sumbawa Island, first/second century CE. Topped by four toads, symbols of fertility, the center of the tympanum features a twelve-branched star, which is a solar symbol; it is surrounded by stylized flying cranes, houses and ceremonial scenes, and geometrical patterns. The costumes of some figures may refer to Han China and India. Horses and elephants are among the animals featured. Diam.: 116 cm, H.: 83.5 cm. National Museum, Jakarta. © National Museum, Jakarta, D. Harahap

Illustration XXXVII
Insular Southeast Asia: the spread of bronze metallurgy

(a) Dancer, bronze, western Java, first half of the first millennium. The statuette reveals an influence from the Dong Son culture. National Museum, Jakarta. © National Museum, Jakarta, D. Harahap

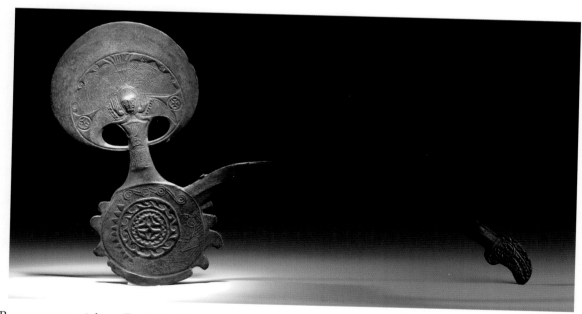

(b) Bronze ceremonial axe, Roti Island. 78 x 41.5 cm. Fragments of an axe head of the same type have been unearthed at Lake Sentani, Irian Jaya. The headdress of the seated man featured on the axe blade is of a type known in Irian Jaya. National Museum, Jakarta, no. 1442. © National Museum, Jakarta, D. Harahap

Illustration XXXVIII
Arabia: the incense roads

(a) Incense burner featuring a camel driver. Alabaster. Shabwa, third century CE. H.: 32 cm. The Sabaean inscription notes that the object was dedicated to a temple. British Museum, ANE 1937-5-7. © The Trustees of the British Museum

Shabwa was built in the vicinity of a salt mine; the city was located along routes leading to Qanî, and to Ma'în.

(b) Relief decorated with a bird pecking grapes. W.: 32 cm, H.: 19 cm. Yemen. Greco-Roman influence. Between the first and third centuries. Louvre, AO5968. © RMN-Grand Palais, Franck Raux

Illustration XXXIX
China: maritime and terrestrial exchanges

(a) Terracotta ship, found in a tomb dating from the Eastern Han period (first century CE), Guangzhou. Guangzhou Museum. The ship shows a central rudder (instead of a two quarter-rudders, as on Southeast Asian and Indian Ocean ships), as well as a cabin for the pilot. The ship probably had one mast. © Cultural Relics Publishing House, Beijing

(b) Chinese bronze mirror with "TLV" decoration, Western Han period (c. second century CE). Musée Guimet, MA1294. © RMN-Grand Palais, Ravaux. A. Parpola has suggested a link between the shape of some buildings from Bactria–Margiana (BMAC culture, late third – early second millennium) (cf. Illustration XI), Tantric mandalas, and Chinese "TLV" mirrors. The decoration of the mirrors primarily expresses Chinese symbolism.

Illustration XL

The Sogdians and the Silk Roads

(a) Flask, Sassanid glass, Famensi (Fufeng, Shaanxi), fifth century. © An Jiayao

Via the Silk Roads, the Sogdians brought in Parthian and later Sassanid glass, metallic vessels, and horses. From China, their primary product was silk. In addition, they contributed to the spread of Buddhism.

(b) Ewer, gilt silver. Of a Sassanid shape, produced in Bactria. H.: 37.5 cm. It features three scenes from the Trojan War. Here we see Helen's abduction. Handles with camel heads. Found in the tomb of General Li Xian and his wife, Northern Zhou dynasty, dated from 569, Guyuan, Ningxia. Guyuan Museum. © Cultural Relics Publishing House, Beijing

12 China: From Kingdoms to Unification

From the Zhou Dynasty to the Warring Kingdoms (1027–221 BCE)

> The great affairs of a state are sacrifices and war.
> (*Zuozhuan*, compiled between 475 and 221 BCE; Liu and Chen, 2012: 253)

Trans-Asian routes were used as early as the third and second millennia BCE (see above), and ships also sailed along the Chinese coasts. Exchange networks grew significantly during the first millennium. Internal development went along with the formation of a state succeeding the Shang state and centered on the Yellow River valley. China became interconnected with Central Asia and India on the one hand, and Southeast Asia, on the other. These changes made China a major pole in the system that was taking shape.

A first period of development occurred during the early first millennium, under the Zhou dynasty. This development reached as far as the plains of the Lower Yangtze and northeastern Shandong. A multitude of small states then recognized the authority of the "Royal Zhou state," whose bureaucracy[1] proved able to exert military and religious leadership. The *Zhuoshizhuan* describes "a hierarchy of domains and family cults, with the royal domain and worship of the Zhou ancestors at its apex ... The capital, Zongzhou (Hao), was the great religious center for the entire community of Zhou cities ... Fiefs were granted to noble families, giving them both religious and military powers over a precisely defined domain" (Gernet 1999: 55). These grants tended to become hereditary. Compared to the previous period, the royal power, however, seems to have grown weaker, acting rather as an arbitrator over many principalities (*guo*, "city") whose leaders were required, in principle, to provide contingents of chariots and soldiers. The Zhou set up vassal states by sending members of the royal family or officials to rule peripheral areas, for example in the state of Yan, in the Beijing region. The Zhou space was in contact with other states, such as Shu, in Sichuan, whose capital was probably the recently discovered city of Jinsha, in the suburbs of the modern city of Chengdu (Qing and Fang 2003). Large quantities of ivory, gold, jade, and bronze items have been excavated. The presence of bronze objects from the Zhou period in regions south of the Yangtze and in Lingnan (Higham 1996a: 90, 92) has

---

[1] The Zhou had a different ethnic origin than the Shang. "They did, however, share the bronze material culture of the Shang," with an emphasis on ritual vessels (Barnes 1999: 134). Their walled royal capital expresses the Zhou ideal of a square city oriented to the four cardinal points, with three gates on each side. There were up to 1,500 principalities. Unlike what has been suggested by Nichols and Charlton (1997), the period of the Zhou dynasty was probably not a hierarchized system of city-states (Hansen 2000c: 598).

already been mentioned.[2] The Zhou were also in contact with "barbarian" populations in the north. The Zhou state formed the core of a world-system where various influences merged; this synthesis in turn had an impact on the vassal regions. Bronzes in the state of Yan thus show stylistic features from both Sichuan and the south (Wucheng), via Gansu and Shaanxi (Sun 2006).

Trade expanded greatly between China and Central Asia. Various cultures of Gansu and Xinjiang reveal influences from the Western Zhou, and also from Inner Asia. Tombs at Cherchen, dated to *ca.* 1000 BCE, on the southern branch of the Silk Roads, have yielded Caucasoid mummies, including a man wearing trousers, an invention associated with horseback riding (the Chinese would adopt trousers at the same time as horseback riding around 400 BCE).[3] Hats either of the "Phrygian" type (Cherchen) or high and pointed (Subeshi, east of Turfan, *c.* fifth century BCE) have been discovered in the tombs; both are reminiscent of Iranian culture (Mallory and Mair 2000: figs. 111 and 125; Barber 2002: 64). In Xinjiang, the introduction of iron technology occurred as early as the end of the second millennium BCE, probably from the Chust culture of Fergana (which was itself connected with southern Turkmenistan and Iran [Sialk]),[4] alongside the development of horseback riding and the appearance of metal objects suggesting connections with Kazakhstan.[5] Various cemeteries have yielded iron artifacts dated to from 1000 BCE onward.[6]

---

[2] The Western Zhou bronzes exceed those of the Shang in variety and number.

[3] Barber 2002: 62. One tomb contained a saddle and horse bones. The cemetery has yielded dates between 1400 and 200 BCE: it was in use over a long period of time (Zhang *et al.* 2007). The cemetery at Qizilchoqa (Wupu, Hami, 1350–1000 BCE) has also yielded Caucasoid "mummies," accompanied by mirrors and combs; they wore clothes of the tartan type (Mallory and Mair 2000: 218) (the cemetery has been redated to between 800 and 530, but it may have been in use during both periods). This type of clothing is known as early as the end of the fourth and beginning of the third millennium between Turkey and the Caucasus, and in the Hallstatt culture at the end of the second millennium; in addition, a loom found at Troy II (*c.* 2600 BCE) made it possible to produce this type of cloth, which was also known in Crete during the second millennium (Barber 1998: 653). Research into the clothing excavated in the Tarim reveals that sheep breeds, exploited for their wool, were different at Krorän (Qumul) and at Cherchen (Good 1998: 656). Part of a spoked wheel has also been discovered at Cherchen. China borrowed from the Indo-Iranian vocabulary used for items of clothing worn by the steppe populations, such as trousers, boots, shirts, and high hats (Kuzmina 2007: 104).

[4] Di Cosmo 2002: 71. The dating of the Chust culture remains debated (Kuzmina 2007: 440); it could be contemporaneous with the Yaz I culture of southern Turkmenistan (which extended as far as southern Afghanistan and southern Uzbekistan) (*c.* 1500–1000 BCE) (Kohl 1984). See Mei and Shell 2002: 230; Wagner 2003: 132. Various Iron Age cultures have been described in Xinjiang, such as the Chawuhugoukou (Charwighul) culture, north of Kurle. The latter shows links with either Gansu and Kazakhstan or southern Tajikistan (Debaine-Francfort 2001: 65). The cemetery at Charwighul has yielded painted pottery reminiscent of the Chust and Vaksh cultures.

[5] The types of bits observed here and some decorative motifs have also been found in Saka territory (Syr Darya and Amu Darya). The Saka culture extended eastward from the eighth or seventh century BCE. The Saka language would dominate along the southern branch of the Silk Roads. In addition, socketed dagger-axes found at Qunbake (west of Kurle, between 800 and 400 BCE) and Banfanggou (Urumqi) suggest contacts with the Tagar culture of Siberia (Altai, Minusinsk) (Mei and Shell 2002: 230). A. Parpola (2002) also relates "horse culture" and iron metallurgy to Proto-Iranians.

[6] A tomb has been dated to 1000 BCE, at Yanbulaq; three datings are between 1000 and 900, six between 900 and 800, and seven between 800 and 700 BCE (Wagner 2003: 130). Wagner points out that Scythian nomads acted as intermediaries in the spread of iron metallurgy, which was introduced from the Fergana

Tombs at Mori contained cowries (950–740 BCE),[7] whereas at Urumqi, other burials exhibited horse bones, as well as human skeletal remains; these are sometimes Caucasoid, sometimes Mongoloid. In Gansu, iron objects have been dated to the eighth or seventh century BCE. In this region, the Shajing culture (starting in the eighth century BCE) has yielded cowries, bronze ornaments showing influences from the steppe cultures, and iron tools (An Zhimin 1996: 331, 335; Di Cosmo 1999b: 937). Shajing and other sites were fortified. Contacts with the central plains of China led to the introduction of iron technology in this area. Artistic forms from the steppes (Karasuk culture, *ca.* 1400–850, and later Scythian culture) can be seen in the assemblages found in China. Slightly later, a glass industry emerged in China during the Spring and Autumn period (770–476 BCE). It may have arisen from contacts with western Asia, but this hypothesis is still debated (Francis Jr. 1986; An Jiayao 1996; see below). Production of the "Han blue" pigment, containing lead and barium, used on faience from the ninth century BCE onward in northwestern China now seems to have been a Chinese invention, whereas it was previously thought to be the result of a transfer of technology.[8] The first types of glass, with lead and/or barium, appeared a few centuries later. The manufacturing of glass in an attempt to imitate jade partially explains the addition of barium characteristic of Chinese glass; moreover, adding lead and potash made it possible to lower the fusion temperature of glass. Other influences arrived in China during the first half of the first millennium, in the musical field: the horizontal angular harp of Central Asia, derived from instruments from Iran and western Asia, was present in Xinjiang and Gansu; this was the ancestor of the Chinese *qin* zither, an instrument Confucius may have played during the sixth century BCE. The first example of *qin* has been discovered in the tomb of Marquis Yi (433 BCE). The iconographic repertoire of these instruments' keys largely borrows from a heritage from the steppes as well as from Iran. Ancient discoveries of horizontal angular harps trace routes connecting the Black Sea and Xinjiang (Lawergren 2003b).

---

valley. The arrival of iron metallurgy via northwestern China implies that "the first iron smelting in China must have been done in bloomeries, rather than in blast furnaces" (Wagner 2003: 129). At Baoji (Shaanxi), a tomb dated to the Spring and Autumn period has yielded various iron items (including some iron–gold objects); the tomb is Chinese, but it contained many objects showing forms typical of the steppe cultures (Wagner 2003: 137–138, 166–169). The cemetery at Yanbulaq has yielded earrings made of spiral cones of wire found in Kazakhstan, in the region of the Ob River and in Fergana. Mirrors with a loop handle on the back, of a type known in Siberia, Kazakhstan, Uzbekistan, and Fergana, have also been excavated (Kuzmina 2007: 263–264). Similar mirrors have been discovered at Anyang and Houjiazhuang. Moreover, Di Cosmo indicates contacts between northeastern China and Transbaikalia, and the introduction of iron technology into China either through exchanges or north/south population movements (2002: 72–73).

[7] Cowries from China have also been excavated in the Alagou I cemetery (mid first millennium BCE) (west of Turfan) and at Yanghai (Turfan basin) (second half of the first millennium BCE); this site has also yielded socketed dagger-axes and a bronze mirror (Mei and Shell 2002: 219, 223).

[8] Berke 2007. The faience beads found in tombs of the Western Zhou period, for example at Baoji (kingdom of Yu) and Beilu (Shaanxi), dated to the beginning of the first millennium BCE, and produced in China, were precursors of Chinese glass (Shixiong 1992: 152). These beads often have a peculiar shape. The beads of the Western Zhou period have sometimes been considered as glass, but they are in fact faience beads (Fukang 1992: 158). According to Fukang, these beads were imports from western Asia. We may also suppose that exchanges with Central Asia initiated and spurred production of this type of bead in China (Rawson 1999: 252–253 provides an example of association with carnelian).

The presence of tripod ceramics in the Transbaikal region during the late second and early first millennia BCE reveals contacts between China and Siberia at this time (Kuzmina 2008: 4), perhaps through the intermediary of northern China, where the Northern Septentrional culture (Upper Xiajiadian culture, late second millennium / early first millennium BCE) shows affinities with the steppe cultures (bronzes decorated with animal and natural motifs, the presence of the domesticated horse, and the practice of horseback riding).[9] Unlike the earlier period, this culture no longer built fortified sites, but the tombs reveal a social hierarchy, with many bronzes, some from the Zhou area; this culture developed pastoralism, a process reinforced by increased aridification (Linduff and Drennan 2002). The Upper Xiajiadian culture entered Korea, where a bronze culture took root, showing Siberian influences. Moreover, the territorial expansion of the Zhou states may have forced coastal populations of China to migrate toward Korea.

Soon thereafter, the Korean bronze culture was introduced into Japan. Rice was transmitted from Korea to the north of Kyushu Island at the start of the first millennium BCE.[10] The site of Kazahari (Tohoku, north of Honshu Island) contained rice and two types of millet, *Setaria italica* (L.) P. Beauv. and *Panicum miliaceum* L. (Crawford 2006: 90), showing the introduction of a series of plants from the continent at this time (millets had already been introduced at Kazahari during the third millennium BCE [D'Andrea *et al.* 1995]). The supposed discoveries of the seeds of *Vigna radiata* and *Vigna mungo* L. (plants of Indian origin) at Nabatake (3230±100 BP) and at Torihama, on the west coast of Honshu (Middle Jomon), respectively, are now rejected (Habu 2004). Other discoveries dated to the Jomon period also seem dubious; examples include barley, hemp, and *Cucumis melo* L. (melon) (found at sites of Torihama and Yamanotera, on Kyushu) (Late Jomon), a plant for which India and China were significant centers of diversity (Crawford 1992: 19, 22, 27ff.). On the other hand, seeds of the gourd *Lagenaria siceraria* (Molina) Standl. (a plant cultivated in ancient China) are well attested at various sites, for example at Torihama and at Sannai Maruyama (northern Honshu).

The late ninth and early eighth centuries saw a decline of northern China due to attacks by foreigners (the Yanyun from the steppes, the Quanrong in the northwest, and so forth) on the one hand,[11] and to a weakening of the royal Zhou state power, on

---

[9] Barnes 1999: 157. One site from this culture (Nanshangen) has yielded a "stirrup-shaped bronze ring adorned with the figures of two hunters on horseback" (Di Cosmo, 2002: 64). In China, the significance of the horse is well known for the Western Zhou period, but horseback riding was attested in the region of Beijing only in the sixth century BCE, and in the fourth century BCE further south (Di Cosmo 1999b: 912). On the region of Chifeng (500 km northeast of Beijing), see Linduff and Drennan 2002.

[10] Rice arrived in Korea during the mid-second millennium. Rice at the site of Oun 1 has been dated to 1900 and 1000 BCE (Crawford and Lee 2003). Rice has been identified at Daecheon-ri, in South Korea, for the beginning of the third millennium, with wheat and barley, but this date is uncertain (Fuller *et al.* 2007). Irrigation systems have been uncovered in Korea for the Early Mumun period (1500–850). In Japan, wet rice culture did not develop until around 400–300 BCE in the Yayoi culture, which spread throughout Japan during the third and second centuries BCE (Crawford 2006: 84, 89). A recent find of rice phytoliths dated to *c.* 6000 BP (Takamiya 2002: 209) shows an earlier rice arrival, without notable consequence. While Takamiya observes that botanical and ethnographic data lead us to believe that rice at Honshu was introduced from the Ryukyu Islands, there is as yet no archaeological proof of this (Takamiya 2002: 216; d'Andrea 2007: 173).

[11] As early as 979 BCE, the Zhou resorted to armed actions against populations of the Ordos region (Barnes 1999: 158). Cf. Di Cosmo 2002: 108ff.

the other (Gernet 1999: 54). Climate deterioration in northern China and Inner Asia during the period 800/700 BCE may have played a role in the devolution observed during the eighth century. The shift of the Zhou capital from Hao (Xi'an) to Chengzhou (Luoyang) around 770 BCE, caused by the threat posed by populations from Inner Asia, marked the transition from the Western to the Eastern Zhou and an overall change in the political and social situation. The Zhou kingdom and its allies were also affected by incursions of populations from northern China during the second half of the seventh century. Various states then tried to arrange peace agreements with these populations. During the sixth century BCE, it became customary for the central states to use troops of foreign origin (Di Cosmo 2002: 123). This period saw the establishment of new relations, with "the incorporation of non-Zhou within the domain of expanding Zhou states" (Di Cosmo 2002: 125). The fragmentation of the central Zhou area during the eighth and seventh centuries contrasts with the formation of progressively larger and more powerful kingdoms at its periphery; these kingdoms were the Qi, Jin, Qin, and Chu (Map 11.14). Some cultural unity was maintained, but the older Zhou networks allowing for the collection of tributes, providing services such as corvées and military help, and redistributing wealth, simply vanished. This political fragmentation led to the coexistence of states of various sizes during the period called "Spring and Autumn" (771–481 BCE).[12] These states expressed a real commitment to developing trade despite near-constant – but often small-scale – conflicts.[13] To the Duke Huan, "who asked him whether or not the state should tax trade or fix prices, " the First Minister of Qi, Guan Zhong, replied: "it would freeze production and hinder economic activity" (Caillé 2005: 123). Along with growth in trade, one observes the social ascension of the merchants, particularly in the state of Zheng, as well as in Wei and Jin, where they played major political roles (Hsu 1999).

It is during this period of change that Confucius (c. 551–479 BCE) lived, in the state of Lu, where he became a magistrate. He taught in a private school that educated future rulers, but was open to everyone. His teaching emphasized personal and governmental morality. For him, restoring harmonious social order would require special observance of the familial order as well as the establishment of an efficient political power that would comply with the five virtues: goodness, righteousness, decency, wisdom, and loyalty. Loyalty to the prince, Confucius said, should go along with admonitions should the latter deviate from the path of righteousness. During this period of trade growth, Confucius warned of the risks linked to the search for profit and the dangers of

[12] Some historians consider the existence of (leagues of) city-states for this period, with the same term *guo* referring to the state and to the capital city. An aristocratic oligarchy formed an assembly headed by the prince or the king, and seems to have ruled the cities, with assemblies of "citizens" more rarely also playing a role (Lewis 2000: 359, 366, 368, 371). For Lewis, even the macro-states of this period, such as Jin, were conglomerates of semi-independent city-states and not true territorial states (2000: 364). The notion of a well-defined territory began emerging during the sixth century BCE. The erection of protective walls in some states from the seventh century onward, however, reveals a real ability to mobilize the labor force at a scale beyond the size of a city.

[13] A debate erupted in 625 BCE at the head of the state of Lu to decide whether or not the various border checkpoints should be suppressed. An agreement between states in 579 BCE stipulated that travelers' movements should not be hampered. See Hsu 1999: 580–581. In addition, Lewis (2000: 367) points to the development of ritualized diplomatic exchanges.

selfishness: "The righteous man understands *yì* [good behaviour, duty to others]; the common man understands *lì* [profit, gain, advantage]." Social harmony arises from a perfection that everyone must develop in himself or herself, and above all, the Emperor. Throughout the history of China, Confucianism – which was largely based on texts written after Confucius's lifetime – would play a role, more or less significant depending on the times, in the functioning of the state, through the values it promoted: respect for social hierarchy and authority; an importance given to agriculture; and the idea of an unchanging natural order.

Growth in trade was accompanied by the development of cities. Chandler estimates that there were six major cities in China in 650 BCE (Mesopotamia had only five); there were five in 800 BCE and three in 1000 BCE. As noted above, however, the number of archaeological discoveries of Shang cities are far fewer than the data given in Chinese texts). Morris (2013: 161) states that Linzi (state of Qi) and Luoyang (the Zhou capital) were the biggest cities, each with approximately 65,000 inhabitants in 600 BCE. The state of Chu, in the Yangtze valley, was at its peak during this period of the eastern Zhou.[14] The remains of its capital, Ying, cover 1600 hectares. In 706, the ruler Xiong Tong, in conflict with Zhou, proclaimed himself king of Chu.[15] A defeat against Jin in 632 at the battle of Chengpu (Henan) does not appear to have caused lasting damage to the Chu kingdom, which won a decisive victory in 597. Its expansion continued until the mid-fifth century. An intensive industry developed, as shown by the remains of the copper mine of Tonglüshan, southeast of Panglongcheng, which had been exploited since at least 1100 BCE.[16] By this time, bronzes no longer had a purely ritual use. They showed various innovations, such as the use of decorations first sculpted on clay; the lost wax technique; and inlays. Scaled-up bronze production boosted trade. Chu primarily encouraged iron metallurgy, which made it possible to manufacture weapons and tools. Finds in Chu tombs reflect the expansion of a glass industry (beads, *bi* discs) and imports along the Yunnan–Burma–India routes (Wu Xiaolong 2004). The opulence of the Chu elites[17] certainly played a major role in the development of trade with southern countries, through the demand by these elites for luxury goods. This trade had a visible impact on the societies of Lingnan (it would become even clearer during the fifth and fourth centuries BCE; see below). Neighboring maritime kingdoms also developed; examples include Wu, at the mouth of the Yangtze, which expanded to the detriment of Chu at the end of the sixth century, and Yue on the coasts of Zhejiang, which annexed the state of Wu in 473 BCE, with the help of Chu (see Map II.15). Yue owned a large fleet: one text reports the defection of Fan Li to Qi in 468 BCE with 300 ships (Deng 1997: 69, after the *Yue Jueshu*, written *c.* 52 CE). Moreover,

---

[14] A cemetery at Changsha contained large tombs equipped with access ramps, like those at the royal Shang tombs at Anyang. Halberds bearing characters in an undeciphered script have been unearthed (Higham 1996a: 70).

[15] As early as the beginning of the ninth century, the Chu ruler rejected the suzerainty of Zhou.

[16] Some shafts reached 20 meters in depth, below the water table, which required an elaborate drainage system. Winches were used from 500 BCE onward (Higham 1996a: 136; Barnes 1999: 149).

[17] The tomb of Marquis Yi of Zeng (Hubei), chief of a principality in the kingdom of Chu, who died in 433 BCE, contained more than ten tons of bronze, including 65 bells, on three levels, as well as chariots. Some items were produced using the new lost-wax technique, borrowed from northern populations (Debaine-Francfort 1999: 80–82).

beads made of soda-lime glass found in Shanxi and dated to the early fifth century reveal growing interactions through the Silk Roads from the sixth century BCE onward. The artistic motifs on various ornaments (winged felines, animal combat scenes, predator–victim "couples") found between Central Asia and China also point to the significance of these interactions. Various authors have suggested an Indian influence on the system of *xieu* lunar mansions – an equivalent of the Indian astronomical system of the *nakxatra*.[18]

The Spring and Autumn period was marked by a crucial innovation: coinage, here cast in molds. During the period of the Western Zhou – as may have been the case during the Shang period – "double strings of cowries" were standards of value and were used to reward services and make gifts.[19] In 925 BCE, a land sale was recorded in these terms: "Citizen Ju Bai received from Qiu Wei one jade tablet worth 80 double strings of cowries for ten fields of his lands." A bronze vase bears this inscription: "The king, having reviewed the governance of the minister Hu, presented him with five double strings of cowries. Wherefore, [Hu] cast this *zun* vase dedicated to his ancestor Ding" (Thierry 2001: 118). Other inscriptions mention payment, in cowries, for work done. Fabrics were also used as currency. The circulation of cowries seems to have increased in China around the end of the eighth century BCE; various "coins" appeared during the late seventh or early sixth century, reflecting both a transformation of the state and the expansion of trade and production: the coins were issued by the rulers of different kingdoms, or by merchants. The first coins (made of bronze) were spade-shaped (*bu*); they have been excavated near Luoyang, the seat of the Zhou court, and in Shanxi in the state of Jin.[20] Knife-shaped *dao* were issued in the states of Qi, Yan, and Zhao. Cowry-shaped *yibi* were produced mostly in the state of Chu.[21] Bronze was well suited to coinage due to its symbolic value, recognized since the Erlitou and Shang periods; bronze vessels were used in rituals in honor of royal ancestors; at the time of the Western Zhou, inscribed bronzes were offered in compensation for services rendered

---

[18] Assyriologists have suggested an ultimate origin of the system in Babylonia, with transmission to India and China at the time of the Persian Empire. Needham (1954), however, suggests that the two systems – Indian and Chinese – formed independently, and later influenced each other.

[19] On a bronze from the Shang period, we read: "On the day *ding-mao*, the king rewarded [Viscount Zu] with a double string of cowries, seized during a campaign against Yong" (Thierry 2001: 118). From the tenth century onward, the money distributed increased, reflecting the growing number of cowries in circulation and rising exchanges with the coasts (Thierry 1997: 44). Note that the term *bi*, "money," also means "gift, made for imperial tribute" (F. Thierry, p.c.). As mentioned above, Y.-T. Li (2003), however, refutes the monetary use of cowries during the Shang period.

[20] The coins' shape reflects a previous period when the tools they represented (spades, and knives) must have been used as currency. Thierry suggests the existence of "primitive monetary spades" without inscriptions, during the Shang period (1997: 49).

[21] Bronze cowries, sometimes gilded, had already appeared during the Shang period; they became more common during the Western Zhou and more importantly the Spring and Autumn periods; these cowries were still without inscription (Thierry 1997: 46). Cowries were also sculpted out of jade and turquoise. "Knives" without inscription were also found in the northern regions (states of Qi and Yan, territories of the Ron, the Di, and the Guzhu). On "spades" issued by the state of Chu in its northern regions, one sometimes reads: "ten bronze cowries" (Thierry 1997: 158), indicating an equivalence between currencies.

to the state. Prior to the appearance of coinage, the state of Wu had used pieces of bronze as currency.[22] The circulation of cowries appears to have diminished from the seventh century BCE onward, following the issuance of coins. As pointed out above, in the states of the Yellow River basin, Chinese money was – as soon as it appeared – a fiduciary type of money: its exchange power was not linked to its intrinsic value. In the state of Chu, by contrast, "money value was linked to the intrinsic value of monetary signs": this meant that money had to be weighed (Thierry 1997: 143).

A crucial change occurred within the state during this period, symbolized by actions taken by the reformers Guan Zhong for Qi, at the end of the seventh century, and Sunshu Ao in Chu, during the late seventh and early sixth centuries. As crafts were developing (salt, iron, bronze, pieces of lacquer ware, and silk), Guan Zhong encouraged the Qi state to commit itself to production, particularly in salt and iron. Chu copied the Zhou hierarchies and rites, but at the same time instituted decisive reforms that reinforced state power and tended to marginalize the aristocracy: Chu was the first kingdom to introduce the administrative district *xian* around 690 BCE, for newly conquered territories;[23] the Qin state would adopt this institution on a larger scale during the fourth and third centuries BCE. This new administrative system met the need to incorporate non-Zhou populations (Di Cosmo 2002: 124). The kingdoms of Lu and Zheng introduced the first forms of agrarian fiscality during the sixth century.[24] At the same time texts of laws appeared, written on bronze.[25] During the fifth century, the First Minister of Chu ordered the registration of arable land and forests and initiated a tax reform. The merchant Fan Li, an advisor to the court of King Goujian of Yue for a time during the first half of the fifth century BCE, showed that the market is a source of wealth in "the Golden Rules of Business Success" (*Jing Shang Bao Dian*):

To know supply and demand and take measures accordingly. See when times of scarcity are coming so you can be ready to act. With these two principles, you control the market. When there is a drought, that is the time to start laying away a stock of boats; and when there is a flood, that is the time to start buying up carts. This is the principle behind the use of goods . . . *To accumulate wealth, you have to use your capital: it should not be sleeping; you must buy and sell without interruption.* Products and goods should circulate constantly just like flowing water . . . If you study the surpluses and shortages of the market, you can judge how much a commodity will be worth. When an article has become extremely expensive, it will surely fall in price, and when it has become extremely cheap, then the price will begin to rise. Dispose of expensive goods as though they were so much filth and dirt; buy up cheap goods as though they were

---

[22] Schaps 2007: 21. "Monetary" finds of "raw bronze" have been made in Henan and, even more significantly, in Zhejiang and Jiangsu (Thierry 1997: 48).

[23] Lewis 2000: 364–365. These districts, however, tended to become hereditary "fiefs" in the state of Wei. It is possible that the state of Qi, under the influence of Guan Zhong, adopted the system of *xian*.

[24] Gernet 1999: 60; Lewis 2000: 370. The encyclopedia *Guanzi*, however, credits Guan Zhong for introducing a uniform tax, collected by the state. The *Guanzi* was not compiled in Qi during the Warring Kingdoms period, as is often thought, but later, during the second century BCE and first century CE.

[25] When money loses its power of compensation for social debts and begins playing a role in trade, according to G. Simmel (1987), a legal evaluation of individuals begins. It is striking that at the time when the first metallic coins used in exchanges appeared in China, the status of the farmers changed, and a code of written laws was proclaimed.

pearls and jade. Wealth and currency should be allowed to flow as freely as water! (*Shiji*, CXXIX, 3256, quoted by Thierry 1997: 38; Watson 1993: 437)

Associated with the state of Yue, the "Book of the Young Master of Accountancy" (*Jinizi*), which may have been written by the master of Fan Li, expresses a new interest in economic thought, and the idea that the state should "be involved in the economic affairs of the nation." "The perception at that time was that economic development marched hand in hand with military expansion" (Milburn 2007: 37). The *Jinizi* proposes to reduce taxes, and to develop agriculture, the silk industry, and trade. "The *Jinizi* is the earliest known text to include the concept of economic cycles, and it stresses the role of investment and savings in economic development, and price stabilization" (Milburn 2007: 19).

Moreover, in various states, ritual innovations reserved a new place for the people, considered as masters of the sacrifice at the "altars of Soil and Grain," and involved in oaths of alliance with the rulers. For Lewis, "the inclusion of new elements of the population in the public realm, the redefinition of the bonds between ruler and ruled . . . show how the process of creating city-states also created the tools for forging the macro-state into which they would be absorbed."[26]

The fragmentation of the Spring and Autumn period was followed by a phase of political reconcentration that began during the second half of the fifth century. Political transformation, economic growth and expanding trade accelerated from the end of the fifth century BCE, thanks to institutional and technical innovations, especially (but not only) in weaponry. The bitter wars between the "Warring Kingdoms" proved to be a period of change, during which a new type of central power developed at the expense of the old aristocracy: the very nature of power was changing at this time. Administrations were set up, with the creation of districts directly controlled by the state. The specific role of the prime minister was recognized; civil and military functions were now distinct from each other. Large kingdoms were formed, of which the most significant were Yan, Qi, and Zhao, in the north, Qin, Han, and Wei, in the central regions; and Chu, in the south. Wei benefited from the reforms of the legist Li Kui, who became first minister in 406. His "Law Codes" (*Fajing*) instituted an impartial law that was valid for all – the ruler of the state being ultimately "the source of all law" (Burbank and Cooper 2010: 46). Suppressing hereditary offices, Li Kui attempted to build a state apparatus based on skills and merit. Large irrigation and drainage systems were developed to increase agricultural production. Allotments of land were distributed to farmers. During the fifth century, the merchant Bai Gui formulated "the first theory of capital accumulation" founded on agricultural and craft production. As a result of the aristocracy's hostile reaction, Wu Qi, a disciple of Li Kui, was exiled to Chu in 382. Declining during the fifth century, the Chu kingdom recovered its vitality following the reforms initiated by Wu Qi, who had become first minister; he renovated the administration, ordered a reversion to the state of lands owned by the aristocracy, and built up an efficient army. Threatened by Qin in the

---

[26] Lewis 2000: 372. The process of social transformation is well described, but it is difficult to follow Lewis in his vision of city-states in China during the Spring and Autumn period.

west, Chu expanded to the east and the south. In 333, it took control of the neighboring state of Yue, which dominated the east Chinese coast from the mouth of the Yangtze to the Zhejiang.[27] It sent an expedition to Yunnan. At the peak of its power, Chu extended from Sichuan to the China Sea, and from central Henan to the Nanling Mountains. The status of farmers changed in various states: they acquired rights to land, and at the same time, a land market took form. Land purchases are mentioned in the states of Wei and Qin during the fourth century BCE. Large estates were formed, and debts were contracted, forcing small peasants to leave their communities and settle on uncleared land. Peasants also provided the labor force needed by flourishing industries.

It was probably in the kingdom of Qin, a neighbor of Chu, centered on the Wei River valley, that the transformation of the state was the most radical. Early on, "a new vision of the state gave Qin a singular identity, marked by the abolition of hereditary aristocracy, the formation of a meritocratic elite," a new military organization and the establishment of a system of taxes (Shelach and Pines 2006: 219). The Qin state would be viewed as "barbarian" (and therefore different) by the other Zhou states (Shelach and Pines 2006: 217). The legist Shang Yang, who became prime minister in 361, was at the heart of the reforms of Qin. These reforms aimed at building an efficient state, increasing agricultural output, and forming a powerful army. Land and men were registered. Roads were improved. The territory was divided into *xian* districts ruled by officials whose activity was controlled and assessed. The administration comprised an eighteen-level hierarchy; officials climbed the social ladder according to their merits and accomplishments, regardless of their social origin. While trade was heavily taxed, its importance was recognized. Qin encouraged immigration, granting lands to farmers from other states in order to attract them. Farmers had the right to acquire land and to sell it, but vagrancy was forbidden. They formed military groups that could be mobilized at any time. The "Eighteen Laws of Qin," found in a tomb dated before Shi Huangdi's reign, reveal an economy already highly monetized, where coinage was used as a means of exchange and a unit of account (Thierry 1997: 163; 2001: 128). Qin benefited from its internal dynamics and from increasing exchanges with Inner Asia.[28] Changes in tombs during the fourth century BCE reflect stronger outside influences and increased transcultural contacts. As early as the fourth and third centuries BCE, silks from Qin were reaching northern India (whence the name Cina used in India for the silk country, and Thinae in the *Periplus*) (Gernet 1999: 74, 122).[29] Changes in China had effects on its neighbors. Growing trade and the aggressive expansion of states – Qin especially tried

---

[27] The state of Yue was in contact with the the island of Kyushu (Japan), where iron was introduced during the Yayoi period around the fourth century BCE (Barnes 1999: 171). The language(s) of the Yue may have belonged to the Austroasiatic family (Boltz 1999: 81–83), but some authors see the Yue as Thai speakers (Marks 1998: 55).

[28] Further east, the Jin state developed a sizeable bronze industry, as shown by the discovery of a huge foundry in its capital (sixth–fifth century BCE).

[29] The term "Cina" figures in the *Laws of Manu* and the *Mahābhārata*. For some researchers, Cina in fact could refer to "the eastern part of India, at the borders of Tibet and Burma" (Boulnois 2001: 163); this agrees with interpretations relating to Ptolemy's Sinae (see above). For Cosmas during the sixth century and Indians during the seventh century, Tsin did refer to China, as did Sin for the Arabs.

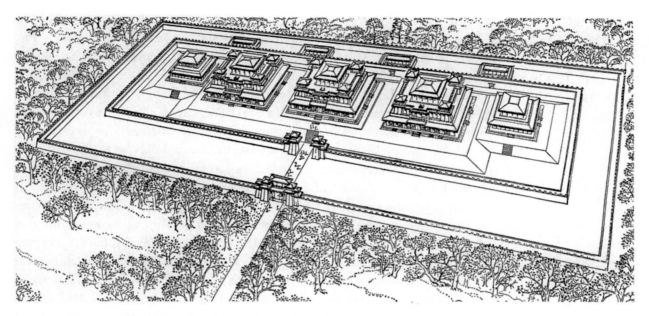

Figure 12.1 Royal mausoleums, Pingshan, state of Zhongshan, fourth century BCE
Reconstruction, Barnhart 2004, after Fu Xinian 1980: 110. Barnhart suggests a possible Greek
influence on Chinese buildings at this time.

to bypass groups of Inner Asia – spurred the formation of a warrior elite among the
Xiongnu nomads, whose tombs have been found at various sites, such as Yulongtai and
Shihuigou (Inner Mongolia).[30]

The formation of a centralized state is deeply connected to a change in war
techniques, with the appearance of cavalry[31] and the increasing significance of infantry,
which reduced the role of chariots and eventually destroyed "the aristocratic mode of
life bound up with the driving of teams" (Gernet 2002: 66). Starting in the seventh
century and more importantly during the fourth and third centuries BCE, walls were
erected between some states, revealing large-scale mobilization of the labor force by the
central power. Walls were also built in the north and in the west by the states of Qin,
Zhao, and Yan. More than reflecting a need for protection from nomads, these walls
reflected the violent expansion of central states into their "barbarian" peripheries.
The walls "were part of a policy of penetration into an alien land," which had several
objectives. It aimed at acquiring horses and pastures, and at enclosing conquered
populations, in order to control their movements and to enrol them in armed forces
(Di Cosmo 2002: 142, 149, 152ff.). The formation of the Xiongnu confederation appears

---

[30] These tombs have yielded iron artifacts inlaid with silver or gold, imported from the Chinese central
plains, and many gold items. Chinese coins were also discovered (Di Cosmo 1999b: 959–960). Sites in the
Ordos area reveal Xiongnu's social complexity and the importance of trade for the aristocracy (Di Cosmo
2002: 85). The first evidence given by texts for direct contact between the Xiongnu and China may go back
to 318 BCE: the Xiongnu were part of a force that attacked Qin. However, there are indications of the
existence of elites in the steppe societies during the early first millennium BCE.

[31] In 307 BCE, the king of Zhao chose to introduce cavalry into his army. The adoption of cavalry starting at
the end of the fourth century BCE is partly a response to growing incursions by nomads from Central Asia.
"The fourth and third centuries BC," also notes Morris, "saw chariots being replaced by cavalry and great
advances in siege warfare" (2013: 214).

largely to have been a defensive response to cope with the aggressiveness of the Chinese states. The frontier did not separate nomads and farmers (the Xiongnu area in fact included populations of farmers); rather, it separated the core from its (semi-) periphery.

The changes we observe were closely connected to the development of iron metallurgy and of the state, itself linked to the rise in trade, because trade was essential for acquiring horses. Contacts with populations of Central Asia speaking Iranian languages – whom Chinese historical sources such as the *Hanshu* allow us to identify as the Saka (Scythians) – probably explain the introduction of iron metallurgy into China (see above), which greatly expanded from the sixth century BCE onward.[32] Some authors (see Wagner 1985), however, have suggested the invention of iron metallurgy in states such as Wu, where bronze was not exclusively reserved for the manufacturing of weapons and ritual vessels, but was also used to produce agricultural tools.[33] Wagner has since changed his mind and now (2003) accepts the idea that iron metallurgy was introduced via northwestern China. The states of Wu and Chu were the first to make significant advances in metallurgy of cast iron (during the fifth century BCE).[34] This type of industry appears to have progressed more rapidly in "peripheral" states than it did in the central states. Barnes (1999: 152) points out that "the weakest of the seven major Late Zhou states, the state of Yan, in the north, produced a greater abundance of iron artifacts than Qin" (Yan yielded the earliest-known iron armor). It was from this state that iron metallurgy spread into Korea around 400 BCE. The ascendancy of this type of metallurgy throughout China is linked to the existence of kilns that could reach temperatures of 1300° as well as to the manufacture of stoneware, in regions where clay was rich in iron (Barnes 1999: 120). The various emerging states controlled a massive production of new weapons such as crossbows, invented in China, and swords, a weapon from the steppes. The prince of Han used crossbows during the fourth century BCE: this weapon must have been developed during the fourth century BCE or perhaps earlier. A text dated to the second century CE goes so far as to place this invention in the seventh century BCE, in the Chu kingdom, but according to

[32] North Korean archaeologists suggest iron introduction into North Korea during the eighth or seventh century, but these dates have not been accepted by South Koreans and western archaeologists (Wagner 2003: 132–133).

[33] Bronze in China during the Zhou and the Spring and Autumn periods is mainly present in the tombs of the elite. G. L. Barnes (1999: 151) notes the production of bronze with a high iron content in the state of Wu, prior to the appearance of iron metallurgy. Bronze agricultural tools must have been expensive and therefore of limited use, which may explain resorting to iron, a cheaper metal.

[34] Wagner 2003: 140ff. At Jingmen, a Chu settlement in Hubei province, iron implements, apparently cast, may date to the late sixth century BCE. Unlike western Asia and Europe, China was therefore able to produce cast iron soon after the introduction of iron metallurgy. Techniques made it possible to lower the melting point by adding "black earth" rich in phosphorus. "The earliest artifacts of smelted iron from a clearly Chinese context were found in the royal tombs of the state of Guo, dated to the early 8th century" or slightly later (Wagner 2003: 135). Moreover, meteoritic iron was used in the central plains as early as the Western Zhou period (site of Shangou) and even in the Late Shang period, at Taixicun (Gaocheng, Hebei) and at Liujiahe (Beijing) (use of iron on bronze axes). We do not know whether this was a Chinese innovation or whether it resulted from influences from Inner Asia (objects in meteoritic iron are dated to 2000 BCE in the Minusinsk basin and the Altai, a region in contact with the cultures of Xinjiang) (Wagner 2003: 134–135 n. 38).

J. Needham, this particular weapon was at best a trigger system and not yet the true crossbow. A Mohist text, *The Book of Master Mo*, describes large crossbows that could shoot several arrows at once. "Multiple-shooting" crossbows were well attested during the Former Han period (Di Cosmo 2002: 235). As early as the third century BCE, the second Qin emperor (*Ershi Huangdi*) could assemble 50,000 archers with crossbows. Artisans producing weapons were required to sign their arms (Brook 1998: 22). We also know that arrow-shooting machines of the crossbow type (called *katapeltikon* by Diodorus of Sicily) were used by the ancient Greeks, for example at Syracuse in 397 BCE, and Hero of Alexandria described an earlier type of crossbow (*gastraphetes*). J. Needham has suggested that this weapon was introduced from China. The crossbow was soon forgotten, but it reappeared in Europe during the tenth century (see below).

Iron led to progress in several sectors of production. Whereas during the preceding period agriculture had not made use of many bronze tools, iron was now used for fashioning plows and hoes. According to Sherratt (2006b), as noted, the introduction of the iron plow may be due to contacts with India, via the Yunnan region. Use of the animal-drawn plow seems to have spread at the same time as iron metallurgy. F. Bray indicates the appearance of the oxen-drawn plow during the fifth century BCE (Needham *et al.* 1988: 141). Its use could only have developed on relatively vast domains. The states encouraged land clearing, the use of manure, drainage of swampy areas, and irrigation of drier lands. Agricultural progress triggered demographic growth, especially during the fourth and third centuries BCE. At least four cities had over 100,000 inhabitants in 300 BCE: Linzi (state of Qi), Qufu (state of Lu), Luoyang (eastern Zhou), Xinzheng (state of Han), and Wuyang (state of Yan) (Morris 2013: 155).

Competition between the "Warring Kingdoms" fostered technical innovations, global economic expansion, and the development of knowledge in various fields. Weapons and war techniques have been mentioned above. The optimization of wind tunnels (with double-acting piston bellows, allowing a continuous stream to be expelled [Temple 2002: 44]) led to steel production perhaps as early as the fifth century BCE. According to Sima Qian, Chinese artisans taught the technique of steel manufacturing to the people of Central Asia and to the Parthians,[35] and this technique spread along the Silk Roads. Around the third century BCE, the Chinese were able to produce malleable cast iron (called "annealed" iron): it was not brittle, and therefore improved the solidity of tools (plows, hoes) and weapons.[36] Improvements were made

---

[35] Boulnois 2001: 216. R. Temple gives a later date for the production of steel: according to J. Needham, the Chinese invented two processes, the first during the second century BCE took the carbon out of cast iron ("decarburization": the procedure is described in a text dated to 120 BCE), and the second (known in Europe as the "Siemens process") during the fifth or sixth century CE melted together cast iron (which has a high carbon content) and wrought iron, which has a very low carbon content (a technique called "cofusion") (Temple 2002: 50, 68–69). Such an early use of the technique in China, however, has been cast into doubt by Craddock (2003: 239). Double-acting piston bellows had been known since the fourth century BCE (Temple 2002: 44–45). We do not know in fact where and when the first method for decarburizing cast iron to convert it into wrought iron was invented (Wagner 2003: 143 and n. 81). Note that double-acting piston bellows were not transmitted to Europe until the sixteenth century.

[36] Temple 2002: 43. Curiously, D. Warburton (2003: 259) writes that states refrained from becoming involved in iron technology, and that technological innovation, in China, was "without consequence."

in horse harnesses and means of transport. The neck yoke was replaced by the breast harness, which allowed horses to tow heavier loads.[37] Shipbuilding began developing at this time. Ships used several layers of planks, held together by pegs and iron nails.[38] Maritime trade connected the Yangtze region and Shandong province. A wide variety of silk fabrics is attested: a tomb in Hebei (*c.* 300 BCE) has yielded more than six kinds of silk.[39]

Social transformations were accompanied by an intellectual effervescence, with the writing of new works, particularly by the "Legists," the formation of the "Confucian tradition" and the Daoist doctrine.[40] The schools of thought of the Mohists and the logicians appeared at this time; they focused their attention on logic, deductive reasoning (from the general to the particular), and inductive reasoning (deriving general principles from specific observations) as ways of searching for knowledge.[41] The school of the Mohists, which opposed Confucian doctrine, would have little influence later in China, probably due to the weight of a powerful state influenced by Confucianism. The Legists, vehemently opposed to the Mohists, first guided the building of the new Chinese state, especially in Qin.[42] They put forward the value of laws and institutions,

---

[37] Two types of harnesses were used in China: the trace harness and the collar harness (see Temple 2002: 20). The trace harness may have appeared during the fourth century BCE and the collar harness during the first century BCE.

[38] Gernet 1999: 67. Deng (1997: 23, 24) also mentions the use of metal hoops to strengthen joints of planks in ships for sea travel, and some standardization of ships (in the ratio of deck length to beam). According to this author, sails became functional only at the time of the Warring Kingdoms (Deng 1997: 32). However, sails had been used on ships since around 4000 BCE: Dahl has reconstructed PAN *laiaɣ*, "sail" (1991). Remember that the Proto-Austronesians went from eastern China (Yangtze region?) to Taiwan around 4000 BCE. In addition, the character *fan* found on oracular bones referred to the sail; the writing of the sign looks like a Melanesian sail held by two masts (double-mast spritsail) (Needham *et al.* 1971: 599) and generally speaking the Oceanic spritsail, one sail that allowed for tacking (Irwin 2008).

[39] Boulnois 2001: 42. In China, silk was used to wrap the bodies of high-status people. The Western Christian world would continue this practice for the corpses of saints and for relics.

[40] The usual dates proposed for Confucius are 551–479 BCE (Gernet 1999: 85ff.). Confucius himself did not leave much written work about his teaching. Elaboration of the Confucian doctrine progressed with Mencius (370–290 BCE) and under the Han, who adopted Confucianism as their official political and moral doctrine. Daoist doctrine refers to Lao-tseu (sixth century BCE); it was developed by Zhuanzi (*c.* 350–275), but would not become a popular religion until the second century CE.

[41] "[These schools of thought] also used the idea of conceptual models" (Ronan 1988: 201–202). The founder of the Mohist school, Mozi (Mo Di) (*c.* 480–390), was probably an official of the Song state. The Mohists developed military defensive techniques. Their writings thus describe the sending of poisonous gases using bellows and a system of pipes used against enemies besieging a town. The Daoists developed research in alchemy, not just aimed at finding "medicines of immortality," but also leading to various discoveries, including that of the propensity for ignition of a mixture of saltpeter and sulphur (Ronan 1988: 251ff.). The processes of sublimation and of distillation using types of "stills" were already being experimented with at this time (Needham *et al.* 1980: 57). The properties of the lodestone were known as early as the fourth century BCE. They would be used by diviners and geomancers, but the *Book of the Devil Valley Master* (written by the philosopher Su Chin, fourth century BCE) also states: "When the people of Cheng go out to collect jade, they carry a south-pointer with them so as not to lose their way" (Temple 2002: 151).

[42] See above. Han Fei (280?–234 BCE), who came from the kingdom of Han, was instrumental in the type of political thought that built the Qin state. The emperor, however, had Han Fei imprisoned. Also worth mentioning is the influence of a text by Shen Buhai (*c.* 337 BCE), prime minister under Marquis Zhao of the state of Han, who advocated the development of a state bureaucracy.

the foundations of the state, and the need for the state to grow rich and to strengthen its army. At the same time, the Legists focused on productivity. They felt that the value of institutions and of agents of the state must be judged on their effective yield (Norel 2005); for the Legists, the principle of equality before the law had to be guaranteed (Gernet 2002: 93). Agriculture was viewed as the source of economic and military power, but the Legists also proposed establishing a policy promoting crafts; an artisanal class emerged, despite the relatively low status usually assigned to craftsmen. Great entrepreneur-traders were influential in the forming of this Legist school of thought.

The use of money expanded, at the same time as a theory on its use was being elaborated. The theorists shed light on the regulatory role that the state could play, setting the value of commodities. During this fiercely competitive period, the states became increasingly aware of the importance of controlling money. Shang Qi, a minister of the Zhou king (540–520 BCE), showed that money does not have a fixed exchange value: value fluctuates "according to the level of prices and standard of living of the population"; Mozi synthesized this in these words: "Monetary knives and goods mutually determine their prices." "The prince, says the *Guanzi*, who can control the balance between grain and money, would be able to conquer the world" (Thierry 2001: 37). Money appears to be fundamentally linked to good governance, when "by manipulating quantities of goods and money, a ruler can adjust the ratios of exchange" and establish an equitable order (von Glahn 1996: 29).[43] The state tried to impose a virtuous cycle; regulating a currency of fluctuating value allowed the state to make both economic and political profits, by intervening in grain markets and markets for other goods and by collecting part of the taxes in cash (Thierry 2001: 35; Schaps 2006: 39). The states still issued "spades," "knives," and also (in Qin especially) round coins[44] (the *banliang*, "half-ounce," was introduced *c.* 210 BCE); the round coins each had a hole, allowing them to be strung on a cord. Qin also recognized a gold ingot (*yi*) as currency. This played a role in interstate trade, and would become a store of value. The state of Chu produced gold plaques bearing various stamps (see below), as well as "spades" and bronze plaques (stamped silver plaques were also known). Gold plaques were weighed at each transaction. One finds small gold squares weighing 4.5 g. The minting of gold was a royal prerogative (Thierry 2001: 132).

The economic and social changes during this period corresponded to a crisis within the aristocratic society; these changes were marked by expanding production and trade, commerce between various regions of China as well as with Inner Asia and overseas countries. At the same time as the state was involved in production, a class of rich merchants was developing who engaged in commerce and craft enterprises, and

---

[43] If the ruler fails to ensure order by maintaining a balance between money and commodities, says the *Guanzi*, "merchants will exploit monetary strategems in order to manipulate the prices of commodities" (von Glahn 1996: 33). "It was the government's function to facilitate the exchange of commodities and, thus, to secure the livelihood of all ... The Pseudo-Guanzi assigns the ruler (or state) to regulate the money supply in order to achieve a balance between the rate of production of goods and the purchasing power of the people" (Zurndorfer 1999: 398). After Rickett (1993), Zurndorfer notes that we have here the first version of the quantity theory of money.

[44] Round coins also appeared in the monetary minting of the "three Jin" (Zhao, Wei, Han) (Thierry 1997: 75). Currencies were issued in many fiefdoms; there were also private monetary workhops (Thierry 1997: 91).

sometimes acted as court advisors. The size of larger cities, which were political and economic centers, increased significantly (Gernet 1999: 72–73).

The growing significance of interactions with Inner Asia during the period of the Warring Kingdoms triggered the emergence of two neighbors of Chu. The first, the state of Qin, has been mentioned above. The second was the kingdom of Shu in Sichuan, which benefited from internal resources and from trade routes connecting it to the Yangtze basin, the Yellow River valley, Southeast Asia, and India (via Yunnan); Shu also appears to have been in contact with populations from the Tarim basin. It is significant that the Chu kingdom decided to launch a military expedition to Sichuan and Yunnan at the beginning of the fourth century. Sichuan yielded many *banliang* coins, probably brought in following its conquest by Qin in 316 BCE. The state of Chu traded with the region of the Xijiang River (Guangxi and Guangdong) and with Sichuan. The issuance by Chu of stamped square gold money may reflect an Indian influence,[45] coming by land (from Yunnan) or by sea. The coasts were gaining new importance, as shown by the invasion of Yue by the armies of Chu. Glass items, first known in the tombs of the Spring and Autumn period, became more abundant at the time of the Warring Kingdoms. Glass (used as inlays on royal swords) found in the coastal states of Wu and Yue was probably imported from the eastern Mediterranean, as well as ocellated beads; other beads, imitating western beads, were produced in China.[46] The discovery of imported glass from western Asia in the states of Yue and Wu appears to reflect maritime traffic via Southeast Asia. This traffic may go back at least to the seventh century BCE if cinnamon *Cinnamomum cassia* Blume was indeed present in Greece at that time (see above). Basing his argument on a Chinese text of the fourth century BCE, Needham has suggested sea journeys by the Yue to the Indian Ocean.[47] In any event, the Yue sailors of Zhejiang and Guangdong must have been in contact with Southeast Asia (Clark 2009: 23). In the north, the kingdom of Yan established relations with Japan.

Exchanges increased between the Yangtze region and Lingnan through maritime and terrestrial routes, encouraging the emergence of local leaders. "The concentration of rich graves in the region where the Xijiang, Beijiang and Suijiang rivers converge above the delta" confirms this process (Higham 1996a: 100), for example at the site of Matougang (late sixth to early fifth century BCE) and at Beilingsongshan, which contained bells and bronze vessels from the state of Chu, local bronzes, and bronze

---

[45] Schaps 2007: 6. These coins were issued between the fifth and third centuries BCE. See Thierry 1997: 146. This gold money has been found in the territories of Chu and Yue (after its conquest by Chu, but perhaps also earlier). Chu was producing gold; moreover, this metal may have come from Sichuan.

[46] Glass inlays decorating the sword of King Goujian (496–465 BCE), of the state of Yue, and that of the king of Wu may be imported glass, as well as the beads found in a tomb at Gushi (Henan), dated to the sixth–fifth century BCE. See An Jiayo 1996: 128–129; Lange Rosenzweig 2004: 13, 16. The chemical composition of these types of glass (with potash and calcium, rather than lead and calcium or lead and barium, as was the case for Chinese glass from this period) reveals that this glass was imported from western Asia; the same can be said for sodo-calcic glass. Beads and *bi* discs of Chinese origin have been excavated from the fifth century BCE onward, especially in the provinces of Hunan, Hubei, Henan, Shaanxi, Hebei, Shandong, and Sichuan (Fukang 1992: 159). Glass "funerary garments" would later be found during the Han period in places such as Yangzhou.

[47] The text "describes the sailors of the Yueh region in southern China [as] being absent from the western regions for years" (Needham 1970: 140).

human-headed staves, symbols of power.[48] It is likely that luxury goods from the southern seas such as kingfisher feathers, rhino horns, and ivory (later enumerated in the Han Annals) had already arrived along the Guangdong coast. Imports of northern origin along the Fujian coast reveal the existence of maritime contacts. Iron metallurgy appeared in Lingnan during the fourth century BCE.[49]

Political changes accelerated at the end of the fourth century BCE: the militaristic Qin state took control of Shu in 316 and then expanded spectacularly at the expense of Chu, which was defeated in 312, 301, and again in 278, when its capital, Ying, was taken. Chu withdrew to its eastern territories, installing a new capital at Chen (Henan), and then at Souchun (Anhui). In northeastern China, Qi was another preeminent state at this time, but during the third century BCE, Qin would be the first to succeed in unifying Chinese territory, with its conquest of Han, Zhao, and Wei, between 230 and 228, and lastly of Chu in 223 and of Qi in 221 BCE.

The Unification of China under the Qin (221–207 BCE), the Western Han (206 BCE – 23 CE), and the Eastern Han (25–220 CE)

> I brought order to the crowd of the creatures and put to the test the acts
> and the facts: everything has its right name.
> (Stela erected by Shi Huangdi)

> The power of a kingdom rests with its horses.
> (Boulnois 2008: 75)

> In the state of the enlightened sovereign there is no literature written on bamboo slips, but the law is the only teaching; there are no quoted sayings of the early kings, but the magistrates are the only instructors. There is no valor through private swords, but slaughter of the enemy is the only courageous deed. As a result, the people, within the boundary, when practicing persuasion and eloquence, always conform to the law; when up and doing, they always aim at meritorious services . . .
> Having stored up the resources of the [kingdom], the sovereign waits for the enemy state to reach an unguarded moment. Those who have surpassed the Five Emperors and compete with the Three Kings have always followed this method.
> (Han Fei, extract from the *Hanfeizi*)

Benefiting from the adoption (*c.* 350 BCE) of a type of administration developed in the state of Chu, with a division of the kingdom into "counties" governed by officials

---

[48] Other tombs, at Nanmendong, south of the Xijiang valley, and at Niaodanshan (fifth or fourth century BCE), southwest of Matougang, contained similar objects. A tomb at Beilingsongshan had particularly rich contents, with over 100 bronzes, and numerous gold and jade ornaments. Bronze staves have also been found in Guangxi; each of their pommels shows a human head; those from central Guangdong have pommels featuring animal heads (Higham 1996a: 100–103).

[49] Iron is present in tombs at the Yinshanling cemetery, in the Guijiang River valley, north of the Xijiang River. In addition, the tombs show bronze vessels in the Chu style and many weapons (five of the six richest tombs contained imports from the Chu state), but agricultural iron tools have also been excavated (Higham 1996a: 104–107).

appointed by the king (see above),[50] the state of Qin triumphed over all its rivals, after great bloodshed. Prince Zheng, who had come to power in 247 BCE when he ascended the throne of Qin, managed to unify China in an empire of a new type. He was then known under the name Shi Huangdi ("First Emperor"). Under his reign, farmers were carefully registered. Shi Huangdi "established the Chinese peasants as independent farmers, but they owed taxes and military service to the state" (Norel 2005). The setting up of massive conscription was deeply ingrained in the new ideology built by the elite of Qin.[51] Three officials, including a military commander, administered each region. Population registration allowed for the collection of taxes; these were higher for merchants than for farmers. Slave owners were heavily taxed. At the same time, the formation of a centralized state, the establishment of "a new graphic norm that replaced the various scripts in use," the standardization of weights and measures,[52] the issuance of "a single type of copper currency using round coins with a square hole in the center";[53] all opened up a new era for exchanges, both within the empire and with foreign countries, via the oases of Central Asia (the Silk Roads), which were under the control of the Yuezhi, and through maritime routes running from China to the south. According to the *Huainanzi*, the emperor of Qin sent armies along five paths to conquer the Lingnan region and the territories of the "Hundred Viets" (*Bai Yue*).[54] The Qin state built roads toward the coasts, and erected the Great Wall, an extension of the fortifications built by the Warring Kingdoms. The state also undertook the digging of canals (the first contour transport canal is dated to this period).[55]

Shi Huangdi's megalomania combined with the tremendous efforts required of the population would bring about the demise of the empire (it is said that 700,000 men helped to build his tomb). Incessant warfare, and the taxes and statutory labor imposed on farmers led to massive revolts. Moreover, the emperor alienated the Confucians and Daoists by having books burned and by forbidding discussion of ancient philosophers. The Qin state did not survive the emperor's death; the Han dynasty succeeded the Qin in 206 BCE.[56] The Han Empire comprised an ensemble of "commanderies" (*jin*) and

---

[50] This reform led to the disappearance of local feudal lords and made power centralization possible. After Yongcheng, the capital of Qin was established further east at Xianyang, facing Chang'an, on the left bank of the Wei River.

[51] This ideology was not just a by-product of statebuilding, however. See Shelach and Pines 2006: 221.

[52] Units of length and capacity followed a decimal system. The state also ensured the uniformization of axle spacing for the carts (Gernet 1999: 102).

[53] According to F. Thierry (1997), the economy was already monetized at the beginning of the empire. At Zhangpu in Shaanxi, a sealed jar was found containing 1,000 *banliang* coins.

[54] As early as 277 BCE, the state of Qin was able to parade a thousand warships (Deng 1997: 69). In 219, Shi Huangdi is said to have launched an expedition to the legendary island of Penglai, the "paradise of the eight immortals" (Pimpaneau 1999: 24–27). Penglai was thought to be "Mount Kunlun, resting upon the back of a tortoise" (Christie 1957: 352) (Christie sees in this mythical image an influence from India). The fleet returned in 210, only to depart again (Cheng Te-K'un 1984: 82).

[55] A canal linked the Xiangjiang and Li rivers (Temple 2002: 181–182). A Mesopotamian influence on Chinese hydraulic techniques, proposed by E. Burke III (2009b: 88), seems improbable.

[56] As was the case for the Egyptian pharaohs of the Fourth Dynasty, a considerable amount of work was invested in Shi Huangdi's tomb, only part of which has been excavated. Although the tombs of the previous kings of Qin cannot be compared to that of Shi Huangdi, those built since the eighth century stand out for their size and their wealth, revealing the willingness of the kings of Qin to present themselves as equal to the Zhou.

vassal kingdoms (whose importance would quickly diminish). Confucianism now served as a reference framework and a standard for social conduct.

While the unification process went along with the internal development of the Chinese plains, it also partially reflected the significance of trade relations with Central Asia during the third century BCE.[57] Note that the first minister of Qin, Lü Buwei, had been a merchant until 237. As mentioned above, parallel to the Qin expansion, a "confederation" of people (Xiongnu)[58] from the steppes was formed in 204 BCE; it remained in place until 43 BCE, when it broke up into two entities. The leader of the Southern Xiongnu married a princess from the harem of the Han emperor Yuandi, Wang Zhaojun, whose history would become a classical theme in Chinese literature (Liu 2010: 5). The Northern Xiongnu were later absorbed by a confederation of Xianbei people from Manchuria (Beckwith 2011: 78). These transformations in the steppes derive from both internal and external processes, and from the interactions of these processes. Recent archaeological research shows that the Xiongnu territory included more than nomads; the political entity that was formed was more strongly structured than previously thought, with advanced interregional integration and marked social stratification. Honeychurch and Amartuvshin have rightly emphasized that the experience of long-distance contacts accumulated by the mobile pastoralist populations of the steppes, implying exchanges with various populations, proved to be an asset for the process of statebuilding (2006: 262, 268). Moreover, ideology certainly played an integrating role. The army was strictly organized, according to a decimal system that would constitute the norm for the "nomadic empires." The Xiongnu power experienced its peak at the time of the Chinese emperor Wendi, who was forced to sign a peace treaty in 162 BCE. A route through the steppes was in use toward Central and western Asia. Tombs at Pazyryk (third century BCE), in the Altai, have yielded embroidered silk, lacquerwork bowls, bronze mirrors, and a Chinese bronze helmet, as well as Indian cotton fabrics, and remnants of carpets and woolen fabrics revealing Iranian influences.[59] This northern route through the steppes, however, was less frequented than the southern routes. On the southern branch of the Silk Roads, a tomb at Niya contained

---

[57] Gills and Frank 1993b: 85. The innovations of the state of Qin in the spheres of public administration and infrastructure also explain the rapid advance of this state (see above). Frank and Gills put forward – on the basis of no evidence – an incorporation of the Chinese complexes into the (western) world-system at the end of the Zhou period (at the same time, they [1993b: 123] note an asynchrony between China and western Asia, China being in expansion during the "B" phase of the western world-system starting in 200 BCE). The appearance of Chinese funerary customs in the Tarim during the third century BCE reveals eastern influences (a silk veil covering the face is one example) (Müller 2003: 53, 62).

[58] This confederation was formed after an expedition conducted by a general of the Qin state into the Ordos in 215 BCE, but it had begun taking shape earlier. Integrated into the Xiongnu state, settlements of sedentary populations practicing agriculture have been unearthed; some of them were surrounded by walls and moats, at Ivolga for example, south of Lake Baikal, where tombs have yielded objects from western Central Asia, such as glass and semiprecious stones. Various fortified sites have also been discovered in Mongolia.

[59] Rudenko 1970; Christian 2000: 15. This silk has been compared to a fabric found in a tomb at Alagou (Xinjiang), and to silks of the Chu kingdom. The decoration of a polychrome fabric from the same kurgan, featuring walking lions, can be related to motifs from Persepolis and Ai Khanum (Francfort 1990: 125). Pazyryk has also yielded coriander and the pelt of a cheetah from western Asia, and a helmet from the Caucasus. The bodies discovered were tattooed, a common practice in the Scythian elite. Francfort also notes the find of sixteen coins from the Bosphorus in Dzungaria, and that of a bronze statuette of a man wearing a high hat of the Phrygian type, at Tuanchang in the Ili river valley (north of the Tianshan) (dated between the fifth and third centuries BCE).

a couple dressed in silk, an item already embedded in regional customs (*c.* 200 BCE) (Barber 2002: 59). Alwighul (Alagou) (near Urumqi) has also yielded silk remnants and lacquered cups, reflecting links with China; numerous gold ornaments exhibit the animal style of the steppes. East of Khotan, silk and cotton fabrics found in the cemetery at Sampul feature a centaur and a "Roman" (probably Saka) portrait (first century BCE) (Mallory and Mair 2000). The Saka who occupied this region were known as Yuezhi by the Chinese. The interconnection with networks linked to India is obvious at Baozidong, north of Akesu (Tarim), where one tomb has yielded 8 carnelian etched beads and 143 glass beads (Mei and Shell 2002: 218). Etched beads have also been unearthed at the fortified site of Djoumboulak Koum (which dates back to the middle of the first millennium BCE), located east of Khotan, where a necropolis has revealed mummies of Caucasoid type (Debaine-Francfort 2001: 66). To the southeast of Lake Baikal, the rich Xiongnu tombs of Noyon Uul (Noin Ula) (first century BCE) contained carpets and embroidered cloth from Sogdiana, Bactria or western Asia, lacquer ware, bronze mirrors, and silk from China (Honeychurch and Amartuvshin 2006: 265).

With the nomads, the Chinese alternated between a policy of appeasement (such as gifts of silks, intermarriages, exchanges of embassies, and organization of border markets) and military operations (for example, between 127 and 119 BCE, and in 97 BCE, when Wudi sent an army of 140,000 infantry and 70,000 cavalry against the Xiongnu). It was probably in order to solicit an alliance against the Xiongnu that Zhang Qian was sent to the Yuezhi in 138 BCE. He reached their court – at that time in Bactria – only in 129 BCE, after spending nine years with the Xiongnu, who had captured him.[60] In Bactria, Zhang Qian was astonished to find bamboo and cloth arriving from Sichuan via Burma and northern India, where the Bactrian merchants had gone to acquire them (the *shu* merchants of Sichuan seem to have brought these products into India, where some of them had settled: this trade was clearly operating on a regular basis).[61] The "Shu fabrics" that Zhang Qian mentioned were perhaps made of hemp: very fine hemp fabrics were stored in large sections of bamboo (Boulnois 2008: 104, 106). Merchants also carried silks along this road. The trade route departed from Chengdu, the capital of Sichuan, then a large city, continued on to Yibin and Kunming, in Yunnan (center of the Dian culture), veered westward and arrived at Yongchang, between the Mekong and the Salween rivers; it then crossed Upper Burma, whence it ran to Assam and Bengal (Boulnois 2008: 154). This discovery prompted Emperor Wudi (141–87 BCE) to launch expeditions to Yunnan in order to control the India-bound trade routes; these were probably seen as alternatives to the Central Asian road and to the maritime route departing from Guangdong (the wealth of Yunnan and Sichuan in precious metals added to this region's appeal).[62] Most of

[60] Boulnois, 2001: 47ff. Despite a treaty concluded with the Han in 162 BCE, the Xiongnu invaded territories south of the Great Wall in the middle of the second century, which led to a counter-onslaught from the Han in 128 BCE. The Xiongnu movements in Gansu and Xinjiang forced the Yuezhi to flee to Bactria during the second century BCE. According to Brown (2001: 72), cool climate conditions and increased aridification help explain these Xiongnu movements; the Han expansion, however, remains their primary cause.

[61] After the *Shiji*, *Historical Records*, written by Sima Qian (135–93 or 86 BCE).

[62] Gernet 1999: 120; Drège 2000: 17. According to the *Shiji*, the mission of another Chinese envoy to the south highlights the existence of a trade route between Canton and Sichuan. The Shu merchants were making use of this route to the coast (Wicks 1992 35). The Qin Empire had tried to control the routes of

Yunnan was incorporated into the Chinese state as of 109 BCE.[63] Moreover, the Han Empire controlled a long corridor in Central Asia, stretching from Mongolia to Turkestan; the Chinese colonies would turn out to be costly, however.

Before Bactria (Daxia), Zhang Qian discovered Dayuan (Fergana, Upper Syr-Darya) and its marvelous horses, which were fed on alfalfa. Zhang Qian also observed plants previously unknown to the Chinese: carrot, sesame, garlic, and grapevine (Boulnois 2008: 91). Dayuan means "Great Yuan," Yuan being a Chinese equivalent of the terms Yona, Yavana, referring to the Greeks in India. Another mission in 115 led Zhang Qian to the Wusun, who were established south and east of Lake Balkhach (Kazakhstan). From there, Zhang Qian sent envoys to the Anxi kingdom (Parthia), with silks. "As a result, there were reciprocal envoys of embassies" and commercial exchanges.[64] It may be true that Chinese silks reached the West following these contacts,[65] but the westward migration of the Yuezhi, who were familiar with Chinese silk, had most likely already facilitated its trade at an earlier time (Liu 2010: 10). Men from Gandhara, Parthia, and Roman Syria arrived in Han China.[66]

On his first journey, Zhang Qian departed from Chang'an, traveled through Lanzhou and Dunhuang, and then followed the northern branch of the Silk Roads, along Lake Lobnor, then north of the Tarim through Karashar, Kuchā, and Kashgar. Another branch of the Silk Roads curved to the south, ran along the northern piedmont of the Altyn and Kunlun mountains, toward Khotan, then Yarkand, whence it joined the other branch at Kashgar. A road further north left from Anxi, northeast of Dunhuang, ran to the Turfan Depression, then north of the Tien Shan mountains, toward Lake Issyk Kul, whence it joined the Syr Darya valley – near the location of the modern city of Tashkent – and Sogdiana.[67]

Contacts with Central Asia allowed various techniques to spread to China, such as tapestry manufacturing,[68] originating in western Asia, and clothing styles: besides trousers, mention should also be made of long-sleeved female clothing, attested in

---

Sichuan. As already mentioned, tombs dated to the second and first centuries BCE in Yunnan have yielded cowries, Indian beads, and Chinese coins, showing the existence of trade with the Bay of Bengal on the one side, and with China on the other. The *Houhanshu* emphasized the economic interest of the country, noting that "the Chinese officials who are there get rich." The tombs also show that Dian notables took advantage of their cooperation with the Chinese officials, especially at the time of the Eastern Han.

[63] Located between the Mekong and the Salween rivers, the Ailo acted as intermediaries between India and China (as shown by the products traded, mentioned by the *Houhanshu*). They submitted to the Han in 69 CE, and Yongchang became the center of a Chinese commandery.

[64] E. de la Vaissière (2002: 222) writes that "the great trade in Central Asia is certainly the result of Chinese diplomatic initiatives," which were also military and commercial.

[65] Boulnois 2001: 55. A Parthian embassy sent between 110 and 100 BCE brought jugglers or magicians from Lijian, which was the name of the Roman territories (still unknown to the Chinese) at this time (Boulnois 2001: 59). One finds a succinct description of Anxi in Sima Qian. The Chinese missions mention Tiaozhi, "near the Western Sea [Mediterranean, or Persian Gulf?], where rice is grown" (probably the Characene, Lower Mesopotamia) (Boulnois 2001: 61) (this word has been related to Tigris [?], or Antioch).

[66] In 120 and 30 BCE, in 87, 101, 120, 13, and 166 CE (Needham *et al.* 1980: 332).

[67] On these itineraries, described in the *Houhanshu*, see Boulnois 2001: 12–13.

[68] Developed in Syria during the third millennium, the tapestry technique was used at Cherchen *c.* 500 BCE. See Barber 2002: 65.

Greece as early as 700 BCE, and in China during the late first millennium BCE.[69] Various language terms of Iranian origin related to divination entered China during the Han period. On the other hand, Chinese techniques spread to the west. The prohibition edicted by a Han emperor during the second century BCE on the export of crossbows and iron was not strictly respected, despite executions of smugglers:[70] the crossbow was found in Sogdiana during the first century BCE.

The southern coasts and their maritime commerce were also of interest to the Chinese Empire. The Qin emperor launched armies toward southern China and Vietnam, and created new commanderies in that region. In 214 BCE, he sent convicts from the north to colonize the south. The appointment of a military commander at Panyu shows that this port was already active in trade. Following the downfall of the Qin dynasty, a Chinese official at the head of "Nanhai province" (Guangdong) proclaimed himself king of Nanyue and installed his capital at Panyu (see Map II.16). His power was acknowledged by the Han emperor Gaozu, but after Gaozu's death (195 BCE), the empress Lü "issued an edict which forbade the export of strategic goods to Nanyue": "gold, iron, weapons, cattle and horses" (Higham 2002: 280). The king of Nanyue later pledged allegiance to the Han emperor Wendi. The tribute sent to China in 179 BCE included kingfishers, peacocks, and other luxury goods coming from the south. The king also sent 500 purple-striped cowries from the China sea.[71] It is probable that ships from Southeast Asia carried these coveted exotic goods, but the Nanyue kingdom was itself active in long-distance trade. Among exotic artifacts, the tomb of the second Nanyue king, Zhao Mo, contained frankincense, a Persian silver box, and five elephant tusks from Africa. The shape of a jade rhyton shows the influence of western artifacts, and the design of an openwork jade ornament with a feline dragon reflects a Persian motif. The *Shanhai jing*, compiled at the end of the first millennium BCE, acknowledges the region of Panyue "as the first one for ship-building." The Han text *Nanyue zhi* also says that "the king of Yue built a great boat, and 3,000 people drowned" (Clark 2009: 23). While the kingdoms of Yue (Fujian) and Nanyue (from Canton to North Vietnam) were annexed in 111 BCE, it is likely that their populations continued trading with the south (Clark 2009: 29). Remember that China south of the Yangtze was still occupied by non-Chinese populations speaking Thai, Austroasiatic, and Tibeto-Burman languages: the Chinese expansion into the south occurred in successive waves, beginning during the Qin period, both under the Han (this expansion benefited from drier and cooler climatic conditions [Brown 2001: 69]) and after the Han, through migrations from the north and sinicization of the southern populations. After the Qin, the Han developed shipbuilding. In 112 BCE, Emperor Wudi may have sent a fleet of 200,000 men to Guangdong in order to subjugate the

---

[69] Barber 2002: 69. See the figure of a female dancer, dated to the second century BCE, in the Metropolitan Museum, New York, ref. 1992.165.19. The long sleeves were meant to evoke wings. The Russian *Radziwill Chronicle*, dated to the fifteenth century CE (copy of an original from the thirteenth century CE), associates these sleeves with dances in honor of nature spirits. Medieval Persian art also shows men with hands covered by long sleeves. They can still be observed today in the Sufi ceremonies of Iranian Kurds.

[70] Thus, in 121 BCE, Emperor Han Wudi sentenced 500 merchants to death because they had been engaged in smuggling (Bentley 1993: 37).

[71] In the south, cowries were used as currency until the thirteenth or fourteenth century (Wicks 1992: 28).

Nanyue; the following year, Han ships contributed to an invasion of northern Vietnam. In addition, a maritime expedition was launched toward Korea in 109 BCE. Korea would be divided into four commanderies. Multiple-decked battleships (*lou-chuan*) with watertight compartments[72] appeared as early as the Qin Empire. Other ships had several masts and bamboo-matting sails, and the technique of sailing with the wind on the quarter was developed.[73] The invention of the central rudder (instead of two side rudders) dates to no later than the first century CE: a tomb from this period has yielded a clay ship model depicting an axial rudder.[74] At least "six treatises on star-guided night navigation were written during this period."[75] The system of monsoons was known at the time of the Han dynasty and their use is attested. A boatyard discovered at Guangzhou "was capable of producing craft ... of a length of about thirty meters" (Clark 2009: 23). Gang Deng states that Chinese ships reached Sri Lanka at the time of the Western Han, then sailed beyond this island during the Eastern Han period (he does not give his sources, however, on these points).[76] The *Qianhanshu* (ch. 8) "provides the first list of maritime routes toward the South Seas and the Indian Ocean during the first century BCE" (see Gernet 2002: 127; Needham *et al.* 1971: 443). The Han's advance southward with the attachment of northern Vietnam to the empire in III BCE shows that the supposed disinterest on the part of the Chinese in regions south does not ring true. Assemblages in the Han tombs of Guangdong province reveal contacts with the regions south of Lingnan.[77] One also discerns a relative sinicization of Lingnan, in the political centers and towns where exchanges took place.

Other (terrestrial) expeditions went to Central Asia, in 108 and 101 BCE (a victory in Fergana – where the army captured 3,000 "celestial horses" [according to the *Shiji*] – opened the trade routes of India and the Caspian Sea to China). Emperor Wudi extended the Great Wall as far as Dunhuang and established fortified posts, settled by

---

[72] Temple (2002: 190–191) considers that watertight compartments in ships appeared during the second century CE at the latest. The Chinese may have been guided by the structure of bamboo. The technique is described by Marco Polo in 1295, but Europe (England) would adopt it only at the end of the eighteenth century.

[73] A text related to the Three Kingdoms period (third century), the *Nanzhou yiwu zhi* (written *c.* 983 CE), describes navigating with the wind on the quarter. "People living near the seas have four sails in line on their ships" (Deng 1997: 43).

[74] Deng 1997: 42; Temple 2002: 185. See Illustration XXXIX. On a textual basis, J. Needham *et al.* (1971: 638–639) show its probable existence as early as the first century BCE. Technological progress would later be made, leading to the balanced-fenestrated rudder, with holes to facilitate its rotation, and by adopting a curved shape toward the interior, following that of the stern. It is astonishing that J. E. McClellan III and H. Dorn (1999: 126) claim that "the sternpost rudder is a recent invention [fifteenth century]." They also repeat the "conventional wisdom" that "China entered late as a major maritime power" (1999: 126).

[75] Deng 1997: 36. Stellar navigation was also practiced in the Indian Ocean, "[it] made sailing along the latitude possible, though finding the longitude was relatively more difficult" (Ray 2002a: 78).

[76] Deng 1997: 41. In the *Nongjiayan*, written under the Han dynasty, monsoons are called "ocean-going ship-driving winds" (*bozhao feng*). The *Shiji* of Sima Qian reveals knowledge of the winds by the Chinese (Deng 1997: 43).

[77] The tombs contained objects reflecting links with networks of the Indian Ocean: for example, lamps carried on the head of a long-nosed man, naked to the waist; agate and glass beads; silver vessels; and ivory. The tomb of the second king of Nanyue was particularly rich in exotic items.

farmer-soldiers, for example at Zhangye and Dunhuang in III BCE. In 59 BCE the Protectorate of Xiyu, meaning "The Western Territories," was created.

Control over trade routes by the Han – until 9 CE – ensured favorable conditions for merchants (although commerce was partly controlled by the state, on the Chinese side). The Silk Roads brought Persian, Sogdian,[78] Greek, and Indian merchants, who carried wool, carpets, brocades, "fabrics that could be washed in fire" (asbestos), "fine cloth which some people say is made from the down of 'water sheep'" (the byssus of *Pinna squamosa*?) (*Houhanshu*, Chavannes 1907: 36, 37 and n. 4), glass, pearls, silver, lapis lazuli, jade, spices, and horses (the importation of horses explains the Han interest in these roads, as horses were obtained mainly in exchange for silks traded by officials or private traders).[79] The *Houhanshu* expresses the supernatural character of these horses:

The heavenly horses arrived from the far west, they have crossed the moving sands, the Nine Barbarians have been overthrown. The heavenly horses arrived, emerging from spring water, like tigers, their backbones are double, they charge like demons. The heavenly horses arrived, passing through places without grass, they covered a distance of one thousand *li*, following the route eastward. The heavenly horses arrived, in the year when Jupiter resided in the *chen* position, are they preparing to soar up into the air, at who knows what moment? (Von Falkenhausen 2011: 12)

Besides silk, China exported iron items, and Chinese metallurgical techniques spread along the Silk Roads. Pliny (XXXIV.145) notes that the best iron is "Chinese iron" (see above). Chinese bronze mirrors have been excavated in Uzbekistan (Tashkent) and in Afghanistan (Tillya Tepe). The dissemination of the crossbow has been mentioned above. Knowledge of Chinese alchemy probably reached Persia. Needham has defended a Chinese origin for the Greek term *chymeia*, found for the first time in Zosimos of Panopolis (late third – early fourth century CE).[80]

The Chinese also established official contacts with foreign powers. In 105 BCE, a Han embassy was received at Seleucia, on the Tigris. Han embassies may have been sent to Huangzhi – Kāñchī, in India – during the second century BCE (under Emperor Wu) and at the beginning of the Christian era (see above). Toward Central Asia, writes the *Shiji*, "there were at most ten missions [each year] sent by the Han, and a minimum of five or six" (de la Vaissière 2002: 35).

Exotic goods from Southeast Asia and the Indian Ocean arrived through the ports of the south. The *Shiji* describes Panyu (Canton), the ancient capital of Nanyue ("southern Yue"), as a city of warehouses, a trading center for pearls, ivory, rhino horns, turtle shells, cowries, fabrics, and slaves from the islands.[81] The *Hanshu* adds

---

[78] The *Shiji* probably provides the first mention of these merchants (de la Vaissière 2002: 31). The Sogdians had the upper hand in the lapis lazuli trade. As early as the Achaemenid period, tablets in Darius's palace at Susa report that Sogdiana sent lapis lazuli (de la Vaissière 2002: 22).

[79] The *Qianhanshu* and the *Shiji* emphasize the efforts of the Chinese government to acquire horses. In addition, the kingdom of Khotan exported jade (Khotan was the main source of jade for China during the Han period).

[80] From the Chinese "*chin i*, 'golden liquid'," which may have been pronounced "*kiem iak*" (Needham *et al.* 1980: 352–353).

[81] For Wilensky (2002: 4), however, there are no references to *kunlun* slaves prior to the fifth century. "An anecdote from a history of the Liu Song dynasty (420–479) describes an emperor who had a *kunlun* slave" (2002: 5), but this account dates back to the Tang period.

silver and copper to this list (Wicks 1992: 21–22). Excavations of Han period tombs in the Canton region have yielded various imported artifacts: "glass, amber, agate, and carnelian" (Gernet 2002: 127). At the time of the Nanyue kingdom, the Chinese emperor was warned by some of his advisers against the destabilizing effects of the growing trade in exotic goods. China exported silk, iron, lacquered items, bronze mirrors,[82] objects made of bamboo, spices and aromatics (ginger, cinnamon), and rhubarb.[83] Imported glass dated to the Han period has been found mostly along the southeastern coasts of China: probably imported by sea, Roman blue glass bowls have been unearthed in various Chinese provinces.[84] During the same period, a local glass industry thrived, producing ornaments and vessels.[85] It is possible that some of the ocellated beads found in the Philippines, Thailand, Sumatra, Kalimantan, and Java and dated to the turn of the Christian era are of Chinese origin. Chemical analyses on seventy cylindrical beads found at Yoshinogari, in Saga Prefecture, Japan, indicate a glass of Chinese origin, but the beads were probably produced in the Japanese archipelago.[86] Blue glass beads found in South Honshu and on Kyushu for the Yayoi period (Japan) (third century BCE – third century CE), however, may reflect exchanges with Southeast Asia. Their provenance from Arikamedu, suggested by P. Francis (2002: 46), still needs to be confirmed.[87] In fact, research on material found in funerary jars from the Fukuoka region (first century BCE, North Kyushu) shows that most of these beads have high contents of lead and barium, as do the Chinese beads.[88] During the following period (Kofun, 250–600), "small beads excavated – in greater number – in the same region may be Funanese imports, according to Francis." Sorghum has been

[82] "Mirrors and seals," notes Barnes (1999: 198), "provide evidence of the integration of surrounding regions into the Han (and later the Wei) tributary system." Mirrors had more than an aesthetic and utilitarian value; in the Zhou period, they were considered as having magical powers to ward off evil (Barnes 1999: 202).

[83] Boulnois 2001: 87. Rhubarb was known in the Muslim world under the name of *rīwand sīnī*.

[84] Three fragments of ribbed bowls have been excavated in a tomb of the Han period, at Canton (around 100 BCE), others come from Hanjiang, in the province of Jiangsu (76 CE). See also the discoveries of "Roman" glass in tombs at Hepu (Western Han period) (Guangxi), Ganjiang (Jiangsu province) (Eastern Han period), and Guixian (Guangxi province). An Jiayao 1992: 15; 1996: 132.

[85] Han China did not limit itself to importing glass; it benefited from transfers of techniques, for example, for the production of yellow opaque glass (Brill *et al.* 1992: 68). Also, China innovated by producing glass with a high content of potash, barium, and lead, a glass of different colors (Henderson 2000: 51; Lange Rosenzweig 2004: 13). Glass was used for new items, vessels, and also on belt buckles and various ornaments. Thirteen glass cups – the oldest glass vessels produced in China known to us – have been excavated in the tomb of Prince Chu (123 BCE), at Xuzhou, in Jiangsu province (An Jiayo 1996: 130). In southern China, glass beads (usually potash glass) have been unearthed in tombs of the elite and also in the tombs of the very poor (Dubussieux 2001: 50). Glass beads of a western type (*dragonfly*, "dragonfly eye"), probably imported, have been excavated in graves of the Western Han of Guangdong and Guangxi.

[86] The sites are dated between 100 BCE and 100 CE. While the glass, with lead and barium, is of the Chinese type, the cylindrical shape of the beads is not common in China. Cylindrical ocellated beads, however, have been found at Niuxengshan dated to the third century BCE (An Jiayao 1996: 129–130).

[87] Beads have a high content of potassium and manganese. See above on the problem of the origin of beads with high potash content. A total of 50,180 Indo-Pacific beads have been discovered in Japan dated to the Yayoi (300 BCE – 250 CE) and Kofun (250–600) periods (Katsuhiko and Gupta 2000), but an analysis of these beads remains to be done. The oldest finds have been made at the site of Yoshitake-Takagi in Fukuoka Prefecture, and at Higashiyamada-Ipponsugi in Saga Prefecture. Importations increased between the first and third centuries (Katsuhiko and Gupta 2000).

[88] Yamasaki and Murozumi 1992: 91–92. These funerary jars also contain bronze mirrors.

discovered at the site of Morooka (district of Kukuoka) during the Yayoi period (300–100 BCE).[89]

In connection with increasing trade, statebuilding, and an interest in agriculture, the Han period shows a series of innovations. Techniques progressed, involving both agriculture and metallurgy. Iron tools were improved upon; ox-drawn ards were used more frequently; iron plows with various types of moldboards appeared;[90] inventions included a multi-tube seed drill, a rotary winnowing fan (functioning with a crank handle), around the second century BCE, and a new form of hoe during the first century BCE. In crafts and industry, various activities progressed: examples include boreholes drilled for brine and natural gas[91] and the invention of the driving belt (used especially in the textile industry in quilling machines, during the first century BCE).[92] It is possible that coal was used at times; a state official may have created a mine around 210 at Bingjingtai. But the first document mentioning this, by the Buddhist traveler Daoan in Xinjiang, dates only as far back as the fourth century CE.[93] The invention of paper may date to the second century BCE.[94] The wheelbarrow appeared around the first century CE. Horse breeding was starting to improve, partly thanks to the introduction of alfalfa from Central Asia during the second century BCE (Zhang Qian may have carried seeds back, along with horses from the Wusun country and from Fergana). The water mill – used for grinding grain – was developed during the first century CE; waterwheels were also used to activate furnace bellows.[95] In addition, interactions with nomads "pushed Chinese leaders into military improvements" (Burbank and Cooper 2010: 56).

[89] Terasawa and Terasawa 1981; Fuller 2003: 256. Another find comes from the district of Yamaguchi (same period).

[90] As early as the fourth century BCE, moreover, plows sometimes used "an adjustable strut which precisely regulated plowing depth by altering the distance between the blade and the beam" (Temple 2002: 18). As J. M. Hobson points out (2004: 194ff.), techniques such as the iron plow with moldboard and the rotary winnowing fan would be adopted in Europe only during the seventeenth or eighteenth century, transmitted through the Jesuits. The Italians did not import the multi-tube seed drill, but knew its principle and reinvented it during the sixteenth century, and later Jethro Tull created his own device, in England, soon after 1700 (Temple 2002: 26; Norel 2008).

[91] Temple 2002: 78–81. As of the second century CE, natural gas was used to heat brine in order to obtain salt. Brine and gas were carried through bamboo pipelines.

[92] Temple 2002: 54. The drive-belt "transmits power from one wheel to another, and produces continuous rotary motion" (Temple 2002: 54). A quilling machine is depicted on a window of the cathedral of Chartres; it arrived in Europe before the spinning wheel (Temple 2002: 120).

[93] Wagner 2001. Some researchers believe that the mine at Fushun (northeastern China) may have been used during the first millennium BCE. Coal would be used in significant amounts only from the eleventh century onward, under the Song.

[94] The first paper was produced from mulberry bark; later, the Chinese used rags. The first paper was a coarse material used for wrapping objects or for clothing; later, paper was used for writing. According to the *Houhanshu*, a man from Sichuan first presented a type of paper suitable for writing to Emperor Hedi, in 105 CE.

[95] Gernet 1999: 127–128. The water mill is mentioned by the *Xinlun* written by Huan Tan (43 BCE – 28 CE). Pacey (1990), as previously noted, believes that the water mill was borrowed from Iran. McClellan and Dorn point out that technological progress was not based on the parallel development of scientific theories. The Han period, however, saw progress in mathematics. As early as the Warring Kingdoms period, positional numeration was used (with a decimal system known since the Shang dynasty). A book dated to the first century BCE, *Nine Chapters on the Mathematical Art*, shows the use of decimal fractions and the extraction of roots, and gives solutions to higher numerical equations (see Chemla and Shuchun

Innovations were organizational as well. The Han dynasty used a large and complex body of officials (the contrast with the Roman Empire here is striking, as Burbank and Cooper have pointed out [2010: 51]). The Han emperors integrated local elites in the service of the state, but they primarily "sponsored the development of an educational system based on Confucian texts and values to produce administrators and bureaucrats."[96] Tests were imposed for entry into the administration, prefiguring the exam system of the Tang period. The power of reason, the idea of a natural order and the importance of the concept known as *laissez-faire* (*wu-wei*) were put forward. Liu An writes in 120 BCE: "What is meant by *wu-wei* is that no personal prejudice interferes with the universal Tao ... Reason must guide action in order that power may be exercised according to the intrinsic properties and natural trends of things" (Hobson 2004: 190).

Large-scale works were also undertaken within China: channels were dug (a 125-kilometer channel linked the Yellow River to the capital, Chang'an), embankments and roads were built,[97] as well as the Great Wall (see above). Populations were deported to northwestern China in order to develop uncultivated land.

Innovations and large-scale works fostered expanded production and trade, accompanied by social transformation. Everywhere in China, rich notables emerged, at the heads of families "who combined agricultural enterprises ..., with industrial undertakings (cloth mills, foundries, lacquer factories), and commercial businesses, and who had at their disposal a very large labor force" (Gernet 2002: 143). Sichuan appears to have been one of the most prosperous and active regions, thanks to its resources and its trade with Upper Burma and India. But the same trend held for other regions. Production for the market, however, remained limited during the Han period, with the government supervising trade. The state took advantage of the expanding trade and tried to limit the power of the notables, who at the same time were providing the empire with many of its administrative executives. During the second century BCE, Emperor Wudi created a tax on boats and carts, and instituted a state monopoly for salt distribution and iron (in 117 BCE),[98] then on alcoholic beverages. In contrast, for silk

2004). The idea of negative numbers is attested during the second century CE (though it may have appeared earlier). A book by Liu Hui from the third century CE indicates the use of algebra in geometry and computes *pi* to five decimals (Temple 2002: 141ff.). McClellan and Dorn (1999: 130) point out that "the overwhelming thrust of Chinese mathematics, however, went toward the practical and utilitarian," as shown by the abovementioned book from the first century BCE. Moreover, a waterwheel was used during the second century CE in an armillary sphere (an astronomical instrument, developed by the Greeks as early as the third century BCE).

[96] Bentley 1993: 35. Access to official positions was not yet based on competition, as in the Tang period, but on recommendation; despite a system of regional quotas, some regions were underrepresented.

[97] The estimate given by Burbank and Cooper (2010: 56) – "China's roads were probably twice as long as Rome's" – however, is debatable.

[98] Private entrepreneurs became rich in the metallurgic industry and in salt exploitation at the beginning of the Han period; they invested their profits in landed estates, which explains the decisions taken by Wudi, partly in order to prevent "salt and iron merchants from developing into powerful families with many peasant dependents" (Sadao 1986: 584).

weaving, "public and private enterprises coexisted."[99] The state owned forty-eight foundries, employing thousands of workers. Crossbows were mass-produced, and this production was a state monopoly.[100] In 144 BCE, the government also set up a monopoly on money.[101] A quantity of coins was issued during the first century BCE[102] and archaeology bears testimony to the growing monetization of the economy. We find coins both in elite tombs and in the tombs of commoners. Each person in the empire was subject to a poll tax, which implies precise censuses of populations. "These measures to control the economy and the hostility to the merchants were closely bound up with the state of the empire's finances" (Gernet 2002: 145): the empire experienced a deficit resulting from an expensive policy of military and diplomatic expansion.[103] It appears that "shops and stands were kept in specific quarters of the cities" (Elvin 1973: 165; Norel 2005). Markets were thus supervised by the government. The term *zhu suan* ("calculation with beads") found in a book from the second century CE seems to refer to the use of the abacus. Merchants frequently encountered animosity in the ancient Chinese civilization. In 199 BCE, measures were taken to limit the merchants' lavish lifestyle. "Silk garments, horses, and the bearing of arms were forbidden for the merchants" (Gernet 2002: 145); these restrictions show just how wealthy this class had become. Already prior to the empire, Confucian and Daoist traditions had come together to condemn luxury.[104] The reasons behind the hostility of the state power, however, were first of all economic and political: merchant activities represented a "factor of social disequilibrium," because the merchants' wealth "enabled them to secure domination over the poor, to buy up peasant lands and to employ as slaves in their mining, iron and steeel, or manufacturing enterprises the cultivators whom they

---

[99] Gernet 1999: 127. Textile crafts would remain largely rural in China, right up to modern times. The state, however, employed thousands of skilled workers in its workshops at Linzi. The economic policy of the state (on the question of limiting landholdings, on monopolies, and on money) and trade with foreign countries was the topic of heated debates between Legists and Confucians in 81 BCE (Loewe 1986: 488–490). In 155 BCE, the Legist Cha Cuo encouraged the state to levy taxes in grain, not in money – this reveals the monetization of the economy.

[100] According to the *Shiji* of Sima Qian, Prince Xiao Wang under the Han (during the second century BCE) "was in charge of arsenals containing several hundred thousand crossbows" (Temple 2002: 220).

[101] A state monopoly on money issuance was already in place in the state of Qin, and from 186 to 175 BCE under the Western Han. On changes in the monetary system, see Sadao 1986: 585ff. Money was made of copper, but the Eastern Han issued silver ingots of standardized size for high-value transactions. For salt and iron, "the advocates of the state monopolies sought their precedents in the action ascribed" to a ruler of Qi during the seventh century BCE (Loewe 1999: 1024).

[102] Between 118 BCE and the first years of the Christian era, the state issued 28 billion coins, which meant 220,000 strings of 1,000 coins [*guan*] per year (during the Tang period, the state issued the equivalent of 327,000 strings of coins per year, which is not much in comparison to the 3 million strings issued per year in 1045, and the 5.86 millions issued in 1080 under the Song). In 175 BCE, the *banliang* cast by the state was devalued compared to those of the Qin period (5.12 g, then 2.56 g, the *banliang* from Qin weighing between 6 and 10 g), in order to increase the supply of money; in 118 BCE, Wudi ordered the issuance of *wuzhou*, "five *zhou*," weighing 3.54 g. Besides the *guan*, the *mo* of 100 coins was another unity of account.

[103] The cost of the wars against the Xiongnu obviously affected the whole empire.

[104] The wealth contained in the tomb of the Marquis of Dai (who died in 186 BCE) at Changsha shows the extent to which some Han officials were becoming extremely wealthy through trade (Barnes 1999: 202).

had reduced to destitution" (Gernet 2002: 144).[105] "The collection of revenue and the enlistment of soldiers were both imperilled by the growth of huge properties" (Elvin 1973: 28). Theoretically, merchants could not purchase land and obtain official positions, but they were not always registered as merchants, especially the great entrepreneur-traders, who had connections to the officials and powerful families of the court (Sadao 1986: 576). It was felt that the power of the notables, when uncontrolled and not put to work for the benefit of the state, threatened the state's authority and its very foundations. The Chinese imperial state "[always] developed a strong interest in peasant welfare, not from an altruistic sense of charity or benevolence but because an economically viable peasantry was understood to be the social base for a politically successful government" (Wong 1997: 77; Norel 2005). However, this vision of a Chinese state hostile toward merchants should not be taken too far: during the second century BCE, Emperor Wudi "held a debate at court about whether the state were best served by competing merchants or government monopolies over crucial goods such as salt and iron" (Pomeranz and Topik 1999: 4), and Sang Hongyang, the architect of the monetary policy under this emperor, admitted: "If merchants do not produce, then the media of exchange will not circulate … When the media of exchange do not circulate, there will be a shortage of wealth" (von Glahn 1996: 38).

The empire appears to have been in trouble toward the end of the first century BCE. Famines occurred under Yuandi's reign (49–33 BCE). The economic, cultural, and military expansion of Han China and the contradictions this engendered deteriorated into an internal crisis at the beginning of the Christian era. At this time, the "usurper" Wang Mang attempted to nationalize the land, to forbid the sale of slaves, and to impose "meritocracy." He was overthrown by a revolt. Then began the reign of the Eastern Han (25–220 CE), who moved their capital to Luoyang. This period recognized the power of a new social class of merchants and notables heading large estates, where poor peasants were forced to find work as sharecroppers (Elvin 1973: 32). Industries and state monopolies were transferred to private ownership, and a process of decentralization was initiated, accompanied by the emergence of local elites. "Even the swords and shields used by the army were purchased from private entrepreneurs" (Ebrey 1987: 609). "The magnates (hao-yu) [a term originally referring to landowners] controlled the supply of horses, driving the price up to two million cash per horse" (Ebrey 1987: 615). Salaries paid in cash are often mentioned, revealing the progress of monetization, supported by regular issuances of coins. Emperor Liu He's tomb (late Western Han period) has yielded 10 tons of Wuzhu bronze coins.[106] Corvée was partially converted into monetary taxation. In agriculture, taxes

---

[105] During the second century BCE, the philosopher Dong Zhongshu protested against a free land market, which allowed wealthy people to form large domains and which deepened the internal disparities between rich and poor. In fact, as early as the seventh century BCE, Shi Dan proposed measures to restrict landed property (Loewe 1999: 1023). In order to pay taxes, small peasants were forced to borrow money, at rates that could reach 200 percent. The land sale contracts at this time would serve as prototypes for those of the Tang period (Brook 1998).

[106] Liu He reigned for one month in 74 BCE. After his deposition, he was made the Marquis of Haihun (Jiangxi). The tomb also contained 285 gold coins, each weighing 250 g, hoof-shaped ingots, and 20 gold plates, each 23 cm long and 10 cm wide (www.thehistoryblog.com/archives/40957). Moreover, a bronze distiller unearthed from the tomb may push the history of distilled liquor in China back 1,000 years (jxnews.com), but this needs further confirmation.

remained low, but farmers had to pay a poll tax (Bang 2009). Great aristocratic families, however, seem to have tried to exempt their clients and servants from taxation and enrolment, thus triggering a progressive financial and military strangulation of the empire, which was then forced to make use of non-Chinese auxiliaries during the second century.[107] At the same time, faced with rising social inequalities and the impoverishment of small farmers, the state provided assistance to the poorest, until the 150s at least. Thereafter, the state was no longer able to provide help.

Technical innovations spurred production in various domains. In agriculture, the square-pallet chain pump used for raising water appeared around the first century CE.[108] The use of a horizontal waterwheel for the operation of blast furnace bellows dates to the same period.[109] According to Needham, the construction of suspension bridges using iron cables also began under the Han. True porcelain probably appeared at this time, in Zhejiang and perhaps in Hebei, but it would not be exported until the Tang period (Temple 2002). Kilns which may have been used for porcelain manufacturing were discovered in 2006 at Duting, in Tangxian County, in Hebei.

Under the Eastern Han, the empire extended and multiplied its connections with the foreign world, using its maritime coastline of Guanxi and Guangdong. In 41–42 CE, a fleet of 2,000 multiple-deck ships was launched against Jiaozhi, and the Han armies reoccupied the Red River valley (see Map II.17). In Central Asia, the Chinese regained control of the oasis from 73 CE. The Shan of Upper Burma sent embassies to Luoyang in 94, 97, and 120. Long-distance trade in horses and other luxury goods also increased during this time. Buddhism arrived in China during the first century CE with merchants of various origins (Parthians, Sogdians, Kushans, and Indians) who came via the Silk

---

[107] Elvin 1973: 34; Adshead 2004: 32. The use of professional soldiers, often from the steppes, may have begun at the end of the first century BCE. The weak integration of the Chinese Empire, compared to that of the Roman Empire, thus had sociological rather than geographical causes. Adshead (1995: 16), however, argues that integration was weaker in China because water transport was less developed there than it was in the Mediterranean world.

[108] Improvements were made to the design of the chain pump during the second century, and it would be adapted for different uses (Temple 2002: 56–57). Treadles were commonly used to operate the chain pumps.

[109] Temple (2002: 55–56) gives the date of 31 CE (see above about the waterwheel). Following J. Needham, the author notes the cumulative and coordinated character of inventions, in fields such as iron metallurgy. There was progress, in fact, in various domains. The astronomer and mathematician Zhang Heng (second century CE), who envisioned the earth as a spherical ball hung in infinite space, is emblematic of this period. Zhang Heng was the inventor of the first known seismograph, using a system of balls, and developed cartography using a grid which made it possible to respect scale and distances. These cartographic accomplishments were clearly relevant for the fields of transport and military art (the first Chinese maps of which we are aware are dated to the fourth century BCE, and have been found in the state of Qin, in Gansu). In addition, Zhang Heng perfected astronomical instruments called "armillary spheres," which had been developed since the first century BCE and were rotated by water power (Temple 2002: 30–33, 37–38, 162–166). Zhang Heng may also have invented the "first cybernetic machine," but this more likely dates to the mid-third century; it was a carriage surmounted by the statue of an "immortal," always pointing toward the south, and it functioned with a train of differential gears (the differential gear was also invented by the Greeks, during the second or first century BCE, as shown in the works of Hero of Alexandria).

Roads,[110] where the southern branch was the most active.[111] Unlike the disdain manifested by Confucianism toward trade, Buddhism – under its Mahāyāna form, from the second century onward – encouraged an increase in mercantile exchanges. The formation of the Kushan Empire played a decisive role in the progress of Buddhism, as well as the Han expansion into Central Asia. Contacts yielded borrowings from India in various fields, especially medicine, mathematics, and astronomy. It is possible that Indian Buddhists also brought with them the practice of script printing on cloth, which later led to the first method of Chinese printing, during the Tang period. The expansion of Buddhism spurred growth in perfume imports, including incense,[112] *bdellium*, storax, and aloeswood, for religious ceremonies. Braziers for incense sometimes borrowed forms known in Central Asia.[113] Cotton (cotton cloth – the plant itself would be cultivated in China much later) arrived in China through Central Asia and through the ports of the China Sea.[114] The importation of cultivated plants from Persia during this period has already been mentioned. Besides the horse, the donkey was introduced into northern China. Curiously, it is likely that the guinea fowl was also introduced (this species is of African origin). A ceramic piece in Boston's Museum of Fine Arts, dated to the Han period, appears to portray this bird, certainly brought via the Silk Roads.

The Han dynasty maintained an active commercial and diplomatic policy, including large gifts of silk, especially to the Xiongnu nomads[115] (the state either obtained this silk from taxes or bought it). "These gifts amounted to tens of thousands of various woven

[110] For the second century, Chinese traditions mention the Parthian (Indo-Parthian?) monk An Shigao, who arrived in 148, and the Parthian merchant An Xuan, who settled in the capital, Luoyang, in 181 (Gernet 1999: 191; Drège 2000: 36), but as early as 65 CE, the existence of a Buddhist community is mentioned in the eastern part of northern Jiangsu. Buddhism was already well established during the first century in the cosmopolitan towns of Gansu and in the capitals, Chang'an and Luoyang (Gernet 1999: 189). During the first centuries, Buddhism remained within the merchant diasporas and spread only very slowly into Chinese society (conversions mainly occurred along China's margins, for example among the Jie and the Toba) (see Bentley 1993: 49–50). After the middle of the fourth century, Chang'an became a center for Buddhist studies. The fifth century was marked by the rise of Buddhism in China, and by the end of this century, the city of Luoyang was a major center for this religion (Gernet 1999: 192, 195).

[111] Whereas money was Chinese or of a Chinese type along the northern branch of the Silk Roads, money in use along its southern branch followed the Indo-Kushan model, with both gold and copper coins (Thierry 2000: 122). After the demise of the Han, the Kushan presence grew at Khotan. Sogdians traveled between China, Sassanid Persia, and Byzantium, combining commerce and diplomacy. They were present in the oases of the south of the Takla-Makan desert in Xinjiang during the third century; their trade networks were little affected by the Turkish invasions of the sixth century (de la Vaissière 2002).

[112] One wonders if the Chinese term *kiuən-liuk* "already known in the third century BCE," a transcription of the Sanskrit *kunduruka* (incense), really corresponds to incense, as E. H. Schafer suggests (1985: 170).

[113] Schafer (1985: 161–162, 316 n. 56) mentions braziers with handles decorated with lions, a form "known in medieval Central Asia and Gandhara, [which] was ultimately, perhaps, derived from ancient Egypt."

[114] The term *bodia*, which would later mean "cotton," is mentioned for the first time in the *Houhanshu*, where it probably refers to hemp cloth; it has been related to the Turkish *pakhta* (Hirth and Rockhill 1911: 218) (cf. Persian *bagtak*, Pali *paṭāka*; Schafer 1985: 205). During the sixth century, the Chinese used the term *gubei*, or *gibei*, related to the Malay *kapas* (from the Sanskrit *karpāsa*, "cotton"). Cotton was cultivated in Yunnan during the Late Han period (by non-Chinese populations) and probably in Lingnan at the time of the Tang dynasty (Schafer 1985: 205, 327 n. 80). Xuanzang, during the seventh century, found large cotton fields in Central Asia.

[115] As in China, silk was used as currency very early on, in the oases of Central Asia. Tombs recently discovered in Xinjiang reveal these exchanges, for example at Yingpan (the tomb of a Sogdian merchant?), and at Sampula (Wieczorek and Lind 2007).

silk fabrics and bales of raw silk. The Xiongnu used part of this silk to barter with other nomad populations situated further west; through 'down-the-line' trade, this silk reached the West" (Drège 2000: 17). A Parthian embassy was received in Luoyang in 87; it was followed by Indian embassies (between 89 and 105), by another Parthian delegation in 101, a Kushan embassy in 158, and so on.[116] In 132 a Javanese embassy was mentioned for the first time. In 159 and 161, Indian embassies arrived via Southeast Asia (*Houhanshu*; Chavannes 1907: 48). Merchant ships from India and Southeast Asia reached either Canton or the mouth of the Yangtze. Further south, Luy Lau, in Jiaozhi, in the Red River valley, became a significant port under the Han. According to the *Houhanshu*, the Jiaozhi country had many precious goods: pearls, kingfisher feathers, rhino horns, elephant tusks, turtle shells, various fragrant woods, and magnificent timberwood. Some of these goods must have come from regions further south. Exotic luxury products were bartered in exchange for gold and silk.[117] The *Houhanshu* mentions various products from Da Qin that certainly arrived in China: gold, silver, red cinnabar, a kind of green jasper, materials of different colors, gold-embroidered textiles, coral,[118] amber, colored glass *biliuli*, and *suhe* perfume.[119] Moreover, according to this text, "in the Da Qin, there are wild silkworms" (probably silk from Cos Island, mentioned by Aristotle in his *History of Animals* [Book V]) (Boulnois 2008: 109). The *Nanfang caomu zhuang* (third century) also mentions *xunlu* incense, a term deriving from the Arabic *kundur*, "incense" (or from the Indian form *kundu* or *kundura*) (Hirth and Rockhill 1911: 196). The *Weilue*, compiled during the third century, refers to glass of ten colors that can be found in Da Qin. Glass arrived from India[120] and from western Asia or Egypt. For the Chinese, the Silk Roads were known as the "Glass Road," at least from the third century on (Thierry 1993: 126). Thousands of imported glass beads dated

---

[116] After defeat against a Chinese army in 86, the Kushans paid tribute to the emperor of China Han He. Under Kanishka (second century), the Kushan Empire controlled part of the Silk Roads, notably Kashgar, Khotan, and Yarkand.

[117] The *Nanshishu* emphasizes the avarice of a merchant called Zhang Jingzhen, who "always calculated carefully the silks and brocades which he used to trade with (the merchants of) the *k'unlun p'o*" (Wang Gungwu 1958: 60). Note that Chinese texts call people from Southeast Asia *Kunlun*.

[118] Coral belongs to the "seven precious materials" of the Buddhists, along with gold, silver, pearls, lapis lazuli, rock crystal, and rubies. Cf. also the "nine precious materials" of Hinduism, linked to the planets. Demand for coral probably increased with the spread of Buddhism (Boulnois 2001: 168). Twigs of coral were offered to the Chinese emperors, mainly red coral from the Mediterranean Sea or other seas. The *Beishi* (written during the seventh century) mentions coral as a product of Persia, because it came through Central Asia. The *Xintangshu* (written during the eleventh century) would provide a good description of the techniques used to collect coral, probably given by Muslim merchants (Boulnois 2001: 171).

[119] For the first centuries of the Christian era, *suhe* may refer to storax (the resin of *Styrax officinalis* L.). The *Liangshu*, for the sixth century, describes this substance as a mixture of fragrant exudates from various trees, from Da Qin. Conversely, the *Suishu* mentions *suhe* as a product from Bosi (Persia) (Hirth and Rockhill 1911: 200–201).

[120] The name *biliuli* (ou *liuli*) given to colored glass comes from the Sanskrit *vaidūrya* or the Pali *veluriya*, referring to beryl (cf. the Greek *beryllos*), emerald or rock crystal. In China also, *liuli* first referred to a precious stone, then to colored glass when the latter was imported. The *Weishu* (*History of the Wei*, written between 551 and 554) connects the introduction of colored glass manufacturing in China, during the fourth century, to people from Da Yuezhi (Central Asia or northern India?) (Hirth and Rockhill 1911: 227). Another word (*boli*, *biboli*) appeared during the fifth century; it referred to a precious stone and later to transparent glass (from the Pali *phalika*, "rock crystal"). The *Beishi* credits Persia with producing colored glass.

Figure 12.2 A square-pallet chain-pump operated by treadles. Illustration from a Chinese book from 1637 (Needham *et al.* 1965: 340, fig. 579). By permission of Cambridge University Press

Figure 12.3 Blowing-engine in a foundry, powered by a waterwheel. Illustration from the *Nung Shu* (1313) (Needham *et al.* 1965: 371, fig. 602). By permission of Cambridge University Press

Figure 12.4 Terracotta guinea fowl, Former Han period. 25.0 x 17.5 x 26.8 cm. Bequest of Charles Bain Hoyt – Charles Bain Hoyt Collection © Museum of Fine Arts, Boston

to the Han period have been unearthed in the Guangzhou region, as well as various kinds of vessels. In 120, moreover, dancers and jugglers from Da Qin (the eastern regions of the Roman Empire), reached the court at Luoyang after traveling by sea from Burma (Gernet 2002: 127). Merchants claiming to be Romans traveled to China in 166, and again in 226 and 284 (the campaign led by Cassius against the Parthians in 163 – the source of the transmission of what was known as the "Antonine plague" – interrupted relations between China and Da Qin and may explain the sea voyages of these "Roman" merchants over subsequent years). Roman coins dated between 14 and 275 have been excavated in Shansi (Adshead 1995: 39). On the other hand, after securing the Tarim,[121] General Ban Chao (the governor of Central Asia installed at Kucha) sent a subordinate, Gan Ying, toward Da Qin, in 97, but the Parthians discouraged Gan Ying from continuing his journey by crossing the "Western Sea" (Persian Gulf, or Mediterranean Sea?).[122] Gan Ying learned that merchants from Da Qin "traded along maritime routes with the kingdom of Parthia and with India, and this commerce brought them profits of 1000% . . . It is from this country that all the various and rare objects from foreign states come" (Boulnois 2008: 117).[123]

Indian products arriving in China – pearls, glass, rock crystal, carnelian, bdellium, costus, myrrh, and pepper – were imported through the roads of Central Asia (note the name *hu jiao* given to pepper), and to a lesser extent through maritime routes. From China, the first product transported to India by the merchants was of course silk, part of which was re-exported (see above), but also adopted in the subcontinent by the aristocracy and for Buddhist rituals. Exchanges led to the use of Indian motifs on Chinese silk (Liu 1988: 75). Recent excavations both in Chang'an (China) and in Ngari (western Tibet) have revealed that tea was already being grown in China, and carried toward central Asia by *c.* 200 CE (Houyuan Lu *et al.* 2016).

The existence of a Chinese fleet and progress in navigation under the Han has been mentioned above. Theirs was not solely a state-owned fleet; some rich families owned as many as 200 ships (Deng 1997). This navy was innovative (with the use of a central rudder), and took advantage of its contacts with the ships of the southern seas, which had sails made for close-hauled sailing (as noted above, however, when the Austronesians left Taiwan during the third or second millennium, they were already using the spritsail, which allowed for tacking).[124] A third-century text by Wan Zhen

---

[121] The *Houhanshu* mentions the fierce repression of a revolt at Yanqi (Karashahr) where Ban Chao killed 5,000 inhabitants and captured 15,000 others, who were then enslaved. It was crucial in order to ensure the safety of the trade roads. Ban Chao and his followers conducted trade and sent exotic products to the court (Liu 1988: 16).

[122] Gernet 1999: 123. After the *Houhanshu*. This chronicle states: "The king of this country [Da Qin] constantly desired to have diplomatic relations with the Han. But Anxi, wanting to be the [only] trader in Chinese silks, opposed this plan and set up obstacles so that there could be no personal communication with China" (Boulnois 2008: 115). Gan Ying was one of the sources of the *Houhanshu* for Da Qin.

[123] It is obvious that the *Houhanshu* sometimes ascribes to Da Qin products which in fact came from Arabia or Persia (for example *suhe*, a mixture of various aromatics). The *Houhanshu* also mentions the gold and silver money of the Da Qin and even gives a ratio of 1:10.

[124] However, W. Mahdi argues that the "double canoe" and the "double-sprit sail on bifid masts" originate in the boat technology of the Negritos from insular Southeast Asia. According to Mahdi, "Austronesians, rather than being the original developers of seagoing watercraft, acquired their maritime mobility from the Negritos who traveled north from insular Southeast Asia" (2016: 26). According to

(*Nanzhou yiwu zhi*, "Strange things of the South")[125] describes the four-masted ships of the "Southerners," "Cantonese or Annamites" according to Needham, but perhaps also Funanese and Austronesians:

The people of foreign parts call ships *bo*. The large ships are more than 20 *zhang* [fifty meters] in length . . . They carry from six to seven hundred persons, with 10,000 *hu* of cargo [260 tons].[126]

The people beyond the barriers, according to the sizes of their ships, sometimes rig [as many as] *four sails* . . . The four sails do not face directly forward, but are set obliquely and so arranged that they can all be fixed in the same direction, to receive the wind and to spill it."[127]

The preceding description, according to Needham *et al.*, evokes "some kind of tall balanced lug-sail" (1971: 601). For this author, this type of trapezoidal sail may have derived from the Indonesian canted square sail.[128]

During the Han period, the Chinese certainly traveled little to the south, and it has often been said that long-distance maritime trade was only of secondary interest to them. Foreigners came to China, attracted by silks, weapons, and aromatics. Han China, writes Adshead, "turned its back on the sea" (2004: 23). But this vision needs qualification. It is certainly not valid for the Yue of Guangdong, who were already trading with the southern countries at the time of the Warring Kingdoms. And how should we interpret the emperors' desire to control southern territories as far as Vietnam? A passage from the *Qianhanshu* also signals that the state organized journeys of Chinese traders to the southern seas, probaby by chartering non-Chinese ships:

There are superintendent interpreters belonging to the civil services personnel, who recruit crews and go to sea to trade for brilliant pearls, glass, strange gems and other exotic products, giving in exchange gold and various silks. Merchant-ships of the barbarians transport them [part of the way] home again. But [these barbarians] also, to get more profit [sometimes] rob people and kill them . . . Even if nothing [of this kind happens, they are] away for several years.[129]

Trade slowed at the end of the second century; at the same time, China's economic and political situation deteriorated, and incursions of nomads threatened the borders of the empire. The powers of provincial governors grew. The years 166–176 were marked by purges against scholars. Revolts burst out from 184 (e.g. revolt of the Yellow Turbans), power struggles caused turmoil at the court, and the roads of Central Asia were cut off

Mahdi, the Negritos also introduced their boat technology into India (2016: 39; see above). The double-spritsail is still in use in Sri Lanka.

[125] The *Nanzhou yiwu zhi* is lost, but parts of the text have been used in the *Taiping yulan*, dated to 983.

[126] Needham *et al.* (1971: 600) give an equivalent of 260 tons, and Manguin 600 tons (1993: 262). Pelliot gave "one thousand metric tons" (1925: 256).

[127] The various masts were not strictly in line, but offset relative to one another, to make best use of the wind's strength.

[128] Needham *et al.* 1971: 599ff., 606. Note that the ships featured on the reliefs at Borobudur show "canted square sails" and "a kind of lug-sail" (Manguin 1993: 263). Manguin (1980) believes that Wan Zhen is describing Austronesian ships, but do the ships described in the second paragraph belong to the *bo* of the first paragraph? For Needham, the "people beyond the barriers" were the sailors of Guangdong or Tonkin. The Indonesian canted square sail showed a type of fore-and-aft rig *sensu largo*.

[129] *Qianhanshu*, ch. 28 B; Needham *et al.* 1971: 443. This text may refer to voyages going back to the first century BCE. Travelers probably followed land routes such as the road of the Three Pagodas Pass.

as of 190. Centrifugal forces triumphed with a rise of regionalism fueled by inequalities between the cores of the empire and its peripheries.[130] In 220, the Han Empire was at last divided into three kingdoms: Wei in the north, Shu in Sichuan, and Wu centered on the lower Yangtze.

This partition ushered in a period of turmoil marked by Turkish, Mongol, and Tibetan invasions. The conflicts appear to be less a cause of the – relative[131] – weakening of the Silk Roads and the Chinese decline than a consequence of both regional and global economic decline,[132] accompanied by famine and social unrest. Climatic changes occurring from the end of the second century in Central Asia and northern China (cooling and aridification) certainly contributed to the sociopolitical developments we have observed.[133] Epidemics were also responsible for the decline; these were, in part, the result of the connections established between distant regions, through the Silk Roads. In 161–162, at the northwestern border of the empire, a Chinese army was decimated. At the beginning of the fourth century, epidemics struck northwestern China, and later a large part of the country (see below).

Cut off from the Silk Roads, the kingdom of Wu (222–280) (Yangtze River valley), which welcomed a flood of refugees from northern regions, pursued an active maritime policy.[134] The king had huge ships built, each holding as many as 3,000 soldiers in sitting position. Ships from Guangzhou "measured 55–60 meters in deck length, each with a capacity of 600 to 700 passengers."[135] As mentioned above, the presence of Chinese envoys in Funan in 245–250[136] was a response to the arrival of Funanese embassies at Nanjing in 225 and 243. The *Sanguozhi* (*History of the Three Kingdoms*), written by Chen Shou during the third century, points out that "the South is an important source of precious rarities from afar"; to the luxury goods already mentioned, it added incense, coral, and lapis lazuli (Wicks 1992: 22; Gernet 1999: 176): these goods came from the western Indian Ocean. Pelliot did not exclude the possibility that during the third century, Chinese envoys reached Alexandria, perhaps mentioned under the

---

[130] The gulf between rich and poor had widened, and this resulted in peasant revolts, at a time when magnates and military commanders acquired more and more autonomy (see V. Hansen 2000: 146–147).

[131] In 224, for example, the rulers of Lobnor, Kucha, and Khotan acknowledged allegiance to the state of Wei. The *Sanguozhi* mentions yearly embassies from Kangju (Sogdiana) under the Wei (220–265) (de la Vaissière 2002: 67).

[132] Gills and Frank 1993b: 168. In contrast, Teggart (1939: 340) believed that these wars caused the closure of the route and the decline of both China and Rome. It has often been written that whenever trade was decreasing or whenever China stopped offering tributes to the nomads, the latter launched raids in order to capture booty. External and internal factors must be taken into account to explain the movements and the developments of the steppe populations. As mentioned above, Di Cosmo (1999) has argued that militarization of pastoralist societies should sometimes be understood as a response to a crisis situation and that this may partially explain the formation of states in the steppes.

[133] J. L. Brooke (2014: 309) notes that the Han Empire disappeared at a time of major disruptions in the monsoon cycle.

[134] The king of Wu sent ships to Taiwan in 230 and to Hainan in 242. The king of Wu still had 5,000 vessels when he surrendered to Jin in 277 (Deng 1997: 69). In northeastern China, the Wei kingdom, moreover, maintained relations with Japan during the third century (Gernet 1999: 176).

[135] Deng 1997: 30. At the beginning of the Jin period (266–420), a large warship was 100 meters long, and held 2,000 soldiers (Deng 1997).

[136] Gernet (1999) gives the date as 228. In addition, Lin Yi (Champa) and Funan sent embassies to the Western Jin (265–316), at Luoyang, in 268, 284, 285, 287, and 289.

name Wuchisan in the *Weilue* (Filesi 1972: 4). Kang Tai mentioned a Chinese merchant, Jia Xiangli, who traded with India.

Buddhism continued its progress and pilgrims traveled to India, through Central Asia, or via southern China (by land or sea). Buddhist scholars arrived, such as Zhi Qian and Dharmaraksa, descendants of Yuezhi families. Along with them came "Parthians, Sogdians, Khotanese, Cachemiris, and Indians" (Boulnois 2001: 221). They often knew several languages and scripts of Central Asia. Moreover, Persians and Sogdians traveled by sea: they were present in Jiaozhi and on the Chinese coasts (Salmon 2004: 29; Grenet 1996). During the third century, the kingdom of Wu welcomed well-known translators, some from Luoyang. The first account known to us by a Chinese pilgrim was written by Faxian (Fa-hsien), who left in 399 through the caravan road of Central Asia, stayed in India for twelve years, and returned to China by sea via Sri Lanka (where he stayed for two years) and Java (see above).

Overall, the third and fourth centuries saw an internal and external decline in trade; demonetization of the economy[137] and the disappearance of many towns. Territorial fragmentation was accompanied by the growth of private estates dependent on semi-servile labor (Lieberman 2009: 500; Lewis 2009). The dynasty of the Western Jin, however, managed to restore the unity of the empire for a brief period – and

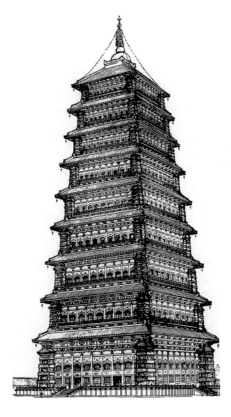

Figure 12.5 Pagoda, temple of Yongning, Luoyang, built in 516 by the empress Ling, Northern Wei. Hypothetical reconstruction (Steinhardt 2002: 84). The origin of the pagoda is Indian, but the architecture in China took a particular form. The character for "pagoda" appeared during the fourth century.

---

[137] The rising price of copper was a difficulty at the end of the Han period; it led to the growing manufacturing cost of the *wuzhou* and other coins, and to the hoarding of these coins. The states of Wu

promoted new exchanges with Central Asia. Invented in the steppes, the stirrup appeared in China, where it was made of cast iron, around the third century CE.[138] This invention revolutionized the practice of war by creating an efficient cavalry. Its use spread rapidly through Europe, with the Avars. Byzantium was using the stirrup at the end of the sixth century (Temple 2002: 90). The spread of the stirrup contributed to the development of chivalry in western Europe. During the fourth century, climatic aridification in northern and southern China[139] was accompanied by economic and political chaos. In 310–312, northwestern China was struck by famines, hordes of grasshoppers, and epidemics, killing a large part of the population. Many Chinese then fled to the south.[140] Sinicized Xiongnu mercenaries looted the capitals, Luoyang and Chang'an, in 311 and 316,[141] bringing the ephemeral empire of the Western Jin to an end. An Eastern Jin dynasty then settled in Nanjing. In 322 geographically greater epidemics, perhaps due to the arrival of a new disease (smallpox?), killed 20 to 30 percent of the population (McNeill 1998b: 146). One of the ancient Sogdian letters found west of Dunhuang by A. Stein in 1907 refers to a fire at Luoyang and gives the Xiongnu looters the name of *xwn*, "Huns" (de la Vaissière 2002: 49). The Sogdian documents as well as a letter from Niya in Prākrit using the Kharoṣṭī script show that the roads to China were practically closed during the early fourth century (de la Vaissière 2002: 57). The Sogdian letters also reveal the existence of well-structured Sogdian networks in Gansu and Inner China at this time; various products were traded on the roads of Central Asia: silk, horses, hemp garments, musk, gold, silver, wine, as well as pepper (from India) and camphor (from Sumatra). The settling of Sogdians in Gansu and China was partly the result of the Han retreat from Central Asia: "When the Han occupied the Tarim, the armies and the Chinese officials received wages paid in silk," which was therefore abundant, but after the Chinese left the Tarim, the Sogdians were then compelled to go and seek silk in China (de la Vaissière 2002).

and northern Zhou took a measure already implemented under Wang Mang's reign, which allowed them to increase the money supply without using more copper: this involved increasing the face value of the coins; the inscriptions no longer referred to the weight of the coins. Other solutions were employed, such as cutting the ancient coins and issuing smaller coins of the same value, as well as changing the counting units *guan* and *mo*; other currencies were used, such as grain and materials. In Lingnan and Jiaozhi, during the sixth century, gold and silver were also used. The Tang would later choose to lower the copper content of their coins (Thierry 2001: 135–137).

[138] The first known depictions are in a Jin tomb at Changsha dated to 302 and in a tomb near Nanjing dated to 322. The stirrup was probably invented in Central Asia. An engraved stone dated to the Kushan period shows a horseman with a kind of stirrup (*c.* 100 CE). At Sānchī (India), representations dated to the end of the second century BCE show leather strips dangling from each side of the saddle. And images of horses in the Dian culture reveal the use of a "proto-stirrup" around the second century BCE (see above).

[139] L. Liu (2004: 254 n. 9) notes that between 200 and 400, the Ji River, a major tributary of the Yellow River, dried out.

[140] In the south, migrants faced other diseases. Over the long term, however, this expansion – and the mixing of populations it implies – gave China "a wider and more varied set of acquired immunities than that enjoyed by any other contemporary center of civilization" (Adshead 2004: 73).

[141] Gernet 1999: 159. For semi-arid China, An and Thompson identify a dry period going from 250 to 625 (with particularly marked aridification between 350 and 450); in semi-humid regions of China, the dry period extended from 320 to 575 (1998: 20). According to J. L. Brooke, the summer monsoon seems to have weakened from 300 to 600, and the winter monsoon intensified between 450 and 600 (2014: 352).

Exchanges along the Silk Roads remained weak throughout the fourth century. "No pilgrim arrived in or left China between 310 and 380" (de la Vaissière 2002: 73). The few "embassies" arriving in China from Central Asia reveal the difficult situation in Inner Asia at this time: the only embassies mentioned were from Fergana in 331, and from Fergana and Kangju (Sogdiana) between 376 and 383 (de la Vaissière 2002) (in addition, as mentioned above, there was the arrival soon after 313 of an "embassy" from the eastern part of the Roman Empire to the Later Liang who controlled Gansu). The Sogdians remained present, however, and "the Tarim maintained strong links with India" (de la Vaissière 2002: 74). An advancing desert and declining trade explain the abandonment of sites such as Loulan and Niya, and traffic along the southern branch of the Silk Roads decreased, to the benefit of the northern branch.

Trade in the China Sea also appears to have been in decline during the fourth century. From 399 to 410, the rebellion of Sun En and of his successor Lu Xun was brewing between Fujian and Guangdong, taking advantage of growing popular indigenous discontent, and of the nautical traditions of the southern populations: according to the *Jinshu*, Lu Xun had "over one thousand 'tower boats' *louchuan*" (Clark 2009: 17). The unstable political situation, marked by the overwhelming might of great families and army commanders, led to the overthrow of the Eastern Jin dynasty, succeeded by the Southern Song in 420.

During the fifth century, changes occurred in Inner Asia. Around 402, in the steppes, a Rouran (Joujan) tribal confederation formed an empire, with an army organized according to the decimal system already set up by the Xiongnu; the Mongols would use this system later. Carrying out raids on China, the Rouran managed to extract tributes. They maintained peaceful relations with the Hephtalites, and this contributed to a trade revival along the Silk Roads, led by the Sogdians. The Rouran Empire disappeared in 552, defeated by the Kök Turks, who then dominated Central Asia as far as Sogdiana and Bactria (Kradin 2005). Meanwhile, the militaristic state of the northern Wei (386–535), led by sinicized Toba (a branch of Xianbei from Manchuria), unified northern China in 439. An economic upswing occurred during the late fifth century. The Wei moved their capital from Datong to Luoyang. The state was transformed, with a sinicization of the elites and the ascent of Buddhism, promoted by the state, which also tried to control it. Persecutions against Buddhists were even perpetrated in 446, and would be repeated in 574, under the Zhou (Gernet 1999: 170, 193ff.). The state encouraged silk production and, at the same time, registered its artisans.

During the same period, the maritime route through Southeast Asia acquired greater importance.[142] From the fourth to the sixth century, the dynasties of the Eastern Jin (317–420), the Song (420–477), the Qi (477–502), and the Liang (502–557) were in contact with Lin-yi (Champa), Funan, Sumatra, Java, India, and Sri Lanka. Between the Han and Tang periods, China welcomed more than one hundred "tributary embassies" from fourteen different Southeast Asian kingdoms (Clark 2009: 23). Moreover, the conquest of Sichuan by the Eastern Jin connected the

---

[142] As mentioned above, however, Sassanid embassies went to China during the sixth century, following the roads of Inner Asia.

southern dynasties with Inner Asia. The Chinese interest in the southern seas and their products must be viewed within the context of an expansion of the Sassanid navy and of commerce along the routes to India and Southeast Asia. Their interest went along with the development of Insulindian states, marked by a spread of Buddhism that was also seen in China.[143] Iranians from Sassanid Persia were present in Funan and perhaps in ports such as Luy Lau and Guangzhou (Canton).[144] A vase with turquoise glaze found at Yangzhou may date to the Sassanid period (Glover 2002: 173). Glass bowls from Persia have been excavated in various Chinese provinces, and also in Japan.[145] Transporters, of course, were not necessarily Persians; the items found in Japan may have been carried by Vietnamese, Funanese, Indians, or the Chinese. Indian and Sinhalese embassies were received at Nanjing (the capital of various successive dynasties).[146] J. Gernet (2002: 197) notes that " Yangtze China's relations with Southeast Asia and the Indian Ocean were to develop from the fourth to the sixth centuries," an expansion heralding developments in the ensuing centuries. An increasing number of foreigners settled in the cities of southern China and of the Yangtze River valley, and Chinese sources emphasize the new importance of insular Southeast Asia. Pepper,[147] incense,[148] spices from the Moluccas, forest products from Southeast Asia, rhino horns, kingfisher feathers, *costus*,[149] storax,[150] and *asafoetida*, all are mentioned as imports.[151] The technique of glassblowing, invented in

[143] Gernet 1999: 162–163. Buddhism was in favor at the Liang court, during the first half of the sixth century, which was a relatively prosperous period. Conversely, the second half of the sixth century was a time of incessant warfare throughout China.

[144] Trade developed in the southern ports despite high levels of corruption, reported for the fourth century by the *Jinshu* ("History of the Jin") (645) and the *Nanshishu* ("History of the Southern Dynasties") (659) (Wicks 1992: 21–23). For the first half of the sixth century, also, the *Liangshu* relates that "the officials of the port of Guangzhou went and bought (the goods of the foreign merchants) at half the market price, and immediately sold them (at the market price). Thus they made profits several times more (than the normal margin). This was so frequently done that it became the usual accepted practice" (Wicks 1992: 23).

[145] A Sassanid glass bowl found in Jiangsu and dated to the "Southern Dynasties" period (420–589) may have been imported by sea. In Japan, Sassanid bowls have been excavated at Kashiharashi (Nara) (fifth century), in the Shōsō-in temple (Nara), and at Osaka (sixth century) (An Jiayao 1996: 133–134). See Whitehouse 2005.

[146] Glass from the "Roman" world has been excavated in various tombs at Nanjing for the period of the Eastern Jin (An Jiayao 1992: 9, 15).

[147] Pepper (*hujiau* in Chinese) is already given by the *Houhanshu* as coming from Tianzhou, India. It may have come by land through Burma, as well as incense. The *Weishu* and the *Suishu* (*History of the Sui*) report pepper as a product of Bosi, Persia (Hirth and Rockhill 1911: 225). The *Suishu* was written between 622 and 656 (Gernet 1999: 242). The *Weishu* also notes as "products from Bosi" "coral, amber, carnelian, pearls, glass (both transparent and opaque), rock crystal, diamonds [?], steel, cinnabar, quicksilver, frankincense, turmeric, storax, *putchuk*, damasks, brocaded muslins, long pepper, black pepper, dates, aconit, . . . a list to which the *Suishu* adds gold, silver, *tush*, lead, sandalwood, various tissues, sugar and indigo" (Hirth and Rockhill 1911: 16 n. 1). It is obvious that many products came from India and Southeast Asia, and not from western Asia or Arabia.

[148] Incense, *hunlu xiang*, is mentioned by the *Suishu* among the products of Bosi, Persia (see above).

[149] *Costus* (in Chinese *mu xiang*) is mentioned by the *Weishu* as a product from Bosi, Persia (Hirth and Rockhill 1911: 221).

[150] According to the *Suishu*, this resin came from Bosi (Hirth and Rockhill 1911: 200).

[151] This resin is given as coming from the kingdom of Qau (in Afghanistan?) (Hirth and Rockhill 1911: 225).

western Asia, appeared in China.[152] Alongside this trade expansion, a growing number of Chinese began to settle in the south.

The presence of Persian ships in the ports of southern China probably goes back to the Sassanid period. Persian ships would become more prevalent – along with Arab ships – after the formation of the Muslim Empire. Ships from India and Southeast Asia also sailed to China. On the other hand, the question of Chinese ventures toward the southern seas and even the western Indian Ocean remains controversial (see below).

The Japanese archipelago benefited from growing maritime trade during this period. The Chinese states of Wu and Wei and the empire of the Western Jin were already in contact with the Japanese principalities.[153] A centralized state took shape during the Yamato period (250–710). Writing and Buddhism developed, both introduced from China via the Korean kingdom of Baekje;[154] these innovations helped the emperor to assert his authority. In 646, land was placed under imperial control and a system of taxation was enforced. Immigrants came from both China and Korea. During the fifth century, Yamato had links with the Liu Song dynasty (China) and maintained contacts with the three Korean kingdoms, Goguryeo, Baekje, and Silla, which had formed at the end of the first century BCE, and with Gaya, a confederacy of small city-states in southern Korea. Gaya notably exported iron and iron artifacts to Baekje and Japan. Ironworking is known in Hongshu during the fifth century CE (and already during the first century CE in Kyushu).

Despite periodic insecurity in Inner Asia from the fourth century onward, merchants, men of religion, and official envoys were traveling along the Silk Roads in increasing numbers during the sixth century.[155] Silk was a luxury item and was used as currency. A flurry of diplomatic activity then took place, with the arrival of Persian embassies (see above), and of envoys from the Hephtalites, Sogdiana, Kuchā, and Khotan; these were clear signs of a trade revival, a prelude to the rise of the late sixth century and of the following century. Zoroastrians were present in China during the sixth century; Persian influences were also mediated by Sogdians and other populations

---

[152] Various blown-glass vessels have been discovered in a stupa at Jingxian, in the state of the Northern Wei (386–534). The technique came from the Roman and Sassanid worlds, but the shape of the vessels is Chinese.

[153] The Chinese chronicle *Records of Three Kingdoms* (c. 297) mentions embassies from "the people of Wa" (Japan).

[154] This kingdom was created at the beginning of the Christian era. In connection with several Chinese kingdoms, it adopted some Chinese features and techniques during the third and fourth centuries especially. Two other kingdoms were formed in Korea after the Western Han period: Goguryeo (North) and Silla (Southeast). Connections between Korea and Japan were significant from the second century onward; they led to the appearance in Japan of cultural elements originating in Inner Asia. Beckwith (2011: 90ff.) suggests a relationship, not universally accepted by linguists, between Proto-Japanese and Puyo-Koguryo languages.

[155] The importation of Sassanid or "Roman" glass into the Ningxia, Hebei, and Liaoning provinces under the Western Jin (265–316), the Northern Yan (409–436), the Northern Wei (386–534), and the Northern Zhou (557–581) attest to this trade (An Jiayao 1992: 14–15; Shimin and Baozhong 1992: 197). Moreover, for the Northern Wei region, Müller (2003) mentions the appearance of a custom consisting in maintaining the jaw of the deceased, known in the Tarim (since the eighth century BCE) and the eastern Mediterranean.

Figure 12.6 Drawing of the central design of a silver plate found at Jingyuan (Gansu), representing Bacchus seated on a lion. Around him, the twelve gods of Olympus, and a design of vines. Of Bactrian origin, sixth century (from Dien 2004: 372)

from Central Asia; these influences can be seen in various domains such as alchemy and Buddhist art (for example, in the paintings at Dunhuang dated to the fifth–sixth century). Moreover, trade relations opened up between the Turkish Empire of Central Asia and Byzantium, via Sogdian merchants: the merchant Maniakh was received by Justin II in 571, who in turn sent an embassy to the Turks. Great Chinese merchants emerged; one was Liu Bao, based at Luoyang, who "had a house built in every provincial capital where he maintained messengers and horses to keep himself informed of price fluctuations . . . His carriage and apparel were as extravagant as that of a prince" (Liu 1988: 50).

Despite political instability and disorder, the period from the third to the sixth century saw technological and institutional progress that would influence subsequent developments. Various transformations in southern and northern China after the Han period paved the way for the reunification of China – by the Sui dynasty – on a new basis. Under the Western Jin (265–311), limits were imposed on land that the wealthy aristocratic families could own. The Toba who ruled the state of Wei (386–535) initiated military and fiscal reforms; with the creation of a heavy cavalry of the Persian type, the army became the "privilege of the aristocracy," with farmers paying the taxes needed by the state for its functioning. The support provided for Daoism and Buddhism allowed the rulers to form new clienteles who counterbalanced those of the

Figure 12.7 Drawing of the design on a gilt bronze goblet, Northern Wei, fifth/sixth century (from Dien 2004: 370)

old aristocratic families. The merchant class was encouraged to develop; in 472, an edict allowed artisans and merchants to buy land. Taxes were levied in silk, the production of which was controlled. The state of the Northern Zhou (557–581) redistributed the land and instituted a military organization influenced by the Toba system, which was based on militias raised from each district; this system was later taken on by the Tang (Elvin 1973: 53). A Zhou general reunified China in 589. In the south, Liang Wudi (542–549) set up a new legal code that reflected the growing influence of Buddhism and the establishment of a more diverse society where the role of the aristocracy was decreasing (Adshead 2004: 34–38). This legal system would influence the future synthesis elaborated by the Tang.

The development of Chinese states and the elites' demand for the luxury goods of western Asia and the southern seas stimulated the forming of exchange networks on the Silk Roads, both terrestrial and maritime. Of course, silk was not the only product transported by the caravans of merchants and ships, but the word "silk" itself places emphasis upon the preeminent position acquired by the Chinese core thanks to technological innovation. From the Qin Empire onward, however, military force also played a significant role. Southeast Asia rapidly emerged as a semi-periphery within the incipient system, taking advantage of its geographic situation at the junction of the China Sea and the Indian Ocean, as well as of its demographic and economic assets (such as rice culture, spices, and perfumes) to set itself up as an interface between the dominant powers of eastern and southern Asia. In the western Indian Ocean, Arabia formed a similar hub between maritime areas and large states, but urban development there happened earlier (although demographic data place Arabia far behind regions such as Java, Thailand, and Cambodia). This may be due to the fact that the western world-system had structured itself earlier than the eastern Asian system had done.

13 Arabia: Maritime Cultures and the Rise of the Caravan Trade

Bordered by three seas – the Persian Gulf, the Indian Sea, and the Red Sea – and not far from the Mediterranean, Arabia was already serving as a bridge between these seas and between continents during the third and second millennia, thanks to the development of seagoing vessels and the organization of caravans, as well as exports in local luxury goods. These processes led to the flowering of an urban culture using writing in western Arabia during the first millennium BCE.

Eastern Arabia

At the beginning of the first millennium BCE, and later during the Neo-Assyrian and Neo-Babylonian periods, trade routes connected Mesopotamia, Iran, and eastern Arabia. The introduction into Oman of irrigation techniques preceded the Achaemenid period by several centuries, suggesting earlier contacts with Iran.[1] These contacts are also revealed by similarities in the pottery and metalwork of the different regions. Agricultural progress underlay demographic growth, as clearly seen in the increasing number of sites in Oman. Archaeological and historical sources for eastern Arabia are limited for the first half of the first millennium BCE. Around 640 BCE, an Assyrian text mentions a tribute sent to Assurbanipal by the king of Dilmun on the one side, and the king of Izkie (Izki), a town located in inland Oman, on the other.[2] A jar found at Muweilah, not far from Tell Abraq (Oman), bears a South Arabian inscription, suggesting contacts with Yemen. Under Nabonidus, Dilmun was a Babylonian province. Oman was integrated into the Achaemenid Empire in 519 BCE.[3] At the end of the Achaemenid period, the Gerrheans, on the coast not far from Bahrain, controlled the caravan routes and traded with Babylonia (see above). The Seleucid king Antiochus III recognized their autonomy, "and the Gerrheans gave him a 'gift' of 500 talents of silver, 1,000 talents of incense and 200 talents of myrrh" (Briant 1996: 782, after Polybius [XIII.9]).

The Omanis and the Arabs of Bahrain played an important role in the trade of the Persian Gulf and beyond, notably during the time of the Achaemenid Empire, and after its fall. The Arab sailors transported "luxury goods," but also wood, foodstuffs,

[1] These techniques, however, are only attested in Iran after the eighth century BCE (see above).

[2] Hoyland 2001: 19. Moreover, a bronze bowl featuring an Assyrian iconography has been discovered at Ed-Dur. The site of Rafaq, in the mountains, has yielded a stone bowl decorated with griffons, and Assyrian cylinder seals (Magee 1998: 57). There was no particularly dominant center in Oman at this time.

[3] Under Darius, a satrap is mentioned at Makkash (cf. Old Persian 'Makā', designating Oman and/or the territory of the United Arab Emirates) (Potts 1990, I: 395).

and cultivated plants. Theophrastus (late fourth century BCE) reveals that wood (possibly teak from India) was imported into Bahrain for shipbuilding. He mentions cotton, tamarind, date palm, grapevine, fig tree, and cereals as being cultivated on the island. These plants were probably introduced before his time, even though archaeology has not yet provided evidence for their earlier arrival. For Potts, new introductions of cultivated plants occurred between the desertion of Saar (Bahrain) (eighteenth century BCE) and the arrival of the Greek admiral Androsthenes in 323 BCE. Introductions apparently came from Mesopotamia and from Iran (grapevine, fig tree), as well as from India (cotton, tamarind) (Potts 1994b: 240). Theophrastus also mentions cotton cultivation in the land of the Ichtyophagi (South Arabia). Early on, Arabs probably transported other Indian plants – such as sugarcane, banana, rice, taro, and *Curcuma* – to the western Indian Ocean. At various times (pre-Islamic and Islamic), different *Citrus* varieties came from Southeast Asia (as evidenced by the Austronesian origin of the Arabic/Persian names for *Citrus*).

We know little about the southern coast of Arabia and navigation between the Red Sea and the Persian Gulf for the period between the fifth and second centuries BCE. Scylax's account mentions Maka (Oman), the Farasan Islands (south of the Red Sea) but strangely ignores South Arabia. However, at Mleiha (United Arab Emirates) inscriptions in the South Arabian script from the third century BCE onward have been found, as well as calcite (often termed "alabaster") vases linked with the trade in ointments, having arrived from South Arabia on caravan routes.[4] "Alabaster" vessels from South Arabia from the first century CE have also been found at the site of ed-Dur. At this time, the ports of Sumhuram (Khor Rorī) and Qanī played an important role in exchanges between the Red Sea and the Persian Gulf (see above and below; Seland 2014).

The fact that the Neo-Assyrian kings designated Ethiopia and northern India under the same name (Meluhha) may indicate that African goods arrived through the Persian Gulf, after having circumnavigated the Arabian Peninsula. These goods, however, could also reach Mesopotamia by traveling through Arabia over caravan routes.

Archaeological data point to the growth of maritime contacts after the beginning of the Christian era. Ed-Dur was involved in maritime trade, as revealed by finds from both the west and the east, such as Characenian, Indian, Roman, and Arabian coins; ceramics similar to Spasinou Charax wares; many glass artifacts (vessels, for example), cast or blown (mainly Roman); decorated carnelian beads; garnets from Sri Lanka and perhaps from Tanzania (imported through Muza); and Indian ceramics.[5] Ed-Dur was supplied with turquoise glazed ware by Characenian tradesmen from southern Mesopotamia. The occurrence of Italian and Eastern Sigillata points to other

---

[4] Mouton 1997: 300. Mleiha has also yielded silver coins from southern Arabia (early first century BCE and first century CE).

[5] Ed-Dur was active between the first century BCE and second century CE; "40% of the diagnostic pottery at the site has Characene analogies" (Ray 2003: 180). Decorated carnelian beads have also been discovered at Dhayah, north of ed-Dur, on the east coast of the Omani peninsula (Dibba, Qalba, Wādī al-Qawr), and in eastern Oman (Rawdah-Muqatta, Samad) (De Waele and Haerinck 2006: 37–38). See also Haerinck 1998. The Roman glass found at ed-Dur probably came from Syria, via Palmyra then Charax, or perhaps from India. The discovery of Nabataean coins also reveals that ed-Dur was linked to caravan roads. Nabataean coins have also been excavated at Thaj and Qatif.

networks: "both Sigillata groups are common along the Red Sea route and on the South Arabian coast, though being else absent at the Persian Gulf. [This suggests that] ed-Dur obtained goods from Roman Egypt through the South Arabian ports" (Schenck 2007: 64). This port has often been identified as the Omana of the *Periplus*, but Omana may also have been Dibba al-Hisn (located on the eastern flank of the Strait of Hormuz), which has yielded Parthian, Roman, and Indian materials from funerary settings of the same period as ed-Dur (Jasim 2006).

Founded during the first century BCE, the Omani port of Sohar played a significant role from the late second century onward. A hoard of Roman coins dated to the period of Tiberius (14–37 CE) has been discovered, and red polished Indian pottery (from Gujarat) was already present in the oldest levels. Another red Indian ceramic was later imported, as well as Sassanian ceramics. Stamped and molded pottery from Banbhore or Gujarat has also been unearthed. Mleiha has yielded orange painted ceramics from Minab (Persia), items from Mesopotamia and the Levant such as glass vessels, Indian jars, Nubian oil lamps, and an Egyptian amphora.[6] These lamps and Mediterranean amphorae have also been excavated at Qanī, on the South Arabian coast, together with ceramics from Minab and black pottery from Mleiha (also found at Socotra) (Mouton 1997: 305–306; see above). Qanī has also yielded Partho-Sassanid ceramics, green-glazed Mesopotamian pottery, and red Indian pottery (Sedov 1996: 26–27; Ray 2003: 198).

Kennet (2005: 116), however, emphasizes the decline in population and activity, and the demise of urban centers in eastern Arabia between the third and seventh centuries, linked to the increased aridity of this region and the global recession in the world-system.

According to a tradition attested in the ninth century, yearly fairs took place in Arabia before the Islamic period; these fairs may have been hosted alternately by various Arabian cities, according to Ibn Habīb (who died in 245 of the Hegira [859 CE]), showing that there was some kind of unification of this region. The tour started in the north, in the month Muharram (first month), after which the fairs moved to the east:

[There was a fair at] al-Muchaqqar, in Hajar ('Umān). It was held the first of Jumāda'l-ākhira until the end of the networks. The Persians used to go there with their merchandise, by crossing the sea. Then [it was] the fair of Suhār, in 'Umān. Then the fair of Dabā, which was one of the two largest ports in Arabia. The merchants used to go there coming from Sind, from Hind (India) and China, people from the Orient as well as people from the Occident . . . Then the fair of Aden. One did not look for an [armed] escort, as it was the land of a kingdom and of a strong government. (Hamidullah 1974: 198)

The veracity of this tradition and the idea of an ancient unity in the region are in fact open to question.

---

[6] Benoist, Mouton, and Schiettecatte 2003. The site has also yielded bitumen from Iraq, wood (possibly remains from pieces of furniture) that probably came from Syria, a green (or blue)-glazed pottery from Mesopotamia or southern Iran (second–fifth century), and carnelian beads (possibly from India). On the wood found at Mleiha, see Tengberg 2002. A Nubian lamp has also been discovered at Arikamedu (Southeast India). Indian brown ceramic is attested at Nevasa and at Navdatoli (western India) between the first century BCE and the third century CE. The fort of Mleiha was occupied between the third century BCE (within the context of an already active long-distance trade) and the fourth century CE.

Western Arabia and the Horn of Africa

> Alexander heard that in their oases cassia grew; and from the trees came myrrh and
> frankincense; and from the bushes, cinnamon was cut; and from their meadows,
> spikenard grew self-sown.
>
> (Arrian VI.20.2; Retsö 2003a)

Western Arabia was involved in the economic revival that marked the early Iron Age in
the Afro-Eurasian world-system as early as the beginning of the first millennium.[7] When
Egypt's relations with Punt waned during the Third Intermediary Period (1070–723 BCE),
the people of southern Arabia took control of the commerce in the Red Sea, where other
mariners, Phoenicians, and Israelites (note the expeditions to Ophir) were also present.
Yemen had at least four assets: its strategic position, incense production from Hadramawt,
an old maritime tradition and intensive agriculture with clever irrigation systems around
the cities located at the edge of the desert.[8] Prior to the upsurge of the caravan trade with
western Asia based around the export of incense (mainly from the eighth century BCE
onward), development of the southern Arabian cities was boosted by commerce with
southern Palestine and with the Horn of Africa. The Yemeni cities implemented a writing
system, probably as early as the eleventh–tenth century BCE (from an Ugaritic and
Palestinian alphabet), and developed monumental architecture at the beginning of the
first millennium BCE.[9] The region of Raybun has yielded ceramics dated to the beginning
of the first millennium BCE, revealing links with Palestine and northwestern Arabia, from
which its inhabitants may have originated. The rise of the Sabaeans after 800 BCE, linked
to their role in the Red Sea, coincides with the disappearance of the kingdom of Punt in
the Egyptian chronicles and with a chaotic situation within Egypt. It also reflects
a reorientation of trade, from Egypt to western Asia, and from maritime to caravan traffic,
corresponding with the Assyrian expansion in western Asia and the formation of the
Qedarite Arab confederation in northwestern Arabia as early as the ninth century BCE.
This reorientation of trade benefited from a cooler and wetter climate after 1000 BCE.[10]

Discoveries of metal and stone objects from after the end of the second millennium
are more numerous at sites located at the edge of the desert (Edens 2002a: 50). Pillars
from the As-Sawdā temple, discovered in the Jawf by R. Audouin and M. Arbach
(2004), feature scenes of Mesopotamian inspiration. Routes led from the Hijaz and
Yemen to Gaza on the Palestinian coast, where Alexander later found large quantities
of myrrh and frankincense when he took the city.[11] The Egyptian attempt to gain

---

[7] In fact, similar pottery has been found at Timna, and in the Hijaz, from as early as the twelfth century,
suggesting contacts between Arabia and Palestine.

[8] The irrigation systems in this region date back to a previous time (see above). Towns, J.-F. Breton writes
(2001a: 23), were established "in the middle of their irrigation systems."

[9] Writing appears on shards dated between the eleventh and the ninth centuries BCE, for example at ed-
Durayb. The inscriptions include Sabaean names or names from northern Arabia (Maigret 1997: 51).
The first inscriptions on monuments appear to date to the beginning of the first millennium BCE (Edens
and Wilkinson 1998: 93, 95, 107). The temple of "Almaqah" (Bar'ān) at Mārib may have been founded as
early as the tenth century BCE (Breton 2001b: 48).

[10] Mitchiner 2004: 70, 84. The improving climate would have made the reintroduction of cattle possible, as
well as the introduction of horses, which were ridden, as depicted on rock carvings.

[11] He purportedly sent 500 talents of incense and 100 talents of myrrh to Leonidas (Retsö 2003a: 265).

control of Palestine under King Sheshonq I (945–924 BCE) probably reflects the growth of trade throughout this region. At the time of the Assyrian king Tikulti-Ninurta II (891–884 BCE), a list of tributes extracted at the end of a trade road in Syria includes myrrh, as well as gold, silver, bronze, and camels.[12] Ivory also arrived along this road, demonstrating the connection between these networks and Africa. An Assyrian text from 859 BCE mentions an Arab leader at the head of 1,000 dromedaries as part of an anti-Assyrian coalition (Kitchen 1994: 117; see above). Tributes and booty seized by the Assyrian kings from the Arab tribes of northwestern Arabia reflect the scale of exchanges during the eighth and seventh centuries. The Assyrian king Tiglath-Pileser III, in a text recounting a campaign led in the Levant in 733 BCE, claims to have killed "9,400 of the warriors of the queen Shamsi of the Arabs" (a queen from northern Arabia) and seized "5,000 bags of spices of all kinds."[13] The Assyrian ruler of Sukhu boasts of having looted a caravan that had failed to pay him allegiance, a caravan of 200 camels from Saba and Taymā' in Syria, loaded with iron, alabaster, and purple dyed wool. The Sabaean ruler It'amara (Yāthi'ī'amar) and "Queen Shamsi" paid tribute to the Assyrian king Sargon II in 716 BCE, and Karībilu (Karib'īl Watār), "the king of Saba," sent precious stones and aromatics to Sennacherib for the foundation of a temple at Assur (Robin 1997b: 61–62). A prince of Karkemish from the eighth century took pride in his knowledge of the "Taymān script." South Arabian inscriptions have also recently been discovered at Jerusalem, dated to the seventh century BCE.[14] The roads of the Arabian Desert toward Palestine, as described by the Bible,[15] went through the oases lining the "incense road" in the west, as far as the Edomite and later Nabatean city of Petra, already mentioned. Major towns and city-states developed on these roads. The first was probably Qurayyah, during the second half of the second millennium. Both Egyptian involvement in the region and a growing caravan trade contributed to its emergence. Taymā', a place mentioned in the Bible (Isaiah 21:14),

---

[12] Retsö 2003a: 122. The camels were certainly dromedaries from Arabia. Retsö assumes, probably incorrectly, that incense did not reach the Levant before the seventh century and that Yemen was not connected to the Levant before the eighth century (2003a: 175).

[13] Retsö 2003a: 133. Sennacherib, Esarhaddon, and Assurbanipal led several military campaigns in northwestern Arabia (see above) (Kitchen 1993: 602; Salles 1996a: 254; Edens and Wilkinson 1998). Various "Egypto-Phoenician" objects (scarabs, small faience amulets) found in the tombs of the Awwām necropolis (used by the Sabaean elite from the eighth century BCE to the fourth century CE) attest to Saba's links to the Levant (Garlach 2001: 50).

[14] Arbach 2001: 14–15. An incense altar has been discovered in the Moab (central Jordan) (c. eighth century BCE). The queen of Saba's visit to Solomon's court recounted in the Bible (Kings 10:1–13) and in the Koran (Sura XVII.20–44) probably never occurred. The kingdom of Saba only truly developed from the eighth century onward (however, the temple of Almaqah at Mārib was built during the tenth century BCE; see above). The account given by the Book of Kings (possibly written around the seventh or sixth century BCE) shows that there were contacts between Saba and the Mediterranean world during the eighth and seventh centuries BCE.

[15] Isaiah 60:6, Genesis 37:25. Palestine also exported spices and aromatics to Egypt and Syria (Genesis 37:25, 43.11; Ezekiel 27:17). A passage in Genesis (25:1–7), listing the names of Abraham's sons by a woman called Qeturah, mentions an incense road going from Hijaz to the Euphrates (cf. Arabic qutār, "smell, fragrance"). Ezekiel (27:21–22) mentions the links between "the princes of Qedar," "the traders from Saba and Rayma," and the city of Tyre (before being captured by Nebuchadnezzar II in 573/572 BCE). Various Arab powers sided with Egypt and the Phoenician cities against the Babylonian Empire during the late seventh and early sixth century.

became a sizeable stopping-point during the first millennium BCE. Assyrian sources mention a tribute paid by the city of Taymā' to King Tiglath-Pileser III. Cuneiform inscriptions dated to the sixth century BCE have been discovered in that city. As noted above, Nabonidus left Babylon and moved his court to Taymā' for a few years; the result of a personal choice, this shift also shows how important the incense route was. The oasis has yielded Aramaic inscriptions from the Achaemenid period. Located north of Mārib, Najrān was another significant center, with a large Jewish community.

Centered around Mārib, where a dam and an irrigation system were built during the seventh century BCE,[16] the kingdom of Saba constituted a major power in southern Arabia. It controlled the coasts of the Red Sea and trade with Ethiopia, where Sabaeans settled. Sabaean merchants traded as far as Egypt: their graffiti have been found along the Wādī Hammamat. The dromedary was probably introduced into Africa within the context of exchanges between Yemen and Ethiopia or Nubia: remains at Qasr Ibrim (southern Egypt) have been dated to the eighth/seventh century BCE.[17] Impressions on pottery and charred plant remains show that plants from western Asia (barley, oat, flax, cumin, and probably grapevine), Africa (tef), and southern Asia (sesame, millet *Panicum miliaceum* L.) were cultivated at Hajar bin Humeid (between 800 and 300 BCE). This site has also yielded evidence of iron metallurgy as early as the tenth century BCE. A ruler called Karib'īl Watār managed to unify southern Arabia; he was the first to bear the title of *mukarrib*, "unifier," a title held by the kings of Saba until the middle of the sixth century BCE.[18] Then the Minaean kingdom, which was centered around the Jawf valley (with Qarnaw [Ma'īn] as its capital) rose to prominence – at least in trade – (Minaean inscriptions have been found in the Hijāz, but also in Egypt and at Delos),[19] as well as the kingdoms of Qatabān (sizeable from the seventh to the first centuries BCE) and Hadramawt. A temple devoted to the Phoenician goddess Athirat has been excavated at Tamna' [Timna'], the capital of Qataban, revealing this region's links with the Levant. South Arabian coinage appears to date back to 350 BCE at Saba. Robin here emphasizes the importance of the religious unity brought about in

---

[16] Some of the great irrigation works at Mārib "probably date to the tenth/ninth century BCE," and others to the eighth/seventh century BCE (Kitchen 2002a: 396). The city of Mārib covered over 100 ha at its peak, for a population of between 10,000 and 30,000 inhabitants.

[17] The dating is 2690 ± 90 BP (Rowley-Conwy 1988). The dromedary was introduced into the Sahara from Egypt. See above.

[18] During the seventh century, Saba captured the capital of a kingdom called Awsān, Hagar Yahirr, located in the Wadi Markha. Drewes (2001), however, translates MKRB as "blessed" (Phillipson 2012: 39).

[19] The Delos texts are dedications made by a Minaean and a man from Hadramawt. Moreover, "the Minaean settlements have yielded texts *in situ* mentioning trade activities in South Arabia, Egypt, on the Mediterranean coast (Tyre and Sidon) and beyond the Euphrates" (Breton 2001a: 29). At Gaza, a Minaean inscription was written by Arab caravan traders who "saved their properties from Egypt during a conflict between the Medes [Persians] and the Egyptians" (Briant 1996: 736). C. J. Robin (1997a: 48–49) considers Ma'īn to have had an important role in the caravan trade between the seventh and second centuries BCE, while remaining under the control of Saba (for example during the fourth and the second centuries BCE), which apparently gave control of the caravan trade to Ma'īn. See Pliny XII.54. After the decline of Ma'īn, the Amir tribe took charge of the trade. The incense road from Ma'īn to the Gulf of Aqaba was described by Eratosthenes during the third century BCE.

the South Arabian trading sphere, providing a basis for its development, and for the security of the people and goods transported.

Shabwa was the capital of Hadramawt, the main "frankincense-bearing land," from the tenth/ninth century BCE onward: the "royal palace" was founded at this time. Around the seventh–sixth century BCE, walls surrounded the city, and large hydraulic systems were constructed. Then, between the sixth and fourth centuries BCE, Shabwa went through a relative decline. The city has yielded Iron Age Syro-Palestinian ceramics and "eastern Greek pottery" from the sixth century BCE. "An inscription indicates the presence of Palmyranes, Indians and Chaldaeans in the third century BCE" (Tomber 2012a: 105). Coinage appeared at the end of the first century BCE. Brown-glazed pottery, also attested at ed-Dur and Susa, may have come from Charax (first century BCE – first century CE). The wealth of the city rose during the first century CE. For this period and the following centuries, archaeologists have recovered Roman pottery from Italy and from Syria, amphorae fragments from Anatolia (dated to the second and third centuries), Aegean amphorae, an Egyptian amphora, and blue or green-glazed ware from Mesopotamia. Around 220–230 CE, Shabwa was looted by the Sabaean army, and then rebuilt. The final destruction of the "palace" took place at the end of the fourth century (Breton 2003: 211).

The Shabwa region was connected to trading ports: Sumhuram (Khor Rorī) (Dhofar, Oman) goes back to the fourth century BCE, but was refounded by colonists from Shabwa during the first century BCE. "The main purpose of Khor Rori was to supply Qana with incense" (Tomber 2012a: 106). "Pottery assemblages show contacts with India, the Persian Gulf, and the Mediterranean" (Seland 2014; Avanzini 2008; Pavan and Schenk 2012). Maintained by the Hadrami central power, the port was active in the metal trade with southeastern Arabia and the Persian Gulf. Indian merchants would land at Khor Rori to spend the winter there, before sailing home to India (*Periplus*; see above). Graffiti found on the city wall depict a two-masted ship quite similar to Indian ships on coins from the second century (Avanzini 2008: 615). Black Ware from Gujarat and Indian Red Polished Ware have been found in the city. Sumhuram went into decline during the fourth century (imported pottery disappeared at the end of this century). Its desertion around the end of the fifth century was partly due to the port silting up, but also linked to "political factors such as competition in the Axumite and Sassanid trade" and the demise of Hadrami autonomy (Avanzini 2008: 613).

As for the trade in South Arabian aromatics, Theophrastus emphasizes the safety of the roads, the warehouses, and markets. The harvest was monopolized by a small number of people: the temple and the king took a significant part of the profits ("the priest, writes Theophrastus, reserves the third of the price for the god"). Aromatics followed well-organized routes. During the first century CE, both Pliny and the *Periplus* mention that incense went through Shabwa ("where the priests take a tenth part in honor of their god") and Tamna'.

Pliny points out that: "The incense can only be exported through the country of the Gebanitae, and for this reason it is that a certain tax is paid for their king as well" (Pliny XII. 63–64; Robin 1997a: 40–41, 47). He adds that the king of Qatabān took for himself one-fourth of the harvest of myrrh.

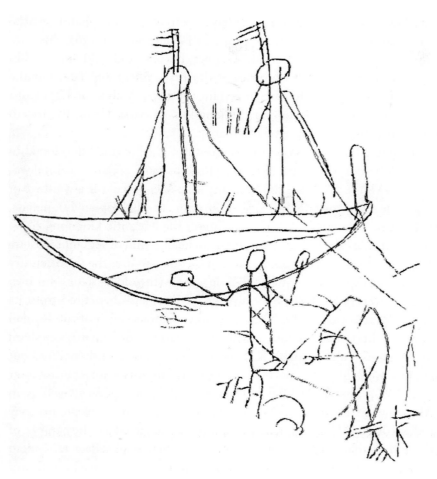

Figure 13.1 Graffiti on an exterior wall of the city of Sumhuram, by A. Avanzini (from Seland 2007: 28 fig. 4)

The Sabaeans' activities extended into Africa. The kingdom of Saba exerted a significant influence over the so-called "Pre-Axumite" culture and the kingdom of Daamat (*D'MT*) (central Eritrea and western Tigray) that emerged around 700 BCE. Urban centers developed at Kaskasé, Matara (central Eritrea), and Yeha, probably the capital of the kingdom (western Tigray). Arabs were settling in Eritrea after 850 BCE, as seen in South Arabian inscriptions. Some authors regard Daamat to have originally been a Sabaean colony. In reality, the kingdom was more the result of the emergence of a local elite influenced by and in contact with Sabaeans who were living in the country.[20] Sabaean was probably the official language of the kingdom. The remains

[20] Fattovich 1997a: 482. According to Fattovich, rock inscriptions in central Eritrea show that "South Arabians were established along the northeastern edge of the Tigrean plateau just before the rise of the Pre-Aksumite kingdom" (1997b: 282–283). The last three rulers of Daamat used the Sabaean title *mukarrib*. "The South Arabian influence is evident in all power manifestation of the elite: monumental architecture, monumental inscriptions, art, votive incense altars, bronze seals, as well as writing" (1997b: 284). Jars from Matara and Yeha appear to be similar to pottery from Subr (Fattovich 2004). Similarities between the architecture of buildings at Yeha and in Ma'īn have also been pointed out (Breton 2002). Inscriptions at the Yeha Great Temple and the site of Maqaber Ga'ewa, 6 km south of Wukro, indicate dedication to Almaqah, the southern Arabian moon god (Phillipson 2012: 26, 29). The oldest layers of the

of a dam exhibiting a South Arabian influence have been excavated at Safra (central Eritrea) (Fattovich 1997a: 487); however, according to Phillipson (2012: 36), this dam "cannot be assumed to date from this period." Copper, bronze, and gold appeared in Eritrea and Ethiopia during the first centuries of the first millennium BCE, but the origins of the technology involved remain uncertain (perhaps Arabia, or Egypt, via Sudan) (Killick 2009b: 412). The decline of the kingdom of Saba during the fourth century BCE coincided with the collapse of Daamat.

Daamat also maintained contacts with the kingdom of Kush, which developed in Upper Nubia as a later heir of the Kerma kingdom (Phillips 1997: 443). The capital was at Napata, and later at Meroe, from the sixth century BCE. Meroe had the advantage of various trade routes, leading toward the African interior, the Ethiopian Highlands, Egypt, and the Red Sea. Strongly influenced by Egypt, the Meroitic kingdom, however, was not organized along the same lines, but was instead a kind of segmentary state (Fuller 2003b). Meroe became a major center for iron metallurgy after the third century BCE (part of the iron was exported through the Nile valley) (the oldest dating for iron smelting at Meroe is 2514±73 BP, Killick 2009b: 496). Meroe also benefited from its access to gold mines located east of the Nile. Like other regions south of the Roman world (South Libya, Nubia), the kingdom grew cotton (African, or Indian) (Clapham and Rowley-Conwy 2006; Fuller 2008b). R. Haaland (2013) has recently pointed out that Indian mahouts were likely to have been present, employed for training war elephants. Depicted in a temple devoted to Apedemak, the war god, as well as in a place called Musawwarat es-sufra, probably a training center, these elephants may have been of Indian origin. The king and the queen are depicted in the temple of Apedemak with clothes that do not look Egyptian but that may reflect an Indian influence (Haaland 2013). A representation of Apedemak emerging from a lotus flower is also reminiscent of India. These connections with South Asia might lead one to conclude that cultivated cotton was perhaps of Indian origin; however, this has yet to be confirmed. Two Roman campaigns against Meroe were launched in 24 BCE and 63 CE. The kingdom was in decline during the third century, and during the fourth century CE the conquest of Meroe by the Axumites sealed the capital's fate.

Moreover, as of the reign of Psamtik I (663–609 BCE), the Egyptians were back in the Red Sea. During the sixth century BCE, Nechao II (609–594 BCE) tried to reopen the canal between the Nile and the Red Sea. He also deployed a naval force in the Red Sea, perhaps to fight the Sabaeans, or Nabataean pirates – who are mentioned for the third century BCE. The Nabataean naval attacks were obviously a reaction to the Egyptians' attempts to bypass the Arab caravan trade. Nechao II's military activities were in any case linked to his commercial goals (the spice trade was a royal prerogative in Egypt) (Salles 1996a: 254).

At this time, the Eritrean coast, together with Yemen, were still crucial in linking Asia and Africa. The sites of the Ona culture are now dated between 800 and 400 BCE. Curiously, they provide little evidence for interaction with Daamat (Schmidt 2006: 267). It remains to be seen, however, whether their development has more to do with an

---

Yeha Great Temple may go back to the eighth century BCE. At Kaskase, "the inscribed pillars and pottery exposed on the surface suggest an age in the mid-first millennium BCE" (Phillipson 2012: 29).

endogenous process or with transregional contacts, as Schmidt suggests (2006). Zebu figurines found at Sembel point to the importance of this type of cattle in the Ona culture's development (2006: 276–277, 283 n. 10). Trade increased in the Indian Ocean from 600–500 BCE, with the development of the Persian Empire, which controlled Asia from the Indus to the Levant and conquered Egypt in 525 BCE. According to stelae discovered at Suez, Darius completed works for digging a canal between the Nile and the Red Sea – a project initiated under Nechao II – and sent twenty-four ships from Suez to Persia: these events appear as the aftermath of the journey made by Scylax between the Indus and the Red Sea.[21] The ascent of Daamat and later of Axum, in connection with South Arabia, facilitated the importation of Asian plants and animals (zebu, dromedary, perhaps also chicken) into Africa. The dromedary was used in Nubia during the early first millennium BCE for transporting merchandise. The zebu figurines of Sembel have already been mentioned here. A bronze figurine representing a zebu has also been unearthed at Zeban Kutur in Eritrea, dated to the second century CE (Marshall 2000: 196, 200).[22] Fragments of zebu skulls have been discovered in Kenya dated between 200 BCE and 100 CE (Marshall 1989). Chickens were raised in Egypt around 330 BCE (McDonald 1993: 587). With regard to plants, Yemen may have acted as a bridge in the introduction of the taro and the banana into Africa. Watson is wrong in rejecting the idea that the taro might have been present in Egypt and Mesopotamia prior to Islam.[23] Pliny's description of a *Colocasia* with a "black" root seems to refer to the taro, as does the description of an *Aron* with a "red, round and big bulb" (XIX.30 and XXIV.143) (Aubaile-Sallenave 1984: 250–251) (however, in XXI.87, Pliny refers to the lotus *Nelumbo nucifera* Gaertn. by the name of *colocasia*). Moreover, Ezekiel (27:24) mentions "blue fabric, embroidered work" traded by the "merchants of Sheba and Raamah," which appears to indicate the use of indigo by Yemeni weavers around the sixth or fifth century BCE: links with India appear to have led to the introduction of indigo (Balfour-Paul 1997) (it is possible, however, that indigo *Indigofera tinctoria* grew wild in Yemen).

During the fifth and fourth centuries BCE, the Arabs of Qedar who occupied the Syro-Arabian desert controlled the incense trade along the oases route.[24] A document in Aramaic dated to the second half of the fifth century BCE refers to a kingdom of Qedar. We know from Herodotus that "Cambyses concluded an agreement with 'the king of the Arabs'" and that "each year, the Arabs [delivered] 1,000 talents of incense to the Persians" (Herodotus III. 7, 9,[25] and 97; Briant 1996: 736). A reference to a Lihyanite

---

[21] The connection with the expedition of Scylax, however, has been put into question by J.-F. Salles (1996a: 254).

[22] N. Boivin and D. Fuller (2009: 140) note that if Asian rhinos were sent to Punt (cf. Meeks 2002), it is possible that zebus were also introduced and reached Africa as early as the second millennium BCE.

[23] Watson 1983: 178–179 n. 6. The Greek name *kolokasion* and the Latin *colocasia* must be related to the Arabic *qulqas*. The etymology of the term seems to be Indian (cf. Sanskrit *kacu-*, "taro"). The first mention of it is in Dioscorides (78 CE) but it may refer to *Faba aegyptiaca* (*Nelumbo nucifera* Gaertn., lotus).

[24] According to Herodotus (III.5), the ports "from Cadytis [Gaza] (which, as I judge, is a city not much smaller than Sardis) to the city of Ienysus [Khan Yunis] the seaports belong to the *arabioi* (Arabians)" (Retsö 2003a: 244). This confederation appears to have been active between the eighth and fourth centuries BCE.

[25] "Cambyses sent messengers to the Arabian and asked and obtained safe conduct, giving to him and receiving from him pledges" (Herodotus III.7).

kingdom centered around Dedān during the fourth century probably corresponds to political changes in Hijaz (Retsö 2003a: 192). Minaeans settled there for a while in order to secure the trade route. A strong Egyptian influence was noticeable during the fourth and third centuries BCE, during a period of expansion under Ptolemy II. Dedān remained prosperous until the first century BCE. Various Arab groups were active participants in the networks. During the fourth century BCE, the Nabataeans were present at Petra, where Antigonus I attacked them without success.[26] According to Diodorus (XIX.94–97), "not a few of them are accustomed to bring down to the sea frankincense and myrrh and the most valuable kinds of spices, which they procure from those who convey them from what is called Arabia Eudaemon."

During the Hellenistic period, the northwestern Arab groups were caught between the Seleucids and the Ptolemies. They provided animal herds, mercenaries, and incense to both of these powers. Arabs settled in central and northern Syria. The Nabataeans, enemies of the pro-Seleucid groups, acquired a growing importance during the second century BCE. Palestine and the Levant, however, were affected by wars between the Seleucids and the Ptolemies during the second century and the first half of the first century BCE, until the bloody conquest achieved by Pompeius in 63 BCE.

During the second and first centuries BCE, under the impetus of the Greeks and later the Romans, maritime commerce partly superseded caravan trade (the two or three centuries preceding the Christian era were a period of increased aridity [Coque-Delhuile 2001: 20], but fluctuations in climate do not appear to have played a significant role in these changes). The southern Arabs not only produced incense and received goods from Southeast Asia and India; they were also active in trade networks. Agatharchides wrote around 120 BCE:

The land of the Sabaeans manifests an abundance in every respect. The people are strong, war-like and excellent sea-farers;[27] they navigate their ships to those countries which produce fragrant products and they establish colonies there. In fact, no people on earth are as rich as the Sabaeans on the Southwestern coast and the Gerrheans on the Eastern coast of Arabia. They are as crafty as the Phoenicians and deal in many wares which bring them huge profits. They have an excess of luxury items – many more than one can find in Europe. In their way of life, they live like kings. (Labib 1974: 226).

A text written on wood (TYA 15) dated to the second or third century contains the term *mskn*, probably designating the Indian musk (Arabic *misk*, Persian *mušk*).[28] It is likely that Indians sailed to the Arab coasts. As mentioned earlier, Indian ceramics have been found at the port of Sumhuram. A Kushan coin from Kanishka I has also

[26] Dated to the reign of Assurbanipal, a text already mentions that: "Natnu, king of Nabayāti, who lives far away, and who has not earlier been subject to Assyria, sends ambassadors and pays tribute to Assurbanipal" (Retsö 2003a: 162–163). Nebayoth is given by Genesis 25:12 as the "elder" of Ismael's sons, before Qedar.

[27] Curiously, J. Pirenne writes (1970: 102): "If we believe what Agatharchides wrote, the Arabs had only very limited maritime activities. The prosperity of the Sabaeans came from profits made from the caravan trade more than earnings from maritime traffic."

[28] Müller 1997: 209. Around 225 CE, moreover, the Sabaeans launched an expedition against Qāni', where they destroyed forty-seven ships, small and large (inscription Ry 533/9) (Robin 1997a: 47).

been recovered at this site, as well as a shard bearing an inscription from Gujarat dated to the fourth century CE (Avanzini 2007).

The expansion of the Roman Empire could not leave the South Arabian kingdoms unaffected. In 25 BCE, in a campaign mentioned by Strabo, Mārib put up successful resistance to a Roman expedition led by the prefect of Egypt, Aelius Gallus. Pliny describes pirates who dwelled in the Farasan Islands, where the Romans finally established a garrison. Two Latin inscriptions found on the Farasan Islands document this Roman military presence in 143–144 CE (Phillips *et al.* 2004). Arab embassies were sent to Rome during the first century by King Charibael (*Periplus*, paragr. 23), "king of the Himyarites and the Sabaeans," and by Hadrami leaders, partly to help prevent future Roman expeditions (Casson 1989: 36). The Romans aimed for direct control over the "incense land," but also hoped to attack the Parthians from the rear, showing here their ignorance of the Arabian peninsula (see Retsö 2003b: 231). The Hadramawt remained prosperous at the turn of the Christian era, but conflicts arose among the various Yemeni kingdoms during the first centuries CE. The Himyarites, who had become independent in 110 BCE, finally gained the upper hand over the Sabaeans and dominated the region after the end of the third century. A strong Jewish influence can be seen during the fourth century, when part of the population adopted Judaism. Under King Abīkarib Asʿad, the Himyarite power extended to a significant part of the Arabian peninsula.[29] The Himyarites certainly played a role in Indian Ocean networks. Imported late Roman Aila/Aqaba amphorae have been discovered at the Himyarite highland capital of Zafar (Damgaard 2009; Seland 2014). However, the presence of "Sabaeans" on the coasts of India and Sri Lanka is improbable (it was once thought that a tradition linked to the Chinese monk Faxian, who visited Sri Lanka in 413 CE, referred to the Sabaeans),[30] and the Himyarite ports on the South Arabian coast "have not been securely identified" (Seland 2014).

The Himyarite power hindered Axum and Byzantium in their attempt to bypass the Sassanids and to gain direct access to Indian commerce (see Procopius, 1.20). From 522 CE, a Jewish prince from Himyar, Yūsuf dhū-Nuwās, organized "persecutions" against Christians (especially at Najrān),[31] which gave the Axumite Empire a pretext for military intervention, although this was primarily motivated by political and economic reasons. The intervention precipitated the decline of the South Arabian cultures. Writing fell into disuse, monumental buildings were no longer built, the maintenance of the irrigation systems appears to have been abandoned, all of which reveals impoverishment and the absence of a strong political power (Gajda 2001: 65). The decline, however, had probably already begun earlier, as South Arabian coinage stopped being produced around 300 CE[32] (the Nabataeans of Petra already appear to have been in

---

[29] He is even credited with mythical expeditions to Iraq and China (Bron 2001: 8).

[30] Due to an erroneous reading of the term "Sabo" (Sa-poh). Hamidullah 1974: 195 n. 13, who quotes Lewicki 1936.

[31] An evangelical movement apparently accompanied the arrival of an envoy of the Roman Empire in 340 CE, Theophilos the Indian (an Arian bishop, and a native of the Maldives), who came with 200 horses "to ask the king of Himyar for permission to build churches" (Boulnois 2001: 249–250).

[32] The first Christians condemned the use of incense as idolatry, which probably contributed to the decline of the South Arabian trade. However, the Christians adopted incense for other purposes, and by the

decline during the second century, with the development of Palmyra on the one side, and the Red Sea maritime routes, on the other).

From the third to the sixth century, the Himyarite kingdom had control of Qanī – the main port of trade for frankincense (see above) – until Axum invaded Yemen. Artifacts from Axum have been found there that are dated later than the fourth century (Mouton 2006). Archaeological data show that "people of different ethnic and religious affiliation" lived together in the city. A synagogue and temple devoted to Sayyin, the supreme god of Hadramawt, have been excavated (Sedov 2010a). A Greek text written by a man called Kosmas (fourth century CE) asks for the protection of the Lord for his caravans and ships. An *ostrakon* with a Greek painted text features a cross at the beginning of the inscription (Sedov 2001: 35). Inscriptions in Greek, Syriac, and Palmyranian appear on ceramics and house walls. In the later period (sixth century), torpedo jars and glazed ware reflect ties with Mesopotamia; eastern Mediterranean and Aqaba amphorae are also present. Shards from the Axumite kingdom (Ethiopia) dominate the record of imported ceramics, reflecting "growing Axumite importance in the Red Sea and the Indian Ocean exchanges as well as Axumite imperial ambitions in southern Arabia at that time" (Seland 2014; Sedov 2010b). Contact with India seems to have declined, but a shard of Chinese green glazed ware has been excavated (Vinogradov 2010), probably reflecting Sassanian contacts with China (Persia took control of southern Arabia in 570 CE, driving the Axumites out of Yemen; see above). The size and importance of Qani decreased during the sixth century and the city was abandoned during the early seventh century, a demise linked to successive political changes, and also to the global recession at that time.

The Axumite kingdom emerged within the context of an expanding Indo-Roman trade, as a leading partner of the Roman Empire and as an interface between the Indian Ocean and the Mediterranean; Phillipson's "Early Aksumite period" starts around 50 CE (2012: 69, 72), but the Axumite kingdom "must have developed by the end of the 2nd century CE" (2012: 79), and coinage began "in the second half of the third century" (2012: 79). The Romans' efforts to weaken the Arabs (in northern Arabia, an expedition sent by Trajan affected the Nabataean land in 105 CE) and the Parthians may have contributed to the rise of Axum.[33] Moreover, a key factor for Axum's success was its capacity to take advantage of routes going into the African interior, toward the Blue Nile, and as far as the Red Sea coast. Ivory exports "contributed to Axum's prosperity" (Phillipson 2012: 71). Axum controlled the port of Adulis, which had the largest ivory market in the Red Sea, as well as South Arabian trade. Slaves were also exported from Adulis. The kingdom sent military expeditions to southern Arabia during the third and fourth centuries CE. Reflecting a growing Byzantine influence in the Red Sea, Axum adopted Christianity as its state religion at

---

fifth–sixth century, incense-burning had come to be part of Christian worship (Ray 2003: 182–183). In any event, it seems that the incense trade declined after the third century.

[33] The tombs excavated in the Wādī Dura (Shabwa), for example the tomb of a warrior chief dated between the first and third centuries, exhibit some Parthian and Sassanid influence, "notably for weapons" (Audouin 2001: 62).

the beginning of the fourth century CE and set up close contacts with Syria.[34] Byzantium had contacts with Axum through trade and diplomacy,[35] and also signed trade treaties with the Himyarites. "Adulis and Aden thus became true Byzantine markets" (Toussaint 1961: 44). Byzantium forbade the sale of iron and copper to the Persians, and the Sassanids increased the price of silk during Justinian's reign. According to Procopius, Justinian decided to cease purchasing silk from the Persians but instead to "trade with Christian monks in India who had learned the art of making silk" (Daryaee 2003: 5). Byzantium's new stance would go on to encourage trade in the Red Sea and in Arabia. The presence of large quantities of ceramics from Aqaba "points toward that port being the main northern trading partner of late period Adulis" (Seland 2014: 381). This also shows "the Axumite kingdom as an actor in ancient Indian Ocean exchange from the first century CE onward but with increased importance in the fourth to early seventh centuries" (Seland 2014: 381).

Indians were already present on the Axumite coasts early on. Beads from India have been found in large numbers at Axum and Matara. Kushan gold coins (104) have been recovered at Debre Damo, in the interior, in a sixth-century context (Pankhurst 1979: 107; Tomber 2012a: 93; see above).[36] Axumite pottery has been found at Kāmrej, in Gujarat, and Axumite coins have been discovered in Sri Lanka and India. According to the Greek author Palladius, who wrote at the end of the fourth century CE, Indians sailed to Adulis, and from there to the Maldives and Sri Lanka. During the fifth century, "a Bishop of Adulis, by name Moses, traveled to India in the company of a Coptic bishop from Egypt, to examine Brahmin philosophy" (Pankhurst www .linkethiopia.org). The Axumite emperor Kaleb is said to have used nine Indian ships when he invaded Yemen around 520 CE.[37] The *Martyrium Sancti Arethae* of Pseudo-Callisthenes mentions nine Indian ships in the Ethiopian port of Gabaza (Adulis) in 525 CE (Pigulevskaya 1951: 300; Kobishanov 1984: 416). Moreover, an ancient text by Heliodorus of Emesa, *Aethiopica*, notes the existence of war elephants in "Ethiopia" led by "Seres" (ninth book), a term which may indicate the presence of Indians at Axum around the third century CE,[38] unless this is a reference to Meroe (see above).

---

[34] A Syrian Christian who was shipwrecked on the Ethiopian coasts around 330 CE "was subsequently instrumental in converting the Aksumite realm to Christianity" (Pankhurst, www .linkethiopia.org/).

[35] Contacts are well attested, especially for the fourth and sixth centuries. According to Procopius, in 530 CE, Justinian sent an embassy to Axum "to urge Kaleb to participate in a Byzantine invasion of Persia" (Phillipson 2012: 205).

[36] Munro-Hay (2002: 336–337) suggests a possible date between the first century BCE and the first century CE.

[37] "Of the 70 ships gathered at Adulis to aid the Aksumite invasion of King Kaleb to South Arabia, 20 came from Clysma [Suez], 15 from Aila [Aqaba], 10 from Adulis and 2 from Berenice, as well as 9 from India and 7 from Farasan" (Tomber 2012a: 162–163). See Glazier and Peacock 2007: 10.

[38] See Janvier 1975b: 122 n. 29. Pliny (VI.54, 88) shows that there was some confusion between the different "Seres," of East Asia or South India. Ptolemy mentions Seres among the people of East Asia, east of Scythia and west of China, with a metropolis called Sera, in the country of Serica, north of the Ottorocoras Mountains, probably Mongolia (Book 6, ch. XVI, p. 146, ed. Stevenson). Moreover, further south there was a river called Serus that ran into a large bay to the east of the Golden Chersonese (Malaysia): this river may correspond to the Mekong (Book 7, ch. II, p. 155, ed.

Axumite power was at its peak between the fourth century (when the kingdom of Meroe collapsed) and the sixth century. There continued to be an active caravan trade in western Arabia. Before Islam, a string of city-states grew up along the main routes; they presented a common culture[39] in which Christianity and Judaism coexisted, until the confrontation initiated by Yūsuf (see above). In 525 CE, Axum invaded southern Arabia, and controlled the region until the conquest of Yemen by the Persians in 570 CE. Yemen's regression at this time – partly due to a worsening climate and also to a plague epidemic (the "Justinian plague") – was marked by the failure of the Mārib dam, in 539 or 542, which was repaired, and later definitively destroyed in 570 CE.[40] Axumite merchants were present as far as Sri Lanka. Numerous Byzantine coins have been recovered in South India, brought there by Axumite traders. Roman coins from the late fourth to the early fifth century have been found at Alangankulam (Tamil Nadu). A hoard of Axumite coins has been collected in Mangalore (western India). Procopius writes that around 530, "the Axumites did not manage to get enough silk from Ceylon to supply the Byzantines. In order to obtain silk, Byzantium [sent monks to the east], who secretly brought back eggs of the silkworm from China [more likely from Central Asia] through terrestrial routes" (Toussaint 1961: 46).

From 570 CE onward, the Persians occupied Yemen (see above) and controlled the Bab-el-Mandeb, at the entrance to the Red Sea. There was a considerable Persian presence in the Hijāz and in the Arabian interior. Al-Hamdānī (tenth century) signals that "thousands of Persians" worked at the silver mine of al-Yam āmah; the Sassanids built a road that crossed Arabia in order to transport silver to Persia (Heck 1999: 368, 383).

During the sixth and seventh centuries, Axum was weakened by problems linked to soil erosion near the capital, declining trade, difficulties due to the empire's over-extension, and internal revolts. Axum may also have been affected by the "Justinianic plague": indeed, the economic decline became apparent after the middle decades of the sixth century (Phillipson 2012: 209). One notes a debasement of gold coins, and Axum ceased its production of coins during the early seventh century. The capital of the kingdom appears to have moved to Kubar, southeast of Axum, although it has not been precisely located (Phillipson 2012: 211). The advent of Islam during the seventh century aggravated the isolation of the Axumite kingdom and its decline. Egypt was conquered by the Arabs in 647, and Muslims settled along the Eritrean and Somali coasts. During

Stevenson). The Greco-Roman world also applied the term Seres to the Chera of the Malabar coast, and even to the Ausar and to the island of Masira in southern Arabia (Schoff 1974: 146, 267). Cosmas Indicopleustes mentions Sri Lanka under the name of Serendip, which has no relation to the Greek term *ser*, "silk" (although Cosmas signals the importation of Chinese silk in Sri Lanka). *Dip* derives from the Sanskrit *dvīpa*, "island." Serendip is linked to the Arabic name for Sri Lanka: Sarandīb, which has been connected to the Sanskrit *simhaladvīpa* (?) (al-Bīrūnī has it as Sangaladīp, and at the time of Yāqūt, we find the form Sīlān) (Bosworth 1997: 39).

[39] Byzantine and Persian coins were in circulation in Mecca prior to the Muslim period.

[40] The dam first broke in 360 CE. Major repairs were implemented in 455 CE. Its destruction around 570 CE may have been caused by flooding, but also undoubtedly was the result of insufficient maintenance. One notes increased aridity after 600 CE (Mitchiner 2004: 69).

the eighth century, Muslim Arabs dominated exchanges in the Red Sea and along the East African coast.

The Arab presence on this coast was not a new phenomenon. The formation of the Pre-Swahili culture on the East African coast at the beginning of the Christian era (or just before), however, cannot be uniquely attributed to the Arabs' presence, as has been previously suggested.

14 East Africa: The Emergence of a Pre-Swahili Culture on the Azanian Coast

> Under the king the people of Mouza hold it [Rhapta] by payment of
> tribute, and send ships with captains and agents who are mostly Arabs,
> and are familiar through residence and intermarriage with the nature
> of the places and their language.
>
> (*Periplus of the Erythraean Sea*; Huntingford 1980: 30)[1]

As has been the case for Southeast Asia, the way in which historians regard the birth and expansion of the coastal cultures of East Africa has changed significantly in recent years. Archaeology has brought forward new knowledge that has caused a reappraisal of traditional accounts of the appearance and rise of settlements on the East African coast. Proponents of an Arab or Persian "colonization" have since given way to the advocates of an African development. However, it seems apparent that the debate cannot be settled in these terms alone. It was the integration of East Africa into the world-system – as a periphery – that led to the emergence of mercantile centers and elites who monopolized contacts with foreign lands; a society was formed which acted as an interface connecting the dominant regions (Arabia, Persia, Egypt) and the terrestrial (the African hinterland) and maritime (the Comoros and Madagascar) margins. However, it seems probable that hunter-gatherers who had settled in Zanzibar long before the Christian era were already engaged in maritime activities in this region (Sinclair 2008). For Chami, these groups went further afield, to the Comoros and Madagascar (2009: 125), a claim confirmed by recent finds.

The existence of East African ports in contact with transoceanic networks probably goes back to the last centuries before the Christian era. However, Chami has suggested that contacts were made earlier (during the first half of the first millennium BCE) between sailors from the Red Sea and India and African communities who were living on the coast, a conclusion drawn from the results of excavations in the Ukunju Cave (Juani Island, near Mafia). Chami unearthed various shards at this site, and tentatively linked them to Indian pottery dated between the fourth century BCE and the fourth century CE as well as red painted pottery of the Gupta period (fourth–sixth century). With the possible exception of a shard from Arikamedu, these identifications ought, however, to be rejected (Sinclair 2008).[2] Other shards have been compared to ceramics of southern

---

[1] Schoff has proposed the following translation: "The people of Muza send thither [to Rhapta] many large ships, using Arab captains and agents who are familiar with the natives and intermarry with them, and who know the whole coast and understand the language [of their inhabitants]" (1974: 28). And Casson (1989: 61) translates: "[The merchants of Muza] send out to it merchant craft that they staff mostly with Arab skippers and agents who, through continual intercourse and intermarriage, are familiar with the area and its language."

[2] The ceramic shards have been examined by S. Gupta and K. Paddaya. S. Gupta corrected his identification of the two "Megalithic" shards from South Asia which he had initially dated to the beginning of the first

Egypt.[3] Glass beads from India and the Mediterranean have also been recovered,[4] but they are "difficult to use as temporal markers" (Sinclair 2008). According to M. Wood (2011: 24–25), none of these beads dates from a period earlier than the eighth or ninth century CE. Recent investigations in Ukunju Cave show "no evidence of any Pre-Middle Iron Age occupation and [ancient] long-distance trade at the site" (Fleisher and Wynne-Jones 2011; Crowther *et al.* 2014: 39), contrary to Chami's assertions. Two shards of Sassanian-Islamic pottery have been discovered, and five of the beads from the lowest excavated level are comparable to beads found at Ugunja Ukuu at Zanzibar, dated between the seventh and tenth centuries (Crowther *et al.* 2014: 37).

Shards found in another cave on Juani Island have been compared with Indian pottery from the first half of the first millennium CE (Sinclair 2008, according to Gupta p.c.): this dating still needs to be confirmed. Moreover, two eye beads have been recovered at Chibuene, in southern Mozambique; however, they probably date to the second half of the first millennium CE.[5]

Moreover, the Machaga Cave (Zanzibar) has yielded animal remains that Chami had identified as chicken bones; however, this identification has now been rejected.[6] This cave also contained items that may recall the Neolithic of the Rift Valley: stone bowl fragments, pottery similar to Narosura pottery (date range *c.* 2800–1400 BP [Lane 2013]), and harpoon remains. The discovery of a rubbing stone or pestle shows that plants (perhaps grains) were prepared, but this does not necessarily point to agricultural practices. Cat bones may also have been discovered, but this has not been confirmed.[7]

Associated with Bantu farmers, the rapid expansion of the Iron Age culture from the Great Lakes toward the coast may have been partly driven by the expansion of coastal trade – involving Late Stone Age groups – and may have followed routes linking the coast and the interior, notably along the Rufiji, to the town of Rhapta (de Maret 2013; Mitchell 2013).[8] The expansion of iron production and of farming

---

millennium BCE. P. Sinclair (2008) has pointed out that specialists in Indian pottery were unable to confirm Chami's claim.

[3] Chami 2006: 134–135. This pottery purportedly belongs to a type called "marled ware" produced in southern Egypt and traded with the Nubian kingdom of Napata (eighth and seventh centuries BCE). This pottery has been examined by P. Sinclair and H. Å. Nordström. One of the problems at the Ukunju site is that the waste area where the excavations have been conducted provides no clear stratigraphy (P. Sinclair, p.c.).

[4] Chami 2003: 77 n. 3; 2006: 135–136. Chami links a type of red (painted) pottery to the Greco-Roman world, as well as three beads in poor condition, including an ocellated glass bead and a banded bead, which he links alongside types produced in the Mediterranean (beads considered to be "Roman" by Chami and dated between 100 BCE and 200 CE have been unearthed on the African coast opposite the island). Remains of stone tools from the Late Stone Age have also been found. Chami also excavated what he considers to be a stone house dating to before the third century at a site on Juani Island (Mafia) (Chami 2000: 210 ff.).

[5] An Egypto-Phoenician origin *c.* 600–400 BCE is unlikely. M. Wood suggests that they were produced in the Mediterranean from the second half of the first millennium CE (P. Sinclair 2008).

[6] The problem is twofold: the identification of the animal and the dating. Most researchers are skeptical about this find (Robertshaw 2009).

[7] Chami 2002: 35ff. Shell beads have been discovered, also at Juani, where they are associated with Kwale pottery (*EIW*). Moreover, pottery from the Pre-Narosura tradition may have been found at Machaga Cave, associated by Chami with a date (/C^{14}) estimated at 2838 BCE (?) (Chami 2003: 75–76): this discovery needs confirmation.

[8] Also Wrigley 1997: 116; Spear 2000: 280; Chami 2001: 94.

communities[9] seem connected to a general growth in trade and an increasing demand for iron in the Mediterranean basin and the Indian Ocean.[10]

Excavations have revealed evidence for the arrival of the Early Iron Age culture on the Tanzanian coast between the Rufiji delta and the Ruvu River at the end of the first millennium BCE (the site of Limbo, near the coast, is dated to a period between the first century BCE and the third century CE).[11] This culture rapidly expanded along the coasts not only via "Bantu migrations," but also thanks to trade contacts and to local groups adopting new technologies (agriculture and ironworking) (de Maret 2013; Mitchell 2013).[12] Twenty or so sites have been discovered in the region of Limbo-Misasa.[13] For Chami, the sizeable scale of iron production suggests that not only local trade, but also overseas exports were being undertaken; however, this interpretation has been rejected by Killick (2009b) and Robertshaw (2009).

This Early Iron Age culture was soon present in the islands off the East African coast, which implies that there was nautical knowledge – an idea already proposed by linguists.[14] This knowledge, evidently acquired from the populations (perhaps partly Cushitic speakers)[15] living on the coasts and the islands,[16] is confirmed by the data given by the *Periplus* about Rhapta. Early Iron Age pottery (EIW) has been excavated on the islands of Kwale (third and fourth centuries), Koma, Mafia, Kilwa, and Zanzibar (Chami 1994, 1998: 199–221; Chami and Kombo 2009; Juma 2004) and in the Comoros (at a site on Moheli and three sites on Grande Comore, notably at Male)

---

[9] Plants cultivated included cereals (pearl millet *Pennisetum glaucum* [L.] R. Br., eleusine *Eleusine coracana* [L.] Gaertner, and sorghum *Sorghum bicolor* [L.] Moench), pulses (*Vigna unguiculata* [L.] Wal. and *Vigna subterranea* [L.] Verdc.), Cucurbitaceae, and probably bananas, brought from the Bantu migrants' region of origin and/or adopted following contacts with Cushitic populations in the region of Lake Nyanza or further north, perhaps as early as the beginning of the first millennium BCE. Communities practiced cattle, goat, and sheep breeding. Most researchers suggest that there was a slow advance through the forest from their center of origin in Cameroon, and that "Eastern Bantus" became differentiated in the region of Lake Nyanza or further south *c.* 1000 BCE (see Ehret 2001; Oliver 2001). The hypothesis that a large migration "of the Eastern Bantus eastward along the northern fringes of the rainforest" reached Lake Victoria "by about 1000 BC" (Bellwood 2005a: 220) is partially abandoned today.

[10] Chami 1999a: 205. Chami (2006), however, argues that agriculture was practiced as early as the third millennium by groups using Nderit type ceramics, which he claims to have unearthed at sites on the Tanzanian coast and on Mafia. D. Q. Fuller (2005: 523) has not excluded the possibility that pastoralism, for the groups with Nderit ceramics, may have been accompanied by "some crop cultivation."

[11] East of Limbo, Misasa has also yielded ancient dates: between the first century BCE and the first century AD: 2470 ± 70 BP, 2910 ± 70 BP, 1960 ± 70 BP [Beta 24619, 24620 and 24621] (Horton 1996: 409 n. 35).

[12] Chami 2001: 11. There was apparently a link between agricultural expansion, ironworking. and the spread of Bantu languages in the eastern part of the continent. Conversely, the connection between these various elements appears to be much more complex than was commonly assumed, on an African continental scale; see Vansina 1995; 2001; Ehret 1998, 2001; Eggert 2005.

[13] See the map and the dates of Early Iron Age sites given by Chami and Msemwa 1997: 674.

[14] Linguists have claimed "that Proto-Sabaki Bantu-speaking peoples arrived on the coast with a well-developed nautical technology" (Kusimba 1999: 76). Besides adopting techniques from coastal populations, Ehret (1998: 57, 276) mentions the existence of nautical traditions on the Great Lakes of the interior.

[15] According to Spear (2000: 270), the South Cushitic languages did not greatly influence Swahili. J. de V. Allen (1993), however, has suggested that the encounter between Cushitic herders and Bantu speakers along the Kenyan coast gave birth to the Swahili culture.

[16] See above for Chami's discoveries on Zanzibar (Machaga Cave) and Mafia (Chami and Kwekason 2003).

(Chami 2009: 108ff.). A Pre-Swahili coastal culture came into being further south, during the first centuries of the Christian era (Mitchell 2013). Sites located in southern Mozambique (Matola, Maputo, Zitundo) have yielded Early Iron Age pottery and traces of ironworking, dated between the beginning and the middle of the first millennium CE (Sinclair 1991: 191). In South Africa, the site of Silver Leaves goes back to the fifth century CE (*c.* 420–545) (Lane 2015: 496). South of the Limpopo River valley, the eastern stream (Kwale pottery) met a western Bantu stream, which may have originated in Angola (Mitchell 2013). Moreover, a type of pottery called Nkope, found in central Tanzania, Zambia, Malawi, Zimbabwe, and northern South Africa, reflects another Bantu stream southward that parallels the coastal stream (Kwale pottery) (Lane 2015: 495; Robertshaw 2015: 108). In the north, on the Somali coast, shards of Kwale pottery have been unearthed in the region of Barawa. Chami has argued for BCE datings for Kwale pottery in Tanzania; BCE dates on Kwale/Matola pottery have been confirmed from southern Mozambique (Kohtamäki 2014).

For T. Spear, the distribution of EIW coincides with that of speakers of the "North East Coast languages," present on the Tanzanian coast during the first centuries of the Christian era, and later with their expansion. The advance of these speakers along the Kenyan coast would have contributed to the formation of the Sabaki languages around the middle of the first millennium (Nurse and Hinnebusch 1993: 491–493; Spear 2000: 258–259, 271). Neologisms in the Proto-North-East Coast (PNEC) languages include terms such as **kisi(l)wa*, "island," **mupunga*, "rice," and perhaps **kitamba(la)*, "cloth" (Nurse and Hinnebusch 1993: 288–289). Words appeared in Proto-Sabaki between 350 and 650 CE, such as **izigu*, "banana," **ikuti*, "leaf of coconut tree," and **mbalazi*, "pigeon-pea" (*Cajanus cajan* [L.] Millsp., a plant of Indian origin) (van der Maesen 1995: 251–252), as well as loanwords from Indian Ocean languages: **mpula*, "steel" (cf. Persian *pulad*, Hindi *faulad*), **muTungi*, "waterpot" (Persian *tung*), **ngamila*, "dromedary" (Arabic *jamil*), **lwavu*, "fishing net" (from Persia or India), and probably **nkamba*, "rope" (Persian *kanaba*), **popoo*, "Areca nut" (Persian *pupal*, Arabic and Hindi *faufal*), **tambulu*, "betel" (Persian *tambuul*, and Arabic *tanbul*, Hindi *tambol*).[17] **Mbalazi* (see above) may be a loanword from the Dravidian languages;[18] it seems likely that **kilazi*, "potato [sic] (yam, or tuber)" is another loanword from languages of the Indian Ocean (Nurse and Hinnebusch 1993: 292). The term *chirāze* noted in Mozambique for "yam" in the nineteenth century probably derives from **kilazi*.[19] The Antemoro dialect (southeastern Madagascar) has *kirary*, "yam" (in Arabic-Malagasy manuscripts),

---

[17] Nurse and Hinnebusch (1993: 316–317) record six likely loanwords and six possible ones. The term **ilema*, "fishing net," is a loanword from the Persian *dam* or from an Indian language (cf. Hindi *dam*); it goes back either to the Proto-Sabaki or the Proto-Swahili (Nurse and Hinnebusch 1993: 295–296).

[18] Nurse and Hinnebusch 1993: 290–292. G. Philippson suggests a (hypothetical) old Bantu word, **mbalawali*, which may be a loanword from Dravidian languages (see below). Moreover, Nurse and Hinnebusch have reconstructed **ncoloko*, "cowpea" (*Vigna unguiculata*) in Proto-Sabaki. In Swahili, however, *mčoroko* (southern Swahili dialects), refers to *Vigna radiata* (L.) Wilczek, as well as the term *voantsoroko* in southern Madagascar, a plant of Indian origin (in contrast, *Vigna unguiculata* is an African plant). One might wonder whether the botanical identification of **ncoloko* was correct, and/or if the term is a loanword. C. Ehret (1998: 329) has suggested a borrowing from South Cushitic languages (PSC **salak^w*, black-eyed pea, *Vigna unguiculata*).

[19] For *chirāze*, see Randles 1975: 71, who quotes A. M. Pacheco 1883.

which may be a loanword from an East African language. There is a visible link between the Proto-Sabaki *kilazi and the Malay keladi, "taro," which is a loanword, that can also be found in other languages (aladi in Makassar, for example) (Blust [1973] has reconstructed the PMP *kala(dDj)i, "a kind of large sized taro," but in support of this reconstruction, he notes only Malay keladi and Hanunoo kaladiq, where the -q is unexplained)).[20] A Dravidian etymology could ultimately be envisaged: one finds kilaru, kilari in Tamil, "to dig (up)" (Burrow and Emeneau 1961, entry 1321). Moreover, the term kērīr has been noted in Yemen for "taro,"[21] and kirre, in Kolami and Naikri (Dravidian languages), means "yam." Southworth has reconstructed *kiẓ, "root, tuber," in Proto-Dravidian (Southworth 2005: 219). An affinity between these terms and *kilazi is however dubious. In any event, across the entire Indian Ocean, linguistic data seem to mix yam and taro.

The Periplus of the Erythraean Sea gives us precious information on trade during the first century. On the African coast, after the Cape of Spices, it describes the ports of Pano, Opōnē, Sarapion, Nikon, the Pyralae Islands [Lamu archipelago], Menuthias [Zanzibar or Pemba], and lastly an emporium called Rhapta, "the very last market-town of the continent of Azania," perhaps located at the mouth of the Ruvu, or more likely the Rufiji River, north of Kilwa, if the island of Menuthias (paragr. 15) can be identified as Zanzibar[22] (see Map II.18). "Each port of trade is administered by its own chief" (Periplus, paragr. 14, Casson 1989: 59): (proto-) city-states were already present along the coast.

The trade in spices at Opōnē and other places, emphasized by the Periplus, has been mentioned above. The Periplus also notes that "better-quality slaves" could be found at Opōnē, "the greater number of which go to Egypt," as well as "tortoiseshell in great quantity and finer than any other"; slaves and tortoiseshell probably came from further south on the East African coast. The slave trade was therefore already active at this time.

Rhapta was clearly of particular significance. The town, according to the Periplus, paid tribute to a Yemeni king who controlled the port of Muza. It seems that the East African coast that the ancients called Azania was "under the domination of whichever was the most powerful Arab state" (Vérin 1994: 49). At Rhapta, one can already observe a situation that became common in later times: a cosmopolitan town, inhabited by a mixed population. The Periplus notes that Rhapta exported ivory (in "large quantity"), rhino horn, turtleshell ("the most in demand after that of India"), products that would later be mentioned in the Arab and Chinese chronicles. The Azanian

---

[20] Expressing an unlikely theory, R. Portères has suggested that keladi is of Sanskrit origin (kala-, "black," and haridra-, Curcuma), via the Bengali kalahaldi referring to "a black-blue Curcuma," Curcuma caesia Roxb. According to Portères (1960: 181), this color would explain the transfer of the name from one plant to another. Haldi is Curcuma longa L. in Bengali (Turner). Kalahaldi is also known in Marathi for Curcuma caesia (Wealth of India). Portères has mentioned a similar Gujarati term, but for Curcuma, the Gujarati language uses more distantly related terms: haldar, haled, haladh (Turner).

[21] There is probably no link with the term kiri-ala (ala referring to tuber in general) for a variety of taro in Sri Lanka (MacMillan 1999 [1935]: 289).

[22] Ptolemy (Book 4, chs. 7 and 8, 1932: 108–109 ed. Stevenson) describes Rhapta as a city located slightly inland along the Raphtus River, north of Cape Rhaptum (Freeman-Grenville gives the name Rhapton for the river and the cape). The distance given between Cape Rhaptum and Cape Prason (Cape Delgado) suggests that Rhapta was located near Bagamoyo. Through a new reading of Ptolemy, some authors such as M. Horton (1996: 20) locate Rhapta on the coast facing the Lamu archipelago. It is unlikely that Rhapta was located on Pemba or Zanzibar, but the site could well be under water today ((Insoll 2003: 145–146).

market's imports were dominated notably by iron tools and weapons, a fact that does not really support Chami's claim that iron was exported by the East African coast. Foreign ships also brought in glass items. Rhapta must have been a center of significant size as it is the only place on the coast that Ptolemy called *metropolis*. The existence of a "metropolis" implies organized systems of exchange with the interior, with trade agreements and groups acting as intermediaries, as would be the case in later periods. As Tomber notices, "Ptolemy presents a more detailed description of the East African coast . . . that may reflect an increased Greco-Roman participation" during the second century (2012a: 98).

According to the *Periplus* (paragr. 18), Arab seamen did not sail further than Rhapta. Ptolemy informs us that the "merchants of Eudaimon Arabia" sailed to the Azanian coast as far as Rhapta, and beyond that as far as Cape Prason, east of which lay Menuthias Island (probably Madagascar). Ptolemy does not seem to be familiar with the coast south of the Delgado Cape. Was the ocean, "further," really "unexplored"? Did the Greco-Roman world know the Comoros Islands and Madagascar? It remains possible that ships sailed south of Rhapta and reached these islands. In this case the arrival of people from Egypt, western Asia, and East Africa in Madagascar and the Comoros ought to be placed at an earlier date. Pliny (VI.152) (first century CE) mentions: *Regio Amithoscatta, Damnia, Mizi maiores and minores, Drimati*, which H. von Wissmann (1968) interprets as referring to "Madagascar, Domoni (on Anjouan Island), the Wamizi Islands (to the north of Mozambique) and the region of Mozambique corresponding to Mrima" (Martin 2010). Chittick (1970) considered Amithoscatta to be northern Madagascar. Allibert (Flacourt 2007: 460–461) has pointed out that the ending *scatta/scutta* for Amithoscatta means "turtle shell" and may refer to the Comoros, but it may well be northern Madagascar, as Chittick suggests (today this region is inhabited by an ethnic group called Antankaraña, from Malagasy *haraña*, "(turtle) shell"). The plausible link established between Damnia and Domoni points to a dual Arabic and Bantu origin; a possible etymology for Domoni is *dumu*, "to go on, to persevere," from the Arabic *dāma*, "to last," with the Bantu locative –*ni*, or the Arabic *dimna*, "vestiges." These suggestions are supported by the recent discovery of East African Iron Age pottery at Comorian sites (see above). A coin dating to Emperor Constantine (306–337 CE) was also discovered at the beginning of the twentieth century in the sands of a promontory near Majunga, but it is difficult to deduce anything from this find (J. and S. Chauvicourt 1968). Note, however, that a shard unearthed on the northern coast of Nosy Be Island, in the hamlet of Ampasindava, might be from a Mediterranean amphora dated to the first half of the first millennium CE (Wright, Radimilahy, and Allibert 2005). Interestingly, the *Periplus* and Ptolemy differ with regard to the location of Menuthias Island. According to the *Periplus*, Menuthias lay 300 stades from the coast, north of Rhapta, or two days' sail away (ch. 16), so it may well refer to Zanzibar. Ptolemy's *Geography* gives Menuthias as located southeast of Cape Prason (Cape Delgado): in this case, it could be Madagascar.[23]

---

[23] Ptolemy, Book 4, ch. 8, 1932: 109, and Horton 1993: 451. Chami (1999a: 207) has suggested locating Ptolemy's Menuthias in the Comoros.

Comorian traditions state that Arab migrants arrived before the advent of Islam: "Our ancestors told us that Gazizad [Ngazija] was first inhabited, after the arrival of the prophet Salomon Ben Daoudou . . . At this time, two Arabs came from the Red Sea with their wives, children and slaves. They settled in Grande Comore. Later, many men arrived, from Africa, the coast of Zanguebar, and they settled in the [Comoro] islands" (Gevrey 1870: 74).

Beyond the "markets of Azania," according to the *Periplus*, "lies unexplored ocean that bends to the west and, extending on the south along the parts of Ethiopia and Libya and Africa that turn away, joins the western sea": seamen, therefore, had sailed around the Cape of Good Hope (*Periplus*, paragr. 18; Casson 1989: 61).

Archaeology provides only limited evidence for artifacts from the Greco-Roman world and from India on the coasts of East Africa. Twenty kilometers away from the mouth of the Rufiji River, the site of Mkukutu-Kibiti has yielded beads considered to be "Roman" by Chami.[24] However, similar beads have been attested for the ninth–tenth century (Sinclair 2008), and M. Wood has rejected these identifications. A bead made of monochrome glass has been found in the Machaga cave excavated at Zanzibar: it may come from Arikamedu.[25] Red pottery similar to Roman pottery attested at Ras Hafun has also been unearthed in the Zanzibar cave, as well as green/ yellow pottery also excavated in the Rufiji delta and at Ras Hafun (Chami and Kwekason 2003: 41). M. Boussac, however, has identified the red pottery as an Indian copy of Roman pottery. Allibert and Vérin (1993b: 66) write that: "Shards of Greco-Roman pottery of a similar type have been found at Ras Hafun (Opōnē in the *Periplus*), at Arikamedu (near Pondicherry) in India, and at Chibuene in Mozambique." In fact, no Greco-Roman pottery has ever been identified at Chibuene, a coastal trading station dating to the late first millennium and early second millennium. It is likely that "Roman" trade went beyond Rhapta, perhaps as far as Natal, but evidence for this is still missing.

Trade routes linked Rhapta to Central Tanzania and the Great Lakes. Beyond these lakes, according to Chami, they probably continued toward the Middle Nile and Meroe, well known for its considerable iron production (Chami 2001: 94). When Nero sent an expedition to explore the sources of the Nile around the middle of the first century CE, "the king of Meroe gave a letter of introduction to be used by the crew of the expedition on the way to the source of the Nile. The king's letter suggests that Meroe had some kind of relationship with the interlacustrine region" (Chami 1999a: 207).[26] These networks led the Greek Diogenes, during the first century CE, to travel inland from Rhapta, where he saw two lakes and the "Mountains of the Moon" (Ruwenzori Mountains) where the Nile takes its source (however, it is possible that

---

[24] Chami 1999b: 239. According to Chami, one of the four beads found (a segmented bead) was produced on the island of Rhodes between 100 BCE and 200 CE (2002: 41; 2006: 134). This bead may actually be dated to the second half of the first millennium CE (Sinclair 2008).

[25] It has been dated by M. Boussac (Lyon) to between 100 BCE and 400 CE. A carnelian bead has also been excavated. As already mentioned, glass beads have been unearthed in a cave on Juani Island (near Mafia) (see above). "Roman" and "Partho-Sassanid" glass beads have been discovered on the Horn of Africa (Axum and Ras Hafun) (Chami 2002: 41).

[26] Before Herodotus, the Egyptians knew of the existence of snow-clad mountains and of a great lake at the source of the Nile (see above).

Diogenes collected information on the sources of the Nile and the "Mountains of the Moon" at Rhapta).[27] Ptolemy's *Geography* shows that some knowledge of the sources of the Nile existed, suggesting connections between the coast, the Great Lakes region, and the Nile (a mountain range – probably the Ruwenzori – provided water for a lake that constituted the source of the Nile).

The Roman presence along the East African coast was obviously intended to short-circuit Arab control over trade.[28] According to the *Periplus* and Latin texts of the fourth and fifth centuries, the king of Himyar kept East Africa under his control.[29] When the Roman Empire went into decline, after the third century CE, Axum dominated the Red Sea, but commerce on the East African coast was in the hands of Arab and then Persian merchants (the Persian Gulf would take on increasing importance until the great period of the eighth–tenth century).

As mentioned above, the *Periplus* named the East African coast *Azania*. Strabo was the first author to use this term; he also wrote of a Zangenae population, although it is not well located. We also find the terms "Zangenae" in Pliny (VI.176) for an African population, "Zinggis" (for a cape) in Ptolemy (I, XVII), and "Zingyon" (for a region) in Cosmas Indicopleustes. Pliny writes of the "Azanian sea," that began around Adulis. The word may be related to the Arabic and Persian *Zanj* or *Zang*, which designated – until the thirteenth century – the East African coast and the black people who lived there.[30] In India, Zanzibar received the name of Kaliyadvipa, "island of the Blacks" (Ray 1999a: 228). The slaves who revolted in Lower Mesopotamia during the ninth century are referred to as "Zanj" (see below). Other etymologies have been suggested, from the Arabic *'ajam* ("foreigner, non-Arab"), or the Greek *azainein* ("to dry, parch"). The term Azania is rendered as Zesan in the Chinese chronicle *Weilue* (third century).

Research in the 1950s and 1960s (see Kirkman 1954, 1970) emphasized the importance of Arabo–Persian arrivals in the development of the East African coast, but recent works have pointed out the African character of the pre-Swahili culture that was forming. It is clear today that the expansion of this culture cannot be uniquely explained by Arabo–Persian "colonization" and the rise of Islam, even though Arabs, particularly Yemenis, had been active for centuries on the African coasts. "Archaeological as well as linguistic and historical evidence, notes Horton, gives no indication of widespread Asiatic settlement in East Africa before the nineteenth century. Notions of Arab colonists establishing trading outposts on the African coast

---

[27] Cary and Warmington 1963: 214; Chami 2001: 16. This mention of the "Mountains of the Moon" is repeated by Marinus of Tyre. The Indian *Puranas*, "written between the 1st and the 4th centuries CE [more likely between 400 and 1000 CE], also mention the Mountains of the Moon" (Schoff 1974: 87–88).

[28] Trajan's expedition in 105 CE against the Nabataean territory, mentioned above, shows that the Roman Empire sometimes attacked Arab merchant bases.

[29] Salles 1998: 67. The king of Himyar was also said to be the "king of the Indians," which may reflect some control over the Persian Gulf, given by Syriac sources of this period as the "Indian Sea" (Salles 1998).

[30] The etymologies of Azania and Zanji given by Chami (2002: 33) are fanciful. Some researchers have suggested a Persian etymology *zang* or *zeng*, from an old term meaning "black" (?) (Schoff 1974: 92). G. Ferrand (1924: 240) also believes that the origin of the term is Persian. C. H. Becker and D. M. Dunlop (1999) give the Zoroastrian Pahlawī *zangik*, "negro." J. Devic (1975) has suggested the Ethiopian *zengua*, "to chatter." P. Dreyer (1980) points to Cushitic terms meaning "brother," *san, zan, zin*. For discussions on the origins of this term, see Popovic 1976: 54–55 and Hilton 1992. One finds different spellings in Arabic: *zanj, zinj, zanji, zinji* (plur. *zunuj*).

are improbable and can be dismissed" (Horton 1996: 407) (see also Chami 1998: 199). The fact remains that Indian Ocean trade, led by Arabs, Persians, Indians, and Austronesians, was crucial to the development of Pre-Swahili towns and probably to the movements of farmers and ironworking groups toward the coast.

The routes linking the coast to the Great Lakes are known thanks to archaeological data. In the 1950s, L. Leakey discovered a carnelian bead of Indian origin and cowries in a Neolithic tomb in the Ngorongoro crater, dated to the seventh century BCE. A small cylindrical faience bead (perhaps of Egyptian or Nubian origin) was also excavated by Leakey at Nakuru (Kenya) in the tomb of a chief dated to 1000–750 BCE.[31] At the site of Seronera (Serengeti, Tanzania, first century BCE), Bower (1973) unearthed 800 glass beads and a faience bead similar to those found in Egypt. At Kondoa, in central Tanzania, red rock paintings (difficult to date, but considered to be earlier than 500 CE), show "two men in cloaks leading a line of chained men, wearing skins with tails,"most likely a depiction of a caravan of slaves, perhaps led by coastal people (possibly foreigners).[32] Rock shelters in Bungule, a site in the Taita-Tsavo region in southeastern Kenya, have yielded cowries that were used as ornaments, dated to the beginning of the first millennium (Kusimba and Kusimba 2005: 409).

Contacts between the East African coast and the maritime networks of the Indian Ocean may go back to earlier times. Previous chapters have mentioned the discovery of copal in Mesopotamia in a third-millennium context, that of faience beads similar to those produced during the Eighteenth Dynasty of Egypt in the Juba country (South Sudan), the exchange of plants between India and Africa during the second millennium BCE, and the introduction of the plantain (see above).

Curiously, the *Periplus of the Erythraean Sea* does not mention any agriculture on the East African coast (for the author of the *Periplus*, agriculture was a common activity, so it may be that it was not worth mentioning). It has been thought that the text spoke of "a little palm oil" [from coconut] being exported from Azania: for this translation, it is necessary to "correct" the word *nauplios* to *nargilios* (cf. Prākrit, Persian: *nargil*, "coconut") (Schoff [1912] 1974: 99), but the word *nauplios* is present in Pliny's work, where it refers to a shellfish "so called as it moves with its shell like a vessel" (nautilus) (Lewis 1998: 1191). The *Periplus* indicates the importation of "honey from the reed called *sacchari*" (sugarcane) from India to the Horn of Africa, but the text does not mention anywhere that sugarcane was grown on the East African coast.[33]

[31] Contrary to Leakey's claim, Beck (1931: 282) does not believe that it is of Egyptian origin. A. Manzo (1999) erroneously indicates a date of 2000 BCE for this bead from Nakuru. Faience objects did not necessarily come from Egypt: its production developed in the Kerma culture at an early time.

[32] Chami 2001: 94; Leakey 1983: 74. Cave art painted in red is considered to be the most ancient. Later, rupestral art used orange, white, and black.

[33] Schoff 1974: 27, 90. However, a passage at paragraph 16 concerning Rhapta has been understood by L. Casson (1989: 61) to refer to "men very great in stature, tillers of the soil;" the last expression translates the word *oratoi*, adjusted to become *arotoi*, but this interpretation has been contested. The *Periplus* mentions the offering of "a little wine and wheat" to the natives, "not for trade but to serve for getting the good-will of the savages" (Schoff 1974: 99). On the term *oratoi* and agricultural practice in the region of Rhapta, see the publications by M. Horton (1990) and C. Wrigley (1997) concerning the translation of the *Periplus* presented by L. Casson (1989). "The *Periplus*," writes Wrigley, "does not require us to posit an agricultural population at the coast in the first century AD" (1997: 115). See in contrast Chami 2001.

From the fourth century on, the region of Zanzibar appears to have been the center of gravity for trade.[34] Among the sites that existed before the Islamic period, Horton mentions, for the north of the Swahili coast, Manda (Manda Island, where the first levels go back to the fifth century),[35] and Shanga (on Pate Island, inhabited since the sixth century, but more sizeable during the eighth and ninth centuries) on the Kenyan coast; Unguja Ukuu and Fukuchani at Zanzibar; and Mkadini, Mzizima, Kunduchi, and Kaole on the coast facing Zanzibar.

A greater number of coastal sites was already noticeable in Tanzania during the "Azanian phase" (Chami), from 300 to 600 CE, and later – with more dispersed settlements – during the "Zanj phase" from 600 to 1000. During the latter period, a type of Tana Ware (Horton) – called "triangular incised ware" (TIW) by Chami – succeeded Early Iron Age culture pottery (see below).

Between the fourth and sixth centuries CE, Axum dominated the Red Sea. The decrease in trade between the Mediterranean and the Indian Ocean may have affected East Africa. Axum itself went into decline after the mid-sixth century. Arabs and, more importantly, Sassanids displaced the Roman, Egyptian, and Axumite merchants in the networks operating along the East African coast. The two ports of Sirāf and Sohar bear witness to the activities of the merchants of the Persian Gulf and Oman in the Indian Ocean even before the Islamic period. Persians and Arabs certainly came to the Azanian coast to acquire ivory and slaves.[36]

For the Pre-Islamic period, imports (in limited quantity) have been unearthed on the Somali, Kenyan, and Tanzanian coasts, but also at sites in the hinterland not far from the coasts: green-blue Sassanid pottery, at Ras Hafun (where it is dated between the first century BCE and the fifth century CE), Fukuchani, Unguja Ukuu,[37] and Kivinja; "eggshell ware" at Ras Hafun (dated to a period between the fifth and seventh centuries);[38] and glass (vessels and beads) (the Kivinja find [north of the mouth of the Rufiji] remains doubtful, but Roman glass has been excavated at Unguja Ukuu).[39] During this period, Unguja Ukuu (Zanzibar) was the most significant center for oceanic exchanges. This site has yielded "a wide variety of imports, from India, the Middle East and the Roman world, all dated to the fifth to seventh century, including pottery, glassware, beads, alabaster, and various kinds of metals" (Juma 1996: 148–154; Chami and Msemwa 1997: 675). Juma has excavated Roman ceramics from

---

[34] We do not know what the size of Rhapta was at this time: the city is mentioned in texts from the first and second centuries, but has not been discovered by archaeologists.

[35] Horton 1996: 408. The oldest northern site is located just south of Mogadishu. Horton then mentions Kiunga (a coastal site north of the Lamu archipelago), Pate and Mbui (on these islands), and the site of Ungwana, near the mouth of the Tana River (1996: 408). Besides Unguja Ukuu and Fukuchani, two other, older sites are attested in Zanzibar, located in the northwestern part of the island: Mkokotoni and Pwani Deburi.

[36] "The first Zanj slaves arrived [in the Persian Gulf] at this time" (Horton and Middleton 2000: 73).

[37] The production of this pottery continued into the early Islamic period, whence its name, "Sassano-Islamic." The production of this type of pottery may go back to the third century BCE (Chami and Msemwa 1997: 675). It is present in the first levels of Unguja Ukuu, where a complete jar has been excavated, with a form similar to that found at Sirāf (Juma 2004). For the East African coast, various authors consider this pottery to date to the Islamic period (Glover 2002; see Sinclair 2008).

[38] This pottery has also been found further south on the Mozambique coast.

[39] A light green glass fragment and a blue glass bead have also been unearthed at the site of Kirungwi-Mkundi, on the small island of Ziweziwe, north of Kisiju (north of Kivinja) (Kessy 1997).

Egypt dated to the fifth or sixth century, which probably came through Ras Hafun with Axumite or Persian merchants, and glass of the same provenance (vessels, beads). Chinese stoneware has been unearthed in layers preceding the Islamic period, for example green-glazed Yue stoneware, and early Changsha pottery (Juma 2004: 107); these finds correspond to the Sassanid expansion in the Indian Ocean and probably in the China Sea. Chloritoschist decorated with dotted circles, a type of decoration already attested in the Persian Gulf during the Bronze Age, has also been discovered. Visits by Indian ships are a possibility: an Indian from the sixth or seventh century tells the story of a merchant who traveled as far as "the island of the Black Yavana," probably on the East African coast (Basham 1967: 227). The remains of domestic cats, which are genetically different from the East African wild cat, have been identified (Ottoni *et al.* 2013). Glass beads made of soda-alumina glass (m-Na-Al 1) found at Unguja Ukuu may come from Mantai (Sri Lanka). Similar beads are present at the Red Sea port of Berenice in contexts dated between the fourth and sixth centuries: "it raises the possibility that a trading circuit that operated between Sri Lanka and the Red Sea also included Unguja Ukuu, in this early period" (Wood 2015: paragr. 20). The m-Na-Al 1 glass (containing more barium and less uranium) was made in Sri Lanka (and possibly South India) between the fifth century BCE and the tenth century CE (Dussubieux *et al.* 2010).

The Zanzibar Museum owns Parthian and Sassanid coins dated between 41 and 241 CE. Their exact provenance is unknown, unfortunately. A gold coin of Ptolemy IX (116–107 BCE) was sold to a tourist at Dar-es-Salaam in 1901. Other discoveries of Ptolemaic, Roman, Axumite, and Byzantine coins have been made at Kimoni (near Tanga); at Bur Gao (Roman coins from the fourth century); in Zanzibar (at Dimbani); in Pemba; but never in stratigraphic contexts. Some of them have been discovered in the interior: a sesterce in the name of Severus Alexander in Uganda; an *antoninianus* of Victorinus at Nairobi; a coin of Antoninus Pius at Umtali in Zimbabwe, where gold was exploited in ancient times; an Indian Kushan coin of the king Huvishka (around 130–150 CE) at Inyanga in Zimbabwe; a coin of Claudius II (268–270) (minted at Alexandria) at Bindura, in Zimbabwe, and so forth.[40] Even though the circumstances of the discoveries raise doubts, their number and their locations (especially in Zimbabwe) seem to be significant.

On the Mozambican coast, the significant site of Chibuene, perhaps already inhabited by the middle of the first millennium, has yielded TIW, as well as a type of pottery belonging to the Gokomere-Ziwa tradition, green-glazed pottery from the Persian Gulf attested at Sohar and Ras Hafun, and "eggshell ware," also discovered at Ras Hafun (see above).[41] Red-slipped pottery with graphite decoration has also been unearthed, a type of pottery found at other East African sites (see below).

The expansion of the Indian Ocean trade south of the Zambezi could be linked to copper and gold exploitation, as these metals are both found in the Zimbabwe region. Copper was already being extracted during the first centuries of the Christian era (Herbert 1984: 25). This metal probably first attracted merchants from the north; gold

---

[40] A list of these finds has been published by Horton 1993: 446–448; also Sheriff 1984: 597–598; Chami 2006: 130–131. A shard probably of Nabataean origin has been found by Chittick at Kisimani Mafia.

[41] Sinclair 1982; 1991: 190. All these ceramics have been found also at Unguja Ukuu in levels Ia (see above). However, T. Spear (2000: 264) is skeptical about a date for Chibuene going back to the middle of the first millennium. He suggests that the first occupation began during the eighth century.

was introduced later into the trade networks (possibly during the seventh/eighth century).[42] Interestingly, among the copper beads that have been found at Mabveni between 180 and 570 CE (Huffman 1980), two were made of high-tin bronze, even though tin bronze appeared in southern Africa only during the second millennium (Thondhlana and Martinón-Torres 2009: 90): either the beads are intrusive or they were imported. As early as the sixth century, "some backwater communities in the Victoria Falls region obtained copper, ostrich eggshell, and even Egyptian glass through trade networks constituted in southern Zambezia" (Pikirayi 2001: 250; Vogel 1990). As was perhaps the case on the Kenyan and Tanzanian coasts, iron may also have been exported. A cowry found at the Iron Age site of Kwali signals connections between southeastern Zimbabwe and the coast during the sixth century (Swan 2007b: 333). Note that within the "Zambian Belt," copper trade expanded around the middle of the first millennium without any significant influence from oceanic networks, but instead within the context of regional developments. Naviundu, at the border between Congo and Zambia, has provided the oldest date for copper objects in eastern Africa with bar-shaped ingot fragments, dated to 345±75 CE (Bisson 2000: 115). Copper was first used for manufacturing prestige goods, and the ingots themselves would later become symbols of power (Swan 2007a: 1001).

An older exploitation of gold cannot be excluded. Some researchers have referred here to Cosmas Indicopleustes, who wrote of a land called Sasu, where the Axumites traveled to trade for gold. However, Cosmas mentions not maritime expeditions, but instead a land journey of "50 stadia." The location of Sasu beyond the Azanian coast is therefore improbable. D. W. Phillipson locates Sasu southwest of Lake Tana, in northwestern Ethiopia (2012: 203).

Along with archaeology and texts, genetic research on commensal animals has also provided evidence for transoceanic contacts. Genetic studies of rats in the islands of the western Indian Ocean and Madagascar "point to origins in India, probably via Arabia or the Middle East" (Tollenaere et al. 2010; Fuller et al. 2011: 552). The mitochondrial DNA of the Malagasy house mouse (*Mus musculus*) has shown that it "probably originated from the Arabian peninsula in a single wave of colonization" (Duplantier et al. 2002) (see below for Madagascar). The Asian house shrew (*Suncus murinus*) originated in South Asia. Its "high morphological variability in East Africa and the Arabian Peninsula suggests multiple introductions directly from South Asia and from early differentiated types of Southeast Asia" (Hingston et al. 2005; Fuller et al. 2011: 552). These different introductions, however, are not well dated.

The emergence of the Pre-Swahili culture, which we have followed here, was not uniquely a result of the connection between expanding East African coastal populations and merchant networks linked to the Red Sea, the South Arabian coast, the Persian Gulf and India. Amongst the people who sailed to the East African coast and contributed to the development of the (pre-)Swahili culture were Austronesians from Southeast Asia: this process provides evidence for the formation of an Afro-Eurasian world-system at the beginning of the Christian era.

---

[42] Swan 1994: 119. Copper bracelets have been excavated at various Zimbabwean sites "between 250 and 550" CE (Miller 2003). In Transvaal, the site of Broederstroom has yielded copper beads and a copper chain (c. sixth century).

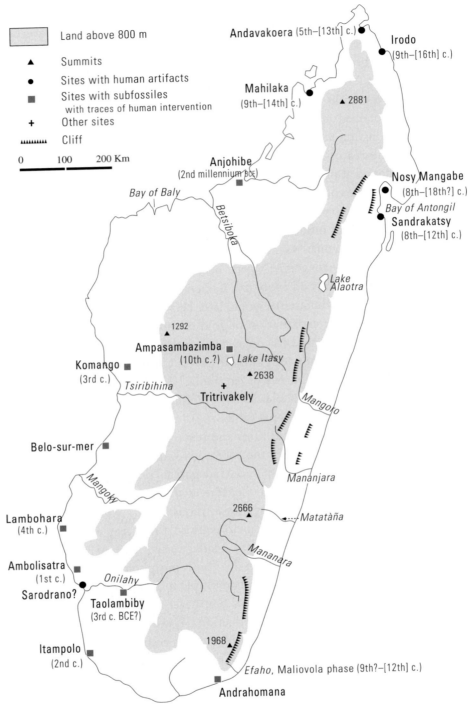

Land above 800 m

▲ Summits

● Sites with human artifacts

■ Sites with subfossiles
with traces of human intervention

+ Other sites

⌢⌢⌢⌢⌢ Cliff

0   100   200 Km

Andavakoera (5th–[13th] c.)

Irodo
(9th–[16th] c.)

Mahilaka
(9th–[14th] c.)

▲ 2881

Nosy Mangabe
(8th–[18th?] c.)

Anjohibe
(2nd millennium BCE)

Bay of Baly

Betsiboka

Bay of Antongil

Sandrakatsy
(8th–[12th] c.)

Lake Alaotra

▲ 1292

Ampasambazimba
(10th c.?) ◊ *Lake Itasy*

Komango
(3rd c.)

Tsiribihina

+
Tritrivakely

▲ 2638

Mangoro

Belo-sur-mer

Mananjara

Mangoky

▲ 2666

·····▶ *Matatàña*

Lambohara
(4th c.)

Mananara

Ambolisatra
(1st c.)

Onilahy

Sarodrano?

Taolambiby
(3rd c. BCE?)

1968 ▲

Itampolo
(2nd c.)

Efaho, Maliovola phase (9th?–[12th] c.)

Andrahomana

Map II.20   Madagascar: ancient sites (first–ninth century CE)

15 The Austronesian Expansion and the First Malagasy Cultures

Austronesians in the Western Indian Ocean

It is certain that Austronesians reached the western Indian Ocean at the end of the first millennium BCE or even earlier (see below). These migrations did not come about by accident, but were based on commercial strategies embedded in evolving exchange networks throughout the Indian Ocean. It is likely that the Austronesians tried to take advantage of the demand from the West – and also from the East – transporting coveted products (above all spices), along routes that bypassed India and allowed them to reach East Africa directly. It may be within this context that Austronesians later settled in the Comoros and Madagascar. These "Pre-Malagasy" Austronesians were probably different from the first Austronesian migrants on the East African coast, however, and the Pre-Malagasy may have migrated for political reasons.

The Austronesians followed various routes from Southeast Asia to the western Indian Ocean:

1. A first route crossed the Bay of Bengal (sailing during the boreal winter) with a stop-over in South India and Sri Lanka; this route might then either follow the coasts, using what has been called "the Sabaean lane" between India and Africa, or continue on directly to East Africa, and/or the Comoros and northern Madagascar, stopping over in the Maldives. Surface currents and winds facilitated journeys from India or Sri Lanka to East Africa in February–March with the northeast monsoon,[1] and from Africa to India or Sri Lanka in August–September with the southwest monsoon (storms in June–July made traveling at this time more dangerous); departures from the East African coast also occurred in April–May, before the rise of the southwest monsoon.[2]

2. A second route went to the Maldives, and on to East Africa, the Comoros and Madagascar from Sumatra, favored by the North Equatorial Current (February–March).

---

[1] During the boreal winter, the North Equatorial current flows along the East African coast, "allowing landing between Cape Gardafui and Zanzibar" (Donque 1965: 57). Ships could also leave India bound for East Africa in December (thus avoiding the strong winds of October–November).

[2] From Arabia to India, ships sailed in both directions with the northeast monsoon. One reads too often that the "voyages [of the Arabs] were made one way with the north-east monsoon, and the other with the south-west, [but] sailing traders in the Indian Ocean had to use the good season – the north-east – for their passages *both* ways, taking care to get back to port before the full force of the south-west monsoon broke on them" (Villiers 1952: 53).

3. A third route went directly to the Comoros and Madagascar via the Chagos from Java and the Sunda Strait, using the South Equatorial Current, which was practicable from May to October. "A coastal arrival may have occurred [in Madagascar] between Antongil Bay and Cap d'Ambre, but by using secondary currents bearing to the southwest from the longitudes 50–60°E, one could reach more southerly regions along the eastern Malagasy coast; it was even possible, by continuing the circumnavigation, to reach the Cap Sainte-Marie-Tulear-Morondava coastal sector" (Donque 1965: 56). The return journey, as P.-Y. Manguin points out (1993: 11), was impossible on this route: ships were required to sail north of the Equator in order to reach the Maldives. Insulindian sailors were probably the only mariners – possibly with the Maldivians – who took this route, as shown by Portuguese texts from the sixteenth century.

Between East Africa and Madagascar, navigation was arduous due to crosscurrents and the frequency of tropical storms during the summer. During the winter, ships could use the Mozambique Channel and take advantage of the weak south–north current flowing along the western coast of Madagascar. By tacking, a northwest–southeast itinerary was possible, toward the Comoros and the northwest of Madagascar. "To come from Southwest Asia," notes however P. Vérin, "it is convenient to take advantage of the steady summer winds. It is not difficult then, by sailing downwind, to reach the Comoros, the northwest, and even the northeast of Madagascar, by benefiting from the diffluence at Cap d'Ambre." "In contrast, the return journey can be more easily accomplished during the cooler season when the trade wind is well established. Moreover, during the cooler season, it is not difficult, coming from the northeast, to round Cap d'Ambre and sail to the northwest [of Madagascar] [and then] on to Africa."[3]

Partially responsible for the "indianization" of Southeast Asia,[4] the spice trade also played a role in Austronesian ventures toward East Africa. The Austronesians sailed to the East African coast to obtain slaves, ivory, panther skins, amber, and turtleshell. Besides spices and aromatics, they brought back edible and fibrous plants, as well as plants used in the magico-religious field. Taro (*Colocasia esculenta* Schott.), great yam (*Dioscorea alata* L.), rice (*Oryza sativa* L.), bananas, and coconut trees were probably introduced into East Africa during the first millennium BCE and/or at the beginning of the Christian era, by Austronesians sailing to the African coasts. The etymology of the Somali word *baris*, "rice," remains debated; it may derive from Malay *beras*, with a metathesis (Witzel 1999: 27), although a Dravidian origin seems more likely: cf.

---

3 Vérin 1972: 17. "From Arabia [toward East Africa], ships departed at the beginning of the Arab winter, which means in October, in order to take advantage of the northeast monsoon which begins at this time . . . The beginning of the trade winds was a favorable time to reach Mombasa and Zanzibar, as the winds at that time are not at their peak. In contrast, to sail further south, one had to wait for the period between December and April; however, the time left for transactions then was short, since the prevailing wind direction changed in April" (Vérin 1979b: 78). According to Ibn Battūta, it took approximately one month to sail from Oman to Kilwa.

4 See Miller 1998; Ellen 1977. See above.

Proto-Dravidian *var-inc, *varici, "rice" (Southworth 2005: 81).[5] The term *mupunga, "rice," was an innovation of the Proto-Northeast Coast (PNEC) languages, as was *nkoWo, "banana" (Nurse and Hinnebusch 1993: 288–289). Various authors have noted that the bananas planted in Uganda were first of all of the AAA type, and that they had certainly come from Indonesia. Bananas of the AA type are mainly present on the coasts, where AAB and AAB triploids can also be found – in a limited number – these were probably more recent introductions (Blench 2009). Taro, however, was cultivated in Egypt during Roman times and may have arrived via Yemen. Moreover, after the first Austronesian settlements – and the arrival of other populations – in Madagascar, plants must have reached the East African coast from this island, at various times.

A number of authors have suggested Austronesian arrivals in the western Indian Ocean at the beginning of the first millennium BCE or even earlier, with the transport of spices such as cinnamon and various plants, notably plantain of the AAB type. Hornell has noted that the distribution of outrigger canoes in the Indian Ocean may indicate an ancient Austronesian presence along the coasts of India and Africa (Hornell 1920: 225–246; Mahdi 1994b: 472 n. 120) (see below). While this distribution is interesting, it cannot be correlated to any precise dates.

We have no evidence that the first Austronesian migrants in the western Indian Ocean reached Madagascar, although this is a possibility. In any event, the fact that the Roman world probably knew of Madagascar during the first centuries of the Christian era (see above) shows that its ships (as well, perhaps, as ships from other regions) went there and that Madagascar was populated earlier than was previously thought (see below).

Archaeological and Genetic Data

We have more data today indicating ancient Asian arrivals, and a body of evidence shows that Austronesians took part in the formation of the Swahili culture. F. Chami's discovery of chicken remains in Machaga Cave (Zanzibar),[6] however, has been refuted (Robertshaw 2009). An analysis of the mitochondrial DNA of chickens from four East African countries (Kenya, Ethiopia, Sudan, and Uganda) has provided evidence for multiple introductions of the domestic chicken into East Africa. "The results indicate a likely Indian subcontinent origin for the commonest haplogroup (D) [also found in West Africa] and a maritime introduction for the next commonest one (A) from Southeast and/or East Asia. The origin of haplogroup E, found in Ethiopia and Sudan, remains unclear being currently observed only outside the African continent in the inland Yunnan Province of China ... The haplogroup A is found only in Kenya, but has also been observed in Zimbabwe (Muchadeyi et al. 2008) and Madagascar (Razafindraibe et al. 2008)" (Mwacharo et al. 2011: 374, 379).[7] Chicken bones have been unearthed at Shanga, on the island of Pate, dated to the eighth century CE, as well as at

---

[5] Southworth relates both the Ngaju bari (Kalimantan) and the Malagasy vari to the Proto-Dravidian.

[6] Chami 2001: 87ff. Chami (2006: 136) claimed to have found chicken bones in the lower levels of the site, dated between 2800 and 800 BCE. Cf. Sutton 2002.

[7] In a more recent analysis of autosomal microsatellite markers genotyped in village chickens from four East African countries (Kenya, Uganda, Ethiopia, and Sudan), Mwacharo et al. (2013) identify three distinct

Manda (on Manda Island) and Chibuene (Mozambique) dated to the same period (Horton 1996: 387). In southern Africa, chicken remains have been found at Ndondondwane (Natal) dated to the eighth century CE, and at Bosutswe (Botswana) dated to the ninth century (Smith 2000: 225). The Bantu name for "chicken" has been connected to Austronesian words: we find koko, "chicken," in To Ntemboan, ko'ko', in To Ndano, and kuku, "clucking of chickens" in Puyuma, but D. Nurse and T. Spear (1985: 109) note k'uku, "chicken," in Proto-Swahili. K'uku does in fact correspond to the sound of chickens clucking; it is therefore difficult to look for an etymology. In Madagascar the term akoho probably comes from the Swahili (as shown by the presence of a prefix a-, as is the case for other animal names borrowed by the Malagasy from Bantu languages).

Recent claims by Chami concerning discoveries of cattle, chicken, and dog bones – and stone tools – at dates going back to the fourth or third millennium BCE in the Kuumbi Cave in Zanzibar, have now been rejected. In addition, Chami has presented a find of chicken remains in a level dating to the first century BCE that also contained two glass beads (Chami 2006: 139; 2009: 48). Here again it has been shown that the bones are those of another (wild) animal. An early human presence in Kuumbi Cave has not been confirmed by recent research (Prendergast et al. 2016; Kourampas et al. 2016).[8]

Chami also claims to have unearthed chicken bones at Misasa, south of Dar-es-Salaam, along with fragments of coconuts in a 500–600 CE context (1994: 64, 68; 2001: 93). It is naturally tempting to connect the possible introduction of the chicken and that of Asian plants such as the banana, the coconut tree, and so on. Prior to the alleged "finds" made by F. Chami in Zanzibar, C. Ehret has been in favor of an introduction of the chicken by Austronesians during the first centuries of the Christian era. According to this author, the Austronesians may have introduced pigs into the Zambezi valley, but he provides no evidence to support this hypothesis (Ehret 1998: 280). Moreover, Blench (2009) notes the existence of a fighting cock of an Indonesian type in Kenya and Malawi. Recent genetic research on Malagasy chickens reveals a double origin, probably Indonesian and African (Razafindraibe et al. 2008).

Aside from these discoveries, material evidence for an Austronesian presence in East Africa and the western Indian Ocean is still lacking (except for Madagascar and Mayotte, with more recent datings), not only because research has been quite limited, but also because the Austronesians used plant materials that left few vestiges. Only a few Austronesian people settled on the islands (Pemba, Zanzibar …) and along the coast. The paucity of data could also result from the fact that archaeologists did not recognize the Austronesian presence due to a lack of knowledge about the Southeast Asian pottery of this period.

Some authors have suggested that elephantiasis (a disease caused by the filarial worm) was introduced into Africa by Austronesians (Laurence 1968; Blench 2007); this hypothesis is disputed, however. A terracotta find from Nok (500 BCE – 500 CE) features a man affected by this disease. If elephantiasis came from Southeast Asia, it

---

autosomal gene pools. The existence of these three gene pools "is compatible with the arrival of three independent waves of domestic chicken in Africa."

[8] Research shows a human presence around 15000 BCE and a later abandonment prior to a reoccupation (Kourampas et al. 2015: 311).

would have been brought even earlier, since a statue of the pharaoh Mentuhotep (*c.* 2000 BCE) depicts a man with the disease. On the other hand, Blench (2007) suggests an ancient introduction of African malaria (due to *Plasmodium falciparum*) into Southeast Asia.

Lastly, the finds of *Musa* phytoliths in Cameroon dated to the middle of the first millennium BCE are noteworthy (this *Musa* was probably an AAB plantain) (Mbida *et al.* 2001, 2004). Blench (2009, 2010a) suggests that Austronesians brought this plant to the Tanzanian coast, as well as taro and the *Dioscorea alata* yam, as early as the late second millennium or the early first millennium BCE (see above).[9] West Africa between Gabon and Nigeria appears to be a center of diversity for the AAB plantain. Moreover, bananas of the AA type were cultivated in West Africa (Gabon) before the arrival of the Portuguese (though their introduction may be relatively recent). Moreover, tetraploids from Southeast Asia (AABB and AAAB, which may have appeared in New Guinea, and ABBB from Southeast Asia), were also present in the Gulf of Benin prior to the arrival of the Portuguese (Blench 2009).

The Ancient Texts

The *Periplus of the Erythraean Sea* does not signal any plant originating in Southeast Asia along the Azanian coast (see above), and contrary to some authors' opinions, the *Periplus* gives no evidence of an Austronesian presence on the East African coast. For the passage concerning Rhapta, a recent edition has amended the older translation of *oratoi* as "pirates" (*oratoi* had been rather freely read as *peiratai*), which had suggested the presence of Austronesian "sea nomads" in the region of Rhapta. The new translation of the term *oratoi*, this time amended to *arotoi* ("tillers of the soil"), is also problematic (Casson 1989: 61, 253). Wrigley (1997: 114–115) proposes reading the term as *horatai*, "overseers, inspectors [of customs]." The Greek text does not refer to agriculture on the East African coast, but this matter is still debated. Archaeological data in fact show that Bantu farmers were already settled on the Tanzanian coast at the time the *Periplus* was written. A dense population existed north of the Rufiji River, where the emporium of Rhapta may have been set up. Excavations at Mkukutu-Kibiti have revealed that a small river there was diverted, perhaps to irrigate fields (Chami 2001: 17).

Based on Hornell's research, Kent interprets the reference of the *Periplus* to sailors using sewn ships at Rhapta as evidence for an Austronesian presence on the East African coast at the beginning of the Christian era (Kent 1979: 139; Hornell 1934: 321–324). The *Periplus*, however, mentions that sewn boats were also used in the Persian Gulf, in India, and on the southern Arabian coasts; the word used is *madarate* (paragr. 36), which is clearly related to the Arabic *muddarra'at*.[10] Moreover, Rhapta is given as the tributary of a Yemeni king (see above).

---

[9] Note that the AAB plantain is quite rare on the East African coast, but there are islands of AAB plantain in western Uganda, surrounded by bananas of the AAA type (Blench 2009).

[10] *Muddarra'at* may mean "fastened with palm fibers" or "things that are armored" (from the root *dara'a*) (Casson 1989). Hornell indicates that the tradition of sewn boats (using fibers of palm trees, especially the coconut tree) was maintained until recently (1946: 234–235). Southeast Asian influences cannot be

Other authors also see an Austronesian influence in the description of fishing techniques in Menuthias (possibly Pemba) given by the *Periplus*:

In this place there are sewn boats and canoes hollowed from single logs, which they use for fishing and catching tortoise. In this island, they also catch them in a peculiar way, in wicker baskets [fish traps], which they fasten across the channel-opening between the breakers. (paragr. 15; Schoff 1974: 28)[11]

The *Periplus* is not the first testimony known to us. A Greek merchant called Iambulos, involved in the spice trade of the Somali coast, probably visited some East African islands soon after 300 BCE. He lived for seven years on an island where the sun was above his head all year long (the island therefore lay below the Equator). The people of this island lived on hunting and fishing, and they practiced various crafts. Expelled from the island, Iambulos sailed to the northeast and after several months, he arrived in India, where he met people speaking Greek, who had taken part in Alexander's expedition (this journey may attest to a knowledge of the monsoon winds for sailing from Africa to India). The island where Iambulos lived could be Pemba or Zanzibar. Iambulos mentions six other islands, inhabited by people of the same tradition.[12]

Pliny mentions "rafts [*rati*]" – probably Indonesian ships (possibly double-hulled canoes with decks) – that brought aromatics to the Horn of Africa (see above).

Ancient Chinese texts mention the existence of Southeast Asian states trading with the Indian Ocean (see above). The ships involved in westward journeys during the first centuries of the Christian era must have belonged to these states: Geying during the third century, and later Gantuoli, in southeastern Sumatra (?), and Heluodan (Ho-lo-tan) in western Java, during the fifth century, all were in contact with India. But we cannot exclude ships from Funan, an empire that was preeminent along the maritime routes of Southeast Asia from the first through the sixth century CE and that at times controlled part of the Thai–Malay peninsula.[13] The language spoken in Funan was probably part of the Khmer subfamily of Austroasiatic languages, but Funanese ships may have employed Austronesian sailors.

What Does Anthropology Teach Us?

Besides archaeology and ancient texts, research has been conducted in anthropology, especially in the fields of navigation and musical instruments, by Hornell (1928, 1934, 1970 [1946]), Sachs (1938), Grottanelli (1947), and Jones (1964, 1972), in an attempt to

---

excluded in the building of the *muddarra'at*, but the techniques in this region were different. The name Rhapta, writes the *Periplus*, derives from the small sewn boats (*rhaptōn ploiariōn*) seen there. It also seems to derive from the Arabic *rabta*, "to tie."

[11] Hornell (1934: 328–329) relates the East African technique of building fishing weirs to Malay practices.

[12] Cary and Warmington 1963: 240–241; Chami 2001: 92. The inhabitants of the "island of the sun" had curious small animals that may have been chickens, according to Chami (2001: 92). Iambulos is mentioned by Theophrastus, Diodorus of Sicily, and Pliny. The island where Iambulos was driven by the winds has sometimes been identified as Sri Lanka.

[13] The languages spoken in the northern part of the Malay peninsula, perhaps as far as Kedah, however, must have been Austroasiatic, not Austronesian languages (Andaya 2001: 327, who quotes G. Benjamin 1997).

identify Austronesian influences on the African coast. Further research on these topics has been scarce, except in navigation (see Prins [1965, 1982]; McGrail [1985]; Manguin [1996, 2000a], and Poumailloux [1999]) and in botany (Hoogervoorst 2012; Beaujard 2017). Synthesis papers have been written by Kent (1979) and Blench (1996, 2009, 2010a). B. Domenichini-Ramiaramanana and J.-P. Domenichini (1983) have related certain cultural features of the East African coast to Austronesian cultures.

The geographical distribution of the double-outrigger canoe,[14] known in Indonesia, the Comoros, East Africa, and Madagascar, may provide support for the thesis that ancient Austronesians arrived in East Africa from Indonesia, and later from Madagascar. Its distribution would appear to reflect routes through the Maldives (Shepherd 1982: 132). As for the single-outrigger canoe, it has a wider geographical distribution, including India's western coast and Sri Lanka (it is not present on the eastern coast of India, however). Hornell notes similarities in shape between pieces of wood linking outriggers and floats on the northern coast of Java and those in Madagascar (Hornell 1946: 254, 259). The double-outrigger canoes of East Africa differ from Malagasy canoes only in minor points: on a Malagasy canoe, the piece of wood connecting boom and float is sometimes peg-shaped, whereas on an African canoe, it has a square section and it is not vertical, but tilted; moreover, the float is flat on an African boat, but cylindrical in Madagascar, as well as in Indonesia.

Hornell has also linked the canoes observed on Lake Nyanza with canoes from Java and Madura (Hornell 1928).[15] Their main peculiarities are the presence of a bifid stem, horns decorating the prow, paddling thwarts extruding through the side planks on the outer side, and "the neat closing of the seams by means of longitudinal battens, held in place by stitching passed through opposed holes in the approximated edges of adjacent planks" (1934: 324). Outrigger canoes from the Philippines and the Minahasa region of Sulawesi also tend to have bifid bows. This transfer of technology implies the existence of a trade route between the African coast, where Austronesians probably settled, and Lake Nyanza (Austronesians may also have settled along the shores of this lake). This route may explain the dissemination of myths and rituals relating the reincarnation of kings as snakes, found in the interlacustrine kingdoms, the Shona country (influences from the coast followed the Zambezi and Save River valleys), and Madagascar (see below). These features of the Nyanza canoes are not observed on the canoes of East Africa or Madagascar, because the latter derive from another type of boat (Hornell 1934: 325).

The parallel distribution of the outrigger canoe and the coco rasp along the East African coast has long been pointed out. The coco rasp has a similar form in East Africa and in Tahiti. Moreover, Prins notes that transporting coconuts was taboo on the East African *mtepe* ships (Prins 1982: 89). This peculiar taboo may be related to

---

[14] According to Hornell, the double-outrigger canoe appeared prior to the single-outrigger canoe, but this idea is debatable.

[15] According to the translation by C. Müller (1883 and 1901) (Freeman-Grenville 1975: 4), Ptolemy speaks of the "Mountains of the Moon, from which the Lake of the Nile [Lake Nyanza ?] receives snow water . . . Above them are the Ethiopians who make sewn boats." The last part of this translation, however, is uncertain. Stevenson suggests: "above these [Mountains of the Moon] are the Rhapsi Aethiopians" (Freeman-Grenville 1975: 109). Some researchers refute the idea of early cultural borrowing.

Austronesian and Indian forays onto the African coasts. Swahili traditions concerning the Wadebuli ("people from Daybul") and the Wadiba ("people of the islands [Maldives]") often link these groups with the transport of coconuts and the culture of the coconut tree (Pouwels 2002: 400; see below). Dick-Read (2005: 92–93) has suggested a connection between the Swahili term *matengo*, "float of the outrigger," and the Konjo (southern Sulawesi) term *tengko*, "outrigger connective piece," but this derivation seems uncertain (Hoogervorst 2012: 242).

Hornell notes the absence of outrigger canoes along the east coast of Madagascar. He relates this absence to "Neo-Indonesian" migrants who did not use outrigger canoes but other ships. The argument is hardly acceptable. It is likely that outrigger canoes disappeared on the east coast, where coastal populations partially abandoned sea navigation, due to its dangers, and in some places outrigger canoes were replaced by sewn boats.

The introduction of double- or single-outrigger canoes does not imply that the Austronesians crossed the ocean on these canoes, only that they brought or transmitted knowledge linked to this type of boat. Larger ships were used. Ships made of "stitched" planks and using outriggers permitted direct crossings to Madagascar, as Hornell points out, without following the coasts. Two-masted sailing ships with massive outriggers are portrayed on the sculptures of the Borobudur temple in Java dated to the ninth century.[16] This type of boat probably influenced the "hybrid" ships known in Sri Lanka under the name *yathra oruwa*, or *yathra dhoni*.[17] An outrigger vessel which had its hull made of "sewn" planks (a technique from the western Indian Ocean) was observed in 1926 by Hornell at Majunga (northwestern Madagascar).

The ancient building techniques of the Maldivian *dhoni* reveal features that connect them to ancient Southeast Asian traditions,[18] unlike those of the Indian subcontinent or western Asia. Rows of thwarts kept the planks of the hull apart; lugs carved out on the internal face of the hull's planks supported the thwarts (these lugs are now merely vestigial). Fastenings held the thwarts together and the frames within the hull. The Chinese traveler Ma Huan (1433) and Portuguese Duarte Barbosa (1518) indicate that the strakes were held together by discontinuous fastenings on the hull's internal side (with ropes made from coconut fibers), as had been the case in Southeast Asia (in Indian and Arab ships, the planks are sewn in a continuous way: the "threads" can be

---

[16] Manguin, however, argues that this type of ship was less well suited for transoceanic journeys than the ships that the Chinese called *kunlun bo* (see above).

[17] Hornell 1946: 256–257. J. Deloche (1996: 204 n. 7) notes that these Sinhalese ships with outriggers keep the memory of contacts with Southeast Asia, but that they are built with "sewn planks," according to the technique of the western Indian Ocean. On the *yathra dhoni* and its hybrid character, see Vosmer 1993: 109–118, and Devendra 2002: 158ff. According to Devendra, the hull shows similarities with ancient Arab and Indian ships; the ship adopted a central rudder (a Chinese feature) and fore-and-aft rig after the ninth century (2002: 149). The model kept in Dodanduwa shows a huge rudder not unlike that of the junks. Speaking of Sinhalese ships, Manguin (2012: 609) has pointed out that "the overall shape of their hull, of the penthouse roofing of palm leaves and of the rig (multiple masts with square sails and foresails) appear to indicate that their shipbuilding tradition was distinct from that of their Arabo-Indian neighbors. Some of these characterisics are reminiscent of traditions that are common further east across the Bay of Bengal, or possibly also of features of ships depicted in ancient Indian iconography and texts" (see above).

[18] Manguin 1993, 2000a. Lashed lug and stitched-plank tradition, already described (see above).

seen on the external face of the hull). The planks were also held together by a system of wooden dowels[19] (the use of dowels was not unique to Southeast Asia, but L. Varadajaran seems to connect this technique, observed on the Lakshadweep Islands, to Indonesia).[20] Coconut fibers were inserted between the ship's planks before the planks were dowelled; these fibers swelled when wet and sealed the hull. To prevent gaps between the planks, the hull was caulked with a mixture of shark oil[21] and *Calophyllum inophyllum* nut, a plant that may have come from insular Southeast Asia, but was spread by the currents along all the shores of the Indian Ocean.[22] Watertight holds were sometimes built between the rows of thwarts, on the *dhoni* of the Maldives as well as on the fishing boats of Southeast Asia.

During the second millennium, building techniques for Austronesian ships evolved, moving away from lashed fastenings between strakes, while pinning with wooden dowels became a technique more often used to hold the planks together. The fastenings between lugs, frames, and thwarts were maintained and later disappeared (except in the ships of eastern Indonesia).[23] The fact that the stitched-plank and lashed-lug tradition was known in the Maldives during the fifteenth and sixteenth centuries suggests that the technique had spread while still largely in use on the big ships of Southeast Asia, namely during the first millennium.[24] The Maldivian *dhoni*

[19] "In the construction of their foreign ships," writes Ma Huan, "they never use nails; they merely bore the holes, and always use these ropes [made of coconut tree fibers] to bind the planks together, employing wooden wedges in addition; afterwards, they smear the seams with foreign pitch" (Ma Huan, ed. Mills, 1970: 149). According to Barbosa, "peoples from the Maldives build many large ships made of palm wood, fastened with fibers" (quoted by Manguin 2000a: 36).

[20] Mentioned by Poumailloux 1999: 284. "While the dowels were not a preeminent feature of Arabo-Indian ships of the western Indian Ocean, they were considered as essential in the Maldivian tradition," which probably reflects an Indonesian influence (Manguin 1985a: 12). In this region, the use of dowels to maintain the planks finally replaced fastenings with palm fibers during the second millennium (see below). But "the word used in Divehi to describe the action of building a boat is *banun*, which literally means 'tying together' or binding (with a rope). The prolonged use of this specific term in the shipbuilding world of the Maldives does hint at the existence of an earlier fastening (sewing or stitching) tradition" (Manguin 2012: 615).

[21] The use of shark or whale oil is certainly an ancient practice in the Indian Ocean. It has been mentioned for various places and at different times: Abū Zayd at Sirāf in the tenth century, Idrīsī in the twelfth century, Ibn Jubayr in the Red Sea during the twelfth century, Ma Huan in 1433, Vasco da Gama on Mozambique Island in 1498, and so forth. Testimonies indicate that "protection was provided to the hull by smearing the inside of it, particularly the coir stitching, with fish oil. The submerged parts of the vessel were kept teredo-free by plastering the outer side of the hull with a mixture of fish-oil, burnt lime and pounded vegetal fiber. This thick white mortar was impenetrable to water and acted as an anti-fouling coating. The term used to refer to it was *galagala* (or cognate forms); it appears in early Western sources as well as in many Southeast Asian and Indian languages" (Manguin 2012: 602). The technique may go back to the third millennium BCE (see above).

[22] Its wood is used for shipbuilding. The Malagasy people of the east coast also use its resin as incense.

[23] The lugs themselves disappeared, as well as the thwarts and all the fastenings, the hulls being "entirely secured by wooden dowels which assemble the strakes together and hold the hull and the frames together" (Manguin 2000a: 40). The thwarts were sometimes maintained: in eastern Java and Madura, today one finds ships without lugs "but with ranges of thwarts dowelled to frames and planks" (Manguin 2000a: 41). On the evolution of the Austronesian ships during the first part of the second millennium, see below.

[24] Manguin 2000a. The Maldives later experienced the same evolution as Southeast Asia with the disappearance of fastenings with sugar palm fibers and the exclusive use of wooden dowels to hold the planks together.

thus reveal an ancient Austronesian presence on these islands, which lay along one of the routes that the Austronesians must have taken en route to East Africa and Madagascar. These boats may also reflect the existence of a shared tradition in the eastern Indian Ocean, reflecting early exchanges between India and Southeast Asia.[25]

The existence in Swahili of an archaic term *sambo*, "ship," used in Madagascar and originating in Southeast Asia, is one argument in favor of Austronesian influences in East Africa.

Some authors have suggested that the *mtepe* built on the Swahili coast in early times derived from the "sewn boats" mentioned by the *Periplus* for Rhapta, and represented the continued existence of an Insulindian type of ship (Allibert and Vérin 1993a: 76). The *mtepe*, however, seem to belong to the tradition of the "sewn boats" of the western Indian Ocean (with continuous sewing), and not to the tradition of the "stitched plank and lashed-lug technique" of the insular Southeast Asian archipelago. The Swahili term *mtepe* certainly derives from the Arabic *mtafieh* (from the Arabic *tāf*, "to float"). C. Allibert, however, suggests links with Dravidian languages: *mitappu*, "ship," de *mita*, "to float" (Allibert 1984: 90 n. 2). Boatbuilders on the East Indian coast constructed a type of catamaran called *teppu* (cf. Telugu *teppa*, "raft") (Poumailloux 1999: 294). Sewn ships, such as the *madarate* mentioned by the *Periplus* as exported by Oman to Kanē (*Periplus*, 30, 36), had been built in the Persian Gulf since early times. Abū Zayd notes that the building of sewn boats was a speciality at Sirāf by the tenth century. An oral tradition, however, attributes the origin of the *mtepe* to a population called Wadiba ("island folk"), who arrived from the Lakshadweep Islands (whose inhabitants speak a Dravidian language) and merged with the Bajun.[26] While Prins links the *mtepe* to an Indian shipbuilding tradition, he recognizes that it is difficult to distinguish between Indian and Arabo-Persian traditions. We must remember that the type of ropes and the wood used in Arabo-Persian shipbuilding originated partly in the Indian peninsula,[27] where shipbuilding probably developed at an early time. The assembly and fastenings of the strakes of the *mtepe* described by Prins (1982) appear to be similar to those observed by L. Varadajaran (1993) on Andrott Island in the Lakshadweep Islands.

Prins also considered the color schemes red, white, and black (which he found along the west coast of India) as Indian features, but these three colors were also the primary colors used along the East African coast as well as in Madagascar (where their symbolism is mainly Austronesian). This makes it hard to determine an origin for this feature of the *mtepe*.[28] These ships also featured red or white flags, or flags combining white and red. In Madagascar, red and white are valued as symbols of the aristocracy. The symbolism these colors

---

[25] Manguin 1996: 191; 2000a: 44. I am indebted to P.-Y. Manguin for the data presented.

[26] Some authors, however, consider the Wadiba as having been Maldivians; the Maldives were called *diba* by the Arabs (we find *diva* in Gujarati, from the Sanskrit *dvipa*). According to a tradition, the Wadiba may have introduced the coconut tree into Pemba (Poumailloux 1999: 298).

[27] Prins 1982: 99; Poumailloux 1999: 282. Note the use of teak from the Malabar coast, and that of the coconut tree (wood, fibers).

[28] It is equally difficult to propose an origin for the bow in the shape of an animal head which Prins considered as another Indian feature of the *mtepe*: this feature is almost universal.

represent probably reflects an evolution from Indonesian concepts under both Indian and Muslim influences; these also left their traces along the East African coast (see Beaujard 1988, and below).

Hornell, however, has identified several features of the *mtepe* that relate them to Indonesian traditions (1934: 322): 1. a head-shaped prow with painted rounded oculi; the stern also usually with two eyes; 2. "a rectangular mat sail, with the upper and lower sides lashed or laced to poles"; 3. "on the bowsprit [was] a row of charms of alternate leaves of *mkindu* (wild date palm) and *mvinji* (*Casuarina*)."[29]

The first two features noted by Hornell can be seen on ships carved on panels of the Javanese temple of Borobudur. Pairs of eyes also feature on outrigger canoes on Pemba, Zanzibar, and the Comoros. According to Hornell, this decorative motif with rounded eyes at both prow and stern of these ships are seen only in Java (Hornell has suggested a Chinese influence for this design, the eyes being those of a dragon), on Zanzibar and on the Comoros (Hornell 1946: 288). Eyes have been noted on ships from the Red Sea, but only on the prow; the ships featured on the Ajanta frescoes (India) also bear eyes painted on the prow (they are elongated, here, not round); Devendra (2002: 156) also mentions an oculus at the prow of *dhoni* of northern Sri Lanka. For Poumailloux, however, the oculi of the *mtepe* evoke the Arab boom: the eye of the prow is featured as a six petaled-rosette; it is accompanied by three moon crescents (on the stern, the rosette sometimes has only five branches, and a half-moon) (Poumailloux 1999: 276).

The transport of coconuts was taboo on the *mtepe*, as mentioned above; this may be linked to Austronesian or Maldivian raids along the East African coast.

Vasco da Gama, who saw *mtepe* on Mozambique Island in 1498, observed the practice of caulking with a plaster made of fish oil mixed with an aromatic resin (Hornell 1946: 235; see above). The caulking inside the hull covered the stitches of the strakes: coir (made of coconut fibres) which had marinated in shark oil was hammered into the seams. This was supplemented by an application of sealant, using crushed bark from mangrove trees, crushed coconut fibers, and the dried crushed veins of palm leaves (Poumailloux 1999: 284). On the Arab boats, the caulking process also used tow from a palm tree, and a mixture of pitch or resin and whale or shark oil to fill the seam holes. It would be interesting to know which resins were used.[30] Manguin notes the use of *Calophyllum* in the Maldives, a tree widespread in South and Southeast Asia. It is obvious that caulking and sealing techniques are similar throughout the Indian Ocean. The Arabic and Persian term for coir is *qayar*, of Dravidian origin (*kāyar* in Malayalam, *kayiru* in Tamil, from which the Portuguese *cairo* is derived).[31]

Migrations and successive contacts along the East African coast necessarily left their mark on the characteristics of ships. Poumailloux, who synthesized the data available, shows that the *mtepe* was like the Swahili culture itself: a hybrid ship, the result of an evolution combining various influences. As Grottanelli has already noted, the *mtepe*

---

[29] "A row of charms, called *mzima*, [was attached on the bowsprit]; [they] were composed of alternate branches of the split and dried leaves of the *mkindu* and *mvinji* trees" (Stigand 1913: 142).

[30] Séverin (1985) speaks of a melted resin of *šundruz*, mixed with coconut oil and crushed shells (Poumailloux 1999: 281).

[31] The ropes used on the ships of Nearchos (fourth century BCE) were already made of coconut fibers, a product that has long been traded in the Indian Ocean (Ray 2003: 60).

was probably "one of the elements of this process of slow cultural collaboration that occurred over the centuries" (1955: 343; Poumailloux 1999: 300). The early existence of large Austronesian ships, which the Chinese chronicles called *bo*, has been mentioned above. It is likely that the Austronesians also used these ships in their journeys westward. Some nautical Malay terms may have been borrowed into Swahili (Blench p.c.).

Research has been conducted in other domains to try to detect the traces of an early Austronesian presence in various locations along the African coast. For Somalia, the Bajun, as well as the Malagasy, used remoras to catch turtles (Grottanelli 1955). But this is not convincing proof of a shared Austronesian origin of this practice. Moreover, Grottanelli (1947: 158) has noted a striking parallel between southern Somalia and Indonesia concerning "a spear made from a long, hollow cane with a leaf-shaped blade fixed to it (the blade is tied to one side)" (Blench 1996: 432) (in Indonesia, this weapon effectively combines the function of blow-pipe and spear).

R. Blench (2010a: 243) notes that the "crossbow traps" known in Southeast Asia and other regions of Asia, are also found in Tanzania, Zanzibar, and Madagascar; they may be another example of cultural spread. M. Walsh (2007: 103) suggests that the consumption of bats on Pemba, in the Comoros, and Madagascar is linked to a shared Austronesian influence.

A. M. Jones has linked the African xylophone to Southeast Asia: the instrument, its tuning, and musical styles, using a technique involving two or three players, are identical on Bali and in Uganda;[32] the use of double playing-sticks can be seen in Africa as well as in Java (Jones 1971: 234ff., 259ff.). Before Jones, "Wachsmann drew attention to the fact that we find a technique of xylophone playing in Uganda, known as Amakonezi (the allocation of the two top keys of the instrument to a special player), which had been reported by Curt Sachs in Madagascar and is also shown in a fourteenth-century relief in a temple at Panataran, in Java" (Allen 1980: 155). Wachsmann has also noted that "the bosses carved on some xylophone keys in Uganda were curiously like the bosses on the Java xylophone" (1967). Studying the xylophone led Jones to link Madagascar to Sulawesi (Jones 1971: 54–56). Reassessing Jones's proposals, Blench has convincingly proposed reversing the direction of the migration: xylophones mounted on frames may have been carried to Indonesia by "Zenj enslaved by Malay raiders" (Blench 1993: 430; 2010a: 245). The instrument was introduced into Indonesia at an early time "Kunst (1973, II: 416–417) shows an image of a wooden xylophone at Borobudur" (Blench 2012: 8). Moreover, the flat-bar stick-zither is known in Africa[33] and Madagascar, where it is called *jejo*, from the Swahili *zeze*. According to Sachs (1938: 47), "this word seems to derive from one of the names for the harp in ancient Egypt, *dede*," but this derivation has been refuted by R. Blench, who notes that "the stick-zither was first represented in India during the 7th century on

---

[32] The various tunes, notes Jones, "are completely interlocked . . . There is no question: the interlocking techniques of Bali and Uganda are identical" (1971: 260).

[33] R. Blench (1984: 168) notes that African stick-zithers "seem to combine elements both of Indian and Southeast Asian stick-zithers."

the temple at Mamallapuram" (2012: 3). From India, it may have spread to Indonesia, and from Indonesia to East Africa, and from there, later, to Madagascar (Blench 2012). The xylophone is is still found today in Sulawesi (Jones 1971: 169). For the xylophone especially, we cannot exclude parallel inventions on both sides of the ocean, but the similarities in mode of tuning are striking.[34] In contrast, the transversely blown conch and bamboo tubes on frames used as wind chimes, known in East Africa and Madagascar, appear to have been linked to Austronesian migrations to the western Indian Ocean.

Moreover, A. M. Jones signals a board game that uses a wooden tablet bearing two or four ranges of six, seven or eight cup-like holes. It is a contest between two players, who use grains or small pebbles. This game is known only in Africa within the xylophone area (Jones 1971: 198–201). Jones suggests an Insulindian origin for this game, noting that the two cupules located at each end of the wooden tablet are used for the game in Indonesia but are not used in Africa, where they are nevertheless present on the board. This game is known in Madagascar under the name of *fanga*, or *katra(ka)*.

In the domain of body adornment, J.-C. Hébert (p.c.) points out that tattoos in Madagascar are made or were made using the technique of dots with needles – not with scarification as in East Africa; this dot technique is known in some populations of Mozambique.

The field of cultivated plants, along with linguistic data concerning taro and banana, leads us to the Kenyan and Tanzanian coasts. Taro may have been carried to Africa along the so-called "Sabaean lane," and also more directly across the ocean (see above). Here, Mas'ūdī's testimony (tenth century) is interesting:

The Zanj [black people from East Africa] eat bananas, which are as common among them as they are in India; but their staple food is millet (dura, sorghum) and a plant called *kalādī* that one digs out of the earth like truffle and the root of elecampane. It is plentiful in Aden and the neighboring part of Yemen near to the town; it is like the colocasia of Egypt and Syria. (Mas'ūdī, 1965, II: 330 [paragr. 872])[35]

Kalādī is obviously related to the Malay *keladi*, "taro." The use of this term seems to support an earlier Malay presence in East Africa. However, the term in Mas'ūdī has sometimes been read as *kalarī*.[36] As noted above, the Malay *keladi* is certainly a loanword.

---

[34] It is even more difficult to assess the direction of transfer for the drum xylophone, observed in Java and West Africa (Jones 1971: 155–157). The linguistic derivations proposed by Jones are usually fanciful, but they are – formally – acceptable for this instrument, called *kele* in Mende, and *kende* in Kissi, terms that Jones relates to the Old Javanese *kele*, "bamboo internode," but this "relation" could be simply a coincidence. The instrument has not been described in Madagascar.

[35] The translation of *dura* as "corn" suggested by the authors is obviously wrong; an American plant, corn (maize) was introduced into Africa much later.

[36] Freeman-Grenville 1975: 16. About this text in Mas'ūdī, Devic (1975: 142 n. 6) has already noted: "*kaladi and* not *kalari*, [this is a term] from which derives the 'caladium' of our botanists" (the French *Dictionnaire Littré* [1880] has "caladion, caladium" for taro).

The discovery of a "wild" banana (related to the *zebrina* subgroup of Java) on Pemba Island suggests that this plant may have been introduced by Austronesians, probably at the same time as other bananas.[37] Many cultivars of AAA type are present in the East African Highlands (subgroup Lujugira-Mutika). These cultivars can only have developed over a long period of time. Their history has been traced back over 1,500 years for the west of the Great Lakes (De Langhe *et al.* 1994–1995: 151), but the time of their arrival may be much older (Perrier *et al.* 2009: 210). The trade routes linking the coast to the interior allowed the spread of these bananas carried by Austronesians and perhaps other populations. We know that the interior of Tanzania, the coast, and the islands were connected through networks open to Indian Ocean trade (Chami 2001). The word *(hu)ti*, which refers to cooking bananas in the Shambala and Bondei languages (Tanzania), is related to the Proto-Malayo-Polynesian (PMP) *punti*, "banana" and Malagasy *fontsy*, which in turn derives from this PMP reconstruction (in these Tanzanian languages, *p > h*) (G. Philippson p.c.) (note that the word *fontsy* was probably introduced into Madagascar later than the Bantu *akondro*, "banana"). Moreover, the term "Buki," referring to Madagascar in Swahili, has sometimes been connected – hypothetically – to the name of the Bugis. It is also important to note that the East African AA bananas (which are cooked) are practically nonexistent in India, a fact that clearly demonstrates their introduction into East Africa via a direct oceanic route.

Linguistics may also provide clues to the existence of relations between Southeast Asia and the East African coast in the field of domestic animals. Blench (2008, 2010a) suggests a possible link between the Western Malayo-Polynesian *kandi* and Bantu terms collected in Kenya (Rabai *kadenge*, "small male-goat," Kamba *kathenge*, Pare *kandhenge, id.*) (terms inherited from *kandi* are known only in a few languages of the Philippines and Kalimantan, and goats were introduced into Southeast Asia at an unspecified time).

The Zambezi valley and its region have been the focus of much attention from comparatist researchers. Austronesian influences, whether from the coast further north or from Madagascar, may have entered Africa through this valley, although the pertinence of the evidence offered can often be questioned.[38] For some historians, cowries may represent the mark of an Austronesian presence. Archaeological East

---

[37] The "wild" banana of Pemba looks morphologically like the *malaccensis* subspecies, but genetically it seems related to the *zebrina* subspecies (E. de Langhe, p.c.). A population of "wild" bananas has also been found in northeastern Madagascar (see below); it would be interesting to compare this wild population with the Pemba banana.

[38] After mentioning the hypothesis (not confirmed by archaeology) of an Austronesian influence on the Gokomere pottery of Zimbabwe, B. Domenichini-Ramiaramanana and J.-P. Domenichini (1983: 13) bravely claim: "from the terrace cultivation to the stone buildings (walls surrounding perched sites and quadrangular-planned houses), toponyms and terms of everyday vocabulary, copper ornaments and various features of the iron metallurgy, etc, there are many clues ... that lead us to suggest ... the existence of a common Wāq-Wāq culture on both shores [of the Mozambique channel, Madagascar and the East African coast], a fact already seen by Idrīsī." In fact, all this remains poorly demonstrated and rather hypothetical.

African sites show the early presence of cowries perhaps from the Maldives: shells have been found at Kumajulo, in the Zambezi valley, a site dated between the fifth and seventh centuries;[39] however, other populations than the Austronesians may have carried cowries to the East African coast. The question of an Austronesian influence on Gokomere-Ziwa-Zhizo pottery (Zimbabwe), linked to the Iron Age (third–eleventh century), and on the development of the Zimbabwe kingdom has sometimes been examined,[40] but remains highly speculative. The presence of glass beads and shells with this type of pottery and at sites further north (Zambezi region), however, does reveal contacts with coastal trade (see above). According to P. Vérin, "Zimbabwe, whose earliest levels go back to the fourth century CE [?], hints at contacts with Indonesians (see the figure of a bird on a roof peak, for example)" (p.c.).[41] These bird sculptures, in fact, probably date to the fourteenth century and Vérin's hypothesis remains most uncertain.

Some words noted in Mozambique may be related to Austronesian terms. At the beginning of the seventeenth century, Father João dos Santos mentions the term *nipa* for a "palm wine," a loanword from Malay *nipah*, the name of a palm tree (a term unknown in Madagascar) (Poumailloux 2002: 61, 277). How and when did this term enter the region?

For the Zambezi and Great Lakes region, moreover, funerary practices concerning kings and the belief in their reincarnation as snakes show similarities with Madagascar. In the Malagasy Highlands, historians have noted striking parallels between ancient beliefs and royal rituals found among the Betsileo people, and those found among the Shona (south of the Zambezi), in Janjero (southern Ethiopia), and in the interlacustrine kingdoms in Rwanda, Burundi, Buhaya, Bushi, Buha, Karagwe, Angkole, and Bunyoro. Upon the death of the Betsileo king, the first worm falling from the corpse was collected. Considered as hosting the soul of the dead king, the worm was placed in a jar, left in the tomb, or immersed in a lake. The worm then was supposed to turn into a snake called *fañany*. In East Africa, the worm collected is fed on milk, which allows its transformation into snake, lion or leopard, according to region (Great Lakes) (Mworoha 1977: 282–290). In a Tañala (southeast of Madagascar) version of the myth "The seven-headed snake," the transformation of the ever-growing snake, kept in bigger and bigger containers, recalls the royal funerary rituals of Burundi (Ndayishinguje 1977: 20; Gahama 1979: 52). In the Zambezi region, Randles mentions the collecting of worms hosting the soul of the dead king, among the Makorekore and the Watonga, and Bourdillon notes for the Shona that pythons are often associated with the guardian spirits of a kingdom. As in Madagascar, the funerary procession on its way to the tomb is accompanied by the sound of a horn; it stops two or three times:

[39] A cowrie shell has been found at the site of Broederstroom (Transvaal) (fifth century) (Duarte 1993: 46–47).

[40] Domenichini and Domenichini-Ramiaramanana 1983; Domenichini-Ramiaramanana 1990.

[41] "At Inyanga, extensive earthworks and irrigation systems for agriculture have been discovered, that may have been externally driven" (Vérin p.c.). Vérin also mentions the site of Engaruka (northern Tanzania), where we have evidence for intensive agriculture, but this site is of much later date (sixteenth century). Other authors also mentioned the royal symbol of the bird (see the photograph of a bird carved in steatite, found at Great Zimbabwe, by P. S. Garlake, in Fagan 1985: 589).

"the corpse is turned around two or three times to make it difficult for the spirit to find its way back to the homestead should the spirit wish to return and scourge the community" (Randles 1975: 110; Bourdillon 1976: 201 n. 5, 233, 258, 293ff.).

While customs such as those (of the Betsileo, etc.) related to the *fañany* snake – a term of Sanskrit origin, widely used in Indonesia – have been interpreted by H. M. Dubois and other authors as evidence of African influences, F. Raison-Jourde has written of "parallel mythico-ritual elaborations" (1983: 31). This "parallel" may also come from Austronesian influences felt in both Madagascar and East Africa (Allibert 1990) (this theory may fit with the idea of later African influences in Madagascar). Allibert has emphasized the use of bamboo (a plant of Asian origin) in East Africa as well as in Madagascar: bamboo allows the maggot from the corpse to leave the royal tomb. Note also that in Rwanda, at the place where the pot stood that contained the liquids from the corpse (and the maggot hosting the soul of the deceased king), a *Ficus* and a kind of *Erythrina* are planted: these plants are commonly used in rituals in the Indonesian world (and Madagascar, for the *Ficus*). Both Lake Nyanza and the Zambezi valley regions may have come into contact with Austronesian people, who settled at the mouths of large rivers, either directly or indirectly through trade networks.

The framework of the myths of the Swallowing Monster – known in East Africa and Madagascar – is unequivocally Bantu, but the motif of the Seven-Headed Snake (five heads in a tale from Mozambique) may have been brought to the African coasts by Indians or Austronesians (Ottino 1977; Beaujard 1991: 489ff.).

The Austronesian influences on the East African coast came either directly, from Southeast Asia, or from the Comoros and/or Madagascar. The colonization of Madagascar by Austronesians is a well-known fact. It is only comprehensible within the framework of the world-system that settled at the beginning of the first millennium CE. Rather than existing as an Austronesian "bridgehead" to the western Indian Ocean (Miller 1969), Madagascar was a marginal land, where local conditions such as significant agricultural potential and sparse population would promote the development of a distinctive Austronesian culture, rapidly mixed with Bantu inflows – and this may have been happening since the area was settled by the first Austronesians, according to some researchers. The Malagasy Austronesians would ply the Mozambique Channel and prove influential, especially in south-eastern Africa.

Madagascar: A Periphery of the World-System Takes Shape

> Une île est toujours veuve d'un continent.
> (A. Césaire)

By the close of the first millennium BCE, Austronesian ships were sailing across the Indian Ocean, an expansion achieved within the context of growing trade based on the Mediterranean demand for spices and aromatics, and on Han China's interest in luxury goods from India, the Roman Empire, and Africa (see above). The Austronesian settlement in the Comoros and Madagascar came later than the

Austronesian arrival in Zanzibar, Pemba, and the African coast, and probably involved populations of different origins. Adelaar – with whom Blench agrees (2007, 2010a) – places the arrival of Austronesian "Pre-Malagasy" from the East African coast, along with Bantu speakers of the Sabaki group ("transported" by the Austronesians), during the Srīwijayan period (Blench 2007: 78). This scenario is poorly supported by current data.

In the Comoros, where Bantus and Arabs also migrated, archaeology reveals no Austronesian influences prior to the eighth–ninth century. It is possible that populations belonging to the Early Iron Age culture of the East African coast reached these islands before the Austronesians: a shard resembling Kwale pottery has been found recently on the surface of a cave on Ndzwani (Anjouan); this find still needs authentification (see Sinclair 2008).

Cultural data suggest an early Austronesian presence in the Comoros: there are toponyms of Austronesian origin, and taboos concerning eels in mountain lakes at Anjouan. The name used for eels (*tona*, a term of Austronesian origin) is the same as the one used in Madagascar, where eels are taboo in various regions. These data may also reflect a (relatively recent) Malagasy influence.

Recent genetic studies have been based on 93 individuals from Grande Comore and a total of 577 persons (381 men and 196 women) from Grande Comore, Anjouan, and Moheli (Msaidie *et al.* 2011). Unsurprisingly, these studies show a dominant Bantu influence, but also an Austronesian impact. "Admixture analysis of the maternal and paternal contributions indicates the gene pool to be predominately African (72%), with significant contributions from Western Asia (17%) [particularly from Iran] and Southeast Asia (11%)" (Msaidie *et al.* 2011: 93). Some Southeast Asian haplogroups are shared with Madagascar; nevertheless, interestingly, "there are several indicators that the Comoros' history of gene flow from SEA is distinct from Madagascar's." Moreover, the studies show a "male-biased gene flow from the Middle East": "the absence of any maternal contribution from Western Eurasia strongly implicates male-dominated trade and religion as the drivers of gene flow from the North" (Msaidie *et al.* 2011: 93).

Madagascar was not an untouched island at the time the Austronesians landed in the north. Recent research has revealed that hunter-gatherers were already present, at least on the west coast. The Austronesians were the first agriculturists, however. They brought with them various plants, but did not introduce any animal (with the possible exception of chickens). They practiced slash-and-burn cultivation and recession agriculture on swamps and on riverbanks. The origin of these Austronesians has long remained an enigma. Although linguistics now provides a partial answer to this question, it can only offer hints of the newcomers' culture and time of arrival. On these points, archaeology and, to a lesser extent, comparative anthropology complement what linguistics can teach us. Recent research does not wholly support G. Ferrand and O. C. Dahl's hypothesis of a "Bantu substratum" in Madagascar. Austronesians may have settled along the East African coast, however, with Bantu groups. Contacts may have been initiated between the "African" Austronesians and the Austronesian colonists of the Comoros and Madagascar.

Age and Diversity of the First Austronesian Arrivals: A Linguistic Approach

The Place of Malagasy among Austronesian Languages

The Southeast Barito Heritage in Malagasy, and Malay, Javanese, and Bugis Loanwords   The link between the Malagasy language and Indonesian languages has been known ever since the Dutch explorer F. de Houtman published his dictionary of the Malagasy language (1606). Specifically which Austronesians landed in Madagascar, when and under what circumstances, all remained to be clarified. Dahl (1951) has shed light on the close affinity between the Malagasy language and languages of the Southeast Barito group of Kalimantan. This comparison involved Maanyan. Adelaar (1995c) has more recently pointed out the affinity of Malagasy with Samihim, a language belonging to the same Kalimantan group.

Beyond the Southeast Barito heritage, linguistic data, however, reveal the geographical and temporal variety of contacts between Pre-Malagasy or Malagasy and various Austronesian languages. Adelaar has shown the importance of Malay (notably Banjarese and Sumatranese Malay) and of Javanese loanwords, which Dahl had under-evaluated (see also Simon [1988] 2006). The links between southern Kalimantan (region of Banjar) and Java probably date back to early times. Banjarese is a Malay dialect, rich in Javanisms (Lombard 1990, vol. I). Some of these Malagasy loanwords bear the stamp of contacts with Bantu languages (occurring soon after the arrival of the Pre-Malagasy[42] in the western Indian Ocean; see below); they show contacts with Comorian in particular. An analysis of these borrowings reveals that the first migrants had been in contact with Malay and Javanese speakers before they left the Javanese Sea to go westwards (see below), on the one hand, and on the other, that contacts between the Malagasy language and other Austronesian languages occurred over a long period of time, since some of the more recent loanwords do not show the transformations of sounds triggered by the first contacts with Bantu languages (Adelaar 1995b: 51ff.; see Table 15.1). These data suggest that the first migrants belonged to groups of Sea People from the Java Sea. This location explains the early contacts with the languages of South Sulawesi. Research has recently shed light on the significance of Malagasy loanwords from South Sulawesi languages (Adelaar 1995a; Beaujard 1998).[43] As for Malay and Javanese, some loanwords reflecting the influence of Bantu languages may go back to the first phase of the Austronesian settlement; these loanwords reinforce the idea of early contacts between the Proto-Bugis and southeastern Kalimantan (see Pelras 1996: 42).

---

[42] The term "Proto-" is used here for a language that is the ancestor to various languages, not for an older stage of a language: the term "Proto-Malagasy," so often used, will be avoided.

[43] W. Mahdi (1988) has emphasized the influence of southern Sulawesi on Malagasy. On the place held by Malagasy and the South-East Barito languages in the Austronesian languages, see Adelaar 2004.
O. Dempwolff (1934, 1937, 1938) was the first to reconstruct an original language, here in fact Proto-Malayo-Polynesian (PMP), by comparing eleven languages. I. Dyen (1963, 1965b) extended the comparison to the languages of Taiwan, thus permitting the reconstruction of PAN, followed by O. C. Dahl (1976, 1981), J. Wolff (1974, 1982), and R. Blust (1993a, 1994a). For the reconstruction of the PAN lexicon, see Blust 1970, 1972a, 1972b, 1973, 1980, 1983–1984, 1986, 1989, and the *Comparative Austronesian Dictionary*. See also Blust 1988a, 1998, and Ross 2002.

Table 15.1 *Sound correspondences between Proto-Austronesian, Malagasy (inherited and borrowed), and Malay (After Adelaar 1995b: 52)*

PAN	Malagasy (inherited)	Malagasy borrowings in Pre-Comorian phase	Malagasy borrowings in Post-Comorian phase	Malay
*a	a	a	a	a
*-a, *-a (q, s, s, h, ʔ, r, l)	-y	-y, -a	-y, -a	a
*ə	e	e, aᵃ	e, a	ə (aᵇ)
*ə (final syllable)	i	a	a	a
*i	i, -y	i, -y	i, -y	i (e)
*u	o	o	o	u (o)
*aw	o	o	o	-aw
*əw	o	o	o	u
*iw, *-əy	-y	-y	-y	-i
*-ay	-y	-y	-y	-ay
*-uy	-o	-i	-i	-i
*b	v	v	v, b	b
*p	f, -ka, -tra	f, -ka, -tra	f, p	p
*g	h	h	g	g
*k	h, -ka	h, -ka	k, -ka	k, -k
*ŋg	k	k	ŋg	ŋg
*ŋk	k	k	ŋk	ŋk
*d, *j	r, -tra	tr, -tra	d	d, -t
*Z	r (lᶜ)	z, j	z, j	j
*nd, *nj	ndr	ndr	nd	nd
*l	l	l	l	l
*li	di, liᵈ	di, li	di, li	li
*-l	-na	-na ?, ø ?	ø ? (-l-)	-l
*t	t, -tra	t, -tra	t, -tra	t, -t
*ti	tsi, tiᵉ	tsi, ti	tsi, ti	ti
*s	ø	s, ø	s	s
*R	ø, z	r	r	r
(*r	r	r, -tra	r, -tra	r)
(*-r		-na, -tra	-tra	-r)
(*cᶠ)	ts	ts	ts	c
*-n, -m, -ŋ	-na	-na	-na	-n, -m, -ŋ

ᵃ *a* in borrowings from Banjarese Malay, *e* in borrowings from Sumatranese Malay
ᵇ *a* in Banjarese Malay
ᶜ *z > l in some cases
ᵈ The western dialects have *li* and *ti*, the Highlands and the east coast have *di* and *tsi*
ᵉ s is sometimes kept in place, notably in words with sVsVC structure
ᶠ c is only reconstructed at the PMP-W level

Other more recent loanwords probably reflect arrivals of South Sulawesi people in Madagascar between the twelfth and fifteenth centuries. Hébert (1996) has tentatively related *Buki*, the Swahili name for Madagascar and its people, to Bugis. The existence of loanwords from Sulawesi languages in the domain of agriculture and cultivated plants should be noted (cf. for example the terms *rofia*, "raphia," *ontsy*, "banana tree," and *voly*, "to plant").

Eastern Indonesia and Madagascar Beyond Sulawesi, some terms may reflect influences from eastern Indonesia. The most significant example of this is the term *taho* applied to the taro, found in the southeast, in Betsileo, and in the southwest; it seems to be related to the word *mutaʔu*, "taro" in various languages of Timor (Naueti, Makasae) (Naueti is an Austronesian language, but not Makasae) (the Marquesan *taʔo* cannot be taken into account, as no historical link has been found between Polynesia and the Indian Ocean). The presence of the *h* in *taho* does not correspond to the glottal *ʔ* of the Timor language (Adelaar 2016), but as in the terms *sahongo*, "taro" (Betsimisaraka, Sakalava), it serves to separate vowels in hiatus. Moreover, Adelaar (2016) points out that the disappearance of the *mu-* of *mutaʔu*, *mutoʔu* remains unexplained; he considers the similarity of *taho* to the terms from Timor as fortuitous. *Mu-* however, may have been considered as a prefix (prefixes are often dropped in loanwords from Bantu languages). A significant plant in the cultures of eastern Indonesia, and earlier throughout Southeast Asia,[44] taro also previously held a higher status in some regions of Madagascar than it does now. D. Coulaud (1973) and M. Bloch have pointed out the significance of taro in the Zafimaniry culture, where rice cultivation is an ancestral taboo. Perhaps there were "taro people" in Madagascar – as was the case in Melanesia – just as there were "yam people" (Bonnemaison 1996; see below). The presence of a taro plant in the northeast corner of the rice field (the northeast being the "direction of the ancestors") has been highlighted in the Vakinankaratra (Betafo region) by C. Blanc-Pamard and H. Rakoto Ramiarantsoa (1998) and M. Randrianera (1995). For Randrianera, "the first culture on a plot is always that of taro, and this practice is called 'continuity of life'." Nowadays cultivated in holes, sometimes manured, and located upstream or above rice fields in small valleys (Imerina, Tañala region), taro may have preceded rice on some wet lands (Blanc-Pamard and Rakoto Ramiarantsoa 1993: 34).

The great yam also held major cultural significance for the ancient Malagasy. Rituals noted in Anosy during the seventeenth century show links between the "white yam" *ovifotsy* (*Dioscorea alata* L.) and the royal power in this region, a link that once again connects Madagascar to eastern Indonesia and Melanesia (Beaujard 1991: 391; 1995; Raison 1992). During the ritual of the "Ramavaha" ("Ramadan"), after the prince "Dian Machicore" [Andriamasikoro] had begun to harvest his rice fields, "the Negroes [each of his vassals] brought for tribute ... four baskets of rice and thirty of yams." Even more interestingly, "Dian Tserongh" sent to Flacourt a yam of

---

44 The inhabitants of the Mentawei Islands still have "taro as staple food" (Walter and Lebot 2003: 16). Rutter (1929) has pointed out the importance of taro amongst the Dusun of northern Kalimantan; this also held true for other groups on this island (Barton and Denham 2011: 22).

such a large size "that two Negroes carried [it] in a tacon [shaft] and were weighed down by the load" (Flacourt 2007: 170, 199). We should note in passing that in Imerina, the cultivation practices and symbolism linked to these tubers of power were later transferred from yam to cassava during the eighteenth century (Callet 1981, II: 809).[45] This interest in increasing the size of yams – symbols of power – echoes cultivation and ritual practices widely known in Melanesia, where "to try and bring one's partner [in a ceremony] to accept a larger yam (and a greater quantity of yams) than what one has been given . . . is not an act of generosity but a way to show one's superiority" and strength (Kaberry 1942: 348; cf. Leenhardt 1980: 133). It seems likely that 'Dian Tserongh"s delivery of "a yam as large as a man's body" to Flacourt reflects the same idea. Such data raise the question of eastern influences – yet certainly not Melanesian – in the settlement process in Madagascar; these influences need not date as far back as the first migrations (see below). However, one can ask whether the importance of yams was necessarily related to eastern Indonesia. During the first millennium and even later, some regions of western Indonesia might have retained cultural traits that are now found only in eastern Indonesia. Like A. Haudricourt, J. Barrau, and G. Condominas, P. Gourou considers that some Asian populations began cultivating rice in what were formerly wet taro fields.[46] In any event, as Bonnemaison (1996: 397) points out, the techniques of intensive yam horticulture "exist only in the cultural areas where yams are dominant." These are so specific that independent "invention" seems less likely than diffusion.

Nowadays, on the whole, tubers (yam, taro, and American plants such as cassava and sweet potato) are symbolically depreciated: they are catalogued into a "black" category (pertaining to natives and dependants) as opposed to rice, which is a "white" food and associated with kings and aristocrats. Nowadays, the culture of yams apparently does not imply any ritual. This decline was probably sparked around the thirteenth/fourteenth century with the arrival of Indonesians (Zafiraminia and the *andriana* ancestors of the Merina kings) who began developing intensive wet rice farming along with rigidly hierarchical royal systems. The depreciation of "black" plants – also linked to Islamic influence – became the general rule, along with the deification of rice. Note that, during the ninth century, Abū Zayd described the plants and food from East Africa as "black," listing sorghum, sugarcane, and some tree products (Miquel 1975: 176).

[45] Flacourt, ed. Allibert 1995a: 160ff., 193. During the eighteenth century, the Imerina region shows a transfer of symbolic value and cultural practices from yam to cassava (Callet 1981 [1908], II: 809).
[46] Gourou 1984: 17–18. "The Indochinese people living in the mountains often plant a ritual yam in the dry field where they will grow rice, and those of the Philippines as well plant a taro in their wet rice fields" (Barrau 1973: 8). Yet many authors refute the idea that the planting of tubers is older than cereal growing in Southeast Asia. The significance of tuber planting could only have resulted from a failure of the cereals to adapt to equatorial conditions at the time the Austroasiatic and Austronesian peoples arrived; new varieties of rice would have been developed later. An ancient spread of taro from its original area of domestication in New Guinea, however, cannot be excluded (the Philippines and Indochina are other likely ancient centers for domestication) (Denham 2010; Blench 2012). The arrival of the Austroasiatics and the Austronesians in the Equatorial zone was certainly accompanied by the near-disappearance of rice: rice varieties brought by the migrants were photosensitive, and therefore not well adapted to the new climatic conditions.

Nor is it certain that the features for yam and taro noted in either Anosy (seventeenth century) or in the Highlands must be linked to the first Austronesian migrations in Madagascar. They may be associated instead with the Indonesian arrivals of the second millennium. The limited extension of the word *taho* certainly reflects a late arrival of this term.

There is another possible indication of an eastern Indonesian influence in Madagascar. P. Ottino noted the use in Timor of the terms *fukun* and *tukun*, corresponding to the Malagasy *foko* ("lineage") and *toko* ("district"), and the parallels that can be drawn between the dual organizations of Timor and Madagascar (see below).[47] It is difficult to assess when these terms reached Madagascar. Moreover, trade networks involving Java operated as far as New Guinea as early as the start of the Christian era. The question therefore arises whether the spread of some terms might be attributable to Sama sailors from Sulawesi, who participated in relations between the Moluccas and southern Sulawesi (Pelras 1996). This may indicate an arrival in Madagascar after the thirteenth century if we accept Pallesen's datings (although this spread could date to an earlier period).[48] A plausible period would be between the thirteenth and fifteenth centuries, when "Javanese" people belonging to the kingdoms controlled the trade routes of eastern Indonesia.[49]

Genetic research based on blood samples from different regions of Madagascar (the West central coast excepted) seems to support the hypothesis of an eastern Indonesian component in the settlement process in Madagascar. Part of the study done by Soodyall *et al.* (1996) has focused on mitochondrial DNA, inherited through the maternal line; twenty-four sequence-specific oligonucleotide (SSO) probes were taken into account, along with the intergenic 9 base pair deletion located between the cytochrome oxydase II and transfer RNA for lysin (COII / tRNALys) genes. SSO-Type n°10, the most prevalent (found in 56% of Malagasy individuals with the intergenic COII / ARNtLys 9 bp deletion), is also the most common between the Samoan Islands and New Guinea. H. Soodyall *et al.* have considered it as rare in Indonesia and Southeast Asia.[50] The Asian contribution for the 9 bp deletion is the highest among the Central Highland groups (27%) and the lowest in southwestern Madagascar (5%) (Soodyall *et al.* 1996: 163, fig. 12.3; 2013: 28).

Among the variants in the mitochondrial DNA used to identify the origin of the Asian contribution in Madagascar, a variant called "Polynesian" associated with the

---

[47] R. Blust connects the Tetun *fuku-n* to the PMP **buku*, "node" (of a bamboo, or a cane); this reinforces the idea of an "eastern" origin for the Malagasy term *foko*.

[48] According to A. K. Pallesen (1985), the Sama may have acted as intermediaries between the Moluccas and western Indonesia after the thirteenth century, but this date should probably be pushed back in time. Blust (2006) has shown that the Sama expansion may have been linked to that of the Malay at the time of Sriwijaya (seventh century) (see below).

[49] Studying Malagasy terminology for domesticated animals, Blench (2008: 27) tentatively links the Sakalava *boroko*, the Shimaore *puruku*, and the Shingazidja *purunku*, with the Proto-Oceanic **boRok*, "pig," but the Portuguese *porco* is a more probable etymology.

[50] The intergenic COII / tRNALys 9 bp deletion is commonly found in East Asia and does not represent a significant marker in itself (Oppenheimer 2004: 597). However, it is interesting to note specific mutations, such as those observed in the "Polynesian motif," although the place of origin of this "motif" remains debated (see below).

intergenic COII / tRNALys 9 bp deletion has been "found in 96% of Malagasy individuals who have SSO-types derived from the Asian source." "The Malagasy show a closer genetic affinity to Polynesians than they do to Indonesians," but Soodyall *et al.* suggest the possibility of the existence of populations harboring high SSO n°10 and the "Polynesian" variant in some regions of Indonesia. Of course, sampling is of crucial importance in these genetic studies. Unlike what these authors write, this "Polynesian" variant is not unknown in southeastern Kalimantan. Oppenheimer notes, however, that it is rare west of the Wallace line, but common beyond: the origin of the "Polynesian motif" may be located in the region of eastern Indonesia, which Oppenheimer calls Wallacea, whence this motif may have spread to the Pacific on the one side, and southeastern Kalimantan and then Madagascar on the other.[51] This motif could be 10,000 years old. For Bellwood, the origin of the "Polynesian motif" may well be located in eastern Indonesia, but the date suggested by Oppenheimer for the mutation is incorrect: it would have occurred during the Austronesian expansion in this region during the second millennium BCE. The Austronesians may also have borrowed the motif from an indigenous – feminine – source in eastern Indonesia (Bellwood 2005a: 270). The widespread distribution of the "Polynesian motif" in the Pacific results from genetic drift linked to the migrations of smaller groups onto unpopulated islands. Bellwood and Sanchez-Mazas (2005) also see a possible heritage of an "ancestral form of the Polynesian motif" from Taiwan as early as the first Austronesian migrations. A more recent study (Soares *et al.* 2011), however, supports an origin of the "Polynesian motif" in the region of the Bismarck archipelago prior to 4000 BCE.

A study by M. E. Hurles *et al.* (2005), which was based on both the Y chromosome, inherited in the paternal line,[52] and on mitochondrial DNA inherited in the maternal line, for the first time (unlike the preceding study by Soodyall *et al.*), provides results that support the linguistic data by locating a Malagasy origin in southeastern Kalimantan. "[For the Y-chromosomal haplogroups], the closest single Island Southeast Asian or Oceanic populations to the Malagasy is that of Banjarmasin [a port in southeastern Kalimantan]." Moreover, "the genetic data provides support for a direct rather than multistep process"; "alternatively, successive waves of migration from Southeast Asia may have brought different sets of lineages into Madagascar"; the Malagasy appear to have greater genetic diversity than that seen in the Pacific Islands (Hurles 2005: 897, 899). "It is intriguing, however, that the majority of Asia-derived mt-DNA types present in the Malagasy do not have exact matches in an extensive database" in [Indonesia] [according to current research]" (Hurles 2005: 900). Consistent with earlier studies, this work emphasizes the African origin of part of

---

[51] Oppenheimer 2004: 597. H. Soodyall *et al.* write: "the most likely explanation is that the original colonists of Madagascar either came directly from Polynesia, or from an Indonesian population who eventually colonized the Pacific Islands ... The absence of the Polynesian motif and mtDNA types found in individuals of Asian descent in Indian and African populations lends more support to the hypothesis that Madagascar was colonised directly from the South Pacific region" (1996: 165). See also Soodyall *et al.* 2013: 27.

[52] The authors used samples from 37 males from four different ethnic groups, Bezanozano (6), Betsileo (18), Merina (10), and Sihanaka (3).

the Malagasy population, while showing no sexual differentiation: the argument that men of Austronesian origin may have married East African women is not supported by this study. While Hurles *et al.* confirm the presence of the "Polynesian motif," they exclude a direct migration from Polynesia, since the Y-chromosomal haplogroups prevalent in Polynesia are not found in Madagascar.

Tofanelli *et al.* (2009) partly disprove Hurles *et al.* Their data reveal no particular connections between the Malagasy and southeastern Kalimantan (while the authors do acknowledge that the Maanyans are not known, genetically speaking). In the end, all studies encounter similar difficulties due to their limitations: small sample sizes, Malagasy samples based on obscure choices (Tofanelli *et al.* have – partially – taken into account four "ethnic" groups: the Merina, Antandroy, Antanosy, and Antesaka), and insufficient genetic data for Indonesia. As for African influences, Tofanelli *et al.* point out that the haplotypes of Central and West African type are more frequent in the Highlands and in Anosy, whereas southern Madagascar (Androy) expresses an influx from southeastern Africa (2009: 2115).[53] The African component reveals higher genetic diversity than does the Indonesian component, for mitochondrial DNA as well as the Y chromosome. This African component is largely predominant among the Antandroy.[54] The proportion of Indonesian to African ancestry is estimated to be "39%:50% for the highland groups, and 20%:74% in the coastal population" (2009: 2114; Soodyall *et al.* 2013: 33). "Thus, in contrast to mtDNA studies, Y chromosome data are consistent with a larger African input to the gene pool of the Malagasy" (Soodyall *et al.* 2013: 33).

Although constrained by similar limitations, recent studies do provide fresh data and open up new research avenues. They assess mtDNA variation in 266 individuals from the Merina, Vezo, and Mikea "ethnic" groups. Ricaut *et al.* (2009) identify five lineages – found in the Mikea and Vezo – belonging to a macro-haplogroup M formed during the migration of *Homo sapiens* out of Africa; these five lineages cluster into a clade – termed M23 – which appears to be restricted to the island of Madagascar and was constituted more than 68,000 years ago. The geographic origin of this M23 branch is unknown, but the authors suggest the circum-Arabia/northwestern Indian Ocean regions (Africa or western Asia). This may illustrate an early pre-Austronesian expansion into Madagascar.

Razafindrazaka *et al.* (2010) have observed a variable frequency in the "Polynesian motif" in the following populations: 50.0 percent in the Merina, 21.8 percent in the Vezo, and 13.4 percent in the Mikea. Interestingly, this "Polynesian motif" shows mutations that identify a "Malagasy motif," unknown – in the current state of research – in Polynesia or in Melanesia (Razafindrazaka *et al.* 2010: fig. 1). Due to limited knowledge of regions that are potential sources in Southeast Asia and in the Pacific, the origin of this "Malagasy motif" remains undetermined.

---

[53] All the "coastal groups" show a southeastern African component in the male line (Tofanelli *et al.* 2009: 2115) (recall, however, that the "coastal groups" in which the authors collected data were limited to the Antandroy, Antanosy, and Antesaka).

[54] It is important to note that the proportion of Indonesian and African components, for mitochondrial DNA, is similar among the Merina (63/37) and the Antanosy (67/33) (Tofanelli *et al.* 2009: 2114).

According to Cox *et al.* (2012: 2766), "the presence of Indonesian mtDNA and Y chromosomes in Madagascar argues for a mixed-sex founder population." The study confirms that "the Polynesian motif, the ancestral lineage of the Malagasy motif, is rare in Indonesia (2%), and with sporadic exceptions, this haplotype is restricted to eastern parts of the archipelago." Estimates "support a model in which Madagascar was settled by a small effective founding population – estimated at only approximately 30 women."[55] Among other hypotheses, the authors suggest that Madagascar may have initially been settled by people "who lost land and power during the rapid expansion of Srivijayan influence."

Kusuma *et al.* (2015), also taking into account both Y chromosome and mitochondrial DNA (giving information on paternal and maternal ancestry), provide important new data that support the idea of diverse Austronesian origins in the Malagasy population. Curiously, the data indicate a weak genetic correlation between the Maanyans and the Malagasy, who appear to be closer to populations from eastern Indonesia (South Sulawesi, Sumba, and Flores).[56] The mitochondrial DNA of the Malagasy, in particular, connects them to groups from eastern Indonesia: "Considering the restricted geographic distribution of the Polynesian motif [in Indonesia], it is most likely that this lineage from Madagascar traces back to eastern rather than western Indonesia … Malagasy women may have originated predominantly from eastern Indonesia" (Kusuma *et al.* 2015: 5). The authors also remind us that the particular Malagasy form of this motif has not been found in Indonesia. They conclude that "the populations involved [in the settlement of Madagascar] may be related to modern sea nomad groups and the ancient Malay Srivijaya trading network." It would be useful to include other populations of Kalimantan and Sea People in the study, and to take into account the fact that the Austronesian arrivals in Madagascar took place over a long period, between the seventh and fifteenth centuries at least. Moreover, D. Pierron (p.c.) rightly points out: "It seems that the genetic markers that were present in Borneo-Sulawesi a thousand years ago have now disappeared, due to demographic changes. These markers are now found only along the margins of eastern Indonesia and Madagascar" (see Pierron *et al.* 2017).

Brucato *et al.* (2016) indicate that "Malagasy Asian Ancestry derives from Southeast Borneo," but also point out that "the higher genetic complexity of the Asian ancestry component in Malagasy likely reflects the fact that more than a single source population was involved in its formation." The authors nevertheless first connect the Proto-Malagasy to a Malay-Southeast Barito admixed group originating in Banjarmasin (southeastern Kalimantan).[57] Due to processes of population replacement in the Java

---

55 According to the authors, "African and Indonesian lineages differ little across all Malagasy ethnic groups screened to date," but other studies clearly show otherwise. Here again, the sampling appears to be problematic. African migrations have occurred constantly over the centuries since the end of the first millennium; this contradicts the idea that "the main episode of African–Indonesian admixture likely occurred at the very beginning of Malagasy history" (2012: 2766). The authors also fail to take into account Austronesian arrivals during the second millennium.

56 "Populations with highest affinity to Malagasy are Mandar (Sulawesi), Flores (Lesser Sunda), Bajo (Sulawesi), and eastern Kalimantan Dayak and Lebbo' (Borneo)" (Kusuma *et al.* 2015: 5).

57 Brucato *et al.* (2016: 2398) write: "the Banjar originated from a Ma'anyan-Malay admixture, at a time preceding the supposed date of migration to Madagascar … the ancestors of the current Banjar would

Sea during the first millennium (see above), however, we will never know if Banjarmasin truly is the place of origin for the Proto-Malagasy, although it seems likely.

The most recent and extensive study on the subject (Pierron *et al.* 2017) has confirmed the link between Malagasy Asian ancestry and southern Kalimantan. The researchers note that "there is no signal of a putative ancient pre-Bantu/pre-Austronesian population." Interestingly, "the northern region of Madagascar has the highest Bantu contribution (Figure 2), and also exhibits the earliest demographic expansion (Figure 1E,: Figure S8) and the highest mtDNA diversity." This agrees with the archaeological evidence. The authors see "a cultural exchange when Austronesians arrived in the western part of the Indian Ocean without significant genetic admixture and later, after the settlement of Madagascar, a genetic admixture." This scenario contradicts "the theories [holding] that already well-mixed populations settled in Madagascar," as suggested by Deschamps, Blench, and Adelaar.

Dating the First Arrivals: How Linguists See It

Using glottochronology (an approach of questionable reliability), Dyen[58] suggests that the Malagasy and Maanyan languages diverged 1,900 years ago. Using the same technique, Vérin *et al.* (1970) propose the beginning of the Christian era for an incipient dialectal differentiation of the Malagasy language. N. Gueunier (1988) has rightly criticized this approach;[59] the estimate of the divergence of the different Malagasy dialects is based on a small sample of words and fails to take into sufficient account interactions between dialects that are geographical neighbors or in historical contact. Gueunier also points out that the study should have taken into consideration the respective influences of various Bantu languages (Comorian, Swahili) on some dialects. Moreover, Madagascar maintained contacts with the Indonesian world until the fifteenth century at least.

In 1951, O. C. Dahl proposed a date of approximately 400 for the Austronesians' arrival, taking into account the following facts: "indianization," in Sumatra, Borneo, and Java, occurred between the second and fifth centuries CE; Indonesian trade with the west progressed during the fifth century; and the Malagasy language contains very few words of Sanskrit or Prākrit origin, mostly arriving via Indonesia (see also Beaujard 2003). These Sanskrit terms dealt primarily with trade, politics, the calendar, or the moral aspects of social life. Research into cultivated plants also reveals some borrowings from Sanskrit, particularly in wet rice cultivation (see below). Loanwords are not necessarily linked to the first Austronesian arrivals, but may correspond to later arrivals, at various times. From the Sanskrit *çuddhi-*, "purity,

---

have contained both Malay and Ma'anyan genetic diversity, and probably linguistic inheritances from both."

[58] Dyen 1953a: 589. Glottochronology is based on the idea suggested by M. Swadesh and R. B. Lees that any replacements in basic vocabulary happen in constant percentages per time elapsed, for all languages: "over a thousand years, the fundamental lexicon, as defined by concepts such as *eating, drinking, man, head,* and consisting of a set of about one hundred words, has lost about 19% of its basic terms" (J. Dubois *et al.* 1973: 237).

[59] See also Dewar 1995: 310, and Poirier 1982, for a refutation of the conclusions of Vérin *et al.*

verification, information," Malay *sudi*, "to try, to test," we find three forms in Malagasy resulting from different borrowings: *sory, sotry*, "to take the appearance of," "to pretend, to turn into," and *asotry*, "dry and cooler season." The Sanskrit *kh*, which corresponds to *k* or *g* in Malay and Javanese, in Malagasy, yielded *h* in one case and *k* in the other loanwords. The Sanskrit *k*, transcribed as *k* in Malay, became *h-* in Malagasy, except for *kala*, a name used when addressing a young girl, probably a more recent loanword (and possibly borrowed directly from India). For other terms that came directly from the Indian subcontinent, as well, Malagasy has retained the *k*, for example in *kida*, "banana," and *katso*, "blue dye." Both are probably "recent" borrowings (after the first millennium), since they do not exhibit the fricativization *k/h* (Beaujard 2003).

P. Ottino has refuted the argument based on the small number of Sanskrit words in Malagasy, noting that indianization in Indonesia first affected the aristocracy, in contrast to a "popular" culture that remained that of the majority. The migrants must have mainly been merchants and sailors, not aristocrats. Indonesian culture, however, could have entered Madagascar in both popular and aristoratic forms. What is more, Indian culture did not influence Indonesia's various regions in the same way.

In 1991, Dahl changed his mind about the date of arrival of the first Austronesians, now proposing 700 CE. Adelaar made the same suggestion by identifying the Malays of Srīwijaya as organizers of the long-distance journeys that took Southeast Barito speakers to Madagascar.[60] Employed as sailors, these Southeast Barito people would have been in a situation of subordination to the Malays. Note that the Malagasy *sambo*, "ship," is related to the Old Malay term *sambu*, which may be of Khmer origin.[61] While the Southeast Barito languages are spoken nowadays by communities living in the interior of Kalimantan, in the past, Southeast Barito speakers lived on the coasts (see below). If journeys were led by Malays, it is unlikely that the latter chose men with no nautical skills for their crews (although specialists other than seamen, such as blacksmiths and cooks, may have been present onboard the ships). Moreover, genetic studies (see above) show that women accompanied the Barito speakers: thus these migrations were probably voluntary.[62]

Adelaar also believes that Malagasy words dealing with space symbolism and navigation are related to Malay. However, we must distinguish between different linguistic strata and, as will be demonstrated in Volume II, some Malay terms certainly arrived after the first Southeast Barito speakers.

In various domains, the existence in the Malagasy language of different terms, inherited and borrowed, reflects the complexity of peopling over time and space.

---

[60] Adelaar 2006. P. Vérin and H. Wright (1999) as well as P. Beaujard (2003) have suggested an earlier Austronesian settlement. In the current state of research, however, there is no evidence for an Austronesian settlement process prior to the eighth century.

[61] Adelaar 1995b. The French–Cambodian dictionary published by M. Moura (1878) indicates *sampou*, "sailing ship." Cf. also Skt. *çambuka* and Middle Persian **sambuk*.

[62] Nor does the absence of the green Chinese pottery termed "Dusun" (found in large quantities at Palembang and at other Malay sites) encourage us to consider the Malays from Srīwijaya as the organizers of the journey(s) of South East Barito speakers toward Madagascar. This pottery has nonetheless been discovered on Mayotte, at the Dembeni site, with its oldest section dated to the ninth–tenth centuries (Allibert 1998) (see below).

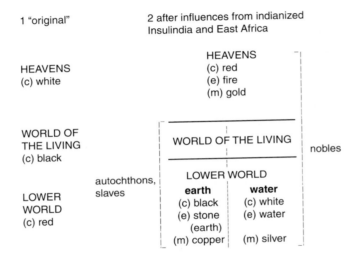

Spatial system

EAST
atsiñanana

UPPER WORLD

upstream

aray

elders

LOWER WORLD

downstream
añava
youngsters

handrefana
WEST

Figure 15.1 Madagascar: symbolic systems inherited from Kalimantan

Ternary representation of the universe

1 "original"   2 after influences from indianized Insulindia and East Africa

HEAVENS
(c) red
(e) fire
(m) gold

HEAVENS
(c) white

WORLD OF
THE LIVING
(c) black

WORLD OF THE LIVING   nobles

autochthons,
slaves

LOWER WORLD

LOWER
WORLD
(c) red

earth	water
(c) black	(c) white
(e) stone	(e) water
(earth)	
(m) copper	(m) silver

Names for the ocean provide a good example,[63] with the inherited terms *taika* (< PMP **tasik*, "sea"; Zorc 1994); *laotse/laotra* (< PAN **laSouth*, "towards the sea"; Adelaar 1989b); and the word *tasik*, found in the name Itasihanaka (<*tasik-anaka) for a lake in the Highlands (Dahl 1991: 27), *tasik* being a loanword from Malay (the *s* was maintained) (*laotra* in *tsimilaotra*, "north or northeast wind," also reveals a borrowing from Malay, one which I consider to be connected to later Indonesian arrivals of people called "Zavaka" or "Zafiraminia," during the second millennium).

---

[63] J.-C. Hébert (1961) has already pointed out the existence of various terms in Malagasy relating to the ocean. The second volume of this book will discuss Austronesian words that have been introduced more recently into the Malagasy language (words related to the Zavaka and Zafiraminia), and study the names of winds and compass directions.

References to spatial orientation in Kalimantan did not make use of cardinal directions, but instead indicated the direction followed by the sun (east/west) and used the oppositions upstream/downstream, or inland/seaward. It would therefore seem likely that Malagasy terms related to the sun's direction and upstream/downstream opposition go back to the first Austronesians' arrival. For "west," the Malagasy has (h)andrefa(na), which may be inherited from PAN *sajep, "to enter, to sink" (Beaujard 1998: 293).[64] The Malagasy word for "east" is atsiñànana, from the radical tsìñana, "rise" (of the new moon) (northern Madagascar atiñana(na), rad. tiñana), that can be tentatively linked to Kagayanen sennaŋan, and sinnaŋan, "whence (the sun) rises," "east" (southern Philippines, Mindanao Island). I have not found any word closer to the Malagasy. However, the Malagasy term does not seem to be a direct loanword from the Kagayanen, since the ŋ and the n are in inverted positions in the terms under consideration (the Malagasy term is most likely a loanword from Jav. Kromo tiñal, "to become visible, appear"; Dahl 1983: 44). Moreover, the se- or si- of the Kagayanen should correspond to a se- or si- in Malagasy.[65] Parallel forms can be found in Tagalog (silàŋan, silaŋànan, "east"), in Cebuano (silaŋan, "east"), and in Hanunóo (sidláŋ, "which rises (celestial body), shines (sun)," sidlaŋ-an, "east").[66]

The Tañala still use the opposition aràɣ/añàva, "upstream/downstream" to orient themselves in space. Ray in aràɣ (a, preposition of location/ray) is a term inherited from PAN *daya, "(toward) the interior (of land)." Ava in añàva (añ-/ava) is related to the Maanyan hawa, and Ngaju awa, ŋawa, "downstream."

The analysis of vocabulary dealing with directions and winds will be discussed further below. As is the case for words belonging to other fields (calendars), these terms demonstrate that several waves of Austronesian arrivals must be distinguished from one another – they may in fact represent a continuum, from the first arrivals until the fifteenth century. In spatiotemporal symbolism, Malay influences were not significant at the time of the first migrations of Southeast Barito speakers. Later, several phases of Malay influence can be seen (see Volume II and Beaujard 2003).

It is interesting to note that the term used for "east" may be linked to a southern Philippines language (new research here is needed), whereas it is generally admitted that the first migrants came from southeastern Kalimantan and the Java Sea. One wonders whether "sea gypsies" sailing between the southern Philippines and Kalimantan might be at the origin of this term in Madagascar. As pointed out already, it may be interesting to compare Malagasy with the languages spoken by the Sama groups (often mistakenly called Bajau)[67] found along the northern coasts of Kalimantan, on the islands between Kalimantan and the Philippines, in the southern Philippines, on the coasts of Sulawesi, and in the Maluku Islands (Moluccas). Today

---

[64] A borrowing from Malay depan, "in front of," suggested by Adelaar, seems less likely.

[65] K. A. Adelaar, p.c. The origin of the Malagasy tsiñana may be the word tiŋan, which is not found in the Philippines. The Sama languages of the Sulu archipelago do not appear to have terms to which the Malagasy tsiñana can be connected.

[66] Cf. also the murut miraŋ, "going up." The root of the Kagayanen sinnaŋan may be unrelated to sinaŋ, "to shine" (< PAN *θiNaŋ, "light"; Tsuchida 1976).

[67] They call themselves Sama (with an exception in the Philippines for the Abaknon and the Yakan), "but their neighbors usually know them under the name of Bajau (southern Philippines and northern Borneo) or Bajo (Indonesia)" (Pelras 1997: 67). On these "sea gypsies," see Sather 1995.

the Sama languages are better known, and R. Blust has recently shown their connection to the Southeast Barito family of southeastern Kalimantan. "The early Sama-Bajaw may well have been drawn into the southern Philippines by the Malay-dominated spice trade": "trade drew both the Malagasy and the Sama-Bajaw out of southeast Borneo" (Blust 2006: 52–53; see also below).[68] We would also need to compare Malagasy with the languages of the Orang Laut, "Sea Peoples" living on the coasts of the Straits of Malacca and in the Riau archipelago.[69]

The Orang Laut and the Sama certainly played major roles in the development of the first thalassocracies mentioned in the Chinese chronicles. During the fifth and sixth centuries, in the kingdom of Gantuoli, the Orang Laut most likely formed a significant minority of the population. "The Orang Laut," C. Pelras points out,[70] "had particular links with the Malay kingdoms, and their spread in the archipelago between the eighth and ninth centuries, as well as that of the Sama-Bajo, far from being the result of simple nomadism, was certainly linked to the trade activity of Srīwijaya and Malayu." These populations may have acted as intermediaries for borrowings from one language to another. The name Vezo for maritime groups in southwestern and western Madagascar may have links with the name Bajaw or Bajo, often used to refer to the Sama. Dahl has noted that Orang Laut groups (the Moken of the Malay peninsula, and the Orang Laut of the Riau-Lingga archipelago) as well as the Vezo of Madagascar deposit their corpses with their heads toward the west (in other Malagasy groups, bodies are laid with their heads toward the east).[71] "The migration of the ancestors of the Malagasy," adds Blench (2008: 20), "can be linked to the dispersal of the Sama-Bajaw during the seventh century or thereabouts, impelled by the expansion of the Srivijaya Malays."

[68] "The specific 'homeland' of the Sama-Bajaw peoples is the area which today forms the basin of the Barito River and its tributaries – the same area from which the Malagasy derive ... Most of the innovations shared exclusively by Sama-Bajaw and the Barito languages favor the Southeast Barito group ... Some of the innovations shared only by the Samalan [Sama] and East Barito languages are almost certainly loanwords. Others, however, are probably not." In addition, Blust notes that Sama-Bajau languages contain many words from Malay, which were borrowed prior to the arrival of the Sama-Bajau speakers in the Philippines.

[69] Orang Laut refers to what Blust terms "aquatic populations" centered on the Strait of Malacca. Aside from Moken, the Orang Laut languages "are Malay dialects," thus they are "clearly distinct from the Sama-Bajau languages" (Blust 2006). According to the linguist Pallesen (1985), the Sama languages of the Sulu archipelago may all derive from the same proto-language; "they cannot be related to the languages of the Philippines, and their original region of dispersion may have been somewhere between the Anambas and Natuna archipelagoes (in the southern China Sea) or in the islands located along the central coast of Sumatra (Riau, Lingga, Bangka, Billiton)" (Pelras 1997: 59). A comparison of the Sama languages of Sulu, Sulawesi, and eastern Indonesia with languages of the Orang Laut of the Malacca Strait remains to be undertaken. According to Pallesen, who uses linguistic evidence, the Sama Bajau were already present in the Sulu archipelago around at least 800 CE (Bellwood 1997: 136). Pallesen places the beginning of the major Sama expansion only at the turn of the second millennium from the Sulu archipelago: this expansion accompanied the development of trade networks, most of them impelled by China under the Song dynasty (Pallesen 1985: 118, 249). Blust (2006) places the Sama expansion earlier, however.

[70] Pelras 1996: 75, after Pallesen 1985: 246–247, 261–266. See also Wolters 1967: 222, 341.

[71] Dahl 1991: 94. Dahl has also considered the Vezo glottal stop that appears in some possessive forms (instead of -n-) as an influence from the Orang Laut languages (tsañoʔao, "your house," instead of tsañonao) (1991: 103).

Interactions between Malays and the people of the Java Sea speaking a language (or languages) of the Southeast Barito type as well as the origin of the Malagasy language are both illuminated by stelae erected by the Srīwijayan king Jayanasa during the late seventh century (see below) in southeastern Sumatra. Linguists have paid special attention to these stelae.[72] Thus, the stela of Kota Kapur, found on Bangka Island, erected in 686, bears two texts written in two different languages; they include a curse against rebels who opposed Srīwijaya. O. C. Dahl has related the first text (written in a language that Damais has termed "B language") to "Old Maanyan," Lom, a dialect on northern Bangka Island, and Malagasy (the stela contains terms having h instead of s in Malay [< *s], and i instead of r in Malay [< *r].[73] In the language of this stela and the Lom language, Dahl saw proof of the existence of a colony of "Maanyans" on Bangka during the seventh century. For Adelaar, however, Lom is simply a Malay dialect, unrelated to Maanyan.[74] The stela at Karang Brahi, in the interior of Sumatra (Jambi), shows a very similar text, with the same beginning in "Old Maanyan." Another inscription at Sebokingking was discovered near a well, near Palembang; like the other stelae, it appears to have been linked to oath-taking rituals, including the drinking of sanctified water. Van Naerssen has conjectured that the "B language" of the stelae may belong to "Orang Laut," a potential ally of the king of Palembang.[75] These stelae were probably set at the boundaries of territory controlled by the king of Srīwijaya. The three stelae include invocations to divinities, curses against those who plot against the king and the kingdom, and the king's blessings on those who submit themselves to his power. Ferrand's and Damais' translations of these texts still show gray areas. As Adelaar notes, interpretation of these stelae can only be speculative, given that these texts are short and difficult to translate. A connection between Malagasy and the language of these stelae, however, can be contemplated (Adelaar 1995a).

One wonders why the part of the text written in "Old Maanyan" is placed at the beginning of each inscription. According to a hypothesis suggested by Dahl, Old Maanyan may have been a sacred language used by diviners (Dahl 1991: 53–54). In fact, we do not know the geographical dispersion of the "Southeast Barito" languages at the start of (and prior to) the seventh century. Trade-oriented groups speaking "Southeast Barito" languages may have lived along the south-southeastern

---

[72] See Kern 1913; Coedès 1930; Ferrand 1932; Aichele 1936, 1954; de Casparis 1956; Dabut 1968; Dahl 1991. G. Ferrand has shown the link between Malagasy and the language used in the first text, but his translation is fanciful.

[73] The rest of the text is written in Old Malay; it contains many Sanskrit words. We observe *s > h only in some languages of Kalimantan and Sulawesi, and in a few smaller neighboring islands (Dahl 1991). One observes h > Ø in Malagasy, and *R > y (usually becoming z) or Ø.

[74] Adelaar 1995a: 339. Dahl also considered the Sekak, living on Bangka Island, as the descendants of Bajau sailors who may have carried other Maanyan to Madagascar. In fact, "we know almost nothing about the language and the society of the Sekak. Their linguistic affiliation with the Bajau is not justified" (Adelaar 1995d: 51).

[75] Nik Hassan Shuhaimi 1990: 66. Above the inscription, a seven-headed snake has been carved. Water spilt on the stone must have been collected in the cavity under the inscription. A ceremony of this type is described in the *Sejarah Melayu*, involving an oath between an envoy of the king and a man representing the king's subjects.

coasts of Kalimantan, on Bangka Island and in southeastern Sumatra.[76] We do not know which languages were spoken in southeastern Sumatra before the Malay expansion (Blust 2006: 34) (eastern and southeastern Sumatra were affected by processes of "linguistic leveling" following the Malay expansion, leading to language extinctions: "an earlier linguistic diversity has been leveled by the expansion of Malayic speakers into southeast Sumatra" [Blust 2006: 34]). Moreover, Malays were present at the mouth of the Barito River, where an inscription in Old Malay perhaps dating to the same period as the stelae of Sumatra and Bangka has been discovered at the site of the temple of Candi Laras. These groups speaking Southeast Barito languages may have been linked to states predating Sriwijaya. The rise of early Malay states may have led to the departure of pre-Malagasy groups toward the western Indian Ocean. According to Blust, the Malays of Sriwijaya began incorporating indigenous groups who were trading products of the jungle in wider exchange networks "during the period 670–800 AD" (2006: 53). In fact, the Malay expansion occurred before Srīwijaya, and contacts made by the inhabitants of Kalimantan with indianized people go back at least to the fourth–fifth century, as shown by the stelae at Kutei (though they had probably begun earlier). In addition, the "B language" of the stelae at Bangka and southern Sumatra dating to the early period of Srīwijaya shows strong connections between the Malays (Srīwijaya and Pre-Srīwijaya) of Sumatra and Southeast Barito speakers before 700. The Austronesians who transported spices and aromatics to China and India as early as the second century BCE may have been Proto-Malays.

It therefore seems possible to envision: 1. Austronesian migrations (possibly of Proto-Malays) to the East African coast, at the turn of the Christian era at the latest; 2. later migrations of Southeast Barito speakers mixed with Malays, to the Comoros and Madagascar; 3. exchanges between Africa and Madagascar involving Austronesians and Bantus, as well as limited cultural blending between Bantus and Austronesians in the Comoros and northern Madagascar, toward the end of the first millennium CE (see Map II.19).

The Archaeological Data

Linguistics can only offer some indication as to the period when the first settlement(s) occurred, or as to the migrants' culture. For its part, archaeology has contributed a great deal of information, by reconsidering subfossil sites, and by discovering and excavating various settlements. Recent research taking palynology and palaeozoogeographical evidence into account has also shed light on the early peopling of Madagascar. However, some gray areas remain.

Subfossil Sites and the Contribution of Palynology

Various sites containing subfossils have been studied, sometimes for extended periods of time; these include Taolambiby (southeast of Tulear) (Walker 1967), Andakatomena

---

[76] The subsequent Malay expansion obliterated this situation. P. Simon ([1988] 2006) also places the "Proto-Malagasy" on the southern coast of Kalimantan; their maritime orientation would explain their contacts in the Java Sea with people speaking "Malayo-Javanese" languages.

(Bay of Saint-Augustine) (Radimilahy *et al.* 2006), Andrahomana (Anosy) (Walker 1967), and Ampasambazimba (Imerina) (where excavations began in 1902). As R. Dewar has pointed out (1984: 581–582; 1986: 29–30), the suggested correlation between objects of human origin and bones of subfossils has often proved problematic, leading to uncertain datings.

At Lambohara (southwest coast), several pierced teeth (possibly parts of a necklace) of an extinct lemur of the genus *Daubentonia* (aye-aye) have been unearthed. Radiocarbon dating shows that the animal was killed between 220 and 440 (MacPhee and Burney 1991). Lambohara, another subfossil site excavated by A. Grandidier at the beginning of the twentieth century, has yielded flint of uncertain dating. A lithic industry, however, cannot be excluded (Battistini 1971: 10; Vérin 1975b: 183; Radimilahy 2011; and below).

More recent research has led to crucial discoveries, revealing a human presence prior to the Christian era. R. MacPhee and D. Burney have shown that several femurs of pigmy hippos from subfossil sites excavated by A. Grandidier show cut marks made by tools: two femurs from Ambolisatra (north of Toliary), two from Lambohara (dated to the first and fourth century CE), and one from Belò-sur-Mer (south of Morondava) (MacPhee and Burney 1991: 696ff.; Burney *et al.* 2004: 53) (see Map II.20). At Taolambiby, a radius of the sloth lemur *Palaeopropithecus ingens* (extinct) with cut marks has been dated to 2325 ± 43 yr BP (2366–2315 cal. yr BP).[77] In addition, a tibiotarsus of *Aepyornis* collected at Itampolo (southwestern coast) shows evidence of human modification; it has been dated to between 30 BCE and 320 CE (Burney 1999).

These finds suggest a permanent human presence in southwestern Madagascar, since at least 300 BCE. It is admitted today that hunter-gatherers from the East African coast (possibly Mozambique) must have come to Madagascar during that time (Bantu agriculturists did not arrive on the Tanzanian coast before the beginning of the Christian era). These hunter-gatherers may have traded with merchants either from the Greco-Roman world (Blench 2007: 72) or from Arabia.[78]

"The phylogeographic histories of rats and mice can be valuable for tracing human history" (Tollenaere *et al.* 2010: 408; see above). Blench (2007) suggests the introduction of rodents into Madagascar – possibly by Greco-Roman ships – before the Austronesians' arrival. "The closest relatives of the specimens of *Rattus rattus* studied [in southern Madagascar] are the rats of the Indian subcontinent," but Hingston *et al.* (2005) point out the lack of data for Africa.[79] Aplin *et al.* (2011) note that genetics indicates a long history of the black rat in Madagascar; it probably arrived during the first millennium BCE. The Malagasy rat is related to a lineage found in Oman and on the western coast of India. "The Arabian Peninsula may be the origin of the black rat colonization of Madagascar" (Tollaere *et al.* 2010: 406). Data suggest that the first arrival of *R. rattus* occurred on the east coast of Madagascar.

---

[77] Burney *et al.* 2004: 32; Perez *et al.* 2005; Blench 2007: 71. There is no sign of human impact on the ecosystems for such an old period.

[78] See also Blench 2010a. The chop marks observed must have been made by stone (quartz?) tools. Iron arrived on the African coast only with the Bantu agriculturists.

[79] "*Rattus rattus* may have spread from India to Egypt during the fourth century BC" (Hingston *et al.* 2005: 1553).

Moreover, Hingston *et al.* have signaled the introduction of the Asian house shrew *Suncus murinus* (an endemic species in South Asia and Pakistan) and of the mouse *Mus musculus gentilulus* (a subspecies found in Yemen) via Africa (at an undetermined time) (2005: 1557). Vasey and Burney (2007) note greater quantities of *Rattus rattus* and *Mus musculus* remains at Andrahomana between 2480 and 1760 BP, to the detriment of endemic species. *Suncus etruscus*, originally from Southeast Asia, was introduced into Madagascar and Mayotte at an undetermined time (Goodman 2013).

A study of lake sediments in southwestern Madagascar, at a level dated to between 10 and 190 CE, has revealed "increases in charcoal associated with a reduction in pollen of woody species and an increase in the pollen of grasses and or weedy herbs."[80] Greater amounts of charcoal dated between 130 and 420 CE have also been noted further north at Lake Komango, in the Manambolo region (west coast) (Burney 1999). "A drastic decrease in spores of the coprophilous fungus *Sporormiella spp.*, a proxy for the presence of megafauna, in sediments dated 1720 ± 40 ^{14}C yr BP (230–410 cal yr CE)" at Ambolisatra indicates a marked decline in megafauna. The same phenomenon has been observed at Belò-sur-Mer for the period between 100 BCE and 110 CE.[81] These declines slightly predate "the concomitant rise in microscopic charcoal particles" (Burney *et al.* 2004: 33).

Fire-setting may have served as a hunting technique. Natural fires, favored by climatic changes, cannot be excluded. Recent finds may lead us to reconsider sixth-century dating suggested by Vérin for the site of Sarodrano, south of Toliary, a dating that had been cast into doubt (Allibert and Vérin 1993a: 38 n. 8).

Hunter-gatherers seem to have arrived much earlier in northwestern Madagascar. Chop marks on the bones of pigmy hippos *Hippopotamus lemerlei* have been identified at the Anjohibe cave, near the bay of Mahajamba; the bones are associated with a date of 2288–2035 cal. BCE (Gommery *et al.* 2011; Dewar *et al.* 2013).

While the impact of these hunter-gatherers on the environment was limited, this situation would change with the arrival of agriculturists and herders during the late first millennium CE. The disappearance of the subfossils, nevertheless, was a slow process, and the extinction of many species occurred only relatively recently, during the second millennium (Dewar *et al.* 2013).

The First Settlements in the North of the Island

In northern Madagascar, excavations in 1986 in the rockshelter of Lakaton'i Anja in the Andavakoera gorge (Antsiranana region) have yielded the date of 420 CE for the lowest level. The archaeological levels contained animal bones (sometimes belonging to extinct species), as well as shells and shards of local pottery (imported pottery has been found only in the upper levels, dated to the tenth century and later). Andavakoera

---

[80] Dewar and Wright 1993: 426, after Burney (1993) on Ambolisatra. A higher amount of charcoal in sediments is noticeable at Belò for a date between 60 and 350 CE but only as of 600 CE at Ambolisatra (Burney *et al.* 2003: 10802). A process of aridification may have affected southwestern Madagascar at the turn of the Christian era (Burney *et al.*, 2004: 31).

[81] Burney *et al.* 2003: 10802; Burney *et al.* 2004: 33; Blench 2007: 72, 2010.

is a site that was visited by small groups engaged in foraging. Recent investigations have led to the discovery of stone tools; "they resemble those known from southern and eastern Africa, southern Arabia, and South Asia, and are unlike those from Southeast Asia" (Dewar *et al.* 2013: 12587). It appears that hunter-gatherers lived in the Andavakoera gorge "during a period between the 3rd and the 7th centuries CE, and possibly prior to this dating" (Dewar *et al.* 2015).[82] "The span of dates from the two sites [Lakaton'i Anja Cave and Ambohiposa Rockshelter] suggest the presence of stone tool producing forager groups in this area from ca. 2000 BCE until 1000–1200 CE" (Ekblom *et al.* 2016).

Research into the sediments of a swamp in the region of Lake Itasy shows an increase in the proportion of grass species, and the presence of charcoal *c.* 100 BCE. H. Straka believed that these changes were in fact the impact of the first agriculturists on the environment, but there is no evidence for this. The forest grew back from around 1000 CE, until 1500 CE, a date Straka links to the arrival of a "second Austronesian wave" (1996: 39).

Straka's observations, however, are in part supported by the find of *Cannabis* pollen *c.* 2200 BP at Lake Tritrivakely and around 500 CE at Lake Kavitaha (Burney 1987c; Gasse and Campo 1998; Burney *et al.* 2004). Burney describes a subsequent increase in charcoal in the sediments around 600 CE at Kavitaha and during the eighth century at Tritrivakely, probably linked to human activity.[83] Indian hemp was certainly introduced by men at an early time in Africa. D. Burney does not exclude the possibility of an early introduction of hemp in Madagascar by sailors, and a human presence on the Malagasy Highlands around 500 CE (Burney 1987a: 141; 1987c: 374). Hemp seeds may even have been dispersed by birds from Africa,[84] although the presence of these seeds during the sixth and seventh centuries in the Itasy region (Lake Kavitaha) and Vakinankaratra (Lake Tritrivakely), respectively, leads one to suspect a link with humans.

Curiously, no settlement has been found in northwestern Madagascar for the period preceding the ninth century, when some of the first Austronesian and Bantu migrants must have landed.[85] Moreover, R. Dewar has correctly pointed out that the objects unearthed from the earliest settlements do not show evidence for an "Austronesian culture": "the dominance of Malagasy as a language and the evidently important contribution of Indonesians to the island's gene pool have yet to find their analogue in the prehistoric material culture" (1995: 315). It is true that shared linguistic elements do not necessarily imply a shared culture.[86] The ceramics that have been unearthed do

---

[82] Stone tools have also been found at the rockshelter of Ambohiposa, in the Bay of Vohemar (Dewar *et al.* 2015). Here, radiocarbon measurements have yielded datings between the ninth and thirteenth centuries BCE.

[83] Burney 1987b; Burney *et al.* 2004. The datings are between 530 and 780 at Lake Kavitaha, and 630–1000 at Lake Tritrivakely.

[84] R. Dewar, p.c. In addition, hemp is a pollen-producing plant, and it is possible to find its pollen in sediments even though the plant is rare.

[85] As mentioned above, a shard found on the northern coast of Nosy Be Island may belong to a Mediterranean amphora from the early first millennium (Wright *et al.* 2005).

[86] I cannot agree with Sutton (1984: 615), who wrote that linguistic definitions and classifications of populations generally offer a maximum of clarity and convenience for anthropologists and historians.

not lead us to establish a definite link with the Austronesian world (Dewar and Wright 1993: 431), partly because little is known about pottery from Kalimantan and other islands for the first millennium CE (Vérin and Wright 1999: 35). But the first sites in northern Madagascar (Andavakoera, Nosy Mangabe, Sandrakatsy, Irodo, for the northeast, and Mahilaka, in the northwest) do reveal coarse *Arca* shell-impressed pottery – of a type also known in the Comoros – that has "few African parallels and may be Southeast Asian" (Vérin and Wright 1999: 39). As mentioned above, *Arca*-impressed ceramic is found in decreasing quantities as one travels westward from the Comoros to East Africa (Wright 1984; Allibert 1992).[87] The dating of this pottery, according to current research, favors Adelaar's hypothesis for an arrival of the Pre-Malagasy around the eighth century.

Comparative Anthropology

In addition to linguistics and archaeology, comparative anthropology has been used to shed light on original peopling. The many Austronesian elements noted in the Malagasy culture, by H. Deschamps for example, relate to concepts such as navigation, agriculture and cultivated plants, breeding, some fishing techniques, the production of bark cloth and mat cloth, house building, spatial orientation, stone constructions in which stone layers are interrupted by vertical slabs, in the corners and at regular intervals,[88] iron metallurgy, the use of the blowpipe, musical instruments, both ternary and dualistic views of the world and of society, funerary practices (such as double funerals) and ancestor worship (forked posts, standing stones, stone tables), ox sacrifice, the importance of cognatism in familial groups, and more.

This comparatism calls for some comments. The "Austronesian" cultural features listed here do not necessarily need to be connected to the first arrivals; some may reflect the impact of more recent migrants, but it is difficult to suggest datings. The wide distribution of most of the cultural characteristics in the Austronesian world prevents us from attributing any to a particular region (it will be shown, however, that some rituals in slash-and-burn cultivation along the east Malagasy coast suggest links with Kalimantan). Moreover, this kind of inventory reflects only the predominant influences in fields that in fact show various syncretisms. Rather than simply attempting to distinguish the juxtaposition of elements of various origins ("African" or "Indonesian"), we should come to an understanding of how various contributions may have merged to elaborate new, constantly evolving cultural schemes. The various features taken into account for comparison should be placed within their overall contexts, through trans-disciplinary research, an approach that has been taken by P. Ottino (1986) and myself (Beaujard 1991, 2003) in the fields of mythology and politics, spatial symbolics, and agriculture.

---

[87] In contrast, red-slipped pottery with silvery graphite decoration unearthed in Madagascar at the beginning of the second millennium, a type of decoration found in the Comoros and at some places along the East African coast, may well be of African origin (see below).

[88] Vérin 1975: 187. This mode of construction has been described on Nias.

Some domains, however, have been explored, using a diachronic perspective, for example ethnomusicology (Sachs 1938) and iron metallurgy (Radimilahy 1988, 1993).

Sachs connected instruments of "Indonesian" origin in Madagascar with a cultural level dated to the beginning of the Christian era (known as the "Sachs 19" level). "The Sachs 20 level, dated to the second half of the first millennium yielded no musical instruments in Madagascar: this island does not know either gongs, or various metallophones, or the brilliant sets of bells that make the musical glory of Java and of the neighboring islands" (Sachs 1938: 76). As instruments of "Indonesian" origin in Madagascar, Sachs listed the split-bamboo clapper, struck bamboo log, bamboo tubes suspended in a frame, the transversely blown conch, a long double-headed drum beaten with three sticks (according to Sachs, outside Madagascar, this can be found only in Sulawesi), a "double headed, conical, laced drum" ("the strings form a Y pattern on the barrel of the drum"), tapped with a hand on one side, and beaten with a stick on the other ("particular to the Malay world") and the tube zither, *valiha*, of Malay tradition (its Malagasy name may not derive from the Sanskrit *vādiya-*, "music instrument," as suggested [Beaujard 2003], but from the Malay *balikan* [Adelaar 2007]).[89] To this list we should add bamboos split and beaten with sticks: these were still being used in Tañala funerary rituals during the 1970s.

The terms related to iron metallurgy are of Austronesian origin, as are related techniques themselves, such as double-pistoned furnace bellows. This type of metallurgy arrived with the first migrants. Characteristic of African metallurgy, "skin-bellows are also present in Madagascar, but used only for precious metals" (Radimilahy 1988: 7).

Data relative to two fields will now be presented: spatial symbolism and agriculture.

The Ternary System: Cosmic and Social Dualism

Spatial symbolism reflects an early Austronesian heritage. The pre-Malagasy brought with them a dual cosmic and social model. Society was divided into two groups, one linked to the upper world and another associated with the lower world; this vision was combined with a ternary system. This division seems to be related to the early spatial symbolism mentioned for Kalimantan (east–west, upstream-downstream). For the Ngju of Kalimantan, Schärer has noted the existence of three worlds (the sky, the world of the living, and the lower world), as well as an opposition between a dominant group (the "whites"), linked to the sky and living in the upper part of the village, and a "poor and inferior" group of "red men," connected to the lower world, living in the lower part of the village (Schärer 1963: 65–66). The three worlds are associated with three colors, white (sky), black (earth), and red (lower world) (Beaujard 2003). Eastern Indonesia offers other examples of cosmic and social dualism, combined with tripartite concepts[90] showing striking parallels

---

[89] R. Blench describes the instrument as "made from a single internode of a broad-diameter bamboo, and the strings are formed from the raised epidermis of the bamboo" (2014: 3) He leaves the question of the etymology of *valiha* open.

[90] Swellengrebel 1960: 41–42. On the ternary/binary system, see also Josselin de Jong 1977.

with Madagascar.[91] However, a number of features shared by eastern Indonesia and Madagascar derive from concepts present in other parts of Indonesia and are almost universal.[92]

Following overhauls caused by new influences (from East Africa, or – more probably – from Indonesia: cf. the alliance of the sky and the waters in what P. Ottino [1986: 64], like J. J. Ras, has called "the original Malay myth"), the Malagasy system differs from the earlier Austronesian model in its split between earth and water (in the middle and lower worlds; this division is connected to the opposition between autochthonous groups and aristocrats), and a complex symbolism based on color. On the east coast and in the Highlands a double – contradictory – symbolism of red, is seen, due to different influences. On the one hand, red is associated with the lower world (for example, the name of "red cloth" *lambamena*, given to the shrouds of the dead in the Highlands; the prohibition on washing washing red cloth in some rivers – linked to "water princesses" *andriambavirano*;[93] and the use of red material to wrap evil charms on the east coast); this connection is shared by many societies of western Indonesia. On the other hand, red is the color of the kings throughout Madagascar (note also the term *volamena*, "red silver," applied to gold, a metal reserved for kings). The adjective *mena* used in Madagascar for the color red may be linked to the Indonesian *hinai*, "henna," from the Arabo-Persian *hinna'*. It is significant that "the color of the king" (red) is the only color in Madagascar whose name is of Arabo-Persian origin, probably via Indonesia (the other color names have an Austronesian etymology); this fact may be connected to the influence of Gujarati Islam in insular Southeast Asia. In the Indian world, where color symbolism is partly the same as in ancient Persia, red is the color of the *kshatriya*. Following the arrival of indianized Austronesians in Madagascar (the groups called Zavaka and Zafiraminia; see below), one notes a new association of these major colors with the three worlds of the universe (red=sky, white=water, black=earth).

The association of the color red with royal power – within the red-white-black triad – may also reflect East African influences. For the Ndembu, Turner has shown the fundamental symbolism of this triad, with red being linked to blood and power, white to milk and life, and black to death and evil.[94]

---

[91]   As in Madagascar, the "sky" is given a cadet position, while at the same time it is the dominant upper half. See Swellengrebel 1960: 39, 41, and F. A. E. Van Wouden, 1963 [1935]: 49, 59–63, 75–76, 102–104, 134, 140, 158.

[92]   In Timor and other islands, a "master of the earth" complements the political chief. Sometimes belonging to the oldest lineage in the region, he is in charge of ceremonies, notably agricultural rituals. These elements recall the position of Malagasy "native" chiefs, called "masters of the earth" (Poirier 1964; Beaujard 1983, 1991; Ottino 1998). This is in fact a nearly universal feature of agrarian societies developing dualist systems.

[93]   Red clothing is believed to attract crocodiles. Among the Ngaju of Kalimantan, crocodiles are the subjects of Djata, the goddess of the lower world of the waters, whose color is red (Stöhr 1968: 32).

[94]   V. Turner 1967: 57, 59ff. Beyond the Ndembu, Turner (1967: 80–81, 83ff.) demonstrates the universal importance of this "archetypal" triad, based on "psycho-biological" experience: everywhere red is associated with blood, white with milk and sperm; in contrast to these two colors, symbols of life, black is linked to bodily substances resulting from metabolism (feces), and therefore to death.

The prows, sterns, and rudders of the ancient sewn boats of the East African coast called *mtepe* were adorned with motifs using red, white, and black (see above). The ships flew red, white, or red and white flags (Poumailloux 1999: 275; Prins 1965: 102).[95] Red was the color of the flag of the sultan of Zanzibar, "as well as the color of flags of early states of the Persian Gulf."[96] This symbolism may prove to be of Persian origin.

The presence of the "three colors" on the cloak (called *lamba telo soratra*, "three-colored cloth" in southeastern Madagascar) worn by kings during ceremonies expresses the kings' universal sovereignty.[97] This ternary system is combined with a binary division. In the Highlands and in southeastern Madagascar, red and white are connected with the aristocracy; red represents political power; white (possibly a Muslim influence) symbolizes purity and religious power. Black is linked to the "masters of the earth (or land)," or "elders on the earth": the autochtonous group (black is also the color of the spirits of the earth). In Anosy, during the seventeenth century, the French administrator E. de Flacourt described a society divided into two hierarchized groups, the "White people" (islamized aristocrats) and the "Black people" (pagan natives), associated with the sky and the earth, respectively. This was a "color" division influenced by Islam, but which obeyed old Austronesian dualism[98] (Java knew an opposition between Muslim "Whites" and pagan "Reds," with red often linked to the lower world in western Indonesia, and white symbolizing the upper world) (for southern Sulawesi, see also Pelras 1996: 81). The Anosy aristocrats were Zafiraminia ("people from Sumatra"), who arrived in Madagascar around the thirteenth century. In Anosy, they show a highly mixed culture (Ottino 1986). This social division between "White" and "Black" people has also been noted, with a variety of modalities, for the countries of Antemoro, Tañala, and Merina. It is linked to an opposition between rice ("white" food) and tubers ("black" food).

Spatial symbolism will be revisited and the later use of of calendars, introduced by the Zavaka and Zafiraminia (in the second millennium), will be discussed in Volume II. We do not have much knowledge about the ways in which early time was reckoned.

---

[95] According to Stigand (1913: 141), the white flag and talismans were meant to counteract the evil influence of sea-devils (*sheitani wa bahari*).

[96] P. Poumailloux, p.c. Since Antiquity, red (or purple) has been the royal color in the Persian Gulf and the Mediterranean.

[97] In Imerina, the king "gives a silver chain, a black silk cloth and a red hat to those who submit themselves" (Callet 1981: 72). We find the same symbolism in Achaemenid Persia, where for clothes, "red is the color of warriors, white that of priests, blue that of peasants. To symbolize its authority over all classes, the king wears clothes mixing these colours" (Huyse 2005: 240).

[98] The opposition of white and black in Anosy during the seventeenth century probably reflects a Muslim influence; however, note that on Bali (an island where Hinduism has remained predominant), the antagonism between the upper and lower worlds is expressed as a white/black opposition (Goris 1960: 98). In Mayotte, traditions recounting the origin of the first *beja* refer to the arrival of a Muslim "white" man and his "black" *waziri*, "a simple African commoner." The two men married two sisters, thus creating two hierarchized lineages, respectively "white" and "black," living in the west and south, and in the east and north of Mayotte, respectively (Blanchy 1997: 115–116).

Agriculture

The first Austronesian migrants brought with them various cultivated plants that were adapted to an equatorial or humid tropical climate: rice, yams, the coconut tree, and turmeric.

Rice, Slash-and-Burn and Wet Rice Types of Cultivation   The first migrants to Madagascar had probably already mastered the techniques of both wet and dry rice farming. The island's Indonesian heritage involves both types, as can be seen in the etymology of its agricultural vocabulary, as well as rituals and farming practices. Rice must have been cultivated during the hot (rainy) season, both on cleared land and along the banks of marshes or rivers. We know that "simple forms of marsh culture require no more commitment than land clearing and can provide higher yields" (Bellwood 1996: 479). There was probably another type of rice cultivation during the colder season, when water levels dropped. If quantities harvested and hours worked are taken into consideration, swidden cultivation would produce higher yields than would be possible when setting out wet rice fields. Moreover, the first Austronesians arrived in Madagascar without cattle; working rice fields with spades alone would have required an enormous amount of energy.

All over Madagascar, the word *vary* refers to the rice plant, the paddy, and cooked rice. *Vary* has been related to several Kalimantan languages; *bari*, meaning "cooked rice," is found in Ngaju, Bakumpai, Katingan, and Ot Danum.[99] These terms are probably loanwords from the Dravidian *vari*,[100] introduced into Indonesia along with rice of the *indica* type. An early borrowing directly from Dravidian may have yielded the form *vary* in Malagasy, yet the other Malagasy terms, as well as rice-related rituals, are clearly connected with the Malay Archipelago and more specifically with Kalimantan (Adelaar 1996 *pace* Ottino 1975).

The first colonists fashioned iron tools for which the Malagasy terms reflect various introductions from Indonesia. For "spade," we find the words *soro* inherited from PMP **suDu*, "spoon" (Wolff 1974), and *sotro*, possibly borrowed from Sulawesi[101] (*sotro* means "spoon" in Merina, in Tañala, and in Betsimisaraka: in the Austronesian languages of insular Southeast Asia and in Malagasy, a series of terms means either "spoon" or "spade").

It has been shown elsewhere (Beaujard 1995, 2012) that certain ceremonies held on freshly cleared ground are similar to the rituals of Kalimantan land clearers in a very precise fashion; they also express ideas related to the "soul" of rice, ideas that have now nearly disappeared in Madagascar.[102] For example, the Tañala ritual of primordial

---

[99] O. C. Dahl (1991), for his part, suggests that *vary* derives from the Malay *beras* with a metathesis. According to R. Blust (p.c.) and K. A. Adelaar (1989a), a borrowing from Kalimantan languages where *bari* exists is more likely.

[100] As already mentioned, F. C. Southworth (2005: 81) relates the Somali *baris*, the Ngaju *bari*, and the Malagasy *vary* to the Proto-Dravidian **var-iñc*, **varici*.

[101] K. A. Adelaar (1989b) has suggested a borrowing from Malay *sudu*, "spoon," but its meaning "spade" – in Antesaka, Zafisoro, and so forth – rather points to languages from Sulawesi.

[102] For the Betsimisaraka, see Fanony 1975: 42; Beaujard 1995: 262.

sowing parallels a ritual found among the Dusun and the Ot Danum:[103] on the chief's field, "soul of rice" seeds were sown into seven holes linked to the seven stars of the Pleiades, which play a part in rice cultivation and myths for many peoples in Indonesia (Beaujard 1995: 257).[104] The Pleiades are linked to rice farming in various regions of Madagascar; in Tañala, their name – Zazamiadidango – means "children fighting over a rice mortar."

The sister of the Tañala land "owner" harvests six (or seven) ears of ripened rice, which are then hung up in the granary or on the eastern wall of the house until the next season (the following year, the rice from these ears is mixed with the seeds). This echoes the seven stalks of rice that the Dusun and the Land Dayak formerly harvested from the central square of each field and then kept in their houses or rice granaries, and which hosted the "soul of rice." The following year, the seeds from these seven ears were mixed with the seeds that were to be spread onto the central square of the new field. Originally, along the southeastern coast of Madagascar, the six or seven ears that were harvested and kept in the house or granary probably also came from the rice sown in the initial "seven" holes.

Among the Tañala, in swidden cultivation, peasants make offerings of grilled green rice (*lango*) on a flat stone set on stalks of rice ears and bran lying on the ground – this represents the "cadaver" that has given birth to the grains. This ritual refers to a myth about the origin of rice that is widespread throughout insular Southeast Asia (Mabuchi 1975), according to which rice is "born" from the corpse of either a sacrificed child or one of the primordial men (here the origin of rice is linked to the origin of death). The ceremony is called the "sweetening of rice" (*fañamamiana vary*) because rice is originally "bitter" (*mafaika*), a term related to the idea of death (Beaujard 1991: 374). Neither the ritual nor the myth can be linked to any particular region.[105] In northeastern Madagascar, the Betsimisaraka and the Tsimihety make an offering of a hen for the "ceremony of the first fruit." Hens are sacrificed at various moments in the rice cycle in swidden cultivation, in both Madagascar and Indonesia (Beaujard 1995: 251 n.1, 257, 258 n. 4).

While wet rice farming vocabulary in the Malagasy language originates in the Malay Archipelago, there are also terms of Indian origin introduced into Madagascar via Indonesia. These data appear to result from new Austronesian arrivals during the second millennium (see Volume II).

Linguistics provides evidence for multiple introductions of rice from various origins at different times in Madagascar's history. In Volume II, we will return to the term *fary* (< *pari*), introduced into Madagascar after the first arrivals.

---

[103] Among the Batak of Sumatra, also, for the first sowing, a priest would make seven holes in the soil using a stick coated with chicken blood (Van der Weijden 1981: 19).

[104] In Bugis, the Pleiades are called *worong-mporong tappitue*, "the seven clumps" (Pelras 1987: 27) (the Sakalava name for the Pleiades – *horonorona*, "gathering, tuft" [Hébert 1965a: 127] – may be reminiscent of the Bugis, although the two terms do not appear to be linguistically related to each other). According to a tale told by the Mori (central Sulawesi), "seven clumps of rice were transformed into men. These seven men were the souls of the rice. One day, they returned to the heavens and became the Pleiades" (van der Weijden 1981: 98).

[105] Beaujard 1995: 259. On this myth, see Beaujard 1991: 374ff.

Yams Apart from, or along with rice, the greater yam (*Dioscorea alata* L.) was probably a major crop among the ancient Malagasy (Raison 1992). During the sixteenth century, Barbosa writes: "Yams are their principal food" (1967 [1516], I: 25). *Ovy*, the Malagasy name for *Dioscorea alata* and other tubers, corresponds to *ubi* in many languages of the Malay Archipelago, from the PMP **qubi(h)* (Dyen 1953b). Virtually unknown along the northern edge of the Indian Ocean, the greater yam must have been brought across the ocean directly into Africa. In the Malagasy Highlands, it is called *ovibe*, "large yam" or "great yam." *Dioscorea esculenta* (Lour.) Burk. is another species of yam, hailing from Southeast Asia and formerly cultivated in Madagascar and Africa. It may have arrived after *Dioscorea alata*.

Among the yams described by E. de Flacourt in Anosy during the seventeenth century, *ovy fotsy* is *Dioscorea alata* L., and the "cambare" yam (*kambary*, *kambaro*) is probably *Dioscorea esculenta* (Lour.) Burk. or perhaps a variety of *Dioscorea alata* (Boiteau 1997). The term *kambaro*, or *kambary*, noted down in various regions of the island, is related to the Bengali *khamalu*, *D. alata* L. The arrival of this term in Madagascar is probably later than that of *ubi/ovy*.

Malagasy myths of sovereignty express an opposition between "black" plants, tubers and sometimes bananas, and the "white" plant, rice (Beaujard 1991: 523). As emphasized, there are symbolic and political dimensions to this opposition, linked to that of the "Whites" (aristocrats) and the "Blacks" (autochthonous groups and dependants) as depicted by Flacourt in Anosy, where this opposition was based on social criteria – as with the *varna* in India – more than upon skin color. The arrival during the second millennium of Indonesians, who began developing intensive wet rice farming along with very hierarchical royal systems, is in fact at the root of this depreciation of the "black" plants, now observed everywhere in Madagascar, and the deification of rice (see Volume II).

One wonders, however, if tubers truly predated rice, as myths would have it and as has sometimes been suggested with regard to Southeast Asia.[106] Flacourt described as many as eleven types of yams (Allibert 1995a: 193–194). Except in some regions (Antongil Bay, the Matatàña River valley, and Anosy), in the sixteenth and seventeenth centuries, testimonies by the earliest travelers suggest that "rice was never the staple food on the coasts: we find in the east, yams and plantains, and in the west, [sorghum] and various tubers" (Raison 1972: 412). Yam cultures diminished after manioc was introduced during the eighteenth century and also with the development of rain-fed rice cultivation. As A. Haudricourt has pointed out (1962: 41 n. 3), "upland rice, when it is known, always replaced yam because it was less labor intensive."

There is also a linguistic argument that sustains the anteriority or special importance of tubers. *Vokatra*, "harvest, production, product of the earth," also means "to dig up, unearth"; it is a loanword from the Malay *bongkar*, representing "the action of drawing from the ground, of digging" (Adelaar 1989) (from PMP **buNkaR*; Wolff 1974) (cf. Dez 1965: 202).

---

[106] "When we consider the 'Indo-Oceanic' domain, it is striking to realize how widespread the primordial cultures of tubers and fruit trees are, wherever rice has not become predominant" (Condominas 1972: 118). See also Barrau 1973.

The relationship between *Dioscorea alata* L. – especially yams of large size obtained using particular techniques – and the royal power in Anosy during the seventeenth century has been mentioned above; this relationship still applies to eastern Indonesia and Melanesia (see also Raison 1992: 202). Madagascar expresses the same sexual masculine symbolism for plants cultivated on rain-fed land (such as yam and manioc) and feminine symbolism for plants cultivated on wet land (such as taro and rice) as they are in insular Southeast Asia and the Pacific (Barrau 1965b: 337).

Nevertheless, although the data do not indicate that yam cultivation occurred prior to that of rice in Madagascar, one can imagine that beyond the symbolism and political construction taking place from perhaps the thirteenth century onward, the opposition between black and white food, bringing together diverse techniques, may encompass contributions made by distinct population groups over the centuries. Austronesian populations of various origins may have practiced various types of agriculture, such as wet and dry rice farming and tuber production, along the coasts and then inland. The coexistence of several farming systems probably also corresponds to different subsistence strategies for groups that were evolving on the island at around this time.

The Coconut Tree   The first Austronesians probably brought along coconuts (see Allibert 1991). The Malagasy term for the coconut palm and its nut is generally *voanio*, etymologically *voa/nio* "fruit of the coconut palm." *Nio* is also found for the tree (in ancient Betsimisaraka, Antemoro, and Antesaka) from the PMP **niuR*, "coconut palm." The name for the coconut palm, and probably the plant itself, seem to have come directly from the Malay Archipelago.

Recent genetic research reveals the Southeast Asian origin of the coconut in Madagascar, but also a genetic admixture with forms linked to India (Gunn *et al.* 2011): "Coconut DNA preserves a record of human cultivation, voyages of exploration, trade and colonization." "Pacific admixture is less pervasive among the samples from the East African coast than in the Indian Ocean island samples [Comoros, Madagascar], but there is nonetheless evidence of some admixture" (K. Olsen, p.c.).

Other terms for the coconut reveal more recent introductions or influences. In northern Madagascar, the coconut is called *dafo*; one also notes *kamba* (Antankaraña) to designate coconut fibers. *Dafo* is identical to the Swahili term *dafu*, "fresh coconut that you drink, which is full of water and whose meat as yet is only white jelly." The term probably derives from the Bengali *dab*, meaning "unripe coconut" (Sacleux 1939: 160). Related to *dafo* are *madrafo*, *majafo* in Vezo, for the "fresh coconut which is drunk, whose water is still abundant and very sweet and whose meat is still in the form of a paste that one scrapes after drinking the water." *Kijavo* in the Malagasy of Mayotte and *sijavo* in Antankaraña, as well as *hijavu* in Comorian, are also related to the abovementioned terms (Gueunier, p.c.).

In northern Madagascar, moreover, *trembo* is the name for a wine made from tapping sap from the inflorescence of coconut palms. The word derives from the Comorian *trembo*, "the coconut sap extracted by slicing the inflorescence; a sweet or fermented palm wine" (in Swahili, *tembo*; Ahmed-Chamanga 1992: 214) (*tembo* in northern Malagasy also designates sperm; the world over, sperm has been related to the juice of certain plants). The Swahili term, however, may derive from the Malay *tebu*, "sugarcane," thus revealing an ancient Austronesian influence on the East African coast.

In his dictionary, Flacourt also gives *harafe*, "coconut wine," the etymology of which seems to be the Old Javanese *karapa*, "coconut" (Zoetmulder 1982, I: 804). One finds *kelapa* in Malay, *kalapa* in Sundanese, "coconut," perhaps from the Sanskrit *kalāpa*, "bunch, packet."[107]

The term *kamba*, "rope," is probably a fairly recent introduction in northern Madagascar, since it has not given rise to the fricativization *k > h* as observed in older loanwords. One finds *kamba* in Swahili, meaning "rope," *kenbār* in Arabic, "a rope made from coconut fibers." Ancient Malagasy probably used coconut fibers for their ships in the same fashion as sailors throughout the Indian Ocean. Yet the techniques for making sewn boats have been lost, except – to a certain extent – in the southeast until the nineteenth century. Indeed, Grandidier and Grandidier (1928) mentioned sewn boats amongst the Rabakara of Farafangana.

Indian Saffron   Indian saffron, *Curcuma domestica* Val. (= *Curcuma longa* Koenig non L.) (Zingiberaceae family) was introduced into Madagascar by Austronesians at a very early stage. Its Malagasy name, *tamotamo*, known throughout the island, probably derives from the Banjar Malay *tamo*, "wild ginger" (Malay *temu*, possibly borrowed from Javanese; Mahdi, p.c.). This is the generic term for *Curcuma sp.* and related plants (Adelaar 1989b). As in Southeast Asia, *Curcuma* is used in Madagascar as a condiment, as a dye, and in the medical and religious domains (turmeric is a protective plant, linked to the earth).

A Phantasmic "Bantu Substrate"

From the eighteenth century, two different Malagasy physical types have been described in opposition to each other, a "fair-skinned" "Indonesian" type, and a black "African" type. This white/black opposition sometimes covers a social dimension, as was the case in Anosy during the seventeenth century or in the Antemoro kingdom. G. Ferrand has put forward the idea of a "Bantu substrate" in Madagascar.[108] We will return to the significance of Bantu contributions on the island; the discussion here will be limited to the linguistic approach to a Bantu substrate, a hypothesis that has received new support.

H. Deschamps for his part has suggested an arrival in Madagascar of "bantuized" Austronesians who settled along the East African coast and in the Comoros; this hypothesis has recently been adopted by Adelaar (2009b).[109]

---

[107] *World Loanword Database* (WOLD), M. Haspelmath and U. Tadmor, http://wold.livingsources.org/

[108] For a good historical presentation of alternative theories on African influences in Madagascar, see Vérin 1974: 103–105.

[109] See also Rafolo 2000: 531. For P. Simon, from the fourth–fifth century CE, the "Proto-Malagasy" present in the Java Sea "conducted incursions along the East African coast." Toward the end of the seventh century, they settled in the Comoros and in Madagascar. Contacts with the African coast brought about the incorporation of Bantu elements, which in turn led to the formation of a language which Simon calls "Paleo-Malagasy," marked by a process of "creolization" with the Bantu languages. This occurred between the seventh and eleventh centuries (Simon 2006: 237–238, 267). As early as the eighth century,

Several features of the Malagasy language have been seen as "proof" of an initial contact of the Malagasy with Bantu languages. Some examples: a vowel added to the final consonants of Indonesian words; *d, *-t, and *-r changed into the affricate phoneme tr [-ts in final position in the dialects of the west]; *nd and *nj changed into the prenasalized affricate ndr; fricativization of the labial consonants p and b, and of the velar consonant k in initial and intervocalic position; and loss of the Maanyan h. These features led O. C. Dahl to elaborate on the notion of a "Bantu substrate" in Malagasy. Dahl writes in 1995: "the Malagasy language can be viewed as Maanyan on a Comorian substrate, . . . the two languages met around 700."[110] More recently, P. Simon (2006) has suggested the existence of a "Bantu substrate" linked to South-Pangani pre-Swahili languages, related to the Pare and Shambala languages (Usambara mountains).

If the Austronesians traveled from the East African coast to Madagascar, along with Africans, how can we explain the absence of Tana pottery (Chami's Triangular Incised Ware) in Madagascar (a type of pottery characteristic of the Swahili sites between the seventh and tenth centuries), except at the southernmost point of the island (Menarandra) (Parker Pearson et al. 2010)? For Mahdi (1988), moreover, the presence of a vowel at the end of Malagasy words may result from influences of South Sulawesi languages (before the Southeast Barito speakers departed for Madagascar) rather than the influence of Bantu languages. Note that the development of a final vowel is not fully effective in Betsimisaraka, Sakalava, and Tañala: here the final consonants -n and -ñ are kept; the Arabic–Malagasy Antemoro manuscripts also contain many examples of words ending in nasal consonants. This phonetic situation, however, may be the result of "recent" Austronesian arrivals on the east coast of Madagascar (between the twelfth and fifteenth centuries), which were also responsible for introducing or rein-troducing Malay or Javanese loanwords such as lambo, "cattle" and fary, "rice" (see below).

A. Crowther et al. (2016) demonstrate that the archaeological sites of the Comorian archipelago and Madagascar dated to between the eighth and fifteenth centuries contain cultivated plants primarily originating in Asia, whereas the East African sites dated to the same period have yielded plants mainly of African origin. This disparity bolsters arguments for an Austronesian arrival mainly in the Comoros and Madagascar (Beaujard 2012 versus Adelaar 2009, 2012).

The arrival of Austronesian people who had settled in Africa and had been in contact with Bantus is not implausible. The African influence on grammar and lexicon, however, appears to be rather limited in Malagasy. Dahl has noted that this influence was felt mainly in terms dealing with cultivated plants, the house and feminine activities, and domesticated animals (Dahl 1978: 126). We will see that plants were

---

the Paleo-Malagasy established in northern Madagascar spread to the southwest coast; during the following centuries, a process of dialectal diversification took place. See Adelaar (1991) for a critical evaluation of Simon's work published in 1988. Tofanelli et al. (2009: 2121) support Deschamps's hypothesis, by proposing an earlier arrival of Bantuized Malagasy into Madagascar (prior to the seventh century); however, they produce no new evidence for this scenario.

[110] Dahl 1995: 42. In 1991, Dahl had already written: "The Malagasy people are Maanyans who came from Borneo around 700 AD. In Madagascar, they merged with a Bantu substrate" (1991: 101).

introduced from Africa early on, with African names, on both the west and east coasts of Madagascar. According to Dahl, the Bantu influence within the sphere of feminine activities suggests that at least some Austronesian migrants took Bantu wives, but a significant number of the words listed arrived in Madagascar at a time when the Bantu languages were no longer influencing the evolution of Malagasy (this is K. A. Adelaar's "Post-Comorian" period): for example, terms such as *kiso, koko,* and *mokary* do not exhibit the fricativization *k/h* observed in older loanwords. Moreover, recent genetic research does not support the idea that the Austronesians arrived without women (see above).

P. Vérin and H. Wright note that terms related to pottery tend to refer rather to Bantu languages. It is possible that the first Austronesian migrants had no true potters among them (1999: 36). Like Dahl, Walsh (2007) and Blench and Walsh (2012) point out that many Malagasy terms referring to wild animals are of Bantu origin, mostly connected to Swahili and to languages belonging to the Sabaki group (this does not tell us anything, however, about when these terms were introduced).

Most of the domestic animals have names of Bantu origin. It seems that the first Austronesian migrants did not bring animals with them, unlike the Austronesians who colonized the Pacific and carried with them pigs, chickens, and dogs (and probably rats, *Rattus exulans*) (Spriggs 2011: 514). The Malagasy language has no word inherited from the PMP **manuk*, "chicken," the PAN **asu/wasu*, "dog," or the PAN **beRek*, "pig." Austronesian migrants may have brought chickens with them, however. Recent genetic research into mitonchondrial DNA has revealed a contribution by Southeast Asia to the genetic pool of the chicken in Madagascar and East Africa, alongside an Indian heritage (Razafindraibe *et al.* 2008; Mwacharo *et al.* 2011; Lyimo *et al.* 2012). In contrast, goats, sheep, and cattle were introduced at an early time by people of African origin, on both the west and east coasts. Yet the practice – of African origin – of notching the ears of oxen (to mark their belonging to a group), however, is unknown in southeastern Madagascar.[III] The existence of several terms for the zebu (see below on *jamoka* and *lambo*) and the goat reveals various arrivals. The goat in Madagascar is called *osy* or *bengy*. For *osy*, Dahl has proposed an etymology from the Proto-Bantu **-búdì*, "goat," Sw., Com. *mbuzi, id.* However, the loss of the *b-* remains unexplained, and the **d > s* transformation is problematic. *Osy* may derive from the PMP **uRsa, Cervinus equinus.* The Persian *buz*, "goat," is at the origin of the Swahili *buzi*. The etymology of the Comorian and Malagasy *bengy, benge* remains uncertain; Blench notes that "it does resemble Malay *kambing*" (2008: 29), but this etymology is speculative.

Along the east coast of Madagascar, in the fields of domesticated plants and animals, Bantu terms sometimes seem to have replaced earlier words of Austronesian origin, which would have been kept in use in some regions. But this reasoning could well be erroneous; the presence of Austronesian terms does not necessarily imply that these terms are ancient. For example, the term *ontsy*, "banana," a loanword from a language

---

[III] On the Tanzanian coast and at Shanga, there is little evidence for goat, sheep, and cattle breeding (because of the tsetse fly) before the end of the first millennium (Horton 1996: 407; Kusimba 1999: 94). On Pate, the remains of cattle have been unearthed in a level dated to the ninth century (Wilson and Lali Omar 1997: 61).

from Sulawesi, is probably not a "relic term," but was brought onto the east coast after the arrival of the first Malagasy. The same can be said of the word *taho*, "taro" (see above), and the name *fontsy*, used for the *ravinala* palm ("traveler's tree," *Ravenala madagascariensis* Sonn., Strelitziaceae family), on the east coast and applied to the banana plant in some regions. It is likely that the term *lambo* was reintroduced during the second millennium. Whereas the first migrants applied the word *lambo* to the bushpig (*Potamochoerus larvatus*) because they arrived without cattle (the term probably took on the meaning of "sacrificial animal"), *lambo* is used to name the zebu in some Tañala and Antemoro expressions (see Volume II), which corresponds to the etymology of the word: *lambo* is a loanword from the Malay *lembu*, "cattle" (Banjarese *lambu*). Adelaar has systematically negated the significance of these introductions by Austronesian newcomers during the second millennium.

The bushpig (*Potamochoerus larvatus*) is of African origin. According to Blench (2008: 22), "it appears to be most closely related to the southern African form *P.l. koiropotamus*, which currently ranges from mid-Tanzania southwards." Blench (2007: 72–73) suggests a voluntary introduction by hunter-gatherers from the East African coast prior to the Austronesian arrival, but D. Gommery considers such an introduction improbable (p.c.). This pig was also present in Mayotte (Walsh 2007: 101). In northern Madagascar, one finds the term *antsanga*, "wild red pig" (Webber), linked by M. Walsh (2007) to the Zanzibari dialect *kitanga*, "boar" (from **ncanga*) (this term may have been introduced into Madagascar recently, however).

Terms of African origin have also been noted for the human body, in the domains of warfare, social life, trade, and religion. Part of the vocabulary relative to the slash-and-burn cultivation technique is also African.

A few words reflect the encounter between the Austronesian and Bantu worlds: for example, one of the names for the spirits of the earth in the southeast, south and southwest of Madagascar is *kokolampo*, related to the Bantu *kuku* and to *rampo*, which in Sulawesi refers to the spirits of the forest.[112]

As P. Vérin has noted, some words of Bantu origin known throughout Madagascar certainly correspond to an early introduction into the vocabulary (while difficult to date precisely). Other words result from more recent borrowings. Vérin (1980) has given an estimate – without evidence – of 7 percent for the proportion of terms of African origin in the Malagasy language. In my Tañala dictionary (Beaujard 1998), the proportion is only 0.8 percent. While some African etymologies have certainly been missed, the percentage in the Tañala lexicon is low. Unsurprisingly, the Sakalava dialects seem far richer in Bantu words than are the dialects of the east coast.

Current linguistic data tend to refute Dahl's idea of a "Bantu substrate," and that of an initial "Creolization" as suggested by Simon and Vérin. Neither do the linguistic and archaeological data support an initial presence of pre-Malagasy Austronesians on

---

[112] *Koko*: cf. Proto-Bantu **kúúkù*, "grandparents, ancestors"; Kagulu, Mambwe *kuku*; Tswa *koko*; Comorian *makoko*, "old, ancestors." For *rampo*, see Adriani and Kruyt, quoted by Allibert 1995a: 493.

the East African coast, a hypothesis put forward by Deschamps and Adelaar.[113] "The Malagasy vocabulary," recognizes Dahl, "is almost totally Austronesian. Examining the words that may have their origin in the substrate, I have found only 50 that I consider as surely of Bantu origin" (1995: 44). Dahl adds that "the grammatical development of Malagasy shows little influence from the substrate." In fact, the Bantus were probably not present in Madagascar when the Austronesians arrived. A Bantu influence on the Malagasy language occurred soon thereafter, in the Comoros and in Madagascar (and perhaps also along the East African coast, as suggested by Deschamps and Adelaar). Contacts then continued over a long period of time (in fact until the nineteenth century), not only via the islamized towns of northern Madagascar, but also via the settlement of African populations on various points along the Malagasy coastlines, notably on the west coast, a process clearly revealed by its toponyms.

A Bantu cultural influence can be seen starting in the eighth century. M. Horton emphasizes the development of a society of sailors on the East African coast in connection with transoceanic trade, even before the Muslim expansion, and then parallel to it.[114] Blench rightly notes that "the main sources of Bantu lexis in Malagasy were drawn from the Swahili language" (2008: 21), but some other sources should be mentioned, notably the Comorian language. Some earlier Bantu arrivals are possible. P. Sinclair has noted that the Comoros and Madagascar have yielded neither Kwale-Matola pottery (Early Iron Age Ware) nor pottery belonging to the Gokomere-Ziwa tradition (Sinclair 1991: 192), but recent finds by Chami *et al.* (2009) show the presence of Early Iron Age Ware at Comorian sites (see above). Ceramics of the Tana tradition Phase A (Chami's TIW), which is a type of pottery characteristic of the Swahili sites between the seventh and tenth centuries, has been found in the Comoros, but not in Madagascar, except in the south (it is not present in Mahilaka) (Horton 1996: 408; Radimilahy 1998: 202). Investigations should be continued, however, in archaeology, linguistics, and genetics, in order to better understand the modalities of the Austronesian and Bantu arrivals and the first stages of hybridization, in the Comoros and Madagascar.

---

[113] H. Deschamps, however, can be credited with pointing out a probable early Austronesian presence on the East African coast. According to him, the "Proto-Malagasy" (Austronesians influenced by Bantu languages) may have come from this coast.

[114] Horton 1993: 440, 454. The excavations led by Horton in East Africa show a development of Swahili cities during the eighth century. See below.

BIBLIOGRAPHY

ABRAHAM, K., 2004, *Business and Politics under the Persian Empire: The Financial Dealings of Marduk-nasir-spli of the House of Egibi*, Bethesda, MD: CDL Press.

ABU-LUGHOD, J., 1989, *Before European Hegemony: The World System AD 1250–1350*, Oxford University Press.

ACHAYA, K.T., 1994, *Indian Food: A Historical Companion*, Delhi: Oxford University Press.

ACOT, P., 2003, *Histoire du climat*, Paris: Perrin.

ADAMS, C., 2007, *Land Transport in Roman Egypt: A Study of Economics and Administration in a Roman Province*, Oxford University Press.

ADAMS, R. MCCORMICK, 1981, *Heartland of Cities: Surveys of Ancient Settlement and Land Use on the Central Floodplain of the Euphrates*, University of Chicago Press.

ADELAAR, K. A., 1985, *Proto-Malayic: The Reconstruction of Its Phonology and Parts of Its Lexicon and Morphology*, Alblasserdam: Offsetdrukkerij Kanters.

1989a, "Les langues austronésiennes et la place du Malagasy dans leur ensemble," *Archipel*, 38, pp. 25–52.

1989b, "Malay influence on Malagasy: linguistic and culture-historical implications," *Oceanic Linguistics*, 28 (1), pp. 1–46.

1991, "New ideas on the early history of Malagasy," in H. Steinhauer (ed.), *Papers in Austronesian Linguistics*, 1 (*Pacific Linguistics*, A-81), Canberra: Pacific Linguistics, pp. 1–22.

1995a, "Asian roots of the Malagasy: a linguistic perspective" (revised version of a paper presented in the symposium "Malagasy cultural identity from an Asian perspective," March 1994, Leiden), *Bijdragen tot de Taal-, Land- en Volkenkunde*, 151 (3), pp. 325–356.

1995b, "Malay and Javanese loanwords in Malagasy, Tagalog and Siraya (Formosa)," *Bijdragen tot de Taal-, Land- en Volkenkunde*, 150 (1), pp. 50–66.

1995c, "L'importance du samihim (Bornéo du Sud) pour l'étymologie malgache," in B. Champion (ed.), *L'étranger intime: Mélanges offerts à Paul Ottino*, Saint-Denis: Université de la Réunion, Océan Éditions, pp. 47–59.

1995d, "Une perspective linguistique sur les origines asiatiques des Malgaches," in S. Evers and M. Spindler (eds.), *Cultures of Madagascar: Ebb and Flow of Influences / Civilisations de Madagascar: Flux et reflux des influences*, Leiden: International Institute for Asian Studies, Working Papers Series 2, pp. 47–55.

1996, "Malagasy culture-history: some linguistic evidence," in J. Reade (ed.), *The Indian Ocean in Antiquity*, London and New York: Kegan Paul, pp. 487–500.

2004, "The Austronesian languages of Asia and Madagascar: a historical perspective," in A. Adelaar and N. P. Himmelmann (eds.), *The Austronesian Languages of Asia and Madagascar*, London: Routledge/Curzon, pp. 1–44.

2006, "The Indonesian migrations to Madagascar: making sense of the multidisciplinary evidence," in T. Simanjuntak, I. H. E. Pojoh, and M. Hisyam (eds.), *Austronesian Diaspora and the Ethnogenesis of People in Indonesian Archipelago*, Jakarta: LIPI Press, pp. 205–232.

2009, "Towards an integrated theory about the Indonesian migrations to Madagascar," in P. N. Peregrine, I. Peiros, and M. Feldman (eds.), *Ancient Human Migrations: A Multidisciplinary Approach*, Salt Lake City: University of Utah Press, pp. 149–172.

2016, "Austronesians in Madagascar: a critical assessment of the works of Paul Ottino and Philippe Beaujard," in G. Campbell (ed.), *Early Exchange between Africa and the Wider Indian Ocean World*, Basingstoke and New York: Palgrave Macmillan, pp. 77–112.

ADSHEAD, S. A. M., 1995, *China in World History*, Basingstoke: Macmillan (1st edn. 1988).

2004, *T'ang China: The Rise of the East in World History*, Basingstoke and New York: Palgrave Macmillan.

AGIUS, D. A., 2002, "Classifiying vessel-types in Ibn Baṭṭūṭa's Riḥla," in D. Parkin and R. Barnes (eds.), *Ships and the Development of Maritime Technology in the Indian Ocean*, London and New York: Routledge/Curzon.

AGLIETTA, M., 2009, "Monnaie et capitalisme," in P. Beaujard, L. Berger, and P. Norel (eds.), *Histoire globale, mondialisations et capitalisme*, Paris: Éditions La Découverte.

AGLIETTA, M. and ORLÉAN, A. (eds.), 1998, *La monnaie souveraine*, Paris: O. Jacob.

2002, *La monnaie entre violence et confiance*, Paris: O. Jacob.

AGRAWAL, D. P. and KHARAKWAL, J. S., 2003, *Bronze and Iron Ages in South Asia*, New Delhi: Aryan Books International.

AHMED-CHAMANGA, M., 1992, *Lexique Comorien (Shindzuani)/Français*, Paris: L'Harmattan.

AHRWEILER, H., 1966, *Byzance et la mer: la marine de guerre, la politique et les institutions maritimes de Byzance aux VIIe–XVe siècles*, Paris: Presses Universitaires de France.

1976, *Byzance: le pays et les territoires*, London: Variorum Reprints.

AICHELE, W., 1936, "Eine neu erschlossene frühindonesische Literatursprache in ihrem Einfluss auf das Altjavanische," *Zeitschrift der Deutschen Morgenländischen Gesellschaft*, 90, pp. 18–19.

1954, "Sprachforschung und Geschichte im Indonesischen Raum," *Oriens Extremus*, 1, pp. 107–122.

AKHUNDOV, T., 2007, "Sites de migrants venus du Proche-Orient en Transcaucasie," in B. Lyonnet (ed.), *Les cultures du Caucase (VIe–IIIe millénaires avant notre ère): leur relations avec le Proche-Orient*, Paris: Editions Recherche sur les Civilisations, pp. 95–121.

Akkadica, 2000, *"Just in time": Proceedings of the International Colloquium on Ancient Near Eastern Chronology (2nd Millennium BCE)*, Ghent July 7–9, 2000, *Akkadica*, 119–120.

AKKERMANS, P. M. and SCHWARTZ, G., 2003, *The Archaeology of Syria: From Complex Hunter-Gatherers to Early Urban Societies (ca. 16,000–300 BCE)*, Cambridge University Press.

ALBRIGHT, W. F., 1956, "Stratigraphic confirmation of the Low Mesopotamian chronology," *Bulletin of the American Schools of Oriental Research*, 144, pp. 26–30.

ALEXANDROVSKYI, A. and ALEXANDROVSKAYA, E. I., 2004, "Changes in palaeoenvironment and human migrations in the centre of the Russian plain," in E. M. Scott, A. Y. Alekseev, and G. Zaitseva (eds.), *Impact of the Environment on Human Migration in Eurasia*, Dordrecht, Boston, and London: Kluwer Academic Publishers, pp. 199–208.

ALGAZE, G., 1993, *The Uruk World System: The Dynamics of Expansion of Early Mesopotamian Civilization*, Chicago University Press.

2001, "The prehistory of imperialism: the case of Uruk period Mesopotamia," in M. S. Rothman (ed.), *Uruk Mesopotamia and Its Neighbors: Cross-cultural Interactions in the Era of State Formation*, Sante Fe: School of American Research; Oxford: James Currey, pp. 27–83.

2008, *Ancient Mesopotamia at the Dawn of Civilization*, University of Chicago Press.

ALIZADEH, A., 2010, "The rise of the highland Elamite state in southwestern Iran," *Current Anthropology*, 51 (3), pp. 353–383.

ALLAM, S., 1998, "Affaires et opérations commerciales," in N. Grimal and B. Menu (eds.), *Le commerce en Égypte ancienne*, Cairo: Institut Français d'Archéologie Orientale, pp. 133–156.

ALLCHIN, F. R., 1969, "Early cultivated plants in India and Pakistan," in P. J. Ucko and G. W. Dimbleby (eds.), *The Domestication and Exploitation of Plants and Animals*, London: Duckworth, pp. 323–329.

1995, *The Archaeology of Early Historic South Asia: The Emergence of Cities and States*, Cambridge University Press.

ALLEN, J. de V., 1980, "Propositions en vue d'études sur l'océan Indien," in *Relations historiques à travers l'océan Indien*, Paris: Unesco, pp. 145–161.

1993, *Swahili Origins: Swahili Culture and the Shungwaya Phenomenon*, London: J. Currey; Nairobi: EAEP; Athens: Ohio University Press.

ALLEN, J. P., 2004, *The Heqanakht Papyri*, New York: Metropolitan Museum of Art.

ALLEN, M., 2005, "Power is in the details: administrative technology and the growth of ancient Near Eastern cores," in C. Chase-Dunn and E. N. Anderson (eds.), *The Historical Evolution of World-Systems*, Riverside: University of California, Palgrave Macmillan, pp. 75–91.

ALLEN, R. C., 1997, "Agriculture and the origins of the state in ancient Egypt," *Explorations in Economic History*, 34, pp. 135–154.

ALLIBERT, C., 1984, *Mayotte, plaque tournante et microcosme de l'océan Indien occidental*, Paris: Anthropos.

1990, *Textes anciens sur la côte est de l'Afrique et l'Océan Indien occidental*, Paris: CEROI-INALCO.

1991, "Waqwaq: végétal, minéral ou humain?" *Études Océan Indien*, 12, pp. 171–189.

1992, "Le monde austronésien et la civilisation du bambou: une plume qui pèse lourd: l'oiseau Rokh des auteurs arabes," *Taloha*, 11, pp. 167–181.

(ed.) 1995a, 2007, *see* Flacourt 1995, 2007.

1995b, "Les mouvements austronésiens vers l'Océan Indien occidental: la tradition arabico-malgache revisitée," in B. Champion (ed.), *L'étranger intime: mélanges offerts à Paul Ottino*, Saint-Denis: Université de la Réunion, Océan Editions, pp. 61–76.

1998, Compte-rendu de M. Horton, *Shanga, the Archaeology of a Muslim Trading Community on the Coast of East Africa*, 1996, *Topoi: Orient-Occident*, 8 (1), pp. 477–486.

ALLIBERT, C. and VÉRIN, P., 1993a, "Linguistique, archéologie et l'exploration du passé malgache," in Ö Dahl (ed.), *Language: A Doorway between Human Cultures. Tributes to Dr. Otto Chr. Dahl on His Ninetieth Birthday*, Oslo: Novus Forlag, pp. 29–38.

1993b, "Les Comores et Madagascar: le premier peuplement," *Archaeologia*, 290, pp. 64–77.

ALPERN, S. B., 2005, "Did they or didn't they invent it? Iron in Sub-Saharan Africa," *History in Africa*, 32, pp. 41–94.

ALSTER, B., 1996, "He who pays with valid money: on the status of merchants in early Mesopotamia," in Ö. Tunca and D. Deheselle (eds.), *Tablettes et images aux pays de Sumer et d'Akkad: Mélanges offerts à Monsieur H. Limet*, Louvain, Peeters, pp. 1–6.

AMIET, P., 1980, *La glyptique mésopotamienne archaïque*, 2nd edn., Paris: Éditions du CNRS.

1986, *L'âge des échanges inter-iraniens, 3500–1700 av. J.-C.*, Paris: Notes et documents des musées de France 11, Réunion des musées nationaux.

1988, *Suse, 6000 ans d'histoire*, Paris: Réunion des musées nationaux.

1997, "La glyptique Transélamite," in A. Caubet (ed.), *De Chypre à la Bactriane: les sceaux du Proche-Orient*, Paris: La Documentation française.

AMIGUES, S., 1996, "Un cinnamome fantomatique," *Topoi: Orient-Occident*, 6 (2), pp. 657–664.

2005, "Végétaux et aromates de l'Orient dans le monde antique," *Topoi: Orient-Occident*, 12–13 (1), pp. 359–383.

AMORE, R. C., 1978, *Two Masters: One Message*, Nashville, TN: Abingdon Press.

AMOURETTI, M.-C., 1987, "La diffusion du moulin à eau dans l'Antiquité," in *L'eau et les hommes en Méditerranée*, Paris: Éditions du CNRS, pp. 13–23.

AMSELLE, J.-L., 1990, *Logiques métisses*, Paris: Payot.

AN, C.-B., TANG, L., BARTON, L., and CHEN, F.-H., 2005, "Climate change and cultural response around 4000 cal yr B.P. in the western part of Chinese Loess Plateau," *Quaternary Research*, 63, pp. 347–352.

AN ZHIMIN, 1996, "The Bronze Age cultures around the Tarim Basin," *Kaogu*, 12, pp. 70–76.

1998, "Cultural complexes of the Bronze Age in the Tarim Basin and surrounding areas," in V. H. Mair (ed.), *The Bronze Age and Early Iron Age Peoples of Eastern Central Asia*, vol. 1: *Archaeology, Migration and Nomadism, Linguistics*, Philadelphia: Institute for the Study of Man, pp. 45–60.

AN, Z. S. and THOMPSON, L. G., 1998, "Paleoclimatic change of monsoonal China linked to global change," in J. Galloway and J. Melillo (eds.), *Asian Change in the Context of Global Climate Change*, Cambridge University Press, pp. 18–41.

ANDAYA, L. Y., 2001, "The search for the 'origins' of Melayu," *Journal of Southeast Asian Studies*, 32 (3), pp. 315–330.

ANDERSON, A., 2006, "Crossing the Luzon Strait: archaeological chronology in the Batanes islands, Philippines and the regional sequence of Neolithic dispersal," *Journal of Austronesian Studies*, 1 (2), pp. 25–44.

ANDERSON, A. and O'CONNOR, S., 2008, "Indo-Pacific migration and colonization – introduction," *Asian Perspectives*, 47, pp. 2–11.

ANDREAU, J., 1988, "Introduction. Antique, moderne et temps présent: la carrière et l'œuvre de Michel Ivanovic Rostovtzeff (1870–1952)," in M. I. Rostovtzeff (ed.), *Histoire économique et sociale de l'Empire romain*, Paris: Laffont, pp. i–lxx.

1994, "La cité romaine dans ses rapports à l'échange et au monde de l'échange," in J. Andreau (ed.), *Économie antique: les échanges dans l'Antiquité: le rôle de l'état*, Musée archéologique départemental de Saint-Bertrand-de-Comminges, pp. 83–98.

1999, "De l'esclavagisme aux esclaves gestionnaires," *Topoi. Orient-Occident*, 9 (1), p. 103–112.

2004a, "Sur les choix économiques des notables romains," in J. Andreau, J. France, and S. Pittia (eds.), *Mentalité et choix économiques des Romains*, Paris and Bordeaux: Ausonius, pp. 71–85.

2004b, "Esclavage antique et rentabilité économique," in H. Bruhns and J. Andreau (eds.), *Sociologie économique et économie de l'Antiquité. À propos de Max Weber, Cahiers du Centre de recherches historiques*, 34, October, pp. 159–166.

2010, *L'économie du monde romain*, Paris: Ellipses.

ANDREAU, J. and MAUCOURANT, J., 1999, "À propos de la rationalité économique," *Topoi. Orient-Occident*, 9 (1), pp. 47–102.

AN JIAYAO, 1992, "The early glass of China," in R. H. Brill and J. H. Martin (eds.), *Scientific Research in Early Chinese Glass*, Corning Museum of Glass, pp. 5–20.

1996, "Glass trade in Southeast Asia," in A. Srisuchat (ed.), *Ancient Trade and Cultural Contacts in Southeast Asia*, Bangkok: Office of the National Culture Commission, pp. 127–138.

ANTHONY, D. W., 2002, "Comments," on C. C. Lamberg-Karlovsky's article, *Current Anthropology*, 43 (1), pp. 75–76.

2007, *The Horse, the Wheel, and Language: How Bronze Age Riders from the Eurasian Steppes Shaped the Modern World*, Princeton University Press.

2009, "The Sintashta genesis: the roles of climate change, warfare, and long-distance trade," in B. K. Hanks and K. M. Linduff (eds.), *Social Complexity in Prehistoric Eurasia: Monuments, Metals, and Mobility*, Cambridge University Press, pp. 47–73.

2012, "Comments" on M. Frachetti's article "Multiregional emergence of mobile pastoralism and nonuniform institutional complexity across Eurasia," *Current Anthropology*, 53 (1), pp. 21–22.

ANTHONY, D. W. and BROWN, D. R., 2003, "Eneolithic rituals and riding in the steppes: new evidence," in M. Levine, C. Renfrew, and K. Boyle (eds.), *Prehistoric Steppe Adaptation and the Horse*, Cambridge: McDonald Institute for Archaeological Research, pp. 55–68.

APERGHIS, G. G., 2004, *The Seleukid Royal Economy: The Finances and Financial Administration of the Seleukid Empire*, Cambridge University Press.

APLIN, K. P. *et al.*, 2011, "Multiple geographic origins of commensalism and complex dispersal history of black rats," *PLoS ONE*, 6 (11), www.plosone.org

APPADURAI, A., 1986, "Introduction: commodities and the politics of value," in A. Appadurai (ed.), *The Social Life of Things: Commodities in Cultural Perspective*, Cambridge University Press, pp. 3–63.

ARBACH, M, 2001, "Le royaume de Saba au 1er millénaire avant J.-C.," *Dossiers d'Archéologie*, 263 (special issue on Yemen), pp. 12–17.

ARDIKA, I. W., 1999, "Ancient trade relation between India and Indonesia," in K. S. Behera (ed.), *Maritime Heritage of India*, New Delhi: Aryan Books International, pp. 80–89.

ARDIKA, I. W., BELLWOOD, P., SUTABA, I. M., and YULIATI, K. C., 1997, "Sembiran and the first Indian contacts with Bali: an update," *Antiquity*, 71 (271), pp. 193–195.

ARNAUD, B. and KINER, A., 2006, "L'Égypte des rois Scorpions," *Sciences et Avenir*, 711, pp. 54–67.

ARNAUD, P., 2012, "Le *Periplus Maris Erythraei*: une œuvre de compilation aux préoccupations géographiques," *Topoi*, suppl. 11, pp. 27–61.

ARRIGHI, G., 1994, *The Long Twentieth Century: Money, Power and the Origins of Our Times*, London and New York: Verso.

ARUZ, J., 2003a and b, "Art and interconnections in the third millennium BCE," and "'Intercultural style' carved chlorite objects," in J. Aruz and R. Wallenfels (eds.), *Art of the First Cities: The Third Millennium BC from the Mediterranean to the Indus*, New York: Metropolitan Museum of Art; New Haven and London: Yale University Press, pp. 239–250 and p. 325.

2008, "The art of exchange," in J. Aruz, K. Benzel, and J. M. Evans (eds.), *Beyond Babylon: Art, Trade, and Diplomacy in the Second Millennium BCE*, New York: Metropolitan Museum of Art; New Haven and London: Yale University Press, pp. 387–394.

ARUZ, J. and WALLENFELS, R. (eds.), 2003, *Art of the First Cities: The Third Millennium BC from the Mediterranean to the Indus*, New York: Metropolitan Museum of Art; New Haven and London: Yale University Press.

ASCALONE, E. and PEYRONEL, L., 2003, "Meccanismi di scambio commerciale e pre-monetaria nell'Asia Media, in India e nel Golfo Persico durante l'età del Bronzo. Spunti per una riflessione sulle sfere di interazione culturale," *Contributi e Materiali di Archeologia Orientale*, 9, pp. 339–438.

ASENSI AMOROS, V., 2003, "L'étude du bois et de son commerce en Égypte: lacunes des connaissances actuelles et perspectives pour l'analyse xylologique," in K. Neumann, A. Butler, and S. Kahlhaber (eds.), *Food, Fuel and Fields: Progress in African Archaeobotany*, Cologne: Heinrich-Barth-Institut, pp. 177–186.

ASKAROV, A. A., 1973, *Sapallitepa*, Tashkent: Fan.

ASOUTI, E. and FULLER, D. Q., 2008, *Trees and Woodlands of South India: Archaeological Perspectives*, Walnut Creek, CA: Left Coast Press.

AUBAILE-SALLENAVE, F., 1984, "L'agriculture musulmane aux premiers temps de la conquête: apports et emprunts, à propos de *Agricultural innovation in the early Islamic world* de Andrew M. Watson," *Journal d'Agriculture Tropicale et de Botanique Appliquée*, 31 (3–4), pp. 245–256.

AUBERT, J.-J., 1999, "Les *institores* et le commerce maritime dans l'empire romain," *Topoi: Orient-Occident*, 9 (1), pp. 145–164.

AUBET, M. E., 2001, *The Phoenicians and the West: Politics, Colonies and Trade*, Cambridge University Press (1st edn. 1987).

2013, *Commerce and Colonization in the Ancient Near East*, trans. Mary Turton, Cambridge University Press.

AUDOUIN, R, 2001, "Les riches tombes du Wādī Dura," *Dossiers d'Archéologie*, 263 (issue on Yemen), pp. 62–63.

AUNG-THWIN, M., 2002, "Lower Burma and Bago in the History of Burma," in J. Gommans and J. Leider (eds.), *The Maritime Frontier of Burma*, Amsterdam: KITLV Press, pp. 25–58.

2005, *The Mists of Rāmañña: The Legend that Was Lower Burma*, Honolulu: University of Hawai'i Press.

AUSTIN, P., MACKAY, A., PALAGUSHKINA, O., and LENG, M., 2007, "A high-resolution diatom-inferred palaeoconductivity and lake level record of the Aral Sea for the last 1600 yr," *Quaternary Research*, 67 (3), pp. 383–393.

AVANZINI, A., 2007, "Sumhuram: a Hadrami port on the Indian Ocean," in E. H. Seland (ed.), *The Indian Ocean in the Ancient Period: Definite Places, Translocal Exchange* (BAR International Series 1593), Oxford: Archaeopress, pp. 23–32.

2008, *Khor Rori Report 2: A Port in Arabia between Rome and the Indian Ocean (3rd C BCE – 5th C. AD)*, Rome: Edizioni Plus.

(ed.), 2011, *Along the Aroma and Spice Routes: The Harbour of Sumhuram, Its Territory and the Trade between the Mediterranean, Arabia and India*, University of Pisa.

AVILOVA, L. I., 2005, "Metall Zapadnoi Azii (Eneolit-Srednii Bronzovyi Vek)," *Opus: Mezhdistsiplinarnye Issledovaniya v Arkheologii*, 4, pp. 11–28.

BACUS, E. A., 2004, "The archaeology of the Philippine archipelago," in I. Glover and P. Bellwood (eds.), *Southeast Asia: From Prehistory to History*, Abingdon and New York: Routledge/Curzon, pp. 257–281.

BADLER, V. R., 2004, "A chronology of Uruk artifacts from Godin Tepe in Western Central Iran and implications for the interrelationships between the local and foreign cultures," in J. N. Postgate (ed.), *Artefacts of Complexity: Tracking the Uruk in the Near East* (Iraq Archaeological Reports 5), Warminster: Aris & Phillips for the British School of Archaeology in Iraq, pp. 79–110 (1st edn. 2002).

BAGLEY, R., 1999, "Shang archaeology," in M. Loewe and E. L. Slaughnessy (eds.), *The Cambridge History of Ancient China: From the Origins of Civilization to 221 BCE*, Cambridge University Press, pp. 124–231.

BAGNALL, R. S., 2003, *Later Roman Egypt: Society, Religion, Economy and Administration*, Aldershot: Ashgate Variorum.

BAGROW, L., 1945, "The origin of Ptolemy's *Geographia*," *Geografiska Annaler*, 27, pp. 318–387.

BAILLIE, M. G. L., 1992, "Dendrochronology and past environmental change," *Proceedings of the British Academy*, 77, pp. 5–23.

1995, *A Slice through Time: Dendrochronology and Precision Dating*, London: B. T. Batsford.

BAINES, J., 2003, "Early definitions of the Egyptian world and its surroundings," in D. T. Potts, M. D. Roaf, and D. L. Stein (eds.), *Culture through Objects: Ancient Near Eastern Studies in Honour of P. R. S. Moorey*, Oxford: Griffith Institute Publications, pp. 27–57.

BAINES, J. and YOFFEE, N., 1998, "Order, legitimacy and wealth in Ancient Egypt and Mesopotamia," in G. M. Feinman and J. Marcus (eds.), *Archaic States*, Santa Fe: School of American Research, pp. 199–260.

BAISHYA, P., 1997, "The putting out system in ancient India," *Social Scientist*, 25 (7–8), pp. 51–66.

BAKELS, C., 2003, "The contents of ceramic vessels in the Bactria-Margiana Archaeological Complex, Turkmenistan," *Electronic Journal of Vedic Studies*, 9 (1c), online.

BAKKER, J. A., KRUK, J., LANTING, A. E., and MILISAUSKAS, S., 1999, "The earliest evidence of wheeled vehicles in Europe and the Near East," *Antiquity*, 73 (282), pp. 778–790.

BALFOUR-PAUL, J., 1997, *Indigo in the Arab World*, Richmond: Curzon Press.

BALLARD, R. and EUGENE, T., 2005, *Les mystères des navigateurs de l'Antiquité: les premières civilisations maritimes*, Washington, DC: National Geographic Books.

BALLET, P, 2001, "Les importations de céramiques sous l'empire romain," *Dossiers d'Archéologie*, 263 (issue on Yemen), pp. 62–63.

BALMUTH, M. S., 1975, "The critical moment: the transition from currency to coinage in the eastern Mediterranean," *World Archaeology*, 6 (3), pp. 293–298.

BAMSHAD, M. *et al.*, 2001, "Genetic evidence on the origins of Indian caste populations," *Genome Research*, 11 (6), pp. 994–1004.

BANCK-BURGESS, J., 1999, *Hochdorf IV. Die Textilfunde aus dem späthallstattzeitlichen Fuerstengrab von Eberdingen-Hochdorf (Kreis Ludwigsburg) und weitere Grabtextilien aus hallstatt- und latènezeitlichen Kulturgruppen*, Stuttgart: K. Theiss.

2012, "Case study: the textiles from the princely burial at Eberdingen-Hochdorf, Germany," in M. Gleba and U. Mannering (eds.), *Textiles and Textile Production in Europe: From Prehistory to AD 400*, Oxford: Oxbow Books, pp. 139–151.

BARAKAT, H. N. and BAUM, N., 1992, *Douch II. La végétation antique. Une approche macrobotanique*, Institut Français d'Archéologie Orientale du Cairo.

BARBARUNOVA, Z. A., 1995, "Early Sarmatian culture," in J. Davis-Kimball, V. A. Bashilov, and L. T. Yablonsky (eds.), *Nomads of the Eurasian Steppes in the Early Iron Age*, Berkeley: Zinat Press, pp. 121–132.

BARBER, E., 1998, "Bronze age cloth and clothing of the Tarim Basin: the Krorän (Loulan) and Qumul (Hami) evidence," in V. H. Mair (ed.), *The Bronze Age and Early Iron Age Peoples of Eastern Central Asia*, vol. II, Washington, DC: Institute for the Study of Man; Philadelphia: University of Pennsylvania Museum Publications, pp. 647–655.

1999, *The Mummies of Ürümchi*, New York, W. W. Norton.

2002, "Fashioned from fiber," in E. Ten Grotenhuis (ed.), *Along the Silk Road*, Washington, DC: A. M. Sackler Gallery, Smithsonian Institution, pp. 57–72.

BARBOSA, D., 1967 [1516], *The Book of Duarte Barbosa: An Account of the Countries Bordering on the Indian Ocean and Their Inhabitants*, English trans. M. L. Dames, 2 vols. Nendeln: Kraus Reprint (new edition, Delhi 1989).

BARD, K. A., 2000, "The emergence of the Egyptian state (c.3200–2686 BCE)," in I. Shaw (ed.), *The Oxford History of Ancient Egypt*, Oxford University Press, pp. 61–88.

BARD, K. A. and FATTOVICH, R. (eds.), 2010, *Mersa/Wadi Gawasis 2009–2010*, www.archeogate.com

BARD, K. A., FATTOVICH, R., and WARD, C., 2007, "Sea port to Punt: new evidence from Marsā Gawāsīs, Red Sea (Egypt)," in J. Starkey, P. Starkey, and T. J. Wilkinson (eds.), *Natural Resources and Cultural Connections of the Red Sea* (BAR International Series 1661), Oxford: British Archaeological Reports, pp. 143–148.

BARFIELD, L., 1994. The Bronze Age of Northern Italy: recent work and social interpretation. In C. Mathers and S. Stoddart (eds.), *The Mediterranean Cultures during the Bronze: Development and Decline in the Mediterranean Bronze Age* (Sheffield Archaeological Monographs 8), Sheffield: J. R. Collis, pp. 129–144.

BARGUET, A. (ed.), 1964: *see* Herodotus.

BARNARD, H., 2009, "The identification of the ancient pastoral nomads on the north-western Red Sea littoral," in L. Blue, J. Cooper, R. Thomas, and J. Whitewright (eds.), *Connected Hinterlands Proceedings of Red Sea Project IV Held at the University of Southampton September 2008* (BAR International Series 2052), Oxford: Archaeopress, pp. 19–28.

BARNES, G. L., 1999, *The Rise of Civilization in East Asia: The Archaeology of China, Korea and Japan*, London: Thames and Hudson (1st edn. 1993).

2004a, "Introduction," in *Textiles in Indian Ocean Societies*, London: Routledge, pp. 1–10.

2004b, "Indian textiles for island taste: Gujarati cloth in eastern Indonesia," *Ars Orientalis*, 34, pp. 135–149.

BARNHART, R. M., 2004, "Alexander in China? Questions for Chinese archaeology," in X. Yang (ed.), *New Perspectives on China's Past*, vol. I, New Haven, CT, and London: Yale University Press, pp. 329–343.

BARRAU, J., 1965a, "Histoire et préhistoire horticoles de l'Océanie tropicale," *Journal de la Société des Océanistes*, 21 (21), pp. 55–78.

1965b, "L'humide et le sec: an essay on ethnobiological adaptation to contrastive environments in the Indo-Pacific Area," *Journal of the Polynesian Society*, 74 (3), pp. 329–346.

1973, "Plantes et comportements des hommes qui les cultivent: l'œuvre ethnobiologique d'André Haudricourt," *La Pensée*, 171, pp. 3–12.

BARTON, H. and PAZ, V., 2007, "Subterranean diets in the tropical rainforest of Sarawak, Malaysia," in T. P. Denham, J. Iriarte, and L. Vrydaghs (eds.), *Rethinking Agriculture: Archaeological and Ethnoarchaeological Perspectives*, Walnut Creek, CA: Left Coast Press, pp. 50–77.

BARTON, H. and DENHAM, T., 2011, "Prehistoric vegeculture and social life in island Southeast Asia and Melanesia," in G. Barker and M. Janowski (eds.), *Why Cultivate? Anthropological and Archaeological Approaches to Foraging-Farming Transitions in Southeast Asia*, Cambridge: McDonald Institute for Archaeological Research, pp. 17–25.

BASA, K. K., 1999, "Early trade in the Indian Ocean: perspectives on Indo-South-East Asian maritime contacts (c. 400 BCE – AD 500)," in K. S. Behera (ed.), *Maritime Heritage of India*, New Delhi: Aryan Books International, pp. 29–71.

BASA, K. K. and BEHERA, K. S., 1999, "Indo-Roman trade," in K. S. Behera (ed.), *Maritime Heritage of India*, New Delhi: Aryan Books International, pp. 15–28.

BASCH, L., 1987, *Le musée imaginaire de la marine antique*, Athens: Institut hellénique pour la préservation de la tradition nautique.

BASELLO, G. P., 2006, "The tablet from Konar Sandal B (Jiroft) and its pertinence to Elamite studies," www.elamit.net

BASHAM, A. L., 1967, *The Wonder That Was India*, 3rd edn., Oxford: Taplinger.

BASS, G. F., 1967, *Cape Gelidonya: A Bronze Age Shipwreck* (Transactions of the American Philosophical Society n.s. vol. 57, part 8), Philadelphia: American Philosophical Society.

1995, "Sea and river craft in the ancient Near East," in J. M. Sasson (ed.), *Civilizations of the Ancient Near East*, vol. III, New York: Scribner's, pp. 1421–1431.

BASU, A. *et al.*, 2003, "Ethnic India: a genomic view, with special reference to peopling and structure," *Genome Research*, 13, pp. 2277–2290.

BATTISTINI, R., 1971, "Conditions de gisement des sites de subfossiles et modifications récentes du milieu naturel dans la région d'Ankazoabo," *Taloha*, 4, pp. 19–27.

BAVAY, L., DE PUTTER, T., ADAMS, B., NAVEZ, J., and ANDRE, L., 2000, "The origin of obsidian in predynastic and Early Dynastic Egypt," *Mitteilungen des Deutschen Archäologischen Instituts, Abteilung Kairo*, 56, pp. 5–20.

BAYLISS-SMITH, T., 1996, "People-plant interactions in the New Guinea highlands: agricultural hearthland or horticultural backwater ?," in D. R. Harris (ed.), *The Origins and Spread of Agriculture and Pastoralism in Eurasia*, London: UCL Press, pp. 499–524.

BEAUJARD, P., 1983, *Princes et paysans: les Tanala de l'Ikongo: un espace social du sud-est de Madagascar*, Paris: L'Harmattan.

1988, "Les couleurs et les quatre éléments dans le sud-est de Madagascar: l'héritage indonésien," *Omaly sy Anio, Hier et Aujourd'hui*, 27, pp. 31–48.

1991, *Mythe et société à Madagascar (Tañala de l'Ikongo): le chasseur d'oiseaux et la princesse du ciel*, preface by G. Condominas, Paris: L'Harmattan.

1995, "Les rituels en riziculture chez les Tañala de l'Ikongo (sud-est de Madagascar): rituels, mythes et organisation sociale," in S. Evers and M. Spindler (ed.), *Cultures of Madagascar: Ebb and Flow of Influences / Civilisations de Madagascar: flux et reflux des influences*, Leiden: International Institute for Asian Studies, pp. 249–279.

1998, *Dictionnaire Malgache–Français (dialecte tañala, sud-est de Madagascar) avec recherches étymologiques*, Paris: L'Harmattan.

2003, "Les arrivées austronésiennes à Madagascar: vagues ou continuum?" *Études Océan Indien*, 35–36, pp. 59–147.

2005, "The Indian Ocean in Eurasian and African world-systems before the sixteenth century," *Journal of World History*, 16 (4), pp. 411–465.

2007, "L'Afrique de l'Est, les Comores et Madagascar dans le système-monde eurasiatique et africain avant le 16e siècle," in D. Nativel and F. Rajaonah (eds.), *L'Afrique et Madagascar*, Paris: Karthala, pp. 29–102.

2009, "Un seul système-monde avant le 16e siècle? L'océan Indien au cœur de l'intégration de l'hémisphère afro-eurasien," in P. Beaujard, L. Berger, and P. Norel (eds.), *Histoire globale, mondialisations et capitalisme*, Paris: Éditions La Découverte, pp. 82–148.

2010a, "From three possible Iron age world-systems to a single Afro-Eurasian world-system," *Journal of World History*, 21 (1), pp. 1–43.

2010b, "L'océan Indien au carrefour du monde," *L'Histoire*, 355 (special issue on "Les Grandes Découvertes"), pp. 30–35.

2011, "Evolutions and temporal delimitations of possible Bronze Age world-systems in western Asia and the Mediterranean," in T. C. Wilkinson, S. Sherratt, and J. Bennet (eds.), *Interweaving Worlds: Systemic Interactions in Eurasia, 7th to 1st Millennia BCE* (Proceedings of the symposium "What Would a Bronze Age World System Look Like? World Systems Approaches to Europe and Western Asia 4th to 1st Millennia BCE," University of Sheffield, April 1–4, 2008), Oxford: Oxbow Books, pp. 7–26.

2012, *Les mondes de l'océan Indien*, vol. I: *De la formation de l'État au premier système-monde afro-eurasien (4e millénaire av. J.-C. – 6e siècle apr. J.-C.)*; vol. II: *L'océan Indien au cœur des globalisations de l'Ancien Monde*, Paris: Armand Colin.

2013, "Ancient world-systems and processes of domination, coevolution, and resistance: the example of the East African coast before the XVIIth century," *Actuel Marx*, 53, pp. 40–62.

2017, *Histoire et voyages des plantes cultivées à Madagascar avant le 16e siècle*, Paris: Karthala.

forthcoming, "World-system cycles since 1000 BCE: temporal boundaries and factors affecting the pulse of the system," in C. Chase-Dunn and H. Inoue (eds.), *Systemic Boundaries: Time Mapping Globalization since the Bronze Age*, New York: Springer.

BEAUJARD, P., BERGER, L., and NOREL, P. (eds.), 2009, *Histoire globale, mondialisations et capitalisme*, Paris: La Découverte.

BEAULIEU, P.-A., 2005, "World hegemony, 900–300 BCE," in D. C. Snell (ed.), *A Companion to the Ancient Near East*, Malden, MA, and Oxford: Blackwell, pp. 48–62.

BECK, H. C., 1931, "Appendix 7: Notes on beads from the Upper Kenyan Aurignacian and the Gumban B cultures," in L. S. B. Leakey (ed.), *The Stone Age Cultures of Kenya Colony*, Cambridge University Press, pp. 281–282.

BECKER, C. H. and DUNLOP, D. M., 1999, "Bahr al-Zandj, " in P. Bearman, T. Bianquis, C. E. Bosworth, E. van Donzel, and W. P. Heinrichs (eds.), *Encyclopedia of Islam*, http://dx .doi.org/10.1163/1573-3912_islam_SIM_1066

BECKMAN, G., 1997, "Real property sales at Emar," in *Studies in Honor of Michael C. Astour on His 80th Birthday*, Bethesda, MD: CDL Press, pp. 95–120.

2000, "Hittite chronology," *Akkadica*, 199–120, pp. 19–32.

BECKWITH, L., 2011, *Empires of the Silk Road: A History of Central Eurasia from the Bronze Age to the Present*, Princeton University Press.

BEDIGIAN, D., 1998, "Early history of sesame cultivation in the Near East and beyond," in A. B. Damania, J. Valkoun, G. Willcox, and C. O. Qualset (eds.), *Origins of Agriculture and Crop Domestication*, Aleppo: ICARDA, pp. 93–101.

BEECH, M., CUTTLER, R., MOSCROP, D., KALLWEIT, H., and MARTIN, J., 2005, "New evidence for the Neolithic settlement of Marawah Island, Abu Dhabi, United Arab Emirates," *Proceedings of the Seminar for Arabian Studies*, 35, pp. 37–56.

BEECH, M., ELDERS, J., and SHEPHERD, E., 2000, "Reconsidering the 'Ubaid of the Southern Gulf: new results from excavations on Dalma Island, U.A.E.," *Proceedings of the Seminar for Arabian Studies*, 30, pp. 41–46.

BEGLEY, V., 1992, "Ceramic evidence for pre-*Periplus* trade on the Indian Coasts," in V. Begley and R. D. De Puma (eds.), *Rome and India: The Ancient Sea Trade*, Delhi: Oxford University Press, pp. 157–196.

BEHERA, K. S., 1999a, "Maritime activities of Orissa," in K. S. Behera (ed.), *Maritime Heritage of India*, New Delhi: Aryan Books International, pp. 162–171.

(ed.), 1999b, *Maritime Heritage of India*, New Delhi: Aryan Books International.

BEJA-PEREIRA, A., ENGLAND, P. R., FERRAND, F., JORDAN, S., BAKHIET, A. O., ABDALLA, M. A., MASHKOUR, M., JORDANA, J., TABERLET, P., and LUIKART, G., 2004, "African origins of the domestic donkey," *Science*, 304 (5678), p. 1781.

BELLINA, B., 1999, "La vaisselle dans les échanges entre le sous-continent indien et l'Asie du Sud-Est à l'époque protohistorique: notes sur quelques marqueurs archéologiques," *Bulletin de l'Ecole française d'Extrême-Orient*, 86, pp. 161–184.

2002, "Le port protohistorique de Khao Sam Kaeo en Thaïlande péninsulaire," *Bulletin de l'École française d'Extrême-Orient*, 89, pp. 329–343.

2003, "Beads, social change and interaction between India and Southeast Asia," *Antiquity*, 77 (296), pp. 285–297.

2005, "La genèse des échanges à longue distance. Apport de l'étude technologique des parures en roches dures," *Dossiers d'Archéologie*, 302, pp. 74–77.

2017, "The inception of the trans-national processes between the Indian Ocean and the South China Sea from an early city-state on the Thai-Malay Peninsula (fourth–second century BCE)," in M.-F. Boussac, S. Roychoudhury, J.-F. Salles, and J.-B. Yon (eds.), *Proceedings of the International Conference "The Ports of the Indian Ocean, from the Red Sea to the Gulf of Bengal,"* Delhi: Primus Books, pp. 463–492.

BELLINA, B., BACUS, E. A. PRYCE, T. O., and WISSEMAN CHRISTIE, J. (eds.), 2010, *50 Years of Archaeology in Southeast Asia: Essays in Honour of Ian Glover*, Bangkok: River Books.

BELLINA, B. and GLOVER, I. C., 2004, "The archaeology of early contacts with India and the Mediterranean world from the fourth century BCE to the fourth century AD," in I. C Glover and P. Bellwood (eds.), *Southeast Asia: From Prehistory to History*, Abingdon and New York: Routledge/Curzon Press, pp. 68–89.

BELLINA-PRYCE, B. and SILAPANTH, P., 2008, "Weaving cultural identities on trans-Asiatic networks: Upper Thai-Malay Peninsula – an early socio-political landscape," *Bulletin de l'École française d'Extrême-Orient*, 93, pp. 257–293.

BELLINA, B., SILAPANTH, P. CHAISUWAN, B., ALLEN, J., BERNARD, V., and BORELL, B. *et al.* 2014, "The development of coastal polities in the Upper Thai-Malay Peninsula in the late first millennium BCE," in N. Revire and S. Murphy (eds.), *Before Siam Was Born: New Insights on the Art and Archaeology of Pre-Modern Thailand and Its Neighbouring Regions*, Bangkok: River Books, pp. 68–89.

BELLWOOD, P., 1978, *The Polynesians: Prehistory of an Island People*, London: Thames and Hudson.

1992, "Southeast Asia before history," in N. Tarling (ed.), *The Cambridge History of Southeast Asia*, vol. I, part. I: *From Early Times to c. 1500*, Cambridge University Press, pp. 55–136.

1996, "The origins and spread of agriculture in the Indo-Pacific region: gradualism and diffusion or revolution and colonization?," in D. R. Harris (ed.), *The Origins and Spread of Agriculture and Pastoralism in Eurasia*, London: UCL Press, pp. 465–498.

1978, *The Polynesians: Prehistory of an Island People*, London: Thames & Hudson.

1997, *Prehistory of the Indo-Malaysian Archipelago*, rev. edn., Honolulu: University of Hawai'i Press (1st edn. 1985).

2004, "The origins and dispersals of agricultural communities in Southeast Asia," in I. Glover and P. Bellwood (eds.), *Southeast Asia: From Prehistory to History*, Abingdon and New York: Routledge/Curzon, pp. 21–40.

2005a, *First Farmers*, Oxford: Blackwell.

2005b, "Examining the language/farming dispersal hypothesis in the East Asian context," in L. Sagart, R. Blench, and A. Sanchez-Mazas (eds.), *The Peopling of East Asia: Putting Together Archaeology, Linguistics and Genetics*, London: Routledge/Curzon, pp. 17–30.

2006, "Early farmers: issues of spread and migration with respect to the Indian subcontinent," in T. Osada (ed.), *Proceedings of the Pre-Symposium of RIHN and 7th ESCA Harvard-Kyoto Roundtable*, Kyoto: Research Institute for Humanity and Nature (RIHN), pp. 58–72.

2007, "Understanding the Neolithic in Northern India," *Pradghara*, 18, pp. 331–346.

BELLWOOD, P., CAMERON, J., VAN VIET, N., and VAN LIEM, B., 2007, "Ancient boats, boat timbers, and locked mortise-and-tenon joints from Bronze/Iron-Age Northern Vietnam," *The International Journal of Nautical Archaeology*, 36 (1), pp. 2–20.

BELLWOOD, P. and GLOVER, I. C., 2004, "Southeast Asia: foundations for an archaeological history," in I. C Glover and P. Bellwood (eds.), *Southeast Asia, from Prehistory to History*, Abingdon and New York: Routledge/Curzon Press, pp. 4–20.

BELLWOOD, P. and NESS, I. (eds.), 2014, *The Global Prehistory of Human Migration*, Oxford: Wiley-Blackwell.

BELLWOOD, P. and SANCHEZ-MAZAS, A., 2005, "Human migrations in continental East Asia and Taiwan: genetic, linguistic and archaeological evidence," *Current Anthropology*, 46 (3), pp. 480–484.

BENECKE, N. and DREISCH, A. VON DEN, 2003, "Horse exploitation in the Kazakh Steppes during the Eneolithic and Bronze Age," in M. Levine, C. Renfrew, and K. Boyle (eds.), *Prehistoric Steppe Adaptation and the Horse*, Cambridge: McDonald Institute for Archaeological Research, pp. 69–82.

BENJAMIN, G. 1997, "Issues in the ethnohistory of Pahang," in N. H. S. Abdul Rahman, M. Abu Bakar, A. H. Khairuddin, and J. Baharuddin (eds.), *Pembangunan Arkeologi Pelancongan Negeri Pahang*, Pekan: Muzium Pahang, pp. 82–121.

BENOIST, A., MOUTON, M., and SCHIETTECATTE, J., 2003, "The artefacts from the fort at Mleiha: distribution, origins, trade and dating," *Proceedings of the Seminar for Arabian Studies*, 33, pp. 59–76.

BENOIT, A., 2003, *Art et archéologie: les civilisations du Proche-Orient ancien*, Paris: Ecole du Louvre, Editions de la Réunion des musées nationaux.

BENSEVAL, R., 1994, "The 1992–1993 field season at Miri-Qalat: new contributions to the chronology of protohistoric settlement in Pakistani Makran," in A. Parpolla and P. Koskikallio (eds.), *South Asian Archaeology 1993*, Helsinki: Suomalian Tiedeakatemia, pp. 81–91.

BENTLEY, J. H., 1993, *Old World Encounters: Cross-Cultural Contacts and Exchanges in Pre-Modern Times*, Oxford University Press.

1996, "Cross-cultural interaction and periodization in world history," *American Historical Review*, 101 (3), pp. 749–770.

BERKE, H., 2007, "The invention of blue and purple pigments in ancient times," *Chemical Society Reviews*, 36, pp. 15–30.

BERKES, F. and FOLKE, C. (eds.), 1998, *Linking Social and Ecological Systems: Management Practices and Social Mechanisms for Building Resilience*, Cambridge University Press.

BERNAL, M., 1991, *Black Athena*, vol. II: *The Archaeological and Documentary Evidence*, London: Free Association Books.

2001, *Black Athena Writes Back: Martin Bernal Responds to his Critics*, London: Free Association Books.

BERNAND, C. and GRUZINSKI, S., 1993, *Histoire du Nouveau Monde,* vol. II: *Les métissages (1550–1640),* Paris: Fayard.

BERNER, K. S., KOÇ, N., GODTSLIEBSEN, F., and DIVINE, D., 2011, "Holocene climate variability of the Norwegian Atlantic Current during high and low solar insolation forcing," *Paleoceanography,* 26, PA2220, doi:10.1029/2010PA002002.

BERTHIER, H., 1933, *Notes et impressions sur les moeurs et coutumes du peuple malgache,* Antananarivo: Imprimerie Officielle.

BERTHOUD, T., 1979, "Étude par l'analyse de traces et la modélisation de la filiation entre minerais de cuivre et objets archéologiques du Moyen-Orient (IVe–IIIe millénaires avant notre ère)," Thèse de Doctorat d'état, Université de Paris VI.

BERTRAND, R., 2007, "Rencontres impériales: l'histoire connectée et les relations euro-asiatiques," *Revue d'histoire moderne et contemporaine,* 54 (4bis), pp. 7–21.

BETTS, A. V. G., BORG, K. VAN DER, JONG, A. DE, MCCLINTOCK, C., and STRYDONCK, M. VAN, 1994, "Early cotton in North Arabia," *Journal of Archaeological Science,* 21 (4), pp. 488–499.

BEZBAKH, P., 2005, *Histoire de l'économie: des origines à la mondialisation,* Paris: Larousse.

BIAGI, P., 2006, "The shell-middens of the Arabian sea and Persian Gulf: maritime connections in the seventh millennium BP?," *Adumatu,* 14, pp. 7–16.

BIAGI, P. and NISBET, R., 1992, "Environmental history and plant exploitation at the aceramic sites of RH5 and RH6 near the mangrove swamp of Qurm (Muscat-Oman)," *Bulletin de la Société Botanique de France,* 139 (2–4), pp. 571–578.

BICKEL, S., 1998, "Commerçants et bateliers au Nouvel Empire: mode de vie et statut d'un groupe social," in *Le commerce en Égypte ancienne,* Cairo: Institut Français d'Archéologie Orientale, pp. 157–172.

BIETAK, M., 2002, "Relative and absolute chronology of the Middle Bronze Age: comments on the present state of research," in M. Bietak (ed.), *The Middle Bronze Age in the Levant,* Vienna: Verlag der Österreichischen Akademie der Wissenschaften, pp. 29–42.

—— 2003, "Science versus archaeology: problems and consequences of high Aegean chronology," in M. Bietak (ed.), *The Synchronisation of Civilisations in the Eastern Mediterranean in the Second Millennium BCE II,* Proceedings of the SCIEM 2000 EuroConference, Haindorf, May 2–7, 2001, Vienna: Verlag der Österreichischen Akademie der Wissenschaften, pp. 23–34.

BIRABEN, J.-N., 2004, "Histoire du peuplement et prévisions," in G. Caselli, J. Vallin, and G. Wunsch (eds.), *Démographie, analyse et synthèse,* vol. V, Paris: INED, pp. 9–32.

BISCIONE, R., 1974, "Relative chronology and pottery connections between Shahr-i Sokhta and Mundigak, eastern Iran," *Memorie dell'Istituto Italiano di Paleontologia Umana,* 2, pp. 131–145.

BISSON, M. S., 2000, "Precolonial copper metallurgy: sociopolitical context," in J. O. Vogel (ed.), *Ancient African Metallurgy: The Sociocultural Context,* Walnut Creek, CA: Altamira, pp. 83–276.

BIVAR, A. D. H., 1971, "A hoard of ingot-currency of the Median Period from Nûsh-i Jân, near Malayir," *Iran,* 9, pp. 97–107.

BLANC-PAMARD, C. and RAKOTO-RAMIARANTSOA, H., 1993, "Les bas-fonds des hautes terres centrales de Madagascar: construction et gestion paysannes," in M. Raunet (ed.), *Bas-fonds et riziculture,* Antananarivo: CIRAD, pp. 31–47.

—— 1998, "Microcosmos, le territoire miniaturisé sur les Hautes Terres centrales de Madagascar," in D. Guillaud, M. Saosset, and A. Walter (eds.), *Le voyage inachevé . . . à Joël Bonnemaison,* Paris: ORSTOM, pp. 643–650.

BLANCHY, S., 1997, "Note sur le rituel d'intronisation des souverains de Mayotte et l'ancien ordre politico-religieux," *Études Océan Indien,* 21, pp. 107–129.

BLAŽEK, V. and BOISSON, C., 1992, "The diffusion of agricultural terms from Mesopotamia," *Archiv Orientální,* 60, pp. 16–37.

BLEIBERG, E., 1995, "The economy of Ancient Egypt," in J. M. Sasson (ed.), *Civilizations of the Ancient Near East*, vol. III, New York: Scribner's, pp. 1373–1385.

2002, "Loans, credit and interest in Ancient Egypt," in M. Hudson and M. van de Mieroop (eds.), *Debt and Economic Renewal in the Ancient Near East*, Bethesda, MD: CDL Press, pp. 257–276.

BLENCH, R., 1984, "The morphology and distribution of sub-Saharan musical instruments of North African, Middle Eastern, and Asian origin," in L. Picken (ed.), *Musica Asiatica*, vol. IV, Cambridge University Press, pp. 155–191.

1996, "The ethnographic evidence for long-distance contacts between Oceania and East Africa," in J. Reade (ed.), *The Indian Ocean in Antiquity*, London and New York: Kegan Paul, pp. 417–438.

2003, "The movement of cultivated plants between Africa and India in prehistory," in K. Neumann, A. Butler, and S. Kahlhaber (eds.), *Food, Fuel and Fields: Progress in African Archaeobotany*, Cologne: Heinrich-Barth-Institut, pp. 273–292.

2004, "Fruits and arboriculture in the Indo-Pacific region," *Bulletin of the Indo-Pacific Prehistory Association*, 24 (The Taipei Papers vol. 2), pp. 31–50.

2006, "A history of fruits on the SE Asian mainland,"paper presented at the International Congress of the EURASEAA (European Association of Southeast Asian Archaeologists), Bougon, September 26, 2006.

2007a, "New palaezoogeographical evidence for the settlement of Madagascar," *Azania*, 42, pp. 69–82.

2007b, "The intertwined history of the silk cotton and baobab," in R. Cappers (ed.), *Fields of Change: Progress in African Archaeobotany*, Groningen: Barkhuis and Groningen University Library, pp. 1–29.

2008, "The Austronesians in Madagascar and their interaction with the Bantu of the East African coast: surveying the linguistic evidence for domestic and translocated animals," *Studies in Philippine Languages and Cultures*, 18, pp. 18–43.

2009, "Bananas and plantains in Africa: re-interpreting the linguistic evidence," *Ethnobotany Research & Applications*, 7, pp. 363–380.

2010a, "Evidence for the Austronesian voyages in the Indian Ocean," in A. Anderson, J. H. Barrett, and K. V. Boyle (eds.), *The Global Origins and Development of Seafaring*, Cambridge: McDonald Institute for Archaeological Research, pp. 239–248.

2010b, "Was there an Austroasiatic presence in Island South-East Asia prior to the Austronesian expansion?," *Bulletin of the Indo-Pacific Prehistory Association*, 30, pp. 130–144.

2012a, "Vernacular names for Taro in the Indo-Pacific region and their possible implications for centres of diversification and spread," in M. Spriggs, D. Addison, and P. J. Matthews (eds.), *Wet Cultivation of Colocasia esculenta in the Indo-Pacific: Archaeological, Technological, Social, and Biological Perspectives* (Senri Ethnological Studies 78), Osaka: Minpaku, pp. 21–43.

2012b, "Almost everything you believed about the Austronesians isn't true," in M. L. Tjoa-Bonatz, A. Reinecke, and D. Bonatz (eds.), *Crossing Borders: Selected Papers from the 13th International Conference of the European Association of Southeast Asian Archaeologists*, vol. 1, Singapore: NUS Press, pp. 128–148.

2014, "Using diverse sources of evidence for reconstructing the prehistory of musical exchanges in the Indian Ocean and their broader significance for cultural prehistory," *African Archaeological Review*, doi: 10.1007/s10437-014-9178-z

BLENCH, R. and WALSH, M., 2009, "Faunal names in Malagasy: their etymologies and implications for the prehistory of the East African coast," http://rb.rowbory.co.uk/Language/Austronesian/Malagasy/

BLOOM, J. M., 2001, *Paper Before Print: The History and Impact of Paper in the Islamic World*, New Haven, CT: Yale University Press.

BLUST, R., 1970, "Proto-Austronesian addenda," *Oceanic Linguistics*, 9, pp. 104–162.

1972a, "Proto-Oceanic addenda with cognates in non-Oceanic Austronesian languages," *Working Papers in Linguistics*, 4 (1), pp. 1–41, Honolulu: Department of Linguistics, University of Hawaii.

1972b, "Additions to 'Proto-Austronesian addenda' and 'Proto-Oceanic addenda with cognates in non-Oceanic Austronesian languages'," *Working Papers in Linguistics*, 4 (8), pp. 1–17, Honolulu: Department of Linguistics, University of Hawaii.

1973, "Additions to 'Proto-Austronesian addenda' and 'Proto-Oceanic addenda with cognates in non-Oceanic Austronesian languages'," part 2: *Working Papers in Linguistics*, 5 (3), pp. 33–61, Honolulu: Department of Linguistics, University of Hawaii.

1976, "Austronesian culture history: some linguistic inferences and their relations to the archaeological record," *World Archaeology*, 8, pp. 19–43.

1980, "Austronesian etymologies I," *Oceanic Linguistics*, 19 (1–2), pp. 1–189.

1983–1984, "Austronesian etymologies II," *Oceanic Linguistics*, 22–23, pp. 29–149.

1986, "Austronesian etymologies III," *Oceanic Linguistics*, 25, pp. 1–123.

1988a, *Austronesian Root Theory: An Essay on the Limits of Morphology*, Amsterdam and Philadelphia: John Benjamins.

1988b, "Malay historical linguistics: a progress report," in M. T. Ahmad and Z. M. Zaim (eds.), *Rekonstruksi dan Cabang-Cabang Bahasa Melayu Induk*, Kuala Lumpur: Dewan Bahasa dan Pustaka, pp. 1–34.

1989, "Austronesian etymologies IV," *Oceanic Linguistics*, 28, pp. 111–180.

1993a, "*S metathesis and the Formosan/Malayo-Polynesian language boundary," in O. Dahl (ed.), *Language: A Doorway between Human Cultures: Tributes to Dr. Otto Christian Dahl on His Ninetieth Birthday*, Oslo: Novus, pp. 178–183.

1993b, "Central and Central-Eastern Malayo-Polynesian," *Oceanic Linguistics*, 32 (2), pp. 241–293.

1994a, "Obstruent epenthesis and the unity of phonological features," *Lingua*, 93, pp. 111–139.

1994b, "The Austronesian settlement of mainland Southeast Asia," in K. L. Adams and T. J. Hudak (eds.), *Papers from the Second Annual Meeting of the Southeast Asian Linguistics Society*, Tempe, AZ: Program for Southeast Asian Studies, Arizona State University, pp. 25–83.

1995, "The prehistory of the Austronesian-speaking peoples: a view from language," *Journal of World Prehistory*, 9 (4), pp. 453–510.

1998, "Ca-reduplication and Proto-Austronesian grammar," *Oceanic Linguistics*, 37 (1), pp. 29–64.

2005, "Borneo and iron: Dempwolff's *besi* revisited," *Bulletin of the IndoPacific*, 25, pp. 31–40.

2006, "The linguistic macrohistory of the Philippines: some speculations," in Hsiu-chuan Liao and C. R. Galvez Rubino (eds.), *Current Issues in Philippine Linguistics and Anthropology: Parangal kay Lawrence A. Reid*, Manila: The Linguistic Society of the Philippines and Summer Institute of Linguistics, Philippines, pp. 31–68.

n.d., *Austronesian Comparative Dictionary*, computer file.

BOCOUM, H., 2002, "La métallurgie du fer en Afrique: un patrimoine et une ressource au service du développement," in H. Bocoum (ed.), *Aux origines de la métallurgie du fer en Afrique: une ancienneté méconnue. Afrique de l'Ouest et Afrique centrale*, Paris: UNESCO, pp. 94–103.

BOGAERT, R., 1966, *Les origines antiques de la banque de dépôt*, Leiden: A. W. Sijthoff.

1998–1999, "Les opérations des banques de l'Égypte ptolémaïque," *Ancient Society*, 29, pp. 49–145.

2007, "La banque à Athènes au IVe siècle: état de la question," in P. Brulé, J. Oulhen, and F. Prost (eds.), *Économie et société en Grèce antique (478–88 BCE)*, Presses Universitaires de Rennes, pp. 405–436.

BOITEAU, P., BOITEAU, M., and ALLORGE-BOITEAU, L., 1997, *Index des noms scientifiques avec leurs équivalents malgaches. Dictionnaire des noms malgaches de végétaux (extrait du Dictionnaire des noms malgaches de végétaux)*, Grenoble: C. Alzieu.

1999, *Dictionnaire des noms malgaches de végétaux*, 4 vols., Grenoble: C. Alzieu.

BOIVIN, N., 2007, "Anthropological, historical, archaeological and genetic perspectives on the origins of caste in South Asia," in M. D Petraglia and B. Allchin (eds.), *The Evolution and History of Human Populations in South Asia: Inter-disciplinary Studies in Archaeology, Biological Anthropology, Linguistics and Genetics*, Dordrecht: Springer, pp. 341–361.

BOIVIN, N., BLENCH, R., and FULLER, D. Q., 2009, "Archaeological, linguistic and historical sources on ancient seafaring: a multidisciplinary approach to the study of early maritime contact and exchange in the Arabian Peninsula," in M. D. Petraglia and J. I. Rose (eds.), *The Evolution of Human Populations in Arabia: Paleoenvironments, Prehistory and Genetics*, Dordrecht: Springer, pp. 251–278.

BOIVIN, N. and FULLER, D., 2009, "Shell middens, ships and seeds: exploring coastal subsistence maritime trade and the dispersal of domesticates in and around the ancient Arabian Peninsula," *Journal of World Prehistory*, 22, pp. 113–180.

BÖKÖNYI, S., 1997, "Horse remains from the prehistoric site of Surkotada, Kutch, late 3rd millennium BC," *South Asian Studies*, 13, pp. 297–307.

BOKOVENKO, N. A., 2004, "Migrations of early nomads of the Eurasian steppe in a context of climatic changes," in E. M. Scott, A. Y. Alekseev, and G. Zaitseva (eds.), *Impact of the Environment on Human Migration in Eurasia*, Dordrecht, Boston, and London: Kluwer Academic Publishers, pp. 21–33.

BOLIKHOVSKAYA, N., KAITAMBA, M., POROTOV, A., and FOUACHE, E., 2004, "Environmental changes of the northeastern Black Sea's coastal region during the Middle and Late Holocene," in E. M. Scott, A. Y. Alekseev, and G. Zaitseva (eds.), *Impact of the Environment on Human Migration in Eurasia*, Dordrecht, Boston, and London: Kluwer Academic Publishers, pp. 209–223.

BOLOHAN, N., 2005, "The Danube, Balkans, and Northern Aegean: trade routes, influences and buffer zones in the Late Bronze Age," in R. Laffineur and E. Greco (eds.), *Emporia: Aegeans in the Central and Eastern Mediterranean*, Proceedings of the 10th International Aegean Conference, Athens, Italyn School of Archaeology, April 14–18, 2004, Aegaeum 25, Annales d'archéologie égéenne de l'Université de Liège and UT-PASP, Université de Liège, University of Texas at Austin, pp. 161–171.

BOLTZ, W. G., 1999, "Language and writing," in M. Loewe and E. L. Slaughnessy (eds.), *The Cambridge History of Ancient China: From the Origins of Civilization to 221 BCE*, Cambridge University Press, pp. 74–123.

BONANI, G., HAAS, H., HAWASS, Z., LEHNER, M., NAKHLA, S., NOLAN, J., WENKE, R., and WÖLFLI, W., 2001, "Radiocarbon dates of Old and Middle Kingdom monuments in Egypt," *Radiocarbon*, 43 (3), pp. 1297–1320.

BOND, G., SHOWERS, W., CHESEBY, M., LOTTI, R., ALMASI, P., DEMENOCAL, P., PRIORE, P., CULLEN, H., HAJDAS, I., and BONANI, G., 1997, "A pervasive millennial-scale cycle in North Atlantic holocene and glacial climates," *Science*, 278 (5341), pp. 1257–1266.

BONGENAAR, A. C. V. M., 1999, "Money in the Neo-Babylonian Institutions," in J. G. Dercksen (ed.), *Trade and Finance in Ancient Mesopotamia (Mos Studies 1). Proceedings of the First Mos Symposium, Leiden 1997*, Nederlands Historisch-Archaeologisch Instituut te Istanbul, pp. 159–174.

BONNEMAISON, J., 1996, "Gens du taro et gens de l'igname," in M. Julien, M. and C. Orliac, B. Gérard, A. and H. Lavondès, and C. Robineau (eds.), *Mémoire de pierre. Tradition et archéologie en Océanie. Hommage à José Garanger*, Paris: Publications de la Sorbonne, pp. 389–404.

BOPEARACHCHI, O., 1996, "Seafaring in the Indian Ocean: archaeological evidence from Sri Lanka," in H. P. Ray and J.-F. Salles (eds.), *Tradition and Archaeology*, New Delhi: Manohar, pp. 60–77 (reissued 2011).

2002, "Archaeological evidence on shipping communities of Sri Lanka," in D. Parkin and R. Barnes (eds.), *Ships and the Development of Maritime Technology in the Indian Ocean*, London and New York, Routledge/Curzon, pp. 92–127.

BORELL, B., 2013, "The glass vessels from Guangxi and the Maritime Silk Road in the Han period 206 BCE – 220 CE," in M. Bloke and V. Degroot (eds.), *Unearthing Southeast Asia's Past*, Singapore: NUS Press, pp. 141–154.

BOROFFKA, N., CIERNY, J., LUTZ, J., PARZINGER, H., PERNICKA, E., and WEISGERBER, G., 2002, "Bronze Age tin from Central Asia: preliminary notes," in K. Boyle, C. Renfrew, and M. Levine (eds.), *Ancient Interactions: East and West in Eurasia*, Cambridge: McDonald Institute for Archaeological Research, pp. 135–159.

BOSTOEN, K., 2014, "Wild trees in the subsistence economy of early Bantu speech communities: a historical-linguistic approach," in C. J. Stevens, S. Nixon, M. A. Murray, and D. Fuller (eds.), *Archaeology of African Plant Use*, Walnut Creek, CA: Institute of Archaeology Publications, Left Coast Press, pp. 129–140.

BOSWORTH, A., 1995, "World cities and world economic cycles," in S. K. Sanderson (ed.), *Civilizations and World Systems: Studying World-Historical Change*, Walnut Creek, CA, London, and New Delhi: Altamira Press, pp. 206–227.

2000, "The evolution of the world-city system, 3000 BCE to AD 2000," in R. A. Denemark, J. Friedman, B. K. Gills, and G. Modelski (eds.), *World System History: The Social Science of Long-Term Change*, London and New York: Routledge, pp. 273–284.

BOUET, A. (ed.), 2005, Aquam in altum exprimere, *les machines élévatrices d'eau dans l'Antiquité*, Pessac: Ausonius.

BOULNOIS, L., 2001, *La Route de la Soie: dieux, guerriers et marchands*, Geneva: Olizane.

2008, *Silk Road: Monks, Warriors and Merchants*, Hong Kong: Odyssey Books.

BOURDILLON, M., 1976, *The Shona Peoples*, Gwelo: Mambo Press.

BOUSSAC, M. F.,. SALLES, J.-F., and YON, J.-B. (eds.), 2012, Autour du *Périple de la mer Érythrée*, *Topoi: Orient-Occident* (Lyon), supplement 11.

BOWEN, R., 1953, "Eastern sail affinities," *The American Neptune*, 13 (2), pp. 81–117.

BOWER, J. R. E., 1973, "Seronera: excavations at a stone bowl site in the Serengeti National Park, Tanzania," *Azania*, 8, pp. 71–104.

BOZEMAN, A. B., 1994, *Politics and Culture in International History: From the Ancient Near East to the Opening of the Modern Age*, 2nd edn., New Brunswick: Transaction Publishers.

BRANIGAN, K., 1970, *The Foundations of Palatial Crete: A Survey of Crete in the Early Bronze Age*, London: Routledge and Kegan Paul.

BRAUDEL, F., 1949, *La Méditerranée et le monde méditerranéen à l'époque de Philippe II*, Paris: Armand Colin.

1958, "Histoire et sciences sociales: la longue durée," *Annales-Économie, Sociétés, Civilisations*, 13 (4), pp. 725–753.

1979, *Civilisation matérielle, économie et capitalisme, XVe–XVIIIe siècle*, vol. I: *Les structures du quotidien*; vol. II: *Les jeux de l'échange*; vol. III: *Le temps du monde*, Paris: Armand Colin.

1981, 1982, 1984, *Civilization and Capitalism, 15th–18th Century*, vol. I: *The Structures of Everyday Life*; vol. II: *The Wheels of Commerce*; vol. III: *The Perspective of the World*, London: Collins.

BRAUN, E., 2001, "Proto, Early Dynastic Egypt, and Early Bronze I–II of the Southern Levant: some uneasy 14C correlations," *Radiocarbon*, 43 (3), pp. 1279–1295.

2002, "Egypt's first sojourn in Canaan," in E. C. M. van den Brink and T. E. Levy (eds.), *Egypt and the Levant: Interrelations from the 4th through the Early 3rd Millennium BCE*, London and New York: Leicester University Press, pp. 173–189.

BREASTED, J. H., 1988, *Ancient Records of Egypt*, vol. II, London: Histories and Mysteries of Man (first published 1906).

BRESSON, A., 2000, *La cité marchande*, Pessac: Ausonius.

BRESSON, A. and BRESSON, F., 2004, "Max Weber, la comptabilité rationnelle et l'économie du monde gréco-romain," in H. Bruhns and J. Andreau (eds.), *Sociologie économique et économie de l'Antiquité. À propos de Max Weber, Cahiers du Centre de recherches historiques*, 34, pp. 91–114.

BRETON, J.-F, 2001a and b, "Les villes du Yémen antique" and "Les sanctuaires de la capitale de Saba, Mārib," *Dossiers d'Archéologie*, 263 (issue on Yemen), pp. 22–29 and pp. 48–49.

2002, "L'architecture antique des deux rives de la mer Rouge: projet de dictionnaire méthodique," *Journal des Africanistes*, 72 (2), pp. 229–240.

2003, "Preliminary notes on the development of Shabwa," *Proceedings of the Seminar for Arabian Studies*, 33, pp. 199–213.

BRETON, S. 2002, "Présentation: monnaie et économie des personnes," *L'Homme*, 162, pp. 13–26.

BRIANT, P., 1982, *Rois, tributs et paysans*, Besançon: Les Belles Lettres.

1994, "Prélèvements tributaires et échanges en Asie Mineure achéménide et hellénistique," in J. Andreau, P. Briant, and R. Descat (eds.), *Les échanges dans l'Antiquité: le rôle de l'état* (Entretiens d'Archéologie et d'Histoire), Musée archéologique departmental de Saint-Bertrand de Comminges, pp. 69–82.

1996, *Histoire de l'empire perse: de Cyrus à Alexandre*, Paris: Fayard.

BRILL, R. H., 1999, *Chemical Analyses of Early Glasses*, Corning, NY: Corning Museum of Glass.

BRILL, R. H., SHI M., JOEL, E. C., and VOCKE, R. D., 1992, "Lead isotope studies of early Chinese glasses," in R. H. Brill and J. H. Martin (eds.), *Scientific Research in Early Chinese Glass*, Corning, NY: Corning Museum of Glass, pp. 65–90.

BRON, F., 1997, "Naissance et destin de l'alphabet sud-arabique," in *Yémen: au pays de la reine de Saba*, Paris: Flammarion, Institut du Monde Arabe, pp. 55–57.

2001a and b, "Les grandes périodes de l'histoire du Yémen préislamique" and "Langues et écriture sudarabiques," *Dossiers d'Archéologie*, 263 (issue on Yemen), pp. 4–8 and p. 9.

BROODBANK, C., 2000, *An Island Archaeology of the Early Cyclades*, Cambridge University Press.

BROOK, T., 1998, *The Confusions of Pleasure: Commerce and Culture in Ming China*, Berkeley: University of California Press.

BROOKE, J. L, 2014, *Climate Change and the Course of Global History: A Rough Journey*, Cambridge University Press.

BROWN, N., 2001, *History and Climate Change: A Eurocentric Perspective*, London and New York: Routledge.

BROWN, R. L. and MacDONNELL, A. M., 1989, "The Pong Tuk lamp: a reconsideration," *Journal of the Siam Society*, 77 (2), pp. 9–20.

BRUCATO, N., KUSUMA, P., COX, M. P., PIERRON, D., PURNOMO, G. A., ADELAAR, S., KIVISILD, T., LETELLIER, T., SUDOYO, H., and RICAUT, F.-X., 2016, "Malagasy genetic ancestry comes from an historical Malay trading post in southeast Borneo," *Molecular Biology and Evolution*, 33, pp. 2396–2400.

BRUHNS, H., 1998, "À propos de l'histoire ancienne et de l'économie politique chez Max Weber," introduction to M. Weber, *Économie et société dans l'Antiquité, précédé de Les causes sociales du déclin de la civilisation antique*, Paris: La Découverte, pp. 9–59.

2001, "La ville bourgeoise et l'émergence du capitalisme moderne. Max Weber: *Die Stadt* (1913/1914–1921)," in B. Lepetit and C. Topalov (eds.), *La ville des sciences sociales*, Paris: Belin, pp. 47–78.

2004, "Max Weber, économie antique et science économique moderne," *Cahiers du Centre de Recherche Historique*, 34, p. 31–45.

BRUINS, H. J., 2001, "Near East chronology: towards an integrated 14 C time foundation," *Radiocarbon*, 43 (3), pp. 1147–1154.

BRUINS, H. J. and PLICHT, J. VAN DER, 2003, "Assorting and synchronizing archaeological and geological strata with radiocarbon: the southern Levant in relation to Egypt and Thera," in M. Bietak (ed.), *The Synchronisation of Civilisations in the Eastern Mediterranean in the Second Millennium BCE II*, Proceedings of the SCIEM 2000EuroConference, Haindorf, May 2–7, 2001, Vienna: Verlag der Österreichischen Akademie der Wissenschaften, pp. 35–42.

BRUINS, H. J., PLICHT, J. VAN DER, and MAZAR, A., 2003, "14C dates from Tel Rehov: Iron-Age chronology, pharaohs, and Hebrew kings," *Science*, 300 (5617), pp. 315–318.

BRYANT, E., 2005, "Concluding remarks," in E. Bryant and L. Patton (eds.), *The Indo-Aryan Controversy*, London: Routledge, pp. 468–506.

BRYCE, T., 2005, *The Kingdom of the Hittites*, New York: Oxford University Press (1st edn. 1999).

BUCCELLATI, G. and KELLEY-BUCCELLATI, M., 1983, "Terqa: the first eight seasons," *Annales Archéologiques Arabo-Syriennes*, 33 (2), pp. 47–67.

BUKHARIN, M. D., 2011, "The notion τὸ πέρας τῆς ἀνακομιδῆς and the location of Ptolemais of the Hunts in the Periplus of the Erythraean Sea," *Arabian Archaeology and Epigraphy*, 22, pp. 219–231.

BULBECK, D., 2004, "Indigenous traditions and exogenous influences in the early history of Peninsular Malaysia," in I. Glover and P. Bellwood (eds.), *Southeast Asia, from Prehistory to History*, Abingdon and New York: Routledge/Curzon, pp. 314–336.

2008, "An integrated perspective on the Austronesian diaspora: the switch from cereal agriculture to maritime foraging in the colonisation of Island South-East Asia," *Australian Archaeology*, 67, pp. 31–52.

BÜNTGEN, U. *et al.*, 2011, "2500 years of European climate variability and human susceptibility," *Science*, 331 (4), pp. 578–582.

BURBANK, J. and COOPER, F., 2010, *Empires in World History: Power and the Politics of Difference*, Princeton University Press.

BURKE III, E., 2009b and c, "The big story: human history, energy regimes, and the environment" and "The transformation of the Middle Eastern environment, 1500 BCE – 2000 CE," in E. Burke III and K. Pomeranz (eds.), *The Environment and World History*, Berkeley, Los Angeles, and London: University of California Press, pp. 33–53 and 81–117.

BURKILL, I. H., 1966, *A Dictionary of the Economic Products of the Malay Peninsula*, 2 vols., Kuala Lumpur: Ministry of Agriculture and Co-operatives (1st edn. 1935).

BURNEY, C., 1994, "Contact and conflict in north-western Iran," *Iranica Antiqua*, 29, pp. 138–153.

BURNEY, D. A., 1987a, "Late Holocene vegetational change in central Madagascar," *Quaternary Research*, 28 (1), pp. 130–143.

1987b, "Late Quaternary stratigraphic charcoal records from Madagascar," *Quaternary Research*, 28 (2), pp. 274–280.

1987c, "Pre-settlement vegetation changes at Lake Tritrivakely, Madagascar," *Paleoecology of Africa*, 18, pp. 357–381.

1993, "Late Holocene environmental changes in arid Southwestern Madagascar," *Quaternary Research*, 40 (1), pp. 98–106.

1999, "Rates, patterns, and processes of landscape transformation and extinction: Madagascar as an experiment in human ecology," in R. MacPhee (ed.), *Extinctions in Near Time: Causes, Contexts, and Consequences*, New York: Plenum, pp. 145–164.

BURNEY, D. A. and MATSUMOTO, K., 1994, "Late Holocene environments at Lake Mitsinjo, northwestern Madagascar," *Holocene*, 4 (1), p. 17–25.

BURNEY, D. A., ROBINSON, G. S., and BURNEY, L. P. 2003. "Spororhoneyla and the late Holocene extinctions in Madagascar," *Proceedings of the National Academy Sciences of the USA*, 100, pp. 10800–10805.

BURNEY, D. A., BURNEY, L. P., GODFREY, L. R., JUNGERS, W. L., GOODMAN, S. M., WRIGHT, H. T., and JULL, A. J. 2004. "A chronology for late prehistoric Madagascar," *Journal of Human Evolution*, 47 (1–2), pp. 25–63.

BURNEY, D. A., VASEY, N., GODFREY, L. R., RAMILISONINA, JUNGERS, W. L., RAMAROLAHY, M., *et al.*, 2008, "New findings at Andrahomana Cave, southeastern Madagascar," *Journal of Cave and Karst Studies*, 70 (1), pp. 13–24.

BURROUGHS, W. J., 2001, *Climate Change in Prehistory: The End of the Reign of Chaos*, Cambridge University Press.

BURROW, T., and EMENEAU, M. B., 1961, *A Dravidian Etymological Dictionary*, Oxford: Clarendon Press.

BUTZER, K. W., 1995, "Environmental change in the Near East and human impact on the land," in J. M. Sasson (ed.), *Civilizations of the Ancient Near East*, vols. I–II, Peabody, MA: Hendrickson Publishers, pp. 123–150.

1997, "Sociopolitical discontinuity in the Near East c. 2000 BCE: scenarios from Palestine and Egypt," in N. Dalfes, G. Kukla, and H. Weiss (eds.), *Third Millennium BCE Climate Change and Old World Collapse* (NATO ASI Series), Berlin and Heidelberg: Springer, pp. 245–296.

CABOURET-LAURIOUX, B., GUILHEMBET, J.-P., and ROMAN, Y., 2009, "Rome et l'Occident: considérations liminaires," in B. Cabouret-Laurioux, J.-P. Guilhembet, and Y. Roman (eds.), *Rome et l'Occident: IIe siècle av. J.-C. – IIe siècle ap. J.-C. Colloque de la SOPHAU, Lyon, May 15–16, 2009* (Pallas: Revue d'Études Antiques, 80), Toulouse: Presses Universitaires du Mirail, pp. 11–32.

CAD: *Chicago Assyrian Dictionary*, see Roth, M. T. *et al.*

CAILLÉ, A., 2005, *Dé-penser l'économique. Contre le fatalisme*, Paris: La Découverte-MAUSS.

CAIN, B. D., 2000, "Dhivehi (Maldivian): a synchronic and diachronic study," Ph. D. dissertation, Cornell University.

CALLEGARIN, L., 2011, "Coinages with Punic and neo-Punic legends of Western Mauritania: attribution, chronology and currency circulation," in A. Dowler and L. R. Galvin (eds.), *Money, Trade and Trade Routes in Pre-Islamic North Africa* (British Museum Research Publication 176), London: British Museum, pp. 42–48.

CALLET, F., 1974, *Histoire des rois*, translation of G. S. CHAPUS and E. RATSIMBA, *Tantara ny andriana*, Antananarivo: Éditions de la Librairie de Madagascar, 3 vols. (1st edn. 1953).

1981, *Tantara ny andriana eto Madagasikara*, 2nd edn., 2 vols., Antananarivo: Imprimerie Officielle (first published 1908).

CALO, A., 2008, "Heger I bronze drums and the relationships between Dian and Dong Son cultures," in E. A. Bacus, I. C. Glover, and P. D. Sharrock (eds.), *Interpreting Southeast Asia's Past: Monument, Image and Text*, Singapore: NUS Press, pp. 208–224.

2009, *The Distribution of Bronze Drums in Early Southeast Asia: Trade Routes and Cultural Spheres* (BAR International Series 1913), Oxford: Archaeopress.

2014, "Ancient trade between India and Indonesia," *Science*, 345 (6202), p. 1255.

CAMERON, J., 2010, "The archaeological textiles from Ban Don Ta Phet in broader perspective," in B. Bellina, E. A. Bacus, T. O. Pryce, and J. Wisseman Christie (eds.), *50 Years of Archaeology in Southeast Asia: Essays in Honour of Ian Glover*, Bangkok: River Books, pp. 140–151.

2011, "Iron and cloth across the Bay of Bengal: new data from Tha Kae, central Thailand," *Antiquity*, 85 (328), pp. 559–567.

CAMERON, E., AGUSTIJANTO INDRAJAYA, and MANGUIN, P.-Y., 2015, "Asbestos textiles from Batujaya (West Java, Indonesia): further evidence for early long-distance interaction between the Roman Orient, Southern Asia and island Southeast Asia," *Bulletin de l'École française d'Extrême-Orient*, 101, pp. 159–176.

CAMPBELL, R. B., 2014, *Archaeology of the Chinese Bronze Age*, Los Angeles: The Cotsen Institute of Archaeology Press.

CAMPS, G., 1978, Compte-rendu de J. Spruytte, *Études expérimentales sur l'attelage: contribution à l'histoire du cheval*, *Revue de l'Occident musulman et de la Mediterranean*, 25, pp. 172–174.

CAPDEPUY, V., 2010, "Entre Méditerranée et Mésopotamie: étude géohistorique d'un entre-deux plurimillénaire," Thèse de doctorat de géographie, Université Paris-Diderot.

CAPOGROSSI, L., 2004, "'Capitalisme' antique et 'capitalisme' médiéval dans l'œuvre de Max Weber," *Cahiers du Centre de Recherche Historique*, 34, pp. 21–30.

CAPPERS, R. T. J., 1999, "Archaeobotanical evidence of Roman trade with India," in H. P. Ray (ed.), *Archaeology of Seafaring: The Indian Ocean in the Ancient Period*, New Delhi: Pragati Publications, pp. 51–69.

2006, *Roman Foodprints at Berenike: Archaeobotanical Evidence of Subsistence and Trade in the Eastern Desert of Egypt* (Cotsen Institute of Archaeology Monograph 55), Los Angeles: Cotsen Institute of Archaeology.

CARLO, A., 2001, "La citoyenneté dans la Grèce antique," conference held at Université Montpellier, March 10, 2001.

CARLSON, D., 2010, "INA in Sri Lanka: Pearl of the Indian Ocean," *INA Annual 2010*, pp. 89–95.

CARNEIRO, R. L., 1970, "A theory of the origin of the state," *Science*, 169 (3947), pp. 733–738.

CARRASCO RUS, J., PACHON ROMERO, J. A., MONTERO RUIZ, I., and GAMIZ JIMENEZ, J., 2012, "Fíbulas de codo 'tipo Huelva' en la Península Ibérica: nuevos datos y comentarios historiográficos," *Trabajos de Prehistoria*, 69 (2), pp. 310–331.

CARTER, A. and LANKTON, J., 2013, "Analysis and comparison of glass beads from Ban Non Wat and Noen U-Loke," in C. F. W. Higham and A. Kinjngam (eds.), *The Origins of the Civilization of Angkor*, vol. VI: *The Excavation of Ban Non Wat: The Iron Age, Summary and Conclusions*, Bangkok: The Fine Arts Department of Thailand, pp. 91–114.

CARTER, A., O'REILLY, D., and SHEWAN, L., 2013, "Think globally, act locally? Exchange and socio-political development in northwest Cambodia as viewed through stone and glass beads," paper presented at the Sealinks Conference "Proto-Globalisation in the Indian Ocean World: Multidisciplinary Perspectives on Early Globalisation," Jesus College, Oxford, November 7–10, 2013.

CARTER, R., 2002, "Ubaid-period boat remains from as-Sabiyah: excavations by the British Archaeological Expedition to Kuwait," *Proceedings of the Seminar for Arabian Studies*, 32, pp. 13–30.

2006, "Boat remains and maritime trade in the Persian gulf during the sixth and fifth millennia BCE," *Antiquity*, 80 (307), pp. 52–63.

CARY, M. and WARMINGTON, E. H., 1963, *The Ancient Explorers*, London: Methuen (1st edn. 1929).

CASAL, J.-M., 1961, *Fouilles de Mundigak*, 2 vols., Paris: Klincksieck.

CASANOVA, M., 1998, "Le lapis-lazuli de l'Asie centrale à la Syrie au Chalcolithique et à l'âge du Bronze," in P. Matthiae, A. Enea, L. Peyronel, and F. Pinnock (eds.), *Proceedings of the First International Congress on the Archaeology of the Ancient Near East*, Rome: Università degli studi di Roma.

1999, "Le lapis-lazuli dans l'Orient ancien," in A. Caubet (ed.), *Cornaline et pierres précieuses: la Méditerranée, de l'Antiquité à l'Islam*, Paris: La Documentation Française, pp. 189–210.

2013, *Le lapis lazuli dans l'Orient ancien: production et circulation du Néolithique au IIe millénaire av. J.-C.*, Paris: Comité des travaux historiques et scientifiques.

CASPARIS, J. G. DE, 1956, *Prasasti Indonesia II: Selected Inscriptions from the 7th to the 9th Century AD*, Bandung: Masa Baru.

1979, "Paleography as an auxiliary discipline in research on Early South-East Asia," in R. B. Smith and W. Watson (eds.), *Early South-East Asia*, New York: Oxford University Press, pp. 380–394.

1983. *India and Maritime South East Asia: A Lasting Relationship*, Kuala Lumpur: University of Malaysia Press.

1988, "Some notes on words of 'Middle-Indian' origin in Indonesian languages (especially Old Javanese)," in L. S. Maria, F. Soenoto Rivai, and A. Sorrentino (eds.), *Papers from the III European Colloqium on Malay and Indonesian Studies*, Naples: Istituto Universitario Orientale, Dipartimento di Studi Asiatici, pp. 51–63.

2000, "The expansion of Buddhism into Southeast Asia (mainly before AD 1000)," in V. Elisseeff (ed.), *The Silk Roads: Highways of Culture and Commerce*, published in association with UNESCO, New York and Oxford: Berghahn Books, pp. 49–68.

CASPARIS, J. G. DE and MABBETT, I. W., 1992, "Religion and popular beliefs of Southeast Asia before c. 1500," in N. Tarling (ed.), *The Cambridge History of Southeast Asia*, vol. I, part I: *From Early Times to c. 1500*, Cambridge University Press, pp. 276–344.

CASSON, L., 1980, "Rome's trade with the East: the sea voyage to Africa and India," *Transactions of the American Philological Association*, 110, pp. 21–36.

(ed.), 1989, *Periplus Maris Erythraei*, Princeton University Press.

1991, *The Ancient Mariners, Seafarers and Sea Fighters of the Mediterranean in Ancient Times*, Princeton University Press.

2001, "New lights on maritime loans: P. Vindob G 40822," in R. Chakravarti (ed.), *Trade in Early India*, Oxford University Press, pp. 228–243 (1st pub. 1990, *Zeitschrift für Papyrologie und Epigraphik*, 84, pp. 195–206).

CASTILLO, C., 2013, "The archaeobotany of Khao Sam Kaeo and Phu Khao Thong: the agriculture of late prehistoric southern Thailand," Ph.D. dissertation, University College London.

CASTILLO, C. and FULLER, D. Q., 2010, "Still too fragmentary and dependent upon chance? Advances in the study of early Southeast Asian archaeobotany," in B. Bellina, E. Bacus, O. Pryce, and J. Wisseman-Christie (eds.), *Studies in Honour of Ian Glover*, Bangkok: River Books, pp. 91–111.

CASTLE, E. W., 1992, "Shipping and trade in Ramessid Egypt," *Journal of the Economic and Social History of the Orient*, 35, pp. 239–277.

CASTLEDEN, R, 2005, *Mycenaeans: Life in Bronze Age Greece*, Abingdon and New York: Routledge.

CAUVIN, J., 1997, *Naissance des divinités. Naissance de l'agriculture. La révolution des symboles au Néolithique*, Paris: CNRS.

CÉSAIRE, A., 1961, *Cadastre*, Paris: Seuil.

CHADWICK, J., 1976, *The Mycenaean World*, Cambridge University Press.

CHAKRABARTI, D. K., 1992, *The Early Use of Iron in India*, New Delhi: Oxford University Press.

2000, "Mahajanapada states of early historic India," in M. H. Hansen (ed.), *A Comparative Study of Thirty City-State Cultures*, Copenhagen: Det Kongelige Danske Videnskabernes Selskab, pp. 375–391.

CHAKRAVARTI, R. (ed.), 2001a, *Trade in Early India* (Oxford in India Readings: Themes in Indian History), Oxford University Press.

2001b and c, "Introduction" and "Monarchs, Merchants, and a Matha in Northern Konkan (c. AD 900–1053)," in R. Chakravarti (ed.), *Trade in Early India* (Oxford in India Readings: Themes in Indian History), Oxford University Press, pp. 1–101 and pp. 257–281 (first published 1990, *Indian Economic and Social History Review*, 27 (2), pp. 189–208).

2002a, "Seafarings, ships and ship owners: India and the Indian Ocean (AD 700–1500)," in D. Parkin and R. Barnes (eds.), *Ships and the Development of Maritime Technology in the Indian Ocean*, London and New York: Routledge/Curzon, pp. 28–61.

2002b, *Trade and Traders in Early Indian Society*, Oxford University Press.

2004, "An enchanting seascape: through epigraphic lens," *Studies in History*, 20 (2), pp. 306–315.

2012, "Merchants, merchandise and merchantmen in the western seaboard of India: a maritime profile (500 BCE – 1500 CE)," in D. P. Chattopadhyaya (ed.), *History of Science, Philosophy and Culture in Indian Civilization*, vol. III, part 7, O. Prakash (ed.), *The Trading World of the Indian Ocean, 1500–1800*, Delhi, Chennai, and Chandigarh: Centre for Studies in Civilizations, pp. 53–116.

CHAMI, F., 1994, *The Tanzanian Coast in the First Millennium AD* (Uppsaliensis SAA 7), Uppsala: Societas Archaeologica Upsaliensis.

1998, "A review of Swahili archaeology," *African Archaeological Review*, 15 (3), pp. 199–218.

1999a, "Graeco-Roman trade link and the Bantu migration theory," *Anthropos*, 94 (1–3), pp. 205–215.

1999b, "Roman beads from the Rufiji Delta: first incontrovertible archaeological link with *Periplus*," *Current Anthropology*, 40 (2), pp. 239–241.

2000, "Further archaeological research on Mafia Island," *Azania*, 35, pp. 208–214.

2001, "Chicken bones from a Neolithic limestone cave site, Zanzibar: contact between East Africa and Asia," in F. Chami, G. Pwiti, and C. Radimilahy (eds.), *People, Contacts and the Environment in the African Past* (Studies in the African Past 1), Dar es Salaam University Press, pp. 84–97.

2002, "People and contacts in the ancient western Indian Ocean seaboard or Azania," *Man and Environment*, 27(1), pp. 33–44.

2004, "The archaeology of the Mafia Archipelago, Tanzania," in F. A. Chami, G. Pwiti, and C. Radimilahy (eds.), *African Archaeology Network: Reports and Views*, Dar es Salaam: University Press, pp. 73–101.

2006, *The Unity of African Ancient History: 3000 BCE to AD 500*, Dar es Salaam: E & D Vision Publishing.

(ed.), 2009, *Zanzibar and the Swahili Coast from c. 30,000 Years Ago*, Dar es Salaam: E & D Vision Publishing.

CHAMI, F. A. and KOMBO, J. K., 2009, "Reconnaissance survey of southern Zanzibar Island," in *Zanzibar and the Swahili Coast from c. 30,000 Years Ago*, Dar es Salaam: E & D Vision Publishing, pp. 95–104.

CHAMI, F. A. and KWEKASON, A., 2003, "Neolithic pottery traditions from the islands, the coast and the interior of East Africa," *African Archaeological Review*, 20 (2), pp. 67–80.

CHAMI, F. A. and MSEMWA, P., 1997, "A new look at culture and trade on the Azanian coast," *Current Anthropology*, 38, pp. 673–677.

CHAMI, F. A., PWITI, G., and RADIMILAHY, C. (eds.), 2001, *People, Contacts and the Environment in the African Past* (Studies in the African Past 1), Dar es Salaam University Press.

CHAMPAKALAKSHMI, R. (ed.), 1996, *Trade, Ideology and Urbanization: South India 300 BCE to AD 1300*, Delhi, Bombay, Calcutta, and Madras: Oxford University Press.

CHANCHALA, S., 1991, "Harappan plant economy in the Rann of Kutch," *Geophytology*, 23 (2), pp. 227–233.

CHANDLER, T., 1987, *Four Thousand Years of Urban Growth: An Historical Census*, Lewiston, Queenston, and Lampeter: Edwin Mellen Press.

CHANG, K.-C., 1999, "China on the eve of the historical period," in M. Loewe and E. L. Slaughnessy (eds.), *The Cambridge History of Ancient China: From the Origins of Civilization to 221 BCE*, Cambridge University Press, pp. 37–73.

CHANKOWSKI, V., 2004, "Quels modèles pour l'économie séleucide?," in V. Chankowski and F. Duyrat (eds.), *Le roi et l'économie: autonomie locale et structures royales dans l'économie de l'empire séleucide. Actes des rencontres de Lille, 23 juin 2003, et d'Orléans, 29–30 janvier 2004,* Topoi suppl. 6, pp. 9–18.

CHARBONNIER, A., 2008, "L'agriculture en Arabie du Sud avant l'islam: une reconstitution des paysages et des systèmes de culture antiques," *Chroniques Yéménites,* 15, pp. 1–28.

CHARLES, M., 1989, "Agriculture in Lowlands Mesopotamia in the Late Uruk/Early Dynastic Period," Ph.D. dissertation, Institute of Archaeology, University College London.

CHARPENTIER, G., 1982, *Recueil de matériaux épigraphiques relatifs à la botanique de l'Égypte antique,* Paris: Trismégiste.

CHARPIN, D., 2005, "Les dieux prêteurs dans le Proche-Orient amorrite," *Topoi: Orient-Occident,* 12–13 (1), pp. 13–34.

CHASE-DUNN, C., 1988, "Comparing world-systems: towards a theory of semi-peripheral development," *Review,* 19, pp. 29–60.

CHASE-DUNN, C. and HALL, T. D., 1997, *Rise and Demise: Comparing World-Systems,* Boulder, CO: Westview Press.

1998, "Ecological degradation and the evolution of world systems," *Journal of World Systems Research,* 3, pp. 403–431.

2000, "Comparing world-systems to explain social evolution," in R. A. Denemark, J. Friedman, B. K. Gills, and G. Modelski (eds.), *World System History: The Social Science of Long-Term Change,* London and New York: Routledge, pp. 85–111.

CHASE-DUNN, C., PASCIUTI, D., ALVAREZ, A., and HALL, T. D., 2006, "Growth/decline phases and semiperipheral development in the ancient Mesopotamian and Egyptian world-systems," in B. K. Gills and W. R. Thompson (eds.), *Globalization and Global History,* London: Routledge, pp. 114–138.

CHASE-DUNN, C., INOUE, H., ALVAREZ, A., ALVAREZ, R., ANDERSON, E. N., and NEAL, T., 2015, "Uneven development: largest cities and empires in world regions and the central international system since the Late Bronze Age," paper, Institute for Research on World-Systems, University of California-Riverside.

CHAUDHURI, K. N., 1985, *Trade and Civilization in the Indian Ocean: An Economic History from the Rise of Islam to 1750,* Cambridge University Press.

CHAUME, F., 2007, "Essai sur l'évolution de la structure sociale hallstattienne," in H. L. Fernoux and C. Stein (eds.), *Aristocratie antique: modèles et exemplarité sociale, actes du Colloque de Dijon 25 novembre 2005,* Dijon: Éditions universitaires dijonnaises, pp. 25–55.

CHAUVICOURT, J. and CHAUVICOURT, S., 1968, "Les premières monnaies introduites à Madagascar," *Numismatique malgache,* fascicule 3, Antananarivo.

CHAVANNES, E., 1907, "Les pays d'Occident d'après le Heou Han Chou," *T'oung-Pao,* series II, 8 (2), pp. 149–234.

CHEMLA, K. and SCHUCHUN, G. (eds.), 2004, *Les neuf chapitres: le classique mathématique de la Chine ancienne et ses commentaires,* Paris: Dunod.

CHENG, C., MOTOHASHI, R., TCHUCHIMOTO, S., FUKUTA, Y., OHTSUBO, H., and OHTSUBO, E., 2003. "Polyphyletic origin of cultivated rice: based on the interspersion patterns of SINEs," *Molecular Biology and Evolution,* 20, pp. 67–75.

CHENG TE-K'UN, 1984, *Studies in Chinese Ceramics,* Hong Kong: The Chinese University Press.

CHERIAN, P. J., 2011, *Kerala Council for Historical Research Annual Report 2010–2011,* Thiruvananthapuram: Kerala Council for Historical Research.

CHERNYKH, E. N., 1992, *Ancient Metallurgy in the USSR: The Early Metal Age,* Cambridge University Press.

(ed.), 2002, *Kargaly,* vol. II, Moscow: Languages of Slavonic Culture.

2009, "Formation of the Eurasian steppe belt cultures viewed through the lens of archaeometallurgy and radiocarbon dating," in B. K. Hanks and K. M. Linduff (eds.), *Social Complexity in Prehistoric Eurasia: Monuments, Metals, and Mobility*, Cambridge University Press, pp. 115–145.

2004, "Ancient metallurgy of northeast Asia: from Ural to the Sain-Altai," in K. M. Linduff (ed.), *Metallurgy in Ancient Eastern Eurasia from Ural to the Yellow River*, Lewiston, NY: Edwin Mellon, pp. 25–30.

CHEW, S. C., 2000, "Neglecting nature: world accumulation and core-periphery relations, 2500 BCE to AD 1990," in R. A. Denemark, J. Friedman, B. K. Gills, and G. Modelski (eds.), *World System History: The Social Science of Long-Term Change*, London and New York: Routledge, pp. 216–234.

2001, *World Ecological Degradation: Accumulation, Urbanization, and Deforestation 3000 BCE–AD 2000*, Walnut Creek, CA: Altamira.

2018, "From the Red Sea to the Indian Ocean and beyond: the maritime 'silk' roads of the Eurasian world economy 200 BC – AD 500," in A. Sarathi (ed.), *Early Maritime Cultures in East Africa and the Western Indian Ocean*, Oxford: Archaeopress, pp. 49–64.

CHILDE, V. G., 1961, *Le mouvement de l'histoire*, Paris: Arthaud.

CHILDS, S. T. and HERBERT, E. W., 2005, "Metallurgy and its consequences," in A. B. Stahl (ed.), *African Archaeology: A Critical Introduction*, Malden, MA, and Oxford: Blackwell, pp. 276–300.

CHIOU-PENG, T., 2004, "Horsemen in the Dian culture of Yunnan," in K. M. Linduff and Y. Sun (eds.), *Gender and Chinese Archaeology*, Walnut Creek, CA: Altamira Press, pp. 289–314.

2008a, "Horses in the Dian culture of Yunnan," in E. A. Bacus, I. C. Glover, and P. D. Sharrock (eds.), *Interpreting Southeast Asia's Past: Monument, Image and Text*, Singapore: NUS Press, pp. 225–238.

2008b, "Dian bronze art: its source and formation," *Indo-Pacific Prehistory Association*, 28, pp. 34–43.

CHITTICK, N., 1970, "Observations on pre-Portuguese accounts on the East African coast," *Sociétés et compagnies de commerce en Orient et dans l'Océan Indien*, Paris: SEVPEN, pp. 129–132.

CHRISOMALIS, S., 2003, "The Egyptian origin of the Greek alphabetic numerals," *Antiquity*, 77 (297), pp. 485–496.

CHRISTIAN, D., 2000, "Silk Roads or Steppe Roads? The Silk Roads in world history," *Journal of World History*, 11 (1), pp. 1–26.

CHRISTIANSEN, B. and LJUNGQVIST, F. C., 2012, "The extra-tropical Northern Hemisphere temperature in the last two millennia: reconstructions of low-frequency variability," *Climate of the Past*, 8, pp. 765–786.

CHRISTIE, A., 1957, "An obscure passage from the *Periplus*," *Bulletin of the School of Oriental and African Studies*, 19, pp. 345–353.

CIARLA, R., 2005, "The Thai-Italian 'Lopburi Regional Archaeological Project': a survey of fifteen years of activities," in I. Piovano (ed.), *La cultura thailandese e le relazioni Italo-Thai: atti del convegno, Torino, 20–21 maggio 2004*, Turin: CESMEO, pp. 77–104.

CIERNY, J., STÖLLNER, T., and WEISGERBER, G., 2005. "Zinn in und aus Mittelasien," in Ü. Yalçin, C. Pulak, and R. Slotta (eds.), *Das Schiff von Uluburun: Welthandel vor 3000 Jahren*, Bochum: Deutsches Bergbau-Museum, pp. 431–448.

CLAPHAM, A. and ROWLEY-CONWY, P., 2006, "Rewriting the history of African agriculture," *Planet Earth Summer 2006*, pp. 24–26 [www.nerc.ac.uk/publications/planetearth/].

CLARK, H. R., 2009, "Frontier discourse and China's maritime frontier: China's frontiers and the encounter with the sea through early imperial history," *Journal of World History*, 20 (1), pp. 1–33.

CLEUZIOU, S., 1992, "The Oman Peninsula and the Indus civilization: a reassessment," *Man and Environment*, 17 (2), pp. 93–103.

2002, "The Early Bronze Age of the Oman Peninsula from chronology to the dialectics of tribe and state formation," in S. Cleuziou, M. Tosi, and J. Zarins (eds.), *Essays on the Late Prehistory of the Arabian Peninsula*, Rome: Instituto Italiano per l'Africa e l'Oriente, pp. 191–236.

2003a, "Early Bronze Age trade in the Gulf and the Arabian Sea: the society behind the boats," *Proceedings of the First Archaeological Conference on the U. A. E.*, pp. 133–149.

2003b, "Jiroft et Tarut: plateau iranien et péninsule arabique," *Dossiers d'Archéologie*, 287, pp. 114–125.

CLEUZIOU, S. and COSTANTINI, L., 1980, "Premiers éléments sur l'agriculture protohistorique de l'Arabie orientale," *Paléorient*, 6, pp. 245–251.

CLEUZIOU, S. and MÉRY, S., 2002, "In-between the Great Powers: Bronze Age Oman Peninsula," in S. Cleuziou, M. Tosi, and J. Zarins (eds.), *Essays on the Late Prehistory of the Arabian Peninsula*, Rome: Istituto Italiano per l'Africa e l'Oriente, pp. 273–316.

CLEUZIOU, S. and TOSI, M., 1989, "The southern frontier of the ancient Near East," in K. Frifelt and P. Sorensen (eds.), *Arabian Archaeology*, London: Curzon Press, pp. 15–44.

1994, "Black boats of Magan: some thoughts on Bronze Age water transport in Oman and beyond from the impressed bitumen slabs of Ra's al-Junayz," in A. Parpola and P. Koskikallio (eds.), *South Asian Archaeology 1993*, vol. 2, Helsinki: Suomalainen Tiedeakatemia, pp. 745–762.

1997a, "Evidence for the use of aromatics in the Early Bronze Age of Oman: Period III at RJ-2 (2300–2200 BCE)," in A. Avanzini (ed.), *Profumi d'Arabia*, Rome: L'Erma di Bretschneider, pp. 57–81.

1997b, "Hommes, climats et environnements de la péninsule arabique à l'Holocène," *Paléorient*, 23 (2), pp. 121–135.

2000, "Ra'as al-Jinz and the prehistoric coastal cultures of the Ja'alān," *Journal of Oman Studies*, 11, pp. 19–73.

2007, *In the Shadow of the Ancestors: The Prehistoric Foundations of the Early Arabian Civilization in Oman*, Oman: Ministry of Heritage and Culture.

CLINE, D., 2013, "Aegean–Near East relations in the second millennium BCE," in *Cultures in Contact: From Mesopotamia to the Mediterranean in the Second Millennium BCE*, New York: Metropolitan Museum of Art, pp. 26–33.

CLIST, B., 2012, "Vers une réduction des préjugés et la fonte des antagonismes: un bilan de l'expansion de la métallurgie du fer en Afrique sud-saharienne," *Journal of African Archaeology*, 10 (1), pp. 71–84

COACM: see GRANDIDIER, A. *et al.*

COEDÈS, G., 1910, *Textes d'auteurs grecs et latins relatifs à l'Extrême-Orient, depuis le IVe siècle av. J.-C. jusqu'au XIVe siècle*, Paris: E. Leroux.

1930, "Les inscriptions malaises de Çrîwijaya," *Bulletin de l'École française d'Extrême-Orient*, 30, pp. 29–80.

1964a, *Les états hindouisés d'Indochine et d'Indonésie*, Paris: De Boccard (1st edn. 1944).

1964b, "A possible interpretation of the inscription at Kedukan Bukit (Palembang)," in J. Bastin and R. Roolvink (eds.), *Malayan and Indonesian Studies: Essays Presented to Sir Richard Winstedt on His Eighty-Fifth Birthday*, Oxford: Clarendon Press, pp. 24–32.

1968, *The Indianized States of Southeast Asia*, Honolulu: East-West Center Press. (English edition of *Les états hindouisés d'Indochine et d'Indonésie*).

1992, "The Malay inscriptions of Sriwijaya," in P.-Y. Manguin and M. Sheppard (eds.), *Sriwijaya: History, Religion and Language of an Early Malay Polity, Collected Studies by G. Coedès and L.-C. Damais* (Monograph of the Malaysian Branch of the Royal Asiatic Society 20), Kuala Lumpur: Academe Art and Printing Services Sdn. Bhd., pp. 41–92 (first published in 1930 as "Les inscriptions malaises de Çrîwijaya," *Bulletin de l'Ecole française d'Extrême-Orient*, 30, p. 29–80).

COEDÈS, G. and DAMAIS, L.-C., 1992, *Sriwijaya. History, Religion and Language of an Early Malay Polity, Collected Studies by G. Coedès and L.-C. Damais*, ed. P.-Y. Manguin and

M. Sheppard (Monograph of the Malaysian Branch of the Royal Asiatic Society 20), Kuala Lumpur: Academe Art and Printing Services Sdn. Bhd.

COHEN, D. J., 1998, "The origins of domesticated cereals and the Pleistocene–Holocene transition in East Asia," *The Review of Archaeology*, 19 (2), pp. 22–29.

COLLEDGE, S. and CONOLLY, J. (eds.), 2007, *The Origins and Spread of Domestic Plants in Southwest Asia and Europe*, Walnut Creek, CA: Left Coast Press.

COLLINS, J. T., 1998, *Malay, World language: A Short History*, Kuala Lumpur: Dewan Bahasa dan Pustaka.

COMPAGNONI, B. and TOSI, M., 1978, "The camel: its distribution and state of domestication in the Middle East during the third millennium BCE in the light of finds from Shar-i Sokhta," in R. H. Meadow and R. H. Zeder (eds.), *Approaches to Faunal Analysis in the Middle East*, Cambridge, MA: Peabody Museum Press, pp. 91–103.

CONDOMINAS, G., 1972, "De la rizière au miir," in J. Thomas and L. Bernot (eds.), *Langues et techniques, nature et société, offert en hommage à André G. Haudricourt à l'occasion de son soixantième anniversaire*, vol. II, Paris: Klincksieck, pp. 115–129.

CONINGHAM, R. A. E., 2002, "Beyond and before the imperial frontiers: early historic Sri Lanka and the origins of Indian Ocean trade," *Man and Environment*, 27 (1), pp. 99–107.

CONINGHAM, R. A. E. and ALLCHIN, F. R., 1995, "The rise of cities in Sri Lanka," in F. R. Allchin (ed.), *The Archaeology of Early Historic South Asia*, Cambridge University Press, pp. 152–184.

CONINGHAM, R. A. E. and SUTHERLAND, T., 1998, "Dwellings or granaries? The pit phenomenon of the Kashmir-Swat Neolithic," *Man and Environment*, 22, pp. 29–34.

CONINGHAM, R. A. E. *et al.*, 1999, 2006, *Anuradhapura: The British-Sri Lankan Excavations at Anuradhapura Salgaha Watta 2*, vol. I (BAR International Series 824); vol. II: *Artefacts* (BAR International Series 1508), Oxford: Archaeopress.

CONNAN, J., LOMBARD, P., KILLICK, R., HØJLUND, F., SALLES, J.-F., and KHALAF, A., 1998, "The archaeological bitumens of Bahrain from the early Dilmun period (c. 2200 BCE) to the 16th century AD: a problem of sources of trade," *Arabian Archaeology and Epigraphy*, 9 (2), pp. 141–181.

CONTI ROSSINI, C., 1906, "Sugli Habas at," *Rendiconti della Reale Accademia dei Lincei*, 15, pp. 39–50.

CONZE, E., 1968, *Thirty Years of Buddhist Studies*, Columbia: University of South Carolina Press.

COOPER, J., 2009, "Egypt's Nile – Red Sea canals: chronology, location, seasonality and function," in L. Blue, J. Cooper, R. Thomas, and J. Whitewright (eds.), *Connected Hinterlands: Proceedings of the Red Sea Project IV* (BAR International Series 2052), Oxford: Archaeopress, p. 195–209.

COOPER, L., 2006, *Early Urbanism on the Syrian Euphrates*, New York: Routledge.

COQUE-DELHUILE, B., 2001, "Les oasis de l'Arabie Heureuse," *Dossiers d'Archéologie*, 263 (issue on Yemen), pp. 18–21.

COQUERY-VIDROVITCH, C., 1969, "Recherches sur un mode de production africain," *La Pensée*, 144, pp. 61–78.

1993, *Histoire des villes d'Afrique Noire: des origines à la colonisation*, Paris: Albin Michel.

2005, *The History of African Cities South of the Sahara*, trans. M. Baker, Princeton: Markus Wiener.

CORDAUX, R., AUNGER, R., BENTLEY, G., NASIDZE, I., SIRAJUDDIN, S. M., and STONEKING, M., 2004, "Independent origins of Indian caste and tribal paternal lineages," *Current Biology*, 14 (3), pp. 231–235.

CORDOVA, C. E., 2005, "The degradation of the Ancient Near Eastern environment," in D. C. Snell (ed.), *A Companion to the Ancient Near East*, Malden, MA, Oxford: Blackwell, pp. 109–125.

COSTANTINI, L., 1979, "Plant remains at Pirak," in J.-F. Jarrige and M. Santoni (eds.), *Fouilles de Pirak*, Paris: De Boccard, pp. 326–333.

1984, "Plant impressions in Bronze Age pottery from Yemen Arab Republic," *East and West*, 34 (1–3), pp. 107–115.

1990a, "Harappan agriculture in Pakistan: the evidence of Nausharo," *South Asian Archaeology*, 1987, pp. 321–332.

1990b, "Ecology and farming of the protohistoric communities in Central Yemeni Highlands," in A. de Maigret (ed.), *The Bronze Age Culture of Halwan at-Tiyal and al-Hada (Republic of Yemen)*, Rome: IsMEO, pp. 187–204.

COSTANTINI, L. and AUDISIO, P., 2000, "Plant and insect remains from the Bronze Age site of Ra's al-Jinz (RJ-2), Sultanate of Oman," *Paléorient*, 26 (1), pp. 143–156.

COSTANTINI, L. and BIASINI, L. C., 1985, "Agriculture in Baluchistan between the 7th and 3rd millennium BC," *Newsletter of Baluchistan Studies*, 2, pp. 16–37.

COULAUD, D., 1973, *Les Zafimaniry: un groupe ethnique de Madagascar à la poursuite de la forêt*, Antananarivo: Fanontam-boky Malagasy.

COURTY, M. A., GUICHARD, F., and WEISS, H., 1995, "Amplitude, duration and societal effects of the abrupt climate change ca. 2200–1900 BC in Mesopotamia," paper presented at the XIVth International INQUA Congress, Berlin.

COX, M. P., NELSON, M. G., TUMONGGOR, M. K., RICAUT, F.-X., and SUDOYO, H., 2012, "A small cohort of Island Southeast Asian women founded Madagascar," *Proceedings of the Royal Society B, Biol. Sci.*, 279, pp. 2761–2768.

CRADDOCK, P. T., 2003, "Cast iron, fined iron, crucible steel: liquid iron in the Ancient World," in P. T. Craddock and Lang (eds.), *Mining and Metal Production through the Ages*, London: British Museum Press, pp. 231–255.

2010, "New paradigms for old iron: thoughts on E. Zangato and A. F. C. Holl's 'On the Iron Front'," *Journal of African Archaeology*, 8 (1), pp. 28–36.

CRAWFORD, G. W., 1992, "Prehistoric plant domestication in East Asia," C. W. Cowan and P. J. Watson (eds.), *The Origins of Agriculture: An International Perspective*, Washington, DC: Smithsonian Institution, pp. 7–38.

2006, "East Asian plant domestication," in S. T. Stark (ed.), *Archaeology of Asia*, Oxford: Blackwell, pp. 77–95.

CRAWFORD, G. W. and LEE, G.-A., 2003, "Agricultural origins in the Korean Peninsula," *Antiquity*, 77 (295), pp. 87–95.

CRAWFORD, H., 1977, *The Architecture of Iraq in the Third Millennium BC*, Copenhagen: Akademisk Vorlag.

1996,"The decline of Dilmun," *Proceedings of the Society of Antiquaries of Scotland*, 26, pp. 13–22.

1998, *Dilmun and Its Gulf Neighbours*, Cambridge University Press.

2004, *Sumer and the Sumerians*, Cambridge University Press (1st edn. 1991).

2005, "Mesopotamia and the Gulf: the history of a relationship," *Iraq*, 67 (2), pp. 41–46.

CREASMAN, P. P., 2005, "The Cairo Dashur boats," M.A. thesis, College Station, Texas A and M. University.

CRONE, P., 2004, *Meccan Trade and the Rise of Islam*, Oxford: Blackwell (1st edn. 1987).

CROWTHER, A., HORTON, M., KOTARBA-MORLEY, A., PRENDERGAST, M., QUINTANA MORALES, E., WOOD, M., et al., 2014, "Iron Age agriculture, fishing and trade in the Mafia Archipelago, Tanzania: new evidence from Ukunju Cave," *Azania*, 49 (1), pp. 21–44.

CROWTHER, A., LUCAS, L., HELM, R., HORTON, M., SHIPTON, C., WRIGHT, H. T., WALSHAW, S. et al., 2016, "Ancient crops provide first archaeological signature of the westward Austronesian expansion," *Proceedings of the National Academy of Sciences of the United States of America (PNAS)*, 113 (24), pp. 6635–6640.

CULLEN, H. M., deMENOCAL, P. B., HEMMING, S., HEMMING G., BROWN, F. H., GUILDERSON, and T. SIROCKO, F., 2000, "Climate change and the collapse of the Akkadian empire: evidence from the deep sea," *Geology*, 28 (4), pp. 379–382.

CUNLIFFE, B., 1994, "Iron Age societies in Western Europe and beyond, 800–140 BC," *The Oxford Illustrated Prehistory of Europe*, Oxford University Press, pp. 336–372.

2015, *By Steppe, Desert and Ocean: The Birth of Eurasia*, Oxford University Press.

CURTIN, P. D., 1984, *Cross-Cultural Trade in World History*, Cambridge University Press.

CURTIS, M. C., 2009, "Relating the ancient Ona culture to the wider northern Horn: discerning patterns and problems in the archaeology of the first millennium BC," *African Archaeological Review*, 26, pp. 327–350.

D'ANDREA, A. C., 2007, "Update: early agriculture in Japan: research since 1999," in T. Denham and P. White (eds.), *The Emergence of Agriculture: A Global View*, London and New York: Routledge, pp. 172–174.

D'ANDREA, A. C., CRAWFORD, G. W., YOSHIZAKI, M., and KUDO, T., 1995, "Late Jomon cultigens from northeastern Japan, " *Antiquity*, 69, pp. 146–152.

D'ANDREA, A. C., KLEE, M., and CASEY, J., 2001, "Archaeobotanical evidence for pearl millet (Pennisetum glaucum) in sub-Saharan West Africa," *Antiquity*, 75 (288), pp. 341–348.

DAHL, J., 2009, "Early writing in Iran: a reappraisal," *Iran*, 47, pp. 23–32.

DAHL, J., PETRIE, C. A., and POTTS, D. T., 2013, "Chronological parameters in the earliest writing system in Iran," in C. A. Petrie (ed.), *Ancient Iran and Its Neighbours: Local Developments and Long-Range Interactions in the 4th Millennium BC*, Oxford: Oxbow Books, pp. 353–378.

DAHL, O. C., 1951, *Malgache et Maanyan: une comparaison linguistique*, Oslo: Egede-Instituttet.

1954, "Le substrat bantou en malgache," *Norsk Tidsskrift for Sprogvidenskap*, 17, pp. 325–362.

1976, *Proto-Austronesian* (Scandinavian Institute of Asian Studies, Monograph Series 15), Lund: Studentlitteratur, Curzon Press.

1977, "La subdivision de la famille barito et la place du Malgache," *Acta Orientalia, Copenhague*, 38, 1977, pp. 77–134.

1978, "Bantu substratum in Malagasy," *Études Océan Indien*, 9 (issue on "Linguistique de Madagascar et des Comores"), pp. 91–132.

1981, *Early Phonetic and Phonemic Changes in Austronesian* (Instituttet for Sammenlignende Kulturforskning, series B, 63), Oslo: Universitetsforlaget.

1991, *Migration from Kalimantan to Madagascar*, Oslo: Institute for Comparative Research in Human Culture.

1995, "L'importance de la langue malgache dans la linguistique austronésienne et dans la linguistique générale," in S. Evers and M. Spindler (eds.), *Cultures of Madagascar: Ebb and Flow of Influences / Civilisations de Madagascar: flux et reflux des influences*, Leiden: International Institute for Asian Studies, pp. 39–45.

DAMAIS, L.-C., 1992, "Language B of the Sriwijaya inscriptions," in P.-Y Manguin and M. Sheppard (eds.), *Sriwijaya: History, Religion and Language of an Early Malay Polity. Collected Studies by G. Coedès and L.-C. Damais* (Monograph of the Malaysian Branch Royal Asiatic Society 20), Kuala Lumpur: Academe Art and Printing Services Sdn. Bhd., pp. 113–165 (first published in 1968 as: "La langue B des inscriptions de Srī Wijaya," *Bulletin de l'Ecole française d'Extrême-Orient*, 54, pp. 523–566).

DAMGAARD, K., 2009, "A Palestinian Red Sea port on the Egyptian road to Arabia: Early Islamic Aqaba and its many hinterlands," in L. Blue, J. Cooper, R. Thomas, and J. Whitewright (eds.), *Connected Hinterlands: Proceedings of Red Sea Project IV Held at the University of Southampton, September 2008* (BAR International Series 2052), Oxford: Archaeopress, pp. 85–98.

DARK, P., 2006, "Climate deterioration and land-use change in the first millennium BC: perspectives from the British palynological record," *Journal of Archaeological Science*, 33 (10), pp. 1381–1395.

DARYAEE, T., 2003a, "The Persian Gulf trade in Late Antiquity," *Journal of World History*, 14, pp. 1–16.

2003b, "The ideal king in the Sasanian world: Ardaxšīr ī Pābagān or Xusrō Anōšagruwān?," *Nāme-ye Irān-e Bāstān, The International Journal of Ancient Iranian Studies*, 3 (1), pp. 33–45.

DAS GUPTA, A. and PEARSON, M. N. (eds.), 1987, *India and the Indian Ocean, 1500–1800*, Calcutta: Oxford University Press.

DATAN, I., 1993, "Archaeological excavations at Gua Sireh (Serian) and Lubang Angin (Gunung Mulu National Park), Sarawak, Malaysia," *Sarawak Museum Journal*, Special Monograph 6.

DAUMAS, F., 1977, "Le problème de la monnaie dans l'Égypte antique avant Alexandre," *Mélanges de l'École Française de Rome. Antiquité*, 89 (2), pp. 425–442.

DAVID, H., 2002, "Soft stone mining evidence in the Oman Peninsula and its relation to Mesopotamia," in S. Cleuziou, M. Tosi, and J. Zarins (eds.), *Essays on the Late Prehistory of the Arabian Peninsula*, Rome: Istituto Italiano per l'Africa e l'Oriente, pp. 317–336.

DAVIS-KIMBALL, J. and YABLONSKY, L. T., 1995, *Kurgans on the Left Bank of the Ilek: Excavations at Pokrovka, 1990–1992*, Berkeley, CA: Zinat Press.

DEBAINE-FRANCFORT, C., 1999, *La redécouverte de la Chine ancienne*, Paris: Gallimard.

2000, "La Néolithisation de la Chine: où, quand, comment?," in J. Guilaine (ed.), *Premiers paysans du monde: naissances des agricultures*, Paris: Éditions Errance, pp. 171–187.

2001, "Xinjiang and Northwestern China around 1000 BC: cultural contacts and transmissions," in R. Eichmann and C. Parzinger (eds.), *Migration und Kulturtransfer: Der Wandel vorder- und zentralasiatischer Kulturen im Umbruch vom 2. zum 1. vorchristlichen Jahrtausend. Akten des Internationalen Kolloquiums Berlin, 23–26 November 1999* (Kolloquien zur Vor- und Frühgeschichte 6), Bonn, pp. 57–70.

DECKER, M., 2009, "Plants and progress: rethinking the Islamic Agricultural Revolution," *Journal of World History*, 20 (2), pp. 187–206.

DE LANGHE, E., 2007, "The establishment of traditional plantain cultivation in the African rain forest: a working hypothesis," in T. Denham, J. Iriarte, and L. Vrydaghs (eds.), *Rethinking Agriculture: Archaeological and Ethnoarchaeological Perspectives* (One World Archaeology 51), Walnut Creek, CA: Left Coast Press, pp. 361–370.

2009, "Relevance of banana seeds in archaeology," *Ethnobotany Research and Applications*, 7, pp. 271–281.

DE LANGHE, E. and DE MARET, P., 1999, "Tracking the banana: its significance in early agriculture," in C. Gosden and J. Hather (eds.), *The Prehistory of Food: Appetites for Change*, London and New York: Routledge, pp. 377–396.

DE LANGHE, E., SWENNEN, R., and VUYLSTEKE, D., 1994–1995, "Plantain in the early Bantu world," *Azania*, 29–39, pp. 147–160.

DE LANGHE, E., VRYDAGHS, L., DE MARET, P., PERRIER, X., and DENHAM, T., 2009, "Why bananas matter: an introduction to the history of banana domestication," *Ethnobotany Research and Applications*, 7, pp. 165–177.

DELOCHE, J., 1996, "Iconographic evidence on the development of boat and ship structures in India (2nd C. BC – 15th C. AD): a new approach," in H. P. Ray and J.-F. Salles (eds.), *Tradition and Archaeology. Early maritime contacts in the Indian Ocean*, Delhi: Manohar, pp. 199–224.

2001, "Geographical considerations in the localization of ancient sea-ports in India," in R. Chakravarti (ed.), *Trade in Early India*, Oxford University Press, pp. 312–325 (first published 1983, *Indian Economic and Social History Review*, 20, 4, pp. 439–448).

DEME, A. and McINTOSH, S. K., 2006, "Excavations at Walalde: new light on the settlement of the Middle Senegal Valley by iron using peoples," *Journal of African Archaeology*, 4 (2), pp. 317–347.

deMENOCAL, P. B., 2001, "Cultural responses to climate change during the Late Holocene," *Science*, 292 (5517), pp. 667–673.

deMENOCAL, P. B., *et al.*, 2000, "Abrupt onset and termination of the African Humid Period: rapid climate response to gradual insolation forcing," *Quaternary Science Reviews*, 19, pp. 347–361.

DEMPWOLFF, O., 1934, 1937, 1938, *Vergleichende Lautlehre des Austronesischen Wortschatzes*: vol. I (1934), *Induktiver Aufbau einer Indonesischen Ursprache*; vol. II (1937), *Deduktive Anwendung des Urindonesischen auf Austronesische Einzelsprachen*; vol. III (1938), *Austronesisches Wörterverzeichnis*, supplements 15, 17, 19, Berlin: Dietrich Reimer.

DENEMARK, R., FRIEDMAN, J., GILLS, B., and MODELSKI, G. (eds.), 2000, *World-System History: The Social Science of Long-Term Change*, London: Routledge.

DENG, G., 1997, *Chinese Maritime Activities and Socioeconomic Development, c. 2100 BC – 1900 AD*, Westport, CT: Greenwood.

DENHAM, T. P., 2004, "The roots of agriculture and arboriculture in New Guinea: looking beyond Austronesian expansion, Neolithic packages and indigenous origins," *World Archaeology*, 36 (4), pp. 610–620.

2010, "From domestication histories to regional prehistory: using plants to reevaluate Early and Mid-Holocene interaction between New Guinea and Southeast Asia," *Food & History*, 8, pp. 3–22.

DENHAM, T. P., HABERLE, S., and LENTFER, C., 2004, "New evidence and revised interpretations of early agriculture in Highland New Guinea," *Antiquity*, 78 (302), pp. 839–857.

DENIAUX, E., 1987a and b, "Rome, cité conquérante et impériale, IVe/Ier siècle av. J.-C." and "Rome et l'intégration d'un monde, Ier siècle av. J.-C./IIIe siècle apr. J.-C.," in P. Vidal-Nacquet (ed.), *Atlas historique: histoire de l'humanité de la préhistoire à nos jours*, Paris: Hachette, pp. 58–59 and 60–61.

2001, *Rome, de la cité-état à l'Empire: institutions et vie politique*, Paris: Hachette.

DERCKSEN, J. G., 1996, *The Old Assyrian Copper Trade in Anatolia*, Istanbul: Nederlands Historisch-Archaeologisch Instituut te Istanbul.

1999a, "On the financing of Old Assyrian merchants," in J. G. Dercksen (ed.), *Trade and Finance in Ancient Mesopotamia: Proceedings of the First Mos Symposium, Leiden 1997* (Mos Studies 1), Nederlands Historisch-Archaeologisch Instituut te Istanbul, pp. 85–100.

(ed.), 1999b, *Trade and Finance in Ancient Mesopotamia Proceedings of the First Mos Symposium, Leiden 1997* (Mos Studies 1), Nederlands Historisch-Archaeologisch Instituut te Istanbul.

DERGACHEV, V. A. and GEEL, B. VAN, 2004, "Large-scale periodicity of climate change during the Holocene," in E. M. Scott, A. Y. Alekseev, and G. Zaitseva (eds.), *Impact of the Environment on Human Migration in Eurasia*, Dordrecht, Boston, and London: Kluwer Academic Publishers, pp. 159–183.

DE ROMANIS, F., 1996, *Cassia, cinnamomo, ossidiana: uomini e merci tra Oceano indiano e Mediterraneo*, Rome: "L'Erma" di Bretschneider.

1997, "Rome and the Notia of India: relations between Rome and southern India from 30 BC to the Flavian period," in F. De Romanis and A. Tchernia (eds.), *Crossings: Early Mediterranean Contacts with India*. New Delhi: Manohar, pp. 80–160.

DESANGES, J., 1975, "L'Afrique noire et le monde méditerranéen dans l'Antiquité (Éthiopiens et Gréco-romains)," *Revue française d'Histoire d'Outre-mer*, 62 (228), pp. 391–414.

1981, "Le point sur le Périple d'Hannon: controverses et publications récentes," *Enquêtes et Documents* (Université de Nantes. Centre de recherches atlantiques), 6, pp. 13–29.

DESCAT, R., 2004, "Max Weber et l'économie de l'esclavage antique," in H. Bruhns and J. Andreau (eds.), *Sociologie économique et économie de l'Antiquité: à propos de Max Weber*, *Cahiers du Centre de recherches historiques*, 34, October, pp. 145–154.

DESCHAMPS, H., 1960, *Histoire de Madagascar*, Paris: Berger-Levrault.

DEUTSCH (ed.), 1982: *see* POLO, M.

DEVENDRA, S., 2002, "Pre-modern Sri Lankan ships," in D. Parkin and R. Barnes (eds.), *Ships and the Development of Maritime Technology in the Indian Ocean*, London and New York: Routledge/Curzon, pp. 128–173.

DEVIC, J., 1975, *Le pays des Zendjs ou la côte orientale d'Afrique au Moyen-Âge*, Amsterdam: Oriental Press (1st edn. 1883).

DEWAR, R. E., 1984, "Extinctions in Madagascar: the loss of the subfossil fauna," in P. S. Martin and R. G. Klein (eds.), *Quaternary Extinctions: A Prehistoric Revolution*, Tucson: University of Arizona Press, pp. 574–593.

1986, "Ecologie et extinctions des subfossiles de Madagascar," trans. P. Vérin, *Taloha*, 10, pp. 25–41.

1995, "Of nets and trees: untangling the reticulate and dendritic in Madagascar's prehistory," *World Archaeology*, 26 (3) (issue on "Colonizations of Islands"), pp. 301–318.

DEWAR, R. E., RADIMILAHY, C., WRIGHT, H. T., JACOBS, Z., KELLY, G. O., and BERNA, F. 2013, "Stone tools and foraging in northern Madagascar challenge Holocene extinction models," *Proceedings of the National Academy of Sciences of the USA*, 110 (31), pp. 12,583–12,588.

DEWAR, R. E., RADIMILAHY, C., and WRIGHT, H. T., 2015, "Campements de cueilleurs-chasseurs dans l'extrême nord de Madagascar: travaux préliminaires à Ambohiposa et Lakaton'i Anja," *Taloha*, 21.

DEWAR, R. E. and WRIGHT, H. T., 1993, "The culture history of Madagascar," *Journal of World Prehistory*, 7 (4), pp. 417–466.

DEYELL, J., 1983, "The China connection: problems of silver supply in medieval Bengal," in J. F. Richards (ed.), *Precious Metals in the Later Medieval and Early Modern Worlds*, Durham, NC: Carolina Academic Press, pp. 207–229 (repr. in SUBRAHMANYAM, 1994, pp. 112–136).

1994: *see* DEYELL, J., 1983.

2001, "The Gurjara-Pratiharas," in R. Chakravarti (ed.), *Trade in Early India*, Oxford University Press, pp. 396–415.

DEZ, J., 1965, "Quelques hypothèses formulées par la linguistique comparée à l'usage de l'archéologie," *Taloha*, 1, pp. 197–214.

DHAVALIKAR, M. K., 1999, "Maritime tradition of western India," in K. S. Behera (ed.), *Maritime Heritage of India*, New Delhi: Aryan Books International, pp. 107–112.

2001, "Green imperialism: monsoon in antiquity and human response," *Man and Environment*, 26 (2), pp. 17–28.

DI COSMO, N., 1999a, "State formation and periodization in Inner Asian history," *Journal of World History*, 10 (1), pp. 1–40.

1999b, "The northern frontier in Pre-Imperial China," in M. Loewe and E. L. Slaughnessy (eds.), *The Cambridge History of Ancient China: From the Origins of Civilization to 221 BCE*, Cambridge University Press, pp. 885–966.

2002, *Ancient China and Its Enemies: The Rise of Nomadic Power in East Asian History*, Cambridge University Press.

DIAKONOFF, I. M., 1974a, "The commune in the ancient Near East," in S. P. Dunn and E. Dunn (eds.), *Introduction to Soviet Ethnography*, vol. II, Berkeley: Highgate Road Social Science Station, pp. 519–548.

1974b, "Slaves, helots and serfs in early antiquity," *ActaAnt*, 22, pp. 45–78.

1996, "Extended family households in Mesopotamia (III–II millennia BC)," in K. R. Veenhof (ed.), *Houses and Households in Ancient Mesopotamia*, Leiden: Nederlands Historisch-Archaeologisch Instituut te Istanbul, pp. 55–60.

DIAMOND, J., 1997, *Guns, Germs, and Steel: The Fates of Human Societies*, New York and London, W. W. Norton.

DIAMOND, J., and BELLWOOD, P., 2003, "Farmers and their languages: the first expansions," *Science*, 300 (5619), pp. 597–603.

DICK-READ, R., 2005, *The Phantom Voyagers: Evidence of Indonesian Settlement in Africa in Ancient Times*, Winchester: Thurlton.

DIEN, A. E., 2004, "Western exotica in China during the Six Dynasties Period," in X. Yang (ed.), *New Perspectives on China's Past: Chinese Archaeology in the Twentieth Century*, vol. I, New Haven, CT: Yale University Press, pp. 362–379.

DIFFLOTH, G., 2005, "The contribution of linguistic palaeontology to the homeland of Austro-Asiatic," in L. Sagart, R. Blench, and A. Sanchez-Mazas (eds.), *The Peopling of East Asia: Putting Together Archaeology, Linguistics and Genetics*, London: Routledge/Curzon, pp. 77–80.

DIGOMBE, L. *et al.*, 1988, "Early Iron Age prehistory in Gabon," *Current Anthropology*, 29 (1), pp. 180–84.

DIRINGER, D., 1982, *The Book Before Printing: Ancient, Medieval and Oriental*, New York: Dover.

DIRKSEN, V. G. and GEEL, B. VAN, 2004, "Mid to late Holocene climate change and its influence on cultural development in South Central Siberia," in E. M. Scott, A. Y. Alekseev, and G. Zaitseva (eds.), *Impact of the Environment on Human Migration in Eurasia*, Dordrecht, Boston, and London: Kluwer Academic Publishers, pp. 291–307.

DOBNEY, K., CUCCHI, T., and LARSON, G., 2008, "The pigs of island Southeast Asia and the Pacific: new evidence for taxonomic status and human-mediated dispersal," *Asian Perspectives*, pp. 59–74.

DOHERTY, C., BEAVITT, P., and KURUI, E., 2000, "Recent observations of rice temper in pottery from Niah and other sites in Sarawak," *Bulletin of the Indo-Pacific Prehistory Association*, 19, pp. 147–52.

DOMENICHINI-RAMIARAMANANA, B., 1990, "Madagascar," in M. El Fasi and I. Hrbek (eds.), *Histoire générale de l'Afrique*, vol. III: *L'Afrique du VIIᵉ au XIᵉ siècle*, Paris: Présence Africaine/Edicef/UNESCO, pp. 727–748.

DOMENICHINI, J.-P. and DOMENICHINI-RAMIARAMANANA, B., 1983, "Madagascar dans l'océan Indien avant le XIIIᵉ siècle," *Nouvelles du Centre d'Art et d'Archéologie*, 1, pp. 5–19.

DONEGAN, P. and STAMPE, D., 2004, "Rhythm and the synthetic drift of Munda," in R. Singh (ed.), *The Yearbook of South Asian Languages and Linguistics 2004*, Berlin: Mouton de Gruyter, pp. 3–36.

DONOHUE, M. and DENHAM, T., 2010, "Farming and language in Island Southeast Asia: reframing Austronesian theory," *Current Anthropology*, 51 (2), pp. 223–256.

DONQUE, G., 1965, "Le contexte océanique des anciennes migrations: vents et courants dans l'océan Indien," *Taloha*, 1, pp. 43–69.

DOUGHERTY, R. P., 1933, *Archives from Erech*, vol. II: *Neo-Babylonian and Persian Periods*, New Haven, CT: Yale University Press.

DOUKI, C. and MINARD, P., 2007, "Histoire globale, histoires connectées: un changement d'échelle historiographique? Introduction," *Revue d'histoire moderne et contemporaine*, 54 (4bis), pp. 7–21.

DOUMAS, C. G., 1988, "EBA in the Cyclades: continuity or discontinuity ?," in E. B. French and K. A. Wardle (eds.), *Problems in Greek Prehistory*, Bristol Classical Press, pp. 21–31.

DRÈGE, J.-P., 1986, *La Route de la Soie: paysages et légendes*, Paris: La Bibliothèque des Arts. 2000, *Marco Polo et la Route de la Soie*, Paris: Gallimard (1st edn. 1989).

DREWES, A. J., 2001, "The meaning of Sabaean MKRB, facts and fiction," *Semitica*, 51, pp. 93–125.

DREWS, R., 1993, *The End of the Bronze Age: Changes in Warfare and the Catastrophe ca. 1200 B.C.*, Princeton University Press.

2004, *Early Riders: The Beginning of Mounted Warfare in Asia and Europe*, New York: Routledge.

DREYER, P., 1980, *Martyrs and Fanatics*, New York: Simon and Schuster.

DRIDI, H., 2002, "Indiens et proche-orientaux dans une grotte de Suqutra (Yemen)," *Journal Asiatique*, 290 pp. 565–610.

DUARTE, R. T., 1993, *Northern Mozambique in the Swahili World* (Studies in African Archaeology 4), Eduardo Mondlane University (Mozambique), Uppsala University (Sweden).

DUBOIS, H. M., 1938, *Monographie des Betsileo*, Paris: Institut d'Ethnologie.

DUBOIS, J., GIACOMO, M., GUESPIN, L., MARCELLESI, C., and MÉVEL, J.-P., 1973, *Dictionnaire de linguistique*, Paris: Larousse.

DUMASY, F., 2005, "L'impérialisme, un débat manqué de l'histoire contemporaine française? Pour une relecture des travaux d'Yvon Thébert dans la perspective de la colonisation," *Afrique et Histoire*, 3 (issue on "Afriques romaines: impérialisme antique, imaginaire colonial (relectures et réflexions à l'école d'Yvon Thébert)"), pp. 57–69.

DUPLANTIER, J.-M., ORTH, A., CATALAN, J., and BONHOMME, F., 2002, "Evidence for a mitochondrial lineage originating from the Arabian peninsula in the Madagascar house mouse (*Mus musculus*)," *Heredity*, 89, pp. 154–158.

DUPREE, L., 1972, *Prehistoric Research in Afghanistan (1959–1966)*, Philadelphia, PA: American Philosophical Society.

DURAND, J.-M. (trans. and ed.), 1983, *Archives royales de Mari*, vol. XXI: *Textes administratifs des salles 134 and 160 du Palais de Mari*, Paris: Librairie Orientaliste Paul Geuthner.

(trans. and ed.), 1998, *Documents épistolaires du palais de Mari*, vol. III, Paris: Éditions du Cerf.

DURING CASPERS, E. C. L., 1994, "Non-Indus glyptics in a Harappan context," *Iranica Antiqua*, 29, pp. 83–106.

1996, "Local MBAC materials in the Arabian Gulf and their manufacturers," *Proceedings of the Seminar for Arabian Studies*, 26, pp. 47–63.

DURRANI, N., 2005, *The Tihamah Coastal Plain of South-West Arabia in Its Regional Context c. 6000 BC – AD 600*, Oxford: Archaeopress.

DUSSUBIEUX, L., 2001, "L'apport de l'ablation laser couplée à l'ICP-MS à la caractérisation des verres: application à l'étude du verre archéologique de l'océan Indien," Thèse de Doctorat, Université d'Orléans.

2010, "Compositional analysis of ancient glass fragments from North Sumatra, Indonesia," in D. Perret and H. Surachman (eds.), *Histoire de Barus III: regards sur une place marchande de l'océan Indien (XIIe – milieu du XVIIe siècle)*, Paris: Association Archipel/EFEO, pp. 385–417.

DUSSUBIEUX, L. and GRATUZE, B., 2001, "Analyse quantitative de fragments de verre provenant de Begram," *Topoi*, 11, pp. 451–472.

2010, "Glass in Southeast Asia" in B. Bellina, E. A. Bacus, T. O. Pryce, and J. Wisseman Christie (eds.), *50 Years of Archaeology in Southeast Asia, Essays in Honour of Ian Glover*, Bangkok: River Books, pp. 247–259.

DYEN, I., 1953a, "Compte rendu de Malgache and Maanjan de Dahl," *Language*, 29, pp. 577–590.

1953b, *The Proto-Malayo-Polynesian Laryngeals*, Baltimore: Linguistic Society of America.

1963, "The position of the Malayo-Polynesian languages of Formosa," *Asian Perspectives*, 7, pp. 261–271.

1965a, "Formosan evidence for some new Proto-Austronesian phonemes," *Lingua*, 14, pp. 285–305.

1965b, *A Lexicostatistical Classification of the Austronesian Languages* (*International Journal of American Linguistics*, Memoir 19), Baltimore: Waverly Press.

DYKMANS, G., 1936, *Histoire économique et sociale de l'Ancienne Egypte*, vol. II: *La vie économique sous l'Ancien Empire*, Paris: Auguste Picard.

EASTON, D. F., HAWKINS, J. D., SHERRATT, A. G., and SHERRATT, E. S., 2002, "Troy in recent perspective," *Anatolian Studies*, 52, pp. 75–109.

EBREY, P., 1987, "The economic and social history of Later Han," in D. Twitchett and M. Loewe (eds.), *Cambridge History of China*, vol. I: *The Ch'in and Han Empires, 221 BC – AD 220*, Cambridge University Press, pp. 608–648.

EDENS, C., 1992, "The dynamics of trade in the ancient Mesopotamian world system," *American Anthropologist*, 94, pp. 118–139.

    1993, "Comments on A. G. Frank's article "Bronze Age world system cycles," *Current Anthropology*, 34 (4), pp. 408–409.

    1995. "Transcaucasia at the end of the Early Bronze Age," *Bulletin of the American Schools of Oriental Research*, 299/300, pp. 53–64.

    2002a, "Looking for connections: Southwest Arabia in late prehistory," *Man and Environment*, 27 (1), pp. 45–55.

    2002b, "Small things forgotten? Continuity amidst change at Godin Tepe," *Iranica antiqua*, 37, pp. 31–45.

EDENS, C. and KOHL, P. L., 1993, "Trade and world-systems in Early Bronze Age western Asia," in C. Scarre and F. Healy (eds.), *Trade and Exchange in Prehistoric Europe*, Oxford: Oxbow Books, pp. 17–34.

EDENS, C. and WILKINSON, T. J., 1998, "Southwest Arabia during the Holocene: recent archaeological developments," *Journal of World Prehistory*, 12 (1), pp. 55–119.

EGBERTS, A., 2001, "Wenamun," *The Oxford Encyclopedia of Ancient Egypt*, vol. III, Oxford, New York, and Cairo: Oxford University Press and The American University in Cairo Press, pp. 495–496.

EGGERT, M. K. H., 2005, "The Bantu problem and African archaeology," in A. B. Stahl (ed.), *African Archaeology: A Critical Introduction*, Malden, MA, and Oxford: Blackwell, pp. 301–326.

EHRET, C., 1998, *An African Classical Age: Eastern and Southern Africa in World History, 1000 BC to AD 400*, Charlottesville: University Press of Virginia; Oxford: James Currey.

    2001, "Bantu expansions: re-envisioning a central problem of early African history," *International Journal of African Historical Studies*, 34 (1), pp. 5–41.

EKBLOM, A., LANE, P., RADIMILAHY, C., RAKOTOARISOA, J.-A., SINCLAIR, P., and VIRAH-SAWMY, M., 2016, "Migration and interaction between Madagascar and eastern Africa, 500 BC–1000 AD: the archeological perspective," in G. Campbell (ed.), *Early Exchange between Africa and the Wider Indian Ocean World*, London: Palgrave Macmillan, https://doi.org/10.1007/978-3-319-33822-4_9

EKHOLM, K., 1972, *Power and Prestige: The Rise and Fall of the Kongo Kingdom*, Uppsala: Skriv Service AB.

EKHOLM, K. and FRIEDMAN, J., 1982, "'Capital' imperialism and exploitation in ancient world systems," *Review*, 4(1), pp. 87–109.

EKHOLM-FRIEDMAN, K., 2000, "On the evolution of global systems, part I: the Mesopotamian heartland," in R. A. Denemark, J. Friedman, B. K. Gills, and G. Modelski (eds.), *World System History: The Social Science of Long-Term Change*, London and New York: Routledge, pp. 153–168.

    2005, "Structure, dynamics, and the final collapse of Bronze Age Civilization," in J. Friedman and C. Chase-Dunn (eds.), *Hegemonic Declines: Present and Past*, Boulder, CO: Paradigm, pp. 51–87.

ELLEN, R. F., 1977, "The trade in spices," *Indonesia Circle*, 12, pp. 21–25.

ELVIN, M., 1973, *The Pattern of the Chinese Past: A Social and Economic Interpretation*, Stanford University Press.

EMBERLING, G., 2002, "Political control in an early state: the Eye Temple and the Uruk expansion in northern Mesopotamia," in L. al-Gailani Werr, J. Curtis, H. Martin, A. McMahon, and J. Reade (eds.), *Of Pots and Plans: Papers on the Archaeology and History of Mesopotamia and Syria Presented to David Oates in Honour of His 75th Birthday*, London: Nabu, pp. 82–90.

EMBERLING, G. and McDONALD, H., 2003, "Excavations at Tell Brak 2001–2002: preliminary report," *Iraq*, 65, pp. 1–75.

ENDICOTT, P., METSPALU, M., and KIVISILD, T., 2007, "Genetic evidence on modern human dispersals in South Asia: Y chromosome and mitochondrial DNA perspectives: the world through the eyes of two haploid genomes," in M. D. Petraglia and B. Allchin (eds.), *The Evolution and History of Human Populations in South Asia*, New York: Springer, pp. 229–244.

ENGLUND, R. K., 1998, "Texts from the late Uruk period," in J. Bauer, R. K. Englund, and M. Krebernik (eds.), *Mesopotamien: Späturuk-Zeit und Frühdynastische Zeit*, Fribourg: Academic Press; Göttingen: Vandenhoeck & Ruprecht, pp. 15–233.

2004, "Proto-Cuneiform account-books and journals," in M. Hudson and C. Wunsch (eds.), *Creating Economic Order: Record-Keeping, Standardization and the Development of Accounting in the Ancient Near East*, Bethesda, MD: CDL Press, pp. 23–46.

ERIKSSON, K. O., 2003, "A preliminary synthesis of recent chronological observations on the relations between Cyprus and other eastern Mediterranean societies during the Late Middle Bronze – Late Bronze II periods," in M. Bietak (ed.), *The Synchronisation of Civilisations in the Eastern Mediterranean in the Second Millennium BC II: Proceedings of the SCIEM 2000 Euro Conference, Haindorf, May 2–7, 2001*, Vienna: Verlag der Österreichischen Akademie der Wissenschaften, pp. 411–430.

ESPER, J., DÜTHORN, E., KRUSIC, P. J., TIMONEN, M., and BÜNTGEN, U., 2014, "Northern European summer temperature variations over the Common Era from integrated tree-ring density records," *Journal of Quaternary Science*, 29 (5), pp. 487–494.

EYRE, C. J., 1987, "Work and the organisation of work in the Old Kingdom," in M. A. Powell (ed.), *Labor in the Ancient Near East*, New Haven: American Oriental Society, pp. 5–47.

1997, "Peasants and 'modern' leasing strategies in Ancient Egypt," *Journal of the Economic and Social History of the Orient*, 40, pp. 367–390.

1999, "The village economy in Pharaonic Egypt," in A. Bowman and E. Rogan (eds.), *Agriculture in Egypt: From Pharaonic to Modern Times: Proceedings of the British Academy 96*, New York: Oxford University Press, pp. 33–60.

FABRE, D., 2004, *Seafaring in Ancient Egypt*, London: Periplus Publishing.

FACEY, W., 2004, "The Red Sea: the wind regime and location of ports," in P. Lunde and A. Porter (eds.), *Trade and Travel in the Red Sea Region: Proceedings of the Red Sea Project I*, Oxford: Archaeopress, pp. 6–17.

FAGAN, B. M., 1985, "Les bassins du Zambèze et du Limpopo (+ 1100 / + 1500)," in D. T. Niane (ed.), *Histoire générale de l'Afrique*, vol. IV: *L'Afrique du XIIe au XVIe siècle*, Paris: UNESCO/ Nouvelles Éditions Africaines, pp. 571–599.

2004, *The Long Summer: How Climate Changed Civilization*, New York: Basic Books.

2009, *Floods, Famines and Emperors: El Niño and the Fate of Civilizations*, New York: Basic Books.

FAHMY, A., 1998, "Artificial pollination: archaeobotanical studies at HK43," *Nekhen News*, www .hierakonpolis.org/resources/nekehn_news.htm

FAIST, B. I., 2001, *Der Fernhandel des Assyrischen Reiches zwischen dem 14. und 11. Jahrhundert v. Chr.*, Münster: Ugarit-Verlag.

FAIVRE, X., 2001, "Peuples de la mer," in F. Joannès (ed.), *Dictionnaire de la civilisation mésopotamienne*, Paris: Laffont, pp. 644–647.

FALKENHAUSEN, L. von, 2003, "The external connections of Sanxingdui," *Journal of East Asian Archaeology*, 5 (1–4), pp. 191–245.

———— 2011, *The Lloyd Cotsen Study Collection of Chinese Bronze Mirrors*, vol. II: *Studies II*, Los Angeles: Cotsen Occasional Press and UCLA Cotsen Institute of Archaeology Press.

FANONY, F., 1975, "La riziculture sur brûlis (*tavy*) et les rituels agraires dans la région de Mananara-Nord," *Terre Malgache*, 17, pp. 29–47.

FARBER, H., 1978, "A price and wage study of northern Babylonia during the Old Babylonian period," *Journal of the Economic and Social History of the Orient*, 21 (1), pp. 1–51.

FATIMI, S. Q., 1996, "History of the development of the kamal," in H. P. Ray and J.-F. Salles (eds.), *Tradition and Archaeology: Early Maritime Contacts in the Indian Ocean*, Delhi: Manohar, pp. 283–292.

FATTOVICH, R., 1990, "Remarks on the Pre-Aksumite period in northern Ethiopia," *Journal of Ethiopian Studies*, 23, pp. 1–33.

———— 1991, "Evidence of possible administrative devices in the Gash Delta (Kassala), 3rd–2nd millennia BC," *Archéologie du Nil Moyen*, 5, pp. 65–78.

———— 1997a, "The Near East and Eastern Africa: their environmental interaction," in J. O. Vogel and J. Vogel (eds.), *Encyclopedia of Pre-Colonial Africa*, London: Sage, pp. 479–484.

———— 1997b, "The contacts between Southern Arabia and the Horn of Africa in late prehistoric and early historic times: a view from Africa," in A. Avanzini (ed.), *Profumi d'Arabia*, Rome: "L'Erma" di Bretschneider, pp. 273–286.

———— 2004, "The 'pre-Aksumite' state in northern Ethiopia and Eritrea reconsidered," in P. Lunde and A. Porter (eds.), *Trade and Travel in the Red Sea Region*, Oxford: BAR International Series, pp. 71–77.

———— 2005a, "Marsā Gawasīs, a Pharaonic coastal settlement by the Red Sea in Egypt," in J. C. M. Starkey (ed.), *People of the Red Sea: Proceedings of Red Sea Project II Held in the British Museum October 2004* (BAR International Series) Oxford: Archaeopress, pp. 15–22.

———— 2005b, "The archaeology of the Horn of Africa," in W. Raunig and S. Wenig (eds.), *Afrikas Horn: Akten der Ersten Internationalen Littman-Konferenz 2*, Wiesbaden: Harrassowitz, pp. 3–29.

———— 2010, "The development of ancient states in the northern Horn of Africa, c. 3000 BC – AD 1000: an archaeological outline," *Journal of World Prehistory*, 23, pp. 145–175.

FAUVELLE-AYMAR, F.-X., 2006, *Histoire de l'Afrique du Sud*, Paris: Seuil.

———— 2013, *Le rhinocéros d'or: histoires du Moyen Âge africain*, Paris: Alma Éditeur.

FELDMAN, M. and KISLEV, M. E., 2007, "Domestication of emmer wheat and evolution of free-threshing tetraploid wheat," *Israel Journal of Plant Sciences*, 55, pp. 207–221.

FENTRESS, E., 2011, "Slavers on chariots," in A. Dowler and E. R. Galwin (eds.), *Money, Trade and Trade Routes in Pre-Islamic North Africa*, London: British Museum, pp. 65–71.

FERJAOUI, A., 1993, *Recherches sur les relations entre l'Orient phénicien et Carthage*, Fribourg: Éditions Universitaires; Göttingen: Vandenhoeck und Ruprecht.

FERNANDEZ-ARMESTO, F., 2006, *The World: A History*, vol. I: *To 1500*; vol. II: *Since 1300*, Upper Saddle River, NJ: Prentice Hall.

FERRAND, G., 1919, "Le K'ouen-Louen et les anciennes navigations interocéaniques dans les Mers du Sud," *Journal Asiatique*, 13, March–April, pp. 239–333; May–June, pp. 431–492; July–August, pp. 5–68; September–October, pp. 201–244 (published as a book, Paris: Imprimerie Nationale, 1919).

———— 1924, "L'élément persan dans les textes nautiques arabes des XVe et XVIe siècles," *Journal Asiatique*, April–June, pp. 193–257.

1932, "Quatre textes épigraphiques malayo-sanskrits de Sumatra et de Bangka," *Journal Asiatique*, 221, p. 271–326.

1987, "Zabag," in *First Encyclopedia of Islam*, vol. VIII, Leiden: E. J. Brill, pp. 1182–1183.

FILESI, T., 1972, *China and Africa in the Middle Ages*, London: Frank Cass (1st edn. 1962).

FILLIOZAT, J., 1956, *Les relations extérieures de l'Inde*, Pondicherry: Institut Français d'Indologie.

1975, "The oldest sea-routes of the Tamil trade," *Bulletin of the Institute of Traditional Cultures*, Madras, pp. 21–28.

1980, "L'Inde de Pline L'Ancien," Appendix in J. André and J. Filliozat (eds.), Pline l'Ancien, *Histoire Naturelle*, Book 6, part 2, Paris: Société d'Edition "Les Belles Lettres,"pp. 143–165.

FINKELSTEIN, I., 1998, "Bible archaeology or archaeology of Palestine in the Iron Age? A rejoinder," *Levant*, 30, pp. 167–173.

FINKELSTEIN, I. and PIASETZKY, E., 2003, "Comment on '14 C dates from Tel Rehov: Iron-Age chronology, pharaohs, and Hebrew kings'," *Science*, 302 (5645), p. 568b.

FISER, I., 2001, "The problem of the Seṭṭhi in Buddhist Jātakas," in R. Chakravarti (ed.), *Trade in Early India*, Oxford University Press, pp. 166–198 (first published 1954, *Archiv Orientalni*, 22, pp. 238–266).

FITZGERALD-HUBER, L. G., 1995, "Qijia and Erlitou: the question of contacts with distant cultures," *Early China*, 20, pp. 17–67.

2003, "The Qijia culture: paths east and west," *The Museum of Far Eastern Antiquities* (Stockholm), 75, pp. 55–78.

FLACOURT, E. de, 1910 [1658], *Dictionnaire de la langue de Madagascar avec un petit recueil des noms et dictons propres des choses qui sont d'une même espèce, plus quelques mots du langage des sauvages de la baie de Saldaigne au Cap de Bonne-Espérance*, Paris, 1658, in A. and G. Grandidier, J. Charles-Roux, C. Delhorbe, and H. Froidevaux (ed.), *Collection des ouvrages anciens concernant Madagascar*, vol. VII, Paris, pp. 206–457.

1995, 2007 [1661], *Histoire de la Grande Isle Madagascar*, ed. C. Allibert, Paris: Karthala-INALCO (1st edn. Allibert 1995a).

FLAD, R., LI, S., WU, X., and ZHAO, Z., 2010, "Early wheat in China: results from new studies at Donghuishan in the Hexi Corridor," *Holocene*, 20, pp. 955–965.

FLEISHER, J., LANE, P., LaVIOLETTE, A., HORTON, M., POLLARD, E., MORALES, E. Q., VERNET, T., CHRISTIE, A., and WYNNE-JONES, S., 2015, "When did the Swahili become maritime?," *American Anthropologist*, 117 (1), pp. 100–115.

FLEISHER, J. and WYNNE-JONES, S. 2011, "Ceramics and the early Swahili: deconstructing the early Tana Tradition," *African Archaeological Review*, 28, pp. 245–278. doi:10.1007/s10437-011-9104-6.

FLEMINGS, M. C., 2002, "Traveling technologies," in E. Ten Grotenhuis (ed.), *Along the Silk Road*, Washington: A. M. Sackler Gallery, Smithsonian Institution, pp. 107–121.

FONTEIN, J. (ed.), 1990, *The Sculpture of Indonesia*, Washington: National Gallery of Art; New York: Harry N. Abrams.

FORD, L. A., POLLARD, A. M., CONINGHAM, R. A. E., and STERN, B., 2005, "A geochemical investigation of the origin of Rouletted and other related south Asian fine wares," *Antiquity*, 79, pp. 909–920, with online supplement available at: www.antiquityac.uk/projgall/ford306/

FOREST, J. D., 2003, "La Mésopotamie et les échanges à longue distance aux IVe et IIIe millénaires," *Dossiers d'Archéologie*, 287, pp. 126–133.

FOSTER, B. R., 1977, "Commercial activity in Sargonic Mesopotamia," *Iraq*, 39, pp. 31–43.

1993, *Before the Muses: An Anthology of Akkadian Literature I–II*, Bethesda, MD: CDL Press.

FOSTER, B. R. and FOSTER, K. P., 2009, *Civilizations of Ancient Iraq*, Princeton University Press.

FOX, J. and LEDGERWOOD, J., 1999, "Dry-season flood-recession rice in the Mekong delta: two thousand years of sustainable agriculture?," *Asian Perspectives*, 38 (1), pp. 37–50.

FRACHETTI, M., 2002, "Bronze Age exploitation and political dynamics of the eastern Eurasian Steppe zone," in K. Boyle, C. Renfrew, and M. Levine (eds.), *Ancient Interactions: East and West in Eurasia*, Cambridge: McDonald Institute for Archaeological Research, pp. 161–170.

2004, "Bronze Age pastoral landscapes of Eurasia and the nature of social interaction in the mountain steppe zone of eastern Kazakhstan," Ph.D. dissertation, University of Pennsylvania.

2009, *Pastoralist Landscapes and Social Interaction in Bronze Age Eurasia*, University of California Press.

2010, "Eurasian pastoralists and their shifting regional interactions at the steppe margin: settlement history at Mukri, Kazakhstan," *World Archaeology*, 42 (4), pp. 622–646.

2012, "Multiregional emergence of mobile pastoralism and nonuniform institutional complexity across Eurasia," *Current Anthropology*, 53 (1), pp. 2–38.

FRACHETTI, M. and ROUSE, L. M., 2012, "Central Asia, the Steppe, and the Near East, 2500–1500 BC," in D. T. Potts (ed.), *A Companion to the Archaeology of the Ancient Near East*, Malden, MA: Wiley-Blackwell, pp. 687–705.

FRACHETTI, M. D., SPENGLER, R. N., FRITZ, G. J., and MAR'YASHEV, A. N., 2010, "Earliest direct evidence for broomcorn millet and wheat in the Central Eurasia steppe region," *Antiquity*, 84, pp. 993–1010.

FRANCAVIGLIA, V. M., 2002, "Some remarks on the irrigation systems of Ancient Yemen," in S. Cleuziou, M. Tosi, and J. Zarins (eds.), *Essays on the Late Prehistory of the Arabian Peninsula*, Rome: Istituto Italiano per l'Africa e l'Oriente, pp. 111–144.

FRANCFORT, H.-P. (ed.), 1989, *Fouilles de Shortughaï: recherches sur l'Asie Centrale proto-historique*, 2 vols., Paris: De Boccard.

1990, "Une proto-route de la soie a-t-elle existé aux 2e–1er millénaires?," in H.-P. Francfort (ed.), *Nomades et sédentaires en Asie Centrale: apports de l'archéologie et de l'ethnologie*, Paris: Éditions du Centre National de la Recherche Scientifique, pp. 121–130.

1993, "Note on some Bronze Age petroglyphs of Upper Indus and Central Asia," *Pakistan Archaeology*, 26, pp. 125–135.

2001a, "The archaeology of Protohistoric Central Asia and the problems of identifying Indo-Europeans and Uralic-speaking populations," in C. Carpelan, A. Parpola, and P. Koskikallio (eds.), *Early Contacts between Uralic and Indo-European: Linguistic and Archaeo-logical Considerations. Papers Presented at an International Symposium Held at the Tvärminne Research Station of the University of Helsinki 8–10 January 1999*, Helsinki: Suomalais-Ugrilainen Seura, pp. 151–168.

2001b, "The cultures with painted ceramics of south Central Asia and their relations with the northeastern steppe zone (late 2nd – early 1st millennium BC," in R. Eichmann and C. Parzinger (eds.), *Migration und Kulturtransfer: Der Wandel vorder- und zentralasiatischer Kulturen im Umbruch vom 2. zum 1. vorchristlichen Jahrtausend. Akten des Internationalen Kolloquiums Berlin, 23–26 November 1999* (Kolloquien zur Vor- und Frühgeschichte 6), Bonn, pp. 221–235.

2005, "La civilisation de l'Oxus et les Indo-Iraniens et Indo-Aryens en Asie centrale," in G. Fussman, J. Kellens, H.-P. Francfort, and X. Tremblay (eds.), *Aryas, Aryens et Iraniens en Asie centrale*, Paris: Collège de France, De Boccard, pp. 253–332.

FRANCIS, P. Jr., 1986, *Chinese Glass Beads: A Review of the Evidence*, Lake Placid, NY: Center for Bead Research.

1989, *Beads and the Bead Trade in Southeast Asia*, Lake Placid, NY: Center for Bead Research.

2001, *Asia's Maritime Bead Trade from ca. 300 BC to the Present*, Honolulu: University of Hawai'i Press.

2002, "Early historic South India and the international maritime trade," *Man and Environment*, 27 (1), pp. 153–161.

2007, *Beads of the World*, Atglen, PA: Schiffer Publishing.

FRANGIPANE, M., 2000, "The development of administration from collective to centralized economies in the Old World: the transformation of an institution from system-serving to self-serving," in J. M. Feinman and L. Manzanilla (eds.), *Cultural Evolution Contemporary Viewpoints*, New York: Kluwer Academic, pp. 215–231.

2001, "Centralization processes in Greater Mesopotamia: Uruk 'expansion' as the climax of systemic interactions among areas of the Greater Mesopotamian region," in M. S. Rothman (ed.), *Uruk Mesopotamia and Its Neighbors*, Santa Fe: SAR Press, pp. 307–347.

2004a, "'Non-Uruk' developments and Uruk-linked features on the northern borders of Greater Mesopotamia," in J. N. Postgate (ed.), *Artefacts of Complexity: Tracking the Uruk in the Near East* (Iraq Archaeological Reports 5), Warminster: Aris & Phillips for the British School of Archaeology in Iraq, pp. 123–148 (1st edn. 2002).

2004b, "Centre de pouvoir du IVe millénaire, Arslantepe en Turquie," *Archéologia*, 417, pp. 60–68.

FRANK, A. G., 1993a, "Bronze Age world system cycles," *Current Anthropology*, 34 (4), pp. 383–405 and 419–430.

1993b, "The world is round and wavy: demographic cycles and structural analysis in the world system. a review essay of Jack A. Goldstone's *Revolutions and Rebellions in the Early Modern World*," in N. Keddie (ed.), *Debating Revolutions*, New York University Press, pp. 200–220.

1998, *ReOrient: Global Economy in the Asian Age*, Berkeley, Los Angeles, and London: University of California Press.

FRANK, A. G. and GILLS, B. K., 1993a and b, "The 5000-year world system: an interdisciplinary introduction" (a), "Rejoinder and conclusions" (b), in A. G. Frank and B. K. Gills (eds.), *The World System: Five Hundred Years or Five Thousand?*, London and New York: Routledge, pp. 3–55 and 297–307.

(eds.), 1993c, *The World System: Five Hundred Years or Five Thousand?*, London and New York: Routledge.

2000, "The five thousand year world system in theory and praxis," in R. A. Denemark, J. Friedman, B. K. Gills, and G. Modelski (eds.), *World System History: The Social Science of Long-Term Change*, London and New York: Routledge, pp. 3–23.

FRANK, A. G. and THOMPSON, W. R., 2005, "Bronze Age economic expansion and contraction revisited," *Journal of World History*, 16, pp. 115–172.

2006, "Early Iron Age economic expansion and contraction revisited," in B. K. Gills and W. R. Thompson (eds.), *Globalization and Global History*, London and Routledge, pp. 139–162.

FRANKE-VOGT, U., 2001, "The Southern Indus Valley during the later 2nd and 1st millennia BC: the Dark Age," in R. Eichmann and H. Parzinger (eds.), *Migration und Kulturtransfer: Der Wandel vorder- und zentralasiatischer Kulturen im Umbruch vom 2. zum 1. vorchristlichen Jahrtausend*, Bonn: Rudolph-Habelt, pp. 247–290.

FRANKFORT, H., 1941, "The origin of monumental architecture in Egypt," *American Journal of Semitic Languages and Literatures*, 58, pp. 329–358.

1969, *The Art and Architecture of the Ancient Orient*, 4th edn., Harmondsworth: Penguin Books.

FREEMAN-GRENVILLE, G. S. P., 1975, *The East African Coast: Select Documents from the First to the Earlier Nineteenth Century*, Oxford: Clarendon Press (1st edn. 1962).

FRENCH-WRIGHT, R., 1983, "Proto-Oceanic horticultural practices," M.A. thesis, University of Auckland, New Zealand.

FRIEDMAN, J., 1994, *Cultural Identity and Global Process*, London: Sage.

2000, "Concretizing the continuity argument in global systems analysis," in R. A. Denemark, J. Friedman, B. K. Gills, and G. Modelski (eds.), *World System History: The Social Science of Long-Term Change*, London and New York: Routledge, pp. 133–152.

2005, "Plus ça change? On not learning from history," in J. Friedman and C. Chase-Dunn (eds.), *Hegemonic Declines: Present and Past*, Boulder, CO: Paradigm, pp. 89–114.

2007, "Globalization," in D. Nugent and J. Vincent (eds.), *A Companion to the Anthropology of Politics*, Malden, MA, and Oxford: Wiley-Blackwell, pp. 179–197.

FRIEDMAN, J. and CHASE-DUNN, C. (eds.), 2005, *Hegemonic Declines: Past and Present*, Boulder, CO: Paradigm.

FRIEDMAN, J. and ROWLANDS, M., 1977, *The Evolution of Social Systems*, London and New York: Duckworth.

FRIEDMAN, R., 2005, "Hiérakonpolis: berceau de la royauté," *Dossiers d'Archéologie*, 307, pp. 62–73.

FRIEDMAN, Z., 2007, "Reply: the Kelenderis ship," *International Journal of Nautical Archaeology*, 36 (2), pp. 417–419.

FRIEDRICH, W., KROMER, B., FRIEDRICH, M., HEINEMEIER, J., PFEIFFER, T., and TALAMO, S., 2006, "Santorini eruption radiocarbon dated to 1627–1600 BC," *Science*, 312 (5773), p. 548.

FU, Y.-B., DIEDERICHSEN, A. and ALLABY, R. G., 2012, "Locus-specific view of flax domestication history," *Ecology and Evolution*, 2 (1), pp. 139–152.

FUKANG, Z., 1992, "Scientific studies of early glasses excavated in China," in R. H. Brill and J. H. Martin (eds.), *Scientific Research in Early Chinese Glass*, Corning, NY: Corning Museum of Glass, pp. 157–166.

FULLER, D. Q., 2003a, "African crops in prehistoric South Asia: a critical review," in K. Neumann, A. Butler, and S. Kahlhaber (eds.), *Food, Fuel and Fields: Progress in African Archaeobotany*, Cologne: Heinrich-Barth-Institut, pp. 239–271.

2003b, "Pharaonic or Sudanic ? Models for meroitic society and change," in D. O'Connor and A. Reid (eds.), *Ancient Egypt and Africa* (Encounters with Ancient Egypt series, ed. P. Ucko), London: UCL Press, pp. 169–184.

2005, "Farming: Stone Age farmers of the savanna," in K. Shillington (ed.), *Encyclopedia of African History*, vol. I: A–G, New York and London: Fitzroy Dearborn, pp. 521–523.

2006a, "Agricultural origins and frontiers in South Asia: a working synthesis," *Journal of World Prehistory*, 20, pp. 1–86.

2006b, "Silence before sedentism and the advent of cash-crops: a status report on early agriculture in South Asia from plant domestication to the development of political economies (with an excursus on the problem of semantic shift among millets and rice)," in T. Osada (ed.), *Proceedings of the Pre-Symposium of RIHN and 7th ESCA Harvard-Kyoto Roundtable*, Kyoto: Research Institute for Humanity and Nature (RIHN), pp. 175–213.

2007, "Non-human genetics, agricultural origins and historical linguistics in South Asia," in M. D. Petraglia and B. Allchin (eds.), *The Evolution and History of Human Populations in South Asia: Inter-disciplinary Studies in Archaeology, Biological Anthropology, Linguistics and Genetics*, New York: Springer, pp. 391–441.

2008a, "Neolithic cultures," in D. M. Pearsall (ed.), *Encyclopedia of Archaeology*, New York: Academic Press, pp. 756–768.

2008b, "The spread of textile production and textile crops in India beyond the Harappan zone: an aspect of the emergence of craft specialization and systematic trade," in T. Osada and A. Uesugi (eds.), *Linguistics, Archaeology and the Human Past*, Kyoto: Indus Project, Research Institute for Humanity and Nature, pp. 1–26.

2011a, "Pathways to Asian civilizations: tracing the origins and spread of rice and rice cultures," *Rice*, 4, pp. 78–92.

2011b, "Finding plant domestication in the Indian subcontinent," *Current Anthropology*, 52 (S4) (issue on "The Origins of Agriculture: New Data, New Ideas"), pp. S347–S362.

2014a, "Agricultural innovation and state collapse in Meroitic Nubia," in C. J. Stevens, S. Nixon, M. A. Murray, and D. Q. Fuller (eds.), *Archaeology of African Plant Use*, London: Institute of Archaeology, University College London, pp. 165–177.

2014b, "Post-Pleistocene South Asia: food production in India and Sri Lanka," in C. Renfrew and P. Bahn (eds.), *The Cambridge World Prehistory*, vol. I: *Africa, South and Southeast Asia and the Pacific*, Cambridge University Press, pp. 389–406.

FULLER, D. Q. and BOIVIN, N., 2009, "Crops, cattle and commensals across the Indian Ocean: current and potential archaeobiological evidence," *Études Océan Indien*, 42–43, pp. 13–46.

FULLER, D. Q., BOIVIN, N., and KORISETTAR, K., 2007, "Dating the Neolithic of South India: new radiometric evidence for key economic, social and ritual transformations," *Antiquity*, 81 (313), pp. 755–778.

FULLER, D. Q., BOIVIN, N., HOOGERVORST, T., and ALLABY, R., 2011, "Across the Indian Ocean: the prehistoric movement of plants and animals," *Antiquity*, 84, pp. 544–558.

FULLER, D. Q., BOIVIN, N., CASTILLO, C. C., HOOGERVORST, T., and ALLABY, R., 2014, "The archaeobiology of Indian Ocean translocations: current outlines of cultural exchanges by proto-historic seafarers," in S. Tripati (ed.), *Maritime Contacts of the Past: Deciphering Connections amongst Communities*, New Delhi: Kaveri Book Service, pp. 1–23.

FULLER, D. Q. and HARVEY, E. L., 2006, "The archaeobotany of Indian pulses: identification, processing and evidence for cultivation," *Environmental Archaeology*, 11 (2), pp. 219–246.

FULLER, D. Q., HARVEY, E. L., and QIN, L., 2007, "Presumed domestication? Evidence for wild rice cultivation and domestication in the fifth millennium BC of the Lower Yangtze region," *Antiquity*, 81 (312), pp. 316–331.

FULLER, D. Q. and HILDEBRAND, E., 2013, "Domesticating plants in Africa," in P. Mitchell and P. Lane (eds.), *The Oxford Handbook of African Archaeology*, Oxford University Press, pp. 507–526.

FULLER, D. Q., MacDONALD, K., and VERNET, R., 2007, "Early domesticated pearl millet in Dhar Nema (Mauritania): evidence of crop processing waste as ceramic temper," in R. Cappers (ed.), *Fields of Change*, Groningen: Barkhuis and Groningen University Library, pp. 71–76.

FULLER, D. Q. and MADELLA, M., 2001, "Issues in Harappan archaeobotany: retrospect and prospect," in S. Settar and R. Korisettar (eds.), *Indian Archaeology in Retrospect*, vol. II: *Protohistory* (Publication of the Indian Council for Historical Research), New Delhi: Manohar, pp. 317–390.

2009, "Banana cultivation in South Asia and East Asia: a review of the evidence from archaeology and linguistics," *Ethnobotany Research and Applications*, 7, pp. 333–351.

FULLER, D. Q. and QIN, L., 2009, "Water management and labour in the origins and dispersal of Asian rice," *World Archaeology*, 41 (1), pp. 88–111.

FULLER, D. Q., SATO, Y.-I., CASTILLO, C., QIN, L., WEISSKOPF, A. R., KINGWELL-BANHAM, E. J., SONG, J., AHN, S.-M., and VAN ETTEN, J., 2010, "Consilience of genetics and archaeobotany in the entangled history of rice," *Archaeological and Anthropological Sciences*, 2, pp. 115–131.

FULLER, D. Q. and WEISSKOPF, A., 2011, "The Early Rice Project: from domestication to global warming," *Archaeology International*, 13/14, pp. 44–51.

FUNICANE, B., MANNING, K., and TOURÉ, M., 2008, "Late Stone Age subsistence in the Tilemsi Valley, Mali: stable isotope analysis of human and animal remains from the site of Karkarichinkat Nord (KN05) and Karkarichinkat Sud (KS05)," *Journal of Anthropological Archaeology*, 27, pp. 82–92.

FUSSMAN, G., 1997, "The *Periplus* and the political history of India," in F. De Romanis and A. Tchernia (eds.), *Crossings: Early Mediterranean Contacts with India*, New Delhi: Manohar, pp. 66–71.

2001, "Fires in temple, fire-temples and Aryan cult practices," *Miras* (Ashgabad, Turkmenistan), 3, pp. 132–138.

FUSSMAN, G., KELLENS, J., FRANCFORT, H.-P., and TREMBLAY, X., 2005, *Aryas, Aryens et Iraniens en Asie Centrale*, Paris: De Boccard.

GAHAMA, A., 1979, *La Reine Mère et ses Prêtres au Burundi*, Nanterre: Laboratoire d'Ethnologie et de Sociologie Comparative.

GAJDA, I., 2001, "L'héritage de l'Antiquité: vers le Yémen Islamique," *Dossiers d'Archéologie*, 263 (issue on "Yémen"), pp. 64–67.

GAMITO, T. J., 1988, *Social Complexity in Southwest Iberia, 800–300 BC: The Case of Tartessos* (BAR International Series 439), Oxford: Archaeopress.

GARLACH, I, 2001, "Édifices funéraires au royaume de Saba," *Dossiers d'Archéologie*, 263 (issue on "Yémen"), pp. 50–53.

GARRIS, A. J., TAI, T. H., COBURN, J., KRESOVICH, S., and McCOUCH, S., 2005, "Genetic structure and diversity in *Oryza sativa* L.," *Genetics*, 169, pp. 1631–1638.

GASCHE, H., ARMSTRONG, J. A., COLE, S. W., and GURZADYAN, V. G., 1998, *Dating the Fall of Babylon: A Reappraisal of Second-Millennium Chronology* (Mesopotamian History and Environment, Series II, Memoirs IV), University of Ghent and the Oriental Institute of the University of Chicago.

GASSE, F. and CAMPO, E. VAN, 1998, "A 40.000-yr pollen and diatom record from Lake Tritrivakely, Madagascar, in the Southern Tropic," *Quaternary Research*, 49 (3), pp. 299–311.

GAT, A., 2002, "Why city-states existed? Riddles and clues of urbanisation and fortifications," in M. H. Hansen (ed.), *A Comparative Study of Six City-State Cultures*, Copenhagen: Det Kongelige Danske Videnskabernes Selskab, pp. 125–139.

GATES, M.-H., 1997, "Archaeology in Turkey," *American Journal of Archaeology*, 101, pp. 241–305.

GAUR, A. S., SUNDARESH, and TRIPATI, S., 2006, "Evidence for Indo-Roman trade from Bet Dwarka waters, west coast of India," *International Journal of Nautical Archaeology*, 35 (1), pp. 117–127.

GELB, I. J., STEINKELLER, P., and WHITING, R. M., 1991, *Earliest Land Tenure Systems in the Near East: Ancient Kuddurus* (Oriental Institute Publications, vol. 104), 2 vols., University of Chicago Press.

GEORGESCU-ROEGEN, N., 1971, *The Entropy Law and the Economic Process*, Cambridge, MA: Harvard University Press.

GERINI, 1909, *Researches on Ptolemy's Geography of Eastern Asia (further India and Indo-Malay Archipelago)*, London: Royal Asiatic Society and Royal Geographic Society.

GERLOFF, S., 1993, "Zu Fragen mittelmeerländischer Kontakte und absoluter Chronologie der Frühbronzezeit in Mittel- und Westgebirge," *Praehistorische Zeitschrift*, 68 (1), pp. 58–102.

GERMER, R., 1979, "Untersuchung über Arzneimittelpflanzen im Alten Ägypten," Ph.D. dissertation, University of Hamburg.

1985, *Flora des pharaonischen Ägypten*, Mainz: Verlag Philipp von Zabern.

GERNET, J., 1999, *Le monde chinois*, Paris: Armand Colin (1st edn. 1972).

2002, *A History of Chinese Civilization*, 2nd edn., London: Folio Society (first published by Cambridge University Press, 1996).

GEVREY, A., 1870, *Essai sur les îles Comores*, Pondicherry: A. Saligny.

GIBBON, E., 1776–1789, *The History of the Decline and Fall of the Roman Empire*, 6 vols., London: Frederick Warne & Co.

GIBBONS, A. 2015, "Nomadic herders left a strong genetic mark on Europeans and Asians," *Science*, doi: 10.1126/science.aac6818

GIBSON, H., 1940, "The use of the cowries as money during the Shang and Chou periods," *Journal of the North China Branch of the Royal Asiatic Society*, 71, pp. 33–45.

GILBOA, A. and SHARON, I., 2001, "Early Iron Age radiometric dates from Tel Dor," *Radiocarbon*, 43 (3), pp. 1343–1351.

GILLS, B. K. and FRANK, A. G., 1991, "5,000 years of world system history: the cumulation of accumulation," in C. Chase-Dunn and T. D. Hall (eds.), *Core/Periphery Relations in Precapitalist Worlds*, Boulder, CO: Westview Press, pp. 67–112.

1993a and b, "The cumulation of accumulation" and "World System cycles, crises, and hegemonic shifts, 1700 BC to 1700 AD," in A. G. Frank and B. K. Gills (eds.), *The World System: Five Hundred Years or Five Thousand?*, London and New York: Routledge, pp. 81–114 and 143–199.

GILLS, B. K. and THOMPSON, W. R. (eds.), 2006, *Globalization and Global History*, London: Routledge.

GIOT, P.-R., BRIARD, J., and PAPE, L., 1995, *Protohistoire de la Bretagne*, Rennes: Ouest-France.

GLASSNER, J.-J., 2000a, *Écrire à Sumer, l'invention du cunéiforme*, Paris: Seuil.

2000b, "Les petits états mésopotamiens à la fin du 4e et au cours du 3e millénaire," in M. H. Hansen (ed.), *A Comparative Study of Thirty City-State Cultures*, Copenhagen: Det Kongelige Danske Videnskabernes Selskab, pp. 35–53.

2001, "Peut-on parler de monnaie en Mésopotamie au IIIe millénaire avant notre ère?," in A. Testard (ed.), *Aux origines de la monnaie*, Paris: Éditions Errance, pp. 61–72.

2002a, *La Mésopotamie*, Paris: Les Belles Lettres.

2002b, "Dilmun et Magan, le peuplement, l'organisation politique, la question des Amorrites et la place de l'écriture: point de vue de l'assyriologue," in S. Cleuziou, M. Tosi, and J. Zarins (eds.), *Essays on the Late Prehistory of the Arabian Peninsula*, Rome: Istituto Italiano per l'Africa e l'Oriente, pp. 337–382.

GLAZIER, D. and PEACOCK, D. 2007, "Historical background and previous investigations," in D. Peacock and L. Blue (eds.), *The Ancient Red Sea Port of Adulis, Eritrea*, Oxford: Oxbow Books, pp. 7–17.

GLEBA, M. and MANNERING, U. (eds.), 2012, *Textiles and Textile Production in Europe from Prehistory to AD 500*, Oxford: Oxbow Books.

GLOVER, I. C., 1986, *Archaeology in Eastern Timor, 1966–67* (Terra Australis, 11), Canberra: Australian National University, Research School of Pacific Studies.

1989, *Early Trade between India and Southeast Asia: A Link in the Development of a World Trade System*, University of Hull, Centre for Southeast Asian Studies (Occasional paper no. 16).

1996, "The archaeological evidence for early trade between South and Southeast Asia," in J. Reade (ed.), *The Indian Ocean in Antiquity*, London and New York: Kegan Paul, pp. 365–402.

2000, "The Southern Silk Road: archaeological evidence of early trade between India and Southeast Asia," in V. Elisseeff (ed.), *The Silk Roads: Highways of Culture and Commerce*, published in association with UNESCO, New York and Oxford: Berghahn Books, pp. 93–121.

2002, "West Asian Sassanian-Islamic ceramics in the Indian Ocean, South, Southeast and East Asia," *Man and Environment*, 27 (1), pp. 165–177.

GLOVER, I. C. and BELLINA, B., 2001, "Alkaline etched beads east of India in the Late Prehistoric and Early Historic periods," *Bulletin de l'Ecole française d'Extrême-Orient*, 88, pp. 191–215.

2003, "Etched alkaline beads in Southeast Asia," in I. Glover, H. Hughes-Brock, and J. Henderson (eds.), *Ornaments from the Past: Bead Studies after Beck*, London and Bangkok: Bead Study Trust, pp. 92–107.

GLOVER, I. C. and HENDERSON, J., 1995, "Early glass in South and South East Asia and China," R. Scott and J. Guy (eds.), *South East Asia and China: Art, Interaction and Commerce*, London: School of Oriental and African Studies , pp. 141–170.

GLOVER, I. C. and HIGHAM, C. F. W., 1996, "New evidence for early rice cultivation in South, Southeast and East Asia," in D. R. Harris (ed.), *The Origins and Spread of Agriculture and Pastoralism in Eurasia*, London: UCL Press, pp. 413–441.

GODARD, A. and TABEAU, M., 2002, *Les climats: mécanismes et répartition*, Paris: Armand Colin (1st edn. 1993).

GOEDICKE, H., 1977, "An Old Kingdom weight," *Journal of the Society for the Study of Egyptian Antiquities*, 7 (3), pp. 6–8.

GOGTE, V. D., 2002, "Ancient maritime trade in the Indian Ocean: evaluation by scientific studies of pottery," *Man and Environment*, 27 (1), pp. 57–66.

GOLDEN, P. B., 2005, "The Turks: a historical overview," in D. J. Roxburgh (ed.), *Turks: A Journey of a Thousand Years, 600–1600*, London: Royal Academy of Arts, pp. 18–31.

GOLDEN, J., 2002, "The origins of the metals trade in the eastern Mediterranean: social organization of production in the early copper industries," in E. C. M. van den Brink and T. E. Levy (eds.), *Egypt and the Levant. Interrelations from the 4th through the Early 3rd Millennium BCE*, London and New York: Leicester University Press, pp. 225–238.

GOLDSTONE, J. A., 2008, *Why Europe? The Rise of the West in World History 1500–1850*, New York: McGraw-Hill Education.

GOLDWASSER, O., 2006, "Canaanites reading hieroglyphs: Horus is Hathor? The invention of the alphabet in Sinai," *Egypt and the Levant: International Journal for Egyptian Archaeology and Related Disciplines*, 16, pp. 121–160.

GOLSON, Y., 1991, "Bulmer phase II: early agriculture in the New Guinea highlands," in A. Pawley (ed.), *Man and a Half*, Auckland: Polynesian Society, pp. 484–491.

GOMMERY, D., RAMANIVOSOA, B., FAURE, M., GUERIN, C., KERLOC'H, P., SENEGAS, F., and RANDRIANANTENAINA, H., 2011, "Les plus anciennes traces d'activités anthropiques de Madagascar sur des ossements d'hippopotames subfossiles d'Anjohibe (Province de Mahajanga)," *Comptes Rendus Palevol*, 10 (4), pp. 271–278.

GONZÁLEZ PONCE, F. J., 2008, *Periplógrafos griegos I: Época arcaica y clásica 1. Periplo de Hanòn y autores de los siglos VI y V a.C.*, Zaragoza: Prensas Universitarias de Zaragoza.

GOOD, I., 1995, "On the question of silk in pre-Han Eurasia," *Antiquity*, 69 (266), pp. 559–568.

1998, "Bronze age cloth and clothing of the Tarim Basin: the Chärchän evidence," in V. H. Mair (ed.), *The Bronze Age and Early Iron Age Peoples of Eastern Central Asia*, vol. II, Washington, DC: Institute for the Study of Man; Philadelphia: University of Pennsylvania Museum Publications, pp. 656–668.

2006, "Textiles as a medium of exchange in third millennium BCE: Western Asia," in V. H. Mair (ed.), *Contact and Exchange in the Ancient World*, Honolulu: Hawaii University Press, pp. 191–214.

forthcoming, *Cloth and Carpet in Early Inner Asia*, Leiden: Brill.

GOOD, I., KENOYER, J. M., and MEADOW, R. H., 2009, "New evidence for early silk in the Indus civilization," *Archaeometry*, 51 (3), pp. 457–466.

GOODMAN, S. M., 2013, "The history of mammal introductions to islands in the western Indian ocean," paper presented at the Sealinks Conference "Proto-Globalisation in the Indian Ocean World: Multidisciplinary Perspectives on Early Globalisation," Oxford, Jesus College, November 7–10, 2013.

GOODY, J., 1996, *The East in the West*, Cambridge University Press.

2001, *The Power of the Written Tradition*, Washington, DC, and London: Smithsonian Institution Press.

2007, *The Theft of History*, Cambridge University Press.

GOPHNA, R. and BRINK, E. C. M. VAN DEN, 2002, "Core–periphery interaction between the pristine Egyptian Nagada IIIb state, Late Early Bronze Age I Canaan, and Terminal A-Group Lower Nubia: more data," in E. C. M. van den Brink and T. E. Levy (eds.), *Egypt and the Levant: Interrelations from the 4th through the Early 3rd Millennium BCE*, London and New York: Leicester University Press, pp. 280–285.

GORIS, P., 1960a and b, "The religious character of the village community" and "Holidays and holy days," in J. L. Swellengrebel *et al.* (eds.), *Bali: Studies in Life, Thought and Ritual*, The Hague and Bandung: W. Van Hoeve, pp. 77–100 and 113–129 (1st edn. 1933).

GÖRSDORF, J., PARZINGER, H., and NAGLER, A., 2004, "14C dating of the Siberian steppe zone from Bronze Age to Scythian time," in E. Scott, M. Alekseev, and A. Yu. Zaitseva (eds.), *Impact of the Environment on Human Migration in Eurasia*, Chelyabinsk Gosudarstvenyi Universitet, pp. 83–89.

GÖRSDORF, J. and VOGT, B., 2001, "Excavations at Ma'layba and Sabir, Republic of Yemen: radiocarbon datings in the period 1900 to 800 cal BC," *Radiocarbon*, 43 (3), pp. 1353–1361.

GOTO, T., 2006, "Asvín- and Nāsatya- in the RgVeda and their prehistoric background," in T. Osada (ed.), *Proceedings of the Pre-Symposium of RIHN and 7th ESCA Harvard–Kyoto Roundtable*, Kyoto: Research Institute for Humanity and Nature (RIHN), pp. 253–283.

GOUROU, P., 1984, *Riz et civilisation*, Paris: Fayard.

GOYON, J.-C., ARCHIER, P., COEN, S., and VIEILLECAZES, V., 1999, "Contribution de la chimie analytique à l'étude de vestiges de la XIIe ou XIIIe dynastie égyptienne," *Studien zur Altägyptischen Kultur*, 27, pp. 107–121.

GRAFF, G., 2002, "Approche de l'iconographie prédynastique. Les peintures sur vases Nagada I-Nagada II: problèmes de lecture et essais d'interprétation," Ph.D. dissertation, Université de Paris IV-Sorbonne.

GRAINGER, J., 1991, *Hellenistic Phoenicia*, Oxford: Clarendon Press.

    1999, "Prices in Hellenistic Babylonia," *Journal of the Economic and Social History of the Orient*, 42 (3), pp. 303–323.

GRANDIDIER, A., CHARLES-ROUX, J. DELHORBE, CL., FROIDEVAUX, H., and GRANDIDIER, G., 1903, 1904, 1905, 1906, 1907, 1910, 1913, *Collection des ouvrages anciens concernant Madagascar (COACM)*, vol. I, *1500–1613*; vol. II, *1613–1640*; vol. III, *1640–1716*; vol. IV, *1701–1720*; vol. V, *1718–1800*; vol. VI, supplement *1598–1741*; vol. VII, *1604–1658*. Paris: Comité de Madagascar et Union Coloniale.

GRANDIDIER, A. and GRANDIDIER, G., 1928, *Histoire physique, naturelle and politique de Madagascar*, vol. IV: *Ethnographie de Madagascar*, book 4: *Agriculture, forêts, élevage, industrie et commerce, travaux publics et moyens de transport, éducation, médecine*, Paris: Hachette, Société d'Editions Géographiques, Maritimes et Coloniales.

GRANDIDIER, G., 1905, "Les animaux disparus de Madagascar," *Revue de Madagascar*, August, pp. 111–128.

GRAS, M., ROUILLARD, P., and TEIXIDOR, J., 1995, *L'univers phénicien*, 2nd edn., Paris: Hachette.

GRASLIN, L. and MAUCOURANT, J., 2005, "Le port de commerce: un concept en débat," *Topoi. Orient-Occident*, pp. 216–257.

GRATALOUP, C., 2003, "Géohistoire," in J. Lévy and M. Lussault (eds.), *Dictionnaire de la géographie et de l'espace des sociétés*, Paris: Belin, pp. 401–402.

GRATUZE, B. and DUSSUBIEUX, L., 2005, "Éléments de parure archéologiques en verre," *Dossiers d'Archéologie*, 302, pp. 68–73.

GREBENART, D., 1988, *Les premiers métallurgistes en Afrique occidentale*, Paris: Éditions Errance.

GREEN, M., 2013, "From enzootics to pandemics: African and Asian origins of disease before 1000 CE," paper presented at the Sealinks Conference "Proto-Globalisation in the Indian

Ocean World: Multidisciplinary Perspectives on Early Globalisation," Oxford, Jesus College, November 7–10, 2013.

GREENFIELD, H. J., 2005, "A reconsideration of the secondary products revolution: 20 years of research in the central Balkans," in J. Mulville and A. Outram (eds.), *The Zooarchaeology of Milk and Fats (Proceedings of the 9th ICAZ Conference, Durham 2002)*, Oxford: Oxbow Books, pp. 14–31.

GRENET, F., 1996, "Les marchands sogdiens dans les mers du Sud à l'époque préislamique," *Cahiers d'Asie Centrale*, 1–2, pp. 65–83.

2005, "Kidarites," *Encyclopædia Iranica* online.

GRIMAL, N. and MENU, B. (eds.), 1998, *Le commerce en Égypte ancienne*, Cairo: Institut Français d'Archéologie Orientale.

GRIMAL, P., 1993, *L'empire romain*, Paris: Le Livre de Poche.

GROTTANELLI, V. L., 1947, "Asiatic influences on Somali culture," *Ethnos*, 4, pp. 153–181.

1955, *Pescatori dell'Oceano Indiano: saggio etnologico preliminare sui Bagiuni, Bagiuni, Bantu costieri dell'Oltregiuba*, Rome: Edizioni Cremonese.

GRUZINSKI, S., 1999, *La pensée métisse*, Paris: Éditions Fayard.

2004, *Les quatre parties du monde: histoire d'une mondialisation*, Paris: Éditions de la Martinière.

GUEUNIER, N., 1988, "Dialectologie et lexicostatistique: cas du dialecte malgache de Mayotte (Comores)," *Études Océan Indien*, 9, pp. 143–167.

GUILLOT, C., 1998, "La nature du site de Lobu Tua à Barus, Sumatra," in C. Guillot, D. Lombard, and R. Ptak (eds.), *From the Mediterranean to the China Sea: Miscellaneous Notes*, Wiesbaden: Harrassowitz, pp. 113–130.

2004, "La Perse et le Monde malais: échanges commerciaux et intellectuels," *Archipel*, 68, pp. 159–192.

GUILLOT, C., D. LOMBARD, and PTAK, R. (eds.), 1998, *From the Mediterranean to the China Sea: Miscellaneous Notes*, Wiesbaden: Harrassowitz.

GUNN, B. F., BAUDOUIN, L., and OLSEN, K. M., 2011, "Independent origins of cultivated coconut (*Cocos nucifera* L.) in the Old World tropics," *PLoS ONE* 6(6): e21143, doi:10.1371/journal.pone.0021143.

GUPTA, A. K., DAS, M., and ANDERSON, D. M., 2005, "Solar influence on the Indian summer monsoon during the Holocene," *Geophysical Research Letters*, 32, L17703, doi:10.1029/2005GL022685.

GUPTA, S., 1998, "Nevasa: a type-site for the study of Indo-Roman trade in western India," *South Asian Studies*, 14, pp. 87–102.

2002, "The archaeo-historical idea of the Indian Ocean," *Man and Environment*, 27 (1), pp. 1–24.

2005, "A historiographical survey of studies on Indo-Roman sea trade and Indian Ocean trade," *Indian Historical Review*, 32, pp. 140–164.

GUPTA, S., WILLIAMS, D., and PEACOCK, D., 2001, "Dressel 2–4 amphorae and Roman trade with India: The evidence from Nevasa," *South Asian Studies*, 17, pp. 7–18.

GUPTA, S. P., GUPTA, S., GARGE, T., PANDE, R., GEETALI, A., and GUPTA, S., 2004, "On the fast track of the Periplus: excavations at Kamrej – 2003," *Journal of Indian Ocean Archaeology*, 1, pp. 9–33.

GUTHERZ, X., and JOUSSAUME, R., 2000, "Le Néolithique de la Corne de l'Afrique," in J. Guilaine (ed.), *Premiers paysans du monde: naissances des agricultures*, Paris: Éditions Errance, pp. 293–320.

GUTHRIE, M., 1967–1972, *Comparative Bantu*, 4 vols., Farnborough: Gregg International.

GUTMAN, P. and HUDSON, B., 2004, "The archaeology of Burma (Myanmar) from the Neolithic to Pagan," in I. Glover and P. Bellwood (eds.), *Southeast Asia: From Prehistory to History*, Abingdon and New York: Routledge/Curzon, pp. 149–176.

GUY, J., 2011, "Tamil merchants and the Hindu Buddhist diaspora in early Southeast Asia," in P.-Y. Manguin, A. Mani, and G. Wade (eds.), *Early Interactions between South and Southeast Asia: Reflections on Cross-Cultural Exchange*, Singapore and New Delhi: ISEA Publishing, Manohar Publishers, pp. 243–262.

HAALAND, R., 1999, "The puzzle of the late emergence of domesticated sorghum in the Nile valley," in C. Gosden and J. Hather (eds.), *The Prehistory of Food: Appetites for Change*, London and New York: Routledge, pp. 397–418.

2013, "Indian impacts on Meroitic civilization: the movement of craftspeople and symbolic styles," paper presented at the Sealinks Conference "Proto-Globalisation in the Indian Ocean World: Multidisciplinary Perspectives on Early Globalisation," Oxford, Jesus College, November 7–10.

HAARER, P., 2001, "Problematising the transition from bronze to iron," in A. J. Shortland (ed.), *The Social Context of Technological Change*, Oxford: Oxbow Books, pp. 255–273.

HABU, J., 2004, *Ancient Jomon of Japan*, Cambridge University Press.

HACKL, J. and PIRNGRUBER, R., 2015, "Prices and related data from northern Babylonia in the Late Achaemenid and Early Hellenistic periods, c. 480–300 BC," in B. van Leeuwen, J. L. van Zanden, and R. van der Spek (eds.), *A History of Market Performance: From Ancient Babylonia to the Modern World*, New York: Routledge, pp. 107–127.

HAERINCK, E., 1998, "International contacts in the southern Persian Gulf in the late 1st century BC/1st century AD: numismatic evidence from Ed-Dur (Emirate of Umm al-Qaiwain, U. A. E.)," *Iranica Antiqua*, 33, pp. 273–302.

HAFFORD, W. B., 2005, "Mesopotamian mensuration balance pan weights from Nippur," *Journal of the Economic and Social History of the Orient*, 48 (3), pp. 345–387.

HAGENS, G., 1999, "An ultra-low chronology for Iron Age Palestine," *Antiquity*, 73 (280), pp. 431–439.

HALL, K. R., 1992, "Economic history of early Southeast Asia," in N. Tarling (ed.), *The Cambridge History of Southeast Asia*, vol. I, part. 1: *From Early Times to c. 1500*, Cambridge University Press, pp. 183–275.

HALL, T. D., 2006, "[Re]periphalization, [re]incorporation, frontiers and non-state societies. Continuities and discontinuities in globalizing processes," in B. K. Gills and W. R. Thompson (eds.), *Globalization and Global History*, London: Routledge, pp. 96–113.

HALLO, W., 2004, "Bookkeeping in the 21st century BCE," in M. Hudson and C. Wunsch (eds.), *Creating Economic Order: Record-Keeping, Standardization and the Development of Accounting in the Ancient Near East*, Bethesda, MD: CDL Press, pp. 89–106.

HAMIDULLAH, M., 1974, "Les escales arabes au début de l'Islam," in J. Pirenne (ed.), *Les grandes escales*, part I: *Antiquité et Moyen-Âge (10e colloque d'Histoire Maritime)*, Brussels: Editions de la Librairie Encyclopédique, pp. 191–206.

HAMMER, C. U., KURAT, G., HOPPE, P., GRUM, W., and CLAUSEN, H. B., 2003, "Thera eruption date 1645 BC confirmed by new ice core data?," in M. Bietak (ed.), *The Synchronisation of Civilisations in the Eastern Mediterranean in the Second Millennium BC II*, *Proceedings of the SCIEM 2000 Euro Conference, Haindorf, May 2–7, 2001*, Vienna: Verlag der Österreichischen Akademie der Wissenschaften, pp. 87–94.

HANDLEY, F., 2011, "The textiles: a preliminary report," in L. Blue and D. Peacock (eds.), *Myos Hormos – Quseir al-Qadim: Roman and Islamic Ports on the Red Sea*, vol. II: *Finds from the Excavations 1999–2003* (BAR International Series 2286), Oxford: Archaeopress, pp. 321–333.

HANKS, B. K., 2014, "The Post-Neolithic of Eastern Europe," in C. Renfrew and P. Bahn (eds.), *The Cambridge World Prehistory*, vol. III: *West and Central Asia and Europe*, Cambridge University Press, pp. 1937–1957.

HANSEN, M. H., 2000a, "Introduction: the concepts of city-state and city-state culture," in M. H. Hansen (ed.), *A Comparative Study of Thirty City-State Cultures*, Copenhagen: Det Kongelige Danske Videnskabernes Selskab, pp. 11–34.

2000b, "The Hellenic polis," in M. H. Hansen (ed.), *A Comparative Study of Thirty City-State Cultures*, Copenhagen: Det Kongelige Danske Videnskabernes Selskab, pp. 141–188.

2000c, "Conclusion: the impact of city-state cultures on world history," in M. H. Hansen (ed.), *A Comparative Study of Thirty City-State Cultures*, Copenhagen: Det Kongelige Danske Videnskabernes Selskab, pp. 597–623.

2000d, "Introduction," in M. H. Hansen (ed.), *A Comparative Study of Six City-State Cultures*, Copenhagen: Det Kongelige Danske Videnskabernes Selskab, pp. 7–21.

HANSEN, V., 2000, *The Open Empire: A History of China through 1600*, New York: W. W. Norton.

HARDING, A. F., 1993, "Europe and the Mediterranean in the Bronze Age," in C. Scarre and F. Healy (eds.), *Trade and Exchange in Prehistoric Europe*, Oxford: Oxbow Books, pp. 153–160.

1994, "Reformation in barbarian Europe, 1300–600 BC," in B. Cunliffe (ed.), *The Oxford Illustrated History of Prehistoric Europe*, Oxford University Press, pp. 304–335.

2000, *European Societies in the Bronze Age*, Cambridge University Press.

2006, "Facts and fantasies from the Bronze Age," *Antiquity*, 80 (308), pp. 463–465.

HARLAN, J. R., 1998, *The Living Fields: Our Agricultural Heritage*, Cambridge University Press (1st edn. 1995).

HARMATTA, J., 1996, "The emergence of the Indo-Iranians: the Indo-Iranian languages," in A. H. Dani and V. M. Masson (eds.), *History of Civilizations of Central Asia*, vol. 1, New Delhi: Motilal Banarsidass, pp. 357–378.

HARRISON, R. and MEDEROS MARTIN, A., 2000, "Patronage and clientship: a model for the Atlantic Final Bronze Age in the Iberian Peninsula," in C. F. E. Pare (ed.), *Metals Make the World Go Round: The Supply and Circulation of Metals in Bronze Age Europe. Proceedings of a Conference Held at the University of Birmingham in June 1997*, Oxford: Oxbow Books, pp. 133–148.

HARROWER, M., 2008a, "Hydrology, ideology and the origins of irrigation in ancient southwest Arabia," *Current Anthropology*, 49 (3), pp. 497–510.

2008b, "Mapping and dating incipient irrigation in Wadi Sana, Hadramawt Yemen," *Proceedings of the Seminar for Arabian Studies*, 38, pp. 187–202.

HARTUNG, U., 2002, "Imported jars from Cemetery U at Abydos and the relations between Egypt and Canaan in predynastic times," in E. C. M. van den Brink and T. E. Levy (eds.), *Egypt and the Levant: Interrelations from the 4th through the Early 3rd Millennium BCE*, London and New York: Leicester University Press, pp. 437–449.

HASEL, M. G., 2004, "Recent developments in Near Eastern chronology and radiocarbon dating," *Origins*, 56, pp. 6–31.

HATKE, G., 2013, *Aksum and Nubia: Warfare, Commerce, and Political Fictions in Ancient Northeast Africa*, New York University Press.

HAUDRICOURT, A., 1962, "Domestication des animaux, culture des plantes et traitement d'autrui," *L'Homme*, 2, pp. 40–50.

HAUPTMANN, M., 2003, "Developments in copper metallurgy during the fourth and third millennia BC at Feinan, Jordan," in P. Craddock and J. Lang (eds.), *Mining and Metal Production through the Ages*, London: The British Museum Press, pp. 90–100.

HAW, G., 2017, "Cinnamon, cassia and ancient trade," *Journal of Ancient History and Archaeology*, 4 (1), DOI: http://dx.doi.org/10.14795/j.v4i1.211

HE, Z., ZHAI, W., WEN, H., TANG, T., WANG, Y., LU, X., GREENBERG, A., HUDSON, R., WU, C., and SHI, S., 2011, "Two evolutionary histories in the genome of rice: the roles of domestication genes," *PLoS Genetics*, 7 (6).

HE JEJIUN, 1999, "Excavations at Chengtoushan in Li County, Hunan Province, China," *Bulletin of the Indo-Pacific Prehistory Association*, 18 (The Melaka Papers 2), pp. 101–103.

HEADLEY, R. K. Jr., 1976, "Some sources of Chamic vocabulary," in P. N. Jenner, L. C. Thompson, and S. Starosta (eds.), *Austroasiatic Studies*, Honolulu: University Press of Hawaii, pp. 453–476.

HÉBERT, J.-C., 1961, "Les mots 'mer' et 'poisson' en malgache," *Bulletin de Madagascar*, 185, pp. 899–916.

1965a and b, "The cosmologie malgache," and "L'énumération des points cardinaux et l'importance du Nord-Est," *Annales de l'Université de Madagascar, Taloha*, 1, pp. 84–149 and 150–195.

HECK, G. W., 1999, "Gold mining in Arabia and the rise of the Islamic state," *Journal of the Economic and Social History of the Orient*, 42 (3), pp. 364–393.

HEIMPEL, W., 1997, "Disposition of households of officials in Ur III and Mari," *Acta Sumerologica*, 19, pp. 63–82.

HEINE-GELDERN, R., 1947, "The drum named Makalamau," *India Antiqua*, Leiden, pp. 167–179.

HELCK, H., and OPPENHEIM, L., 1972, *Lexikon der Ägyptologie*, Wiesbaden: Harassowitz (reissued in 6 vols. 1986).

HELMS, M. W., 1988, *Ulysses' Sail: An Ethnographic Odyssey of Power, Knowledge, and Geographical Distance*, Princeton University Press.

1993, *Craft and the Kingly Ideal: Art, Trade and Power*, Austin: University of Texas Press.

HELTZER, M., 1979, "A recently discovered Phoenician inscription and the problem of the guilds of metal-casters," *Atti del Congresso Internazionale di Studi fenici e punici*, Rome: Conziglio Nazionale della Ricerche, pp. 119–123.

1996, "The symbiosis of public and private sectors in Ugarit, Phoenician, and Palestine," in M. Hudson and B. A. Levine (eds.), *Privatization in the Ancient Near East and Classical World*, Cambridge, MA: Peabody Museum of Archaeology and Ethnology, Harvard University, pp. 171–196.

1999, "The economy of Ugarit," in W. G. E. Watson and N. Wyatt (eds.), *Handbook of Ugaritic Studies* (Handbuch der Orientalistik, vol. 39), Leiden: Brill, pp. 423–454.

HELWING, B., 2013, "Some thoughts on the mode of culture change in the fourth-millennium BC," in C. A. Petrie (ed.), *Ancient Iran and Its Neighbours: Local Developments and Long-Range Interactions in the Fourth Millennium BC*, Oxford: Oxbow Books, pp. 75–91.

HEMPHILL, B. E. and MALLORY, J. P. 2004, "Horse-mounted invaders from the Russo-Kazakh steppe or agricultural colonists from western Central Asia? A craniometric investigation of the Bronze Age settlement of Xinjiang," *American Journal of Physical Anthropology*, 124 (3), pp. 199–222.

HENDERSON, J., 2000, *The Science and Archaeology of Materials: An Investigation of Inorganic Materials*, London and New York: Routledge.

HENDRICKX, S. and BAVAY, L., 2002, "The relative chronological position of Egyptian Predynastic and Early Dynastic tombs with objects imported from the Near East and the nature of interregional contacts," in E. C. M. van den Brink and T. E. Levy (eds.), *Egypt and the Levant: Interrelations from the 4th through the Early 3rd Millennium BCE*, London and New York: Leicester University Press, pp. 58–81.

HENNING, W. B., 1977, *Selected Papers*, 2 vols., Acta Iranica, 14–15, Leiden: Brill.

HERBERT, E. W., 1984, *Red Gold of Africa: Copper in Precolonial History and Culture*, Madison and London: University of Wisconsin Press.

HERODOTUS, 1964, *L'enquête*, trans. A. Barguet, in A. Barguet and D. Roussel (eds.), Hérodote–Thucydide, *Oeuvres complètes*, Paris: La Pléiade, pp. 3–654.

HERRENSCHMIDT, C., 2004, "De la monnaie frappée et du mythe d'Artémis," *Techniques et culture*, 43–44, "Mythes. L'origine des manières de faire," online April 15, 2007: http://tc.revues.org/document1222.html

HEUSCH, L. de, 1997, "The symbolic mechanisms of sacred kingship: rediscovering Frazer," *Journal of the Royal Anthropological Institute*, 3 (2), pp. 213–232.

HIEBERT, F. T., 1994, *Origins of the Bronze Age Oasis Civilization in Central Asia* (American School of Prehistoric Research Bulletin 42), Cambridge, MA: Peabody Museum of Archaeology and Ethnology, Harvard University.

2000, "Bronze Age Central Eurasian cultures in their steppe and desert environments," in G. Bawden and R. Reycraft (eds.), *Environmental Disaster and the Archaeology of Human Response*, Albuquerque: University of New Mexico, pp. 51–62.

2001, "The recently discovered Bronze Age inscription (2300 BC) from Anau, Central Asia," paper presented at the Third Harvard Round Table on the Ethnogenesis of South and Central Asia, May 12–14 (www.fas.harvard.edu/~sanskritRoundTableSchedule.html).

2002, "Bronze Age interaction between the Eurasian Steppe and Central Asia," in K. Boyle, C. Renfrew, and M. Levine (eds.), *Ancient Interactions: East and West in Eurasia*, Cambridge: McDonald Institute for Archaeological Research, pp. 237–248.

HIGHAM, C., 1996a, *The Bronze Age of Southeast Asia*, Cambridge University Press.

1996b, "Archaeology and linguistics in Southeast Asia: implications of the Austric Hypothesis," *Bulletin of the Indo-Pacific Prehistory Association*, 14 (Chang Mai Papers, vol. 1), pp. 110–118.

2001, *The Civilization of Angkor*, Berkeley: University of California Press.

2002, *Early Cultures of Mainland Southeast Asia*, Bangkok: River Books.

2003, "Languages and farming dispersals: Austroasiatic languages and rice cultivation," in P. Bellwood and C. Renfrew (eds.), *Examining the Language/Farming Dispersal Hypothesis*, Cambridge: McDonald Institute for Archaeological Research, pp. 223–232.

2004, "Mainland Southeast Asia from the Neolithic to the Iron Age," in I. Glover and P. Bellwood (eds.), *Southeast Asia: From Prehistory to History*, Abingdon and New York: Routledge/Curzon, pp. 41–67.

2009a, b, "East Asian agriculture and its impact" and "Complex societies of East and Southeast Asia," in C. Scarre (ed.), *The Human Past*, 2nd edn., London: Thames and Hudson, pp. 234–263 and 552–594.

2010, "The Iron Age of Thailand: trends to complexity," in B. Bellina, E. A. Bacus, T. O. Pryce, and J. Wisseman Christie (eds.), *50 Years of Archaeology in Southeast Asia, Essays in Honour of Ian Glover*, Bangkok: River Books, pp. 128–139.

2014, *Early Mainland Southeast Asia. From First Humans to Angkor*, Bangkok: River Books.

HIGHAM, C., CAMERON, J., CHANG, N., CASTILLO, C., HALCROW, S., O'REILLY, D., PETCHEY, F., and SHEWAN, L., 2014, "The excavation of Non Ban Jak, northeast Thailand – a report on the first three seasons," *Journal of Indo-Pacific Archaeology*, 34, pp. 1–41.

HIGHAM, C. and HIGHAM, T., 2009, "A new chronological framework for prehistoric Southeast Asia, based on a Bayesian model from Ban Non Wat," *Antiquity*, 82, pp. 1–20.

HIGHAM, C., HIGHAM, T., CIARLA, R., KIJNGAM, A., and RISPOLI, F., 2011, "The origins of the Bronze Age of Southeast Asia," *Journal of World Prehistory*, DOI 10.1007/s10963-011-9054-6

HIGHAM, C. F. W., HIGHAM, T. F. G., and KIJNGAM, A., 2011, "Cutting a Gordian knot: the Bronze Age of Southeast Asia: origins, timing and impact," *Antiquity*, 85 (328), pp. 583–598.

HIGHAM, C. and LU, T. L.-D., 1998, "The origins and dispersals of rice cultivation," *Antiquity*, 72 (278), pp. 867–877.

HIGHAM, C. and THOSARAT, R., 1998, *The Excavation of Nong Nor, a Prehistoric Site in Central Thailand* (University of Otago Studies in Prehistoric Anthropology 18), Oxford: Oxbow Books.

HILL, J. E., 2003, *The Western Regions according to the* Hou Hanshu. *The Xiyu juan, 'Chapter on the Western Regions', from Hou Hanshu 88*, trans. John E. Hill, http://depts.washington.edu/silkroad/texts/hhshu/hou_han_shu.html

2004, The peoples of the west: from the Weilue from Yu Huan, http://depts.washington.edu/silkroad/texts/weilue/weilue.html

HILTON, J., 1992, "Azania. Some etymological considerations," *Acta Classica*, 35, pp. 151–159.

HINGSTON, M., GOODMAN, S. M., GANZHORN, J. U., and SOMMER, S., 2005, "Reconstruction of the colonization of southern Madagascar by introduced *Rattus rattus*," *Journal of Biogeography*, 32, pp. 1549–1559.

HIRSCHFELD, Y., 2004, "A climatic change in the Early Byzantine period? Some archaeological evidence,"*Palestine Exploration Quarterly*, 136 (2), pp. 133–149.

HIRST, K., 2011, "Domestication and dispersal of coconuts," http://archaeology.about.com/od/domestications/ss/Coconut-Domestication_3.htm

HIRTH, F. and ROCKHILL, W. W., 1911, *Chau-Ju-Kua: His Work on the Chinese and Arab Trade in the Twelfth and Thirteenth Centuries, Entitled Chu-fan chi*, St. Petersburg: Printing Office of the Imperial Academy of Sciences.

HJELMQVIST, H., 1979, "Some economic plants and weeds from the Bronze Age of Cyprus," *Studies in Mediterranean Archeology*, 45 (5), pp. 110–113.

HOBSON, J. M., 2004, *The Eastern Origins of Western Civilisation*, Cambridge University Press.

HOCART, A. M., 1952, *The Life-Giving Myth and Other Essays*, New York: Grove Press.

1954, *Social Origins*, London: Watts and Co.

1970, *Kings and Councillors: An Essay in the Comparative Anatomy of Human Society*, University of Chicago Press (1st edn. 1936).

HODGSON, M. G. S., 1954, "Hemispheric interregional history as an approach to world history," *Unesco Journal of World History/Cahiers d'Histoire Mondiale*, 1 (3), pp. 715–723.

1963, "The interrelations of societies in history," *Comparative Studies in Society and History*, 5, pp. 227–250.

HOGENDORN, J. and JOHNSON, M., 1986, *The Shell Money of the Slave Trade*, Cambridge University Press.

HÖLBL, G., 2001, *A History of the Ptolemaic Empire*, London and New York: Routledge.

HOLL, A. F. C., 1993. "Late Neolithic cultural landscape in southeastern Mauritania: an essay in spatiometrics," in A. F. C. Holl and T. E. Levy (eds.), *Spatial Boundaries and Social Dynamics*, Ann Arbor, MI: International Monographs in Prehistory, pp. 95–133.

2009, "Early West African metallurgies: new data and old orthodoxy," *Journal of World Prehistory*, 22, pp. 415–438.

HONEYCHURCH, W. and AMARTUVSHIN, C., 2006, "States on horseback: the rise of Inner Asian confederations and empires," in M. T. Stark (ed.), *Archaeology of Asia*, Malden, MA, and Oxford: Blackwell, pp. 255–278.

HONG, Y. T., HONG, B., LIN, Q. H., ZHU, Y. X., SHIBATA, Y., HIROTA, M., UCHIDA, M., LENG, X. T., JIANG, H. B., XU, H., WANG, H., and YI, L., 2003, "Correlation between Indian Ocean summer monsoon and North Atlantic climate during the Holocene," *Earth and Planetary Science Letters*, 211 (3–4), pp. 371–380.

HOOGERVOORST, T., 2012, "Southeast Asia in the ancient Indian Ocean World. Combining historical linguistic and archaeological approaches," Ph.D. dissertation, Oxford University.

HOPKINS, K., 2009, "The political economy of the Roman Empire," in I. Morris and W. Scheidel (eds.), *The Dynamics of Ancient Empires: State Power from Assyria to Byzantium*, New York: Oxford University Press, pp. 178–204.

HORNBORG, A. and CRUMLEY, C. (eds.), 2007, *The World System and the Earth System: Global Socioenvironmental Change and Sustainability since the Neolithic*, Walnut Creek, CA: Left Coast Press.

HORNELL, J., 1920, "The origins and ethnological significance of Indian boat designs," *Memoirs of the Asiatic Society of Bengal*, 7, pp. 139–256.

1928, "Indonesian culture in East Africa," *Man*, 28 (1), pp. 1–4.

1934, "Indonesian influence on East African culture," *Journal of the Royal Anthropological Institute*, 64, pp. 305–332.

1946, *Water Transport: Origins and Early Evolution*, Cambridge University Press (reissued 1970).

HORNUNG, E., KRAUSS, R., and WARBURTON, D., 2006, "Chronological table for the Dynastic Period," in E. Hornung, R. Krauss, and D. Warburton (eds.), *Ancient Egyptian Chronology*, Leiden: Brill, pp. 490–495.

HORRIDGE, A., 1982, *The Lashed-Lug Boat of the Eastern Archipelagoes*, London: National Maritime Museum.

1995, "The Austronesian conquest of the sea – upwind," in P. Bellwood, J. Fox, and D. Tryell (eds.), *The Austronesians: Historical and Comparative Perspectives*, Canberra: Australian National University, pp. 143–160.

HORTON, M. C., 1990, "The *Periplus* and East Africa," *Azania*, 25, pp. 95–99.

1993, "Swahili architecture, space and social structure," in M. Parker Pearson and C. Richards (eds.), *Architecture and Order*, London: Routledge, pp. 147–169.

1996, *Shanga: The Archaeology of a Muslim Trading Community on the Coast of East Africa*, London: British Institute in Eastern Africa.

HORTON, M. and MIDDLETON, J., 2000, *The Swahili, the Social Landscape of a Mercantile Society*, Oxford: Blackwell.

HOUYUAN LU *et al.*, 2016, "Earliest tea as evidence for one branch of the Silk Road across the Tibetan Plateau," *Scientific Reports*, doi: 10.1038/srep18955, www.nature.com/scientificreports

HOYLAND, R. G., 2001, *Arabia and the Arabs, from the Bronze Age to the Coming of Islam*, London: Routledge.

HSU, C.-Y., 1999, "The Spring and Autumn Period," in M. Loewe and E. L. Slaughnessy (eds.), *The Cambridge History of Ancient China: From the Origins of Civilization to 221 BC*, Cambridge University Press, pp. 885–966.

HSU, K.-J., 1998, "Did the Xinjiang Indo-Europeans leave their home because of global cooling?," in V. H. Mair (ed.), *The Bronze Age and Early Iron Age Peoples of Eastern Central Asia*, vol. II, Washington, DC: The Institute for the Study of Man; Philadelphia: University of Pennsylvania Museum Publications, pp. 683–696.

HUDSON, B., 2004, "The origins of Bagan," Ph.D. dissertation, Archaeology, University of Sydney, http://setis.library.usyd.edu.au/adt/public_html/adt-NU/public/adt-NU20050721.144907/index.html

HUDSON, M., 1996, "The dynamics of privatization, from the Bronze Age to the present," in M. Hudson and B. A. Levine (eds.), *Privatization in the Ancient Near East and Classical World*, Cambridge, MA: Peabody Museum of Archaeology and Ethnology, pp. 33–72.

2000, "How interest rates were set, 2500 BC – 1000 AD: *máš, tokos* and *fœnus* as metaphors for interest accruals," *Journal of the Economic and Social History of the Orient*, 43 (2), pp. 132–161.

2002, "Reconstructing the origins of interest-bearing debt and the logic of clean slates," in M. Hudson and M. van de Mieroop (eds.), *Debt and Economic Renewal in the Ancient Near East*, Bethesda, MD: CDL Press, pp. 7–58.

2004a and b, "Introduction: the role of accounting in civilization's economic takeoff," and "The development of money-of-account in Sumer's temples," in M. Hudson and C. Wunsch (eds.), *Creating Economic Order: Record-Keeping, Standardization and the Development of Accounting in the Ancient Near East*, Bethesda, MD: CDL Press, pp. 1–22 and 303–329.

2004c, "The archaeology of money: debt versus barter theories of money's origins," in L. R. Wray (ed.), *Credit and State Theories of Money: The Contributions of A. Mitchell Innes*, Cheltenham: Edward Elgar, pp. 99–127.

2005, "A free-entreprise critique of ancient economies," *Journal of the Economic and Social History of the Orient*, 48 (1), pp. 119–122.

HUFFMAN, T. N., 1980, "Ceramics, classification and Iron Age entities," *African Studies*, 39 (2), pp. 123–174.

HUGHES, J. D., 2009, *An Environmental History of the World: Humankind's Changing Role in the Community of Life*, London: Routledge (1st edn. 2001).

HUNG, H.-C. and BELLWOOD, P., 2010, "Movement of raw materials and manufactured goods across the South China Sea after 500 BCE: from Taiwan to Thailand, and back," in B. Bellina, E. A. Bacus, T. O. Pryce, and J. Wisseman Christie (eds.), *50 Years of Archaeology in Southeast Asia, Essays in Honour of Ian Glover*, Bangkok: River Books, pp. 234–245.

HUNG, H.-C., IIZUKA, Y., BELLWOOD, P., NGUYEN, K. D., BELLINA, B., SILAPANTH, P., DIZON, E., SANTIAGO, R., DATAN, I., and MANTON, J. H., 2007, "Ancient jades map 3,000 years of prehistoric exchange in Southeast Asia," *Proceedings of the National Academy of Sciences (USA)*, 104 (50), pp. 19745–19750.

HUNTINGFORD, G. W. B., 1980, *The Periplus of the Erythraean Sea*, London: Hakluyt Society.

HUOT, J.-L., 2004, *Une archéologie des peuples du Proche-Orient*, vol. I: *Des premiers villages aux peuples des cités-états (Xe–IIIe millénaires av. J.-C.)*, vol. II: *Des hommes des Palais aux sujets des Premiers Empires (IIe–Ier millénaire av. J.-C.)*, Paris: Errance.

HURLES, M. E., SYKES, B. C., JOBLING, M. A., and FORSTER, P., 2005, "The dual origin of the Malagasy in island Southeast Asia and East Africa: evidence from maternal and paternal lineages," *The American Society of Human Genetics*, 16, pp. 894–901.

HUYSE, P., 2005, *La Perse antique*, Paris: Éditions Les Belles Lettres.

IBN BATTŪTA, 1958–1994, *Travels of Ibn Battuta, AD 1325–1354*, trans. H. A. R. Gibb, with revisions and notes, from the Arabic text ed. C. Defrémery and B. R. Sanguinetti, vol. I (1958); vol. II (1959); vol. III (1971); vol. IV (trans. C. F. Beckingham, 1994), Cambridge University Press, for the Hakluyt Society.

2002, *The Travels of Ibn Battuta*, ed. T. Mackintosh-Smith, London: Picador.

IBN KHURDADBEH, 1865, *Le livre des routes et des provinces*, ed. C. Barbier de Meynard, *Journal Asiatique*, March–April and May–June, pp. 227–296 and 446–532.

INDRAWOOTH, P., 2004, "The archaeology of the early Buddhist kingdoms of Thailand," in I. Glover and P. Bellwood (eds.), *Southeast Asia: From Prehistory to History*, Abingdon and New York: Routledge/Curzon, pp. 120–146.

INIZAN, M.-L., 1999, "La cornaline de l'Indus et la voie du Golfe au IIIe millénaire," in A. Caubet (ed.), *Cornaline et pierres précieuses: la Méditerranée, de l'Antiquité à l'Islam*, Paris: La Documentation Française, pp. 125–138.

INOUE, H., ÁLVAREZ, A., LAWRENCE, K., ROBERTS, A., ANDERSON, E. N., and CHASE-DUNN, C., 2012, "Polity scale shifts in world-systems since the Bronze Age: a comparative inventory of upsweeps and collapses," *International Journal of Comparative Sociology*, http://cos.sagepub.com/content/53/3/210.full.pdf+html

INSOLL, T., 2003, *The Archaeology of Islam in Sub-Saharan Africa*, Cambridge University Press.

IRWIN, G., 2008, "Pacific seascapes, canoe performance, and a review of Lapita voyaging with regard to theories of migration," *Asian Perspectives*, 47, pp. 12–27.

ISAAKIDOU, V., 2006, "Ploughing with cows: Knossos and the Secondary Products Revolution," in, D. Serjeantson and D. Field (eds.), *Animals in the Neolithic of Britain and Europe*, Oxford: Oxbow Books, pp. 95–112.

JACOBSEN, T., 1987, *The Harps that Once . . . Sumerian Poetry in Translation*, New Haven, CT: Yale University Press.

JACOMY, B., 1990, *Une histoire des techniques*, Paris: Seuil.

JACQ-HERGOUALC'H, M., 2002, *The Malay Peninsula: Crossroads of the Maritime Silkroad (100 BC – AD 1300)*, Leiden: Brill.

JACQ-HERGOUALC'H, M., SRISUCHAT, T., SUPAJANYA, T., and KRISANAPOL, W., 1996, "La région de Nakhon Si Thammarat (Thaïlande péninsulaire) du Vᵉ au XIVᵉ siècle," *Journal Asiatique*, 284 (2), pp. 361–435.

JACQ-HERGOUALC'H, M., SUPAJANYA, T., and KRISANAPOL, W., 1998, "Une étape maritime de la route de la soie: la partie méridionale de l'isthme de Kra au IXᵉ siècle," *Journal Asiatique*, 286 (1), pp. 235–320.

JAHAN, S. H., 2002, "Early maritime trade network of Bengal," *Man and Environment*, 27 (1), pp. 127–138.

JAIN, V. K., 2001, "Trading community and merchant corporations," in R. Chakravarti (ed.), *Trade in Early India*, Oxford University Press, pp. 344–369 (first published 1989 in *Trade and Traders in Western India 1000–1300*, Delhi, pp. 209–232).

JAMES, P., THORPE, I. J., KOKKINOW, N., MORKOT, R., and FRANKISH, J., 1993, *Centuries of Darkness: A Challenge to the Conventional Chronology of Old World Archaeology*, preface by C. Renfrew, Brunswick, NJ: Rutgers University Press.

JANIK, L., 2002, "Wandering weed: the journey of buckwheat (*Fagopyrum* sp.) as an indicator of human movement in Eurasia," in K. Boyle, C. Renfrew, and M. Levine (eds.), *Ancient Interactions: East and West in Eurasia*, Cambridge: McDonald Institute for Archaeological Research, pp. 299–307.

JANSSEN, J. J., 1975, *Commodity Prices for the Ramessid Period*, Leiden: Brill.

    1994, "Debts and credit in the New Kingdom," *Journal of Egyptian Archaeology*, 80, pp. 129–136.

JANVIER, Y., 1975a, "La géographie gréco-romaine a-t-elle connu Madagascar?," *Omaly sy Anio (Hier et Aujourd'hui)*, 1–2, pp. 11–41.

    1975b, "Histoire ancienne et océan Indien dans les perspectives malgaches," *Omaly sy Anio (Hier et Aujourd'hui)*, 1–2, pp. 211–226.

JARRIGE, J.-F., 1985, "Les relations entre Asie centrale méridionale, le Baluchistan et la vallée de l'Indus à la fin du 3ᵉ et au début du 2ᵉ millénaire," in *L'archéologie de la Bactriane ancienne*, Paris: Editions du CNRS, pp. 105–117.

    (ed.), 1988, *Les cités oubliées de l'Indus – Archéologie du Pakistan*, Paris: Musée National des Arts Asiatiques Guimet.

    1997, "From Nausharo to Pirak: continuity and change in the Kachi/Bolan region from the 3rd to the 2nd millennium BC," in R. and B. Allchin (eds.), *South Asian Archaeology 1995*, New Delhi and Oxford: IBH Publishing, pp. 11–32.

JARRIGE, J.-F., SANTONI, M., LE CHEVALLIER, M., COSTANTINI, L., MEADOW, R., and JARRIGE, C., 1979, *Fouilles de Pirak*, vol. I: *Texte*, Paris: De Boccard.

JARRIGE, J.-F. and TOSI, M., 1981, "The natural resources of Mundigak," in H. Hartel (ed.), *South Asian Archaeology 1979*, Berlin: Reimer, pp. 115–142.

JASIM, S. A., 2006, "Trade centres and commercial routes in the Arabian Gulf: post-Hellenistic discoveries at Dibba, Sharjah, United Arab Emirates," *Arabian Archaeology and Epigraphy*, 17, pp. 214–237.

JAVALOYAS MOLINA, D., 2006, "Contactos culturales en el Mediterráneo a fines del II milenio
  A.C.," *ArqueoWeb – Revista sobre Arqueología en Internet*, 8 (1).

JOANNÈS, F., 1989, "Distribution de médailles par Hammurabi," *Nouvelles Assyriologiques Brèves
  and Utilitaires (NABU)*, 108, pp. 80–81.

  1995, "Private commerce and banking in Achaemenid Babylon," in J. M. Sasson (ed.),
  Civilizations of the Ancient Near East, vol. III, New York: Scribner's, pp. 1475–1485.

  1999, "Structures et opérations commerciales en Babylonie à l'époque néo-babylonienne," in
  J. G. Dercksen (ed.), *Trade and Finance in Ancient Mesopotamia Proceedings of the First Mos
  Symposium, Leiden 1997* (Mos Studies 1). Nederlands Historisch-Archaeologisch Instituut
  te Istanbul, pp. 175–194.

  2000, *La Mésopotamie au premier millénaire avant J.-C.*, Paris: A. Colin.

  (ed.), 2001a, *Dictionnaire de la civilisation mésopotamienne*, Paris: Laffont.

  2001b, "Alphabet," "Chronologie," in F. Joannès (ed.), *Dictionnaire de la
  civilisation mésopotamienne*, Paris: Laffont, pp. 36–37, 184–188.

  2005, "L'argent des dieux babyloniens," *Topoi: Orient–Occident*, 12–13 (1), pp. 35–53.

  2006a, *Les premières civilisations du Proche-Orient*, Paris: Belin.

  2006b, "Compte rendu de M. Hudson and M. Van de Mieroop (éditeurs), *Debt and Economic
  Renewal in the Ancien Near East* (2002)," *Topoi: Orient–Occident*, 14 (2), pp. 405–414.

  2010, "Le plus vieux récit du monde," *L'Histoire*, 356, pp. 44–51.

JOFFE, H., 2000, "Egypt and Syro-Mesopotamia in the 4th millennium: implications of the New
  Chronology," *Current Anthropology*, 41 (1), pp. 113–123.

JONES, A. M., 1959, "Indonesia and Africa: the xylophone as a culture indicator," *Journal of the
  Royal Anthropological Institute*, 89, (2), pp. 155–168.

  1971, *Africa and Indonesia: The Evidence of the Xylophone and Other Musical and Cultural Factors*,
  Leiden: E. J. Brill (1st edn. 1964).

  1972, "Elephantiasis and music," *African Music Society Journal*, 5 (2), pp. 46–49.

JONES, P. D. and MANN, M. E., 2004, "Climate over past millennia," *Reviews of Geophysics*, 42
  (2), pp. 1–42.

JOSHI, J. P. and PARPOLA, A. (eds.), 1987, *Corpus of Indus Seals and Inscriptions*, vol. 1: *Collections
  in India*, Helsinki: Suomalainen Tiedeakatemia.

JOSSELIN DE JONG, J. P. B., de, 1977, "The Malay Archipelago as field of ethnological study," in
  P. E. de Josselin de Jong (ed.), *Structural Anthropology in the Netherlands*, The Hague:
  Springer, pp. 164–182 (1st edn. 1935).

JOUANNÈS, C., 2001, "La 'Sufālīya': un poème du maître-pilote Shihab ad-Dīn Aḥmad
  bin Mājid. Essai de traduction, notes et commentaires. D'après le manuscrit W992
  du fonds de répartition des manuscrits de l'Institut des Études Orientales de l'Académie
  des Sciences de Russie à St Petersbourg. Feuillets 83 r à 96 r," *Études Océan Indien*, 31,
  pp. 35–114.

  2007a, "En Océan Indien Occidental, les saisons du voyage selon Ibn Mâjid, pilote hauturier
  arabe de la fin du 15e siècle," *La Lettre des Paquebots*, 61, pp. 23–26.

  2007b, "Les moyens de la navigation arabe vers la fin du 15e siècle en Océan Indien occidental,"
  La Lettre des Paquebots, 63, pp. 18–23.

  forthcoming, "L'instrument de mesure des hauteurs d'étoiles," *La Lettre des Paquebots*.

JOUKOWSKY, M. S., 1996, *Early Turkey: An Introduction to the Archaeology of Anatolia from
  Prehistory through the Lydian Period*, Dubuque, IA: Kendall/ Hunt.

JUMA, A. M., 1996, "The Swahili and the Mediterranean worlds: pottery of the late Roman
  period from Zanzibar," *Antiquity*, 70 (267), pp. 148–154.

  2004, *Unguja Ukuu on Zanzibar: An Archaeological Study of Early Urbanism* (Studies in Global
  Archaeology 3), Uppsala University.

JURSA, M., 2002, "Debts and indebtedness in the Neo-Babylonian period: evidence from the institutional archives," in M. Hudson and M. van de Mieroop (eds.), *Debt and Economic Renewal in the Ancient Near East*, Bethesda, MD: CDL Press, pp. 197–220.

2005, "Money-based exchange and redistribution: the transformation of the institutional economy in first millennium Babylonia," in P. Clancier, F. Joannès, P. Rouillard, and A. Tenu (eds.), *Autour de Polanyi: vocabulaires, théories et modalités des échanges*, Paris: De Boccard, pp. 171–186.

2010, with contributions by J. HACKL, B. JANKOVIC, K. KLEBER, E. E. PAYNE, C. WAERZEGGERS, and M. WESZELI, *Aspects of the Economic History of Babylonia in the First Millennium BC: Economic Geography, Economic Mentalities, Agriculture, the Use of Money and the Problem of Economic Growth*, Münster: Ugarit-Verlag.

2014, "Economic development in Babylonia from the late 7th to the late 4th century BC: economic growth and economic crises in imperial contexts," in H. D. Baker and M. Jursa (eds.), *Documentary Sources in Ancient Near Eastern and Greco-Roman Economic History*, Oxford: Oxbow Books, pp. 113–138.

2015, "Market performance and market integration in Babylonia in the long sixth century BC," in R. J. Van der Spek, Jan Luiten van Zanden, and Bas van Leeuwen (eds.), *A History of Market Performance: From Ancient Babylonia to the Modern World*, London and New York: Routledge, pp. 83–106.

JURSA, M. and MORENO GARCIA, J. C., 2015, "The Ancient Near East and Egypt," in A. Monson and W. Scheidel (eds.), *Fiscal Regimes and the Political Economy of Premodern States*, Cambridge University Press, pp. 115–165.

KABERRY, P., 1942, "Law in the Abelam tribe," *Oceania*, 12 (4), pp. 331–363.

KAJALE, M. D., 1989, "Mesolithic exploitation of wild plants in Sri Lanka: archaeobotanical study at the cave site of Beli-Lena," in D. R. Harris and G. C. Hillman (eds.), *Foraging and Farming: The Evolution of Plant Exploitation*, London: Routledge, pp. 269–281.

KANAKASABHAI, V., 1904, *The Tamils Eighteen Hundred Years Ago*, Madras and Bangalore: Higginbotham.

KANGINAKUDRU, S., METTA, M., JAKATI, R. D., and NAGARAJU, J., 2008, "Genetic evidence from Indian red jungle fowl corroborates multiple domestication of modern day chicken," *BMC Evolutionary Biology*, doi: 10.1186/1471-248-8-174.

KANIUTH, K., 2007, "The metallurgy of the Late Bronze Age Sapalli culture (southern Uzbekhistan) and its implications for the 'tin question'," *Iranica Antiqua*, 42, pp. 24–40.

KAPOOR, D., 1995, *Opium Poppy: Botany, Chemistry and Pharmacology*, Binghamton, NY: Haworth Press.

KARASHIMA, N., 1995, "Indian commercial activities in ancient and medieval South East Asia," paper presented in the Plenary Session of the VIIIth International Conference – Seminar of Tamil Studies, Thanjavur.

(ed.), 2002, *Ancient and Medieval Commercial Activities in the Indian Ocean: Testimony of Inscriptions and Ceramic Sherds*, Tokyo: Taisho University Press.

KATSUHIKO, O. and GUPTA, S., 2000, "The Far East, Southeast and South Asia: Indo-Pacific beads in Yayoi tombs as indicators of early maritime exchanges," *South Asian Studies*, 16, pp. 73–88.

KEALHOFER, L. and PIPERNO, D. R., 1994, "Early agriculture in Southeast Asia: phytolith evidence from the Bang Pakong Valley, Thailand," *Antiquity*, 68 (260), pp. 564–572.

KEALL, E. J., 1998, "Encountering megaliths on the Tihama coastal plain of Yemen," *Proceedings of the Seminar for Arabian Studies*, 28, pp. 139–147.

2004, "Possible connections in antiquity between the Red Sea coast of Yemen and the Horn of Africa," in P. Lunde and A. Porter (eds.), *Trade and Travel in the Red Sea Region: Proceedings of the Red Sea Project I* (BAR International Series 1269), Oxford: Archaeopress, pp. 43–55.

KEARNEY, M., 2004, *The Indian Ocean in World History*, New York: Routledge.

KEAY, J., 2005, *The Spice Route*, London: The Folio Society.

KEIGHTLEY, D. N., 2006, "Marks and labels: early writing in Neolithic and Shang China," in M. T. Stark (ed.), *Archaeology of Asia*, Malden, MA, and Oxford: Blackwell, pp. 177–201.

KEMPINSKI, A., 1994, "Tel Kabri: l'influence crétoise dans un palais de Canaan," *Le Monde de la Bible*, 89, pp. 1–38.

KENNEDY, J., 2008, "Pacific bananas: complex origins, multiple dispersals?," *Asian Perspectives*, 47 (1), pp. 75–94.

KENNET, D., 2005, "On the eve of Islam: archaeological evidence from Eastern Arabia," *Antiquity*, 79, pp. 107–118.

2007, "The decline of eastern Arabia in the Sasanian period," *Arabian Archaeology and Epigraphy*, 18 (1), pp. 86–122.

2009, "Report on the TGP from Pattanam excavation 2007 Season," KCHR, Trivandrum.

KENOYER, J. M., 1998, *Ancient Cities of the Indus Valley Civilization*, Karachi: Oxford University Press.

2003, "Beads of the Indus valley," in J. Aruz and R. Wallenfels (eds.), *Art of the First Cities, The Third Millennium B.C. From the Mediterranean to the Indus*, New York: Metropolitan Museum of Art; New Haven, CT, and London: Yale University Press, pp. 395–413.

2006, "The origin, context and function of the Indus script: recent insights from Harappa," in T. Osada (ed.), *Proceedings of the Pre-Symposium of RIHN and 7th ESCA Harvard–Kyoto Roundtable*, Kyoto: Research Institute for Humanity and Nature (RIHN), pp. 9–27.

2008, "Indus and Mesopotamian trade networks: new insights from shell and carnelian artifacts," in E. Olijdam and R. H. Spoor (eds.), *Intercultural Relations between South and Southwest Asia. Studies in Commemoration of E. C. L. During Caspers (1934–1996)* (BAR International Series 1826), Oxford: Archaeopress, pp. 19–28.

2009, "Carts and wheeled vehicles of the Indus civilization: new evidence from Harappa, Pakistan," in T. Osada and A. Uesugi (eds.), *Linguistics, Archaeology, and the Human Past: Occasional Paper 9*, Kyoto: Research Institute for Humanity and Nature, pp. 1–34.

2014, "The Indus civilization," in C. Renfrew and P. Bahn (eds.), *The Cambridge Prehistory*, Cambridge University Press, pp. 407–432.

KENOYER, J. M. and MEADOW, R. H., 2008, "The early Indus script at Harappa: origins and development," in E. Olijdam and R. H. Spoor (eds.), *Intercultural Relations between South and Southwest Asia. Studies in Commemoration of E. C. L. During Caspers (1934–1996)* (BAR International Series 1826), Oxford: Archaeopress, pp. 124–131.

KENT, R., 1979, "Possibilité de colonies indonésiennes en Afrique, avec référence spéciale à Madagascar," *Omaly sy Anio (Hier et Aujourd'hui)*, 9, pp. 129–150.

KERN, H., 1913, "Inscriptie van Kota Kapur (eiland Bangka)," *Bijdragen tot de Taal-, Land- en Volkenkunde / Journal of the Humanities and Social Sciences of Southeast Asia*, 67, pp. 393–400.

KERVRAN, M., 1999, "Multiples ports at the mouth of the River Indus: Barbarike, Deb, Daybul, Lahori Bandar, Diul Sinde," in H. P. Ray (ed.), *Archaeology of Seafaring: The Indian Ocean in the Ancient Period*, New Delhi: Pragati, pp. 70–153.

KESSY, E. T., 1997, "Archaeological sites Survey from Kisiju to Dar es Salaam," *Nyame Akuma*, 48, pp. 57–69.

KHALIDI, L., 2009, "Holocene obsidian exchange in the Red sea region," in M. Petraglia and J. Rose (eds.), *Paleoenvironments, Prehistory and Genetics: The Evolution of Human Populations in Arabia*, New York: Springer, pp. 272–291.

KHOMUTOVA, T. E., 2007, "An assessment of changes in properties of steppe kurgan paleosols in relation to prevailing climates over recent millennia," *Quaternary Research*, 67 (3), pp. 328–336.

KHOURY, I., 1982, "The poem of Sofala' by Ahmad ibn Mâjid," *Boletim da Biblioteca da Universidade de Coimbra*, 37, pp. 201–332.

1985–1986, "Les poèmes nautiques d'Ahmad Ibn Majid, 2ᵉ partie: Les poèmes à rime unique," *Bulletin d'Études Orientales*, 37–38, pp. 163–276.

KILLICK, D., 2004, "What do we know about African iron working?," *Journal of African Archaeology*, 2 (1), pp. 97–112.

2009a, "Agency, dependency and long-distance trade: East Africa and the Islamic world, ca. 700–1500 CE," in S. Falconer and C. Redman (eds.), *Polities and Power: Archaeological Perspectives on the Landscapes of Early States*, Tucson: University of Arizona Press, pp. 179–207.

2009b, "Cairo to Cape: the spread of metallurgy through eastern and southern Africa," *Journal of World Prehistory*, 22, pp. 399–414.

2016, "A global perspective on the pyrotechnologies of Sub-Saharan Africa," *Azania, Archaeological Research in Africa*, 51 (1), pp. 62–87.

KIRKMAN, J., 1954, *The Arab city of Gedi: Excavations at the Great Mosque, Architecture and Finds*, London: Oxford University Press.

1970, "The coast of Kenya as a factor in the trade and culture of the Indian ocean," *Actes du 8e Colloque International d'Histoire Maritime (Beyrouth, 5–10 septembre 1966)*, Paris: SEVPEN, pp. 247–253.

KITCHEN, K. A., 1993, "The land of Punt," in T. Shaw, P. Sinclair, B. Anday, and A. Okpoko (eds.), *The Archaeology of Africa: Food, Metals and Towns*, London: Routledge, pp. 587–607.

1994, *Documentation for Ancient Arabia. Part I. Chronological Framework and Historical Sources*, Liverpool University Press.

1996, *The Third Intermediate Period in Egypt (1100–650 BC)*, Oxford: Oxbow Books (1st edn. 1972).

1999, "Further thoughts on Punt and its neighbours," in A. Leahy and J. Tait (eds.), *Studies in Ancient Egypt, in Honour of H. S. Smith*, London: Egypt Exploration Society, pp. 173–178.

2000, "Regnal and genealogical data of ancient Egypt (absolute chronology I): the historic chronology of ancient Egypt, a current assessment," in M. Bietak (ed.), *The Synchronisation of Civilisations in the Eastern Mediterranean in the Second Millennium BC I*, Vienna: Denkschriften der Gesamtakademie, pp. 39–52.

2002a, "Egypt, Middle Nile, Red Sea and Arabia," in S. Cleuziou, M. Tosi, and J. Zarins (eds.), *Essays on the Late Prehistory of the Arabian Peninsula*, Rome: Istituto Italiano per l'Africa e l'Oriente, pp. 383–402.

2002b, "Ancient Egyptian chronology for Aegeanists," *Mediterranean Archaeology and Archaeometry*, 2 (2), pp. 5–12.

2004, "The elusive land of Punt revisited," in P. Lunde and A. Porter (eds.), *Trade and Travel in the Red Sea Region* (BAR International Series), Oxford: Achaeopress, pp. 25–31.

2009, "Ancient polities and interrelations along the Red Sea and its western and eastern hinterlands," in L. Blue, J. Cooper, R. Thomas, and J. Whitewright (eds.), *Connected Hinterlands: Proceedings of the Red Sea Project IV* (BAR International Series 2052), Oxford: Archaeopress, p. 3–8.

KIVISILD, T. *et al.*, 2003, "The genetic heritage of the earliest settlers persists both in Indian tribal and caste populations," *American Journal of Human Genetics*, 72, pp. 313–332.

KLENGEL, H., 1992, *Syria 3000 to 300 BC: A Handbook of Political History*, Berlin: Akademie Verlag.

KLIMBURG-SALTER, D. E., 1999, "From an art historical perspective: problems of chronology in the Kuṣāna period," in M. Alram and D. E. Klimburg-Salter (eds.), *Coins, Art and Chronology. Essays on the Pre-Islamic History of the Indo-Iranian Borderlands*, Vienna: Verlag der Österreichischen Akademie der Wissenschaften, pp. 3–17.

KLINGER, J., 2006, "Chronological links between the cuneiform world of the ancient Near East and ancient Egypt," in E. Hornung, R. Krauss, and D. Warburton (eds.), *Ancient Egyptian Chronology*, Leiden: Brill, pp. 304–324.

KOBISHANOV, Y. M., 1984, "Axoum: du Ier au IVe siècle, économie, système politique, culture," in G. Mokhtar (ed.), *Histoire générale de l'Afrique*, vol. II: *Afrique ancienne*, Paris: Jeune Afrique/UNESCO, pp. 407–428.

KOEHLER, L. and BAUMGARTNER, W., 1967–1996, *Hebräisches und aramäisches Lexikon zum Alten Testament*, Leiden: Brill, 6 vols.

KOGAN, A. I., 2005, *Dardskie yazyki. Geneticheskaya kharakteristika*, Moscow: Vostochnaya literatura.

KOHL, P. L., 1975, "The importance of long-distance exchange for the emergence of civilization in southwest Asia," paper presented in the Symposium held by the Department of Sociology and Anthropology, Wellesley College, February 1975.

1984, *Central Asia: Palaeolithic Beginnings to the Iron Age / L'Asie Centrale des origines à l'Âge du fer*, Paris: Éditions recherches sur les civilisations.

1987, "The ancient economy, transferable technologies and the Bronze Age world-system: a view from the northeastern frontier of the ancient Near East," in M. Rowlands, M. Larsen, and K. Kristiansen (eds.), *Centre and Periphery in the Ancient World*, Cambridge University Press, pp. 13–24.

1989, "The use and abuse of world systems theory: the case of the 'pristine' west Asian state," in C. C. Lamberg-Karlowsky (ed.), *Archaeological Thought in America*, Cambridge University Press, pp. 218–240.

1995, "Central Asia and the Caucasus in the Bronze Age," in J. M. Sasson (ed.), *Civilizations of the Ancient Near East*, vols. I–II, Peabody, MA: Hendrickson Publishers, pp. 1051–1065.

2001, "Reflections on the production of chlorite at Tepe Yahya: 25 years later," in D. T. Potts (ed.), *Excavations at Tepe Yahya, Iran, 1967–1975, the Third Millennium* (Bulletin of the American School of Prehistoric Research 45), Cambridge, MA: Peabody Museum of Archaeology and Ethnology, Harvard University, pp. 209–230.

2002, "Archaeological transformations: crossing the pastoral/agricultural bridge," *Iranica Antiqua*, 37, pp. 151–189.

2007, *The Making of Bronze Age Eurasia*, Cambridge University Press.

2009a, "The Maikop singularity: the unequal accumulation of wealth on the Bronze Age Eurasian steppe?," in B. K. Hanks and K. M. Linduff (eds.), *Social Complexity in Prehistoric Eurasia: Monuments, Metals, and Mobility*, Cambridge University Press, pp. 91–104.

2009b, "Perils of carts before horses: linguistic models and the underdetermined archaeological record," *American Anthropologist*, 111 (1), pp. 109–111.

KOHL, P. L., GADZHIEV, M. G., and MAGOMEDOV, R. G., 2002, "Between the steppe and the sown: cultural developments on the Caspian littoral plain of southern Daghestan, Russia, c. 3600–1900 BC," in K. Boyle, C. Renfrew, and M. Levine (eds.), *Ancient Interactions: East and West in Eurasia*, Cambridge: McDonald Institute for Archaeological Research, pp. 113–128.

KOHL, P. L. and TRIFONOV, V., 2014, "The prehistory of the Caucasus: internal developments and external interactions," in C. Renfrew and P. Bahn (eds.), *The Cambridge World Prehistory*, vol. III: *West and Central Asia and Europe*, Cambridge University Press, pp. 1571–1595.

KOHTAMÄKI, M. 2014. "Transitions: a landscape approach to social and cultural changes in southern Mozambique, 500 BC – 800 AD," Ph.D. dissertation, Uppsala University.

KONISHI, M. A., 1994, *Ain Umm-es-Sujur: An Interim Report 1993/4*, Tokyo: Shonan Good.

KORISETTAR, R., 2004, "Origins of plant agriculture in South India," in H. P. Ray and C. M. Sinopoli (eds.), *Archaeology as History in Early South Asia*, New Delhi: Aryan Books, pp. 162–184.

KORYAKOVA, L. and EPIMAKHOV, A., 2007, *The Urals and Western Siberia in the Bronze and Iron Ages*, Cambridge University Press.

KORYAKOVA, L. and KOHL, P. L., 2000, "Complex societies of Central Eurasia from the 3rd to the 1st millennia BC: regional specifics in the light of global models," *Current Anthropology*, 41, pp. 638–642.

KOSAMBI, D. D., 1956, *An Introduction to the Study of Indian History*, Bombay.

1965, *The Culture and Civilisation of Ancient India in Historical Outline*, London: Routledge & Kegan Paul.

KOUCHOUKOS, N. and WILKINSON, T., 2007, "Landscape archaeology in Mesopotamia: past, present, and future," in E. C. Stone (ed.), *Settlement and Society: Essays Dedicated to Robert McCormick Adams*, Los Angeles: UCLA Cotsen Institute of Archaeology, pp. 1–18.

KOULKOVA, M. A., 2004, "Applications of geochemistry to paleoenvironmental reconstruction in Southern Siberia," in E. M. Scott, A. Y. Alekseev, and G. Zaitseva (eds.), *Impact of the Environment on Human Migration in Eurasia*, Dordrecht, Boston, and London: Kluwer Academic Publishers, pp. 255–274.

KOURAMPAS, N., *et al.*, 2015, "Late Quaternary speleogenesis and landscape evolution in a tropical carbonate island: Pango la Kuumbi (Kuumbi Cave), Zanzibar," *International Journal of Speleology*, 44 (3), pp. 293–314.

KOVACH, M. J., CALINGACION, M. N., FITZGERALD, M. A., and MCCOUCH, S. R., 2009, "The origin and evolution of fragrance in rice (*Oryza sativa* L.)," *Proceedings of the National Academy of Sciences of the United States of America*, 106 (34), pp. 14444–14449.

KOVACH, M. J., SWEENEY, M. T., and MCCOUCH, S. R., 2007, "New insights into the history of rice domestication," *Trends in Genetics*, 23 (11), pp. 578–587.

KRADIN, N. N., 2005, "From tribal confederation to empire: the evolution of the Rouran society," *Acta Orientalia*, 58 (2), pp. 149–169.

KRAMER, S. N., 1952, *Enmerkar and the Lord of Aratta: A Sumerian Epic Tale of Iraq and Iran*, Philadelphia: University of Pennsylvania.

KRAUSS, R., 2003, "Arguments in favor of a low chronology for the Middle and New Kingdom in Egypt," in M. Bietak (ed.), *The Synchronisation of Civilisations in the Eastern Mediterranean in the Second Millennium BC II: Proceedings of the SCIEM 2000 EuroConference, Haindorf, May 2–7, 2001*, Vienna: Verlag der Österreichischen Akademie der Wissenschaften, pp. 175–198.

2006, "Egyptian Sirius/Sothic dates and the question of the Sirius based lunar calendar," in E. Hornung, R. Krauss, and D. Warburton (eds.), *Ancient Egyptian Chronology*, Leiden: Brill, pp. 439–457.

KRAUSS, R. and WARBURTON, D., 2006, "Conclusions and a postscript to Part II, Chapter 1," in E. Hornung, R. Krauss, and D. Warburton (eds.), *Ancient Egyptian Chronology*, Leiden: Brill, pp. 475–489.

KRISTIANSEN, K., 1993, "Comments" on A. G. Frank's article "Bronze Age world system cycles," *Current Anthropology*, 34 (4), p. 415.

1998, *Europe Before History*, Cambridge University Press.

2007, "Eurasian transformations: mobility, ecological change, and the transmission of social institutions in the third millennium and the early second millennium BCE," in A. Hornborg and C. Crumley (eds.), *The World System and the Earth System. Global Socioenvironmental Change and Sustainability since the Neolithic*, Walnut Creek, CA: Left Coast Press, pp. 149–162.

KRISTIANSEN, K. and LARSSON, T. B., 2005, *The Rise of Bronze Age Society. Travels, Transmissions and Transformations*, Cambridge University Press.

KROMER, B., KORFMANN, M., and JABLONKA, P., 2003, "Heidelberg radiocarbon dates for Troia I to VIII and Kumtep," in G. A. Wagner, E. Pernicka and H.-P. Uerpmann (eds.), *Troia and the Troad. Scientific Approaches*, Berlin, Heidelberg, and New York: Springer, pp. 43–54.

KUČAN, D., 1995, "Zur Ernährung und dem Gebrauch von Pflanzen im Heraion von Samos im 7 Jahrhundert v. Chr," *Jahrbuch des Deutschen Archäologischen Instituts*, 10, pp. 10–64.

KUHRT, A., 1994–1995, *The Ancient Near East, c. 3000–330 BC*, 2 vols., London and New York: Routledge.

KUIPER, F. B. J., 1948, *Proto-Munda Words in Sanskrit*, Amsterdam: N. V. Noord-Hollandsche Vitgevers Maatschappij.

KULKE, H., 1990, "Indian colonies, Indianization or cultural convergence? Reflections on the changing image of India's role in South-East Asia," in H. S. Nordholt (ed.), *Onderzoek in Zuidoost-Azie: Agenda's voor de Jaren Negentig*, Leiden: Rijksuniversiteit te Leiden, pp. 8–32.

　　1993, *Kings and Cults: State Formation and Legitimation in India and Southeast Asia*, New Delhi: Manohar.

KULKE, H. and ROTHERMUND, D., 1995, *A History of India*, London and New York: Routledge (1st edn. 1986, reissued 2004).

KUNST, J., 1973, *Music in Java, Its History, Its Theory and Its Technique*, The Hague: Martinus Nijhoff.

KUSIMBA, C. M., 1999, *The Rise and Fall of Swahili States*, Walnut Creek, CA: Altamira Press.

KUSIMBA, C. M. and KUSIMBA, S. B., 2005, "Mosaics and interactions: East Africa, 2000 b.p. to the present," in A. B. Stahl (ed.), *African Archaeology: A Critical Introduction*, Malden, MA, and Oxford: Blackwell, pp. 392–419.

KUSUMA, P., BRUCATO, N., COX, M. P., PIERRON, D., RAZAFINDRAZAKA, H., ADELAAR, A., SUDOYO, H., LETELLIER, T., and RICAUT, F.-X., 2016, "Contrasting linguistic and genetic influences during the Austronesian settlement of Madagascar," *Scientific Reports* 6:26066, doi: 10.1038/srep26066

KUSUMA, P., COX, M. P., PIERRON, D., RAZAFINDRAZAKA, H., BRUCATO, N., TONASSO, L., SURYADI, H. L., LETELLIER, T., SUDOYO, H., and RICAUT, F.-X., 2015, "Mitochondrial DNA and the Y chromosome suggest the settlement of Madagascar by Indonesian sea nomad populations," *BMC Genomics*, 16 (191), doi: 10.1186/s12864-015-1394-7.

KUZMINA, E. E., 1994, *Okuda prishli Indo Arii*, Moscow: Académie des Sciences de Russie.

　　2007, *The Origin of the Indo-Iranians*, ed. J. P. Mallory, Leiden and Boston: Brill.

　　2008, *The Prehistory of the Silk Road*, ed. V. H. Mair, Philadelphia: University of Pennsylvania Press.

KWASMAN, T. and PARPOLA, S., 1991, *Legal Transactions of the Royal Court of Nineveh. Part I. Tiglat-Pileser through Esarhaddon* (State Archives of Assyria vol. 6), Helsinki University Press.

LABIB, S. Y., 1974, "Medieval Islamic maritime policy in the Indian Ocean Area," in J. Pirenne (ed.), *Les grandes escales. 1re partie: Antiquité et Moyen-Âge (10e colloque d'Histoire Maritime)*, Brussels: Éditions de la Librairie Encyclopédique, pp. 225–241.

LACAU, P., 1949, "Une stèle juridique de Karnak," *Supplément aux Annales du Service des Antiquités de l'Égypte (ASAE)* 13, pp. 1–54.

LAFONT, B., 2010, "Gilgamesh a-t-il existé ?," *L'Histoire*, 356, pp. 44–51.

LAFONT, S., 2001, "Taxes," in F. Joannès (ed.), *Dictionnaire de la civilisation mésopotamienne*, Paris: Laffont, pp. 832–834.

LAIOU, A. E. and MORRISON, C., 2007, *The Byzantine Economy*, Cambridge University Press.

LAL, B. B., 1997, *The Earliest Civilization of South Asia (Rise, Maturity and Decline)*, New Delhi: Aryan Books International.

2002. *The Sarasvati Flows On*, New Delhi: Aryan Books International.

LALUEZA-FOX, C., SAMPIETRO, M. L., GILBERT, M. T. P., CASTRI, L., FACCHINI, F., PETTENER, D., and BERTRANPETIT, J., 2004, "Unravelling migrations in the steppe: mitochondrial DNA sequences from ancient Central Asians," *Proceedings of the Royal Society Biological Sciences*, 271, pp. 941–947.

LAM THI MY DZUNG, 2009, "Sa Huynh regional and inter-regional interactions in the Thu Bon valley, Quang Nam province, Central Vietnam," *Bulletin of the Indo-Pacific Prehistory Association*, 29, pp. 68–75.

LAMB, H. H., 1995, *Climate, History and the Modern World*, London: Routledge (1st edn. 1982).

LAMBERG-KARLOVSKY, C. C., 1977, "Foreign relations in the third millennium at Tepe Yahya," in J. Deshayes (ed.), *Le plateau iranien et l'Asie Centrale des origines à la conquête islamique. Leurs relations à la lumière des documents archéologiques* (Colloques internationaux du CNRS, no. 567), Paris: Éditions du CNRS, pp. 33–43.

1993, "Comments on A. G. Frank's article 'Bronze Age world system cycles'," *Current Anthropology*, 34 (4), pp. 415–416.

1996, "The archaeological evidence for international commerce: public and/or private enterprise in Mesopotamia," in M. Hudson and B. A. Levine (eds.), *Privatization in the Ancient Near East and Classical World*, Cambridge, MA: Peabody Museum of Archaeology and Ethnology, pp. 73–108.

1999, "Households, land tenure, and communications systems in the 6th–4th millennia of Greater Mesopotamia," in M. Hudson and B. Levine (eds.), *Urbanization and Land Ownership*, Cambridge, MA: Peabody Museum of Archaeology and Ethnology, Harvard University, pp. 167–202.

2001a, "Afterword," in D. T. Potts (ed.), *Excavations at Tepe Yahya, Iran, 1967–1975, the Third Millennium* (Bulletin of the American School of Prehistoric Research 45), Cambridge, MA: Peabody Museum of Archaeology and Ethnology, Harvard University, pp. 269–280.

2001b, "Comments on S. Ratnagar's article 'The Bronze Age: unique instance of a pre-industrial world system?'," *Current Anthropology*, 42 (3), pp. 368–369.

2002, "Archaeology and language: the Indo-Iranians," *Current Anthropology*, 43 (1), pp. 63–75 and 83–84.

2003, "To write or not to write," in D. T. Potts, M. D. Roaf, and D. L. Stein (eds.), *Culture through Objects: Ancient Near Eastern Studies in Honour of P. R. S. Moorey*, Oxford: Griffith Institute Publications, pp. 59–75.

LANDSTRÖM, B., 1970, *Ships of the Pharaohs: 4000 Years of Egyptian Shipbuilding*, Garden City, NY: Doubleday.

LANE, P., 2013, "The archaeology of pastoralism and stock-keeping in East Africa," in P. Mitchell and P. Lane (eds.), *The Oxford Handbook of African Archaeology*, Oxford University Press, pp. 581–597.

2015, "Early agriculture in sub-Saharan Africa to ca. AD 500," in G. Barker and C. Goucher (eds.), *Cambridge World History*, vol. II: *A World with Agriculture*, Cambridge University Press, pp. 736–773.

LANGE ROSENZWEIG, D., 2004, "Chinese glass technology," in E. Byrne Curtis (ed.), *Pure Brightness Shines Everywhere: The Glass of China*, Aldershot and Burlington, VT: Ashgate, pp. 11–19.

LANKTON, J. W. and DUSSUBIEUX, L., 2006, "Early glass in Asian maritime trade: a review and an interpretation of compositional analyses," *Journal of Glass Studies*, 48, pp. 121–144.

LANKTON, J., DUSSUBIEUX, L., and REHREN, T., 2008, "A study of mid-first millennium CE Southeast Asian specialized glass beadmaking traditions," in E. Bacus, I. Glover, and P. Sharrock (eds), *Interpreting Southeast Asia's Past: Monument, Image and Text*, vol. II, National University of Singapore, pp. 335–356.

LANKTON, J. and GRATUZE, B., 2013, "Agents of exchange and technology transfer: new insight from glass compositional data," paper presented at the Sealinks Conference "Proto-Globalisation in the Indian Ocean World: Multidisciplinary Perspectives on Early Globalisation," Oxford, Jesus College, November 7–10, 2013.

LAPE, P. V., 2002, "On the use of archaeology and history in island Southeast Asia," *Journal of the Economic and Social History of the Orient*, 45 (4), pp. 468–491.

LARSEN, C. E., 1983, *Life and Land Use on the Bahrein Islands*, University of Chicago Press.

LARSEN, M. T., 1976, *Old Assyrian City-State and Its Colonies*, Copenhagen: Akademisk Forlag.

1987, "Commercial networks in the ancient Near East," in M. Rowlands, M. Larsen, and K. Kristiansen (eds.), *Centre and Periphery in the Ancient World*, Cambridge University Press, pp. 47–56.

2000a, "The Old Assyrian city-state," in M. H. Hansen (ed.), *A Comparative Study of Thirty City-State Cultures*, Copenhagen: Det Kongelige Danske Videnskabernes Selskab, pp. 77–87.

2000b, "The city-states of the early Neo-Babylonian period," in, M. H. Hansen (ed.), *A Comparative Study of Thirty City-State Cultures*, Copenhagen: Det Kongelige Danske Videnskabernes Selskab, pp. 117–127.

LARSON, G. *et al.*, 2007, "Phylogeny and ancient DNA of *Sus* provides new insights into Neolithic expansion in Island Southeast Asia and Oceania," *Proceedings of the National Academy of Sciences*, 104 (12), pp. 4834–4839.

2010, "Patterns of East Asian pig domestication, migration, and turnover revealed by modern and ancient DNA," *Proceedings of the National Academy of Sciences*, 107 (17), pp. 7686–7691.

LATOUCHE, S., 2004, *Survivre au développement*, Paris: Mille et Une Nuits.

2005, *L'invention de l'économie*, Paris: Albin Michel.

LAURENCE, B. R., 1968, "Elephantiasis and Polynesian origins," *Nature*, 219 (5154), pp. 53–56.

LAUFER, B., 1919, *Sino-Iranica: Chinese Contributions to the History of Civilisation* (Field Museum of Natural History Publication 201, Anthropological Series 15/3), Chicago: Field Museum.

LAUM, B., 2006, *Heiliges Geld: eine historische Untersuchung über den sakralen Ursprung des Geldes*, Berlin: Semele Verlag (1st edn. 1924).

LA VAISSIÈRE, E. DE, 2002, *Histoire des marchands sogdiens*, Paris: Collège de France, Institut des Hautes Études Chinoises (2nd edn. 2004).

2006, "Xiongnu," *Encyclopædia Iranica* online.

2008, "Les Sogdiens, un peuple de commerçants au cœur de l'Asie," www.clio.fer/BIBLIOTHEQUE/

LAWERGREN, B., 2003a, "Oxus trumpets, ca. 2200–1800 BCE: material overview, usage, societal role, and catalog," *Iranica Antiqua*, 38, pp. 41–118.

2003b, "Western influences on the early Chinese *Qin*-Zither," *The Museum of Far Eastern Antiquities* (Stockholm), 75, pp. 79–109.

LAWLER, A., 2006, "North versus south, Mesopotamian style," *Science*, 312 (6191), pp. 1458–1463.

2012, "The ingredients for a 4000-year-old proto-curry," *Science*, 337, p. 288.

2014, "Sailing Sindbad's seas," *Science*, 344, pp. 1440–1445.

LE RIDER, G., 1997, "Le monnayage des Séleucides," *Histoire économique et monétaire de l'Orient hellénistique, Annuaire du Collège de France, 1996–1997*, Paris, pp. 811–828.

2001, *La naissance de la monnaie: pratiques monétaires de l'Orient ancien*, Paris: Presses Universitaires de France.

LE RIDER, G. and CALLATAY, F. de, 2006, *Les Séleucides et les Ptolémées: l'héritage monétaire et financier d'Alexandre le Grand*, Paris: Éditions du Rocher.

LE THI LIEN, 2005, "Gold plaques and their cultural contexts in the Oc Eo culture," *Bulletin of the Indo-Pacific Prehistory Association*, 25 (The Taipei Papers vol. 3), pp. 145–157.

LE XUAN DIEM, DAO LINH CON, VO SI KHAI, and VAN HOA, 1995, *Oc Eo: Oc Eo Cultures, Recent Discoveries*, Hanoi: Social Science Publishing House (in Vietnamese).

LEAKEY, M. D., 1966, "Excavation of burial mounds in Ngorongoro Crater," *Tanzania Notes and Record*, 66, pp. 123–135.

1983, *Africa's Vanishing Art: The Rock Paintings of Tanzania*, London: Hamish Hamilton.

LEBOT, V., 1999, "Biomolecular evidence for plant domestication in Sahul," *Genetic Resources and Crop Evolution*, 46, pp. 619–628.

LEEMANS, W. F., 1960, *Foreign Trade in the Old Babylonian Period as Revealed by Texts from Southern Mesopotamia*, Leiden: Brill.

LEENHARDT, M., 1980, *Notes d'ethnologie néo-calédonienne*, Paris: Institut d'Ethnologie (1st edn. 1930).

LEFEBVRE DES NOËTTES, C., 1931, *L'attelage, le cheval de selle à travers les âges, contribution à l'histoire de l'esclavage*, Paris: A. Picart.

LEJJU, B. J., ROBERTSHAW, P., and TAYLOR, D., 2006, "Africa's earliest bananas?," *Journal of Archaeological Science*, 33, pp. 102–113.

LEMAIRE, A., 1987, "Les Phéniciens et le commerce entre la Mer Rouge et la Méditerranée," in E. Lipinski (ed.), *Phoenicia and East Mediterranean in the First Millennium*, Leuven: Vitgeverij Peeters, pp. 49–60.

2007, "La diffusion des écritures alphabétiques (*ca.* 1700–500 av. N.E.)," *Diogène*, 218, pp. 57–70.

LEROUXEL, F. and ZURBACH, J., 2006, Compte rendu de *Autour de Polanyi: Vocabulaire, théories et modalités des échanges* (Colloque Nanterre, 12–14 juin 2004, Paris: De Boccard, 2005, 290 p.), *Topoi: Orient–Occident*, 14 (2), pp. 349–360.

LEVEAU, P., 1978, "La situation coloniale de l'Afrique romaine," *Annales ESC*, 33, pp. 89–92.

2008, "Conduire l'eau et la contrôler: l'ingénierie des aqueducs romains," in M. Molin (ed.), *Archéologie et histoire des techniques du monde romain: Actes du Colloque de la Société Française d'Archéologie Classique, Paris, I.N.H.A., 15 novembre 2006*, Paris: de Boccard, pp. 133–163.

LÉVI, S., 1900, "Ceylan et la Chine," *Journal Asiatique*, 15, pp. 411–429.

1936, "Kaniska et Satavahana: deux figures symboliques de l'Inde au premier siècle," *Journal Asiatique*, pp. 61–121.

LÉVI-STRAUSS, C., 1964, *The Raw and the Cooked*, New York: Harper Torch Books.

LEVINE, M., and KISLENKO, A., 2002, "New Eneolithic and Early Bronze Age radiocarbon dates for North Kazakhstan and South Siberia," in K. Boyle, C. Renfrew, and M. Levine (eds.), *Ancient Interactions: East and West in Eurasia*, Cambridge: McDonald Institute for Archaeological Research, pp. 131–134.

LEVINE, M. A., RENFREW, A. C., and BOYLE, K. (eds.), 2003, *Prehistoric Steppe Adaptation and the Horse*, Cambridge: McDonald Institute for Archaeological Research.

LEVY, T. E., and BRINK, E. C. M. van den, 2002, "Interaction models: Egypt and the Levantine periphery," in E. C. M. van den Brink and T. E. Levy (eds.), *Egypt and the Levant: Interrelations from the 4th through the Early 3rd Millennium BCE*, London and New York: Leicester University Press, pp. 3–38.

LEWICKI, T., 1936, "Les premiers commerçants arabes en Chine," *Rocznik Orjentalistyczny* (Lwow), 11, pp. 173–186.

1974, *Arabic External Sources of the History of Africa to the South of Sahara*, London: Curzon Press; Lagos: Pilgrim Books (1st edn. 1969).

LEWIS, M. E., 2000, "The city-state in Spring-and-Autumn China," in M. H. Hansen (ed.), *A Comparative Study of Thirty City-State Cultures*, Copenhagen: Det Kongelige Danske Videnskabernes Selskab, pp. 359–373.

2009, *China between Empires*, Cambridge, MA: Belknap Press of Harvard University Press.

LI, C. *et al.*, 2015, "Analysis of ancient human mitochondrial DNA from the Xiaohe cemetery: insights into prehistoric population movements in the Tarim Basin, China," *BMC Genetics*, 16, doi: 10.1186/s12863-015-0237-5

LI, S., 2002, "The interaction between Northwest China and Central Asia during the second millennium BC: an archaeological perspective," in K. Boyle, C. Renfrew, and M. Levine (eds.), *Ancient Interactions: East and West in Eurasia*, Cambridge: McDonald Institute for Archaeological Research, pp. 171–182.

2003, "Ancient interactions in Eurasia and Northwest China: revisiting Johan Gunnar Andersson's legacy," *Museum of Far Eastern Antiquities* (Stockholm), 75, pp. 9–30.

LI, X.-Q., ZHOU, X. Y., ZHOU J., *et al.*, 2007, "The earliest archaeobiological evidence of the broadening agriculture in China recorded at Xishanping site in Gansu Province," *Science China Series D: Earth Sciences*, 50 (11), pp. 1707–1714.

LI, Y.-T, 2003, "On the function of cowries in Shang and western Zhou China," *Journal of East Asian Archaeology*, 5 (1–4), pp. 1–26.

LICHTENBERG, R. J., and THUILLIEZ, A. C., 1981, "Sur quelques aspects insolites de la radiologie de Ramsès II," *Bulletins et Mémoires de la Société d'Anthropologie de Paris*, 8 (3), pp. 323–330.

LICHTHEIM, M., 2006, *Ancient Egyptian Literature*, University of California Press.

LIEBERMAN, V., 2003 and 2009, *Strange Parallels. Southeast Asia in Global Context, c. 800–1830*, vol. I: *Integration on the Mainland*; vol. II: *Mainland Mirrors: Europe, Japan, China, South Asia, and the Islands*, Cambridge University Press.

LINDUFF, K., 2000, *The Beginnings of Metallurgy in China*, Lewiston, NY: Edwin Mellen Press.

2002, "At the eastern edge: metallurgy and adaptation in Gansu (PRC) in the 2nd millennium BC," in K. Jones-Bley and D. G. Zdanovich (eds.), *Complex Societies of Central Eurasia from the 3rd to the 1st Millennium BC: Regional Specifics in Light of Global Models* (Journal of Indo-European Studies Monograph Series 45, vol. II), Washington, DC: Institute for the Study of Man, pp. 595–611.

LINDUFF, K. M., DRENNAN, R. D., and SHELACH, G., 2002–2004, "Early complex societies in Northeast China: the Chifeng International Collaborative Archaeological Research Project," *Journal of Field Archaeology*, 29 (1/2), pp. 45–73.

LIPINSKI, E., 1979, "Les temples néo-assyriens et l'origine du monnayage," in E. Lipinski (ed.), *State and Temple Economy*, vol. II, Leiden: Brill, pp. 565–588.

2004, *Itineraria Phoenicia*, Leuven: Peeters.

2010, "Hiram of Tyre and Solomon," in A. Lemaire, B. Halpern, and M. J. Adams (eds.), *The Book of Kings*, Leiden: Brill, pp. 251–272.

LIPKE, P., 1984, *The Royal Ship of Cheops* (BAR International Series 225), Oxford: Archaeopress.

LIU, L., 2003, "'The products of minds as well as of hands': production of prestige goods in the Neolithic and Early States Periods of China," *Asian Perspectives*, 42 (1), pp. 1–40.

2004, *The Chinese Neolithic: Trajectories to Early States*, Cambridge University Press.

LIU, L. and CHEN, X., 2003, *State Formation in Early China*, London: Duckworth.

2006, "Sociopolitical change from Neolithic to Bronze Age China," in M. T. Stark (ed.), *Archaeology of Asia*, Malden, MA, and Oxford: Blackwell, pp. 149–176.

2012, *The Archaeology of China: From the Late Paleolithic to the Early Bronze Age*, Cambridge University Press.

LIU, L., XU, L., and CUI, H., 2002, "Holocene history of desertification along the woodland-steppe border in northern China," *Quaternary Research*, 57, pp. 259–270.

Liu, X., 1988, *Ancient India and Ancient China: Trade and Religious Exchanges AD 1–600*, Delhi: Oxford University Press.

2010, *The Silk Road in World History*, Oxford University Press.

Liu, Y. P., Zhu, Q., and Yao, Y. G., 2006a, "Genetic relationship of Chinese and Japanese gamecocks revealed by mtDNA sequence variation," *Biochemical Genetics*, 44, pp. 18–28.

Liu, Y. P., Wu, G.-S., Yao, Y.-G., Miao, Y.-W., Luikart, G., Baig, M., Beja-Pereira, A., Ding, Z.-L., Gounder Palanichamy, M., and Zhang, Y. P., 2006b, "Multiple maternal origins of chickens: out of the Asian jungles," *Molecular Phylogenetics and Evolution*, 38 (1), pp. 12–19.

Liverani, M., 1990, *Prestige and Interest: International Relations in the Near East ca. 1600–1100 BC* (History of the Ancient Near East, Studies 1), Padua: Sargon SRL.

1991, "The trade network of Tyre according to Ez.27," in M. Cogan and I. Ephal (eds.), *Ah Assyria . . . Studies in Assyrian History and Ancient Near Eastern Historiography Presented to Hayim Tadmor* (Scripta Hierosolymitana, vol. 33), Hebrew University of Jerusalem, pp. 65–79.

2005, "Historical overview," in E. D. Snell (ed.), *A Companion to the Ancient Near East*, Oxford: Blackwell, pp. 3–19.

2014, *The Ancient Near East: History, Society and Economy*, New York: Routledge.

Lo, J., 1970, "Chinese shipping and East–West trade from the tenth to the fourteenth century," in M. Mollat (ed.), *Sociétés et Compagnies de commerce en Orient et dans l'Océan Indien*, Paris: SEVPEN, pp. 215–225.

Loewe, M., 1986, "The structure and practice of government," in D. Twitchett and M. Loewe (eds.), *The Cambridge History of China*, vol. I, Cambridge University Press, pp. 463–490.

1999, "The heritage left to the empires," in M. Loewe and E. L. Slaughnessy (eds.), *The Cambridge History of Ancient China: From the Origins of Civilization to 221 BC*, Cambridge University Press, pp. 967–1032.

Loewe, M. and Shaughnessy, E. L. (eds.), 1999, *The Cambridge History of Ancient China: From the Origins of Civilization to 221 BC*, Cambridge University Press.

Lombard, D., 1990, *Le carrefour javanais: essai d'histoire globale*, vol. I: *Les limites de l'occidentalisation*; vol. II: *Les réseaux asiatiques*; vol. III: *L'héritage des royaumes concentriques*, Paris: EHESS.

Lombard, M., 1971, *L'Islam dans sa première grandeur VIIIe–XIe siècles*, Paris: Flammarion (reissued 1980).

Londo, J. P., Chiang, Y., Hung, K., Chiang, T., and Schaal, B. A., 2006, "Phylogeography of Asian wild rice, *Oryza rufipogon*, reveals multiple independent domestications of cultivated rice, *Oryza sativa*," *Proceedings of the National Academy of Sciences of the United States of America*, 103, pp. 9578–9583.

Loofs-Wissowa, H., 1991, "Dong Son drums: instruments of shamanism or regalia?," *Arts Asiatiques*, 46, pp. 39–49.

Loret, V., 1892, *La flore pharaonique d'après les documents hiéroglyphiques et les spécimens découverts dans les tombes*, Paris: E. Leroux.

Löw, I., 1924–1934, *Die Flora der Juden*, 4 vols., Vienna: R. Löwit.

Lu, T. L.-D., 2005, "The origin and dispersal of agriculture and human diaspora in East Asia," in L. Sagart, R. Blench, and A. Sanchez-Mazas (eds.), *The Peopling of East Asia*, London and New York, Routledge/Curzon, pp. 51–62.

Lubec, G., Holaubek, J., Feld, C., Lubec, B., and Strouhai, E., 1993, "Use of silk in ancient Egypt," *Nature*, 362 (6145), p. 25.

Ludden, D., 1999, *An Agrarian History of South Asia*, Cambridge University Press.

Luikart, G., Gielly, L., Excoffier, L., Vigne, J.-D., Bouvet, J., and Taberlet, P., 2001, "Multiple maternal origins and weak phylogeographic structure in domestic goats," *Proceedings of the National Academy of Sciences of the United States*, 98, pp. 5927–5932.

LYIMO, C. M., WEIGEND, A., JANßEN-TAPKEN, U., MSOFFE, P. L., SIMIANER, H., and WEIGEND, S., 2012, "Assessing genetic diversity of five Tanzanian chicken ecotypes using microsatellite markers and mitochondrial DNA D-loop sequencing," paper presented at the conference on "International Research on Food Security, Natural Resource Management and Rural Development," Göttingen, September 19–21, 2012.

LYONNET, B., 2005, "Another possible interpretation of the Bactro-Margiana Culture (BMAC) of Central Asia: the tin trade," in C. Jarrige and V. Lefèvre (eds.), *South Asian Archaeology 2001*, vol. I: *Prehistory*, Paris: adpf-Éditions Recherche sur les Civilisations, pp. 191–200.

LYONNET, B. and KOHL, P. L., 2008, "By land and by sea: the circulation of materials and peoples, ca. 3500–1800 BC," in E. Olijdam and R. H. Spoor (eds.), *Intercultural Relations between South and Southwest Asia: Studies in Commemoration of E.C.L. During Caspers (1934–1996)* (BAR International Series 1826), Oxford: Archaeopress, pp. 29–42.

MA HUAN, 1970, *Ying-yai Sheng-lan: "The Overall Survey of the Ocean's Shores"* [1433], trans. and annotated by J. V. G. Mills, Cambridge: Hakluyt Society.

MABUCHI, T., 1975, "Tales concerning the origin of grains in the insular areas of eastern and southeastern Asia," in *Ethnology of the Southwestern Pacific: The Ryu-kyus Taiwan-Insular Southeast Asia*, Taipei: The Orient Cultural Service.

McCLELLAN, J. E. and DORN, H., 1999, *Science and Technology in World History: An Introduction*, Baltimore, MD: Johns Hopkins University Press.

McCORMICK, M. *et al.*, 2012, "Climate change during and after the Roman Empire: reconstructing the past from scientific and historical evidence," *Journal of Interdisciplinary History*, 43 (2), pp. 169–220.

McCORRISTON, J., 1997, "The fiber revolution: textile extensification, alienation, and social stratification in Ancient Mesopotamia," *Current Anthropology*, 38 (4), pp. 517–549.

McCORRISTON, J. and MARTIN, L., 2009, "Southern Arabia's early pastoral population history: some recent evidence," in M. Petraglia and H. Rose (eds.), *Paleoenvironments, Prehistory and Genetics: The Evolution of Human Populations in Arabia*, New York: Springer, pp. 237–250.

McCORRISTON, J., OCHES, O., WALTHER, D., and COLE, K., 2002, "Investigating the roots of agriculture in Holocene highland southern Arabia and the archaeological-palaeoecological record," *Paléorient*, 28 (1), pp. 61–78.

McCRINDLE, J. W. (ed.), 1877, *Ancient India as Described by Megasthenes and Arrian, Being a Translation of the Fragments of the Indika of Megasthenes collected by Dr Schwanbeck, and of the First Part of the Indika of Arrian*, Calcutta, Bombay, and London: Thacker and Co., Trübner and Co.

MacDONALD, K. C., 1993, "Chickens in Africa: the importance of Qasr Ibrim," *Antiquity*, 67 (256), pp. 584–590.

1998, "Before the Empire of Ghana: pastoralism and the origins of cultural complexity in the Sahel," in G. Connah (ed.), *Transformations in Africa: Essays on Africa's Later Past*, London: Leicester University Press, pp. 71–103.

2000, "The origins of African livestock: indigenous or imported?," in R. Blench and K. C. MacDonald (eds.), *The Origins and Development of African Livestock: Archaeology, Genetics, Linguistics and Ethnography*, London: UCL Press, pp. 2–17.

2011, "A view from the south: sub-Saharan evidence for contacts between North Africa, Mauritania and the Niger, 1000 BC – AD 700," in A. Dowler and E. R. Galvin (eds.), *Money, Trade and Trade Routes in Pre-Islamic North Africa*, London: British Museum Press, pp. 72–82.

MacDONALD, K. C. and MacDONALD, R. H., 2000, "The origins and development of domesticated animals in arid West Africa," in R. Blench and K. C. MacDonald (eds.), *The Origins and Development of African Livestock: Archaeology, Genetics, Linguistics and Ethnography*, London: UCL Press, pp. 127–162.

MacDonald, K. C., Vernet, R., Martinon-Torres, M., and Fuller, D. Q., 2009, "Dhar Néma: from early agriculture to metallurgy in southeastern Mauritania," *Azania*, 44 (1), pp. 3–48.

MacDonald, M. C. A., 1997, "Trade routes and trade goods at the northern end of the 'Incense Road' in the first millennium BC," in A. Avanzini (ed.), *Profumi d'Arabia*, Rome: "L'Erma"di Bretschneider, pp. 333–350.

McDowall, D. W., 1996, "The evidence of the gazetteer of Roman artefacts in India," in H. P. Ray and J.-F. Salles (eds.), *Tradition and Archaeology*, New Delhi: Manohar, pp. 79–95.

MacEachern, S., 2005, "Two thousand years of West African history," in, A. B. Stahl (ed.), *African Archaeology: A Critical Introduction*, Malden, MA, and Oxford: Blackwell, pp. 441–466.

2013, "Genetics and archaeology," in P. Mitchell and P. Lane (eds.), *The Oxford Handbook of African Archaeology*, Oxford University Press, pp. 65–76.

McGovern, P. E., 2003, *Ancient Wine: The Search for the Origins of Viniculture*, Princeton University Press.

McGrail, S., 1985, "Towards a classification of water transport," *World Archaeology*, 16, pp. 289–303.

2001, *Boats of the World: From the Stone Age to Medieval Times*, Oxford University Press.

2015, *Early Ships and Seafaring: Water Transport beyond Europe*, Barnsley: Pen and Sword.

McIntosh, J. R., 2005, *Ancient Mesopotamia: New Perspectives*, Santa Barbara, CA: ABC-CLIO.

MacIntosh, S. K., 1999, "Modelling political organization in large-scale settlement clusters: a case study from the inland Niger Delta," in S. K. MacIntosh (ed.), *Beyond Chiefdoms: Pathways to Complexity in Africa*, Cambridge University Press, pp. 66–79.

2005, "Archaeology and the reconstruction of the African past," in J. Philips (ed.), *Writing African History*, University of Rochester Press, pp. 51–85.

McKinnon, E. E., 1994, "The Sambas hoard: bronze drums and gold ornaments found in Kalimantan in 1991," *Journal of the Malayan Branch of the Royal Asiatic Society*, 67 (1), p. 9–28.

2000, "Buddhism and the pre-Islamic archaeology of Kutei in the Mahakama valley of East Kalimantan," in N. A. Taylor (ed.), *Studies in Southeast Asian Art: Essays in Honour of Stanley J. O'Connor*, Ithaca, NY: Cornell University Press, pp. 217–240.

McLaughlin, R., 2010, *Rome and the Distant East: Trade Routes to the Ancient Lands of Arabia, India and China*, London, Oxford, and New York: Bloomsbury.

2014, *The Roman Empire and the Indian Ocean: The Ancient World Economy and the Kingdoms of Africa, Arabia and India*, Barnsley: Penn and Sword.

McMahon, A., Oates, J. *et al.*, 2007, "Excavations at Tell Brak 2006–2007," *Iraq*, 69, pp. 145–171.

McMahon, A., Soltysiak, A., and Weber, J., 2011, "Cities and conflict: Late Chalcolithic mass graves at Tell Brak, Syria (3800–3600 BC)," *Journal of Field Archaeology*, 36 (3), pp. 201–220.

MacMillan, H. F., 1999, *Tropical Planting and Gardening with Special Reference to Ceylon*, New Delhi and Madras: Asian Educational Services (1st edn. 1935).

McNeill, W. H., 1963, *The Rise of the West: A History of the Human Community*, Chicago University Press.

1990, "*The Rise of the West* after twenty-five years," *Journal of World History*, 1 (1), pp. 1–21.

1998a, "World history and the rise and fall of the West," *Journal of World History*, 9 (2), pp. 215–236.

1998b, *Plagues and Peoples*, New York: Anchor Books (1st edn. 1976).

2000, "Transportation nets in world history," in R. A. Denemark, J. Friedman, B. K. Gills, and G. Modelski (eds.), *World System History: The Social Science of Long-term Change*, London and New York: Routledge, pp. 201–215.

MacPhee, R. D. E. and Burney, D. A., 1991, "Dating of modified femora of extinct dwarf Hippopotamus from southern Madagascar: implications for constraining human colonization and vertebrate extinction events," *Journal of Archaeological Science*, 18, pp. 695–706.

MacPherson, K., 1998, *The Indian Ocean: A History of People and the Sea*, Delhi: Oxford University Press.

Madella, M., 2003, "Investigating agriculture and environment in South Asia: present and future contributions from opal phytoliths," in S. Weber and W. R. Belcher (eds.), *Indus Ethnobiology: New Perspectives from the Field*, Lanham, MD: Lexington Books, pp. 199–249.

Madella, M. and Fuller, D. Q., 2006, "Palaeoecology and the Harappan civilisation of South Asia: a reconsideration," *Quaternary Science Reviews*, 25, pp. 1283–1301.

Madjidzadeh, Y., 2003a, b, and c, "La découverte de Jiroft," "La première campagne de fouilles à Jiroft dans le bassin du Halil Roud (janvier et février 2003)," and "Photorama," *Dossiers d'Archéologie*, 287, pp. 19–26, 65–75, and 135–142.

2003d, "Au berceau de la civilisation orientale: le mystérieux 'pays d'Aratta'?," *Archéologia*, 399, pp. 36–45.

2008, "Excavations at Konar Sandal in the region of Jiroft (2002–2008)," *Iran*, 46, pp. 69–104.

Maekawa, K., 1987, "Collective labor service in Girsu-Lagash: the Pre-Sargonic and Ur III Periods," in M. A. Powell (ed.), *Labor in the Ancient Near East*, New Haven, CT: American Oriental Society, pp. 49–71.

Magee, P., 1998, "Settlement patterns, polities and regional complexity in the Southeast Arabian Iron Age," *Paléorient*, 24 (2), pp. 49–59.

2005, "The chronology and environmental background of Iron Age settlement in southeastern Iran and the question of the origins of the Qanat irrigation system," *Iranica Antiqua*, 40, pp. 217–231.

2010, "Revisiting Indian Rouletted Ware and the impact of Indian Ocean trade in early historic South Asia," *Antiquity*, 84, pp. 1043–1054.

2014, *The Archaeology of Prehistoric Arabia: Adaptation and Social Formation from the Neolithic to the Iron Age*, Cambridge University Press.

Magee, D. A., Mannen, H., and Bradley, D. G., 2007, "Duality in *Bos indicus* mtDNA diversity: support for geographical complexity in zebu domestication," in M. D. Petraglia and B. Allchin (eds.), *The Evolution and History of Human Populations in South Asia* (Interdisciplinary Studies in Archaeology, Biological Anthropology, Linguistics and Genetics), Dordrecht: Springer, pp. 385–391.

Magnavita, S., 2003, "The beads of Kissi," *Journal of African Archaeology*, 1 (1), pp. 127–138.

2008, "The oldest textiles from Sub-Saharan West Africa: woolen facts from Kissi, Burkina Faso," *Journal of African Archaeology*, 6 (2), pp. 243–257.

Magnavita, S., Breunig, P., Ameje, J., and Posselt, M., 2006, "Zilum: a mid-first millennium BC fortified settlement near Lake Tchad," *Journal of African Archaeology*, 4 (1), pp. 153–169.

Mahadevan, I., 1996, "Old Sinhalese inscriptions from Indian ports: new evidence for ancient India-Sri Lanka contacts," *Journal of the Institute of Asian Studies*, 14 (1), pp. 55–67.

Mahdi, W., 1988, *Morphophonologische Besonderheiten und historische Phonologie des Malagasy. Veröffentlichungen des Seminars für Indonesische und Südseesprachen der Universität Hamburg*, vol. XX, Berlin and Hamburg: Dietrich Reimer.

1994 and b, "Some Austronesian maverick protoforms with culture-historical implications," *Oceanic Linguistics*, 33 (1), pp. 167–229, and 33 (2), pp. 421–490.

1998, "Linguistic data on transmission of South-East Asian cultigens to India and Sri Lanka," in R. Blench and M. Spriggs (eds.), *Archaeology and Language II: Archaeological Data and Linguistic Hypotheses*, London and New York: Routledge, pp. 390–415.

1999a, "The dispersal of Austronesian boat forms in the Indian Ocean," in R. Blench and M. Spriggs (eds.), *Archaeology and Language III: Artefacts, Languages and Texts*, London and New York: Routledge, pp. 144–179.

1999b, "Linguistic and philological data towards a chronology of Austronesian activity in India and Sri Lanka," in R. Blench and M. Spriggs (eds.), *Archaeology and Language IV: Language Change and Cultural Transformation*, London and New York: Routledge, pp. 160–242.

2008, "Yavadvipa and the Merapi volcano in West Sumatra," *Archipel*, 75, pp. 111–143.

2016, "Origins of Southeast Asian shipping and maritime communication across the Indian Ocean," in G. Campbell (ed.), *Early Exchanges between Africa and the Wider Indian Ocean World*, London: Palgrave Macmillan, pp. 25–49.

MAI, H. *et al.*, 2016, "Characterization of cosmetic sticks at Xiaohe Cemetery in early Bronze Age Xinjiang, China," *Scientific Reports*, 6 (18939), doi: 10.1038/srep18939.

MAIGRET, A. DE, 1997, "L'aube de l'histoire dans le Yémen intérieur," in *Yémen: au pays de la reine de Saba*, Paris: Flammarion, Institut du Monde Arabe, pp. 50–51.

MAIR, V., 2005, "The northwestern peoples and the recurrent origins of the 'Chinese State'," in J. A. Fogel (ed.), *The Teleology of the Modern Nation-State: Japan and China*, Philadelphia: University of Pennsylvania Press.

MAIRS, R., 2012, "Glassware from Roman Egypt at Begram (Afghanistan) and the Red Sea trade," *British Museum Studies in Ancient Egypt and Sudan*, 18, pp. 61–74.

MALAMAT, A., 1998, *Mari and the Bible*, Leiden: Brill.

MALHAO PEREIRA, J. M., 2003, *The Stellar Compass and the Kamal: An Interpretation of Its Practical Use*, Lisbon: Academia de Marinha.

MALININE, M., 1953, *Choix de textes juridiques en hiératique 'anormal' et en démotique (XXVe–XXVIIe dynasties)*, Paris: Champion.

MALLERET, L., 1959–1963, *L'archéologie du delta du Mékong*, 4 vols., Paris: École française d'Extrême-Orient.

MALLORY, J. P., 1998, "A European perspective on Indo-Europeans in Asia," in V. Mair (ed.), *The Bronze Age and Early Iron Age Peoples of Eastern Central Asia*, vol. 1, Washington, DC: Institute for the Study of Man, pp. 175–201.

2002, "Archaeological models and Asian Indo-Europeans," *Proceedings of the British Academy*, 116, pp. 19–42.

MALLORY, J. P. and MAIR, V. H., 2000, *The Tarim Mummies, Ancient China and the Mystery of the Earliest Peoples from the West*, London: Thames and Hudson.

MALONEY, B. K., 1994, "The prospects and problems of using palynology to trace the origins of tropical agriculture: the case of Southeast Asia," in J. G. Hather (ed.), *Tropical Archaeobotany: Applications and New Developments*, London and New York: Routledge, pp. 139–171.

MANGUIN, P.-Y., 1980, "The Southeast Asian ship: an historical approach," *Journal of Southeast Asian Studies*, 11 (2), pp. 266–276.

1985a, "Late mediaeval Asian shipbuilding in the Indian Ocean: a reappraisal," *Moyen Orient & Océan indien, XVIe–XIXe s / Middle East & Indian Ocean*, 2 (2), pp. 1–30.

1985b, "Sewn-plank craft of South-East Asia: a preliminary survey," in S. McGrail and E. Kentley (eds.), *Sewn Planked Boats: Archaeological and Ethnographic Papers Based on those Presented to a Conference at Greenwich in November, 1984* (Archaeological Series 10 / BAR International Series 276), Oxford: National Maritime Museum, Greenwich, pp. 319–343.

1988, "Review of Kenneth R. Hall, *Maritime Trade and State Development in Early Southeast Asia*, Honolulu, University of Hawaii Press, 1985," *Journal of the Economic and Social History of the Orient*, 31 (3), pp. 327–333.

1993, "Trading ships of the South China Sea: shipbuilding techniques and their role in the history of the development of Asian trade networks," *Journal of the Economic and Social History of the Orient*, 36, pp. 253–279.

1996, "Southeast Asian shipping in the Indian Ocean during the first millennium AD," in H. P. Ray and J.-F. Salles (eds.), *Tradition and Archaeology: Early Maritime Contacts in the Indian Ocean*, Delhi: Manohar, pp. 181–196.

2000a, "Les techniques de construction navale aux Maldives originaires d'Asie du Sud-Est," *Techniques et culture*, 35–36, pp. 21–47.

2000b, "Shipshape societies: boat symbolism and political systems in Insular Southeast Asia," *Techniques et culture*, 35–36, pp. 373–400.

2000c, "City-states and city-state cultures in pre-15th century Southeast Asia," in M. H. Hansen (ed.), *A Comparative Study of Thirty City-State Cultures*, Copenhagen: Det Kongelige Danske Videnskabernes Selskab, pp. 409–416.

2000d, "Les cités-états de l'Asie du Sud-Est côtière: de l'ancienneté et de la permanence des formes urbaines," *Bulletin de l'Ecole française d'Extrême-Orient*, 87, pp. 151–182.

2002, "The amorphous nature of coastal polities in Insular Southeast Asia: restricted centres, extended peripheries," *Moussons*, 5, pp. 73–99.

2004a, Notices on "Sriwijaya," "Oc Eo," "Shipbuilding," and "Firearms," in Ooi Keat Gin (ed.), *Southeast Asia: A Historical Encyclopedia, From Angkor Wat to East Timor*, 3 vols., Santa Barbara, CA: ABC-Clio.

2004b, "The archaeology of the early maritime polities of Southeast Asia," in P. Bellwood and I. Glover (eds.), *Southeast Asia: From Prehistory to History*, London: Routledge Curzon, pp. 282–313.

2005, "Nouvelles recherches dans le delta du Mékong: le site de Oc Eo," *Dossiers d'Archéologie*, 302, pp. 78–81.

2010, "Pan-regional responses to South Asian inputs in early Southeast Asia," in B. Bellina, E. A. Bacus, T. O. Pryce, and J. Wisseman Christie (eds.), *50 Years of Archaeology in Southeast Asia: Essays in Honour of Ian Glover*, Bangkok: River Books, pp. 170–181.

2012, "Asian ship-building traditions in the Indian Ocean at the dawn of European expansion," in O. Prakash (ed.), *The Trading World of the Indian Ocean, 1500–1800*, Delhi and Chennai: Centre for Studies in Civilizations, pp. 597–629.

2016, "Austronesian shipping in the Indian Ocean: from outrigger boats to trading ships," in G. Campbell (ed.), *Early Exchange between Africa and the Wider Indian Ocean World*, London: Palgrave Macmillan, pp. 51–76.

MANI, B. R., 2004, "Further evidence on Kashmir Neolithic in light of recent excavations at Kanishkapura," *Journal of Interdisciplinary Studies in History and Archaeology*, 1 (1), pp. 137–142.

MANN, M., 1986, *The Sources of Social Power*, vol. 1: *A History of Power from the Beginning to AD 1760*, Cambridge University Press.

MANN, M. E. and JONES, P. D., 2003, "Global surface temperatures over the past two millennia," *Geophysical Research Letters*, 30 (15), p. 1820.

MANN, M. E, ZHANG, Z., HUGHES, M. K., et al., 2008, "Proxy-based reconstructions of hemispheric and global surface temperature variations over the past two millennia," *Proceedings of the National Academy of Sciences of the United States of America*, 105, pp. 13252–13257.

MANNING, J. G., 2003, *Land and Power in Ptolemaic Egypt: The Structure of Land Tenure*, Cambridge University Press.

MANNING, K. and FULLER, D. Q., 2014, "Early millet farmers in the Lower Tilemsi Valley," in C. J. Stevens, S. Nixon, M. A. Murray, and D. Fuller (eds.), *Archaeology of African Plant Use*, Walnut Creek, CA: Left Coast Press, Institute of Archaeology Publications, pp. 73–81.

MANNING, K., PELLING, R., HIGHAM, T., SCHWENNINGER, J.-L., and FULLER, D. Q., 2010, "4500-year old domesticated pearl millet (*Pennisetum glaucum*) from the Tilemsi valley, Mali: new insights into an alternative cereal domestication pathway," *Journal of Archeological Science*, doi: 10.1016/j.jas.2010.09.007.

MANNING, S. W., 2006, "Radiocarbon dating and Egyptian chronology," in E. Hornung, R. Krauss, and D. Warburton (eds.), *Ancient Egyptian Chronology*, Leiden: Brill, pp. 327–355.

MANNING, S. W. and RAMSEY, C. B., 2003, "A Late Minoan I-II absolute chronology for the Aegean: combining archaeology with radiocarbon," in M. Bietak (ed.), *The Synchronisation of Civilisations in the Eastern Mediterranean in the Second Millennium BC II, Proceedings of the SCIEM 2000 EuroConference, Haindorf, May 2–7, 2001*, Vienna: Verlag der Österreichischen Akademie der Wissenschaften, pp. 111–134.

MANZO, A., 1999, *Échanges et contacts le long du Nil et de la mer Rouge dans l'époque protohistorique (IIIe et IIe millénaires avant J.-C.): une synthèse préliminaire* (BAR International Series 782), Oxford: Archaeopress.

MARCUS, E., 2002a, "The southern Levant and maritime trade during the Middle Bronze IIA period," in E. D. Oren and S. Ahituv (eds.), *Aharon Kempinski Memorial Volume. Studies in Archaeology and Related Disciplines*, Ben-Gurion University of the Negev, pp. 241–263.

2002b, "Early seafaring and maritime activity in the southern Levant from prehistory through the third millennium BCE," in E. C. M. Van den Brink and T. E. Levy (eds.), *Egypt and the Levant: Interrelations from the 4th through the Early 3rd Millennium BCE.*, London: Leicester University Press, pp. 403–417.

MARCUS, J., 1998, "The peaks and valleys of ancient states: an extension of the Dynamic Model," in G. M. Feinman and J. Marcus (eds.), *Archaic States*, Santa Fe: School of American Research, pp. 59–94.

MARET, P. DE, 2013, "Archaeologies of the Bantu expansion," in P. Mitchell and P. Lane (eds.), *The Oxford Handbook of African Archaeology*, Oxford University Press, pp. 627–644.

MARFOE, L., 1987, "Cedar forest to silver mountain: social change and the development of long-distance trade in early Near Eastern societies," in M. Rowlands, M. Larsen, and K. Kristiansen (eds.), *Centre and Periphery in the Ancient World*, Cambridge University Press, pp. 25–35.

MARGARITI, C., PROTOPAPAS, S., and ORPHANOU, V., 2010, "Reviewing past analyses and introducing new data to the Kerameikos HTR-73 excavated textile find," *Journal of Archaeological Science*, 38 (3), pp. 522–527.

MARGARITI, R. E., 2007, *Aden and the Indian Ocean Trade: 150 Years of the Life of a Medieval Arabian Port*, Chapel Hill: The University of North Carolina Press.

MARGUERON, J.-C., 2004, *Mari, métropole de l'Euphrate au IIIe et au début du IIe millénaire*, Paris: Picard/Éditions Recherche sur les Civilisations.

MARGUERON, J.-C. and PFIRSCH, L., 2001, *Le Proche-Orient et l'Égypte antiques*, Paris: Hachette (1st edn. 1996).

MARK, S., 1998, *From Egypt to Mesopotamia: A Study of Predynastic Trade Routes*, College Station: Texas A&M University Press.

MARKS, R. B., 1998, *Tigers, Rice, Silk and Silt. Environment and Economy in Late Imperial South China*, Cambridge University Press.

MARLIER, S. and POMEY, P., 2008, "La construction navale à l'époque romaine: permanences et évolutions," in M. Molin (ed.), *Archéologie et histoire des techniques du monde romain, Actes du Colloque de la Société Française d'Archéologie Classique, Paris, I.N.H.A., 15 novembre 2006*, Paris: de Boccard, pp. 105–118.

MARRO, C., 2007, "Upper-Mesopotamia and Transcaucasia in the Late Chalcolithic period (4000–3500 BC)," in B. Lyonnet (ed.), *Les cultures du Caucase (VIe–IIIe millénaires avant notre ère): leurs relations avec le Proche-Orient*, Paris: Éditions Recherche sur les Civilisations, pp. 77–94.

MARSHALL, F., 1989, "Rethinking the role of *Bos indicus* in Sub-Saharan Africa," *Current Anthropology*, 30, pp. 235–240.

2000, "The origins and spread of domestic animals in East Africa," in R. Blench and K. C. MacDonald (eds.), *The Origins and Development of African Livestock. Archaeology, Genetics, Linguistics and Ethnography*, London: UCL Press, pp. 191–221.

MARTIN, N., 2010, "Les productions céramiques de l'océan Indien occidental: implications culturelles au carrefour d'influences," Thèse, Institut National de Langues et Civilisations Orientales.

MARTIN-PUERTAS, C. *et al.*, 2012, "Regional atmospheric circulation shifts induced by a grand solar minimum," *Nature Geoscience*, 5, pp. 397–401.

MASETTI-ROUAULT, M. G., 2008, "Économie de redistribution et économie de marché au Proche-Orient ancien," in Y. Roman and J. Dalaison (eds.), *L'économie antique, une économie de marché?, Actes de deux Tables rondes tenues à Lyon en 2004*, Paris: de Boccard, pp. 55–152.

MASICA, C., 1979, "Aryan and Non-Aryan elements in north Indian agriculture," in M. Deshpande and P. Hook (eds.), *Aryan and Non-Aryan in India*, Ann Arbor, MI: Center for South and Southeast Asian Studies, University of Michigan, pp. 55–152.

MASSON, V. M., 1996a and b, "The Bronze Age in Khorasan and Transoxania" and "The decline of the Bronze Age civilization and movements of the tribes," in A. H. Dani and V. M. Masson (eds.), *History of Civilizations of Central Asia*, vol. I, New Delhi: Motilal Banarsidass, pp. 225–245 and 337–356.

MAS'ŪDĪ, 1841, *The Meadows of Gold and Mines of Gems*, vol. I, trans. from the Arabic by Aloys Sprenger, London: Printed for the Oriental Translation Fund of Great Britain and Ireland.

1962, 1965, *Les prairies d'or*, trans. Barbier de Meynard and Pavet de Courteille, ed. C. Pellat, Paris: Société Asiatique, vols. I and II.

MATHEW, G., 1975, "The dating and the significance of the *Periplus of the Erythrean Sea*," in N. Chittick and R. Rotberg (eds.), *East Africa and the Orient*, London and New York: Holmes and Meier, Africana Publishing Co., pp. 147–163.

MATHIEU, B., 2004, "Les travaux de l'Institut Français d'Archéologie Orientale en 2003–2004," *Bulletin de l'Institut Français d'Archéologie Orientale*, 104, pp. 585–762.

MATTHEWS, R., 2003, *The Archaeology of Mesopotamia: Theories and Approaches*, London and New York: Routledge.

2013, "The power of writing: administrative activity at Godin Tepe, central Zagros, in the later 4th millennium BC," in C. A. Petrie (ed.), *Ancient Iran and Its Neighbours*, Oxford: Oxbow Books, pp. 327–350.

MATTINGLY, D. J., 2011, "The Garamantes of Fazzan: an early Libyan state with trans-Saharan connections," in A. Dowler and E. R. Galwin (eds.), *Money, Trade and Trade Routes in Pre-Islamic North Africa*, London: British Museum, pp. 49–60.

MATTINGLY, D. J., DANIELS, C. M., DORE, J. N., EDWARDS, D., and HAWTHORNE, J., 2007, *The Archaeology of Fezzan*, vol. II: *Gazetter, Pottery and Other Finds*, London and Tripoli, Society for Libyan Studies.

MATTINGLY, D. J., DORE, J., and WILSON, A. I., 2003, *The Archaeology of Fezzan*, vol. I: *Synthesis*, London and Tripoli: Society for Libyan Studies.

MATTINGLY, D. J., OREJAS, A., and CLAVEL-LÉVÊQUE, M. (eds), 2009, *From Present to Past through Landscape*, Madrid: CSIC.

MAUCOURANT, J., 2004, "Karl Polanyi, les marchés et le Marché," *Actes du colloque Karl Polanyi et le marché du 12 juin 2003, Nanterre*, MSH René-Ginouvès/Les Colloques en ligne, www.mae.u-paris10.fr/fx/detail.php?ID=72&query=

2008, "Figures du néomodernisme: le 'marché' est-il un 'signifiant vide'?," in Y. Roman and J. Dalaison (eds.), *L'économie antique, une économie de marché?, Actes de deux Tables rondes tenues à Lyon en 2004*, Paris: de Boccard, pp. 17–47.

MAYRHOFER, M., 1986–2001, *Etymologisches Wörterbuch des Altindoarischen*, Heidelberg: Carl Winter Universitätsverlag.

MAZZARINO, S., 1997, "The Hypalum of Pliny," in F. De Romanis and A. Tchernia (eds.), *Crossings: Early Mediterranean Contacts with India*, New Delhi: Manohar, pp. 72–79.

MAZOYER, M. and ROUDART, L., 1998, *Histoire des agricultures du monde du Néolithique à la crise contemporaine*, Paris: Seuil.

MBIDA, C. M., DOUTRELEPONT, H., VRYDAGHS, L., SWENNEN, R. L., SWENNEN, R. J., BEECKMAN, H., DE LANGHE, E. A. L., and DE MARET, P., 2001, "First archaeological evidence of banana cultivation in central Africa during the third millennium before present," *Vegetation History and Archaeobotany*, 10 (1), pp. 1–6.

MBIDA, C. M., DOUTRELEPONT, H., VRYDAGHS, L., SWENNEN, R. L., SWENNEN, R. J., BEECKMAN, H., DE LANGHE, E. A. L., and DE MARET, P., 2004, "Oui, il y avait bien des bananiers au Cameroun il y a 2000 ans," *Infomusa*, 13 (1), pp. 40–42.

MBIDA, C. M., DE LANGHE, E., VRYDAGHS, J., DOUTRELEPONT, H., SWENNEN, R., VAN NEER, W., and DE MARET, P., 2006, "Phytolith evidence for the early presence of domesticated banana (Musa) in Africa," in M. A. Zeder, D. G. Bradley, E. Emshwiller, and B. D. Smith (eds.), *Documenting Domestication: New Genetic and Archaeological Paradigms*, Berkeley: University of California Press, pp. 68–81.

MEADOW, R. H., 2002, "The chronological and cultural significance of a steatite wig from Harappa," *Iranica Antiqua*, 37, pp. 191–202.

MEDEROS, A. and LAMBERG-KARLOVSKY, C. C., 2004, "Weight systems and trade networks in the Old World (2500–1000 BC)," in M. Hudson and C. Wunsch (eds.), *Creating Economic Order: Record-Keeping, Standardization and the Development of Accounting in the Ancient Near East*, Bethesda, MD: CDL Press, pp. 199–214.

MEEKS, D., 1993, "Migration des plantes, migration des mots dans l'Égypte ancienne," in M.-C. Amouretti and G. Comet (eds.), *Des hommes et des plantes: plantes méditerranéennes, vocabulaire et usages anciens* (Cahier d'Histoire des Techniques 2), Université de Provence, pp. 71–92.

—— 1997, "Navigation maritime et navires égyptiens: les éléments d'une controverse," D. Meeks and D. Garcia (eds.), *Techniques et économie antiques et médiévales*, Paris: Érrance, pp. 175–194.

—— 2002, "Coptos et les chemins de Pount," *Topoi*, Supplément 3, pp. 267–335.

—— 2006, "L'Égypte ancienne et l'histoire des techniques: Égyptiens et égyptologues entre tradition et innovation," in B. Mathieu, D. Meeks, and M. Wissa (eds.), *L'apport de l'Egypte à l'histoire des techniques: méthodes, chronologie et comparaisons*, Cairo: Institut Français d'Archéologie Orientale, pp. 1–13.

MEI, J., 2003, "Qijia and Seima-Turbino: the question of early contacts between North-West China and the Eurasian Steppe," *The Museum of Far Eastern Antiquities* (Stockholm), 75, pp. 31–54.

MEI, J. and SHELL, C., 1999, "The existence of Andronovo cultural influence in Xinjiang during the second millennium BC," *Antiquity*, 73 (281), pp. 570–578.

MEI, J., XU, J., CHEN, K., SHEN, L., and WANG, H., 2012, "Recent research on early bronze metallurgy in northwest China," in P. Jett, B. McCarthy, and J. Douglas (eds.), *Scientific Research on Ancient Asian Metallurgy. Proceedings of the Fifth Forbes Symposium at the Freer Gallery of Art*, Washington, DC: Archetype Publications in association with the Freer Gallery of Art, Smithsonian Institution, pp. 37–46.

—— 2002, "The Iron Age cultures in Xinjiang and their steppe connections," in K. Boyle, C. Renfrew, and M. Levine (eds.), *Ancient Interactions: East and West in Eurasia*, Cambridge: McDonald Institute for Archaeological Research, pp. 213–234.

MEIJER, D. J. W., 2001, "Long-distance trade. some remarks on the ancient Syrian economy," in W. H. van Soldt, J. G. Dercksen, N. J. C. Kouwenberg, and T. J. H. Krispijn (eds.), *Veenhof*

Anniversary Volume: Studies Presented to Klaas R. Veenhof on the Occasion of His Sixty-Fifth Birthday, Leiden: Nederlands Instituut voor het Nabue Oosten, pp. 325–341.

MENU, B., 1998, *Recherches sur l'histoire juridique, économique et sociale de l'ancienne Égypte* (Institut Français d'Archéologie Orientale, Bibliothèque d'Étude, 122), Cairo: Institut Français d'Archéologie Orientale.

2001a "La monnaie des Égyptiens de l'époque pharaonique," in A. Testard (ed.), *Aux origines de la monnaie*, Paris: Éditions Errance, pp. 73–108.

2001b "Economy: overview," in *The Oxford Encyclopedia of Ancient Egypt*, vol. 1, Oxford University Press, pp. 422–426.

METSPALU, M. *et al.*, 2004, "Most of the extant mitDNA boundaries in South and Southwest Asia were likely shaped during the initial settlement of Eurasia by anatomically modern humans," *BMC Genetics*, 5 (26), doi: 10.1186/1471-2156-5-26.

MEYER, J. C., 2007, "Roman coins as a source for Roman trading activities in the Indian Ocean," in E. H. Seland (ed.), *The Indian Ocean in the Ancient Period: Definite Places, Translocal exchange* (BAR International Series 1593), Oxford: Archaeopress, pp. 59–68.

MEYER, C., TODD, J. M., and BECK, C. W., 1991, "From Zanzibar to Zagros: a copal pendant from Eshnunna," *Journal of Near Eastern Studies*, 50, pp. 289–298.

MICHAILIDOU, A., 2005, *Weight and Value in Pre-coinage Societies, an Introduction*, Paris: de Boccard.

MICHALOWSKI, P., 2003, "The earliest scholastic tradition," in J. Aruz and R. Wallenfels (eds.), *Art of the First Cities: The Third Millennium B.C. From the Mediterranean to the Indus*, New York: The Metropolitan Museum of Art; New Haven, CT, and London: Yale University Press, pp. 450–478.

2008, "The mortal kings of Ur: a short century of divine rule in ancient Mesopotamia," in N. Brisch (ed.), *Religion and Power: Divine Kingship in the Ancient World and Beyond*, University of Chicago Press, pp. 33–46.

MICHEL, C., 2001a, "Commerce des grands organismes," and "Commerce international," in F. Joannès (ed.), *Dictionnaire de la civilisation mésopotamienne*, Paris: Laffont, pp. 194–196 and 196–199.

2001b *Correspondance des marchands de Kaniš au début du IIe millénaire avant J.-C.*, Paris: Éditions du Cerf.

2001c "Le lapis-lazuli des Assyriens au début du IIe millénaire av. J.-C.," in W. H. van Soldt, J. G. Dercksen, N. J. C. Kouwenberg, and T. J. H. Krispijn (eds.), *Veenhof Anniversary Volume: Studies Presented to Klaas R. Veenhof on the Occasion of His Sixty-Fifth Birthday*, Leiden: Nederlands Instituut voor het Nabue Oosten, pp. 341–359.

MIELANTS, E. H., 2007, *The Origins of Capitalism and the 'Rise of the West'*, Philadelphia, PA: Temple University Press.

MIGEOTTE, J., 2007, *L'économie des cités grecques de l'archaïsme au Haut Empire romain*, 2nd edn., Paris: Ellipses Marketing.

2008, "Les cités grecques: une économie à plusieurs niveaux," in Y. Roman and J. Dalaison (eds.), *L'économie antique, une économie de marché?*, *Actes de deux Tables rondes tenues à Lyon en 2004*, Paris: de Boccard, pp. 69–86.

MIKSIC, J., 2004, "The classical cultures of Indonesia," in I. Glover and P. Bellwood (eds.), *Southeast Asia: From Prehistory to History*, Abingdon and New York: Routledge/Curzon, pp. 234–256.

MILBURN, O., 2007, "The *Book of the Young Master of Accountancy*: an ancient Chinese economics text," *Journal of the Economic and Social History of the Orient*, 50 (1), pp. 19–40.

MILLER, D. 2002, "Smelter and smith: Iron Age metal fabrication technology in southern Africa," *Journal of Archaeological Science*, 29 (10), pp. 1083–1131.

2003, "Indigenous copper-mining and smelting in pre-colonial southern Africa," in P. Craddock and J. Lang (eds.), *Mining and Metal Production through the Ages*, London: British Museum Press, pp. 101–110.

MILLER, J. I., 1998, *The Spice Trade of the Roman Empire, 29 BC to AD 641*, Oxford: Clarendon Press (1st edn. 1969).

MILLS, J. V. G. (ed.), 1970: *see* MA HUAN, 1970.

MIN-SHAN KO, A., CHEN, C.-Y., FU, Q., DELFIN, F., LI, M., CHIU, H.-L., STONEKING, M., and KO, Y.-C., 2014, "Early Austronesians: into and out of Taiwan," *American Journal of Human Genetics*, 94, pp. 426–436.

MIQUEL, A., 1967, 1975, 1980, *La géographie humaine du monde musulman jusqu'au milieu du 11e siècle*, vol. I: *Géographie et géographie humaine dans la littérature arabe des origines à 1050*, vol. II: *Géographie arabe et représentation du monde: la terre et l'étranger*, vol. III: *Le milieu naturel*, Paris and The Hague: Mouton et École des Hautes Études en Sciences Sociales.

MIROSCHEDJI, P. DE, 2002, "The socio-political dynamics of Egyptian-Canaanite interaction in the early Bronze Age," in E. C. M. van den Brink and T. E. Levy (eds.), *Egypt and the Levant. Interrelations from the 4th through the Early 3rd Millennium BCE*, London and New York: Leicester University Press, pp. 39–57.

2003, "Susa and the highlands: major trends in the history of Elamite civilization," in N. F. Miller and K. Abdi (eds.), *Yeki bud, Yeki nabud: Essays on the Archaeology of Iran in Honor of William M. Sumner*, Los Angeles: Cotsen Institute of Archaeology, University of California, pp. 17–38.

MITCHELL, P., 2002, *The Archaeology of Southern Africa*, Cambridge University Press.

2013, "Early farming communities of southern and south-central Africa," in P. Mitchell and P. Lane (eds.), *The Oxford Handbook of African Archaeology*, Oxford University Press, pp. 657–670.

MITCHINER, M., 2000, *The Land of Water: Coinage and History of Bangladesh and Later Arakan*, London: Hawkins Publications.

2004, *Ancient Trade and Early Coinage*, vol. 1, London: Hawkins Publications.

MITTAL, S. N., 2004, *Kautiliya Arthasastra Revisited*, New Delhi: Centre for Studies in Civilizations.

MOBERG, A., SONECHKIN, D. M., HOLMGREN, K., DATSENKO, N. M., and KARLEN, W., 2005, "Highly variable Northern Hemisphere temperatures reconstructed from low- and high-resolution proxy data," *Nature*, 433 (7026), pp. 613–617.

MODELSKI, G., 2003, *World Cities: –3000 to 2000*, Washington, DC: Faros 2000.

MOLIN, M., 2009, "Circulations, transports et déplacements en Europe occidentale (IIe siècle av. J.-C. – IIe siècle ap. J.-C.): données indigènes et apports romains," in B. Cabouret-Laurioux, J.-P. Guilhembet, and Y. Roman (eds.), *Pallas: Revue d'Études Antiques* ("Rome et l'Occident: IIe siècle av. J.-C.– IIe siècle ap. J.-C.," Colloque de la SOPHAU, Lyon, May 15–1, 2009), Toulouse: Presses Universitaires du Mirail, pp. 205–221.

MOLINA, J., *et al.*, 2011a, "Molecular evidence for a single evolutionary origin of domesticated rice," *Proceedings of the National Academy of Sciences of the United States of America*, 108 (20), pp. 8351–8356.

2011b, "Reply to Ge and Sang: a single origin of domesticated rice," *Proceedings of the National Academy of Sciences of the United States of America*, 108 (39), E756, doi: 10.1073/pnas.1112466108

MONROE, C. M., 2005, "Money and trade," in D. C. Snell (ed.), *A Companion to the Ancient Near East*, Malden and Oxford: Blackwell, pp. 155–168.

MOOKERJI, R. K., 1999, *Indian Shipping: A History of the Sea-Borne Trade and Maritime Activity of the Indians from the Earliest Times*, New Delhi: Munshiram Manoharlal (1st edn. 1912).

MOORE, E. H., 2007, *Early Landscapes of Myanmar*, Bangkok: Riverbooks.

Moore, K. and Lewis, D., 1999, *Birth of the Multinational – 2000 Years of Ancient Business History from Ashur to Augustus*, Copenhagen: Copenhagen Business School Press.

2009, *The Origins of Globalization*, New York and London: Routledge.

Moorey, P. R. S., 1994, *Ancient Mesopotamian Materials and Industries*, Oxford: Clarendon Press.

1995, "Did Easterners sail round Arabia to Egypt in the fourth millennium BC?" in J. M. Sasson (ed.), *Civilizations of the Ancient Near East*, vols. I-II, Peabody, MA: Hendrickson Publishers, pp. 189–206.

2001, "The mobility of artisans and opportunities for technology transfer between Western Asia and Egypt in the Late Bronze Age," in A. J. Shortland (ed.), *The Social Context of Technological Change in Egypt and the Near East, 1650–1550 BC*, Oxford: Oxbow Books, pp. 1–14.

Moran, W. L., 1987, *Les Lettres d'Amarna*, Paris: Le Cerf.

1992, *The Amarna Letters*. Baltimore, MD: Johns Hopkins University Press.

Morgunova, N. L. and Kokhlova, O. S., 2006, "Kurgans and nomads: new investigations of mound burials in the southern Urals," *Antiquity*, 80 (308), pp. 303–317.

Morin, E., 1990, *Science avec conscience*, Paris: Fayard (1st edn. 1982).

Morris, I., 1987, *Burial and Ancient Society: The Rise of the Greek City-State*, Cambridge University Press.

2009, "The Greater Athenian State," in I. Morris and W. Scheidel (eds.), *The Dynamics of Ancient Empires: State Power from Assyria to Byzantium*, Oxford University Press, pp. 99–177.

2013, *The Measure of Civilization*, Princeton University Press.

Moulherat, C., Mille, B., Tengberg, M., and Haquet, J.-F., 2002, "First evidence of cotton at Neolithic Mehrgarh, Pakistan: analysis of mineralized fibres from a copper bead," *Journal of Archaeological Science*, 29, pp. 1393–13401.

Moulins, D. d., Phillips, C., and Durrani, N., 2003, "The archaeobotanical record of Yemen and the question of Afro-Asian contacts," in K. Neumann, A. Butler, and S. Kahlhaber (eds.), *Food, Fuel and Fields: Progress in African Archaeobotany*, Cologne: Heinrich-Barth-Institut, pp. 213–228.

Moura, M., 1878, *Vocabulaire Français–Cambodgien et Cambodgien–Français*, Paris: Challamel.

Mouton, M., 1997, "Les échanges entre l'Arabie du Sud et la péninsule d'Oman du 3e siècle av. J.-C. au 4e siècle apr. J.-C.," in A. Avanzini (ed.), *Profumi d'Arabia*, Rome: "L'Erma" di Bretschneider, pp. 297–313.

2006, "Le port sud-arabique de Qânî: paléogéographie et organisation urbaine," *Comptes rendus de l'Académie des Inscriptions et Belles-Lettres*, pp. 3–34.

Msaidie, S., Ducourneau, A., Boëtsch, G., Longepied, G., Papa, K., Allibert, C., Yahayaa, A., Chiaroni, J., and Mitchell, M. J., 2011, "Genetic diversity on the Comoros Islands shows early seafaring as major determinant of human biocultural evolution in the Western Indian Ocean," *European Journal of Human Genetics*, 19 (1), pp. 89–94.

Muchadeyi, F. C., Eding, H., Simianer, H., Wollny, C.B.A., Groeneveld, E., and Weigend, S., 2008, "Mitochondrial DNA D-loop sequences suggest a Southeast Asian and Indian origin of Zimbabwean village chickens," *Animal Genetics*, 39, pp. 615–622.

Muhly, J. D., 1993, "Comments on A. G. Frank's article 'Bronze Age world system cycles'," *Current Anthropology*, 34 (4), pp. 417–418.

1995, "Mining and metalwork in ancient western Asia," in J. M. Sasson (ed.), *Civilizations of the Ancient Near East*, vol. III, New York: Scribner's, pp. 1501–1521.

Mukherjee, A., Rossberger, E., James, M. A., Pfälzner, P., Higgitt, C. L., White, R., Peggie, D. A., Azar, D., and Evershed, R. P., 2008, "The Qatna lion: scientific confirmation of Baltic amber in Late Bronze Age Syria," *Antiquity*, 82 (315), pp. 49–59.

MUKHERJEE, B. N., 1999, "The maritime contacts between eastern India and South-east Asia: new epigraphic data," in K. S. Behera (ed.), *Maritime Heritage of India*, New Delhi: Aryan Books International, pp. 201–205.

———— 2001, "Coastal and overseas trade in Pre-Gupta Vanga and Kalinga," in R. Chakravarti (ed.), *Trade in Early India*, Oxford University Press, pp. 199–227 (first published 1996 in S. Chakravarti [ed.], *Vinayatoshini: Benoytosh Centenary Volume*, Calcutta: Benoytosh Centenary Committee, pp. 181–192).

MÜLLER, S., 2003, "Chin-straps of the Early Northern Wei: new perspectives on the trans-Asiatic diffusion of funerary practices," *Journal of East Asian Archaeology*, 5 (1–4), pp. 27–71.

MÜLLER, W. W., 1997, "Namen von Aromata im Antiken Süd-arabien," in A. Avanzini (ed.), *Profumi d'Arabia*, Rome: "L'Erma" di Bretschneider, pp. 193–210.

MÜLLER-KARPE, A., 1994, *Altanatolisches Metallhandwerk*, Neumünster: Wachholtz.

MÜLLER-WOLLERMANN, R., 1985, "Warenaustausch im Ägypten des Alten Reiches," *Journal of the Economic and Social History of the Orient*, 28, pp. 138–148.

MUNRO-HAY, S. C. H., 1996, "Aksumite overseas interests," in J. Reade (ed.), *The Indian Ocean in Antiquity*, London and New York: Kegan Paul, pp. 403–416.

———— 2002, *Ethiopia. The Unknown Land: A Cultural and Historical Guide*, London: I. B. Tauris.

MURDOCH, G. P., 1959, *Africa. Its Peoples and Their Culture History*, New York, Toronto, and London: McGraw-Hill.

MURILLO-BARROSO, M., PRYCE, T. O., BELLINA, B., and MARTINON-TORRES, M., 2010, "Khao Sam Kaeo: an archaeometallurgical crossroads for trans-asiatic technological traditions," *Journal of Archaeological Science*, 37 (7), pp. 1761–1772.

MUSCARELLA, O. W., 2001, "Jiroft and 'Jiroft-Aratta': a review article of Yousef Madjidzadeh, *Jiroft: The Earliest Oriental Civilization*, *Bulletin of the Asia Institute*, 15, pp. 173–198.

MWACHARO, J. M., BJØRNSTAD, G, MOBEGI, V., NOMURA, K., HANADA, H., AMANO, T., JIANLIN, H., and HANOTTE, O., 2011, "Mitochondrial DNA reveals multiple introductions of domestic chicken in East Africa," *Molecular Phylogenetics and Evolution*, 58, pp. 374–382.

MWACHARO, J. M., NOMURA, K., HANADA, H., HAN, J. L., AMANO, T., and HANOTTE, O., 2013, "Reconstructing the origin and dispersal patterns of village chickens across East Africa: insights from autosomal markers," *Molecular Ecology*, 22 (10), pp. 2683–2697.

MWOROHA, E., 1977, *Peuples et rois de l'Afrique des lacs: le Burundi et les royaumes voisins au XIXe siècle*, Dakar and Abidjan: Nouvelles Editions Africaines.

MYRDAL, G., 1970, *The Challenge of World Poverty: A World Anti-Poverty Program in Outline*, New York: Pantheon Books.

NADIS, S., 2001, "Ice Man," *Archaeology*, November–December, pp. 28–33.

NAERSSEN, F. H. VAN, 1947, "The Cailendra interregnum," in J. P. Vogel (ed.), *India Antiqua*, Leiden: Brill, pp. 249–253.

NALESINI, O., 2009, "History and use of an ethnym: Ichthyophagoi," in L. Blue, J. Cooper, R. Thomas, and J. Whitewright (eds.), *Connected Hinterlands: Proceedings of the Red Sea Project IV* (BAR International Series 2052), Oxford: Archaeopress, pp. 9–18.

NAMDAR, D., GILBOA, A., NEUMANN, R., FINKELSTEIN, I., and WEINER, S., 2013, "Cinnamaldehyde in early Iron Age Phoenician flasks raises the possibility of Levantine trade with South East Asia," *Mediterranean Archaeology and Archaeometry*, 13 (2), pp. 1–19.

NASU, H., MOMOHARA, A., YASUDA, Y., and HE, J., 2007, "The occurrence and identification of *Setaria italica* (L.) P. Beauv. (foxtail millet) grains from Chengtoushan site (*ca.* 5800 cal. B.P.) in Central China, with reference to the domestication centre in Asia," *Vegetation History and Archaeobotany*, 16 (6), pp. 481–494.

NAVILLE, H. E., 1895–1908, *The Temple of Deir el Bahari*, London: Egypt Exploration Fund.

1906, *The Tomb of Hâtshopsîtû: Theodore M. Davis' Excavations, Bibân El Molûk*, London: A. Constable.

NAYAR, N. M., 1995, "Sesame (*Sesamum*; Pedaliaceae)," in J. Smartt and N. W. Simmonds (eds.), *Evolution of Crop Plants*, London and New York: Longman, pp. 404–407.

NDAYISHINGUJE, P., 1977, *L'intronisation d'un mwami: La royauté capture les rois*, Nanterre: Laboratoire d'Ethnologie et de sociologie comparative.

NEEDHAM, J., 1970, "Abstract of material presented to the International Maritime History Commission at Beirut," in M. Mollat (ed.), *Sociétés et Compagnies de commerce en Orient et dans l'Océan Indien*, Paris: SEVPEN, pp. 139–165.

NEEDHAM, J. *et al.* (eds.), 1954–, *Science and Civilisation in China*, Cambridge University Press. Vol. I: *Introductory Orientations*, ed. J. NEEDHAM and Wang LING (1956); vol. II: *History of Scientific Thought*, ed. J. NEEDHAM and Wang LING (1956); vol. III: *Mathematics and the Sciences of the Heavens and Earth*, ed. J. NEEDHAM and Wang LING (1959); vol. IV (2): *Mechanical Engineering*, ed. J. NEEDHAM and Wang LING (1965); vol. IV (3): *Civil Engineering and Nautics*, ed J. NEEDHAM, Wang LING, and Lu GWEI-DJEN (1971); vol. V (4): *Chemistry and Chemical Technology: Spagyrical Discovery and Invention: Apparatus, Theories and Gifts*, ed. J. NEEDHAM, Ho PING-YU, Lu GWEI-DJEN, and N. SIVIN (1980); vol. V (7): *Military Technology: The Gunpowder Epic*, ed. J. NEEDHAM, Ho PING-YU, Lu GWEI-DJEN, and Wang LING (1987); vol. V (9): *Textile Technology: Spinning and Reeling*, D. KUHN (1986). vol. VI (2): *Agriculture*, ed. F. BRAY (1988), vol. VI (6): *Biology and Biological Technology: Medicine* (2000).

NEGEV, A., 1990, *The Archaeological Encyclopedia of the Holy Land*, New York: Prentice Hall.

NEUMANN, H., 1999, "Ur-Dumuzida and Ur-Dun: reflections on the relationship between state-initiated foreign trade and private economic activity in Mesopotamia towards the end of the third millennium BC," in J. G. Dercksen (ed.), *Trade and Finance in Ancient Mesopotamia Proceedings of the First Mos Symposium, Leiden 1997* (Mos Studies 1). Nederlands Historisch-Archaeologisch Instituut te Istanbul, pp. 43–53.

NEUMANN, K. and HILDEBRAND, E., 2009, "Early bananas in Africa: the state of the art," *Ethnobotany Research & Applications*, 7, pp. 353–362.

NEWTON, L. and ZARINS, J., 2000, "Aspects of Bronze Age art of southern Arabia: the pictorial landscape and its relation to economic and socio-political status," *Arabian Archaeology and Epigraphy*, 11, pp. 154–179.

NEZAFATI, N., PERNICKA, E., and MOMENZADEH, M., 2006, "Ancient tin: old question and a new answer," *Antiquity*, 80 (308), pp. 308–311.

NG, N. Q., 1995, "Cowpea. *Vigna unguiculata* (Leguminosae-Papilionideae)," in J. Smartt and N. W. Simmonds (eds.), *Evolution of Crop Plants*, London and New York: Longman, pp. 326–332.

NGUYEN, K. D., 2001, "Jewelry from late prehistoric sites recently excavated in South Viet Nam," *Bulletin of the Indo-Pacific Prehistory Association*, 21 (The Melaka Papers vol. 5), pp. 107–113.

2017, "The Sa Huynh culture in ancient regional trade networks: a comparative study of ornaments," in P. J. Piper, H. Matsumura, and D. Bulbeck (eds.), *New Perspectives in Southeast Asian and Pacific Prehistory*, Canberra: ANU Press, pp. 311–332.

NGUYEN, K. S., PHAM, M. H., and TONG, T., 2004, "Northern Vietnam from the Neolithic to the Han period," in I. Glover and P. Bellwood (eds.), *Southeast Asia, from Prehistory to History*, Abingdon and New York: Routledge/Curzon, pp. 177–208.

NICHOLS, D. L. and CHARLTON, T. H. (eds.), 1997, *The Archaeology of City-States: Cross-Cultural Approaches*, Washington, DC: Smithsonian Institution Press.

NICOLET, C., 1988, *Rendre à César: économie et société dans la Rome antique*, Paris: Gallimard.

2000, *Censeurs et publicains: économie et fiscalité dans la Rome antique*, Paris: Fayard.

NICOLET-PIERRE, H., 2002. *Numismatique grecque*. Paris: Armand Colin.

NIEMEYER, H. G., 2000, "The early Phoenician city-states on the Mediterranean: archaeological elements for their description," in M. H. Hansen (ed.), *A Comparative Study of Thirty City-State Cultures*, Copenhagen: Det Kongelige Danske Videnskabernes Selskab, pp. 89–115.

NIK HASSAN SHUHAIMI BIN NIK ABDUL RAHMAN, 1990, "The kingdom of Srīvijaya as socio-political and cultural entity," in, J. Kathirithamby-Wells and J. Villiers (eds.), *The Southeast Asian Port and Polity: Rise and Demise*, Singapore University Press, pp. 61–82.

NISBET, R., 1985, "Evidence of sorghum at site RH5, Qurm, Muscat," *East and West*, 35 (4), pp. 415–417.

NISHIMURA, M., 2005, "Settlement patterns on the Red River plain from the late prehistoric period to the 10th century AD," *Bulletin of the Indo-Pacific Prehistory Association* 25 (The Taipei Papers vol. 3), pp. 99–107.

NISSEN, H. J., 1988, *The Early History of the Ancient Near East, 9000–2000 B.C.*, University of Chicago Press.

2001, "Cultural and political networks in the Ancient Near East during the fourth and third millennia BC," in M. S. Rothman (ed.), *Uruk Mesopotamia and Its Neighbors: Cross-cultural Interactions in the Era of State Formation*, Sante Fe, School of American Research; Oxford: James Currey, pp. 149–180.

2004, "Uruk: key site of the period and key site of the problem," in J. N. Postgate (ed.), *Artefacts of Complexity: Tracking the Uruk in the Near East* (Iraq Archaeological Reports 5), Warminster: Aris & Phillips for the British School of Archaeology in Iraq, pp. 1–16 (1st edn. 2002).

NITTA, E., 2007, "Heger I drums, bronze halberds and ranked societies in the Mekong Basin," *Bulletin of the Indo-Pacific Prehistory Association*, 25, pp. 125–128.

NIWINSKI, A., 1999, "Amber in ancient Egypt," in B. Kosmowska-Ceranowicz and H. Paner (eds.), *Investigations into Amber: Proceedings of the International Interdisciplinary Symposium: Baltic Amber and Other Fossil Resins, 2–6 September 1997, Gdansk*, Gdansk: Muzeum Ziemi and the Archaeological Museum in Gdansk, pp. 115–119.

NOREL, P., 2004, *L'invention du marché: une histoire économique de la mondialisation*, Paris: Seuil.

2005, "Le développement est-il né en Asie?," *Économies et sociétés, série développement, croissance et progrès*, 43, pp. 415–459.

2008, "Réseaux commerciaux polarisés et innovation technologique," in O. Bouba-Olga and J. Léonard (eds.), *Globalisation, gouvernance et innovation, économies et sociétés*, 42 (8), pp. 1369–1390.

2009a "Dynamique smithienne et création des institutions du capitalisme: une analyse des mondialisations antérieures à 1860," in P. Beaujard, L. Berger, and P. Norel (eds.), *Histoire globale, mondialisations et capitalisme*, Paris: La Découverte, pp. 374–402.

2009b, *L'histoire économique globale*, Paris: Seuil.

NOREL, P. and TESTOT, L. (eds.), 2012, *Une histoire du monde global*, Auxerre: Éditions Sciences Humaines.

NOUR, Z., OSMAN, S., IZKANDER, Z., and MOUSTAFA, A. Y., 1960, *The Cheops Boat. Part I*, Cairo: General Organisation for Government Printing Offices.

NURSE, D., 1983, "A linguistic reconsideration of Swahili origins," *Azania*, 18, pp. 127–150.

NURSE, D. and HINNEBUSCH, T. J., 1993, *Swahili and Sabaki: A Linguistic History*, with an addendum by Gérard Philippson, Berkeley, Los Angeles, and London: University of California Press.

NURSE, D. and SPEAR, T., 1985, *The Swahili: Reconstructing the History and Language of an African Society, 800–1500*, Philadelphia: Pennsylvania University Press.

OATES, J., 1978, "The balance of trade in southwestern Asia in the mid-third millennium," *Current Anthropology*, 13, pp. 480–481.

2001, "Equid figurines and chariot models," in D. Oates, J. Oates, and H. McDonald (eds.), *Excavations at Tell Brak 2: Nagar in the Third Millennium BC*, Cambridge: McDonald Institute for Archaeological Research, pp. 279–293.

2003, "A note on the early evidence for horse in Western Asia," in M. Levine, C. Renfrew, and K. Boyle (eds.), *Prehistoric Steppe Adaptation and the Horse*, Cambridge: McDonald Institute for Archaeological Research, pp. 115–125.

2004, "Tell Brak: the 4th millennium sequence and its implications," in J. N. Postgate (ed.), *Artefacts of Complexity: Tracking the Uruk in the Near East* (Iraq Archaeological Reports 5), Warminster: Aris & Phillips for the British School of Archaeology in Iraq, pp. 111–122 (1st edn. 2002).

2014a and b, "The rise of cities in Mesopotamia and Iran" and "Mesopotamia: the historical periods," in C. Renfrew and P. Bahn (eds.), *The Cambridge World Prehistory*, vol. III: *West and Central Asia and Europe*, Cambridge University Press, pp. 1474–1497 and 1498–1507.

OATES, J., McMAHON, A., KARSGAARD, P., AL QUNTAR, S., and UR, J., 2007, "Early Mesopotamian urbanism: a new view from the north," *Antiquity*, 81 (313), pp. 585–600.

OATES, D. and OATES, J., 1976, *The Rise of Civilization*, New York: Elsevier Phaidon.

1993, "Excavations à Tell Brak 1992–93," *Iraq*, 40, pp. 155–199.

2004, "The role of exchange relations in the origins of Mesopotamian civilization," in J. Cherry, C. Scarre, and S. Shennan (ed.), *Explaining Social Change: Studies in Honour of Colin Renfrew*, Cambridge: McDonald Institute for Archaeological Research, pp. 177–92.

OKAFOR, E. E., 2002, "La réduction du fer dans les Bas-Fourneaux – une industrie vieille de 2500 ans au Nigeria," in H. Bocoum (ed.), *Aux origines de la métallurgie du fer en Afrique*, Paris: Editions UNESCO, pp. 35–48.

OLCK, F., 1899, "Kasia," in G. Wissowa *et al.* (eds.), *Paulys Realencyclopädie des Classischen Altertumswissenschaft*, Munich: A. Druckenmüller Verlag, pp. 1638–1651.

OLDFATHER, C. H., 1939, *Diodorus of Sicily*, London: Loeb Classical Library, vols. III and V.

OLIVER, R., 2001, "Comments on Ehret, 'Bantu expansions'," *International Journal of African Historical Studies*, 34 (1), pp. 43–45.

OLMER, F., 2008, "L'aristocratie romaine, le vin et le marché gaulois," in Y. Roman and J. Dalaison (eds.), *L'économie antique, une économie de marché?*, Lyon and Paris: de Boccard.

OLSEN, S. L., 2003, "The exploitation of horses at Botai, Kazakhstan," in M. Levine, C. Renfrew, and K. Boyle (eds.), *Prehistoric Steppe Adaptation and the Horse*, Cambridge: McDonald Institute for Archaeological Research, pp. 83–103.

OMAR, H., ADAMSON, E. A. S., BHASSU, S., GOODMAN, S. M., SOARIMALALA, V., HASHIM, R., *et al.*, 2011, "Phylogenetic relationships of Malayan and Malagasy pygmy shrews of the genus *Suncus* (Soricomorpha: Soricidae) inferred from mitochondrial cytochrome *b* gene sequences," *The Raffles Bulletin of Zoology*, 59 (2), pp. 237–243.

OPPENHEIM, A. L., 1969, "Mesopotamia – land of many cities," in I. M. Lapidus (ed.), *Middle Eastern Cities: A Symposium on Ancient, Islamic and Contemporary Middle Eastern Urbanism*, Berkeley: University of California Press, pp. 3–18.

OPPENHEIMER, S., 2004, "The 'Express Train from Taiwan to Polynesia': on the congruence of proxy lines of evidence," *World Archaeology*, 36 (4), pp. 591–600.

ORSOY DE FLINES, E. W. VAN, 1949, *Gids voor de Keramische Verzameling (Uitheemsch Keramiek)*, Batavia: Koninklijk Bataviaasch Genootschap Van Kunsten En Wetenschappen.

OSADA, T., 2006, "How many Proto-Munda words in Sanskrit? With special reference to agricultural vocabulary," in T. Osada (ed.), *Proceedings of the Pre-Symposium of RIHN and 7th ESCA Harvard-Kyoto Roundtable*, Kyoto: Research Institute for Humanity and Nature (RIHN), pp. 151–174.

O'Shea, J., 1992, "A radiocarbon-based chronology for the Maros Group of southeast Hungary," *Antiquity*, 66 (250), pp. 97–102.

Ottino, P., 1974a, "L'Océan Indien comme domaine de recherche," *L'Homme*, 3–4, pp. 143–151.

1974b, *Madagascar, les Comores et le sud-ouest de l'océan Indien*, Antananarivo: Centre d'Anthropologie culturelle et sociale, Université de Madagascar.

1975, "L'origine dravidienne du vocabulaire du riz et de certains termes de riziculture à Madagascar," *Annuaire des Pays de l'Océan Indien*, CERSOI, pp. 104–121.

1977, "Le thème du Monstre Dévorant dans les domaines malgache et bantou," *ASEMI*, 8, 3–4 (issue on "Langues, cultures et sociétés de l'océan Indien"), pp. 219–251.

1986, *L'étrangère intime: essai d'anthropologie de la civilisation de l'ancien Madagascar*, Paris: Éditions des Archives Contemporaines, 2 vols.

1998, *Les champs de l'ancestralité à Madagascar: parenté, alliance et patrimoine*, Paris: Karthala/ORSTOM.

Ottoni, C., Van Neer, W., Boivin, N., Prendergast, M., Grange, T., and Geigl, E.-M., 2013, "Ancient DNA from cats hints to early trade in the Indian Ocean world," paper presented at the Sealinks Conference "Proto-Globalisation in the Indian Ocean World: Multidisciplinary perspectives on early globalisation," Oxford, Jesus College, November, 7–10.

Oumar, I, Mariac, C., Pham, J.-L., and Vigouroux, Y., 2008, "Phylogeny and origin of pearl millet (*Pennisetum glaucum* [L.] R. Br.) as revealed by microsatellite loci," *Theoretical and Applied Genetics*, 117 (4), pp. 489–497.

Outram, A. K. *et al.*, 2009 "The earliest horse harnessing and milking," *Science*, 323 (5919), pp. 1332–5.

Özdogan, M., 2014, "3.9 Anatolia: from the Pre-Pottery Neolithic to the end of the Early Bronze Age (10,500–2000 BCE)," in C. Renfrew and P. Bahn (eds.), *The Cambridge World Prehistory*, vol. III: *West and Central Asia and Europe*, Cambridge University Press, pp. 1508–1544.

Pacey, A., 1990, *Technology in World Civilization*, Cambridge, MA: MIT Press.

Pacheco, A. M., 1883, "Uma viagem de Tete ao Zumbo: diario de Albino Manoel Pacheco," *Boletim official do Governo Geral da Provincia de Moçambique*, Lourenço Marques: Imprensa Nacional, pp. 120–270.

Palat, R., 2015, *The Making of an Indian Ocean World-Economy, 1250–1650: Princes, Paddy Fields and Bazaars*, London: Palgrave Macmillan.

Pallesen, A. K., 1985, *Culture Contact and Language Convergence*, Manilla: Linguistic Society of the Philippines.

Panaino, A., 2004, "Commerce and conflicts of religions in Sasanian Iran between social identity and political ideology," in R. Rollinger and C. Ulf (eds.), *Commerce and Monetary Systems in the Ancient World: Means of Transmission and Cultural Interaction*, Stuttgart: Franz Steiner Verlag, pp. 385–401.

Panchenko, D. V., 1998, "'Scylax' circumnavigation of India and its interpretation in early Greek geography, ethnography and cosmography, I," *Hyperboreus*, 4 (2), pp. 211–242.

2003, "Scylax' circumnavigation of India and its interpretation in early Greek geography, ethnography and cosmography, II," *Hyperboreus*, 9 (2), pp. 274–294.

Pankhurst, R., 1979, "The 'Banyan' or Indian presence at Massawa, the Dahlak islands and the Horn of Africa," in *Mouvements de populations dans l'Océan Indien, Actes du 4e Congrès de l'Association Historique Internationale de l'Océan Indien et du 14e Colloque de la Commission Internationale d'Histoire Maritime (Saint-Denis de la Réunion, septembre 1972)*, Paris: Champion, pp. 107–128.

Paranavitana, S., 1961, *A Concise History of Ceylon*, Colombo: Ceylon University Press.

PARE, C. F. E., 2000, "Bronze and the Bronze Age," in C. F. E. Pare (ed.), *Metals Make the World Go Round: The Supply and Circulation of Metals in Bronze Age Europe*, Proceedings of a Conference Held at the University of Birmingham in June 1997, Oxford: Oxbow Books, pp. 1–38.

PARKER, A. G., GOUDIE, A. S., STOKES, S., WHITE, K., HODSON, M. J., MANNING, M., and KENET, D., 2006, "A record of Holocene climate change from lake geochemical analyses in southeastern Arabia," *Quaternary Research*, 66 (3), pp. 465–476.

PARKER, G., 2002, "Ex Oriente Luxuria: Indian commodities and Roman experience," *Journal of the Economic and Social History of the Orient*, 45 (1), pp. 39–95.

PARKER PEARSON, M., 2010, *Pastoralists, Warriors and Colonists: The Archaeology of Southern Madagascar* (BAR International Series 2139), Oxford: Archaeopress.

PARKIN, D. and BARNES, R. (eds.), 2002, *Ships and the Development of Maritime Technology in the Indian Ocean*, London and New York: Routledge/Curzon.

PARKINSON, W. A. and GALATY, M. L., 2007, "Secondary states in perspective: an integrated approach to state formation in the prehistoric Aegean," *American Anthropologist*, 109 (1), pp. 113–129.

PARPOLA, A., 1977, "The Meluhha village: evidence of acculturation of Harappan traders in late third millennium Mesopotamia?," *Journal of the Economic and Social History of the Orient*, 20 (2), pp. 129–165.

1994a, *Deciphering the Indus Script*, Cambridge University Press.

1994b, "Harappan inscriptions: an analytical catalogue of the Indus inscriptions from the Near East," in F. Højlund and H. H. Andersen (eds.), *Qala'at al-Bahrain*, vol. I: *The Northern City Wall and the Islamic Fortress*, Aarhus University Press, pp. 304–315.

1995, "The problem of the Aryans and the Soma: the archaeological evidence," in G. Erdosy (ed.), *The Indo-Aryans of Ancient South Asia: Language, Material Culture and Ethnicity*, Berlin and New York: De Gruyter, pp. 353–381.

2002, "Pre-Proto-Iranians of Afghanistan as Initiators of Sākta Tantrism: on the Scythians/ Saka Affiliation of the Dāsas, Nuristanis and Magadhans," *Iranica Antiqua*, 37, pp. 233–324.

2003, "Assyria's expansion in the 8th and 7th centuries and its long-term repercussions in the West," in W. G. Dever and S. Gitin (eds.), *Symbiosis, Symbolism and the Power of the Past*, Winona Lake, OH: Eisenbrauns, pp. 99–111.

2006, "A new Indus seal excavated at Gonur," in T. Osada (ed.), *Proceedings of the Pre-Symposium of RIHN and 7th ESCA Harvard-Kyoto Roundtable*, Kyoto: Research Institute for Humanity and Nature (RIHN), pp. 53–57.

PARPOLA, A., PANDE, B. M., and KOSKIKALLIO, P. (eds.), 2010, *Corpus of Indus Seals and Inscriptions*, vol. III: *New Material, Untraced Objects and Collections outside India and Pakistan*, part 1: *Mohenjo-daro and Harappa*, with R. H. Meadow and J. M. Kenoyer, Helsinki: Suomalainen Tiedeakatemia.

PARTINGTON, J. R., 1999, *A History of Greek Fire and Gunpowder*, Baltimore, MD: Johns Hopkins University Press (1st edn. 1960).

PARZINGER, H., 2003, "Zinn in der Bronzezeit Eurasiens," in H. Parzinger and N. Boroffka (eds.), *Das Zinn der Bronzezeit in Mittelasien, I: Archäologie in Iran und Turan*, Mainz, pp. 287–296.

2014, "Central Asia before the Silk Road," in C. Renfrew and P. Bahn (eds.), *The Cambridge World Prehistory*, vol. III: *West and Central Asia and Europe*, Cambridge University Press, pp. 1617–1637.

PATYAL, H. C., 1979, "Etymology and *Sanskrit dictionary on historical principles*," *Indian Linguistics*, 40, pp. 115–122.

PAUTREAU, J.-P., MORNAIS, P., COUPEY, A.-S., MAITAY, C., PELLE, F., and AUNG KYAW, A., 2005, "Vallée de la Samon: recherches sur les sépultures de l'âge du fer," *Dossiers d'Archéologie*, 302, pp. 56–58.

PAUTREAU, J.-P., MORNAIS, P., and DOY-ASA, T., 2005, "Thaïlande du Nord: les sépultures protohistoriques," *Dossiers d'Archéologie*, 302, pp. 60–66.

PAVAN, A. and SCHENK, H., 2012, "Crossing the Indian Ocean before the *Periplus*: a comparison of pottery assemblages at the sites of Sumhuram (Oman) and Tissamaharama (Sri Lanka)," *Arabian Archaeology and Epigraphy*, 23, pp. 191–202.

PAZ, V., 2005, "Rock shelters, caves, and archaeobotany in Island Southeast Asia," *Asian Perspectives*, 44 (1), pp. 107–118.

PEACOCK, D., 2011, "Glass," in D. Peacock and L. Blue (eds.), *Myos Hormos – Quseir al-Qadim: Roman and Islamic Ports on the Red Sea*, vol. II: *Finds from the Excavations 1999–2003* (BAR International Series 2286), Oxford: Archaeopress, pp. 57–78.

PEACOCK, D. and BLUE, L. (eds.), 2007a, *The Ancient Red Sea Port of Adulis, Eritrea: Report of the Eritro–British Expedition, 2004–2005*, Oxford: Oxbow Books.

(eds.), 2007b, "Incense and the port of Adulis," in D. Peacock, D., Williams, and S. James (eds.), *Food for the Gods: New Light on the Ancient Incense Trade*, Oxford: Oxbow Books, pp. 135–140.

(eds.), 2011, *Myos Hormos – Quseir al-Qadim. Roman and Islamic Ports on the Red Sea*, vol. II: *Finds from the Excavations 1999–2003* (BAR International Series 2286), Oxford: Archaeopress.

PEACOCK, M., 2013, *Introducing Money: Economics as Social Theory*, Abingdon and New York: Routledge.

PEARSALL, D. M., 2000, *Paleoethnobotany: A Handbook of Procedures*, 2nd edn., New York: Academic Press (1st edn. 1989).

PEARSON, M. N., 2003, *The Indian Ocean*, London and New York: Routledge.

(ed.), 2015, *Trade, Circulation, and Flow in the Indian Ocean World*, London: Palgrave.

PEET, T. E., 1932, "The Egyptian words for 'money', 'buy' and 'sell'," in R. Mond (ed.), *Studies Presented to F. L. Griffith*, London: Egypt Exploration Society, pp. 122–127.

1934, "L'unité de valeur š'ty dans le Papyrus Bulaq II," *Mélanges Maspéro I*, Cairo: Imprimerie de l'Institut Français d'Archéologie Orientale, pp. 185–199.

PEJROS, I. and SHNIRELMAN, V., 1998, "Rice in South-East Asia: a regional interdisciplinary approach," in R. Blench and M. Spriggs (eds.), *Archaeology and Language II. Archaeological Data and Linguistic Hypotheses*, London and New York: Routledge, pp. 379–389.

PELLING, R., 2005, "Garamantian agriculture and its significance in a wider North African context: the evidence of the plant remains from the Fazzan project," *Journal of North African Studies*, 10 (3–4), pp. 397–411.

2008, "Garamantian agriculture: the plant remains from Jarma, Fazzan," *Libyan Studies*, 39, pp. 41–71.

PELLIOT, P., 1903, "Le Fou-nan," *Bulletin de l'École française d'Extrême-Orient*, 3, pp. 248–333.

1904, "Deux itinéraires de Chine en Inde à la fin du VIIIe siècle," *Bulletin de l'École française d'Extrême-Orient*, 4, pp. 131–413.

1925, "Quelques textes chinois concernant l'Indochine hindouisée," *Études Asiatiques*, 2, pp. 243–263.

PELON, O., 2001, "Les tombes royales d'Alaca Hüyük et les Hattis d'Anatolie," *Clio*. www.clio.fr

PELRAS, C., 1987, "Le ciel et les jours: constellations et calendriers agraires chez les Bugis," Koechlin, F. SIGAU., J. M. C. Thomas, and G. Toffin (eds.), *De la voûte céleste au terroir, du jardin au foyer: textes offerts à Lucien Bernot*, Paris: EHESS, p. 19–39.

1996, *The Bugis*, Oxford: Blackwell.

1997, "Populations aquatiques de la peninsule malaise ('Orang Laut')" and "Groupes Sama," in V. Arnaud and H. Campagnolo (eds.), *Lexique thématique plurilingue de trente-six langues et dialectes d'Asie du Sud-Est insulaire*, Paris and Montréal: LASEMA/CNRS/ L'Harmattan, vol. I, pp. 59–66 and 67–80.

PELTENBURG, E., 2007, "East Mediterranean interactions in the 3rd millennium BC," in S. Antoniadou and A. Pace (eds.), *Mediterranean Crossroads*, Athens: Pierides Foundation, pp. 141–161.

PEREGRINE, P., 1991, "Prehistoric chiefdoms on the American mid-continent: a world system based on prestige goods," in C. Chase-Dunn and T. D. Hall (eds.), *Core/Periphery Relations in Precapitalist Worlds*, Boulder, CO: Westview Press, pp. 193–211.

PEREZ, V. R., GODFREY, L. R., NOWAK-KEMP, N., BURNEY, D. A., RATSIMBAZAFY, J., and VASEY, N., 2005, "Evidence of early butchery of giant lemurs in Madagascar," *Journal of Human Evolution*, 49, pp. 722–742.

PERNICKA, E., EIBNER, C., ÖZTUNALL, E., and WAGNER, G. A., 2003, "Early Bronze Age metallurgy in the northeast Aegean," in G. A. Wagner, E. Pernicka, and H.-P. Uerpmann (eds.), *Troia and the Troad: Scientific Approaches*, Berlin, Heidelberg, and New York: Springer, pp. 143–172.

PERRIER, X., BAKRY, F., CARREEL, F., JENNY, C., HORRY, J.-P., LEBOT, V., and HIPPOLYTE, I., 2009, "Combining biological approaches to shed light on the evolution of edible bananas," *Ethnobotany Research & Applications*, 7, pp. 199–216.

PERRIER, X., DE LANGHE, E., DONOHUE, M., LENTFER, C., VRYDAGHS, L., BAKRY, F., *et al.* 2011, "Multidisciplinary perspectives on banana (*Musa sp.*) domestication," *Proceedings of the National Academy of Sciences USA*, 108 (28), pp. 11311–11318.

PERROT, J. and MADJIDZADEH, Y., 2005, "L'iconographie des vases et objets en chlorite de Jiroft (Iran)," *Paléorient*, 31 (2), pp. 123–151.

PERSSON, J., 2005, "Escaping a closed universe: world-system crisis, regional dynamics, and the rise of Aegean palatial society," in J. Friedman and C. Chase-Dunn (eds.), *Hegemonic Declines: Present and Past*, Boulder, CO: Paradigm, pp. 7–50.

PETERS-DESTÉRACT, M., 2005, *Pain, bière et toutes bonnes choses . . . L'alimentation dans l'Égypte ancienne*, Paris: Éditions du Rocher.

PETRAGLIA, M. D. and ALLCHIN, B. (eds.), 2007, *The Evolution and History of Human Populations in South Asia. Interdisciplinary Studies in Archaeology, Biological Anthropology, Linguistics and Genetics*, Dordrecht: Springer.

PETRIE, C. A., 2013a and b, "Ancient Iran and its neighbours: the state of play" and "Ancient Iran and its neighbours: emerging paradigms and future directions," in C. A. Petrie (ed.), *Ancient Iran and Its Neighbours: Local Developments and Long-range Interactions in the 4th Millennium BC*, Oxford: Oxbow Books, pp. 1–24, and 385–412.

PFÄLZNER, P., WISSING, A., and HUBNER, C., 2004, "Urbanismus in der Unterstadt von Urkeš: Ergebnisse einer geomagnetischen Prospektion und eines archäologischen Surveys in der südostlichen Unterstadt von Tall Mozan im Sommer 2002," *Mitteilungen der Deutschen Orient-Gesellschaft zu Berlin*, 136, pp. 41–86.

PHAM HUY THONG *et al.* (eds.), 1990, *Dong Son Drums in Vietnam*, Hanoi: The Vietnam Social Science Publishing House.

PHILIP, G., 2004, "Contacts between the 'Uruk' world and the Levant during the fourth millennium BC: evidence and interpretation," in J. N. Postgate (ed.), *Artefacts of Complexity: Tracking the Uruk in the Near East* (Iraq Archaeological Reports 5), Warminster: Aris & Phillips for the British School of Archaeology in Iraq, pp. 207–236 (1st edn. 2002).

PHILIPPSON, G., 1981, "Glossaire des noms des principales plantes cultivées sur la côte d'Afrique orientale," *Bulletin des Études africaines de l'Inalco*, 1 (1), pp. 89–100.

PHILIPPSON, G. and BAHUCHET, S., 1994–1995, "Cultivated crops and Bantu migrations in Central and Eastern Africa: a linguistic approach," *Azania*, 29–30, pp. 103–120.

PHILLIPS, C., VILLENEUVE, F., and FACEY, W., 2004, "A Latin inscription from South Arabia," *Proceedings of the Seminar for Arabian Studies*, 34, pp. 239–250.

PHILLIPS, J., 1997, "Punt and Aksum: Egypt and the Horn of Africa," *Journal of African History*, 38, p. 423–457.

PHILLIPSON, D. W., 2012, *Foundations of an African Civilisation: Aksum and the Northern Horn 1000 BC – AD 1300*, Woodbridge: James Currey.

PHILLIPSON, J., 2013, *C. P. Cavafy Historical Poems: A Verse Translation with Commentaries*, Bloomington, IN: AuthorHouse UK.

PIACENTINI, V. F., 2002, "Arab expeditions overseas in the seventh century AD – working hypotheses on the dissolution of the Sasanian state apparatus along the eastern seaboard of the Arabian Peninsula," *Proceedings of the Seminar for Arabian Studies*, 32, pp. 165–173.

PIERRAT-BONNEFOIS, G., 1999, "Les objets en lapis-lazuli dans le trésor de Tôd," in A. Caubet (ed.), *Cornaline et pierres précieuses: la Méditerranée, de l'Antiquité à l'Islam*, Paris: La Documentation Française, pp. 285–302.

PIERRON, D. *et al.*, 2017, "Genomic landscape of human diversity across Madagascar," *PNAS*, www.pnas.org/cgi/doi/10.1073/pnas.1704906114

PIGOTT, V. C., 1999, *The Archaeometallurgy of the Asian Old World*, Philadelphia: University of Pennsylvania Museum.

   2011, "Tin-bronze as a Pan-Asian technological phenomenon," in P. P. Betancourt and S. C. Ferrence (eds.), *Metallurgy: Understanding How, Learning Why, Studies in Honor of James D. Muhly*, Philadelphia, PA: INSTAP Academic Press, pp. 273–291.

   2012a, "Looking East: the coming of tin-bronze in the context of Bronze Age trans-Eurasian exchange – an overview," in P. Jett, B. McCarthy, and J. Douglas (eds.), *Scientific Research on Ancient Asian Metallurgy: Proceedings of the Fifth Forbes Symposium at the Freer Gallery of Art*, Washington, DC: Archetype Publications in association with the Freer Gallery of Art, Smithsonian Institution, pp. 85–100.

   2012b, "On ancient tin, its sources and trade: further comments," in V. Kassianidou and G. Papasavvas (eds.), *Eastern Mediterranean Metallurgy and Metalwork in the Second Millennium BC*, Oxford: Oxbow Books, pp. 222–236.

PIGOTT, V. C. and CIARLA, R., 2007, "On the origins of metallurgy in prehistoric Southeast Asia: the view from Thailand," in S. La Niece, D. Hook, and E. P. Craddock (eds.), *Metals and Mines: Studies in Archaeometallurgy*, London: British Museum, pp. 76–88.

PIGULEVSKAYA, N., 1951, *Byzantium on the Roads to India: A History of Byzantine Trade with the East in the 4th to 6th Centuries*, Moscow and Leningrad: Izdatelstvo Akademii Nauk SSSR (in Russian).

PIKIRAYI, I., 2001, *The Zimbabwe Culture: Origins and Decline in Southern Zambezian States*, Walnut Creek, CA: Altamira Press.

PIMPANEAU, J., 1999, *Chine, mythes et dieux de la religion populaire*, Arles: Philippe Picquier.

PIRAZZOLI-T'SERSTEVENS, M., 1988, "Les cultures du Sichuan occidental à la fin de l'âge du Bronze et leurs rapports avec les steppes," in *L'Asie centrale et ses rapports avec les civilisations orientales des origines à l'Âge du Fer, Actes du colloque franco-soviétique, Paris 1985*, Paris: de Boccard, pp. 183–196.

PIRENNE, J., 1944–1956, *Les grands courants de l'histoire universelle*, 7 vols., Neuchâtel: Éditions de la Baconnière.

   1961, *Histoire de la civilisation de l'Ancienne Égypte*, Paris: Albin Michel; Neuchâtel: À la Baconnière.

1970, "Le développement de la navigation Égypte-Inde dans l'Antiquité," *Sociétés et compagnies de commerce en Orient et dans l'océan Indien, Actes du 8e Colloque International d'Histoire Maritime (Beyrouth, 5–10 septembre 1966)*, Paris: SEVPEN, pp. 100–119.

PITTMAN, H., 2001a, "Glyptic art of period IV," in D. T. Potts (ed.), *Excavations at Tepe Yahya, Iran, 1967–1975: The Third Millennium* (Bulletin of the American School of Prehistoric Research 45), Cambridge, MA: Peabody Museum of Archaeology and Ethnology, Harvard University, pp. 231–268.

2001b, "Mesopotamian intraregional relations reflected through glyptic evidence in the Late Chalcolithic 1–5 periods," in M. S. Rothman (ed.), *Uruk Mesopotamia and Its Neighbors. Cross-cultural Interactions in the Era of State Formation*, Sante Fe: School of American Research; Oxford: James Currey, pp. 403–443.

2003, "La culture du Halil Roud," *Dossiers d'Archéologie*, 287, pp. 78–87.

2013, "Imagery in administrative context: Susiana and the west in the fourth millennium BC," in C. A. Petrie (ed.), *Ancient Iran and Its Neighbours: Local Developments and Long-Range Interactions in the Fourth Millennium BC*, Oxford: Oxbow Books, pp. 293–336.

PITTS, M. and VERSLUYS, M. J. (eds.), 2014, *Globalisation and the Roman World*, Cambridge University Press.

PLINY THE ELDER / Pline l'Ancien, 1949, *Histoire naturelle*, Book 12, ed. and trans. A. Ernout, Paris: Société d'Edition "Les Belles Lettres" (text written *c.* 70 AD).

1980, *Histoire naturelle*, Book 6, part 2 (l'Asie centrale et orientale, l'Inde), ed. and trans J. André and J. Filliozat, Paris: Société d'Edition "Les Belles Lettres."

POIRIER, J., 1970, "Les Bezanozano, contribution à l'étude des structures sociales d'une population malgache," thèse sous la direction de H. Deschamps.

POIRIER, J., with J. DEZ, 1982, "Glottochronologie et histoire culturelle malgache," *Taloha*, 8, pp. 97–120.

POLANYI, K., 1957a, *The Great Transformation: The Political and Economic Origins of Our Time*, Boston, MA: Beacon Press (1st edn. 1944).

1957b, "Marketless trading in Hammurabi's time," in C. Arensberg, H. W. Pearson, and K. Polanyi (eds.), *Trade and Market in Early Empires*, Glencoe, IL: Free Press, pp. 12–26.

1975, "Traders and trade," in J. A. Sabloff and C. C. Lamberg-Karlovsky (eds.), *Ancient Civilization and Trade*, Albuquerque: University of New Mexico Press, pp. 133–154.

1981, *The Livelihood of Man*, ed. H. W. Pearson, New York: Academic Press.

POLLOCK, S., 1996, "The Sanskrit cosmopolis, 300–1300: transculturation, vernacularization, and the question of ideology," in J. E. M. Houben (ed.), *Ideology and Status of Sanskrit*, Leiden: Brill, pp. 197–247.

1999. *Ancient Mesopotamia: The Eden that Never Was*, Cambridge University Press.

2006, *The Language of the Gods in the World of Men: Sanskrit, Culture, and Power in Premodern India*, Berkeley, Los Angeles, and London: University of California Press.

POLO, M., 1980, *Le devisement du monde. Le livre des merveilles*, 2 vols., ed. A.-C. Moule and P. Pelliot, trans. L. Hambis, introduction and notes by S. Yerasimos, Paris: Maspéro.

1982, *The Travels of Marco Polo*, London: André Deutsch (1st edn. 1959).

1998, *La description du monde*, ed. and trans. P.-Y. Badel, Paris: Librairie générale française.

2003, *The Travels of Marco Polo the Venetian*, ed. J. Masefield, New Delhi, Chenai: Asian Educational Services (1st edn. 1931).

2005, *The Travels of Marco Polo*, trans. into English from the text of L. F. Benedetto, ed. A. Ricci, London and New York: RoutledgeCurzon (1st edn. 1931).

2009, *Le devisement du monde. Tome VI. Livre d'Ynde. Retour vers l'Occident*, ed. P. Ménard, D. Boutet, T. Delcourt, and D. James-Raoul, Geneva: Droz.

POMERANZ, K., 2000, *The Great Divergence: China, Europe and the Making of the Modern World Economy*, Princeton University Press.

POMERANZ, K. and TOPIK, S., 1999, *The World that Trade Created: Society, Culture and the World Economy, 1400 to the Present*, Armonk, NY: M. E. Sharpe.

POMEY, P., 2006, "Le rôle du dessin dans la conception des navires antiques: à propos de deux textes akkadiens," in B. Mathieu, D. Meeks, and M. Wissa (eds.), *L'apport de l'Égypte à l'histoire des techniques: méthodes, chronologie et comparaisons*, Cairo: Institut Français d'Archéologie Orientale, pp. 239–251.

PONTING, C., 1991, *A Green History of the World: The Environment and the Collapse of Great Civilizations*, London: Penguin.

POPOVIC, A., 1976, *La révolte des esclaves en Iraq au IIIe/IXe siècle*, Paris: P. Geuthner.

PORTÈRES, R., 1960, "La sombre Aroïdée cultivée: *Colocasia antiquorum* Schott. ou taro de Polynésie. Essai d'étymologie sémantique," *Journal d'Agriculture Tropicale et de Botanique Appliquée*, 7, 4–5, pp. 169–192.

POSSEHL, G. L., 1996, "Meluhha," in J. Reade (ed.), *The Indian Ocean in Antiquity*, London and New York: Kegan Paul, pp. 132–208.

1998, "Sociocultural complexity without the state: the Indus Civilization," in G. M. Feinman and J. Marcus (eds.), *Archaic States*, Santa Fe: School of American Research, pp. 261–291.

1999a, *Indus Age: The Beginnings*, Philadelphia: University of Pennsylvania Press.

1999b, "The transformation of the Indus civilization," *Man and Environment*, 24 (2), pp. 1–33.

2002a, *The Indus Civilization: A Contemporary Perspective*, Walnut Creek, CA: Altamira Press.

2002b, "Indus-Mesopotamian trade: the record in the Indus," *Iranica Antiqua*, 37, pp. 325–342.

POSTGATE, J. N., 1985, "The 'oil-plant' in Assyria," *Bulletin on Sumerian Agriculture*, 2, pp. 33–38.

1987, "Notes on fruit in the Cuneiform sources," *Bulletin on Sumerian Agriculture*, 3, pp. 115–144.

2003, *Early Mesopotamia. Society and Economy at the Dawn of History*, London and New York: Routledge (1st edn. 1992).

POTTIER, C., 2005, "Avant Angkor: découvertes récentes," *Dossiers d'Archéologie*, 302, pp. 82–87.

POTTIER, M.-H., 1984, *Matériel funéraire de la Bactriane Méridionale de l'Âge du Bronze*, Paris: Éditions du CNRS.

POTTS, D. T., 1990, *The Arabian Gulf in Antiquity*, vol. I: *From Prehistory to the Fall of the Achaemenid Empire*, vol. II: *From Alexander the Great to the Coming of Islam*, Oxford University Press.

1993a, "Rethinking some aspects of trade in the Arabian Gulf," *World Archaeology*, 24, pp. 423–440.

1993b, "The Late Prehistoric, Protohistoric, and Early Historic periods in Eastern Arabia (ca. 5000–1200 BC)," *Journal of World Prehistory*, 7 (2), pp. 163–212.

1994a, *Mesopotamia and the East: An Archaeological and Historical Study of Foreign Relations 3400–2000 BC*, Oxford University Committee for Archaeology.

1994b, "Contributions to the agrarian history of Eastern Arabia. I. Implements and cultivation techniques, II. The cultivars," *Arabian Archaeology and Epigraphy*, 5 (3), pp. 158–168, and 5 (4), pp. 236–275.

1995, "Distant shores: Ancient Near Eastern trade with South Asia and Northeast Africa," in J. M. Sasson (ed.), *Civilizations of the Ancient Near East*, vol. III, New York: Scribner's, pp. 1451–1462.

1996, "The Parthian presence in the Arabian Gulf," in J. Reade (ed.), *The Indian Ocean in Antiquity*, London and New York: Kegan Paul, pp. 269–286.

1997, *Mesopotamian Civilization: The Material Foundations*, Ithaca, NY: Cornell University Press.

1999, *The Archaeology of Elam: Formation and Transformation of an Ancient Iranian State*, Cambridge University Press.

2001, "Situating Tepe Yahya in time and space," in D. T. Potts (ed.), *Excavations at Tepe Yahya, Iran, 1967–1975: The Third Millennium* (Bulletin of the American School of

Prehistoric Research 45), Cambridge, MA: Peabody Museum of Archaeology and Ethnology, Harvard University, pp. 195–207.

POTTS, D. T., 2002, "Total prestation in Marhashi–Ur relations," *Iranica Antiqua*, 37, pp. 343–357.

2003a, "Tepe Yahya, Tell Abraq and the chronology of the Bampur Sequence," *Iranica Antiqua*, 38, pp. 1–11.

2003b, "The Gulf: Dilmun and Magan," in J. Aruz and R. Wallenfels (eds.), *Art of the First Cities, The Third Millennium BC From the Mediterranean to the Indus*, New York: Metropolitan Museum of Art; New Haven, CT, and London: Yale University Press, pp. 307–375.

2003c, "A soft-stone genre from southeastern Iran: 'zig-zag' bowls from Magan to Margiana," in D. T. Potts, M. D. Roaf, and D. L. Stein (eds.), *Culture through Objects: Ancient Near Eastern Studies in Honour of P. R. S. Moorey*, Oxford: Griffith Institute Publications, pp. 77–91.

2004, "Camel hybridization and the role of *Camelus Bactrianus* in the Ancient Near East," *Journal of the Economic and Social History of the Orient*, 47 (2), pp. 143–165.

2005, "In the beginning: Marhashi and the origins of Magan's ceramic industry in the middle of the 3rd millennium BC," *Arabian Archaeology and Epigraphy*, 16, pp. 67–78.

2008, "Arabian Peninsula," in D. Pearsall (ed.), *Encyclopedia of Archaeology*, New York: Elsevier, pp. 827–834.

2014, "Elamite monumentality and architectural scale," in J. F. Osborne (ed.), *Approaching Monumentality in Archaeology*, Albany: State University of New York Press, pp. 23–38.

POTTS, D. T., PARPOLA, A., PARPOLA, S., and TIDMARSH, J., 1996, "Guhlu and guggulu," *Wiener Zeitschrift für die Kunde des Morgenlandes*, 86, pp. 291–305.

POTTS, D. T., PHILLIPS, C. S., and SEARIGHT, S. (eds.), 1998, *Arabia and Its Neighbours: Essays on Prehistorical and Historical Developments Presented in Honour of Beatrice de Cardi*, Turnout: Brepols.

POUMAILLOUX, P., 1999, "Le 'mtepe', bateau cousu des Swahili, suivi d'un glossaire technique," *Études Océan Indien*, 27–28 (issue on "Navires, ports, itinéraires"), pp. 227–328.

2002, "Une étude raisonnée de la côte orientale d'Afrique à la fin du XVIe siècle, à travers l'*Ethiopia Oriental* du Père João dos Santos," Thèse de Doctorat, Institut National des Langues et Civilisations Orientales.

POUWELS, R. L., 2002, "Eastern Africa and the Indian Ocean to 1800: reviewing relations in historical perspective," *International Journal of African Historical Studies*, 35 (2–3), pp. 385–425.

POWELL, M. A., 1976, "The antecedents of Old Babylonian place notation and the early history of Babylonian mathematics," *Historia Mathematica*, 3, pp. 414–439.

1977, "Sumerian merchants and the problem of profit," *Iraq*, 39, pp. 23–29.

1990, "Identification and Interpretation of long term price fluctuations in Babylonia: more light on the history of money in Mesopotamia," *Altorientalischen Forschungen*, 17, pp. 76–99.

1996, "Money in Mesopotamia," *Journal of the Economic and Social History of the Orient*, 39, pp. 224–242.

1999, "Wir müssen alle unsere Nische nutzen: monies, motives and methods in Babylonian economics," in J. G. Dercksen (ed.), *Trade and Finance in Ancient Mesopotamia Proceedings of the First Mos Symposium, Leiden 1997* (Mos Studies 1). Nederlands Historisch-Archaeologisch Instituut te Istanbul, pp. 5–24.

PRAMUAL, P., MEEYEN, K., WONGPAKAM, K., and KLINHOM, U., 2013, "Genetic diversity of Thai native chicken inferred from mitochondrial DNA sequences," *Tropical Natural History*, 13 (2), pp. 97–106.

PRÉAUX, C., 2002, *Le monde hellénistique*, Paris: Presses Universitaires de France.

PRENDERGAST, M. E., *et al.*, 2016, "Continental island formation and the archaeology of defaunation on Zanzibar, Eastern Africa," *PLOS*, http://dx.doi.org/10.1371/journal .pone.0149565.

PRIMAS, M., 2002, "Early tin bronze in Central and Southern Europe," in M. Bartelheim, E. Pernicka, and R. Krause (eds.), *Die Änfänge der Metallurgie in der Alten Welt*, Rahden: Verlag Marie Leidorf, pp. 303–314.

2007, "Innovationstransfer vor 5000 Jahren Knotenpunkte an Land- und Wasserwegen zwischen Vorderasien und Europa," *Eurasia Antiqua*, 13, pp. 1–19.

PRINS, A. H. J., 1965, *Sailing from Lamu: A Study of Maritime Culture in Islamic East Africa*, Assen: Van Gorcum.

1970, *A Swahili Nautical Dictionary*, Dar es Salaam: Cho cha Uchunguzi wa Lugha ya Kiswahili.

1982, "The *mtepe* of Lamu, Mombasa and the Zanzibar sea," *Paideuma*, 28, pp. 85–100.

PROUST, C., 2006, "Les mathématiques en Mésopotamie," *CultureMATH*, http://culturemath .ens.fr/

PRYCE, T. O., BELLINA-PRYCE, B., and BENNETT, A. T. N., 2006, "The development of metal technologies in the Upper-Thai-Malay Peninsula: initial interpretation of the archaeometallurgical evidence from Khao Sam Kaeo," *Bulletin de l'École française d'Extrême-Orient*, 93, pp. 295–315.

PRYCE, T. O., PIGOTT, V. C., MARTINÓN-TORRES, M., and REHREN, T., 2010, "Prehistoric copper production and technological reproduction in the Khao Wong Prachan Valley of Central Thailand," *Archaeological and Anthropological Sciences*, 2, pp. 237–264.

PRYCE, T. O. *et al.*, 2014, "More questions than answers: the Southeast Asian Lead Isotope Project 2009–2012," *Journal of Archaeological Science*, 42, pp. 273–294.

PRZYLUSKI, J., 1975, "Non-Aryan loans in Indo-Aryan," trans. P. C. Bagchi, in S. Lévi, J. Przyluski, and J. Bloch (eds.), *Pre-Aryan and Pre-Dravidian in India*, University of Calcutta, pp. 1–32 and 149–160 (1st edn. 1921).

PTOLEMY, 1883–1901, *Claudii Ptolemaei Geographia*, ed. K. Müller and C. T. Fischer, 2 vols., Paris.

1991, *Geography of Claudius Ptolemy*, trans. E. L. Stevenson, New York: Dover Publications (1st edn. 1932).

2000, *Ptolemy's Geography*, trans. J. L. Berggren and A. Jones, Princeton University Press.

PULAK, C., 1998, "The Uluburun shipwreck: an overview," *International Journal of Nautical Archaeology*, 27, pp. 188–224.

PULLEN, D., 2008, "The Early Bronze Age in Greece," in C. W. Shelmerdine (ed.), *The Aegean World*, Cambridge University Press, pp. 19–46.

PUSALKER, A. D., 2007, "Economic ideas of the Hindus," in K. B. Janardan (ed.), *Economic History of Ancient India*, New Delhi: Arise Publishers, pp. 19–38.

PYDYN, A., 2000, "Value and exchange of bronzes in the Baltic area and in north-east Europe," in C. F. E. Pare (ed.), *Metals Make the World Go Round: The Supply and Circulation of Metals in Bronze Age Europe, Proceedings of a Conference Held at the University of Birmingham in June 1997*, Oxford: Oxbow Books, pp. 225–232.

QING, Z. and FANG, W., 2003, "The Jinsha site: an introduction," *Journal of East Asian Archaeology*, 5 (1–4), pp. 247–276.

QUALLS, C., 1981, "Boats of Mesopotamia before 2000 BC," Ph.D. dissertation, Columbia University (Ann Arbor: University Microfilms International no. 8222473).

QUÉCHON, G., 2002, "Les datations de la métallurgie du fer à Termit (Niger): leur fiabilité, leur signification," in H. Bocoum (ed.), *Aux origines de la métallurgie du fer en Afrique, une ancienneté méconnue. Afrique de l'Ouest et Afrique Centrale*, Paris: Éditions de l'UNESCO, pp. 105–114.

RADIMILAHY, C., 1988, *L'ancienne métallurgie du fer à Madagascar*, Oxford: Archaeopress.

1993, "Origine des villes: le cas de Mahilaka dans le Nord-Ouest de Madagascar," in *Données Archéologiques sur l'Origine des Villes à Madagascar* (Project Working Papers), Antananarivo: Musée d'Art et d'Archéologie, pp. 1–44.

1998, *Mahilaka: An Archaeological Investigation of an Early Town in Northwestern Madagascar*, Department of Archaeology and Ancient History, Uppsala University.

2011, "Contribution à l'archéologie du Sud-Ouest de Madagascar," in *Civilisations des mondes insulaires (Madagascar, îles du canal de Mozambique, Mascareignes, Polynésie, Guyanes). Mélanges en l'honneur du Professeur Claude Allibert*, Paris: Karthala, pp. 825–853.

RADIMILAHY, C., MANJAKAHERY, B., and RAKOTOZAFY, L. 2006, "Archaeology of St. Augustine's Bay. Lower and Middle Onilahy Valley, southwestern Madagascar," in J. Kinahan and J. Kinahan (eds.), *Studies in the African Past 5*, Windhoek: Dar es-Salaam University Press, pp. 60–95.

RADNER, K., 1999a and b, "Traders in the Neo-Assyrian period" and "Money in the Neo-Assyrian Empire," in J. G. Dercksen (ed.), *Trade and Finance in Ancient Mesopotamia Proceedings of the First Mos Symposium, Leiden 1997* (Mos Studies 1), Nederlands Historisch-Archaeologisch Instituut te Istanbul, pp. 101–126 and 127–158.

2009, "Tyre and the other Phoenician city-states," *Assyrian Empire Builders*, University College London, www.ucl.ac.uk/history2/sargon/essentials/countries/Phoenicians/

2012, "The King's Road – the imperial communication network," *Assyrian Empire Builders*, University College London, www.ucl.ac.uk/sargon/essentials/governors/thekingsroad/

RAEPSAET, G., 2008a, "Techniques de traction et de transport terrestre dans l'Antiquité. Bilan et avancées expérimentales," in M. Molin (ed.), *Archéologie et histoire des techniques du monde romain, Actes du Colloque de la Société Française d'Archéologie Classique, Paris, I.N.H.A., 15 novembre 2006*, Paris: de Boccard, pp. 87–94.

2008b, "Land transport, Part 2: Riding, harnesses, and vehicles," in J. P. Oleson (ed.), *The Oxford Handbook of Engineering and Technology in the Classical World*, Oxford University Press, pp. 580–605.

RAFFAELE, F., 2003, "Dynasty 0," *Aegyptiaca Helvetica*, 17, pp. 99–141.

RAFOLO, A., 2000, "Mixed cultures of Madagascar and the other islands of the Indian Ocean," in M. A. Al-Bakhit, L. Bazin, and S. M. Cissoko (eds.), *History of Humanity*, vol. IV: *From the Seventh to the Sixteenth Century*, Paris: UNESCO, pp. 531–537.

RAHMSTORF, L., 2006a, "In search of the earliest balance weights, scales and weighing systems from the East Mediterranean, the Near and Middle East," in *Weights in Context. Bronze Age Weighing Systems of Eastern Mediterranean. Chronology, Typology, Material and Archaeological contexts, Proceedings of the International Colloquium Rome 22–24 November 2004*, Rome: Istituto Italiano di Numismatica, pp. 9–45.

2006b, "Zur Ausbreitung vorderasiatischer Innovationen in die frühbronzezeitliche Ägäis," *Praehistorische Zeitschrift*, 81 (1), pp. 49–96.

RAISON-JOURDE, F., 1983a and b, "Introduction" and "De la restauration des talismans royaux au baptême de 1869 en Imerina. Une tentative de légitimation des rapports entre pouvoir royal dominé et pouvoir d'état hova dominant au milieu du XXe siècle," in F. Raison-Jourde (ed.), *Les souverains de Madagascar: l'histoire royale et ses résurgences contemporaines*, Paris: Karthala, pp. 7–68 and 337–369.

(ed.), 1983, *Les souverains de Madagascar: l'histoire royale et ses résurgences contemporaines*, Paris: Karthala.

RAISON, J. -P., 1972, "Utilisation de l'espace et organisation de l'espace en Imerina ancienne," *Études de Géographie Tropicale offertes à Pierre Gourou*, Paris and The Hague: Mouton, pp. 407–425.

1992, "Le noir et le blanc dans l'agriculture ancienne de la côte orientale malgache," *Études Océan Indien*, 15 (issue on "Le scribe et la grande maison: études offertes au professeur J. Dez"), pp. 199–216.

RAJAN, K., 2002, "Maritime trade in early historic Tamil Nadu," *Man and Environment*, 27(1), pp. 83–98.

RAJGOR, D., 1998, *History of the Traikūṭakas: Based on Coins and Inscriptions*, New Delhi: Harman.

RAKOTO RAMIARANTSOA, H., 1998, "Mérinité du paysage et comportements d'alliances: des signes de l'ascendance austronésienne à Madagascar," in D. Guillaud, M. Seysset, and A. Walter (eds.), *Le voyage inachevé . . . A Joël Bonnemaison*, Paris: Editions de l'ORSTOM, PRODIG-CNRS, pp. 651–656.

RAMASWAMY, V., 2002, "Interactions and encounters: Indian looms and crafts traditions abroad – a South Indian perspective," in D. P. Chattopadhyaya (ed.), *History of Science, Philosophy and Culture in Indian Civilization*, vol. III, part 2, A. Rahman (ed.), *India's Interaction with China, Central and West Asia*, of Delhi: Oxford University Press, pp. 428–444.

RANDLES, W. G. L., 1975, *L'empire du Monomotapa du XVe au XIXe siècle*, Paris: Mouton.

RANDRIANERA, M., 1995, "Lignages et eau: une dynamique liée. Fokontany de Vakinifasina, Betafo-Antsirabe, Vakinankaratra," Mémoire de Capen, Université de Tananarive, Ecole Normale Supérieure.

RANGAN, H., CARNEY, J., and DENHAM, T., 2012, "Environmental history of botanical exchanges in the Indian Ocean world," *Environment and History*, 18, p. 311–342.

RAO, K. P., 2000, "Megalithic anthropomorphic statues: meaning and significance," *Bulletin of the Indo-Pacific Prehistory Association*, 19, pp. 111–114.

RAO, S. R., 1999, *The Lost City of Dvaraka*, New Delhi: Aditya Prakashan.

RAS, J. J., 1968, *Hikayat Banjar: A Study in Malay Historiography*, The Hague: M. Nijhoff.

RASCHKE, M. G., 1975, "Papyrological evidence for Ptolemaic and Roman trade with India," in *Proceedings of the 14th International Congress of Papyrologists, Oxford, 24–31 July 1974*, pp. 241–246.

RASSAMAKIN, Y., 2002, "Aspects of Pontic steppe development (4550–3000 BC) in the light of the new cultural-chronological model," in K. Boyle, C. Renfrew, and M. Levine (eds.), *Ancient Interactions: East and West in Eurasia*, Cambridge: McDonald Institute for Archaeological Research, pp. 49–73.

RATHBONE, D., 1991, *Economic Rationalism and Rural Society in Third-Century AD Egypt: The Heroninos Archive and the Appianus Estate*, Cambridge University Press.

2003, "Economic rationalism and the Heroninos Archive," *Topoi. Orient-Occident*, 12–13, pp. 261–269.

2004, "Weber et la comptabilité, Bücher et l'industrie," in H. Bruhns and J. Andreau (eds.), *Sociologie économique et économie de l'Antiquité: à propos de Max Weber, Cahiers du Centre de recherches historiques*, 34, October, pp. 133–142.

RATNAGAR, S., 1991, *Enquiries into the Political Organization of Harappan Society*, Pune: Ravish.

2000, *The End of the Great Harappan Tradition*, New Delhi: Manohar.

2001a, "Harappan trade in its 'world-context'," in R. Chakravarti (ed.), *Trade in Early India*, Oxford University Press, pp. 102–127 (first published 1994 in *Man and Environment*, 19, 1–2, pp. 115–127).

2001b, "The Bronze Age: unique instance of a pre-industrial world system?," *Current Anthropology*, 42 (3), pp. 351–379.

2004, *Trading Encounters: From the Euphrates to the Indus in the Bronze Age*, Oxford University Press.

RAWLINSON, H., 1901, *Babylonian and Assyrian Literature*, New York: P. F. Collier and Son.

RAWSON, J., 1999, "Jade pei pectoral," in X. Yang (ed.), *The Golden Age of Chinese Archaeology: Celebrated Discoveries from the People's Republic of China*, Washington, DC: National

Gallery of Art; Kansas City: The Nelson-Atkins Museum of Art; New Haven, CT, and London: Yale University Press, pp. 252–253.

RAY, H. P., 1988, "The Yavana presence in Ancient India," *Journal of the Economic and Social History of the Orient*, 31 (2), pp. 311–325.

1989, "Early maritime contacts between South and South-East Asia," *Journal of South-East Asian Studies*, 20 (1), pp. 42–54.

1991, "In search of Suvarnabhumi," *Bulletin of the Indo-Pacific Prehistory Association*, 10, pp. 357–365.

1994, *The Winds of Change: Buddhism and the Maritime Links of Early South Asia*, New Delhi: Manohar.

1996, "Early coastal trade in the Bay of Bengal," in J. Reade (ed.), *The Indian Ocean in Antiquity*, London and New York: Kegan Paul, pp. 351–364.

1999a, "Orissa in Chinese historical records," in K. S. Behera (ed.), *Maritime Heritage of India*, New Delhi: Aryan Books International, pp. 225–235.

1999b and c, "Preamble" and "The legacy of Childe and the archaeology of coastal sites," in H. P. Ray (ed.), *Archaeology of Seafaring: The Indian Ocean in the Ancient Period*, New Delhi: Pragati, pp. 1–21 and 313–324.

(ed.), 1999, *Archaeology of Seafaring: The Indian Ocean in the Ancient Period*, New Delhi: Pragati.

2001, "South and Southeast Asia: the commencement of a long lasting relationship," in M. J. Klokke and K. R. Van Kooij (eds.), *Fruits of Inspiration: Studies in Honour of Prof. J. G. De Casparis, Retired Professor of the Early History and Archeology of South and Southeast Asia at the University of Leiden, the Netherlands, on the Occasion of His 85th Birthday*, Groningen: Egbert Forstein, pp. 407–421.

2002a and b, "Shipping in the Indian Ocean: an overview" and "Seafaring in Peninsular India in the Ancient Period: of watercraft and maritime communities," in D. Parkin and R. Barnes (eds.), *Ships and the Development of Maritime Technology in the Indian Ocean*, London and New York: Routledge/Curzon, pp. 1–27 and 62–91.

2003, *The Archaeology of Seafaring in Ancient South Asia*, Cambridge University Press.

2006a, "The Axial Age in South Asia: the archaeology of Buddhism (500 BC–AD 500)," in M. T. Stark (ed.), *Archaeology of Asia*, Malden, MA, and Oxford: Blackwell, pp. 303–323.

2006b, "Inscribed pots, emerging identities: the social milieu of trade," in P. Olivelle (ed.), *Between the Empires: Society in India 300 BCE to 400 CE*, Oxford University Press, pp. 113–143.

RAY, H. P. and SALLES, J.-F., 1996, *Tradition and Archaeology: Early Maritime Contacts in the Indian Ocean*, New Delhi: Manohar.

RAZAFINDRAIBE, H., MOBEGI, V. A., OMMEH, S. C., RAKOTONDRAVAO, M. L., BJØRNSTAD, G., HANOTTE, O., and HAN JIANLIN, 2008, "Mitochondrial DNA origin of indigenous Malagasy chicken," *Annals of the New York Academy of Sciences*, 1149, pp. 77–79.

RAZAFINDRAZAKA, H., RICAUT, F.-X., COX, M. P., MORMINA, M., DUGOUJON, J.-M., RANDRIAMAROLAZA, L.-P., GUITARD, E., TONASSO, L., LUDES, B., and CRUBÉZY, E., 2010, "Complete mitochondrial DNA sequences provide new insights into the Polynesian motif and the peopling of Madagascar," *European Journal of Human Genetics*, 18 (5), pp. 575–81.

READE, J. (ed.), 1996, *The Indian Ocean in Antiquity*, London and New York: Kegan Paul.

2001, "Assyrian king-lists, the royal tombs of Ur, and Indus origins," *Journal of Near Eastern Studies*, 60 (1), pp. 1–29.

2008, "The Indus–Mesopotamian relationship reconsidered," in E. Olijdam and R. H. Spoor (eds.), *Intercultural Relations Between South and Southwest Asia: Studies in Commemoration of*

E.C.L. During Caspers (1934–1996) (BAR International Series 1826), Oxford: Archaeopress, pp. 12–18.

REICHEL, C., 2002, "Administrative complexity in Syria during the 4th millennium BC: the seals and sealings from Tell Hamoukar," *Akkadica*, 123, pp. 35–56.

REID, A., 2001, "Understanding *Melayu* (Malay) as a source of diverse modern identities," *Journal of Southeast Asian Studies*, 32 (3), pp. 295–330.

2005, "The current status of Austric: a review and evaluation of the lexical and morphosyntaxic evidence," in L. Sagart, R. Blench, and A. Sanchez-Mazas (eds.), *The Peopling of East Asia: Putting Together Archaeology, Linguistics and Genetics*, London: Routledge/Curzon, pp. 132–160.

REINECKE, A., 1996, "Ohrringe mit Tierkopfenden in Südostasien," *Beiträge zur Allgemeinen und Vergleichenden Archaeologie*, 16, pp. 5–51.

REINECKE, A. and NGUYEN THI THANH LUYEN, 2009, "Recent discoveries in Vietnam: gold masks and other precious items," *Arts of Asia*, 39, pp. 58–67.

REINECKE, A., LAYCHOUR, V., and SONETRA, S., 2012, "Prohear: an Iron Age burial site in Southeastern Cambodia: preliminary report after three excavations," in M. L. Tjoa-Bonatz, A. Reinecke, and D. Bonatz (eds.), *Crossing Borders: Selected Papers from the 13th International Conference of the European Association of Southeast Asian Archaeologists*, National University of Singapore Press, pp. 268–285.

RENFREW, C., 1975, "Trade as action at a distance: questions of integration and communication," in J. A. Sabloff and C. C. Lamberg-Karlovsky (eds.), *Ancient Civilization and Trade*, Albuquerque: University of New Mexico Press, pp. 3–59.

2002, "Pastoralism and interaction: some introductory questions," in K. Boyle, C. Renfrew, and M. Levine (eds.), *Ancient Interactions: East and West in Eurasia*, Cambridge: McDonald Institute for Archaeological Research, pp. 1–10.

RENFREW, C. and BAHN, P., 2000 *Archaeology: Theories, Methods and Practice*, 3rd edn., London: Thames and Hudson (1st edn. 1991).

RENGER, J. M., 1994, "On economic structures in Ancient Mesopotamia," *Orientalia*, 63, pp. 157–208.

1995, "Institutional, communal, and individual ownership or possession of arable land in Ancient Mesopotamia from the end of fourth to the end of the first millennium BC," *Chicago Kent Law Review*, 71, pp. 269–319.

2003, "Trade and market in the Ancient Near East: theoretical and factual implications," in C. Zaccagnini (ed.), *Mercanti e politica nel mondo antico*, Rome: "L'Erma" di Bretschneider, pp. 15–39.

RETSÖ, J., 2003a, *The Arabs in Antiquity: Their History from the Assyrians to the Umayyads*, London and New York: Routledge.

2003b, "When did Yemen become *Arabia Felix?*," *Proceedings of the Seminar for Arabian Studies*, 33, pp. 229–235.

RHOUMA, S., DAKHLAOUI-DKHIL, S., OULD MOHAMED SALEM, A., ZEHDI-AZOUZI, S., RHOUMA, A., MARRAKCHI, M., and TRIFI, M., 2008, "Genetic diversity and phylogenic relationships in date-palms (*Phoenix dactylifera* L.) as assessed by random amplified microsatellite polymorphism markers (RAMPOs)," *Scientia Horticulturae*, 117, pp. 53–57.

RICAUT, F.-X., RAZAFINDRAZAKA, H., COX, M.P., DUGOUJON, J.-M., GUITARD, E., SAMBO, C., MORMINA, M., MIRAZON-LAHR, M., LUDES, B., and CRUBÉZY, E., 2009, "A new deep branch of Eurasian mtDNA macrohaplogroup M reveals additional complexity regarding the settlement of Madagascar," *BMC Genomics*, 10, p. 605.

RICE, M., 1994, *The Archaeology of the Arabian Gulf, c. 5000–323 BC*, London and New York: Routledge.

RICHARDS, J. F. (ed.), 1983, *Precious Metals in the Later Medieval and Early Modern Worlds*, Durham, NC: Carolina Academic Press.

1983a and b, "Introduction" and "Outflows of precious metals from early Islamic India," in J. F. Richards (ed.), *Precious Metals in the Later Medieval and Early Modern Worlds*, Durham, NC: Carolina Academic Press, pp. 3–26 and 185–205.

RISPOLI, F., CIARLA, R., and PIGOTT, V. C., 2013, "Establishing the prehistoric cultural sequence for the Lopburi region, Central Thailand," *Journal of World Prehistory*, 26 (2), pp. 101–171.

ROACH, B. T., 1995, "Sugar cane. *Saccharum* (Gramineae)," in J. Smartt and N. W. Simmonds (eds.), *Evolution of Crop Plants*, 2nd edn., London and New York: Longman, pp. 160–166.

ROAF, M., 2001, "Continuity and change from the Middle to the Late Assyrian period," in R. Eichmann and C. Parzinger (eds.), *Migration und Kulturtransfer: Der Wandel vorder- und zentralasiatischer Kulturen im Umbruch vom 2. zum 1. vorchristlichen Jahrtausend, Akten des Internationalen Kolloquiums Berlin, 23–26 November 1999* (Kolloquien zur Vor- und Frühgeschichte 6), Bonn: Habelt, pp. 357–369.

ROBERTSHAW, P., 2009, "African archaeology in world perspective," in S. Falconer and C. Redman (eds.), *Polities and Power: Archaeological Perspectives on the Landscapes of Early States*, Tucson: University of Arizona Press, pp. 208–220.

2015, "Sub-Saharan Africa: archaeology," in P. Bellwood (ed.), *The Global Prehistory of Human Migration*, Oxford and Malden, MA: Wiley Blackwell, pp. 107–114.

ROBIN, C. J., 1997a, "Arabie méridionale: l'état et les aromates," in A. Avanzini (ed.), *Profumi d'Arabia*, Rome: "L'Erma" di Bretschneider, pp. 37–56.

1997b, "La chronologie et ses problèmes," in *Yémen: Au pays de la reine de Saba*, Paris: Flammarion, Institut du Monde Arabe, pp. 60–62.

1997c, "The date of the *Periplus of the Erythraean Sea* in the light of South Arabian evidence," in F. De Romanis and A. Tchernia (eds.), *Crossings: Early Mediterranean Contacts with India*, New Delhi: Manohar, pp. 41–65.

2005–2006, "Chrétiens de l'Arabie Heureuse et de l'Arabie déserte: de la victoire à l'échec," *Archéologia*, 309, pp. 24–35.

ROBSON, E., 2008, *Mathematics in Ancient Iraq: A Social History*, Princeton University Press.

ROHL, D., 1995, *A Test of Time: The Bible from Myth to History*, London: Arrow.

ROMAN, D. and ROMAN, Y., 1998, *Histoire de la Gaule, VIe siècle av. J.-.C. – 1er siècle ap. J.-C.*, Paris: Le Grand Livre du Mois.

ROMAN, Y., 2009a, "Avant-propos," in Y. Roman (ed.), *Rome et l'Occident. 197 BC à 192 ap. J.-C.*, Paris: Ellipses, pp. 5–8.

2009b, "Entre Rome et Gaules, le commerce, vecteur de romanisation," in B. Cabouret-Laurioux, J.-P. Guilhembet, and Y. Roman (eds.), *Pallas: Revue d'Études Antiques*, "*Rome et l'Occident: IIe siècle av. J.-C. – IIe siècle ap. J.-C.*," Colloque de la SOPHAU, Lyon, 15–16 mai 2009, Toulouse: Presses Universitaires du Mirail, pp. 245–277.

RONAN, C. A., 1986, *The Shorter Science and Civilisation in China: An Abridgment of Joseph Needham's Original Text*, vol. III, Cambridge University Press.

1988, *Histoire mondiale des sciences*, Paris: Seuil (1st edn. 1983).

ROSEN, A. M., 2007, *Civilizing Climate. Social Responses to Climate Change in the Near East*, Lanham, MD: Altamira Press.

ROSS, M. D., 2002, "The history and transitivity of Western Austronesian voice and voice marking," in F. Wouk and M. D. Ross (eds.), *The History and Typology of Western Austronesian Voice Systems*, Canberra: Pacific Linguistics, p. 17–62.

ROSTOVTZEFF, M., 1988, *Histoire économique et sociale de l'Empire romain*, Paris: Robert Laffont (1st edn. 1926).

    1998, *The Social and Economic History of the Roman Empire*, 2 vols., Oxford University Press (1st edn. 1926).

    1989, *Histoire économique et sociale du monde hellénistique*, Paris: Robert Laffont (1st edn. 1941).

ROTH, M. T., BIGGS, R. D., BRINKMAN, J. A., CIVIL, M., FARBER, W., GELB, I. J., LANDSBERGER, B., OPPENHEIMER, L., and REINER, E., 1964–2006, *The Assyrian Dictionary of the Oriental Institute of the University of Chicago*, Chicago: The Oriental Institute; Glückstadt: J. J. Augustin-Verlagsbuchhandlung.

ROTHMAN, M. S., 2001a and b, "The local and the regional: an introduction" and "The Tigris Piedmont, Eastern Jazira, and Highland Western Iran in the fourth millennium BC," in M. S. Rothman (ed.), *Uruk Mesopotamia and Its Neighbors: Cross-Cultural Interactions in the Era of State Formation*, Sante Fe: School of American Research; Oxford: James Currey, pp. 3–24 and 349–402.

    2004, "Tepe Gawra: chronology and socio-economic change in the foothills of northern Iraq in the era of state formation," in J. N. Postgate (ed.), *Artefacts of Complexity: Tracking the Uruk in the Near East* (Iraq Archaeological Reports 5), Warminster: Aris and Phillips for the British School of Archaeology in Iraq, p. 49–63 (1st edn. 2002).

    2013, "Interpreting the role of Godin Tepe in the 'Uruk expansion'," in C. A. Petrie (ed.), *Ancient Iran and Its Neighbours: Local Developments and Long-Range Interactions in the Fourth Millennium BC*, Oxford: Oxbow Books, pp. 75–91.

ROUGEULLE, A., 1996, "Medieval trade networks in the western Indian ocean (8–14th centuries): some reflections from the distribution pattern of Chinese imports in the Islamic world," in H. P. Ray and J.-F. Salles (eds.), *Tradition and Archaeology: Early Maritime Contacts in the Indian Ocean*, Delhi: Manohar, pp. 159–180.

    2007, "A medieval trade entrepôt at Khor Rori? The study of the Islamic ceramics from al-Hamra al-Sharqiya," in A. Avanzini (ed.), *A Port in Arabia between Rome and the Indian Ocean (3rdC. BC – 5thC. AD)* (Khor Rori Report 2), Rome: "L'Erma" di Bretschneider, pp. 645–667.

ROVIRA, S. and MONTERO, I., 2003, "Natural tin–bronze alloy in Iberian peninsula metallurgy: potentiality and reality," in A. Giumlia-Mair and F. Lo Schiavo (eds.), *Le problème de l'étain à l'origine de la métallurgie. Colloque Âge du Bronze en Europe et en Méditerranée, Actes du XIVe congrès UISPP, Université de Liège, Belgique, 2–8 septembre 2001* (BAR International Series 1199), Oxford: Archaeopress, pp. 15–22.

ROWLANDS, M., 1987, "Centre and periphery: a review of a concept," in M. Rowlands, M. Larsen, and K. Kristiansen (eds.), *Centre and Periphery in the Ancient World*, Cambridge University Press, pp. 1–11.

ROWLANDS, M., LARSEN, M., and KRISTIANSEN, K., (eds.), 1987. *Centre and Periphery in the Ancient World*, Cambridge University Press.

ROWLEY-CONWY, P., 1988, "The camel in the Nile valley: new radiocarbon accelerator (AMS) dates from Qasr Ibrim," *Journal of Egyptian Archaeology*, 74, pp. 245–248.

    1991, "Sorghum from Qasr Ibrim, Egyptian Nubia, c. 800 BC – AD 1811: a preliminary study," in J. Renfrew (ed.), *New Light on Early Farming*, Edinburgh University Press, pp. 191–212.

ROWLEY-CONWY, P., DEAKIN, W., and SHAW, C. H., 1997, "Ancient DNA from archaeological sorghum (*Sorghum bicolor*) from Qasr Ibrim, Nubia: implications for domestication and evolution and a review of the archaeological evidence," *Sahara*, 9, pp. 23–34.

RUDENKO, S. I., 1970, *Frozen Tombs of Siberia*, Berkeley: University of California.

Ruiz-Gálvez Priego, M. (ed.), 1995, *Ritos de paso y puntos de paso: la ría de Huelva en el mundo del Bronce Final Europeo* (*Complutum*, special issue 5). Madrid.

2000, "Weight systems and exchange networks in Bronze Age Europe," in C. F. E. Pare (ed.), *Metals Make the World Go Round: The Supply and Circulation of Metals in Bronze Age Europe, Proceedings of a Conference Held at the University of Birmingham in June 1997*, Oxford: Oxbow Books, pp. 267–272.

Rutter, O., 1929. *The Pagans of North Borneo*, London: Hutchinson & Co.

Sachs, C., 1938, *Les instruments de musique à Madagascar*, Paris: Institut d'Ethnologie.

Sacleux, C., 1939, *Dictionnaire Swahili–Français*, Paris: Institut d'Ethnologie.

Sadao, N., 1986, "The economic and social history of the Former Han," in *The Cambridge History of China*, vol. 1, Cambridge University Press, pp. 545–607.

Sagart, L., 2003, "The vocabulary of cereal cultivation and the phylogeny of East Asian languages," *Bulletin of the Indo-Pacific Prehistory Association*, 23, pp. 127–136.

2005a, "Sino-Tibetan-Austronesian: an updated and improved argument," in L. Sagart, R. Blench, and A. Sanchez-Mazas (eds.), *The Peopling of East Asia: Putting Together Archaeology, Linguistics and Genetics*, London: Routledge/Curzon, pp. 161–176.

2005b, "Tai-Kadai as a subgroup of Austronesian," in L. Sagart, R. Blench, and A. Sanchez-Mazas (eds.), *The Peopling of East Asia: Putting Together Archaeology, Linguistics and Genetics*, London: Routledge/Curzon, pp. 177–181.

2008, "Reply to Matisoff on the *Handbook of Proto-Tibeto-Burman: System and Philosophy of Sino-Tibetan Reconstruction*," *Diachronica*, 25 (1), pp. 153–155.

2011, "How many independent rice vocabularies in East Asia?," *Rice*, 4 (4), pp. 121–133.

Sagart, L., Blench, R., and Sanchez-Mazas, A., 2005, "Introduction," in L. Sagart, R. Blench, and A. Sanchez-Mazas (eds.), *The Peopling of East Asia: Putting Together Archaeology, Linguistics and Genetics*, London: Routledge/Curzon, pp. 1–14.

Saletore, R. N., 1994, *Early Indian Economic History*, London: Sangam Books.

Salles, J.-F. (ed.), 1988, *L'Arabie et ses mers bordières*, Lyon: Maison de l'Orient.

1993, "*The Periplus of the Erythraean Sea* and the Arab-Persian Gulf," *Topoi: Orient-Occident*, 3 (2), pp. 493–524.

1996a, "Achaemenid and Hellenistic trade in the Indian ocean," in J. Reade (ed.), *The Indian Ocean in Antiquity*, London and New York: Kegan Paul, pp. 251–268.

1996b, "Hellenistic seafaring in the Indian Ocean: a perspective from Arabia," in H. P. Ray and J.-F. Salles (eds.), *Tradition and Archaeology: Early Maritime Contacts in the Indian Ocean*, Delhi: Manohar, pp. 293–310.

1998, "Antique maritime channels from the Mediterranean to the Indian Ocean," in C. Guillot, D. Lombard, and R. Ptak (eds.), *From the Mediterranean to the China Sea*, Wiesbaden: Harassowitz, pp. 45–68.

2004, "Archaeology and history of Bangladesh: recent perspectives," in H. P. Ray and C. M. Sinopoli (eds.), *Archaeology as History in Early South Asia*, New Delhi: Aryan Books, pp. 185–218.

2012, "Le Golfe Persique dans le *Périple de la mer Erythrée*: connaissances fondées et ignorances réelles," *Topoi* supplement 11, pp. 293–328.

Salles, J.-F., Boussac, M.-F., and Breuil, J.-Y., 2002, "Mahasthangarh (Bangladesh) and the Ganges valley in the Mauryan period," in G. Sengupta and S. Panja (eds.), *Archaeology of Eastern India*, Kolkata: Centre for Archaeological Studies and Training, pp. 527–550.

Salles, J.-F. and Sedov, A. V. (eds.), 2010, *Qâni': le port antique du Hadramawt entre la Méditerranée, l'Afrique et l'Inde. Fouilles russes 1972, 1985–1989, 1991, 1993–1994*, Turnhout: Brepols.

Salmon, C., 2004, "Les Persans à l'extrémité orientale de la route maritime (IIe A.E. – XVIIe siècles)," *Archipel*, 68, pp. 23–58.

2009, "Malay (and Javanese) loanwords in Chinese as a mirror of cultural exchanges," *Archipel*, 78, pp. 181–208.

SALVATORI, S. and TOSI, M., 2005, "Shar-i Sokhta revised sequence," in C. Jarrige and V. Lefèvre (eds.), *South Asian Archaeology 2001*, Paris: Éditions Recherche sur les Civilisations, pp. 281–292.

SANG, T. and GE, S., 2007, "The puzzle of rice domestication," *Journal of Integrative Plant Biology*, 49, pp. 760–768.

SANLAVILLE, P., 1992, "Changements climatiques dans la péninsule arabique durant le Pléistocène Supérieur et l'Holocène," *Paléorient*, 18, pp. 5–26.

SARASWAT, K. S., 1993, "Plant economy of Late Harappan at Hulas," *Puratattva*, 23, pp. 1–12.

2005, "Agricultural background of the early farming communities in the Middle Ganga Plain," *Pragdhara*, 15, pp. 145–177.

SARASWAT, K. S. and POKHARIA, A. K., 2003, "Palaeoethnobotanical investigations at early Harappan Kunal," *Pragdhara*, 13, pp. 105–140.

SARASWAT, K. S. SHARMA, N. K., and SAINI, D. C., 1994, Plant economy in ancient Narhan (ca. 1,300 B.C. – 300/400 A.D.), in P. Purushottam Singh (ed.), *Excavations at Narhan (1984–1989)*, Varanasi: Banaras Hindu University, pp. 255–346.

SARIANIDI, V. I., 1994a, "Preface," in F. T. Hiebert (ed.), *Origins of the Bronze Age Oasis Civilization in Central Asia* (American School of Prehistoric Research Bulletin 42), Cambridge, MA: Peabody Museum of Archaeology and Ethnology, Harvard University, pp. xxxi–xxxiv.

1994b, "Temples of Bronze Age Margiana: traditions of ritual architecture," *Antiquity*, 68 (259), pp. 388–397.

1996, "Afghanistan," in A. H. Dani and J.-P. Mohen (eds.), *History of Humanity*, vol. II: *From the Third Millennium to the Seventh Century BC*, London and New York: Routledge; Paris: UNESCO, pp. 232–237.

2001, "The Indo-Iranian problem in the light of the latest excavations in Margiana," *Studia Orientalia*, 94, pp. 417–441.

2002, *Margush: Ancient Oriental Kingdom in the Old Delta of the Murghab River*, Ashgabat: Türkmendöwlethabarlary.

2006, "Le plus ancien sacrifice de poulain au Proche-Orient," *Dossiers d'Archéologie*, 317, pp. 34–39.

2007, *Necropolis of Gonour*, Athens: Kapon Editions.

SARKAR, K. R., 2003, *Public Finance in Ancient India*, New Delhi: Abhinav Publications.

SARTRE, M., 2001, *D'Alexandre à Zénobie: Histoire du Levant Antique, IVe siècle av J.-C. – IIIe siècle apr. J.-C.*, Paris: Fayard.

SASTRI, K. A. NILAKANTA, 1949, *History of Srivijaya*, University of Madras.

SATHER, C., 1995, "Sea nomads and rainforest hunter-gatherers," in P. Bellwood, J. J. Fox, and D. T. Tryon (eds.), *The Austronesians: Comparative and Historical Perspectives*, Canberra: Department of Anthropology, Research School of Pacific and Asian Studies, pp. 229–268.

SATO, Y.-I., 2005, "Rice and Indus civilization," in T. Osada (ed.), *Linguistics, Archaeology and Human Past*, Kyoto: Research Institute for Humanity and Nature, pp. 213–214.

SAUER, C. O., 1952, *Agricultural Origins and Dispersals*, New York: American Geographical Society.

SAVE-SÖDERBERGH, T., 1946, *The Navy of the Eighteenth Egyptian Dynasty*, Uppsala: Lundequistska bokhandeln.

SAXENA, A., PRASAD, V., SINGH, I. B., CHAUHAN, M. S., and HASAN, R., 2006, "On the Holocene record of phytoliths of wild and cultivated rice from Ganga Plain: evidence for rice-based agriculture," *Current Science*, 90 (11), pp. 1547–1552.

SCARRE, C. (ed.), 2000, *The Times Archaeology of the World*, London: Times Books.

SCHAFER, E. H., 1985, *The Golden Peaches of Samarkand: A Study of T'ang Exotics*, Berkeley, Los Angeles, and London: University of California Press (1st edn. 1963).

SCHAPS, D., 2004, *The Invention of Coinage and the Monetization of Ancient Greece*. Ann Arbor: University of Michigan Press.

2007, "The invention of coinage in Lydia, in India, and in China," *Bulletin du Cercle d'Études Numismatiques*, 44, (part 1) pp. 281–300; (part 2) pp. 313–322.

SCHÄRER, H., 1963, *Ngaju Religion: The Conception of God among a South Borneo People*, The Hague: M. Nijhoff (1st edn. 1946).

SCHEIDEL, W., 1999, "The slave population of Roman Italy: speculations and constraints," *Topoi: Orient-Occident*, 9, pp. 129–144.

SCHENK, H. 2006, "The dating and historical value of Rouletted ware," *Zeitschrift für Archäologie Außereuropäischer Kulturen*, 1, pp. 123–53.

2007, "Parthian glazed pottery from Sri Lanka and the Indian Ocean trade," *Zeitschrift für Archäologie Aussereuropäischer Kulturen*, 2, pp. 57–90.

2014, "Tissamaharama, Sri Lanka. Die Keramiksequenz und ihre Bedeutung für den frühhistorischen Fernhandel im Indischen Ozean," *Forschungsberichte des DAI 2014*, Faszikel 2, urn:nbn:de:0048-DAI-EDAI-F.2014-2–3.

SCHETTLER, G., LIU, Q., MINGRAM, J., STEBICH, M., and DULSKI, P., 2006, "East-Asian monsoon variability between 15 000 and 2000 cal. yr BP recorded in varved sediments of Lake Sihailongwan (northeastern China, Long Gang volcanic field)," *The Holocene*, 16 (8), pp. 1043–1057.

SCHIETTECATTE, J., 2010, "L'Arabie à la veille de l'islam," *L'Archéo-Théma*, 9, pp. 46–49.

2011, *D'Aden à Zafar: villes de l'Arabie du Sud préislamique* (Orient et Méditerranée, 6), Paris: de Boccard.

2013, "À la veille de l'islam: effondrement ou transformation du monde antique?," in C. Robin and J. Schiettecatte (eds.), *Les préludes de l'islam: ruptures et continuités des civilisations du Proche-Orient, de l'Afrique orientale, de l'Arabie et de l'Inde à la veille de l'islam* (Orient et Méditerranée, 11), Paris: de Boccard, pp. 9–36.

SCHMIDT, P. R., 2006, *Historical Archaeology in Africa: Representation, Social Memory, and Oral Traditions*, Lanham, MD: Altamira Press.

SCHMITT, P., 1987, "Le monde grec archaïque, VIIIe/VIe siècle av. J.-C.," in P. Vidal-Nacquet (ed.), *Atlas historique: histoire de l'humanité de la préhistoire à nos jours*, Paris: Hachette, pp. 42–43.

SCHNEIDER, J., 1977, "Was there a pre-capitalist world-system?," *Peasant Studies*, 6 (1), pp. 20–29 (repr. 1991 in C. Chase-Dunn and T. D. Hall [eds.], *Core/Periphery Relations in Precapitalist Worlds*, pp. 45–66).

SCHOFF, W. H., 1920, "Cinnamon, cassia and Somaliland," *Journal of the American Oriental Society*, 40, pp. 260–270.

1974, *The Periplus of the Erythraean Sea*, New Delhi: Oriental Books Reprint Corp (1st edn. 1912).

SCHOFIELD, L., 2007, *The Mycenaeans*, London: British Museum Press.

SCHORTMAN, E. M. and URBAN, P. A., 1987, "Modeling interregional interaction in prehistory," *Advances in Archaeological Method and Theory*, 11, pp. 37–95.

SCHOTTENHAMMER, A., 1999, "The maritime trade of Quanzhou (Zaitun) from the ninth through the thirteenth century," in H. P. Ray (ed.), *Archaeology of Seafaring: The Indian Ocean in the Ancient Period*, Delhi: Pragati, pp. 271–290.

SCHREIDEN, J., 1979, *La découverte d'Ophir et le canal de Psammétique*, Wetteren: Editions Cultura.

SCHWARTZ, H. M., 1994, *States versus Markets*, New York: St. Martin's Press.

SCORA, R. W., 1975, "On the history and origin of *Citrus*," *Bulletin Torrey Botanical Club*, 102, pp. 369–375.

SCUBLA, L., 2003, "Roi sacré, victime sacrificielle et victime émissaire," *La Revue du MAUSS*, 22, pp. 197–221.

SEDOV, A., 1996, "Qana' [Yemen] and the Indian Ocean: the archaeological evidence," in H. P. Ray and J.-F. Salles (eds.), *Tradition and Archaeology: Early Maritime Contacts in the Indian Ocean*, Delhi: Manohar, pp. 11–36.

2001, "Qanî, ancien port du Hadramaout," *Dossiers d'Archéologie*, 263 (issue on "Yémen"), p. 32–35.

2007, "The port of Qana' and the incense trade," in D. Peacock, D. Williams, and S. James (eds.), *Food for the Gods: New Light on the Ancient Incense Trade*, Oxford: Oxbow, pp. 71–111.

2010a and b, "Les fouilles de secteur 3: la synagogue" and "Place of Qani' in the Rome-Indian sea-trade," in J.-F. Salles and A. V. Sedov (eds.), *Qani: le port antique du Hadramawt entre la Méditerranée, l'Afrique et l'Inde. Fouilles russes 1972, 1985–1989, 1991, 1993–1994*, Brepols: Turnhout, pp. 87–122 and 453–474.

SELAND, E. H., 2007, "Ports, Ptolemy, *Periplus* and poetry: Romans in Tamil South India and on the Bay of Bengal," in E. H. Seland (ed.), *The Indian Ocean in the Ancient Period: Definite Places, Translocal Exchange* (BAR International Series 1593), Oxford: Archaeopress, pp. 69–82.

2010, *Ports and Power in the Periplus: Complex Societies and Maritime Trade on the Indian Ocean in the First Century AD* (BAR International Series 2102), Oxford: Archaeopress.

2011, "The Persian Gulf or the Red Sea? Two axes in ancient Indian Ocean trade, where to go and why," *World Archaeology*, 43, pp. 398–409.

2014, "Archaeology of trade in the western Indian Ocean, 300 BC – AD 700," *Journal of Archaeological Research*, doi: 10.1007/s10814-014-9075-7.

SELVAKUMAR, V., SHAJAN, K. P., and TOMBER, R., 2009, "Archaeological investigations at Pattanam, Kerala," New evidence for the location of ancient Muziris, in R. Tomber, L. Blue, and S. Abraham (eds.), *Migration, Trade and Peoples*, part 1: *Indian Ocean Commerce and the Archaeology of Western India*, London: British Association for South Asian Studies, The British Academy, pp. 29–41.

SERGENT, B., 1997, *Genèse de l'Inde*, Paris: Payot.

SERPICO, M. and WHITE, R., 2000, "The botanical identity and transport of incense during the Egyptian New Kingdom," *Antiquity*, 74 (286), pp. 884–897.

SEVERIN, T., 1985, "Constructing the Omani Boom Sohar," in S. McGrail and E. Kentley (eds.), *Sewn Plank Boats, Archaeological and Ethnographic Papers Based on Those Presented to a Conference at Greenwich in November, 1984* (Archaeological Series no. 10, BAR International Series 276), Greenwich: National Maritime Museum, pp. 280–285.

1985, *The Jason Voyage: The Quest for the Golden Fleece*, New York: Simon and Schuster.

SHAH, S. G. M. and PARPOLA, A. (eds.), 1991, *Corpus of Indus Seals and Inscriptions*, vol. II: *Collections in Pakistan*, Helsinki: Suomalainen Tiedeakatemia.

SHAHID, I., 2000, "Tayyi'," in P. Bearman, T. Bianquis, C. E. Bosworth, E. van Donzel, and W. P. Heinrichs (eds.), *Encyclopedia of Islam*, vol. X, Leiden: Brill, p. 62.

SHAHMIRZADI, S. M., 2004, "Sialk und seine Kultur. Ein Überblick," in T. Stöllner, R. Slotta, and A. Vatandoust (eds.), *Persiens Antike Pracht: Bergbau – Handwerk – Archäologie*, Bochum: Deutsches Bergbau Museum, vol. I, p. 200–208.

SHAIKH, N., 2000, "The Indus–Gulf relations: a reassessment in the light of new evidence," in V. Elisseeff (ed.), *The Silk Roads, Highways of Culture and Commerce*, published in association with UNESCO, New York and Oxford: Berghahn Books, pp. 81–92.

SHAJAN, K. P., TOMBER, R., SELVAKUMAR, V., and CHERIAN, P. J., 2004, "Locating the ancient port of Muziris, fresh findings from Pattinam," *Journal of Roman Archaeology*, 17, pp. 351–359.

SHAOWU, W., 2006, "Abrupt climate change from pre-Xia to Xia Dynasty and the formation of Ancient Chinese civilization," *Advances in Climate Change Research*, 2 (suppl. 1), pp. 64–67.

SHARIF, M. and THAPAR, B. K., 1992, "Food producing communities in Pakistan and Northern India," in A. H. Dani and V. M. Masson (eds.), *History of Civilizations of Central Asia*, vol. 1: *The Dawn of Civilization: Earliest Times to 700 BC*, Paris: UNESCO, pp. 127–151.

SHARMA, R. S., 1987, *Urban Decay in India (c. 300 – c. 1000)*, New Delhi: Munshiram Manoharlal.

2005, *Indian Feudalism, AD 300–1200*, 3rd rev. edn., Delhi: Macmillan (1st edn. 1965).

SHAW, B., 1979, "The camel in Roman North Africa and the Sahara: history, biology, and human economy," *Bulletin de l'IFAN (séries B)*, 41, pp. 663–721.

SHAW, G. W., 1989, "Phoenicians in southern Crete," *American Journal of Archaeology*, 93 (2), pp. 165–183.

SHAW, I., 2000, "Egypt and the outside world," in I. Shaw (ed.), *The Oxford History of Ancient Egypt*, Oxford University Press, pp. 314–329.

SHELACH, G. and PINES, Y., 2006, "Secondary state formation and the development of local identity: change and continuity in the state of Qin (770–221 BC)," in M. T. Stark (ed.), *Archaeology of Asia*, Malden, MA, and Oxford: Blackwell, pp. 202–230.

SHEN FUWEI, 2002, "Chitu Guo Lishi Tanyuan" ("Une exploration des sources sur l'histoire du royaume de Chitu"), *Wenshi*, 61, pp. 84–100.

SHEPHERD, G., 1982, "The making of the Swahili: a view from the southern end of the east African coast," *Paideuma*, 28, pp. 129–147.

SHEPPARD, E. and MCMASTER, R. B. (eds.), 2004, *Scale and Geographic Inquiry: Nature, Society, and Method*, Oxford: Blackwell.

SHERIFF, A., 1984, "La côte d'Afrique orientale et son rôle dans le commerce maritime," in G. Mokhtar (ed.), *Histoire générale de l'Afrique*. vol. II: *Afrique ancienne*, Paris: Jeune Afrique/UNESCO, pp. 595–611.

2002, "Navigational methods in the Indian Ocean," in D. Parkin and R. Barnes (eds.), *Ships and the Development of Maritime Technology in the Indian Ocean*, London and New York: Routledge/Curzon, pp. 209–226.

SHERRATT, A., 1981, "Plough and pastoralism: aspects of the secondary products revolution," in I. Hodder, G. Isaac, and N. Hammond (eds.), *Pattern of the Past: Studies in Honour of David Clarke*, Cambridge University Press, pp. 261–305.

1993, "'Who are you calling peripheral?' Dependence and independence in European prehistory," in C. Scarre and F. Healy (eds.), *Trade and Exchange in Prehistoric Europe*, Oxford: Oxbow Books, pp. 245–255.

1994a, "What would a Bronze Age world system look like? Relations between temperate Europe and the Mediterranean in later Prehistory," *Journal of European Archaeology*, 1 (2), pp. 1–57.

1994b, "Core, periphery and margin: perspectives on the Bronze Age," in C. Mathers and S. Stoddart (eds.), *Development and Decline in the Mediterranean Bronze Age*, Sheffield: J. R. Collins, pp. 325–345.

1994c and d, "The transformation of early agrarian Europe: the Later Neolithic and Copper Ages, 4500–2500 BC" and "The emergence of elites: earlier Bronze Age Europe, 2500–1300 BC," in B. Cunliffe (ed.), *The Oxford Illustrated History of Prehistoric Europe*, Oxford University Press, pp. 167–201 and 244–276.

1997, *Economy and Society in Prehistoric Europe: Changing Perspectives*, Edinburgh University Press.

2003, "The horse and the wheel: the dialectics of change in the circum-Pontic region and adjacent areas," in M. Levine, C. Renfrew, and K. Boyle (eds.), *Prehistoric Steppe Adaptation and the Horse*, Cambridge: McDonald Institute for Archaeological Research, pp. 233–252.

2004, "Material resources, capital, and power: the coevolution of society and culture," in G. M. Feinman and L. M. Nicolas (eds.), *Archaeological Perspectives on Political Economies*, Salt Lake City: University of Utah Press, pp. 79–103.

2006a, "La traction animale et la transformation de l'Europe néolithique," in P. Pétrequin, R-M. Arbogast, A-M. Pétrequin, S. van Willigen, and M. Bailly (eds.), *Premiers chariots, premiers araires: la diffusion de la traction animale en Europe pendant les IVe et IIIe millénaires avant notre ère*, Paris: Éditions du CNRS, pp. 329–360.

2006b, "The Trans-Eurasian exchange: the prehistory of Chinese relations with the West," in V. H. Mair (ed.), *Contact and Exchange in the Ancient World*, Honolulu: Hawaii University Press, pp. 30–61.

SHERRATT, A. and SHERRATT, S., 1991, "From luxuries to commodities: the nature of Mediterranean Bronze Age trading systems," in N. H. Gale (ed.), *Bronze Age Trade in the Mediterranean*, Jonsered: Paul Aströms Förlag, pp. 351–386.

1993, "The growth of the Mediterranean economy in the early first millennium BC," *World Archaeology*, 24 (3), pp. 361–378.

2001, "Technological change in the East Mediterranean Bronze Age: capital, resources and marketing," in A. J. Shortland (ed.), *The Social Context of Technological Change in Egypt and the Near East, 1650–1550 BC*, Oxford: Oxbow Books, pp. 15–38.

SHERRATT, S., 2000, "Circulation of metals and the end of the Bronze Age in the eastern Mediterranean," in C. F. E. Pare (ed.), *Metals Make the World Go Round: The Supply and Circulation of Metals in Bronze Age Europe, Proceedings of a Conference Held at the University of Birmingham in June 1997*, Oxford: Oxbow Books, pp. 82–98.

2003, "The Mediterranean economy: 'globalization' at the end of the second millennium BCE," in W. G. Dever and S. Gitin (eds.), *Symbiosis, Symbolism and the Power of the Past*, Winona Lake, IN: Eisenbrauns, pp. 37–62.

SHI MEIGUANG, HE OULI, and ZHOU FUZHENG, 1987, "Investigation on some Chinese potash glasses excavated in Han dynasty tombs," in H. C. Bhardwaj (ed.), *Archaeometry of Glass, Proceedings of the Archaeometry Session of the XIV International Congress on Glass, 1986, New Delhi*, Calcutta: Indian Ceramic Society, pp. 15–26 (part II).

SHIMIN, F. and BAOZHONG, Z., 1992, "Some glass in the Museum of Chinese History," in R. H. Brill and J. H. Martin (eds.), *Scientific Research in Early Chinese Glass*, Corning, NY: Corning Museum of Glass, pp. 193–200.

SHINNIE, P. L., 1991, "Trade routes of the ancient Sudan 3000 BC – AD 350," in W. V. Davies (ed.), *Egypt and Africa: Nubia from Prehistory to Islam*, London: British Museum Press and Egypt Exploration Society, pp. 49–53.

SHIRAZI, R., 2007, "Figurines anthropomorphes du Bronze Ancien de Shar-i Sokhta, Période II (Séistan, Sud-Est de l'Iran): approche typologique," *Paléorient*, 33 (2), pp. 147–162.

SHISHLINA, N. I., 2004, "North-west Caspian Sea steppe: environment and migration crossroads of pastoral culture population during the third millennium BC," in E. M. Scott, A. Y. Alekseev, and G. Zaitseva (eds.), *Impact of the Environment on Human Migration in Eurasia*, Dordrecht, Boston, and London: Kluwer Academic Publishers, pp. 91–106.

SHISHLINA, N. I., ORFINSKAYA, O. V., and GOLIKOV, V. P., 2003, "Bronze Age textiles from the North Caucasus: new evidence of fourth millennium BC fibres and fabrics," *Oxford Journal of Archaeology*, 22 (4), pp. 331–344.

SHIXIONG, W., 1992, "Scientific studies of early glasses excavated in China: a compilation of lead isotope ratios of some ores from China published by Chen Yuwei, Mao Cunxiao, and Zhu Bingquan," R. H. Brill and J. H. Martin (eds.), *Scientific Research in Early Chinese Glass: Proceedings of the Archaeometry of Glass Sessions of the 1984 International Symposium on Glass, Beijing, September 7, 1984, with supplementary papers*, Corning, NY: Corning Museum of Glass.

SHORTLAND, A. J., 2001, "Social influences on the development and spread of glass technology," in A. J. Shortland (ed.), *The Social Context of Technological Change in Egypt and the Near East, 1650–1550 BC*, Oxford: Oxbow Books, pp. 211–222.

SIDEBOTHAM, S. E., 1996, "Roman interests in the Red Sea and Indian Ocean," in J. Reade (ed.), *The Indian Ocean in Antiquity*, London and New York: Kegan Paul, pp. 287–308.

—— 2011, *Berenike and the Ancient Maritime Spice Route*, Berkeley: University of California Press.

SIDWELL, P. J., 2005, "Acehnese and the Aceh-Chamic language family," in A. P. Grant and P. J. Sidwell (eds.), *Chamic and Beyond: Studies in Mainland Austronesian Languages*, Canberra: Pacific Linguistics, pp. 211–246.

SIDWELL, P. J. and BLENCH, R., 2011, "The Austroasiatic Urheimat: the southeastern riverine hypothesis," in N. J. Enfield (ed.), *Dynamics of Human Diversity: The Case of Mainland Southeast Asia*, Canberra: Pacific Linguistics, pp. 317–345.

SILVER, M., 1983, "Karl Polanyi and markets in the Ancient Near East: the challenge of the evidence," *Journal of Economic History*, 43 (4), pp. 795–829

—— 1985, *Economic Structures of the Ancient Near East*, London: Croom-Helm.

—— 1995, *Economic Structures of Antiquity*, Westport, CT: Greenwood Press.

—— 2002, "Land markets in the Ancient Near East: a critique of the primitivist perspective," http://members.tripod.com/~sondmor/index-9.html

—— 2004a, "Ancient economies. Topic III: Evidence for Pre-Lydian coin and currency," http://members.tripod.com/~sondmor/index-7.html

—— 2004b, "Modern ancients," in R. Rollinger and C. Ulf (eds.), *Commerce and Monetary Systems in the Ancient World: Means of Transmission and Cultural Interaction*, Stuttgart: Franz Steiner Verlag, pp. 65–87.

—— 2004c, "Review of D. Schaps, *The Invention of Coinage and the Monetization of Ancient Greece*," EH.net, Economic History Services, http://eh.net/bookreviews/library/0772

—— 2007a, "Redistribution and markets in the economy of Ancient Mesopotamia: updating Polanyi," *Antiguo Oriente*, 5, pp. 89–112.

—— 2007b, "Grain funds in the Roman Near East: market failure or murder of the market?," *Ancient History Bulletin*, 21 (1–2), pp. 95–104.

SIMKIN, C. G. F., 1968, *The Traditional Trade of Asia*, London: Oxford University Press.

SIMMEL, G., 1987, *Philosophie de l'argent*, Paris: PUF (1st edn. 1900).

SIMON, P., 2006, *La langue des ancêtres: Ny Fitenin-dRazana*, Paris: L'Harmattan (1st edn. 1988, *Ny fiteny fahizany: reconstitution et périodisation du malgache ancien jusqu'au XIVe siècle*, Travaux et Documents 5 du CEROI, Paris: Institut National des Langues et Civilisations orientales).

SIMONNOT, P., 2002, *Vingt-et-un siècles d'économie: en vingt-et-une dates-clés*, Paris: Les Belles Lettres.

SINCLAIR, P., 1982, "An early trading site in southern Mozambique," *Paideuma*, 28, pp. 149–164.

—— 1987, *Space, Time and Social Formation: A Territorial Approach to the Archaeology and Anthropology of Zimbabwe and Mozambique c. 0–1700 AD*, Uppsala: Societas Archaeologica Upsaliensis.

—— 1991, "Archaeology in Eastern Africa: an overview of current chronological issues," *Journal of African History*, 32, pp. 179–219.

—— 2008, "What is the archaeological evidence for external trading contacts on the East African coast in the first millennium BC?," paper presented at the Sealinks Project Workshop at York, December 5.

SINCLAIR, P., EKBLOM, A., and WOOD, M., 2012, "Trade and society on the south-east African coast in the latter first millennium AD: the case of Chibuene," *Antiquity*, 86, pp. 723–737.

SINGH, U., 2008, *A History of Ancient and Early Medieval India: From the Stone Age to the 12th century*, Delhi: Dorling Kindersley / Pearson Education.

SINHA, B. K., 2000, "Golbai: a protohistoric site on the coast of Orissa," in K. K. Basa and P. Mohanty (eds.), *Archaeology of Orissa*, Delhi: Pratibha Prakashan, pp. 322–355.

SINOPOLI, C., 2006, "Imperial landscapes of South Asia," in M. T. Stark (ed.), *Archaeology of Asia*, Malden, MA, and Oxford: Blackwell, pp. 324–349.

SLAMET-VELSINK, I. E., 1995, *Emerging Hierarchies*, Leiden: KITLV.

SMITH, A., 1961, *An Inquiry into the Nature and Causes of the Wealth of Nations*, 2 vols., London: Methuen.

1991, *La richesse des nations*, 2 vols., Paris: Flammarion.

SMITH, A. B., 2000, "Origins of the domesticated animals of southern Africa," in R. Blench and K. C. MacDonald (eds.), *Origins and Development of African Livestock: Archaeology, Genetics, Linguistics and Ethnography*, London: UCL Press, pp. 222–238.

SMITH, B. D., 1998, *The Emergence of Agriculture*, New York: Scientific American Library (1st edn. 1995).

SMITH, M. L., 2002, "The role of local trade networks in the Indian subcontinent during the early historic period," *Man and Environment*, 27 (1), pp. 139–151.

SMITH, M. and WRIGHT, H. T., 1988, "The ceramics from Ras Hafun in Somalia: notes on a Classical maritime site," *Azania*, 33, pp. 115–141.

SMYTH, F., 1998, "Égypte-Canaan: quel commerce?," in N. Grimal and B. Menu (eds.), *Le commerce en Égypte ancienne*, Cairo: Institut Français d'Archéologie Orientale, pp. 5–17.

SNAPE, S., 2000, "Trade in the Late Bronze Age," in P. G. Bahn (ed.), *Atlas of World Archaeology*, London: B. T. Batsford, pp. 80–81.

SNELL, D., 1982, *Ledgers and Prices: Early Mesopotamian Merchant Accounts*, New Haven, CT: Yale University Press, 283 p.

1991, "Marketless trading in our time," *Journal of the Economic and Social History of the Orient*, 34, pp. 129–141.

1995, "Methods of exchange and coinage in ancient western Asia," in J. M. Sasson (ed.), *Civilizations of the Ancient Near East*, vol. III, New York: Scribner's, pp. 1487–1496.

SOARES, P., RITO, T., TREJAUT, J., MORMINA, M., HILL, C., TINKLER-HUNDAL, E., BRAID, M., CLARKE, D. J., LOO, J.-H., THOMSON, N., DENHAM, T., DONOHUE, M., MACAULAY, V., LIN, M., OPPENHEIMER, S., and RICHARD, M. B., 2011, "Ancient voyaging and Polynesian origins," *The American Journal of Human Genetics*, 88, pp. 239–247.

SOLHEIM , W. G., II, 1983, "The development of metallurgy in Southeast Asia: another reply to Loofs-Wissowa," *Journal of Southeast Asian Studies*, 14 (1), pp. 18–25.

1990, "Earthenware pottery, the T'ai and the Malay," *Asian Perspectives*, 29, pp. 25–36

SOMBART, W., 1926, *Le bourgeois: contribution à l'histoire morale et intellectuelle de l'homme économique moderne*, Paris: Payot (1st edn. 1913).

SONAWANE, V. H., 2000, "Early farming communities of Gujarat, India," *Bulletin of the Indo-Pacific Prehistory Association*, 19, pp. 137–146.

SOODYALL, H., JENKINS, T., HEWITT, R., KRAUSE, A., and STONEKING, M., 1996, "The peopling of Madagascar," in A. J. Boyce and C. G. N. Mascie-Taylor (ed.), *Molecular Biology and Human Diversity*, Cambridge University Press, pp. 157–170.

SOODYALL, H., MORAR, B., and JENKINS, T., 2013, "The genetic trail to Madagascar," in S. Evers, G. Campbell, and M. Lambek (eds.), *Contest for Land in Madagascar*, Leiden: Brill, pp. 21–40.

SORREL, P., POPESCU, S.-P., KLOTZ, S., SUC, J.-P., and OBERHÄNSLI, O., 2007, "Climate variability in the Aral Sea basin (Central Asia) during the late Holocene based on vegetation changes," *Quaternary Research*, 67 (3), pp. 357–370.

SOUTHWORTH, F. C., 2005, *Linguistic Archaeology of South Asia*, London and New York: Routledge.

2006, "Proto-Dravidian agriculture," in T. Osada (ed.), *Proceedings of the Pre-Symposium of RIHN and 7th ESCA Harvard-Kyoto Roundtable*, Kyoto: Research Institute for Humanity and Nature (RIHN), pp. 121–150.

SOUTHWORTH, W. A., 2001, "The origins of Campa in central Vietnam: a preliminary review," Ph.D. dissertation, School of Oriental and African Studies, University of London.

2004a, "The coastal states of Champa," in I. Glover and P. Bellwood (eds.), *Southeast Asia, From Prehistory to History*, Abingdon and New York: Routledge/Curzon, pp. 209–233.

2004b and c, "Funan" and "Sailendras: a Javanese Buddhist dynasty," in Ooi Keat Gin (ed.), *Southeast Asia: A Historical Encyclopedia, from Angkor Wat to East Timor*, Santa Barbara, CA: ABC-Clio, vol. I, pp. 529–530, and vol. III, 1167–1168.

SOUTHWORTH, W. A. and PRIOR, R., 2010, "History and archaeology at Tra Kieu," in B. Bellina, E. A. Bacus, T. O. Pryce, and J. Wisseman Christie (eds.), *50 Years of Archaeology in Southeast Asia: Essays in Honour of Ian Glover*, Bangkok: River Books, pp. 182–193.

SPEAR, T., 2000, "Early Swahili history reconsidered," *International Journal of African Historical Studies*, 33 (2), pp. 257–290.

SPENGLER, R., FRACHETTI, M., DOUMANI, P., ROUSE, L., CERASETTI, B., BULLION E., and MAR'YASHEV, A., 2014, "Early agriculture and crop transmission among Bronze Age mobile pastoralists of Central Eurasia," *Proceedings of the Royal Society*, 281, http://rspb.royalsocietypublishing.org/content/281/1783/20133382.full.html#ref-list-1

SPENS, R. DE, 1998, "Droit international et commerce au début de la XXIe dynastie: analyse juridique du rapport d'Ounamon," in N. Grimal and B. Menu (eds.), *Le commerce en Égypte ancienne*, Cairo: Institut Français d'Archéologie Orientale, pp. 105–128.

SPRIGGS, M., 2011, "Archaeology and the Austronesian expansion: where are we now?," *Antiquity*, 85, pp. 510–528.

SPRIGGS, M. and D. MILLER, 1988, "A previously unreported bronze kettledrum from the Kai Islands, eastern Indonesia," *Indo-Pacific Prehistory Association Bulletin*, 8, pp. 79–89.

SPRUYTTE, J., 1977, *Études expérimentales sur l'attelage: contribution à l'histoire du cheval*, Paris: Crepin Lebond.

SRINIVASAN, S., 2010, "Megalithic high-tin bronzes and peninsular India's living prehistory," in B. Bellina, E. A. Bacus, T. O. Pryce, and J. Wisseman Christie (eds.), *50 Years of Archaeology in Southeast Asia, Essays in Honour of Ian Glover*, Bangkok: River Books, pp. 260–271.

SRISUCHAT, A., 1996, "Merchants, merchandise, markets: archaeological evidence in Thailand concerning maritime trade interaction between Thailand and other countries before the 16th century AD," in A. Srisuchat (ed.), *Ancient Trade and Cultural Contacts in Southeast Asia*, Bangkok: The Office of the National Culture Commission, pp. 237–274.

STACUL, G., 2001, "The Swat Valley in the late 2nd and early 1st millennium BC," R. Eichmann and C. Parzinger (eds.), *Migration und Kulturtransfer: Der Wandel vorder- und zentralasiatischer Kulturen im Umbruch vom 2. zum 1. vorchristlichen Jahrtausend. Akten des Internationalen Kolloquiums Berlin, 23–26 November 1999* (Kolloquien zur Vor- und Frühgeschichte 6), Bonn: Rudolf Habelt, pp. 237–2.

STARK, M. T., 1998, "The transition to history in the Mekong Delta: a view from Cambodia," *International Journal of Historical Archaeology*, 2 (3), pp. 175–203.

2006, "Early Mainland Southeast Asian landscapes in the first millennium AD," *Annual Review of Anthropology*, 35, pp. 407–432.

STARK, M. T. and SOVATH, B., 2001, "Recent research on emergent complexity in Cambodia's Mekong," *Bulletin of the Indo-Pacific Prehistory Association*, 21 (The Melaka Papers vol. 5), pp. 85–97.

STAUBWASSER, M., SIROCKO, F., GROOTES, P., and SEGL, M., 2003, "Climate change at the 4.2 ka BP termination of the Indus valley civilization and Holocene south Asian monsoon variability," *Geophysical Research Letters*, 30, pp. 1425–1431.

STAUBWASSER, M. and WEISS, H., 2006, "Holocene climate and cultural evolution in late prehistoric–early historic West Asia," *Quaternary Research*, 66, p. 372–387.

2007, "Corrigendum to 'Introduction: Holocene climate and cultural evolution in late prehistoric–early historic West Asia'," *Quaternary Research*, 68 (1), p. 175.

STEIN, G. J., 1994, "Economy, ritual, and power in Ubaid Mesopotamia," in G. Stein and M. Rothman (eds.), *Chiefdoms and Early States in the Near East: The Organizational Dynamics of Complexity*, Madison, WI: Prehistory Press, pp. 35–46.

1999, *Rethinking World Systems. Diasporas, Colonies, and Interaction in Uruk Mesopotamia*, Tucson: University of Arizona Press.

2004, "The Uruk expansion in Anatolia: a Mesopotamian colony and its indigenous host community at Hacınebi, Turkey," in J. N. Postgate (ed.), *Artefacts of Complexity: Tracking the Uruk in the Near East* (Iraq Archaeological Reports 5), Warminster: Aris & Phillips for the British School of Archaeology in Iraq, pp. 149–172 (1st edn. 2002).

2009, "Tell Zeidan (2008)," *Oriental Institute Annual Report 2008–2009*, University of Chicago Oriental Institute Publications, pp. 126–137.

STEINHARDT, N. S. (ed.), 2002, *Chinese Architecture*, New Haven, CT: Yale University and World Press.

STEINKELLER, P., 1993, "Early political development in Mesopotamia and the origins of the Sargonic Empire," in M. Liverani (ed.), *Akkad, the First World Empire: Structure, Ideology, Traditions*, Padua: Sargon, pp. 107–129.

1999, "Land-tenure conditions in third-millennium Babylonia: the problem of regional variation," in M. Hudson and B. Levine (eds.), *Urbanization and Land Ownership*, Cambridge, MA: Peabody Museum of Archaeology and Ethnology, Harvard University, pp. 289–329.

2002, "Money-lending practices in Ur III Babylonia: the issue of economic motivation," in M. Hudson and M. van de Mieroop (eds.), *Debt and Economic Renewal in the Ancient Near East*, Bethesda, MD: CDL Press, pp. 109–138.

2004, "The function of written documentation in the administrative praxis of early Babylonia," in M. Hudson and C. Wunsch (eds.), *Creating Economic Order: Record-Keeping, Standardization and the Development of Accounting in the Ancient Near East*, Bethesda, MD: CDL Press, pp. 65–88.

STERLING BERRY, T., 1997, *Christianity and Buddhism: A Comparison and a Contrast*, New Delhi: Asian Educational Services.

STERN, E., "The silver hoard from Tel Dor," in M. Balmuth (ed.), *Hacksilver to Coinage*, New York: American Numismatic Society, pp. 19–26.

STEVENS, M. E., 2006, *Temples, Tithes, and Taxes: The Temple and the Economic Life of Ancient Israel*, Grand Rapids, MI: Baker Academic.

STIGAND, C. H., 1913, *The Land of Zinj*, London: Constable.

STÖHR, W., 1968, "Les religions archaïques d'Indonésie et des Philippines," in W. Stöhr and P. Zoetmulder (eds.), *Les religions d'Indonésie*, Paris: Payot, pp. 9–255.

STOL, M., 1982, "Review of Feigin 1979," *Journal of the American Oriental Society*, 102, pp. 161–63.

STONE, E. R., 2008, "Some Begram ivories and the South Indian narrative tradition: new evidence," *Journal of Inner Asian Art and Archaeology*, 3 (3), pp. 45–59.

STRAKA, H., 1996, "Histoire de la végétation de Madagascar oriental dans les derniers 100 millénaires," in W. R. Lourenço (ed.), *Biogéographie de Madagascar*, Paris: ORSTOM, pp. 33–47.

STRAUCH, I., 2012, *Foreign Sailors on Socotra: The Inscriptions and Drawings from the Cave Hoq*, Bremen: Hempen.

STRAUCH, I., and BUKHARIN, M. D., 2004, "Indian inscriptions from the cave Hoq on Suqutra (Yemen)," *AION*, 46, pp. 121–138.

STRECK, M., 1978, "Kalah," in *Encyclopédie de l'Islam*, vol. IV, new edn., Paris: Maisonneuve and Larose; Leiden: Brill, pp. 488–489.

SUBRAHMANYAM, S., 1996, "Iranians abroad: intra-Asian elite migration and early modern state formation," in S. Subrahmanyam (ed.), *Merchant Networks in the Early Modern World*, Aldershot: Variorum, pp. 72–95 (first published 1992, *Journal of Asian Studies*).

    2005a, *Explorations in Connected History: Mughals and Franks*, New Delhi: Oxford University Press.

    2005b, *Explorations in Connected History: From the Tagus to the Ganges*, New Delhi: Oxford University Press.

SUN, Y., 2006, "Cultural and political control in North China: style and use of the bronzes of Yan at Liulihe during the early Western Zhou," in V. H. Mair (ed.), *Contact and Exchange in the Ancient World*, Honolulu: Hawaii University Press, pp. 215–237.

    2017, "Identity and artifacts on the north central and northeastern frontier during the period of state expansion in the late second and the early first millennium BCE," in K. Linduff, Y. Sun, W. Cao, and Y. Liu (eds.), *Ancient China and Its Eurasian Neighbors: Artifacts, Identity and Death in the Frontier, 3000–700 BCE*, Cambridge University Press, pp. 72–145.

SUTTON, J. E. G., 1984, "Irrigation and soil conservation in African agricultural history," *Journal of African History*, 25 (1), pp. 25–41.

    1990, *A Thousand Years of East Africa*, Nairobi: British Institute in East Africa.

    2002, "A review of people, contact(s) and the environment in the African past," *Journal of African History*, 43, pp. 503–505.

SWADLING P., 1996, "Plumes from Paradise: trade cycles in outer Southeast Asia and their impact on Papua New Guinea until 1920," Papua New Guinea Museum and Robert Brown and Associates, Queensland.

SWAN, L. M., 1994, *Early Gold Mining on the Zimbabwean Plateau* (Studies in African Archaeology 9), Uppsala: Societas Archaeologica Upsaliensis.

    2007a, "Economic and ideological roles of copper ingots in prehistoric Zimbabwe," *Antiquity*, 81 (314), pp. 999–1012.

    2007b, "Early iron manufacturing industries in semi-arid, south-eastern Zimbabwe," *Journal of African Archaeology*, 5 (2), pp. 315–338.

SWEENEY, M. and McCOUCH, S., 2007, "The complex history of the domestication of rice," *Annals of Botany*, 100 (5), pp. 951–957.

SWELLENGREBEL, J. L. *et al.*, 1960, *Bali: Life, Thought, and Ritual*, The Hague: W. van Hoeve.

TAAGEPERA, R., 1978, "Size and duration of empires: systematics of size" and "Size and duration of empires: growth-decline curves, 3000 to 600 BC," *Social Science Research*, 7, pp. 108–127 and 180–196.

TACITUS, 1985, *Vie d'Agricola*, ed. E. de Saint-Denis, Paris: Belles Lettres.

TAKAMIYA, 2002, "Introductory routes of rice to Japan: an examination of the southern route hypothesis," *Asian Perspectives*, 40, pp. 209–226.

TANNO, K. I. and WILLCOX, G., 2006, "How fast was wild wheat domesticated?," *Science*, 311 (5769), p. 1886.

TARLING, N. (ed.), 1992, *The Cambridge History of Southeast Asia*, vol. I, part 1: *From Early Times to c. 1500*, Cambridge University Press.

TATELMAN, J., 1999, *Glorious Deeds of Purna: A Translation and Study of the Purnavadan*, London: Curzon.

TAYLOR, T., 1994, "Thracians, Scythians, and Dacians, 800 BC – AD 300," in B. Cunliffe (ed.), *The Oxford Illustrated History of Prehistoric Europe*, Oxford University Press, pp. 373–410.

    2001, "Believing the ancients: quantitative and qualitative dimensions of slavery and the slave trade in later prehistoric Eurasia," *World Archaeology*, 33 (1), pp. 27–43.

TCHERNIA, A., 1997, "Winds and coins: from the supposed discovery of the monsoon to the denarii of Tiberius," in F. De Romanis and A. Tchernia (eds.), *Crossings. Early Mediterranean Contacts with India*, New Delhi: Manohar, pp. 250–276.

1999, "Arikamedu et le graffito naval d'Alagankulam," *Topoi: Orient-Occident*, 8, pp. 447–463.

TEGGART, F., 1939, *Rome and China: A Study of Correlations in Historical Events*, Berkeley, University of California Press.

TEMIN, P., 2001, "A market economy in the early Roman Empire," *Journal of Roman Studies*, 91, pp. 169–181.

2004, "The labour market of the early Roman Empire," *Journal of Interdisciplinary History*, 34, pp. 513–538.

TEMPLE, R., 2002, *The Genius of China, 3000 Years of Science, Discovery and Invention*, Foreword by J. Needham, London: Prion Books (1st edn. 1986).

TENGBERG, M., 2002, "The importation of wood to the Arabian Gulf in antiquity: the evidence from charcoal analysis," *Proceedings of the Seminar for Arabian Studies*, 32, pp. 75–81.

2003, "Archaeobotany in the Oman peninsula and the role of Eastern Arabia in the spread of African crops," in K. Neumann, A. Butler, and S. Kahlhaber (eds.), *Food, Fuel and Fields: Progress in African Archaeobotany*, Cologne: Heinrich-Barth-Institut, pp. 229–237.

2004, "Research into the origins of date palm domestication," in *The Date Palm: From Traditional Resource to Green Wealth*, Abu Dhabi: Emirates Center for Strategic Studies and Research, pp. 51–62.

TERASAWA, K. and TERASAWA, T., 1981, "The basic study of the Yayoi plant food: for the research on the early agricultural society," *Kohkogaku Ronkoh (The Kashihara Institute for Archaeological Research)*, 5, pp. 1–129 [in Japanese].

TESTARD, A., 2001, "Moyen d'échange/moyen de paiement: des monnaies en général et plus particulièrement des primitives," in A. Testard (ed.), *Aux origines de la monnaie*, Paris: Éditions Errance, p. 11–60.

2004, *L'origine de l'état: la servitude volontaire II*, Paris: Editions Errance.

THAPAR, R., 1984, *A History of India*, vol. I, London: Penguin Books.

1997, "Early Mediterranean contacts with India: an overview," in F. De Romanis and A. Tchernia (eds.), *Crossings: Early Mediterranean Contacts with India*, New Delhi: Manohar, pp. 11–40.

2004, *Early India: From the Origins to AD 1300*, Berkeley: University of California Press.

2007, "The rise of the mercantile community 200 BC – 300 AD," in K. B. Janardan (ed.), *Economic History of Ancient India*, New Delhi: Arise Publishers, pp. 264–291.

THAPLYAL, K. K., 2001, "Guilds in Ancient India (antiquity and various stages in the development of guilds up to AD 300)," in G. C. Pande (ed.), *Life Thoughts and Culture in India*, Delhi: Munshiram Manoharlal, pp. 995–1006.

THEOPHRASTUS, 1988, *Recherches sur les plantes*, trans. S. Amigues, vol. 1: Books I–II, LVIII; 1989, vol. 2: Books III–IV.10; 1993, vol. 3: Books V–VI. XII; 2003, vol. 4: Books VII–VIII. 12; 2006, vol. 5: Book IX. Index.

THEUNISSEN, R., GRAVE, P., and BAILEY, G., 2000, "Doubts on diffusion: challenging the assumed Indian origin of Iron Age agate and cornalian beads in Southeast Asia," *World Archaeology*, 32 (1), pp. 84–105.

THEURL, E., 2004, "Konkurrierende Theorien der Geldentstehung: einige Überlegungen zur Vereinbarkeit," in R. Rollinger and C. Ulf (eds.), *Commerce and Monetary Systems in the Ancient World: Means of Transmission and Cultural Interaction*, Wiesbaden: Franz Steiner Verlag, pp. 33–53.

THIERRY, F., 1993, "Sur les monnaies sassanides trouvées en Chine," in R. Gyselen (ed.), *Circulation des monnaies, des marchandises et des biens (Res Orientales, 5)*, Bures-sur-Yvette: Groupe pour l'Étude de la Civilisation du Moyen-Orient, pp. 89–139.

1997, *Monnaies chinoises*, vol. 1: *L'antiquité préimpériale*, Paris: Bibliothèque Nationale de France.

2000, "Entre Iran et Chine, la circulation monétaire en Sérinde du Ve au IXe siècle," in J.-P. Drège (ed.), *La Sérinde, terre d'échanges: art, religion, commerce du Ier au Xe siècle*, Paris: La Documentation Française, pp. 121–147.

2001, "Sur les spécificités fondamentales de la monnaie chinoise," in A. Testard (ed.), *Aux origines de la monnaie*, Paris: Éditions Errance, pp. 109–144.

THOMAS, P. K. and JOGLEKAR, P. P., 1994, "Holocene faunal studies in India," *Man and Environment*, 19 (1–2), pp. 179–203.

THOMAS, R., 2012, "Port communities and the Erythrean Sea trade," *British Museum Studies in Ancient Egypt and Sudan*, 18, pp. 170–199.

THOMPSON, C. M., 2003, "Sealed silver in iron age Cisjordan and the 'invention' of coinage," *Oxford Journal of Archaeology*, 22 (1), pp. 67–107.

THOMPSON, G. B., 1996, *The Excavation of Khok Phanom Di, a Prehistoric Site in Central Thailand*, vol. IV: *Subsistence and Environment: The Botanical Evidence* (Research Reports of the Society of Antiquaries of London, 53), London: Society of Antiquaries.

THOMPSON, W. R., 2005, "Eurasian C-wave crises in the first millennium BC," in C. Chase-Dunn and E. N. Anderson (eds.), *The Historical Evolution of World-Systems*, Riverside: University of California, Palgrave Macmillan, pp. 20–51.

2017, "Incursions, climate change, and early globalization patterns," in C. Chase-Dunn and H. Inoue (eds.), *Systemic Boundaries: Time Mapping Globalization since the Bronze Age*, New York: Springer.

THOMPSON, L. G., MOSLEY-THOMPSON, E., DAVIS, M. E., HENDERSON, K. A., BRECHER, H. H., ZAGORODNOV, V. S., MASHIOTTA, T. A., PING-NAN LI, MIKHALENKO, V. N., HARDY, D. R., and BEER, J., 2002, "Kilimanjaro ice core records: evidence of Holocene climate change in tropical Africa," *Science*, 298 (5593), pp. 589–593.

THONDHLANA, T. P. and MARTINÓN-TORRES, M., 2009, "Small size, high value: composition and manufacture of second millennium and copper-based beads from northern Zimbabwe," *Journal of African Archaeology*, 7 (1), pp. 79–97.

THOURY, M., MILLE, B., SÉVERIN-FABIANI, T., ROBBIOLA, L., RÉFRÉGIERS, M., JARRIGE, J.-F., and BERTRAND, L., 2016, "High spatial dynamics-photoluminescence imaging reveals the metallurgy of the earliest lost-wax cast object," *Nature Communications*, 7, doi:10.1038/ncomms13356.

THUESEN, I., 2000, "The city-state in ancient western Syria," in M. H. Hansen (ed.), *A Comparative Study of Thirty City-State Cultures*, Copenhagen: Det Kongelige Danske Videnskabernes Selskab, pp. 55–65.

2002, "The Neo-Hittite city-states," in M. H. Hansen (ed.), *A Comparative Study of Six City-State Cultures*, Copenhagen: Det Kongelige Danske Videnskabernes Selskab, pp. 43–55.

THURGOOD, G., 1999. *From Ancient Cham to Modern Dialects: Two Thousand Years of Language Contact and Change* (Oceanic Linguistics Special Publication no. 28), Honolulu: University of Hawai'i Press.

TIBBETTS, G. R., 1971, *Arab Navigation in the Indian Ocean before the Coming of the Portuguese, Being a Translation of* Kitāb al Fawā'id fī uṣūl al-baḥr wa'l-qawā'id *of Aḥmad b. Mājid al-Najdī*, London: Luzac (2nd edn. 1981).

1979, *A Study of the Arabic Texts Containing Material on South-East Asia*, Leiden: Brill.

TOFANELLI, S., BERTONCINI, S., CASTRI, L., LUISELLI, D., CALAFELL, F., DONATI, G., and PAOLI, G., 2009, "On the origins and admixture of Malagasy: new evidence from high-resolution analyses of paternal and maternal lineages," *Molecular Biology and Evolution*, 26 (9), pp. 2109–2124.

TOLLENAERE, C., BROUAT, C., DUPLANTIER, J.-M. RAHALISON, L., RAHELINIRINA, S., PASCAL, M., MOORE, H., MOUAHID, G., LIERS, H., and COSSON, J.-F., 2010, "Phylogeography of the introduced species *Rattus rattus* in the western Indian Ocean, with special emphasis on the colonization history of Madagascar," *Journal of Biogeography*, 37, pp. 398–410.

TOLMACHEVA, R., 1980, "On the Arab system of nautical orientation," *Arabica*, 27 (2), pp. 180–192.

TOMBER, R., 2002, "Indian fine wares from the Red Sea coast of Egypt," *Man and Environment*, 27 (1), pp. 25–31.

2005, "Troglodites and trogodites: exploring interaction on the Red Sea during the Roman period," in J. C. M. Starkey (ed.), *People of the Red Sea: Proceedings of Red Sea Project 2* (BAR International Series 1395), Oxford: Archaeopress, pp. 41–49.

2012a, *Indo-Roman Trade: From Pots to Pepper*, London: Bloomsbury (1st edn. 2008).

2012b, "From the Roman Red Sea to beyond the Empire: Egyptian ports and their trading partners," *British Museum Studies in Ancient Egypt and Sudan*, 18, pp. 201–215.

TOMBER, R., CARTWRIGHT, A. C., and GUPTA, S., 2011, "Rice temper: technological solutions and source identification in the Indian Ocean," *Journal of Archaeological Science*, 38, pp. 360–366.

TORRES ORTIZ, M., RUIZ-GÁLVEZ PRIEGO, M., and RUBINOS, A., 2005, "La cronología de la Cultura Nurágica y los inicios de la Edad del Hierro y de las colonizaciones históricas en el Mediterráneo Centro-occidental. Una aproximación desde la cronología radiocarbónica y el registro arqueológico," in M. Ruiz-Galvez Priego (ed.), *Territorio nurágico y paisaje antiguo. La meseta de Pranemuru (Cerdeña) en la Edad del Bronce*, Madrid: Universidad Complutense de Madrid, pp. 169–174.

TOSI, M., 2001, "The Harappan civilization beyond the Indian Subcontinent," in R. Chakravarti (ed.), *Trade in Early India*, Oxford University Press, pp. 128–151 (first published 1991 in G. L. Possehl [ed.], *The Harappan Civilization: A Recent Perspective*, New Delhi: Oxford University Press and IBH, pp. 365–378).

TOSI, M. and LAMBERG-KARLOVSKY, C. C., 2003, "Pathways across Eurasia," in J. Aruz and R. Wallenfels (eds.), *Art of the First Cities: The Third Millennium BC from the Mediterranean to the Indus*, New York: The Metropolitan Museum of Art; New Haven, CT, and London: Yale University Press, pp. 347–350.

TOSI, M., SHAHMIRZADI, S. M., and JOYENDA, M. A., 1996, "Bronze Age in Iran and Afghanistan," in A. H. Dani and V. M. Masson (eds.), *History of Civilizations of Central Asia*, vol. 1, New Delhi: Motilal Banarsidass, pp. 191–223.

TOUSSAINT, A., 1961, *Histoire de l'océan Indien*, Paris: Presses Universitaires de France.

TRAUTMANN, T. R., 1971, *Kautilya and the Arthasastra: A Statistical Investigation of the Authorship and Evolution of the Text*, Leiden: Brill.

TREYDTE, K. S., SCHLESER, G. H., HELLE, G., FRANK, D. C., WINIGER, M., HAUG, G. H., and ESPER, J., 2006, "The twentieth century was the wettest period in northern Pakistan over the past millennium," *Nature*, 440 (7088), pp. 1179–1182.

TRIFONOV, V., 2004, "Die Majkop Kultur und die ersten Wagen in der südrussischen Steppe," in M. Fansa and S. Burmeister (eds.), *Rad und Wagen: Der Ursprung einer Innovation: Wagen im Vorderen Orient und Europa*, Mainz: Zabern, pp. 167–176.

TRIPATHI, S., 2004, "An ancient harbour at Dwarka: study based on the recent underwater explorations," *Current Science*, 86 (9).

TRIPATHI, V., 2001, *The Age of Iron in South Asia: Legacy and Tradition*, New Delhi: Aryan International.

TSANG, C.-H., 2005, "Recent discoveries at the Tapenkeng culture sites in Taiwan: implications for the problem of Austronesian origins," in L. Sagart, R. Blench, and A. Sanchez-Mazas (eds.), *The Peopling of East Asia*, London: New York, Routledge/Curzon, pp. 63–73.

TSUCHIDA, S., 1976, *Reconstruction of Proto-Tsouic Phonology*, Tokyo: Institute for the Study of Languages and Cultures of Asia and Africa, Tokyo Gaikokugo Daigaku.

TURNER, H. R., 1997, *Science in Medieval Islam: An Illustrated Introduction*, Austin: University of Texas Press.

TURNER, R. L., 1962–1966, *A Comparative Dictionary of the Indo-Aryan Languages*, Oxford University Press.

   1969–1985, Supplements to *A Comparative Dictionary of the Indo-Aryan Languages*, Oxford University Press.

TURNER, V. W., 1967, *The Forest of Symbols: Aspects of Ndembu Ritual*, Ithaca, NY: Cornell University Press.

UDOVITCH, A., 1979, "Bankers without banks: commerce, banking and society in the Islamic world in the Middle Ages," in Center for Medieval and Renaissance Studies, University of California (ed.), *The Dawn of Modern Banking:*, New Haven, CT: Yale University Press, pp. 255–273.

UERPMANN, H. P., 2001, "Remarks on the animal economy of Tell Abraq (Emirates of Sharjah and Umm al-Qaywayn) UAE," *Proceedings of the Seminar for Arabian Studies*, 31, pp. 227–234.

   2008, "Animal domestication," in D. M. Pearsall (ed.), *Encyclopedia of Archaeology*, vol. III, New York: Academic Press, pp. 434–445.

UR, J. A., 2010, "Cycles of civilization in Northern Mesopotamia, 4400–2000 BC," *Journal of Archaeological Research*, 18 (4), pp. 387–431.

   2014, "Households and the emergence of cities in Ancient Mesopotamia," *Cambridge Archaeological Journal*, 26 (2), pp. 1–24.

USOSKIN, I. G., 2013, "A history of solar activity over millennia," *Living Reviews in Solar Physics*, 10 (1), www.livingreviews.org/lrsp-2013-1, doi:10.12942/lrsp-2013-1

USOSKIN, I. G., SOLANKI, S. K., and KOVALTSOV, G. A., 2012, "Grand minima of solar activity during the last millennia," D. Webb and C. Mandrini (eds.), *Proceedings IAU Symposium No. 286: Comparative Magnetic Minima: Characterizing Quiet Times in the Sun and Stars*, Cambridge University Press, pp. 372–382.

VALBELLE, D., 2005, "Économie. Égypte," in J. Leclant (ed.), *Dictionnaire de l'Antiquité*, Paris: Presses Universitaires de France, p. 732.

VALLAT, F., 2003a and b, "La civilisation proto-élamite 3100–2600" and "L'origine orientale de la ziggurat," *Dossiers d'Archéologie*, 287, pp. 88–91 and 92–95.

VALLET, E., 2010, *L'Arabie marchande, état et commerce sous les sultans rasûlides du Yémen (626–858/1229–1454)*, Paris: Publications de la Sorbonne.

VAN DE MIEROOP, M., 1992, *Society and Enterprise in Old Babylonian Ur*, Berliner Beiträge zum Vorderen Orient, Berlin: Reimer.

   1999, *The Ancient Mesopotamian City*, Oxford University Press.

   2002, "A history of near eastern debt ?," in M. Hudson and M. van de Mieroop (eds.), *Debt and Economic Renewal in the Ancient Near East*, Bethesda, MD: CDL Press, pp. 59–94.

   2004, "Economic theories and the ancient Near East," in R. Rollinger and C. Ulf (eds.), *Commerce and Monetary Systems in the Ancient World: Means of Transmission and Cultural Interaction*, Stuttgart: Franz Steiner Verlag, pp. 54–64.

   2014, "Silver as a financial tool in ancient Egypt and Mesopotamia," in P. Bernholz and R. Vaubel (eds.), *Explaining Monetary and Financial Innovation: A Historical Analysis*, Heidelberg, New York, Dordrecht, and London: Springer, pp. 17–30.

VAN DER MAESEN, L. J. G., 1995, "Pigeonpea *Cajanus cajan* (Leguminosae-Papilionideae)," in J. Smartt and N. W. Simmonds (eds.), *Evolution of Crop Plants*, 2nd edn., Harlow: Longman, pp. 251–255.

VAN DER SPEK, R. J., 2004, "Palace, temple and market in Seleucid Babylonia," in *Le roi et l'économie: autonomies locales et structures royales dans l'économie de l'empire séleucide, Actes des rencontres de Lille (23 juin 2003) et d'Orléans (29–30 janvier 2004) (Topoi: Orient–Occident,* suppl. 6), Paris: de Boccard, pp. 303–332.

2006, "How to measure prosperity? The case of Hellenistic Babylonia," in R. Descat (ed.), *Approches de l 'économie hellénistique* (Entretiens d'archéologie et d'histoire 7), Musée archéologique departmental de Saint-Bertrand de Comminges, pp. 287–310.

2015, "Money, prices and market in the Ancient Near East," Yale University, Economics Department.

VAN DER SPEK, R. J. and VAN LEEUWEN, B., 2014, "Quantifying the integration of the Babylonian economy in the Mediterranean world using a new corpus of price data, 400–50 BC," in F. de Callataÿ and A. Wilson (eds.), *Long-Term Quantification in Ancient History,* Bari: Edipuglia, available online: www.cgeh.nl/sites/default/files/WorkingPapers/CGEHWP47_vanderspekvanleeuwen.pdf

VAN DER VEEN, M., with contributions by A. COX, R. GALE, D. HAMILTON, J. MORALES, and D. ÜBEL, 2011, *Consumption, Trade and Innovation: Exploring the Botanical Remains from the Roman and Islamic Ports at Quseir al-Qadim* (Journal of African Archaeology Monograph Series 6), Frankfurt-am-Main: Africa Magna Verlag.

VAN DER WEIJDEN, G., 1981, *Indonesische Reisrituale* (Basler Beiträge zur Ethnologie Band 20), Basel: Ethnologisches Seminar der Universität und Museum für Völkerkunde.

VAN DRIEL, G., 2000, "Institutional and non-institutional economy in ancient Mesopotamia," in A. C. V. M. Bongenaar (ed.), *Interdependency of Institutions and Private Entrepreneurs Proceedings of the Second MOS Symposium (Leiden 1998)* (MOS Studies 5), Leiden: Nederlands Historisch-Archaeologisch Instituut te Istanbul, pp. 5–23.

2002, *Elusive Silver: In Search of a Role for a Market in an Agrarian Environment: Aspects of Mesopotamia's Society,* Leiden: Nederlands Instituut voor het Nabije Oosten.

VAN DRIEM, G., 1998, "Neolithic correlates of ancient Tibeto-Burman migrations," in R. Blench and M. Spriggs (eds.), *Archaeology and Language II. Archaeological Data and Linguistic Hypotheses,* London and New York: Routledge, pp. 67–102.

2005, "Tibeto-Burman vs. Indo-Chinese: implications for population geneticists, archaeologists and prehistorians," in L. Sagart, R. Blench, and A. Sanchez-Mazas (eds.), *The Peopling of East Asia: Putting Together Archaeology, Linguistics and Genetics,* London: Routledge/Curzon, pp. 81–106.

VAN GEEL, B., BOKOVENKO, N. A., BUROVA, N. D., CHUGUNOV, K. V., DERGACHEV, V. A., DIRKSEN, V. G., KULKOVA, M., NAGLER, A., PARZINGER, H., VAN DER PLICHT, J., VASILIEV, S. S., and ZAITSEVA, G. I., 2004, "The Sun, climate change and the expansion of the Scythian culture after 850 BC," in E. M. Scott, A. Y. Alekseev, and G. Zaitseva (eds.), *Impact of the Environment on Human Migration in Eurasia,* Dordrecht, Boston, and London: Kluwer Academic, pp. 151–158.

VAN HEEKEREN, H. R., 1958, *The Bronze-Iron Age of Indonesia,* The Hague: Nijhoff.

VAN KOPPEN, F., 2004, "The geography of the slave trade and northern Mesopotamia in the Late Old Babylonian period," in H. Hunger and R. Pruzsinszky (eds.), *Mesopotamian Dark Age Revisited, Proceedings of an International Conference of SCIEM2000 (Vienna 8–9 November 2002),* Vienna: Verlag der Österreichischen Akademie der Wissenschaften, pp. 9–33.

VAN LEUR, J. C., 1955, *Indonesian Trade and Society,* The Hague: W. van Hoeve.

VANSINA, J., 1995, "New linguistic evidence and 'the Bantu Expansion'," *Journal of African History,* 36, pp. 173–195.

2001, "Comment on C. Ehret, 'Bantu expansions: re-envisioning a central problem of early African history'," *International Journal of African Historical Studies*, 34, pp. 52–54.

2004, "Bananas in Cameroon c. 500 BCE? Not proven," *Azania*, 38, pp. 174–176.

2006, "Linguistic evidence for the introduction of ironworking into Bantu-speaking Africa," *History in Africa*, 33, pp. 321–361.

VAN ZEIST, W., 1985, "Pulses and oil crop plants," *Bulletin on Sumerian agriculture*, 2, pp. 33–38.

1987, "The plant remains," in A. Vila (ed.), *Le cimetière Kermaique d'Ukma Ouest*, Paris: Éditions du CNRS, pp. 247–255.

VAN ZEIST, W. and WATERBOLK-VAN ROOIJEN, W., 1992, "Two interesting floral finds from third millennium BC Tell Hammam et-Turkman, northern Syria," *Vegetation History and Archaeobotany*, 1, pp. 157–161.

VARADAJARAN, L., 1993, "Indian boat building traditions: the ethnological evidence," *Topoi Orient-Occident*, 3 (2), pp. 547–568.

VARBERG, J., KAUL, F., and GRATUZE, B., 2014, "Danish Bronze Age glass beads traced to Egypt," *ScienceNordic*, December 8.

VARGYAS, P., 1999, "Money in the Ancient Near East before and after coinage," *American Schools of Oriental Research, Newsletter*, 49 (3), pp. 15–16.

2001, *A History of Babylonian Prices in the First Millennium BC*, vol. 1: *Prices of the Basic Commodities* (Heidelberger Studien zum alten Orient, ed. Hartmut Waetzoldt and Harald Hauptmann, vol. 10), Heidelberg: Heidelberger Orientverlag.

2004, "La monétisation de l'économie rurale en Babylonie et en Egypte pendant le 1er millénaire av. J.-C.," in B. Menu (ed.), *La dépendance rurale dans l'Antiquité égyptienne et proche-orientale, Colloque Aidea Banyuls-sur-Mer 2001*, Cairo: Institut Français d'Archéologie Orientale, pp. 109–120.

VARTAVAN, C. DE and ASENSI AMOROS, V., 1997, *Codex of Ancient Egyptian Plant Remains / Codex des restes végétaux de l'Égypte ancienne*, London: Triade Exploration.

VASEY, N. and BURNEY, D. A., 2007, "Subfossil rodent species assemblages from Andrahomana Cave, southeastern Madagascar: evidence of introduced species and faunal turnover," poster at the conference "Rats, Humans, and Their Impacts on Islands," Hawai'i.

VAUGHAN, D. A., LU, B.-R., and TOMOOKA, N., 2008, "The evolving story of rice evolution," *Plant Science*, 174, pp. 394–408.

VEENHOF, K. R., 1972, *Aspects of Old Assyrian Trade and Its Terminology*, Leiden, Brill, 487 p.

1987, "'Dying tablets' and 'hungry silver': elements of figurative language in Akkadian commercial terminology," in M. Mindlin, M. J. Geller, and J. E. Wansbrough (eds.), *Figurative Language in the Ancient Near East*, London: School of Oriental and African Studies, pp. 41–75.

1997, "'Modern' features in old Assyrian trade," *Journal of the Economic and Social History of the Orient*, 40 (4), pp. 336–366.

1999, "Silver and credit in old Assyrian Trade," in J. G. Dercksen (ed.), *Trade and Finance in Ancient Mesopotamia Proceedings of the First Mos Symposium, Leiden 1997* (Mos Studies 1), Nederlands Historisch-Archaeologisch Instituut te Istanbul, pp. 55–83.

2003, "Archives of Old Assyrian Traders," in M. Brosiu (ed.), *Ancient Archives and Archival Traditions: Concepts of Record-Keeping in the Ancient World*, Oxford University Press, pp. 78–123.

VÉRIN, P. (ed.), 1972, *Histoire ancienne du nord-ouest de Madagascar, Taloha 5*, Antananarivo: Musée d'Art et d'Archéologie.

1975, "Austronesian contributions to the culture of Madagascar: some archaeological problems," in N. Chittick and R. Rotberg (eds.), *East Africa and the Orient*, London, and New York: Holmes and Meier, Africana Publishing, pp. 164–191.

1979a, "Le problème des origines malgaches," *Taloha*, 8, pp. 41–55.

1979b, "Aspects de la civilisation des échelles anciennes du Nord de Madagascar," in *Mouvements de populations dans l'Océan Indien, Actes du 4e Congrès de l'Association Historique Internationale de l'Océan Indien et du 14e Colloque de la Commission Internationale d'Histoire Maritime (Saint-Denis de la Réunion, septembre 1972)*, Paris: Champion, pp. 61–90.

1980, "Les apports culturels et la contribution africaine au peuplement de Madagascar," in *Relations historiques à travers l'océan Indien: compte-rendu de la réunion d'experts de 1974* (Histoire générale de l'Afrique, Études et Documents 3), Paris: UNESCO, pp. 103–124.

1994, *Les Comores*, Paris: Karthala.

VÉRIN, P., KOTTAK, C., and GORLIN, P., 1970, "The glottochronology of Malagasy speech communities," *Oceanic Linguistics*, 8(1), pp. 26–83.

VÉRIN, P. and WRIGHT, H. T., 1999, "Madagascar and Indonesia: new evidence from archaeology and linguistics," *Bulletin of the Indo-Pacific Prehistory Association*, 18, pp. 35–42.

VERNET, R., 1993, *Préhistoire de la Mauritanie*, Paris and Nouakchott: Sepia.

VERTESALJI, P. P., 1992, "Le manche de couteau de Gebel el-'Arak dans le contexte des relations entre la Mésopotamie et l'Égypte," in F. Charpin and F. Joannès (eds.), *La circulation des biens, des personnes et des idées dans le Proche-Orient ancien*, Paris: Éditions Recherche sur les Civilisations, pp. 29–41.

VICKERY, M., 1998, *Society, Economics and Politics in Pre-Angkor Cambodia: The 7th-8th Centuries*, Tokyo: Centre for East Asian Cultural Studies for Unesco.

2003–2004, "Funan reviewed: deconstructing the ancients," *Bulletin de l'École française d'Extrême-Orient*, 90–91, pp. 101–143.

VILÀ, C., LEONARD, J. A., GÖTHERSTRÖM, A., MARKLUND, S., SANDBERG, K., LIDEN, K., WAYNE, R. K., and ELLEGREN, H., 2001, "Widespread origins of domestic horse lineages," *Science*, 291 (5503), pp. 474–477.

VILÀ, C., LEONARD, J. A., and BEIJA-PEREIRA, A., 2006, "Genetic documentation of horse and donkey domestication," in M. A. Zeder, D. G. Bradley, E. Emshwiller, and B. D. Smith (eds.), *Documenting Domestication: New Genetic and Archaeological Paradigms*, Berkeley: University of California Press, pp. 342–354.

VILLARD, P., 2001, "Arabie," in F. Joannès (ed.), *Dictionnaire de la civilisation mésopotamienne*, Paris: Laffont, pp. 61–63.

VILLIERS, A., 1952, *The Indian Ocean*, London: Museum Press.

1957, *Wild Ocean*, New York: McGraw-Hill.

VINOGRADOV, I. V., 1991, "The Predynastic Period and the Early and the Old Kingdoms in Egypt," in I. M. Diakonoff and P. L. Kohl (eds.), *Early Antiquity*, University of Chicago Press, pp. 137–157.

VINOGRADOV, J. G., 2010, "Une inscription grecque sur le site de Bir 'Alī (Qāni')," in J.-F. Salles and A. V. Sedov (eds.), *Qāni' – le port antique du Ḥaḍramawt entre la Méditerranée, l'Afrique et l'Inde* (Indicopleustoi. Archaeologies of the Indian Ocean 6), Turnhout: Brepols, pp. 389–392.

VINOGRADOV, Y. A., 2011, "An important archaeological discovery on the island of Socotra," *Vestnik Drevnej Istorii*, 4, pp. 99–105.

VISICATO, G., 2000, *The Power and the Writing: The Early Scribes of Mesopotamia*, Bethesda, MD: CDL Press.

VITHARANA, V., 1999, "Kalinga-Sri Laṅkā relations," in K. S. Behera (ed.), *Maritime Heritage of India*, New Delhi: Aryan Books International, pp. 179–187.

VOGEL, H. U., 1993, "Cowry trade and its role in the economy of Yünnan: from the ninth to the mid-seventeenth century," part 1, *Journal of the Economic and Social History of the Orient*, 36 (3), pp. 211–251.

VOGEL, P., 1990, "The cultural basis: development and influence of a socially mediated trading corporation in southern Zambezia," *Journal of Anthropological Archaeology*, 9, pp. 104–147.

VOGT, B. and SEDOV, A., 1998, "The Sabir culture and coastal Yemen during the second millennium BC – the present state of discussion," *Proceedings of the Seminar for Arabian Studies*, 28, pp. 261–270.

VON GLAHN, R., 1996, *Fountain of Fortune: Money and Monetary Policy in China, 1000–1700*, Berkeley, Los Angeles, and London: University of California Press.

VOSMER, T., 1993, "Boat ethnography: the *yathra dhoni* of Sri lanka," in J. Green and S. Devendra (eds.), *Maritime Archaeology in Sri Lanka: The Galle Harbour Project, 1992*, Archaeological Department of Sri Lanka, The Central Cultural Fund, Western Australian Maritime Museum and Postgraduate Institute of Archaeology, Colombo.

1999, "Maritime archaeology, ethnography and history in the Indian Ocean: an emerging partnership," in H. P. Ray (ed.), *Archaeology of Seafaring. The Indian Ocean in the Ancient Period*, Delhi: Pragati, pp. 291–312.

2000, "Ships in the ancient Arabian Sea: the development of a hypothetical reed model," *Proceedings of the Seminar for Arabian Studies*, 30, p. 235–242.

VRYDAGHS, L., BAKRY, F., BOIVIN, N., CROWTHER, A., DE MARET, P., DE LANGHE, E., DENHAM, T., DONOHUE, M., FULLER, D., GARCIA-GRANERO, J. J., LANCELOTTI, C., MADELLA, M., PERRIER, X., and WOLLSTONECRAFT, M., 2013, "The banana: insights into an Indian Ocean odyssey," paper presented at the Sealinks Conference "Proto-Globalisation in the Indian Ocean World: Multidisciplinary Perspectives on Early Globalisation," Oxford, Jesus College, November 7–10, 2013.

WACHSMANN, J., 1967, "Pen-equidistance and accurate pitch: a problem from the source of the Nile," in L. Fischer and C.-K. Mahling (eds.), *Festschrift für Walter Wiora zum 30, Dez. 1966*, Kassel, pp. 583–592.

WACHSMANN, K. P., 1950, "An equal-stepped tuning in a Ganda harp," *Nature*, 165, pp. 40–41.

1957, "A study of norms in tribal music of Uganda," *Ethnomusicology Newsletter*, 1 (11), pp. 9–16.

WAETZOLDT, H., 1972, *Untersuchungen zur neusumerischen Textilindustrie*, Rome: Centro per le Antichità e la Storia dell'Arte del Vicino Oriente.

WAGNER, D. B., 1985, *Dabieshan: Traditional Chinese Iron-Production Techniques Practised in Southern Henan in the Twentieth Century* (Scandinavian Institute of Asian Studies Monograph Series 52), London and Malmö: Curzon Press.

2001, "Blast furnaces in Song-Yuan China," *East Asian Science, Technology, and Medicine*, 18, pp. 41–74.

2003, "The earliest use of iron in China," *Bulletin of the Museum of Far Eastern Antiquities* (Stockholm), 75, pp. 127–169.

WAGNER, G. A., GENTNER, N., GROPENGIESSER, H., and GALE, N. H., 1980, "Early Bronze Age lead-silver mining and metallurgy in the Aegean: the ancient workings on Siphnos," in P. T. Craddock (ed.), *Scientific Studies in Early Mining and Extractive Metallurgy*, London: British Museum, pp. 63–80.

WAGNER, G. A., PERNICKA, E., and UERPMANN, H.-P. (eds.), 2003, *Troia and the Troad: Scientific Approaches*, Berlin, Heidelberg, and New York: Springer.

WAGNER, W., 1993, *Antike Technologie: Die Sabäische Wasserwirtschaft von Marib. Teil 2: Bodenkundliche Untersuchungen in der Oase von Marib* (Deutsches Archäologisches Institut Sana'a, Archäologische Berichte aus dem Yemen 6), Mainz: Verlag Philipp von Zabern.

WALKER, A. C., 1967, "Patterns of extinction among the subfossil Madagascan lemuroids," in P. S. Martin and H. Wright (eds.), *Pleistocene Extinctions: The Search for a Cause*, New Haven, CT: Yale University Press, pp. 425–432.

WALL-ROMANA, C., 1990, "An areal location of Agade," *Journal of Near Eastern Studies*, 49 (3), pp. 205–245.

WALLERSTEIN, I, 1974a, "The rise and future demise of the world capitalist system: concepts for comparative analysis," *Comparative Studies in Society and History*, 16 (4), pp. 387–415.

1974b, 1980, 1988, *The Modern World-System*, vol. I, *Capitalist Agriculture and the Origins of the European World-Economy in the Sixteenth Century*, vol. II, *Mercantilism and the Consolidation of the European World-Economy, 1600–1750*, vol. III, *The Second Era of Great Expansion of the Capitalist World-Economy 1730–1840s*, New York: Academic Press.

WALSH, M., 2007, "Island subsistence: hunting, trapping and the translocation of wildlife in the Western Indian ocean," *Azania*, 42, pp. 83–113.

WALTER, A. and LEBOT, V., 2003, *Jardins d'Océanie*, Paris: IRD Éditions-CIRAD.

WANG, Y., 2001, "Royal hunting on the Shang border," paper presented at the Annual Conference of the Association for Asian Studies, Chicago.

WANG, Y., CHENG, H., EDWARDS, R. L., HE, Y., KONG, X., AN, Z., WU, J., KEY, M. J., DYKOSKI, C. A., and LI, X., 2005, "The Holocene Asian monsoon: links to solar changes and North Atlantic climate," *Science*, 308 (5723), pp. 854–857.

WANG GUNGWU, 1998, *The Nanhai Trade: The Early History of the Chinese Trade in the South China Sea*, Singapore: Times Academic Press (1st edn. 1958).

WANG YI, 2003, "Prehistoric walled settlements in the Chengdu plain," *Journal of East Asian Archaeology*, 5 (1–4), pp. 109–148.

WARBURTON, D., 1997, *State and Economy in Ancient Egypt*, Fribourg University Press; Göttingen: Vandenhoeck & Ruprecht.

2000a, "Before the IMF: the economic implications of unintentional structural adjustment in Ancient Egypt," *Journal of the Economic and Social History of the Orient*, 43 (2), pp. 65–131.

2000b, "State and economy in ancient Egypt," in R. A. Denemark, J. Friedman, B. K. Gills, and G. Modelski (eds.), *World System History: The Social Science of Long-Term Change*, London and New York: Routledge, pp. 169–184.

2003, *Macroeconomics from the Beginning: The General Theory, Ancient Markets, and the Role of Interest*, Neuchâtel and Paris: Recherches et Publications.

2005, "Le marché en Égypte Ancienne (à l'Âge du Bronze, 2500–1200 av. J.-C.)," in G. Bensimon (ed.), *Histoire des représentations du marché*, Paris: Michel Houdiard Éditeur, pp. 631–651.

2007a, "Work and compensation in Ancient Egypt," *Journal of Egyptian Archaeology*, 93, pp. 175–194.

2007b, "What happened in the Near East ca. 2000 BC?," in E. H. Seland (ed.), *The Indian Ocean in the Ancient Period: Definite Places, Translocal Exchange* (BAR International Series 1593), Oxford: Archaeopress, pp. 9–22.

2013, "Integration by price in the Bronze Age," in D. Frenez and M. Tosi (eds.), *South Asian Archaeology 2007*, vol. I: *Prehistoric Periods* (BAR International Series 2454), Oxford: Archaeopress, pp. 287–296.

WARD, C. A., 2003, "Sewn planked boats from Early Dynastic Abydos, Egypt," in C. Beltrane (ed.), *Boats, Ships and Shipyards, Proceedings of the Ninth International Symposium on Boat and Ship Archaeology, Venice 2000*, Oxford: Oxbow Books, pp. 19–23.

2004, "Boatbuilding in Ancient Egypt," in F. M. Hocker and C. A. Ward (eds.), *The Philosophy of Shipbuilding: Conceptual Approaches to the Study of Wooden Ships*, College Station: Texas A&M University Press, pp. 13–24.

2006, "Boatbuilding and its social context in early Egypt: interpretations from the First Dynasty boat-grave cemetery at Abydos," *Antiquity*, 80 (307), pp. 118–129.

WARD, C. A. and ZAZZARO, C., 2010, "Evidence with Pharaonic seagoing ships at Mersa/Wadi Gawasis, Egypt," *International Journal of Nautical Archaeology*, 39 (1), doi:10.1111/j.1095-9270.2009.00229.x

WARMINGTON, B. H., 1984, "La période carthaginoise," in G. Mokhtar (ed.), *Histoire générale de l'Afrique*, vol. II: *Afrique ancienne*, Paris: Jeune Afrique/UNESCO, pp. 475–499.

WARMINGTON, E. H., 1974, *The Commerce between the Roman Empire and India*, London: Curzon Press; New York: Octagon Books (1st edn. 1928).

WARNIER, J.-P., 2008, "Les politiques de la valeur," *Sociétés politiques comparées*, 4. www .fasopo.org

WASYLIKOWA, K., and VAN DER VEEN, M., 2004, "An archaeobotanical contribution to the history of watermelon, *Citrullus lanatus* (Thunb.) Matsum. & Nakai (syn. *C. vulgaris* Schrad.)," *Vegetation History and Archaeobotany*, 13, pp. 213–217.

WATRIN, L., 2002, "Tributes and the rise of a predatory power: unraveling the intrigue of EBI Palestinian jars found by E. Amélineau at Abydos," in E. C. M. van den Brink and T. E. Levy (eds.), *Egypt and the Levant: Interrelations from the 4th through the Early 3rd Millennium BCE*, London and New York: Leicester University Press, pp. 450–463.

WATSON, A. M., 1983, *Agricultural Innovation in the Early Islamic World: The Diffusion of Crops and Farming Techniques, 700–1100*, Cambridge University Press.

The Wealth of India: A Dictionary of Indian Raw Materials and Industrial Products, 1948–1976, New Delhi: Council of Scientific and Industrial Research, 11 vols.

WEBBER, R. P., 1853, *Dictionnaire malgache–français rédigé selon l'ordre des racines, par les Missionnaires Catholiques de Madagascar et adapté aux dialectes de toutes les provinces*, Ile Bourbon: Etablissement Malgache de Notre-Dame de la Ressource.

WEBER, E., 1999, "The Tabula Peutingeriana and the Madaba Map," in M. Piccirillo and E. Alliata (eds.), *The Madaba Map Centenary 1897–1997: Travelling through the Byzantine Umayyad Period. Proceedings of the International Conference Held in Amman, 7–9 April 1997* (SBF Collectio Maior 40), Jerusalem, pp. 41–46.

WEBER, M., 1921/1972, "Die Stadt: eine soziologische Untersuchung," *Archiv von Socialwissenschaft und Sozialpolitik*, 47, pp. 621–772; published as chapter 8 in *Wirtschaft und Gesellschaft*, 5th edn. (Tübingen, 1972), pp. 727–814.

1978, *Economy and Society: An Outline of Interpretive Sociology*, University of California Press.

1998, *Économie et société dans l'Antiquité*, preceded by *Les causes sociales du déclin de la civilisation antique*, Paris: La Découverte (1st edn. 1909).

WEBER, S. A., 1998, "Out of Africa: the impact of millets in South Asia," *Current Anthropology*, 39, pp. 267–274.

WEBER, S. A., LEHMAN, H., BARELA, T., HAWKS, S., and HARRIMAN, D., 2010, "Rice or millets: early farming strategies in Central Thailand," *Archaeological and Anthropological Sciences*, 2, pp. 79–88.

WEEKS, L. R., 2003, *Early Metallurgy of the Persian Gulf: Technology, Trade and the Bronze Age World*, Boston and Leiden: Brill.

2008, "The 2007 Early Iranian metallurgy workshop at the University of Nottingham," *Iran*, 46, pp. 335–345.

2013, "Iranian metallurgy of the fourth millennium BC in its wider technological and cultural contexts," in C. A. Petrie (ed.), *Ancient Iran and Its Neighbours: Local Developments and Long-Range Interactions in the Fourth Millennium BC*, Oxford: Oxbow Books, pp. 75–91.

WEEKS, L., KEALL, E., PASHLEY, V., EVANS, Y., and STOCK, S., 2008, "Lead isotopes analyses of Bronze Age copper base artefacts from al-Midamman, Yemen: towards the identification of an indigenous metal production and exchange system in the southern Red Sea region," *Archaeometry*, 51 (1), pp. 576–597.

WEISS, H., 2000, "Beyond the younger days: collapse as adaptation to abrupt climate change in ancient western Asia and the eastern Mediterranean," in G. Bawden and R. M. Reycraft (eds.), *Environmental Disaster and the Archaeology of Human Response*, Albuquerque, NM: Maxwell Museum of Anthropology, pp. 75–99.

WEISSKOPF, M., 1989, *The So-called 'Great Satraps' Revolt', 366–360 BC: Concerning Local Instability in the Achaemenid Far West*, Wiesbaden: F. Steiner.

WEITZMAN, M., 2012, "GHG targets as insurance against catastrophic climate damages," *Journal of Public Economic Theory*, 14 (2), pp. 221–244.

WENDRICH, W. Z., TOMBER, R. S., SIDEBOTHAM, S. E., HARRELL, J. A., CAPPERS, R. T. J., and BAGNALL, R. S., 2003, "Berenike cross-roads: the integration of information," *Journal of the Economic and Social History of the Orient*, 46 (1), pp. 46–87.

WENGROW, D., 2006, *The Archaeology of Early Egypt: Social Transformations in North-East Africa, c. 10,000 to 2,650 BC*, Cambridge University Press.

WESTENHOLZ, A., 1975, *Old Sumerian and Old Akkadian Texts in Philadelphia, Chiefly from Nippur. Part 1: Literary and Lexical Texts and the Earliest Administrative Documents from Nippur, Bibliotheca Mesopotamica*, 1, Malibu: Undena Publications.

2002, "The Sumerian city-state," in M. H. Hansen (ed.), *A Comparative Study of Six City-State Cultures*, Copenhagen: Det Kongelige Danske Videnskabernes Selskab, pp. 23–42.

WESTERN, A. C. and MCLEOD, W., 1995, "Woods used in Egyptian bows and arrows," *Journal of Egyptian Archaeology*, 81, pp. 77–94.

WET, J. M. J. DE, 2000, "Sorghum," in K. F. Kiple and K. C. Ornelas (eds.), *Cambridge World History of Food*, vol. I, Cambridge University Press, pp. 152–157.

WETTERSTROM, W., 1996, "La chasse-cueillette et l'agriculture en Égypte: la transition de la chasse et de la cueillette à l'horticulture dans la vallée du Nil," *Archéo-Nil*, 6, pp. 27–50.

WHEATLEY, P., 1961, *The Golden Chersonese: Studies in the Historical Geography of the Malay Peninsula before A.D. 1500*, Kuala Lumpur: University of Malaya Press.

1983, *Nagara and Commandery: Origins of the Southeast Asian Urban Traditions*, University of Chicago Press.

WHEELER, M., 1968, *The Indus Civilization*, 3rd edn., Cambridge University Press.

WHITE, J. C., 1986, "A revision of the chronology of Ban Chiang and its implications for the prehistory of Northeast Thailand," Ph.D. thesis, University of Pennsylvania, Philadelphia.

1997, "A brief note on new dates for the Ban Chiang cultural tradition," *Bulletin of the Indo-Pacific Prehistory Association*, 16, pp. 103–106.

WHITE, J. C., PENNY, D., KEALHOFER, L., and MALONEY, B., 2004, "Vegetation changes from the late Pleistocene through the Holocene from three areas of archaeological significance in Thailand," *Quaternary International*, 113, pp. 111–132.

WHITEHOUSE, D., 1989, "Begram, the *Periplus* and Gandharan art," *Journal of Roman Archaeology*, 3, pp. 93–100.

1996, "Sasanian maritime activity," in J. Reade (ed.), *The Indian Ocean in Antiquity*, London and New York: Kegan Paul, pp. 339–350.

2005, *Sassanian and Post-Sassanian Glass in the Corning Museum of Glass*, Corning, NY: Corning Museum of Glass.

WICK, L., LEMCKE, G., and STURM, M., 2003, "Evidence of Late glacial and Holocene climatic change and human impact in eastern Anatolia: high resolution pollen, charcoal, isotopic and geochemical records from the laminated sediments of Lake Van," *Holocene*, 13, pp. 665–675.

WICKS, R. S., 1992, *Money, Markets and Trade in Early Southeast Asia: The Development of Indigenous Monetary Systems to AD 1400*, New York and Ithaca, NY: Cornell University Press.

WIDELL, M., 2005, "Some reflections on Babylonian exchange during the end of the third millennium BC," *Journal of the Economic and Social History of the Orient*, 48 (3), pp. 388–400.

WIECZOREK, A. and LIND, C., 2007, *Ursprünge der Seidenstraße: sensationelle Neufunde aus Xinjiang, China. Begleitbuch zur Ausstellung*, Stuttgart: Konrad Theiss.

WIESEHÖFER, J., 2009, "The Achaemenid Empire," in I. Morris and W. Scheidel (eds.), *The Dynamics of Ancient Empires: State Power from Assyria to Byzantium*, Oxford University Press, pp. 66–98.

WILCKE, C., 2003, *Early Ancient Near Eastern Law. A History of Its Beginnings: The Early Dynastic and Sargonic Periods*, Munich: Verlag der Bayerischen Akademie der Wissenschaften.

WILD, J. P. and WILD, F. C., 2007, "Chapter 11: Textiles," in S. E. Sidebotham and W. Z. Wendrich (eds.), *Berenike 1999/2000*, Cotsen Institute of Archaeology, University of California, Los Angeles, pp. 225–227.

WILENSKY, J., 2002, "The Magical Kunlun and 'Devil Slaves': Chinese perceptions of dark-skinned people and Africa before 1500," in V. H. Mair (ed.), *Sino-Platonic Papers*, Philadelphia: University of Pennsylvania, pp. 1–50.

WILKINSON, D., 1995a and b, "Central civilization" and "Civilizations are world systems!," in S. K. Sanderson (ed.), *Civilizations and World Systems: Studying World-Historical Change*, Walnut Creek, CA, London, and New Delhi: Altamira Press, pp. 46–74 and 234–246.

WILKINSON, T. A. H., 1999, *Early Dynastic Egypt*, London: Routledge.

2002, "Reality versus ideology: the evidence for 'Asiatics' in Predynastic and Dynastic Egypt," in E. C. M. van den Brink and T. E. Levy (eds.), *Egypt and the Levant: Interrelations from the 4th through the Early 3rd Millennium BCE*, London and New York: Leicester University Press, p. 514–521.

2003, *Genesis of the Pharaohs*, London: Thames and Hudson.

2004, "Uruk into Egypt: imports and imitations," in J. N. Postgate (ed.), *Artefacts of Complexity: Tracking the Uruk in the Near East* (Iraq Archaeological Reports 5), Warminster: Aris & Phillips for the British School of Archaeology in Iraq, pp. 237–247 (1st edn. 2002).

WILKINSON, T. C., SHERRATT, S., and BENNET, J. (eds.), 2011, *Interweaving Worlds: Systemic Interactions in Eurasia, 7th to the 1st Millennia BC (Proceedings of the Symposium "What Would a Bronze Age World System Look Like? World Systems Approaches to Europe and Western Asia 4th to 1st Millennia BC," University of Sheffield, 1–4 April 2008)*, Oxford: Oxbow Books.

WILKINSON, T. J., 1999, "Settlement, soil erosion and terraced agriculture in highland Yemen: a preliminary statement," *Proceedings of the Seminar for Arabian Studies*, 29, pp. 183–191.

1999–2000, 2001–2002, Project for the Archaeology of Yemeni Terraced Agriculture, 1999–2000 and 2001–2002. Annual Reports.

2003, "The organization of settlement in highland Yemen during the Bronze and Iron Ages," *Proceedings of the Seminar for Arabian Studies*, 33, pp. 157–168.

2005, "Soil erosion and valley fills in the Yemen highlands and southern Turkey: integrating settlement, geoarchaeology, and climate change," *Geoarchaeology*, 20 (2), pp. 169–192.

WILL, E. L., 1992, "The Mediterranean shipping amphoras from Arikamedu," in V. Begley and R. D. De Puma (eds.), *Rome and India: The Ancient Sea Trade*, Delhi: Oxford University Press, pp. 151–156.

WILLCOX, G., 1991, "Carbonised plant remains from Shortughai, Afghanistan," in J. M. Renfrew (ed.), *New Light on Early Farming: Recent Developments in Palaeoethnobotany*, Edinburgh University Press, pp. 139–153.

1994, "Archaeobotanical finds," in F. Højlund and H. Anderson (eds.), *Qalaat al Bahrain*, vol. 1, Jutland Archaeological Society Publications, pp. 459–462.

WILLIAMSON, K., 2000, "Did chicken go west?," in R. M. Blench and K. C. MacDonald (eds.), *The Origins and Development of African Livestock. Archaeology, Genetics, Linguistics and Ethnography*, London: UCL Press, pp. 368–448.

WILSON, A. I., 2005, "Foggara irrigation, early state formation and Saharan trade: the Garamantes of Fazzan," *Schriftenreihe der Frontinus Gesellschaft 26, Internationales Frontinus-Symposium, Wasserversorgung aus Qanaten – Qanate als Vorbilder im Tunnelbau, 2.-5. Oktober 2003, Walferdange, Luxemburg*, pp. 223–234.

WILSON, T. H. and OMAR, A. L., 1997, "Archaeological investigations at Pate," *Azania*, 32, pp. 31–76.

WINKELMANN, S., 2008, "Ein baktrischer Edelmetall-Hortfund und noch einmal zur Frage der Quellen baktrischer Compartimentsiegel," in E. Olijdam and R. H. Spoor (eds.),

Intercultural Relations between South and Southwest Asia: Studies in Commemoration of E. C. L. During Caspers (1934–1996) (BAR International Series 1826), Oxford: Archaeopress, pp. 184–199.

WINTER, I. J., 1999, "The aesthetic value of lapis lazuli in Mesopotamia," in A. Caubet (ed.), *Cornaline et pierres précieuses: la Méditerranée, de l'Antiquité à l'Islam*, Paris: La Documentation Française, pp. 43–58.

2008, "Touched by the gods: visual evidence for the divine status of rulers," in N. Brisch (ed.), *Religion and Power: Divine Kingship in the Ancient World and Beyond*, University of Chicago, pp. 75–102.

WISSA, M., 2006, "Du rouleau de cuir au parchemin: réflexion sur l'évolution d'une technique en Égypte, depuis les origines jusqu'au début de l'ère islamique," in B. Mathieu, D. Meeks, and M. Wissa (eds.), *L'apport de l'Égypte à l'histoire des techniques: méthodes, chronologie et comparaisons*, Cairo: Institut Français d'Archéologie Orientale, pp. 277–292.

WISSEMAN CHRISTIE, J., 1990, "Trade and state formation in the Malay Peninsula and Sumatra, 300 BC – AD 700," in J. Kathirithamby-Wells and J. Villiers (eds.), *The Southeast Asian Port and Polity: Rise and Demise*, Singapore University Press, pp. 39–60.

1995, "State formation in early maritime Southeast Asia," *Bijdragen tot de Taal-, Land- en Volkenkunde*, 151 (2), pp. 235–288.

1999, "Asian sea trade between the tenth and the thirteenth centuries and its impact on the states of Java and Bali," in H. P. Ray (ed.), *Archaeology of Seafaring: The Indian Ocean in the Ancient Period*, New Delhi: Pragati, pp. 221–270.

WISSMANN, H. VON, 1968, "Zanganae," *Paulys Realencyclopädie der Classischen Altertumswissenschaft*, Supplementband XI, pp. 1337–1348.

WITTFOGEL, K. A., 1957, *Oriental Despotism: A Comparative Study of Total Power*, New Haven, CT, and London: Yale University Press.

WITZEL, M., 1999, "Substrate languages in Old Indo-Aryan (Rgvedic, Middle and Late Vedic)," *Electronic Journal of Vedic Studies (EJVS)*, pp. 1–67.

2005, "Central Asian roots and acculturation in South Asia: linguistic and archaeological evidence from Western Central Asia, the Hindukush and Northwestern South Asia for early Indo-Aryan language and religion," in T. Osada (ed.), *Linguistics, Archaeology and the Human Past*, Kyoto: Research Institute for Humanity and Nature (RIHN), pp. 87–211.

2006a, "South Asian agricultural terms in Old Indo-Aryan," in T. Osada (ed.), *Proceedings of the Pre-Symposium of RIHN and 7th ESCA Harvard–Kyoto Roundtable*, Kyoto: Research Institute for Humanity and Nature (RIHN), pp. 96–120.

2006b, "Early loanwords in Western Central Asia: indicators of substrate populations, migrations, and trade relations," in V. H. Mair (ed.), *Contact and Exchange in the Ancient World*, Honolulu: Hawaii University Press, pp. 158–190.

WOLF, E. R., 1982, *Europe and the People without History*, Berkeley: University of California Press.

WOLFF, J., 1974, "Proto-Austronesian *r and *d," *Oceanic Linguistics*, 13, pp. 77–121.

1982, "Proto-Austronesian *c, *z, *g and *t," *Pacific Linguistics*, series C, 75, pp. 1–30.

WOLTERS, O. W., 1967, *Early Indonesian Commerce: A Study of the Origins of Srivijaya*, Ithaca, NY: Cornell University Press.

1979, "Studying Srivijaya," *Journal of the Malaysian Branch of the Royal Asiatic Society*, 52 (2), pp. 1–32.

1999, *History, Culture, and Religion in Southeast Asian Perspectives* (Southeast Asian Program Publications 26), Ithaca, NY: Cornell University Press (1st edn. 1982).

WONG, R. B., 1997, *China Transformed: Historical Change and the Limits of European Experience*, Ithaca, NY: Cornell University Press.

WOOD, M., 1996, *In Search of the Trojan War*, London: Penguin Books (1st edn. 1985).

WOOD, M. 2011, *Interconnections: Glass Beads and Trade in Southern and Eastern Africa and the Indian Ocean — 7th to 16th Centuries AD*, Uppsala: Uppsala University, Department of Archaeology and Ancient History.

2015, "Divergent patterns in Indian Ocean trade to East Africa and Southern Africa between the 7th and 17th centuries CE: the glass bead evidence," *Afriques*, 6, http://afriques.revues.org

WOODHOUSE, J., 1998, "Iron in Africa: metal from nowhere," in G. Connah (ed.), *Transformations in Africa: Essays on Africa's Later Past*, London: Leicester University Press, pp. 160–185.

WOUDEN, F. A. E. VAN, 1963 [1935], *Types of Social Structure in Eastern Indonesia*, Leiden: J. Ginsberg.

WRIGHT, H. T., 1984, "Early seafarers of the Comoro Islands: the Dembeni Phase of the IXth-Xth centuries AD," *Azania*, 11, pp. 13–59 (with contributions from C. Sinopoli, L. Wojnaroski, E. S. Hoffman, S. L. Scott, R. W. Redding, and S. M. Goodman).

2001, "Cultural action in the Uruk world," in M. S. Rothman (ed.), *Uruk Mesopotamia and Its Neighbors: Cross-Cultural Interactions in the Era of State Formation*, Sante Fe: School of American Research; Oxford: James Currey, pp. 123–148.

2013, "A bridge between worlds: south-western Iran in the fourth millennium BC," in C. A. Petrie (ed.), *Ancient Iran and Its Neighbours: Local Developments and Long-Range Interactions in the Fourth Millennium BC*, Oxford: Oxbow Books, pp. 75–91.

WRIGHT, H. T., RADIMILAHY, C., and ALLIBERT, C., 2005, "L'évolution des systèmes d'installation dans la baie d'Ampasindava et à Nosy-Be," *Taloha*, 14–15, www.taloha.info/document.php?id=137

WRIGHT, H. T. and RUPLEY, E. S. A., 2001, "Radiocarbon age determinations of Uruk-related assemblages," in M. S. Rothman (ed.), *Uruk Mesopotamia and Its Neighbors: Cross-Cultural Interactions in the Era of State Formation*, Sante Fe: School of American Research; Oxford: James Currey, pp. 85–122.

WRIGHT, R. P., REID, A. B., and SCHULDENREIN, J., 2008, "Water supply and history: Harappa and the Beas regional survey," *Antiquity*, 82, pp. 37–48.

WRIGLEY, C., 1997, "The *Periplus* and related matters," *Azania*, 32, pp. 112–116.

WU XIAOLONG, 2004, "Exotica in the funerary debris in the state of Zhongshan: migration, trade, and cultural contact," K. Linduff (ed.), *Silk Road Exchange in China, Sino-Platonic Papers*, 142, pp. 6–16.

WUNSCH, C., 2002, "Debt, interest, pledge and forfeiture in the Neo-Babylonian and Early Achaemenid period: the evidence from private archives," in M. Hudson and M. van de Mieroop (eds.), *Debt and Economic Renewal in the Ancient Near East*, Bethesda, MD: CDL Press, pp. 221–256.

2010, "Neo-Babylonian entrepreneurs," in D. S. Landes, J. Mokyr, and W. J. Baumol (eds.), *The Invention of Enterprise: Entrepreneurship from Ancient Mesopotamia to Modern Times*, Princeton University Press, pp. 40–61.

WYNNE-JONES, S., 2016, *A Material Culture: Consumption and Materiality on the Coast of Precolonial East Africa*, Oxford University Press.

YAMAGATA, M., 2007, "The early history of Lin-i viewed from archaeology," *Acta Asiatica*, 92, pp. 1–30.

YAMAGATA, M. and NGUYEN KIM DUNG, 2010, "Ancient roof tiles found in central Vietnam," in B. Bellina, E. A. Bacus, T. O. Pryce, and J. Wisseman Christie (eds.), *50 Years of Archaeology in Southeast Asia: Essays in Honour of Ian Glover*, Bangkok: River Books, pp. 195–205.

YAMAGATA, M., PHAM DUC MANH, and BUI CHI HOANG, 2001, "Western Han bronze mirrors recently discovered in central and southern Viet Nam," *Bulletin of the Indo-Pacific Prehistory Association*, 21 (The Melaka Papers Volume 5), pp. 99–106.

YAMASAKI, K. and MUROZUMI, M., 1992, "Similarities between Ancient Chinese glasses and glasses excavated in Japanese tombs," in R. H. Brill and J. H. Martin (eds.), *Scientific Research in Early Chinese Glass*, Corning, NY: Corning Museum of Glass, pp. 91–98.

YANG, R., YANG, Y., LI, W., ABUDURESULE, Y., HU, X., WANG, C., and JIANG, H., 2014, "Investigation of cereal remains at the Xiaohe Cemetery in Xinjiang, China," *Journal of Archaeological Science*, 49, pp. 42–47.

YANG, X. (ed.), 2004, *New Perspectives on China's Past: Chinese Archaeology in the Twentieth Century*, 2 vols., New Haven, CT: Yale University Press.

YANG BAO, BRAEUNING, A., JOHNSON, K. R., and YAFENG SHI, 2002, "General characteristics of temperature variation in China during the last two millennia," *Geophysical Research Letters*, 29, 1324.

YANG SHAO-YUN, n.d., "The origins of Sriwijaya reconsidered: a review of Shen Fuwei's 'Chitu Guo Lishi Tanyuan'," www.chinahistoryforum.com/lofiversion/index.php/t9606.html

YINZENG, G., 2006, "Deep footprints of Odyssey: Chinese sources of India–China civilisational dialogue," *China Report*, 42 (2), pp. 117–121.

YOFFEE, N., 1995a, "The collapse of ancient Mesopotamian states and civilization," in N. Yoffee and G. L. Cowgill (eds.), *The Collapse of Ancient States and Civilizations*, Tucson: University of Arizona Press, pp. 44–68.

1995b, "The economy of ancient western Asia," in J. M. Sasson (ed.), *Civilizations of the Ancient Near East*, vol. III, New York: Scribner's, pp. 1387–1399.

YOFFEE, N. and CLARK, J. J. (eds.), 1993, *Early Stages in the Evolution of Mesopotamian Civilization: Soviet Excavations in Northern Iraq*, Tucson: University of Arizona Press.

YOFFEE, N. and COWGILL, G. L. (eds.), 1995, *The Collapse of Ancient States and Civilizations*, 2nd edn., Tucson: University of Arizona Press.

YOUNG, G. K., 2001, *Rome's Eastern Trade: International Commerce and Imperial Policy*, London and New York: Routledge.

YULE, P., RATH, B. K., and HOJGAARD, K., 2000, "Sankarjang," in K. K. Basa and P. Mohanty (eds.), *Archaeology of Orissa*, vol. I, New Delhi: Pratibha Prakashan, pp. 285–321.

ZAITSEVA, G. I. and VAN GEEL, B., 2004, "The occupation history of the southern Eurasia steppe during the Holocene: chronology, the calibration curve and methodological problems of the Scythian chronology," in E. M. Scott, A. Y. Alekseev, and G. Zaitseva (eds.), *Impact of the Environment on Human Migration in Eurasia* (NATO Science Series, IV. Earth and Environmental Sciences, 42), Dordrecht: Springer, pp. 63–82.

ZANGATO, E., 1999, *Sociétés préhistoriques et mégalithes dans le nord-ouest de la République centrafricaine* (Bar International Series 768; Cambridge Monographs in African Archaeology 46), Oxford: Archaeopress.

ZANGATO, E. and HOLL, A. F. C., 2010, "On the Iron Front: new evidence from north-central Africa," *Journal of African Archaeology*, 8 (1), pp. 7–23.

ZARINS, J., 1989, "Ancient Egypt and the Red Sea trade: the case for obsidian in the Predynastic and Archaic periods," in A. Leonard and B. B. Williams (eds.), *Essays in Ancient Civilization*, Chicago: Oriental Institute, pp. 339–368.

1990, "Obsidian and the Red Sea trade: prehistoric aspects," *South Asian Archaeology 1987*, pp. 507–541.

1997, "Mesopotamia and frankincense: the early evidence," in A. Avanzini (ed.), *Profumi d'Arabia*, Rome: "L'Erma" di Bretschneider, pp. 251–272.

2002, "Dhofar, frankincense, and Dilmun precursors to the Iobaritae and Omani," in S. Cleuziou, M. Tosi, and J. Zarins (eds.), *Essays on the Late Prehistory of the Arabian Peninsula*, Rome: Istituto Italiano per l'Africa e l'Oriente, pp. 403–438.

2008, "Magan shipbuilders at the Ur III Lagash state dockyards (2062–2025 BC)," in E. Olijdam and R. Spoor (eds.), *Intercultural Relations between South and Southwest Asia*.

Studies in commemoration of E. C. L. During Caspers (1934–1996), Oxford: Archaeopress, pp. 209–229.

ZARINS, J. and ZAHRANI, A., 1985, "Recent archaeological investigations in the southern Tihama Plain: the sites of Athar and Sihi," *Atlal*, 9, pp. 65–107.

ZAZZARO, C., 2013, *The Ancient Red Sea Port of Adulis and the Eritrean Coastal Region. Previous Investigations and Museums Collections* (BAR International Series 2569), Oxford: Archaeopress.

ZAZZARO, C., COCCA, E., and MANZO, A., 2014, "Towards a chronology of the Eritrean Red Sea port of Adulis (1st – early 7th century ad)," *Journal of African Archaeology*, 12 (1), pp. 43–73.

ZDANOVICH, G. B. and ZDANOVICH, D. G., 2002, "The 'Country of Towns' of Southern Trans-Urals and some aspects of steppe assimilation in the Bronze Age," in K. Boyle, C. Renfrew, and M. Levine (eds.), *Ancient Interactions: East and West in Eurasia*, Cambridge: McDonald Institute for Archaeological Research, pp. 249–263.

ZEEB, F., 2004, "The history of Alalah as a testcase for an ultrashort chronology of the mid-2nd millennium BCE," in H. Hunger and R. Pruzsinszky (eds.), *Mesopotamian Dark Age Revisited, Proceedings of an International Conference of SCIEM 2000* (Vienna November 8–9, 2002), Vienna: Verlag der Österreichischen Akademie der Wissenschaften, pp. 81–94.

ZETTLER, R. L., 2003, "Reconstructing the world of Ancient Mesopotamia: divided beginnings and holistic history," *Journal of the Economic and Social History of the Orient*, 46 (1), pp. 3–45.

ZHANG, C. and HUNG, H., 2010, "The emergence of agriculture in southern China," *Antiquity*, 84 (323), pp. 11–25.

ZHANG, D. D., ZHANG, J, LEE, H. F., and HE, Y-Q., 2007, "Climate change and war frequency in eastern China over the last millennium," *Human Ecology*, 35 (4), pp. 403–414.

ZHANG, L., 2009, "Metal trade in Bronze Age Central Asia," in J. Mei and T. Rehren (eds.), *Metallurgy and Civilisation: Eurasia and Beyond*, London: Archetype Publications, pp. 17–25.

ZHANG, Q.-B. and HEBDA, R., 2005, "Abrupt climate change and variability in the past four millennia of the southern Vancouver Island, Canada," *Geophysical Research Letters*, 32, L 16708.

ZHOUYONG SUN et al. 2014, "The Shimao site in Shenmu County, Shaanxi," *Chinese Archaeology*, 14 (1), pp. 18–26.

ZIDE, A. and ZIDE, N. H., 1976, "Proto-Munda cultural vocabulary: evidence for early agriculture," in P. N. Jenner, L. C. Thompson, and S. Starosta (eds.), *Austroasiatic Studies*, Honolulu: University Press of Hawaii, pp. 1295–1334.

ZIEGLER, N., 2001, "Amorrite," in F. Joannès (ed.), *Dictionnaire de la civilisation Mésopotamienne*, Paris: Laffont, pp. 40–42.

ZOETMULDER, P. J., 1982, *Old Javanese-English Dictionary*, with the collaboration of S. O. Robson, 2 vols., Leiden and The Hague: Martinus Nijhoff.

ZOHARY, D. and HOPF, M., 2000, *Domestication of Plants in the Old World*, 3rd edn., Oxford University Press.

ZOHARY, D., HOPF, M., and WEISS, E., 2012, *Domestication of Plants in the Old World*, 4th edn., Oxford University Press.

ZOHARY, M., 1982, *Plants of the Bible*, Cambridge University Press.

ZORC, R., 1994, "A glossary of Austronesian reconstructions," in D. Tryon (ed.), *Comparative Austronesian Dictionary: An Introduction to Austronesian Studies*, part 1, fascicle 2, New York and Berlin: Mouton de Gruyter, pp. 1105–1197.

ZURNDORFER, H. T., 1999, "Another look at China, money, silver, and the 17th century crisis," *Journal of the Economic and Social History of the Orient*, 42 (3), pp. 396–412.

INDEX OF GEOGRAPHICAL NAMES

NAME INDEX

SUBJECT INDEX